COMPREHENSIVE
HANDBOOK OF
SOCIAL WORK
AND
SOCIAL WELFARE

Volume
3

COMPREHENSIVE HANDBOOK OF SOCIAL WORK AND SOCIAL WELFARE

SOCIAL WORK PRACTICE

Volume Editors
William Rowe   Lisa A. Rapp-Paglicci

Editors-in-Chief
Karen M. Sowers   Catherine N. Dulmus

WILEY
John Wiley & Sons, Inc.

KH

Library of Congress Cataloging-in-Publication Data:

Comprehensive handbook of social work and social welfare /
     editors-in-chief, Karen M. Sowers and Catherine N. Dulmus.
          p.   cm.
     Includes bibliographical references.
     ISBN 978-0-471-76997-2 (cloth) Volume 1: The Profession of Social Work
     ISBN 978-0-471-76272-0 (cloth) Volume 2: Human Behavior in the Social Environment
     ISBN 978-0-471-76280-5 (cloth) Volume 3: Social Work Practice
     ISBN 978-0-471-76998-9 (cloth) Volume 4: Social Policy and Policy Practice
     ISBN 978-0-471-75222-6 (cloth) 4-Volume set
     1. Social service.   2. Social service—Practice.   3. Public welfare.   4. Social policy.
     I. Sowers, Karen M. (Karen Marlaine)   II. Dulmus, Catherine N.

  HV40.C66   2008
  361—dc22   2007026315

Printed in the United States of America.

10 9 8 7 6 5 4 3 2 1

10/5/09

Our lives are rich tapestries woven with relationships and experiences. The thread begins with our parents—relationships that color the work of art that we become. For this reason, and many more, I would like to dedicate this volume to my mother, Charlotte (Kitty) Rowe (1924–2007).

William Rowe

There are people who touch our lives, help to shape and inspire us and then there are others who make a profound impact on us. There are those, whose spirits are so potent that their imprint remains with us even when they are no longer here. I would like to dedicate this volume to my husband, one of those intense spirits whose impact cannot be measured nor forgotten, David Paglicci (1963–2006).

Lisa A. Rapp-Paglicci

Contents

Handbook Preface ──────────────────────

The profession of social work spans more than 100 years. Over this period, the profession has changed in scope and depth. Despite the varied functions and methods of our profession, it has always been committed to social justice and the promotion of well-being for all. The profession has made great strides and is experiencing a resurgence of energy, commitment, and advancement as we face new global realities and challenges and embrace new and innovative technologies.

In considering how the field of social work has evolved over the past century with the resulting explosion of new knowledge and technologies, it seemed imperative to create a resource (*Comprehensive Handbook of Social Work and Social Welfare*) that provides a manageable format of information for researchers, clinicians, educators, and students. Our editors at John Wiley & Sons, the volume editors (Ira Colby, William Rowe, Lisa Rapp-Paglicci, Bruce Thyer, and Barbara W. White) and we as editors-in-chief, developed this four-volume handbook to serve as a resource to the profession.

The *Comprehensive Handbook of Social Work and Social Welfare* includes four volumes (*The Profession of Social Work, Human Behavior in the Social Environment, Social Work Practice,* and *Social Policy and Policy Practice*). Each volume editor did an outstanding job of assembling the top social work scholars from around the globe to contribute chapters in their respective areas of expertise. We are enormously grateful to the chapter authors who have contributed their expert knowledge to this work. Each volume includes a Preface written by the respective volume editor(s) that provides a general overview to the volume. In developing the *Comprehensive Handbook,* we attempted to focus on evidence supporting our theoretical underpinnings and our practice interventions across multiple systems. Content was designed to explore areas critically and to present the best available knowledge impacting the well-being of social systems, organizations, individuals, families, groups, and communities. The content is contemporaneous and is reflective of demographic, social, political, and economic current and emerging trends. Authors have paid close attention to contextual factors that shape the profession and will have a future impact on practice. Our profession strives to understand the dimensions of human difference that we value and engage to ensure excellence in practice. These dimensions of diversity are multiple and include factors such as disability, religion, race, culture, sexual orientation, social class, and gender. Each of the volumes addresses how difference characterizes and shapes our profession and our daily practice. New knowledge, technology, and ideas that may have a bearing on contemporary and future social work practice are infused throughout each of the volumes.

We challenged the chapter authors to not only provide an overview of specific content, but to feel free to raise controversial issues and debates within the profession. In the interest of intellectual freedom, many of our chapter authors have done just that in ways that are intriguing and thought provoking. It was our objective to be comprehensive but not encyclopedic. Readers wishing to obtain even greater specificity are encouraged to access works listed in the references for each chapter.

The *Handbook*'s focus on evidence should assist the reader with identifying opportunities to strengthen their own understanding of the amount of science that does or does not support our social work theory and practice. Social work researchers must expand the scientific evidence that supports social work theory and practice as well as informing policy, and enhance their functional scope to overcome the more than 10-year lag between research and practice. We are rightfully proud of our social work history, and its future will be driven by our success in demonstrating that as a profession we can achieve credible and verifiable outcomes across the spectrum of services that utilize our skills. As a profession, we must assure we value science so that even the most vulnerable populations receive the best available services.

We hope that you find this *Handbook* useful. We have endeavored to provide you, the reader and user, with a comprehensive work that will serve as a guide for your own work in this wonderful profession. We welcome your comments and suggestions.

KAREN M. SOWERS
CATHERINE N. DULMUS

Acknowledgments

An endeavor of this magnitude required the efforts of many people, and we are indebted to their unique and valuable contributions. First, we would like to thank Tracey Belmont, our initial editor at John Wiley & Sons, for recognizing the importance of this project to the profession of social work and for her commitment to making it a reality. It was Tracey's vision that allowed this project to get off the ground, and we are grateful to her. A special thanks to Lisa Gebo, our current editor at John Wiley & Sons, who provided us with expert guidance and technical support to see this project to fruition. Others to thank at John Wiley & Sons include Isabel Pratt and Sweta Gupta who assisted us with all aspects of the contractual and prepublication processes. They were invaluable in assisting with a project of this size, and we are grateful to them.

Most important, we would like to thank the volume editors and contributors who made this *Handbook* a reality. The volume editors did an excellent job of developing their respective volumes. We particularly thank them for their thoughtful selection and recruitment of chapter contributors. The contributor lists for each volume read like a "Who's Who" of social work scholars. We are pleased that each contributor recognized the importance of a seminal piece such as this *Handbook* for the profession of social work and willingly contributed their time and knowledge. We extend a special debt of gratitude to these eminent contributors from around the globe who so graciously and willingly shared their expertise with us. It is the work of these scholars that continues to move our profession forward.

K. M. S.
C. N. D.

Preface

The field of social work has made dramatic changes since its inception. Trends and fads in practice have come in and out of vogue, some lasting a decade or so and others only a blink of an eye. These movements did not persist long in the field because they were not based in solid theory, did not have empirical verification and were not bound to a core ethical standard of the field. Evidence-based practice however is different. It is not simply a practice technique, rather it is a philosophical, theoretical, ethical, and practice approach, and its inception has changed the field of social work in a profound manner.

Evidence-based practice (EBP) has affected social workers from caseworkers to clinicians, modifying their practice skills and more importantly transforming their thinking about problems, planning, and intervention. EBP has also clarified the ethical principle requiring social workers to practice using effective interventions. These are the qualities of a movement that inform us that evidence-based practice is no whim.

Evidence-based practice was not openly welcomed at first in the field. However, over time it has become well understood and acknowledged and is revolutionary to the field. But the increased speed by which clinicians are bombarded with information and the sheer volume of information can make practitioners' tasks of rapidly identifying high-quality studies seem overwhelming. Ironically, clinicians previously had little or no evidence-based guidelines to work from, now the formidable number of studies and information often leads to the same result: A continued difficulty in application of evidence-based practice.

This volume addresses this concern by compiling an enormous amount of state-of-the-art information on EBP utilizing renowned international experts throughout the world. Its use for practitioners, researchers, educators, and students is incalculable, yet it is practically written for manageable access. It includes two sections: the first comprising information about basic social work skills such as interviewing, planning, advocacy, and termination and the second encompassing assessment and intervention for various populations like children, adolescents, elderly, families, groups, and communities. The chapters summarize EBP in a large variety of domains and populations and are extremely efficient to use. This volume is also a frontrunner in providing information about EBP in assessment and in providing outstanding chapters from social work authorities around the world.

Evidence-based practice has been accepted by a vast number of social workers and will continue to transform the field of social work if sustained. In this time of rapid information and technological change, this volume is immediately invaluable by its comprehensiveness, ease of use, and distinctiveness in the field of social work.

WILLIAM ROWE
LISA A. RAPP-PAGLICCI

Contributors

Paula Allen-Meares, PhD
School of Social Work
University of Michigan
Ann Arbor, Michigan

Michael J. Austin, PhD
School of Social Welfare
University of California, Berkeley
Berkeley, California

Katharine Briar-Lawson, PhD
School of Social Welfare
State University of New York—Albany
Albany, New York

Elaine Congress, PhD, DSW, LCSW
Fordham University Graduate School of
    Social Service
New York, New York

Cecilia Lai Wan Chan, PhD
Center on Behavioral Health and
Department of Social Work and Social
    Administration
University of Hong Kong
Hong Kong, China

Lena Dominelli, PhD
School of Applies Social Sciences
Durham University
Durham, United Kingdom

Sophia F. Dziegielewski, PhD, LISW
School of Social Work
University of Cincinnati
Cincinnati, Ohio

Cynthia Franklin, PhD
School of Social Work
University of Texas—Austin
Austin, Texas

Don M. Fuchs, PhD
Faculty of Social Work
University of Manitoba
Winnipeg, Manitoba, Canada

Leon Fulcher, PhD
Dunfermline, Fife, Scotland

Eileen Gambrill, PhD
School of Social Welfare
University of California—Berkley
Berkley, California

Charles Glisson, PhD
College of Social Work
University of Tennessee—Knoxville
Knoxville, Tennessee

Wendy Grainger, MHSA
Ohio State University Hospital
Columbus, Ohio

John Heckman, DMin
School of Social Work
University of Georgia
Athens, Georgia

Michael J. Holosko, PhD
School of Social Work
University of Georgia
Athens, Georgia

Valerie Holton, MSW
School of Social Work
Virginia Commonwealth University
Richmond, Virginia

Laura Hopson, MSW
School of Social Work
University of Texas—Austin
Austin, Texas

Heather K. Horton, PhD
School of Social Welfare
State University of New York—Albany
Albany, New York

Catheleen Jordan, PhD
School of Social Work
University of Texas—Arlington
Arlington, Texas

Chi Kwong Law, PhD
Department of Social Work and Social
    Administration
University of Hong Kong
Hong Kong, China

Craig Winston LeCroy, PhD
School of Social Work
Arizona State University
Tucson, Arizona

Samuel A. MacMaster, PhD
College of Social Work
University of Tennessee
Nashville, Tennessee

Robyn Munford, PhD
School of Health and Social Services
Massey University
Palmerston North, New Zealand

William R. Nugent, PhD
College of Social Work
University of Tennessee—Knoxville
Knoxville, Tennessee

Gregory J. Paveza, MSW, PhD
School of Health and Human Services
Southern Connecticut State University
New Haven, Connecticut

D. Mark Ragg, PhD
School of Social Work
Eastern Michigan University
Ypsilanti, Michigan

Lisa A. Rapp-Paglicci, PhD
School of Social Work
University of South Florida
Tampa, Florida

Michael Reisch, PhD
School of Social Work
University of Michigan
Ann Arbor, Michigan

Albert R. Roberts, PhD
Criminal Justice Department
School of Arts and Sciences
Rutgers University
Piscataway, New Jersey

Brian Roland, MSW
School of Social Welfare
State University of New York—Albany
Albany, New York

William Rowe, DSW
School of Social Work
University of South Florida
Tampa, Florida

David Royse, PhD
College of Social Work
University of Kentucky
Lexington, Kentucky

Mary C. Ruffolo, PhD, LMSW
School of Social Work
University of Michigan
Ann Arbor, Michigan

Jackie Sanders, PhD
School of Health and Social Services
Massey University
Palmerston North, New Zealand

Sara Sanders, PhD
School of Social Work
University of Iowa
Iowa City, Iowa

David W. Springer, PhD, LCSW
School of Social Work
University of Texas—Austin
Austin, Texas

Bruce A. Thyer, PhD
College of Social Work
Florida State University
Tallahassee, Florida

Francis J. Turner, PhD
Professor and Dean Emeritus
School of Social Work
Wilfrid Laurier University
Waterloo, Ontario, Canada

Catherine M. Vu, MPA, MSW
School of Social Welfare
University of California—Berkeley
Berkeley, California

Joseph Walsh, PhD
School of Social Work
Virginia Commonwealth University
Richmond, Virginia

Michael E. Woolley, PhD
Schools of Social Work and Education
University of Michigan
Ann Arbor, Michigan

Kenneth R. Yeager, PhD
Department of Psychiatry
Ohio State University
Columbus, Ohio

Section I

ASSESSMENT AND INTERVENTION OVERVIEW

Chapter 1

EVIDENCE-INFORMED PRACTICE

Eileen Gambrill

Evidence-based practice (EBP) describes a philosophy and process designed to forward effective use of professional judgment in integrating information regarding each client's unique circumstances and characteristics, including their preferences and actions, and external research findings. It involves the "integration of best research evidence with clinical expertise and [client] values" (Sackett, Straus, Richardson, Rosenberg, & Haynes, 2000, p. 1):

> Without clinical expertise, practice risks becoming tyrannized by external evidence, for even excellent external evidence may be inapplicable to or inappropriate for an individual patient. Without current best external evidence, practice risks becoming rapidly out of date, to the detriment of patients. (Sackett, Richardson, Rosenberg, & Haynes, 1997, p. 2)

Evidence-informed practice is a guide for thinking about how decisions should be made (Haynes, Devereaux, & Guyatt, 2002). It requires the "conscientious, explicit and judicious use of current best evidence in making decisions about the care of individual [clients]" (Sackett et al., 1997, p. 2). It is a process for handling the uncertainty surrounding decisions that must be made in real life, in real time. Sources of uncertainty include limitations in current knowledge, lack of familiarity with what knowledge is available, and difficulties in distinguishing between personal ignorance and lack of competence and actual limitations of knowledge (Fox & Swazy, 1974). Uncertainties may be related to lack of information about problem-related causes, clients' ambivalence about pursuit of certain goals, and whether resources are available to help clients. A willingness to acknowledge that "I don't know," combined with taking steps to see if needed information is available, increases the likelihood that important uncertainties can be decreased or identified (Chalmers, 2004). This helps us to honor ethical obligations to involve clients as informed participants.

Evidence-informed practice involves a shift in paradigms. Intuition and unsystematic clinical expertise are considered insufficient grounds on which to make decisions. On the other hand, the "value-laden nature of clinical decisions" (Guyatt & Rennie, 2002, p. 4) implies that we cannot rely on evidence alone:

> Thus, knowing the tools of evidence-based practice is necessary but not sufficient for delivering the highest quality of [client] care. In addition to clinical expertise, the clinician requires compassion, sensitive listening skills, and broad perspectives from the humanities and social sciences. These attributes allow understanding of [clients' concerns] in the context of their experience, personalities, and cultures. (p. 9)

... any external guideline must be integrated with individual clinical expertise in deciding whether and how it matches the [client's] clinical state, predicament, and preferences and thus whether it should be applied. (Sackett et al., 1997, p. 2)

The philosophy of evidence-based practice encourages practitioners to be effective advocates for their clients: "physicians concerned about the health of their patients as a group, or about the health of the community, should consider how they might contribute to reducing poverty" (Guyatt & Rennie, 2002, p. 9). The National Association of Social Workers (NASW) encourages social workers to "Stand up for others" (*NASW News*, 2006, p. 11). Service is the first value described in NASW's Code of Ethics (1999). A key characteristic of EBP is breaking down the division between research and practice, for example, highlighting the importance of clinicians critically appraising research reviews and developing a technology to help them do so: "the leading figures in EBM ... emphasized that clinicians had to use their scientific training and their judgment to interpret [guidelines] and individualize care accordingly" (Gray, 2001b, p. 26).

Although its philosophical roots are old, the blooming of EBP as a process attending to evidentiary, ethical, and application issues in all professional venues (education, practice/ policy, and research), is fairly recent, facilitated by the Internet revolution. Critical thinking is integral to this process. In both critical thinking as well as EBP, attention is given to ethical issues. If we examine the intellectual traits inherent in critical thinking suggested by Paul (1993) such as courage, integrity, and perseverance, we see that they reflect the philosophies of EBP described by the originators of EBP. Honesty and transparency (clear description of what is done to what effect) are emphasized in both. This applies to all venues of interest in the helping professions: professional education, practice and policy (what is done to what effect), and related research (its design, conduct, and reporting).

Evidence-based practice and health care arose because of troubling gaps between available knowledge and what is used by professionals. It suggests and explores ways to decrease gaps both at the level of clinical practice and decision making about groups or populations, for example, purchasing services (Gray, 2001a, 2001b). It is as much about the ethics of educators and researchers as it is about the ethics of practitioners and agency administrators. Gray (2001a) suggests that, at present, the helping process has the following characteristics:

1. Overenthusiastic adoption of interventions of unproven efficacy or even proven ineffectiveness;
2. Failure to adopt interventions that do more good than harm at a reasonable cost;
3. Continuing to offer interventions services demonstrated to be ineffective;
4. Adoption of interventions without adequate preparation such that the benefits demonstrated in a research setting cannot be reproduced in the ordinary service setting;
5. Wide variation in the rates at which interventions are adopted or discarded. (p. 366)

Descriptions of EBP differ in their breadth and attention to ethical issues ranging from the broad, systemic philosophy and related evolving technology envisioned by its originators (e.g., Gray, 1997; Sackett et al., 1997) to narrow views (use of practice guidelines) and total distortions (Gambrill, 2003). For example, many descriptions of evidence-based decision making ignore hallmarks of this process such as involving clients as informed participants. Given these many different views, it is important to review the vision of EBP and health care as described by its creators. Otherwise, potential benefits to clients and professionals may be lost. Recently, more attention has been given to client preferences and actions because what clients do (e.g., carry out agreed-on tasks or not) often differs from their stated preferences and estimates of preferences are often wrong (Haynes et al., 2002).

EBP describes a process for and a new professional educational format (problem-based learning) designed to help practitioners to link evidentiary, ethical, and application issues. It is assumed that professionals often need information to make decisions, for example, concerning risk assessment or what services are most likely to help clients attain outcomes they value. Sackett et al. (1997) estimated that about two questions arise for every three patients physicians see and that 30% of all questions remain unanswered (p. 8). We do not know how many questions arise in the course of other professionals' work or how many of these remain unanswered. As Gray (2001a, p. 354) suggests, when evidence is not used, important failures in decision making occur:

- Ineffective interventions are introduced;
- Interventions that do more harm than good are introduced;
- Interventions that do more good than harm are not introduced;
- Interventions that are ineffective or do more harm than good are not discontinued.

Clinical expertise includes use of effective relationship skills and the experience of individual helpers to rapidly identify each client's unique circumstances, characteristics, and "their individual risks and benefits of potential interventions and their personal values and expectations" (Sackett et al., 2000, p. 1). Using clinical expertise, practitioners integrate information about a client's characteristics and circumstances with external research findings, client expectations and values, and their preferences and actions (Haynes et al., 2002; Sackett et al., 1997). Sackett and his colleagues (1997) suggest that: "Increased expertise is reflected in many ways, but especially in more effective and efficient [assessment] and in the more thoughtful identification and compassionate use of individual [clients'] predicaments, rights and preferences in making clinical decisions about their care" (p. 2). Client values refer to "the unique preferences, concerns and expectations each [client] brings to a clinical encounter and which must be integrated into clinical decisions if they are to serve the [client]" (Sackett et al., 2000, p. 1). Evidence-based health care refers to use of best current knowledge as evidence in decision making about groups and populations (see Gray, 2001a). Professional codes of ethics call for key characteristics of EBP such as drawing on practice- and policy-related research and involving clients as informed participants.

AN ALTERNATIVE TO AUTHORITY-BASED PRACTICE

Evidence-based decision making arose as an alternative to authority-based decision making in which consensus, anecdotal experience, or tradition are relied on to make decisions (see Table 1.1).

Table 1.1   Differences between Authority-Based and Evidence-Based Practitioners

Authority-Based Decision Making	Evidence-Based Decision Making
Clients are not informed or are misinformed.	Clients are involved as informed participants.
Ignores client preferences (e.g., "We know best.").	Seeks and considers client values and preferences.
Does not pose specific questions about important decisions that must be made and does not search for and critically appraise what is found and share results with clients.	Poses clear questions related to information needs, seeks related research findings, critically appraises them, and shares what is found with clients and others.
Motivated to appear well informed, to preserve status and reputation.	Motivated to help clients and be an honest and competent broker of knowledge and ignorance.
Ignores errors and mistakes.	Seeks out errors and mistakes; values criticism as vital for learning.
Accepts practice- and policy-related claims based on misleading criteria such as tradition and expert consensus.	Relies on rigorous criteria to appraise practice claims and select practices and policies (e.g., those that control for biases).
Relies solely on self-report of clients or anecdotal observations to evaluate progress.	Uses objective as well as subjective measures to evaluate progress with a focus on outcomes of concern to clients.

Although misleading in the incorrect assumption that EBP means only that decisions made are based on evidence of their effectiveness, use of the term does call attention to the fact that available evidence may not be used or the current state of ignorance shared with clients. It is hoped that professionals who consider related research findings regarding decisions and inform clients about them will provide more effective and ethical care than those relying on criteria such as anecdotal experience, available resources, or popularity. The following examples illustrate reliance on authority-based criteria for selection of service methods:

> Ms. Riverton has just been to a workshop on eye movement desensitization therapy. The workshop leader told the participants that this method "works and can be used for a broad range of problems." Ms. Riverton suggests to her supervisor at the mental health clinic where she works that agency staff should use this method. When asked why, she said because the workshop leader is a respected authority in the field.

> Mr. Davis read an editorial that describes the DARE programs as very effective in decreasing drug use. No related empirical literature was referred to. He suggests to his agency that they use this method.

In the first example, the authority of a workshop leader is appealed to. In the second, the authority of an author of an editorial is appealed to. Evidence-based decision making involves use of quite different criteria. A key one is information about the accuracy of practice and policy-related claims. EBP draws on the results of systematic, rigorous, critical appraisals of research related to different kinds of questions such as "Is eye movement desensitization effective for certain kinds of problems? Are DARE programs effective?" For example, review groups in the Cochrane and Campbell Collaborations prepare comprehensive, rigorous reviews of all research related to a question (see later descriptions).

THREE PHILOSOPHIES OF EVIDENCE-BASED PRACTICE

Evidence-based practice and social care involve a philosophy of ethics of professional practice and related enterprises such as research and scholarly writing, a philosophy of science (epistemology—views about what knowledge is and how it can be gained), and a philosophy of technology. Ethics involves decisions regarding how and when to act; it involves standards of conduct. Epistemology involves views about knowledge and how to get it or if we can. The philosophy of technology involves questions such as: Should we develop technology? What values should we draw on to decide what to develop? Should we examine the consequences of a given technology? Evidence-informed practice encourages the integration of research and practice, for example, by highlighting the importance of clinicians critically appraising research reviews and developing a technology to help them to do so; "the leading figures in EBM . . . emphasized that clinicians had to use their scientific training and their judgment to interpret [guidelines] and individualize care accordingly" (Gray, 2001b, p. 26). It encourages clinicians to think for themselves—to develop critical appraisal skills. It offers practitioners and administrators a philosophy that is compatible with obligations described in professional codes of ethics as well as an evolving technology for integrating evidentiary, ethical, and practical issues. The uncertainty associated with decisions is acknowledged, not hidden.

EBP requires considering research findings related to important practice/policy decisions and sharing what is found (including nothing) with clients. Transparency and honesty regarding the evidentiary status of services is a hallmark of this philosophy. For example, on the back cover of the seventh edition of *Clinical Evidence* (2002), the continually updated book distributed to physicians, it states that "it provides a concise account of the current state of knowledge, ignorance, and uncertainty about the prevention and treatment of a wide range of clinical conditions." In what books describing practices in psychology, psychiatry, or social work do we find such a statement? To the contrary, we find books titled *What Works in Child Welfare* (Kluger, Alexander, & Curtis, 2002) and *A Guide to Treatments That Work* (Nathan & Gorman, 2002).

Steps in Evidence-Based Practice

Steps in EBP include the following:

1. Convert information needs related to practice decisions into answerable questions.
2. Track down, with maximum efficiency, the best evidence with which to answer them.
3. Critically appraise that evidence for its validity, impact (size of effect), and applicability (usefulness in practice).
4. Integrating the critical appraisal with our clinical expertise and with our client's unique characteristics and circumstances, including their preferences and values. This involves deciding whether evidence found (if any) applies to the decision at hand (e.g., is a client similar to those studied, is there access to services described) and considering client values and preferences in making decisions as well as other applicability.
5. Evaluate our effectiveness and efficiency in carrying out steps 1 to 4 and seek ways to improve them in the future (Straus, Richardson, Glasziou, & Haynes, 2005, pp. 3–4).

Questions that arise in the fourth step include: Do research findings apply to my client? That is, is a client similar to clients included in related research findings? Can I use this practice method in my setting (e.g., Are needed resources available?)? If not, is there some other access to programs found to be most effective in seeking hoped-for outcomes? What alternatives are available? Will the benefits of service outweigh harms of service for this client? What does my client think about this method? Is it acceptable to clients? What if I don't find anything (Glasziou, Del Mar, & Salisbury, 2003)? What is the number needed to treat, that is, how many people must receive a service for one person to be helped? (See Sinclair, Cook, Guyatt, Pauker, & Cook, 2001.) What is the number needed to harm? Evidence-informed practitioners take advantage of efficient technology for conducting electronic searches to locate the current best evidence regarding a specific question; information literacy and retrivability are emphasized (Gray, 2001a, 2001b).

DIFFERENT KINDS OF QUESTIONS

Different questions require different kinds of research methods to critically appraise proposed assumptions (e.g., Greenhalgh, 2006; Guyatt & Rennie, 2002; Straus et al., 2005). These differences are reflected in the use of different "quality filters" to search for research findings that reflect the particular terms associated with research likely to offer critical tests of questions. Kinds of questions include the following:

- *Effectiveness:* Do job training programs help clients get and maintain jobs?
- *Prevention:* Do Head Start programs prevent school drop out?
- *Screening (risk/prognosis):* Does this measure accurately predict suicide attempts?
- *Description/assessment:* Do self-report data provide accurate descriptions of parenting practices?
- *Harm:* Does (or will) this intervention harm clients?
- *Cost:* How much does this program cost compared to others?
- *Practice guidelines:* Are these practice guidelines valid and are they applicable to my client/agency/community?
- *Self-development:* Am I keeping up-to-date? How can I keep up-to-date?

Sackett et al. (1997, 2000) suggest posing four-part questions that describe the population of clients, the intervention you are interested in, what it may be compared to (including doing nothing), and hoped-for outcomes (PICO questions). Gibbs (2003) refers to these as COPES questions. They are **C**lient **O**riented. They are questions clinicians pose in their daily practice that affect clients' welfare. Second, they have **P**ractical importance. They concern problems that arise frequently in everyday practice and that are of concern to an agency. For example, child protective service workers must assess risk. Asking the question about what types of clients present the greatest immediate risk for child abuse is a critical one. Third, COPES (PICO) questions guide an **E**lectronic search for related research findings. The process of forming a specific question often begins with a vague general question and then proceeds to a well-built question. Fourth, hoped-for outcomes are identified. **S**ynonyms can be used to facilitate a search (e.g., see Gibbs, 2003; Glasziou et al., 2003). For example, if abused children are of concern, other terms for this may be "maltreated children," "neglected children," "mistreated children." Sackett et al. (1997) suggest that a well-formed question should meet the following criteria:

- It concerns a problem of concern to clients.
- It affects a large number of clients.
- It is probably answerable by searching for related research findings.

A careful search requires actively seeking information that challenges or disconfirms our assumptions as well as for information that supports them. In addition to the development of the systematic review, the availability of the Internet has revolutionized the search for information making it more speedy and more effective. The Cochrane Collaboration prepares, maintains, and disseminates high-quality reviews of research related to a particular practice question. The Cochrane Library is an electronic publication designed to supply high-quality evidence to those providing and receiving care and those responsible for research, teaching, funding, and administration at all levels. The Cochrane database includes thousands of systematic reviews. It is distributed on a subscription basis. Abstracts of reviews are available without charge and can be searched. Both published and unpublished content (the gray literature) is sought in all languages, and journals are hand-searched. Reviews are prepared by people who are also responsible for identifying and incorporating new evidence as it becomes available. Entries include completed reviews, available in full text, as well as protocols that are expressions of intent and include a brief outline of the topic and a submission deadline. Reviews are prepared and maintained, based on standards in *The Reviewers' Handbook*, which describes the process of creating Cochrane systematic reviews (Higgins & Green, 2005). It is revised often to ensure that it remains up to date. The Cochrane Collaboration focuses on health concerns, however, many reviews are relevant to a wide variety of professionals. Examples are "Psychoeducation for Schizophrenia" (Pekkala & Merinder, 2004) and "Psychological Debriefing for Preventing Posttraumatic Stress Disorder" (Rose, Bisson, Churchill, & Wessely, 2000). The Cochrane Library also includes a Controlled Trials Register and the Cochrane Review Methodology Database that is a bibliography of articles concerning research synthesis and practical aspects of preparing systematic reviews.

The Campbell Collaboration, patterned after the Cochrane Collaboration, prepares reviews related to education, social intervention, and criminal justice. Coordinating groups include communication and dissemination, crime and justice, education, social welfare, and a methods group. Like the Cochrane Collaboration, detailed instructions are followed for preparing high-quality reviews, and reviews are routinely updated. They, like the Cochrane Collaboration, have an annual conference and both are attended by methodologists as well as those interested in particular problem areas (www.campbellpenn.com).

DIFFERENT STYLES OF EVIDENCE-BASED PRACTICE

Sackett and his colleagues (2000) distinguish among three different styles of EBP, all of which require integrating evidence with a client's unique personal and environmental circumstances. All require step 4 (see prior list of steps in EBP) but they vary in how other steps are carried out. They suggest that for problems encountered on an everyday basis, you should invest the time and energy necessary to carry out both searching and critical appraisal of reports found. For level 2 (problems encountered less often), they suggest that you seek out critical appraisals already prepared by others who describe and use explicit criteria for deciding what evidence they select and how they decide whether it is valid. Here, step 3 can be omitted and step 2 restricted to sources that have already undergone critical appraisal. A third style applies to problems encountered very infrequently in which we "blindly seek, accept, and apply the recommendations we receive from authorities" (p. 5). As they note, the trouble with this mode is that it is "blind" to whether the advice received from the experts "is authoritative (evidence-based, resulting from their operating in the appraising mode) or merely authoritarian (opinion-based, resulting from pride and prejudice)" (p. 5). One clue they suggest to distinguish which style is being used is uncritical documentation with a reluctance to describe what is in the documentation. Lack of time may result in using style 2 with most problems. Guyatt and Rennie (2002) recommend the highest possible skill levels: "Only if you develop advanced skills in interpreting the [practice- and policy-related] literature will you be able to determine the extent to which these attempts are consistent with the best evidence. Second, a high level of EBP skills will allow you to use the original literature effectively, regardless of whether preappraised synopses and evidence-based recommendations are available" (p. 208).

EXAMPLES OF EVIDENCE-BASED DECISION MAKING

Dr. Price works in a mental health crisis center. The administrator of this agency sent a memo around to staff that he had heard that brief psychological debriefing was effective in decreasing posttraumatic stress disorder following a crisis and suggested that his staff use this method. Dr. Price decided to see if this was accurate. He formed the following question: In clients experiencing a potentially traumatic event, is brief (one hour) psychological debriefing compared to no service more effective in preventing post traumatic stress disorder? This is an effectiveness question. He looked in the Cochrane Database and found the systematic review prepared by Rose et al. (2000). To his surprise, this review concluded that not only was this method not effective, there was some indication that it had harmful effects; one study reported that those receiving such counseling were *more* likely to experience stressful reactions a year later. Based on this review, he sent an e-mail to his colleagues questioning the use of this method for clients.

Richard works in a child protection agency that requires him to use a risk assessment measure to estimate the likely recurrence of child abuse among parents alleged to have abused their children. The method used by his agency is a consensus-based instrument, that is, it is based on the opinions of a group of experts on what they consider risk factors. His question is as follows: Among parents alleged to have abused their children, are actuarial- compared to consensus-based measures most accurate in predicting the likelihood of future abuse? Notice again that this is a four-part question: (1) a client group, (2) a particular predictive measure, (3) another kind of risk measure, and (4) the hoped for outcome. He looked in www.childwelfare.com and located an article by Baird and Wagner (2000) that compared the reliability and validity of these two kinds of risk measures. This article concluded that the actuarial method was the most accurate. Actuarial measures are based on empirical relationships between certain factors and the likelihood of an outcome such as abuse.

These examples illustrate distinctive features of evidence-informed decision making. The clinicians posed well-structured questions related to their information needs that guided an effective, efficient electronic search. Searches can be done in the office with modem-equipped computers using appropriate search methods including Boolean logic (and/or), relevant databases, and quality filters designed to locate the best evidence for a particular kind of question. Critical appraisal skills are used to review what is found (see, e.g., Altman et al., 2001). Many sources are available to guide this appraisal that include user-friendly checklists for different kinds of questions (e.g., Greenhalgh, 2006). A search for research findings may reveal that a practice method is harmful. We may discover that there is no research that critically appraises the effectiveness of a practice or policy or that the research is too weak to draw an inference. All these are findings related to important decisions that must be made. If no research findings are available that provide guidance, decisions must be based on other criteria, such as an empirically grounded practice theory. This is a finding and is shared with clients.

Implications of evidence-informed practice for assessment include: (a) drawing on available problem-related research, for example, about related factors; (b) selecting empirically grounded assessment frameworks that reflect research findings regarding outcomes of interest; (c) using reliable, valid assessment measures including measures designed to assess risk of certain outcomes, such as suicide or child maltreatment; (d) avoiding common errors in integrating data from multiple sources; and (e) involving clients as informed participants and considering their values and preferences. Implications for intervention include using practices and policies found via critical appraisal to do more good than harm and accurately informing clients concerning the evidentiary status of methods used. Implications for evaluation include using methods that accurately reflect degree of change and keeping track of progress on an ongoing basis. The more one reads about current-day practices in the helping professions, the clearer it is that helping efforts do not have the characteristics of EBP. Literature suggests that professionals do not draw on practice-related research findings to inform practice decisions (see, e.g., Mullen & Bacon, 2004; Rosen, Proctor, Morrow-Howell, & Staudt, 1995). Not keeping up with new research findings related to important decisions renders the practitioner's knowledge increasingly out of date. As a result, decisions may be made that harm rather than help clients (e.g., see Jacobson, Foxx, & Mulick, 2005; Lilienfeld, Lynn, & Lohr, 2003; Ofshe & Watters, 1994). Many clinicians do not honor obligations described in professional codes of ethics regarding informed consent (e.g., see Braddock, Edwards, Hasenberg, Laidley, & Levinson, 1999). Lack of transparency regarding limitations of research remains common as does the publication of incomplete, uncritical reviews that provide an overly rosy picture of alleged effectiveness of practice methods (Schulz, Chalmers, Hayes, & Altman, 1995).

ORIGINS OF EVIDENCE-BASED DECISION MAKING

Sackett and his colleagues (2000) suggest four realizations made possible by five recent developments for the rapid spread of evidence-based medicine. Realizations include (1) practitioner need for valid information about decisions they make; (2) the inadequacy of traditional sources for acquiring this information (e.g., because they are out of date, frequently wrong, overwhelming in their volume, variable in their validity); (3) the gap between assessment skills and clinical judgment "which increase with experience and our up-to-date knowledge and performance which decline" (p. 2); and (4) lack of time to locate, appraise, and integrate this evidence (p. 2). Traditional forms of continuing education were not effective (O'Brien et al., 2001). There were increasing gaps between information available on the Internet that could be of value to clients and clinicians in making informed decisions and what was drawn on. Five developments allowed improvement in this state of affairs:

1. The development of strategies for efficiently tracking down and appraising evidence (for its validity and relevance);
2. The creation of systematic reviews and concise summaries of the effects of health care (epitomized by the Cochrane Collaboration);
3. The creation of evidence-based journals of secondary publication;
4. The creation of information systems for bringing the forgoing to us in seconds;
5. The identification and application of effective strategies for lifelong learning and for improving our clinical performance. (Sachett et al. 2000, p. 3)

Study of Variations in Services Offered

EBP and health care originated in medicine in part because of variations in services offered and their outcomes (Wennberg, 2002). Variations in services naturally raise questions such as "Are they of equal effectiveness?" "Do some cause harm?"

Gaps among Ethical, Evidentiary, and Application Concerns

Services found to be effective are often not used and services of little value are often offered. Although interlinked in professional codes of ethics and accreditation standards, ethical and evidentiary issues are often worlds apart in practice. Sheldon and Chilvers (2000) found that 18% of social workers surveyed ($n = 2,285$) had read nothing related to practice within the past 6 months. If professionals are not familiar with the evidentiary status of alternative practices and policies, they cannot pass this information on to their clients; they cannot honor informed consent obligations. If some alternatives are more effective than others in helping clients, and practice proceeds in ignorance of this information, clients are deprived of opportunities to achieve hoped-for outcomes. How can clients exercise self-determination if they are uninformed or misinformed about the evidentiary status of recommended services? Currently, gaps between what research suggests is effective and what services are provided are hidden. For example, rarely do child protection staff compare services offered by agencies to which they refer clients for parent training with what research suggests is effective and share this information with clients. Clients are typically not informed that recommended services have not been critically tested or have been found to be ineffective or harmful.

Increased Attention to Harm in the Name of Helping

The history of the helping professions shows that common practices thought to help people were found to harm them (e.g., see Blenkner, Bloom, & Neilson, 1971; McCord, 2003; Sharpe & Faden, 1998; Valenstein, 1986). Such reports increased awareness that services designed to help clients, including assessment measures, may result in negative effects. For example, routine use of mammograms results in a high rate of false positives with consequent unnecessary anxiety and invasive procedures such as biopsies for many individuals (Gigerenzer, 2002; Schwartz & Woloshin, 2007; Thornton, Edwards, & Baum, 2003).

Limitations of Traditional Methods of Knowledge Dissemination

Gray (2001a) highlights the role of troubling gaps between obligations of researchers to report limitations of research, prepare systematic reviews, and accurately describe well-argued alternative views and what we find in published literature. We find:

- Inflated claims: Professional propaganda.
- Biased estimates of the prevalence of a concern: Propagandistic advocacy in place of careful weighting of evidence.
- Hiding limitations of research.
- Preparing fragmented, incomplete literature reviews.
- Ignoring counterevidence to preferred views.
- Ignoring well-argued alternative perspectives and related evidence.
- Pseudoinquiry: Poor match between questions addressed and methods used to address them (e.g., see Rubin & Parrish, 2007).
- Ad hominem rather than ad rem argument.
- Ignoring unique knowledge of clients and service providers in making decisions about the appropriateness of a practice guideline.

Poor quality research continues to appear in professional journals (Altman, 2002). There are many reasons for this including the special interests of those who fund research such as pharmaceutical companies and censorship of findings (e.g., see Angell, 2004; Bodenheimer, 2000).

In discussing the origins of EBP, Gray (2001b) emphasized the increasing lack of confidence in data of potential use to clinicians: peer review which he subtitled feet of clay; flaws in books, editorials, and journal articles. Examples include submission bias, publication bias, methodological bias, abstract bias, and framing bias. In place of critical, systematic reviews of research, we find incomplete, uncritical reviews (e.g., see Oxman & Guyatt, 1993). Most reviews do not tell us how they researched, where they searched, what criteria they used to review studies and do not search for published as well as unpublished reports. Conclusions drawn based on unsystematic reviews are often quite misleading. As Rosenthal (1994) suggests in his description of hyperclaiming (telling others that proposed research is likely to achieve goals that it will not) and causism (implying a causal relationship when none has been established), "Bad science makes for bad ethics" (p. 128). Chalmers

(1990) argues that failure to accurately describe research methods used is a form or scientific misconduct.

Evolution of the Systematic Review

Recognition of limitations in narrative reviews of research related to practice questions encouraged development of the systematic review for synthesizing research findings (see Table 1.2). Such reviews "state their objectives, ascertain as much of the available evidence as possible, use explicit quality criteria for inclusion or exclusion of the studies found, use explicitly stated methods for combining data, [and] produce reports which describe the processes of ascertainment, inclusion and exclusion, and combining data" (Gray, 2001b, p. 24). (See Egger, Smith, & O'Rourke, 2001 as well as the *Cochrane Reviewers' Handbook*.)

The Internet Revolution

As Gray (2001b) notes, "The Internet stimulated the development of a number of software tools which allowed international organizations such as the Cochrane Collaboration to function effectively" (p. 25). The Internet provides rapid access to research related to practice guidelines including databases that facilitate speedy searches. New search methods using Boolean terms (and/or) facilitate searches on the Internet.

Other Factors

Gray (2001b) attributes part of the appeal of EBP to clinicians and to clients:

> It also came as a shock that even the knowledge, where it was available, was often deficient (or commonly not even utilized by doctors who had been left behind the knowledge frontier). They therefore welcomed EBM enthusiastically and it is remarkable how quickly that access to information has turned the table on professional expertise and power. It is no longer feasible to feign knowledge: patients are just as likely to have searched for the evidence before they consult a clinician. (p. 27)

Table 1.2   Examples of Difference between Systematic Reviews and Traditional Reviews

Traditional Reviews	Systematic Reviews
The search process is not described.	The search process is clearly described.
The review omits many related studies.	All currently available research related to a practice question, both published and unpublished in all languages, is sought.
Criteria used to review research regarding different kinds of practice questions are not described.	Criteria used to appraise research related to different kinds of practice questions are clearly described.
Criteria used to appraise the quality of studies are not rigorous.	Criteria used to appraise research are rigorous (e.g., Were evaluators of outcome blind to group assignment?).
Readers are not provided with sufficient information about each study to judge its quality for themselves.	Readers are provided with enough information about each study to judge its quality for themselves.
Claims of effectiveness and validity are inflated.	Claims are accompanied by descriptions of related evidence.

Economic considerations were a factor. No matter what system of care exists, resources are limited with subsequent pressures to use them justly and wisely including considering both individuals and populations (Do all residents with a particular need have access to similar quality care?). Gray (2001b) also notes the contributions of key individuals such as David Sackett (e.g., see Sackett et al., 1997) and the role of the National Health Service Research and Development Program in encouraging an evaluative culture.

HALLMARKS AND IMPLICATIONS OF THE PHILOSOPHY OF EVIDENCE-BASED PRACTICE AND CARE

The philosophy and related technology of EBP has implications for all individuals and institutions involved with helping clients, including educators, researchers, practitioners/policy makers, and those who provide funding. Research, practice, and educational issues are closely intertwined. For example, poor quality reviews of research related to practice and policy questions may result in bogus practice guidelines that result in poor quality services for clients. Clinicians may be misinformed about the evidentiary status of practice and policy claims and so harm rather than help clients. Hallmarks and implications are interrelated. For example, promotion of transparency contributes to both knowledge flow and honoring ethical obligations.

Move Away from Authoritarian Practices and Policies

The key contribution of EBP is moving from authority-based professions to those in which ethical obligations to clients and students are honored and critical appraisal and honest brokering of knowledge and ignorance thrive (Gambrill, 1999). A preference for authoritarian beliefs and actions is by no means limited to clinicians. It flourishes among researchers and academics as well. Examples include misrepresenting views, hiding limitations of research studies, ignoring counterevidence to preferred views, and not involving clients and clinicians as informed participants in decisions made (e.g., about whether to use a certain practice guideline). Indicators of the authority-based nature of practice include large gaps between what is said and what is done (e.g., professional codes of ethics and current practices and policies—basing decisions on criteria such as consensus and tradition, lack of informed consent, and censorship of certain kinds of knowledge such as variations in services and their outcomes; Gambrill, 2001).

Honor Ethical Obligations

Evidence-informed practice has ethical implications for practitioners and policy makers as well as for researchers and educators. Hallmarks include focusing on client concerns and hoped-for outcomes, attending to individual differences in client characteristics and circumstances, considering client values and expectations, and involving clients as informed participants in decision making (see prior list of steps). Ignoring practice- and policy-related research findings and forwarding bogus claims of effectiveness violates our obligation to provide informed consent and may result in wasting money on ineffective services, harming clients in the name of helping them, and forgoing opportunities to attain hoped-for outcomes. A striking characteristic of EBP and related developments is the extent to which clients are involved in many different ways (e.g., see Edwards & Elwyn, 2001; Entwistle, Renfrew, Yearley, Forrester, & Lamont, 1998; Entwistle, Sheldon, Sowden, & Watt, 1998). One is in the attention given to individual differences in client characteristics, circumstances, actions, values, and preferences in making decisions (e.g., see earlier description of EBP). Considerable attention has been devoted to creation of decision aids (O'Conner et al., 2001). A second is helping clients to develop critical appraisal skills. A third is encouraging client involvement in the design and critique of practice- and policy-related research (e.g., Hanley, Truesdale, King, Elbourne, & Chalmers, 2001). A fourth is attending to outcomes clients value and a fifth is involving them as informed participants. A sixth is recognizing their unique knowledge in relation to application concerns.

The client focused nature of evidence-informed decision making requires helpers to attend to client interests: What are *their* desired outcomes, What information would *they* like, what are *their* preferences regarding practices and policies? Sharpe and Faden (1998) describe the struggle in medicine, a continuing one, to focus on client outcomes and highlight how recent this focus is and what a contentious issue it has been and continues to be. A concern for involving clients in making decisions that affect their lives emphasizes the importance of informed (in contrast to uninformed or misinformed) consent. EBP involves sharing responsibility for decision making in a context of recognized uncertainty. Although professional codes of ethics call on practitioners to inform clients regarding risks and benefits of recommended services and alternatives, this is typically not done (e.g., see Braddock et al., 1999). Decisions concerning the distribution of scarce resources is a key ethical concern in the helping professions; this requires consideration of populations as well as individuals (Gray, 2001a). Decisions concerning populations may pose hardships for individual clients. EBP encourages programmatic research regarding error, both avoidable and unavoidable, its causes and consequences for clients and other involved parties, and exploration of methods designed to minimize avoidable errors including agency-wide risk management programs (e.g., see Reason, 1997, 2001). A careful review of the circumstances related to mistakes allows us to plan how to minimize avoidable ones. Such attention helps us to minimize harming in the name of helping.

Making Practices, Policies, and Their Outcomes Transparent

Evidence-informed practice encourages transparency of what is done to what effect in all venues of interest including practice and policy, research, and professional education. It is a democratic endeavor in which clients are apprised of the evidentiary status of services (e.g., the likelihood that they will do more good than harm). There is candidness and clarity in place of secrecy and obscurity (Chalmers, 2003). These characteristics are at odds with authority-based practice (Chalmers, 1983; Gambrill, 1999). For example, is there evidence for the following claims:

- Scared straight programs decrease delinquency.
- Psychological debriefing prevents posttraumatic stress syndrome.
- Eyewitness testimony can be trusted.
- Genograms contribute to accurate assessment.
- Screening programs for depression do more good than harm.
- Anger management programs for adolescents are effective.

Transparency calls for blowing the whistle on pseudoscience, fraud, quackery, and professional propaganda (see, e.g., Jacobson et al., 2005; Lilienfeld et al., 2003; Sarnoff, 2001). It will highlight gaps between resources needed to attain hoped-for outcomes as suggested by related research and what is used and thus may (and should) encourage advocacy on the part of clients and professionals for more effective services. It will reveal services that are ineffective, allowing a more judicious distribution of scarce resources (see Eddy, 1994a, 1994b). For example, why pay for unneeded training or ineffective services? It will highlight gaps between causes of client problems (e.g., poverty) and interventions used and promoted to have value (see, e.g., Lindsey's, 2004, critique of the residual nature of the child welfare system). Identification of gaps will suggest ways to rearrange resources. Transparency will reveal the extent to which different kinds of ethical obligations are met, such as involving clients as informed participants. It will reveal impossible tasks; consider the unrealistic expectation to "ensure" that no child in protective care be harmed. This cannot be done. Transparency encourages clear language that should discourage propagandistic ploys that hide what is done to what effect. There is no longer a need to veil the lack of evidentiary status for practices and policies, or the lack of focus on client outcomes and failure to consider client preferences.

Increased transparency also has implications for the conduct, reporting, and dissemination of research findings. It requires accurate description of well-argued alternative views and related evidence and encourages rigorous testing of claims. Biases intrude both on the part of researchers when conducting and reporting research and when preparing research reviews (e.g., see MacCoun, 1998) as well as on the part of practitioners when making decisions. The use of rigorous criteria to evaluate research studies is encouraged by the prevalence of incomplete reviews resulting in faulty conclusions that mislead both helpers and clients. EBP calls for candid descriptions of limitations of research studies and use of methods that critically test questions addressed; it calls for systematic reviews (see Cochrane and Campbell Collaborations protocols). A key contribution of EBP is discouraging inflated claims of knowledge that mislead involved parties and hinder the development of knowledge. Consider terms such as *well established* and *validated* that convey a certainty that is not possible. Bogus claims based on uncritical appraisals of related research hinder exploration and may result in harmful practices and policies.

Encourage a Systemic Approach for Integrating Practical, Ethical, and Evidentiary Issues

Evidence-informed practice describes a process designed to encourage integration of ethical, evidentiary, and application concerns. It advocates a systemic approach to improving the quality of services: (a) efforts to educate professionals who are lifelong learners, (b) involving clients as informed participants, (c) attending to management practices and policies that influence practice (i.e., evidence-based purchase of services), (d) considering the implications of scarce resources, and (e) attending to application challenges. Quality of services are unlikely to improve in a fragmented approach, that is, without attending to *all* links in the system of service provision. Gray (2001a, p. 354) suggests that performance (P) is directly related to an individual's motivation (M) and competence and inversely related to the barriers (B) that individual has to overcome: $P = (M \times C)/B$. EBP encourages the creation of tools and training programs designed to develop and encourage use of critical appraisal skills. Related literature describes a wide variety of efforts to address application concerns.

Maximize Knowledge Flow

EBP and social care are designed to maximize knowledge flow. Exploring ways to diffuse and disseminate knowledge encourages knowledge flow and related literature is rich in the variety of efforts described. In a culture in which knowledge flow is free, puffery (inflated claims of knowledge) is challenged and such challenges are welcomed. Evidence-informed decision making emphasizes the importance of collaboration among interested parties including clients, and its advocates have actively pursued the development of a technology and political base to encourage this, for example, involving clients in the design and interpretation of research (Hanley, Truesdale, King, Elbourne, & Chalmers, 2001). Gray (2001a) notes that evidence-based organizations should include systems that are capable of providing evidence and promoting the use of evidence including both explicit (created by researchers) and tacit (created by clinicians, clients, and managers). Clinicians and clients are involved as informed participants—there is no privileged knowledge in the sense of not sharing information about the evidentiary status of recommended practices and policies. Such sharing poses a direct threat to those who forward bogus claims and carry out pseudo inquiry, perhaps to gain funding and maintain status. Benefits of a free, efficient, knowledge market include:

- Critical appraisal of knowledge claims.
- Honoring informed consent obligations.
- Increased staff moral because decisions will be more informed and staff are rewarded for sharing knowledge and are free to discuss problems including errors and learn from colleagues and others throughout the world.
- Increase in the ratio of informed to uninformed or misinformed decisions.
- Recognizing uncertainty. This is often swept under the rug resulting in blaming staff for not acting on knowledge that does not (or did not) exist.
- Reducing bogus claims of knowledge that may result in harm to clients among all parties including researchers. We often find little match between questions addressed and use of methods that can critically test them together with hiding limitations and inflated claims of effectiveness regarding what has been found.
- Lack of censorship of well-argued alternative views and counterevidence regarding popular views.

Identifying errors, mistakes, and related factors and using this information to minimize avoidable mistakes contributes to knowledge flow. Thus, we have an obligation to recognize and learn from our mistakes (Popper, 1998, pp. 64–65). We learn from our mistakes, and we lose valuable learning opportunities by overlooking opportunities to "educate our intuition" (Hogarth, 2001). Research regarding errors shows that systemic causes including quality of staff training and agency policies contribute heavily to mistakes and errors (Reason, 1997, 2001). Accountable complaint systems are another way to maximize knowledge flow. Evidence-informed agencies encourage knowledge flow by using services found to maximize the likelihood of attaining outcomes clients value and not using services of unknown effectiveness or those found to do more harm than good.

EDUCATIONAL IMPLICATIONS

The importance of developing professionals who are lifelong learners is highlighted by research that shows that the typical professional program produces graduates who do not keep up with the literature, and this results in knowledge becoming rapidly out of date, with all the implications of this for clients (Sackett et al., 2000). Problem-based learning (PBL) was initiated at the McMaster University Faculty of Health Sciences in Canada. This involves a totally different form of professional education in which students are placed in small groups of five or seven, together with a tutor who is trained in group process as well as in skills involved in evidence-informed practice such as posing well-structured questions and searching effectively and efficiently for related literature. This kind of problem-based learning in medicine has spread throughout the world. It provides repeated opportunities for corrective feedback that is so vital for learning. In the traditional format of education, students are given the *products* of the process of investigation rather than being involved in the *process* of creating the products themselves so that they can not only understand this process, but experience the excitement and the challenges of wrestling with problems that make a difference in the lives of their clients.

A problem focus grounds content squarely on practice concerns, highlights key decisions and related questions and options, and links curriculum areas in a manner required when making decisions "on-the-job" including research and practice, policy and practice, and knowledge about human behavior and the environment. It emphasizes the unstructured and uncertain nature of problem solving and provides repeated opportunities to help students learn how to handle this. Focusing on problems of concern to clients and/or significant others in no way implies that client strengths are overlooked. It would be a poor problem solver indeed who did not take advantage of available resources. Yet another implication is describing methodological and conceptual controversies related to topics discussed so students are informed and thus can accurately inform clients as required by our code of ethics. That this does not occur is suggested by reviews of course outlines (e.g., see Lacasse & Gomory, 2003).

OBJECTIONS TO EVIDENCE-BASED PRACTICE

All innovations have advantages and disadvantages; evidence-informed practice is no exception. Many challenges confront helpers who want to make evidence-informed decisions such as gaining access to research findings related to important questions and critically appraising this knowledge in a timely manner. Straus and McAlister (2000) note that some limitations of EBP are universal in helping efforts such as lack of scientific evidence related to decisions and challenges in applying evidence to the care of individuals. Barriers they suggest include the need to develop new skills and limited funds and resources. Some objections result from misunderstandings of EBP. Others result from distortions of EBP (see Gibbs & Gambrill, 2002).

CONTROVERSIES REGARDING EVIDENCE

The degree of rigor that should be used to evaluate claims of effectiveness and the extent to which clients should be involved as informed participants are key controversies reflected in material in which the title "evidence-based practice" appears as revealed for example by use of hierarchies of evidence of different degrees of rigor (Gambrill, 2006). Both the origins of EPB and objections to it reflect different views of "evidence." Concerns about inflated claims of effectiveness based on biased research studies was a key reason for the origin of EBP and health care. Inflated claims obscure uncertainties that, if shared, may influence client decisions. When do we have enough to recommend a practice or policy? Do criteria for "having enough" differ in relation to different kinds of decisions? There are many kinds of evidence. Davies (2004) suggests that a broad view of evidence is needed to review policies including (a) experience and expertise, (b) judgment, (c) resources, (d) values, (e) habits and traditions, (f) lobbyists and pressure groups, and (g) pragmatics and contingencies. He argues that we should consider all of these factors in making decisions about whether or not to implement a policy. Davies identifies six kinds of research related to evidence of policy impact: (1) implementation, (2) descriptive analytical, (3) attitudinal, (4) statistical modeling, (5) economic/econometric, and (6) ethical.

Different Criteria for Evaluating Practice and Policy Claims

Different opinions about how much "we know" reflects use of different criteria. The Clinical Psychology Taskforce (1995) of the American Psychological Association suggested that two well-designed RCTs showing positive outcomes represent an "empirically validated treatment." A more measured statement would be to say that a claim has been critically tested in two high-quality randomized controlled trials (see Altman et al., 2001) and has passed both tests; this keeps uncertainty in view (Popper, 1994). Given the history of the helping professions (e.g., bogus claims of effectiveness and harming in the name of helping), isn't the most ethical road to make measured rather than inflated claims so that professionals are not misled and, in turn, mislead clients?

Research suggests that professionals rely on weaker criteria when evaluating the evidentiary status of claims that affect their clients than they rely on when evaluating claims that affect their personal well-being (see Gambrill & Gibbs, 2002). Differences of opinion regarding what evidence is can be seen in the professional literature as well as in the media. Consider the book *What Works in Child Welfare* (Kluger et al., 2002). The editors say they originally had a question mark after the title but: "We decided to eliminate the question mark from the title because, despite its limitations, this book is a celebration of what works in child welfare" (p. xix). Leaving off the question mark is a red flag that the rigor of appraisal reflected in a book is quite different than that found in Cochrane and Campbell Collaboration reviews, for example. The authors do not clearly describe where they searched, how they searched, or what criteria were used to critically appraise different kinds of research reports. We are given no information at many points as to the length of follow-up. Contrast such a grandiose title with the statement on the back of the seventh edition of *Clinical Evidence* (2002) described earlier. Has social work outstripped the field of medicine and health care in what it knows about what works?

Systematic Compared to Unsystematic Reviews of Research

A key way in which views of evidence-informed practice differ is in the degree of rigor in evaluating knowledge claims illustrated by the different conclusions concerning the effectiveness of multisystemic therapy (MST; Henggeler, Schoenwald, Borduin, & Swenson, 2006; Littell, 2005). MST is widely touted as effective (see, e.g., Lehman, Goldman, Dixon, & Churchill, 2004). Based on a critical appraisal of reviews of MST, Littell (2005) concluded that such programs have few if any significant effects on measured outcomes compared with usual services or alternative treatment. Littell followed the guidelines developed by the Campbell and Cochrane Collaborations in preparing her review. She found that few reviews reported information on attrition in primary studies, whether outcome measures were blind or included an intent-to-treat analysis. Concerns identified in the eight studies that met inclusion criteria and that were included in a subsequent analysis were inconsistent reports on the number of cases randomly assigned, unyoked designs, unstandardized observation periods within studies, unclear randomization procedures, and subjective definitions of treatment completion. Only one study met the criterion of a full intent-to-treat analysis with a well-defined follow-up (see also Littell, 2006; Littell, Popa, & Forsythe, 2005). This review, as well as many others, show that unsystematic reviews come to different conclusions than do systematic reviews; typically, the former conclude that an intervention was successful when systematic reviews conclude that there is no evidence for claims of effectiveness.

Another term used is *best evidence*. For example, if there are no randomized controlled trials regarding an effectiveness question, then we may consult a hierarchy of evidence in relation to the rigor of critical appraisal of a claim and move down the list. This indeed is what we must do in the everyday world since most interventions have not been critically tested. Thus, instead of well-designed randomized controlled trials regarding an intervention, we may have to rely on findings from a pre/post test. As this example illustrates, the term *best evidence* could refer to tests that differ greatly in their ability to critically test a claim.

OBSTACLES

Obstacles lie at many different levels ranging from dysfunctional organizational cultures and climates in which errors are hidden and staff are punished for blowing the whistle on inadequate or harmful practices and policies to personal characteristics such as arrogance and flawed self-assessments (Dunning, Heath, & Suls, 2004) continue biases such as wishful thinking (Gambrill, 2005) and preferences for ideologies rather than evidentiary status (Gorman, 1998). Challenges include gaining timely access to external research findings related to important practice and policy questions and critically appraising this knowledge (see, e.g., Greenhalgh, Robert, Macfarlane, Bate, & Kyriakidou, 2004; Oxman & Flottorp, 1998). Inflated claims are more the rule than the exception in the helping professions, misleading clients and others. Money may not be available for computers allowing rapid access to needed databases or for knowledge resource personnel who can help staff locate valuable research related to information needs in a timely manner. The steps in EBP may sound as if they are easy to carry out but that is often not the case. Literature concerning

EBP suggests that posing well-structured questions can be difficult. Thus, one obstacle is thinking it is easy and giving up when difficulty occurs. Special training, repeated guided practice, and related tools and resources are needed to carry out the steps of EBP in real time. Even then, many obstacles remain, such as authoritarian agency cultures. Skills are needed in evidence management, searching, appraisal, and storage (Gray, 2001a). And competence does not guarantee good performance; the distinction between performance and competence is an old and continuing concern. Developing technology to address application problems has been a key contribution of evidence-informed practice. This is an ongoing challenge. A review of 102 trials of interventions designed to help health professionals deliver services more effectively and efficiently shows that there are "no magic bullets" (Oxman, Thomson, Davis, & Haynes, 1995).

A lack of assessment knowledge and skills may contribute to posing misleading questions and overlooking important individual differences in a client's circumstances or characteristics. For example, posing an effectiveness question before discovering factors that contribute to depression (such as "In adults who are depressed, is cognitive-behavioral therapy, compared to medication, most effective in decreasing depression?") may overlook the fact that, for this client, recent losses in social support are uppermost, which suggests a different question, such as "In adults who are depressed because of a recent loss in social support, is a support group or individual counseling more effective in decreasing depression?" A reluctance to candidly acknowledge controversy, both conceptual and methodological, is a key obstacle that compromises fulfillment of ethical obligations to accurately inform clients and to draw on practice and policy related research. Consider critiques of practice guidelines (see Norcross, Beutler, & Levant, 2006). If it is true, as Wampold (2006) suggests, that the particular intervention contributes little to outcome, what are the implications for evidence-informed practice?

CHOICES AHEAD

This overview of EBP suggest choices ahead including the view of EBP favored—a broad, systemic view or a narrow view such as use of practice guidelines (Gambrill, 2006). Choices include how transparent to be regarding controversies (both methodological and conceptual), whether to involve clients as informed participants, and whether to advocate for better services in the face of need. (See the introduction to this chapter.) Individuals in organizations such as clearinghouses for EBP will make decisions about how transparent to be regarding the evidentiary status of current and proposed practices and policies. Choices will also be made about who to involve in selecting key questions to focus on. Will it be clients and line staff on the front lines of care? Or will it be researchers and administrators who make such decisions for clients and line staff? Who will be trained in critical appraisal skills? Will the vision of EBP promoted forward client involvement as informed participants? Will social workers be "conscientious, judicious and explicit" (Sackett, Rosenberg, Gray, Haynes, & Richardson, 1996) regarding decisions that must be made? To what extent do the chapters in this volume reflect such characteristics? The key choice will be whether and to what extent to honor obligations described in our professional codes of ethics.

CONCLUSION

EPB offers practitioners and administrators a philosophy that is compatible with obligations described in professional codes of ethics and educational accreditation policies and standards (e.g., for informed consent and to draw on practice and policy-related research findings) as well as an evolving technology for integrating evidentiary, ethical, and practical issues. Related literature highlights the interconnections among evidentiary, ethical, and application concerns in making decisions and suggests specific steps that can be taken (a technology) to decrease gaps among them in all professional venues including practice and policy (e.g., drawing on related research as required in professional codes of ethics), research (e.g., preparing systematic reviews and clearly describing limitations of studies), and professional education (e.g., exploring the value of problem-based learning in developing practitioners who are lifelong learners). Transparency and honesty regarding the evidentiary status of services is a hallmark of this philosophy. The uncertainty associated with decisions is highlighted not hidden. Evidence-informed decision making calls for honest brokering of knowledge and ignorance, for example, clear description of criteria used to make decisions. It encourages us to attend to ethical obligations (to draw on practice- and policy-related literature, to involve clients as informed participants, to focus on outcomes clients value), and to be systemic (e.g., address application obstacles such as agency cultures). Professional codes of ethics require characteristics of EBP such as drawing on practice- and policy-related research and involving clients as informed participants.

The idea of integrating practice and research in professional contexts is not new, nor is attention to ethical issues as they relate to evidentiary ones. What is new about EBP and care is the description of an evolving philosophy and process designed to interlink evidentiary, ethical, and evidentiary concerns in all professional venues (practice/policy, research, and professional education). Key steps in EBP include posing well-formed, questions regarding information needed to make important decisions, searching efficiently and effectively electronically for related research, critically appraising what is found (or drawing on high-quality critical reviews prepared by others), using practice expertise to integrate diverse sources of information including knowledge about the clients' values, expectations and preferences and available resources, and making a decision together with clients about what to do, trying it out, evaluating what happens, and learning from this experience how to do better next time. These steps increase the likelihood that all involved parties will be well informed about the uncertainties associated with decisions.

As with all innovations, objections will and should be raised. It is important to distinguish between objections based on incorrect views of EBP and those based on an accurate understanding. Otherwise, we may prematurely discard promising approaches and lose opportunities to address real challenges. Differences of opinion regarding how rigorous to be in reviewing practice- and policy-related research will continue. There are many challenges to evidence-informed practice, including those involved in learning new skills and acquiring access to needed resources, such as high-quality training programs and needed databases and arranging for ongoing feedback to keep skills well honed. Although the steps involved in evidence-informed practice may sound simple and straight forward, they are often difficult and sometimes impossible to carry out successfully in the real world. Access to a skilled informatist and to efficient search engines are vital. The more the guided practice and provision of needed tools, the more likely the steps can be carried out in a way that honors ethical obligations to make well-reasoned decisions and to accurately inform clients regarding the evidentiary status of recommended services. In the everyday world, "best practice" may have to be based on shaky evidentiary grounds. Evidence-informed practice and policy encourages professionals to be honest about these grounds so clients are involved as informed participants in decisions made. Perhaps the greatest challenge is a willingness to acknowledge gaps in our current knowledge regarding decisions that must be made and what may be "out there." A willingness to say "I don't know" and a commitment to clients to discover what is out there (including nothing) are vital. So, too, is a willingness and the courage to "stand up for others."

REFERENCES

Altman, D. G. (2002). Poor-quality medical research: What can journals do? *Journal of the American Medical Association*, *287*, 2765–2767.

Altman, D. G., Schulz, K. F., Moher, D., Egger, M., Davidoff, F., Elbourne, D., et al. (2001). The revised CONSORT statement for reporting randomized trials: Explanation and elaboration. *Annals of Internal Medicine*, *134*, 663–694. Available from www.consort-statement.org.

Angell, M. (2004). *The truth about drug companies: How they deceive us and what to do about it.* New York: Random House.

Baird, C., & Wagner, D. (2000). The relative validity of actuarial and consensus-based risk assessment systems. *Child and Youth Services Review*, *22*, 839–871.

Blenkner, M., Bloom, M., & Nielson, M. (1971). A research and demonstration project of protective services. *Social Casework*, *52*, 483–499.

Bodenheimer, T. (2000). Disease management in the American market. *British Medical Journal*, *320*, 563–566.

Braddock, C. H., Edwards, K. A., Hasenberg, N. M, Laidley, T. L., & Levinson, W. (1999). Informed decision making in outpatient practice: Time to get back to basics. *Journal of the American Medical Association*, *282*, 2313–2320.

Chalmers, I. (1983). Scientific inquiry and authoritarianism in perinatal care and education. *Birth*, *10*, 151–166.

Chalmers, I. (1990). Underreporting research limitations is scientific misconduct. *Journal of the American Medical Association*, *263*, 1405–1408.

Chalmers, I. (2003). Trying to do more good than harm in policy and practice: The role of rigorous, transparent, up-to-date evaluation. *Annals of the American Academy of Political and Social Science*, *589*, 22–40.

Chalmers, I. (2004). Well-informed uncertainties about the effects of treatment. *British Medical Journal*, *328*, 425–426.

Clinical evidence: The international source of the best available evidence for effective health care. (2002). (7th Issue). London: BMJ Publishing Group.

Clinical Psychology Taskforce. (1995). Training in and dissemination of empirically validated psychological treatment: Report and recommendations of the task force on Promotion and Dissemination of Psychological Procedures of Division 12 (Clinical Psychology, American Psychological Association). *Clinical Psychologist*, *48*, 3–23.

Davies, P. (2004, February). *Is evidence-based government possible?* Jerry Lee lecture, 4th annual Campbell Collaboration Colloquium, Washington, DC.

Dunning, D., Heath, C., & Suls, J. M. (2004). Flawed self-assessment: Implications for health, education, and the workplace. *Psychological Science in the Public Interest*, *5*, 69–106.

Eddy, D. M. (1994a). Principles for making difficult decisions in difficult times. *Journal of the American Medical Association*, *271*, 1792–1798.

Eddy, D. M. (1994b). Rationing resources while improving quality. *Journal of the American Medical Association*, *373*, 817–824.

Edwards, A., & Elwyn, G. (Eds.). (2001). *Evidence-based patient choice: Inevitable or impossible?* New York: Oxford University Press.

Egger, M., Smith, G. D., & O'Rourke, K. (2001). Rationale, potentials, and promise of systematic reviews. In M. Egger, G. D. Smith, & D. G. Altman (Eds.), *Systematic reviews in health care: Meta-analysis in context* (pp. 3–19). London: BMJ Publishing Group.

Entwistle, V. A., Renfrew, M. J., Yearley, S., Forrester, J., & Lamont, T. (1998). Lay perspectives: Advantages for health research. *British Medical Journal*, *316*, 463–466.

Entwistle, V. A., Sheldon, T. A., Sowden, A., & Watt, I. S. (1998). Evidence-informed patient choice: Practical issues of involving patients in decisions about health care technologies. *International Journal of Technology Assessment in Health Care*, *14*, 212–225.

Fox, R. C., & Swazey, J. P. (1974). *The courage to fail: A social view of organ transplants and dialysis*. Chicago: University of Chicago Press.

Gambrill, E. (1999). Evidence-based practice: An alternative to authority-based practice. *Families in Society: Journal of Contemporary Human Services*, *80*, 341–350.

Gambrill, E. (2001). Social work: An authority-based profession. *Research on Social Work Practice*, *11*, 166–175.

Gambrill, E. (2003). Evidence-based practice: Sea change or the emperor's new clothes? *Journal of Social Work Education*, *39*, 3–23.

Gambrill, E. (2005). *Critical thinking in clinical practice* (2nd ed.). Hoboken, NJ: Wiley.

Gambrill, E. (2006). Evidence-based practice: Choices ahead. *Research on Social Work Practice*, *16*, 338–357.

Gambrill, E., & Gibbs, L. (2002). Making practice decisions: Is what's good for the goose good for the gander? *Ethical Human Services and Services*, *4*, 31–46.

Gibbs, L. (2003). *Evidence-based practice for the helping professions*. Pacific Grove, CA: Brooks/Cole.

Gibbs, L., & Gambrill, E. (2002). Arguments against evidence based practice. *Research on Social Work Practice*, *14*, 452–476.

Gigerenzer, G. (2002). *Calculated risks: How to know when numbers deceive you*. New York: Simon & Schuster.

Glasziou, P., Del Mar, C., & Salisbury, J. (2003). *Evidence-based medicine workbook*. London: BMJ Publishing Group.

Gorman, D. M. (1998). The irrelevance of evidence in the development of school-based drug prevention policy, 1986–1996. *Evaluation Review*, *22*, 118–146.

Gray, J. A. M. (1997). *Evidence-based health care: How to make health policy and management decisions*. New York: Churchill Livingstone.

Gray, J. A. M. (2001a). *Evidence-based health care: How to make health policy and management decisions* (2nd ed.). New York: Churchill Livingstone.

Gray, J. A. M. (2001b). Evidence-based medicine for professionals. In A. Edwards & G. Elwyn (Eds.), *Evidence-based patient choice: Inevitable or impossible?* (pp. 19–33). New York: Oxford University Press.

Greenhalgh, T. (2006). *How to read a paper: The basics of evidence-based medicine* (3rd ed.). London: BMJ Publishing Group.

Greenhalgh, T., Robert, G., Macfarlane, F., Bate, P., & Kyriakidou, O. (2004). Diffusion of innovations in service organizations: Systematic review and recommendations. *Milbank Quarterly*, *82*, 581–629.

Guyatt, G., & Rennie, D. (2002). *Users' guide to the medical literature: A manual for evidence-based clinical practice* (Evidence-Based Medicine Working Group Journal of the American Medical Association and Archives). Chicago: American Medical Association Press.

Hanley, B., Truesdale, A., King, A., Elbourne, D., & Chalmers, I. (2001). Involving consumers in designing, conducting, and interpreting randomised controlled trials: Questionnaire survey. *British Medical Journal, 322,* 519–523.

Haynes, R. B., Devereaux, P. J., & Guyatt, G. H. (2002, March/April). Clinical expertise in the era of evidence-based medicine and patient choice [Editorial]. *ACP Journal Club, 136*(A11), 1–7.

Henggeler, S. W., Schoenwald, S. K., Borduin, C. M., & Swenson, C. C. (2006). Methodological critique and meta-analysis as Trojan horse. *Children and Youth Services Review, 28,* 447–457.

Higgins, J. P. T., & Green, S. (Eds.). (2005, March). Cochrane handbook for systematic reviews of interventions 4.2.4. In *Cochrane Library* (Vol. 2). Chichester, West Sussex, England: Wiley.

Hogarth, R. M. (2001). *Educating intuition.* Chicago: University of Chicago Press.

Jacobson, J. W., Foxx, R. M., & Mulick, J. A. (Eds.). (2005). *Controversial therapies for developmental disabilities: Fads, fashion, and science in professional practice.* Mahwah, NJ: Erlbaum.

Kluger, M. P., Alexander, G., & Curtis, P. A. (2002). *What works in child welfare.* Washington, DC: Child Welfare League of America Press.

Lacasse, J. R., & Gomory, T. (2003). Is graduate social work education promoting a critical approach to mental health practice? *Journal of Social Work Education, 39,* 383–408.

Lehman, A. F., Goldman, H. H., Dixon, L. B., & Churchill, R. (2004). *Evidence-based mental health treatments and services: Examples to inform public policy.* New York: Millbank Memorial Fund.

Lilienfeld, S. O., Lynn, S. J., & Lohr, J. M. (Eds.). (2003). *Science and pseudoscience in clinical psychology.* New York: Guilford Press.

Lindsey, D. (2004). *The welfare of children* (2nd ed.). New York: Oxford University Press.

Littell, J. H. (2005). Lessons from a systematic review of effects of multisystemic therapy. *Children and Youth Services Review, 27,* 445–463.

Littell, J. H. (2006). The case for multisystemic therapy: Evidence or orthodoxy? [Letter to the editor]. *Children and Youth Services Review, 28,* 458–472.

Littell, J. H., Popa, M., & Forsythe, B. (2005). Multisystemic therapy for social, emotional, and behavioral problems in youth aged 10–17. In *Cochrane Database of Systematic Reviews* (Vol. 3). Chichester, West Sussex, England: Wiley.

MacCoun, R. (1998). Biases in the interpretation and use of research results. *Annual Review of Psychology, 49,* 259–287.

McCord, J. (2003). Cures than harm: Unanticipated outcomes of crime prevention programs. *The Annals of the American Academy of Political and Social Science, 587,* 16–30.

Mullen, E. J., & Bacon, W. (2004). A survey of practitioner adoption and implementation of practice guidelines and evidence-based treatments. In A. R. Roberts & K. Yeager (Eds.), *Evidence-based practice manual: Research and outcome measures in health and human services* (pp. 210–218). New York: Oxford University Press.

Nathan, P. E., & Gorman, J. M. (2002). *A guide to treatments that work* (2nd ed.). New York: Oxford University Press.

National Association of Social Workers. (1999). *Code of ethics.* Silver Spring, MD: Author.

Norcross, J. C., Beutler, L. E., & Levant, R. F. (Eds.). (2006). *Evidence-based practices in mental health: Debate and dialogue on the fundamental questions.* Washington, DC: American Psychological Association.

O'Brien, M. A., Freemantle, N., Oxman, A. D., Wolf, F., Davis, D. A., & Herrin, J. (2001). Continuing education meetings and workshops: Effects on professional practice and health care outcomes. In *Cochrane Database in Systematic Review* (Issue 1). Chichester, West Sussex, England: Wiley.

O'Conner, A. M., Stacey, D., Entwistle, V., Rovner, D., Holmers-Rovner, M., Tait, V., et al. (2001). Decision aids for people facing health treatment or screening decisions (Cochrane Review). In *Cochrane Database of Systematic Reviews* (Issue 3). Chichester, West Sussex, England: Wiley.

Ofshe, R., & Watters, E. (1994). *Making monsters: False memories, psychotherapy, and sexual hysteria.* New York: Scribner.

Oxman, A. D., & Flottorp, S. (1998). An overview of strategies to promote implementation of evidence based health care. In C. Silagy & A. Haines (Eds.), *Evidence based practice in primary care* (pp. 91–109). London: BMJ Publishing Group.

Oxman, A. D., & Guyatt, G. H. (1993). The science of reviewing research. In K. S. Warren & F. Mosteller (Eds.), *Doing more good than harm: The evaluation of health care interventions* (pp. 125–133). New York: New York Academy of Sciences.

Oxman, A. D., Thomson, M. A., Davis, D., & Haynes, R. B. (1995). No magic bullets: A systematic review of 102 trials of interventions to improve professional practice. *Canadian Medical Association Journal, 153*, 1423–1431.

Paul, R. (1993). *Critical thinking: What every person needs to survive in a rapidly changing world* (3rd ed.). Sonoma, CA: Foundation for Critical Thinking. Available from www.criticalthinking .org.

Pekkala, E., & Merinder, L. (2004). Psychoeducation for schizophrenia (Cochrane Review). In *Cochrane Library* (Vol. 4). Chichester, West Sussex, England: Wiley.

Popper, K. (1994). *The myth of the framework: In defense of science and rationality* (M. A. Notturno, Ed.). New York: Routledge.

Popper, K. (1998). *The world of parmenides: Essays on the pre-Socratic enlightenment.* New York: Routledge.

Reason, J. (1997). *Managing the risks of organizational accidents.* Brookfield, VT: Ashgate.

Reason, J. (2001). Understanding adverse events: The human factor. In C. Vincent (Ed.), *Clinical risk management: Enhancing patient safety* (2nd ed., pp. 9–30). London: BMJ Publishing Group.

Rose, S., Bisson, J., Churchill, R., & Wessely, S. (2000). Psychological debriefing for preventing post traumatic stress disorder (PTSD). In *Cochrane Database in Systematic Reviews* (Issue 1). Chichester, West Sussex, England: Wiley.

Rosen, A., Proctor, E. K., Morrow-Howell, N., & Staudt, M. (1995). Rationales for practice decisions: Variations in knowledge use by decision task and social work service. *Research on Social Work Practice, 15*, 501–523.

Rosenthal, T. (1994). Science and ethics in conducting, analyzing, and reporting psychological research. *Psychological Science, 5*, 127–134.

Rubin, A., & Parrish, D. (2007). Problematic phrases in the conclusions of published outcome studies: Implications for evidence-based practice. *Research on Social Work Practice, 17*, 334–347.

Sackett, D. L., Richardson, W. S., Rosenberg, W., & Haynes, R. B. (1997). *Evidence-based medicine: How to practice and teach EBM.* New York: Churchill Livingstone.

Sackett, D. L., Rosenberg, W. M. C., Gray, J. A. M., Haynes, R. B., & Richardson, W. S. (1996). Evidence-based medicine: What it is and what it isn't [Editorial]. *British Medical Journal, 312*, 71–72.

Sackett, D. L., Straus, S. E., Richardson, W. C., Rosenberg, W., & Haynes, R. M. (2000). *Evidence-based medicine: How to practice and teach EBM* (2nd ed.). New York: Churchill Livingstone.

Sarnoff, S. K. (2001). *Sanctified snake oil: The effect of junk science on public policy.* Westport, CT: Praeger.

Schulz, K. F., Chalmers, I., Hayes, R. J., & Altman, D. G. (1995). Empirical evidence of bias: Dimensions of methodological quality associated with estimates of treatment effects in controlled trials. *Journal of the American Medical Association, 273*, 408–412.

Schwarz, L. M., & Woloshin, S. (2007). Participation in mammography screening: Women should be encouraged to decide what is right for them, rather than being told what to do. *British Medical Journal, 335*, 731–732.

Sharpe, V. A., & Faden, A. I. (1998). *Medical harm: Historical, conceptual, and ethical dimensions of iatrogenic illness.* New York: Cambridge University Press.

Sheldon, B., & Chilvers, R. (2000). *Evidence-based social care: A study of prospects and problems.* Lyme Regis: Russell House.

Sinclair, J. C., Cook, R. J., Guyatt, G. H., Pauker, S. G., & Cook, D. J. (2001). When should an effective treatment be used? Derivation of the threshold number needed to treat and the minimum event rate for treatment. *Journal of Clinical Epidemiology, 54*, 253–262.

Straus, S. E., & McAlister, D. C. (2000). Evidence-based medicine: A commentary on common criticisms. *Canadian Medical Journal, 163*, 837–841.

Straus, S. E., Richardson, W. S., Glasziou, P., & Haynes, R. D. (2005). *Evidence-based medicine: How to practice and teach EBP* (3rd ed.). New York: Churchill Livingston.

Thornton, H., Edwards, A., & Baum, M. (2003). Women need better information about routine mammography. *British Medical Journal, 327*, 101–103.

Valenstein, E. S. (1986). *Great and desperate cures: The rise and decline of psychosurgey and other medical treatments for mental illness.* New York: Basic Books.

Wampold, B. E. (2006). The psychotherapist. In J. C. Norcross, L. E. Beutler, & R. F. Levant (Eds.), *Evidence-based practices in mental health: Debate and dialogue on the fundamental questions* (pp. 202–207). Washington, DC: American Psychological Association.

Wennberg, J. E. (2002). Unwarranted variations in healthcare delivery: Implications for academic medical centers. *British Medical Journal, 325*, 961–964.

Chapter 2

INTERVIEWING SKILLS

Francis J. Turner

Regardless of where we might find ourselves in today's world and regardless to whom we were speaking, a component of their image of the social worker would most probably be someone who talks to others. Indeed, whether a correct or full picture of today's social worker, it is true that much of the work of a modern social worker is to talk to people about their problems or problems of others and help them with those problems. Talking to people in a formal and purposeful way is called interviewing and it is the skills of interviewing that are discussed in this chapter.

But social workers are not the only people who interview. In fact, to survive in today's world, no matter who we are, we have to be able to interview if by interview we mean a purposeful conversation. In the complex situations in which most us live, in our daily activities, we need to be able to open a conversation, to listen to others, to ask questions, to begin, to control, to focus, to refocus, and to end. Probably we rarely think of our mundane, daily, conversations as having all of these parts. However, if we studied them in detail we would find each of these facets of an interview to be present. We would also notice that we and the people with whom we converse implement the various tasks and roles in interviewing in a broadly differential qualitative way.

But not everyone is a social worker. We need to ask then what is so special about what social workers do in interviewing that sets us apart? Much of what we do in our interviewing activities is done by everybody else in the world in one way or another. Social workers differ in that we do these things in a more structured, targeted, and conscious manner with specific goals and specific deliberate strategies. But because of the similarity to the day-to-day components of our interviews, one of our biggest challenges is to learn to make skilled use of interviews to help persons, our clients, to achieve better and more satisfying psychosocial functioning.

It is because we do what everybody else does—talk to others in a purposeful way—that it is challenging to talk about our interviewing in social work in an analytic professional way. But even when we talk about professional interviewing and attempt to set it apart from our day-to-day interaction with the person at the corner market, there is still a great lack of clarity as to what makes our interviewing different. What is it that distinguishes us and makes us more skilled in this process than someone we meet socially?

There is great conviction among people from a wide variety of professions that professional interviewing is different and does require special skills. Also it is commonly believed that we can learn how to interview in a professional manner and can learn how to make our interviews more effective. A visit to any bookstore will show that there are many experts in professional interviewing in many different areas. This is manifest in the wide range of readily available books of the "how to" variety: how to interview for a job, how to make a good impression, how to win friends and influence people, how to sell a car, how to talk to your physician, how to talk to your teenager, how to talk to your partner, and so on.

However, in spite of the universal requirement that we all need to know how to interview, there is still not a great amount of empirical data as to what makes for an effective interview, that is, one that achieves its goal in a mutually satisfactory and timely way. There is an abundance of information about what makes for effective interviewing in social work. However, the majority of this material falls into the category of practice wisdom and is written by practitioners known to be good interviewers or acknowledged to be so.

This is not to disparage practice wisdom as a source of knowledge, especially when there is a high degree of consensus about interviewing between and among persons identified as skilled interviewers. Indeed, not only is there consensus within our profession, but there is also a high degree of consensus among professions, especially those we usually designate as the helping professions.

The test of quality interviewing rests with the outcome of our interviewing. Do we, for the most part in our practice, attain the goal of our interviews? Are our clients more effective and satisfied human beings as a result of our interactions with them?

Much research has been carried out on the effectiveness of social work intervention, and although there is still much to be done, the overall findings are that the interventions of social workers have a positive effect on their clients (Brothers, 2002; Thomlison, 1984.) That is, social work does work. Social workers do help their clients. Thus, what we do in our interviews must be helpful. If we begin from this basic assumption, then our task in this chapter is to try and identify what makes a good or effective interview.

By having an overview on what makes a good interview, we can apply this overview to ourselves. You can look at your personal profile of interviewing strategies and ask what is it you do best and what are your areas of difficulty? Does changing your style change the impact you have on your clients? It there anything you can do to improve your efficiency? What can you do to have a different impact?

DEFINITION

In beginning our discussion, we first define just what we mean by a social work interview. Then we look at its parts and formats. From the perspective of social work, we define an interview as a verbal exchange between one or more clients and one or more social workers in which the social workers involved draw on their knowledge, skills, and techniques to better understand and make judgments as to how to assist a client to enhance his or her psychosocial functioning.

These judgments include an assessment of the person (such things as what are their significant system resources and stresses, what do they hope to attain from this process, and how can I or others be of assistance?). Included as well is the process of identifying what and where resources exist to which I have access either directly or indirectly that will assist the client.

Everyone with whom a social worker has an interview is not a client in a technical sense. However, we use the term *client* in our discussion here in a very broad sense to refer to anyone with whom a social worker is interacting with.

INTERVIEWING AS AN ART

Quality and effective interviewing is not a science. Rather it is an art in which we learn to make use of our knowledge, skills, and techniques to attain the therapeutic goals we and the clients seek. Much of what we know about interviewing comes from other related professions. That is, we learn much from colleagues who share with us their understanding of what makes for good interviewing. Also, in developing the art of interviewing, we draw on what we have learned and what we can learn from formal research.

The art of interviewing focuses on communications among people, both verbal and nonverbal. Each of us interacts with others in different ways. However, it is important to remember that interviewing is an art based on knowledge that is practiced by professionals. Thus, as with other professional activities, there are things we can learn from each other that will help us to make our individual skills more creative and effective. Nevertheless, there will be differences in the way we make use of these skills.

A skilled pianist or painter learns much from other pianists and painters about the theory and techniques of making music or producing paintings. Yet in using this knowledge and skill, what is produced by each artist carries with it the mark or the individuality of the artist involved. The art of interviewing is no different.

CHALLENGES OF INTERVIEWING

One of the challenges facing us as we attempt to enhance our interviewing skills is finding a balance between spontancity and very deliberative interviewing and the use of interviewing techniques. This skill comes from practice. Just as practice for the athlete or artist result in skills that, when well learned, become spontaneous and automatic when playing or painting. Usually it is only after completing an artistic piece that they are aware of making use of some other technique. But it was only because they knew and understood the technique well that they were able to make use of it in a spontaneous way. So, too, in our interviewing. What appears to be a smooth almost seamless process of professional interviewing is in fact the skillful and spontaneous use of a wide range of strategies and techniques.

A further challenge facing anyone wishing to develop effective interviewing skills in social work is to develop that special kind of discipline that permits us to push the content and process of one interview from our consciousness and turn at once to another one just as complex, serious, and demanding as the one before. This is a highly important skill that we need to develop so we can turn our full attention to our next client. We need to be free for a time from the critical diagnostic and assessment processes we needed and used to attend in an earlier interview so we can apply these same skills and processes to our next interview.

An important component of this needed skill is to become adept at brief summary recording immediately following an interview in which the essential data of the interview and our initial diagnostic thinking are addressed. Rarely does it happen in practice that we go directly from one interview to the next without some kind of break, albeit a short one. Some practitioners find it useful to make use of short-term meditative skills between interviews. Such a process aids in helping to turn from a prior interview, to relax briefly to prepare for the next interview, and to clear or refocus our attending skills. This is necessary to ensure that our next client also receives our full ability to listen, to hear, and to understand.

Thus learning to listen is the sine qua non of interviewing. It is essential that we convey to the client that we are hearing what is being said. This ability to listen and to convey to someone that we are listening is one of the attributes of a professional interview that clearly separates it from many social conversations where much of what is said is not heard or even listened to.

THE HELPING RELATIONSHIP

Interviewing in social work has frequently been described as the process of establishing, maintaining, and drawing on the latent potential of the helping relationship. This term, *the helping relationship*, is frequently found in the literature and is a concept endowed with great respect. At times, discussions of the helping relationship convey the feeling that this relationship has almost a quasi-mystical quality to it. The term indicates a belief and understanding of the power that is present in the worker/client relationship. The goal of this relationship is to seek to have the client experience the social worker as a safe, understanding, empathetic, knowledgeable person able to be helpful in a wide range of psychosocial situations.

The helping relationship is understood to be very much a one-way process from the perspective of gratification. That is, it is something that exists for the client with no expectation of gratification or rewards for the worker. (This, of course, apart from the gratification of experiencing a job well done.) It is this quality that marks the professional relationship as a separate experience from other relationships.

Colleagues of a psychodynamic orientation view this helping relationship from the perspective of the concept of *transference*. This is a Freudian term that describes the process in which the client begins to view and to respond to the therapist as if he or she were someone significant from their past, most frequently a parental figure, and presumes a broad range of potential unconscious wishes and desires (Coady, 2002, pp. 122–124; Perlman, 1971, pp. 76–78). Others minimize the importance or even the existence of transference and view the helping relationship as still powerful but viewed from a more present-centered, real perspective.

In the early development of social work therapy, there was great interest invested in identifying just what were the factors that went into the development of this all important helping relationship, which is viewed as the basis of effective interviewing and the achievement of enhanced psychosocial growth. Carl Rogers, who was both a social worker and a psychologist, contributed greatly to a helpful and clear understanding of how this process developed and what requisite factors were needed to ensure the successful development of this relationship.

Dr. Rogers was very committed to research that examined therapeutic relationships with a view to identifying their essential qualities. Similar important work was done by both Perlman (1971) and Hollis (1972). Within this work, there is a remarkable degree of consensus about these qualities. These are usually described as warmth, acceptance, empathy caring, concern, and genuineness. These six attributes are seen as the qualities that need to be present for the establishment of the helping relationship. They are not referred to as techniques, however, because techniques describe the ways and strategies we use to achieve these attributes.

It has long been taught that each of us as therapists needs to learn to develop this profile of qualities in our work with clients and to find, both from our colleagues and in the idiosyncratic use of ourselves, ways that lead the client to experience these qualities. Again, although there is great stress on understanding these qualities or necessary conditions for the establishment of a therapeutic climate, there has not been a great deal of research that aims at identifying specific techniques for doing so apart from some general strategies for effective interviewing. There is much written about such things as eye contact, body language, being attentive, reflecting back our understanding of what has been said, offering support, and making use of mild challenges and the discreet use of opinion and authority.

TECHNIQUES OR VALUES

Authenticity is an important issue that the social work literature seems not to have viewed as important, or perhaps avoided as heretical, in looking at the necessary qualities of the helping relationship.

The question is whether these sought-for feelings, attitudes, and qualities need to actually be present in the therapist or is it sufficient for the client to feel or believe that they are present? In a less value-laden way, the question can be put differently: Do we have to have internalized all of these qualities ourselves? Do they need to be a part of our psyche? Or can we learn to feign them?

Social work has devoted much attention over the decades to the development of our body of knowledge. A great portion of this has included a conviction that there is a set of values intrinsic in each social worker. Admirable as this may be, is it realistic to expect this value set in each member of the profession? How would we test for or measure such a set?

Is it not sufficient that a profession operates from a set of values to which its members subscribe and work to demonstrate their existence in their practice? This is a viewpoint highly unacceptable in the profession because it is strongly believed by many that to be an effective interviewer, it is also necessary to be a helping therapist. This value set needs be a part of each of us.

A different position says that effective interviewing consists of a set of specific actions that can be learned and that differentially impact the client. Our skill, and hence effectiveness as a practitioner, then hinges on our ability to project the necessary qualities mentioned earlier whether we feel them or subscribe to them in our lives. Could we, for example, thoroughly dislike a client and still be a highly effective therapist for them by means of our ability to utilize a cluster of techniques that conveys empathy, concern, genuineness, and so on?

Before we reject this position, we need to remember the power of the actor who can convey to us in a most convincing way virtually every human emotion and, from the stage, make us both love him and hate him. We have all attended theatrical performances where we were brought to tears by the skill of the actor or actress. Similarly we hear from time to time of sociopathic persons with no feelings for their clients (apart from perhaps curiosity) who function as social workers or physicians and who, even when discovered, still have strong support from their clients and patients.

This question is raised not to question the importance of the sought-for qualities of effective interviewing in which we believe and which we seek to instill and convey to our students and colleagues. Nor am I suggesting that we should minimize the importance of our profession's value base but rather continue to seek to reflect it to our clients and reinforce it in ourselves.

This discussion is raised to bring an added focus to the question of technique as a topic that is not considered of great importance in the social work interviewing literature. Although some research indicates that technique only appears to contribute minimally to the effectiveness of an interview (Coady, 2002), it may be that we have underestimated to a great extent the fact that everything we do in an interview is a discrete and describable action, that it is a technique (Fischer, 1978, pp. 60–61). If we are interested in addressing more research to improve our interviewing effectiveness, we need to pay much more attention to the minutiae of our interventions—that is, the very complex yet varied actions that make up an interview. If we continue to see effective interviewing as the projection of a set of values and qualities, it would mean that anyone who had the desired set of attitudes and characteristics would make an effective interviewer, and those without these values would be incompetent interviewers, regardless of technique.

But all of us know from our practices that although the conveying of positive attitudes is important, there is much more to be learned about interviewing. We are aware that some colleagues are much more effective in working with certain kinds of clients. We know that there are techniques to be learned that facilitate the development of the relationship. We soon experience in our practice that different clients respond to different strategies in our interviewing. We understand that particular problems and difficulties better respond to some types of intervention than others. Thus, we know that it is important that we devote much more time and attention to studying how to make our interviewing more effective, that is, how to enhance our interviewing skills.

AN ETHICAL ISSUE

If we begin to put more emphasis on technique than attitudes or values, then we need to address a related ethical issue. To ensure our effectiveness, we have a responsibility to assess the differential impact of various techniques. However, this raises the question: How do I try out a technique that has not been tested or proven to be useful in practice? How do I, or rather how does the profession, test out new techniques without using them on clients? This is not unlike the challenge faced by the medical profession in regard to new medications. How do we know if a medication is going to do what it is supposed to do if we do not try it out? But how do we find out if it is going to be effective without trying it out on patients?

We really have not addressed this in social work principally because we have tended to see interviewing as a process between the social worker and the involved clients rather than seeing it as a series of individual actions or techniques. Our literature is replete with descriptions of the many techniques or activities that colleagues have used in their practice. These usually include descriptions of the presumed impact of the technique. It is in this way that the range of techniques expands in our profession. However, as mentioned earlier, there is often little evaluation of the import of the technique apart from descriptions of its apparent impact as viewed by the author of the technique in regard to a specific group of clients or problems.

But let us not be too critical. We need to remember that there are evaluative processes going on and reported in the body of the professional literature. As mentioned, it is through the publication of professional literature that new techniques get promulgated or old techniques get evaluated.

There appear to be at least three kinds of evaluation: There is the evaluation of the expert, that is, persons well known in the profession who comment on some interviewing technique that has been described in the literature and either support it as a positive contribution or challenge its usefulness and appropriateness. Second, there is the less frequent but highly necessary article that formally assesses the use of some techniques. As we get increasingly sophisticated in our research, this type of article is going to be one of the important ways in which interviewing techniques will be evaluated. Third, there is the response of the profession to the announcement or description of a new interviewing technique—the sociopolitical factor. There may be general acceptance of some technique, or there may be rejection of it as not being appropriate for the profession or not helpful to clients. Or there may be debate about it as practitioners express differing opinions as to the perceived utility and/or appropriateness of what is being suggested. But as yet there is no formal process that gives legitimization or approbation to individual techniques.

Certainly all of these evaluative methods for interviewing techniques are important. They do and will help us expand our knowledge of what makes for effective interviewing. However, encapsulated within this type of evaluation by the expertise of the profession is the need to address the ethical question as to how to establish whether a particular technique in interviewing is helpful without trying it out on clients. In the meantime, we need to continue our pragmatic approach that says we will try things out and see what happens with the understanding that if it doesn't work or if it appears to be harmful in some situations we will no longer use it. We do this when we try one strategy with a client, see that it is ineffective, and move immediately to a different one.

At the same time, we need to keep very much before us our essential need to move on two fronts. The first, that we focus strong efforts on identifying what are the component parts of an interview. What are the individual pieces of the interview from which the process is shaped. In other words, what are the techniques that are used in interviewing? Second, once we are clear about the segments that make up an interview, we need to focus efforts on attempting to assess the differential impact of each segment. In talking of the segments or pieces of an interview, we must continue to follow the example of colleagues in other professions who seek to identify the smallest segments or units of their sphere of study. Already some of this is happening; for example, there are articles that discuss the importance of such things as body position and eye contact in an interview.

INTERVIEWING MODALITIES

We next look at the principal kinds of interviews in which we become involved as practitioners and comment very briefly on some differences in each. In this discussion, we focus of the types of interviews in which there is only one social worker involved. This with the understanding that there are situations when, for various therapeutic reasons, we would have more than one therapist conducting the interview. Again we will take as given that we are talking about our interactions with clients, realizing that there will also be interviews with other persons in a client's life, and with other professionals.

From this perspective, we can talk about one-to-one interviews, dyadic interviews where there are two persons and one social worker involved, family interviews, and group interviews. Although there is much that is common to each of these interviews, there are important differences that need to be discussed if we are to make optimum use of each modality.

One-to-One Interviews

This is the type that we think of most often when discussing interviewing. From the social worker's perspective, it has the advantage of only having to focus on one person, although there may be ghosts of significant others in the room. Having only a single client lets us adjust the setting to meet the client's preferences and needs with respect to comfort, furnishings, sound light, and so on. The client can be assured of confidentiality in that no one other than the therapist will hear the content. Also the client can be assured of privacy from the perspective of what is discussed as well as the emotional level and emotional response that may accompany any disclosure or content. The client has the social worker all to him- or herself and need not share the social worker's interest or attention as happens in other modalities. The social worker can adjust the speed and content of the interview as well as the level of speech and intensity of content and direct the interview, as appropriate, to be where the client is and where and when the client is ready to go or not go. In addition, the therapist can elect to use techniques that are targeted to the individuality of the client.

However, there are limitations to this form of interviewing. Interviewing one person limits the depth of the information provided. There is always the possibility that the client is misrepresenting a situation either deliberately or as he or she views it or believes it to be. There is the further challenge that may come from the balance of power, that is, the client may attribute a negative factor of power and control to the situation that inhibits his or her ability to invest fully into a therapeutic relationship.

Joint or Dyadic Interviewing

This is a modality of interviewing about which the least has been written and perhaps that has been practiced the least. The majority of the writing about this modality focuses on couple interviewing, that is, situations where the clients know each other and are in some kind of relationship; often the clients are married couples. However, there are many other dyadic situations where this type of interviewing could be and should be used, such as two siblings, two friends, or even two strangers who have gone through a similar experience or have something in common.

The advantages of this type of interviewing is that from the client's perspective there can be a sense of enhanced power that minimizes the perceived power of the therapist and gives the client the feeling that he or she is better able to influence the relationship. Some clients may be fearful of the prospect of a one-on-one situation and thus choose to have someone else present.

This is a somewhat different situation than when both persons in the interview are designated clients. Even here both persons present may feel more at ease and more able to share material. There is an advantage in having two perceptions or viewpoints on the various presenting situations that may comprise the interview content. From the perspective of the therapist, it helps to understand the situation better from two sources. It can also be helpful from the client's viewpoint in that it may present him or her with a different perspective on a situation that may be helpful both in understanding it and in seeking alternative solutions.

But as with each methodology, there are limitations. First, as is known from group theory, triadic groups are difficult to manage because there is always the risk of two of the members pairing against the other. This could be the two clients in power struggles with the therapist or a more complex pairing when the therapist and one client form, or fall into, a relationship that excludes the other client or when one client assumes the role of assistant therapist. The struggle between two clients need not be a power struggle but could reflect that each of the clients is vying for the attention of the therapist, and if this takes on elements of transference it can become very complex. A further difficulty for the social worker is keeping a balance between the attention given to the problems or wishes of each of the clients.

As mentioned, one of the strengths of this type of interviewing is that it provides an opportunity for two clients to mutually aid each other by sharing in understanding and finding mutually satisfying solutions. However, when this process gets off track, a great deal of the therapist's time and efforts can get taken up in keeping the relationship moving forward.

Family Interviews

One of the developments in social work practice that quickly achieved high status in the late 1950s, was that of family therapy—a modality that involved having the whole family present for the interview. The theory and method drew heavily on systems theory and the idea of mutually influencing subsystems. This reflected the theoretical understanding that many problems that clients brought to us involved difficulties in family dynamics and that these were best dealt with when the entire family was present and all viewed as the client. As social workers became more comfortable with this form of treatment, it was found to be a powerful medium for family change.

Family therapy views the family as a system in which each member carries specific roles. Thus by having all family members involved in the process of dealing with problems as family issues, much progress could be made. Everyone in the family could have an opportunity to speak and to hear how others view various family situations. This modality makes it difficult for individual family members or subsets of the family to hide, scapegoat, or to overinfluence or overblame the situation. The family interview provides a safe place where family matters can be discussed openly.

It is a type of interviewing that requires considerable comfort and discipline on the part of the interviewer. The family is a powerful unit that can exclude the social worker from family dynamics and family secrets. Family dynamics are very powerful and a social worker can feel very isolated by the family even though the family has sought help. There is also the risk of the therapist being co-opted by some members of the family or some subsets in the family. Rivalries can develop within the family for the attention and approval of the social worker, and such rivalries and power struggles can complicate the process of family healing. Because of the complexities of family dynamics, much work has been done by having family interviews observed by another therapist or group of therapists as a way of keeping the process on track.

Group Interviews

Working with groups has long been recognized as an essential part of social work practice. Thus the process of group interviewing is a most important modality. Group interviews are a powerful medium to achieve a broad range of objectives, such as helping a group achieve a particular external goal or helping the members of a group in some personal, therapeutic, or educative way. For many people, the possibility of working on a particular project with others is highly appealing while for others a group is intimidating and inhibiting.

The strengths of this type of interviewing are many. As a group begins to develop its identity, a strong sense of group loyalty and group support that can be extremely helpful to all its members can quickly develop. Within a group, members can learn much about themselves and their own potential by listening to others and by experiencing the power of the group. In addition, people can find strength in themselves when they are able to help others.

Successful group interviewing requires an understanding of group processes and their complexities and an ability to assess the functioning of the group as well as the individual members of which it is comprised. As group leader, it is important to stress the development of the group process as the medium of growth and development and to avoid falling into or being pushed into roles that work against this.

Groups can have many goals and purposes and thus are a constant challenge for the social worker leading the group. The leader must be cognizant of the established goals of the group and be aware that goals can change as the group develops. Shifts in goals and purpose may be in a direction that is not acceptable to all group members. As with other forms of multiple client situations, individual members of the group or subsets of the group may develop complex relationships or power relationships with either the group leader or other group members. Thus, there is an ongoing responsibility for the group leader to be aware of the relationship factors that are present and to ensure that individuals or subsystems are not being ignored or harmed. Not everyone is able to work with groups and a requisite skill for the social worker is to assess accurately this capability and interest.

OTHER MODALITIES

Telephone Interviewing

Another form of interviewing that requires attention in this discussion of interviewing skills is that of telephone interviews.

In recent years, the spread of the availability of the telephone worldwide has been dramatic. More and more of our interactions with others are by telephone. We are often unwilling listeners to others' cell phone conversations, increasing our awareness of the necessity for privacy in our own conversations. In our practice, we find that many more of our interactions with clients are by telephone, and the need for privacy on both ends of the conversation is important.

As with each interviewing modality, there are strengths and limitations. Clearly, time is one advantage in that the phone can put the client and therapist in contact very quickly. This often permits issues to be dealt with in a prompt and convenient way for both parties. For some of our clients, there is an element of safety in using the phone. For some, the phone gives them an element of power and control because they can terminate an interview at any time. Some people are able to talk about very intimate or charged material by phone, talking from a comfortable setting surrounded by their various security objects. These may be topics they are not able to talk about in a face-to-face interview situation. One other potential of the phone is that it can greatly facilitate involving more than one person in an interview; this may not be possible if we are trying to set up an in-office situation. With our enhanced technology, it is possible to have several persons involved in conference calls.

However, there are also limitations to telephone interviews. Until recently, at least one of the difficulties about phone interviewing was that you could not see the client. We know that many of our cues in treatment come from our being able to observe the person(s) we are interviewing. However, even this is changing with the newer technology that permits you to see the person to whom you are speaking. Seeing a person's face, however, does not allow you to observe their body fully, so you may be missing important cues such as foot tapping or hand twisting.

Neither does a phone interview permit you to control the setting in which the interview takes place, at least from the perspective of the client. This could result in situations where the client is in a situation of high disruption making the ability to discuss important matters or concentrate very difficult, if not impossible. Although most therapists prefer a face-to-face situation, we should be open to the potential of the phone as a modality of interviewing.

Video Interviews

A further type of interview follows from the discussion of phone interviews especially phones with video capacities—video interviews. As mentioned with phone interviews, advances in technology have greatly facilitated the availability and cost of interactive video conferencing. This format of interviewing allows us to interview individuals, dyads, families, and groups from a distance. In many situations, this is the only way that it is possible to be in contact with some clients. This may be of special importance in rural settings or where clients are in distant places and a contact is needed. Experience with this format of interviewing gives the therapist the sense of being in the direct presence of the client(s), and very intense and complex situations can be addressed.

Even with the enhanced capabilities and availabilities of this interviewing format, the persons involved in the interview have to be at or go to a specific setting where the appropriate resources are available. This can mean that people are not in a therapeutic interviewing setting but more of a studio. This raises the question of confidentiality because technicians may be required. In addition, the setting may lack a sense of intimacy and confidentiality. There are many potential uses for this type of resource; and with growing availability of these resources, we need to develop and promulgate as much experience as possible about how to make maximum use of this modality of interviewing.

USE OF INTERPRETERS

As our caseloads become increasingly diverse, we may be dealing with clients who do not speak a language in which we are fluent. Most of us at some time or another have had to conduct interviews through an interpreter. Most of us have found such interviews to be very unsatisfactory and difficult for several reasons. Often persons we have called on to translate may have the language ability that we need but do not understand the role of the interpreter. However, because some of the world's most sensitive issues are negotiated through the services of interpreters, we know that it is possible to deal with the most complex and highly charged material using an interpreter.

What is essential is to understand that interpreting is a profession, and when you conduct an interview with the assistance of a *professional interpreter* much can be accomplished. It is probable that there are a few situations when we cannot deal with the assistance of a professional interpreter. However, we need to gather and share considerably more experience with this format.

Unfortunately, for many of us the reality will be that professional interpreting services are not available, and we will need to rely on persons with language skills but not interpreting skills. In these situations, we need to make strenuous efforts to ensure that persons functioning as interpreters understand their role—they are to be our voice and the client's voice only; they must be competent in the needed language skills; they must be acceptable to the client from a sociopolitical perspective; and they must understand that they are to convey what is being said by you and the client *without* embellishment, explanations, or side discussions either with the worker or the client.

It is equally important that the therapist understands the role of the interpreter and when this resource is needed so that consultative services are available to assist in orienting persons who may have the language facility but not the interpreter skills.

As mentioned in the discussion of dyadic interviewing, one of the challenges of using an interpreter in a one-on-one client situation is that it creates a triadic situation with all the potential difficulties that go with it. Nevertheless, this format of interviewing is rapidly becoming a reality in all areas of practice, and social work could well lead the way in developing therapeutic expertise in its use.

INTERVIEW OVERVIEW

Not only do we need to be skilled in each of these interviewing modalities, we need to learn to use them differentially. We still have much to learn in this area. At present, therapists seem to differ in the use of modalities more from their interviewing preferences rather than clients' needs and preferences. And perhaps more importantly in today's practice, we are becoming increasingly aware that cultural differences and all forms of diversity have important implications on what interviewing skills, techniques, and knowledge we use.

INTERVIEW SETTING

In spite of a great deal of experience in interviewing, we have given minimal attention to the physical settings in which we interview. From time to time in the literature, there have been suggestions as to what physical resources contribute to effective interviewing but there appears to have been little effort made to address this important topic in anything but a cursory way. There seems to have been an idea that since the essence of the interview was the establishment, maintenance, and utilization of the helping relationship, this is where we needed to focus. If we could do this well, then where we held the interview and how we equipped the area where we did the interview was less important. This seems to be reflected in a presumption that if you are a good interviewer, you can interview anywhere.

As we said at the outset, one of the most frequent human activities is the process of having conversations with others. We know that where we hold such conversations impacts considerably on the quality and comfort of a conversation. Thus, because an interview is simply a focused conversation with the purpose of helping one of the participants, we assume this would also apply to an interview.

The following comments focus on the situation of a single client; however, they also apply to multiple client situations. Although we have conversations with one another in all kinds of settings, in matters of importance, if we have a choice, we prefer the setting to be comfortable. It would follow that where we interview professionally should also be a physically comfortable situation for both the client and the worker. This seems obvious. However, over the years, I have seen such an amazing range of uncomfortable chairs in waiting rooms and interviewing rooms that I have been led to conclude that for many of us comfort does not seem important. I disagree; even as basic a piece of equipment as the chairs need to be carefully considered. Because we are all different in our tastes and needs, I think it important that there be a choice of chairs for the client that provides comfort for different people. There still seems to be an attitude in some parts of the profession that where we practice and interview should not be too comfortable or attractive.

Another area of important consideration is where do we, the therapist, sit. In our culture, the across-the-desk position is often seen as a symbol of authority and hence presumed to be uncomfortable for the client and thus to be avoided. Thus, some therapists have gotten rid of their desk, viewing it as a barrier between them and the client and as a way of lessening any power issues that may be present without fully appreciating the dimensions of this issue.

However, we need to be careful not to blindly follow a set of rules. Even though for some the desk can be a power symbol, for others it is a safety barrier and indeed a desired barrier for some clients who need the protection of the desk at least until they have a better understanding of who we are and what the process is going to be like. One of the problems in any discussion of the "ideal" interviewing setting is that different things have different meanings for different people. This is especially so in our increasingly differentiated client population so that for some a desk would be an expected and desired part of an interviewing space. For others, it would be an unwelcome sign of authority.

The answer to this and similar kinds of questions is that we have a variety of possible seating arrangements in our offices that permit a choice for the client. If we are uncertain as to what the client would prefer, especially in regard to new clients, it is much easier to start with formality and move from a formal setting to a less formal one.

The offices in which we interview should assure privacy, confidentiality, and safety both for us and the client. Thus, as basic a thing as not having client files on our desks or obvious to the client is a facet of this privacy issue. (With more and more of our record keeping being in an electronic format, there is less of this risk.) The color of the walls and pictures and overall decor should convey warmth, competence, security, and safety as should all the furniture and furnishings. Washroom facilities should be convenient and private and their location known to the client. Telephone resources need be present but in a manner that ensures there are no unnecessary interruptions. Coat racks, a mirror, writing equipment for both parties, necessary forms, and reference materials should all be highly accessible.

The question of whether we should display our degrees and professional membership certification is often debated. It is a practice I encourage as a symbol of our qualifications and assurance of competence and legitimacy.

To add privacy, and for its soothing and relaxing qualities, many practitioners like having appropriate background music. Although there is abundant evidence that the proper music and the appropriate sound level does contribute to helping many persons relax, there are those who find music distracting and unprofessional; thus, it should be possible to turn it off.

We need also to be careful about having too much personal material in sight, such as family pictures. This can take away from a sense of privacy and some colleagues have suggested that having pictures of one's children could be a security risk. In addition, unhappily in this day of worldwide violence, there should also be some unobtrusive way of calling for help, such as a panic button of some sort.

The lighting in our offices is also important and considerable professional help is available to help us create the safe therapeutic mood that we seek. Once again, there should be a variety of lighting arrangements to set the tone we seek for individual clients.

Overall, if we really wish to establish as therapeutic a setting as possible, we need to devote much more time and attention to a study of all the physical factors that contribute to this process. In addition, we need to study in much more detail the differential importance of each.

What we must seek in our physical settings where we interview is as much diversity and flexibility as possible so that we are able to adjust the interview setting to suit the client and the situation. Much more data are required to assess both the importance of the setting in interviewing as well as how to vary the many aspects of an office setting to bring about the maximum desirable impact on the client.

In addition to the more formal office setting, we need to give attention *where* to conduct our interview. The majority of our discussion about setting has thus far related to the formal offices where we practice. However, there are other choices open to us where we may elect to interview, such as home visits, informal settings such as a coffee shop, or less structured settings such as a walk in the park or a visit to a museum. There are many opportunities open to us in this regard that we may choose for various therapeutic reasons. Each of these various settings offers us particular interviewing opportunities, yet each has its limitations.

The decision of where to do an interview in each case is a strategic move on our part and needs to be carefully thought through. It is much more complex than a value issue on our part. For example, deciding to meet a client for a cup of coffee in some downtown restaurant could greatly strengthen the relationship in a manner that permits the client to develop a more relaxed and trusting attitude. Also it could be totally misunderstood by the client and reenforce his or her view of the relationship as being something more than it is, a sign from us that we want something other than the therapist/patient relationship. Again, we have not directed sufficient attention to this aspect of interviewing nor studied the potential positives and negatives of our choice of location.

One area to which we have given some formal attention came from our experience in family therapy. In the early days of family therapy, the home visit was viewed as important.

Seeing where the family lived and seeing how they interacted in their home was viewed as having diagnostic and assessment utility on the part of the therapist. The home visit has the same positive potential for other modalities, such as couple and individual work.

Again, although it is a technique not without its risks of being misunderstood or in some instance of putting an unnecessary burden on the client, the use of home visits needs to be a strategic diagnostic decision rather than something we always choose to do or don't do.

TECHNIQUE

Throughout this discussion about interviewing, we have referred to the concept of technique. As mentioned earlier, it is our view that to date in our profession we have tended to view interviewing as a process in which a discrete number of procedures are used to develop, maintain, and utilize the helping relationship. This stress on process as the interaction between two people has led us to stress the responsibility of social workers to understand themselves, the effect of the client on them, and the tenor of the interaction. However, we need to recognize that by putting the stress on the relationship, we have overlooked that what goes on between two people in an interview consists of a series of discrete actions between the persons involved, that is, a series of techniques (Fischer, 1978). This position leads us to begin to consider interviewing as a series of actions that can be observed, individually manipulated, and ultimately measured and assessed for impact.

It is important to pay much more attention to technique than we have. Unfortunately, we have been less than precise about the meaning of the term *technique* and hence often use it imprecisely.

By technique, we mean the use in therapeutic practice of an ethical, observable action or object to achieve a particular therapeutic outcome. It is something that can be observed by others and can be replicated by others and has received a level of professional affirmation. We can view an interview as a series of such actions—as a series or combination of a cluster of techniques. Thus, we talk of such things as the empty chair, use of games, food, music, gifts, reflection, advice, and so on. In considering techniques, the qualities and characteristics of each needs to be understood to learn how to use them differentially. In so doing, we need to avoid a position that says if you want to accomplish this, do this. We need to understand the potential of each technique and learn to use it in our own idiosyncratic way for the good of the client.

We need to incorporate this thinking into our ideas of interviewing and learn to measure, not just report. What is critical for us is to begin to focus on the concept that an interview is a series of diverse yet discrete acts, that is, techniques, and to begin to identify these and focus more on evaluating their impact rather than only reporting on use of them in practice.

CONCLUSION

For over 100 years, social workers have been engaged in the process of professional interviewing. In this time, we have developed a rich repertoire of techniques and skills in their use. We know a great deal about interviewing and may of us are very good at it. The great majority of social workers become skilled interviewers in a very short time in practice. But they do so on almost a trial-and-error basis. Most of what we know is in the form of practice wisdom.

If we are going to become even more proficient and effective in the art and science of interviewing, we need to become more precise and objective. We need to be able to look at our interviews and identify what we did, why we did it, and with what resulted. We need to become more comfortable in having others look at our interviewing to enhance our ability to identify the techniques that had the most impact.

Because so much of the content of our work deals with the minutiae of our clients' everyday lives, we need to become more comfortable and skilled in making use of a much broader repertoire of the objects and processes of daily living. This will enrich our interviewing skills so that we can assist individuals, couples, groups, and families to achieve their optimum potential as humans in the complex societies in which we all live.

ADDITIONAL READINGS

Carrillo, D. F., & Thyer, B. A. (1994, Fall). Advanced standing and two-year program MSW students: An empirical investigation of foundation interviewing skills. *Social Work Education, 30,* 377–387.

Coady, N. F. (1991). The association between complex types of therapist intervention and outcomes in psychodynamic psychotherapy. *Research on Social Work Practice, 1,* 257–277.

Coady, N. F. (1995). A reflective/inductive model of practice: Emphasizing theory building for unique cases versus applying theory to practice. In G. Rogers (Ed.), *Social work field education: Views and visions* (pp. 139–151). Dubuque, IA: Kendall/Hunt.

Cournoyer, B. (1991). *The social work skills workbook.* Belmont, CA: Wadsworth.

De Jong, P., & Miller, S. D. (1995, November). How to interview for client strengths. *Social Work, 40*(6), 176–193.

Diggins, M. (2004). *Teaching and learning communication skills in social work education.* Social Care Institute for Excellence. London: Social Care Institute for Excellence. Available from www.scie.org.uk/.

Egan, G. (1994). *The skilled helper: A problem-management approach to helping.* Pacific Grove, CA: Brooks/Cole.

Epstein, L. (1990). *Talking and listening: A guide to the helping interview.* St. Louis, MO: Times Mirror/Mosby College Publishing.

Evans, D., Hearn, M., Uhlemann, M., & Ivey, A. (1998). *Essential interviewing: A programmed approach to effective communication* (5th ed.). Pacific Grove, CA: Brooks/Cole.

Fox, E., Nelson, M., & Bolman, W. (1969). The termination process: A neglected dimension in social work. *Social Work, 14*(4), 53–63.

Garrett, A. (1972). *Interviewing: Its principles and methods* (2nd rev. ed.). New York: Family Service Association of America.

Gelso, C., & Carter, J. (1985). The relationship in counseling and psychotherapy: Components, consequences, and theoretical antecedents. *Counseling Psychologist, 13,* 155–243.

Goldstein, H. (1990). The knowledge base of social work practice theory, wisdom, analogue, or art? *Families in Society, 35,* 32–43.

Gordon, R. L. (1992). *Basic interviewing skills.* Itasca, IL: Peacock.

Ivey, A., Gluckstem, N., & Ivey, M. (1997). *Basic attending skills* (3rd ed.). North Amherst, MA: Microtraining Associates.

Ivey, A., Ivey, M. B., & Marx, R. (1998). *Intentional interviewing and counseling: Facilitating client development in a multicultural society.* Pacific Grove, CA: Brooks/Cole.

Kadushin, A. (1972). *The social work interview.* New York: Columbia University Press.

Kadushin, A., & Kadushin, G. (1995). *The social work interview: A guide for human services professionals*. New York: Columbia University Press.

Maidment, J., & Egan, R. (Eds.). (2004). *Practice skills in social work and welfare: Inure than just common sense*. Crows Nest, New South Whales: Allen and Unwin.

Matarazzo, R. G., & Patterson, D. R. (1986). Methods of teaching therapeutic skill. In S. L. Garfield & A. E. Bergin (Eds.), *Handbook of psychotherapy and behavior change* (3rd ed., pp. 821–843). New York: Wiley.

May, R. (1989). *The art of counseling* (Rev. ed.). New York: Gardner Press.

Okun, B. F. (1991). *Effective helping, interviewing and counseling techniques* (4th ed.). Pacific Grove, CA: Brooks/Cole.

Perlman, H. H. (1979). *Relationship: The heart of helping people*. Chicago: University of Chicago Press.

Rogers, C. R. (1957). The necessary and sufficient conditions of therapeutic personality change. *Journal of Consulting Psychology*, *21*, 95–103.

Rowe, W. (1986). Client-centered theory. In F. J. Turner (Ed.), *Social work treatment: Interlocking the theoretical approaches* (pp. 407–431). New York: Free Press.

Shulman, L. (1992). *The skills of helping individuals and groups* (3rd ed.). Itasca, IL: Peacock.

Thompson, N. (2003). *Communication and language. A handbook for practitioners*. London: MacMillan.

Trevithick, P., Richards, S., Ruth, G., & Moss, B. (2004). *Teaching and learning communication skills in social work education*. London: Social Care Institute for Excellence. Available from www.scie.org.uk/.

Turner, F. J. (1978). *Psychosocial therapy*. New York: Free Press.

Wolgien, C. S., & Coady, N. F. (1997). Good therapists' beliefs about the development of their helping ability: The wounded healer paradigm revisited. *Clinical Supervisor*, *15*(2), 19–35.

REFERENCES

Brothers, C. (2002). The process of interviewing. In F. J. Turner (Ed.), *Social work practice* (2nd ed., pp. 191–203). Toronto Ontario, Canada: Prentice Hall.

Coady, N. F. (2002). The helping relationship. In F. J. Turner (Ed.), *Social work practice* (2nd ed., pp. 116–130). Toronto Ontario, Canada: Prentice Hall.

Fischer, J. (1978). *Effective casework practice: An eclectic approach*. New York: McGraw-Hill.

Hollis, F. (1972). *Casework: A psychosocial therapy*. New York: Random House.

Perlman, H. H. (1971). *Social casework: A problem-solving process*. Chicago: University of Chicago Press.

Thomlison, R. J. (1984, January/February). Something works: Evidence from practice effectiveness studies. *Social Work*, *29*, 51–58.

Chapter 3

ASSESSMENT AND DATA COLLECTION

William R. Nugent

Assessment is a topic widely written about and discussed by social workers, and a variety of definitions have been offered. Assessment has been defined as referring to "the interpretation of information (data) collected about the client's problem" (Nugent, Sieppert, & Hudson, 2001, p. 62). It has also been conceptualized as referring to "a process occurring between practitioner and client in which information is gathered, analyzed, and synthesized to provide a concise picture of the client and his or her needs and strengths" (Hepworth, Rooney, & Larsen, 2002, p. 187). Others have argued that, "Assessment consists of procedures and tools used to collect and process information from which the entire helping program is developed" (Cormier & Nurius, 2003, p. 175). Cormier and Nurius (2003) go on to note that, during the collection of data about the client's problems, strengths, and environment, the social worker must engage in important tasks of making sense of all of the data gathered:

> Equally important is the helper's own mental (covert) activity that goes on during the process. The helper typically gathers a great amount of information from client's during this stage of helping. Unless the helper can integrate and synthesize the data, they are of little value and use. (p. 175)

Gambrill (1997) described what she called a "contextual assessment," a process with a number of important characteristics, including: (a) an individually tailored focus on the client; (b) an emphasis on the formulation of conjectures about the client, with these conjectures regarded as tentative hypotheses in need of testing; (c) a demand that valid measurement and assessment methods be used; and (d) a recognition of a close relationship between assessment and intervention.

Common to these definitions is the notion that assessment requires the collection of information or data about the client and then the use of this information to make inferences about her or him. Given this commonality, assessment is defined in this chapter as:

> the imperfect process of obtaining fallible information from and about a client (or clients), the aggregation of these data into a provisional picture of the client-environment context and fit, and then the use of this picture to: (1) make fallible, probabilistic inferences about the client's (clients') problems, strengths, needs, and environmental fit; (2) make service related decisions and intervention selections; and (3) use the obtained information and tentative picture as a baseline to evaluate the outcomes of services provided.

The emphasis in this definition on the fallible and provisional nature of the data collected and the inferences made during assessment implies that this endeavor must be conducted within a critical thinking context (Gambrill, 1997).

COMMON INFERENTIAL ERRORS

Assessment must be done within a critical thinking framework (Gambrill, 1997). An important component of this framework is awareness of ways in which human beings err when observing their environment and then making inferences from the information gleaned. Social work (and other professional) practitioners make these errors not only in their everyday, personal lives, but also in their professional practice efforts. An important step in reducing the problems that such observational and inferential errors introduce into social work practice is the ability to recognize them. The following discussion is by no means comprehensive; see such sources as Gilovich (1993), Garb (1998), and Gambrill (1997) for additional information.

Practitioners can first make errors in how and what they observe. One problem is information that is laden with errors. This occurs when poor observational methods are used. Another problem is biased information. Biased data can result from any number of problems with how the practitioner observes and gathers information about her or his client. One significant problem is *observational bias*. Observational bias can occur when the practitioner, usually without awareness, looks at the client through conceptual lenses provided by the society and culture to which the practitioner belongs. These observational lenses are referred to as *frames*. Informal social and cultural frames that social workers learn from the cultural groups they are a part of can predispose them to *prejudices* and *stereotypes* that make them vulnerable not only to observational biases, but also *diagnostic*, or *interpretive*, *biases*. One example of such a frame is the notion that human beings have different levels of worth and can be rank ordered from higher to lower worth dependent on such things as occupation, gender, or color. Another is the idea that some human beings "deserve" or "are worthy of" being denied certain resources or services, or even being dealt with violently, if they have certain characteristics or have behaved in certain ways. An example of diagnostic or interpretive prejudice is when practitioners make biased diagnoses with respect to age, gender, and race (Garb, 1996). The effects of informal social and cultural frames on how practitioners observe and interpret client behaviors and information can be subtle and difficult to recognize.

Another common and important error that occurs in practice is what Garb (1998) and others refer to as *context effect*. This form of error occurs when the context in which a social worker practices influences what the practitioner pays attention to and how he or she interprets the information obtained from and about a client. A related problem is that practitioners in mental health settings tend to *overperceive psychopathology* and have a difficult time recognizing normality (Garb, 1996). What this means is that a practitioner will be vulnerable to interpreting normal behavior, thoughts, and actions as being indicators of psychopathology. For example, suppose that a social worker is a psychotherapist in an out-patient mental health clinic. A part of this context—psychotherapy done in an out-patient mental health clinic—can predispose the social worker to interpret client complaints as a mental health problem in need of psychotherapy, without considering alternative explanations for the client's complaints. Suppose that a client complains of being run down and tired, feeling depressed and anxious, feeling frequently irritable, and no longer enjoying things that he or she used to. The practitioner—in the context of a mental health center in which the social worker does psychotherapy—will be predisposed to interpret the client's complaints as symptoms of depression or of an anxiety disorder *without considering alternative possibilities,* such as the possibility of a health problem. In fact, as shown in Table 3.1, a number of physical disorders produce symptoms that can be easily misinterpreted as depression or anxiety disorders, such as anemia, endocrinopathies (e.g., hyperthyroidism), and various forms of cancer (Barlow, 2002; Martin, 1983; Morrison, 1999). Of course, the opposite is true as well: Mental health problems can be misinterpreted as physical disorders (Barlow, 2002), so practitioners in health settings need to be cautious about predispositions to interpret mental health problems as physical problems.

Practitioners also tend to make diagnostic type decisions rather quickly, based on initial impressions and minimal information (Garb, 1996). They are then unlikely to stray very far from this initial judgment, a phenomena known as *anchoring* (Gilovich, 1993). Once a practitioner has made a judgment, say a determination that the client is depressed, he or she is vulnerable to one of several *confirmation biases.* A confirmation bias is a tendency to look for and pay attention to evidence that confirms a belief while *not* looking for and considering contradictory evidence. This can be manifested most simply by failing to look for evidence that would disprove a belief or by refusing to consider the possibility of alternate possibilities. Another form of confirmation bias is a tendency to remember events, situations, or evidence that confirms a belief. On occasion, we can even mentally manufacture "memories" that confirm a belief, memories that are not real (Garb, 1996). A third form of confirmation bias occurs when a person accepts at face value evidence that

Table 3.1   Physical Disorders That Have Depression-Like and Anxiety-Like Symptoms

Depression-Like	Anxiety-Like
Chronic illness	Endocrine disorders
Chronic fatigue syndrome	–Hypoglycemia
Diabetes	–Hyperthyroidism
Fibromyalgia	–Cushing's syndrome
Heart disease/heart failure	–Pheochromocytoma
Respiratory insufficiency	Cardiovascular disorders
Parkinson's disease	–Mitral valve prolapse
Brucellosis (acute phase especially)	–Cardiac arrhythmias
Thyroid disorders	–Hypertension
Postpolio syndrome	Respiratory disorders
Hypersensitivity pneumonitis	–Chronic obstructive
Hyperparathyroidism	–Pulmonary disease
Hypoadrenocorticism	Neurological disorders
Adrenal disorders	–Epilepsy
Adrenal insufficiency	–Huntington's disease
Addison's disease	–Vestibular disorders
Celiac disease	Substance-related anxiety

Sources: Anxiety and Its Disorders, second edition, by D. Barlow, 2002, New York: Guilford Press; "The Risk of Misdiagnosing Physical Illness as Depression" (pp. 93–112), by M. Gold, in *The Hatherleigh Guide to Managing Depression,* F. Flach (Ed.), 1996, New York: Hatherleigh; "A Brief Review of Organic Diseases Masquerading as Functional Illness," by M. Martin, 1983, *Hospital and Community Psychiatry, 34*(4), pp. 328–332; *When Psychological Problems Mask Medical Disorders,* by J. Morrison, 1999, New York: Guilford Press.

confirms a belief, while evaluating and challenging contradictory evidence in an extremely critical manner until some reason is found to discount it (Gilovich, 1993). The effects of confirmation biases can be seriously enhanced by *practitioner overconfidence* in the validity of the decisions that he or she has made.

The practitioner is also vulnerable to erring through a *labeling effect*, a tendency to interpret what a client says and does through the lens of an inference that someone else has made about the client or a label that someone else has placed upon the client. In the words of Rosenhan (1973, p. 253), "Once a person is designated abnormal, all of his other behaviors and characteristics are colored by that label." One example of this is to be overly influenced by a psychiatric diagnosis given to a client by another practitioner (Garb, 1996; Gilovich, 1993). This kind of error can also occur and be compounded if the other person's inference or label comes to the practitioner as *second-hand information*. Second-hand information comes to the practitioner through one or more intermediaries. For example, practitioner A makes a diagnosis that practitioner B learns about in some manner, and then practitioner B conveys this information to practitioner C. In this process information is *sharpened* and *leveled*. Sharpening refers to a person emphasizing and possibly embellishing some aspects of the information they have received, while downplaying or even omitting other aspects. The children's game "telephone" or "gossip" is a good example of this process. The information received by the last person in the process has been altered and distorted, possibly in ways that have completely altered what the first person in the process conveyed (Gilovich, 1993).

Another form of error that practitioners are vulnerable to is the failure to recognize that the inferences he or she is making about a client are almost certainly based on *incomplete or missing data*. There will always be some amount of missing information, and this incomplete picture can easily lead the practitioner to make erroneous inferences. The practitioner must recognize that all of her or his inferences about a client are based on limited, fallible, and incomplete data and that this can lead to inaccurate conclusions about client's problems, needs, strengths, and so on.

Practitioners can also err by overreliance on theory, and this can occur when a theory, model, or other set of practice principles has the *aura of plausibility*. The aura of plausibility error occurs when we accept something as true simply because it sounds plausible or reasonable. So, if a theory or intervention model sounds good, fits with other beliefs that one holds, and just seems to make good sense, then, on this basis alone the theory or intervention model may be accepted by a practitioner as being true. In this manner, a practitioner may end up using interventions that are not only ineffective, but also harmful. The growing evidence on *iatrogenic effects*—harmful outcomes that result from treatments and interventions—should raise flags of caution for all social workers and highlight the great need for practice to be based on models that have substantial bodies of supporting evidence. The first part of Whitaker's (2002) book *Mad in America: Bad Science, Bad Medicine, and the Enduring Mistreatment of the Mentally Ill* contains numerous examples of how we have used horrific treatments for those in need, with little more justification than a plausible sounding theoretical argument. Iatrogenic outcomes may be the third leading cause of death in the United States (Starfield, 2000), and iatrogenic outcomes may occur in as many as one-third of cases in mental health settings (Lilienfeld, Lohr, & Lynn, 2003).

Practitioners also frequently *do not take into account base rates* or *prevalence rates* when doing assessments and making inferences about client problems. This can lead to a number of errors and misjudgments, including a *misunderstanding of probability* and the *probabilistic nature of diagnostic inferences*. Given how commonly forms of diagnosis are made in social work practice, this problem is considered in detail later in this chapter.

In summary, there are numerous ways in which social workers can jump to erroneous conclusions when doing assessments in social work practice. Good assessment methods and critical thinking help to decrease the likelihood of these types of errors. Errors can, of course, never be completely eliminated. However, they can be reduced and, hopefully, minimized. The principles of critical thinking and of data collection and assessment discussed next can help the social worker to minimize these errors of observation and judgment.

CRITICAL THINKING

Much could be written here about critical thinking (see, e.g., Gambrill, 1990, 1997; Gibbs & Gambrill, 1999; Paul, 1993). However, in the interest of brevity, the focus will be not on in-depth coverage of this topic, but rather on questions that the social worker can continually use to help herself or himself avoid the errors of observation and inference that can lead to problematic assessments. Assessment should be an ongoing process throughout the course of service provision, ending only when services have been completed. The social worker should always keep in mind that her or his knowledge about the client is most likely biased in some manner and to some degree; is based on limited, incomplete, and error laden data; and that the inferences and conclusions that he or she is making may be to a greater or lesser degree in error. Thus, the social worker should always be in the process of gathering new information; should be critically questioning and evaluating the information already obtained; and should be continually asking, and actively seeking answers to, the following questions:

- What information am I missing that, if I had it, might lead me to an alternate understanding about what is going on with my client?
- What biases are there in my data collection that I am not aware of, and how are these biases affecting how I make sense of the information I have obtained so far?
- What alternative interpretations and understandings are there for the information I have obtained so far? What other pictures might I be able to build, using the information I have, about what is going on with my client?
- What evidence supports my current interpretation of what is going on with my client, and what is the quality of this evidence?
- What evidence contradicts my current interpretation of what is going on with my client, and what is the quality of this evidence?
- What have I failed to consider that might lead me to a different interpretation? The social worker should, in particular, be actively seeking information that will contradict, or be inconsistent with, the provisional understanding that he or she currently has about the what is going on with her or his client. The process of seeking to answer these questions and the active search for evidence contradicting current tentative judgments, done within the context of humility about what the social worker believes he or she knows, can help decrease the likelihood of assessment errors.

A BIOPSYCHOSOCIAL PERSPECTIVE

The general perspective, or assessment *Weltanshauung* (worldview), within which the assessment needs to be conducted is *biopsychosocial*. This means that the social worker will gather her or his data—the information about her or his client—from a biopsychosocial perspective and will ultimately aggregate the information obtained into a coherent picture of her or his client's situation using a biopsychosocial framework, that is, the social worker endeavors to build a complete and total picture of the client's unique person-environment context (Gambrill, 1997). The social worker gathers information about the client's current physical state, including data on any physical symptoms or complaints the client has; medications the client is taking; any medical problems the client may have and whether and how they are being treated, and by whom; and information on when the client last had a physical exam. The social worker also gathers information on the client's psychological and emotional state, including data on any troubling emotions, such as anxiety, fear, anger, or depression. Information is also obtained on the social context within which the client is currently embedded, including data about important interpersonal relationships the client is involved in, especially relationships with intimate partners and family. The social worker needs to obtain information about the client's relationships with various social groups and organizations, such as schools, work, and recreation. The social worker also needs to look at the client's economic status, as well as her or his current living context, including the environment in which he or she lives. In short, the social worker must endeavor to obtain a comprehensive picture of the client's physical, psychological, emotional, interpersonal, economic, social, and physical living circumstances. The biopsychosocial perspective demands comprehensive consideration of, and gathering data about, all aspects of the client's current life situation. This perspective will help to decrease the likelihood of falling prey to the narrow perspectives engendered by the contexts within which social workers practice. Once the social worker has gathered these data, he or she then aggregates the information obtained into a coherent picture of the client's current person-environment situation. This aggregation is guided by the general philosophy that the practitioner's task is to build as accurate and complete a picture of the client's current physical, psychological, emotional, interpersonal, social, economic, and living circumstances and conditions as possible, *with no preferred arena of focus*; that is, with no preset aspect of the client's person-environment constellation that the social worker intends to narrowly focus on. This biopsychosocial perspective helps to minimize the biases created by the social worker's professional work context and other personal and social factors, such as those discussed previously.

Once the social worker has built this picture of the client's current person-environment circumstances, he or she works collaboratively with the client to develop a service plan, with a prioritization of service and intervention needs. Special attention needs to be paid to the pieces of information obtained from the measurement and assessment methods with the highest levels of validity (see validity discussion that follows) since this information will have the soundest base for making decisions about the client. The social worker should always keep in mind as he or she conducts the assessment that one of her or his most important responsibilities is to protect their client from harm and to protect others in the client's environment from harm at the hands of the client. For this reason, the practitioner should always make a preliminary suicide risk assessment a normal part of the assessment process. If he or she detects any signs of suicidal ideation, then he or she will need to conduct a more comprehensive suicide risk assessment (Bongar, 2002). The social worker will also need to consider the physical safety of the client's current living situation. For example, if the client lives in a neighborhood in which gunfire is a normal and common occurrence, and persons are regularly the victims of gunshots, then an important concern will be the client's physical safety. Other safety concerns to keep in mind as the social worker conducts her or his assessment are the client's safety from intimate-partner and/or family violence and violence that the client may perpetrate upon others in her or his environment. Safety issues need to be addressed first.

PRINCIPLES OF MEASUREMENT

Good quality information can be obtained during assessment by paying attention to measurement issues. Measurement is fundamental to assessment. In fact, it is impossible to adequately gauge the nature and severity of a client's problem(s) without some form of measurement. No one can tell how far he or she has progressed or deteriorated without some form of measurement. Measurement can be, and often is, conducted in an informal, subjective manner. However, more formal measurement procedures greatly enhance assessment and data collection. In a technical sense, measurement is the use of numbers, words, or other symbols, according to well-specified rules, to represent attributes and characteristics of persons (Crocker & Algina, 1986; Lord & Novick, 1968; Nunnally, 1978). In simpler terms, though, measurement is a process of representation or description. Any time the social worker seeks to describe or represent some characteristic of a client, he or she is seeking to measure the client in some way. A measurement procedure produces a "score" that is composed of words (as in a *DSM-IV* diagnosis, for example), numbers (such as a score on a measure of clinical depression), or both. Blythe and Tripodi (1989) characterized measurement as a process that involves: (a) identifying a concept (construct) to be measured; (b) specifying an indicator (or set of indicators) of the concept; (c) operationally defining relevant data and a way of ordering the data (such as determining how to assign levels from low to high, and so on); and (d) determining the validity and reliability of the scores produced by the resultant measurement procedure.

Two aspects of this definition need to be pointed out. Measurement is a process of (a) identifying and evaluating properties or characteristics (b) by the use of indicators. This means, first of all, that measurement involves looking at particular *characteristics* of persons. In many cases, the property or characteristic is not directly observable in the same way that something like "weight" or "hair color" would be. For example, "depression" is a problem commonly experienced and reported by clients, yet "depression" is not a thing that can be seen on the top of a client's head or sitting in a chair next to the client. No one can directly observe it in quite the same way that they can observe, for example, a client's hair color. Depression involves, to a great extent, a set of private events experienced by a client, though it is also manifested in some behaviors that are directly observable by others. In such cases the social worker must look for the presence of behaviors or physiological states that point to the presence and severity of "depression." These behaviors or physiological states are called *indicators* (Nunnally, 1978). When asking clients directly about their problems, the practitioner can ask questions about, and look and listen for, various indicators that will help to pinpoint the nature and severity of the problems and challenges the client faces, as well as the strengths the client brings that can be used to help deal with these challenges.

Characteristics of Good Measurement Procedures

Good measurement procedures can help to minimize the errors of observation discussed earlier and to provide good quality information on which to base inferences and decisions about a client. There are a number of characteristics that must be considered when selecting a measurement procedure for use in assessment. Some of these are general attributes that make certain measurement procedures more appropriate or easier to use in particular situations. Others are more specific and relate to the psychometrics of the measurement method. *Psychometric* is a term that refers to the science of measuring psychological, behavioral, and social phenomena.

First and foremost, any measure used for assessment and to monitor and evaluate practice should be easy to use. This has a number of implications for selecting measurement procedures. They should be as short as possible, and should be easy to use, so as to fit well within the social work practice context. They should be easy for clients to understand and, if the measurement procedure is self-report, it should be easy to complete. They should be easy for the practitioner to understand, and easy to describe and explain to clients. Good measures also provide good referents so that the practitioner can anchor her or his interpretations consistently. The measurement procedure should produce scores sufficiently sensitive to detect meaningful changes in the characteristic, problem, or situation being monitored.

Most of all, however, measurement procedures selected and used in assessment need to meet the following two key criteria: First, they need to be appropriate for the type of client being assessed, in terms of age, cognitive functioning, language capabilities, cultural background, and so on. Second, good measures must focus directly on the client objectives collaboratively established by the social worker and client. Without meeting these two criteria, all others are meaningless. The best measurement procedures also facilitate an important aspect of monitoring and service evaluation. They allow for repeated measurements over time, without undue distortion or bias. This is important because basic practice evaluation methods, such as single-case designs (Bloom, Fischer, & Orme, 2005; Nugent et al., 2001), cannot be implemented without the ability to detect emerging patterns in client functioning. The social worker should be able to integrate the measurement procedure into normal assessment and monitoring procedures without adding too much extra work for either herself or himself or for the client.

Some measurement instruments are simply too large or complex to fit into this framework. This is particularly true if regular, repeated measurement is desired over a relatively short period of assessment and intervention. For all of the these reasons, many have advocated the use of short-form instruments that are quickly and easily administered, scored, and interpreted. Such instruments are often called *rapid assessment instruments* (RAIs; Bloom et al., 2005). These RAIs can have as few as 4 to 25 items, and take only a few minutes to complete (Nugent et al., 2001). There are two other critically important criteria for judging the worth of measurement procedures that must be discussed. These are the psychometric properties of *reliability* and *validity.*

Reliability and Relative Inferences

Reliability concerns the ability of a measure to produce scores, whether qualitative or quantitative, that have very little measurement error; said another way and more generally, reliability concerns measurement error. Ideally, a measurement procedure implemented repeatedly to assess the same person, under the condition that the level of the characteristic possessed by the person and measured by the procedure remains constant, will produce very nearly the same score every time (Lord & Novick, 1968). This means the instrument must resist the influence or contamination of random factors external to the phenomenon being measured that might influence results from one application to another.

The central concept in classical reliability theory is the *reliability coefficient*. The reliability coefficient is a number ranging from 0 to +1.0 that indicates how good a job the scores produced by the measurement procedure do in allowing the practitioner to place a client relative to others with respect to the characteristic being measured (Crocker & Algina, 1986; Lord & Novick, 1968; Nunnally, 1978). Said another way, the reliability coefficient tells the social worker how much error there is when he or she compares a person's score against the scores of others (or against a set of scores obtained from this same person at different points in time) for the purpose of deciding whether this person has more of, or less of, the characteristic than the other persons (or more of or less of the characteristic than the person did at other points in time).

For example, the client responds to the items on a depression inventory, which produces scores ranging from 0 to 25, with higher scores presumably indicative of greater magnitude depression and vice versa. The client has a score of 16 on October 1. The practitioner then compares this score for the client against a set of scores for this same client from four prior administrations of this measurement procedure: June 1, 21; July 1, 19; August 1, 20; and September 1, 18. The closer the reliability coefficient is to 1.0, the less error there is in the practitioner's judgment that the person's score is lower on October 1 than her or his previous four scores.

There are four principal methods for estimating the classical reliability coefficient: test-retest, alternate forms, split-halves, and coefficient alpha. These methods are described in detail in most research texts (e.g., Rubin & Babbie, 2007). The test-retest method produces a correlation between scores from the measurement procedure, interpreted as an estimate of the reliability coefficient, at two different points in time, and is often considered to be an indicator of the *stability* of scores from the measurement procedure. The alternate forms method also produces a correlation, in this case between the two different forms of the measurement procedure, that is also interpreted as an estimate of the reliability coefficient. This form of reliability estimate is sometimes referred to as an *equivalence coefficient*. The split-halves method produces a correlation between two halves of the measurement procedure, a correlation that is stepped-up in value to characterize the reliability of scores from the entire measurement procedure. This form of estimate is often referred to as an *internal consistency index* since it makes use of the extent to which the items on the measure are intercorrelated. Finally, coefficient alpha gives an estimate of the mean of all possible split halves estimates of the reliability coefficient. These forms of estimates of the reliability coefficient for scores from standardized measures are reported in journal articles, technical manuals, and books describing specific measurement tools and procedures (see, e.g., Corcoran & Fischer, 2000a, 2000b).

The reliability coefficient is an appropriate index of measurement error when the practitioner intends to make what are referred to as relative comparisons or inferences; or, alternatively, when the measurement he or she makes is a *norm-referenced measurement*. Norm-referenced measurement is the use of scores from a measurement procedure to make relative or comparative inferences or decisions (Crocker & Algina, 1986). Again, a relative or comparative inference is one in which the social worker compares a person's score against those of other persons (or against scores from the same person at different points in time) for the purpose of deciding whether or not the person has more or less of the characteristic of interest than the other persons (or whether the person has more of or less of the characteristic now than he or she did at different points in time).

A related index of measurement error appropriate for characterizing the error involved in making relative inferences or comparisons is the *standard error of measurement*. The standard error of measurement is defined as the standard deviation of errors of measurement (Lord & Novick, 1968). It is really just another way of making use of the reliability coefficient since the two indices are related by a simple equation (see Crocker & Algina, 1986; Lord & Novick, 1968). The standard error of measurement is just another way of describing how much error is involved in comparing one person's score against those of other persons (or against other scores from the same person obtained at different points in time). It gives an estimate of how much of the difference between two scores is attributable to measurement error. The standard error of measurement is, in classical measurement theory, the square root of the classical error variance, which is another indicator of measurement error.

The concept of the classical error variance is a form of *relative error variance*, which is, again, a way of characterizing the error involved in making relative or comparative decisions based on persons' scores (Brennan, 2001). Estimates of the standard error of measurement associated with scores from standardized measurement procedures can be found in the same sources (technical manuals, journal articles, etc.) as the estimates of reliability coefficients mentioned previously.

Absolute Inferences

There is a second form of decision made from scores in social work practice, and that is the so-called *absolute decision*, and the form of measurement involved in making such decisions is referred to as *criterion-referenced measurement*. An absolute decision or inference involves a determination about either: (a) which of two or more categories a person belongs to with respect to some characteristic (such as which of several diagnostic categories the person belongs in with respect to a mental disorder), or (b) the absolute level of magnitude of some characteristic of the person (such as how much knowledge the person has about clinical social work practice and is it enough knowledge to be licensed as a clinical social worker; Crocker & Algina, 1986)? Criterion-referenced measurement is simply the use of scores to make absolute decisions.

One way this is done is by the establishment and use of some form of *cut score*. A cut score is some score produced by a measurement procedure that serves as a criterion for placing persons into categories. For example, a measure used to assess the level of depression may have a *clinical cutting score*. Scores above this cutting score lead the practitioner to infer that the client has a clinically significant problem with depression (see, e.g., Hudson, 1982). A second example would be a social worker taking a licensing exam who must obtain a certain minimum passing score, say 80% correct, in order to be licensed. If she obtains a score at or above the passing score of 80%, then she is placed into the category "licensable." Say the social worker received a score of 86% correct. This percentage, 86%, would also serve as an absolute estimate of her knowledge of a well-defined universe of content on social work practice (Brennan, 2001).

When absolute decisions are to be made via use of criterion-referenced measurement procedures, then the *absolute error variance* is the relevant variance indicator of error associated with these decisions (Brennan, 2001). The square root of the absolute error variance would give an *absolute standard error of measurement* that could be used to characterize the measurement error involved in such classification decisions. An important result from the measurement theory underpinning these notions (generalizability theory; see Brennan, 2001) is that *absolute error variance is never less than the relative error variance; it is, except in the most unusual of circumstances, greater than the relative error variance.* This means that the measurement error associated with absolute decisions or inferences will, except in the most unusual and unlikely of circumstances, be greater than the measurement error associated with relative or comparative decisions. This has a number of implications for assessment that are discussed later.

There are indices analogous to the reliability coefficient that are appropriate for describing the measurement error associated with classification decisions. One has been called the *Brennan-Kane dependability index* (Brennan & Kane, 1977) and has been symbolically represented in generalizability theory treatments as $\Phi(\lambda = L)$, where λ represents a specific cutting score (Brennan, 2001). This index ranges from 0 to 1.0 and can be interpreted as an index describing the agreement in decisions based on alternate versions of the measurement procedure and its associated cut score (Brennan, 1983). The closer the index is to 1.0, the more dependable (i.e., the less error there is in) the classification decisions made on the basis of the scores from the measurement procedure. Brennan (2001) describes procedures for estimating this index. A second index for characterizing the reliability of classification decisions based on a measurement procedure is the index Φ described in generalizability theory treatments (see Brennan, 1983, 2001). This index also ranges from 0 to 1.0, and gives the extent to which the measurement procedure contributes to classification decisions over and above chance expectations (Brennan, 1983). It can be interpreted, technically, as the expected agreement in scores across randomly parallel versions of the measurement procedure, controlling for chance agreement (Brennan, 2001). It can therefore be used as an index describing the reliability of classification decisions, based on the measurement procedure, taking chance agreement in classification into account. Methods for estimating this index are described by Brennan (2001).

Issues of reliability are central to good practice. An unreliable set of scores is infused with variability that is unrelated to the construct the social worker is trying to measure and use for decisions about her or his client. One product of an unreliable set of scores is, therefore, a flawed and invalid client assessment (Allen & Yen, 2001; Crocker & Algina, 1986; Hudson, 1982; Lord & Novick, 1968; Nunnally, 1978). The social worker has an ethical obligation to avoid such risks by using measurement procedures known to be capable of producing a reliable set of scores.

Validity

Validity concerns the degree to which the measurement procedure being used to produce scores allows the social worker to accurately make the inferences he or she wants to make (Messick, 1989). The question of validity is often stated in a somewhat simplified manner as, "Do the scores from this measurement procedure allow the type of inferences desired to be meaningfully made to the construct of interest?" If the answer is no, then the inferences made from the scores are not valid, and the client assessment is flawed. For example, if the social worker wants to know how depressed a client is, he or she needs a measure that produces scores that allow her or him to accurately infer the client's level of depression. In this case the practitioner wants to make inferences from the client's score to her or his level of depression.

It is important to realize that this simple notion refers to more than just pencil and paper scales. The concept of validity applies to any act of assessment or measurement. Questions of validity are as applicable and critical to practitioner's observations, interview questions, intuitive hunches, and so on, as they are to any standardized measure (see Nugent et al., 2001; Messick, 1989). If the social worker fails to obtain information that allows her or him to make accurate inferences to the characteristic that he or she desires to measure, the result is a misdirected and potentially dangerous (mis-) understanding of the client.

The general notion of validity is relatively simple. The scores from a measurement procedure should allow the social worker to make a certain type of inference to a construct or concept of interest. However, the determination of validity is complex in that it requires multiple types of evidence to support claims that the scores produced by a measurement instrument are valid for making specific inferences. These forms of evidence have often been conceptualized as "types" of validity (Messick, 1989). Researchers and psychometricians speak about such things as "face validity," "content validity," "predictive validity," "concurrent validity," "convergent validity," and "divergent validity." Each of these "types" of validity is actually a form of evidence used to support a claim that the particular measurement procedure produces scores allowing the user to make a specific inference (Messick, 1989). To "validate" a measurement tool means to gather evidence that bears on the appropriateness of the use of the scores produced by the measure to make specific inferences.

The validation of a measurement procedure is an evolving and ongoing process that, in a sense, never ends. It is critical to note that the best measures will have all of the above types of evidence supporting the validity of specific uses of the scores they produce (Messick, 1989). Perhaps most important of all of the previously discussed types of evidence is that for convergent and divergent validity (Nugent et al., 2001).

It is beyond the scope of this chapter to give a full and detailed discussion of how to establish validity. For more information, see the very detailed treatment of validity given by Messick (1989). Other excellent references are Crocker and Algina (1986), Nunnally (1978), and Hudson (1982).

Also important is the issue of differential validity, or bias, in measurement. Differential validity concerns the extent to which the manner in which we interpret scores from a measurement procedure *for different types of persons (male and female, majority and minority, etc.) remains invariant*. This topic is discussed in depth by Cole and Moss (1989), and Masters and Keeves (1999) discussed this topic in the context of social work research and practice. Setting standards for validity is not as easy as it is for reliability. In terms of reliability the social worker would want a set of scores with a reliability or dependability coefficient close to 1.0. However, since there are a variety of types of evidence necessary to support validity claims, it is not possible to give a single number that can be used as a standard for comparison that practitioners can use to make selections of measurement procedures. The situation is further complicated by the fact that validation is an ongoing, ever-evolving process. This makes any determination of the "better validated measure" a comparative process that is time dependent. At the risk of over simplifying a complex process, the best measurement procedure to use is the one that *currently has the best and most complete evidence supporting its use for making the type of inference the practitioner needs to make.*

Evidence for validity is often (though by all means not always) given in the form of a correlation coefficient and, when used in this manner, the correlation coefficient is referred to as a *validity coefficient*. A correlation coefficient is a numerical index that ranges from -1 to $+1$ and that tells the extent to which the scores from two measures are related. A correlation of $+1$ indicates that the scores from the two measures are perfectly related and that a high score on one of the measures is accompanied by high scores on the second (and vice versa). A correlation of -1 indicates that the scores are perfectly related, but that high scores on one of the measures is accompanied by low scores on the second (and vice versa). As the correlation coefficient approaches 0, it indicates that the scores are unrelated; knowing a person's score on one measure tells nothing about her or his score on the second measure. Whether a validity coefficient should be large of small in magnitude depends on the type of validity evidence being put forth. Validity coefficients for measurement procedures are often reported in the technical manuals, journal articles, books, and so on, described earlier that report information on reliability coefficients for standardized measurement procedures.

The past 3 decades has seen greatly improved knowledge and procedures related to the construction of clinical measures. This enhanced ability has lead to evolving validity standards. Practitioners looking for valid instruments should find those for which the full range of evidence supporting validity has been reported. There should be evidence for face validity; content validity; if appropriate, predictive validity; concurrent validity; convergent validity; and divergent validity. The most demanding form of evidence for validity is the combination of convergent and divergent validity. The prudent practitioner will make sure that evidence for the convergent and divergent validity of scores produced by a measurement procedure exists before using the measure in practice.

Ways of Describing Clients and Their Problems

There are essentially two ways to measure some characteristic of a client and/or the problems that he or she faces: by observing them or by asking them. The first of these procedures refers to *direct observation*, while the second refers to *self-report*. The social worker could, of course, obtain collateral information (i.e., information from others) from the client's parents, spouse or partner, children, or some other person or persons familiar with her or him. Each of these other reporters, however, can only have obtained this information by either direct observation or self-report from the client (or both of these). This distinction helps the practitioner determine which form of data collection is most appropriate for the measurement task he or she faces with the client.

There is another distinction that can be made between measurement procedures. This distinction concerns the manner in which characteristics of the client and her or his problems can be described. There are four basic dimensions of characteristics that a measurement process can tap (Nugent et al., 2001):

1. *Its binary or categorical status*—That is, whether the characteristic is present or absent, or which of several categories it belongs to. For example, what is your client's gender? Religious preference? Occupation?

2. *Its frequency*—That is, how often does the characteristic, such as a behavior or experience, occur during some specified interval of time. For example, if the client reports experiencing headaches, how frequent are these headaches?

3. *Its duration*—That is, how long does the characteristic, such as a behavior or event, last from its onset to some other point in time. For example, the client reports that when angry at her partner she gives her or him the "silent treatment." When she does this, how long does the silent treatment generally last?

4. *Its magnitude*—That is, in a quantitative sense, how "large" or "small" is the characteristic. For example, if the client reports being depressed, to what degree or relative magnitude is your client depressed? If he or she experiences headaches, how intense are each of the headaches when they occur?

Measurement procedures that can be used as a part of the assessment process can be used to obtain one or more of these types of descriptive information about the client and her or his problem(s), strengths, situation, and so on.

Measurement Methods

There are a wide range of measurement procedures that the practitioner might choose to use. These include interview techniques that are structured, semistructured, and unstructured; standardized scales, both self-report and other-report; self-report and other-report methods that are unstandardized (e.g., individualized rating scales); observational procedures, both self-observation and other-observation; physical methods, such as blood tests, blood pressure cuffs, and so on. The measurement procedures that the social worker elects to use depends to a great extent on the practice setting and context in which he or she works. These procedures are so many and varied that it is impossible to describe them all in detail in this chapter. However, the following is a brief overview. The reader interested in a specific measurement method should consult the references cited.

Standardized Scales

Some measurement methods are *standardized*, meaning they have a specific fixed format with well-specified and detailed instructions for use, scoring, and interpretation. Standardized measurement procedures, like any measurement method, can be described as either *unidimensional* or *multidimensional*. Unidimensional measurement procedures are those that allow inferences to a single construct, such as depression or anxiety. An example of a standardized unidimensional measure is Hudson's Generalized Contentment Scale (GCS; Hudson, 1982; Nugent et al., 2001). A multidimensional measurement procedure allows for inferences to be made from scores over subsets of items, or over subscales, to multiple constructs. For example, Hudson's Multi-Problem Screening Inventory (MPSI; Nugent et al., 2001) produces scores on 27 different unidimensional subscales that allow inferences to 27 different constructs. As noted earlier, some standardized measurement procedures are referred to as RAIs. These are short standardized instruments, usually unidimensional, with relatively few items, commonly 30 or less. Hudson's GCS is an example of an RAI.

Standardized measures can have any of a number of formats. A typical format is the so-called *Likert-type* scale. This format presents a client with several *items*—short sentences or phrases the content of which serves as an indicator of the construct to which inferences are to be made. The client is asked to respond to each item by placing a number next to the item, with the numbers "anchored" to some descriptive phrase denoting a quantitative level of meaning. For example, an item might read, "I feel sad." The client would be asked to respond to the item by placing one of the following numbers, with the specified meaning, next to the item: 1 = never; 2 = some of the time; 3 = a good part of the time; 4 = all, or nearly all, of the time. This set of numbers and their attendant defined meanings constitutes a *frequency category partition;* that is, a frequency continuum is partitioned into ordered categories that persons responding to the item can use to indicate the relative frequency with which they have the experience indicated in the item. Hudson's GCS is an example of a Likert-type scale with a frequency category partition. Another frequently used type of category partition used in Likert-type measures is the categorization of an agree-disagree continuum.

There are other formats for standardized scales, such as *semantic differential, Thurstone, Guttman,* and *adjective checklist* (see, e.g., Allen & Yen, 2001; Grinnell, 2001; Neuman, 2006; Nunnally & Bernstein, 1994; Rubin & Babbie, 2007). A catalog of standardized measurement procedures for use in social work practice can be found in Corcoran and Fischer (2000a, 2000b).

Self-Anchored Scales/Individualized Rating Scales

A form of measurement procedure often discussed in the context of practice evaluation is the so-called *individualized rating scale* (Bloom et al., 2005) or what is also referred to as the *self-anchored scale* (Nugent et al., 2001). An individualized rating scale is a nonstandardized measurement procedure created for use with a specific client, sometimes to try and measure a unique problem that the client reports. The practitioner, in collaboration with her or his client, will create and tailor the individualized rating scale for this particular client. In-depth discussion on how to create an individualized rating scale can be found in Bloom et al. (2005) and Nugent et al. (2001). There is research on the reliability and validity characteristics of these forms of measurement procedure reported in Bloom et al. (2005).

Informal Scales

An informal scale or measurement procedure is one created by a practitioner, many times without any specific plan, for a unique situation or client. This form of measurement tool has a format unique to the practitioner, setting, and client. It can be something as basic as the social worker asking her or his client how he or she is doing relative to the last time the practitioner met with her or him: Is he or she better? The same? Worse? This verbal, informal approach produces an ordinal ranking, from the client's viewpoint (so it is a form of self-report) as to how he or she is doing relative to the last session. The practitioner might make her or his own assessment using the same ordinal ranking (i.e., the client is either better, the same, or worse). The problem with such approaches to measurement is that the information obtained is vulnerable to all of the types of error discussed earlier. Further, such approaches to measurement lack any evidence concerning reliability and validity. Garb (1998) gives an in-depth discussion of research on the reliability and validity of practitioner judgment, with and without the use of formal, standardized measurement and assessment tools. While it is probably safe to say that this form of measurement is common in both everyday life and in professional practice, the prudent practitioner will, if it is to be used, always augment such measurement methods with formal, standardized measurement procedures.

Interview Methods

Interview methods are very common in social work practice. Interview methods for measuring client characteristic, problems, strengths, and so on can be described along a dimension that concerns how structured versus unstructured the process is. A *free style interview* has the least amount of formal structure to it. In this type of interview, the social worker asks whatever questions come to mind, usually in response to the client's responses to prior questions. The information obtained from this form of interview has the lowest levels of reliability and validity (Garb, 1998). *Semi-structured interviews* have some degree of formal structure to them, with some specific questions required, yet retain the flexibility inherent in the free-style interview in that the social worker will be free to ask other, unscripted questions that seem appropriate. A *structured interview* is a formal, standardized interview protocol that specifies which questions are to be asked, in what order, and under what circumstances. The information obtained from structured interviews has the highest levels of reliability and validity of the interview methods (Garb, 1998). An example of a formal structured interview is the Anxiety Disorders Interview Schedule for *DSM-IV* (ADIS-IV; Di Nardo, Brown, & Barlow, 1994). The scores from this interview schedule, for example, lead to diagnoses of anxiety disorders with, perhaps, the highest levels of reliability currently available (Barlow, 2002).

Thought/Feeling Listing

A qualitative measurement approach, which could readily be used to provide quantitative information as well, is the *thought listing technique* (Cacioppo & Petty, 1981; Goldberg & Shaw, 1989). In this procedure, your client makes a listing of thoughts that he or she has in relevant and important circumstances that you the practitioner specify. For example, you might have a client who is afraid to confront a coworker about a problem write out a list of thoughts that he or she has when contemplating speaking with the coworker about these issues.

Research has suggested this measurement approach can have reliability coefficients on the order of .80 or better, and that the thought lists obtained can be sensitive to change associated with interventions (Cacioppo & Petty, 1979; Cacioppo, Sandman, & Walker, 1978; Petty & Cacioppo, 1979; Petty, Wells, & Brock, 1976). Nugent (1992) used a variation of thought listing—feeling listing—in research on the affective impact of interviewing styles. In this method, you would have your client make a list of the emotions that he or she experiences in a relevant and important situation or setting. You could also, of course, have your client do a combined thought and feeling listing as well. The thought and feeling listing techniques are closely related to some of the cognitive restructuring techniques found in cognitive-behavior therapy (see Beck, 1995).

Behavioral Observations

Another measurement approach would be to have your client keep count of the frequency and/or intensity of problematic behaviors, troubling emotions and/or thoughts, or other problematic occurrences. For example, if your client appears to have problems with panic attacks you might have your client keep a daily count of the occurrence of panic attacks. You might also have your client keep track of the intensity of each panic attack, for example on a 0 (zero intensity) to 100 (the most intense panic attack imaginable) rating scale. As another example, you might have your client keep a daily count of the number of times that he becomes angry, along with a rating of the intensity of the anger felt each occurrence, while driving. Such counts and ratings can be kept on 3 × 5 note cards. In-depth descriptions of how to have your client do behavioral counts can be found in such sources as Bloom et al. (2005); Nugent et al. (2001); and Johnston and Pennypacker (1993).

It should be noted that the reliability of behavioral counts is usually reported as some form of *interrater agreement*. Interrater agreement concerns the extent to which two independent observers agree in terms of the occurrence of a behavior; the frequency with which the behavior occurs; and so on. Interrater agreement is usually expressed as the percentage of the time the different observers agree, or as a chance-corrected interrater agreement index called *kappa*. For example, suppose that two different observers are keeping track of whether or not a child hits her or his sibling during a particular day. An interrater agreement index of 85% would tell the social worker that the two observers agreed 85% of the time about whether or not the child hit her or his sibling. In contrast, a kappa value can range in value from −1 to +1, and is interpretable as the extent to which two observers agree *over and above the level of agreement expected by chance*. Thus, a kappa of +.85 would indicate that the two observers agreed 85% over and above the agreement expected just by chance. A kappa of 0 would indicate that the two observers were agreeing at a level expected just by chance. Details about how to create and implement observational procedures for assessing behaviors can be found in sources such as Bloom et al. (2005); Nugent et al. (2001); Johnston and Pennypacker (1993); and any books on behavior therapy or applied behavior analysis.

Books of Measures   There are a number of books devoted to collections and descriptions of measures for use in practice. Probably one of the relevant for clinical practice is Corcoran and Fischer's (2000a, 2000b) two volume set, *Measures for Clinical Practice*. Other sources are *Family Assessment: A Guide to Methods and Measures* (Grotevant & Carlson, 1989); *Measures of Family Functioning for Research and Practice* (Sawin, Harrigan, & Woog, 1995); and *The Sixteenth Mental Measurements Yearbook* (Spies, Plake, & Murphy, 2005). You can search through these sources for standardized procedures for use in measuring a wide range of client characteristics and problems.

Context and Demand Characteristics

The practitioner needs to keep in mind that the environment into which clients are placed during assessment is usually at least a little (if not a lot) foreign to them. They may be asked to enter a strange environment, sit down with someone they barely (or do not) know, and then talk about sensitive and troubling aspects of their lives. They might be nervous about coming to see a social worker, therapist, or a doctor; and these context factors can sometimes lead clients to give misleading self-reports, either consciously or unconsciously. The context factors associated with the measurement process that can create a pressure on the client to respond in possibly biased ways are referred to as *demand characteristics* and should be minimized as much as possible (Nunnally & Bernstein, 1994). The social worker should also keep in mind the numerous factors, discussed earlier (see also Dawes, 1996; Garb, 1998; Gilovich, 1993), that can bias perceptions and questions in such a way as to lead the practitioner to erroneous conclusions. The social worker should structure the measurement process so as to minimize these effects.

Triangulation

It is also important to recognize that no measurement or assessment method is infallible. Thus, rather than relying on one or two methods, it is best to use as many methods as possible, a methodology referred to as *triangulation*, a term meaning that multiple and different measurement and assessment methods are used in an effort to triangulate on the construct of interest. For example, the social worker might have her client complete a set of self-report scales, obtain information from the client's family members, and gather information from a one-on-one interview with her client. The information from these multiple methods would be combined with the data obtained from one method complementing that obtained from another. In this way, the weaknesses of one method are rectified by the strengths of another.

The need for triangulated data collection was clearly illustrated for the author several years ago. The author was helping a family service agency incorporate the Multi-Problem Screening Inventory (MPSI; Nugent et al., 2001), into the agency's routine assessment procedures. One of the agency's counselors worked with a young female adolescent brought to the agency by her mother. The young woman had been in a residential facility being treated for suicidal depression, and the residential facility had just released the teenager as "cured," coincidentally on the same day that her insurance benefits had terminated. The young woman's mother brought her to the family service agency because she was (justifiably) concerned that her daughter might still be depressed and suicidal. The counselor conducted an in-depth, free-style interview with the teenager and her mother together. The main purpose of the interview was to determine whether, and to what degree, the young woman was still suicidal. During the interview the teenager repeatedly and convincingly told the counselor and her mother that she was no longer contemplating suicide. The teenager convinced both the counselor and her mother that she was feeling better and that she was no longer suicidal. The counselor had her complete, as part of a triangulation approach, the MPSI, and then sent her home with her mother.

After the interview, the counselor scored the MPSI and was both scared and confused. The MPSI contains a suicidal ideation subscale. The young woman's score on this subscale was 96, nearly the highest score possible, which is 100. The score implied that she was, contrary to her verbal expressions to the contrary, extremely suicidal. The counselor immediately telephoned the young woman and asked her to help him resolve his confusion: Her words said that she was okay, while her score on the suicidal ideation subscale told a different story. The teenager informed him that she was still suicidal but had not wanted to reveal this in the interview because she had not wanted to upset her mother.

The use of the standardized measure as a triangulated source of information complementing that obtained in the interview allowed the counselor to obtain critical information that the interview had failed to obtain. Triangulation of data collection is considered a critical component of an adequate standard of care (Fremouw, Perczel, & Ellis, 1990).

Measuring Strengths

One other aspect of description should be mentioned. Practitioners often focus on the issues and problems that clients face. Client's problems do not have to be the only things practitioners focus on. Measurement can also help to describe the assets, strengths, and accomplishments that clients bring to the helping context. For instance, the social worker could monitor a depressed, emotionally withdrawn client's ability to express her or his feelings to her or his companion animal. This could be done throughout the helping process. The act of measuring strengths can be very empowering for clients.

THE PROBABILISTIC NATURE OF DIAGNOSIS

As noted earlier, practitioners have been criticized for not taking prevalence rates into account during assessment. This is especially true when practitioners make inferences that lead to a "diagnosis," an inference that a client belongs to a specific class (such as person's who have experienced abuse) or has a particular disease or disorder (e.g., a mental disorder). Ignoring base rates, or what are referred to as *prevalence rates*, can lead to biases and errors (see, e.g., Arkes, 1991; Dawes, 1986; Finn, 1982). Gibbs and Gambrill (1999, p. 135) pointed out that ignoring prevalence rates can lead social worker to the erroneous belief that the same assessment procedure will identify individuals with some disorder just as well in a low prevalence context as in a high prevalence context.

In this section, probability theory is used to explore the roles that prevalence rates and the sensitivity and specificity of an assessment procedure have on the probability that a client actually has a disorder that he or she has been diagnosed as having, a number sometimes referred to as the *positive predictive value* of an assessment procedure, and the probability that a client does *not* have a disorder that he or she has judged to *not* have, a number referred to as the *negative predictive value*. These notions are critically important for any social worker who makes any type of diagnosis, such as that of the presence of a mental disorder, and for any social worker whose client has been given some form of mental health diagnosis or has been diagnosed as having a particular disease. Web sites that may help the reader to understand these notions are: www.musc.edu/dc/icrebm/sensitivity.html and www.fpnotebook.com/PRE17.htm.

It will be assumed in the following discussion that the particular disorder exists and is real in the sense that a person can develop and suffer from it independent of any social convention concerning its existence. For example, a person can develop and suffer from kidney failure, regardless of whether the social group to which the person belongs recognizes and identifies the disease. In other words, the disorder is more than just a socially constructed, reified entity.

Positive Predictive Value

Let's first review several important concepts important to subsequent discussion. Table 3.2 shows both reality and the outcomes of an assessment inference made by a practitioner on the basis of results from some assessment procedure. The labels above the cells of the box represent reality: A client either has (yes), or does not have (no), a particular disease or disorder. The labels on the side of the box represent the inferences made by a practitioner from the results of the assessment procedure: The practitioner either infers that the client has the particular disorder (yes), or that the client does not (no). The terms within the cells of the box describe the inferences made by the social worker. If the client does *not* have the disease or disorder, and the practitioner infers that the client does not have the disorder (upper left cell in the box), then this correct inference is called a *true negative*. The proportion of persons who do not have a disorder who are correctly inferred to not have the disorder, on the basis of the results of the assessment procedure, is referred to as the *specificity* of the assessment procedure.

If the client *does* have the disorder, and the practitioner infers that the client does indeed have the disorder (lower right cell), then this correct inference is referred to as a *true positive*. The proportion of persons who have a disorder who are correctly inferred to have the disorder on the basis of the results of the assessment procedure is referred to as the *sensitivity*. Table 3.2 shows a representation of the outcomes of assessment inferences. The columns represent the two possibilities concerning whether a client has or does not have a specific disorder, while the rows represent the two possible outcomes of assessment inferences about whether or not the client has the specific disorder.

If the client does *not* have the disorder, but the practitioner infers that the client *does* have the disorder (lower left cell), then this erroneous inference is referred to as a *false positive*. The proportion of persons who do not have a disorder incorrectly inferred to have the disorder on the basis of the results of some assessment procedure is referred to as the *false positive rate* of the assessment procedure. If the client *does* indeed have the disorder, but the practitioner infers that the client *does not* have the disorder, then this incorrect inference is referred to as a *false negative*. The proportion of persons who have a disorder who are incorrectly inferred to not have the disorder on the basis of the results of some assessment procedure is referred to as the *false negative rate* of the assessment procedure.

Now suppose that an assessment or diagnostic procedure produces results that are positive, leading a practitioner to infer that a client has some disorder, call it disorder X. What is the probability that the client actually has disorder X given that he or she has been diagnosed as having it? This important probability is referred to as the *positive predictive*

Table 3.2   Inference from Assessment Results: Does Client Have the Disorder?

		Reality	
		No	Yes
Assessment Procedure	No	True Negative	False negative
	Yes	False Positive	True positive

value (PPV) of the diagnosis. This probability can be computed using the diagram in Figure 3.1 (see Ash, 1993, pp. 58–61; also, Mendenhall, 1975, pp. 80–82), which represents the outcomes, already shown in Table 3.2, of an assessment procedure. First, the client either has, or does not have, disorder X. Figure 3.1 represents this state of affairs by showing two paths, path A and path B. Path A represents the situation in which a person has disorder X, while path B shows the situation in which the person does *not* have disorder X. A number is placed in parentheses next to the letter A to represent the prevalence of the disorder in a given population or subpopulation. The *prevalence* is the proportion (or percentage) of a given population (or subpopulation) that has the disorder (see later discussion).

Let's assume, for purposes of explication, that the prevalence is .05, so the number .05 is placed in the parentheses in Figure 3.1 next to the letter A. A number can also be placed next to the letter B to represent the prevalence of "not having disorder X." This number will be $1 - p$, where p is the prevalence of disorder X, so if the prevalence is .05, then the prevalence of "not having disorder X" will be .95, as shown in Figure 3.1.

The path in Figure 3.1 marked with the letter C represents the situation in which a person who has disorder X is identified via some assessment procedure as having disorder X, and a number can be placed next to the letter C to represent the true positive rate, or the sensitivity, of the assessment procedure. The sensitivity can be interpreted as the probability that a person who has disorder X is identified by use of the assessment procedure as having disorder X. Similarly, the path labeled with the letter D in Figure 3.1 shows the situation in which a person who has disorder X is incorrectly inferred, from the assessment, to *not* have the disorder. This event is of course a false negative and a number can be placed next to the letter D to represent this rate. The false negative rate, FNR, which is the proportion of persons who have disorder X who are erroneously inferred as *not* having this disorder, is related to the sensitivity by, FNR = 1 − Sensitivity. For example, since the sensitivity in Figure 3.1 is .95, the FNR would be $1 - .95 = .05$.

The path labeled E in Figure 3.1 represents the state of affairs in which the person does *not* have disorder X but is incorrectly inferred from the results of the assessment procedure

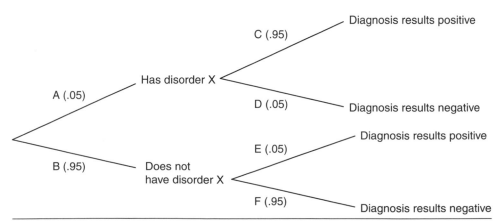

Figure 3.1   A tree diagram representing assessment inferences as a two-stage process. The number in parentheses next to the letter A represents the prevalence of a disorder or problem; the number in the parentheses next to the letter C represents the sensitivity of an assessment method; and the number in parentheses next to the letter F represents the specificity of the assessment method.

to have the disorder. This situation is a false positive and a number can be placed next to the letter E to represent the false positive rate, which gives the proportion of persons who do *not* have disorder X who are erroneously inferred as having the disorder. Finally, the path labeled F represents the situation in which the person who does *not* have disorder X is correctly determined to not have the disorder. This is referred a true negative, and the number representing the specificity—the proportion of persons who have disorder X who are accurately inferred to have the disorder—of the assessment procedure can be placed next to the letter F to represent this rate. The false positive rate, FPR, is related to the specificity by, FPR $= 1 -$ Specificity. For example, since the specificity in Figure 3.1 is .95, the FPR will be $1 - .95 = .05$.

Figure 3.1 shows a hypothetical assessment procedure with a sensitivity of .95 (FNR = .05), and a specificity of .95 (FPR = .05), for detecting the presence or absence of disorder X. This assessment procedure is being used in the context of a disorder with a prevalence rate of .05. The question thus becomes, "If a client is inferred to have disorder X from the results of the assessment procedure, what is the probability that the client does, in fact, have disorder X?" In other words, what is the PPV of the diagnosis, "The client has disorder X?" An equation discussed in Nugent (2004) can be used to compute this probability. This probability depends on (a) the sensitivity of the assessment procedure for detecting the presence of disorder X, (b) the specificity of the assessment procedure for detecting the absence of disorder X, and (c) on the prevalence of disorder X.

So, assuming that the sensitivity and specificity are both .95 as in Figure 3.1, and that the prevalence of disorder X is .05, then, using the formula discussed in Nugent (2004), the probability that a client actually has disorder X given that he or she has been diagnosed as having it—the PPV of the diagnosis—will be .50. Thus, even though the sensitivity and specificity of this assessment procedure are each .95, the odds that the client really has disorder X, given that he or she has been diagnosed with it, are only 50/50. The reason for this perhaps counter-intuitive result for the probability that the client has disorder X given that he or she has been diagnosed as having the disorder through use of the assessment procedure, in this context of the high sensitivity and specificity values for the assessment procedure, is the low prevalence rate. Note that if the sensitivity and specificity both remain at .95, *but the prevalence rate of disorder X increases to .50* (i.e., 50% of the population has the disorder), then the probability that the client has disorder X given that he or she has been diagnosed with it from the results of the assessment procedure will increase to .95. This shows how the same assessment procedure works differently in high and low prevalence rate contexts.

The Negative Predictive Value

In a similar vein, the probability that a client does *not* have disorder X given that the assessment procedure produces results that lead the practitioner to infer that he or she does *not* have the disorder, the negative predictive value (NPV), is given by a second equation in Nugent (2004). For the situation in Figure 3.1, using the appropriate formula in Nugent (2004), it can be seen that the probability that a client does not have disorder X given that the assessment results suggest he or she does not have it—the NPV—will be .997. Note that in this context, where the prevalence of disorder X is .05, the prevalence of *not* having disorder X is $1 - .05 = .95$. This high prevalence context of not having disorder X is why the assessment procedure leads to such a high NPV associated with the absence of the diagnosis of disorder X.

Common Misunderstandings

When asked what the probability is that a client has the disorder that he or she has been diagnosed as having, many of the author's students have responded by saying that this probability is the same as the sensitivity of the assessment procedure or, equivalently, the same as the true positive rate. For example, if the sensitivity (true positive rate) is .95, then students have said that the probability that a client has disorder X given that he or she has been diagnosed as having the disorder will also be .95. However, this is incorrect, as can be seen by closely considering the various formulae in Nugent (2004). The formula for the PPV can be written in a form in which the numerator gives the number of persons who have disorder X who have been (accurately) inferred as having disorder X by use of the assessment procedure, while the denominator gives the *total number of persons who have been diagnosed as having disorder X.* In contrast, the formula for the sensitivity can be written in a form in which the numerator, as in the formula for the PPV, is the number of persons who have disorder X who have been (accurately) inferred as having disorder X by use of the assessment procedure, while, in contrast, the denominator is the *total number of persons who have disorder X in the population.* Thus, the formulae for the PPV and the sensitivity, while sharing the same numerator, have different denominators. A similar line of reasoning will show that the NPV and the specificity (true negative rate) will not be the same since the formulae for the NPV and the specificity have different denominators (see discussion in Nugent, 2004).

What Are the PPV and NPV of Assessment Inferences Made in Practice?

The previous discussion immediately raises questions about what the probabilities that clients actually have the disorder with which they have been diagnosed as having and what the probabilities that clients actually do *not* have the disorders that they have been inferred as *not* having, might actually be in social work practice. Before considering these probabilities, we first need to determine the best estimates of the prevalence rates of specific disorders and of the sensitivities and specificities of commonly used assessment procedures and then use these in calculations of the PPV and the NPV.

Prevalence Estimates

As noted earlier, the prevalence of a disorder is the proportion or percentage of persons in a given population that have the disorder. The prevalence of a disorder in a given population can be specified as the proportion (or percentage) of the population that has the disorder at a *given point in time,* a so-called *point estimate;* over a *specific duration of time,* a so-called *period estimate;* or *over a person's lifetime,* a so-called *lifetime estimate* (Banks & Kerns, 1996). For example, Eaton, Dryman, and Weissman (1991) reported data from the Epidemiologic Catchment Area (ECA) study (see later) suggesting that the point prevalence of Panic Disorder (PD) in the general U.S. population is .0053 (.53%); the 1-year prevalence is .0091 (.91%); and the life-time prevalence is .0157 (1.57%). Generally a point estimate will be lower than a 1-year prevalence, while the 1-year prevalence will be lower than a lifetime prevalence (Banks & Kerns, 1996).

A number of epidemiologic investigations on the prevalence of various mental disorders have been conducted. Two of the largest have been the ECA study, which involved a probability sample of over 12,000 community residents, and the National Comorbidity Study (NCS), which involved a probability sample of over 8,000 community residents (see Barlow, 2002). Recently, Reiger, Narrow, and Rae (as cited in Barlow, 2002, p. 22) used the data from these two epidemological studies to provide best estimates of the 1-year prevalence of a number of disorders. These estimates suggested, for example, that .049 (4.9%) of the overall U.S. population suffer from agoraphobia; 5.3% from Major Depressive Disorder; and 3.6% from Posttraumatic Stress Disorder at some point over a 1-year period. Other studies have suggested that a point estimate of the prevalence of Major Depression among adolescents is 3.4%, while a lifetime prevalence is 24.8% (Lewinsohn, Hops, Roberts, Seeley, & Andrews, 1993).

As noted earlier, numerous writers have argued that practitioners need to take into account prevalence rates when making assessment and diagnostic inferences. Consideration of general population prevalence rates when making inferences from assessment results assumes that these rates are the same as those in the population of persons actually seeking services. However, the prevalence of some disorders and problems appears to be greater within specific subpopulations than in the general population. For example, within the population of persons with certain physical diseases the prevalence of major depression may be higher than that in the general population. Studies have led to estimates of the prevalence of Major Depressive Disorder (MDD) of 23% among women recently diagnosed with cancer (Evans et al., 1986), 14% among persons who suffered a stroke within the past 2 months (Morris, Robinson, & Raphael, 1990), and as high as 54% among chronic pain patients (Banks & Kerns, 1996).

Other lines of research have suggested that prevalence rates among persons seeking services will differ from general population rates. For example, it has been estimated that only 10% of those who experience depression actually seek services (NIH, 2001). Some epidemiologic research has suggested that only about 13% of persons with a single diagnosable disorder actually seek treatment (Blazer, Kessler, McGonagle, & Swartz, 1994). Thus, the prevalence rate of those suffering from a particular disorder in the general population, or in specific subpopulations, may not be the same as that among those seeking services. The prevalence rate among those seeking services could be either higher or lower than in the general population, could be either higher or lower than in specific subpopulations, and in many cases may not be known.

A caveat is in order concerning these (as well as all other) prevalence estimates: They are only as accurate as the methodology on which they are based. While the ECA and NCS prevalence estimates were based on probability samples, and therefore may be reasonably accurate, the other prevalence estimates reported earlier may be less sound, and the reader is referred to the original studies for details of the methodologies on which the estimates are based. Another concern is that prevalence estimates are themselves based on fallible assessment procedures. Thus, all prevalence estimates are vulnerable to measurement error inherent in the results of the assessment procedures. The implications of these uncertainties are considered later.

Sensitivity and Specificity of Commonly Used Assessment Methods

For illustrative purposes, let's consider the sensitivity and specificity of various assessment procedures for determining whether a person has a Major Depressive Disorder (MDD). Recently, Williams, Pignone, Ramirez, and Stellato (2002) synthesized the results of 38 studies, involving 32,000 participants, on the sensitivity and specificity of 16 different measures of depression used in primary care settings to identify persons with MDD. The median sensitivity was .85, and the median specificity was .74, and the results suggested that there were no significant differences between any of the 16 instruments. These sensitivity and specificity values were used to compute the probability that a client actually has a MDD given that he or she has been diagnosed as having a MDD (i.e., the PPV)—and the probability that the client does, in fact, *not* have a MDD given that he or she has been inferred as *not* having a MDD (i.e., the NPV)—for five different prevalence rates: .05, .15, .25, .54, and .70. The results of these computations are shown in Table 3.3. The prevalence value of .05 is approximately equal to the 1-year prevalence of MDD in the general population; the .54 value represents an upper boundary for the relatively high rates of MDD that have been estimated for chronic pain patients; while the .70 value represents a prevalence exceeding any found in the literature for special populations and is used to illustrate PPV and NPV values in this highest of prevalence contexts. The range .05 to .70

Table 3.3   PPV and NPV Values for the Diagnosis of Major Depressive Disorder for Five Prevalence Rates and Three Assessment Procedures

	Prevalence =	.05	.15	.25	.54	.70
Williams et al. (2002) results for sixteen measurement scales						
Sensitivity = .85	PPV =	.15	.37	.52	.79	.88
Specificity = .74	NPV =	.99	.97	.94	.81	.67
Noerholm et al. (2001) results for the Major Depression Inventory (MDI)						
Sensitivity = .92	PPV =	.26	.54	.69	.88	.94
Specificity = .86	NPV =	.99	.98	.97	.90	.82
Murphy et al. (2000) results for the Diagnostic Interview Schedule (DIS)						
Sensitivity = .55	PPV =	.22	.54	.65	.87	.93
Specificity = .90	NPV =	.97	.92	.86	.63	.46
Eaton et al. (2000) results for the Diagnostic Interview Schedule (DIS)						
Sensitivity = .25	PPV =	.40	.69	.81	.94	.97
Specificity = .98	PPV =	.96	.88	.80	.65	.36

Sources: "Identifying Depression in Primary Care: A Literature Synthesis of Case-Finding Instruments," by J. Williams et al., 2002, *General Hospital Psychiatry, 24*(4), pp. 225–237; "A Comparison of Diagnostic Interviews for Depression in the Stirling County Study," by J. Murphy, R. Monson, N. Laird, A. Sobol, and A. Leighton, 2000, *Archives of General Psychiatry, 57*(3), pp. 230–236; "A Comparison of Self-Report and Clinical Diagnostic Interviews for Depression: Diagnostic Interview Schedule and Schedules for Clinical Assessment in Neuropsychiatry in the Baltimore Epidemiologic Catchment Area Follow-Up," by W. Eaton, K. Neufeld, L. Chen, and G. Cai, 2000, *Archives of General Psychiatry, 57*(3), pp. 217–222; "The Sensitivity and Specificity of the Major Depression Inventory, Using the Present State Examination as the Index of Diagnostic Validity," by P. Bech, N. Rasmussen, R. Olsen, V. Noerholm, and W. Abildgaard, 2001, *Journal of Affective Disorders, 66*(2–3), pp. 159–164.

likely captures the range of prevalence rates of MDD among many populations seeking services in health and mental health settings.

The uppermost entries in Table 3.3 show the values of the PPV and NPV computed from the Williams et al. (2002), sensitivity and specificity estimates for the five prevalence rates. For example, given the sensitivity of .85 and the specificity of .74, and a prevalence of .05, then PPV = .15; and NPV = .99. As can be seen in Table 3.3, PPV values range from .15 to .88, and NPV values range from .67 to .99.

In another study, Bech, Rasmussen, Olson, Noerholm, and Abildgaard (2001) investigated the sensitivity and specificity of the Major Depression Inventory (MDI) for detecting MDD. The authors reported an upper value for the sensitivity of the MDI of .92, and an upper value for the specificity of .86, for detecting MDD. The second set of entries in Table 3.3 show the PPV and NPV values. The PPV values range from .26 to .94, and the NPV values range from .82 to .99. The PPV and NPV values are somewhat higher than those for the depression measures in the first example because the sensitivity and specificity estimates are higher for the MDI.

The Diagnostic Interview Schedule (DIS) is a highly structured interview for use in identifying mental health problems, such as depression, and for making *DSM* type diagnoses (Robins, Helzer, Croughan, & Ratcliff, 1981). Murphy et al. (2000) reported a sensitivity for the DIS of .55, and a specificity of .90, for identifying MDD. The third set of entries in Table 3.3 shows PPV and NPV values for the DIS under the five different prevalence rates. In a second study, Eaton et al. (2000) estimated the sensitivity of the DIS at .25, while the specificity was estimated to be .98. Note that in this study the estimated sensitivity was lower, .25 versus .55, than that estimated by Murphy et al. (2000), while the specificity was a bit higher, .98 versus .90.

The fourth set of entries in Table 3.3 show the PPV and NPV values based on the Eaton et al. (2000) sensitivity and specificity estimates. It is important to note here that even though the estimated sensitivity of the DIS is lower in this second study, .25, versus .55 in the previous study, the probabilities that a client diagnosed as having a MDD actually has MDD are uniformly higher across the range of prevalence values. This illustrates the importance of attempts to gather evidence inconsistent with a particular diagnosis or assessment result, thereby increasing the specificity, a topic discussed in detail later. Note also that as the prevalence of the disorder increases the prevalence of *not* having the disorder decreases, so as PPV values increase, NPV values decrease, and vice versa. This again illustrates the important role that prevalence plays in interpreting what the results of an assessment tell the practitioner.

In summary, these results should be quite sobering. These results imply that even in the exceedingly high prevalence rate context of 70%, as many as 64% of clients may be misdiagnosed in the sense that they have been determined to *not* have MDD, when in fact they do. The actual rates of misdiagnosis are likely higher than implied in Table 3.3 for two reasons. First, in all but the most unusual of circumstances the prevalence rates of disorders in populations of persons seeking services are most likely *less* than .70. This means that the values in Table 3.3 for the prevalence rates less than .70 are most likely representative of the PPV and NPV values found in actual practice. Second, the most common assessment approaches used in actual practice are most likely unstructured approaches (Garb, 1998; see discussion immediately following). Since the sensitivity and specificity values for unstructured approaches are almost certainly lower than for structured approaches (Garb,

1998; Nugent, 2004), this second consideration implies that the actual diagnostic error rates found in clinical practice are almost certainly higher than those implied by the numbers in Table 3.3. This is not a happy outcome for either practitioner or client.

Research on Unstructured Assessments by Practitioners

Unstructured assessment methods, within the context of the free style interview, may be the most common form of assessment conducted by practitioners (Garb, 1998). Research on these types of assessment inferences made by practitioners is, therefore, an important research topic. Research has suggested that clinicians make assessment decisions, such as diagnoses, very quickly, frequently after gathering very little information (see Ambady & Rosenthal, 1992; Gambrill, 1997; Garb, 1998; Houts & Galante, 1985). Further, practitioners frequently do not attend to diagnostic criteria when they are conducting assessments (e.g., Jampala, Spears, & Neubauer, 1988; Rubinson, Asnis, & Friedman, 1988; see also the discussion in Garb, 1998). For example, in one study, replicated by Blashfield and Herkov (1996), Morey and Ochoa (1989) compared the criteria used by clinicians to make *DSM-III* diagnoses with the actual *DSM-III* criteria. The results showed that the agreement, expressed as a kappa coefficient, between the criteria used by clinicians and the actual *DSM-III* criteria ranged from only .05 to .59. As noted earlier, practitioners also engage in a number of cognitive processes that focus on confirming impressions already formed, and they do not appear to explicitly search for information contradicting initial clinical impressions and diagnostic decisions (Garb, 1998). This confirmation bias makes diagnostic error much more likely (Garb & Boyle, 2003).

Evidence That Increases PPV and NPV Values

An important question concerns what types of information can help the practitioner to increase either the PPV or the NPV. Nugent (2004) derived equations that implied that: (a) if a practitioner has made a tentative inference based on the results of an assessment procedure that a client *has* disorder X, then subsequent efforts to obtain new information *inconsistent with the diagnosis of disorder X* will lead to greater increases in the PPV than will efforts to obtain information consistent with the diagnosis, and (b) if a practitioner has made a tentative inference that a client does *not* have disorder X based on the results of an assessment procedure, then subsequent efforts to obtain new information *inconsistent with the inference*—that is, consistent with the client having disorder X—will lead to grater increases in the NPV. The equations in Nugent (2004) are consistent with the conclusions of many writers (e.g., Garb, 1998; Gibbs & Gambrill, 1999; Gilovich, 1993) that *one of the most important activities that a practitioner can engage in is the search for information that contradicts a belief, inference, or conclusion.*

These results also imply that practitioners, contrary to what appears to be common practice (see Garb, 1998), should view assessment as an ongoing process that ends only when the services being provided to the client have ended. Again, research suggests that practitioners make diagnoses very quickly, based on limited information, and then tend not to seek information that would contradict the practitioner's initial impressions. In many cases, once a diagnosis has been made, there are no subsequent efforts to obtain new information that could lead to reconsideration of the validity of the diagnosis. This approach to assessment, in which assessment is actualized as a brief, time-limited process that essentially ends with the making of a diagnosis and the initiation of some treatment or intervention, is fraught with the risk of erroneous inferences about clients' problems and disorders (Garb & Boyle, 2003). However, if assessment is operationalized as an ongoing process throughout the provision of services, the assessment inferences made from the constantly accruing information can be constantly updated and altered as necessary. This ongoing assessment process may thereby lead to increases in specificity and sensitivity and attendant increases in the probabilities represented by the PPV and NPV.

Make and Use Diagnoses with Great Caution

The foregoing clearly suggests that social workers should avoid making categorical inferences if at all possible. Earlier it was noted that relative inferences will have greater measurement error than absolute inferences—such as diagnoses—except in the most unusual and unlikely of circumstances. Assessments that lead to categorical inferences will almost certainly have more error in them than those in which relative inferences are to be made. This is why standardized categorical assessment procedures, such as diagnostic methodologies, are now beginning to appear that make use of relative ordering aspects (Barlow, 2002). However, it is likely that diagnoses of various forms are unavoidable in social work practice. Thus, it is incumbent on the practitioner to make and use diagnoses only with the greatest of caution and humility as to what they are telling the social worker. First, it must be recognized that any diagnosis is a probabilistic statement, not a statement of fact. If the practitioner can find reasonable estimates of the sensitivity and specificity of the assessment procedures to be used, as well as good estimates of the prevalence of the disease(s) or disorder(s) that are under consideration, then the practitioner can use the methods in Nugent (2004) to obtain estimates of the PPV and NPV of diagnoses made or not made. These estimates can help the practitioner to make treatment decisions well informed by the probabilities associated with a particular diagnosis—the PPV of the diagnosis, and/or the probabilities associated with the absence of a diagnosis—the NPV. Unfortunately, these estimates of the sensitivity and specificity of the assessment procedures to be used may not be available or even known; and estimates of the prevalence of the disease(s) or disorder(s) of focus will most likely not be known for the particular population seeking services in a given social work practice context. Thus, the practitioner is in the unenviable position of having to make use of a probabilistic tool, the diagnosis, without any real sense of the PPV or NPV values. It is a probability game without the player (the practitioner) being given the probabilities of either winning or losing. Humility about what a diagnosis tells the social worker is clearly in order!

CONCLUSION

Assessment is fundamental to social work practice. A good assessment will be an ongoing process throughout the provision of services and will be conducted within a biopsychosocial and critical-thinking framework. The social worker must be constantly vigilant to look for information and evidence that contradicts judgments, inferences, and conclusions that he or she has made. Measurement procedures with evidence concerning reliability and validity should be used and, if at all possible, relative inferences should be made in lieu of absolute inferences because the former will have less measurement error than the latter. If diagnoses of some type must be made or used, the social worker should make attempts to find good estimates of the sensitivity and sensitivity of the assessment or diagnostic methods to be used, as well as estimates of the prevalence of the disorders or diseases of concern in the relevant populations. The PPV and NPV of diagnoses made or not made can then be estimated, helping the practitioner to more clearly understand what a particular diagnosis, or absence of diagnosis, tells her or him. If these values cannot be obtained, then the practitioner must be extremely cautious about what a diagnosis tells her or him since it is a probability game being played without knowledge of the probabilities involved. Finally, the practitioner must approach assessment—indeed the entire helping process—with humility about what he or she believes that he or she knows. This humility can help keep the social work practitioner from making assessment errors that lead to iatrogenic outcomes for her or his clients.

REFERENCES

Allen, M., & Yen, W. (2001). *Introduction to measurement theory*. Long Grove, IL: Waveland.

Ambady, N., & Rosenthal, R. (1992). Thin slices of expressive behavior as predictors of interpersonal consequences: A meta-analysis. *Psychological Bulletin*, *111*(2), 256–274.

Arkes, H. (1991). Costs and benefits of judgment errors: Implications for debiasing. *Psychological Bulletin*, *110*(3), 486–498.

Ash, C. (1993). *The probability tutoring book*. New York: Wiley.

Banks, S., & Kerns, R. (1996). Explaining high rates of depression in chronic pain: A diathesis-stress framework. *Psychological Bulletin*, *119*(1), 95–110.

Barlow, D. (2002). *Anxiety and its disorders* (2nd ed.). New York: Guilford Press.

Bech, P., Rasmussen, N., Olsen, R., Noerholm, V., & Abildgaard, W. (2001). The sensitivity and specificity of the major depression inventory: Using the present state examination as the index of diagnostic validity. *Journal of Affective Disorders*, *66*(2–3), 159–164.

Beck, J. (1995). *Cognitive therapy: Basics and beyond*. New York: Guilford Press.

Blashfield, R., & Herkov, M. (1996). Investigating clinician adherence to diagnosis by criteria: A replication of Morey and Ochoa (1989). *Journal of Personality Disorders*, *10*, 219–228.

Blazer, D., Kessler, R., McGonagle, K., & Swartz, M. (1994). The prevalence and distribution of major depression in a national community sample: The National Comorbidity Survey. *American Journal of Psychiatry*, *151*(7), 979–986.

Bloom, M., Fischer, J., & Orme, J. (2005). *Evaluating practice: Guidelines for the accountable professional* (5th ed.). Boston: Allyn & Bacon.

Blythe, B., & Tripodi, T. (1989). *Measurement in direct practice*. Thousand Oaks, CA: Sage.

Bongar, B. (2002). *The suicidal patient: Clinical and legal standards of care* (2nd ed.). Washington, DC: American Psychological Association.

Brennan, R. (1983). *Elements of generalizability theory*. Iowa City, IO: ACT.

Brennan, R. (2001). *Generalizability theory*. New York: Springer Verlag.

Brennan, R., & Kane, M. (1977). An index of dependability for mastery tests. *Educational Measurement*, *14*, 277–289.

Cacioppo, J., & Petty, R. (1979). The effects of message repetition and position on cognitive response, recall, and persuasion. *Journal of Personality and Social Psychology*, *37*, 97–109.

Cacioppo, J., & Petty, R. (1981). Social psychological procedures for cognitive response assessment: The thought listing technique. In T. V. Merluzzi, C. Glass, & M. Genest (Eds.), *Cognitive assessment* (pp. 308–342). New York: Guilford Press.

Cacioppo, J., Sandman, C., & Walker, B. (1978). The effects of operant heart rate conditioning on cognitive elaboration and attitude change. *Psychophysiology, 15,* 330–338.

Cole, N., & Moss, P. (1989). Bias in test use. In R. Linn (Ed.), *Educational measurement* (3rd ed., pp. 201–220). New York: Macmillan.

Corcoran, K., & Fischer, J. (2000a). *Measures for clinical practice: A source book: Vol. 1. Couples, families, and children* (3rd ed.). New York: Free Press.

Corcoran, K., & Fischer, J. (2000b). *Measures for clinical practice: A source book: Vol. 2. Adults* (3rd ed.). New York: Free Press.

Cormier, S., & Nurius, P. (2003). *Interviewing and change strategies for helpers: Fundamental skills and cognitive behavioral interventions* (5th ed.). Pacific Grove, CA: Thomson.

Crocker, L., & Algina, J. (1986). *Introduction to classical and modern test theory.* Belmont, CA: Wadsworth.

Dawes, R. (1986). Representative thinking in clinical judgement. *Clinical Psychology Review, 6*(5), 425–441.

Dawes, R. (1996). *House of cards: Psychology and psychotherapy built on myth.* New York: Free Press.

Di Nardo, P., Brown, T., & Barlow, D. (1994). *Anxiety disorders interview schedule for DSM-IV.* San Antonio, TX: Psychological Corporation/Graywind Publications.

Eaton, W., Dryman, A., & Weissman, M. (1991). Panic and phobia. In L. N. Robins & D. A. Regier (Eds.), *Psychiatric disorders in America: The Epidemiological Catchment Area study.* New York: Free Press.

Eaton, W., Neufeld, K., Chen, L., & Cai, G. (2000). A comparison of self-report and clinical diagnostic interviews for depression: Diagnostic interview schedule and schedules for clinical assessment in neuropsychiatry in the Baltimore epidemiologic catchment area follow-up. *Archives of General Psychiatry, 57*(3), 217–222.

Evans, D. L., McCartney, C. F., Nemeroff, C. B., Raft, D., Quade, D., & Golden, R. N., et al. (1986). Depression in women treated for gynecological cancer: Clinical and neuroendocrine assessment. *American Journal of Psychiatry, 143*(4), 447–452.

Finn, S. (1982). Base rates, utilities, and DSM-III: Shortcomings of fixed rule systems of psychodiagnosis. *Journal of Abnormal Psychology, 91*(4), 294–302.

Fremouw, W., Perczel, M., & Ellis, T. (1990). *Suicide risk.* Elmsford, NY: Pergamon.

Gambrill, E. (1990). *Critical thinking in clinical practice.* San Francisco: Jossey-Bass.

Gambrill, E. (1997). *Social work practice: A critical thinker's guide.* New York: Oxford University Press.

Garb, H. (1996). The representativeness and past-behavior heuristics in clinical judgement. *Professional Psychology: Research and Practice, 27,* 272–277.

Garb, H. (1998). *Studying the clinician: Judgement research and psychological assessment.* Washington, DC: American Psychological Association.

Garb, H., & Boyle, P. (2003). Understanding why some clinicians use pseudo-scientific methods: Findings from research on clinical judgement. In S. Lilienfeld, J. Lohr, & S. Lynn (Eds.), *Science and pseudoscience in clinical psychology* (pp. 17–38). New York: Guilford Press.

Gibbs, L., & Gambrill, E. (1999). *Critical thinking for social workers: Exercises for the helping professions.* Thousand Oaks, CA: Pine Forge Press.

Gilovich, T. (1993). *How we know what isn't so.* New York: Free Press.

Gold, M. (1996). The risk of misdiagnosing physical illness as depression. In F. Flach (Ed.), *The Hatherleigh guide to managing depression* (pp. 93–112). New York: Hatherleigh.

Goldberg, J., & Shaw, B. (1989). The measurement of cognition in psychopathology. In A. Freeman, K. Simon, L. Beutler, & H. Arkowitz (Eds.), *Comprehensive handbook of cognitive therapy* (pp. 37–59). New York: Plenum Press.

Grinnell, R. (2001). (Ed.). *Social work research and evaluation: Quantitative and qualitative approaches* (6th ed.), Itasca, IL: Peacock.

Grotevant, H., & Carlson, C. (1989). *Family assessment*. New York: Guilford Press.

Hepworth, D. H., Rooney, R. H., & Larsen, J. A. (2002). *Direct social work practice: Theory and skills* (6th ed.). Pacific Grove, CA: Brooks/Cole.

Houts, A., & Galante, M. (1985). The impact of evaluative disposition and subsequent information on clinical impressions. *Journal of Social and Clinical Psychology*, *3*, 201–212.

Hudson, W. (1982). *The clinical measurement package*. Homewoood, IL: Dorsey.

Jampala, V., Spears, S., & Neubauer, D. (1988). The use of DSM-III in the United States: A case of not going by the book. *Comprehensive Psychiatry*, *29*, 39–47.

Johnston, J., & Pennypacker, H. (1993). *Strategies and tactics of behavioral research*. Mahwah, NJ: Erlbaum.

Lewinsohn, S., Hops, H., Roberts, R., Seely, J., & Andrews, J. (1993). Adolescent psychopathology: I. Prevalence and incidence of depression and other DSM-R disorders in high school students. *Journal of Abnormal Psychology*, *102*(1), 133–144.

Lilienfeld, S., Lohr, J., & Lynn, S. (Eds.). (2003). *Science and pseudoscience in clinical psychology*. New York: Guilford Press.

Lord, F., & Novick, M. (1968). *Statistical theories of mental test scores*. New York: Addison-Wesley.

Martin, M. (1983). A brief review of organic diseases masquerading as functional illness. *Hospital and Community Psychiatry*, *34*(4), 328–332.

Masters, G., & Keeves, J. (Eds.) (1999). *Advances in measurement in educational research and assessment*. Tarrytown, NY: Pergamon Press.

Mendenhall, W. (1975). *Introduction to probability and statistics* (4th ed.). Belmont, CA: Wadsworth.

Messick, S. (1989). Validity. In R. Linn (Ed.), *Educational Measurement* (3rd ed., pp. 13–104), New York: Macmillan.

Morey, L., & Ochoa, E. (1989). An investigation of adherence to diagnostic criteria: Clinical diagnosis of the DSM-III personality disorders. *Journal of Personality Disorders*, *3*(3), 180–192.

Morris, P. L. P., Robinson, R. G., & Raphael, B. (1990). Prevalence and course of depressive disorders in hospitalized stroke patients. *International Journal of Psychiatric Medicine*, *20*(4), 349–364.

Morrison, J. (1999). *When psychological problems mask medical disorders*. New York: Guilford Press.

Murphy, J., Monson, R., Laird, N., Sobol, A., & Leighton, A. (2000). A comparison of diagnostic interviews for depression in the Stirling County study. *Archives of General Psychiatry*, *57*(3), 230–236.

National Institutes of Health. (2001). Depression can differ in men and women. *NIH Record*, *53*(10). Available from www.nih.gov/news/NIH-Record/05_15_2001/story08.htm#top/.

Neuman, W. (2006). *Social research methods: Qualitative and quantitative methods*. Boston: Pearson.

Nugent, W. (1992). The affective impact of a clinical social worker's interviewing style: A series of single-case experiments. *Research on Social Work Practice*, *2*(1), 6–27.

Nugent, W. (2004). The role of prevalence, sensitivity, and specificity on diagnostic accuracy: Rolling the dice in social work process. *Journal of Social Service Research*, *31*(2), 51–75.

Nugent, W., Sieppert, J., & Hudson, W. (2001). *Practice evaluation for the 21st century*. Belmont, CA: Wadsworth.

Nunnally, J. (1978). *Psychometric theory* (2nd ed.) New York: McGraw-Hill.

Nunnally, J., & Bernstein, I. (1994). *Psychometric theory* (3rd ed.). New York: McGraw-Hill.

Paul, R. (1993). *Critical thinking*. Santa Rosa, CA: Foundation for Critical Thinking.

Petty, R., & Cacioppo, J. (1979). Issue involvement can increase or decrease persuasion by enhancing message relevant cognition. *Journal of Personality and Social Psychology*, *37*, 1915–1926.

Petty, R., Wells, G., & Brock, T. (1976). Distraction can enhance or reduce yielding to propaganda: Thought disruption versus effort justification. *Journal of Personality and Social Psychology*, *34*, 874–884.

Robins, L. N., Helzer, J. E., Croughan, J., & Ratcliff, K. S. (1981). National institute of mental health diagnostic interview schedule: Its history, characteristics and validity. *Archives of General Psychiatry, 38*, 381–389.

Rosenhan, D. (1973). On being sane in insane places. *Science, 179*, 250–258.

Rubin, A., & Babbie, E. (2007). *Research methods for social work* (6th ed.). Pacific Grove, CA: Wadsworth.

Rubinson, E., Asnis, G., & Friedman, J. (1988). Knowledge of diagnostic criteria for major depression: A survey of mental health professionals. *Journal of Nervous and Mental Diseases, 176*, 480–484.

Sawin, K., Harrigan, M., & Woog, P. (1995). *Measures of family functioning for research and practice.* New York: Springer.

Spies, R., Plake, L., & Murphy, L. (2005). *The sixteenth mental measurements yearbook.* Lincoln: University of Nebraska Press.

Starfield, B. (2000). Is U.S. health really the best in the world? *Journal of the American Medical Association, 284*(4), 483–485.

Whitaker, R. (2002). *Mad in America.* Cambridge, MA: Perseus.

Williams, J., Pignone, M., Ramirez, G., & Stellato, C. (2002). Identifying depression in primary care: A literature synthesis of case-finding instruments. *General Hospital Psychiatry, 24*(4), 225–237.

Chapter 4

PROBLEM IDENTIFICATION, CONTRACTING, AND CASE PLANNING

Sophia F. Dziegielewski

With the rapid growth of behavioral-based or evidence-based care, social workers and other human service workers employed in health and mental health settings are now expected to be keenly skilled in identifying, planning, and documenting the needs of clients. This makes correct and complete documentation and accurate record keeping essential for effective practice (Dziegielewski, Green, & Hawkins, 2002). According to Dust (1996), when accurate records are prepared and utilized, "a clinician can examine the past and prepare for the future" (p. 50). Furthermore, to keep these skills up to date all human service professionals need specific exposure with subsequent application to the latest trends for documenting in the profession. This exposure allows the professional to further develop and refine problem-solving skills thereby avoiding therapeutic setbacks and limited helping interventions.

For the evidence-based practitioner, the most effective intervention plan for a client is directly influenced by the need to measure the overall efficacy, necessity, and effectiveness of social services provided, while clearly ascertaining the variables that can be linked directly to outcome success and client change (Auerbach & Kilmann, 1977; Dziegielewski, 2004; Dziegielewski & Roberts, 2004; Dziegielewski, Shields, & Thyer, 1998; Evans, Smith, Hill, Albers, & Neufeld, 1996; Hartman & Sullivan, 1996; Koss & Butcher, 1986). Therefore, to avoid pitfalls in formulating the evidence-based or practice-based case plan, documentation is needed that clearly outlines the problem while explaining the actual differences between the intervention approaches utilized (Monette, Sullivan, & DeJong, 2005; Neimeyer & Pfeffier, 1994; Nugent, Sieppert, & Hudson, 2001). The individual treatment or intervention plans that are needed to address each situation can make clearly establishing the success of change efforts difficult (Dziegielewski, 2005). The limitation rests in the fact that client or system change behavior and the resulting case plan can be seen as subjective. Controlling for subjectivity becomes even more complicated because client systems can change over time even without any therapeutic intervention (Bergin & Suinn, 1975). Furthermore, the identified problem itself is not static and can change as well. Regardless of the struggles inherent with achieving organized and complete client records, the impetus toward achieving evidence-based procedures remains unavoidably strong. Without clear progress records, helping professionals simply cannot accurately document the services that they provide (Kagle, 2002) nor can they stand behind the interventions that have been delivered. Furthermore, with the increased emphasis on accountability, documentation that cannot show evidence-based changes may result in system-related negative effects such as the loss of insurance coverage from third-party payers (Dziegielewski & Leon, 2001).

When working in the practice environment, all human service workers are hired with the expectation that they have good problem identification, contracting, and case planning skills. This expectation of preexisting skill may also send an inaccurate message to administrators: Since these employees already have skills when they are hired, only limited agency funds will be needed for updating or refining skill development in this area. Since agencies are not rewarded for providing training on case planning unless it is directly related to reimbursement practices, human service workers may be forced to seek their own training. Or worse, when training is provided, the focus may be related directly to meeting agency standards, rather than for enhancing quality care while improving service delivery. To assist in bridging this gap, this chapter provides tips for evidence-based intervention efforts that are based on sound case planning and the subsequent documentation of all problem-solving efforts.

HISTORICAL BACKGROUND

According to Kagle (1993), inadequate record keeping often results from professionals not being properly trained in documentation. This lack of training can make it difficult for human service workers to meet record-keeping requirements for a growing number of clients. Furthermore, Kagle (2002) believes that many social workers simply do not recognize the importance of keeping sound records. When a trial-and-error approach is used to document case plan services, the worker may be uncertain about the nature, duration, and outcomes of the therapeutic encounter.

Developing a complete case plan can be hampered further by the methodological limitations inherent in most forms of time-limited interventions especially when searching for the overall effectiveness of/and between competing intervention approaches (Monette et al., 2005; Neimeyer & Pfeffier, 1994; Nugent et al., 2001). Methodological limitations such as clearly identifying the time needed to comprehensively assess the problem can hamper helping efforts.

In addition, some social workers may resist the extra time and effort needed to ensure that they have complete and accurate records. This resistance is related directly to their belief that this extra effort will result in less quality time spent with clients. At times, social service workers may place minimal importance on documentation because they do not consider this activity an integral part of the therapeutic process (Moreland & Racke, 1991; Rock & Congress, 1999; Wilson, 1980). This resistance and subsequent anxiety can result in a strong desire by many social workers to postpone or defer documentation to a later time. To quell these fears, the service provider must recognize his or her current level of skill in this area, have the desire to improve, and be willing to focus attention on the importance of identifying and documenting behavioral outcomes, as well as involvement in using these outcomes to formulate and document intervention plans.

IMPORTANCE OF EVIDENCE-BASED DOCUMENTATION SKILLS

Since service documentation remains an essential part of human service work, learning to identify and record problem behaviors remains a basic requirement of all educational training efforts (Dziegielewski & Leon, 2001). Yet, as the profession continues to struggle with establishing specific treatment goals and objectives, it is no surprise that evidence-based documentation continues to lag behind. Furthermore, since there are no national policies regarding documentation guidelines for many mental health conditions, professionals in the field often struggle with how best to document the case plan ("APA Practice," 2007).

Given the importance of this type of skills training, many graduate and undergraduate human service programs have been compelled to teach documentation from an evidence-based perspective. To develop this skill, the traditional approach may be for colleges and universities to offer a specific course on problem-focused documentation. This trend can be problematic, however, if it simply restricts this information to just one or two courses. Evidence-based documentation needs to be covered in conjunction with all courses across the curriculum and limiting this exposure can result in a lack of emphasis on the direct application of these principles in the practice setting as well as disrupting the continuity of care (Dziegielewski, 2005). Furthermore, teaching this skill from such a limited perspective can result in beginning professionals having inadequate knowledge or limited skill in evidence-based documentation when they enter the workforce. Whether a human services worker is involved in indirect practice (focusing on policy, planning, administration, and community organization) or direct practice (involving assessment, intervention, prevention, and alleviation of negative situations) with individuals, couples, families, or groups, the development of problem identification skills reflective of the case plan remains essential for quality intervention.

Limited resources and specific program guidelines make it imperative that social workers remain responsive to growing expectations of accountability and improved program effectiveness. Despite this imperative, some educational programs still do not view integration of these principles across all practice courses as a critical component for achieving this. Nevertheless, with the influx and importance of evidence-based interventions, it makes sense that most human service agencies will expect their new employees to know how to identify problems and set up case plans that are clearly documented and included in the case files (Gelman, Pollack, & Weiner, 1999; Moreland & Racke, 1991; Wilson, 1980).

An exhaustive literature search of this topic identified little specific information on any type of documentation training provided to social service workers. In fact, Kaczmarek and Barclay (1996) stated that there was a desperate need for more controlled studies in this area. Snider (1987) also made a similar observation about the lack of research on documentation when he noted that there are few resources on client record keeping, despite the recognition that documentation is an essential clinical skill. Although this trend may be changing, we still have a long way to go (Dziegielewski, 2002, 2004).

When specifically addressing the needs of social workers, several articles and texts addressed the issue of how to clearly identify problem behaviors and document this accordingly in the human services; however, few reported the results of specific training provided to practitioners on this topic. Several articles did, however, stress the importance of training professionals on documentation to prevent problems with managed care and accountability. For example, Blue Cross Blue Shield of Michigan (1992) published the following guidelines: "High standards of record keeping are required to support professional claims ... third party payers such as BCBSM must be sure they are paying for therapy and procedures that actually were provided and that were reasonable and necessary" (pp. A1–A2). According to Callahan (1996), behavior that is inconsistent with these Blue Cross Blue Shield guidelines is negligence, and clear documentation is a demonstration that the clinician was not negligent.

Kaczmarek and Barclay (1996) conducted a study on documentation training. They asserted that accurate record keeping needed to include information such as clinical summaries, diagnosis, treatment plans, case progress notes, written contracts, and a termination summary. When they surveyed 235 psychologists about their record keeping practices, Kaczmarek and Barclay found great variability in the styles of client documentation that were reported. They related this variation to a lack of appropriate standards and training. According to Kaczmarek and Barclay, "in this age of rising malpractice litigation, managed care, and the need for professionals to demonstrate treatment outcomes, it is increasingly important that academic training programs provide more emphasis on client documentation" (p. 78). These authors advocated for more counselors training on documentation and urged that this content be covered in professional education. They suggested that the content be presented first in an introductory course and then again built on and reinforced in all subsequent assessment and treatment courses.

In the introductory courses, they recommended that teaching techniques include: (a) reviewing current research on documentation to become familiar with new strategies in recording, (b) teaching at least one structured note system, (c) having students write notes on videotapes of counseling sessions, and (d) developing a diagnosis and a treatment plan from a vignette. These suggestions were intended to help students become familiar with current documentation strategies. In addition, Kaczmarek and Barclay (1996) suggested strategies that could be helpful for more advanced study, such as starting growth groups where poorly written case notes could be presented and improved. Kaczmarek and Barclay noted that: "academic training programs need to be proactive and incorporate more systematic skill training on client documentation within existing course work. Specific teaching strategies have been provided to implement more systemic training; however, research is needed to demonstrate their effectiveness" (p. 85). Kaczmarek and Barclay, consistent with the findings of Boylan, Malley, and Scott (1988), concluded that the absence of a systemic approach to documentation training could translate into inaccurate records and ineffective treatment interventions.

Although continuing education to provide human service workers with evidence-based documentation training is assumed to be critical, there appears to be a paucity of controlled studies on this topic. Dziegielewski et al. (2002) engaged in a study to measure whether specific training could increase the human service professionals' confidence in their documentation abilities after introducing options for specific evidenced-based methods for measuring treatment effectiveness. Fifty-six professionals attended a 1-day, 6-hour seminar on social work record keeping, treatment planning, and documentation. All of the participants responded to pretest and posttest questions that measured their level of comfort and skill in documentation. Topics covered during the workshop included problem identification that was linked to evidence-based treatment planning and measurement such as use of self-report instruments to support problem-solving efforts.

Information presented in the workshop addressed the professional changes based on reimbursement practices as well as skills for record keeping, treatment planning, and documentation. Workshop content stressed the knowledge and skills needed to develop specific treatment objectives and related interventions from a behaviorally based, managed care perspective. On completion of the workshop, the competencies to be enhanced included:

- Gain an understanding of the diversity, necessity, and limitations that can result from using specific preplanned treatment interventions.
- Become familiar with how to document and develop treatment plans reflective of the "specific" needs or identified problems of the client served.
- Describe the importance of, and be able to utilize, time-limited concrete intervention strategies that address specific behavioral treatment objectives.
- Be familiar with use of a multi-axis assessment system as a guide for concrete problem assessment and subsequent behavior change.
- Introduce the participant to a specific type of problem-oriented record keeping and considerations for how best to use this method.
- Understand the importance of clear documentation and appropriate intervention contracts (e.g., no-suicide agreement) as part of the therapeutic process.
- Become familiar with several different models for concrete treatment planning that can be used to address common problems encountered in social work practice.

The pretest/posttest instrument revealed that these social workers wanted more training on problem identification, record keeping, treatment planning, and documentation. Because these professionals are required to document clinical records on a regular basis, participating in this continuing education seminar helped to provide them with an opportunity to improve both their comfort and skill when documenting the services provided. Although social workers initially reported feeling that documentation was important, their assessments of its importance increased after participating in the workshop. When examining the written comments, many of these social workers reported that they were not aware of how much was involved in defining behaviorally based goals and objectives and relating them to the appropriate intervention regimes. Nor were they aware of the degree to which standardized measures could support the acquisition of the case plan and practice effectiveness. This study, similar to Kaczmarek and Barclay's (1996), found that social workers almost unanimously (97%) felt that professional educational training programs need to include more updated content and information on documentation and record keeping. Providing information on this content to human service workers can only result in an improvement in their attitudes about its importance, their confidence in their skills to document, and their level of efficiency in record keeping activities.

USING EVIDENCE-BASED PRINCIPLES IN PROBLEM IDENTIFICATION AND CASE PLANNING

Each of the chapters in Section II of this book discusses the application of evidence-based practice principles with different populations at risk. Regardless of the population or the problem being identified, Bergin (1971) cautioned that one general premise that should always be applied is that "it is essential that the entire therapeutic enterprise be broken down into specific sets of measures and operations, or in other words, be dimensionalized"

(p. 253). This ideal is still supported and considered essential in documenting evidence-based case planning that resulting in a multifaceted assessment process (Dziegielewski & Roberts, 2004). In addition, the importance of individualizing all intervention efforts and basing all helping activity on this premise cannot be overestimated (Dziegielewski, 2005, 2006).

For the evidence-based practitioner, any discussion on problem identification, case planning, and documentation strategy must clearly relate to measuring treatment effectiveness (O'Hare, 2005). From a traditional standpoint, Kagle (1993) reported that case records needed to focus on understanding the client in context, with a special emphasis on documenting the client's social history, current relationships, and describing and analyzing the process of intervention and change. This is somewhat different than evidenced-based principles where the focus starts and ends with direct observation, exploration, and intervention all related to the identified problem behavior(s). The evidence-based practitioner starts with the identification of the problem behavior and then links this behavior to the treatment plan (Klott & Jongsma, 2006). Understanding the problem is clearly related to ascertaining the variables that can be linked directly to client change (Auerbach & Kilmann, 1977; Dziegielewski, 2004; Dziegielewski & Roberts, 2004; Dziegielewski et al., 1998; Evans et al., 1996; Hartman & Sullivan, 1996; Koss & Butcher, 1986). From this perspective, the evidence-based practitioner identifies the problem as clearly and concisely as possible and relates the problem directly to the behavior change. When this connection is not clear, third-party reviewers who monitor records for quality control and service utilization may reject even the best-intended helping efforts. Furthermore, when problem behaviors are not clearly linked to positive behavior change, these reviewers have the power to terminate treatment on the basis that what is provided does not clearly reflect the continuity, effectiveness, and the need for continued services (Corcoran & Boyer-Quick, 2002). In this managed care environment, the documentation for continued care must clearly correspond with medical necessity (Wiger, 2005). Therefore, to avoid issues, all case plan progress must always reflect the evidence-based interventions being implemented and link these interventions to whether the services are medically necessary.

This clear linkage between problem intervention and outcome connects the relevance of the intervention to the problem, creating a pathway for the acknowledgment and achievement of intervention success. The social worker must clearly identify in each record the client's problem(s), the need for service, goals and objectives to be achieved, plans to be achieved, service attitudes, activities, and the impact of the situation on the client. Although this newer approach to case planning and record keeping may be unfamiliar to many social workers, it is imperative for developing new and innovative approaches for ensuring practice effectiveness.

In viewing client problems from an empirical standpoint, the various dimensions of the intervention experience need to be treated as a complex network of functional relationships within which there occurs a series of interactions among the primary factors (i.e., the independent and dependent variables). Simply stated, in any functional relationship, the independent variables operate as presumed causes and dependent variables operate as the presumed effects (Neuman & Kreuger, 2003). Therefore, when documenting a client problem, an important first step in the evaluation process is to sort out what is believed to be the causal connection operating in any given problem situation. This involves identifying a series of interdependent problem-solving steps that logically flow from the presenting problem (Powers, Meenaghan, & Toomey, 1985). It is at this point that the social worker needs to ascertain which of the problem behaviors need to be addressed in order to yield the most relevant and important therapeutic gain. The identified behaviors to be addressed must also be part of a mutually negotiated plan.

CREATING THE PROBLEM STATEMENT

Embedded in the logic of this problem-identification and solving process is an implied hypothesis that can be stated as follows:

> In problem situations, if X is employed as an intervention strategy (i.e., the independent variable), then it is expected that Y (i.e., obtain desired functioning level) will be the predicted outcome (i.e., the dependent variable).

Evidence-based documentation is based on identifying and linking the problem statement in this way. In this format, the problem statement is clearly related to the implied hypothesis. This requires stating clearly what it is that he or she intends to do with or on behalf of the client, as well as the expected consequences of those actions. In order to do this, the identified problem statement must correspond to both the case plan and the outcome; and all must be defined in operational or measurable terms.

To accomplish this, vague concepts such as "emotional support will result in enhanced client self-esteem" need to be avoided. Although on the surface this statement may appear very important for guiding practice strategy, when stated in such global terms, it simply cannot adequately operationalize testable hypotheses or problem statements identified. Evidence-based practice documentation requires that vague concepts be linked to constructs that involve the measurement of self-esteem and how an increase of this concept will be obtained.

Although the task of operationally defining concepts is not easy, many researchers concur that it is essential to the effective evaluation of the intervention, regardless of one's theoretical orientation (Bisman & Hardcastle, 1999; Bloom, Fischer, & Orme, 2003; Monette et al., 2005). Furthermore, the value and subsequent recognition of our clinical practice efforts will prove to be only as good as the empirical observations on which they are based. This makes the use of measurement instruments designed to help operationalize this concept central. Picking a standardized instrument to assist with identifying problem behaviors will help to achieve greater accuracy and objectivity in measuring some of the more commonly encountered clinical problems.

MEASURING THE PROBLEM BEHAVIOR

The most notable development in assisting the eveidence-based practitioner has been the emergence of numerous brief pencil-and-paper assessment devices known as rapid assessment instruments (RAIs). As standardized measures, RAIs share a number of characteristics. These measurements are brief, relatively easy to administer, score, and interpret, and require very little knowledge of testing procedures on the part of the clinician. For the most part, these self-report measures can be completed by the client, usually within 15 minutes, RAIs are independent of any particular theoretical orientation, and as such, can be used with a variety of intervention methods (Dziegielewski & Powers, 2005). These instruments provide a systematic overview of the client's identified problem(s) and can be used to stimulate discussion related to the information elicited by the instrument itself. The score that is generated provides an operational index of the frequency, duration, or intensity of the problem. Most RAIs can be used as repeated measures and thus are adaptable to the methodological requirements of both research design and goal assessment purposes. In addition to providing a standardized means by which change can be monitored over time with a single client, RAIs can also be used to make equivalent comparisons across clients experiencing a common problem (e.g., marital conflict).

RAIs can assist in providing information concerning reliability and validity. Reliability refers to the stability of a measure and whether the questions mean the same thing to the individual answering them at different times, as well as whether different individuals inter-pret like questions similarly. Unless an instrument yields consistent data, it is impossible for it to be valid. But even highly reliable instruments are of little value unless their validity can also be demonstrated. Validity speaks to the general question of whether an instrument does in fact measure what it purports to measure. Although both are important, validity tends to be a little more elusive than reliability. There are several different approaches to establishing validity (Chen, 1997; Cone, 1998; Dziegielewski & Powers, 2005; Powers et al., 1985; Schutte & Malouff, 1995), each of which is designed to provide information regarding how much confidence we can have in the instrument as an accurate indicator of the problem under consideration. While levels of reliability and validity vary greatly among available instruments, it is very helpful to the social work professional to know in advance the extent to which these issues have been addressed. Information concern-ing reliability and validity, as well as other factors related to the standardization process (e.g., the procedures for administering, scoring, and interpreting the instrument), can help the professional make informed judgments concerning the appropriateness of any given instrument.

The key to selecting the best instrument for the intervention is knowing where and how to access the relevant information concerning potentially useful measures. Fortunately, there are a number of excellent sources available to the clinician to help facilitate this process. One such compilation of standardized measures is *Measures for Clinical Practice* by Corcoran and Fischer (2000) and another is *Sourcebook of Adult Assessment Strategies* by Schutte and Malouff (1995). These reference texts can serve as valuable resources for identifying useful rapid-assessment instruments suited for the kinds of problems most commonly encountered in clinical social work practice. Schutte and Malouff provide a list of mental health related measures for adults and guidelines for their use with different types of practice-related problems. In addition to an introduction to the basic principles of measurement, these books discuss various types of measurement tools, including the advantages and disadvantages of RAIs. Corcoran (2001) also provides some useful guidelines for locating, selecting, evaluation, and administering prospective measures. The availability of these, as well as numerous other similar references related to special interest areas, greatly enhances the social work professional's options with respect to monitoring and evaluation practice (Buros, 1978; Mitchell, 1983a, 1983b). Overall, the RAIs can serve as valuable adjuncts for the social work professional's evaluation efforts.

Another type of measurement used to enhance documentation that helps to record a client's functioning level are the therapist-directed rating scales provided in the *DSM-IV-TR* on Axis V (Generalized Assessment of Functioning [GAF]). The scale provides individual rating scores for each client served. In this method, ratings of a client's functioning are assigned at the outset of therapy and again on discharge. The scales allow for assigning a number that represents a client's behaviors. The scales are designed to enable the worker to differentially rank identified behaviors from 0 to 100, with higher ratings indicating higher overall functioning and coping levels. By rating the highest level of functioning a client has attained over the past year and then comparing it to his or her current level of functioning, helpful comparisons can be made. Utilizing this scale can help professionals to both quantify client problems and document observable changes that may be attributable to the counseling relationship. This allows the worker to track performance variations across behaviors relative to client functioning. See the *DSM-IV-TR* published by the American Psychiatric Association (2000) for a copy of the scale.

Also, in the *DSM-IV-TR* "Criteria Sets and Axes Provided for Further Study," there are two scales that are not required for the formal multi-axial diagnosis yet can provide a format for ranking function that might be particularly helpful to social work professionals. The first of these optional scales is the relational functioning scale termed the Global Assessment of Relational Functioning (GARF). This index is used to address the status of family or other ongoing relationships on a hypothetical continuum from competent to dysfunctional. The second index is the Social and Occupational Functioning Assessment Scale (SOFAS). With this scale, the individual's level of social and occupational functioning can be addressed (American Psychiatric Association, 2000). The complimentary nature of these scales in identifying and assessing client problems is evident in the fact that all three scales, the GAF, GARF, and SOFAS use the same rating system. The rankings for each scale range from 0 to 100, with the lower numbers representing more severe problems. The uses of all three of these tools have been encouraging for obvious reasons. Collectively, they provide a viable framework within which human service workers can apply concrete measures to a wide variety of practice situations. They also provide a multi-dimensional perspective that permits workers to document variations in levels of functioning across system sizes, including the individual (GAF), family (GARF), and social (SOFAS) perspective.

In summary, tools to help document client change are essential in problem identification and case planning and these measures can help to quantify the resultant progress and reporting of these accomplishments. To further address use of these measurement tools, specific concrete goals and objectives need to also incorporate a number of direct behavioral observation techniques that are identified by the self-administered RAIs or other types of therapist-directed rating scales. Space limitations do not permit a more thorough discussion of these methods in this chapter. However, there are a number of excellent sources available that discuss in detail the kinds of information one would need in order to make informed decisions regarding their selection and application to specific cases (Bloom et al., 2003). To further supplement these efforts, scales such as the GAF, GARF, and SOFAS can be used to assist in behaviorally based outcome measures. Overall, once the problem behavior is identified, case plan development can use this wide array of measures to operationally define the various dimensions of the intervention process.

DEVELOPING THE SERVICE OR CASE PLAN

Once the problem statement is outlined and how it will be assessed has been developed, the task now becomes integrating the problem behavior with the appropriate service or case planning strategies. This integration needs to encompass a seamless and synergistic bond (Dziegielewski & Powers, 2005). In evaluating the service or case planning, evidence-based practice dictates that the problem statement, the behavioral-based goals and objectives, and the accompanying intervention plan coincide completely. For the new practitioner, coordinating all of these parts into an integrated whole can be both frustrating and confusing. Therefore, to effectively implement such a case plan the process must be clearly linked to the outcome. And, this linkage must occur in an informed and sensitive manner, where the practitioner is well versed in the following procedures.

In selecting the practice strategy, it must be firmly based within the reality of the environment. This can present a particular problem for the evidence-based practitioner as the pressure to select a method of intervention may be influenced and subsequently trapped within a system that is driven by social, political, cultural, and economic factors. It is obvious to the social worker that the bottom line is most often cost reduction and containment (Fiesta, 1995; Franklin, 2002). In conjunction with cost-saving strategy, the guidelines and practices developed through quality improvement programs can also be used as preestablished criteria for service delivery. These preestablished criteria for practice delivery can limit the treatment plans and types of case planning strategy utilized (Dziegielewski, 2004).

This is further complicated by the need to individualize each case plan so that it reflects the unique symptoms and needs the client is experiencing. When the case plan clearly delineates the intervention plan, families and friends of the client may feel more at ease and may actually agree to participate and assist in any behavioral interventions that will be applied. Factors that influence the case plan strategy are numerous with the most important being the general use of traditional methods of time-limited intervention, lack of a formal space for counseling, and time and/or agency constraints. A further complication when selecting a structure for practice intervention is defending the type of intervention in the best interest of the client. In the practice environment, reality dictates that the duration of most therapeutic sessions, regardless of the intervention used or the orientation of the social worker. In social work practice, most of these therapeutic encounters generally range from six to eight sessions to as long as 20 sessions. Generally speaking, the least number of sessions is one, and the greatest number is 20. For the evidence-based practitioner, an intervention plan carried out in one session and monitored periodically over time can provide attraction for funding sources.

It is beyond the scope of this chapter to review all possible modes of practice strategy that can be implemented to support the case plan. Yet, regardless of the method used, all helping efforts must include a viable time-limited approach with mutually negotiated concrete and realistic goals, a clear problem statement, and a plan for measuring effectiveness, as well as a specific time frame for conducting and completing the service. Furthermore, regardless of the method selected, in the *initial phase* of the case plan, a hopeful environment is created where the client begins to feel confident that his or her problem can and will be addressed. The role of the social worker is clear in helping the client to break down problems into concrete terms that once identified, establish the groundwork for the development of concrete goals and objectives. For the evidence-based practitioner, a written case plan that shows a clear understanding of what will transpire is essential. If measurement scales are not implemented to serve as a baseline, an initial ranking to compare client functioning at the beginning and end of intervention is suggested.

At the root of this process is the establishment of a positive and supportive working relationship with the client and therefore building rapport is considered part of the process of problem identification. This process is greatly facilitated by the articulation of a set of mutually negotiated, realistic and specific time-limited goals and objectives. When the problem behavior is clearly articulated, the objectives can flow accordingly and ambiguousness and confusion on expectations and/or outcomes is controlled. These goals and objectives should be clearly outlined in relation to client's identified needs and capacities and this in turn creates a functional relationship between the independent variables and the dependent variables (Neuman & Kreuger, 2003). Furthermore, social workers need to remain mindful of the personal, cultural, and environmental circumstances that can directly or indirectly affect the problem behavior and how these dynamics may impact the problem-solving process. This awareness correlates nicely with recognizing the person in his or her environment or situation creating a comprehensive case plan. From this perspective, the social workers' role is one of action and direction, particularly when individuals are in the early phases of problem identification. It is essential to realize that for individuals, the problem impairment can result in a type of crisis where frustration and an inability to start the process are prominent. At times, especially in the beginning of the problem-solving process, clients may seek the input of the social worker for help in seeing the connection between the problem behaviors and the outlined behavior change. Once identified, the case plan often referred to as the treatment or intervention plan is formulated. This initial phase ends with an agreed-on time frame for service provision, and in the initial phase, the measurement of effectiveness will be finalized. It is here that the social worker must decide and plan for implementation of how she or he will measure the effectiveness of the intervention strategy employed.

The *main phase of intervention* is generally based on the model and format chosen in the initial phase. This is the most active of the stages because this is when concrete problem solving actually occurs. In this phrase, individualized case plans reflect the concrete efforts to address the problem. It is here the foundation is made for the case plan and the benchmarks for completion to be linked. According to Whitlock, Orleans, Pender, and Allan (2002), the case plan always starts with identifying the five As (assess, advise, agree, assist, and arrange). To take this further, the main phase of the intervention needs to formulate the treatment plan into several critical steps (Jongsma & Peterson, 2006).

First, problem behaviors, which are interfering with functioning, must be identified or selected. Second, once selected, the problems must be defined (Klott & Jongsma, 2006). The role of the social worker is to *assess* and *advise* along therapeutic lines. In practice, it is considered essential that the client and his or her family *agree* to participate and assist in this selection process as much as possible in terms of identifying the issues, problem behaviors, and coping styles that are either causing or contributing to the client's discomfort. Of all the problem behaviors a client may be experiencing, it is important to clearly select the ones that should receive the most attention—those behaviors that impair independent living skills or cause difficulties in completing tasks of daily living or impair usual occupational of social functioning.

The role of the human service professional is clear in helping to *arrange* a course of action and to help the client to complete the tasks assigned. Third is goal formulation and development coupled with an objective interpretation of the problem. In order to measure progress in the case plan, the social worker must start with clear and behaviorally specific goals. The more precisely they are defined in measurable terms, the easier it is to verify if and when they are achieved. Identification of the goals allows for further refinement in terms of more specific immediate, intermediate, and long-term objectives. When the problem behavior has been clearly identified, the case plan flows from it. Once all related factors have been identified, the reported problems are then prioritized so that goals, objectives, and action tasks may be developed. This step constitutes the basis for the case plan. Furthermore, these goals must be broken down into specific objective statements that reflect target behaviors to be changed and ways to measure the client's progress on each objective. As subcomponents to the objectives, the case plan needs to include the action tasks that clearly delineate the steps to be taken by the client and the helping professional to ensure successful completion of each objective must be included. For example, if the problem behavior is ambivalent feelings that impair general task completion, the main goal may be to help the client reduce feelings of ambivalence. An objective that clearly articulates a behavioral definition of ambivalence is articulated along with the ways that the ambivalence will be decreased (Dziegielewski & Powers, 2005). This provides the mechanisms used to determine if the behavior has been changed. For example, a client is able to demonstrate the ability to express his or her feelings toward a significant other. In this case, the therapeutic intervention involves assisting the client to develop specific and concrete tasks that are geared toward increasing this behavior and consequently meeting the objective. The outcome measure simply becomes establishing whether the task was completed.

Fourth, once the goals and specific objectives are identified and the social worker and the client have mutually agreed on them, the intervention strategy must be selected. To start this process, a partnership of mutual respect needs to be formed. In this relationship, agreement and support starts with the belief that the client will succeed, and the practitioner can help provide the necessary foundation for progress within the case plan. Basically, no matter what evaluation strategy is selected, it is likely to be meaningful only if it is initiated early and brought to closure fairly quickly (Dziegielewski & Powers, 2005). In addition, the methodology itself should not be experienced by the client as being in any way intrusive to the helping process. Ideally, the purposes of both the intervention and the evaluation should be compatible and mutually supportive making all efforts at establishing a treatment plan a team effort. Once the client agrees, the client can determine whether the goals and objectives sought are consistent with his or her own culture and values. The responsibility of developing the structure and intervention strategy rests with the practitioner; however, emphasis on mutuality is a joint effort between the practitioner and the client where the practitioner may take an active role in the beginning.

Measurement is an important aspect of problem identification but the importance of practice wisdom when creating the case plan cannot be underestimated. To facilitate effective planning, the human service worker must be aware of what is likely to work for a particular client, and possess the theoretical knowledge necessary to justify the selection and application of appropriate techniques. Theory informs practice by providing a plausible framework within which critical intervention and evaluation issues can be simultaneously raised and interpreted. Therefore, the more we know about the theoretical underpinnings of any given problem-solving focused counseling strategy, the better informed we will be in our efforts to document what is predicted and/or explained. As stated earlier, practice wisdom often dictates how best to proceed in helping a client, given the specific nature of the situation and the surrounding circumstances. It can also help the practitioner decide when to apply and/or withdraw the various components of the treatment package throughout the course of the intervention process.

One technique that can aid the evidence-based practitioner is *summarization*. In summarization, regardless of the model chosen, each session is planned in advance and reviewed in the session, remaining open and flexible if renegotiation needs to occur in regard to the problem-solving process. In this phase, regardless of how many sessions are being implemented, the summarization should be incorporated into each session (Dziegielewski, 2004). In this process, each formal encounter is dedicated to the client actually stating the agreed-on problem statement and objectives to be addressed. This allows both client and social worker to quickly focus on the task at hand. Summarization should also be practiced at the end of each session. This allows the client to recapitulate what she or he believes has transpired in the session and how it relates to the stated objectives. Clients should use their own words to summarize what has transpired. In acknowledging and summarizing the content and objectives of the session, (a) the client takes responsibility for his or her own actions, (b) repetition allows the session accomplishments to be highlighted and reinforced, (c) the client and the social worker ascertain that they are working together on the same objectives, and (d) the therapeutic environment remains flexible and open for renegotiation of contracted objectives.

Last, after the problem behavior has been identified, the goals and/or objectives of intervention have been established, and practice strategy has been determined, the difficult task now becomes evaluating the clinical intervention in standardized or operationally based terms. Now outcomes will need to be articulated in terms of realistic goals that can be easily converted to operationally defined objectives that avoid vague and nebulous language. As stated earlier, this is a much easier task when subjective terms such as stress, anxiety, and depression that are often used to describe important facets of a client's social/psychological functioning have been assessed beyond their usual subjective connotations. Specific definitions are essential as when semantic elusiveness exists it makes it very difficult to establish reliable measures of change (Whitlock et al., 2002).

In the *final phase* of the intervention process, follow-up contact is established. Here the social worker either meets the client in person for intermittent sessions or arranges for telephone communication to review and evaluate current client progress and status. A recommended time lapse of no more than 1 to 4 months is recommended (Dziegielewski, 1997). The social worker should prepare in advance for this meeting to continue and reaffirm previous measurement strategies. In this final phase, measuring practice effectiveness and reaching the stated outcomes typically involves a process designed to determine whether or to what extent mutually negotiated goals and objectives have been met. These changes need to be documented through concrete measurement that is indicative of client progress. Dziegielewski (2002, 2004) suggests that this process can be greatly facilitated by establishing clear-cut treatment contracts with clients who, in turn, provide a viable foundation for a variety of individual and/or group evaluation designs. Once the treatment agreement is in place, standardized instruments can be used as repeated measures to gather consistent data from baseline through termination and follow-up.

In summary, it is important to note, however, that no case plan is designed to be all-inclusive. Rather each case plan is designed to provide the guidelines for effective documentation of the assessment and intervention process. Each case plan must be individualized for the client, outlining the specific problem behaviors and how each of these behaviors can be addressed. Once problems are identified and a case plan is being formulated, input from the client's support system needs to be included. This input can enhance communication between the client and his or her family members. Involving the family and support system in treatment plan formulation and application can be especially helpful and productive because at times individuals experiencing mental confusion and distortions of reality may exhibit bizarre and unpredictable symptoms. If support systems are not included in the intervention planning process, and the client's symptoms worsen, the client-family system environment may become characterized by increased tension, frustration, fear, blame, and helplessness. To avoid support systems that withdraw from the client thereby decreasing the available support, family members and key support system members need to either be involved or at a minimum made aware of the treatment plan goals and objectives that will be utilized if the client consents to their involvement. Family education and supportive interventions for family and significant others can be listed as part of the treatment plan for an individual client. It is beyond the scope of this chapter to discuss the multiple interventions available to the family members; however, interested readers are encouraged to study the applications described in the remainder of this book.

RECORD KEEPING AND THE PROBLEM-ORIENTED RECORD

Sound documentation is at the root of intervention success and clear problem-oriented case recording can facilitate this process. Traditionally, one of the most popular type of recording formats has been the problem-oriented recording (POR; Dziegielewski, 2002, 2006). Still often used widely in health care or medical settings, this type of recording was originally formulated to encourage multidisciplinary and interdisciplinary collaboration and to train medical professionals (Weed, 1969). What most professionals report is that for multidisciplinary or interdisciplinary teams, helping professionals find that problem-oriented case documentation enables them to maintain documentation uniformity while remaining active within a team approach to care. For the evidence-based practitioner, this focus on the problem along with the clear outlining of attempts to bring about change fits well within this data-based framework.

To use POR from an evidence-based perspective, it must clearly emphasize accountability through brief and concise documentation of client problems, services, or interventions as well as client responses. Although there are numerous formats for problem-oriented case recording, the underlying principle is always keep comments brief, concrete, measurable, and concise. This provides a relevant practitioner-friendly format that corresponds well to making connections to increased client caseloads, the use of rapid assessment instruments to measure problem behaviors, and implementing time-limited treatment options. Brief and problem-focused notes help to provide detailed summaries of the intervention progress. Generally, use of the POR is often based on agency choice as well as the need for accountability.

One element that all POR recording formats share is that all formats start with a problem list that is clearly linked to the behavioral-based biopsychosocial interventions (Dziegielewski, 2004). Data-based documentation related directly to the identified problem helps guide the case plan, allowing the social worker to focus on the strategies needed to address presenting problems and coping styles. Maintaining a clear focus on all documentation efforts helps to limit abstractions and vague clinical judgments. In addition, an inventory that reflects the current active problems to be addressed needs to be periodically updated. Therefore, when a problem is resolved, it can be crossed off the list with the date of resolution clearly designated. Note that the behavioral-based objectives that the evidence-based practitioner uses to describe the client problem are considered the basic building blocks for POR recording.

Although numerous POR formats for progress note documentation can be selected, the subjective-objective-assessment-plan (SOAP) is the most commonly used. The SOAP first became popular in the 1970s. In this format, the **S** (subjective) records the data relevant to the client's request for service and the things the client says and feels about the problem (Dziegielewski, 2002, 2004). This section allows some degree of clinical judgment and skilled diagnostic impression that may not be based on clear data. Some professionals prefer to document this information in terms of major themes or general topics addressed, rather than making specific statements about what the practitioner thinks is happening. Generally, in this section, intimate personal content or details of fantasies and process interactions should not be included. When charting in this section of the SOAP, the social worker needs to examine whether his or her statements could be open to misinterpretation. If statements are in fact vulnerable to misinterpretation or resemble a personal rather than professional reaction to the problem identified, these comments should not be included. For the evidence-based practitioner, this section will probably be the shortest and is provided to introduce the objective information to follow.

The **O** (objective) includes observable and measurable criteria related to the problem. These are symptoms, behaviors, and descriptors related to the client-focused problems observed directly by the worker during the assessment and intervention process. Here the independent and dependent variables are identified and described. In addition, some agencies, clinics, and practices have started to include client statements in this section as well. If a client statement is to be utilized as objective data, however, exact quotes must be used. For example, if in the session a client states that he will not harm himself, the practitioner must document exactly what the client has said and in the client's exact words how it relates to the behavioral outcome. What is said must be enclosed within quotation marks.

This section may also include the introduction of standardized assessment instruments designed to measure psychological or social functioning. As the notes progress, it makes sense to also include the results of these measures as well.

In each part of the objective section, clearly defined goals and objectives need to be linked to clear descriptors of what is happening. The frequency, intensity, and duration of each behavior are highlighted.

The **A** (assessment) includes the therapist's assessment of the underlying problems, which in the mental health setting might include a *DSM-IV-TR* multi-axial system. Since application of this framework is beyond the scope of this chapter, please see Dziegielewski (2002) for more detail.

In **P** (plan), the practitioner records how treatment objectives will be carried out, areas for future interventions, and specific referrals to other services needed by the client. A clear behavioral assessment is needed to establish the plan to follow. The plan must also provide a method for follow-up or for tracking changes and time frames. This will allow the evidence-based practitioner to clearly document the changes and the time frames in which the changes occurred.

The traditional format of the SOAP has been extended in some settings to answer issues related to implementation and evaluation. To address this, new areas have been added to the original SOAP format (Dziegielewski & Leon, 2001). This extension referred to as SOAPIE identifies the first additional term as **I** that stands for the *implementation* considerations of the service to be provided. Exactly how, when, and who will implement the service is explained. In the last section, an **E** represents service provision *evaluation* (Dziegielewski, 2002).

This has become a popular addition to treatment plan formulation and development that can be tracked on the service note. Specific actions are evaluated that relate to the progress achieved after any interventions are provided. When treatment is considered successful, specific outcomes-based objectives established early in the treatment process are documented as progressing or checked off as attained. In some agencies, a modified version of the SOAPIE has been introduced and referred to as SOAPIER. In this latest version, the **R** stands for the client's *response* to the intervention provided.

The SOAP is only one type of POR, yet regardless of the type of POR used, the same principles should always be applied. A second type of POR is the data, assessment, and plan (DAP) format. The DAP identifies only the most salient elements of a practitioner's client contact. Using the **D** (data), objective client data and statements are recorded that relate to the presenting problem and the focus of the therapeutic contact. The **A** is used to record the diagnostic assessment intervention from the multi-axial format, the client's reactions to the service and intervention, and the human service worker's assessment of the client's overall progress toward the treatment goals and objectives. Specific information on all tasks, actions, or plans related to the presenting problem and to be carried out by either the client or the helping professional is recorded under P (plan). Also recorded under **P** (plan) is information on future issues related to the presenting problem to be explored at the next session and the specific date and time of the next appointment (Dziegielewski, 2002). Again, similar to the SOAP, the DAP format has also undergone some changes. For example, some counseling professionals who generally use the DAP are now being asked to modify this form of record keeping to add an additional section. This changes the DAP into the DAPE and adds a section where documentation under the **E** reflects what type of educational and evaluative services have been conducted.

Two other forms of problem-based case recording formats often used in health and mental health setting are the problem, intervention, response, and plan (PIRP) and the assessed information, problems addressed, interventions provided, and evaluation (APIE). Similar to the SOAP and the DAP, a comparison structure is employed. All four of these popular formats of problem-oriented case recording have been praised for supporting increased problem identification and the standardization of how client behaviors and coping styles are reported. In effect, the formats provide a greater understanding of health and mental health problems and the various methods of managing them. This type of problem-oriented record brings the focus of clinical attention to an often neglected aspect of recording that involves the recognition of a client's problems by all helping professionals to quickly familiarize themselves with a client's situation (Starfield, 1992). Utilizing a problem-focused perspective must go beyond merely recording information that is limited to the client's problems because when the focus is limited to gathering only this information, important strengths and resources that clients bring to the therapeutic interview may not be validated. Furthermore, partialization of client problems presents the potential risk that other significant aspects of a client's functioning will be overlooked in treatment planning and subsequent practice strategy. Therefore, problem-oriented forms of case recording need to extend beyond the immediate problem regardless of whether insurance reimbursement requires it (Dziegielewski, 2002).

As the use of computer-generated notes continue to become more common varying forms of problem-oriented case recording will be linked directly into computerized databases (Gingerich, 2002; Starfield, 1992). In terms of convenience, this can mean immediate access to fiscal and billing information as well as client intervention strategy, documentation, and treatment planning. When working with computerized records, Bernstein and Hartsell (1998) suggest the following: (a) when recording client information on a hard drive or disk be sure storage is in a safe and secure place; (b) be sure to secure any passwords from detection; (c) if you are treating a celebrity or a famous individual, use a fictitious name and be sure to keep the "key" to the actual name in a protected place; (d) always maintain a back-up system and keep it secure; (e) be sure that everyone who will have access to the client's case file reads and signs an established protocol concerning sanctity, privacy, and confidentiality of the records; and (f) take the potential of computer theft or crash seriously and establish a policy that will safeguard what will need to happen if this should occur. The convenience of records and information now being easily transmitted electronically produces one major concern. Since clinical case records are so easy to access and are portable, there is a genuine problem represented by the vulnerability of unauthorized access of the recorded information, and every precaution should be taken to safe guard the information that is shared. In addition, since clinical records are kept for the benefit of the client, access to the record by the client is generally allowed. When engaging in any type of disclosure or transfer to either the client or third parties, however, a written client consent form is usually obtained.

In closing, documentation in the case plan should always be clearly sequenced and easy to follow. If a mistake occurs, never change a summary note or intervention plan without acknowledging it. When changes need to be made to the clinical case record, the intervention plan, or any other type of case recording, clearly indicate that a change is being made by drawing a thin line through the mistake and dating and initialing it. Records that are legible and cogent limit open interpretation of the services provided. In addition, the mental health practitioner will always be required to keep clinical case records (including written records and computerized back-up files) safeguarded in locked and fireproof cabinets; and often, after a service is terminated, many health and mental care facilities prefer to use archival types of storage systems such as microfiche or microfilm to preserve records and maximize space.

CONCLUSION

Helping human service practitioners to become better equipped with problem identification and case planning skills by utilizing an evidence-based perspective allows for a higher level of comfort and confidence with their ability to be efficient, effective, and accountable. In addition to providing a clear record of the intervention, clear and concise documentation serves to protect the client, the professional worker, and the human service agency. Since practitioners assist a variety of social and human service agencies as well as other professionals with the treatment of clients, identifying client problems and providing clearly articulated case plans are critical because it is this written record that is often used to justify treatment for the clients served.

The evolution of evidence-based practice has changed the expectations of what should be contained in the case plan and the subsequent documentation effects that follow. Evidence-based practice principles go beyond general theoretical approaches and provide a procedural framework that uses scientific methodology along with qualitative and quantitative practice methods. Professional training in this area is essential, and practice application highlights the importance of uniting problem identification with the case plan using a process that clearly leads to the outcome.

REFERENCES

American Psychiatric Association. (2000). *Diagnostic and statistical manual of mental disorders* (4th ed., text rev.). Washington, DC: Author.

APA practice Documentation. (2007). *APA Online.* Available from www.apa.org/practice/meddocum.html.

Auerbach, S. M., & Kilmann, P. R. (1977). Crisis intervention: A review of outcome research. *Psychological Bulletin, 84,* 1189–1217.

Bergin, A. E. (1971). The evaluation of therapeutic outcomes. In A. E. Bergin & S. L. Garfield (Eds.), *Handbook of psychotherapy and behavior change* (pp. 217–270). New York: Wiley.

Bergin, A. E., & Suinn, R. M. (1975). Individual psychotherapy and behavior therapy. *Annual Review of Psychology, 26,* 509–555.

Bernstein, B. E., & Hartsell, T. L. (1998). *The portable lawyer for mental health professionals.* New York: Wiley.

Bisman, C. D., & Hardcastle, D. A. (1999). *Integrating research into practice.* Belmont, CA: Brooks/Cole and Wadsworth.

Bloom, M., Fischer, J., & Orme, J. (2003). *Evaluating practice: Guidelines for the accountable professional* (4th ed.). Boston: Allyn & Bacon.

Blue Cross Blue Shield of Michigan. (1992, March 1). Payment determinations are based on appropriate documentation. *Facility News,* pp. A1–A4.

Boylan, J., Malley, P., & Scott, J. (1988). *Practicum and internship.* Muncie, IN: Accelerated Development.

Buros, O. K. (Ed.). (1978). *The eighth mental measurements yearbook* (Vols. 1 & 2). Highland Park, NJ: Gryphon Press.

Callahan, J. (1996). Documentation of client dangerousness in a managed care environment. *Medical Social Work, 21,* 202–208.

Chen, S. (1997). *Measurement and analysis in psychosocial research.* Brookfield, VT: Avebury.

Cone, J. D. (1998). Psychometric considerations: Concepts, contents and methods. In A. S. Bellack & M. Hersen (Eds.), *Behavioral assessment: A practical handbook* (4th ed., pp. 22–46). Boston: Allyn & Bacon.

Corcoran, K. (2001). Locating instruments. In B. Thyer (Ed.), *The handbook of social work research methods* (pp. 69–80). Thousand Oaks, CA: Sage.

Corcoran, K., & Boyer-Quick, J. (2002). How clinicians can effectively use assessment tools to evidence medical necessity and throughout the treatment process. In A. R. Roberts & G. J. Greene (Eds.), *Social workers' desk reference* (pp. 198–204). New York: Oxford University Press.

Corcoran, K., & Fischer, J. (2000). *Measures for clinical practice: A source book* (4th ed., Vols. 1 & 2). New York: Free Press.

Dust, B. (1996). Training needs. *Training and Development*, *50*, 50–51.

Dziegielewski, S. F. (1997). Time limited brief therapy: The state of practice. *Crisis Intervention and Time Limited Treatment*, *3*(3), 217–228.

Dziegielewski, S. F. (2002). *DSM-IV-TR*™ *in action*. Hoboken, NJ: Wiley.

Dziegielewski, S. F. (2004). *The changing face of health care social work: Professional practice in managed behavioral health care*. New York: Springer.

Dziegielewski, S. F. (2005). *Substance addictions: Assessment and intervention*. Chicago: Lyceum Books.

Dziegielewski, S. F. (2006). *Psychopharmacology handbook for the non-medically trained*. New York: Norton.

Dziegielewski, S. F., Green, C. E., & Hawkins, K. (2002). Improving clinical record keeping in brief treatment: Evaluation of a documentation workshop. *Brief Treatment*, *2*(1), 1–10.

Dziegielewski, S. F., & Leon, A. (2001). Time-limited case recording: Effective documentation in a changing environment. *Journal of Brief Therapy*, *1*(1), 51–56.

Dziegielewski, S. F., & Powers, G. T. (2005). Procedures for evaluating time-limited crisis intervention. In A. Roberts (Ed.), *Crisis intervention handbook* (3rd ed., pp. 742–774). New York: Oxford University Press.

Dziegielewski, S. F., & Roberts, A. R. (2004). Health care evidenced-based practice: A product of political and cultural times. In A. R. Roberts & K. R. Yeager (Eds.), *Handbook of practice-focused research and evaluation* (pp. 200–204). New York: Oxford University Press.

Dziegielewski, S. F., Shields, J. P., & Thyer, B. A. (1998). Short-term treatment: Models, methods, and research. In J. B. Williams & K. Ell (Eds.), *Advances in mental health research: Implications for practice* (pp. 287–308). Washington, DC: National Association of Social Workers Press.

Evans, W., Smith, M., Hill, G., Albers, E., & Neufeld, J. (1996). Rural adolescent views of risk and protective factors associated with suicide. *Crisis Intervention and Time-Limited Treatment*, *3*(1), 1–13.

Fiesta, J. (1995). Managed care: Whose liability? *Nursing Management*, *26*, 31–32.

Franklin, C. (2002). Developing effective practice competencies in managed behavioral health care. In A. R. Roberts & G. J. Greene (Eds.), *Social workers' desk reference* (pp. 3–10). New York: Oxford University Press.

Gelman, S. R., Pollack, D., & Weiner, A. (1999). Confidentiality of social work records in the computer age. *Social Work*, *44*(3), 243–252.

Gingerich, W. J. (2002). Computer applications for social work practice. In A. R. Roberts & G. J. Greene (Eds.), *Social workers' desk reference* (pp. 23–28). New York: Oxford University Press.

Hartman, D. J., & Sullivan, W. P. (1996, October). Residential crisis services as an alternate to inpatient care. *Families in Society: Journal of Contemporary Human Services*, 496–501.

Jongsma, A. E., & Peterson, L. M. (2006). *The complete adult psychotherapy treatment planner* (4th ed.). New York: Wiley.

Kaczmarek, P., & Barclay, D. (1996). Systematic training in client documentation: Strategies for counselor educators. *Counselor Education and Supervision*, *36*, 77–85.

Kagle, J. D. (1993). Record keeping: Directions for the 1990s. *Social Work, 38*, 190–197.

Kagle, J. D. (2002). Record-keeping. In A. R. Roberts & G. J. Greene (Eds.), *Social workers' desk reference* (pp. 28–37). New York: Oxford University Press.

Klott, J., & Jongsma, A. E. (2006). *The co-occurring disorders: Treatment planner*. Hoboken, NJ: Wiley.

Koss, M. P., & Butcher, J. N. (1986). Research on brief psychotherapy. In S. L. Garfield & A. E. Bergin (Eds.), *Handbook of psychotherapy and behavior change* (pp. 627–670). New York: Wiley.

Mitchell, J. V. (1983a). *Ninth mental measurement yearbook*. Lincoln: University of Nebraska Press.

Mitchell, J. V. (1983b). *Tests in print III*. Lincoln: University of Nebraska Press.

Monette, D. R., Sullivan, T. J., & DeJong, C. R. (2005). *Applied social research: A tool for human services*. Belmont, CA: Books/Cole-Thompson Learning.

Moreland, M. E., & Racke, R. D. (1991). Peer review of social work documentation. *Quality Review Bulletin*, 236–239.

Neimeyer, R. A., & Pfeiffer, A. M. (1994). Evaluation of suicide intervention effectiveness. *Death Studies, 18*, 131–166.

Neuman, W., & Kreuger, L. (2003). *Social work research: Qualitative and quantitative applications*. Boston: Allyn & Bacon.

Nugent, W. R., Sieppert, J. D., & Hudson, W. W. (2001). *Practice evaluation for the 21st century*. Belmont, CA: Brooks/Cole-Thomson Learning.

O'Hare, T. (2005). *Evidence-based practices for social workers: An interdisciplinary approach*. Chicago: Lyceum Books.

Powers, G. T., Meenaghan, T., & Toomey, B. (1985). *Practice-focused research*. Englewood Cliffs, NJ: Prentice Hall.

Rock, B., & Congress, E. (1999). The new confidentiality for the 21st century in a managed care environment. *Social Work, 44*(3), 253–262.

Schutte, N. S., & Malouff, J. M. (1995). *Sourcebook of adult assessment strategies*. New York: Plenum Press.

Snider, P. (1987). Client records: Inexpensive liability protection for mental health counselors. *Journal of Mental Health Counseling, 9*, 134–141.

Starfield, B. (1992). *Primary care, concept, evaluation and policy*. New York: Oxford University Press.

Weed, L. (1969). *Medical records, medical evaluation, and patient care*. Cleveland, OH: Case Western Reserve University Press.

Whitlock, E. P., Orleans, T., Pender, N., & Allan, J. (2002). Evaluating primary care counseling interventions: An evidence-based approach. *American Journal of Preventive Medicine, 22*(4), 267–284.

Wiger, D. E. (2005). *The psychotherapy documentation primer*. Hoboken, NJ: Wiley.

Wilson, S. J. (1980). *Recording guidelines for social workers*. New York: Free Press.

Chapter 5 ———————————————————————————

PRACTICE EVALUATION

Bruce A. Thyer

Practice evaluation refers to the efforts made by individual social workers to appraise the results of their interventions with clients. This chapter is limited to a review of evaluation efforts that are practicable when undertaken by clinicians operating within the domain of direct practice—efforts at interpersonal helping focused on the problems and situations of individuals, couples, marriages, families, and small groups. Even more narrowly, this chapter focuses on efforts made to empirically ascertain the actual outcomes of practice, on how people's lives have been changed following their experience of services by a professional social worker. And, in some circumstances, how it may be possible to determine not only the possible changes in peoples' lives, but to empirically determine if these observed changes can plausibly be attributed to have been *caused* by the client's receipt of social work services. These efforts, when successful, constitute the highest form of scientifically credible evidence relating to empirically demonstrating a cause-and-effect relationship between intervention and outcome.

The term *clients,* as used in this chapter, refers not simply to individuals but also to couples, families, and so on. The term *intervention* is used synonymously with *treatment.* The evaluation practices described in this chapter can be employed with all types of clients, the very young and the very old, with people of all races and ethnicities, and, equally importantly, by practitioners using virtually any type of social work intervention. It does not matter if you are a psychodynamically oriented clinician, a cognitive-behaviorist, a client-centered practitioner, or a solution-focused therapist; the evaluation methods described herein are genuinely *atheoretical*—they are not derived from any particular formal theory of behavior or of mind. They are *methods of evaluation* capable of being adopted by any practitioner who hopes that his or her interventions will produce pragmatic changes in the way clients think, feel, act, or cope with their environment.

This chapter, by focusing on evaluating your interpersonal practice with clients, omits several other areas of evaluating social work intervention. It does not present various methods to conduct client needs assessments, to undertake formative or summative evaluations of a service program, or to conduct sweeping appraisals of the overall results of program outcomes. Nor is attention given to evaluating social work interventions at a more macro level, for example, by the analysis of the effects of social welfare policies (e.g., changes in the well-being of welfare clients as the nation transitioned from AFDC to TANF). Also omitted are efforts using nomothetic (e.g., group) research designs such as preexperimental studies, quasi-experiments, or randomized controlled trials to evaluate practice outcomes. While these are all admittedly important and engaging topics, they are beyond the more limited scope of the present chapter (e.g., see Royse, Thyer, Padgett, & Logan, 2006; Thyer & Myers, 2007 for more encompassing reviews of evaluation research methods).

This chapter focuses on the use of single-system research designs, also known as single-subject designs (SSDs), defined as:

> A research procedure often used in clinical situations to evaluate the effectiveness of an intervention. Behavior of a single subject, such as an individual client, is used as a comparison and as a control. Typically the results of progress or change are plotted graphically. Single-system design is also known as $N = 1$ design or single system design. (Barker, 2003, p. 398)

Keep in mind that the term *client* is used not only for an individual person, but also for larger systems such as couples, families, and small groups. It is also important to keep in mind the inclusive definition of *behavior:*

> Any action or response by an individual, including observable activity, measurable physiological changes, cognitive images, fantasies, and emotions. (Barker, 2003, p. 40)

Behavior does not only refer to the observable actions of clients. It refers to everything they publicly or privately experience.

BRIEF BACKGROUND

From the very beginnings of professional social work in North America, individual practitioners have been concerned with obtaining credible evidence as to whether social work clients actually benefit from the services they received. Mary Richmond's (1917) classic text *Social Diagnosis* was one early attempt to teach social workers how to gather systematic and reliable information on client circumstances and functioning, so as to better serve clients and to evaluate outcomes more credibly. A few decades later, social workers began experimenting with an outcome measure called the Hunt-Kogan Movement Scale, a way of assessing client functioning and measuring changes occurring during and after social work intervention with individual clients. Although some formal studies were undertaken on this instrument's reliability and validity (see Gershenson, 1952; Hunt, Blenkner, & Kogan, 1950; Kogan, Kogan, & Hunt, 1952; Wessel, 1953), it never really became widely used. This scale was cited by Wolins in an early social work book chapter devoted to the topic of practice evaluation. Wolins also noted that one very legitimate focus of social work evaluation is "the effect of the caseworker in a minute operation with a single client" (1960, p. 248).

The earliest known published study authored by a social worker who used an SSD to evaluate practice appeared in 1965, written by Arthur Staats (a psychologist) and William Butterfield, a social worker, and involved evaluating the results of providing academic tutoring to an Hispanic juvenile delinquent. Since that time, many SSDs have appeared in the social work literature (see Thyer & Thyer, 1992).

EVIDENCE-BASED INFORMATION ON PRACTICE EVALUATION

There are actually only two essential features needed to undertake single-system research designs useful to evaluate your own practice, and to some extent these are consistent with the dictates of sound practice in general. The first is to be able to locate and apply one or more reliable and valid outcome measures pertinent to the client's problem and/or situation. And the second prerequisite is to then actually apply this outcome measure repeatedly over time. All SSDs are simply variants on these two principles, which are discussed in sequence.

All social worker therapists make use of outcome measures in their practice. Most commonly we rely on what clients tell us during clinical interviews. The client lives his or her life, encountering other people, circumstances, and events, and then comes to see us for 50 minutes or so each week. During these therapy sessions, we invite the client to relate the week's events, what they did, how they felt, and what they thought. From such primary source material, we make inferences about client functioning, their possible progress or deterioration, and adjust our interventions accordingly. Occasionally we also seek information from others involved in the client's life—a parent, a spouse, a partner, more rarely coworkers, employers, or friends. And even more rarely we may obtain more objective information from agency records, health-care facilities, schools, and so forth. As noted previously, Mary Richmond's (1917) *Social Diagnosis* laid the empirical foundations for clinical interviewing by professional social workers, and its most contemporary parallel is *Clinical Assessment for Social Workers* (Jordan & Franklin, 2003).

Rather striking advances have been made in assessment methodology in the past few decades, advances that have the potential to markedly improve the reliability, validity, and pragmatic usefulness of the information we can obtain from our interactions with and on behalf of clients. For example, rapid assessment instruments (RAIs) have been developed that consist of short standardized questionnaires or inventories focused on particular problem areas or strengths. Sometimes these are related to specific disorders, such as depressive conditions, anxiety disorders, trauma, alcohol abuse, or psychosis, and an overall score is calculated that provides a systematic if approximate quantitative measure of the problem. Others deal with more complex issues, such as domestic violence, child abuse or neglect, social support, life satisfaction, or quality of life. These RAIs can be completed by clients periodically—weekly, biweekly, or monthly—and the results used to augment our judgments heretofore solely informed from our clinical interviews. Fischer and Corcoran (2007) have assembled a comprehensive listing of such RAIs, including copies of the actual scales, how to score them, and where to obtain more primary information about them. Walter Hudson developed a couple of dozen such instruments for use in evaluating social work practice, and these are available at www.walmyr.com. Useful RAIs can be found for virtually any clinical problem encountered, and new ones are constantly being developed and published. The journal *Research on Social Work Practice* usually has several reports of new or expanded RAIs appearing in each of its bimonthly issues.

Another development in clinical assessment related to practice evaluation has been the considerable advances made in the systematic measurement of client behavior via direct observation. Virtually all conditions for which clients seek help from social workers present with important behavioral manifestations. These may be behavioral excesses such as drinking too much (alcoholism), weeping too much (depression), or talking too long or rapidly (manic behavior). Others are behavioral deficits, such as a lack of social skills on the part of the schizophrenic, a failure to get out of bed on the part of the catatonic, or an inability to find a job on the part of the unemployed. A client may suffer from a lack of appropriate stimulus control in behaviors that are displayed at the wrong time, place, or circumstance, but are otherwise appropriate (e.g., randomly giggling). Social workers of all theoretical persuasions are keenly interested in helping clients change their behavior along more functional lines. Even those practitioners who theorize that overt behavior is a primarily a symptom of intrapsychic processes that are the true focus of treatment endorse the principle that at some point therapeutic gains should be manifested as positive behavioral change. Within the social literature, Rosen and Polansky (1975) and Polster and Collins (1993) provide very good, if a bit dated, overviews of behavioral assessment, whereas Baer, Harrison, Fradenburg, Petersen, and Milla (2005) have published a more contemporary presentation.

The third domain that may be the focus of clinical assessment for the purposes of practice evaluation consists of selected physiological indicators. Urine screens, blood tests, and hair analyses are sometimes used to assess client's use of illegal (or abused but legal) drugs. Medical social workers sometimes examine clients' charts for records of blood pressure or blood sugar to assess compliance with health-care regimens. Some social workers make use of biofeedback instrumentation that assesses various indicators of anxiety (e.g., muscle tension, skin temperature, perspiration, brain waves) to help clients acquire skills in becoming less stressed.

CASE STUDIES

The case study or history is the oldest method of appraising the outcomes of social work practice. It is a primarily a qualitative evaluation methodology that uses verbal narratives, diagrams, and pictures to assess and evaluate client changes. Gilbert and Franklin (2003), Brandell and Varkas (2001), and Gilgun (1994) provide reviews of this approach specific to social work, while Yin (1989) provides a more general description. Almost all social work journals regularly publish case histories or studies of clients that have been used for a variety purposes—to illustrate practice technique, to enrich clinical theory, and to try and document client changes. Historically and currently, many prominent social workers and psychotherapists have achieved great acclaim and recognition through their publication of clinical case studies. Case studies many be grounded in the epistemologies of mainstream or conventional science (e.g., positivism) or based on alternative philosophical perspectives (e.g., postmodernism and constructivism. The approach is not intrinsically linked to either orientation although it is more closely associated with the methodologies collectively known as qualitative research. Narrative case studies can be as brief as a few pages or as long as an entire book. I have published a number of them myself, illustrating the usefulness that I personally place on this form of practice evaluation (Cameron & Thyer, 1985; Koepke & Thyer, 1985; Pergeron, Curtis, & Thyer, 1986; Thyer, 1980, 1981; Thyer & Stocks, 1986). Many new schools of psychotherapy begin to establish their research foundations with the publication of case studies and some approaches such as classical psychoanalysis remain strongly linked to this approach as the primary method of evaluating practice outcomes (e.g., Colby, 1960).

The strengths of the case study are in its apparent ability to place clinical events in their situational contexts, which greatly facilitates making inferences about etiology and response to treatment. Many case studies can be considered classics—think of the influence of some of Sigmund Freud's case histories, the conditioning studies of John Watson the behavioral psychologist, or the sexual dysfunction cures achieved by Masters and Johnson.

Very rarely can the results of individual case studies be aggregated in an attempt to produce more generalizable findings, but usually case histories are narratively presented as isolated instances of some phenomenon.

In a paper titled "Drawing Valid Inferences from Case Studies," psychologist Alan Kazdin (1981) is appropriately cautious regarding the internal validity of the single narrative case study, noting:

> Despite its recognized heuristic value, the case study is usually considered to be inadequate as a basis for drawing valid scientific inferences. Relationships between independent and dependent variables are difficult to discern in a typical case study because of the ambiguity of the factor(s) responsible for the performance. For example, treatment for a particular clinical case may be associated with therapeutic change. However the basis for the change cannot be determined from an uncontrolled case study. Even if treatment were responsible for change, several alternative interpretations of the case might be proposed. These alternative interpretations have been catalogued under the rubric of "threats to internal validity." (p. 184)

Kazdin goes on to discuss some special design features by which the case study can be strengthened so that valid causal inferences regarding the effects of treatment may become more legitimate, consisting of practices such as gathering more objective data, repeatedly assessing client functioning using these more objective indicators, taking baseline measures of client functioning prior to treatment, observing immediate and marked changes in the clients immediately after treatment is initiated, repeating this methodology across a number of similar cases and hopefully obtaining similar results. This discussion of Kazin leads us to the topic of single-system research designs, which forms the balance of this chapter's presentation on clinician-friendly approaches to practice evaluation.

THE B DESIGN

To begin with, imagine the typical narrative case study of social work intervention with a client, but with the addition of some more objective indicator of functioning obtained prior to the beginning of treatment, and again after treatment has been terminated. For some clinical issues, the choice of such outcome measures is obvious and noncontroversial. If a client is seeking assistance in losing weight, weighing him or her once at the beginning of therapy and again at its conclusion provides a rather obvious way to look at clinical success (or its lack). Or if a client is seeking assistance in abstaining from cocaine, a urine test can be administered upon initial assessment (a positive result would indicate recent cocaine ingestion) and again after termination (a negative result, hopefully). But outcome measures need not be so blunt. For example, a depressed client could complete the well-known Beck Depression Inventory (BDI) pre- and posttreatment. Measures such as these would add to the narratively provided clinical evidence of treatment success.

The limitations of such singularly administered outcome assessments are obvious, however. Prior to treatment, the client's problem may be very labile and an isolated measure may not accurately reflect long-term functioning. The same caveat applies to posttreatment assessments. Also, many clients tend to seek treatment when problems reach a crisis and in the natural ebb and flow of life's circumstances the passage of time alone, or the tendency for extreme variations to regress to average or more normative functioning, means that any single pretreatment assessment will, if repeated after some time has passed, likely indicate lessened severity of the presenting problem. One possible solution to these barriers to making causal inferences about the true effects of social work intervention is to obtain *repeated* assessments of the client's state over time. In this way, trends can be determined in a more reliable fashion than relying on a single benchmark pre- and posttreatment. This approach is also congruent with the advice of Richmond (1917) who asserted:

> Special efforts should be made to ascertain whether abnormal manifestations are *increasing* or *decreasing* in number and intensity, as this often has a practical bearing on the management of the case (p. 435, italics in original).

What could be a clearer historical precedent for what has become known as single-system research designs.

The simplest form of an SSD can be called the B design, and refers to the social worker beginning treatment and formal assessment with one or more structured outcome measures at the same time. As an example, during an initial assessment session the social worker has a depressed client tell his or her story; conducts a psychosocial assessment; offers empathy, support, and encouragement; and concludes with arriving at a formal treatment contract (verbal or written) with the client and the client is asked to complete a Beck Depression Inventory (BDI). Evidence-based psychosocial treatment begins the following week and continues with weekly sessions. At the beginning of each session, the client is asked to once again complete the BDI. These BDIs are scored by the social worker and depicted on a graph, with the vertical axis indicating the BDI score and the horizontal axis the time intervals, say weeks or treatment sessions. Over time it will be evident if the client's BDI scores are remaining stable (depressed), improving, or growing worse. This information, combined with the usual rich clinical narrative material disclosed in therapy, augments the social worker's ability to judge whether the client is getting any better. After a reasonable period of time, lack of progress may call for a reevaluation of the treatment being provided. Please note that the more objective measure is never intended to supplant the social worker's clinical judgment. If BDI scores and the client's narrative do not jibe, this can serve to direct attention in treatment to the apparent disparity.

Previously, I noted that simply taking a single assessment pre- and posttreatment would not constitute an SSD, so that leaves us with the question of how many data points are needed? This is a murky area. The general rule is that the more the better. Two is better than one, but you need at least three to infer any trend. Four is better than three, five is better than four, and so on. Any inferences made using this approach to practice evaluation are very much qualitative in nature. There are no widely applied quantitative tests to add in this process. If you do observe a trend, the best check on the reliability of your judgment is to show the graph to one or more colleagues and ask what they think, after you fill them in on the clinical background material. If your colleagues concur with your views, then you have a rough form of interrater agreement. But if they disagree with you, or among each other, then the clarity of inference you had hoped for is absent, and you'd best defer drawing any conclusions or, more conservatively, infer that no changes are obvious. If the clinical situation permits, then simply continuing treatment and gathering more data is the best option. This rough guide to making inferences from data presented on line graphs can be called the "intra-ocular trauma test," that is, the conclusion must jump out at you and hit you between the eyes. Lacking such striking changes, it is best to infer nothing. Which is itself informative—knowing that the outcome measure does not clearly indicate any client improvement.

Outcome measures in SSDs need not be quantitative. For example, weekly urine screens of illicit drug use can be depicted on a line graph using "Yes" or "No" using a pair of labels on the vertical axis and the dates of the tests labeled on the horizontal axis. Over time, you would hope that with successful treatment for substance abuse, the frequency of the Yes test results (indicating that the client had used drugs) would diminish and be replaced with an eventual succession of No results. A child might be asked to indicate his or her mood by placing adhesive smiley or frowney faces on a graph each week. Such an approach to an SSD would render this a purely qualitative method of outcomes assessment.

The absence of a formal baseline period wherein assessments are systematically made prior to beginning actual treatment makes the B design rather ineffectual for trying to determine if the client improved *because* of social work intervention but it can be an excellent way to more objectively document the client's status throughout the course of treatment. Wong and his colleagues used a B design to see how an institutionalized psychotic individual's problematic behavior diminished over a 35-week period (Wong, Woolsey, & Gallegos, 1987). Vonk used a B design to see how a client's previously intractable sexual phobia changed over several months of treatment (Vonk & Thyer, 1995). These SSDs are obviously more than a simple case history. The use of more systematic assessments of client functioning adds to the richness of the narrative and background material and augments your ability to infer meaningful change. But the B design does not usually allow the worker to make *causal* inferences about the effects of treatment. To do that, more stringent design requirements are needed, like the one discussed next.

THE AB DESIGN

The AB design builds on the features of the B design by adding one further element, and that is the repeated assessment of client functioning *before* social work intervention formally begins. This is an operationalization of the social work dictum, "Beginning where the client is at." This baseline phase—an A phase of a single system design—attempts to exclude the possibility that the client's functioning is so labile that it would be hard to determine if any meaningful change occurred following treatment. In the best of all circumstances (in an inferential sense), several baseline measures of some reliable and valid outcome measure indicate that a serious problem is present and that the values of the outcome measure are neither fluctuating wildly nor trending in the direction of improvement or give signs of regression to the mean. Then treatment is initiated and measurement of the client's problem/situation continues as before, using the same reliable and valid outcome indicator(s). If, in the best of all possible worlds (in an inferential sense), the client's situation immediately and markedly improves and stays better during this treatment or B phase of the AB design, you are marginally in a better position to tentatively claim that intervention caused this change. This ability to make such as inference is enhanced by having a larger rather than a small number of baseline measurements, by having a very stable baseline, and by the presence of an abrupt and clinically important improvement at the beginning of the B phase, an improvement that is maintained or even enhanced throughout the entirety of the B phase. Such inferences are also affected by the nature of the problem. Serious issues known to be generally intractable, or whose natural history does not indicate that improvements are likely, or problems not known to be responsive to placebo or nonspecific treatment factors all augment the strength of the inferences that can potentially be drawn.

Over 25 years ago, Stanley Witkin, the distinguished social worker and past-editor of the NASW journal *Social Work,* illustrated the use of AB designs in his evaluations of social work practice in the field of marital counseling. He provided a very favorable appraisal of this approach, saying:

> This chapter recounts how in a marital intervention training program for social workers in a public agency . . . intervention and evaluation was highly compatible with the exigencies and needs of the workers and couples served. Assessment was clear and provided clients and workers with ongoing feedback. Intervention was directive and action-oriented; evaluation was straightforward and relevant. . . . Measurement of intervention efficacy provided accountability data. (Witkin, 1981, p. 286)

THE ABA DESIGN

The next incrementally complex SSD can be called the ABA design. An ABA design consists of conducting a regular AB design and then discontinuing treatment while continuing to assess your outcome measure(s). ABA designs begin to approximate what have been called *experiments.* Here are some definitions of this term:

> A study in which an intervention is deliberately introduced to observe its effects. (Shadish, Cook, & Campbell, 2002, p. 12)

> One or more independent variables are manipulated to observe their effects on one or more dependent variables. (Shadish et al., 2002, p. 12)

> **Experiment.** The manipulation of one or more independent variables conducted under controlled conditions to test one or more hypotheses, especially for making inferences of a cause-effect character. Involves the measurement of one or more dependent variables. (Corsini, 2002, p. 351, bold in original)

Digging deeper into our indigenous social work literature we find a similar definition:

> Manipulation of subject and/or intervention is the essence of experimental method. . . . The demands of science and of practice have lead to a whole array of experiments. They include experiments designed . . . with the subjects serving as controls for themselves. (Wolins, 1960, p. 255)

Although you may associate the term *experiment* with the use of research designs involving large numbers of participants, perhaps randomly selected from some population on interest and perhaps randomly assigned to active treatment and to control groups, such group research designs are only one type of experiment. Certain forms of SSDs also qualify.

The landmark book *Evidence-Based Medicine* (Straus, Richardson, Glasziou, & Haynes, 2005, pp. 172–175) discusses the use of $N = 1$ studies as an important component of evidence-based practice. In fact, selected forms of SSDs are asserted in the *Users' Guide to the Medical Literature: Essentials of Evidence-Based Clinical Practice* (Guyatt & Rennie, 2002, p. 12) to be the *strongest* form of evidence to make treatment decisions, rated superior to systematic reviews or randomized controlled trials. If this flies in the face of everything you have been taught about any presumptive hierarchy of research evidence, I encourage you to read primary sources on this methodology to help you in understanding the inferential logic behind such assertions (e.g., Guyatt & Rennie, 2002; Hersen & Barlow, 1985; Sidman, 1960; Straus et al., 2005; Thyer & Myers, 2007). The issue relates to a person's direction of inference. If you are attempting to make an inference about the effects of social work treatment for *this particular client,* then an SSD is indeed a superior form of evidence. If you wish to make inferences from a sample of clients who responded favorably to a specific social work treatment to a larger population of interest (e.g., everyone with problem X), then larger scale group studies will usually provide a stronger evidentiary foundation for such inferences. Curiously a single randomized controlled trial or even a comprehensive systematic review of the effects of some intervention for problem X may actually provide *little* guidance on how to care for an individual with that problem who sits in your consulting room. Friston, Homles, and Worsley (1999, p. 1) addressed this issue in their paper titled "How Many Subjects Constitute a Study?" "A critical distinction that determines the number of subjects included in a ... study is between inferences about *the particular subjects studied* and inferences that pertain to *the population* from which these subjects came" [italics added]. To see if treatment X really helped Mr. Smith, an SSD is needed. To see if treatment X is reliably effective for many clients with the same problem that Mr. Smith experienced requires a group outcome study with a sample of clients representative of folks with that problem. Given that social workers in direct practice are primarily concerned with evaluating the outcomes of the interventions they provided to *their* clients, you can grasp the superiority of using SSD methodology in practice evaluation relative to group research designs.

Going back as far as Aristotle, we find references to the idea that gaining evidence by deliberately introducing or removing a purported cause and systematically observing its apparent effects, provides the most credible evidence for making cause-and-effect determinations. The experimental SSDs make use of this principle. Take a baseline (the A phase). Introduce social work treatment (B phase). Remove social work treatment (restore the conditions of the A phase). If (happily) the problem gets better when B is introduced and then relapses (unhappily) when B is removed and A reinstated, we have considerably stronger evidence of the causal role of B in bringing about these changes than with the more simple AB design alone. This design, the ABA, was used in landmark investigations by Truax and Carkhuff (1965) to evaluate the processes of Rogerian psychotherapy.

The ABA design is primarily useful when the effects of intervention are predicted to be short lived, not durable. Yet, many social work treatments can be anticipated to produce durable changes. For example, the insights achieved via psychotherapy do not evaporate if therapy is halted. If the client is taught a social or academic skill, these will not vanish. If a client has been cured of a phobia via exposure therapy, the phobic condition is unlikely to return. In instances of treatments producing well-maintained effects, the experimental logic of the ABA design and other SSDs using withdrawal phases will collapse. If during the second A phase, client gains seen during the B phase are maintained, then you have, logically, only the results of an AB design in terms of making causal inferences about treatment. This is good clinically, but not for experimental demonstration purposes. This is okay for the direct practitioner who would undoubtedly prefer, as would the client, that gains made via intervention be maintained after treatment is terminated. Such designs do, after all, provide a good test of how genuinely successful treatment was. But if the client does relapse during the second A phase, then the opportunity for a more rigorous experimental demonstration of the effects of social work treatment becomes possible, as discussed next.

THE ABAB DESIGN

The ABAB design is simply a continuation of the principles outlined previously. If the client regresses during the second baseline (A phase), reinstate treatment B. If the problem resolves again, you have three consecutive demonstrations of an apparent cause-effect relationship between treatment and outcome. The first is the improvement seen during the first B phase when the client gets better after treatment begins. The second is the deterioration when treatment is removed, during the second A phase. The third is the second demonstration of improvement when the treatment is reapplied during the second B phase. Such shifts in the data pattern, clearly linked to the introduction or the removal of treatment, provides a very high level of confidence in inferring that treatment was responsible for these changes. The ABAB design was used by Thyer, Irvine, and Santa (1984) to examine the effects of a reinforcement program on promoting aerobic exercise among individuals with chronic mental illness.

MULTIPLE BASELINE DESIGNS

Multiple baseline (MBL) designs make use of the same experimental logic as withdrawal designs such as the ABA and ABAB SSDs, namely attempting to see if a problem improves when, and only when, a given social work intervention is provided to clients. And to demonstrate such an apparent relationship several times, with each successful replication enhancing confidence that treatment caused improvements. There are three major variations of the MBL designs, outlined next.

Multiple Baseline Design across Clients

This novel design requires that the social worker have access at the same point in time to two or more clients with the same problem who will receive the same intervention. Although this may sound unlikely, in many cases, it is not. How many social workers have two clients with major depression seek treatment during the same week, or month? If you do, then using this type of design might be one way to evaluate your practice outcomes. As with all SSDs, you must choose a reliable and valid outcome measure and begin a baseline for your clients (2, 3, or even more clients) around the same time. Prepare an AB graph at the top of the page, and label this *Client 1*. The values of the outcome measure appear on the left vertical axis, and the dimension of time (date, week, session, etc.) is depicted on the bottom axis. Obtain a baseline (the A phase) consisting of a certain number of data points (e.g., 3, 4, 5, whatever), then begin the intervention (the B phase). Continue monitoring the outcome measure(s). When you begin baselining Client 1, also begin baselining Client 2 on a second AB graph positioned or drawn on the page directly under Client 1's graph with the bottom axes aligned so that the labels for both graphs refer to the same time periods (date, week, session, etc.). Now, for Client 2, have his or her baseline extend beyond that of Client 1, so that, say if Client 1's baseline was four data points, Client 2's is six or eight data points. After the extended baseline without treatment, provide Client 2 with the same treatment that you delivered to Client 1. In ideal circumstances, you are looking for a situation wherein Client 1 has a baseline indicating a stable, serious problem; and when treatment is provided, his or her outcome measure indicates a rapid, meaningful improvement. However, Client 2's baseline remains stable, indicating continuing problems. If, when you subsequently provide the same intervention to Client 2 and problem resolution/improvement is also immediately observed, you have two demonstrations of the treatment application resulting in problem improvement. This replicated effect is more convincing evidence than a single AB study, and the lengthier baseline of Client 2, which remains unchanged when Client 1's treatment data reflects improvement, serves as a partial control for some sort of historical event (spring break, Christmas, etc.) as being responsible for these improvements. If you conduct this MBL across clients with three rather than two clients, the evidence can be even more persuasive. Besa (1994) used this type of design with several families to evaluate the effects of narrative therapy, a study he used as his doctoral dissertation. Pinkston, Howe, and Blackman (1987) also used a MBL design across clients to assess the effectiveness of social work intervention designed to help nursing home residents achieve a greater degree of urinary continence.

Multiple Baseline Design across Problems

In the MBL across problems approach to practice evaluation, the social worker must have one client with two or more problems or difficulties that will be treated using the same intervention. Appropriate outcome measures will be selected for each problem and graphed on separate AB designs, aligned one over the other. Like before, the horizontal axis reflects the dimension of time and the vertical axes measure the different problems. As an example, let says that our client, Allen, suffers from three different phobias, to dogs, snakes, and bugs, each of which will be treated *sequentially,* not concurrently. The top graph is an AB design measuring Allen's fear of dogs. The social worker locates reliable and valid measures of phobic anxiety (they do indeed exist). A baseline is taken and then a specific treatment, say graduated real-life exposure therapy, is undertaken involving dogs. No therapy is applied to snakes or bugs, but concurrent baseline measures are taken of these fears while treatment for the dog phobia is applied. After a longer baseline than that of the dog phobia, treatment begins for Allen's snake phobia. But his bug phobia is not yet treated, and the bug phobia baseline is continued. Then following a longer baseline than that used for snake fears, the social worker begins treatment for the bug phobia. In the ideal situation, all baselines display stable, profound levels of fear for their specific phobic stimulus. When treatment, exposure therapy, is applied to the dog phobia, this problem quickly improves but the snake and bug fear baselines remain unchanged. Then, a bit later when the snake fear is treated again with exposure therapy, snake fears quickly improve but bug fears remain. Last, treatment begins for the bug phobia, and it too rapidly resolves. In this example, three distinct problems remain intact until they are individually treated, and then and only then are they resolved. This provides three demonstrations of an apparent treatment effect. You can do a MBL across problems with only two problems, and this is stronger in terms of internal validity than a single AB study.

Multiple Baseline Design across Situations

This variation of SSDs requires a client with a particular problem that manifests itself across several different circumstances, and sequentially applies the same intervention to this problem in these differing settings, so as to provide a convincing demonstration that it was indeed treatment that caused these (hopefully) observed improvements. Allen (1973) provides a nice illustration of this design to evaluate a psychosocial intervention targeting bizarre speech in a youth with brain damage residing at a summer camp. Baselines were made of the child's frequency of odd speech in four different settings while he was at a summer camp:

1. While walking on a trail during evening activities.
2. In the dining hall.
3. In the cabin where the boy lived.
4. During education classes.

A 6-day baseline was taken of bizarre talk while on the trail, then intervention began on day 7. Bizarre talk quickly reduced in frequency. But the baselined bizarre talk in the other three settings continued unabated. After 12 days of baseline, intervention was also applied in the dining hall. Bizarre talk again declined. Bizarre talk was baselined for 16 days in the cabin, then intervention was applied, and the bizarre talk declined, and last, following 20 days of baseline, intervention was introduced during education classes, and again, for the fourth demonstration, peculiar talk subsided to near zero levels. Such a data pattern is rather convincing evidence that for this child, with this problem, this intervention was causally responsible for the improved behavior.

ALTERNATING TREATMENT DESIGN

The alternating treatment design is an innovative approach to examine the relative effectiveness of two of more interventions with the same client. Following a baseline period, assessing some problem or situation, a coin is tossed and the client is provided with one of, say two, possible treatments (call them Treatment X or Treatment Y), based on the random fall of the coin. The next session, the coin is tossed again to determine if the client receives Treatment X or Y. This process is repeated. The experimental logic is that if X and Y are differentially effective, a line connecting the data points for the session when Treatment X was provided and another line connecting the data points for the sessions when Treatment

Y was provided, will not overlap and indeed show marked divergence. This ADT is only appropriate for treatments with effects that are expected to be immediate and pronounced.

Wong and his colleagues used such an approach with a 37-year-old man called Tom who was diagnosed with schizophrenia and who resided at a state mental hospital. One of Tom's problems was that he rather constantly engaged in mumbling or solitary laughter, behaviors that hindered his ability to be placed in a less restrictive community setting. Tom's occurrence of mumbling and solitary laughter was measured in the hospital dayroom setting for 5 sessions. Following the baseline, the client was randomly presented, at the beginning of free-time periods in the dayroom, with the opportunity to select from a variety of magazines. In other words, given something interesting to do (his history indicated he enjoyed reading) or not given anything to do and just left to his own devices in the dayroom with other patients (similar to the baseline period). During the baseline period and during the similar sessions when baseline and reading opportunities were randomly alternated, Tom displayed stereotypic vocalizations about 77% of the time when he had nothing to do. However, when he was provided with magazines to read, mumbling and solitary laughter declined to about 24% of the time, a rather marked and clinically significant decline. This was striking evidence that providing Tom (and perhaps others suffering from chronic mental illnesses) the opportunity to engage in something interesting to do, rather than being bored, can produce dramatic reductions in bizarre symptoms (see Wong, Terranova, et al., 1987, for a fuller description of this SSD).

The ATD is similar to what is labeled an $N = 1$ randomized controlled trial within the field of evidence-based practice, although they have been in use with psychology and education for decades prior to their discovery by medicine (Guyatt et al., 1986; Janosky, 2005). Kent, Camfield, and Camfield (1999) demonstrate their usefulness with 50 families of children diagnosed with Attention-Deficit/Hyperactivity Disorder (ADHD). The families were provided with bottles of identical capsules containing either standard medication (Ritalin) or placebo. The child, family, teacher, and physician were unaware of the true content of the capsules, administered in random order each day to the child. Careful assessment was made of ADHD symptoms during the baseline and during 3 weeks of treatment. Sometimes (randomly) the children got placebo and sometimes Ritalin. After 3 weeks of daily treatment, data were analyzed to see if medication was really having an effect on the children's behavior. This approach was extremely useful in determining the real effects of Ritalin versus placebo on ADHD. A similar $N = 1$ randomized trial (an ATD) was conduced by McBride (1988) and the medical literature is rapidly embracing this method of practice evaluation to compare the effects of two of more treatments.

This brief overview just touched on the general principles of conducting single system designs. Before attempting these designs, consult various book-length treatments of the topic to be found in the social work literature, such as Thyer and Myers (2007); Bloom, Fischer, and Orme (2006); Kazi (1998); and Tripodi (1994).

IS THERE A HIERARCHY OF RESEARCH EVIDENCE?

There have been several attempts to conceptualize research evidence in terms of its credibility and usefulness in informing clinical practice. In the mid-1950s, a group of psychiatrists were invited to participate in one of the first-ever randomized controlled trials of the effects of psychotropic medication. Their reaction? "The psychiatrists immediately betrayed their skepticism by declaring the supremacy of knowledge acquired by doctors at the bedside and clinical intuition to be above any other methodology" (Tansella, 2002, p. 4). Another similar statement made with respect to the treatment of clinical depression is representative of the evidentiary hierarchy prevalent at the time:

> There is no psychiatric illness in which bedside knowledge and long clinical experience pays better dividends and we are never going to learn how to treat depression properly from double blind sampling. (Sargant, as cited in Tansella, 2002, p. 4, from a 1965 letter in the *British Medical Journal*)

Thus, 50 years ago clinical observations, practitioner intuition, and experience were widely viewed as the most credible sources of information to guide the care of individual clients. Suffice it say, although such views continue to be maintained by a minority of social workers, most contemporary professionals acknowledge the limitations of clinical experience alone as a guide to evaluating practice and accept the general idea that scientific investigations of the effects of interventions have something to contribute as well and in many instances can provide more valid and useful information.

One of the more recent efforts to develop an explicit hierarchy of research evidence was undertaken by members of Division 12 (Clinical Psychology) of the American Psychological Association, who comprised a Task Force on Treatments That Work, formed in the early 1990s. This group was charged with three ambitious projects—to determine what amount of evidence would suffice to claim that a given psychosocial treatment was empirically supported, to create lists of such empirically supported treatments, and to help disseminate these empirically supported treatments to the practice community. The first task was completed (not without considerable contention), and their results appear in Table 5.1. Please note the rather unconventional equating of a large (≥ 9 participants) series of well-designed SSDs with the results of two well-designed randomized controlled group studies as the standard needed to be met to label an intervention a well-established treatment (in terms of its evidentiary foundations) and similarly equivalent but more modest standards to label a treatment as probably efficacious. These criteria strikingly illustrate the sometimes superior ability of SSDs to arrive at causal knowledge regarding the effects of social work treatments, relative to group outcome studies.

Another hierarchy of research evidence developed by the proponents of evidence-based practice appears in the *Users' Guides to the Medical Literature: Essentials of Evidence-Based Clinical Practice* (Guyatt & Rennie, 2002). Contained in this volume is a small section called "A Hierarchy of Evidence" in which the authors lay out the following position:

> What is the nature of the "evidence" in EBM? We suggest a broad definition: any empirical observation about the apparent relation between events constitutes potential evidence. Thus the unsystematic observations of the individual clinician constitute one source of evidence.... Unsystematic observations can lead to profound insight, and experienced clinicians develop a healthy respect for the insights of their senior colleagues.... At the same time, unsystematic clinical observations are limited by small sample size and more importantly, by deficiencies in human processes of making inferences. Given the limitations of unsystematic clinical observations ... EBM suggests a hierarchy of evidence. (p. 11)

Table 5.1   Criteria for Empirically-Validated Treatments

Well-Established Treatments

I. At least two good between-group design experiments demonstrating efficacy in one or more of the following ways:
   A. Superior (statistically significantly so) to pill or psychological placebo or to another treatment.
   B. Equivalent to an already established treatment in experiments with adequate sample sizes.

Or

II. A large series of single-case design experiments ($n \geq 9$) demonstrating efficacy. These experiments must have:
   A. Used good experimental designs and
   B. Compared the intervention to another treatment as in I.A.

Further criteria for both I and II:

III. Experiments must be conducted with treatment manuals.
IV. Characteristics of the client samples must be clearly specified.
V. Effects must have been demonstrated by at least two different investigators or investigating teams.

Probably Efficacious Treatments

I. Two experiments showing the treatment is superior (statistically significantly so) to a waiting-list control group.

Or

II. One or more experiments meeting the Well-Established Treatment Criteria I.A or I.B, III, and IV, but not V.

Or

III. A series of single-case design experiments ($n \geq 3$) otherwise meeting Well-Established Treatment Criteria II, III, and IV.

Source: "Update on Empirically Validated Therapies," part II, by D. L. Chambless et al., 1998, *Clinical Psychologist, 51*(1), pp. 3–16. Reprinted with permission.

These authors' suggested hierarchy is presented in Table 5.2. However, they do include cautionary language regarding the interpretation of this framework:

> This hierarchy is not absolute. If treatment effects are sufficiently large and consistent, for instance, observational studies may provide more compelling evidence than most RCTs. . . . The hierarchy implies a clear course of action for (clinicians) addressing patient problems: They should look for the highest available evidence from the hierarchy. The hierarchy makes clear that any statement to the effect that there is no evidence addressing the effect of a particular treatment is a nonsequitur. The evidence may be extremely weak—it may be the unsystematic observation of a single clinician or a generalization from physiological studies that are related only indirectly—but there is always evidence. (pp. 13–14)

It is very important to stress this point, EBP prefers stronger evidence over weaker evidence and suggests that clinicians should not only seek out the highest levels of evidence, but clearly indicates that additional forms of evidence of lesser internal validity should also be appraised. It is important to stress the inclusive nature of all of the evidence being consulted because the misperception is widespread that EBP only relies on studies of the highest quality, as in the following definition for EBP found in *The Social Work Dictionary:* "The use of the best available scientific knowledge derived from randomized controlled outcome studies and meta-analyses of existing outcome studies" (Barker, 2003,

Table 5.2   A Hierarchy of Strength of Evidence for Treatment Decisions

$N = 1$ randomized controlled trial
Systematic reviews of randomized trials
Single randomized controlled trial
Systematic review of observational studies addressing patient-important outcomes
Single observational study addressing patient-important outcomes
Physiologic studies
Unsystematic clinical observations

Note: These criteria are listed in order of descending strength.
Source: "Introduction: The Philosophy of Evidence-Based Medicine" (p. 12), by G. Guyatt et al., in *Users' Guides to the Medical Literature: Essentials of Evidence-Based Clinical Practice,* G. Guyatt and D. Rennie (Eds.), 2002, Chicago: American Medical Association. All rights reserved. Reprinted with permission.

p. 149). Given that substantial domains of social work field of practice have yet to have their interventions investigated by well-designed RCTs, the hapless social worker reading such misleading descriptions may shrug his or her shoulders and conclude (incorrectly) that the process of EBP has little to offer clinicians in their area of practice. If there are no experimental SSDs, look for systematic reviews. If there are none of these, look for randomized controlled trials of interventions applied to persons similar to your client with similar problems. If none can be located, drill down the evidentiary strata to the quasi-experiments, then consensus-based practice guidelines perhaps, then case studies. The most comprehensive systematic reviews of this nature may be located on the web sites of the Cochrane (related to health and mental health) and Campbell (related to social welfare, education, and criminal justice) Collaborations, available at www.cochrane.org and www.campbellcollaboration.org, respectively. Although some forms of evidence may be deemed of greater credibility that others, EBP suggests that all forms of relevant evidence be judiciously considered and critically reviewed. Anyone who implies that EBP focuses only on randomized controlled trials, meta-analyses, or systematic reviews is simply ignorant.

LIMITATIONS OF THIS APPROACH

Twenty-five years ago the Council on Social Work Education (CSWE) accreditation standards stated that training in practice skills needed to include "data gathering . . . and evaluation relevant to social work practice" (p. 10) and that the content on research should incorporate ". . . designs for the systematic evaluation of the student's own practice" (CSWE, 1982). Soon some social work programs did indeed begin including such content. Nowadays the CSWE's *Educational Policy and Accreditation Standards* (CSWE, 2002, p. 8) continues to include as a foundation program objective the requirement that students demonstrate the ability to "Evaluate research studies, apply research findings to practice, and evaluate their own practice interventions." In the concentration year, the research objectives state that "The content prepares students to develop, use, and effectively communicate empirically based knowledge, including evidence-based interventions. Research knowledge is used by students . . . to evaluate their own practice" (CSWE, 2002, p. 10). On paper these are fine aspirations. But there is relatively little evidence to suggest that we are doing a good job at this. In the 1980s there was a flurry of articles that followed up on the post-MSW graduation use of SSDs in real-life practice, which found that they were relatively rarely used (e.g., Cheatham, 1987), but I am aware of no such studies conducted in recent years. A recent survey on a related topic, the extent to which social work programs actually provide didactic instruction and clinical supervision in empirically supported treatments, found them to be very rarely taught indeed (Bledsoe et al., 2007; Weissman et al., 2006). One is tempted to conclude that if the CSWE accreditation standard mandating teaching empirically supported interventions as well as research designs to evaluate one's own practice found that the former is infrequently taught, then it seems likely that the latter is not well covered either. About 20 years ago, I reported on a survey of the extent to which training in SSDs was covered in MSW programs (Thyer & Maddox, 1988). At that time, a large majority appeared to ignore this content, but these old results cannot be extrapolated to the present. However, I venture to speculate that training in SSDs remains rarely taught and when it is covered is perhaps not well addressed or applied during internships.

Another limitation is the strong association between SSDs and the approach to practice called behavioral social work. This is important because behavioral social work has a long history of being misrepresented, to its detriment, within the social work literature to such an extent that the model is often viewed with disfavor. By inaccurately linking the use of SSDs with behavioral methods, the former topic is tainted by the latter (see Thyer, 1991, 2005). The reality is that the atheoretical methodology of SSDs originated in early nonbehaviorist psychological research and within medicine, physiology, and related disciplines during the late 1800s. In the middle of the last century, researchers began advocating for using SSDs to examine the outcomes and processes of nonbehavioral psychotherapy (e.g., Chassan, 1967; Shapiro, 1961; Shapiro & Ravenette, 1959) and the person-centered therapy developed by Carl Rogers was subjected to analysis using ABA SSDs (e.g., Truax & Carkhuff, 1965). Within social work, SSDs have been used to evaluate the outcomes of psychodynamic therapy (e.g., Broxmeyer, 1978), task-centered practice (e.g., Tolson, 1977), and treatment informed by communication theory (Nelsen, 1978). The fact that behaviorally oriented practitioners have admittedly made greater use of SSDs should not overshadow the fact that these research techniques can and should be used to evaluate the outcomes of all forms of practice.

It also cannot be denied, in discussing limitations of using SSDs, that some of the designs possess fairly restrictive methodological requirements (e.g., staggered baselines, withdrawal phases) that are difficult to meet, which limits their applicability. Also most agencies seem to provide little in the way of organizational support to reinforce practitioner efforts to undertake these designs, and, as we well know, that which has not been reinforced in the past is much less likely to be engaged in.

IMPLICATIONS FOR SOCIAL WORK ON MICRO-, MEZZO-, AND MACROLEVELS

At the microlevel, it will be obvious that I advocate the wider use of SSDs by social workers to evaluate the outcomes of their own practice. This is not only congruent with what is required by the CSWE, such evaluations are also compatible with the practice standards and the Code of Ethics promulgated by the National Association of Social Workers that call for social workers to engage in such systematic practice evaluations (these standards are reviewed in Royse et al., 2006, p. 16). I encourage practitioners to start with relatively simple designs, such as the B or AB, prior to undertaking more complex SSDs, so that your skills in applying these research methods can be honed. Try it with one client, then perhaps another. No one, certainly not me, is suggesting social workers should be required to use these designs with all clients. Advocates of SSDs are simply urging their gradual incorporation into some cases. Quite apart from the desirability of enhancing this aspect of professional practice, if greater numbers of social workers undertook such SSDs, they would be in a better position to submit such cases to the various professional journals that welcome examples of such evaluations. It would certainly be a good thing for our professional journals to have greater representation from the practice community among its published authors.

Supervisors also can encourage their supervisees to undertake SSDs and incorporate a review of graphed data into their supervisory sessions with social workers (see Artelt & Thyer, 1998). As Gambrill has aptly noted: "The quality of services you offer should be enhanced by the supervision you receive and supervisors should be evaluated by reviewing the outcomes achieved by those whom they supervise" (1983, pp. 400–401). This is a very radical idea! There are a few examples of social workers receiving supervision that incorporated the use of SSDs (e.g., Isaacs, Embry, & Baer, 1982; Jones, Morris, & Barnard, 1986), so this approach is not without precedent nor is it impractical.

Artelt and Thyer (1998, pp. 419–420) provided three even more directive recommendations:

1. Supervisors should encourage social workers to use, as first-choice assessment options, empirically supported methods of assessment, where such knowledge is available.
2. Supervisors should encourage social workers to repeatedly gather quantitative and qualitative data on the client's situation throughout the course of treatment. This information should be presented in records as an up-to-date graph.
3. Supervisors should encourage social workers to use as first-choice treatment options empirically supported methods of intervention, where such knowledge is available.

Again, such recommendations can be seen as compatible with contemporary practice standards and ethical admonitions. See Myers and Thyer (1997) for an expanded argument for the client's right to receive empirically supported treatments.

Earlier, Thyer (1995, p. 95) provided the following statement as a proposed addition to the NASW's Code of Ethics:

> Clinicians should routinely gather empirical data on client's relevant behavior, affect, and reports of thoughts, using reliable and valid measures, where such measures have been developed. These measures should be repeated throughout the course of treatment, and used in clinician decision making to supplement professional judgments pertaining to the alteration or termination of treatment.

This recommendation, of course, is identical with using SSDs in your own practice.

At the macrolevel, several larger-scale practices suggest themselves. The CSWE could strengthen its required content related to research so that each student specializing in direct practice would be expected to actually undertake a SSD during his or her clinical internship. This is not a requirement at present. So we have the very odd accreditation standard situation wherein students are supposed to be taught something (how to evaluate their own practice), but they are not ever required to actually do so. An even stiffer standard for individual programs to adopt, if not the CSWE, would be for each direct practice student to be required, during his or her internship, to provide convincing evidence that he or she has helped at least one client! When, over the years, I have voiced this suggested requirement among groups of students or faculty, it is usually met with grins or nervous laughter. I wonder why?

Going up the mezzo/macro scale of implications, third-party vendors (e.g., insurance companies) who pay for clinical social work services could adopt some of these suggestions—such as requiring clinical social workers to provide objective data of client functioning presented via graphs. Many already ask for some information from clinicians such as client diagnoses, time and duration of therapy sessions, and the nature of treatment being provided. Asking for additional data related to client functioning before, during, and perhaps after the social work services they are paying for could exert a significant leavening effect on the field.

CONCLUSION

Social work practice can be evaluated using a variety of methodological tools. Single-system designs are one very good tool for evaluating practice outcomes. They have been advocated within social work for the past 40 years, and a rather substantial literature describing the methodology of SSDs, as well as hundreds of real-life examples of using them in direct social work practice, is available (Thyer & Thyer, 1992). SSDs can range in internal validity from the very weak to the very strong. Some practitioners within the empirically supported treatments and evidence-based practice communities consider well-conducted SSDs to be among the strongest forms of evidence available for practitioners to make causal inferences about the effects of treatment with their individual clients.

SSDs can be used by practitioners operating from any conceivable theoretical framework, and they can be usefully employed to evaluate outcomes across all the client systems encountered in direct practice—individuals, couples, families, and small groups. There is much that our major professional organizations could do to promote the greater use of SSDs in social work practice, but individual clinicians need not wait for external contingencies to be established to begin experimenting with applying these approaches to practice evaluation. So using SSDs has the potential to help clients more effectively, to contribute to the knowledge base of the field, and to more tightly knit the art of social work practice with the science of human behavior.

REFERENCES

Allen, G. J. (1973). Case study: Implementation of behavior modification in summer camp settings. *Behavior Therapy*, *4*, 570–575.

Artelt, T., & Thyer, B. A. (1998). Empirical approaches to social work supervision. In J. S. Wodarski & B. A. Thyer (Eds.), *Handbook of empirical social work practice: Vol. 2. Social problems and practice issues* (pp. 413–431). New York: Wiley.

Baer, D. M., Harrison, R., Fradenburg, L., Petersen, D., & Milla, S. (2005). Some pragmatics in the valid and reliable recording of directly observed behavior. *Research on Social Work Practice*, *15*, 440–451.

Barker, R. (Ed.). (2003). *The social work dictionary* (5th ed.). Washington, DC: National Association of Social Workers Press.

Besa, D. (1994). Evaluating narrative family therapy using single-system designs. *Research on Social Work Practice*, *4*, 309–325.

Bledsoe, S. E., Weissman, M. M., Mullen, E. J., Betts, K., Gameroff, M. J., Verdeli, H., et al. (2007). Empirically supported psychotherapy in social work training: Does the definition of evidence matter? *Research on Social Work Practice*, *17*, 1–7.

Bloom, M., Fischer, J., & Orme, J. (2006). *Evaluating practice: Guidelines for the accountable professional* (5th ed.). Boston: Allyn & Bacon.

Brandell, J. R., & Varkas, T. (2001). Narrative case studies. In B. A. Thyer (Ed.), *Handbook of social work research methods* (pp. 293–307). Thousand Oaks, CA: Sage.

Broxmeyer, N. (1978). Practitioner-research in treating a borderline child. *Social Work Research and Abstracts*, *14*(4), 5–10.

Cameron, O. G., & Thyer, B. A. (1985). Treatment of pavor nocturnus with alprazolam [Letter]. *Journal of Clinical Psychiatry*, *46*, 504.

Chambless, D. L., Baker, M. J., Baucom, D. H., Beutler, L. E., Calhoun, K. S., Crits-Critsoph, P., et al. (1998). Update on empirically validated therapies (Pt. II). *Clinical Psychologist*, *51*(1), 3–16.

Chassan, J. B. (1967). *Research design in clinical psychology and psychiatry*. New York: Appleton-Century-Crofts.

Cheatham, J. M. (1987). The empirical evaluation of clinical practice: A survey of four groups of practitioners. *Journal of Social Service Research*, *10*(2/3/4), 163–177.

Colby, K. M. (1960). *An introduction to psychoanalytic research*. New York: Basic Books.

Corsini, R. J. (2002). *The dictionary of psychology*. New York: Brunner-Routledge.

Council on Social Work Education. (1982). Curriculum policy for the master's degree and the baccalaureate degree programs in social work education. *Social Work Education Reporter*, *30*(3), 5–12.

Council on Social Work Education. (2002). *Educational policy and accreditation standards*. Alexandria, VA: Author.

Fischer, J., & Corcoran, K. (Eds.). (2007). *Measures for clinical practice* (4th ed.). New York: Free Press.

Friston, K. J., Homles, A. P., & Worsley, K. J. (1999). How many subjects constitute a study? *NeuroImage*, *10*, 1–5.

Gambrill, E. (1983). *Casework: A competency approach*. Englewood Cliffs, NJ: Prentice Hall.

Gershenson, C. P. (1952). The reliability of the movement scale. *Social Casework*, *33*, 294–300.

Gilbert, D. J., & Franklin, C. (2003). Qualitative assessment methods. In C. Jordan & C. Franklin (Eds.), *Clinical assessment for social workers* (2nd ed., pp. 139–178). Chicago: Lyceum Books.

Gilgun, J. (1994). A case for case studies in social work research. *Social Work*, *39*, 371–380.

Guyatt, G., Haynes, B., Jaeschke, R., Cook, D., Greenhalgh, T., Meade, M., et al. (2002). Introduction: The philosophy of evidence-based medicine. In G. Guyatt & D. Rennie (Eds.), *Users' guides to the medical literature: Essentials of evidence-based clinical practice* (pp. 5–20). Chicago: American Medical Association.

Guyatt, G., & Rennie, D. (Eds.). (2002). *Users' guides to the medical literature: Essentials of evidence-based clinical practice*. Chicago: American Medical Association.

Guyatt, G., Sackett, D., Taylor, D. W., Chong, J., Roberts, R., & Pugsley, S. (1986). Determining optimal therapy: Randomized trials in individual patients. *New England Journal of Medicine*, *314*, 889–892.

Hersen, M., & Barlow, D. H. (1985). *Single case experimental designs*. New York: Pergamon Press.

Hunt, J., Blenkner, M., & Kogan, L. S. (1950). A field test of the movement scale. *Social Casework*, *31*, 267–277.

Isaacs, C. D., Embry, L. H., & Baer, D. M. (1982). Training family therapists: An experimental analysis. *Journal of Applied Behavior Analysis*, *15*, 505–520.

Janosky, J. E. (2005). Use of the single subject design for practice-based primary care research. *Postgraduate Medicine Journal*, *81*, 549–551.

Jones, H. H., Morris, E. K., & Barnard, J. D. (1986). Increasing staff completion of civil commitment forms through instructions and graphed group performance feedback. *Journal of Organizational Behavior Management*, *7*(3/4), 29–43.

Jordan, C., & Franklin, C. (Eds.). (2003). *Clinical assessment for social workers* (2nd ed., pp. 139–178). Chicago: Lyceum Books.

Kazdin, A. E. (1981). Drawing valid inferences from case studies. *Journal of Consulting and Clinical Psychology*, *49*, 183–192.

Kazi, M. A. F. (1998). *Single-case evaluation by social workers*. Aldershot, England: Ashgate.

Kent, M. A., Camfield, C. S., & Camfield, P. R. (1999). Double-blind methylphenidate trials: Practical and highly endorsed by families. *Archives of Pediatric and Adolescent Medicine*, *153*, 1292–1296.

Koepke, J., & Thyer, B. A. (1985). Behavioral treatment of failure to thrive in a two-year-old infant. *Child Welfare*, *64*, 511–516.

Kogan, N., Kogan, L. S., & Hunt, J. (1952). Expansion and extension of use of the movement scale. *Social Casework*, *33*, 10–12.

McBride, M. (1988). An individual double-blind cross-over trial for assessing methylphenidate response in children with attention deficit disorder. *Journal of Pediatrics*, *113*, 137–145.

Myers, L. L., & Thyer, B. A. (1997). Should clients have the right to effective treatment? *Social Work*, *42*, 288–298.

Nelsen, J. (1978). Use of communication theory in single-subject research. *Social Work Research and Abstracts*, *14*(4), 12–19.

Pergeron, J. P., Curtis, G. C., & Thyer, B. A. (1986). Simple phobia leading to suicide: A case study [Letter]. *Behavior Therapist*, *9*, 134–135.

Pinkston, E. M., Howe, M. W., & Blackman, D. K. (1987). Medical social work management of urinary incontinence in the elderly. *Journal of Social Service Research*, *10*(2/3/4), 179–194.

Polster, R. A., & Collins, D. (1993). Structured observation. In R. M. Grinnell (Ed.), *Social work research and evaluation* (4th ed., pp. 244–261). Itasca, IL: Peacock.

Richmond, M. (1917). *Social diagnosis*. New York: Sage.

Rosen, S., & Polansky, N. A. (1975). Observation of social interaction. In N. A. Polansky (Ed.), *Social work research* (2nd ed., pp. 154–181). Chicago: University of Chicago Press.

Royse, D., Thyer, B. A., Padgett, D. K., & Logan, T. K. (2006). *Program evaluation: An introduction* (4th ed.). Belmont, CA: Thomson-Brooks/Cole.

Shadish, W. R., Cook, T. D., & Campbell, D. T. (2002). *Experimental and quasi-experimental designs for generalized causal inference*. New York: Houghton Mifflin.

Shapiro, M. B. (1961). The single-case in clinical-psychological research. *British Journal of Medical Psychology*, *34*, 255–263.

Shapiro, M. B., & Ravenette, A. T. (1959). A preliminary experiment of paranoid delusions. *Journal of Mental Science*, *105*, 295–312.

Sidman, M. (1960). *Tactics of scientific research: Evaluating experimental data in psychology*. New York: Basic Books.

Staats, A. W., & Butterfield, W. (1965). Treatment of nonreading in a culturally deprived juvenile delinquent. *Child Development*, *36*, 925–942.

Straus, S. E., Richardson, W. S., Glasziou, P., & Haynes, R. B. (2005). *Evidence-based medicine: How to practice and teach EBM*. New York: Elsevier.

Tansella, M. (2002). The scientific evaluation of mental health treatments: An historical perspective. *Evidence-Based Mental Health*, *5*, 4–5.

Thyer, B. A. (1980). Phobia sufferers take a journey into fear. *Practice Digest*, *3*(3), 8–10.

Thyer, B. A. (1981). Prolonged in-vivo exposure therapy with a 70-year-old woman. *Journal of Behavior Therapy and Experimental Psychiatry*, *12*, 47–51.

Thyer, B. A. (1991). Behavioral social work: It is not what you think. *Arete*, *16*(2), 1–9.

Thyer, B. A. (1995). Promoting an empiricist agenda in the human services: An ethical and humanistic imperative. *Journal of Behavior Therapy and Experimental Psychiatry*, *26*, 93–98.

Thyer, B. A. (2005). The misfortunes of behavioral social work: Misprized, misread, and miscon- strued. In S. A. Kirk (Ed.), *Mental disorders in the social environment: Critical perspectives* (pp. 230–243). New York: Columbia University Press.

Thyer, B. A., Irvine, S., & Santa, C. (1984). Contingency management of exercise among chronic schizophrenics. *Perceptual and Motor Skills*, *58*, 419–425.

Thyer, B. A., & Maddox, K. (1988). Behavioral social work: Results of a national survey of graduate curricula. *Psychological Reports*, *63*, 239–242.

Thyer, B. A., & Myers, L. L. (2007). *A social worker's guide to evaluating practice outcomes*. Alexandria, VA: Council on Social Work Education.

Thyer, B. A., & Stocks, J. T. (1986). Exposure therapy in the treatment of a phobic blind person. *Journal of Visual Impairment and Blindness*, *80*, 1001–1003.

Thyer, B. A., & Thyer, K. B. (1992). Single system research designs in social work practice: A bibliography from 1965–1990. *Research on Social Work Practice*, *2*, 99–116.

Tolson, E. (1977). Alleviating marital communication problems. In W. Reid & L. Epstein (Eds.), *Task-centered practice* (pp. 100–112). Chicago: University of Chicago Press.

Tripodi, T. (1994). *A primer on single-subject design for clinical social workers*. Washington, DC: National Association of Social Workers Press.

Truax, C. B., & Carkhuff, R. R. (1965). Experimental manipulation of therapeutic conditions. *Journal of Consulting Psychology*, *29*, 119–124.

Vonk, E. M., & Thyer, B. A. (1995). Exposure therapy in the treatment of vaginal penetration phobia. *Journal of Behavior Therapy and Experimental Psychiatry*, *29*, 359–363.

Weissman, M. M., Verdeli, H., Gameroff, M., Bledsoe, S. E., Betts, K., Mufson L., et al. (2006). A national survey of psychotherapy training programs in psychiatry, psychology, and social work. *Archives of General Psychiatry*, *63*, 925–934.

Wessel, S. L. (1953). A study of the Hunt Movement Scale at family service of Philadelphia. *Smith College Studies in Social Work*, *24*, 7–40.

Witkin, S. (1981). Preparing for marital counseling in nontraditional settings. In S. P. Schinke (Ed.), *Behavioral methods in social welfare* (pp. 269–286). New York: Aldine de Gruyter.

Wolins, M. (1960). Measuring the effect of social work intervention. In N. A. Polansky (Ed.), *Social work research* (pp. 247–272). Chicago: University of Chicago Press.

Wong, S. E., Terranova, M. D., Bowen, L., Zarate, R., Massel, H. K., & Liberman, R. P. (1987). Provid- ing independent recreational activities to reduce stereotypic vocalizations in chronic schizophren- ics. *Journal of Applied Behavior Analysis*, *20*, 77–81.

Wong, S. E., Woolsey, J. E., & Gallegos, E. (1987). Behavioral treatment of chronic psychiatric patients. *Journal of Social Service Research*, *10*(2/3/4), 7–35.

Yin, R. K. (1989). *Case study research: Design and methods*. Newbury Park, CA: Sage.

Chapter 6

PROGRAM EVALUATION: ITS ROLE AND CONTRIBUTION TO EVIDENCE-BASED PRACTICE

David Royse

Social workers who are directly intervening with clients or dysfunctional families must keep foremost in their minds the tasks and responsibilities required in the performance of their jobs. Often practitioners are so caught up in the delivery of service and the demands on their time that they do not have occasion to view their own efforts or those of others from a program evaluation perspective. Indeed, it is not unusual to hear social workers express criticisms of management or administration when their agencies announce that a research or evaluation study is about to be conducted.

Practitioners who are already overburdened sometimes react negatively to any additional paperwork or reporting that takes time away from directly serving their clients. Evaluation of service can seem like a real luxury or wasteful extravagance of time when we have a caseload of clients with immediate needs (i.e., obtaining necessary medication and shelter or protection from an abusive partner). What practitioners can fail to recognize is the essential nature of the feedback loop that evaluation provides.

Consider, for a moment, an individual who wants to give a compliment to another coworker. Let's say that Bob wants Sue to understand that she did a great job with the Smith case. He says, "Sue, you were masterful with the Smiths! What a wonderful job of turning that family around! I can hardly believe the improvement they've made in just six weeks!"

If you are Bob, you'll be looking for some kind of acknowledgment from Sue. But say that Sue does not look up or respond and continues eating her lunch. Bob is left with a quandary. He must either conclude that she didn't hear him, or he walks away believing that Sue did not appreciate his remark—that somehow perhaps she thought that he meant it sarcastically.

How would we know if a compliment was received the way we intended it if there was no smile or verbal acknowledgment from the other party? In a similar way, how are social workers to know that they are actually helping the majority of their clients if there is no objective evaluation to affirm that clients make or are making satisfactory improvement?

Sadly, because of limited financial resources and restrictions of service from third-party payers and agency policies, practitioners must regularly close cases or terminate services even though the practitioner might prefer to see the client longer to ensure that the intervention had the desired effect or that the client was able to maintain progress toward treatment goals. In other words, practitioners must often discharge clients without knowing if clients (especially the more difficult ones) have improved or have improved enough to sustain continued change. In these situations (frequently found in all fields of social work practice), it is particularly important to know if the implemented therapies or interventions worked. This can be even more of an issue when brief therapies are employed and there are even fewer sessions with which to monitor client progress. When our interventions don't work, we owe it to our clients to identify other approaches. We cannot ever lose sight of the fact that social work exists to improve the lives of our clients—that is, and must continue to be, the central focus of all our efforts.

Without knowing if we have lessened our clients' problems or made a positive difference, we cannot assume success. Without some kind of a verification, affirmation, or acknowledgment from a client, the client's family or significant others, other professionals, or the community, we are shooting in the dark, hoping that we have hit the target problem, but remain unable to achieve confirmation.

The provision of social services is often chaotic and not as well planned as we would like it to be. Emergencies can arise that pull a practitioner away from a case at a critical juncture. Practitioners may have to deal with a hospitalization or suicide attempt. Clients also routinely don't show up for appointments. This can be especially problematic when the last session, planned to assess progress and close the case, is missed. To complicate matters even more, even if clients do show up for their final sessions, they may be less than honest. They may, for instance, be motivated to say that their problems have become manageable when, in fact, the clients are merely trying to get out from under a court mandate for treatment.

Subjective assessments of client progress are also not always that reliable. A suicidal client who is smiling more may, instead of progressing, have decided on a definite date, chosen a method, and achieved peace of mind because a decision has been made. Because practitioners may desperately want to see progress when it doesn't actually exist, their own biases may cause them to misinterpret or view otherwise insignificant activities (i.e., cleaning up one's house) as clinically significant and therefore indicative of progress.

Service to clients is seldom like following a recipe from a cookbook. Clients are unique and present problems in distinctive ways that vary because of differences in life experiences, as well as physical, emotional, familial, and intellectual resources. They may or may not like or respect their service providers. They can be uncooperative, nonverbal, resistant to change or anxious; they can also be compliant, easy to work with, and highly motivated to change. Even those with the same problem can present it initially in different ways or with varying levels of urgency. As a rule of thumb, clients seldom have a simple problem like just needing a place to live, but more often than not have a cornucopia of problems (i.e., PTSD, alcoholism, anger-control issues, lack of education, unemployment, legal charges from failing to pay child support).

In some settings, it may seem that clients are all so unique as to make any program evaluation effort worthless, if not completely impossible. And yet, if we have the proper perspective (a colleague of mine says, "able to view the landscape from 20,000 feet"), then certain commonalities among clients can be found. Let's take a moment to consider how we might get around the problem of seeing, first and foremost, the uniqueness of clients and their dissimilarities instead of how they might be viewed as clientele of a specific program.

A program can be defined as "an organized collection of activities designed to reach certain objectives" (Royse, Thyer, Padgett, & Logan, 2006, p. 5). Programs generally exist to address specific problems and are considered to be potent enough to have a positive impact or benefit to the client. They are not a haphazard collection of activities but are part of a thoughtful, planned effort that might revolve around some conceptual or theoretical model. Ideally, the program has an evidence-based foundation—it is not simply a way of doing things because they have always been done that way, but the activities or tasks of the practitioner have a logic and organizing principle that can be followed by others.

A program doesn't attempt to fix all of the problems of all of the clients but focuses very specifically and selectively on a well-defined group. For instance, hospice might run a program designed to help bereaved family members to adjust to the loss of a loved one. A mental health agency might run another somewhat different group program for family members whose grief stems from the suicide or murder of a loved one.

To take another example: Within an outpatient mental health agency, there will, of course, be interventions (or programs) for clients with *acute*, situational depression (i.e., divorce, loss of employment), and those interventions will be different from clients who have *chronic* schizophrenia and who are in need of day treatment or partial hospitalization. Sometimes, programs can be "found" when we begin to think about the interventions designed to address the problems of a certain class or category of clients (i.e., those with substance abuse issues). Yes, most clients are unique in the way they look and express themselves and their problems, but when we begin to think about the primary reason that they have come to our agencies, we can often see the need for different interventions or programs.

Well-planned program evaluations do not necessarily require a great deal of individual practitioner's time. That is, evaluation efforts can be designed so that clients complete self-assessments in the waiting room or the therapy office immediately prior to or after being seen by the therapist. Such data gathered from a random sampling (or the whole population of current clients) at the beginning and end (or close to the end) of treatment can provide important information about clients' welfare and experience with the treatment provided by the agency. Program directors and agency administrators can then use this information to make program improvements as needed.

For instance, if certain kinds of clients or problems do not show as much improvement as might be expected, it may be that the staff needs additional training or continuing education. It could also be that different treatment modalities ought to be tried or that a program overhaul is needed. This may mean that a consultant should be brought in or even that an ad hoc committee ought to be formed to review recent literature and make recommendations to help adjust or fine tune the program so that clients will receive a better benefit.

In this age of extremely limited resources for social services, practitioners must, absolutely must, be able to convincingly show that the efforts of social workers make a difference. If we assume that society knows how successful we are, but we cannot demonstrate it; if we assume that other professions value our interventions, but we cannot document how effective we are, then there will be fewer and fewer social work positions over time. Others (i.e., nurses and associate degreed human service technicians) will perform activities that we have thought of as belonging exclusively to social work. The only way that the status and prestige of social work will improve is when we can conclusively demonstrate that our interventions are both needed and effective. It is a much easier task to show that clients need services than to show that a real impact has been made on their problems—and that is the major challenge accompanying program evaluation. Who should be evaluated? When—at what point in the intervention process or when afterwards should the evaluation be conducted? For what purpose—how will the information be used? These and many other questions can seem like insurmountable obstacles at times because answers often depend on the funding available, the staff resources and expertise for helping with the study, the support of staff and supervision, the time line, and so forth. Nonetheless, evaluating a program does not involve magic or any skills that cannot be locally obtained. What is needed more than anything is a motivation and an interest in examining the helping process.

Computers have made the evaluation of the feedback loop not only possible, but imperative. It is the rare agency that does not have the ability to look at the productivity of its workers. Most agencies are sophisticated enough to pull up data to show how many clients each worker had contact with last week or month and the disposition of those cases. Many agencies closely monitor the "billable" and "nonbillable" hours of their staff.

This is not to say, however, that every social service agency has the wherewithal to perform competent and useful program evaluation. Indeed, it is the purpose of this chapter to help practitioners, directors, and managers see how program evaluation fits into successful service delivery. Evaluation is not just a part of the managerial process, it is a vital component that helps practitioners know that clients improve, assists management to better perform its supervisory and oversight functions, can inform the community about the quality of care provided, and communicate to the profession the advantages of one program over another.

Most MSW social workers have received sufficient preparation in their master's programs to at least have some beginning idea how they might design a program evaluation for some facet of their own agency. Most MSW programs teach research methods, but it is not clear to what extent faculty help students see that the same scientific process used in basic research can be very successfully employed as a program evaluation. So, let's take a moment to discuss the similarities and differences between these two concepts.

SCIENTIFIC PROCESS APPLIED TO PROGRAM EVALUATION

Both basic research and program evaluation follow the same logical, orderly steps of the scientific process. They both normally involve a question or hypothesis to be examined, require familiarity with the relevant literature, and follow some sort of a basic methodological blueprint known as either a research design or evaluation design. These designs frequently involve one or more groups. Group research designs are generally classified as *pre-experimental* (a pretest is administered to the same group of clients prior to and then after treatment), *quasi-experimental* (where a second or additional group is brought in for comparison. This helps answer the question of whether those without intervention improved as much as the group that received it), or *experimental* (where clients are randomly assigned to either the intervention group or the control group that does not receive any treatment). The control group helps to eliminate any alternative explanations regarding clients' improvement. Would clients have improved even without the intervention? These designs usually employ instruments or scales with known psychometric properties (i.e., reliability and validity) that allow the investigators to have confidence in the concepts that they are measuring. There is not sufficient time or space in this chapter to review or discuss all that we must know about research designs, measurement instruments, and sampling (i.e., the trade-offs between convenience samples and more scientific random sampling). For a review of this material, any of a number of research methods texts are available (i.e., Royse, 2008).

Research is generally associated with efforts that allow scientists to build on or extend established knowledge. Thus, the goal of new research is to allow for generalization so that others can use the findings. A metaphor is that research lays foundation stones or creates steps to new knowledge. Unlike research, program evaluation does not set out to create knowledge for its own sake or to test theory, but to create useful, applied knowledge that can improve services provided to clients. In contrast, a metaphor for program evaluation is that it is like creating a peephole in a solid door so that the viewer can see what is taking place in the other room. What is going on there may or may not be of interest to others outside the agency because programs are often very specific; however, many times other agencies or practitioners are definitely interested because they, too, have clients with the same problems.

Program evaluations are not usually designed to generalize knowledge but are conducted to answer pragmatic questions such as:

- Are our clients being helped?
- Has the program made any real difference?
- Does the program deserve the money spent on it?
- How should we improve this program?

The answers to questions like these would be useful at the local agency level. It should be apparent that the specifics associated with a particular agency and its clientele in a given geographical location might not be generalizable. For instance, a community education intervention on a Native American reservation may not work quite the same way in Detroit, Michigan, or Cincinnati, Ohio. If, however, the program is strongly successful in one location, it may be reasonable to assume that it might be successful in another location (perhaps with some modification)—especially if both locations share similar characteristics in clientele, agency structure, and so forth.

You might wonder if the major purpose of evaluation is to inform at the local level and not specifically to add to our scientific knowledge, then what is the point? The answer is that we all need information that addresses our immediate needs. We want to know what the price of the cell phone is now, when we are interested in purchasing a new one. Similarly, we want to know: How many miles does the warranty on the new car cover; How much will my health insurance cost if I change jobs? Program evaluation primarily answers questions needed at the local level about the worth of programs. Evaluation has as its goal the assessment of the value of a program or intervention. It allows the evaluator to make recommendations regarding the program. For instance, should the program be continued? Is the program more or less effective than other interventions? How does its cost compare to other treatment modalities?

Evaluation is focused on helping decision makers make informed choices regarding programs (i.e., cut their funding because they are ineffective, expand them because of good client outcomes, or make improvements/modifications and continue to monitor the program's success rates). Because questions about a program may stem from concerns that it is not performing as desired (these might come from formal complaints from clients, lack of referrals from other helping professionals, or even subjective impressions from key staff), evaluators may be directed to investigate certain questions and not others. In this way, evaluators have less control over the application-oriented questions that drive the evaluation than do researchers who create their own theoretical or applied questions. Most often, evaluators are concerned with issues of program worth, merit, or quality. Thus, program evaluation is usually focused on improvement of programs and not knowledge development for its own sake.

Although program evaluation can be conducted on a statewide or national level, as a rule program evaluation efforts are of much smaller scale and are intended only for in-house agency use. Typically, their results might be conveyed to a funding source (i.e., United Way), to the agency's board of directors or managers, and sometimes to staff and clientele. When findings are especially compelling (i.e., 95% of clients say that they would refer others to the agency for help), this information can be used for marketing purposes, for educating the community and taxpayers (especially important when social services are supported by local tax levies), or to inform potential new clients that the services are of good quality.

Program evaluation is not practice evaluation and does not use single-system research designs (SSRD). SSRD might be used with 1 to 3 clients (for instance, to pilot test an intervention for possible adoption), or by a practitioner to check how he or she is faring with a particular client, or even to gather some preliminary performance data in the absence of a program evaluation effort. However, SSRD should never be considered to be a stand-in or an acceptable substitute for program evaluation.

In brief, program evaluation is a management tool that provides information about the impact or outcomes produced by a set of organized activities on clients who are program participants or recipients. Program evaluation informs policy makers so that they can make better decisions. Better decisions mean less waste of financial and human resources and, ultimately, better service to clients.

HISTORICAL BACKGROUND

The exact origin of program evaluation is a bit difficult to pin down. Guba and Lincoln (1981) claim that "Evaluation is not new; indeed, the emperor of China instituted proficiency requirements for his public officials, to be demonstrated in formal tests, as early as 2200 B.C." (p. 1). It is, however, entirely possible that down through the ages countless rulers and governors have employed astute persons to evaluate various approaches to solving the problems (like hunger or possible starvation) facing them. At some point in the beginning of civilization, it must have been noticed that some farming practices produced more yield than other practices. For example, crop rotation was mentioned in Roman literature as well as "referred to by the great civilizations in Africa and Asia" ("Crop Rotation," n.d.).

In some ways, it is not fruitful to try and identify the earliest historical roots of evaluation. It makes much more sense to examine recent influences.

Many early proponents of program evaluation in this country have come from the field of education. Madaus, Scriven, and Stufflebeam (1983) have noted that:

> perhaps the earliest formal attempt to evaluate the performance of schools took place in Boston in 1845. This event is important in the history of evaluation because it began a long tradition of using pupil test scores as a principal source of data to evaluate the effectiveness of a school or instructional program. (p. 5)

Horace Mann introduced the written essay exam to replace the oral examination that was viewed as unfair because it could not be standardized for all pupils (Madaus et al., 1983). Also, prior to 1890 Joseph Rice conducted, "what is generally recognized as the first formal educational program evaluation in America. He carried out a comparative study on the value of drill in spelling instruction across a number of school districts" (p. 6).

Perloff, Perloff, and Sussna (1976), while acknowledging the influence of "what was later to become the U.S. Office of Education" state that evaluation began in its "present form" with "the development of programs started during the New Deal era of Franklin D. Roosevelt" (p. 571).

Other significant events include the founding of the Educational Testing Service in 1947.

Weiss (1987) has claimed that the first federal program to require evaluation was the juvenile delinquency program enacted by Congress in 1962. Others like Wholey (1986, see also Wholey & White, 1973) point to the Manpower Development and Training Act of 1962 and Senator Robert Kennedy's 1965 rider to the Title I section of the Elementary and Secondary Education Act that provided major set-aside funding for evaluation efforts. The 1967 amendments to the Economic Opportunity Act of 1964 directed the Government Accountability Office (GAO) to examine the progress antipoverty programs were making and how well they were carrying out their objectives. Congress was glad to learn of the progress that the antipoverty programs had made and affirmed the GAO's move into program evaluation in the Legislative Reorganization Act of 1970 and the Congressional Budget and Impoundment Control Act of 1974 (Government Accountability Office, n.d.).

About this same time (1963), a book was written by Campbell and Stanley that has been rated as more influential than any other evaluation work or concept (Shadish, Cook, & Leviton, 1991). *Experimental and Quasi-Experimental Designs for Research* has been studied by tens of thousands of graduate students in the social sciences. Donald Campbell is also noted for writing "perhaps the single most influential article in the evaluation field" (Rossi, Freeman, & Lipsey, 1999, p. 29). In that article, "Reforms as Social Experiments" in the 1969 *American Psychologist*, Campbell argued that "policy and program decisions should emerge from continual social experimentation that tests ways to improve social conditions" (Rossi et al., 1999, p. 29). Campbell challenged social scientists to take their experiments out of the laboratory and to improve society by investigating real problems and ways to solve them.

A short time later, another major book that would be greatly influential, Carol Weiss's (1972) *Evaluation Research: Methods for Assessing Program Effectiveness* became a staple in many graduate departments. The late 1960s was a time when a number of important books on evaluation were written. Among these were: R. W. Tyler, R. M. Gagne, and M. Scriven's (1967) *Perspectives of Curriculum Evaluation* and E. A. Suchman's (1967) *Evaluative Research: Principles and Practice in Public Service and Social Action Programs.* Other prominent figures who were writing and conceptualizing evaluation approaches include

Robert Stake, Daniel Stufflebeam, and later, Michael Patton. This is not by any means an exhaustive listing but a brief synopsis of some of the key shapers and molders of evaluation thought.

Within social work, a landmark article by Joel Fischer in 1973 challenged "the idea that social work services were, invariably, worthwhile and effective" (Ginsberg, 2001, p. 13). Fischer examined the literature that he could find on the effectiveness of social work and tossed out 70 of the studies because they contained no control group. With the remaining 11 studies, he discovered that it was difficult to show that social work intervention had a positive effect overall. In fact, about half of those receiving a social work intervention seemed to be worse off despite their treatment. Ginsberg notes that although the article provoked controversy, "it became clear that social work would have to change its approaches to helping and to evaluating the effectiveness of its work" (p. 14).

A number of new journals focusing on evaluation came to life in the 1970s. These were *Evaluation Review, Evaluation and Program Planning,* and *New Directions for Program Evaluation*. In the January 1973 issue of *Psychological Abstracts*, the term "Program Evaluation" was added as an index term (Perloff et al., 1976, p. 572). The *Evaluation Studies Review Annual* was first published in 1976. In that same year, two new professional societies were formed: the Evaluation Research Society and the Evaluation Network. In 1985, they joined to form the American Evaluation Association.

Federal funding for evaluation activities began to take a dip as the 1970s wound down, and this trend continued into the 1980s under the Republican administration of Ronald Reagan. Categorical funding for evaluation began to be replaced with block grants with no evaluation requirements.

Although it cannot be said that every elected politician is a firm believer in the necessity for funding program evaluation, it can be said that most decision makers recognize that good data is very powerful. The problem appears to be that some of our elected leaders believe they know the right course of action whether or not they have solid, reliable data to support their political beliefs or philosophical views. Despite being in a political era when new, large-scale social programs are not being launched or seen as valuable experiments, program evaluation methodology is maturing, the literature is growing impressively, and the decline in federal funding has led to "the development of a richer and fuller approach to determining merit and worth" (Fitzpatrick, Sanders, & Worthen, 2003, p. 41). While program evaluation studies and reports have always been dominated by positivist, quantitative approaches, there has been greater recognition in recent years of the value of "mixed methods" which allow the investigator to utilize qualitative interviews to provide more detail and depth to the quantitative findings.

The broad interest and recognition of the value of evidence-based practice in the past several years will continue to further develop and strengthen the role of program evaluation. The next section discusses evidence-based practice and its relationship to program evaluation.

EVIDENCE-BASED PRACTICE AND PROGRAM EVALUATION

Zayas, Gonzalez, and Hanson (2003) have noted that in the infancy of the social work profession practice, wisdom was passed from supervisor to trainee through an oral tradition that was later written down by early social work authors. These interventions that were taught and transmitted to the next generation of social workers were "poorly defined" and not submitted to "rigorous empirical scrutiny" (p. 60).

Unfortunately, there has not been a great deal of testing of social work practice interventions at any level (micro, mezzo, or macro). So while there may exist some very effective treatments that work exceptionally well in some locations with certain diagnoses or clients, by and large the social work profession has emphasized practice knowledge to the detriment of larger scale program evaluations that would provide credible scientific evidence of effectiveness.

This situation has been well-documented in social work literature by major figures in the field (Rosen, Proctor, & Staudt, 1999; Thyer, 1996). McNeece and Thyer (2004) note that "recent attention" to evidence-based practice (EBP) inside the profession could easily mislead those outside the profession into believing that "social workers commonly use the current best scientific evidence available, rather than solely relying on practice wisdom, tradition, or 'common sense' in deciding how to assist a client" (pp. 8–9).

As they go on to point out, the social work literature on EBP has been developing at a slow pace and consists mostly of articles asserting why social workers should be engaged in EBP and explanations on why studies of EBP are not found in the literature. This is not to say, however, that all of the literature on EBP is calling the profession to arms instead of producing the studies that are need to substantiate good practice. While the research supporting EBP might have gotten off to a slow start in the history of the profession, there is, as mentioned earlier, a growing body of literature regarding clinical applications.

A search in the Library of Congress Online Catalog listed 83 books on January 11, 2006, that contained "evidence based" in the title. The earliest was a medical text written in 1997. The vast majority of these 83 titles are written for health-care professionals. Keeping in mind that the evidence-based practice movement originated in the field of medicine, a field with a longer and stronger tradition of science-based practice, social work has not lagged far behind.

In 1998, Thyer and Wodarski published the *Handbook of Empirical Social Work Practice: Volume I: Mental Disorders* that reviewed existing scientific information for working with a particular set of clients. Their book was followed by Corcoran's (2000) *Evidence-Based Practice with Families*; McDonald's (2001) *Effective Interventions for Child Abuse and Neglect: An Evidenced-Based Approach to Planning and Evaluating Interventions*; Nathan and Gorman's (2002) *A Guide to Treatments that Work*; Corcoran's (2003) *Clinical Applications of Evidence-Based Family Interventions*; Gibbs' (2003) *Evidence-Based Practice for the Helping Professions: A Practical Guide*; Springer, McNeece, and Mayfield Arnold's (2003) *Substance Abuse Treatment for Criminal Offenders: An Evidence-Based Guide for the Practitioner*; Roberts and Yeager's (2004) *Evidence-Based Practices Manual: Research and Outcome Measures in Health and Human Service's*; Sommerfeld and Herzog's (2005) *Evidence-Based Social Work: Toward a New Professionalism*; and O'Hare's (2005) *Evidence-Based Practices for Social Workers: An Interdisciplinary Approach*. Clearly, there is an expanding collection of information that is being systematized and made available to practitioners.

Unfortunately, social workers who go to *Social Work Abstracts* and attempt to find articles to guide their interventions will find that the number of articles in any one field of practice is somewhat disappointing. A key word search of "evidence-based" in titles listed in *Social Work Abstracts'* database on January 11, 2006, produced only 40 articles for the whole profession—from child welfare to renal social work. The earliest one was Gambrill's 1999 article titled "Evidence-Based Practice: An Alternative to Authority-Based Practice."

Social workers who might want to find evidence-based literature to guide their practice will have better luck by searching in the Medline database. Using the same key words "evidence" and "based" in the titles, a search on January 11, 2006, produced over 7,000 "hits." Of course, many of these articles would not be useful to social workers, but there would also be many that could be directly relevant. An alternative and probably more efficient use of your browsing time to find pertinent material would be to harness the power of PsycINFO. A key word search of "evidence" and "based" in the titles on January 11, 2006, produced almost 1,200 "hits." Again, these databases show that while the smallest (*Social Work Abstracts*) does not provide the breadth of the other two, one should not conclude that EBP is a passing fad. Indeed, the evidence is quite to the contrary and suggests that professionals in the helping professions like psychology and health care have strongly embraced the concept of examining which interventions work and which ones are less effective.

LIMITATIONS OF EVIDENCE

Thus far in this chapter we have defined evaluation, examined its historical development, discussed the need for it, and briefly highlighted the progress EBP is making in our literature. At this point, you have undoubtedly come to understand the importance of being able to draw on interventions and programs that have been shown to be effective. The arguments for using only tried-and-proven treatments have to do with worker competence (using interventions with unknown or poor effectiveness would not only be unethical, but also indicate incompetence), and with our desire to improve the client's quality of life with a minimum of wasted time and effort.

When practitioners provide the most appropriate intervention and clients improve, everyone benefits—the client, the practitioner (from the recognition of others such as coworkers, supervisors, and others), and the community (when tax-supported services are able to assist clients with conquering their problems and becoming productive wage-earners and citizens). Ultimately, even the profession itself benefits from increased recognition resulting from delivery of effective interventions and communication of those results to other professionals and decision makers in policy-making agencies. Along this line, Witkin and Harrison (2001) have stated that EBP creates a "scientifically based social work" that "aligns social work with other, more prestigious professions like medicine" (p. 295).

There is virtually no one who would want to be known as an incompetent practitioner, and yet without employing program evaluation or, at a minimum, some form of practice evaluation to assess our efforts, then there is always the possibility that the practitioner is less successful than he or she believes. Without systematic evidence of successful interventions, we cannot assume or call our efforts effective.

Why can't we use intuition or our own subjective impressions to conclude that our work with clients is successful? To view this issue from a scientist's perspective, the problem is, first of all, that a conclusion of this nature must be based on data or evidence. A worker's impression or subjective judgment that a client has improved is not considered good evidence because of the strong possibility that personal bias (e.g., my wanting to believe that I did a good job in working with Client X). If the process of gathering the data is somehow less than fair, not impartial and not random, then there is a distinct possibility that our own biases and desire to see ourselves as being successful may, in fact, affect the selection of clients and their perceived outcomes. Researchers and evaluators have to be aware of threats to the internal validity of their studies. When the "evidence" that represents client progress flows from observations that do not involve standardized measuring instruments or samples of clients that may reflect some favoritism (e.g., not be representative), the resulting findings will be distorted and not reflect reality. While we may not want to think it, most of us might be tempted to influence the findings of a study by pushing our most successful cases to the front—especially if we knew that a poor showing would cause us to lose our jobs—which could happen under some circumstances. A scientific approach requires that investigators maintain a great deal of control over who is included or excluded from the study and how success or change is to be measured. The goal is to make the whole process, from start to finish, as objective and impartial as possible. When this is achieved, the evidence from a controlled, scientific investigation can be considered "good" or credible, whether or not the program, intervention, or treatment was a success.

Our subjective impressions regarding client success are also subject to another source of error. Clients may have reasons to be less than honest (i.e., to deny that they are continuing to drink or use drugs). Even if they are not fabricating the truth, they may feel that their anger-management problem has improved when there has been no "test" of their new learning or management skills. They may also be embarrassed by their problem (e.g., sexual addiction or gambling) and find it so difficult to discuss that they want to get out of or end the treatment as quickly as possible—even if they haven't quite gotten complete control over the problem. Clients can come into treatment for a lot of different reasons—at the demand of a spouse or loved one or the mandate of a judge. If the client is not motivated to improve and is eager to conclude treatment—only complying to make an intimate partner happy or to get the legal system off his or her back—the client might have reasons to minimize the extent of the problem after being in treatment for a while. Sadly, there are also clients whose most important human relationship is with their therapist, and they do not want to improve or get better for fear of losing that relationship. These are just a few of the ways that clients can frustrate the assessment of their progress.

Without a rigorous evaluation or research methodology in place to provide the data needed to determine the extent of success with a given program, practitioners ought to support their practice by relying on meta-analyses or systematic reviews of the literature concerning effective interventions. (For more information on how to do meta-analysis see Forness & Kavale, 1994.) The problem with using only established literature to inform one's practice is that often times the articles do not contain enough information to allow one to completely duplicate or replicate the intervention in another location. Even when there is a treatment manual to follow, programs differ in their clients' characteristics, the eligibility policies for inclusion/exclusion of clients, the preparation of the practitioners (the credentials, training, and experience), the extent of supervision, and so forth.

Treatment fidelity is a term applied to how accurately or faithfully a program is reproduced from a manual, protocol, or model (Royse et al., 2006). Even when all the staff or treatment providers have been well-trained and provided with a manual, programs can drift when policies and procedures evolve, and staff do not consistently follow the way the intervention has been prescribed. Even slight deviations by individual therapists, over time, can result in clients within the same agency having completely different experiences because the standardized approach has been compromised. Treatment fidelity is threatened any time deviations occur.

In brief, it should be noted that any program assessment using less than a randomized controlled trial (RCT) is likely to yield biased, if not flawed, data that will limit any derived conclusions. This does not mean that important data about whether clients are progressing in treatment cannot be determined from less rigorous approaches (i.e., pre-experimental and quasi-experimental designs), but it does lead us to a topic not usually discussed in association with evidence-based practice—the limitations of evidence.

That assumptions arising from less than rigorous assessments of one's practice or program may be flawed can be easily seen when one considers that even scientific evidence is imperfect (Brownson, Baker, Leet, & Gillespie, 2003). How is this possible?

Consider, first, the statistical problem of heterogeneity of treatment effects (HTE). HTE may be present when the treatment provides a range of results in patients. That is, some might show major benefit, some minor benefit, and others no benefit at all. Yet, the group data from pre- to posttest comparisons could lead one to conclude that because the *average* score improved for the group, everyone must have shown at least a modest benefit (Kravitz, Duan, & Braslow, 2004). In medicine, this situation is well acknowledged because individuals vary widely in their rate of metabolism, rate of drug absorption, and responsiveness to drugs. Because randomized controlled trials are designed with very specific inclusion criteria, the heterogeneity of treatment effects may be vastly underestimated with researchers "misled into thinking that their results are more generalizable than they actually are" (p. 667). Patients involved in clinical effectiveness studies may not be representative of patients in the target population. To the extent that the sample is not representative, but homogeneous, a successful intervention might suggest a uniform effect and overestimate its benefit for the larger target population. Thus, practitioners who are drawing on an existing study to inform their own practice need to be attentive to the range and diversity of the patients participating in the study and should look for any analysis that might indicate that improvement was not uniform.

Second, even when evidence exists that an intervention is effective, the practitioner must keep in mind that statistically significant improvement (e.g., major reduction in the number or severity of symptoms) while giving rise to the belief that clients would stand to benefit from the intervention, is not the same as clinical improvement. That is, statistical significance is not to be confused with clinical significance. For instance, a substance-abusing client might cut down on the frequency of his or her use but still engage in dangerous weekend binging behavior. A depressed client might rate his or her symptoms as less severe but still be too depressed to leave home and look for a job. In studies where sample sizes are large, it is easy to have statistically significant results that are not clinically important (Deeks, 1999).

Third, evidence that exists for decision making is almost always a product of situations that are beyond the investigator's control. Often studies involve judgments that in retrospective might have been made differently by other practitioners or investigators. The better the study, the more scientific control, the more certainty that the investigator has that the variables are pure and uncompromised—that they truly represent the concept being measured. This speaks to the importance of employing reliable and valid measurement instruments. Instruments vary a great deal in how well the measurements hold up over time (i.e., test-retest reliability) and the amount of research that exists to support their validity. Diagnostic instruments vary with regard to their sensitivity (how good a positive result test is at identifying those with a problem) and specificity (how good a negative test result is at identifying those without a problem). Thus, knowledge of both sensitivity and specificity allows the investigator to estimate true positives and false negatives (sensitivity) as well as true negatives and false positives (specificity). Studies that have been conducted with weak instruments or are biased in the way their client samples were obtained will generate data that are not trustworthy.

Although most peer-reviewed journals serve as a fairly effective screen for keeping out poorly constructed, inadequately analyzed, and flawed studies, the reader of program evaluation studies can have more confidence in studies that are in well-established, professional journals that employ a rigorous blind review (like *Research on Social Work Practice*) than in unpublished papers or brand new journals that may not have a good pool of initial papers to choose from. Whatever the source, the reader should not suspend his or her curiosity about how the study was conducted and ways the results might have been shaped or influenced by certain decisions that were made about client selection, the process of implementing the intervention, and the determination that a client made major, moderate, or minor improvement. When questions arise that are not answered in reading an evaluation report, readers should probably not give that study as much authority as reports that clearly flesh out every part of the intervention evaluation and leave few unanswered questions.

In general, a single study promoting the effectiveness of an intervention should (all other factors being equal) not be valued as much as several studies showing the same general level of effectiveness—and is not as good as five studies, for example, where two show little or no improvement and three show major or definite improvement. This also means that without confirming studies to support the claims of a single study, the program developer or adaptor should be cautious. Not only that, but the person interested in transferring the program and implementing it locally is required to view evidence for its effectiveness with somewhat more suspicion than when multiple studies exist making the same claim.

Because there may be several studies on the same intervention that do not agree regarding its potency for creating change in clients, practitioners need to look for meta-analyses or reviews of literature that attempt to bring together all the pertinent studies examining that treatment. Statistical techniques, like examining the proportion of variance explained (PVE), can help those comparing studies of the same intervention to understand how much of the change or improvement in scores was due to the intervention. (For a brief discussion of this approach, see Royse et al., 2006.)

Last, practitioners would do well to keep in mind that information that a given intervention was effective with a given population should not be employed in a "one-size-fits-all manner" (Jutai & Teasell, 2003, p. 72). That is, the practitioner is also obligated to look for indications that a given approach might not work well with a particular client or client grouping (i.e., clients not compliant with medication, the clients who won't talk in group settings). As Jutai and Teasell suggest, EBP has a focus on the treatment of a group of clients or patients. Aggregate data sometimes masks the fact that not every individual will show improvement.

It is for this reason that Gambrill (1999), among others, has called for social workers to seek their clients' input regarding the choice of interventions. Holmes (2000) and Zayas et al. (2003) argue, relying solely on "evidence-based treatments overlooks the complexities of problems brought by clients" and the historical and sociological forces "that influenced their lives" (p. 64). Practitioners should not apply research findings at the expense of establishing rapport and a healthy worker-client relationship that could be jeopardized when a given treatment is forced on a client. Clients need to be brought into the discussion concerning the range of alternative treatments available. They need to know what evidence exists concerning the benefits of each intervention so that they can make informed decisions. Along this line, clients should understand if the research findings about the treatment would apply to them. In other words, how similar are they to the clients who showed improvement from the intervention? Are they a good fit or a weak fit? They would benefit from knowing the range of expected improvement—indeed, how much improvement can they expect? It is not always easy to provide answers to questions such as these, and it may be that in some instances the practitioner will need to present highlights of the study or evaluation to his or her clients.

If the trend focusing more and more attention within health care and social services on EBP continues, more evaluative studies of intervention will be conducted at the local agency level. The day is not too far off when practitioners will be relying more on their own studies and those being conducted in their agencies than relying solely on evaluative studies conducted elsewhere and reported in professional journals.

IMPLICATIONS FOR SOCIAL WORK

Program evaluation has become a topic of interest to policy makers, program developers and planners, managers and administrators, as well as clients and consumers of services. Each of these groups may have a vested interest in learning about how well certain programs perform.

Program evaluation is not a topic discussed only by academics and doctoral students; instead, it is a vital and fundamental component in a human service management model (See, for instance, Lewis, Lewis, Packard, & Souflee, 2001.) This is true whether the practitioner is employed by an organization to practice at the micro-, mezzo-, or macrolevel. (If the practitioner is self-employed or in a private practice where programs do not exist in the same way as they do in social and human service agencies, the practitioner should conceptualize evaluation in terms of practice evaluation and not program evaluation.) While the lion's share of information flowing from EBP literature deals only with micro or clinical problems, this is not to say that EBP and program evaluation should be limited to the micro and mezzo arenas. Indeed, community programs (social action, locality development, etc.) should also be evaluated because society can only benefit when we learn which programs are effective and which ones are not.

What are the implications for social work? Ginsberg (2001) notes that "What some call a revolution in accountability is among the most important influences on social work and other human services professions" (p. 3). Computers are such an indispensable part of our world that we are never going to be less accountable—barring a worldwide cataclysmic energy shortage. They are going to be with us each and every day for the rest of our lives and in the future will become even more enmeshed in our lives than they are now. Because they are tools that can provide valuable information, each practitioner and employee of a social or human service agency should begin now to plan for ways in which computers can be used to provide useful information about one's practice or program. Social workers should be proactive and not have to be dragged kicking and screaming sometime in the not-too-distant future into defending programs for which no information exists about their effectiveness.

There are several challenges for practitioners who are interested in making greater use of EBP and program evaluation:

- As anyone who has attempted an electronic literature search (or even a Google search) in the past several years knows, the databases are so large that at times the impression we can get is that there is too much information available. The thoughtful practitioner needs to learn how to pare down and shift through the inconsequential and useless "hits" and to find the articles that will be informative. A review of the literature is often the first place evaluators and social scientists turn to familiarize themselves with the issues, the variables, and the extent of the available knowledge about given programs. Any practitioner who is not skilled at literature searching may want to consult a colleague or a professional librarian to learn how to acquire the skills need to find useful material and avoid being buried under an avalanche of fruitless and unproductive but somehow distantly related articles.

- As Pfeffer and Sutton (2006) point out, trying to bring the best evidence to bear on decisions can also result in feeling or discovering that there is not enough good evidence and/or that the evidence doesn't quite apply. In situations like this, the practitioner needs to consider whether the studies are "close enough" to apply and give direction. If they are not, then the practitioner must either expand the search or begin planning for a study or evaluation for his or her own program or practice.

- Although perhaps we all yearn for a "cookbook" that will provide us with a recipe for evaluating this or that program in this or that agency or with a particular client population, each program evaluation must be tailored to the organizational makeup of the program and the host agency. This is what Rossi et al. (1999) have to say on the matter:

> The availability of administrative cooperation and support; the ways in which program files and data are kept and access permitted to them; the character of the services provided; the nature, frequency, duration, and location of the contact between program and client; and numerous other such matters must be taken into consideration in the evaluation design. . . . Modifications, perhaps even compromises, may be necessary in the types, quantity, or quality of the data collected as a result of unanticipated practical or political obstacles. (p. 24)

The implication for practitioners is that if we do not have a solid foundation in research methodology, then it may be necessary to involve colleagues who are more knowledgeable in this arena, or the agency may need to hire a consultant. Simply stated, it is not going to be possible to find a recipe for a program evaluation that will fit every, or even most, situations.

- Anecdotes and personal stories are very persuasive and one person's retelling of a dismal failure or tremendous success with a given approach should not be given more credibility than it deserves—especially if it runs counter to the studies and quantitative evidence available. However, if even a small number of clients are seeking out management or someone trusted in the agency to complain about a therapist or something not working well within a program, then attention should definitely be paid to such complaints. In fact, every complaint should be investigated; practitioners can learn as much or more from mistakes as from successes.

Thomas Davenport in a special issue on decision making (2006) in the *Harvard Business Review* goes a bit further. He suggests that competitive companies should "not only avidly consume data but also seize every opportunity to generate information, creating a 'test and learn' culture" (p. 106). While for-profit business enterprises do not always serve as the best models for nonprofit social services, practitioners in the social and human services can learn from this kind of stance.

While the bulk of this chapter has probably come across as conceptualizing program evaluation as a single or solitary event that occurs after much planning and design, if not physical effort—much like climbing Kilimanjaro—it is also valuable to consider what might be learned if program evaluation were not viewed as such a big endeavor. What might we discover about our programs, their success, and the characteristics of those successful if we seized "every opportunity to generate information"? How might this dynamic view of program evaluation change services to clients and the way society views the social work profession?

CONCLUSION

Social work is firmly situated in a discipline that draws from such allied fields as nursing, psychology, and psychiatry. The movement toward evidence-based practice in these fields is a strong current that will continue to pull social work in the direction of greater examination of interventions. While not every social worker will feel comfortable in conducting program evaluation, we must not be closeminded and fight opportunities to study and evaluate our helping processes. This chapter has attempted to provide a perspective for the practitioner to not only understand the importance of evidence-based practice and program evaluation, but also to think conceptually about these topics and how one might start exploring the success (or lack of it) of interventions. Program evaluation supplies important information for managers and decision makers. To the extent that we use EBP, we align our profession with those that are science based, admired, and respected in our society.

Suggestions were provided in this chapter to help practitioners consider the nature of evidence that an intervention works and the limitations of existing evidence. Practitioners were cautioned to not assume that even programs supported by empirical evidence provides the same level of benefit to every client.

Critical thinking is called for. O'Hare (2005) has written, "scientific evidence does not speak for itself. Some inference and interpretation is involved in understanding and applying a professional knowledge base" (p. 9). Practitioners cannot simply order a program evaluation like one might order a hamburger and fries in a fast-food restaurant. Program evaluation cannot be created overnight or in a single staff meeting. Evaluators need a firm understanding of research methodology and the scientific process. Even when literature exists on how well programs perform, the practitioner must evaluate the findings and consider whether the program is a good fit for the agency being considered. The study methodology must also be assessed in terms of the assumptions made and the investigator's control over the variables. Finally, a determination must be made that the study population is a reasonable or similar facsimile of the agency's target population.

Because we not only live in an era of accountability, but in an age where consumers are strong advocates for themselves and want to know exactly what they are getting, practitioners will increasingly be asked about the effectiveness of interventions being applied. Because we understand so little about human nature and why some interventions bring about change and others don't, because the science of helping persons with emotional, mental, or adjustment problems is not as advanced as certain other fields (pharmaceutical research), program evaluation will continue to be somewhat of a challenge in human services. But at the same time, it is a worthy endeavor and goal.

Every practitioner should aspire to use only evidence-based interventions and where sufficient data are not available to convince a reasonably well-informed layperson, then it is time for each and every practitioner to roll up his or her sleeves and go to work to create or bring about the kind of information that is needed. We social workers cannot abdicate our responsibilities to our clients and society. Without credible scientific data to support our efforts, we are simply practicing the "friendly visiting" that characterized social work at its very beginning.

REFERENCES

Brownson, R. C., Baker, E., Leet, T., & Gillespie, K. (2003). *Evidence-based public health.* New York: Oxford University Press.

Campbell, D. T., & Stanley, J. C. (1963). *Experimental and quasi-experimental designs for research.* Skokie, IL: Rand McNally.

Corcoran, J. (2000). *Evidence-based social work practice with families: A lifespan approach.* New York: Springer.

Corcoran, J. (2003). *Clinical applications of evidence-based family interventions.* New York: Oxford University Press.

Crop Rotation. (n.d.). Retrieved January 5, 2006, from http://en.wikipedia.org/wiki/Crop_rotation/.

Davenport, T. H. (2006, January). Competing on analytics. *Harvard Business Review,* 98–107.

Deeks, J. J. (1999). Using evaluations of diagnostic tests: Understanding their limitations and making the most of available evidence. *Annals of Oncology, 10,* 761–768.

Fitzpatrick, J. L., Sanders, J. R., & Worthen, B. R. (2003). *Program evaluation: Alternative approaches and practical guidelines.* Boston: Allyn & Bacon.

Forness, S. R., & Kavale, K. (1994). Meta-analysis in intervention research: Methods and implications. In J. Rothman & E. J. Thomas (Eds.), *Intervention research: Design and development for human services* (pp. 117–132). Binghamton, NY: Haworth Press.

Gambrill, E. (1999). Evidence-based practice: An alternative to authority-based practice. *Families in Society, 80*(4), 341–350.

Gibbs, L. E. (2003). *Evidence-based practice for the helping professionals: A practical guide.* Pacific Grove, CA: Brooks/Cole-Thomson Learning.

Ginsberg, L. H. (2001). *Social work evaluation: Principles and methods.* Boston: Allyn & Bacon.

Government Accountability Office. (n.d.). *Legislative Reorganization Act of 1970 and the Congressional Budget and Impound Control Act of 1974.* Retrieved September 13, 2005, from www.gao.gov/about/history/gaohist_1966–1981.htm.

Guba, E. G., & Lincoln, Y. S. (1981). *Effective evaluation.* San Francisco: Jossey-Bass.

Holmes, J. (2000). Narrative in psychiatry and psychotherapy: The evidence? *Journal of Medical Humanities, 26,* 92–96.

Jutai, J. W., & Teasell, R. W. (2003). The necessity and limitations of evidence-based practice in stroke rehabilitation. *Topics in Stroke Rehabilitation, 10*(1), 71–78.

Kravitz, R. L., Duan, N., & Braslow, J. (2004). Evidence-based medicine, heterogeneity of treatment effects, and the trouble with averages. *Milbank Quarterly, 82*(4), 661–687.

Lewis, J. A., Lewis, M. D., Packard, T., & Souflee, F. (2001). *Management of human service programs.* Belmont, CA: Brooks/Cole.

Madaus, G. F., Scriven, M. S., & Stufflebeam, D. L. (1983). Program evaluation: A historical overview. In G. F. Madaus, M. Scriven, & D. L. Stufflebeam (Eds.), *Evaluation models: Viewpoints on educational and human services evaluation* (pp. 3–18). Boston: Kluwer-Nijhoff.

McDonald, G. (2001). *Effective interventions for child abuse and neglect: An evidenced-based approach to planning and evaluating interventions.* Chichester, West Sussex, England: Wiley.

McNeece, C. A., & Thyer, B. A. (2004). Evidence-based practice and social work. *Journal of Evidence-Based Social Work, 1*(1), 7–25.

Nathan, P. E., & Gorman, J. M. (2002). *A guide to treatments that work.* New York: Oxford University Press.

O'Hare, T. (2005). *Evidence-based practices for social workers: An interdisciplinary approach.* Chicago: Lyceum Books.

Perloff, R., Perloff, E., & Sussna, E. (1976). Program evaluation. *Annual reviews of psychology.* Retrieved September 13, 2005, from arjournals.annualrefiews.org.

Pfeffer, J., & Sutton, R. I. (2006, January). Evidence-based management. *Harvard Business Review,* 63–74.

Roberts, A. R., & Yeager, K. (2004). *Evidence-based practice manual: Research and outcome measures in health and human services.* New York: Oxford University Press.

Rosen, A., Proctor, E. K., & Staudt, M. (1999). Social work research and the quest for effective practice. *Social Work Research, 23,* 4–14.

Rossi, P. H., Freeman, H. E., & Lipsey, M. W. (1999). *Evaluation: A systematic approach.* Thousand Oaks, CA: Sage.

Royse, D. (2008). *Research methods in social work.* Pacific Grove, CA: Brooks/Cole.

Royse, D., Thyer, B. A., Padgett, D. K., & Logan, T. K. (2006). *Program evaluation: An introduction.* Belmont, CA: Brooks/Cole.

Shadish, W. R., Cook, T. D., & Leviton, L. C. (1991). *Foundations of program evaluation: Theories of practice.* Newbury Park, CA: Sage.

Sommerfeld, P., & Herzog, P. (2005). *Evidence-based social work: Toward a new professionalism.* New York: Peter Lang.

Springer, D., McNeece, C. A., & Mayfield Arnold, E. M. (2003). *Substance abuse treatment for criminal offenders: An evidence-based guide for practitioners.* Washington, DC: American Psychological Association.

Suchman, E. A. (1967). *Evaluative research: Principles and practice in public service and social action programs.* New York: Russell Sage Foundation.

Thyer, B. A. (1996). Forty years of progress toward empirical clinical practice? *Social Work Research, 20,* 77–82.

Thyer, B. A., & Wodarski, J. S. (1998). *Handbook of empirical social work practice: Vol. 1. Mental disorders.* New York: Wiley.

Tyler, R. W., Gagne, R. M., & Scriven, M. (1967). *Perspectives of curriculum evaluation*. Chicago: Rand McNally.

Weiss, C. H. (1987). Evaluating social programs: What have we learned? *Society*, *25*(1), 40–45.

Weiss, C. H. (1972). *Evaluation research: Methods for assessing program effectiveness*. Englewood Cliffs, NJ: Prentice Hall.

Wholey, J. S. (1986). Using evaluation to improve government performance. *Evaluation Practice*, *7*, 5–13.

Wholey, J. S., & White, B. F. (1973). Evaluations impact on Title I elementary and secondary education program management. *Evaluation*, *1*, 73–76.

Witkin, S. L., & Harrison, W. D. (2001). Whose evidence and for what purpose? *Social Work*, *46*(4), 293–296.

Zayas, L. H., Gonzalez, M. J., & Hanson, M. (2003). "What do I do now?": On teaching evidence-based interventions in social work practice. *Journal of Teaching in Social Work*, *23*(3/4), 59–72.

Chapter 7

CASE MANAGEMENT

Joseph Walsh and Valerie Holton

DEFINITION OF THE TOPIC

While there is not a single, generally accepted definition of the term, *case management* can be defined as an approach to social service delivery that attempts to ensure that clients with multiple, complex problems and disabilities receive the services they need in a timely, appropriate fashion (Rubin, 1992). It is practiced in such fields as mental health, child welfare, aging and long-term care, alcohol and drug treatment, health care, and the public welfare system. Case managers, who may be social workers, nurses, psychologists, and members of other health-care professions, may work independently or as members of coordinated teams. Service objectives in case management include continuity of care, accessibility, accountability, and efficiency. Many years ago, Roberts-DeGennaro (1987) observed that case managers must possess the traditional social work practice skills of casework, group work, and community organization because any of these may take priority with clients in community systems. The concept of case management emerged in mental health literature during the 1970s, but the practice can be understood as the modern application of social casework techniques that have a century-old tradition in social work and nursing.

The case manager is responsible for service coordination and helping the client hold elements of the service system accountable for adequate service delivery. Two driving principles of case management practice are that clients tend to get lost, frustrated, and may drop out of treatment without a central point of integration and that the community contains many resources that can meet the needs of clients. These two principles are sometimes conflicting because improving the quality of care for vulnerable populations may be at odds with controlling the costs of such care (Frankel & Gelman, 2004).

The National Association of Social Workers (2006) has established standards for case management that stress the importance of the case manager's appropriate knowledge base, educational background, and skill level. The case manager should work for the benefit of the client, involve the client in all levels of the case management process, hold client information as confidential, and participate in all levels of the service delivery system, including advocating for appropriate service delivery and evaluating services.

While case management can be utilized with a variety of client populations, the remainder of this chapter focuses on its uses with clients who have serious mental illnesses.

The authors would like to thank Jessica Cann, MSW, for contributing her example of case management brokerage.

MODELS OF CASE MANAGEMENT

Case management can be organized in a variety of ways, depending on the nature of the client population, the host agency, and the financial and staff resources available. Moxley (1996) differentiates *system-driven* from *consumer-driven* case management. System-driven case management may be practiced in areas where practitioners must rely on limited outside services (such as medical care, job training, and recreation), whereas consumer-driven case management may be exercised in areas where many services are available in coordination with the practitioner's agency, and clients can choose from among them. In either situation, clients can be helped to experience *service empowerment,* or participation in service decisions and reciprocity in their relationships with case managers (Crane-Ross, Lutz, & Roth, 2006). Research has shown that service empowerment is a significant predictor of recovery outcomes across all models of case management.

Fiorentine and Grusky (1990) propose a *role-contingency* approach to case management, stating that the priorities case managers give to the functions of counseling, linkage, intervention, and services integration vary depending on the nature of the service system and the policies of the employing organization. When case managers perceive community services to be adequate for clients, they primarily perform linkage activities. More intensive worker intervention is required when case managers perceive that outside services are not adequate.

Strengths-based case management focuses on needs assessments and goal setting that empower the client (Rapp, 2002). The focus is on client strengths rather than pathology. For example, people with major mental illnesses are valued as people who can continue to grow, learn, and reach goals, and interventions are based on client self-determination. The community is seen as providing a wealth of resources, and aggressive outreach is the preferred mode of intervention. The most important part of strengths-based case management is the engagement and relationship with the client. The relationship should be based on the social work value of unconditional positive regard and include the use of empathy, genuineness, and positive reinforcement. Rapp (1998) states that the case manager-client relationship must be purposeful, reciprocal, friendly, trusting, and empowering. It helps if the social worker meets the client in neutral settings of the client's choice, maintains a conversational focus, jointly attends to concrete tasks, and delineates the roles that each member will play in the relationship. In this model, purposeful self-disclosure is viewed as being helpful in establishing a trusting relationship, as is modeling the appropriate expression of emotion, providing alternate views of how challenging situations can be handled, and normalizing the client's feelings or concerns. Accompanying clients to first-time appointments and helping them with new tasks can also alleviate anxiety and demonstrate the case manager's commitment to helping clients.

Consumer case management is a rapidly developing area of client-centered services (Craig, Doherty, & Jamieson-Craig, 2004). It occurs when "consumers" (in this case, persons with mental illness) are employed as full-fledged case managers or aides for clients to assist them with obtaining needed social, vocational, financial, and other supports. The use of these consumers provides gainful employment for clients and also taps into the expertise of persons who have a unique appreciation for the challenges faced by persons with mental illness. In these programs, consumers usually work under the supervision of another professional.

Some researchers and theorists have specified models of case management. While there is variety in how the models are described and differentiated, we summarize them into the following three models.

The Broker Model

In the broker model, which is the most "basic" type of case management, individual case managers are responsible for connecting their clients to appropriate resources in the community. Case manager tasks include assessment, planning, linking, monitoring, and perhaps advocacy on behalf of the client (Walsh, 2002). Case managers who operate under the broker model do not have financial responsibility for clients and so may not assume responsibility for how well their referrals will result in desired service delivery (Austin & McClelland, 2002). For instance, a case manager might refer a client to receive therapy services; however, the client may not have a clear working relationship with the therapist and thus may have no influence on how that referral might be implemented. Nor does the case manager have the authority to negotiate the cost of that service.

Case Example: Hospital Broker

Jessica works in a university medical center as a hospital social worker in the spinal cord rehabilitation unit where there is a team of physical therapists, occupational therapists, recreation therapists, speech therapists, rehabilitation psychologists, nurses, doctors, and social workers. The role of the social worker is to help patients prepare for life outside of the unit. When the patient leaves the unit, the team needs to make sure his or her support system is in place to ensure safety and well-being. Jessica's job as a social worker/case manager involves planning for a patient's discharge by linking the patient and family with ongoing rehabilitative and medical resources in the community. In order to achieve this, Jessica completes a biopsychosocial assessment during the initial interaction to find out what the patient has in place and what is needed. Prior to discharge, Jessica checks in with the patient and family to see how they are mentally preparing for the next step and if there are any concerns about being able to follow through with any of her referrals. She offers to help clients and families if they have any difficulty with referral sources after discharge, but has no scheduled contacts with them.

Assertive Community Treatment

Assertive community treatment (ACT) is carried out in multidisciplinary teams with five or more members who share a caseload of about 100 clients with serious mental illness (Hangan, 2006). This model was initially developed in the late 1970s by Leonard Stein and Mary Ann Test in Madison, Wisconsin (Lehman et al., 2003; Test & Stein, 1985). Their initial experiment essentially moved the treatment team of the state hospital into the community setting. Rather than connecting their clients with services in the community, ACT staff attempt to provide the majority of the services themselves. All members are cross trained to the extent possible and provide services to their clients in the community as opposed to meeting in office settings. Additionally, all team members are equally responsible for working with all the clients. It is a model of direct, intensive, and aggressive outreach to clients. The model emphasizes a person's strengths in adapting to community life and providing consultation and support to a person's natural support networks including families, employers, peers, friends, and community agencies (Lehman et al., 2004; McReynolds, Ward, & Singer, 2002).

King (2006) lists the following as key features of ACT programs:

- A clear program identity and structured program processes.
- Team-based service delivery and responsibility for ensuring continuity and effectiveness.
- Mobile responsive services delivered in the home or local environment of the client.
- Extended hours service response and capacity to deal with crises at any time.
- High contact frequency (usually several times per week) that is not dependent on client initiative.
- Clinical, rehabilitation, and social support needs are closely integrated.
- Close liaison with family members and other client supports.

The ACT model's philosophy of intervention has remained fairly constant over the years, although staff, client ratios, and resources vary across programs. The terms programs of assertive community treatment (PACT) and assertive community treatment (ACT) are frequently used interchangeably to describe this model; other terms include enhanced community management and mobile intensive treatment (NAMI, 2007).

Case Example: Community Treatment Team

Vicki, the mental health agency's treatment team leader, began her Monday as usual calling the five-member team meeting to order at 8:30. Vicki had a master's degree in social work and was especially skilled at client assessment and linkage with financial aid services in the midwestern city. She maintained a highly professional demeanor and was known as the "best" team member with the administrative tasks of meeting other service providers, helping them understand the needs of clients, and emphasizing the cooperative relationship they could expect with the team. Paul was the housing specialist. Barbara, a registered nurse, conducted health assessments and had good relationships with medical personnel and pharmacists in the area. Jeff had a background in vocational counseling. Abby was the team's a recreational specialist and loved to organize social activities for members of the 100-client caseload.

On this Monday morning, the team reviewed client "events" over the weekend. It had been Jeff's turn to be on call and he reviewed the six clients whom he had visited over the weekend and how he had dealt with their needs, which ranged from needing cooking appliances to having lost a bottle of psychotropic medication. He had coordinated several of his activities with staff at the nearby hospital emergency services unit. Following this update, Vicki informed the team about the new referrals that were expected from the psychiatric hospital this week, and she made assignments to the team members regarding who would assume primary responsibility for entering those clients onto the team caseload and making the first community contacts. Barbara would arrange for their initial appointments with the agency physician. Before the meeting ended, Abby reminded staff of the picnic that was planned for later that week and for all staff to invite their clients to attend. When the meeting ended, all of the team members left the agency in their cars to begin making client home visits. Six clients would be transported that day to scheduled appointments in the community at the housing authority and social services departments.

Intensive Case Management with Individual Case Managers

This model of intensive case management (ICM) bears similarities to the ACT model except that it is delivered by one case manager rather than a team (King, 2006). This model may be utilized in agencies with relatively small numbers of overall staff or in communities where there is not a high number of clients with mental illness. It goes well beyond the broker role in that the case manager is responsible for spending much time with clients, including being available or arranging for another contact person's availability during evenings and weekends. The case manager also works primarily in the community to help clients successfully establish themselves in stable life structures. Using King's (2006) characteristics of ACT as a basis, ICM provides the same range of services except that there is no team and the case manager cannot provide as many services to the clients himself or herself. Referrals are more common within this model, although unlike the broker model, the case manager will spend much time developing relationships with referral sources and following clients through their referral processes.

Case Example: "Mobile Home" Visitor

Family preservation services (FPS) provides time-intensive in-home counseling and case management services to families who have been identified as "at risk" for serious health, mental health, or social functioning problems. Social workers go to clients' homes three or four times per week, spending time with all family members to help them with problems that are considered to be serious and potentially long term. An average visit is 2 or 3 hours long, and the full intervention process can take 6 months or more. Andy worked with the McCurdy family for a full year. The mother, her live-in boyfriend, two adolescent sons, and adolescent daughter came to the attention of several legal and human service agencies because of their physical violence with one another. The mother had filed assault charges against each of her sons, but she also initiated fights with them and with her daughter. The family had recently moved

(continued)

from another state into a small, two-bedroom trailer in an isolated rural area. The family members were estranged from each other and disconnected from the nearby community. FPS hoped to teach them alternative ways to work out conflicts.

The entire family was ambivalent about Andy's visits, which is typical of FPS clients. In-home services are highly invasive so the social worker's engagement and relationship-building skills are essential. Andy's clinical assessment skills are also important in developing an intervention plan that will address each family member's psychosocial as well as material needs. The McCurdy's made good progress during the months that followed through Andy's teaching, conflict mediation, cognitive-behavioral interventions, role-playing, and modeling activities. Andy also made decisions about appropriate social, educational, and vocational referrals to make for various members of the family. The McCurdys' use of violence fell markedly and they seemed to increase their sense of contentment with each other. They were able to step back and think about their behaviors more clearly and became better at controlling their impulses. Reports from the referring agencies, with whom Andy kept in regular contact, were positive. During the final months, Andy initiated a "step-down" process, in which he gradually reduced his amount of contact with the family.

Clinical Case Management

One type of case management that is closely associated with the individual intensive model is clinical case management. Clinical case management integrates elements of clinical social work and traditional case management practices and is generally provided by a single professional (Walsh, 2000, 2002). The social worker combines the interpersonal skill of the psychotherapist with the creativity and action orientation of the environmental architect. The practice gives priority to the quality of the relationship between the client and social worker as a prerequisite for the client's personal growth. Further, due to the inherent problems with role confusion and authority in traditional case management, the client is considered to be best served if the worker functions as the primary therapeutic resource. Clinical case management draws in part on psychodynamic theories that help the social worker attend to transference, countertransference, and boundary issues, but also utilizes other intervention perspectives that draw from cognitive, behavior, and social support theories.

Clinical case management includes the following 13 activities within four areas of focus:

1. Initial phase—engagement, assessment, and planning.
2. Environmental focus—linking with community resources, consulting with families and caregivers, maintaining and expanding social networks, collaboration with physicians and hospitals, and advocacy.
3. Client focus—intermittent individual psychotherapy, independent living skill development, and client psychoeducation.
4. Client-environment focus—crisis intervention and monitoring (Kanter, 1996a).

The client/case manager relationship provides a context in which the full range of medical, rehabilitative, educational, and social interventions can be effectively implemented (Buck & Alexander, 2006). The other clinical skills needed for long-term work with clients having mental illness include the ability to:

5. Make ongoing judgments about the intensity of one's involvement with a client.
6. Assess and recognize a client's fluctuating competence and changing needs.
7. Titrate support so as to maximize a client's capacity for self-directed behavior.
8. Differentiate the biological and psychological aspects of mental illness.
9. Help family members cope with their troubled relative.
10. Appreciate the effects of social factors on a client's sense of competence.
11. Understand how clients both shape and internalize their environments.
12. Appreciate a client's conscious and unconscious motives for behavior.
13. Develop a longitudinal view of the client's strengths, limitations, and symptoms (Harris & Bergman, 1988; Kanter, 1995, 1996a).

With this overview of current models of case management, we now consider how the modality has evolved over the past century.

HISTORICAL BACKGROUND OF CASE MANAGEMENT

Social Casework

Between 1890 and 1920, social casework was the hallmark of the young social work profession, which was then focused on alleviating the urban problems of poverty and illness. Its mediating and linkage functions included any activities designed to influence behavior and improve client welfare (Lubove, 1965). Mental health became a field of social work practice at this time as well, due to the crowding of the large public institutions that had once held the promise of "curing" mental maladies. With the influence of Freud's writings during the 1920s, however, the treatment of mental illness in social work became more psychoanalytic and less social (Ehrenreich, 1985). Practitioners invested more of their professional energy into working with clients in the community who could benefit from long-term analytic therapies. The most seriously impaired clients still spent much time in state hospital facilities, and these were not well coordinated with community services (Fellin, 1996).

Since World War II, however, partly in response to demands for mental health care for war veterans, social welfare policy has been characterized by a gradual shift from the hospital to the community as the preferred locus of care for persons with mental illness (Grob, 1991). Federal initiatives culminated in the 1963 Community Mental Health Centers Act. Reformers anticipated that these centers would make effective mental health intervention accessible to all who needed it, with far less reliance on state hospitals. The appeal to economy, however, was equally strong in the evolution of community care. State hospitals were viewed as anachronistic institutions and drains on the public purse. There was hope that the mental health centers would result in public savings.

Until the mid-1970s there was federal support for community mental health center development through matching grants with local communities. However, states and communities did not participate to the extent planned, and eventually the federal formula policy was terminated after fewer than half the projected 1,500 centers were established (Levine, 1981). The mental health centers came under attack from some professionals and family advocacy groups for serving clients with relatively minor emotional problems. As late as 1975, only 20% of mental health center clients had ever been hospitalized, and from 1970 to 1978 the percentage of persons with schizophrenia served by agencies actually dropped from 19% to 10% (Mechanic, 1999). Thus, community and state hospital systems coexisted without a mandate for a unified system of care. This resulted in a lack of central planning, organizational barriers, service duplications, and service gaps despite community center availability, the new availability of psychotropic medication, increased attention to patients' rights, and the new federal money for persons with disabilities (Medicaid, Medicare, and Social Security Disability funds). By 1989, the average daily state hospital population was 130,000, but the rate of admissions had declined by only 10% since 1970, indicating a "revolving door" phenomenon (Mechanic, 1999).

Policy makers who valued the idea of community care became disillusioned with the ongoing difficulties clients with mental illness faced in trying to become established in their communities. By 1980, enthusiasm about the mental health centers was waning (Grob, 1991). Some of this was related to President Reagan's desire to reduce the scope of the federal government and institute discretionary state block grants for social services. Community mental health centers became a lower priority among state legislators because they were costly and voters demanded lower taxes.

Still, federal policy continued to be influential in addressing the perceived inadequacies of community mental health centers. The assumption that community care was more effective and less expensive than hospital care persisted. In 1963, 96% of public funding for persons with mental illness came from the states, but by 1985 only 53% was state provided, with 38% coming from federal programs (Torrey, 1988). Seventy percent of public mental health resources remained in hospitals, despite emerging research on the comparable effectiveness of community-based treatment alternatives.

Emergence of Community-Based Case Management

The emergence of community-based case management was spurred in part by National Institute of Mental Health policies introduced in 1978 to make support services available for clients who were not being adequately served through traditional agency systems (Turner & TenHoor, 1978). Community care problems at the time included a lack of clarity of mental health service system goals, fragmentation of responsibility for client interventions, the lack of a systematic approach to financing, inadequate agency commitments to clients, and a need for government leadership in planning for mental health service delivery. Case management was identified as a means of enhancing assistance to clients with mental illness, including greater access to entitlements, crisis stabilization services, psychological rehabilitation and other support services, medical care, support to families and friends, and protection of clients' rights.

The Community Mental Health Centers Act had bypassed state governments, but by 1981 most control of programs was returned to the states in the form of block grants. The Omnibus

Budget Reconciliation Act, a product of President Reagan's antifederalist inclinations, expanded the state's power to make choices about how certain federal funds would be allocated (Rochefort & Logan, 1989). Community centers became more dependent on state funding policies. By 1991, 64% of center funds were coming from the states in the form of revenues, block grants, Medicaid, and user fees. These developments made the enhancement of service for persons with mental illness, with the hope of cost reductions, the top priority of state mental health directors (Ahr & Holcomb, 1985). Financial incentives were expected to reduce state mental hospital use, resulting in innovative case management programs at the local level.

Innovative program developers, such as Test and Stein (1985) in Wisconsin, demonstrated that community-based programs characterized by assertive case management could reduce psychiatric hospitalizations and improve the social functioning of persons with mental illness, allegedly at a lower cost. Their interventions acknowledged the chronic nature of mental illness and focused on rehabilitation rather than cure. Service goals focused on normalizing the lives of clients by providing them with case management support in securing jobs, housing, socialization opportunities, and access to medical care. This approach was implemented in other sites across the country.

Many state departments, impressed by the efforts of community support programmers and faced with the need to reduce hospital costs, turned over considerable budgeting and planning responsibility to community agencies. The State Comprehensive Mental Health Service Plan Act of 1986 was a federal initiative requiring states to develop and implement plans for achieving an organized system of community-based care for persons with mental illness. A 1990 amendment required the same coordination of children's services (Davis, Yelton, Katz-Leavy, & Lourie, 1995).

With the policy shift to community care, case management gained momentum as a favored treatment modality, with its potential to help clients develop productive lifestyles. Through case management, clients could be linked with informal supports (friends, neighbors, recreation centers, etc.) as well as with formal systems. The social value of community care was one rational for shifting money from the state to the community mental health centers; such care was also ostensibly less expensive. Early experiments in community care tended to confirm this, but later the issue of reduced cost was challenged (Mechanic, 1999). Case managers came under pressure from administrators to keep out of the hospital even those clients who might benefit from a short in-patient experience. In geographic areas with few alternative funding sources, agencies had difficulty providing supportive services to clients even when hospital stays were reduced. Still, by 1996 there were 397 ACT programs in the United States (Mueser, Bond, Drake, & Resnick, 1998). As described earlier, other kinds of case management programs shared some characteristics of the ACT model.

The Present

Mental illness continues to represent a major social problem in the United States as evidenced by the numbers of people who experience it and who endure its associated costs. The precise prevalence of mental illness is unknown, but the National Institute of Mental Health (2006a, 2006b) estimates that 26.2% of Americans over 18 years old suffer from a diagnosable mental disorder (not including substance abuse). In 2004, 57.7 million people suffered from a mental health disorder. The most significant burden of mental illness is experienced by the 6% of the adult population who suffer from a serious mental illness. Each year, about 6.7% of adults (14.4 million) suffer from Major Depressive Disorder and 2.6% (5.7 million) suffer from Bipolar Disorder. About 18% (40 million) of adults experience Anxiety Disorders, and these frequently co-occur with depressive and substance abuse disorders. Additionally, 1.1% (2.4 million) adults suffer from Schizophrenia in a given year. Nearly half (45%) of those with any mental disorder meet criteria for two or more co-occurring disorders. One in 10 children suffer from a mental disorder severe enough to cause some level of impairment.

The concept of managed care has also advanced in response to this problem. Managed care refers to organizational arrangements that alter treatment decisions that would otherwise be made by clients or providers (Mechanic, Schlesinger, & McAlpine, 1995). Its goals are to contain costs, efficiently allocate resources, monitor care, and improve the quality of care. All models of managed care seek to control *who* shall receive *what services* with *what frequency,* over *what duration* from *what providers* (regarding discipline and experience), in pursuit of *what outcomes* (Sherman & Dahlquist, 1996). In an ideal situation, the client receives the best care for the fewest dollars. The philosophy of managed care is quite consistent with, and supportive of, the service modality of case management.

The primary reason for the public mental health system's shift toward forms of managed care is Medicaid program cost increases (Edgar, 1996). Although 16% of Medicaid recipients have physical or mental disabilities, they account for 32% of Medicaid costs. Elders and disabled people make up 30% of recipients and 70% of costs, with the largest proportion of funds going to nursing homes. Certain underinsured groups might also benefit from managed care strategies. For example, persons with mental illness living in rural areas face difficulties in receiving adequate mental health care because they have limited access to service providers. Health-care reform may benefit these clients, as consolidating services within a benefits package might encourage their use of alternative treatment to crisis care (Shelton & Frank, 1995).

Case management interventions with persons having mental illness have the capacity to streamline service delivery in keeping with managed care objectives. Managed care providers support only short-term hospitalization and greater client use of community support or recovery groups when warranted (Davis, 1996). The modality can ration service while efficiently using formal and informal resources. The case manager's involvement of significant others (friends and family) in a client's treatment is another way of reducing the amount of professional service that must be provided. Further, the process of carefully coordinating intervention plans with clients and other professionals can reduce projected costs of treatment (Kanter, 1996b).

Cost control is not synonymous with low-quality care, but the ability to provide high-quality service in a managed care context is another argument for skilled case management. Costs should not override the value of helping clients achieve a decent overall quality of life, defined as one's life satisfaction, living situation, daily activities, family and social relations, financial status, occupation, safety, and physical and mental health status (Lehman, 1988). Some policy makers assert that there should be special managed care corporations for persons with mental illness based on case management models of intervention (Scheffler, Grogan, Cuffel, & Penner, 1993). Eligibility for such an HMO would be determined by criteria including diagnosis, level of disability, and duration of illness. In this way, case managers, working individually or on teams, might successfully integrate services and provide effective continuity of care for the most disabled clients.

A recent trend toward cost containment and expanded service quality is the privatization of case management (Merrick, Horgan, & Garnick, 2006). Historically, case management has been provided through public agencies and staff through "purchase of service" agreements. However, in some states Medicaid dollars now "follow the client," rather than being given directly to agencies, enabling private case management agencies to compete with public providers. Many people consider this a positive development because competition is promoted.

Case management, then, has "face validity" as a practice that can maximize clients' adaptations to community life and also contain the costs of health care. In the next section, we see if these goals in fact are achieved.

SUMMARY OF CURRENT EVIDENCE-BASED INFORMATION ON CASE MANAGEMENT

Given the enthusiasm for case management programs among policy makers, it is not surprising that government and academic organizations have sponsored much evaluation research on the modality. The focus of these evaluations is both on the process of implementation and client outcomes. Appropriate research questions include the following:

- What clients can be best served with case management?
- How can its implementation be assessed?
- Which of its many components are most crucial?
- How can it be modified to meet the needs of special populations?
- Is it more effective than other models of service?
- Can clients eventually move from more to less intensive forms of care? (Drake & Burns, 1995)

Implementation Research

Process evaluation is important because administrators need to know whether the service provided matches those that are prescribed. For example, case managers do not always function in the ways program developers intend because of the unpredictable effects of the service environment on practice (Floersch, 2002). Perhaps the most intensive evaluation of a community support system program to date was made through the Robert Wood Johnson Foundation Program on Chronic Mental Illness, conducted in nine major cities across the United States in the late 1980s and early 1990s. The program's five goals were to ensure continuity of care, create a flexible financing system, develop a range of housing options, provide a range of psychosocial and vocational rehabilitation supports, and improve client outcomes (Morrissey et al., 1994). This was primarily a service system intervention, focused on the development of local mental health authorities.

The research team concluded that a local authority can be created and the continuity of case management improved in all sites, but it was more difficult to document improvements in client outcomes (Lehman, Postrado, Roth, McNary, & Goldman, 1994). They found that structural change reforming mental health services for persons with serious mental illness was not sufficient by itself to produce improvements in clients' quality of life

(Goldman, Morrissey, & Ridgely, 1994). That is, no direct correlation exists between case management program implementation and improved quality-of-life outcomes. Devising strategies for helping clients achieve their goals requires ongoing financial investments from administrators and policy makers, as well as the creative ideas of skilled case managers.

Outcome Research

Research on the effects of case management on client outcomes dates back to the early 1980s. Initially, case management services were compared with "traditional," or office-bound, interventions. Draine (1997) reviewed eight experimental studies conducted between 1981 and 1993 and noted that while early studies of case management focused on broad models of community care, research over time has focused on narrower applications of the modality, including those for special populations. Case management has advanced from a generic approach to a range of different applications to special client circumstances. By 1999, the comparative impact of types of case management programs became more of a focus for study. This is because of the great variability found in programs with regard to staffing, types of clients, and resources (Mueser et al., 1998). In all instances, results have been mixed for a variety of outcome indicators such as costs, use of hospitals, client vocational status, and life satisfaction. These results do not necessarily reflect on the value of case management; rather, they suggest that researchers need to refine methodologies and distinguish between the activities of case managers in different sites.

Several meta-analyses have found encouraging results for all types of case management. Gorey, Leslie, Morris, Carruthers, and Chacko (1998) conducted a meta-analysis of 24 studies published between 1980 and 1996 and concluded that 75% of clients who participate in case management programs do better than clients who do not. Positive outcomes were noted in the areas of functional status, rehospitalization, quality of care, cost of care, range of services received, emergency room visits, intervention compliance, social networks, and jail time. They found no differences, however, among models. In a recent review of 75 studies, Marshall and Lockwood (2003) found that both ACT and other types of case management were more effective than other forms of intervention in helping clients stay in contact with services, spend fewer days in the hospital, secure employment, and express life satisfaction. There were no clear differences, however, in measures of mental status and social functioning. Case management was superior to other interventions with regard to client use of hospitalization, but differences were not clear on the other measures.

Reviewers have tended to find that client gains persist only as long as comprehensive services are continued. This raises the question as to whether clients are acquiring skills and resources that promote permanent improvement or are showing short-term gains reflective of intensive support. We now look more closely at evaluations of particular types of case management programs and their impact on clients.

Assertive Community Treatment/Intensive Case Management

Studies have consistently demonstrated the efficacy of the ACT model in both improving the living conditions for persons with mental illness and reducing symptoms and the length of hospitalizations (Bond, Drake, Mueser, & Latimer, 2001; Lehman, Dixon, Kernan, DeForge, & Postrado, 1997). Gains in both quality of life and functional status are also frequently reported as outcomes (Dixon, 2000). Phillips et al. (2001) found similar results: that ACT improves the quality of life and increases housing stability for people experiencing the most severe and persistent forms of mental illness (Phillips et al., 2001). Mueser et al. (1998) reviewed the literature on ACT programs with serious mental illness, including 75 studies that were either comparative studies or single programs with pre- and posttest measures. Increased housing stability was indicated in 9 out of 11 studies. A decrease in the amount of time spent in the hospital occurred in 14 of 22 studies. Few of the studies compared models with each other. Case management was effective in reducing hospital time, improving housing stability, and, to a lesser degree, reducing symptoms and improving quality of life. It had little effect on social functioning, arrests, time in jail, and vocational functioning. The available evidence for ACT also suggests that it is a less costly intervention for high mental health service users and participants report high levels of satisfaction with services (Lauriello, Bustillo, & Keith, 1999; Mueser & McGurk, 2004). Less evidence exists for demonstrating ACT's impact on social functioning and competitive employment (Lauriello, Lenroot, & Bustillo, 2003).

Rapp and Goesha (2004) examined 21 case management studies employing quasi-experimental or experimental designs to identify the common denominators of intervention that produced statistically significant positive outcomes for people with psychiatric disabilities, including persons with schizophrenia. They conclude the strengths model of case management demonstrated desired impacts on nonhospitalization outcomes, such as symptoms, housing, social functioning, vocational, quality of life, leisure time, and social contacts. They found the simpler broker model of case management, which relies only on indirect service coordination, to be ineffective.

While ICM has been widely considered to be an evidenced-based and cost-effective form of service to people struggling with severe mental health disorders, recent studies have begun to show a decrease in its effectiveness. King (2006) used a narrative analytic procedure to analyze five independent studies from the United States, the United Kingdom, Australia, and the Netherlands. Surprisingly, he found that none of the studies reported significant differences in frequency of acute hospital admission between ICM and usual care. He also found that an additional three studies found mixed results regarding the impact of ICM on service costs. Overall, King asserts that while the first and second generation of studies found benefits for the use of ICM, more current studies are finding lesser effects. Similarly, program costs are either not significantly different or more costly than usual care unless usual care includes lengthy hospital admission. In conclusion, King encourages the use of ICM for clients who consume about 50 days or more of hospitalization per year, when standard case management does not allow for flexible and assertive treatment, and when resources from inpatient services can be shifted to ICM.

Clinical Case Management

When compared to standard care, clinical case management has shown mixed results. When compared with no case management, clinical case management is more effective for people who have been hospitalized but are not dependent on substances (Havassy, Shopshire, & Quigley, 2000). Another set of researchers found that clinical case management significantly improved the substance-dependent client outcomes on alcohol use, medical status, employment, family relations, and legal status (McLellan et al., 1999). The addition of clinical case management to other therapy services has also been shown to be beneficial. For instance, Miranda, Azocar, Organista, Dwyer, and Areane (2003) found that the use of clinical case management with cognitive-behavior treatment for impoverished, depressed patients improved retention rates and outcomes, especially for the Spanish-speaking clients.

Ziguras and Stuart (2000) conducted a meta-analysis to study the effectiveness of case management based on 44 published studies between 1980 and 1998, specifically to compare clinical case management and ACT outcomes. For both modalities, similar positive outcomes were reported with regard to family satisfaction with services, family burden, and cost of care, compared to other interventions.

Specialized Programs

In a meta-analysis of 15 empirical studies of interventions with clients who have dual diagnoses of mental illness and substance abuse, it was found that intensive case management was associated with the greatest effect size and that smaller effect sizes were found for standard practices (Dumaine, 2003). Interestingly, there were no correlations found between levels of practitioner training or staff-to-client ratios and client outcomes. Calsyn (2003) found that a modified ACT intervention was more effective in finding stable housing for homeless individuals who were mentally ill than the drop-in center, outpatient treatment, and brokered case management. Those clients also expressed greater satisfaction with the ACT intervention. Jerrell and Ridgely (1995) compared the effectiveness of a 12-step, behavioral skills management program with a case management program for persons with the dual disorders of mental illness and substance abuse. While clients in the behavior skills intervention functions best overall, both programs offered useful interventions and could be effectively combined.

Several case management models have been used effectively in interventions for persons who have mental illness and are homeless. In the NIMH McKinney Project, 894 homeless mentally ill adults in four cities were exposed to rehabilitation, assertive community treatment, or intensive case management services, depending on which model was offered in each city (Shern et al., 1997). Though the specific intervention models differed, all of them used teams of case managers and assertive outreach. The project report noted a 47.5% increase in individuals living in community housing among those who received the intervention. Additionally, 78% of clients had been housed in permanent sites by the end of the program. While the focus of this study was on housing outcomes for those who were homeless, the multisite project did a randomized experimental design in concluding that the services were effective. As with other studies of case management, residential stability, independence, and daily life functions seemed to improve with the duration of service provision.

Macias, Kinney, Farley, Jackson, and Vos (1994) studied the combined effects of case management and psychosocial rehabilitation services (including scheduled dialing activities, staff assistance with social activities, and counseling) to case management alone and found that the experimental group demonstrated better mental and physical health, fewer mood or thought problems, a higher sense of well-being, and less family burden. The two types of service were mutually supportive. Walsh (1994) compared two variations of a single case management program (in one clients received group interventions, and in the other they received individual interventions) with regard to natural social support outcomes. The clients receiving group interventions developed more extensive friendship networks.

The literature also includes examples of consumers working as advocates or peer specialists on case management teams. Solomon and Draine (1995) report on the 1-year outcomes of a randomized trial of consumer case management with 91 clients with serious mental illness using a pre- and posttest experimental design. They found that consumers who received services from a consumer case management team had the same outcomes as consumers who received services from a nonconsumer team on quality of life and various clinical and social outcomes such as housing, homelessness, size of social network, and level of functioning, and behavioral symptoms. Dixon, Krauss, and Lehman (1994) reported on the experience of employing two full-time consumer advocates as part of an experimental ACT team that provided services to persons who were homeless and had a severe mental illness. Consumer-advocates served as role models for recovery and played an important role in the engagement of clients and sensitizing team staff to consumer experiences. Felton et al. (1995) examined 104 clients served by teams that included these peer specialists and found a reduction in the number of major life problems experienced and greater improvement in multiple areas of quality of life.

Cost Containment

Policy makers and agency administrators are concerned with how well case management services achieve the goals of cost containment and service quality. Scott and Dixon (1995) reviewed 13 major studies conducted between 1981 and 1994 and concluded that assertive community treatment clearly reduces the rates and duration of hospitalization and may be less costly over the short-term than other service approaches. Still, client improvements in community functioning and resource access were not achieved in all studies, and program costs seem to increase in the long run. Research findings across sites may differ because programs are modified when transferred from one setting to another. One theme across studies is that, with new programs, the amount of time required to make significant differences in the lives of clients may be 2 years or more. The authors recommend that family well-being be adopted as an additional outcome indicator and that researchers include the perspectives of the client, family, and case manager as data sources.

Several studies have demonstrated that "capitated" case management programs can control health-care costs for persons with mental illness. In a New York study, clients in one program used the psychiatric hospital less than a control group of clients receiving free-for-service case management, with no observed differences in symptoms or functional status (Cole, Reed, Babigham, Brown, & Fray, 1994). Differences in case manager behavior in the two groups appeared to result from the flexibility in client care made possible by the capitation system. That system inspired case managers to develop new services, and case managers became more adept at crisis intervention. Program costs were reduced by 13.8% in year 1 and 14.5% in year 2 of the capitated program. In a New Hampshire study, fee-for-service case management was compared with an approach that confined capitation with fee-for-service schemes to evaluate the impact of flexibility on community-based treatment (Clark, Drake, McHugo, & Ackerson, 1995). Results indicated a shift from office to community-based practice in the capitation group, although total case management time provided by the groups did not differ. It was not apparent whether these changes had an impact on client outcomes. McCrone, Beecham, and Knapp (1994) compared case management costs with those in a more traditional community psychiatric nursing service in Britain. They identified short-term savings (on hospital care, community health and mental health services, education, law enforcement, social care services, employment services, and housing) with the innovative program, but these did not persist beyond 6 months, implying that the institution of new community services is not inexpensive.

Limitations of the Evidence

Several methodological limitations are evident in the previous studies. First, the independent variable of case management is difficult to define clearly enough to make comparisons across studies. Given the reliance on links with other service providers, the case managers, the programs, or the adjunctive community service, it might be useful to evaluate each of these components distinctly. Further, researchers have tended to overlook the impact of individual case manager's skill on service outcomes. Because case management was initially conceptualized rather generically, and is frequently delivered in teams, it is not often considered that differences in outcomes may be due to individual case managers. The work of Ryan, Sherman, and Judd (1994) is one exception to this trend. They studied the implementation of three community support programs and found that, while all were effective, case managers themselves significantly influenced client outcomes when the type of service was controlled.

One critic of the PACT approach states that the research is biased by authors who support the program philosophy and that evaluators may be confusing workers' efforts for clients' efforts (Gomory, 1999). That is, some positive outcomes may be due to administrators refusing some services such as hospitalization to clients as an option, and practitioners may be coercing clients to behave in ways that are consistent with program values. In summary, ACT programs and other forms of intensive community intervention for persons with schizophrenia do produce positive outcomes, but some questions remain as to the influence of resource availability (fewer hospital beds, more short-term crisis residences) and the more pervasive presence of case managers in clients' lives.

IMPLICATIONS FOR SOCIAL WORK ON MICRO-, MEZZO-, AND MACROLEVELS

Based on the previous research review, we now outline some implications for case management at three systems levels. The microlevel of practice refers to direct service delivery to clients. The mezzolevel reflects operations at the agency or local system level, while the macrolevel refers to the larger policy level.

Microlevel

Because the practice of case management involves many services provided by many agency practitioners in distinctive community service systems, it is difficult to confidently generalize findings from one program to another program. For this reason, it is important to acknowledge the role of the individual case manager in helping programs meet overall objectives and helping clients to meet their goals. In short, people deliver services, not programs. At the microlevel, it is important to utilize highly skilled case managers who will have access to ongoing supervision, training, and continuing education opportunities. Case managers also need to be given the flexibility to titrate their activities to address the particular characteristics of their clients and community systems (Floersch, 2002).

Mezzolevel

Agency administrators need to be aware that case management practice is often stressful, frustrating, and conflict riddled. Administrators need to be able to provide their case managers with an agency atmosphere that is supportive of their work, concretely values their work (via salaries, benefits, recognition, advancement opportunities), and actively deals with the possibility of worker burnout. While the benefits to clients and public budgets are clear, the short half-life of case managers is also well known (Frankel & Gelman, 2004). Administrators can help to support the work of case managers by offering competitive compensation packages, agreeable working conditions, adequate agency material supports, close access to referral providers such as agency physicians, reasonable caseload sizes, and opportunities for professional advancement. Recently, Glissen, Dukes, and Green (2006) have developed an availability, responsiveness, and continuity organizational intervention strategy to minimize caseworker turnover and improve the working climate and cultures in one case management system.

Macrolevel

All policy makers hope that their case management programs are effective across a range of client goals that include quality of life and that those programs are cost-effective in comparison to treatment alternatives. Given the various ways in which case management programs "play out" in different service systems, it is still hard to understand *what works* for *what clients* under *what circumstances*. Further, when a program is implemented, it cannot be assumed that it will unfold in precisely the manner that the policy makers have intended. Policy makers should ensure that case management programs are available in all localities for persons with mental illness, but they should be hesitant about promoting "exact" replications from one service setting to another. Further, the interests of cost containment and quality of life may best be achieved if policy makers allow for competitive markets to develop along the lines of privatization as well. It seems that this can be best achieved if the dollars follow the client, rather than being provided to various providers in purchase of service agreements.

LIMITATIONS

Case management is thriving as a method of service delivery that spans many client populations, but it does seem to have several inherent limitations. Case managers possess only a modest level of authority in some community service systems. If the case manager is responsible for linking clients with a variety of service providers, it follows that he or she should have some authority over how those services are delivered, including decision making about which are adequate. But though case managers generally have college degrees in a variety of human service professions, many do not have graduate degrees, which tends to limit their recognized authority in interdisciplinary work. For example, a case manager might decide that a certain vocational counselor's work with a given client is, for some reason, inappropriate. Should the case manager approach the counselor about changing the treatment modality? Many providers would question whether a professional with lesser credentials should make judgments about the quality of his or her work, but the case manager's monitoring and evaluation of services are considered to be essential roles.

Other limitations of the approach include unclear expectations for job performance and problems with attrition (McClelland, Austin, & Schneck, 1996). The case management modality risks failure because of such issues as role ambiguity, inadequate resources, a lack of administrative authority, and low salaries. Case managers function best when their roles are clearly delineated, and opportunities for professional growth and advancement within their positions might enhance retention and job satisfaction.

Caseload size is often cited as a determining factor of the nature of case manager activity. Caseloads generally range from 15 to 50 clients per worker (Rothman & Sager, 1998). Rose and Moore (1995) point to the irony that as the complexity of client needs increases, caseload size also tends to increase, and educational standards for employment are lowered.

CONCLUSION

The practice of case management has become a professionally and politically preferred means of providing and coordinating social services to clients with multiple needs. Even as social service delivery becomes more streamlined and unified, there will always be a need for professionals who are adept at assessing clients' broad needs and knowing how to pull together those services in complex social environments. The profession of social work has always been uniquely positioned to undertake the challenges of case management, given its holistic perspective on people and its biopsychosocial framework for assessment. Developing systems of care that are specifically effective with clients of various needs in various service systems will always be a challenge for programmers and administrators, and clients will be best served if social workers are at the forefront of those processes.

REFERENCES

Ahr, P. R., & Holcomb, W. R. (1985). State mental health directors' priorities for mental health care. *Hospital and Community Psychiatry, 31*(1), 47–52.

Austin, C., & McClelland, R. W. (2002). Case management with older adults. In A. Roberts & G. Greene (Eds.), *Social workers' desk reference* (pp. 502–506). Oxford: Oxford University Press.

Bond, G. R., Drake, R. E., Mueser, K. T., & Latimer, E. (2001). Assertive community treatment for people with severe mental illness: Critical ingredients and impact on clients. *Disease Management and Health Outcomes, 9*, 141–159.

Buck, P. W., & Alexander, L. B. (2006). Neglected voices: Consumers with serious mental illness. *Administration and Policy in Mental Health and Mental Health Services, 33*(4), 470–481.

Calsyn, R. J. (2003). A modified ESID approach to studying mental illness and homelessness. *American Journal of Community Psychology*, *32*(3/4), 319–331.

Clark, R. E., Drake, R. E., McHugo, G. J., & Ackerson, T. H. (1995). Incentives for community treatment: Mental illness management services. *Medical Care*, *33*(7), 729–738.

Cole, R. E., Reed, S. K., Babigham, H. M., Brown, S. W., & Fray, J. (1994). A mental health capitation program: Pt. I: Patient outcomes. *Hospital and Community Psychiatry*, *45*(11), 1090–1096.

Craig, T., Doherty, I., & Jamieson-Craig, R. (2004). The consumer-employee as a member of a mental health assertive outreach team: Pt. I: Clinical and social outcomes. *Journal of Mental Health*, *13*(1), 59–69.

Crane-Ross, D., Lutz, W. J., & Roth, D. (2006). Consumer and case manager perspectives of service empowerment: Relationship to mental health recovery. *Journal of Behavioral Health Services and Research*, *33*(2), 142–155.

Davis, K. (1996). *Managed care and social work practice*. Richmond: Virginia Commonwealth University School of Social Work.

Davis, M., Yelton, S., Katz-Leavy, J., & Lourie, I. S. (1995). Unclaimed children revisited: The status of state children's mental health service systems. *Journal of Mental Health Administration*, *22*(2), 147–166.

Dixon, L. (2000). Assertive community treatment: Twenty-five years of gold. *Psychiatric Services*, *51*(6), 759–765.

Dixon, L., Krauss, N., & Lehman, A. F. (1994). Consumers as service providers: The promise and challenge. *Community Mental Health Journal*, *30*(6), 615–625.

Draine, J. (1997). A critical review of randomized field trials of case management for individuals with serious and persistent mental illness. *Research on Social Work Practice*, *7*(1), 32–52.

Drake, R. E., & Burns, B. J. (1995). Special section on assertive community treatment: An introduction. *Hospital and Community Psychiatry*, *46*(7), 667–668.

Dumaine, M. L. (2003). Meta-analysis of interventions with co-occurring disorders of severe mental illness and substance abuse. *Research on Social Work Practice*, *13*(2), 142–165.

Edgar, E. (1996). Managed care basics. *NAMI Advocate*, *18*(2), 6–16.

Ehrenreich, J. H. (1985). *The altruistic imagination: A history of social work and social policy in the United States*. Ithaca, NY: Cornell University Press.

Fellin, P. (1996). *Mental health and mental illness: Polices, programs, and services*. Itasca, IL: Peacock.

Felton, C. J., Stastny, P., Shern, D., Blanch, A., Donahue, S. A., Knight, E., et al. (1995). Consumers as peer specialists on intensive case management teams: Impact on client outcomes. *Psychiatric Services*, *46*(10), 1037–1044.

Fiorentine, R., & Grusky, O. (1990). When case managers manage the seriously mentally ill: A role-contingency approach. *Social Service Review*, *64*, 79–93.

Floersch, J. (2002). *Meds, money, and manners: The cased management of severe mental illness*. New York: Columbia University Press.

Frankel, A. J., & Gelman, S. R. (2004). *Case management* (2nd ed.). Chicago: Lyceum Books.

Glissen, C., Dukes, D., & Green, P. (2006). The effects of the ARC organizational intervention on caseworker turnover, climate, and culture in children's service systems. *Child Abuse and Neglect*, *30*, 855–880.

Goldman, H. H., Morrissey, J. P., & Ridgely, M. S. (1994). Evaluating the Robert Wood Johnson Foundation program on chronic mental illness. *Milbank Quarterly*, *72*(1), 37–47.

Gomory, T. (1999). Programs of assertive community treatment: A critical review. *Ethical Human Sciences and Services*, *1*(2), 147–163.

Gorey, K. M., Leslie, D. R., Morris, T., Carruthers, W. V., John, L., & Chacko, J. (1998). Effectiveness of case management with severely and persistently mentally ill people. *Community Mental Health Journal*, *34*(3), 241–250.

Grob, G. (1991). *From asylum to community: Mental health policy in modern America*. Princeton, NJ: Princeton University Press.

Hangan, C. (2006). Introduction of an intensive case management style of delivery for a new mental health service. *International Journal of Mental Health Nursing*, *15*(3), 157–162.

Harris, M., & Bergman, H. C. (1988). Clinical case management for the chronically mentally ill: A conceptual analysis. In M. Harris & L. Bachrach (Eds.), *Clinical case management* (pp. 5–13). San Francisco: Jossey-Bass.

Havassy, B. E., Shopshire, M. S., & Quigley, L. A. (2000). Effects of substance dependence on outcomes of patients in a randomized trial of two case management models. *Psychiatric Services*, *51*(5), 639–644.

Jerrell, J. M., & Ridgely, M. S. (1995). Comparative effectiveness of three approaches to service people with severe mental illness and substance abuse disorders. *Journal of Nervous and Mental Diseases*, *183*(9), 566–576.

Kanter, J. (Ed.). (1995). *Clinical issues in case management*. San Francisco: Jossey-Bass.

Kanter, J. (1996a). Case management with long-term patients. In S. M. Soreff (Ed.), *Handbook for the treatment of the seriously mentally ill* (pp. 259–275). Seattle, WA: Hogrefe & Huber.

Kanter, J. (1996b). Case management and managed care: Investing in recovery. *Psychiatric Services*, *47*(7), 699–701.

King, R. (2006). Intensive case management: A critical re-appraisal of the scientific evidence for effectiveness. *Administration and Policy in Mental Health and Mental Health Services Research*, *33*(5), 529–535.

Lauriello, J., Bustillo, J., & Keith, S. J. (1999). A critical review of research on psychosocial treatment of schizophrenia. *Biological Psychiatry*, *46*, 1409–1417.

Lauriello, J., Lenroot, R., & Bustillo, J. R. (2003). Maximizing the synergy between pharmacotherapy and psychosocial therapies for schizophrenia. *Psychiatric Clinics of North America*, *26*, 191–211.

Lehman, A. F. (1988). A quality of life interview for the chronically mentally ill. *Evaluation and Program Planning*, *11*, 51–52.

Lehman, A. F., Buchanan, R. W., Dickerson, F. B., Dixon, L. B., Goldberg, R., Green-Paden, L., et al. (2003). Evidence-based treatment for schizophrenia. *Psychiatric Clinics of North America*, *26*(4), 939–954.

Lehman, A. F., Dixon, L. B., Kernan, E., DeForge, B. R., & Postrado, L. T. (1997). A randomized trial of assertive community treatment for homeless persons with severe mental illness. *Archives of General Psychiatry*, *54*, 1038–1043.

Lehman, A. F., Kreyenbuhl, J., Buchanan, B. W., Dickerson, F. B., Dixon, L. B., Goldberg, R., et al. (2004). The schizophrenia Patient Outcomes Research Team (PORT): Updated treatment recommendations 2003. *Schizophrenia Bulletin*, *30*(2), 193–217.

Lehman, A. F., Postrado, L. T., Roth, D., McNary, S. W., & Goldman, H. H. (1994). Continuity of care and client outcomes in the Robert Wood Johnson Foundation program on chronic mental illness. *Milbank Quarterly*, *72*(1), 105–122.

Levine, M. (1981). *The history and politics of community mental health*. New York: Oxford University Press.

Lubove, R. (1965). *The professional altruist: The emergence of social work as a career, 1880–1930*. Cambridge, MA: Harvard University Press.

Macias, C., Kinney, R., Farley, O. W., Jackson, R., & Vos, B. (1994). The role of case management within a community support system: Partnership with psychosocial rehabilitation. *Community Mental Health Journal*, *30*(4), 323–339.

Marshall, M., & Lockwood, A. (2003). Early intervention for psychosis. *Cochrane Database of Systematic Reviews*, *2* (Art. No: CD004718).

McClelland, R. W., Austin, C. D., & Schneck, D. (1996). Practice dilemmas and policy implications in case management. In C. C. Austin & R. W. McClelland (Eds.), *Perspectives on case management practice* (pp. 257–278). Milwaukee, WI: Families International.

McCrone, P., Beecham, J., & Knapp, M. (1994). Community psychiatric nurse teams: Cost-effectiveness of intensive support versus generic care. *British Journal of Psychiatry*, *165*(2), 218–221.

McLellan, A. T., Hagan, T. A., Levine, M., Meyers, K., Gould, F., Bencivengo, M., et al. (1999). Does clinical case management improve outpatient addition treatment? *Drug and Alcohol Dependence*, *55*(1/2), 91–103.

McReynolds, C. J., Ward, D. M., & Singer, O. (2002). Stigma, discrimination, and invisibility: Factors affecting successful integration of individuals diagnosed with schizophrenia. *Journal of Applied Rehabilitation Counseling*, *33*(4), 32–39.

Mechanic, D. (1999). *Mental health and social policy: The emergence of managed care*. Boston: Allyn & Bacon.

Mechanic, D., Schlesinger, M., & McAlpine, D. D. (1995). Management of mental health and substance abuse services: State of the art and early results. *Milbank Quarterly*, *73*(1), 19–55.

Merrick, E. L., Horgan, C. M., & Garnick, D. W. (2006). Managed care organizations' use of treatment management strategies for outpatient mental health care. *Administration and Policy in Mental Health and Mental Health Services Research*, *33*(1).

Miranda, J., Azocar, F., Organista, K., Dwyer, E., & Areane, P. (2003). Treatment of depression among impoverished primary care patients from ethnic minority groups. *Psychiatric Services*, *54*(2), 219–225.

Morrissey, J. P., Calloway, M., Bartko, W. T., Ridgely, M. S., Goldman, H. H., & Paulson, R. I. (1994). Local mental health authorities and service system change: Evidence from the Robert Wood Johnson program on chronic mental illness. *Milbank Quarterly*, *72*(1), 49–80.

Moxley, D. P. (1996). *Case management by design: Reflections on principles and practices*. Chicago: Nelson-Hall.

Mueser, K. T., Bond, G. R., Drake, R. E., & Resnick, S. G. (1998). Models of community care for severe mental illness: A review of research on case management. *Schizophrenia Bulletin*, *24*(1), 37–70.

Mueser, K. T., & McGurk, S. R. (2004). Schizophrenia. *Lancet*, *363*, 2063–2072.

National Alliance on Mental Illness. (2007). *Assertive Community Treatment (ACT)*. Retrieved January 25, 2007, from www.nami.org/Template.cfm?Section=ACT-TA_Center/.

National Association of Social Workers. (2006). *NASW standards for the practice of clinical social work*. Silver Spring, MD: Author.

National Institute of Mental Health. (2006a). *NASW standards for social work case management*. Retrieved September 8, 2006, from www.socialworkers.org/practice/standards/sw_case_mgmt.asp.

National Institute of Mental Health. (2006b). *The numbers count: Mental disorders in America*. Retrieved January 26, 2007, from www.nimh.nih.gov/publicat/numbers.cfm#Intro/.

Phillips, S., Burns, B., Edgar, E., Mueser, K. T., Linkins, K. W., Rosenheck, R. A., et al. (2001). Moving assertive community treatment into standard practice. *Psychiatric Services*, *52*(6), 771–779.

Rapp, C. (1998). *The strengths model: Case management with people suffering from severe and persistent mental illness*. New York: Oxford University Press.

Rapp, C. (2002). A strengths approach to case management with clients with severe mental disabilities. In A. Roberts & G. Greene (Eds.), *Social workers' desk reference* (pp. 486–489). New York: Oxford University Press.

Rapp, C., & Goesha, R. J. (2004). The principles of effective case management of mental health services. *Psychiatric Rehabilitation Journal*, *27*(4), 319–333.

Roberts-DeGennaro, M. (1987). Developing case management as a practice model. *Social Casework*, *68*, 416–420.

Rochefort, D. A., & Logan, B. (1989). Mental illness and mental health as public policy concerns. In D. A. Rochefort (Ed.), *Handbook on mental health policy in the United States* (pp. 143–167). Westport, CT: Greenwood.

Rose, S. M., & Moore, V. L. (1995). Case management. In R. L. Edwards & J. G. Hopps (Eds.), *Encyclopedia of social work* (19th ed., pp. 335–340). Washington, DC: National Association of Social Workers Press.

Rothman, J., & Sager, J. S. (1998). *Case management: Integrating individual and community practice.* Boston: Allyn & Bacon.

Rubin, A. (1992). Case management. In S. M. Rose (Ed.), *Case management and social work practice* (pp. 5–24). New York: Longman.

Ryan, C. S., Sherman, P. S., & Judd, C. M. (1994). Accounting for case manager effects in the evaluation of mental health services. *Journal of Consulting and Clinical Psychology*, *62*(5), 965–974.

Scheffler, R., Grogan, C., Cuffel, B., & Penner, S. (1993). A specialized mental health plan for persons with severe mental illness under managed competition. *Hospital and Community Psychiatry*, *44*(10), 937–942.

Scott, J. E., & Dixon, L. B. (1995). Assertive community treatment and case management for schizophrenia. *Schizophrenia Bulletin*, *21*(4), 657–668.

Shelton, D. A., & Frank, R. (1995). Rural mental health coverage under health care reform. *Community Mental Health Journal*, *31*(6), 539–552.

Sherman, P. S., & Dahlquist, B. L. (1996). Managed care viewpoint. *NAMI Advocate*, *18*(1), 4–6.

Shern, D. L., Felton, C. J., Hough, R. L., Lehman, A. F., Goldfinger, S., Valencia, E., et al. (1997). Housing outcomes for homeless adults with mental illness: Results from the second-round McKinney program. *Psychiatric Services*, *48*, 239–241.

Solomon, P., & Draine, J. (1995). Consumer case management and attitudes concerning family relations among persons with mental illness. *Psychiatric Quarterly*, *66*(3), 249–261.

Test, M., & Stein, L. (Eds.). (1985). *The training in community living model: A decade of experience.* New directions for mental health services. San Francisco: Jossey-Bass.

Torrey, E. F. (1988). *Nowhere to go: The tragic odyssey of the homeless mentally ill.* New York: Harper & Row.

Turner, J., & TenHoor, W. (1978). The NIMH community support program: Pilot approach to a needed social reform. *Schizophrenia Bulletin*, *4*, 319–334.

Walsh, J. (1994). Social support resource outcomes for the clients of two community treatment teams. *Research in Social Work Practice*, *4*, 448–463.

Walsh, J. (2000). *Clinical case management with persons having mental illness: A relationship-based perspective.* Pacific Grove, CA: Wadsworth-Brooks/Cole.

Walsh, J. (2002). Clinical case management. In A. Roberts & G. Greene (Eds.), *Social workers' desk reference* (pp. 472–476). New York: Oxford University Press.

Ziguras, S. J., & Stuart, G. W. (2000). *A meta-analysis of the effectiveness of mental health case management over 20 years.* Psychiatric Services, *51*(11), 1410–1421.

Chapter 8

ADVOCACY

Cecilia Lai Wan Chan and Chi Kwong Law

When there is change, there is movement. When there is movement, there is friction that is needed to make the movement possible. When there is friction between different fronts, there is conflict. When there is conflict, there is heat. For changes to take place, there is inevitably movement, friction, conflict, and heat. To make changes happen, there are mechanisms to lubricate the movement, reduce friction, contain the heat, and manage the differences between interfaces. Social work intervention can initiate change and movement and reduce conflict and heat simultaneously.

Common concepts of change in chemistry and physics can be applied to human interaction and system change: for example, catalysts to facilitate interaction and crystallization of good ideas to bring about desired interpersonal relations, and mechanical systems to move heavy weights by small actions of lobbying and persuasion. Advocacy is one good example of lubrication for movement and change.

The term *advocacy* is used in many fields: law, medicine, education, urban planning, culture and art, politics, environmental protection, and social work. In this chapter, we explore the role of advocacy in social work. While there is no widely agreed on definition of advocacy in social work, we can find similarities in the description of various elements of advocacy and in the explanation of what advocacy means.

ADVOCACY AS A SOCIAL WORK FUNCTION

A useful starting point for exploring the meaning of advocacy in social work is the concept of "roles of social workers." The most frequently mentioned roles include enabler, broker, mediator, advocate, resource person, gate keeper, educator and trainer, which overlap to various degrees. For example, being a teacher, educator, or trainer is very similar to being an enabler. A change agent can be an enabler or an advocate. The description of roles helps social work students conceptualize the diverse fields and purposes of social work practice into a relatively parsimonious framework, without which they will be lost in the complex web of social work practice. This conceptual instrument, the roles of social workers, is built on various combinations of actions, relationships, and systems in the context of social work practice. For instance, the advocate role of the social worker involves actions of advocating or doing advocacy. In the case of helping a client to obtain a service, once denied, the social worker acts on behalf of clients (involving relationships) to negotiate (involving actions) with the relevant service provider (involving service delivery systems) to ensure that their human rights are protected. Thus, to look for the meaning of advocacy, we would have to examine relevant relationships, actions, and systems.

The most common definition we find in dictionaries for the word *advocacy* is "to speak on behalf of." In advocacy, speaking takes different forms, including writing position papers or feature articles, making petitions, and holding press conferences. Communication is a key component of advocating. The purpose is to induce change, the object of which may be an attitude, an entrenched practice, a social policy, or a piece of legislation.

HISTORICAL DEVELOPMENT

Schneider and Lester (2001) provided a detailed account of advocacy in the history of social work in the United States beginning from the 1870s with the settlement house, the Charity Organization Society (COS) movement as well as actions to alter the legislative process for system change. Not only would social workers working in communities and neighborhoods advocate for their clients, but clinical social workers under the Code of Ethics would also advocate for their clients. It is the social worker's obligation to see justice being done and injustice against clients removed.

Through the Reform Period, the New Deal, and the War on Poverty, social workers took on leadership roles in political and collective actions to advocate for humanitarian social policies to meet the needs of citizens who were suffering in silence and in pain. Such activities were coherent with the commitment to human rights to welfare services (Schneider & Lester, 2001). With the New Federalism and the War on Terrorism, resources on human rights protection are being channeled to military actions. Welfare efforts and establishments are so eroded that the unmet needs of vulnerable groups have become more apparent in the recent decade (Haynes & Mickelson, 2006).

Similar developments can be found from the Victorian Era to the Poor Law period, moving from community development for colonies all over the world, into National Health Services, settlements, and a universal welfare system from cradle to grave for all in the United Kingdom. Social workers' role in social change, advocacy, mediation, and counseling was seen as an integrated whole (Bailey & Brake, 1975; Craig, 1998).

As the population ages, issues of old age protection, pension, health care, employment, and quality of life attract more public attention. In the contemporary postmodern society, with widening gaps between the rich and the poor after globalization and internationalization, issues of war, HIV/AIDS, drugs, domestic violence, persons with different abilities and gender orientations, lifelong learning, income protection, housing, health, education, crime, discrimination, and human rights are all seen as critical and in need of immediate action. The War on Poverty has to be revitalized because of the growing gaps between the rich and the poor.

ADVOCACY BY HUMAN SERVICE PROFESSIONALS

Human service professionals other than social workers, such as lawyers, doctors, nurses, and pharmacists, also are very active in serving as advocates for their users (Bastian, 1998; Bell & Goodman, 2001; Grabenstein, Hartzema, Guess, Johnston, & Rittenhouse, 1992).

Students in various professional schools are trained to serve as advocates for their clients so that they can gain firsthand experience helping and caring. Professionals also help train survivors, volunteers, and retirees to serve as advocates.

In dealing with domestic violence, nurses are playing a leading role in the promotion of training lay advocates in emergency rooms to help victims (Sullivan & Bybee, 1999). Sullivan and her colleagues conducted a long-term follow-up in a community-based advocacy for women with abusive partners. Among the women who were supported and followed up by an advocate, long-term reduction of violent behavior was evidenced (Bybee & Sullivan, 2002; Sullivan, 2003). Nurses are also leading innovative projects for the promotion of women's help through volunteers, nursing students, and practicing nurses (Gillette, 1988). Emergency room advocacy programs to help battered women better utilize community resources are being launched in different projects and hospitals (Muelleman & Feighny, 1999).

The illness experience can be greatly disempowering (Illich, 1977). Advocacy programs were established in clinics, hospitals, and community health centers so that patients and their caregivers can be assisted in steering their way smoothly through the health-care system (Tauber & Houston, 1977). The initiation of a patient advocacy program in a private psychiatric hospital in 1980 was found to be effective in reducing the rate of hospital discharge against medical advice (Targum, Capodanno, Hoffman, & Foudraine, 1982). There are web-based guides to help users negotiate the mental health system through advocacy as well (Hunt & Osher, 2006). (Details can be found in www.tapartnership.org/Regions/RegionI_docs/A_Family_Guide_to_%20Achieving_the_Promise.pdf.)

Professionals also establish programs to empower and enable users in asserting their rights in the legal process. Doueck, Weston, Filbert, Beekhuis, and Redlich (1997) reported caretakers' and professionals' views on a child witness advocacy program that allowed the voices of children who were victims of sexual abuse to be heard. Law students are being trained to serve as advocates for children in care and battered women (Wan, 2000). These programs serve the oppressed and the voiceless. In addition, participating law students take on more affirmative attitudes and become more committed toward anti-oppression and fighting for social justice.

Womock and Sata (1975) promoted a child advocacy project, which was developed much further, subsequently. Besides finding an advocate for children, there are also projects to mobilize teenagers and young persons to serve as advocates to combat drug abuse, HIV/AIDS, high-risk behaviors, and smoking (Winkleby, Feighery, Altman, Kole, & Tencati, 2001; Winkleby et al., 2004). The U.S. Air Force reported the success of family advocacy programs in terms of significant reductions of domestic violence, suicide, and accidents (Brewster, Milner, Mollerstrom, Saha, & Harris, 2002).

There are users who cannot advocate for themselves. The pain of frail and sick persons may go unnoticed, and their voices may not be heard. Partnership and advocacy in palliative care for dying patients are mushrooming in different parts of the world (Kapo, Morrison, & Liao, 2007; Lee, 2002). Eng (2002) proposed a program called Program of All-Inclusive Care for the Elderly (PACE) to serve older adults in palliative care. Gitlin, Miller, and Boyce (1999) established a community-based program to help frail elderly renters modify their bathrooms, the domestic site with the highest risk of falling and injury. The advocacy involved negotiation with the landlord as well as the health authorities to make home modifications possible.

There are advocates who would like to promote individual self-discipline and control, as in the case of mothers who are drug or alcohol abusers and who feel that advocates are able to help them much more than their case managers (Grant, Ernst, Streissguth, Phipps, & Gendler, 1996). In confronting death, there are also organ transplant (e.g., liver, kidney, cornea, bone, skin) advocates in hospitals to promote organ donation (Anderson-Shaw et al., 2005). Advocates can also help alter public discrimination against marginal groups, such as drug abusers, teenage mothers, and populations who are HIV positive (Lenton & Phillips, 1997). Archer (1996) reported positive changes in the relations between communities and the medical campus achieved through a community health advocacy program. Medical students as well as professors who served as advocates experienced a fresh perspective from the patients' point of view. Not only were patients empowered, but professionals and students were transformed.

Users with limited mental capacities also need professionals and their family members to advocate for them. Lennox et al. (2004) advocated for the development of health advocacy intervention for adults with intellectual disabilities and their general practitioners. Patients with mood disorders often have to wait for a very long time before they obtain appropriate services. Patients who have an advocate can have their rights to services better protected (Christiana et al., 2000). The mental health survivors' movement is weak, and services for persons with mental health problems often have long waiting lists. Patients are widely discriminated against in terms of job opportunities, employment, education, and access to services. The family members' movement is growing to ensure that public policy and service provision can match growing needs (Sommer, 1990). Empowerment packages are developed for chronic mental patients (Linhorst, 2006).

An organization called ParkinSons and Daughters consists of children who advocate for their parents suffering from Parkinson's disease. There are users who turn themselves into advocates for fellow sufferers and people in similar situations. Through their active partici-pation in self-help activities, many of the leaders report that the experience of advocacy can foster their own spiritual growth and personal transformation (Armstrong, 2001). Instead of being absorbed in self-pity and self-blame, users find their adversities and sufferings turned into escalators to authentic happiness and fulfillment (Chan, Ho, & Chan, 2007; Chan, Ho, Fu, & Chow, 2006; Ho, Chan, & Ho, 2004).

Facilitating User-Led Advocacy

User-led advocacy movements among persons with disability, survivors of mental illness or domestic violence, adult survivors of childhood sexual abuse, cancer survivors, divorced people, and other groups are gathering momentum in bringing about changes in society. Many small user groups are actively participating in advocacy and forming themselves into communal or district coalitions, national alliances, and ultimately international platforms for social and policy changes. The first author contributed to the establishment of a patients' mutual help movement in Hong Kong. With groups of social work students, she mobilized patients to form themselves into self-help groups. The groups were organized to form an alliance of patients' mutual help organizations (Wong & Chan, 1994). She was also instrumental in the formation of grassroots organizations and the mobilization for support of environmental improvement projects (Chan & Hills, 1993).

Social workers can serve as support and coaches for users to form themselves into user-led advocacy groups or organizations. At the same time, social work professional organizations or groups can form alliances with advocacy users' groups to promote desirable social reform in social systems, policies, policy implementations, and priorities in resource allocation. It is crucial for social workers to be equipped with knowledge and skills in staying in the background while helping our clients use advocacy for change.

SOCIAL WORK AND ADVOCACY

Advocacy has always been part of professional social work practice, including social workers' contribution and participation in networking, capacity building, resource mobilization, advocacy of rights without neglecting responsibilities, policy change, and attitude change among the public. However, with increasing professionalization and privatization of services, social workers view themselves more and more as gatekeepers to protect clients from unjust service delivery systems. There are intense debates in the profession regarding a fundamental reexamination of social workers' role in advocacy and system change (Beresford & Harding, 1993; Dominelli, 1996).

Social workers are historically linked to orchestrating changes in people's lives through collective action, advocacy for effective social policy, empowerment through community development, fostering communication through family interventions, and individual case work. Schneider and Lester (2001, pp. 58–64) identified the key dimensions of advocacy as (a) pleading or speaking on behalf of others, (b) representing another, (c) taking action, (d) promoting change, (e) accessing rights and benefits, (f) serving as a partisan, (g) demonstrating influence and political skills, (h) securing social justice, (i) empowering clients, (j) identifying with the client, and (k) establishing a legal basis. They defined social work advocacy as "the exclusive and mutual representation of a client(s) or a cause in a forum, attempting to systematically influence decision making in an unjust or unresponsive system(s)" (p. 65).

Fueled by the passion to serve humanity, social workers, social work academics, and students often launch programs to advocate for and empower disadvantaged and underprivileged populations, such as new immigrants; ethnic minorities; elderly persons; single parents; and persons with disabilities, physical, or mental illnesses (Carter, 2006; Linhorst, 2006; Pardeck, 2006; St. Angelo, 1982; Sullivan, Campbell, Angelique, Eby, & Davidson, 1994). The settlement housing, antipoverty legislation and campaigns in the United Kingdom and United States, and international movements among persons with disabilities or different sexual orientations are examples of advocacy efforts by social workers and human rights activists (Bateman, 2006; Haynes & Mickelson, 2006).

Advocacy in Macro Social Work

Motivation for advocacy in macro social work is an ethics of zero tolerance to injustice. The International Federation of Social Workers (IFSW) head office is located in Geneva, Switzerland. Social workers attempt to represent clients' interests through constant presence in the UN task forces and activities. Social workers also play important roles in the formation of international lobby, advocacy, and service organizations such as Amnesty International, UNICEF, Oxfam, and World Vision.

Social workers are instrumental in the establishment of national coalitions for underprivileged populations. Those who work with clients who are powerless and oppressed have to be creative in finding ways to help those clients move out of unjust social circumstances and situations. They form, together with clients, national organizations, such as the National Association of Child Advocates, the National Clearinghouse on Child Abuse and Neglect, the National Foster Parent Association, HungerWeb, and the Family Caregiver Alliance; they also initiate neighborhood projects to mobilize attitude change and collective actions for the betterment of communities (Pardeck, 2006; Stone, 1999).

In macro practice, social workers actively participate in research and problem analysis, community organization and development, service planning and delivery, research, policy advocacy, public mobilization, and collective action for building a better world for all. With the rapid transformation of communication in the Internet era, users and social workers take on international advocacy. The recent international collective actions against the World Trade Organization in different cities of the world were made possible by the Internet and e-mail systems. The wide Internet access and rapid dissemination of information are vital forces toward knowledge dissemination and democratization of collective participation. World Wide Web advocacy resources can easily be found in books on advocacy (Haynes & Mickelson, 2006, pp. 214–223; Schneider & Lester, 2001, appendix A).

Advocacy in Clinical Social Work

Advocacy in clinical social work is motivated by an ethics of care. Social workers do not tolerate second-class service for their clients or deprivation of essential social and human services for clients. Craig (1998) edited a book on advocacy, counseling, and mediation in social casework. There were interesting cases of advocacy for children, students, mental health consumers, health-care users, persons with disabilities, and persons going through traumatic experiences. Clinical social workers can take on an active role to speak on behalf of clients who do not have the ability to express their needs effectively. Peer and lay volunteers are also involved in advocacy especially in community acceptance of disadvantaged groups, public health education, and prevention of social problems or illnesses.

Social workers can advocate for or help users fight for their welfare rights (Bateman, 2006). Individuals can also advocate for themselves after being empowered by social workers. Working with people who are stressed by poor housing conditions and crime in the neighborhood, social workers help clients by advocating appropriate social policy or community infrastructural alterations that can reduce systematic oppression on the poor and disadvantaged. Critical social policies of safety, public hygiene, housing, poverty alleviation and relief, child labor, crime reduction, and education were targets of advocacy in the early twentieth century. Social workers crusaded for social reforms and protection of basic human rights for victims of injustice and exploitation.

Social workers have a duty and commitment to actively pursue social equality and equity for their clients. Not only should social workers connect their clients with necessary social and community resources so as to ensure their safety and optimal functioning, social workers should also fight for such resources if they are not available. As in the case of social workers who work with rape victims, the general awareness of the neighborhood crime statistics and safety on public transport and the streets cannot be ignored. A flexible and holistic awareness from case to policy aptitude is required of professional social workers to keep abreast of newly emerging social problems in contemporary society.

MOTIVATION AND ETHICS OF ADVOCACY

Before discussing strategies, skills, and tactics of advocacy, it is essential for us to review the motivation and ethical position of social workers in advocacy. What is the motivation behind each advocacy action and the philosophical assumptions of the ethical position?

Motivation for Advocacy

People make history. There are individuals who are altruistically driven and are committed to social justice and equity for all. Their commitment to building a better world for everyone becomes their motivation to bring about change. Unpleasant experiences of being oppressed, discriminated against, or unjustly treated can also be motivating forces behind advocacy. Likewise, trauma and suffering can motivate people to have a lifelong commitment to justice.

Experience of grief and loss can fuel a lifelong commitment to collective actions. For example, Mothers Against Drunk Driving (MADD) organized themselves into a strong lobby for educating young persons about the dangers of drinking and driving; they supported legislation against and tight monitoring of drunk driving. This group started as a group of mothers who had lost children in car accidents caused by drunk driving. By collaborating with the health and transport authorities, MADD has become internationally known for their efforts. Turning grief and sorrow into a motivating force is common among user-led advocacy groups. Social workers have to be self-reflective to ensure that the motivation behind each advocacy action is for an altruistic goal for all.

Ethics of Advocacy

In the process of advocacy, it is imperative that there be a commitment to a philosophical position that we call TECNA which stands for:

Trust the strength and ability of the people.

Establish realistic goals.

Celebrate even the smallest achievements.

Never give up because advocacy for the vulnerable is a life mission.

Appreciate that system change requires a long time.

Trust the strength and ability of the people. Trust the strength of the users and adopt an empowerment approach in advocacy. Chan, Ho, and Chow (2001) adopted a body-mind-spirit approach to empower divorced women to regain their sense of confidence and sense of efficacy in being single parents. Advocacy projects for women to promote women's health and well-being are highly effective (Carter, 2006; Chan, Chan, & Lou, 2002; Hung, Kung, & Chan, 2003). Through systematic training of advocates and users, strengths can be enhanced and new advocacy programs can be launched to exercise the human rights of disempowered groups (Baker, Leitner, & McAuley, 2001; Morgan & David, 2002).

Establish realistic goals. The coaching and support that peer advocates can offer cannot be replaced by professional services. The peer support and sharing from advocates can enhance self-confidence through a supportive relationship of unconditional acceptance. Set small, achievable goals in advocacy so that there are positive achievements to celebrate—small and realistic achievements and goals, such as compiling convincing background data and presenting it to a selected audience, or organizing human stories so that touching episodes can be shared with people in power. If these people can be touched by the stories, they will eventually make appropriate decisions.

Celebrate even the smallest achievements. Advocates can be friends who provide much needed social and emotional support. Cancer patients, battered women, mental patients, and frail elderly persons living alone all need support. Even if it is not possible to actually gain access to special services or get the legislation changed, users appreciate the efforts of advocates. Volunteers who are trained to serve as advocates get positive experience through helping persons in need (Davis, Salo, & Redman, 2001). Celebrate every achievement, no matter how small. Every achievement serves as a boost for the team to keep going. Policy and legislative change takes a long time; it is important to keep momentum going. Thus, setting small achievable goals and celebrating small successes is crucial.

Never give up because advocacy for the vulnerable is a life mission. There will be new problems and new frustrations among our clients and disadvantaged populations whom we serve. After one successful project, there will be another unjust issue that needs to be tackled.

Appreciate that system change requires a long time. Besides appreciating a lifelong commitment, it is also essential for us to understand that all change take time. Sometimes, changing a piece of legislation may take 10 years. As in the case of training more competent professionals, it may take more than a decade to ensure that there are sufficient jobs with ample opportunities for postgraduate training or specialization. System change takes time.

ADVOCACY INTERVENTION

Social workers need to use advocacy to defend the welfare rights and benefits of clients, irrespective of the type of service, organizational structure, and mode of service delivery. Advocacy is necessary because clients are often quiet or voiceless despite their suffering and pain. Advocacy aims at influencing policy and behavior of decision makers so as to benefit client groups whom social workers serve.

Levels of Change

There are five levels of influence that social workers want to achieve through advocacy. They are:

1. *Intrapersonal advocacy for fundamental values and ethics of clients.* At times, some clients may deliberately harm themselves and their loved ones. Social workers, especially clinical social workers, will have to advocate for the clients' best interests. By bringing to the clients an awareness of their own needs and self-abusive behavior,

social workers help clients to make decisions to take better care of themselves and their loved ones.

2. *Intrafamilial advocacy to communicate clients' needs and thoughts to other family members so that the family functioning and interactions can be modified and improved.* Family and intimate relationships are most important to our clients. Miscommunication and familial conflicts can be devastating to individuals. Changing behavior within the family can alter the dynamics and interaction in the family to enhance resilience and capacity of the family to deal with hardship.

3. *Interpersonal advocacy with teachers, school principals, employers, landlords, government officials, legislators, and persons in authority whose decisions can influence our clients.* When the client is a member of a group, collective actions can be adopted to bring about changes in mode of operation, rules, and regulations governing the interaction of clients and decision makers who have power over the clients.

4. *Communal and organizational advocacy for welfare rights, working hours, access to health care/housing/education/old age protection, bureaucratic procedures, and legislation so as to foster a supportive environment for all.* Culture and traditions as well as bureaucratic procedures can be oppressive, especially to disadvantaged groups such as women, children, persons with disabilities, the elderly, and legal or illegal immigrants. Advocacy aimed at changing organizational culture, rules, and regulations would benefit our clients whose needs are often not taken into consideration during service planning.

5. *National and international advocacy involves issues such as global warming, pollution and sustainability, fair trade, war and victimization, racial conflict and disharmony, migration, trafficking of women and children, and human rights and international justice in the midst of globalization.* Advocacy with a global perspective often is not restricted by national boundaries. Social workers may also participate in national and international advocacy movements.

Strategies of Advocacy

It is essential to have clear goals and objectives in advocacy so that the most appropriate strategies can be planned. Individuals may be motivated by the ethics of care or by the ethics of justice in altruistic actions. The commitment to justice and a high standard of caring is often the main force behind professional involvement in advocacy. Social workers who are dedicated to promoting a healthy and happy society cannot support substandard service provision and oppressive policies. Regardless of motivation, objectives have to be stated explicitly.

It is common for social workers to advocate through: (1) collaborative and persuasive strategies, (2) public education and campaign strategies, and (3) contesting and confrontational strategies. It is also possible for social workers to use more than one of these strategies.

Collaborative and Persuasive Strategies

Soft tactics of persuasion and collaboration can often lead to positive results in bringing in new resources, lubricating bureaucratic mechanisms to reduce inefficiencies and hurdles.

Advocates have to work with gatekeepers within the same organization or other service providers. People skills and effective communication, such as conveying the hardship and why a particular client deserves early attention and priority, are very helpful to get things done.

Storytelling, production of photo albums, person-to-person conversation and conference, and other written forms of advocacy can be useful in persuasion. Recruitment of professionals and decision makers into interest groups, charity organizations, task forces, and advisory committees are often effective tactics to cultivate a big supportive team and wide social networks. Friendly social relationships can dissolve unnecessary suspicions and get the bureaucracies to walk an extra mile.

Public Education and Campaign Strategies

Public education and campaigns can be described as a process of pedagogy of hope. Paulo Friere (1996) highlighted the importance of empowering pedagogy for the oppressed, powerless, and hopeless population so as to offer hope. It is certainly important for social workers to plant faith, confidence, hope, trust, and strength among their clients. The process of pedagogy has to be enjoyable, full of fun activities, with highly relevant contents and practical techniques. To be able to launch pedagogy of hope, advocates have to be filled with positive experiences in bringing about social change. Touching stories of personal growth and empowerment among clients and advocates should be carefully documented. With the use of multimedia, success stories and dreams can be disseminated.

The outcomes of advocacy are often good practices and new policies. Cultural change in society can be brought about through creating public expectations, affirming new norms of higher standards of service, and promoting best practices, both local and international. When the poor and underprivileged population is educated about ways to help themselves, their life circumstances can improve dramatically. When administrators and policy makers are aware of what has worked in other countries, if it will not add huge costs, such innovations can be tried.

In accordance with the five levels of advocacy, we need to be educated and change as well. Interpersonal relationships and interorganizational relationships can be altered by promoting creative innovations and good ideas that work elsewhere. Government departments and legislators often try to compare their own practice with established standards and innovations by their competitors or counterparts. Promoting competition among decision makers can be a soft tactic that can bring in new energy for change.

The establishment of new advocacy groups and nongovernment organizations can effect change. Charities and groups that serve persons whose issues may not attract public attention are good at institutionalizing change through an organizational approach. New forms of social problems have appeared, such as drug abusers, suicide and mental health problems, orphans as a result of HIV/AIDS, and abandoned and abused children. Investigation reports, commission studies, and pilot project results are commonly used advocacy mechanisms to raise public awareness. With enhanced public concern, new resources can be channeled into programs for dealing with these new problem areas.

Professional organizations can serve as platforms for advocacy. The National Association of Social Workers (NASW), the Council of Social Work Education (CSWE), the International Federation of Social Workers (IFSW), the International Council of Social

Welfare (ICSW), and the International Association of Schools of Social Work (IASSW) are good examples of national and international professional organizations that work to uphold a high professional standard and to advocate for the underprivileged. The Association of Oncology Social Workers (AOSW), for example, systematically organizes all their members to advocate for service standards and provision of psychosocial care for cancer patients in the United States.

Contest and Confrontational Strategies

Not all decision makers, politicians, or government officials can be easily persuaded. The use of peoples' power and confrontational strategies may be necessary in situations of gross discrimination and oppression. Collective action is a common social work tactic to empower the powerless and to advocate for equity of services. With social segregation and institutional barriers created to protect the rich and powerful, the hardships and sufferings of the poor are often invisible in society. Social workers who work with victims of violence, discrimination, abuse, asylum seekers, prisoners of war, drug addicts, new immigrants, and low-income populations will inevitably have to use collective action as a catalyst for social change. Creative collective actions, usually in collaboration with the media, can attract public concern and attention. When voters are keen to see that injustices and discriminations are being rectified, legislators are put under pressure to act in order to get reelected.

Collective action can also aim at altering the legislative process. It is important for social workers to be involved in ensuring that problems be dealt with through legislation to protect the feeble, the elderly, women and children under threats of violence, and so forth. With rapidly increasing family breakdowns and teenage pregnancies, the rights to custody and those of custodial visits have to be carefully balanced. Both tenants and landlords have rights that should be safeguarded. Legislative advocacy is also included in the field of psychosocial oncology. A large number of oncology and medical social workers are serving as patient advocacy managers. The AOSW organized toolboxes in advocacy for all of its members so that oncology social workers can be involved in advocating for psychosocial support services for cancer patients. Social workers represent the voiceless in our population; it is essential to get their views across and to ensure that their voices are heard.

Mixed and Multiple Strategies

There are social workers who define themselves by their action tactics such as community worker, agency administrator, health educator, caseworker, and group worker. One strategy may be more relevant under a certain circumstance, while another strategy may be more relevant under another circumstance. Thus, it is advisable that social workers be flexible; they may adopt dynamic and multiple strategies to achieve multilevel desired changes (see Table 8.1).

We can certainly utilize all five levels of appeal. Through touching stories, we can appeal to most of these levels. Television documentary and investigation reports in newspapers or magazines can use stories to appeal to the sense of justice and to cultivate intolerance of injustice. Following international standards and best practice, efficacy studies and

Table 8.1   Levels of Appeal, Focus and Strategies, and Tactics in Advocacy

Levels of Appeal	Focus and Strategies	Tactics in Advocacy
Emotions	Touch people's hearts and minds by appealing to their emotions, agitate public discontent, find sympathetic audiences, increase sense of we-feelings.	Touching stories, heart-breaking episodes to promote zero tolerance, heart-warming episodes to demonstrate that change is possible.
Senses	Use movement and senses to effect change to demonstrate body-mind connection.	Physical exercise can lead to joy, tasting bitter tea and looking for a sweet aftertaste.
Reason	Review of policy objectives, program evaluation, impact assessment, speak with authorities based on detailed research and investigation.	Surveillance, actuarial projects, numbers and statistics, prevalence and incidence rates, use professionals as spokespersons.
Public morality	Public interests, appeal to sense of injustice, cultivate public expectations on what is right and standard, advertise, community mobilization.	Compare local situation with international best practice, focus on basic rights and acceptable social standards.
Pragmatic interests	Convenience, cost benefit analysis, feasible financial and administrative arrangements.	Incentive systems, rewards, being aware of co-option, mobilization to fight against external conflict and to lead to internal cohesion.

cost-benefit analysis can help to convince the public and policy makers that change is relatively painless and benefits are obtainable.

Spirituality of Advocacy

Furman, Benson, Grimwood, and Canda (2004) proposed a model of advocacy based on spirituality of reciprocity rather than alienation. It is very easy for us to fall into the trap of polarization and targeting the person whom we want to influence as our opponent or enemy. "In this enemy mentality, . . . we exploit, damage, or diminish others in our efforts for victory on behalf of the client, we become exactly what we opposed. This is a sin of omission—committing acts of violence or dehumanization. . . . And in returning indignity and harm to that opponent, we become just like the enemy. This approach does not afford any possibility of reconciliation or mutual benefit" (p. 203).

We can complement advocacy with reciprocity by seeking mutual growth and benefit through creative solutions: "We respect all parties, even when we disagree or are in conflict. When conflict is unresolvable, we find ways to continue the conflict in a humane manner, or to forgive and move on. Mahatma Ghandi and Rev. Martin Luther King Jr. were excellent examples of social activist who strove to put this ideal into action . . . the ideals of compassion, forgiveness, reconciliation, service and nonviolence" (Furman et al., pp. 203–204).

In the reconciliatory style of advocacy, social workers treat clients, government officials, and opponents with respect and work toward win-win solutions in a persistent and collaborative manner. Principles and steps for win-win strategy for change in advocacy:

1. Try to bring all parties into a dialogue based on mutual respect and willingness to understand each other. Assume the altruistic nature of all parties involved.
2. Do not reduce people to problems or enemies. Get to know each other as fellow people. Try to establish a genuine and warm relationship so that collaboration is possible.
3. Identify shared vision, aspirations, and interests, common commitments and passion as well as different positions of all parties concerned. Service the most important principles and aspirations underlying their behavior and actions so that the deeper meaning can be established.
4. Feelings touch feelings. Help each party to articulate their feelings because the process will result in mutual appreciation from each other's point of view.
5. Create a platform so that different parties can brainstorm to discover alternative solutions in which all parties would feel a sense of ownership to proposed solutions and feel that they have won.
6. Accept a process of give and take. Stay in a continuous process of negotiation and communication. Select solutions that are ultimately acceptable to all parties.
7. Develop an action plan and roles involving cooperative teamwork by representatives of all parties.
8. Follow up implementation of the plan, evaluating success in terms of common interests and different standards.
9. Examine collaboratively the long-term impacts of the change and revise activities as necessary (Furman et al., 2004, p. 205).

The proposed spirituality of advocacy can be seen as a checklist for adopting a flexible and collaborative style of negotiation and advocacy. A rigid adherence to a fixed strategy is often not the most effective. A focus on finding win-win situations for all would guarantee success in the long run.

DISCUSSION AND IMPLICATIONS FOR SOCIAL WORK PRACTICE

There is increasing awareness of the rights of consumers, patients, and persons who are intellectually disadvantaged or mentally disordered. In the process of protecting rights, advocates and community support services are being developed. The rapid development of the Internet has empowered the general public by giving them easy access to information. Online self-help groups and support are transforming the lives of persons who are frail or have mobility difficulties, enabling them to reach persons who have similar problems. In the process of advocacy intervention, basic social work techniques in communication and taking care of players' emotions contribute to negotiation and conflict resolution. Emotions and reason are actually connected. The use of jokes, artistic activities, rituals, and celebrations can nurture positive emotions that can help in resolving conflicts and arriving at commonly desired goals (Maiese, 2006).

Barriers to Advocacy in Social Work

Brill (2001) identified a great discrepancy between what is stated in the NASW Code of Conduct and actual professional practice. There is less concern for social injustice, inequity, and oppression as the profession has claimed to care for the "population at risk." Professional social work practice, especially clinical services, is increasingly restricted by organizational constraints and guidelines that place emphasis on helping clients to accept limitations caused by insufficient resources instead of focusing on forming coalitions or networks that can bring about change in the unjust sociopolitical system. With increasing budget constraints, there is also a strong tendency for social workers to opt for new kinds of services that can be sustained by a fee-for-service mode of operation. In order to work with other professionals, social workers tend to adopt more collaborative strategies and are becoming more willing to compromise for the sake of gaining support from interdisciplinary teams. There may be an unintentional domination by professionals of the service users (Foucault, 1973).

There is a general misconception that social workers should avoid confrontational strategies and advocacy that will inevitably lead to conflict. Such uncomfortable feelings toward conflict may deter social workers from participating in advocacy to bring about necessary changes in social policies and legislature. The protection of whistle blowers and advocates in public organizations is usually not explicitly stated, and procedures for protection are far from elaborate. Many social workers feel torn between their commitment to protect clients and having to protect themselves. The lack of systematic training on advocacy and system change may be the reason why social workers feel so uncomfortable with advocacy and interacting with politicians and legislators (Haynes & Mickelson, 2006). Such hesitation to use advocacy for disadvantaged populations and empowerment of users has ignited debates in the profession for reform (Beresford & Harding, 1993; Dominelli, 1996). The profession is actively responding to these barriers and therefore many international advocacy organizations are being established. Social workers can form professional organizations, special interest groups, and watchdog groups so as to ensure that continuous advocacy efforts can be sustained.

Citizen and Political Advocacy

Social workers can participate in advocacy by taking on political roles (Hayes & Mickelson, 2006). As in the case of the second author, C. K. Law was a legislator for 6 years in the Legislative Council of Hong Kong. He conducted surveys of needs and analyzed population trends to generate a clear and persuasive demographic understanding of the citizens he served. In the process of systems change, he used case examples, statistics, evidence of practice overseas, and cost-benefit analysis to convince the administrators and other legislators in supporting new bills and budgets for new modes of services. Besides relying on public finance, he also established new nongovernment organizations to respond to new needs in the community. For example, he set up an organization to provide home phone and emergency services for elderly living alone. In 10 years of service, this organization grew into an effective social enterprise that served tens of thousands of senior citizens in Hong Kong. Advocacy at the macrolevel is closely linked to policy analysis, needs studies, and outcome and impact assessments of innovative projects, before lobbying and legislative reforms are possible.

Social workers have contributed to the training and support for self-advocacy in consumer movements, family members serving as advocates, peer advocacy, volunteer advocacy, and professional advocacy. Unlike international corporations who can hire professional political and legislative lobbyists, social workers often have to use mass education, mobilization, public morality, and grassroots mobilization to effect change. There are social workers who eventually become politicians themselves or join advocacy organizations to work full time on system change.

Social Worker as Targets of Advocacy

It would be wrong if we assume social workers are always on the side of the service users. At times, social workers may become targets of change by advocacy groups and service users. The social work bureaucracy may not be sensitive to the needs of clients all the time. Social workers and agency administrators are often operating under constraints of limited resources and overwhelming demands for services. As a result, social work administrators and policy makers may become targets of change in user-led advocacy actions. Thus, social workers have to not only learn to empower clients in advocacy, be involved in advocacy, but also to respond appropriately in case of being targeted by advocacy actions to change. The commitment to redistributive justice and constant critical review of service delivery is fundamental for social workers who must welcome communication with advocacy groups so as to constantly revitalize service delivery mechanisms and procedures. It is essential to be willing to get our hands and feet dirty, experience the painstaking process of gaining access to services, and be well grounded in a lifelong commitment to service.

CONCLUSION

Social workers are committed to finding ways to help improve services for the underprivileged and oppressed. Advocacy is part and parcel of professional social work practice, involving tasks, procedures, skills, and efficacy measures. Making all parties feel good about the process of advocacy can reduce resistance to change. Through mutual accommodation and collaborative and creative attitudes, the process of advocacy can be enjoyable as well. By working hard and playing hard, social workers can increase the elements of fun by sharing jokes, humor, and food. Only through a mutually gratifying process can we recreate meaning and nurture resilience, of ourselves, our target of change, and our clients.

REFERENCES

Anderson-Shaw, L., Schmidt, M. L., Elkin, J., Chamberlin, W., Benedetti, E., & Testa, G. (2005). Evolution of a living donor liver transplantation advocacy program. *Journal of Clinical Ethics*, *16*(1), 46–57.

Archer, D. (1996). The community health advocacy program: Changing the relations between communities and the medical campus. *Medicine and Health Rhode Island*, *79*(12), 420–421.

Armstrong, L. (2001). *It's not about the bike: My journey back to life*. London: Yellow Jersey Press.

Bailey, R., & Brake, M. (Eds.). (1975). *Radical social work*. London: Arnold.

Baker, P., Leitner, J., & McAuley, W. J. (2001). Preparing future aging advocates: The Oklahoma Aging Advocacy Leadership Academy. *Gerontologist*, *41*, 394–400.

Bastian, H. (1998). Speaking up for ourselves: The evolution of consumer advocacy in health care. *International Journal of Technology Assessment in Health Care*, *14*, 3–23.

Bateman, N. (2006). *Practising welfare rights*. London: Routledge.

Bell, M. E., & Goodman, L. A. (2001). Supporting battered women involved with the court system: An evaluation of a law school-based advocacy intervention. *Violence against Women*, *7*(12), 1377–1404.

Beresford, P., & Harding, T. (1993). *A call to change*. London: National Institute for Social Work.

Brewster, A. L., Milner, J. S., Mollerstrom, W. W., Saha, B. T., & Harris, N. (2002). Evaluation of spouse abuse treatment: Description and evaluation of the Air Force family advocacy programs for spouse physical abuse. *Military Medicine*, *167*(6), 464–469.

Brill, C. K. (2001). Looking at the social work profession through the eye of the NASW code of ethics. *Research on Social Work Practice*, *11*(2), 223–234.

Bybee, D. I., & Sullivan, C. M. (2002). The process through which an advocacy intervention resulted in positive change for battered women over time. *American Journal of Community Psychology*, *30*(1), 103–132.

Carter, C. S. (2006). *Social work and women's health: Resources on health empowerment, advocacy, and literacy*. Alexandria, VA: Council on Social Work Education.

Chan, C., Chan, Y., & Lou, V. (2002). Evaluating an empowerment group for divorced Chinese women in Hong Kong. *Research on Social Work Practice*, *12*(4), 558–569.

Chan, C., & Hills, P. (Eds.). (1993). *Limited gains: Grassroots mobilization and environmental management in Hong Kong*. Hong Kong: University of Hong Kong, Centre of Urban Planning and Environmental Management.

Chan, C., Ho, P. S. Y., & Chow, E. (2001). A body-mind-spirit model in health: An eastern approach. *Social Work in Health Care*, *34*(3/4), 261–282.

Chan, C., Ho, R. T. H., Fu, W., & Chow, A. Y. M. (2006). Turning curses into blessings': An eastern approach to psychosocial oncology. *Journal of Psychosocial Oncology*, *24*(4), 15–32.

Chan, T. H. Y., Ho, R. T. H., & Chan, C. L. W. (2007). Developing an outcome measure for meaning-making intervention with Chinese cancer patients. *Psycho-Oncology*, *16*, 1–8.

Christiana, J. M., Gilman, S. E., Guardino, M., Mickelson, K., Morselli, P. L., Olfson, M., et al. (2000). Duration between onset and time of obtaining initial treatment among people with anxiety and mood disorders: An international survey of members of mental health patient advocate groups. *Psychological Medicine*, *30*, 693–703.

Craig, Y. J. (Ed.). (1998). *Advocacy, counselling and mediation in casework*. Philadephia: Jessica Kingsley.

Davis, C., Salo, L., & Redman, S. (2001). Evaluating the effectiveness of advocacy training for breast cancer advocates in Australia. *European Journal of Cancer Care*, *10*, 82–86.

Dominelli, L. (1996). Deprofessionalizing social work. *British Journal of Social Work*, *26*(2), 153–175.

Doueck, H. J., Weston, E. A., Filbert, L., Beekhuis, R., & Redlich, H. F. (1997). A child witness advocacy program: Caretakers' and professionals' views. *Journal of Child Sexual Abuse*, *6*(1), 113–132.

Eng, C. (2002). Future consideration for improving end-of-life care for older persons: Program of All-inclusive Care for the Elderly (PACE). *Journal of Palliative Medicine*, *5*(2), 305–309.

Foucault, M. (1973). *The birth of a clinic*. London: Tavistock.

Friere, P. (1996). *The pedagogy of hope*. New York: Continuum.

Furman, L. D., Benson, P. W., Grimwood, C., & Canda, E. (2004). Religion and spirituality in social work education and direct practice at the millennium: A survey of U.K. social workers. *British Journal of Social Work*, *3*(6), 767–792.

Gillette, J. (1988). Advocacy and nursing: Implications for women's health care. *Australian Journal of Advanced Nursing, 6,* 4–11.

Gitlin, L. N., Miller, K. S., & Boyce, A. (1999). Bathroom modifications for frail elderly renters: Outcomes of a community-based program. *Technology and Disability, 10*(3), 141–149.

Grabenstein, J. D., Hartzema, A. G., Guess, H. A., Johnston, W. P., & Rittenhouse, B. E. (1992). Community pharmacists as immunization advocates: Cost-effectiveness of a cue to influenza vaccination. *Medical Care, 30*(6), 503–513.

Grant, T. M., Ernst, C. C., Streissguth, A. P., Phipps, P., & Gendler, B. (1996). When case management isn't enough: A model of paraprofessional advocacy for drug- and alcohol-abusing mothers. *Journal of Case Management, 5*(1), 3–11.

Haynes, K. S., & Mickelson, J. S. (Eds.). (2006). *Affecting change: Social workers in the political arena.* Boston: Pearson/Allyn & Bacon.

Ho, S. M. Y., Chan, C. L. W., & Ho, R. T. H. (2004). Post-traumatic growth in Chinese cancer survivors. *Psycho-Oncology, 13*(6), 377–389.

Hung, S. L., Kung, W. W., & Chan, C. L. (2003). Women coping with divorce in the unique sociocultural context of Hong Kong. *Journal of Family Social Work, 7*(3), 1–22.

Hunt, P., & Osher, T. (2006). *A guide to achieving the promise: Transforming mental health care in America through advocacy!* Available from www.tapartnership.org/Regions/RegionI_docs/A_Family_Guide_to_%20Achieving_the_Promise.pdf.

Illich, I. (1977). *Limits of medicine: Medical nemesis the expropriation of health.* Hammondsworth, England: Penguin.

Kapo, J., Morrison, L. J., & Liao, S. (2007). Palliative care for the older adult. *Journal of Palliative Medicine, 10*(1), 185–209.

Lee, K. F. (2002). Future end-of-life care: Partnership and advocacy. *Journal of Palliative Medicine, 5*(2), 329–334.

Lennox, N., Taylor, M., Rey-Conde, T., Bain, C., Boyle, F. M., & Purdie, D. M. (2004). Ask for it: Development of a health advocacy intervention for adults with intellectual disability and their general practitioners. *Health Promotion International, 19*(2), 167–175.

Lenton, S., & Phillips, M. (1997). Mobilizing public support for providing needles to drug injectors: A pilot advocacy intervention. *International Journal of Drug Policy, 8*(2), 101–110.

Linhorst, D. M. (2006). *Empowering people with severe mental illness: A practical guide.* New York: Oxford University Press.

Maiese, M. (2006). Engaging the emotions in conflict intervention. *Conflict Resolution Quarterly, 24*(2), 187–195.

Morgan, R. E., & David, S. (2002). Human rights: A new language for aging advocacy. *Gerontologist, 42,* 436–442.

Muelleman, R. L., & Feighny, K. M. (1999). Effects of an emergency department-based advocacy program for battered women on community resource utilization. *Annals of Emergency Medicine, 33*(1), 62–66.

Pardeck, J. T. (2006). *Children's rights: Policy and practice.* New York: Haworth Social Work Practice Press.

Schneider, R. L., & Lester, L. (2001). *Social work advocacy: A new framework for action.* Belmont, CA: Brooks/Cole.

Sommer, R. (1990). Family advocacy and the mental health system: The recent rise of the alliance for the mentally ill. *Psychiatric Quarterly, 61*(3), 647-668.

St. Angelo, D. (1982). Aging advocacy: The cozy triangle's hesitant angle. *Journal of Applied Gerontology, 1*(1), 115–125.

Stone, K. (1999). *To stand beside: The advocacy for inclusion training manual.* Canberra, Australia: Stone and Associates.

Sullivan, C. M. (2003). Using the ESID model to reduce intimate male violence against women. *American Journal of Community Psychology, 32*(3/4), 295–303.

Sullivan, C. M., & Bybee, D. I. (1999). Reducing violence using community-based advocacy for women with abusive partners. *Journal of Consulting and Clinical Psychology, 67*(1), 43–53.

Sullivan, C. M., Campbell, R., Angelique, H., Eby, K. K., & Davidson, W. S. (1994). An advocacy intervention program for women with abusive partners: Six-month follow-up. *American Journal of Community Psychology, 22*(1), 101–122.

Targum, S. D., Capodanno, A. E., Hoffman, H. A., & Foudraine, C. (1982). An intervention to reduce the rate of hospital discharges against medical advice. *American Journal of Psychiatry, 139*, 657–659.

Tauber, D., & Houston, J. (1977). The advocacy program. *Hospital Community Psychiatry, 28*, 360–361.

Wan, A. M. (2000). Battered women in the restraining order process: Observations on a court advocacy program. *Violence against Women, 6*(6), 606–632.

Winkleby, M. A., Feighery, E. C., Altman, D. A., Kole, S., & Tencati, E. (2001). Engaging ethnically diverse teens in a substance use prevention advocacy program. *American Journal of Health Promotion, 15*(6), 433–436.

Winkleby, M. A., Feighery, E. C., Dunn, M., Kole, S., Ahn, D., & Killen, J. D. (2004). Effects of an advocacy intervention to reduce smoking among teenagers. *Archives of Pediatric Adolescent Medicine, 158*(3), 269–275.

Womock, W. M., & Sata, L. S. (1975). The first year of a child advocacy project. *Hospital Community Psychiatry, 26*, 819–822.

Wong, D., & Chan, C. (1994). Advocacy on self-help for patients with chronic illness: The case of Hong Kong (Special volume in Self-Help Groups). *Prevention in Human Services, 11*(1), 17–139.

Chapter 9

CRISIS INTERVENTION

Kenneth R. Yeager, Albert R. Roberts, and Wendy Grainger

Crisis is a term that is used frequently. Pick up the daily newspaper and you will read something about the oil crisis, the AIDS crisis, or the citrus fruit crisis. While some usage of the word may be journalistic grandstanding, the fact remains that we live in a world in which sudden and unpredictable events are part of our existence. Every day, millions of people are negatively impacted by crisis-inducing events that they are not capable of resolving on their own. When such an event occurs, a crisis intervenor can provide assistance. Crisis intervenors come from a variety of backgrounds (e.g., mental health workers, police or fire responders, nurses, social workers, or physicians) and are skilled in addressing the various aspects of trauma. Crisis intervenors are called on to work in a variety of situations, including violent crime, natural disasters, traumatizing accidents, domestic violence, violence perpetrated upon children, the emergence of a severe mental illness, or the loss of a loved one to physical illness, accident, or suicide. The list of problems is long and varied.

Correspondingly, the crisis intervenor must tailor the approach to the problem to best meet the needs of the individual. What is the best way to achieve success? How does a professional provide a consistently effective approach to crisis intervention, regardless of the root event? One answer lies in Roberts' seven-stage model of crisis intervention. Using current best practices and an evidence-based framework, Roberts' model provides a consistent and comprehensive approach that providers can apply to a variety of crisis situations, and it is the focus of this chapter.

TRENDS IN CRISIS INTERVENTION

Since the publication of the first edition of *The Crisis Intervention Handbook: Assessment, Treatment and Research* (Roberts, 1991) there has been a remarkable increase in interest in the appropriate methods to address crisis response, intervention, management, and stabilization. Expanding media coverage of large-scale crises such as school shootings, terrorist attacks, and natural disasters have raised the awareness of both professionals and the general public of the need for rapid, effective approaches to all kinds of critical events. As a result, crisis intervention practices and programs have become increasingly sophisticated and complex.

Crisis intervention programs have mushroomed in the past 20 years. There are now over 1,400 grassroots crisis centers and units affiliated with the American Association of

Suicidology or local community mental health centers. There are also over 11,000 victim assistance programs, rape crisis programs, child sexual and physical abuse intervention programs, police-based crisis intervention programs, and programs for survivors and victims of domestic violence (Roberts, 2005). The method for treating acute mental health problems has also changed drastically. In 1990, the average length of stay (ALOS) for an inpatient mental health disorder was over 30 days. By 2005, the ALOS had shortened to 8 days. At the same time, inpatient medical hospitalizations shifted from inpatient treatment models to outpatient forms of treatment (Yeager & Roberts, 2005).

The shift to outpatient care led to the development of crisis centers that are pivotal in providing persons in crisis with access to crisis information, assessment, and intervention. Crisis center personnel routinely assist callers with problems such as depression, substance dependence, health issues, and victimization by providing initial information and, when appropriate, triage. In addition, the staff and resources of crisis hotlines, hospital emergency departments, and first responders have been thoroughly tested because of their round-the-clock availability, rapid access, and ability to provide immediate, yet temporary, assistance (Roberts, 2005).

To complicate matters, trends show that an increasing number of persons have no health-care insurance or the ability to pay for mental health services. Between 1998 and 2004, an annual percentage increase of 5.5% (95% confidence interval = 5.17% to 5.92%) of the population was unable to obtain medical care due to cost. When this kind of societal pattern emerges, crisis intervention centers become the access portals that link the caller to appropriate community resources.

PREVALENCE AND IMPACT OF EMOTIONAL TRAUMA

Mental Health and Trauma

A look at widely circulated information such as the *Surgeon General's Report,* the *U.S. Department of Health and Human Services Report* (1996), and updates from the *National Institute of Mental Health* (Drake et al., 2001) paints a broader picture of the impact of emotional trauma:

- 17% of the population has been victim to physical assault but not diagnosed with Posttraumatic Stress Disorder (PTSD).
- 40% of the population has *witnessed* serious violence.
- Among adolescents aged 12 to 17, an estimated 8% are victims of serious sexual abuse. Millions more suffer from a far less obvious condition, namely, the aftermath of trauma that stems from poor parental attachment in infancy.
- Mental disorders account for more than 15% of the overall burden of disease, slightly more than the burden associated with all forms of cancer and second only to cardio-vascular disease. One in five Americans is affected by mental illness.
- Eleven million Americans become depressed every year. Twice as many women as men suffer depression.
- Twelve million Americans under age 18 suffer from some form of mental illness, with lifetime prevalence rates as high as 17%.

- More than 16 million adults in the United States aged 18 to 54 have anxiety disorders.
- The number of Americans encountering suicidal depression some time in their lives has increased from under 10% for baby boomers and their parents to as much as 25% for the post-baby boomer generations.
- The United States is the world's largest market for antidepressants with annual sales estimated at $7.2 billion. However, these medications are not reducing mental health problems. There is a 50% chance of recurrence after an individual's first episode of depression, 70% after the second, and 95% after the third.

Crisis Response and Crisis Intervention

A crisis can be defined as a period of psychological disequilibrium experienced as a result of a hazardous event or situation and constitutes a significant problem that cannot be remedied by using familiar coping strategies. The main cause of a crisis is an intensely stressful, traumatic, or hazardous event that is accompanied by two other conditions: (1) the individual perceives the event as the cause of considerable upset and/or disruption, and (2) the individual is unable to resolve the disruption by previously used coping methods (Roberts, 2005).

These two factors combine with the event to create an upset in the steady state of the individual experiencing the crisis. While all crises are unique to the individual, each crisis episode has similar components. Episodes are usually comprised of five components: (1) a hazardous or traumatic event, (2) a vulnerable state, (3) a precipitating factor, (4) an active crisis state, and (5) the resolution of the crisis (Roberts, 2005).

A crisis reaction refers to the acute stage, which usually occurs shortly following the hazardous event. An individual may experience various forms of reactions during the acute phase, including, but not limited to confusion, shock, disbelief, feelings of helplessness, hopelessness, hurt, loss, shame, shock, and anger. There is often an emergent state of depression or, in lesser severity, an impact on the level of self-confidence and self-esteem. A person who has recently experienced a crisis may appear confused and disorganized. They may experience an agitated, anxious, or volatile state. This stage is when the individual is most receptive to assistance and is generally aware that usual coping mechanisms are not going to be sufficient to resolve the crisis they have just experienced (Golan, 1978; Roberts, 2005).

Crisis intervention provides both challenges and opportunities for the clinician and the patient. The individual is challenged to apply new coping strategies. The clinician is challenged to help the patient maintain the level of motivation and risk-taking necessary to sustain the patient's acceptance of new and challenging tasks to aid in recovery. According to Roberts and Dziegielewski (1995), crisis clinicians are encouraged to examine psychological and situational crises in terms of "both danger and opportunity." The aftermath of a crisis often results in a significant change in the individual's ability to function. Immediate, effective crisis intervention can minimize the amount of psychological distress experienced by the individual and support optimal functioning during the time of crisis. The use of Roberts' seven-stage model facilitates crisis resolution, cognitive mastery, and personal growth at a critical time (Yeager & Roberts, 2005).

Helping a person in crisis requires an exceptional amount of emotional sensitivity, active listening skills, and the ability to effectively communicate genuine caring and understanding, while, at the same time, gathering information to facilitate effective decision making throughout intervention, assessment, and treatment. The clinician is challenged to rapidly establish rapport with an individual who may be emotionally guarded and, at best, marginally available psychologically for clinical interventions. The structure provided by Roberts provides the framework for establishing processes applied to the individual case in a systematic manner to support the individual's coping skills.

HISTORICAL BACKGROUND

Physicians emphasized the significance of a hazardous life event as far back as 400 BC Roberts (2005) notes that Hippocrates defined a crisis as a sudden state that gravely endangers life. However, the emergence of a comprehensive theory on the impact of crisis did not emerge until early in the twentieth century. Among the first to provide crisis services was the National Save-a-Life Center in New York City, which focused on suicide prevention. The current approach to crisis intervention emerged in the 1940s and was influenced primarily by the work of Erich Lindemann and, later on, by Gerald Caplan.

Lindemann and his associates were employed by Massachusetts General Hospital in Boston, Massachusetts. On the night of November 28, 1942, approximately 1,000 persons, many of whom were preparing to go overseas on military duty, were at the Coconut Grove nightclub in Boston when a tragic fire erupted that took the lives of 492 persons. Many more were seriously injured. Evidence indicates an employee using a lighted match to provide light while he changed a lightbulb ignited flammable decorations that rapidly spread the fire. In the aftermath, it was discovered that the two revolving doors at the main entrance had bodies stacked four and five deep (Lindemann, 1944).

Lindemann and colleagues based their emerging crisis theory on observations of the acute and delayed reactions of the survivors and grief-stricken relatives and friends of the victims. They noted that many individuals experiencing acute and delayed responses to grief and trauma demonstrated five related reactions:

1. Somatic distress.
2. Preoccupation with the image of the deceased.
3. Guilt.
4. Hostile reactions.
5. Loss of patterns of conduct.

Lindemann's observations led to an increased understanding of what became known as *grief work*. His major finding was that the duration of the grief reaction appeared to be dependent on the degree to which the bereaved person was able to conduct her or his mourning. In general, it was believed that grief work included actions toward emancipation from the deceased, adjustment to living within the environment from which the loved one is now absent, and developing new relationships. Lindemann's work taught us that people need to be encouraged to permit time for mourning in order to effectively respond to the loss and adjust to life without their loved one. Further, negative outcomes of crises develop if the normal grieving process is delayed. Lindemann's work was also applied in interventions with World War II veterans who were suffering from "combat neuroses" and bereaved family members.

Caplan (1964), who was also affiliated with Massachusetts General Hospital and Harvard School of Public Health, expanded on the groundbreaking work of Lindemann throughout the 1940s and 1950s. Caplan explored a variety of developmental crisis situations, for example, accidental and health-related crisis and death. He was the first to link the concept of homeostasis to crisis intervention. In 1961, he noted that crisis is an upset of a steady state in which the individual encounters an obstacle (usually to significant life goals) that cannot be overcome through traditional problem-solving activities. Caplan noted there was a homeostatic balance between affective and cognitive experience for each individual. Psychological functioning is threatened when opposing physiological, psychological, or social forces disrupt the balance. A crisis state will ensue if these forces overcome an individual's innate coping skill. Caplan further defined a crisis as an individual response to "stimuli which signals danger to a fundamental need satisfaction . . . and the circumstances are such that habitual problem-solving methods are unsuccessful within the time span of past expectation for success" (p. 39). Additionally, four stages of crisis reaction were described:

1. The initial rise of tension that comes from the precipitating event.
2. An increased level of disruption to daily living as the individual is unable to resolve the crisis quickly.
3. The potential emergence of depressive or other primary mental health issues, that if unattended result in stage 4.
4. A complete mental collapse or acute mental health episode *or* an alternative of partial resolution of the crisis, resulting in functioning for extended periods of time with diminished emotional skills and responses.

J. S. Tyhurst (1957) contributed to the crisis knowledge base through his study of transition states; for example, migration, retirement, civilian disaster, and the like. Based on his studies of individual patterns in response to community disaster, Tyhurst concluded that there are three overlapping phases, each with it own unique manifestation of stress:

1. A period of impact.
2. A period of recoil.
3. A posttraumatic period of recovery.

Tyhurst recommended state-specific intervention that focused on reinforcing the relationship network and not removing persons experiencing transitional crisis from their life situation.

L. Rapoport (1962) expanded on the concept of disruption of the homeostasis by indicating that the "upset of a steady state" (p. 212) placed the individual in a hazardous condition. The crisis situation results in a problem frequently perceived as a threat, loss, or challenge and is linked to three interrelated factors that function to create or exacerbate the crisis:

1. A hazardous event.
2. A threat to life goals.
3. An inability to respond with adequate coping mechanisms.

Rapoport was the first to clinically conceptualize and apply a crisis intervention process. She asserted that persons experiencing crisis must have immediate access to the crisis worker stating, "A little help, rationally directed and purposefully focused at a strategic time, is more effective than more extensive help given at a period of less emotional accessibility" (Rapoport, 1967, p. 38). Additionally, Rapoport connected the process of establishing a primary diagnosis during the initial crisis assessment combined with conveying a sense of hope and optimism to the victim, in an effort to support the individual in the development of new problem-solving skills, along with clearly delineated goals and tasks. The result was the establishment of the initial working structure between the client and the therapist to resolve a crisis. Parad added the concept that the crisis is not the situation itself; rather, it is the person's perception of the event combined with the individual response to the situation that dictates the degree of reaction (Parad, 1971, p. 197).

N. Golan (1978) echoed the concepts set forth by Rapoport. Golan concluded that a person is frequently more amenable to suggestions and change during a state of active crisis. Golan noted that intensive, brief, appropriately focused treatment when the client is motivated produces more effective change than in long-term therapy when motivation and emotional accessibility may be lacking.

ROBERTS' SEVEN-STAGE PRACTICE MODEL FOR CRISIS INTERVENTION

Several practice models have emerged for crisis intervention work, which build on and synthesize the works of Caplan (1964), Rapoport (1962, 1967), Parad (1971), and Golan (1978). Each of the models focus on therapeutic techniques designed to resolve immediate problems and emotional conflicts within a time-limited, goal-directed framework. Crisis-oriented treatment is designed to minimize the need for long-term treatment by capitalizing on the immediate emotional crisis and motivation that is present as a result of the crisis, thus providing optimal impact in a brief, time-limited approach. Roberts' (1991) seven-stage model of crisis intervention has been utilized for helping persons in acute psychological and situational crisis. Roberts' model has been tested and applied for 15 years with successes in numerous venues, including, but not limited to addictions, psychiatric treatment, child welfare, domestic violence, battered women, school crisis health, and community crisis (Roberts, 2005, p. 20). The seven stages are:

1. Plan and conduct a thorough assessment (including lethality, dangerousness to self or others, and immediate psychosocial needs).
2. Make psychological contact, establish rapport, and rapidly establish the relationship (conveying genuine respect for the client, acceptance, reassurance, and a nonjudgmental attitude).
3. Examine the dimensions of the problem in order to define it (including the "last straw" or precipitating event).
4. Encourage an exploration of feelings and emotions.
5. Generate, explore, and assess past coping attempts.
6. Restore cognitive functioning through implementation of an action plan.
7. Follow up and leave the door open for booster sessions 3 and/or 6 months later.

Discussion

Plan and Conduct a Thorough Assessment

Experienced clinicians frequently complete Stages 1 and 2 concurrently. However, it is most important to assess the individual's risk for harm to self or others and the potential for rescue. The first and foremost task for the crisis intervenor is gathering basic information related to individual needs, experiences, perceptions, and plans to determine potential risk. Counselors, social workers, physicians, psychologists, and nurses are likely to encounter a full range of self-destructive individuals in crisis, including those who have taken potentially lethal actions to end their lives. Clinical staff dealing with crisis calls, or individuals in crisis centers or emergency rooms, often face cases where there is "some" potential danger for harm, but the individual is not forthcoming with enough information to determine the level of risk. In these situations, it is important to evaluate the patient in the following areas:

1. Need for medical attention (e.g., drug overdose, suicide attempt, or victim of domestic violence).

2. Examination of general thoughts, specific plans, actions, or gathering of items that suggests a plan of self-harm. Ask about the patient's age, recent major life events, physical health, history of psychiatric diagnosis, family history, history of substance abuse, sexual orientation, previous attempts at self-harm, and personal beliefs related to self-harm. (Note: Risk factors for self-harm do not necessarily equal potential for self-harm, but must be carefully considered against environmental protective factors such as positive outlook on life, cultural beliefs that view suicide as negative, presence of positive coping skills, presence of positive social supports, and a positive relationship with family members. (For a complete assessment of at-risk patients see the American Psychiatric Association Practice Guidelines for the Assessment and Treatment of Patients with Suicidal Behaviors.)

3. Determine if any children are involved and are in danger.

4. Does the victim require emergency transportation to a hospital or shelter?

5. Is the crisis caller under the influence of alcohol or drugs?

6. Determine the potential for domestic violence and if there are any violent persons living in the residence. (Roberts, 2005, pp. 21–22)

Make Psychological Contact, Establish Rapport, and Rapidly Establish the Relationship

Stage 2 involves the initial contact between the professional and the patient. The priority of the clinician is to rapidly establish rapport with the individual based on interactions that communicate respect for, and acceptance of, the person seeking assistance. In most cases, it is helpful to engage active listening skills. Taking time to hear and assess the individual's story, smiling, questioning, and coming from a position of interest are all important factors in establishing rapport with the individual experiencing crisis. Frequently, persons seeking assistance require assurance that they are going to be able to cope with the issues they are facing. Providing assurance and examples of approaches to help the person to stabilize assist the person in feeling he or she has "come to the right place" to address individual needs. It is important to remember that persons in crisis feel as if they are the first to have ever faced this issue or situation. It is essential that the care provider offer assurance of the potential for recovery (Roberts, 2005, p. 22).

Examine the Dimensions of the Problem in Order to Define It

It is useful to identify contributing factors to the crisis event. Questions that assist the clinician in understanding the patient's experience are paramount. For example, ask a leading question, such as, "What is it that made today different from other difficult days you have experienced?" Examine the "last straw" or precipitating event. Ask the patient about previous coping methods, previous experiences with health-care providers, previous experiences with treatments, and the success or failure of prior hospitalizations or therapeutic interactions. Use open-ended questions to examine the dimensions of the problem. Focus on the "now and how" of resolving the crisis rather than what has happened (Roberts, 2005, p. 23).

Encourage an Exploration of Feelings and Emotions

Stage 4 is closely related to Stage 3, particularly when focusing on the precipitating event. It is presented here as a separate step because some therapists might be tempted to gloss over it in an effort to complete the assessment in a timely manner. Effective assessment takes time. Simply asking a few "key" questions cannot sum up the assessment of the situation. The intervenor must permit the client to express feelings and emotions in an accepting and supportive, confidential, nonjudgmental manner. Frequently, important clues for stabilizing the patient begin to emerge (Roberts, 2005, p. 23).

Generate, Explore, and Assess Past Coping Attempts

Most youth and adults have established coping mechanisms. Some are more effective, some less effective, and some are completely inadequate or maladaptive. For example, substance abuse is frequently considered to be a common maladaptive coping mechanism. It is important to work with the patient to assess the presence of both positive and negative coping attempts and their relative application to the current crisis situation. The skilled clinician will be able to formulate an effective treatment plan building on the successful experiences of the client, working from a strengths perspective. Consider the use of solution-focused therapy at this stage of crisis intervention. Solution-focused therapy emphasizes working with existing client strengths to establish a pathway toward resolving the crisis through a series of agreed-on steps between the clinician and the patient. Both strengths perspective and solution-focused therapy view the patient as resilient. Both methods offer a two-pronged approach that is an effective tool for assessing past coping mechanisms that were effective and can again be applied to empower the patient to assume an active problem-solving role in the recovery process (Roberts, 2005, pp. 23–24).

Restore Cognitive Functioning through Implementation of an Action Plan

Integral to the crisis intervention process is the restoration of cognitive stability, which involves three phases:

> *Phase 1:* Establishment of a realistic understanding of what happened and what led to the crisis. Frequently, details surrounding the crisis are unclear. Establishing a clear understanding of what happened, how and why it happened, persons involved, and extenuating circumstances establishes the foundation on which cognitive mastery will be established.

Phase II: Evaluate the patient's understanding of the events' specific meanings. Crisis episodes tend to shatter an individual's future outlook. In an instant, everything the patient had understood as the pathway to the future can actually or appear to be uncertain. Examining how the situation conflicts with his or her expectations, life goals, and belief systems will assist the individual in understanding and addressing current reality. Resist the temptation to identify the patient's irrational beliefs, but rather permit the client to discover cognitive distortions and/or irrational beliefs.

Phase III: Restructure or replace irrational beliefs. This phase frequently is completed in individual sessions, but can include homework assignments, journaling assignments, support groups, or other processes that assist the patient in formalizing thoughts and beliefs related to the crisis situation (Roberts, 2005, pp. 24–25).

Follow Up

Closing sessions provide the client with opportunities to explore the progress they have made in therapy. Patients can examine the support systems available to them and discuss with group members how they can access ongoing support within the community. Offer follow-up sessions to support ongoing recovery processes. Make patients aware of potential trigger events, anniversaries of the crisis, and other high-risk times that may require additional support (Roberts, 2005, p. 25).

SUMMARY OF CURRENT EVIDENCE-BASED INFORMATION ON CRISIS INTERVENTION

Remarkable strides have been made within the past decade to clarify knowledge, practices, and processes supporting evidence-based approaches to crisis intervention. One simplistic, but straightforward approach to understanding the increase in readily available knowledge related to evidence-based crisis intervention is to begin searching on the Internet. A recent Google search for "Evidence-Based Crisis Intervention" retrieved 1,180,000 sites. Certainly, this is a broad brushstroke.

Using a sharper tool of focus, the next sample, which queried PsycINFO for both psychology and evidence-based appearing together in an abstract, located 70 hits. A quick substitution of "social work" for "psychology" returned 156 hits. While this approach may be a rather crude measure to estimating a field's attention level to a topic, it does provide a basic framework for understanding. It is increasingly clear that social work is committed as a profession to improving understanding, implementation, and measurement of evidence-based approaches.

As one continues to refine the search, a clearer picture emerges regarding the advancements of evidence-based approaches. Searching the Cochrane Database of Systematic Reviews for Social Work displayed 69 records from the fourth quarter of 2006. The wide variety of areas where knowledge is expanding to address evidence-based social work include, but are not limited, to:

- Crisis intervention for people with severe mental illnesses.
- Validation therapy for dementia.

- Vitamin E for neuroleptic-induced tardive dyskinesia.
- Therapy-based rehabilitation services for stroke patients at home.
- Telephone follow-up, initiated by a hospital-based health professional, for postdischarge problems in patients discharged from hospital to home.
- Supported housing for people with severe mental disorders.
- Specialist outreach clinics in primary care and rural hospital settings.
- Services for reducing duration of hospital care for acute stroke patients.
- Psychosocial interventions for depression in dialysis patients.
- Psychosocial combined with agonist maintenance treatments versus agonist maintenance treatments alone for treatment of opioid dependence.
- Psychological therapies for people with Borderline Personality Disorder.
- Preventing occupational stress in health-care workers.
- Pharmacotherapy for Posttraumatic Stress Disorder.
- Therapy for social, emotional, and behavioral problems in youth aged 10 to 17. [Systematic Review] Cochrane Developmental, Psychosocial and Learning Problems Group.
- Media-based behavioral treatments for behavioral problems in children.
- Interventions for treating depression after stroke.
- Individual behavioral counseling for smoking cessation.
- Independent living programs for improving outcomes for young people leaving the care system.
- Home visits during pregnancy and after birth for women with an alcohol or drug problem.
- Hospital at home for acute exacerbations of chronic obstructive pulmonary disease.
- Effectiveness and cost effectiveness of counseling in primary care.
- Cognitive-behavioral training interventions for assisting foster careers in the management of difficult behavior.
- Cognitive-behavioral interventions for children who have been sexually abused.
- Case management for people with severe mental disorders.
- Provider training and experience for people living with HIV/AIDS.
- Parenting programs for improving the parenting skills and outcomes for incarcerated parents and their children.
- Multidisciplinary rehabilitation interventions for joint replacement.

Examination of the data indicates there are great strides being made in increased awareness, knowledge base, application issues, integration of services, and needs management across time. It is clear to see by review of the data that evidence-based practice (EBP) is a world-wide undertaking, encompassing not only a great diversity of subjects but a wide diversity of persons, situations, and innovative approaches to care for persons experiencing physical health, mental health, social, and behavioral problems.

Many new concepts for care have emerged from the EBP initiative. The most important is the use of EBP to improve care through application of the best available evidence. However, a close second is the concept of an integrative care approach. An integrative approach is one in which all disciplines interact to provide the best care to meet the individualized needs and preferences of the patient who presents in crisis. Current evidence has shown that rapid responses to trauma lead to more rapid recoveries and offer opportunities for practitioners to collaborate in ways not previously imagined.

One of the areas experiencing increasing integration is the crossroads of physical and mental health. Evidence-based practice guidelines for the treatment and management of common mental disorders were first introduced in the 1990s. These guidelines described effective treatments for mental illnesses commonly seen within the primary health-care setting (Roberts & Yeager, 2004; Schulberg, Katon, Simon, & Rush, 1998). However, mental illness is not neatly packaged as a single diagnosis. Frequently, depression is complicated by substance dependence. Additionally, many persons who present with co-occurring physical and mental illness also report additional somatic symptoms. Despite the guidelines and other diagnostic aids, as many as 75% of primary care providers indicate that they feel unprepared to address co-occurring diseases within the primary care setting (Wiest et al., 2002).

Evidence-based techniques can fill this knowledge gap and direct the implementation of collaborative care between medical and behavioral health providers. One group of studies has focused on "stepped care." Stepped care begins in the primary care office with low-intensity interventions and steps up the resistant patient to more intensive levels of care as necessary (Katon, Von Korff, Lin, & Simon, 2001; Katon et al., 1995, 1996, 1997; Von Korff & Tiemens, 2000).

Current literature report several studies that demonstrate the potential for utilization of collaborative care models to improve patient compliance, outcome, and communication among care providers, patients, and families in crisis. Still unclear is the exact framework and/or nature of these collaborative efforts. Within the literature, there appears to be a range of what can best be referred to as "co-located services." Best practice models are recommending a "continuum of collaboration" between a variety of care providers, such as physicians, psychiatrists, and nurses, yet the degree to which collaboration actually occurs within current health-care structures remains to be seen. However, as evidence increases and systems evolve over time, there will emerge a new model of service delivery that will encompass a variety of disciplines working to resolve the critical issues of the individual in carefully constructed, evidence-based interventions (Badamgarav et al., 2003; Schoenbaum, Miranda, Sherbourne, Duan, & Wells, 2004; Schoenbaum et al., 2002; Simon et al., 2001, 2002; Von Korff, Unutzer, Katon, & Wells, 2001; Wagner, Austin, & Von Korff, 1996).

Another key component of evidence-based crisis intervention is the utilization of technology. Since 1996, systematic reviews prepared and maintained by the Cochrane Collaboration have been published in the Cochrane Library, along with bibliographic and quality-assessed material on the effects of health-care interventions submitted by others. Cochrane reviews have been published in the Cochrane Database of Systematic Reviews. These reviews are regularly updated as information becomes available and in response to comments and criticism. The reviews are now widely regarded as being of better quality, on average, than their counterparts in print journals (Roberts & Yeager, 2004). For evidence to be effective, technology must be available to deliver decision support. The emergence of decision support programs like the Cochrane Collaboration signifies remarkable progress in the application of evidence-based practices in all areas of crisis intervention.

As technology grows so does the complexity of analysis. Decision-support and technical groups are growing rapidly. Evidence-based technology centers have been established in numerous areas of government, university, and private business sectors, such as:

- Blue Cross and Blue Shield Association, Technology Evaluation Center
- Duke University
- Agency for Healthcare Research and Quality
- Johns Hopkins University
- McMaster University
- Oregon Health & Science University
- RTI International, University of North Carolina
- Southern California
- Tufts University, New England Medical Center
- University of Alberta, Edmonton, Alberta, Canada
- University of Minnesota, Minneapolis, MN
- University of Ottawa, Ottawa, Canada

The formation of decision-support systems and the means to access them is an important component to expanding evidence-based approaches to treatment. The process is one of a logical sequence of events:

1. As information on EBP becomes readily available, care providers are more likely to incorporate evidence-based approaches and protocols.
2. Inclusion of an interdisciplinary approach to crisis situations will move the knowledge base forward through the examination of outcomes, thus closing the loop.
3. New evidence will be examined and weighed against previously established best evidence.

Additional sources for the advancement of EBPs are the establishment of practice-based research groups who are applying evidence-based approaches following a crisis. It is important to note that evidence-based knowledge development is not a one-way street flowing from the scientific bench to the crisis situation. The practitioner has an equally important role in assessing and understanding the applicability of evidence in the management of crisis situations. Practitioners serve an important role of not only testing the protocols, but also improving the evidence as applied to crisis situations.

As you read and learn more about evidence-based approaches, you may find yourself wanting more information about your specific area of expertise, such as Police Crisis Intervention Teams (CIT), Crisis Intervention with HIV patients, or Children's Protective Services Crisis Intervention. Here is an exercise to try:

1. Stop for just a moment and think about what you have just read. Then ask yourself, "Can I replicate the process described?" "Can I formulate a question in my area of interest that I want answered?"
2. Next Google the area of interest. Look at the information available. Appraise the level of evidence you find.

3. Now refine your search in a more comprehensive manner by examining the Cochrane Collaboration, or InfoPOEMS, or any other evidence-based resource.
4. Now ask yourself the following questions:

    "Does the information apply to my patient or problem of interest?"

    "Does the information influence my approach to treatment?"

    "How does the information assist in diagnosis?"

    "Is there information about risk factors?"

    "Is there a comparison of treatment approaches?"

    "Can I use the information to develop a target for outcome measurement?"
5. Consider what information is still needed and search for those answers. Keep completing the process until you feel comfortable with your answers.
6. Review your findings with your team, colleagues, or supervisor.

While it is virtually impossible to cover all aspects of evidence-based crisis intervention within a single chapter, it is possible to provide resources that will assist you in developing the skills to conduct your own search for evidence. As we have said previously, crisis is a very broad term. The best approach is to provide a road map that gives each provider the means to answer his or her own questions.

The information on crisis intervention is growing and changing daily. Evidence-based crisis intervention is a field in transition. Best practices exist in some areas but are absent in others. The challenge to the clinician is to develop and evaluate the evidence in a systematic method, apply the information in his or her practice, and measure the outcomes to further inform yourself and others. As with any new methodology, barriers exist that impact establishment and acceptance. Commonly encountered challenges and possible remedies are discussed next.

CHALLENGES IN IMPLEMENTING EVIDENCE-BASED PRACTICE

The emergence of the evidence-based approach has presented challenges across the physical and behavioral health continuum. Some of the major challenges to implementing evidence-based practices for crisis intervention are discussed next.

Consumer Information Overload

We live in a scientific age in which new medical and social science advances are reported almost daily. The pace of change is breathtaking. Consumers are bombarded with information about medications, surgeries, alternative health-care approaches, and psychological interventions that are "guaranteed" to ease their burden and enhance their lives each time they open their e-mail, postal box, turn on the TV, or surf the Internet. Individuals are faced with choices of herbal remedies, gadgets, intrusive physical interventions, and intriguingly named psychological treatments to manage everything from life-threatening illness to unappealing aspects of their appearance. People naturally apply information they hear to their problems and seek clarification from their care providers. This need for clarification usually comes in the form of a question like ... "I saw this product on television; the ad said I should talk to you." Or, "I read about this in a magazine." It is the responsibility of the care provider to keep up with innovations, but what is the best method of evaluation? The answer: evidence-based approaches (Roberts & Yeager, 2004).

Professional Information Overload

Professionals are flooded with an overwhelming volume of information on a daily basis. Rosenthal (2004) estimates the average professional must read an estimated 19 articles per day in his or her field just to keep up with the advances in clinical research (p. 20). The process required to do a thorough evidence-based search only adds to the burden. This process is generally defined as having five well-defined steps (Rosenthal, 2004; Sackett, Rosenberg, Gray, Haynes, & Richardson, 1996):

1. Format structured, clear, and answerable clinical questions about a patient's problem or information needed.
2. Search the literature for relevant clinical articles that might answer the question.
3. Conduct a critical appraisal on the selected research articles and rank the evidence for its validity and usefulness (clinical applicability).
4. Formulate and apply a clinical intervention based on the useful findings, or "best evidence."
5. Conduct clinical audits to determine if the protocol was implemented properly (identify issues/problems).

Lack of Standardized Instruments

While the recurring emphasis in the literature is on assessment, there is a notable lack of standardized instruments with strong psychometric properties available to practitioners (Aguilera, 1998; Kanel, 1999; Roberts & Greene, 2002; Yeager & Roberts, 2005). Few studies have tested intervention models based on crisis theory (Aguilera, 1998; Kanel, 1999; Roberts, 1996; Slaikeu, 1984). Measurement instruments designed to objectively assess the degree of an individual's crisis state are not available (Corcoran & Roberts, 2000). The scales that have been developed are not capable of measuring the magnitude of a crisis state from the client's viewpoint (Roberts & Lewis, 2001). The science of EBP frequently does not transition well from the "bench to the bedside." Strategies are needed that will connect trusted psychometric measures to real-world referents and eliminate arbitrariness.

Effectiveness Training and Skill Set

Another challenge to implementation of EBPs in crisis intervention relates to workforce training. The objective of the National Survey of Psychotherapy Training in Psychiatry, Psychology, and Social Work was to determine the amount of evidence-based treatment taught in accredited training programs in these areas to identify whether the training was elective or required and presented as didactic (coursework) or clinical supervision. The major findings were as follows:

- Training programs offered a range of psychotherapies (mostly non-evidence-based practice [non-EBP]) as electives and often did not require the gold standard of didactic and clinical supervision for EBP. However, more recently, training programs have been seen offering a higher percentage of EBP courses that meet the training gold standard.
- The two disciplines with the largest number of students and the emphasis on training for clinical practice (PsyD and MSW) required the lowest percentage of gold standard training in EBP. Although all of the disciplines offered elective courses in a range of psychotherapies, including EBP, the required clinical supervision training was largely in non-EBP, particularly in psychiatry. Among the EBPs, cognitive behavioral therapy (CBT) remained the best disseminated among all the disciplines. In psychiatry, this was likely due to the psychiatry accreditation board CBT requirement. Even though psychiatry reported the highest percentage of obstacles to EBP, more than 90% of the psychiatry residency programs were complying. Accreditation requirements, rather than voluntary changes, seemed to be effective in changing practice.
- The PhD clinical psychology programs were the most positive about EBP. This acceptance may be due to the success of CBT, which was developed in close collaboration with PhD psychologists who were often involved in the trials. Twenty percent of psychiatry training directors mentioned that EBP training was "too time-consuming." Non-EBP may be less time consuming to teach because it may require less precision (Weissman et al., 2006, p. 930).

Finally, the provider who performs an effective evidence-based crisis intervention assessment must possess a skill set that involves being able to find, rank, and analyze the best current evidence in a timely manner. Some providers will need continuing professional development education to become more comfortable with methods to incorporate these skills into daily practice.

Organizational Culture and Climate

The degree to which EBP is implemented in crisis intervention is complex and based on the reaction of those within the organization. Several recently proposed models target organizational factors that may support or hinder implementation of EBP and innovation in mental health settings (Aarons, 2004; Burns & Hoagwood, 2005). Additionally, a number of studies have identified certain constructs that are believed to be important in effective implementation of any innovation in organizations (Damanpour, 1991; Frambach & Schillewaert, 2002; Glisson, 2002).

Organizational culture and climate are two factors thought to influence attitudes toward adoption of new and innovative approaches in general, including EBP (Aarons, 2004). Although definitions vary, organizational culture can be defined as the organizational norms and expectations regarding how people behave and how things are done in an organization (Glisson & James, 2002). In contrast, organizational climate is more accurately a reflection of the staff's perceptions and emotional responses to, not only the work environment, but also the potential impact that proposed changes may have on the workplace, workload, and overall functionality of the agency (Glisson & James, 2002). Thus, culture and climate are believed to be major contributing factors to attitudes in the workplace. These characteristics are likely to impact dissemination and adoption of EBP (Gotham, 2004).

Studies across social work and mental health delivery systems have shown organizational culture and climate are important contributors to the quality and outcomes of services provided. For example, organizational culture influences staff attitudes (e.g., job satisfaction, organizational commitment), service quality, turnover rate, and morale of the institution (Glisson & James, 2002). Constructive cultures are characterized by established organizational norms that are both reflective and rewarding of achievement, motivation, and individual accomplishment and satisfaction, combined with supportive and ethical approaches to all aspects of the workplace. Constructive cultures encourage supportive interactions and approaches to tasks that aid staff in meeting their goals for the task at hand and their individual satisfaction goals. In contrast, defensive cultures are characterized by seeking approval and consensus, requiring pre-established conventions, conforming, and a degree of subservient dependence. Defensive cultures encourage or implicitly require interaction with people in ways that will not threaten personal security (Cooke & Szumal, 2000). Carmazzi and Arrons (2003) found that staff working in child and adolescent mental health agencies with more positive cultures had more positive attitudes toward the adoption of EBP, whereas those with more negative cultures had more negative attitudes toward adoption of EBP.

Additionally, organizational culture has been shown to impact organizational change by facilitating or hindering the change process. When an organization's cultural values are in conflict with change, the result can be a lack of support, cooperation, and innovation (Feldman, 1993). Therefore, it is important to understand how organizational culture affects organizational change, including the implementation of EBP.

Studies in mental health service agencies and programs have examined a number of organizational-level factors that affect clinician attitudes. A positive organizational climate correlates positively with better organizational processes, work attitudes, and outcomes. A positive organizational climate is also associated with better long-term treatment outcomes (Schoenwald, Sheidow, Letourneau, & Liao, 2003). Work attitudes are also important contributing factors because they tend to mediate the effects of climate on employee performance and motivation (Parker et al., 2003). Positive organizational characteristics tend to positively correlate to employees' commitment to their organization and their job satisfaction (Glisson & Durick, 1988; Morris & Bloom, 2002). By developing a clearer understanding of the culture of an organization, it becomes possible to identify potential positive or negative attitudes that may affect the implementation of EBPs.

Provider Demographics

It is important to make an effort to consider and control for individual-level variables such as provider demographics when attempting to implement any innovation to a practice environment. Gotham (2004) suggests that provider demographics and attitudes can be influential in the willingness to adopt and implement an innovation such as EBPs. Levels of individual receptivity to change can be an important determinant of innovation success. Rogers (1995) suggested that higher levels of formal education among staff and favorable attitudes toward change and science are associated with increased adoption of innovation.

Remember to take the provider's level of professional development into consideration, as well as the time that has passed since completion of training, when attempting to introduce change into the practice environment. Findings suggest that psychiatric interns in specialty mental health clinics report more positive attitudes to using evidence-based assessment protocols (Garland, Kruse, & Aarons, 2003) and endorse more positive attitudes toward adopting EBPs than more experienced clinicians (Aarons, 2004; Ogborne, Wild, Braun, & Newton-Taylor, 1998). While senior leadership may decide to adopt an innovation, individual buy-in is the key element to acceptance, implementation, and development. Without the support of clinic staff, the implementation of any innovation is frequently long and less than effective (Moore, 2002; Rogers, 1995).

EBPs affect the structure and function of the agency and must be carefully considered in light of the patient population. Changes that may affect the patients need to be carefully thought out, planned, communicated, and tested. Current evidence demonstrates that positive consumer attitudes toward EBP can be achieved as a result (Roberts & Yeager, 2004).

CONCLUSION

Crisis intervention is a field that has expanded and evolved throughout the past 64 years. This expansion will continue as our understanding of the nature of crisis and the individual response to crisis evolves. There is an opportunity within each major crisis episode to improve professional practice and provide additional data to the applied form of crisis intervention. As with many forms of health and mental health interventions, the focus on evidence-based practice is still widely dispersed. Only moderate levels of evidence support the findings. However, the tide appears to be changing. Practitioners, educators, administrators, consumers, and researchers are becoming increasingly aware of the principals of evidence-based practice. Within each area, studies of varying sophistication are being developed to inform the evidence base.

The goals of this chapter are threefold. The first goal is to present an overview of the current issues and trends in evidence-based crisis intervention. The second goal is to provide the reader with a knowledge base of practical application. The third goal is to inform and inspire the practitioner to take up the challenges of evidence-based approaches, both in crisis intervention and in other practice areas. It is our belief that crisis intervention and evidence-based approaches have the potential to touch all areas of clinical practice. The body of evidence and knowledge will grow as practitioners apply systematic program evaluations, as researchers develop greater numbers of randomized control studies, and as consumer organizations provide data related to client satisfaction with services provided. We are confident that practitioners, when provided with the right tools, can produce compelling evidence that will direct the continued development of effective crisis intervention treatment.

REFERENCES

Aarons, G. A. (2004). Mental health provider attitudes toward adoption of evidence-based practice: The Evidence-Based Practice Attitude Scale (EBPAS). *Mental Health Services Research, 6*, 61–74.
Aguilera, D. (1998). Crisis intervention: Theory and methodology. St. Louis, MO: Mosby.

Badamgarav, E., Weingarten, S. R., Henning, J. M., Knight, K., Hasselblad, V., Gano, A., Jr., et al. (2003). Effectiveness of disease management programs in depression: A systematic review. *American Journal of Psychiatry, 160*(12), 2080–2090.

Burns, B. J., & Hoagwood, K. E. (Eds.). (2005). Evidence-based practice: Pt. II. Effecting change [Special issue]. *Child and Adolescent Psychiatric Clinics of North America, 14*(2).

Caplan, G. (1964). *Principles of preventive psychiatry.* New York: Basic Books.

Carmazzi, A., & Aarons, G. A. (2003, February). *Organizational culture and attitudes toward adoption of evidence-based practice.* Presented at the NASMHPD Research Institute's 2003 Conference on State Mental Health Agency Services Research, Program Evaluation, and Policy, Baltimore.

Cooke, R. A., & Szumal, J. L. (2000). Using the organizational culture inventory to understand the operating cultures of organizations. In N. M. Ashkanasy, C. P. M. Wilderom, & M. F. Peterson (Eds.), *Handbook of organizational culture and climate* (pp. 147–162). Thousand Oaks, CA: Sage.

Corcoran, J., & Roberts, A. R. (2000). Research on crisis intervention and recommendations for future research. In A. R. Roberts (Ed.), *Crisis intervention handbook: Assessment treatment and research* (2nd ed., pp. 453–483). New York: Oxford University Press.

Damanpour, F. (1991). Organizational innovation: A meta-analysis of effects of determinants and moderators. *Academy of Management Journal, 34,* 555–590.

Drake, R. E., Goldman, H. H., Leff, H. S., Lehman, A. F., Dixon, L., Mueser, K. T., et al. (2001). Implementing evidence-based practices in routine mental health service settings. *Psychiatric Services, 52,* 179–182.

Feldman, S. P. (1993). How organizational culture can affect innovation. In L. Hirschhorn & C. K. E. Barnett (Eds.), *The psychodynamics of organizations: Labor and social change* (pp. 85–97). Philadelphia: Temple University Press.

Frambach, R. T., & Schillewaert, N. (2002). Organizational innovation adoption: A multi-level framework of determinants and opportunities for future research. [Special issue]: *Marketing Theory in the Next Millennium, Journal of Business Research, 55,* 163–176.

Garland, A. F., Kruse, M., & Aarons, G. A. (2003). Clinicians and outcome measurement: What's the use? *Journal of Behavioral Health Services and Research, 30,* 393–405.

Glisson, C. (2002). The organizational context of children's mental health services. *Clinical Child and Family Psychology Review, 5,* 233–253.

Glisson, C., & Durick, M. (1988). Predictors of job satisfaction and organizational commitment in human service organizations. *Administrative Science Quarterly, 33,* 61–81.

Glisson, C., & James, L. R. (2002). The cross-level effects of culture and climate in human service teams. *Journal of Organizational Behavior, 23,* 767–794.

Golan, N. (1978). *Treatment in crisis interventions.* New York: Free Press.

Gotham, H. J. (2004). Diffusion of mental health and substance abuse treatments: Development, dissemination, and implementation. *Clinical Psychology: Science and Practice, 11,* 161–176.

Kanel, K. (1999). *A guide to crisis intervention.* Pacific Grove, CA: Brooks/Cole.

Katon, W., Robinson, P., Von Korff, M., Lin, E., Bush, T., Ludman, E., et al. (1996). A multifaceted intervention to improve treatment of depression in primary care. *Archives of General Psychiatry, 53*(10), 924–932.

Katon, W., Von Korff, M., Lin, E., & Simon, G. (2001). Rethinking practitioner roles in chronic illness: The specialist, primary care physician, and the practice nurse. *General Hospital Psychiatry, 23*(3), 138–144.

Katon, W., Von Korff, M., Lin, E., Unutzer, J., Simon, G., Walker, E., et al. (1997). Population-based care of depression: Effective disease management strategies to decrease prevalence. *General Hospital Psychiatry, 19*(3), 169–178.

Katon, W., Von Korff, M., Lin, E., Walker, E., Simon, G. E., Bush, T., et al. (1995). Collaborative management to achieve treatment guidelines: Impact on depression in primary care. *Journal of the American Medical Association, 273*(13), 1026–1031.

Lindemann, E. (1944). Symptomology and management of acute grief. *American Journal of Psychiatry, 101*, 141–148.

Moore, G. A. (2002). *Crossing the chasm: Marketing and selling high-tech products to mainstream customers*. New York: HarperCollins.

Morris, A., & Bloom, J. R. (2002). Contextual factors affecting job satisfaction and organizational commitment in community mental health centers undergoing system changes in the financing of care. *Mental Health Services Research, 4*, 71–83.

Ogborne, A. C., Wild, T. C., Braun, K., & Newton-Taylor B. (1998). Measuring treatment process beliefs among staff of specialized addiction treatment services. *Journal of Substance Abuse Treatment, 15*, 301–312.

Parad, H. J. (1971). Crisis intervention. In R. Morris (Ed.), *Encyclopedia of social work* (16th ed., Vol. 1, p. 197). New York: National Association of Social Workers Press.

Parker, C. P., Baltes, B. B., Young, S. A., Huff, J. W., Altmann, R. A., Lacost, H. A., et al. (2003). Relationships between psychological climate perceptions and work outcomes: A meta-analytic review. *Journal of Organizational Behavior, 24*, 389–416.

Rapoport, L. (1962). The state of crisis: Some theoretical considerations. *Social Service Review, 36*, 211–217.

Rapoport, L. (1967). Crisis-oriented short-term casework. *Social Service Review, 41*, 31–43.

Roberts, A. R. (1991). Conceptualizing crisis theory and the crisis intervention model. In A. R. Roberts (Ed.), *Contemporary perspectives on crisis intervention and prevention* (pp. 3–17). Englewood Cliffs, NJ: Prentice Hall.

Roberts, A. R. (1996). Epidemiology and definitions of acute crisis in American society. In A. R. Roberts (Ed.), *Crisis management and brief treatment: Theory, technique and applications* (pp. 16–33). Chicago: Nelson-Hall.

Roberts, A. R. (2005). Bridging the past and present to the future of crisis intervention and crisis management. In A. R. Roberts (Ed.), *Crisis intervention handbook: Assessment, treatment, and research* (3rd ed., pp. 3–34). New York: Oxford University Press.

Roberts, A. R., & Dziegielewski, S. F. (1995). Foundation skills and applications of crisis intervention and cognitive therapy. In A. R. Roberts (Ed.), *Crisis intervention and time limited cognitive treatment* (pp. 3–27). Thousand Oaks, CA: Sage.

Roberts, A. R., & Greene, G. J. (2002). *Social workers' desk reference*. New York: Oxford University Press.

Roberts, A. R., & Lewis, S. (2001). Crisis assessment tools: The good, the bad and the available. *Brief Treatment and Crisis Intervention, 1*, 17–28.

Roberts, A. R., & Yeager, K. R. (2004). Systematic reviews of evidence-based studies and practice-based research: How to search for, develop and use them. In A. R. Roberts & K. R. Yeager (Eds.), *Handbook of evidence-based practice: Research and outcome measures in health and human services* (pp. 3–14). New York: Oxford University Press.

Rogers, E. M. (1995). *Diffusion of innovations* (4th ed.). New York: Free Press.

Rosenthal, R. N. (2004). Overview of evidence-based practice. In A. R. Roberts & K. R. Yeager (Eds.), *Handbook of evidence-based practice: Research and outcome measures in health and human services* (pp. 20–29). New York, Oxford University Press.

Sackett, D. L., Rosenberg, W. M. C., Gray, J. A. M., Haynes, R. B., & Richardson, W. S. (1996). Evidence based medicine: What it is and what it isn't. *British Medical Journal, 312*, 71–72.

Schoenbaum, M., Miranda, J., Sherbourne, C., Duan, N., & Wells, K. (2004). Cost-effectiveness of interventions for depressed Latinos. *Journal of Mental Health Policy and Economics, 7*(2), 69–76.

Schoenbaum, M., Unutzer, J., McCaffrey, D., Duan, N., Sherbourne, C., & Wells, K. B. (2002). The effects of primary care depression treatment on patients' clinical status and employment. *Health Services Research, 37*(5), 1145–1158.

Schoenwald, S. K., Sheidow, A. J., Letourneau, E. J., Liao, J. G. (2003). Transportability of multisystemic therapy: Evidence for multilevel influences. *Mental Health Services Research, 5*, 223–239.

Schulberg, H. C., Katon, W., Simon, G. E., & Rush, A. J. (1998). Treating major depression in primary care practice: An update of the Agency for Health Care Policy and Research Practice Guidelines. *Archives of General Psychiatry, 55*(12), 1121–1127.

Simon, G. E., Katon, W. J., Von Korff, M., Unutzer, J., Lin, E. H., Walker, E.A., et al. (2001). Cost-effectiveness of a collaborative care program for primary care patients with persistent depression. *American Journal of Psychiatry, 158*(10), 1638–1644.

Simon, G. E., Von Korff, M., Ludman, E. J., Katon, W. J., Rutter, C., Unutzer, J., et al. (2002). Cost-effectiveness of a program to prevent depression relapse in primary care. *Med Care, 40*(10), 941–950.

Slaikeu, K. (1984). *Crisis intervention: A handbook for practice and research.* Boston: Allyn & Bacon.

Tyhurst, J. S. (1957). The role of transition states—including disasters—in mental illness. In *Symposium on preventive and social psychiatry* (pp. 1–23). Washington, DC: Walter Reed Army Institute of Research.

U.S. Department of Health and Human Services. (1996). *A report of the surgeon general.* Atlanta, GA: National Center for Chronic Disease Prevention and Health.

Von Korff, M., & Tiemens, B. (2000). Individualized stepped care of chronic illness. *Western Journal of Medicine, 172*(2), 133–137.

Von Korff, M., Unutzer, J., Katon, W., & Wells, K. (2001). Improving care for depression in organized health care systems. *Journal of Family Practice, 50*(6), 530–531.

Wagner, E. H., Austin, B. T., & Von Korff, M. (1996). Improving outcomes in chronic illness. *Managed Care Quarterly, 4*(2),12–25.

Weissman, M. M., Verdeli, H., Gameroff, M. J., Bledsoe, S. E., Betts, K., Mufson, L., et al. (2006). A national survey of psychotherapy training in psychiatry, psychology, and social work. *Archives of General Psychiatry, 63*(8), 925–934.

Wiest, F. C., Ferris, T. G., Gokhale, M., Campbell, E. G., Weissman, J. S., & Blumenthal, D. (2002). Preparedness of internal medicine and family practice residents for treating common conditions. *Journal of the American Medical Association, 288*(20), 2609–2614.

Yeager, K. R., & Roberts, A. R. (2005). Differentiating among stress, acute stress disorder, acute crisis episodes, trauma and PTSD: Paradigm and treatment goals. In A. R. Roberts (Ed.), *Crisis intervention handbook: Assessment, treatment, and research* (3rd ed., pp. 90–119). New York: Oxford University Press.

Chapter 10 ───────────────────────────────

TERMINATION, STABILIZATION, AND CONTINUITY OF CARE

Samuel A. MacMaster and Sara Sanders

Termination and stabilization are quite possibly the most important phases in the entire clinical process. It is in these phases that changes initiated during the course of services are solidified, the individual or client system envisions a future in this new state, and the groundwork is laid for any future service use with the current or any other service provider. Yet, despite the overall importance of these critical phases of treatment, there is a paucity of literature dedicated to the ending of clinical services and the maintenance of any changes that have been realized.

Both termination and stabilization have been broadly defined within the social work literature and are often conceptualized as two closely and interrelated processes. This chapter treats them as two phases of what is essentially the same process. In an ideal world, once the client stabilizes, and has met all goals, services naturally come to an end. Therefore, stabilization is the process that indicates an ending point or termination of services.

Ideally, stabilization and termination are linear processes in which a stabilized client who has met the treatment goals and experienced a resolution to the presenting problem initiates an ending to services with interpersonal growth. However, stabilization and termination are rarely carried out in this fashion. Depending on the mode of service delivery and, unfortunately, more often than not, external environmental factors, service termination, and stabilization may not always occur as a smooth transition or may even be related to each other.

This chapter provides a brief overview of the historical trends of termination and stabilization and an overview of termination and stabilization from a trantheoretical perspective. We discuss the importance of these phases for the overall clinical process, provide a discussion of stabilization beyond the settling of a crisis, introduce ideal termination process, discuss perspectives on planned and unplanned terminations, and finally provide perspectives of termination and stabilization in areas of social work practice that do not follow the idealized clinical process.

HISTORICAL TRENDS

As argued by many clinicians and clinical researchers, preparation for stabilizing the client and terminating the clinical relationship starts from the first day of treatment (Woods & Hollis, 1990). The need for this type of practice approach has become more pronounced as the requirements for documenting clinical outcomes, justifying ongoing treatment and reimbursement have taken a prominent role in clinical practice. With reductions in mental health care in an attempt to control climbing fees for service (Anderson, 2000; Ligon, 1997; Strom, 1992), it is becoming more critical to develop intervention plans that are geared toward timely termination and long-term client stabilization.

Third-party reimbursement has received criticism for the impact that it has on the clinical relationship between the social worker and client in all phases of the treatment process, but also at termination. The result is that clients often have a reduced length of treatment (i.e., termination too soon) because of the inability to justify the continued need for treatment (Strom, 1992). This was further echoed by Petryshen and Petryshen (1992) as they discussed the drive toward fiscally responsible lengths of treatment. Third-party reimbursement has also created concern about premature termination because of the lack of insurance funding. This has ramifications for the client who loses insurance before treatment has been completed. Does the social worker continue the treatment process knowing that the client is unable to pay; thus, the social worker loses financially? Or does the social worker terminate the therapeutic relationship with the client prior to client stabilization (Strom, 1992)? These questions create an ethical dilemma for social workers as they continue to strive to provide cost-effective treatment and positive clinical outcomes.

A BROADER PERSPECTIVE ON SERVICE DELIVERY

A discussion of stabilization and termination requires a broader view of not only the clinical process, but also incorporating what we know about the process of behavior change. Any change stabilized and ultimately maintained throughout and after termination must first be initiated in the early stages of the clinical process. Through research and practice experiences, it has become clear that individuals rarely make behavior changes rapidly in response to professional interventions, but rather changes occur through a slow and steady ongoing process with the *assistance of* professional interventions. This conceptualization of the change process has become known as the stages of change or transtheoretical model (Table 10.1). Developed by Prochaska and DiClemente (1983), the transtheoretical model helps explain how both self-initiated and professionally assisted changes occur for individuals with problematic behavior. Prochaska and DiClemente put forth a five-stage theory based on a review of all empirical research on professionally assisted behavior change. The basic premise of their work is that stages of change are temporal dimensions that determine when particular shifts in attitudes, intentions, and behaviors occur within a much larger dynamic process.

In general, each stage represents a period of time, as well as a set of tasks needed for movement to the next stage. Although the time an individual spends in each stage may vary, tasks to be accomplished are assumed to be uniform. With regard to implications for stabilization and termination, it is important to note that the vast majority of people are neither highly motivated nor are they in the action stage. However most social work interventions are oriented toward individuals seeking services in an action stage of change or minimally assume an action orientation toward the presenting problem. Studies indicate that of the individuals seeking professional services only 10% to 15% are prepared for action; 30% to 40% are in the contemplation stages; and the majority, 50% to 60%, are

Table 10.1   Transtheoretical Model

1. Precontemplation Stage

No intention to change in the foreseeable future.

Unaware or under aware that there is even a problem.

Present to treatment because of outside influences.

May even demonstrate change while pressure is on.

Resistance to recognizing or modifying a problem is the hallmark, for example, "I don't have any problems."

2. Contemplation Stage

Aware problem exists—seriously thinking about overcoming it, but have not yet made a commitment to take action.

May be stuck here for a long time.

"Knowing where you want to go, but not quite ready yet."

Weigh pros and cons of problem and solution—struggle with positive evaluations of their addiction and the amount of energy, effort, and loss it will cost to overcome the problem.

3. Preparation Stage

Combines intention and behavioral criteria, for example, individuals in this stage are intending to take action in the next month and have unsuccessfully taken action in the past year.

Typically will report some action such as a decrease in the behavior—but have not yet reached a criterion for effective action.

They are, however, intending to take such action in the future.

4. Action Stage

Individuals modify their behavior, experiences, or environment to overcome their problems.

Involves the most overt behavioral changes and requires considerable commitment of time and energy.

Modifications here tend to be the most visible and receive greatest external recognition.

Do not confuse this stage with change, which often happens, as you will overlook the requisite work that prepares changers for action and important efforts necessary to maintain the changes following action.

They have successfully altered the behavior for a period of 1 day to 6 months, for example, reaching a certain criterion.

Modification of the target behavior to an acceptable criterion and significant overt efforts to change are the hallmarks of action.

5. Maintenance

People work to prevent relapse into the changed behavior and consolidate the gains attained during action.

Maintenance is not static and is viewed as a continuation of change. It extends from about 6 months to an indeterminate period past the initial action—for some, it's a lifetime of change.

Being able to remain free of the behavior and being able to consistently engage in new, incompatible behavior for more than 6 months are the criteria for this stage.

Stabilizing behavior change and avoiding relapse into old behavior patterns are the hallmarks of maintenance.

Since relapse into old behaviors is the rule rather than exception, cannot conceptualize this model as a linear model with people neatly going from one stage to another, rather the authors present it as a spiral pattern.

In relapse to old behavior patterns, some return to the stage before relapse. Others begin again somewhere in the middle. The majority recycle back to later stages, that is, they potentially learn from their mistakes.

In a cohort of individuals, the number of successes continues to increase gradually over time, but a large number stay in the precontemplation and contemplation stages.

in the precontemplation stages (Prochaska, DiClemente, & Norcross, 1992) Therefore, most social workers and social work programs will underserve, misserve, or not serve the majority of their target populations in the beginning stages of services and set up problems that will continue until the ending stages. The amount of measurable progress clients make following an intervention tends to be a function of their pretreatment stage of change.

Research has also shown that if clients progress from one stage to the next in the first month of treatment, they can double their chances of taking actions during the initial 6 months of services. It is important for social workers to remember that action-oriented treatment with definitive beginnings and endings may be ideal and may work with people who initially present in the preparation or action stages. However this assumption will lead to a mismatch between the intervention and the stage change and will likely be totally ineffective with individuals in the precontemplation or contemplation stages. Just as individuals will be poorly conceptualized to be in preparation or action stages at the beginning of services, it is often quite common for misconceptions to continue with the assumption that individuals are in the maintenance stage. Therefore, it is quite likely that services will end with little hope of stabilization, and termination will not be the smooth end to an idyllic process, but services are likely to end abruptly and/or prematurely (Prochaska & Velicer, 1997; Prochaska, Velicer, DiClemente, & Fava, 1988; Prochaska, Velicer, DiClemente, Guadagnoli, & Rossi, 1991).

There are clear markers for determining where an individual may be relative to their stage of change. In the precontemplative stage, people processed less information about their problems, devoted less time and energy to reevaluating themselves and experienced fewer emotional reactions to the negative aspects of their problems. These clients tended to be less open with others about their problems and did little to shift their attention or their environment in the direction of overcoming problems—they were the most resistant and least active patients. In the contemplation stage, they were most open to consciousness-raising techniques, such as confrontations or educational processes. They reevaluated themselves more and struggled with questions such as "How do I think and feel about living in a deteriorating environment that places my families or friends at increasing risk for disease, poverty, or imprisonment?" In the preparation stage, people began to take small steps toward action—this is where is it appropriate to use counterconditioning and stimulus-control techniques to begin reducing the targeted behavior. During the action stage, individuals endorsed higher levels of self-liberation, believed they had the autonomy to change their lives, and relied increasingly on support and understanding from helping relationships. In the maintenance stage, clients relied on all the processes that came before it. This stage entails an assessment of the conditions under which a person was likely to relapse into the old behaviors and development of alternative responses for coping with such conditions.

This broader perspective on social work practice clearly suggests the need to assess the stage of a client's readiness for change and to tailor interventions accordingly throughout the clinical process. Ultimately, effective and efficient professionally assisted change depends on doing the right things (processes) at the right time (stages). While not assuming a linear process through these stages, the stabilization of client gains and the termination of services do rely on the accomplishment of certain markers in the previous stages. The lack of awareness or lack of recognition of these markers by clinicians will determine the ability to effectively stabilize targeted behaviors and ultimately the experience of both the service recipient and the service provider in the termination of services.

IMPORTANCE OF TERMINATION AND STABILIZATION

While a great deal of literature, training, research, and resources are dedicated to the beginning stages of treatment in which a social worker engages with the client, it is quite clear that the ending stages of the same services are just as, if not more, important for the long-term health of the client. The manner in which the clinician handles these interrelated processes has significant implications for the client long after formal professional services are complete. Woods and Hollis (1990) describe five features that highlight the importance of this stage and the need for heightened skill, care, and sensitivity to the client or client system.

The most important feature is the crisis focus that many clients seeking services present with at the beginning of treatment. When entering the stabilization and termination phases, this crisis may have abated and the motivation to continue to seek growth may decrease. The first struggle for a social worker working with a client in this phase is that as the momentum decreases, it becomes necessary to assist the client in maintaining focus and continuing to seek and foster growth.

Heightened sensitivity to client's emotional reactions to services is also necessary at this time. As services are initiated, discussions of the relationship between the client and the social worker naturally occur; however, as stabilization begins to occur and termination may be seen as imminent, clients may have heightened emotions regarding the therapeutic relationship and transference and countertransference issues may arise. Unlike the beginning stages of services, clients at this point may experience less awareness of these issues and are much less likely to acknowledge these feelings.

Increased vigilance at this point in the relationship is also necessary because it is a very vulnerable time for clients. This vulnerability is related to both the new growth experienced in services and the nature of the transitional period, which may heighten a desire to return to ineffective coping mechanisms. If handled poorly, this transition may negate any growth developed during the therapeutic process, and more important it may be so damaging that the client may be reluctant to reconnect with services in the future. Mistakes made at this time are also further exacerbated because there may be little time to become aware and/or correct any issues that arise.

Another factor that is often overlooked when planning and beginning services is that very few clients actually follow an ideal pattern of stabilization and termination. There are a host of issues that may be completely unplanned that often cause an individual to prematurely end services. As a result, there may little or no time for stabilization and/or a formal termination process. Likewise the nature of the event or factor that leads to the ending or reduction of the length of services is also important. The way that this is viewed within the therapeutic relationship has a definitive impact on the opportunities for stabilization and termination. Who initiates the ending of services, whether this is planned or unplanned, and the reasoning behind it may influence how this is viewed within the relationship, particularly if these events are not conceptualized by both parties in the same way.

While these previous factors are discussed in the literature on stabilization and termination, Woods and Hollis (1990) make particular mention of the difficulties in the process from the vantage point of the social worker. They suggest that unresolved ambivalence around both the client and the nature of therapeutic process with the system will impact stabilization and termination. The social worker will likely have increased emotions around both issues that he or she may not recognize. More important they suggest that the re-lationship the social worker has with separation will directly impact this stage. Again, similar to the other previously mentioned issues, the social worker is likely to have less self-awareness at the ending of services versus the beginning; and at the same time the potential impact that these issues have for the overall health of the client is much greater. Because of the nature of delivering social work services over time, social workers, unless extremely self-aware, are likely to somewhat deny the impact of termination on emotions simply because these emotions may be experienced on a regular basis, and they may not connect these experiences to their own potential issues around separation or attachment.

Stabilization and termination are potentially the most important stages of the therapeutic process because it is here that the potential for real-world growth of the client is developed. Despite this importance, stabilization and termination are frequently overlooked and rarely focused on. Intensifying the potential for problems at this stage of the process is the need for the clinician to be aware of and plan for the complex set of factors that serve as barriers to a smooth transition to stabilization and from stabilization to termination. Dorfman (1996) refers to this as a time for mourning or a time for celebration; however, it is important for social workers to be aware of all of these factors so that they can adequately address the grief or the celebration.

STABILIZATION

Typically, writings on social work practice assume a linear process conceptualizing the interactions between a social worker and a client system, which has a beginning, middle and an end. There are many of these models in the social work and other related literatures (Corey, 1991; Northen, 1995; Woods & Hollis, 1990), which tend to be closely related on a conceptual basis to the one posited by Hepworth, Rooney, and Larsen (2002) that suggests a three-phase process of a beginning, described as exploration, assessment, and planning; followed by a middle stage, described as implementation and goal attainment; and a final or ending stage or termination. While there are many such conceptualizations for these processes, they often overlook the all-too-important stage of stabilization. It is within this stage that a client is able to incorporate changes to overcome the presenting problem, return to a new state of homeostasis, and develop new mechanisms for coping with the environment that include any gains and/or new skills developed as a direct result of the received services. Stabilization is not an event—signaling the need for termination—but is rather a process unto itself.

Contrasting with the previously described conceptualization of stabilization is another broader perspective that takes in both the individuals and environmental factors over a longer period of time. From this perspective, services are not complete when a presenting crisis is over and/or has been successfully dealt with through an intervention. For many individuals seeking social work services, the presenting issue rarely exists in a vacuum, but is often symptomatic of an extended, often lifelong, pattern of poor coping with environmental stressors. However, most service recipients seek services during a crisis and through this myopia are only able to be aware of the presenting problem. When the crisis is resolved, individuals often seek to terminate services. However, for true stabilization to occur, a skilled social worker must assist the individual in identifying these underlying patterns and working toward their abatement.

A four-stage model for conceptualizing this broader perspective has been posited by Smets (1988). This model includes an incubation phase, the crisis, the development of an intervention plan, and finally stabilization. The inclusion of an early, pretreatment seeking phase of incubation provides a conceptualization that is more in line with what we know about behavior change from the transtheoretical model's stages of change. This conceptualization from a broader perspective also assists clinicians in providing services that will be more efficient because they are tailored to the underlying issue and not the immediate crisis, thus interventions are specifically directed at the root cause and not symptoms of the issue and are tailored to the appropriate stage of change. Clinicians will also therefore be more effective at achieving the treatment goal both in the short term, but more importantly over the long term.

Usually services are initiated at the high point of the crisis phase, which naturally passes with time. It is the clinicians' responsibility to not assume stabilization once this crisis has passed, but to direct services to the underlying issues that incubated the presenting problem (Smets, 1988). Within this model, stabilization and termination occur in stage four—only after the client and the social worker have mutually achieved stabilization of the underlying issue. This model assumes that true stabilization of the client or client system rarely occurs because the focus is on stabilizing the crisis and not on the stabilization of the underlying issue.

In order to effectively stabilize a client, the clinician must first have the long-term perspective of the nature of presenting problems. Similarly, the clinician must be willing and able to take services to a deeper level beyond the superficial crisis. From an environmental perspective, an opportunity must exist for the client to engage with a service provider over a long enough time period for the underlying issue or issues to emerge. The social worker's time is often the most frequently discussed resource in service delivery; however, the client too must have the available time and energy to devote to this endeavor. Similarly, the client must maintain motivation toward change. However, regardless of how high the motivational state may be, it is the opportunity that is most lacking and creating the most barriers for vulnerable client populations. Once the clinician and client both possess the opportunity, willingness, and perspective, stabilization can occur, but only if the clinician maintains vigilance against the issues previously raised that so often interfere with ideal stabilization.

CASE MANAGEMENT, BRIEF THERAPY, AND CRISIS INTERVENTION

Much of the literature on stabilization and termination in social work practice assumes a highly clinical or therapeutic style of service delivery, which is most often typified by weekly outpatient office visits where time is not a constraining resource. While this type of service delivery is in no way typical of the work that all, or even most, social workers perform, it is the type of service that is described when ideal therapeutic processes are presented in the literature. To fully describe stabilization and termination as it relates to social work practice, there are some areas that need special attention because of time constraints or the nature of the service delivery mechanism.

Case Management

Case management is a primary social work service for frail elders, children and youth, individuals with cognitive or physical disabilities, individuals with physical or mental health problems, and those who are experiencing poverty or other disabling life circumstances (Fiene & Taylor, 1991; Levine et al., 2006). Through the roles of brokering, counseling, educating, and advocating, case managers strive to enhance the functioning of the client through locating and securing necessary support services from the community (Fiene & Taylor, 1991; Moxley, 1989). The coordination of services looks different based on the client and his or her needs. For some, the case management may be simply assessing the clients needs and then connecting them to other providers of services, but for others it may be more intensive, including counseling, interdisciplinary assessment and care planning, scheduling and transporting to appointments, monitoring medications and follow-up with medical care, serving as a liaison between the client and other providers, and ensuring that daily needs, including activities of daily living, are being met. The length of time that clients receive case management services will also vary based the clients' needs, the structure of the case management program, and agency resources.

Stabilization and termination also look different based on the case management program. For instance, in health-care related case management programs, termination of client services is based on client progress and reimbursement issues. In home health care, for example, if the patients' condition stabilizes, many insurance programs cease paying for services. As found in the work of Levine and colleagues (2006), the decision to terminate services may occur within 24 to 48 hours, giving the patient and family little time to make alternative care arrangements. The ramification of this type of termination is that family support systems often do not have time to prepare for losing assistance, thus, termination occurs before stabilization happens in the home.

In the area of child welfare, termination may also occur prior to stabilization. For instance, case managers within the child welfare system work with families to obtain resources to strengthen their family unit and address individual needs, such as substance abuse, domestic violence, and parenting skills. If the family system is strengthened, termination will occur with the child returning to or remaining in the home. However, if these goals are not accomplished, it is determined that stabilization within the family unit has not occurred. Thus, termination of parent rights or continued work will occur.

With other client populations, social service agencies work on stabilization and termination simultaneously. This has been seen predominantly in the areas of substance abuse and criminal justice, where clients are terminated from one type of treatment program when they reach a certain level of stabilization only to then be enrolled in a case management program to ensure long-term stabilization. Rich and colleagues (2001) presented a program such as this for ex-offenders who have HIV. As ex-offenders left prison, they enrolled in a community-based case management program to assist them in maintaining their involvement with medical care. These researchers concluded that through this case management program, ex-offenders were able to remain connected to the medical services they needed and maintain stabilization postprison.

A variant of this form of termination and stabilization process has also been found to be effective in work with older adults. Naleppa and Reid (1998) used a task-focused case management program with older adults. They found that within a few weeks, the needs of most older adults were met. At this point, they could be transferred into a longer-term case management program or discharged completely from case management services. Morrow-Howell, Becker-Kemppainen, and Judy (1998) also found that older adults, following an intensive telephone-based case management program, had fewer unmet needs and improved life situations at termination. The relationships that had been formed through the case management referrals created stabilization over time.

Finally, some case management programs place a greater emphasis on client stabilization with the hopes of keeping the clients from leaving the program. This model has been seen in the areas of mental health and substance abuse. Noel (2006) found that in adolescent substance abusers, premature termination from the case management program was more associated with programmatic elements than frequency of case management service. Thus, for some populations, stabilization through case management has to be related to client motivation; otherwise, they may opt for prematurely terminating the program. This could also apply to the area of child welfare.

As case management services continue to grow, particularly state-funded case management programs, stabilization and termination needs to be given greater attention. Although stabilization and termination may look different based on the case management program and the population that is being served, considering these two elements of practice early in the case management process are essential for long-term client outcomes.

Brief Therapy

Brief therapy has become a common form of treatment for clients of all ages because of issues relating to reimbursement, insurance, and managed care (Anderson-Klontz, Dayton, & Anderson-Klontz, 1999). Instead of having a relationship with a therapist that lasts years, brief therapy on average lasts 5.5 sessions over a period of less than 4 months (Lee, 1997). Other estimates suggest that brief therapy lasts no more than eight sessions. While there are different schools of brief therapy, including solution-focused or Adlerian, the stabilization and termination process of brief therapy models is similar. These concepts will be discussed in general, instead of focusing specifically on one form of brief therapy.

Brief therapy is based on a treatment model to enable clients to work on "achievable goals within a limited time period" (Anderson-Klontz et al., 1999, p. 115). As a result of this approach, brief therapy models have received criticism for not providing sufficient time for a thorough exploration of client problems; instead, problems are examined at a "surface level" (Walter & Peller, 1992). It has been suggested that brief therapy approaches restrict clients from working through the emotions related to their problems as well as discovering unresolved issues that may inhibit stabilization in the future.

Professionals who provide brief therapy are often hesitant to use the word "termination" when working with a client. Some brief therapy models, specifically Adlerian brief therapists, use the word "interrupted" instead of "terminated" at the end of a client period (Bitter & Nicoll, 2000). From this perspective, interruption leaves the door open for the client and therapist to reconnect in the future to continue to work on problematic issues. Others have focused less on the "finished product" or the long-term sustainable outcomes and instead on the incremental changes that were seen during the therapeutic process (Watts & Pietrzak, 2000, p. 445). Thus, sustainable change is not necessarily the goal; instead, the focus is on the change process and client growth.

The effectiveness of brief therapy approaches for creating long-term client stabilization is starting to be documented (Gingerich & Eisengart, 2000) with some researchers suggesting that short-term approaches are as effective as long-term approaches in creating client stabilization (Smyrnios & Kirby, 1993; Weisz, Thurber, Sweeney, Proffitt, LeGagnoux, 1997). However, the sophistication of the intervention models has made this a slow process (Gingerich & Eisengart, 2000).

Research has also suggested that long-term stabilization of clients following brief therapy may be hard to obtain without adequate follow-up plans. Allison, Roeger, Dadds, and Martin (2000) found that 27% of children who received brief therapy for mental health problems were still experiencing difficulty posttermination. It was suggested that maintaining contact with the parents of the child via telephone posttermination may have led to greater stabilization of the children because treatment could have been re-initiated before the problem escalated to pretreatment levels. One way to address issues of stabilization posttermination from brief therapy may be what Shakeshaft, Bowman, Burrows, Doran, and Sanson-Fisher (1997) proposed. They proposed that following brief therapy for alcohol abuse, individuals who need more intensive intervention or follow-up could start into a longer term cognitive behavioral program.

The rates of stabilization postbrief therapy have varied. Lee (1997) found that brief therapy had a 65% success rate in achieving treatment outcomes in children with mental health problems. While this rate was lower than what was found in other studies (de Shazer, 1991), it does provide some evidence of the effectiveness of brief therapy approaches for client stabilization, at least in the short term. Franklin, Biever, Moore, Clemons, and Scamardo (2001) found that brief therapy, specifically solution-focused, was effective with children in school-based settings who were experiencing learning and behavioral problems. In this study, only one student at follow-up had returned to preintervention clinical levels.

Brief intervention models have also been found to be effective in creating stabilization in adolescents admitted to psychiatric hospitals. Balkin and Roland (2007) found that adolescent stabilization was connected to the attainment of therapeutic goals. Stabilization occurred as the adolescents became better at articulating their problems and committing to follow-up posthospitalization as determined by a reduction in psychiatric symptoms. This obviously played an important role as the patient was preparing for discharge or termination from the hospital program.

Finally, brief therapy has also been found to be effective in stabilization in adult populations. Barkham, Shapiro, Hardy, and Rees (1999) presented a two-plus-one brief therapy model for adults with depression, as measured by the Beck's Depression Inventory (Beck, Ward, & Mendelson, 1961). They found that gains made by the clients were still evident up to 1 year posttreatment, thereby suggesting client stabilization.

While brief therapy has been found to have short-term effectiveness in resolving client issues, long-term client stabilization rates are not known. As brief therapy receives more empirical attention, focus should be given to documenting client stabilization over time.

Crisis Intervention Therapy

Stressful life events lead to crises when individuals feel as though they have lost control over their particular circumstances. Depending on the person's coping ability and resolution of previous crises, life crises can lead to dysfunctional and at times self-destructive behavior. Crisis intervention therapy is frequently provided to individuals who experience distress following "normal" life stressors. Crisis intervention therapy can also be provided to individuals who experience significant trauma; however, crisis intervention in this context may appear different and include additional forms of intervention.

When considering termination and stabilization in a crisis intervention format, it is critical to consider the person's history of crisis, functional ability following a crisis, use and effectiveness of coping strategies, available formal and informal support systems, and ability to access additional assistance should a crisis stage reoccur. Anthony (1992) found that individuals who had been admitted to a crisis inpatient psychiatric unit were more successful at discharge if they had greater support from families and greater compliance with treatment protocols.

For stabilization postcrisis, part of crisis intervention is working with the client to determine how to prevent the next crisis, as well as how to respond when the next crisis occurs (Smets, 1988). Equally important to long-term stabilization postcrisis is considering ways to prepare clients for resolving future crises that may or may not be related to the same stressful event. Following crises, clients are reluctant to hear that the problems that led to the crisis may reappear, but part of termination and ensuring a stabilized client is being cognizant of how prepared the client is for the reoccurrence of events that precipitated the crisis in his or her life (Smets, 1988).

Research on crisis intervention has been found within multiple areas of social work including health care, child welfare, suicide and mental health, and substance abuse. This literature, while rich and informative, has yet to provide sufficient detail into how termination and stabilization are assessed and evaluated within a crisis situation. However, the literature emphasizes the importance of the person in crisis having the opportunity to work on time-limited tasks and developing some form of follow-up plan to future intervention if necessary (Poindexter, 1997).

Research on the effectiveness of crisis intervention therapy has found mixed results for creating stabilization in client. Rossi (1992) suggested that family preservation programs that provided crisis intervention were not successful with families who were experiencing extreme amounts of stress. However, Ruffin and colleagues (Ruffin, Spencer, Abel, Gage, & Miles, 1993) determined that a crisis stabilization program that consisted of daytime crisis work, after-hours assistance, and the ability to broker additional services that were beyond outpatient and inpatient care was effective in reducing the number of youth who were admitted to psychiatric facilities. Evans et al. (2003) found that in-home intensive crisis services for children and their families were successful in creating family cohesion by termination, as well as increased social support at termination and follow-up. Thus, as seen in this research, stabilization over time did occur following crisis-based services.

CONCLUSION

Greater attention needs to be directed to discussing termination and stabilization within the therapeutic process. Termination and stabilization are critical phases in the therapeutic relationship between the social worker and the client; however, they frequently receive scant empirical and clinical attention. While these two processes may appear different based on the clinical model and the client's circumstances, termination and stabilization should be incorporated into all phases of treatment and not introduced only at the end of therapy.

REFERENCES

Allison, S., Roeger, L., Dadds, V., & Martin, G. (2000). Brief therapy for children's mental health problems: Outcomes in a rural setting. *Australian Journal of Rural Health*, *8*, 161–166.

Anderson, C. E. (2000). Dealing constructively with managed care: Suggestions from an insider. *Journal of Mental Health Counseling*, *22*, 343–354.

Anderson-Klontz, B. T., Dayton, T., & Anderson-Klontz, L. S. (1999). The use of psychodramatic techniques within solution-focused brief therapy: A theoretical and technical integration. *Action Methods*, 113–120.

Anthony, D. J. (1992). A retrospective evaluation of factors influencing successful outcomes on an inpatient psychiatric crisis unit. *Research on Social Work Practice*, *2*, 56–64.

Balkin, R. S., & Roland, C. B. (2007). Reconceptualizing stabilization for counseling adolescents in brief psychiatric hospitalization: A new model. *Journal of Counseling and Development*, *85*, 64–72.

Barkham, M., Shapiro, D. A., Hardy, G. E., & Rees, A. (1999). Psychotherapy in two-plus-one sessions: Outcomes of a randomized control trail of cognitive-behavioral and psychodynamic-interpersonal therapy for subsyndromal depression. *Journal of Consulting and Clinical Psychology*, *67*, 201–211.

Beck, A. T., Ward C., & Mendelson, M. (1961). Beck Depression Inventory (BDI). *Archives of General Psychiatry*, *4*, 561–571.

Bitter, J. R., & Nicoll, W. G. (2000). Alderian brief therapy with individuals: Process and practice. *Journal of Individual Psychology*, *56*, 31–44.

Corey, G. (1991). *Theory and practice of counseling and psychotherapy*. Pacific Grove, CA: Brooks/Cole.

de Shazer, S. (1991). *Putting difference to work*. New York: Norton.

Dorfman, R. (1996). *Clinical social work: Definition, practice, and wisdom*. New York: Brunner/Mazel.

Evans, M. E., Boothroyd, R. A., Armstrong, M. I., Greenbaum, P. E., Crown, E. C., & Kuppinger, A. D. (2003). An experimental study of the effectiveness of intensive in-home crisis services for children and their families: Program outcomes. *Journal of Emotional and Behavioral Disorders*, *11*, 92–104.

Fiene, J. I., & Taylor, P. A. (1991). Serving rural families of developmentally disabled children: A case management model. *Social Work*, *36*, 323–327.

Franklin, C., Biever, J., Moore, K., Clemons, D., & Scamardo, M. (2001). The effectiveness of solution-focused therapy with children in a school setting. *Research on Social Work Practice*, *11*, 411–434.

Gingerich, W. J., & Eisengart, S. (2000). Solution-focused brief therapy: A review of the outcome research. *Family Processes*, 477–498.

Hepworth, D., Rooney, R., & Larsen, J. (2002). *Direct social work practice: Theory and skills*. Pacific Grove, CA: Brooks/Cole.

Lee, M. (1997). A study of solution-focused brief family therapy: Outcomes and issues. *American Journal of Family Therapy*, *25*, 3–17.

Levine, C., Albert, S. M., Hokenstad, A., Halper, D. E., Hart, A. Y., & Gould, D. A. (2006). "This case is closed": Family caregivers and the termination of home health care services for stroke patients. *Milbank Quarterly*, *84*, 305–331.

Ligon, J. (1997). Brief crisis stabilization of an African American woman: Integrating cultural and ecological approaches. *Journal of Multicultural Social Work*, *6*, 111–122.

Morrow-Howell, N., Becker-Kemppainen, S., & Judy, L. (1998). Evaluating an intervention for the elderly at increased risk for suicide. *Research on Social Work Practice*, *8*, 28–46.

Moxley, D. P. (1989). *The practice of case management*. Newbury Park, CA: Sage.

Naleppa, M. J., & Reid, W. J. (1998). Task-centered case management for the elderly: Developing a practice model. *Research on Social Work Practice, 8*, 63–85.

Noel, P. E. (2006). The impact of therapeutic case management on participation in adolescent substance abuse treatment. *American Journal of Drug and Alcohol Abuse, 32*, 322–327.

Northen, H. (1995). *Clinical social work: Knowledge and skills.* New York: Columbia University Press.

Petryshen, P. R., & Petryshen, P. M. (1992). The case management model: An innovative approach to the delivery of patient care. *Journal of Advanced Nursing, 17*, 1188–1194.

Poindexter, C. (1997). In the aftermath: Serial crisis intervention for people with HIV. *Health and Social Work, 22*, 23–35.

Prochaska, J. O., & DiClemente, C. C. (1983). Stages and processes of self-change of smoking: Toward an integrative model of change. *Journal of Consulting and Clinical Psychology, 51*, 390–395.

Prochaska, J. O., DiClemente, C. C., & Norcross, J. C. (1992). In search of how people change: Applications to addictive behaviors. *American Psychologist, 47*(9), 1102–1114.

Prochaska, J. O., & Velicer, W. F. (1997). The transtheoretical model of health behavior change. *American Journal of Health Promotion, 12*, 38–48.

Prochaska, J. O., Velicer, W. F., DiClemente, C. C., & Fava, J. L. (1988). Measuring the processes of change: Applications to the cessation of smoking. *Journal of Consulting and Clinical Psychology, 56*, 520–528.

Prochaska, J. O., Velicer, W. F., DiClemente, C. C., Guadagnoli, E., & Rossi, J. (1991). Patterns of change: A dynamic typology applied to smoking cessation. *Multivariate Behavioral Research, 26*, 83–107.

Rich, J. D., Holmes, L., Salas, C., Macalino, G., Davis, D., Ryczek, J., et al. (2001). Successful linkage of medical care and community services for HIV-positive offenders being released from prison. *Journal of Urban Health, 78*, 279–289.

Rossi, P.H. (1992). *Using theory to improve program and policy evaluations.* Westport, CT: Greenwood.

Ruffin, J. E., Spencer, H. R., Abel, A., Gage, G, & Miles, L. (1993). Crisis stabilization services for children and adolescents: A brokerage model to reduce admissions to state psychiatric facilities. *Community Mental Health Journal, 29*, 433–441.

Shakeshaft, A. P., Bowman, J. A., Burrows, S., Doran, C. M., & Sanson-Fisher, R. W. (1997). Community-based alcohol counseling: A randomized clinical trail. *Addictions, 97*, 1449–1463.

Smets, A. C. (1988). What to do when the crisis is over? *Journal of Strategic and Systemic Therapies, 4*, 20–29.

Smyrnios, K. X., & Kirby, R. J. (1993). Long-term comparison of brief versus unlimited psychodynamic treatments with children and their parents. *Journal of Consulting and Clinical Psychology, 61*, 1020–1027.

Strom, K. (1992). Reimbursement demands and treatment decisions: A growing dilemma for social workers. *Social Work, 37*, 398–404.

Walter, J. L., & Peller, J. E. (1992). *Becoming solution-focused in brief therapy.* New York: Brunner/Mazel.

Watts, R. E., & Pietrzak, D. (2000). Adlerian encouragement and the therapeutic process of solution-focused brief therapy. *Journal of Counseling and Development, 78*, 442–227.

Weisz, J. R., Thurber, C. A., Sweeney, L., Proffitt, V. D., & Le Gagnoux, G. L. (1997). Brief treatment of mild-to moderate children depression using primary and secondary control enhancement training. *Journal of Consulting and Clinical Psychology, 65*, 703–707.

Woods, M., & Hollis, F. (Eds.). (1990). *Casework: A psychosocial therapy.* New York: McGraw-Hill.

ASSESSMENT AND INTERVENTION WITH SPECIFIC POPULATIONS

Chapter 11

ASSESSMENT OF CHILDREN

Michael E. Woolley

Social workers are vital members of teams delivering services to children across a variety of settings including, but not limited to, child welfare agencies, family service organizations, schools, health-care providers, and mental health settings. The struggles and challenges faced by children served by those social workers covers a broad spectrum from day-to-day struggles to life altering trauma. In all those settings and struggles, beginning the social work intervention process with a systematic and comprehensive effort to gather information about the child, the social contexts of the child, and the presenting struggle or challenge is a critical first step to providing professional, appropriate, and effective services to children who have been impacted by issues ranging from sexual abuse or mental illness to brain tumors or learning disabilities.

Social work has been increasingly called on, from both outside and inside the profession, to demonstrate the effectiveness of its practices. This scrutiny provides the impetus to engage in research to develop evidence-based practice (EBP) strategies and approaches (Gambrill, 1999). The needs for quality assessment tools and strategies as a fundamental task within that effort are twofold. First, all practice activities should start with and be informed by an assessment process. Second, gathering evidence as to the effectiveness of an intervention requires assessing the target of that intervention before and after that intervention is delivered; therefore, reliable and valid assessment measures are a fundamental tool in the pursuit of evidence to support practice.

This chapter first defines what is involved in performing a systematic and comprehensive social work child assessment process. The accumulated social work practice knowledge in the area of child assessment emerging across the first 100 years of professional social work is discussed. We then outline the current prevailing framework used to gather, organize, and present assessment information about children. More recent developments in the assessment of children are then added to that framework, for example, the necessity of gathering information from multiple informants and using multiple information-gathering tools when assessing children. Within that evolving assessment framework, a growing effort in social work (and other helping professions) is to strive to utilize evidence-based strategies and tools in practice. What is meant by evidence-based practice and how that effort can inform the most effective and efficient assessment of children is explored. The limitations to the evidence in support of our current assessment strategies with children, as well as promising ways to reduce those limitations, are detailed. Finally, current trends and developments in the assessment of children in social work practice settings including child protection, schools, and mental health are presented.

DEFINING ASSESSMENT

Assessment is used to describe an assortment of activities and processes in the social sciences and human services, that involve gathering information about a client(s) and the presenting circumstances leading to an evaluation, determination, or plan of action focused on that client or client system. In social work practice, some aspects of assessment are driven by the practice setting, the population being served, and the practice model being applied by the social worker. However, this chapter offers a framework for social work assessment with children that, while embedded within the evolution of the social work perspective and the current effort to situate social work practice on an evidence-base, can be applied by any direct practitioner regardless of setting, population, practice level, or model. In this chapter, a descriptive and evolving definition of assessment in the context of providing social work services to children is offered. As a starting framework, assessment in social work with children is defined as including three key components: (1) data collection, (2) informed by a contextual perspective, (3) leading to a prevention or intervention plan.

Data Collection

First, assessment of children is in large part defined by a range of activities used to gather information about a child, a struggle or challenge confronting that child, and relevant information about that child's social environments. Those activities can include but are not limited to: (a) clinical interviews, (b) structured interviews, (c) self-report instruments, (d) direct observations, and (e) reviews of existing records. Those data collection activities may elicit information from multiple informants including the child, parents/guardians, other family members and key individuals in the child's life, and professionals with direct experience with the child.

Contextual Perspective

The second component is illustrated by an enlightening distinction about assessment in social work practice made by Clifford (1998). He referred to "social assessment" as opposed to psychological or medical assessment, in that social assessment "is centered on a social explanation—and will draw on social research and social science concepts" in identifying the service needs of an individual, small group, or community. While social workers clearly also draw on, and are informed by, psychological and medical aspects of and explanations for client struggles, Clifford's focus on the social aspects of the client and his or her struggles distinguishes assessment in social work from assessment in other disciplines. This focus on contextual factors in social work can be seen in many assessment orientations in social work, for example, the person-in-environment perspective, psychosocial models, the widespread use of ecological systems thinking, and the pervasive structuring of assessment information into a biopsychosocial assessment document.

Prevention or Intervention Planning

Third, child assessment in social work will also be defined as having as the central goal in gathering that information, to inform the development of a social work prevention or intervention plan to help that child or group of children. While systematic information about a child and his or her social environments may be gathered for other reasons—such as part of a research endeavor or eligibility evaluation—unless the ultimate goal is a formulation leading to the implementation of a social work service plan, then the gathering of that information does not constitute an assessment as it will be referred to in this chapter.

Thus, a social work assessment of a child involves: (a) data collection defined as a systematic gathering of information about the child, a struggle or challenge facing that child, and that child's multiple social environments; (b) pursued from a contextual perspective oriented to how the child's social environments influence the child, the struggle or challenge, and efforts to resolve that struggle or challenge; and (c) developing an intervention plan to assist that child with that struggle or challenge as the primary goal of that data collection effort.

The application of systemic and comprehensive assessment strategies has become more important given profession-wide efforts to build an evidence-based approach to social work services (Gambrill, 1999). Since service delivery activities start with and are built on the assessment process, reliable and valid assessment strategies and tools are fundamental to identifying, developing, evaluating, and providing evidence-based interventions. For example, reliable and valid assessments provide a vehicle to evaluate interventions, thereby establishing evidence as to when and with whom such interventions can be effective. Further, the application of interventions with already established bodies of evidence as to their effectiveness should only be utilized after the application of systematic, comprehensive, reliable, and valid assessment strategies and tools to inform the selection of interventions appropriate for a specific child in a specific situation. Additionally, the results of a systematic assessment should influence the provision of the interventions chosen, thereby following long-established social work practice principles such as *starting where the client is* and *treat each client as an individual* and provide individualized services (Hepworth, Rooney, & Larsen, 2002; Pilsecker, 1994).

The wide variety of settings in which social workers serve children, the larger array of struggles and challenges faced by those children, and the wide range of what and who social workers are actually assessing—for example, the child, a potential home placement, the risk of a caregiver to abuse or neglect, the appropriateness of a classroom setting—all make a truly comprehensive discussion of assessment of children in social work seem daunting. Therefore, one goal of this chapter is to set the current state of assessment of children in social work in an historical context. That historical overview will present our collective professional knowledge informing the assessment of children as a framework on which to add recent advancements.

HISTORICAL BACKGROUND

Mary Richmond, in her seminal book *Social Diagnosis* (1917), presented the first comprehensive treatise on the assessment process in social work. Although she used the term *diagnosis,* which for most social workers today means something quite different than assessment, what she was referring to as a social diagnosis 90 years ago meets the three criteria for social work assessment offered earlier. In fact, for those who have not read all or even parts of her book, it is truly worth the time, and you may find it contains surprisingly still-relevant insights on assessment and social casework and prescient glimpses of things to come. For example, Richmond described her preparation to write *Social Diagnosis* as including systematically reviewing social work case records and recording interviews with caseworkers across five different sites over the course of a year "to bring to light the best social work practice that could be found" (p. 7). Is that not an effort to build a body of evidence about what works? Richmond further described her efforts in the preparation of the book, "the most difficult of all my problems has been to make a presentation on the handling of evidence" (p. 9) in the assessment process. Richmond's book culminates in a series of structured interview protocols for the assessment of various clients and situations.

Best Practice? Evidence? Structured Protocols?

The pursuit of providing clients with the best possible social work services available at a given point in time, basing assessment on gathering the best evidence possible, and collecting that evidence in a systematic manner are distinctly not new endeavors in the social work profession. In fact, social work has a rich history of professional knowledge development in the area of assessment.

Central to that accumulation of knowledge in the assessment of children has been the conceptual perspective of a child as embedded in a set of social contexts. Mary Richmond articulated that fundamental perspective 90 years ago. Jane Addams and the Hull House staff were also guided by that perspective. For example, in the area of juvenile delinquency, Hull House rejected dominant theories based on heredity, and asserted that the most important factors leading to juvenile delinquency were environmental (Hart, 1990). With respect to assessment, that clearly means the gathering of information about, and analysis of, the social environment that a child inhabits in an effort to understand that child's struggles and behavior.

The history of that perspective can be traced to today by examining social work textbooks over the decades detailing the state of the art and science of casework practices. For example, Hamilton (1951) stated assessment is an attempt to understand the client, the problem, and the situation; and authors such as Perlman (1957), Hollis (1964), and Pincus and Minahan (1973) iterated that triad of assessment. Hollis stated this perspective succinctly when she pointed out that in assessment "strengths as well as weaknesses in both the person and the situation are important considerations" (p. 261). Hepworth et al. (2002) offered a similar triad, assessment they suggested is a process "to gather information and formulation of that information into a coherent picture of the client and his or her circumstances" leading to "our inferences about the nature and causes of the client's difficulties" (p. 187). They did, however, describe a meaningful shift in one aspect of that triad in that they stressed the assessment of the *needs* and the *strengths* of the client, as much as the *difficulties* of the client. This strengths perspective continues to guide the development of structured assessment instruments for practice, for example, a strength-based and culturally informed reliable and valid assessment tool for practice with Native American youth, their families, and communities (Gilgun, 2004). This sort of melding of the long-evolving social work ecological, strengths, and culturally informed orientation to helping clients, with more recent and rigorous assessment methodology, seems like a promising trajectory in social work assessment with children.

The focus on strengths has grown in part from the long-standing fundamental humanistic perspective in social work that all clients are doing their best and have resources and that where clients struggle it is because of a deficit in those available resources. Such resources can be both internal and environmental, and clients can call on those resources—social workers can likewise call on those resources in the assessment process—to help meet challenges and struggles clients face (McQuaide & Ehrenreich, 1997). Such a strengths perspective grows out of social work's values and ethical orientation to clients: (a) as persons of worth, (b) who have a fundamental right to choose their goals in the helping process, (c) how they go about working on those goals, and (d) who are capable of solving their own problems with appropriate support (Loewenberger & Dolgoff, 1985). The strengths perspective also stands in contrast to the still pervasive medical model of diagnosing and labeling limitations, particularly prevalent in mental health practice (Cox, 2006). The strengths perspective and the focus on the social environments of a client are reflected in the ubiquitous development of an ecological systems orientation in social work practice.

EVOLVING ECOLOGICAL SYSTEMS PERSPECTIVE

A seminal application of the ecological perspective in social work is the introduction of the life model of practice by Germain and Gitterman in 1980. As they put it, "the social purpose [of social work] calls for a practice method that is designed to engage people's strengths and the forces pushing them toward growth, and to influence organizational structures, other social systems, and physical settings so they will be more responsive to people's needs" (p. 2). In the 1980s, the ecological perspective was increasingly used to articulate the social work approach to assessment and service delivery. Further, some authors started adding concepts from the general systems theory to that ecological perspective to create what was termed the ecosystems perspective (Greif & Lynch, 1983).

The adaptation of systems thinking introduced several helpful theoretical concepts into social work thinking. Those concepts are especially helpful in assessment, as they offer insights into how social systems—the interactions between a client and his or her environment—work. For example, *equilibrium,* a concept that states that systems (read families) tend toward establishing a balance that can be maintained, whether that balance is good or not so good for the members of the system. That *boundaries,* such as between members of the family, between the family and other systems like the school or neighborhood are critical is the flow of information, resources, and support within and among systems. Social work has long asserted that assessing and attending to these dynamic processes is critical to effective assessment of a child and his or her social systems (Germain & Gitterman, 1980).

Another notable step in the evolution of the contextual orientation to assessment in social work is the person-in-environment (PIE) system, introduced by Karls and Wandrei (1992). The PIE system offered a common language and structure for social workers to use in formulating assessments from the unique orientation of social work. One goal in the development of the PIE system was to design an assessment structure that focused on the "social well-being" of a client, which was identified as "different than physical or mental well-being" (p. 81), that assertion being supported by research about those three domains. The PIE assessment approach was systematic and comprehensive and included information about the client, the problem, and the client's social environment. Therefore, possessing many of the characteristics described earlier for an effective assessment. It also introduced a coding system for client problems, with codes for duration, severity, and coping, as a way to quantify assessment information. The basic structure of the PIE system includes four factors: Factor 1: Social Role Problems, Factor 2: Environmental Problems, Factor 3: Mental Disorders, and Factor 4: Physical Disorders. This system shares some structural characteristics with the *Diagnostic and Statistical Manual of Mental Disorders* (American Psychiatric Association, 2000) diagnostic format, and although not widely used today, the PIE system was an important development in social work's quest to build a professionally unique and uniform structure to assessment. Additionally, the PIE perspective continues to evolve, for example, the person-environment practice approach, as described by Kemp, Whitaker, and Tracy (1997), offers an ecological competence-oriented practice model that stresses the importance of ongoing assessment, social support, empowerment, and collective action.

Other developments in social assessment have also yielded systematic formats to gather and organize information. For example, there are two diagrammatic assessment tools that have seen widespread use in social work practice with children and families, the eco-map and the genogram (Hartman, 1995). Both tools grew out of the ecological systems perspective and gained popularity in social work practice in the 1980s. Either or both can be drawn by a social worker in concert with a child and family during the assessment process and used as tools to elicit and synthesize information from the child and family as they help complete each diagram. Either can then be used to analyze family dynamics, gain a comprehensive picture of the family circumstances related to the struggle or challenge, used to search for strengths and possible resources, and for ongoing collection of assessment information.

Hartman (1995), a social worker, first developed the eco-map for use in child welfare practice. An eco-map has at its center the child and family, drawn as a circle (Figure 11.1). Then surrounding the family and child is a system of circles representing other important people, resources, or activities, for example, extended family; friends of the child and parents/guardians; activities such as recreation, sports, or hobbies; organizations such as schools, churches, neighborhood groups, or workplaces; or other agencies such as health-care providers, mental health providers, or juvenile court. Care should be taken to include not just circles related to the presenting challenge or struggle, but that also represent strengths and resources to the child and family, and other struggles or possible barriers to solving the presenting issue. Once all the needed circles have been drawn, various types of lines are drawn between the circles to represent the nature of the connection between the child and family and each particular circle. For example, a solid line depicts a strong relationship, a dashed line represents a tenuous connection, while a line with hash marks across it suggests a stressful connection. Arrows are drawn along the connections to indicate the direction of flow of support, resources, and energy.

Bowen (1978), a psychiatrist who was a pioneer in the field of family therapy, developed the genogram as an assessment tool. Carter and McGoldrick (1980), social workers who have been at the forefront of the evolution of family therapy over the past 25 years, particularly with respect to gender and ethnicity issues, introduced the use of genograms in social work. In drawing a genogram, three or even four generations of the family are depicted (Figure 11.2). Males are drawn as squares and females as circles and a system of lines are utilized to connect family members and indicate the nature of their kinship. A genogram has levels for each generation, such that family members in the same generation are on

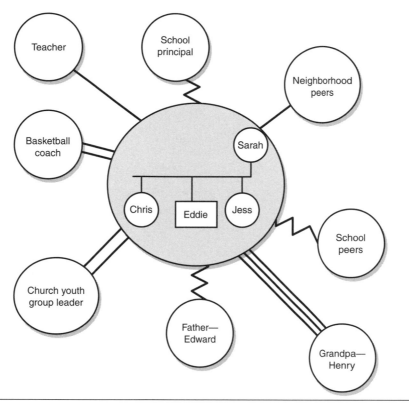

Figure 11.1   Example of an eco-map for Eddie: A 10-year-old boy with behavior problems

the same level across the page. Once all the multigenerational members of the family are included and kinship lines drawn, other aspects of the family dynamics and circumstances can be included such as marriages and divorces, deaths and illnesses, alcohol or drug use, significant events in the family history, religion, occupation, education, mental health problems, or any important events or family dynamics. Similar to the eco-map, various types of lines can also be added that characterize the nature of the relationships between family members. A genogram is used in practice not just as an assessment tool to identify family patterns, strengths and resources, and unresolved issues, but as an ongoing tool to identify strengths and resources in intervention planning and implementation. A comprehensive discussion of the use of genograms as an assessment and intervention tool is beyond this chapter; for more detail see McGoldrick, Gerson, and Shellenberger (1999).

Another important step in the evolution of the ecological perspective in social work is the incorporation of a focus on risk and protective factors and the vulnerability or resilience to the impact of environmental stressors that such factors may offer (Fraser, Richman, & Galinsky, 1999). From this perspective, the characteristics of the physical environment and social relationships may act as risk or protective factors with respect to child and family functioning. Risk factors are environmental characteristics that predict undesirable developmental outcomes, while protective factors are promotive of positive developmental outcomes or may compensate for the negative impact of certain risk factors (Richman, Bowen, & Woolley, 2004). Central to this perspective is the concept of *resilience,* which has been defined as the dynamic interplay of environmental, social, and individual

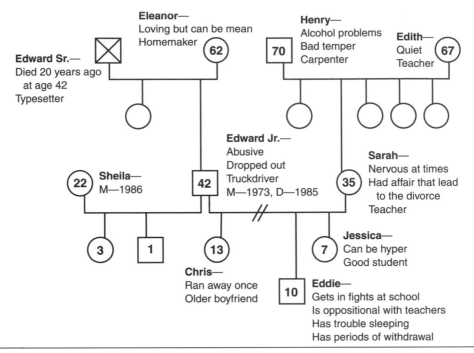

Figure 11.2   Example of a genogram for Eddie: A 10-year-old boy with behavior problems

protective factors, in the context of risk exposure, leading to positive adaptation and desirable developmental outcomes for youth (Luthar, Cicchetti, & Becker, 2000).

Bringing many of these concepts together in a manner that makes them applicable to assessment with children is the eco-interactional developmental (EID) perspective as described by Richman et al. (2004). This framework is informed by: (a) the ecological systems perspective in terms of the centrality of the social environment, (b) the risk and resilience perspective in how that environment influences children, all within (c) a developmental orientation whereby child functioning can only be meaningfully interpreted in the context of that child's developmental trajectory and current developmental level, needs, and struggles. Within this ecological framework, there are three key environmental contexts that must be assessed in social work practice with children: family, neighborhood, and school. As described by Bronfenbrenner (2005), these *microsystems* are the environmental settings that directly influence a child, while *mezzosystems* represent the connections among those key microsystems. Examples of mezzosystems would include the nature of the relationship between a child's family and a teacher or the relationships between the family and neighborhood residents and organizations. The larger social, cultural, and political environments that children and their families inhabit, and the characteristics of those systems, constitute the *macrosystem*.

Social work also has a rich history in stressing issues of cultural and ethnic diversity and historic and current forms of discrimination and oppression that emerge within a family's macrosystem and the various microsystems and mezzosystems surrounding a child and his or her family. Building on the ecological and strengths-oriented PIE assessment system described earlier, Appleby, Colon, and Hamilton (2007) have comprehensively approached the effects of race, culture, and social class in the dynamics of oppression and discrimination (including racism, sexism, homophobia, ableism, and religious bigotry) on healthy development and social functioning. Since a fundamental goal in social work assessment is to take a contextual perspective, it seems imperative to attend to the impact of such issues with respect to child clients and their families who may be members of currently or historically oppressed or discriminated groups. For example, the authors point out that culture is often seen as static, when in fact it is dynamic, changing as it develops much like an individual develops and changing as the result of interactions with the environment and other cultures. Therefore, the culture in which the child client and his or her family are members is changing, as are the other cultures that child is surrounded by, and the dominant or majority culture, if that is different than the child's culture. Those multiple changing cultural contexts can at once serve as developmental settings for the child and family, a source of strengths and resources, mediators of struggles and challenges, or sources of oppression and discrimination, all potentially profoundly impacting child and family adaptation and functioning.

The pursuit of *social justice* has become an overarching framework in social work practice that refers to activities to reduce the causes and sequelae on clients, groups, and society associated with oppression and discrimination. Finn and Jacobsen (2003) have offered a social work practice model that synthesizes on well-established practice values, professional ethics, client engagement and professional relationship principles, and the PIE orientation to assessment, while focused on the impact of traditionally unjust structures and processes and the pursuit of socially just outcomes for clients. A comprehensive discussion of the impact on the child assessment process of social justice issues associated with current or historical oppression and discrimination is beyond the scope of this chapter, and readers are encouraged to consult the literature starting with the references cited here. In fact, much research and intervention development and evaluation yet needs to be done related to the impact of issues of gender, race, ethnicity, culture, mental or physical ability, age, socioeconomic class, religion, family structure, sexual orientation, gender identity or expression, and citizenship status on clients and the social work helping process. However, a couple of examples may offer tangible reference points to illustrate that ambitious research and practice strategy development agenda.

In the context of working with Latino clients, Colon, Appleby, and Hamilton (2007) warn us that traditional models of social work practice "ignore the interdependent, mutually supportive aspects of Latino group norms and individual values" (p. 302): For example, the centrality of familism (*familismo*) in the provision of social and economic support, and the importance of dignity (*dignidad*) and respect (*respeto*) in the dynamics of Latino families. Likewise, Colon and colleagues assert there are important practice implications to the historical racism experienced by African Americans, which today accounts for reduced access to socioeconomic resources, poor health and mental health outcomes, and limited access to social services, much of which is maintained by ongoing structural racism, particularly inequitable access to educational opportunity (Orfield, Losen, Wald, & Swanson, 2004). Finn and Jacobsen (2003) suggest that the application of the *empowerment* approach, an approach with a strong tradition in social work with respect to helping oppressed groups (Gutierrez & Lewis, 1999; Simon, 1994), presents a significant addition to an ecologically PIE-oriented framework to assessment in the pursuit of socially just outcomes for clients.

Identifying and building evidence to support the understanding of the practice assessment implications of such cultural and social justice dynamics that impact children and families requires ongoing research efforts. For example, researchers (Ogbu, 1991, 1998; Oyserman, Bybee, & Terry, 2006; Oyserman, Terry, & Bybee, 2002; Woolley & Bowen, 2007; Woolley & Grogan-Kaylor, 2006) have empirically studied and furthered our knowledge (evidence) base about what and how children who are members of historically oppressed and discriminated groups struggle in school and how to reduce long-standing gaps in school achievement for such groups. However, such efforts must find the balance between making broad, or even stereotypical, assertions about members of certain cultural or ethnicity groups and identifying and explicating important cultural patterns impacting social functioning, assessment, and service delivery. The task for individual social work practitioners is to actively seek and synthesize knowledge about the client groups she or he is serving, from understanding cultural practices and norms to emerging research informing evidence-based assessment and intervention activities.

In sum, an effective assessment of a child in need of social work services not only requires data about the child's struggles, challenges, and functioning, and the social microsystems—family, neighborhood and school—in which that child is embedded, but also the mezzosystem cultural dynamics of that child and his or her family along with the current and historical implications of that culture within the wider macrosystemic cultural context. Once such data has been gathered, it must be organized into a coherent format for analysis and synthesis in order to inform intervention planning. A biopsychosocial assessment offers a format for such organization and synthesis.

BIOPSYCHOSOCIAL ASSESSMENT REPORT

Organizing the data collected in a systematic and comprehensive social work assessment of a child involves bringing together these various elements that have evolved with the accumulation of social work practice knowledge. Reflecting the pervasive impact of the ecological perspective in social work, an assessment report of a child is most frequently termed a *biopsychosocial assessment* (Lukas, 1993), although some authors have referred to it as a *psychosocial study* (Cooper & Lesser, 2002) or a *multidimensional assessment* (Hepworth et al., 2002). The outline of a biopsychosocial assessment reflects the social work ecological orientation, including information about various aspects of the child, the presenting challenge, the child's environment, that need to be attended to in the developing an effective service plan. Table 11.1 is a suggested biopsychosocial assessment outline that reflects the evolution of social work thinking over the past 100 years as it relates to assessment. Some sections will not be called for depending on the setting for practice, the child's developmental stage, the presenting struggle, and a child's particular circumstances. Further, additional sections may be needed in some situations to address specific issues that are relevant to a comprehensive assessment study of a specific child.

We have reviewed the evolution of the ecosystems perspective informing assessment in social work over the past 100 years: assessment tools that have grown out of that perspective like the PIE system, genograms, and eco-maps; the recognition of the critical role of issues in assessment such as cultural diversity and oppression; and the organization of ecological assessment information into a systematic and comprehensive biopsychosocial assessment. These accumulated forms of social work assessment knowledge and strategies with children are still useful today across the very wide range of settings where social workers serve children. However, there are setting- and situation-specific assessment tools that have more

Table 11.1   Biopsychosocial Assessment Outline

Identifying Information
Child's name, age, race/ethnicity, physical appearance, religion
Child's place of residence, school, other important settings
Referral source and referral information

Presenting Struggle(s)
Child's definition
Parent/guardian's definition
Social worker's definition

History of the Struggle(s)
When did it start, how frequently, with whom, and where does it occur?
What social, emotional, psychological, learning, or medical/physical risk factors contribute to, or
    are key factors in this struggle?
What are the consequences of the struggle to the child and family?
Results from assessment instruments: child-reports, adult-reports, and structured interviews
What attempts have been made to resolve this struggle:
—By the child or family?
—With the assistance of professional helpers?

Safety Concerns
Abuse or neglect concerns
Suicide or homicide risk

Developmental History
Current developmental challenges
Previous developmental challenges the child
Role of developmental issues in the presenting challenge

Family History
Multigeneration background of child's family setting
Ethnocultural issues: Acculturation stressors, language concerns, immigration/refugee status
Genogram

Strengths and Resilience Factors
The child's talents, resources, skills, and protective factors
Family strengths, resources, and protective factors
Extended family resources
Communal resources: Neighborhood, religious organization, ethnocultural organizations
Eco-map

Results, Interpretations, and Implications of Structured Assessment Instruments
Self-report instruments
Adult-report instruments
Structured interviews

Child and Family Needs
Economic: Income, housing, food, clothing, transportation
Social/emotional: Peer interaction, recreation
Educational: Appropriate school services
Medical: Health care, medication
Sociocultural: Translator, cultural specific support, community, advocacy
Legal: Guardian ad litem, current court involvement, advocacy

(continued)

Table 11.1   *(Continued)*

Mental Status Exam
Snapshot of child's social, psychological, cognitive, and behavioral functioning
Most often used in mental health settings (see Cooper & Lesser, 2002)

Mental Health Diagnosis
DSM Five Axis Diagnosis—most often used in mental health and other clinical settings, see the
    DSM-IV-TR (American Psychiatric Association, 2000)
Results from mental health assessment instruments

Initial Contacts with Child and Family
Brief description of first meetings and actions taken
Child's and family's orientation to the social worker and helping process

Summary Statement
A paragraph or two summing up the key information

Initial Service Plan
Identify focus of initial service efforts
Goals and objectives for those efforts
Who will be involved, how, when, and for what purpose?

Note: This outline was informed by Cooper and Lesser (2002); Fraser, Richman, and Galinsky (1999); Hepworth, Rooney, and Larson (2002); and Lukas (1993).

recently evolved since social work adopted the application of measurement theory in the 1970s and sought to develop more valid and reliable assessment tools for practice and research (Hudson, 1997). In the sections that follow, some of those assessment strategies for use in settings such as child welfare, schools, mental health, and health are detailed. This brings us into the 1990s and the emergence of the movement in social work toward evidence-based practice (Gambrill, 1999). This movement has been calling for increased practice evaluation and research efforts to build evidence supporting the effectiveness of social work practice. Fundamental tasks toward that end are the development and application of evidence-based assessment strategies.

SUMMARY OF CURRENT EVIDENCE-BASED ASSESSMENT OF CHILDREN

Since Mary Richmond reviewed case records and interviewed social workers over 90 years ago, members of the social work profession have endeavored to identify, disseminate, and increase the widespread use of what we have evidence to believe works best for clients. Over those many decades, our methodological tools to measure: (a) the struggles our clients face; (b) the functioning levels of children and families across social, emotional, and behavioral domains; and (c) the impact of our professional efforts to help have steadily advanced. Those advancements have increased the profession's ability to determine what works best for clients, and our expectations for the evidence in support of those determinations should therefore likewise progress. The pursuit of EBP is the latest effort toward that progression (Gambrill, 1999). However, efforts to move toward an evidence-based approach to the assessment of children are only just beginning; while there has been an increasing focus on evidence-based intervention approaches for use with children, less attention has been given to assessment (Mash & Hunsley, 2005). While it does seem true that limited effort has gone into evaluating and synthesizing the assessment tools and strategies available for specific situations for children from an evidence-based perspective, there are many tools out there with supporting evidence that can be identified and applied. Next, a process to identify such tools and strategies is offered.

Defining what qualifies as *evidence* in support of child assessment tools and strategies evokes issues of epistemology, paradigmatic orientation, and research and practice methodologies, a comprehensive discussion of which is beyond the scope of this chapter. Social work has been historically epistemologically diverse, valuing different ways of knowing (Fraser, Taylor, Jackson, & O'Jack, 1991). Within that historical context, the paradigm of *pragmatism*—which supports the application of the research or practice methods that work best for a question or client—and a *mixed methods* approach—combining quantitative and qualitative tools, which in the case of assessment means using both clinical interview techniques and empirically tested self-report instruments or structured interviews—provides the epistemological foundation for this chapter (Tashakkori & Teddlie, 2003).

Fitting within the definition of what can qualify as evidence, Gambrill (1999) has offered a hierarchy of possible evidence in support of interventions that can be adapted to assessment tools and strategies for use with children. Gambrill described six levels; however, the last two were cases of the evidence indicating that an intervention would not be beneficial or even harmful. Therefore, the top four levels of evidence will be adapted here:

1. Evidence level one, rigorously developed structured assessment instruments, which attended to the developmental and cognitive characteristics of children, with resulting strong evidence of validity and reliability, demonstrated with multiple samples including in practice settings substantially similar to the targeted population.

2. Evidence level two, well-developed assessment tools or strategies with some evidence of reliability and validity with at least one sample similar to the targeted population.

3. Evidence level three, includes child assessment tools or strategies with reliability and validity evidence from samples somewhat similar to the targeted population, or, assessment tools with anecdotal or clinical evidence of utility with clients similar to the targeted population.

4. Finally, level four consists of tools or strategies that appear promising but for which no evidence exists as to their utility with the targeted population.

However, locating the practice approach for any given situation with the best supporting evidence requires some effort. Applying EBP is more of a process or goal than a destination. A five-step process emerging from the medical field to locate the best evidence has been applied to child welfare practice (see Shlonsky & Wagner, 2005). Applying that five-step process to the various social work practice contexts where assessment of children is needed, can inform a systematic approach to deciding what assessment approaches would be best in a given setting, with a specific population of children, experiencing a certain range of struggles or challenges:

1. State the assessment needs in the situation of interest as a question that can be answered. For example, what is the best approach to assess depression in elementary-aged children in schools?

2. Search for the best evidence with which to answer that question. In the current example, that process might start with searching the literature for assessment tools and

strategies that have been shown to be reliable and valid—see the following section for a discussion of the reliability and validity of assessment instruments—with latency-aged children, accessible to school social workers, and, which would effectively and efficiently assess potentially large numbers of children.

3. Evaluate the tools and strategies found in light of the available evidence in support of their utility, in this case, comparing reliability and validity results and evaluating descriptions of their application in elementary school settings.

4. Relying on the clinical experience and judgment of the practitioners involved, integrate the results of the evaluation of the available tools and strategies with the specific characteristics and needs of the clients who will be assessed.

5. Appraise the performance of the previous four steps with the goal of making the next search for needed assessment tools and strategies more streamlined and effective.

With the state of our knowledge and evidence in support of our practices ever advancing, this process may need to be done with some regularity so current practices in an agency or utilized by a social worker do not fall significantly behind the current state of the evidence. That process points out that one of the advantages of EBP is the constant pursuit of providing the best services to clients, which is in sync with the ethical values of social work. Other advantages include encouraging ongoing professional development and transparency of the effectiveness of social work services that maximizes practitioners providing clients with the opportunity to make informed consent about services (Gambrill & Shlonsky, 2001). Although such a process is needed to find the best currently available assessment tools for a specific situation, some general principles of an evidenced-based approach to the assessment of children can be gleaned from our accumulating knowledge. One is the use of multiple informants in the assessment of children.

Multiple Informants

As asserted earlier, the central goal in the assessment of a child is the formulation of an intervention plan. To effectively inform that intervention, an evidence-based assessment is using the best available tools and strategies to gather information about the child, the presenting struggle or challenge, and the critical microsystems that child inhabits such as his or her family, school, and neighborhood. The accumulating evidence supports the conclusion that the most effective strategy is to collect that information from multiple informants who know and interact with that child (N. K. Bowen, Bowen, & Woolley, 2004; Pelham, Fabiano, & Massetti, 2005). Multiple informants (such as the child, parents/guardians, and teachers) typically do not agree on important aspects of the child's functioning because those multiple informants will have different perspectives emerging from different settings, all of which may hold "truths" about the child (Bidaut-Russell, Valla, Thomas, Bergeron, & Lawson, 1998; Ivens & Rehm, 1988; March, Parker, Sullivan, Stallings, & Conners, 1997; Montgomery, 1994; Tinsley & Holtgrave, 1997; Wright-Strawdermann & Watson, 1992; Yugar & Shapiro, 2001). This is a very important point; no reporter providing assessment data about a child—the child, parent, foster-parent, sibling, teacher, police officer, probation officer, and so on—should be seen as the gold standard or without merit. The type of data sought, the knowledge and experiences pertaining to the child of the possible reporters, the apparent veracity of those reporters, any complicating factors impacting the data provided by those reporters, as well as a myriad of other possible situational factors must be included in the evaluation and utilization of assessment data collected. Still, the most effective strategy is to gather assessment data about a child from multiple informants.

Child

Children have often been assessed by gathering information only from adults such as parents/guardians and teachers. However, research has found that children often report higher rates or severity of social or emotional problems than adult informants, for example, depression, which is experienced internally and not easily observed (Breton, Bergeron, Valla, Berthiaume, & Gaudet, 1999; Wood, Kroll, Moore, & Harrington, 1995). Further, it has been found that children as young as 6 provide assessment data that can be more predictive of future functioning than adult-report assessment data (Ialongo, Edelsohn, & Kellam, 2001). These findings should lead clinicians and researchers to discontinue assessing children solely or even primarily by adult report. Clearly, assessing a child should include gathering data directly from that child.

Parent/Guardian

There are many important aspects of the child's functioning for which the caregiving adults can provide vital information. It also seems self-evident that parent/guardians can provide important information about the family situation, information that is not appropriately gathered from the child, such as financial issues, parent/guardian health, mental health, substance abuse struggles, or marital conflicts negatively impacting parenting behaviors. Parent/guardians may also observe improvements, such as in behavior, mood, or other functioning, before the child does.

Other Family

Informed by the ecological systems perspective, family therapists have long observed that other family members may provide valuable assessment information about a presenting challenge or struggle with a child (Haley, 1987). For example, a sibling may have a perspective on a child's problem or functioning that is not available to the child or parents/guardians. Similarly, cultures with strong extended families, such as extended family caregiving networks, may mean that grandparents, aunts, uncles, even cousins may be vital participants in a child's life and provide important assessment data (Paniagua, 2005).

Teachers

How a child functions at school is an important question in any assessment of a child because school performance is a vital developmental outcome for children (Woolley & Grogan-Kaylor, 2006). Teacher input is a valuable source of data about the child's school functioning, and that is why teachers are an important reporter in several well-validated child assessment instruments for elementary school-aged children (e.g., N. K. Bowen et al., 2004; Essex et al., 2002).

Multiple Data Collection Strategies

Clinical Interviews

Assessment interviews are the traditional method of collecting assessment data in social work with children and their families. This is still a foundation strategy for assessing and intervening with children and will likely always be. A clinical interview is required as a starting point to determine what other assessment tools and strategies may be appropriate. While the more structured assessment tools described next can collect reliable and valid data about children, the interpretation of those tools, the application to the presenting struggle or challenge, and the formulation of a plan for intervention are still tasks that can only be accomplished the skills, experience, and judgment of a trained social worker. Additionally, once more structured assessment tools have been administered and scored, a social worker can use his or her clinical skills to gather more information from the child and family about what the scores may mean.

Structured Survey Instruments

Self-report instruments are completed by the child or other informant and mathematically represent the child's or informant's—parent/guardian, other family, teacher—perception about the extent or level of a struggle or challenge by assigning it a number. In the case of a child self-report instrument assessing depression for example, each question or item measures the presence and/or extent of a depression-related symptom. Therefore, a depression self-report measure relies on a child or other reporter to accurately answer questions about the child's behaviors, thoughts, beliefs, feelings, attitudes, and/or perceptions. Self-report assessment instruments typically consist of multiple questions or items with two or more response options. Most instruments include subgroups of items designed to measure different underlying symptoms impacting the child. Each such group of items constitutes a *scale,* and an assessment instrument may contain one or multiple scales (DeVellis, 2003). As discussed previously, the quality of such an instrument is a function of the evidence in support of its reliability and validity.

Reliability is the extent to which an assessment tool is consistent. When an instrument is consistent across time, it will result in similar depression scores at two different points in time with the same child (assuming the level of depression has not changed). That type of reliability is referred to as *test-retest* reliability. When an instrument is consistent across items in a scale, groups of items designed to measure the same underlying depression construct will show a pattern of similar answers within any given report. That type of reliability is known as *internal consistency reliability,* which is the most often reported form of instrument reliability and is usually estimated with Cronbach's formula for alpha (Cronbach, 1990).

Reliability coefficients range from .0 to 1.00. The closer to 1.00 the coefficient is, the more consistent the instrument is from administration to administration or among the items in the scale. A reliability coefficient can also be interpreted as revealing the percentage of an individual score that is attributable to the true score. In other words, if an instrument has an alpha of .80, 80% of the score is attributable to the child's level of depression, and 20% is attributable to something other than depression, in other words, sources of error. The reliabilities of child-report instruments are typically lower than for adult instruments. In general, reliabilities above .80 are considered good, with above .70 considered acceptable.

However, given that an instrument with a reliability of .70 includes 30% error, then scores with such an instrument must be interpreted in that light. For example, if an intervention is anticipated to have a 30% effect on a struggle or challenge, and the assessment tool used to measure change in the client before and after that intervention has a 30% proportion of measurement error, then the assessment tool being used will be limited in its ability to consistently detect true change. Reliability is the most often reported characteristic of instrument quality, and while good reliability is a necessary characteristic of a quality instrument, it is not by itself sufficient to evaluate an instrument. For an instrument to be judged to have level one or two evidence as defined previously, evidence as to its validity must also be available.

Validity is the extent to which an assessment tool measures what it is supposed to measure for a given individual at a given point in time. An instrument can be shown to be valid if it is shown to result in scores similar to a previously validated instrument or is predictive of outcomes or other variables with known relationships to the measured struggle or challenge. If an assessment tool is shown to result in similar scores to other tools that are known to be valid, it is said to have *criterion validity*. If an assessment tool is shown to be associated with related constructs in the predicted manner, the assessment tool is said to have *construct validity*. Assessing the validity of child depression instruments can be difficult because there are often a limited number of quality instruments available for use with children for a given purpose. Developing reliable and valid assessment tools requires careful and rigorous research. When developing assessment tools for use with children, the combination of the developmental level and limited cognitive ability of children makes that process even more difficult.

In terms of the example of assessing depression in children, such an assessment tool would be the Mood and Feelings Questionnaire (MFQ)—a 33-question self-report instrument designed for children ages 8 to 18. Statements describing depressive symptoms within the past 2 weeks are rated on a 3-point scale by the child. In addition to the child form, there is also a parent form to collect multi-informant data. Studies have shown good reliability for both the child (alpha = .90 to .94) and parent (alpha = .90 to .92) forms of the MFQ (Angold et al., 1995; Wood et al., 1995). The correlation between the child and parent forms has been found to range from .51 to .65, which represents higher interreporter correlation than typically found (Kent, Vostanis, & Feehan, 1997; Wood et al., 1995). The child form has been shown to have significantly higher diagnostic validity (Wood et al., 1995). Efforts to merge child and parent data have failed because no combination was more valid than the child data alone, which emphasizes the importance of gathering assessment information directly from children.

Structured Interview Instruments

Structured interview instruments consist of a set of scripted assessment questions that are asked of an informant by the social worker, with the responses to the questions indicated on the instrument form. The answers to the questions lead to a score, which will quantify specific struggles or symptoms that the child may be experiencing. Structured interview instruments are evaluated utilizing the same reliability and validity criteria used to evaluate the evidence in support of survey instruments. An example of such a tool is the Diagnostic Interview Schedule for Children (DISC), which is designed to assess for 30 different mental disorders in children. The DISC includes both a child and parent interview form and has been shown to have good reliability and validity in the assessment of mental disorders in children from disruptive behavior disorders to anxiety and depressive disorders (Shaffer, Fisher, Lucas, Dulcan, & Schwab-Stone, 2000). However, few such structured interview instruments have been developed for social work practice settings despite being a potentially reliable and valid strategy to collect assessment data, while still utilizing the interview skills of a social worker and interactions embedded within the social work relationship with a child and family.

Direct Observation

In many social work practice settings such as schools, residential treatment facilities, and inpatient psychiatric hospitals, social workers can directly observe children being assessed. Such observations can be made in various settings, structured and unstructured, and in interactions with various significant others, such as peers, teachers, parent/guardians, and other family. This allows the social worker to collect data about child functioning not filtered through the perceptual process of the child or other reporter. Such observation can be done in a systematic and structured manner utilizing observation protocols that can quantify the frequency and extent of targeted behaviors. For example, in the assessment of school behavioral struggles—referred to as a functional behavioral assessment—it is standard procedure for the social worker to observe the child in multiple circumstances at school, chosen in light of the behavioral struggles (Gresham, Watson, & Skinner, 2001). The data collected in those observations is vital to identifying the child and con-textual factors that lead to and emerge from the behavior, informing strategies to create behavioral change.

Limitations of the Evidence

One limitation to the application of assessment tools with supporting evidence is the limited number of such tools for use with children. For example, in Corcoran and Fischer's (2000) widely used sourcebook of assessment tools for use in social work practice and research, there are 265 instruments listed for use with adults, while only 49 are listed for use with children. On closer examination of the instruments listed for children, 21 are for use exclusively with adolescents, 5 are completed by adults about youth, and 2 do not specify an age range or age information about the normative sample. This leaves only 21 child-report assessment tools presented as appropriate for use with children.

In terms of using the instruments that are available for use with children, significant limitations to the collection of reliable and valid assessment data can be seen as a function of three factors: first, the limited cognitive ability of children according to their age and developmental level to provide such assessment data, while still often being the best, or only, source of assessment data about many childhood struggles and challenges, second, while adults can provide assessment data about many important targets of assessment, their reports are limited to their observations of the child and are filtered through their own perceptual processes, which are subject to distortion and bias, third, the quality of research methods applied to develop assessment tools to collect valid and reliable data directly from children. Next we discuss the limitations of children to provide assessment data followed by emerging and promising methods to develop better assessment tools for use with children.

Childhood can be separated into three phases: infancy, early childhood, and middle childhood (Ashford, LeCroy, & Lortie, 2001). Gathering assessment data about infants is limited to adult-report and observation of the infant. Children under the age of 6—early childhood—present cognitive limitations that severely constrain providing assessment information and the reliability of such information can be difficult to determine. So for children in early childhood, assessment is largely limited to adult reports and observational data. However, as our methods improve and our understanding of child cognitive capacity continues to advance, we may yet develop tools to collect reliable and valid assessment data from children under 6.

In middle childhood (6 to 12 years), children develop their own culture, characterized by social rules, familiar games, interpersonal reciprocity, and attention to fairness (Ashford et al., 2001). This is a critical time in development when physical skills, social skills, and academic skills are acquired at a rapid rate. It is in this phase that children first have the cognitive ability to reliably and validly self-report perceptions, feelings, beliefs, and experiences. However, the cognitive ability of children in middle childhood is still much lower than adults, and careful attention to developmental issues is necessary in order to gather quality information (Chorpita, Albano, & Barlow, 1998; Garbarino, Stott, & Faculty of the Erikson Institute, 1989). Still, recent research indicates that children have a mostly positive reaction to providing assessment data such as filling out self-report assessment instruments, more positive than adolescents, and that girls are also more positive than boys (Saldana & DuBois, 2006).

However, the quality of evidence in support of assessment tools and strategies for use with children 6 to 12 is limited. The tools that are available typically have lower levels of reliability and validity evidence than seen for adult instruments. Childhood is a time of rapid growth, and children, as a function of their age and emerging cognitive ability, have limitations in their capacity to reliably and validly self-report perceptions, feelings, beliefs, experiences, and behaviors (N. K. Bowen et al., 2004; Chorpita et al., 1998; Woolley et al., 2004).

Clearly, the cognitive demands of self-report instruments for children in middle childhood, including format and wording, are critical features in the development and selection of valid self-report instruments for children (N. K. Bowen et al., 2004). Instruments that meet these criteria are considered developmentally valid, which has been defined as when the cognitive demands of an instrument—vocabulary, length and complexity of items, level of abstraction, nature of measured concepts—fall within the cognitive ability of children in the targeted age range (Woolley et al., 2004). These developmental issues impact the reliability and validity of child self-report instruments. However, the emerging use of *cognitive methods* to assess and advance the validity of assessment tools for use with children holds great promise to advance the validity of such instruments.

EMERGING TRENDS IN CHILD ASSESSMENT

Child struggles and challenges that are the attention of social work services can be measured with self-report assessment instruments. However, for the development of such instruments to lead to reliable and valid tools, that development process must follow consistent and rigorous methods. DeVellis (2003) has detailed a step-by-step procedure to construct reliable and valid assessment tools (Table 11.2).

Table 11.2   Assessment Instrument Development Procedure

Step	Task
1	Identify what struggle or challenge you want to assess.
2	Generate a pool of questions.
3	Determine the format for the assessment tool.
4	Seek review of question pool by experts in the specific area of practice.
5	Administer assessment tool to a pilot sample.
6	Statistically evaluate questions and overall assessment tool performance.
7	Optimize assessment tool length.

Based on *Scale Development: Theory and Applications* (pp. 51–86), by R. F. DeVellis, 2003, Thousand Oaks, CA: Sage.

Such a procedure outlines the typical assessment tool development process; however, such a procedure does not take into account the developmental level of children and the associated cognitive limitations of children to provide assessment data about themselves. Cognitive methods are a group of strategies used in the development of self-report questions used to assess the validity of assessment questions by collecting data directly from respondents about how they interpret and respond to such questions.

Cognitive methods emerged from a seminar held in 1983 that included cognitive psychologists and survey methodologists. The goal of that meeting was to develop a methodology to increase the validity of self-report questions through the application of theories of human cognition. Since that meeting cognitive methods have been applied with adults (Jabine, Straf, Tanur, & Tourangeau, 1984; Jobe & Mingay, 1989), although only more recently with children (N. K. Bowen et al., 2004; Woolley et al., 2004). Cognitive interviewing is the cognitive method that is most applicable with children and involves interviewing a child while he or she reads and responds to an assessment question in order to collect data about four steps in the self-report process: (1) comprehension (reading and interpreting the item accurately), (2) retrieval (adopting the appropriate perspective for the item), (3) judgment (understanding the response continuum and the response options within the context of the item), and (4) response (providing an answer and demonstrating an ability to provide a rationale for the answer; DeMaio & Rothgeb, 1996; Jobe & Mingay, 1989; Tourangeau, Rips, & Rasinski, 2000). Table 11.3 details an example of an interview procedure to collect such data from children. That data is used to evaluate the validity of the information gathered from children with respect to the intent of the self-report questions tested and to inform changes to the questions in order to increase the validity of child responses.

Once cognitive interview data have been collected about an assessment tool under development from children who are members of the targeted population, that data can be analyzed to determine the validity of the interpretation of assessment question meanings and chosen answers by that sample of children. That analysis is best guided by the construction of a validity codebook, which defines the acceptable ranges of question interpretations and rationale for chosen responses (Woolley, Bowen, & Bowen, 2006).

This approach has been used with promising results in the development of an assessment tool for use with children in school settings, the Elementary School Success Profile (N. K. Bowen et al., 2004; Woolley et al., 2006). N. K. Bowen and colleagues found that the methodology revealed significant validity problems in assessment questions for children that would not have otherwise been identified and that the methodology could be applied

Table 11.3   Cognitive Interview Procedure

Step	Ask the Child
1	To read the assessment question out loud.
2	To describe what he or she thinks the question is trying to find out and/or what reading the question made the child think about.
3	To read the answer options out loud.
4	To pick the best answer option to the question for him or her.
5	To explain his or her answer.
6	If he or she can give an example of why he or she chose that answer.

Based on "Constructing and Validating Assessment Tools for School-Based Practitioners: The Elementary School Success Profile" (pp. 509–517), by N. K. Bowen, G. L. Bowen, and M. E. Woolley, in *Evidence-Based Practice Manual: Research and Outcome Measures in Health and Human Services,* A. R. Roberts and K. Y. Yeager (Eds.), 2004, New York: Oxford University Press; and "Cognitive Pretesting and the Developmental Validity of Child Self-Report Instruments: Theory and Applications," by M. E. Woolley, G. L. Bowen, and N. K. Bowen, 2004, *Research on Social Work Practice, 14*, pp. 191–200.

systematically and with reliable results (Woolley et al., 2006). This line of research suggest that the application of cognitive methods, specifically cognitive interviewing, in the development of assessment tools for use with children will result in more reliable and valid instruments and better evidence to support those qualities. More widespread application of this method will lead to better assessment tools available to social workers for practice purposes in the varied settings in which children are served.

IMPLICATIONS FOR SOCIAL WORK ON MICRO-, MEZZO-, AND MACROLEVELS

Child Protection

Few practice settings involve the level of potential consequences to the decisions made at the end of the assessment process than in child protection work. While correct decisions can save children's lives, literally and metaphorically, wrong decisions can lead to death or long-term damage from traumatically removing children from their families when not necessary. Therefore, in the practice of child protection today, the primary goal is to assess *risk*. That risk comes from the behavior of the caretakers of that child, but as in all areas of child assessment, should include assessing the child, the caretakers, the social environment, and how those three interact. The risk being assessed can take on two forms: the child being seriously mistreated in the immediate future, or the cumulative negative impact on that child's developmental outcomes. However, much as in other areas of child assessment, there is tension between the two assessment strategies, clinical interview or structured instrument, or in this context referred to as "actuarial and clinical" (Munro, 2002). Traditionally, assessment in child protection was clinical in nature and relied on the experience, judgment, and evolving practice wisdom of caseworkers. Over the past 20 years, that evolving practice wisdom has informed the development and empirical evaluation of risk assessment actuarial instruments, which have consistently demonstrated higher predictive validity (Baird & Wagner, 2000). Table 11.4 lists factors often included in child maltreatment risk assessment instruments.

Table 11.4   Child Protection Risk Assessment Factors

Adult Factors
Number and severity of previous child maltreatment events
Developmental history
   Instability
      Childhood—frequent moves, change in household members, parental absences
      Adolescence—substance abuse, mental illness, criminal behavior
      Inadequate parental nurturing or supervision
   Abuse history
      Victim of coercive, hostile, or neglectful parenting
      Was he or she a victim or witness of abuse as a child
      Nature, duration, frequency of that abuse
Alcohol or drug abuse
   Currently using
   Failed attempts at treatment
Mental health or cognitive problems
   Mood disorder or personality disorder
   Insecure adult attachment style (ambivalent or avoidant)
   Low self-esteem
   Violent behavior toward others or suicide attempts
   Learning disability
   Low intellectual functioning
   Cognitive distortions in terms of the use of violence
   Noncompliance with treatment or medications
Poor problem-solving skills
Age 20 or less at birth of first child
Gender—males at higher risk of reoccurrence
Single parent
Partner not biological parent of child
Lack of social support
Lack of knowledge about parenting or child development
   Lack of insight into or failure to anticipate the child's needs
   Unrealistic expectations for child behavior
   Lack of or poor supervision of child
Place own needs above the needs of the child
External locus of control
Chronic illness
Previous use and availability of weapons
Previous service contacts

Family Situation Factors
History of family violence
Attachment difficulties
   Lack of concern or warmth toward the child
   Negative attitude toward pregnancy
   Prolonged separation(s) of mother and child
Less than 18 months between births of children
High levels of family stress
Family feels isolated
Family targeted or exploited by local community

Table 11.4   *(Continued)*

Family members emotionally supportive of each other
Is the house dirty, cluttered, or disorganized
Have other professional helpers felt intimidated or had needed services rejected
Any children under 18 not living at home
Previously found abuse or neglect
Economic struggles
   Unemployment
   Poor housing—unsafe, lack of privacy, residential instability
Parental discipline
   Coercive parenting
      Yelling, shouting, or criticizing
      Hostile or threatening
   Random punishment
   Few positive strategies used to reinforce or change behavior

Child Factors
Unplanned child
History of attachment difficulties
Being younger (especially under age 5)
Adopted, foster child, or stepchild
Being premature, low birth weight, or currently underweight
Chronic illness, developmental delay, or birth defect
Difficult to comfort, cries frequently, or difficult temperament
Mental or physical disability
Gender
   Girls more likely to be sexually abused
   Boys are more likely to be seriously physically abused
Poor school attendance or frequent tardiness
Appearance
   Inappropriately dressed
   Looks tired, unkempt, or neglected
Child complaining about care or treatment at home

Note: This list of risk factors was informed by Corby (2000); Fowler (2003); Munro (2002); and Righthand, Kerr, and Drach (2003).

The tension between clinical and actuarial risk assessment has spawned a debate in the literature that has been referred to as the "risk assessment wars" (Johnson, 2006). However, such an either/or debate about the relative merits of clinical versus actuarial assessment represents a false dichotomy leading to a pointless turf war—a false dichotomy because it implies the need to chose one or the other, while ignoring the differential and complementary merits of each. It also ignores the fact that neither by itself has proven to be reliably effective in assessing risk for maltreatment so far, defined as both high rates of sensitivity and specificity (Munro, 2002). In fact, still quite limited research has examined the predictive validity of risk assessment instruments for child protection, and some have shown marginal performance (Camasso & Jagannathan, 2000; Rittner, 2002). Such research has offered suggestions about how to improve the validity and utility of risk assessments including making them shorter, easier to score and interpret, multilevel risk classification as opposed to binary in nature, better training of caseworkers in the science informing their development and use, and more input of clinical wisdom to their design (Baird & Wagner, 2000; Baumann, Law, Sheets, Grant, & Graham, 2005; Camasso & Jagannathan, 2000). Still, actuarial approaches have shown clear utility, and it is reasonable to anticipate that ongoing research will continue to advance their utility and predictive validity in the years to come. Alternatively, it seems illogical to remove the benefits of clinical information gathering and judgment informed by experience from the important work of protecting children while assessing and helping the huge diversity of families confronted by child protection systems with respect and dignity.

In the general discussion of evidence-based assessment with children, the use of both multiple information sources and data-gathering strategies was advocated. Shlonsky and Wagner (2005) have called for just such an integrated approach in child protection assessment. They assert that actuarial risk assessment has the best potential to predict future reoccurrence of child maltreatment, while clinical, or contextual assessment of child and family functioning as they call it, is the most effective way to identify treatment factors that need to be addressed and the services that would most benefit the family. The authors describe this *structured decision-making* process, which integrates actuarial risk assessment combined with clinical judgment. In this approach, an actuarial risk assessment determines the initial response, while clinical assessment of the child and family determine case planning and services provided. That clinical assessment includes gathering information about family struggles as well as strengths in areas such as family relationships, social support, health, mental health, substance abuse, and housing. Other sections of this chapter, and volume, can be consulted for guidelines to assess these areas of child and family functioning and needs.

Forty states have adopted the use of structured risk-assessment instruments at various points in the child protection service process, which may include many points from deciding to open a case, removing a child from the home, returning a child, or closing a case (Camasso & Jagannathan, 2000). Still, the process to gather the information and fill out the risk assessment instrument, as well as assess the current situation and functioning of the child and family, relies on the clinical skills, judgment, and experience of caseworkers. The future of assessment in child protection hopefully will bring the development of more predictive and utilitarian risk assessment instruments, and integration of those instruments with clinical skills and judgment, informing a more evidence-based approach to the vital work of child protection.

Schools

Schools are one of the few settings where social workers can practice on micro-, mezzo-, and macrolevels. For example, a child who is being teased and bullied can be addressed on a microlevel to increase that child's ability to cope and respond when bullied, on the mezzolevel to reduce bullying in a classroom, or on a macrolevel to implement a program to change the social climate of a school system to reduce teasing and bullying throughout the district (Woolley, 2006). Because schools serve all children, including those in need of services from child protection, mental health, and health-care providers, school social workers provide assessment, referral, and intervention services literally to the whole population of children in a given area. Therefore, the assessment tools and strategies needed by school social workers bridge the needs of social workers from many other settings that serve children, and the trends discussed in other sections of this chapter may also be informative to school practice.

However, school social workers also have the unique task of completing an ecologically oriented systematic and comprehensive assessment of a child or groups of children, the findings of which can inform prevention or intervention planning to reduce the impact of specific struggles or challenges that negatively impact school success. To that end, there are assessment tools that have been rigorously developed and have level one or two evidence to support their use with children in schools. One such tool is the School Success Profile (SSP; G. L. Bowen, Woolley, Richman, & Bowen, 2001) for use with middle and high school students, and another is the Elementary School Success Profile (ESSP; N. K. Bowen et al., 2004) for use with children in third through fifth grades.

The SSP is an ecologically oriented self-report assessment instrument for use in school-based practice that includes 220 questions. Those questions gather assessment information about the risk and protective factors in a child's life across five domains affecting school outcomes, including school, family, peers, neighborhood, and health and well-being. The SSP has gone through multiple revisions over more than 10 years of research and practice use, and its reliability and validity has been demonstrated (G. L. Bowen, Rose, & Bowen, 2005). The SSP can be used to inform micro-, mezzo-, or macrolevel practice because scoring the instrument can result in both individual student and group (classroom, grade, school) results that can then be used to inform prevention and intervention planning for students at risk of school failure.

Emerging from the development and use of the SSP, the ESSP includes three forms—child, parent/guardian, and teacher—so fits within the use of multiple informants of information about children suggested earlier. Cognitive interviewing methods were applied in the rigorous development of the ESSP, and the child form is computerized and animated to appeal to younger children and hold their attention. For more information about the SSP or ESSP, please go to www.schoolsuccessprofile.org.

Mental Health

The area of mental health practice with children has the benefit of the most attention in terms of developing assessment tools. Partly as a benefit of the medical model, which is built on arriving at a diagnosis for the purpose of insurance and publicly funded health care, there are assessment instruments for many childhood mental health problems. Such instruments have varied levels of evidence as to their reliability and validity and include assessment tools to measure childhood depression (Angold et al., 1995), anxiety (Silverman & Ollenbeck, 2005), behavior problems (Macgowan, Nash, & Fraser, 2002), thought disorders (Kaufman et al., 1997), attention problems (Pelham et al., 2005), suicide risk (Reynolds & Mazza, 1999), trauma (Balaban, 2006), and multiple mental health struggles (Shaffer et al., 2000). Social workers practicing in mental health settings with children should have success in finding assessment tools with level one or two evidence for most mental health issues with children by following the procedures outlined previously. However, many of those instruments have been developed by professionals from other disciplines, such as psychology or psychiatry, with few being developed from the unique perspective of social work practice. That is also the case, although less so, in other areas of social work practice.

In order for social work to develop its own assessment tools and strategies informed by a social work perspective that have supporting evidence, more social work researchers and practitioners need to engage in the work of developing assessment tools.

An example of a social work constructed assessment tool is the Carolina Child Checklist, developed by Fraser and colleagues (2005) as part of an overall intervention research project to prevent aggression and behavior problems in children ages 8 to 12. This teacher-report instrument was developed utilizing rigorous methods, has demonstrated reliability and validity, identifies both male and female forms of aggression in children, and was developed not just as an assessment tool, but as a research tool to be sensitive enough to provide evidence as to the effectiveness of a manualized preventive intervention for use with third-grade children and their families (Macgowan et al., 2002). Fraser and colleagues' work, from the construction of assessment tools to intervention development, implementation, and evaluation, presents a meritorious model for the pursuit of evidence-based practice in social work.

CONCLUSION

To paraphrase Shakespeare, for something to go well, it must start well. Assessment is the starting point of all social work practice activities. Social workers provide services in a multitude of settings to children and their families, who are facing a broad range of struggles and challenges. To serve children in the most ethical and effective manner, social workers must identify and apply the best assessment tools and strategies available. That goal is best accomplished by identifying the assessment tools and strategies with the best available evidence supporting their use and quality. This chapter reviewed the history of the social work orientation to the assessment of children over the past 100 years. The wisdom accumulated over that century informs the current approach to such assessment offered here, including the format for organizing that assessment information into a biopsychosocial assessment report and the best available current tools and strategies to collect that information.

The approach to child assessment offered in this chapter includes an ecological systems framework, which means: (a) collecting data from the child, parent/guardians, and others such as teachers; (b) using multiple data collection tools such as clinical interviews, self-report instruments, structured interview instruments; and (c) direct observations of the child. The significant limitations—in number and quality—of the currently available assessment tools for use with children was described, and a process to identify what is available and how good the evidence for specific practice applications was offered. Emerging assessment tool development methods were reviewed that promise to lead to more reliable and valid child assessment tools in the future. Finally, social work practice setting specific assessment issues in the arenas of child protection, school, and mental health practice were reviewed.

In closing, social work has much work to do to develop more reliable and valid tools and strategies to assess children across all practice settings. If we are to move toward more evidence-based practices, then the need for assessment tools that start those services well and can effectively be used to measure the efficacy of prevention and intervention activities must be a primary focus of ongoing research and practice efforts.

REFERENCES

American Psychiatric Association. (2000). *Diagnostic and statistical manual of mental disorders* (4th ed., text rev.). Washington, DC: Author.

Angold, A., Costello, E. J., Messer, S. C., Pickles, A., Winder, F., & Silver, D. (1995). Development of a short questionnaire for use in epidemiological studies of depression in children and adolescents. *International Journal of Methods in Psychiatric Research, 5*, 237–249.

Appleby, G. A., Colon, E., & Hamilton, J. (2007). *Diversity, oppression, and social functioning: Person-in-environment assessment and intervention* (2nd ed.). Boston: Allyn & Bacon.

Ashford, J. B., LeCroy, C. W., & Lortie, K. L. (2001). *Human behavior in the social environment: A multidimensional perspective*. Belmont, CA: Wadsworth.

Baird, C., & Wagner, D. (2000). The relative validity of actuarial- and consensus-based risk assessment systems. *Children and Youth Services Review, 22*, 839–871.

Balaban, V. (2006). Psychological assessment of children in disasters and emergencies. *Disasters, 30*, 178–198.

Baumann, D. J., Law, J. R., Sheets, J., Grant, R., & Graham, C. (2005). Evaluating the effectiveness of actuarial risk assessment models. *Children and Youth Services Review, 27*, 465–490.

Bidaut-Russell, M., Valla, J.-P., Thomas, J. M., Bergeron, L., & Lawson, E. (1998). Reliability for the terry: A mental health cartoon-like screener for African American children. *Child Psychiatry and Human Development, 28*, 249–263.

Bowen, G. L., Rose, R. A., & Bowen, N. K. (2005). *The reliability and validity of the school success profile*. Philadelphia: Xlibris Press.

Bowen, G. L., Woolley, M. E., Richman, J. M., & Bowen, N. K. (2001). Brief intervention in schools: The school success profile. *Brief Treatment and Crisis Intervention, 1*, 43–54.

Bowen, M. (1978). *Family therapy in clinical practice*. New York: Aronson.

Bowen, N. K., Bowen, G. L., & Woolley, M. E. (2004). Constructing and validating assessment tools for school-based practitioners: The elementary school success profile. In A. R. Roberts & K. Y. Yeager (Eds.), *Evidence-based practice manual: Research and outcome measures in health and human services* (pp. 509–517). New York: Oxford University Press.

Breton, J.-J., Bergeron, L., Valla, J.-P., Berthiaume, C., & Gaudet, N. (1999). Quebec Child Mental Health Survey: Prevalence of DSM-III-R mental health disorders. *Journal of Child Psychology and Psychiatry and Allied Disciplines, 40*, 375–384.

Bronfenbrenner, U. (Ed.). (2005). *Making human beings human: Bioecological perspectives on human development*. Thousand Oaks, CA: Sage.

Camasso, M. J., & Jagannathan, R. (2000). Modeling the reliability and predictive validity of risk assessment in child protection services. *Children and Youth Services Review, 22*, 873–896.

Carter, B., & McGoldrick, M. (1980). *The family life cycle*. New York: Gardner Press.

Chorpita, B. F., Albano, A. M., & Barlow, D. H. (1998). The structure of negative emotions in a clinical sample of children and adolescents. *Journal of Abnormal Psychology, 107*, 74–85.

Clifford, D. (1998). *Social assessment theory and practice: A multidisciplinary framework*. Brookfield, VT: Ashgate.

Colon, E., Appleby, G. A., & Hamilton, J. (2007). Affirmative practice with people who are culturally diverse and oppressed. In G. A. Appleby, E. Colon, & J. Hamilton (Eds.), *Diversity, oppression, and social functioning: Person-in environment assessment and intervention* (pp. 294–311). Boston: Allyn & Bacon.

Cooper, M. G., & Lesser, J. G. (2002). *Clinical social work practice*. Boston: Allyn & Bacon.

Corby, B. (2000). *Child abuse: Towards a knowledge base* (2nd ed.). Philadelphia: Open University Press.

Corcoran, K. J., & Fischer, J. (2000). *Measures for clinical practice: A sourcebook*. New York: Free Press.

Cox, K. F. (2006). Investigating the impact of strength-based assessment on youth with emotional or behavioral disorders. *Journal of Child and Family Studies, 15,* 287–301.

Cronbach, L. J. (1990). *Essentials of psychological testing* (5th ed.). New York: HarperCollins.

DeMaio, T. J., & Rothgeb, J. M. (1996). Cognitive interviewing techniques: In the lab and in the field. In N. Schwartz & S. Sudman (Eds.), *Answering questions: Methodology for cognitive and communicative processes in survey research* (pp. 177–196). San Francisco: Jossey-Bass.

DeVellis, R. F. (2003). *Scale development: Theory and applications.* Thousand Oaks, CA: Sage.

Essex, M. J., Boyce, W. T., Goldstein, L. H., Armstrong, J. M., Kraemer, H. C., & Kupfer, D. J. (2002). The confluence of mental, physical, social, and academic difficulties in middle childhood: Developing the MacArthur Health and Behavior Questionnaire. *Journal of the Academy of Child and Adolescent Psychiatry, 41,* 588–603.

Finn, J. L., & Jacobsen, M. (2003). *Just practice.* Peosta, IA: Eddie Bowers.

Fowler, J. (2003). *A practitioners' tool for child protection and the assessment of parents.* Philadelphia: Jessica Kingsley.

Fraser, M. W., Galinsky, M. J., Smokowski, P. R., Day, S. H., Terzian, M. A., Rose, R. A., et al. (2005). Social information-processing skills training to promote social competence and prevent aggressive behavior in third grade. *Journal of Consulting and Clinical Psychology, 73,* 1045–1055.

Fraser, M. W., Richman, J. M., & Galinsky, M. J. (1999). Risk, protection, and resilience: Toward a conceptual framework for social work practice. *Social Work Research, 23*(3), 131–143.

Fraser, M. W., Taylor, M. J., Jackson, R., & O'Jack, J. (1991). Social work and science: Many ways of knowing. *Social Work Research and Abstracts, 27*(4), 5–15.

Gambrill, E. (1999). Evidence-based practice: An alternative to authority based practice. *Families in Society: Journal of Contemporary Human Services, 80,* 341–350.

Gambrill, E., & Shlonsky, A. (2001). The need for comprehensive risk management systems in child welfare. *Children and Youth Services Review, 23,* 79–107.

Garbarino, J., Stott, F. M., & Faculty of the Erikson Institute. (1989). *What children can tell us: Eliciting, interpreting, and evaluating information from children.* San Francisco: Jossey-Bass.

Germain, C. B., & Gitterman, A. (1980). *The life model of social work practice.* New York: Columbia University Press.

Gilgun, J. F. (2004). The 4-d: Assessment instruments for youth, their families, and communities. *Journal of Human Behavior in the Social Environment, 10,* 51–73.

Greif, G. L., & Lynch, A. A. (1983). The eco-systems perspective. In C. H. Meyer (Ed.), *Clinical social work in the eco-systems perspective* (pp. 35–71). New York: Columbia University Press.

Gresham, F. M., Watson, T. S., & Skinner, C. H. (2001). Functional behavioral assessment: Principles, procedures, and future directions. *School Psychology Review, 30,* 156–172.

Gutierrez, L., & Lewis, E. (1999). Working with women of color: An empowerment perspective. *Social Work, 35,* 149–153.

Haley, J. (1987). *Problem-solving therapy* (2nd ed.). San Francisco: Jossey-Bass.

Hart, S. L. (1990). Working with the juvenile delinquent. In M. L. M. Bryan & A. F. Davis (Eds.), *100 years at Hull House* (pp. 145–150). Bloomington: Indiana University Press.

Hartman, A. (1995). Diagrammatic assessment of family relationships. *Families in Society, 76*(2), 111–122.

Hepworth, D. H., Rooney, R. H., & Larsen, J. A. (2002). *Direct social work practice: Theory and skills* (6th ed.). Pacific Grove, CA: Brooks/Cole.

Hollis, F. (1964). *Casework: A psychosocial therapy.* New York: Random House.

Hudson, W. W. (1997). Assessment tools as outcome measures in social work. In E. J. Mullen & J. Magnabosco (Eds.), *Outcome measures in the human services: Cross-cutting issues and methods* (pp. 68–80). Washington, DC: National Association of Social Workers Press.

Ialongo, N. S., Edelsohn, G., & Kellam, S. G. (2001). A further look at the prognostic power of young children's reports of depressed mood and feelings. *Child Development, 72,* 736–747.

Ivens, C., & Rehm, L. P. (1988). Assessment of childhood depression: Correspondence between reports by child, mother, and father. *Journal of American Academy of Child and Adolescent Psychiatry, 27,* 738–741.

Jabine, T. B., Straf, M. L., Tanur, J. M., & Tourangeau, R. (1984). *Cognitive aspects of survey methodology: Building a bridge between disciplines.* Washington, DC: National Academy Press.

Jobe, J. B., & Mingay, D. J. (1989). Cognitive research improves questionnaires. *American Journal of Public Health, 79,* 1053–1055.

Johnson, W. (2006). The risk assessment wars: A commentary response to "evaluating the effectiveness of actuarial risk assessment models." *Children and Youth Services Review, 28,* 704–714.

Karls, J. M., & Wandrei, K. E. (1992). Pie: A new language for social work. *Social Work, 37,* 80–85.

Kaufman, J., Birmaher, B., Brent, D., Rao, U., Flynn, C., Moreci, P., et al. (1997). Schedule for Affective Disorders and Schizophrenia for School-Age Children-Present and Lifetime (K-SADS-PL): Initial reliability and validity. *Journal of the American Academy of Child and Adolescent Psychiatry, 36,* 980–988.

Kemp, S. P., Whittaker, J. K., & Tracy, E. M. (1997). *Person-environment practice: The social ecology of interpersonal helping.* New York: Aldine de Gruyter.

Kent, L., Vostanis, P., & Feehan, C. (1997). Detection of major and minor depression in children and adolescents: Evaluation of the Mood and Feelings Questionnaire. *Journal of Child Psychology and Psychiatry, 38,* 565–573.

Loewenberger, F., & Dolgoff, R. (1985). *Ethical decisions for social work practice.* Itasca, IL: Peacock.

Lukas, S. R. (1993). *Where to start and what to ask: An assessment handbook.* New York: Norton.

Luthar, S. S., Cicchetti, D., & Becker, B. (2000). The construct of resilience: A critical evaluation and guidelines for future work. *Child Development, 71,* 543–562.

Macgowan, M. J., Nash, J. K., & Fraser, M. W. (2002). The Carolina Child Checklist of risk and protective factors for aggression. *Research on Social Work Practice, 12,* 253–276.

March, J. S., Parker, J. D. A., Sullivan, K., Stallings, P., & Conners, C. K. (1997). The Multidimensional Anxiety Scale for Children (MASC): Factor structure, reliability, and validity. *Journal of the Academy of Child and Adolescent Psychiatry, 36,* 554–565.

Mash, E. J., & Hunsley, J. (2005). Evidence-based assessment of child and adolescent disorders: Issues and challenges. *Journal of Clinical Child and Adolescent Psychology, 34,* 362–379.

McGoldrick, M., Gerson, R., & Shellenberger, S. (1999). *Genograms: Assessment and intervention.* New York: Norton.

McQuaide, S., & Ehrenreich, J. H. (1997). Assessing client strengths. *Families in Society, 78,* 201–212.

Montgomery, M. S. (1994). Self-concept and children with learning disabilities: Observer-child concordance across six context-dependent domains. *Journal of Learning Disabilities, 27,* 254–262.

Munro, E. (2002). *Effective child protection.* Thousand Oaks, CA: Sage.

Ogbu, J. U. (1991). Low school performance as an adaptation: The case of Blacks in Stockton, California. In M. A. Gibson & J. U. Ogbu (Eds.), *Minority status and schooling: A comparative study of immigrant and involuntary minorities* (pp. 249–285). New York: Garland Press.

Ogbu, J. U. (1998). Voluntary and involuntary minorities: A cultural-ecological theory of school performance with some implications for education. *Anthropology and Education Quarterly, 29,* 155–188.

Orfield, G., Losen, D., Wald, J., & Swanson, C. B. (2004). *Losing our future: How minority youth are being left behind by the graduation rate crisis.* Cambridge, MA: Civil Rights Project at Harvard University and the Urban Institute. Available from www.urban.org/url.cfm?ID=410936/.

Oyserman, D., Bybee, D., & Terry, K. (2006). Possible selves and academic outcomes: How and when possible selves impel action. *Journal of Personality and Social Psychology, 91,* 188–204.

Oyserman, D., Terry, K., & Bybee, D. (2002). A possible selves intervention to enhance school involvement. *Journal of Adolescence, 25,* 313–326.

Paniagua, F. A. (2005). *Assessing and treating culturally diverse clients: A practical guide.* Thousand Oaks, CA: Sage.

Pelham, W. E., Fabiano, G. A., & Massetti, G. M. (2005). Evidence-based assessment of attention deficit hyperactivity disorder in children and adolescents. *Journal of Clinical Child and Adolescent Psychology, 34,* 449–476.

Perlman, H. H. (1957). *Social casework: A problem solving approach.* Chicago: University of Chicago Press.

Pilsecker, C. (1994). Starting where the client is. *Families in Society, 75,* 447–452.

Pincus, A., & Minahan, A. (1973). *Social work practice: Model and method.* Itasca, IL: Peacock.

Reynolds, W., & Mazza, J. (1999). Assessment of suicidal ideation in inner-city children and young adolescents: Reliability and validity of the Suicidal Ideation Questionnaire—JR. *School Psychology Review, 28,* 17–30.

Richman, J. M., Bowen, G. L., & Woolley, M. E. (2004). School failure: An eco-interactional developmental perspective. In M. W. Fraser (Ed.), *Risk and resilience in childhood: An ecological perspective* (2nd ed., pp. 133–160). Washington, DC: National Association of Social Workers Press.

Richmond, M. E. (1917). *Social diagnosis.* New York: Sage.

Righthand, S., Kerr, B., & Drach, K. (2003). *Child maltreatment risk assessments.* Binghamton, NY: Haworth Press.

Rittner, B. (2002). The use of risk assessment instruments in child protection services case planning and closures. *Children and Youth Services Review, 24,* 189–207.

Saldana, L., & DuBois, D. L. (2006). Youth reactions to participation in psychological assessment procedures. *Journal of Clinical Child and Adolescent Psychology, 35,* 155–161.

Shaffer, D., Fisher, P., Lucas, C. P., Dulcan, M. K., & Schwab-Stone, M. E. (2000). NIMH Diagnostic Interview Schedule for Children Version IV (NIMH DISC-IV): Description, differences from previous versions, and reliability of some common diagnoses. *Journal of the American Academy of Child and Adolescent Psychiatry, 39,* 28–38.

Shlonsky, A., & Wagner, D. (2005). The next step: Integrating actuarial risk assessment and clinical judgment into an evidence-based practice framework in CPS case management. *Children and Youth Services Review, 27,* 409–427.

Silverman, W. K., & Ollenbeck, T. H. (2005). Evidence-based assessment of anxiety and its disorders in children and adolescents. *Journal of Child and Adolescent Psychology, 34,* 380–411.

Simon, B. L. (1994). *The empowerment tradition in American social work: A history.* New York: Columbia University Press.

Tashakkori, A., & Teddlie, C. (2003). Major issues and controversies in the use of mixed methods in the social and behavioral sciences. In A. Tashakkori & C. Teddlie (Eds.), *Handbook of mixed methods in the social and behavioral sciences* (pp. 3–50). Thousand Oaks, CA: Sage.

Tinsley, B. J., & Holtgrave, D. R. (1997). A multimethod analysis of risk perceptions and health behaviors in children. *Educational and Psychological Measurement, 57,* 197–209.

Tourangeau, R., Rips, L. J., & Rasinski, K. (2000). *The psychology of survey response.* Cambridge: Cambridge University Press.

Wood, A., Kroll, L., Moore, A., & Harrington, R. (1995). Proper ties of the mood and feelings questionnaire in adolescent psychiatric outpatients: A research note. *Journal of Child Psychology and Psychiatry, 36,* 327–334.

Woolley, M. E. (2006). Advancing a positive school climate for students, families, and staff. In C. Franklin, M. B. Harris, & P. Allen-Meares (Eds.), *The school services sourcebook* (pp. 777–784). New York: Oxford University Press.

Woolley, M. E., & Bowen, G. L. (2007). In the context of risk: Supportive adults and the school engagement of middle school students. *Family Relations, 56,* 92–104.

Woolley, M. E., Bowen, G. L., & Bowen, N. K. (2004). Cognitive pretesting and the developmental validity of child self-report instruments: Theory and applications. *Research on Social Work Practice, 14,* 191–200.

Woolley, M. E., Bowen, G. L., & Bowen, N. K. (2006). The development and evaluation of procedures to assess child self-report item validity. *Educational and Psychological Measurement, 66,* 687–700.

Woolley, M. E., & Grogan-Kaylor, A. (2006). Protective family factors in the context of neighborhood: Promoting positive school outcomes. *Family Relations, 55,* 95–106.

Wright-Strawdermann, C., & Watson, B. L. (1992). The prevalence of depressive symptoms in children with disabilities. *Journal of Learning Disabilities, 25,* 258–264.

Yugar, J. M., & Shapiro, E. S. (2001). Elementary children's school friendship: A comparison of peer assessment methodologies. *School Psychology Review, 30,* 568–587.

Chapter 12

INTERVENTION WITH CHILDREN

Mary C. Ruffolo and Paula Allen-Meares

Intervening in the lives of children and their families is a challenging and dynamic process. Selecting evidence-based interventions that will help children who are at risk for emotional and behavioral problems to confront adversity and promote resiliency is a critical task facing social workers across the child-serving systems. Protecting children from harm and poor developmental outcomes involves not only targeting the child's behavior but also the family, school, and neighborhood environments that often contribute to challenges that the child faces. Interventions that evolve into evidence-based practices (EBPs) can facilitate the process of promoting positive outcomes for children in need of treatment in real-world settings. While children who are at risk for emotional or behavioral problems often experience impaired functioning at home, in school, or in their neighborhood, EBP provides hope that these youth will experience better outcomes in many of these functioning areas.

Recent reports from the New Freedom Commission on Mental Health (2003) and the U.S. Surgeon General (1999, 2001) highlight the need to improve mental health services for children and their families by developing and using more evidence-based interventions. Several federal and national organizations have developed lists of evidence-based or empirically supported interventions for work with children and their families in order to promote the use of those that have demonstrated success. For example, the Substance Abuse and Mental Health Services Administration (SAMHSA) compiled an expert consensus review of published and unpublished evaluations and a web-based listing of science-based prevention programs that may be replicated. They grouped these programs as models, effective, and promising practices (www.modelprograms.samhsa.gov).

This chapter examines the development of EBPs with children at risk of emotional and behavioral problems, summarizes EBPs that are currently being used across child-serving systems, explores the limitations of implementing EBP interventions and discusses the implications for social work intervention practice with children who are at risk for emotional and behavioral problems and who face adversity.

DEVELOPMENT OF EVIDENCE-BASED PRACTICES FOR CHILDREN AT RISK FOR EMOTIONAL OR BEHAVIORAL PROBLEMS

The current child-serving systems have evolved from primarily an institutional-based system to a community-based system of care for children and their families. While more children are served in community-based programs, the majority of expenditures on services for children are for institutional-based services (U.S. Surgeon General, 1999). Most children receiving intervention services in institutional-based settings are in residential treatment programs operated through the child welfare or juvenile justice systems (Lyons, 2004). Although little evidence exists to support residential treatment approaches in work with children, there is some evidence that indicates these approaches actually harm instead of helping children (Dishion, Bullock, & Granic, 2002).

The child-serving systems today are not comprehensive or integrated, resulting in many children in need of treatment getting inappropriate services, inadequate services, or no services. In addition, for those children who have access to intervention services, 40% to 60% may discontinue services before completing the treatment (Kazdin, 1997). Social work professionals who intervene with children often find themselves dealing with service systems that are unresponsive to emerging child and family needs. Furthermore, these professionals have limited access to EBPs that promote successful engagement and positive child outcomes. The need to address effective interventions for children at risk for emotional and behavioral problems across service system settings is urgent.

For an EBP to be effective in work with children at risk for emotional and behavioral problems, attention to developmental changes, age-related changes, the family context, and the service setting where the intervention is being delivered (e.g., schools, mental health organizations, juvenile justice centers) is critical (Hoagwood, Burns, Kiser, Ringeisen, & Schoenwald, 2001). The social work profession, like other disciplines has looked to the experiences in the health field to better understand ways to improve intervention outcomes for children and increase the use of EBPs across service settings.

The Institute of Medicine (IOM) defines EBP as "the integration of best research evidence with clinical expertise and patient values" (IOM, 2001). This definition involves three critical elements: best research evidence, clinical expertise, and patient values. Based on this definition, when intervening in the lives of children, social workers using the EBP model need to have access to the best intervention research evidence available, use clinical expertise to guide the intervention process, and partner with children and families in understanding their values and preferences in intervention work. EBP involves a collaborative process where children and families are involved in defining the problem, determining what outcomes that the intervention will achieve, integrating and applying evidence to design the initial practice strategy, modifying the initial practice strategy based on child and family preferences and practice expertise, applying the tailored strategy, and evaluating the outcomes (Fraser, 2003). The challenge for social workers is to understand how the child and family values and preferences affect the decision-making process and seek to balance these factors with the best available clinical and empirically supported evidence.

The recent Institute of Medicine (IOM) report "Crossing the Quality Chasm: A New Health System in the 21st Century" (2001) highlights priority conditions for evidence-based practice in health care. These priority conditions include: ongoing analysis and synthesis of the medical evidence, delineation of specific practice guidelines, the identification of best practices, the dissemination efforts to communicate evidence and guidelines, the development of decision support tools to assist clinicians and patients in applying the evidence, and the establishment of goals for improvement in care (IOM, 2001).

For social workers, using EBPs maximizes the likelihood of achieving child and family hoped-for outcomes and minimize the potential for harm. Gambrill (2003) identifies 20 interrelated contributions of EBP for the social work profession. These include the following: focuses on client concerns and hoped-for outcomes; encourages a comprehensive, systemic approach to the provision of effective, efficient, and ethical services; describes a process for integrating evidentiary, ethical, and application concerns; promotes transparency and honesty; encourages rigorous testing and appraisal of practice/policy-related claims; promotes the preparation and dissemination of critical appraisals of practice/policy-related research findings; highlights applicability challenges; attends to individual differences; discourages inflated claims; describes and takes proactive steps to minimize errors, accidents, and mistakes; welcomes criticism; recognizes our ignorance and consequent uncertainty; honors a professional code of ethics; increases available knowledge; considers both populations and individuals; minimizes harm in the name of helping; blows the whistle on pseudoscience, propaganda, quackery, and fraud; creates educational programs that develop lifelong learners; and explores how to decrease obstacles to EBP (Gambrill, 2003).

Efforts over the past 20 years to promote evidence-based social work practice, such as the evolution of program evaluation methods; encouraging social workers to read, synthesize, and apply intervention research in practice; and encouraging practitioners to use single subject designs to inform practice have often resulted in significant resistance from social work professionals (Kirk, 1999). In the child-serving organizations, social work professionals have been strongly encouraged to use EBPs in their work with children, but organizations often do not have the resources to train and implement emerging EBPs. In addition, the readiness of many emerging evidence-based child interventions for large-scale dissemination is limited (Hoagwood et al., 2001).

Because evidence-based interventions often address the "average" child experiencing a problem condition, many social work practitioners do not find the information helpful since the research does not necessarily address what intervention is best for the child at hand. In fact, child populations encountered in many social work service settings are often excluded from randomized controlled trials (RCT) because of the complexity of needs experienced by these youth. The development of practice guidelines for specific interventions and programs for children has been viewed as an important factor in helping social workers implement EBPs across various service settings. Practice guidelines are "systematically developed statements to assist practitioner and patient decisions about appropriate care for specific clinical circumstances" (IOM, 1990, p. 27). Use of practice guidelines increases "the predictability of practice around a set of standardized 'best practices' and reduce variability between social workers" in their work with children and families (Rosen & Proctor, 2003, p. 5). In addition to practice guidelines, evidence-based interventions develop treatment manuals that are more specific and provide guidelines for establishing the therapeutic relationships, suggestions for sequencing activities, monitoring outcomes, and addressing implementation issues in real-world settings (Fraser, 2003).

CURRENT EVIDENCE-BASED PRACTICES WITH CHILDREN

Although the state of EBPs in work with children and their families is expanding and new practices are being studied as they arise, this chapter focuses primarily on existing EBPs that have demonstrated positive outcomes for children at risk for emotional and behavioral problems and their families across child-serving systems. Some of the EBPs operate at a program level and others at the clinical level. These EBPs often involve child, family, and system-level changes in order to enhance positive outcomes for children.

The primary organizing framework for current evidence-based social work interventions with children who experience emotional or behavioral problems builds on an ecological, developmental, family-centered, resiliency-based, multisystem perspective (Fraser, 2004; Friesen & Stephens, 1998).

The ecological systems perspective encourages social workers to incorporate a transactional and dynamic approach to understanding children within their environmental contexts. Children are viewed within their social ecology that consists of interdependent and often nested systems (Bronfenbrenner, 1986). The developmental perspective highlights the need for social workers to assess a child's developmental level within their environmental contexts and use developmentally sensitive intervention techniques. The developmental course for children varies and the youth's cognitive-developmental level may limit or enhance the degree to which a youth engages in change efforts (Holmbeck, Greenley, & Franks, 2003).

Social workers who use EBP interventions for children not only use empirically supported interventions, but also integrate the child and family's perspective into the design of the intervention strategy. A family-centered orientation encourages social workers to involve families as partners in all aspects of all interventions: planning, intervention strategies, outcome determination, and effectiveness evaluation (Duchnowski, Kutash, & Friedman, 2003).

A resiliency-based perspective requires that social workers understand children at risk within their environmental and cultural contexts. Resiliency is a dynamic process and is defined as "observing a normal or even exceptional positive developmental outcome in spite of exposure to major risk for the development of serious social and health problems" (Fraser, 2004, p. 22). Resilience has been defined as the dynamic interplay of individual, social, and environmental protective factors, in the context of risk exposure, resulting in positive developmental outcomes and adaptation (Luthar, Cicchetti, & Becker, 2000). A resiliency-based framework requires that social workers who intervene with children look holistically at risk and protective factors present within the child, the family, the school, the neighborhood, as well as the child-serving delivery system, and intervene to support child functioning and healthy development. Risk factors are any influence that increases the probability of harm, contributes to a more serious state, or maintains a problem condition (Coie et al., 1993; Fraser, 2004). Risk factors may frequently occur together, and as the number of risk factors increases the chance for negative developmental outcomes for children increases (Dishion, Capaldi, & Yeager, 1999; Hawkins, Catalano, & Miller, 1992; Luthar, 1991). Protective factors can be defined as "both internal and external resources that modify risk" (Fraser, 2004, p. 28). Three main categories of protective factors have been identified by Garmezy (1985): (1) dispositional attributes, such as temperamental factors; (2) social orientation and responsiveness to change; and (3) cognitive abilities and coping skills.

Finally, social workers using a multisystems perspective when working with children with emotional and behavioral problems assess and intervene within family systems and across child-serving systems to improve outcomes. Essentially, child-serving systems have the overall goal of keeping children at home, in school, and in the community with improved functioning in critical life domains. Although social workers recognize that many of the children they serve are involved in more than one child-serving system, current funding streams for child services have resulted in fragmented, uncoordinated service delivery systems with different traditions and often conflicting approaches to work with children and their families. The president's New Freedom Commission on Mental Health (2003) recommends that child-serving systems promote early screening for behavioral and emotional problems in children, improve access to quality care that is culturally competent, and develop individualized plans of care that involve families as partners. In addition, the Surgeon General's Conference on Children's Mental Health (U.S. Surgeon General, 2001) recommends four guiding principles for the development of responsive child-serving systems to meet the needs of children with behavioral and emotional problems: (1) promoting the recognition of mental health as an essential part of children's health; (2) integrating family, child, and youth-centered mental health services into all systems that serve children and youth; (3) engaging families and incorporating the perspectives of children and youth in the development of all mental health-care planning; and (4) developing and enhancing a public-private health infrastructure to support these efforts to the fullest extent possible. In addition, this report recommends that in order to improve services for children at risk of emotional and behavioral problems, it is important to continue to develop, disseminate, and implement scientifically proven prevention and treatment services in the field of children's mental health and work to eliminate racial/ethnic and socioeconomic disparities in access to needed mental health services across child-serving systems.

The EBPs selected address the complex needs of children at risk for emotional and behavioral problems and their families, have been implemented by social workers, and have demonstrated success in the real-world child service system settings. These evidence-based interventions have practice principles or intervention manuals that support replication and promote ways to assess fidelity to the intervention model. The EBPs reviewed are divided into emerging evidence-based individual child and family interventions and school-wide/community interventions (see Table 12.1). For each intervention reviewed, the key components of the intervention are presented, as well as the status of the empirical evidence to support this intervention with targeted child populations.

Child- and Family-Based Interventions

The child- and family-based intervention programs involve not only intervening with the child, but also engaging the family in the work of promoting positive outcomes for the child. While some of the interventions, such as cognitive-behavioral therapy, could be implemented without a family or parent component, in this chapter only the cognitive-behavioral interventions that involve the child and the parents or families are discussed.

Table 12.1   Key Evidence-Based Practices across Child-Serving Systems

Child- and Family-Based Interventions
Cognitive-behavioral therapy
Parent management training models and multidimensional therapeutic foster care
Multisystemic therapy
Brief strategic family therapy
Schoolwide/Community Interventions
Families and Schools Together
Strengthening Families Program
Project Achieve

Cognitive-Behavioral Therapy

Cognitive-behavioral therapy (CBT) approaches have been used successfully to address a range of internal and external emotional/behavioral disorders in children (Barrett, 1998; Kendall et al., 1997; Shortt, Barrett, & Fox, 2001). These problems include living with anxiety, depression, or conduct disorders. Involving parents in the interventions enhances positive outcomes for the youth and family. CBT focuses on the relationship among cognitions, affect, and behavior. The process in CBT is to assist a child in moving from a dysfunctional cycle of thoughts (overly negative, self-critical), feelings (anxious, depressed, angry), and behavior (avoid, give up, act out inappropriately) to a functional system of thoughts (more positive, acknowledge success, recognize strengths), feelings (relaxed, happy, calm), and behavior (confront, try, appropriate; Stallard, 2002). Most CBT interventions involve at least eight sessions, focus on skills-based learning, and address current problems. Children learn how to monitor thoughts; identify cognitive distortions; develop alternative cognitive processes; learn new cognitive skills; learn affective monitoring and management; conduct behavioral experiments; use role-playing, modeling, exposure, and rehearsal skills; and engage in positive reinforcement and rewards (Stallard, 2002).

A Cochrane Collaboration Review of CBT for anxiety disorders in children found that CBT appears to be an effective treatment for children (over the age of 6 years) and adolescents (Soler & Weatherall, 2005). Thirteen studies of children and adolescents experiencing anxiety disorders met the criteria for inclusion in this review. The criteria included that the study had to be a randomized trial, conform to CBT principles through the use of a protocol, and comprise at least eight sessions (Soler & Weatherall, 2005). Over 50% of youth who received CBT for anxiety disorders showed improvement in their anxiety symptoms even 3 or more months after the intervention was completed (Soler & Weatherall, 2005).

One CBT family-based program, called FRIENDS (Barrett, Lowry-Webster, & Turner, 2000), illustrates the steps involved in delivering CBT interventions. The acronym FRIENDS highlights the strategies taught in this intervention:

F: Feeling worried?

R: Relax and feel good.

I: Inner thoughts.

E: Explore plans.

N: Nice work so reward yourself.

D: Don't forget to practice.

S: Stay calm, you know how to cope now.

FRIENDS focuses on working with children experiencing anxiety disorders and their parents and was part of the Cochrane Review of CBT for anxiety disorders in children and adolescents conducted by Soler and Weatherall (2005). This CBT family-based program could be delivered in community-based settings, schools, mental health clinics, or family/social service agencies.

In the FRIENDS program, cognitive distortions are seen as central to the maintenance of anxiety symptoms (Barrett & Shortt, 2003). Parents are involved in the intervention in order to facilitate new experiences for the child to test cognitive distortions and to assist the child in processing these new experiences on a daily basis (Barrett & Shortt, 2003).

According to Barrett and Shortt (2003, p. 103), the FRIENDS program encourages children to:

1. Think of their body as their friend because it tells them when they are feeling worried or nervous by giving them clues;
2. Be their own friend, and reward themselves when they try hard;
3. Make friends, so that they can build their social support networks; and
4. Talk to their friends when they are in difficult or worrying situations.

Parents are enlisted to help change the child's environment to reduce the child's anxiety and promote positive change.

This intervention is conducted in a group format and has two versions based on the developmental level of the child or adolescent. One group version is designed for children ages 7 to 11 years and the other for adolescents ages 12 to 16 years. Both versions involve 10 sessions and 2 booster sessions (1 month and 3 months following completion of the sessions). Each session runs for approximately 1 hour and is conducted weekly. The family skills or parenting component of the program usually runs 1 hour and 30 minutes for a total of 6 hours using a group format over four sessions. In the family skills component, parents learn about the steps of FRIENDS; explore their own thoughts and ways to challenge thoughts; how to reinforce learning; how to establish appropriate reward structures and strategies for promoting strengths in the youth, parent(s), and family.

The FRIENDS group format for youth involves teaching seven key skills. The skill taught in the *F-Feeling Worried?* segment of the intervention involves helping the child identify physiological and behavioral indicators of anxiety. In this skill area, a child might focus on the connection between how one feels (sick, faint) and what one does (avoid school or friend activities). The *R-Relax and Feel Good* skill teaches youth to engage in enjoyable activities when feeling worried or sad. The *I-Inner Thoughts* skill teaches youth how the way they talk to themselves influences how they feel and what they do. The *E-Explore Plans* skill teaches youth how to use the six block problem-solving plan (what is the problem; list all possible solutions; list what might happen with each solution; select the best solution based on consequences; make a plan and do it; and evaluate the outcome). The *N-Nice Work so Reward Yourself* skill helps youth evaluate successes, set reasonable goals, and establish rewards for success. The *D-Don't Forget to Practice* skill encourages youth to role-play, rehearse, and practice new behaviors and ways to handle their anxieties or worries. The *S-Stay Calm* skill reminds youth that they have the skills to handle their worries and anxieties.

The CBT approaches used for youth with depressive symptoms or conduct disorders employs similar strategies but educates the youth about their specific problem area instead of anxiety disorders.

Parent Management Training Models and Multidimensional Therapeutic Foster Care

Parent management training models have evolved over several decades and current models are based on successful findings from several clinical and prevention trials (Kazdin, 2005; Patterson, 2004). Parent management training (PMT) involves manualized interventions in which parents are taught social learning techniques to change the behavior of their children (Kazdin, 2005). In addition, PMT approaches do not assume that the solution to problem behaviors lies within the child but that it lies within the social environment (Patterson, 2005). Successful PMT approaches target working with parents of children experiencing antisocial behavior, oppositional or conduct disorders, delinquent behavior, attention-deficit/hyperactivity disorders, and who are at risk for substance use (Kazdin, 2005; Patterson, 2005). Kazdin reports that research studies of PMT approaches have demonstrated effectiveness in improving youth academic behavior and classroom performance, increasing prosocial behavior, preventing deviant behavior, and improving adherence to medication treatment.

PMT approaches are based primarily on operant conditioning methods and social learning techniques. These methods emphasize the control that environmental events exert on behavior. Kazdin (2005, p. 23) identified four key principles of operant conditioning used in PMT approaches. These principles include:

1. *Reinforcement* (presentation or removal of an event after a response that increases the likelihood of probability of that response),
2. *Punishment* (presentation or removal of an event after a response that decreases the likelihood or probability of that response),
3. *Extinction* (no longer presenting a reinforcement event after a response that decreases the likelihood or probability of the previously reinforced response), and
4. *Stimulus control and discrimination* (reinforcing the response in the presence of one stimulus but not in the presence of another).

In operant conditioning, the main focus is on examining the contingencies of reinforcement, and this involves describing antecedent events (A), behaviors (B), and consequences (C) and altering the sequence to promote desired outcomes. Parents learn how to track behavior using the A-B-C formula. For example, a parent might document that the antecedent event (A) was asking the child to clean the room, the behavior (B) of the child might be picking up toys, and the consequence (C) is that the parent gives the child verbal praise. The reinforcers used in PMT might include food or consumables, social reinforcers (e.g., attention, praise, and physical contact), privileges and activities, and tokens. The essential ingredients to make reinforcement programs successful involve the following factors: contingent application of consequences, immediacy of reinforcement, continuous reinforcement, magnitude or amount of the reinforcer, quality or type or the reinforcer, varied and combined reinforcers, use of prompts, shaping, and practice trials (Kazdin, 2005).

PMT interventions involve working directly with the parent(s) who implement effective parenting skills at home using social learning techniques. According to Forgatch, Patterson, and DeGarmo (2005, p. 4), the core parenting skills taught in the PMT training work at the Oregon Learning Center involve:

1. *Skill encouragement*—promotes prosocial development through scaffolding techniques (e.g., breaking behavior into small steps, prompting appropriate behavior) and contingent positive reinforcement (e.g., praise and incentives).
2. *Discipline* (i.e., limit setting)—decreases deviant behavior through the appropriate and contingent use of mild sanctions (e.g., time-out, privilege removal).

3. *Monitoring* (i.e., supervision)—involves tracking youngsters' activities, associates, whereabouts and transportation.
4. *Problem-solving*—skills help families negotiate disagreements, establish rules, and specify consequences for following or violating rules.
5. *Positive involvement*—reflects the many ways that parents provide their youngsters with loving attention.

In general, PMT approaches involve several meetings with the parent(s). PMT approaches alter not only what the parent does in managing their child but also alters how the parent thinks and feels about parenting (Patterson, 2004). Kazdin (2005) in his review of PMT approaches identified the following format for the core sessions: (1) a pretreatment introduction and orientation; (2) defining, observing, and recording behavior; (3) positive reinforcement; (4) time-out from reinforcement; (5) attending and planned ignoring; (6) shaping and school program; (7) review and problem solving; (8) family meeting; (9) low-rate behaviors; (10) reprimands; (11) compromising; and (12) skill review. Each core session involves a review of the previous week and how the behavior-change program is working or not, presentation of a principle or theme, practice in role-playing with the therapist and/or the youth, and the addition of some assignment or changes in the program that will be implemented at home for the next week.

The Oregon multidimensional treatment foster care (MTFC) model is a specialized community-based PMT program that has been used with children with antisocial problems involved in the juvenile justice, mental health, and child welfare systems (Chamberlain & Smith, 2003). The MTFC model uses a comprehensive treatment approach that creates opportunities for youth to live successfully in their communities while providing them with intensive supervision, support, and skill development. Many of these youth would be placed in group homes or residential placement settings if they did not enter a MTFC program. The effectiveness of this model has been documented with a range of youth and in a variety of child-serving settings (Chamberlain & Reid, 1991; Fisher, Ellis, & Chamberlain, 1999).

Youth are placed in foster homes where the foster parents are trained to be the primary treatment agents and the youth's biological/step/adoptive/relative families help shape the youth's treatment plan and participate in family therapy and home visits throughout placement to prepare for reunification with their youth at the program's end (Fisher & Chamberlain, 2000).

In order to deliver the MFTC program, a team consisting of the MTFC parent(s), program supervisor, family therapist for the biological/adoptive or relative family, individual therapist for the youth, behavioral support specialist, and consulting psychiatrist works together to conduct the treatment intervention (Chamberlain & Smith, 2003). Each team member has a separate role and specialized responsibilities.

The specific targets of treatment in MFTC include reinforcing normative and prosocial behavior of the youth, providing youth with close supervision, closely monitoring peer associations, specifying clear and consistent limits, following through on rule violations, encouraging youth to develop positive work habits and academic skills, supporting family members to increase the effectiveness of their parenting skills, decreasing conflict between family members, and teaching youth new skills for forming relationships with positive peers and for bonding with adult mentors and role models (Fisher & Chamberlain, 2000).

MTFC parents participate in a 20-hour preservice training where they are taught a four-step approach to analyzing behavior (knowing when a problem is a problem, developing a clear behavioral description of that problem, identifying what precedes the behavior, and identifying antecedents to the behavior; Chamberlain & Smith, 2003; Fisher & Chamberlain, 2000). MTFC parents also learn how to implement an individualized daily program with the youth and how to work with the youth's biological family.

After training, the MFTC parents and youth are matched and an individualized program is developed by the team. The individualized program is detailed and includes a behavior management program within the foster home. The youth has opportunities to earn points for satisfactory performance and receive frequent positive feedback from the MFTC parents about his or her progress (Fisher & Chamberlain, 2000).

MFTC parents receive daily telephone calls from program staff to monitor the interventions and provide support. In addition, program staff visit each MFTC home once a week and are available to foster parents 24 hours a day to provide back-up support.

The MTFC program is individually tailored to meet the needs of each youth and family and changes over time based on the individual child's progress and family readiness to handle the challenges of their youth (Chamberlain, 2002).

Another specialized PMT program with a strong evidence base is the Incredible Years Training Series for parents of young children, ages 3 to 8 years, who have conduct problems. The Incredible Years Training Series is designed to promote social competence and prevent, reduce, and treat conduct problems by working with parents, teachers, and children using developmentally appropriate curricula (Webster-Stratton, 2001). The parent training component of this training series teaches parents skills in how to play with children, how to give praise and rewards, effective limit setting, strategies to handle misbehavior, improving communication, anger management, problem solving, ways to get and give support, and how to promote children's academic skills. The training program uses video vignettes to help parents learn these new skills (Webster-Stratton, 1994). Children in this intervention develop skills in emotional literacy, empathy or perspective taking, friendship, anger management, interpersonal problem solving, school rules, and how to succeed in school. Teacher training helps teachers use effective classroom management skills that involve positive attention; giving praise and encouragement; use of incentives for difficult behavior problems; how to manage inappropriate classroom behaviors; and how to teach empathy, social skills, and problem solving in the classroom.

Multisystemic Therapy

Multisystemic therapy (MST) is an ecologically based, short-term, intensive home and community-based intervention program for families of youth with severe psychosocial and behavioral problems (Henggeler, Schoenwald, Borduin, Rowland, & Cunningham, 1998; Henggeler, Schoenwald, Rowland, & Cunningham, 2002; Swenson, Henggeler, Taylor, & Addison, 2005). MST provides an alternative to out-of-home placement of children and youth.

The MST program uses a family preservation service delivery model that provides time-limited, intensive services to the child and their family over a period of 4 to 6 months (Henggeler et al., 1998). Therapists work with the youth and their families as a treatment team. The treatment team usually consists of three or four mental health professionals with masters or doctoral degrees who share responsibility for the treatment and provide services to about 50 families a year. The MST program model involves being available to the youth and family 24 hours a day, 7 days a week. The treatment team model allows for families to have more than one therapist to relate to over time to address the serious challenges that they face raising a youth with severe psychosocial and behavioral problems. In addition, the treatment team has the opportunity to provide each other instrumental and affective support and coverage for one another during vacation or personal time off (Schoenwald & Rowland, 2002).

MST usually involves work not only with the child and the family but also work with other social systems including neighborhoods, schools, and peer groups (Swenson et al., 2005). In MST, the child and the family may receive a range of interventions that are individualized to address specific needs. The individual and family interventions may focus on cognitive and/or behavioral change, communication skills, parenting skills, family relations, peer relations, school performance, and/or social networks (Littell, Popa, & Forsythe, 2005).

The MST program is manualized and includes measures to ensure fidelity through supervision and organizational quality improvement efforts. The MST program has nine principles that guide and organize the treatment team's work with the child and family. The nine principles that guide the assessment and intervention process include:

1. The primary purpose of assessment is to understand the fit between the identified problems and their broader systemic context.
2. Therapeutic contacts emphasize the positive and should use systemic strengths as levers for change.
3. Interventions are designed to promote responsible behavior and decrease irresponsible behavior among family members.
4. Interventions are present-focused and action-oriented, targeting specified and well-defined problems.
5. Interventions target sequences of behavior within and between multiple systems that maintain the identified problems.
6. Interventions are developmentally appropriate and fit the developmental needs of the youth.
7. Interventions are designed to require daily or weekly effort by family members.
8. Intervention effectiveness is evaluated continuously from multiple perspectives, with providers assuming accountability for overcoming barriers to successful outcomes.
9. Interventions are designed to promote treatment generalization and long-term maintenance of therapeutic change by empowering caregivers to address family members' needs across multiple systemic contexts. (Henggeler et al., 1998, p. 23)

According to Schoenwald and Rowland (2002), the MST treatment team engages in an analytical process designed to:

• Gain a clear understanding for the reasons for referral;
• Assess and develop overarching treatment goals that build on the strengths of the child, the family, and other relevant social systems;
• Establish intermediary treatment goals that are linked to the overarching treatment goals; and
• Engage in an ongoing assessment of advances and barriers to intervention effectiveness.

MST has a relatively robust evidence base with several randomized controlled trials (RCTs). Eight MST RCTs met the selection criteria for inclusion in a rigorous Cochrane Collaborative Review conducted by Littell et al. (2005). While many of the MST studies published in professional journals tend to show positive outcomes for children, Littell et al. (2005) concluded in their review that there may be no significant differences between the MST population and the usual services population. More studies are needed to assess the impact of MST. MST Services, Inc. was formed to standardize the dissemination of MST and to ensure fidelity to the model. MST has been replicated in several sites across the United States, Canada, and Norway.

Brief Strategic Family Therapy

The brief strategic family therapy (BSFT) is a culturally appropriate intervention that focuses on addressing substance abuse risks as it relates to Latino youth (ages 6 to 17 years) and their family members (Robbins et al., 2003; Szapocznik, Hervis, & Schwartz, 2003). This BSFT intervention uses a problem-focused and a family systems therapy approach. It usually involves 12 to 16 weekly sessions. The intervention was first developed for work with Latino youth involved with drugs and their families. BSFT is a manualized intervention and has been extensively evaluated for more than 25 years. The evaluation research supports that BSFT is effective in work with youth with substance abuse and conduct problems.

In BSFT, the family is viewed as the primary context for work. Three central themes guide the work in BSFT. These themes include: *system, structures*, and *strategy* (Szapocznik & Kurtines, 1989). A family is a *system* comprised of individuals whose behavior affects other family members; *structures* are repetitive patterns of interaction and involve content and process; and *strategy* are the interventions that are practical, problem focused, and deliberate (Robbins et al., 2003). *Content* refers to what family members talk about and *process* involves family interaction behaviors (Szapocznik et al., 2003).

According to Robbins et al. (2003, p. 409), the key assumptions that guide BSFT include:

1. Changing the family is the most effective way of changing the individual;
2. Changing an individual and then returning him or her to a detrimental or negative environment does not allow the individual changes to remain in place; and
3. Changes in one central or powerful individual can result in changes in the rest of his or her family.

BSFT involves the whole family in treatment. Family sessions typically take place once a week and each session runs 1 to $1\frac{1}{2}$ hours. The first step in BSFT is *joining* (building a therapeutic relationship with each family member and addressing barriers to engagement), followed by *diagnosing family strengths and weaknesses, developing a treatment plan*, and *restructuring* (implementing change strategies needed to transform family relations; Robbins et al., 2003). Change strategies include cognitive restructuring; directing, redirecting, or blocking communication; shifting family alliances; placing parents in charge; helping families to develop conflict resolution skills; developing effective behavior management skills; and fostering parenting and parental leadership skills (Robbins et al., 2003). The restructuring techniques used are: working in the present, reframing negativity, reversals, working with boundaries and alliances, detriangulation, and opening up closed systems and tasks (Szapocznik et al., 2003).

BSFT can be delivered in office or community-based and in-home settings. The BSFT therapist works with 10 to 12 families.

Schoolwide/Community Interventions

There are numerous schoolwide prevention programs that have demonstrated initial success in early evaluation studies across the county for children, especially as it relates to improving attendance and academic performance. In fact, many of the programs target behaviors that place students at risk for emotional and behavioral problems. Some of these programs focus on bullying behavior, anger management, and prevention of gang activity and substance misuse. Resilience research cites that positive school experiences for youth and having a parent who promotes the importance of education can serve as key protective factors (Luthar et al., 2000). Three specific prevention programs are discussed in this section that involve schools and communities in helping children and their families. The three programs include Families and Schools Together, Strengthening Families, and Project Achieve.

All three programs address the key principles of effective prevention programs. These program principles include: (a) being comprehensive; (b) using varied teaching methods; (c) providing sufficient dosage to produce desired effects; (d) are theory driven; (e) provide exposure to adults and peers in a way that promotes strong, positive relationships; (f) are initiated early enough to have an impact; (g) are socioculturally relevant; (h) include evaluation of outcomes; and (i) train staff to implement the program with fidelity (Nation et al., 2003).

Families and Schools Together

The Families and Schools Together (FAST) program is a "developmental, risk focused, early intervention/prevention program built on the knowledge that effective prevention programs must reduce cumulative risks and combinations of factors that increase risk for children, as well as enhance protective factors in families that buffer children from such multiple risks" (Coote, 2000, p. 2). The FAST program has been implemented in 45 states in the United States, as well as in Australia, Canada, Germany, and Russia (Soydan, Nye, Chacon-Moscosco, Sanchez-Meca, & Almeida, 2005).

In the FAST program, child well-being is viewed as linked to family and community functioning. The FAST program model, through early intervention with at-risk children living in impoverished conditions, supports families and integrates community development with family and individual clinical approaches to reduce substance abuse, violence, delinquency, and school failure (McDonald, Billingham, Conrad, Morgan, & Payton, 1997).

FAST engages parents of at-risk elementary school youth in an 8-week, multifamily group that involves structured activities aimed at enhancing family functioning, building social connections, and reducing parent /family isolation (Coote, 2000; McDonald et al., 1997). The FAST program integrates concepts from family stress theory, community development theory, parent-mediated play therapy, and behavioral parent management strategies to help parents, families, and communities meet the needs of at-risk children (McDonald et al., 1997). FAST has the ultimate goal of "increasing the likelihood of the child being successful in the home, in the school and in the community" (Coote, 2000, p. 5). The specific outcome goals embedded in the program model include: (a) preventing school failure,

(b) enhancing family functioning, (c) reducing everyday stress by developing an ongoing support group for parents, and (d) preventing substance abuse (Fischer, 2003).

The first phase of the FAST program involves teachers in the elementary school identifying children with behavioral, emotional, or learning problems who are at risk of academic and social problems. The FAST team that includes FAST parent graduates visits the homes of the identified children to invite the parent(s) and family to participate in the FAST program. When 8 to 10 families have agreed to join the FAST program, these families begin an 8-week, multifamily group. The multifamily group uses a structured, interactive format to empower parents to address the behavioral, emotional, and learning needs of their children. The $2\frac{1}{2}$ hour weekly meetings are led by a trained team that includes a parent, a school professional (e.g., the school social worker), a clinical social worker from a mental health agency, and a substance-abuse counselor (McDonald et al., 1997). Each session includes six basic elements: (1) a shared family meal, (2) family games involving communication tactics, (3) a group discussion for parents separate from a play session for the children, (4) play-focused time involving parent and target child, (5) a family lottery in which each family wins once to serve as the host for the next FAST session, and (6) a closing ceremony with singing and recognition of family and individual accomplishments (Fischer, 2003). Some of the specific strategies used in the FAST sessions include making a family flag; a FAST hello where each family is welcomed by another family; singing the FAST song; creating individual pictures out of scribbles for positive family communication; feelings charades where children and parents act out their feelings and others guess; buddy time for adults where couples and parents are paired up to share their day, their hassles and what happened without the other person giving advice; special play time where the parent is coached by the FAST team to follow the child's lead; a door prize for one family each week; and special topic sessions to talk about hard to discuss issues such as alcohol and drug use (Coote, 2000; McDonald et al., 1997). At the end of the 8-week, multifamily group, a graduation ceremony is held with certificates presented to the parents from the school principal. Linkages to community services are also made for parents and families based on need. The parents then become a part of the next phase of the FAST program. The next phase is called FASTWORKS. Families are invited to participate for 2 years in this phase of the program. FASTWORKS involves monthly meetings designed to provide continued family support and networking. These meetings are run by a parent-advisory council of graduates. Attendance at these meetings for parents is voluntary but encouraged by the FAST team.

Several evaluations and at least five randomized controlled studies have been conducted on the FAST program with promising results. In some of the studies, a significant positive overall effect of FAST on the child's academic performance at 2 years based on teacher's report was noted, and families sustained their positive changes for over 6 months after completing the multifamily group. A systematic review of the FAST effects is currently being conducted as part of the Cochrane Collaboration (Soydan et al., 2005).

Strengthening Families Program

The Strengthening Families Program (SFP) is designed for youth ages 6 to 14 years and their families. The program targets improving family relationships, parenting skills, and youth's social and life skills (Kumpfer & Alvardo, 2003). It was originally developed for children of parents who abuse drugs (Kumpfer, Alvardo, Tait, & Turner, 2002). There are different versions of this program. The SFP uses a biopsychosocial vulnerability model (Kumpfer & Alvardo, 2003) and a resiliency-based framework to guide all program interventions.

The SFP for youth ages 6 to 12 years involves families in a 14-week training session using family systems and cognitive-behavioral approaches to increase protective factors and decrease risk factors in the youth and their families. These sessions are held at the school. This version of the SFP involves parents and youth attending 14 sessions that run for 2 hours each session. The SFP sessions are structured and involve three components: family life skills training, parent skills training, and child problem-solving and social skills training (Kumpfer et al., 2002). Parents meet separately from the youth for 1 hour and this component is facilitated by two group leaders. The focus of the session is to help parents learn ways to increase positive behavior in their children, use discipline and limit setting effectively, improve parent-child communication, develop problem-solving skills, and address substance use. During this time, the youth meet with two children's trainers to learn about feelings, how to control anger, resist peer pressure, use problem solving, and develop social skills. In the second hour of each session, families meet together to engage in structured family activities and practice skills. After completing the sessions, families are invited to participate in a 6-month and a 12-month booster session to maintain intervention gains (Kumpfer et al., 2002).

The SFP for youth ages 10 to 14 years is video-based, addressing substance abuse and problem behavior in youth. This SFP is a universal prevention program, the objectives of which are to (a) build skills in youth to reduce risk and build protective factors, (b) improve parenting practices known to reduce risk in youth, and (c) build stronger family units to support and monitor youth (Molgaard & Spoth, 2001). This version of SFP consists of seven sessions plus four booster sessions for parents and youth. Similar to the SFP for youth ages 6 to 12 years, this version separates parents and youth for the first hour and the second hour is spent in supervised family activities. Three group leaders are needed: one to lead the parent session and two to lead the youth session. The group leaders shift roles from teacher to facilitator for the second half of each session.

The SFP uses incentives, family meals, and other rituals to foster engagement and attendance at the sessions. Research on SFP has consistently found positive results for youth in reducing substance use risk and increasing protective factors in the youth and families, even at 5-year follow-up measures (Kumpfer & Alvardo, 2003).

Project Achieve

Project Achieve is a school-based program that focuses on academic work, school safety, and positive climate and parent involvement outcomes (Knoff & Batsche, 1995). According to Knoff, Finch, and Carlyon (2004, p. 6), Project Achieve's ultimate goal "is to help design and implement effective school and schooling processes to maximize the academic and social/emotional/behavioral progress and achievement of all students." It has a primary prevention focus but also will intervene with students in difficulty. The six primary goals of Project Achieve include: (1) enhancing the problem-solving skills of teachers and other educators; (2) improving classroom and behavior management skills of school personnel; (3) intervening with students who are not performing at their expected levels; (4) increasing social and academic progress of students by increasing parent involvement and linking to community resources; (5) engaging in a comprehensive improvement process; and (6) creating a school climate in which every teacher, school staff member, and parent shares responsibility for building community (Knoff et al., 2004).

Project Achieve has seven major, interdependent components that focus on building a schoolwide positive behavioral self-management system:

1. *Strategic planning and organizational analysis:* This component focuses on assessing the organizational climate, administrative style, and decision-making processes in the school.

2. *Referral questioning consultation (RQC):* RQC is a problem-solving approach that links the problem assessment to intervention. All staff are trained in this technique.

3. *Classroom teacher/staff development:* Assists teachers in securing the needed skills to implement various instructional styles to maximize student learning.

4. *Instructional consultation and curriculum-based assessment/intervention:* Emphasizes direct instruction and a mastery model perspective in academic outcomes.

5. *Behavioral consultation and behavioral interventions:* This component focuses on establishing a schoolwide positive behavioral self-management system that addresses behavioral interventions designed to resolve students' behavioral problems or to improve teachers' classroom management procedures. A major part of this component is implementing the Stop and Think Social Skills Program (Knoff, 2001). The Stop and Think Social Skills Program teaches students over 60 behavioral skills (e.g., listening, problem solving, asking for help, responding to teasing). There are five steps in the Stop and Think Social Skills Program. These steps include: (1) Stop and think. (2) Are you going to make a good choice or bad choice? (3) What are your choices or steps? (4) Do it! and (5) Good job! (Knoff et al., 2004).

6. *Parent training, tutoring, and support:* Focuses on building an ongoing home-school collaboration and making parents an integral part of the school. Parent training sessions are conducted that help parents learn how to transfer the social skills and discipline/behavior management approaches used in the school into the home.

7. *Research and accountability:* Addresses the evaluation of the program and ways to improve outcomes.

The implementation of Project Achieve components is sequenced over a 3-year period. Several schools have implemented this program and initial evaluations of this schoolwide initiative indicate positive outcomes for youth in school engagement and prosocial skill development.

LIMITATIONS OF THE EVIDENCE

Despite the availability of EBP for work with children and their families, many of these EBPs are not widely used in social work practice. The gap between research and practice continues to be a challenge for the social workers involved in delivering interventions in public child-serving systems. While this chapter addressed a few of the EBPs that have a solid research base, there are many other emerging practices that also have promise for work with children and their families such as motivational interviewing, parent-child interaction therapy, and wraparound services. All of these EBPs require that social workers be trained to deliver the interventions with fidelity, and this requires ongoing supervision, monitoring of the implementation process, and measurement of relevant clinical outcomes.

The EBPs discussed in this chapter involve multiple strategies at different system levels to produce positive outcomes for children and their families. There are similar elements/strategies in each of the EBPs, especially as it relates to the use of behavioral and cognitive-behavioral techniques. In many of the interventions, parents are involved in learning new skills to facilitate management of child problem behaviors.

For some social workers, one of the limitations of EBPs is the use of prescriptive manuals that often do not allow for individualizing the intervention to better meet the needs of a child and family with multiple problems, and they may limit the opportunity to engage in collaborative work with families.

While the EBPs presented in this chapter address multiple problem areas and are multicomponent, the social worker still needs to understand how and why the interventions work. In addition, more work is needed on how to tailor the interventions to include preferences of families based on, but not limited to, gender, ethnicity, culture, race, sexual orientation, gender identity, religion, and spirituality differences. The New Freedom Commission (2003) specifically identified the need to tailor interventions for culturally diverse populations as one of the goals of transforming the mental health system. The evaluation of the EBPs should include a range of child and family outcomes in order to assess the impact of the interventions over time.

CONCLUSION

For the greatest possibility of success, it is imperative that we use and continue to develop EBPs for children. Despite the many benefits of using these types of interventions, both practitioners and clients often are hesitant to employ them. While practitioners prefer providers to use best evidence when they are clients, they feel that evidence-based interventions do not provide enough direction in their own practice. Pollio (2006) attributes this to the fact the EBP training and practice represents researchers and academics talking to practitioners rather than an open dialogue between the two groups. In addition, many practitioners feel that academics simply explain how EBP can be applied generically into practice rather than providing guidance on how to apply these interventions based on the specific circumstances of the case. Likewise, clinical practitioners report that their clients have often had negative experiences with evidence-based interventions that were ineffective and are uncomfortable implementing complicated data collection methods. Their clients' preconceptions can make it difficult to utilize an evidence-based intervention during the treatment process.

While these complaints and hesitations are certainly valid, it is important that practitioners are not discouraged, but rather supported in analytically investigating the quality of the evidence undergirding the intervention. Furthermore, they need to determine for whom the intervention will be most effective and under what conditions, which in turn should be communicated clearly to the client. It is also important to remember that families and the various child-serving systems are a part of the solution. This keeps the family and child factors in the forefront of any EBP and allows for contextualization given the needs of the child and/or family.

Another aspect of the analytical process is understanding the psychometric properties and characteristics of the target population associated with the evidence, for example, ethnicity/race, culture, sexual orientation, and economic situation of the client. Attention should also be paid to the relevant theories that guide the various evidence-based interventions.

For EBP to be most effective, it must be integrated into the micro-, mezzo- and macrolevels of social work. A microsystem is defined as the interpersonal interactions within an individual's immediate environment, such as the school or workplace. A mezzosystem, on the other hand, involves the way two or more microsystems interact with one another, for example, between one's school and home environments. Overarching both of these is the macrosystem, or the ideologies and values governing a society (Bronfenbrenner, 1986, as cited in Neville & Mobley, 2001).

On the microlevel, a comprehensive training and dissemination system including manuals, guidelines, web sites, and adequate consideration of treatment fidelity issues would provide a solid base for more fully integrating EBP into the social work profession. Continuing education and outreach is necessary for success on the mezzolevel. This will enable practitioners to remain up to date on interventions and relevant literature, as well as receive guidance from professionals trained in EBP to ensure they appropriately implement the interventions in the most effective and efficient manner. Agencies need to not only address ways to support the training and implementation of EBPs to ensure fidelity but agencies also need to sustain these efforts over time. Finally, on the macrolevel, there are a variety of ways to inform the policy makers and funding agencies in order to heighten their awareness of the advantages of EBP, so they can act accordingly. This can range from informing local leaders who influence and assist in propagating information to practitioners, calling attention to effective practices/interventions before congressional groups, advocating quality improvement at the organizational level, or by utilizing technology or mass media campaigns to educate clients about their treatment options (Allen-Meares, 2006).

Replication of interventions in different contexts and with diverse children groups is vital for advancing our practice knowledge. By adequately addressing needs at all levels, the result will be a broader understanding and more widespread use of EBP in a number of practice settings and organizational levels. The larger implications of reliance on EBP include a move toward recognition of professional standards and an element of measurability in the results. Drawing on the examples prevalent in the health-care fields, EBP should be viewed as a way to increase effectiveness and quality of care by defining the best practices for the profession through wide dissemination of the subsequent findings (Sharts-Hopko, 2003).

REFERENCES

Allen-Meares, P. (2006). Where do we go from here? Mental health workers and the implementation of an evidence-based practice. In C. Franklin, M. B. Harris, & P. Allen-Meares (Eds.), *The school services sourcebook: A guide for school-based professionals* (pp. 1189–1194). New York: Oxford University Press.

Barrett, P. M. (1998). Evaluation of cognitive-behavioral group treatments for childhood anxiety disorders. *Journal of Clinical Child Psychology, 27*, 459–469.

Barrett, P. M., Lowry-Webster, H., & Turner, C. (2000). *FRIENDS program for children: Group leaders manual*. Brisbane, Australia: Australian Academic Press.

Barrett, P. M., & Shortt, A. L. (2003). Parental involvement in the treatment of anxious children. In A. E. Kazdin & J. R. Weisz (Eds.), *Evidence-based psychotherapies for children and adolescents* (pp. 101–119). New York: Guilford Press.

Bronfenbrenner, U. (1986). Ecology of the family as a context to human development: Research perspectives. *Development Psychology, 22,* 723–742.

Chamberlain, P. (2002). Treatment foster care. In B. J. Burns & K. Hoagwood (Eds.), *Community treatment for youth: Evidence-based interventions for severe emotional and behavioral disorders* (pp. 117–138). New York: Oxford University Press.

Chamberlain, P., & Reid, J. (1991). Using a specialized foster care treatment model for children and adolescents leaving the state mental hospital. *Journal of Community Psychology, 19,* 266–276.

Chamberlain, P., & Smith, D. K. (2003). Antisocial behavior in children and adolescents: The Oregon Multidimensional Treatment Foster Care Model. In A. E. Kazdin & J. R. Weisz (Eds.), *Evidence-based psychotherapies for children and adolescents* (pp. 282–300). New York: Guilford Press.

Coie, J. D., Watt, N. F., West, S. G., Hawkins, J. D., Asarnow, J. R., Markman, H. J., et al. (1993). The science of prevention: A conceptual framework and some directions for a national research program. *American Psychologist, 48,* 1013–1022.

Coote, S. (2000). *Families and Schools Together (FAST).* Paper presented at the conference reducing criminality: Partnerships and best practice, Australian Institute of Criminology, Perth, Australia.

Dishion, T. J., Bullock, B. M., & Granic, I. (2002). Pragmatism in modeling peer influence: Dynamics, outcomes, and change processes. *Development and Psychopathology, 14,* 969–981.

Dishion, T. J., Capaldi, D. M., & Yeager, K. (1999). Middle childhood antecedents to progressions in male adolescent substance use: An ecological analysis of risk and protection. *Journal of Adolescent Research, 14*(2), 175–205.

Duchnowski, A. J., Kutash, K., & Friedman, R. M. (2003). Community-based interventions in a system of care and outcomes framework. In B. J. Burns & K. Hoagwood (Eds.), *Community treatment for youth: Evidence-based interventions for severe emotional and behavioral disorders* (pp. 16–37). New York: Oxford University Press.

Fischer, R. L. (2003). School-based family support: Evidence from an exploratory field study. *Families in Society, 84*(3), 339–347.

Fisher, P. A., & Chamberlain, P. (2000). Multidimensional treatment foster care: A program for intensive parenting, family support, and skill building. *Journal of Emotional and Behavioral Disorders, 8*(3), 155–164.

Fisher, P. A., Ellis, B. H., & Chamberlain, P. (1999). Early intervention foster care: A model for preventing risk in young children who have been maltreated. *Children Services: Social Policy, Research and Practice, 2*(3), 159–182.

Forgatch, M. S., Patterson, G. R., & DeGarmo, D. S. (2005). Evaluating fidelity: Predictive validity for a measure of competent adherence to the Oregon Model of Parent Management Training. *Behavior Therapy, 36,* 3–13.

Fraser, M. W. (2003). Intervention research in social work: A basis for evidence-based practice and practice guidelines. In A. Rosen & E. K. Proctor (Eds.), *Developing practice guidelines for social work intervention: Issues, methods and research agenda* (pp. 17–36). New York: Columbia University Press.

Fraser, M. W. (2004). The ecology of childhood: A multisystems perspective. In M. W. Fraser (Ed.), *Risk and resilience in childhood: An ecological perspective* (2nd ed., pp. 1–12). Washington, DC: National Association of Social Workers Press.

Friesen, B. J., & Stephens, B. (1998). Expanded family roles in the system of care: Research and practice. In M. H. Epstein, K. Kutash, & A. J. Duchnowski (Eds.), *Outcomes for children and youth with behavioral and emotional disorders: Programs and evaluation best practices* (pp. 231–253). Austin, TX: ProEd.

Gambrill, E. (2003). Evidence-based practice: Implications for knowledge development and use in social work. In A. Rosen & E. K. Proctor (Eds.), *Developing practice guidelines for social work intervention: Issues, methods and research agenda* (pp. 37–58). New York: Columbia University Press.

Garmezy, N. (1985). Stress-resistant children: The search for protective factors. In J. E. Stevenson (Ed.), *Recent research in developmental psychopathology* (pp. 213–233). Tarrytown, NY: Pergamon Press.

Hawkins, J. D., Catalano, R. F., & Miller, J. Y. (1992). Risk and protective factors for alcohol and other drug problems in adolescence and early adulthood: Implications for substance abuse prevention. *Psychological Bulletin, 112*, 64–105.

Henggeler, S. W., Schoenwald, S. K., Borduin, C. M., Rowland, M. D., & Cunningham, P. B. (1998). *Multisystemic treatment of antisocial behavior in children and adolescents.* New York: Guilford Press.

Henggeler, S. W., Schoenwald, S. K., Rowland, M. D., & Cunningham, P. B. (2002). *Serious emotional disturbance in children and adolescents: Multisytemic therapy.* New York: Guilford Press.

Hoagwood, K., Burns, B. J., Kiser, L., Ringeisen, H., & Schoenwald, S. K. (2001). Evidence-based practice in child and adolescent mental health services. *Psychiatric Services, 52*, 1179–1189.

Holmbeck, G. N., Greenley, R. N., & Franks, E. A. (2003). Developmental issues and considerations in research and practice. In A. E. Kazdin & J. R. Weisz (Eds.), *Evidence-based psychotherapies for children and adolescents* (pp. 21–41). New York: Guilford Press.

Institute of Medicine. (1990). *Guidelines for clinical practice: From development to use.* Washington, DC: National Academy Press.

Institute of Medicine, Committee on Quality of Health Care in America. (2001). *Crossing the quality chasm: A new health system for the 21st century.* Washington, DC: National Academy Press.

Kazdin, A. E. (1997). A model for developing effective treatments: Progression and interplay of theory, research, and practice. *Journal of Clinical Child Psychology, 26*, 114–129.

Kazdin, A. E. (2005). *Parent management training: Treatment for oppositional, aggressive and antisocial behavior in children and adolescents.* New York: Oxford University Press.

Kendall, P. C., Flannery-Schroeder, E., Panichelli-Mindel, S. M., Southam-Gerwo, M., Henin, A., & Warman, M. (1997). Therapy for youths with anxiety disorders: A second randomized clinical trial. *Journal of Consulting and Clinical Psychology, 65*, 366–380.

Kirk, S. (1999). Good intentions are not enough: Practice guidelines for social work. *Research on Social Work Practice, 9*, 302–310.

Knoff, H. M. (2001). *The Stop and Think Social Skills Program (preschool, grade 1, grades 2/3, grades 4/5, middle school 6/8).* Longmont, CO: Sopris West.

Knoff, H. M., & Batsche, G. M. (1995). Project ACHIEVE: Analyzing a school reform process for at-risk and underachieving students. *School Psychology Review, 24*(4), 579–603.

Knoff, H. M., Finch, C., & Carlyon, W. (2004). Project ACHIEVE and the development of school-wide positive behavioral self-management systems- prevention, intervention, and intensive needs approach. In K. E. Robinson (Ed.), *Advances in school-based mental health interventions: Vol. 19. Best practices and program models* (pp. 1–28). Kingston, NJ: Civic Research Institute.

Kumpfer, K. L., & Alvarado, R. (2003). Family-strengthening approaches for the prevention of youth problem behaviors. *American Psychologist, 58*(6/7), 457–465.

Kumpfer, K. L., Alvarado, R., Tait, C., & Turner, C. (2002). Effectiveness of school-based family and children's skills training for substance abuse prevention among 6–8 year old rural children. *Psychology of Addictive Behaviors, 16*(4S), 565–571.

Littell, J. H., Popa, M., & Forsythe, B. (2005). Multisytemic therapy for social, emotional and behavioral problems in youth aged 10–17. *Cochrane Database of Systemic Reviews* (Issue 4, Art. No: CD004797.pub4, DOI:10.1002/15671838.CD004797.pub4.)

Luthar, S. S. (1991). Vulnerability and resilience: A study of high-risk adolescents. *Child Development, 62*, 600–616.

Luthar, S. S., Cicchetti, D., & Becker, B. (2000). The construct of resilience: A critical evaluation and guidelines for future work. *Child Development, 71*(3), 543–562.

Lyons, J. S. (2004). *Redressing the emperor: Improving our children's public mental health system.* Westport, CT: Praeger.

McDonald, L., Billingham, S., Conrad, T., Morgan, A. O. N., & Payton, E. (1997). Families and Schools Together (FAST): Integrating community development with clinical strategies. *Families in Society, 78*(2), 140–155.

Molgaard, V., & Spoth, R. (2001). The Strengthening Families Program for Young Adolescents: Overview and outcomes. In S. I. Pfeiffer & L. A. Reddy (Eds.), *Innovative mental health interventions for children: Programs that work* (pp. 15–29). New York: Haworth Press.

Nation, M., Crusto, C., Wandersman, A., Kumpfer, K. L., Seybolt, D., Morrissey-Kane, E., et al. (2003). What works in prevention: Principles of effective prevention programs. *American Psychologist, 58*(6/7), 449–456.

Neville, H. A., & Mobley, M. (2001). Social identities in contexts: An ecological model of multicultural counseling psychology processes. *Counseling Psychologist, 29*(4), 471–486.

New Freedom Commission on Mental Health. (2003). *Achieving the promise: Transforming mental health care in America* (SMA 03-3832). Rockville, MD: Substance Abuse and Mental Health Administration.

Patterson, G. R. (2004). Systematic changes in families following prevention trials. *Journal of Abnormal Child Psychology.* Retrieved February 20, 2006, from www.findarticles.com/p/articles/mi_m_0902/is_6_32/ai_n8590486/.

Patterson, G. R. (2005). The next generation of PMTO models. *Behavior Therapist,* 27–33.

Pollio, D. E. (2006). The art of evidence-based practice. *Research on Social Work Practice, 16*(2), 224–232.

Robbins, M. S., Szapocznik, J., Santisteban, D. A., Hervis, O. E., Mitrani, V. B., & Schwartz, S. J. (2003). Brief strategic family therapy for Hispanic youth. In A. E. Kazdin & J. R. Weisz (Eds.), *Evidence-based psychotherapies for children and adolescents* (pp. 407–424). New York: Guilford Press.

Rosen, A., & Proctor, E. K. (2003). Practice guidelines and the challenge of effective practice. In A. Rosen & E. K. Proctor (Eds.), *Developing practice guidelines for social work intervention: Issues, methods and research agenda* (pp. 1–14). New York: Columbia University Press.

Schoenwald, S. K., & Rowland, M. D. (2002). Multisystemic therapy. In B. J. Burns & K. Hoagwood (Eds.), *Community treatment for youth: Evidence-based interventions for severe emotional and behavioral disorders* (pp. 91–116). New York: Oxford University Press.

Sharts-Hopko, N. C. (2003). Evidence-based practice: What constitutes evidence? *Journal of the Association of Nurses in AIDS Care, 14*(3), 76.

Shortt, A. L., Barrett, P. M., & Fox, T. L. (2001). Evaluating the FRIENDS program: A cognitive-behavioral group treatment for anxious children and their parents. *Journal of Clinical Child Psychology, 30,* 525–535.

Soler, J. A., & Weatherall, R. (2005). Cognitive behavioural therapy for anxiety disorders in children and adolescents. *Cochrane Database of Systematic Reviews* (Issue 4, Art. No: CD004690.pub2, DOI:10.1002/14651858.CD004690.pub2.)

Soydan, H., Nye, C., Chacon-Moscoso, S., Sanchez-Meca, J., & Almeida, C. (2005). Families and Schools Together (FAST) for improving outcomes of school-aged children and their families (Protocol). *Cochrane Database of Systematic Reviews* (Issue 2, Art. No: CD005210, DOI: 10.1002/14651858.CD005210.)

Stallard, P. (2002). *Think good-feel good: A cognitive behaviour therapy workbook for children and young people.* Hoboken, NJ: Wiley.

Swenson, C. C., Henggeler, S. W., Taylor, I. S., & Addison, O. W. (2005). *Multisystemic therapy and neighborhood partnerships: Reducing adolescent violence and substance abuse.* New York: Guilford Press.

Szapocznik, J., Hervis, O., & Schwartz, S. (2003). *Brief strategic family therapy for adolescent drug abuse*. (NIH Pub. No. 03-4751). Bethesda, MD: U.S. Department of Health and Human Services, National Institutes of Health, National Institute of Drug Abuse.

Szapocznik, J., & Kurtines, W. M. (1989). *Breakthroughs in family therapy with drug abusing and problem youth*. New York: Springer.

U.S. Surgeon General. (1999). *Mental health: A report to the Surgeon General*. Washington, DC: Department of Health and Human Services.

U.S. Surgeon General. (2001). *Report of the United States Surgeon General's Conference on children's mental health: A national action agenda*. Washington, DC: Department of Health and Human Services.

Webster-Stratton, C. (1994). Advancing videotape parent training: A comparison study. *Journal of Consulting and Clinical Psychology, 62*(3), 583–593.

Webster-Stratton, C. (2001). The incredible years: Parents, teachers, and children training series. In S. I. Pfeiffer & L. A. Reddy (Eds.), *Innovative mental health interventions for children: Programs that work* (pp. 31–48). New York: Haworth Press.

Chapter 13 ─────────────────────────

ASSESSMENT OF ADOLESCENTS

David W. Springer

"They love too much and hate too much, and the same with everything else. They think they know everything; and are always quite sure about it; this, in fact, is why they overdo everything." These words were written by Aristotle, the ancient Greek philosopher, over 2,300 years ago (*Rhetoric, Book II*). Today's scientific study of adolescence can be traced back to the work of G. Stanley Hall (1904), who wrote a two-volume work on adolescence in which he proposed that adolescence was a separate stage of development. Now fast-forward 100 years.

As recently as 2005, the *Journal of Clinical Child and Adolescent Psychology* devoted a special section on developing guidelines for the evidence-based assessment of child and adolescent disorders, where evidence-based assessment (EBA) is "intended to develop, elaborate, and identify the measurement strategies and procedures that have empirical support in their behalf" (Kazdin, 2005, p. 548). In this special issue on evidence-based assessment, Mash and Hunsley (2005) emphasize the great importance of assessment as part of intervention but acknowledge that the development of evidence-based assessment has not kept up with the increased emphasis on evidenced-based treatment. In fact, there is a significant disconnect between evidence-based assessment and evidence-based treatment. This is no small problem for those in the field. Several studies spanning different geographical locations (such as the United States, Puerto Rico, Canada, and New Zealand) have produced consistent results on the prevalence of disorders among children and adolescents, with estimates indicating that 17% to 22% suffer significant developmental, emotional, or behavioral problems (U.S. Congress, 1991; World Health Organization [WHO], 2001; as cited in Kazdin & Weisz, 2003).

The developmental tasks associated with adolescence only serve to complicate matters because the practitioner must take into account many interrelated domains of the adolescent's life. Some behaviors may be considered quite normal at one age but later cross a threshold that suggests mental illness or impairment in functioning. In addition to the importance placed on recognizing the developmental tasks of adolescence during the assessment process, this chapter adopts the assumptions about assessment presented by Jordan and Franklin (1995): "(1) assessment is empirically based, (2) assessment must be made from a systems perspective, (3) measurement is essential, (4) ethical practitioners evaluate their clinical work, and (5) well-qualified practitioners are knowledgeable about numerous assessment methods in developing assessments" (p. 3). These assumptions serve as a guide for social workers when determining what type of assessment protocol to implement with adolescents (and their families).

Assessment is the first active phase of treatment (Springer, McNeece, & Arnold, 2003). Without a thorough and complete assessment, the social worker cannot develop a treatment plan that will serve the youth and his or her family. In this chapter, various methods of assessment, such as interviews and the use of standardized instruments that may be useful in assessment with adolescents, are reviewed. For a more comprehensive review of assessment methods and tools for youth, see other excellent sources, including a compilation of rapid assessment instruments for children and families (K. Corcoran & Fischer, 2007), an overview of tools and methods for assessment with children and adolescents (Shaffer, Lucas, & Richters, 1999), and a guide to empirically based measures of school behavior (Kelley, Reitman, & Noell, 2003). The special section of *Journal of Clinical Child and Adolescent Psychology* referred to earlier is another excellent resource, as it examines the evidence-based assessment of pediatric biopolar disorder (Youngstrom, Findling, Youngstrom, & Calabrese, 2005); anxiety disorders (Silverman & Ollendick, 2005); depression (Klein, Dougherty, & Olino, 2005); ADHD (Pelham, Fabiano, & Massetti, 2005); conduct problems (McMahon & Frick, 2005); learning disabilities (Fletcher, Francis, Morris, & Lyon, 2005); and autism spectrum disorders (Ozonoff, Goodlin-Jones, & Solomon, 2005).

After reviewing each of the articles in the special issue mentioned earlier, Kazdin (2005, p. 549) provided a commentary where he identified common themes in child and adolescent clinical assessment:

1. There is no gold standard to validate assessment.
2. Multiple measures need to be used to capture diverse facets of the clinical problem.
3. Multiple disorders or symptoms from different disorders ought to be measured because of high rates of comorbidity.
4. Multiple informants are needed to obtain information from different perspectives and from different contexts.
5. Adaptive functioning, impairment, or more generally how individuals are doing in their everyday lives are important to assess and are separate from symptoms and disorders.
6. Influences (or moderators) of performance need to be considered for interpreting the measures, including sex, age or developmental level, culture, and ethnicity, among others.

These themes are certainly critical to the assessment of adolescents, and will be revisited throughout the remainder of the chapter.

EVIDENCE-BASED ASSESSMENT WITH ADOLESCENTS

There are various methods of assessment available to social work practitioners that can be used with adolescents. These include, but are not limited to, interviews, self-observation, and observation by others, family sculpting, individualized rating scales, rapid assessment instruments, and standardized assessment tools. The focus of this chapter is primarily on the use of standardized assessment tools and interviews with adolescents.

Interviews

The assessment process typically starts with a face-to-face interview (e.g., psychosocial history) with the adolescent. The family should also be involved for at least part of this interview. The interview serves several purposes, such as an opportunity to establish rapport with the client and allow the client to tell his or her story. Recall that one key assumption of conducting a good assessment is to operate from a systems perspective. Involving the family during part of the interview may help meet this goal because family members provide varying perspectives and are more often than not a key factor in an adolescent's life.

Morrison and Anders (1999) have written a useful book on interviewing children and adolescents, in which they advocate for a blended interviewing style that uses both directive and nondirective techniques. "In general, nondirective, open-ended style of questioning is important during the early stages of an initial interview, when you want to give the respondent greatest leeway to volunteer important observations concerning the child's or adolescent's behavior and emotional life. Later on, as you come to understand the scope of your respondent's concerns, use questions that require short answers to increase the depth of your knowledge" (p. 20).

Consider the following case for illustration purposes. Ramon, a 16-year-old Hispanic male who has been diagnosed with ADHD and oppositional defiant disorder (ODD), is brought into your agency by his parents because he is "failing 11th-grade Spanish and precalculus, and he won't listen." Ramon also has threatened to run away from home on more than one occasion. In addition to obtaining information from Ramon's parents typically covered in a psychosocial history (e.g., medical, developmental, social, and family history), some areas that the social worker may cover with Ramon's parents during an initial interview are as follows:

- Presenting problem and specific precipitating factor (e.g., Tell me in your own words what prompted you to bring Ramon in for help at this point in time?)
- Attempts to deal with the problem (e.g., What has your family done to try to deal with this problem(s)? What have you tried that has worked?)
- Hopes and expectations (e.g., What do you hope to get out of coming here for services? If you could change any one thing about how things are at home, what would it be?)

In addition to the these areas (with variations of the corresponding sample questions), consider some questions that the social worker may ask Ramon individually:

- Peer relationships (e.g., Tell me about your friends. What do you like to do together?)
- School (e.g., What are your favorite [and least favorite] classes at school? What about those classes do you like [not like]?)
- Suicide risk (e.g., When you feel down, do you ever have any thoughts of hurting/killing yourself? Do you ever wish you were dead? How would you end your life?)
- Substance use (What do you drink/use? When was the last time you had a drink/used? How much did you have? Have you ever unsuccessfully tried to reduce your substance use?)
- Targeted behavior/goal setting (e.g., If there was any thing that you could change about yourself/your life, what would it be? What do you like most about yourself?)

These questions are meant only to illustrate the range of questions that you might ask during an interview. A complete psychosocial history would need to be conducted with Ramon.

J. Corcoran and Springer (2005) emphasize a strengths-and-skills-based approach to engage the adolescent client in the treatment process. This approach pulls primarily from solution-focused therapy, motivational interviewing, and cognitive-behavioral therapy. Youths, especially those with externalizing behavioral disorders like Ramon, have often experienced a range of life stressors, such as poverty, overcrowded living conditions, parental divorce, incarceration of parents, community violence, and parental substance use. The practitioner's attempt to explore the adolescent's feelings and thoughts around such issues is often met with resistance. Rather than getting into a struggle with adolescents or trying to push them in a certain direction, the strengths-and-skills-based approach underscores building on strengths and past successes rather than correcting past failures and mistakes. Accordingly, the interviewer focuses on positives and solutions over negative histories and problems. Consider some of the following interviewing tips provided by J. Corcoran and Springer (2005).

They propose the following options for dealing with the "I don't know" stance that adolescents take:

1. Allow silence (about 20 to 30 seconds).
2. Rephrase the question.
3. Ask a relationship question (adolescents sometimes feel put on the spot by having to answer questions about themselves but can take the perspective of others to view their behavior).
4. Say, "I know you don't know, so just make it up," which bypasses teens' resistance or fear that they don't know or don't have the right answer. Or, using presuppositional language, say, "Suppose you did know . . ."
5. Speak hypothetically about others: "What would [pro-social peers that teens respect] say they do to keep out of trouble [get passing grades or get along with their parents]?" (p. 136)

J. Corcoran and Springer (2005) go on to point out that asking evocative questions may help adolescent clients increase their readiness for change, and they provide a recommended line of questioning to explore the disadvantages of the status quo (e.g., "What difficulties or hassles have you had in relation to ____?" "What is there about ____ that you or other people might see as reasons for concern?") as well as the advantages of change (e.g., "What would you like your life to be like 5 years from now?" "If you could make this change immediately, by magic, how might things be better for you?" "What would be the advantages of making this change?").

Social workers like Saleebey (1997) and Clark (1998) recommended that practitioners incorporate a strengths-based perspective into their assessment approach with adolescents. Cowger (1997, pp. 69–71) proposes specific exemplars for assessment of client strengths in five areas: cognition (e.g., is open to different ways of thinking about things); emotion (e.g., is positive about life); motivation (e.g., wants to improve current and future situations); coping (e.g., has dealt successfully with related problem in the past); and interpersonal (e.g., makes sacrifices for friends, family members, and others). For the complete listing of exemplars, see Cowger (1997). Indeed, a thorough assessment includes a deliberate examination of the client's unique strengths that in turn can be amplified over the course of treatment.

In addition to these interviewing strategies, more structured and systematic interview protocols for use with adolescents are also available to practitioners. The Diagnostic Interview Schedule for Children (DISC) is one such interview.

The Voice Diagnostic Interview Schedule for Children

The Diagnostic Interview Schedule for Children (DISC) is a computerized respondent-based interview that assesses over 30 common diagnoses found among children and adolescents, including anxiety disorders, eating disorders, mood disorders, attention-deficit and disruptive behavior disorders, and substance use disorders (Shaffer, Fisher, & Lucas, 1999; Shaffer, Fisher, Lucas, Dulcan, & Schwab-Stone, 2000). It was developed to be compatible with the *DSM-IV, DSM-III-R,* and the *International Classification of Diseases (ICD-10),* and is organized into six diagnostic modules that measure the major Axis I disorders and impairment. The DISC-IV includes assessment for three time frames—the present (past 4 weeks), the last year, and ever—with parallel versions existing for youth ages 9 to 17 (DISC-Y) and for parents or caretakers of youth ages 6 to 17 years (DISC-P). The present-state assessment is considered to be the most accurate because it minimizes the risk of bias due to telescoping (Shaffer, Fisher, & Lucas, 1999). The DISC-IV is scored by algorithms that apply Boolean logic (i.e., "and" and "ors") to combine answers to component questions and is "an ideal candidate for computerization, given the highly structured nature of the interview, the limited response options, the complicated branching and skipping instructions, and the need for the interviewer to keep close track of an informant's answers to numerous symptoms in order to ask onset and impairment questions correctly" (Shaffer, Fisher, & Lucas, 1999, p. 23). A recent voiced adaptation allows youth to hear the interview over headphones (while also reading questions on the computer screen) and key in responses via computer.

The Center for the Promotion of Mental Health in Juvenile Justice at Columbia University is spearheading efforts to administer the voice version of the DISC-IV. It has already been tested in three states (Illinois, South Carolina, and New Jersey) with youth recently admitted to juvenile correction institutions, with the primary aims to more accurately assess rates of mental health disorders among incarcerated juveniles, and to test the feasibility of using this type of structured, self-administered mental health assessment with this population (Ko & Wasserman, 2002). The Voice DISC-IV provides a "provisional" diagnosis for youth assessed. Findings from initial feasibility studies indicate that the instrument is tolerated well by youth, parents, and agency staff and support its validity, revealing that information on psychiatric status matches existing justice system information regarding current substance offenses (Wasserman, McReynolds, Lucas, Fisher, & Santos, 2002). Adaptations for detention, correctional, and community juvenile justice sites are ongoing in 10 other states. The DISC-IV has also been translated into a Spanish version (Bravo et al., 2001).

For sites that are willing and capable, the Center for the Promotion of Mental Health in Juvenile Justice will provide the Voice DISC-IV assessment software program, provide training for key personnel, offer ongoing technical support via phone and e-mail, assist with data interpretation and preparation of reports/presentations, and provide guidelines for appropriate mental health referral. For more detailed information, see www .promotementalhealth.org/voicedisc.htm.

Information gathered from the face-to-face interview can subsequently be used to inform a more in-depth assessment in targeted areas, which in turn guides treatment planning. Rapid assessment instruments and other standardized assessment protocols may prove useful for this purpose.

Rapid Assessment Instruments and Standardized Assessment Tools

Rapid assessment instruments (RAIs; Levitt & Reid, 1981) are short-form, pencil-and-paper assessment tools that are used to assess and measure change for a broad spectrum of client problems (Bloom, Fischer, & Orme, 2006; K. Corcoran & Fischer, 2007; Hudson, 1982). RAIs are used as a method of empirical assessment, are easy to administer and score, are typically completed by the client, and can help monitor client functioning over time. Given the proliferation of RAIs and standardized tools in recent years that measure various areas of adolescent functioning, it can be an overwhelming task to select a tool for use with an individual client. Thus, some guidelines are provided next.

The social worker practitioner needs to take several factors into consideration when choosing an RAI or standardized protocol for use with clients, such as the tool's reliability, validity, clinical utility, directness, availability, and so on (K. Corcoran & Fischer, 2007). To the extent that an RAI has sound psychometric properties, it helps practitioners measure a client's problem consistently (reliability) and accurately (validity). Using reliable and valid tools becomes increasingly critical as one considers the complexities surrounding assessment with adolescents who (potentially) have comorbid disorders. A brief overview of reliability and validity is provided next; however, the reader is referred to the following sources for a more detailed exposition on these topics (K. Corcoran & Fischer, 2007; Crocker & Algina, 1986; Hudson, 1982; Nunnally & Bernstein, 1994; Springer, Abell, & Hudson, 2002; Springer, Abell, & Nugent, 2002).

Reliability

A measurement instrument is reliable to the extent that it consistently yields similar results over repeated and independent administrations. A tool's reliability is represented through reliability coefficients, which range from .0 to 1.0. What constitutes a satisfactory level of reliability depends on how a measure is to be used. For use in research studies and scientific work, a reliability coefficient of .60 or greater is typically considered acceptable (Hudson, 1982). However, for use in guiding decision making with individual clients, a higher coefficient is needed. Springer, Abell, and Nugent (2002) provide the following guidelines for acceptability of reliability coefficients for use with individual clients to aid in clinical decision making:

$$< .70 = \text{Unacceptable}$$
$$.70 \text{ to } .79 = \text{Undesirable}$$
$$.80 \text{ to } .84 = \text{Minimally acceptable}$$
$$.85 \text{ to } .89 = \text{Respectable}$$
$$.90 \text{ to } .95 = \text{Very good}$$
$$> .95 = \text{Excellent}$$

The greater the seriousness of the problem being measured (e.g., suicidal risk) and the graver the risk of making a wrong decision about a client's level of functioning, the higher the standard should be adopted.

Validity

Where reliability represents an instrument's degree of consistency, validity represents how accurately an instrument measures what it is supposed to measure. There are various ways to determine an instrument's validity: content validity (which subsumes face validity), criterion-related validity (concurrent and predictive), and construct validity (convergent and discriminant).

The social worker must make decisions about a measure's validity in relationship to its intended use. In other words, the social worker must determine if the measure is valid for that particular client in a particular setting at a given time. A measure may be valid for one client but not for another.

Additional Considerations in Selecting Scales

Age and Readability

Practitioners must take into consideration the client's age and reading ability when selecting a scale. Scales are developed, validated, and normed for an intended population and for specific uses. It a scale is developed for use with adult clients, and a practitioner administers the scale to a 13-year-old client with a fifth-grade reading level, then this scale is not being administered properly and the results obtained from the scale are potentially meaningless and clinically irrelevant.

Ethnic and Cultural Diversity

A second consideration is to fully respect a client's ethnic and cultural background when using scales in practice. Ethnicity and culture affect all aspects of an adolescent's life, and acculturation experiences among minority youth can also have a significant impact on a youth's development and functioning (Jordan & Hickerson, 2003).

Consider the following challenges, for example, associated with assessing substance-abusing adolescents. An increasingly important issue in adolescent substance abuse treatment is "amenability to treatment," which concerns the identification of subgroups of individuals in a target population who are likely to be the most amenable or responsive to a treatment (i.e., what interventions work for whom under what conditions; Kazdin, 1995). Family influences on substance use may be particularly profound for Latino and African American youth due to important ethnic variations in family rules and monitoring of children in relation to risk behaviors such as substance use. In fact, some research suggests that these variations may decrease risk behaviors among Latino and African American youth (Catalano, Hawkins, & Krenz, 1993; Li, Fiegelman, & Stanton, 2000; Vega & Gil, 1998). The Latino preference for close family proximity may result in vulnerability when emigration from the country of origin causes family disruption (Vega, 1990). Moreover, there is evidence that traditional familistic values can serve as a protective factor mitigating against adolescent maladjustment (Vega, Gil, Warheit, Zimmerman, & Apospori, 1993). Gil, Wagner, and Vega (2000) have shown that the loss of familism and parental respect that accompanies greater acculturation among Latino adolescents has negative impacts on predispositions toward deviant behaviors and alcohol use. So, while it seems clear that ethnicity and acculturation are likely to impact multiple aspects of the substance abuse treatment process (Collins, 1993), there is a paucity of knowledge about the assessment (and subsequent treatment) of substance use among ethnic minorities.

Additionally, standardized measurement instruments may be biased against certain ethnic and cultural groups. For example, Mercer (1979) documented that African American children routinely scored 10 points lower than European American children on the Weschler Intelligence Scale for Children—Revised (WISC-R), indicating a cultural bias in the WISC-R when administering it to African American children. Practitioners should exercise cultural sensitivity throughout the assessment and treatment process with clients.

Overall Clinical Utility

In addition to these factors, the overall clinical utility of a scale refers to several factors. Is the scale sensitive to changes in client functioning over time? Are the items direct and easy to understand? Is the length of the scale appropriate given its intended use by the practitioner? Lengthy scales may not be appropriate to administer in crisis situations, for example. Is the scale accessible at a reasonable cost? In addition to examining a scale's psychometric properties, these are all factors that must be considered when selecting a scale for use with a given population in a given setting.

The number of standardized tools developed specifically for use with adolescents has grown considerably in recent years, and it is impossible to review them all here. However, selected standardized tools that may be useful in assessing for comorbid disorders in adolescents are briefly reviewed next. Each tool reviewed has sound psychometric properties and can be used to help guide treatment planning and to monitor client progress over the course of treatment.

Problem Oriented Screening Instrument for Teenagers

The Problem Oriented Screening Instrument for Teenagers (POSIT) was developed by a panel of experts as part of the comprehensive Adolescent Assessment/Referral System (AARS) for use with 12- to 19-year-olds (Rahdert, 1991). The POSIT is a 139-item, self-administered tool. Items are measured on a dichotomous (yes/no) scale. The POSIT is intended to be used as a screening tool. It is not designed to measure treatment progress or outcomes. A more complete diagnostic evaluation requires that the practitioner implement another component of the AARS, called the Comprehensive Assessment Battery (CAB). The POSIT provides independent scores in ten areas of functioning: substance use/abuse, physical health, mental health, family relations, peer relations, educational status, vocational status, social skills, leisure/recreation, and aggressive behavior and delinquency. The National Clearinghouse for Alcohol and Drug Information (NCADI) offers the AARS (National Institute on Drug Abuse [NIDA], 1991, DHHS Publication No. ADM 91-1735), which contains the POSIT, free of charge. (Contact NCADI, P.O. Box 2345, Rockville, MD 20847; 800-729-6686.)

Drug Use Screening Inventory—Revised

The Drug Use Screening Inventory—Revised (DUSI-R; Tarter & Hegedus, 1991) is a 159-item multidimensional pencil-and-paper instrument, measured on a dichotomous (yes/no) scale that has recently been created to assess the severity of problems of adolescents and adults. Like the Addiction Severity Index (ASI; McLellan et al., 1985) and the POSIT (Rahdert, 1991), this instrument addresses areas in addition to substance abuse. The 10 domains of the DUSI-R are drug and alcohol use, behavior patterns, health status, psychiatric

disorder, social competence, family system, school performance/adjustment, work adjustment, peer relationships, and leisure/recreation. A "lie scale" documents reporting validity.
The information obtained from the completed DUSI-R can be used to develop an individualized treatment plan; however, scores do not indicate specific types of treatment needed.
That decision is left to the clinical judgment of the practitioner. The instrument's developers report that it is able to identify adolescents (and adults) with *DSM-IV* substance use
disorders, including those with and without psychiatric disorders. In a sample of 191 adolescents with alcohol and drug abuse problems, internal reliability coefficients averaged .74
for males and .78 for females across the 10 life problem areas. In a sample of polysubstance
abusing adolescents, the mean test-retest coefficients (1 week) were .95 for males and .88
for females (NIDA, 1994).

The DUSI-R is available from the Gordian Group, P.O. Box 1587, Hartsville, SC 29950;
(803) 383-2201. The instrument is copyrighted and is available in three formats: (1) paper
questionnaire for manual scoring ($3 each); (2) computer administration and scoring system
($495); and (3) Opscan administration and scoring (25 tests for $100).

Child and Adolescent Functional Assessment Scale

The Child and Adolescent Functional Assessment Scale (CAFAS; Hodges, 2000) is a
popular standardized multidimensional assessment tool that is used to measure the extent to
which a youth's (age 7 to 17) mental health or substance use disorder impairs functioning.
It is completed by the practitioner and requires specialized training. Like the POSIT, a
major benefit of the CAFAS in helping practitioners determine a youth's overall level of
functioning is that it covers eight areas: school/work, home, community, behavior toward
others, moods/emotions, self-harmful behavior, substance use, and thinking. The youth's
level of functioning in each domain is then scored as severe, moderate, mild, or minimal.
Additionally, an overall score can be computed. These scores can be graphically depicted
on a one-page scoring sheet that provides a profile of the youth's functioning. This makes
it easy to track progress over the course of treatment. The CAFAS also contains optional
strengths-based and goal-oriented items (e.g., good behavior in classroom, obeys curfew)
that are not used in scoring, but are helpful in guiding treatment planning.

The psychometric properties of the CAFAS have been demonstrated in numerous studies
(cf. Hodges & Cheong-Seok, 2000; Hodges & Wong, 1996). One study on the predictive
validity of the CAFAS indicates that this scale is able to predict recidivism in juvenile
delinquents (Hodges & Cheong-Seok, 2000). Higher scores on the CAFAS are associated
with previous psychiatric hospitalization, serious psychiatric diagnoses, below average
school performance and attendance, and contact with law enforcement (Hodges, Doucette-
Gates, & Oinghong, 1999). The CAFAS is available from Dr. Kay Hodges, 2140 Old
Earhart Road, Ann Arbor, Michigan 48105; (734) 769-9725; e-mail: hodges@provide.net.

The CAFAS would be a useful assessment tool to use with a client like Ramon, who
presents with impaired functioning in multiple areas, to help monitor treatment progress.

Based on the scores for each domain (see Table 13.1), Ramon's impairment in functioning could be interpreted as follows: severe (score of 30), moderate (score of 20), mild (score
of 10), or minimal (score of 0). The overall scores can also be computed as severe (140 to
240), marked (100 to 130), moderate (50 to 90), mild (20 to 40), or minimal to no (0 to 10)
impairment in functioning. Using these clinical cutting scores, the CAFAS results indicate

Table 13.1   Ramon's CAFAS Scores: Intake and Termination

CAFAS Domain	Intake	Termination
School/work	30	10
Home	30	10
Community	30	0
Behavior toward others	30	10
Moods/emotions	20	10
Self-harmful behavior	0	0
Substance use	30	10
Thinking	10	0
Overall functioning	180	50

that Ramon made clinically meaningful progress over the course of treatment, moving from "severe impairment in functioning" at intake to the low range of "moderate impairment in functioning" at termination.

The Substance Abuse Subtle Screening Inventory for Adolescents

The Substance Abuse Subtle Screening Inventory (SASSI; Miller, 1985; Miller, Miller, Roberts, Brooks, & Lazowski, 1997) is a 67-item pencil-and-paper instrument. There is also an updated adolescent version of the SASSI, referred to as the SASSI-A2, which is composed of 32 new items and 40 true/false items from the original adolescent version of the SASSI. The SASSI-A2 has been empirically validated as a screening tool for both substance dependence and substance abuse among adolescents, based on a sample of adolescents ($n = 2,326$) from treatment and criminal justice programs. Like the SASSI, an appealing feature of the SASSI-A2 is that it contains both face-valid items that directly address alcohol and drug use and subtle true/false items that do not inquire directly about alcohol or drug use. Administering the subtle true/false items to an adolescent client before the more direct items related to alcohol and drug use may help minimize defensiveness and lead to more accurate responses. Research findings revealed that 95% of adolescents with a substance use disorder were correctly identified with a "high probability" result in the SASSI-A2 decision rule, while 89% of adolescents without a substance use disorder were correctly classified with a "low probability" decision rule. (All of the SASSI instruments are available from the SASSI Institute at www.sassi.com or 800-726-0526.)

Adolescent Concerns Evaluation

The Adolescent Concerns Evaluation (ACE; Springer, 1998), a 40-item, multidimensional rapid assessment instrument, measures the degree to which a youth may be at risk of running away (see Table 13.2). Items are scored on a five-point Likert scale, and there are four separate yet interdependent domains: family, which addresses the youth's perception of relations and functioning of his or her family; school, which addresses the youth's self-esteem as it relates to school; peer, which addresses the youth's self-esteem as it relates to his or her peer relations; and individual, which addresses the youth's level of depression. The relevant literature on runaway youth, the ecological perspective (Germain & Gitterman,

Table 13.2   Adolescent Concerns Evaluation (ACE)

Name:_____ **Today's Date:**_____

This questionnaire is designed to measure how you see the world around you. Since these are your personal views, there are no right or wrong answers. Please answer as honestly as possible. Some items ask about relationships with parents. If you are not living with a parent, then for those items think about your primary adult caretaker(s).

Please rate how strongly you agree or disagree with each statement by placing a number beside each one as follows:

1 = strongly disagree
2 = disagree
3 = neither agree nor disagree
4 = agree
5 = strongly agree

First, think about your family life.
____ I am not comfortable talking to my parents about my problems.
____ My mother and I get along well.
____ My father and I get along well.
____ My parents do not understand me.
____ I enjoy spending time with my family.
____ I do not feel safe at home.
____ I am not listened to in my family.
____ My feelings are respected in my family.
____ My parents demand too much from me.
____ The rules in my family are not fair.
____ I feel my parents trust me.
____ All in all, I like my family.

Now, think about your experiences with school.
____ I have good relationships with my teachers.
____ My teachers are hard on me.
____ I get into trouble at school.
____ School is easier for other people than it is for me.
____ Finishing high school is important to me.
____ School is helping me prepare for my future.
____ I am not usually happy with my grades.
____ My friends generally do not go to school.
____ I do not enjoy school.

Now, think about your experiences with your peers.
____ I am well liked by my peers.
____ I do not fit in with my peers.
____ My peers seem to respect me.
____ I do not feel like part of the group.
____ My parents do not approve of my peers.
____ My peers seem to care about me.
____ I have a lot of fun with my peers.

Table 13.2   *(Continued)*

Finally, think about your feelings about your life.
___ I feel depressed a lot of the time.
___ I feel hopeless about my situation.
___ I think about suicide.
___ I feel worthless.
___ I can't do anything right.
___ I handle my problems well.
___ I feel trapped.
___ I feel good about myself.
___ I deal well with stress.
___ I feel angry a lot of the time.
___ I do not feel like I have control over my life.
___ I feel that others would be glad if I wasn't around.

1980), and the domain sampling model of measurement (Nunnally & Bernstein, 1994) provided the theoretical framework for the development of the ACE.

Participants in the validation study consisted of a clinical (youth at a runaway shelter; $n = 110$) and a nonclinical (students in grades 6 through 12, $n = 117$) sample. Each domain has excellent alpha and SEM values: Family (alpha = .9497, SEM = .206); School (alpha = .8884, SEM = .265); Peer (alpha = .9048, SEM = .222); and Individual (alpha = .9491, SEM = .214), indicating excellent internal consistency and low error for each domain. The ACE has excellent known-groups validity, discriminating significantly (a = .05) between members of the clinical and nonclinical samples (Family Eta = .656, School Eta = .630, Peer Eta = .528, Individual Eta = .610). There is evidence of factorial validity using the Multiple Groups Method (Nunnally & Bernstein, 1994), as well as convergent and discriminant construct validity. The ACE performed very well in a discriminant function analysis, often (87% of the time) classifying subjects correctly. The ACE is available for use from the chapter author at no cost from dwspringer@mail.utexas.edu.

The ACE is scored by summing the item scores in each domain and collectively. After the client has completed the ACE, the practitioner reverse scores the items listed at the bottom of the ACE (2, 3, 5, 8, 11, 12, 13, 17, 18, 22, 24, 27, 28, 34, 36, 37). For example, if Ramon rated item 2 ("My mother and I get along well") with a score of 4 (agree), the practitioner would recode it as a 2 (disagree). Higher scores reflect a higher risk of running away. The possible range of scores for each domain on the ACE is listed in Table 13.3.

Table 13.3   Scoring the ACE

ACE Domain	Range of Scores
Family domain	12 to 60
School domain	9 to 45
Peer domain	7 to 35
Individual domain	12 to 60
Overall score	40 to 200

Table 13.4   Ramon's ACE Scores

ACE Domain	Intake	Termination
Family domain	55	20
School domain	35	15
Peer domain	30	12
Individual domain	45	15
Overall score	165	62

Ramon was potentially at risk of running away from home due to conflict with his parents, and as indicated by his repeated verbal threats to run away. Accordingly, it would be appropriate for the social worker to administer the ACE to Ramon at the beginning of treatment to assess his risk of running away. Of course, the social worker would also want to administer the ACE to Ramon throughout the course of treatment to determine if this risk increased, decreased, or stayed the same. Ramon's scores on the ACE (see Table 13.4) reveal that over the course of treatment, his risk of running away decreased considerably.

Additional Rapid Assessment Instruments

In addition to the standardized tools reviewed, there are numerous RAIs that can be used with adolescents to measure functioning across various areas, such as suicidal tendencies (e.g., Multi-Attitude Suicide Tendency Scale), conduct-problem behaviors (e.g., Eyeberg Child Behavior Checklist), family functioning (e.g., Family Assessment Device, Index of Family Relations), and peer relations (Index of Peer Relations), to name just a few (K. Corcoran & Fischer, 2007). There are also standardized general behavior rating scales (e.g., Louisville Behavior Checklist, Child Behavior Checklist, and Conners Rating Scales) and tools that are useful for measuring the degree of functional impairment (e.g., Children's Global Assessment Scale; Shaffer, Lucas, & Richters, 1999).

Having provided an overview of standardized assessment tools, a word of caution is in order. Recall Kazdin's (2005) common themes listed earlier in the chapter, where he underscored the notion that multiple measures need to be used to capture diverse facets of the clinical problem, and that multiple informants are needed to obtain information from different perspectives and different contexts. It is ill advised for a practitioner to rely solely on self-report measures when determining diagnostic impressions and a course of treatment for youth. Youth can easily present themselves as they wish to be perceived by others on such measures. Thus, clinical decisions should be supplemented by a thorough psychosocial history (which should include information gathered from external sources such as parents, physicians, and teachers when at all possible), a mental status exam (when appropriate), and direct observation of the client. Indeed, there exists no gold standard of assessment with adolescents.

LIMITATIONS OF EVIDENCE-BASED ASSESSMENT WITH ADOLESCENTS

Mash and Humsley (2005) note that most practitioners routinely use traditional and accepted forms of assessment, even though very little evidence exists for the clinical utility of the measures. That is, although assessment measures are frequently evaluated for their psychometric criteria (reliable and valid), they are rarely examined for their applied value and accuracy in assessing the clinical populations they are intended to measure.

Understanding evidence-based assessment for adolescents is especially daunting, given the multifaceted nature of assessment with youth, including developmental issues and the role of family and peer groups. Assessing adolescents with comorbid disorders only adds to these complexities, amplifying the conceptual soup surrounding systematic assessment of youth with multifaceted presenting problems. The terms *comorbid disorders* and *coexisting disorders* are frequently used interchangeably to describe adolescents who have two or more coexisting diagnoses on Axis I or Axis II of the *DSM-IV-TR* (American Psychiatric Association, 2000), while the term *dual diagnosis* is often reserved to refer to clients with at least one Axis I diagnosis and a substance abuse problem. Approximately half of all adolescents who receive mental health services have coexisting substance abuse problems; common coexisting disorders are depression, conduct disorder, and Attention-Deficit/Hyperactivity Disorder (ADHD; McBride, VanderWaal, Terry, & VanBuren, 1999).

Given the prevalence of coexisting disorders in clinical settings and the seriousness of making false-positive or false-negative diagnoses, it is critical that social work practitioners assess for the presence of comorbid disorders in a deliberate manner rather than making "on the spot" diagnoses. A social worker's assessment often helps guide treatment planning. Misdiagnosing an adolescent as not having (or having) a certain set of problems (e.g., mistaking acting out behaviors related to poverty as conduct disorder, confusing symptoms of ADHD with pediatric bipolar disorder) can pose serious consequences for the course of treatment (e.g., the wrong medications may be prescribed, adolescents and their families may be turned off to treatment owing to repeated treatment "failures"). Unfortunately, in many respects, our methods of assessment for youth with comorbid disorders are not as sophisticated as the adolescents that we're treating.

More generally speaking, standardized assessment measures have many strengths: They are quick and efficient to use, they are easy to score and interpret, and they provide other sources of data than can be gained in a client interview in that they measure or screen for specific client problems or characteristics. Yet, these measures do have some practical weaknesses other than possible limitations in their psychometric properties. Springer and Franklin (2003) identified the following limitations.

First, standardized assessment measures are subject to demand characteristics or social desirability. Clients may answer the questions on the measure to cast themselves in a favorable or unfavorable light.

Second, most rapid assessment instruments present a narrow band of information and are not able to assess the whole client picture. Critics believe the measures have limited usefulness because they treat characteristics of clients as if they are static, instead of forever changing in response to environmental contingencies.

Third, standardized measures have been criticized for focusing on client problems instead of strengths. In this regard, standardized methods are believed to pathologize clients without pointing to their unique motivation and capacities. Some assessment measures, however, have begun to include scales on coping abilities or problem solving. For example, the Behavioral and Emotional Rating Scale (BERS; Epstein & Sharma, 1998) is a 52-item tool that measures functioning in youth ages 11 to 18 across five areas: interpersonal strength, involvement with family, intrapersonal strength, school functioning, and affective strength. Items are scored on a 4-point Likert scale (ranging from "very much like the child" to "not at all like the child"). It can be completed by teachers, parents, and practitioners and is easily scored and recorded on a summary/response form. A key feature that distinguishes the BERS from other standardized tools (e.g., Achenbach's widely used Child Behavior Checklist [CBCL]) is that it is truly based on a strengths perspective (in contrast to a deficit model), and the wording of the items reflects this perspective. Some sample items are:

- Maintains positive family relationships.
- Accepts responsibility for own actions.
- Pays attention in class.
- Identifies own feelings.

This makes the BERS popular among practitioners operating from a strength-based perspective, as well as with parents and teachers.

Finally, standardized assessment measures have been criticized for their inability to make direct linkages between client problems and interventions, that is, the measure does not prescribe a useful treatment plan, which is the main purpose of assessment.

Building on this last critique, there is also too often a disconnect between screening, assessment, and treatment planning. This is a truism across outpatient, inpatient, school-based, and juvenile justice settings. In response to this challenge, a recent meeting of juvenile justice assessment experts, dubbed the "Consensus Conference," produced recommendations for screening and assessment of mental health needs in the juvenile justice system (Wasserman, Jensen, et al., 2002). The Consensus Conference attendees suggest that screening mental health problems and identifying needs with an eye to long-term service planning should occur for all youth prior to court disposition (Potter & Jenson, 2007; www.promotementalhealth.org/practices.htm). Developing a treatment plan involves practitioners using information gathered from screening and assessment tools, and more important, their own cognitive abilities to map out a set of tasks to undertake with the client. The section that follows addresses this task.

TREATMENT GOALS

Treatment plans and treatment goals are established collaboratively between the social worker and the adolescent and help focus their work together. Goals specify what the adolescent wants to work on in treatment and the treatment plan serves as a "game plan" for how these goals will be obtained. Treatment goals and treatment plans are a critical component of effective social work practice, for without them, both social workers and clients run the risk of aimlessly "stumbling around in the dark" until they happen on a "problem" that needs to be addressed. As consumers of care, we expect our primary care physicians to deliver services with some sense of purpose, direction, and expertise. We should expect no less from social workers and the care that they provide.

The first step in establishing treatment goals with any client is to conduct a thorough assessment, as has been discussed throughout this chapter. This entails allowing the client to tell his or her story, conducting a psychosocial history, and using standardized assessment tools and rapid assessment instruments as needed. Clients may also need to be referred for medical and/or psychological testing. Following a thorough assessment, the social worker and client work together to establish goals for the client. In this sense, goals link the assessment and treatment process.

The following guidelines are helpful in establishing treatment goals. The goals should be (a) clearly defined and measurable; (b) feasible and realistic; (c) set collaboratively by the social worker and the client; (d) stem directly from the assessment process; and (e) stated in positive terms, focusing on client growth. Treatment goals "should specify *who, will do what, to what extent and under what conditions*" (Bloom et al., 2006, p. 104).

Treatment goals need to be defined clearly and stated in such a way that progress toward the goals can be measured. If goals are stated too ambiguously, clients may become discouraged or feel as if the goals are "out of reach." For example, compare the ambiguous goal of "Improve family communication" with the more concrete goal of "Ramon will have at least two 10-minute positive conversations per day with his parents over the next two weeks." The latter goal is more likely to be meaningful and obtainable to Ramon and his parents.

This leads to the second element of establishing treatment goals, which is that they must be feasible and realistic. "Improving family communication" is not only vague, it may not be feasible or realistic because it potentially covers so much ground. Additionally, little discussion between the social worker and the adolescent is needed to create vague goals. By contrast, concrete goals require a serious dialogue to take place between the worker and the client so that conceptual ideas about client functioning can be "wrestled to the ground" in clear day-to-day terms.

To the extent that adolescent clients participate in this discussion, the more likely it is that they will feel a sense of ownership over the established goals, which in turn means that they are more likely to follow through with the treatment plan. Clients (especially adolescents) will experience less "buy-in" to the treatment process if goals are imposed on them by a social worker or parent. Thus, goal setting needs to be a truly collaborative process among the social worker, adolescent, and his or her parents (when appropriate).

Treatment goals need to stem directly from the assessment process. The assessment should be thorough, empirically based, and grounded in a systems perspective. This minimizes the likelihood that the worker is creating treatment goals based solely on gut feeling or an on-the-spot diagnosis.

Finally, treatment goals need to be stated in positive terms. In other words, the goal should state what the client will do rather than what the client will not do. For example, a client will be more motivated and goal directed by a goal that states "Attend the entire school day every day for the next two weeks" in comparison to a goal that states "Stop skipping school."

IMPLICATIONS FOR SOCIAL WORK

Adolescents present with multiple needs, and these needs must be adequately captured in the assessment process so that interventions are practical and relevant. Regardless of the method of assessment and intervention used, one truism rings loud and clear: *The assessment and intervention process with youths must be conducted in a therapeutic relationship that is driven by worker genuineness, warmth, empathy, and understanding.* In other words, youth need to connect with a caring adult. Wolkind's (1977) seminal study of 92 children in residential care supports this notion, where he found that prolonged contact with the same houseparent was associated with lower rates of psychiatric disorder and acting out behavior.

It is critical that researchers continue their efforts to partial out what methods of assessment are the most effective with adolescents and to subsequently relay any relevant findings to workers and policy makers in a meaningful and user-friendly manner. Mash and Hunsley (2005) propose that it might also be important for evidence-based assessment to appraise therapeutic relationship and client satisfaction variables across specific disorders and assessment constructs. More systematic guidelines are needed to inform practitioners in their assessment with adolescents. "Ivory-tower pleas to use multiple perspectives from multiple contexts in the absence of specific guidelines for translating these recommendations into clinical practice are not close to the mark regarding what is needed or feasible based on the way current clinical practice is structured" (Kazdin, 2005, p. 556).

CONCLUSION

The field continues to make progress in developing user-friendly standardized assessment tools with sound psychometric properties that can be used in assessment with adolescents. While these tools should not take the place of a face-to-face psychosocial history, they should be used to complement the assessment process and to track progress in client functioning over the course of treatment. It is important to emphasize that a standardized tool does not take the place of a solid therapeutic helping relationship. A limitation of RAIs is that clients may answer items in a way that presents themselves in a certain light to the social worker. This risk is minimized to the extent that rapport has been established between the social worker and the adolescent and to the extent that the adolescent understands the importance of the assessment process and how it will be used to help them make desired changes.

Social workers have an ethical obligation to utilize empirical assessment protocols and standardized tools whenever possible rather than relying solely on gut feeling when conducting assessments with adolescents. The potential consequences of misdiagnosing a client, such as Ramon described earlier, can be severe. Thus, social work practitioners are encouraged to utilize available empirically based assessment tools within a systems framework to guide treatment planning, to monitor client functioning, and to evaluate the effectiveness of their interventions. In sum, while the practice of evidence-based assessment with youth is itself in its adolescence, the field is maturing.

REFERENCES

American Psychiatric Association. (2000). *Diagnostic and statistical manual of mental disorders* (4th ed., text rev.). Washington, DC: Author.

Bloom, M., Fischer, J., & Orme, J. G. (2006). *Evaluating practice: Guidelines for the accountable professional* (5th ed.). Boston: Allyn & Bacon.

Bravo, M., Ribera, J., Rubio-Stipec, M., Canino, G., Shrout, P., Ramírez, R., et al. (2001). Test-retest reliability of the Spanish version of the Diagnostic Interview Schedule for Children (DISC-IV). *Journal of Abnormal Child Psychology, 29*(5), 433–444.

Catalano, R. F., Hawkins, J. D., & Krenz, C. (1993). Using research to guide culturally appropriate drug abuse prevention. *Journal of Consulting and Clinical Psychology, 61*(5), 804–811.

Clark, M. D. (1998, June). Strength based practice: The ABC's of working with adolescents who don't want to work with you. *Federal Probation Quarterly*, 46–53.

Collins, L. R. (1993). Sociocultural aspects of alcohol use and abuse: Ethnicity and gender. *Drugs and Society*, 8, 89–116.

Corcoran, J., & Springer, D. W. (2005). Treatment of adolescents with disruptive behavior disorders. In J. Corcoran (Ed.), *Strengths and skills building: A collaborative approach to working with clients* (pp. 131–162). New York: Oxford University Press.

Corcoran, K., & Fischer, J. (2007). *Measures for clinical practice: Vol. 1. A sourcebook* (4th ed.). New York: Free Press.

Cowger, C. (1997). Assessing client strengths: Assessment for client empowerment. In D. Saleebey (Ed.), *The strengths perspective in social work practice* (2nd ed., pp. 59–73). New York: Longman.

Crocker, L., & Algina, J. (1986). *Introduction to classical and modern test theory*. Ft. Worth, TX: Harcourt Brace Jovanovich.

Epstein, M. H., & Sharma, J. M. (1998). *Behavioral and Emotional Rating Scale: A strength-based approach to assessment* [Examiner's manual]. Austin, TX: ProEd.

Fletcher, J. M., Francis, D. J., Morris, R. D., & Lyon, G. R. (2005). Evidence-based assessment of learning disabilities in children and adolescents. *Journal of Clinical Child and Adolescent Psychology*, 34(3), 506–522.

Germain, C. B., & Gitterman, A. (1980). *The life model of social work practice*. New York: Columbia University Press.

Gil, A. G., Wagner, E. F., & Vega, W. A. (2000). Acculturation, familism and alcohol use among Latino adolescent males: Longitudinal relations. *Journal of Community Psychology*, 28(4), 443–458.

Hall, G. S. (1904). *Adolescence*. New York: Appleton.

Hodges, K. (2000). *The Child and Adolescent Functional Assessment Scale self training manual*. Ypsilanti: Eastern Michigan University, Department of Psychology.

Hodges, K., & Cheong-Seok, K. (2000). Psychometric study of the Child and Adolescent Functional Assessment Scale: Prediction of contact with the law and poor school attendance. *Journal of Abnormal Child Psychology*, 28, 287–297.

Hodges, K., Doucette-Gates, A., & Oinghong, L. (1999). The relationship between the Child and Adolescent Functional Assessment Scale (CAFAS) and indicators of functioning. *Journal of Child and Family Studies*, 8, 109–122.

Hodges, K., & Wong, M. M. (1996). Psychometric characteristics of a multidimensional measure to assess impairment: The Child and Adolescent Functional Assessment Scale. *Journal of Child and Family Studies*, 5, 445–467.

Hudson, W. W. (1982). *The clinical measurement package: A field manual*. Homewood, IL: Dorsey Press.

Jordan, C., & Franklin, C. (1995). *Clinical assessment for social workers: Quantitative and qualitative methods*. Chicago: Lyceum Books.

Jordan, C., & Hickerson, J. (2003). Children and adolescents. In C. Jordan & C. Franklin (Eds.), *Clinical assessment for social workers: Quantitative and qualitative methods* (2nd ed., pp. 179–213). Chicago: Lyceum Books.

Kazdin, A. E. (1995). Scope of child and adolescent psychotherapy research: Limited sampling of dysfunctions, treatments, and client characteristics. *Journal of Clinical Child Psychology*, 24, 125–140.

Kazdin, A. E. (2005). Evidence-based assessment for children and adolescents: Issues in measurement development and clinical application. *Journal of Clinical Child and Adolescent Psychology*, 34(3), 548–558.

Kazdin, A. E., & Weisz, J. R. (2003). Context and background of evidence-based psychotherapies for children and adolescents. In A. E. Kazdin & J. R. Weisz (Eds.), *Evidence-based psychotherapies for children and adolescents* (pp. 3–20). New York: Guilford Press.

Kelley, M. L., Reitman, D., & Noell, G. R. (Eds.). (2003). *Practitioner's guide to empirically based measures of school behavior*. New York: Kluwer Academic/Plenum Press.

Klein, D. N., Dougherty, L. R., & Olino, T. M. (2005). Toward guidelines for evidence-based assessment of depression in children and adolescents. *Journal of Clinical Child and Adolescent Psychology*, *34*(3), 412–432.

Ko, S. J., & Wasserman, G. A. (2002). Seeking best practices for mental health assessment in juvenile justice settings. *Report on Emotional and Behavioral Disorders in Youth*, *2*(4), 88–99.

Levitt, J., & Reid, W. (1981). Rapid-assessment instruments for practice. *Social Work Research and Abstracts*, *17*(1), 13–19.

Li, X., Fiegelman, S., & Stanton, B. (2000). Perceived parental monitoring and health risk behaviors among urban low-income African-American children and adolescents. *Journal of Adolescent Health*, *27*, 43–48.

Mash, E., & Hunsley, J. (2005). Evidence-based assessment of child and adolescent disorders: Issues and challenges. *Journal of Clinical Child and Adolescent Psychology*, *34*(3), 362–379.

McBride, D. C., VanderWaal, C. J., Terry, Y. M., & VanBuren, H. (1999). *Breaking the cycle of drug use among juvenile offenders*. Washington, DC: National Institute of Justice. Available from www.ncjrs.org.

McLellan, A. T., Luborsky, L., Cacciola, J., Griffith, J., Evans, F., Barr, H. L., et al. (1985). New data from the addiction severity index: Reliability and validity in three centers. *Journal of Nervous and Mental Diseases*, *173*, 412–423.

McMahon, R. J., & Frick, P. J. (2005). Evidence-based assessment of conduct problems in children and adolescents. *Journal of Clinical Child and Adolescent Psychology*, *34*(3), 477–505.

Mercer, J. R. (1979). *System of multicultural pluralistic assessment technical manual*. San Antonio, TX: Psychological Corporation.

Miller, G. A. (1985). *The Substance Abuse Subtle Screening Inventory manual*. Bloomington, IN: Substance Abuse Subtle Screening Inventory Institute.

Miller, G. A., Miller, F. G., Roberts, J., Brooks, M. K., & Lazowski, L. G. (1997). *The SASSI-3*. Bloomington, IN: Baugh Enterprises.

Morrison, J., & Anders, T. F. (1999). *Interviewing children and adolescents: Skills and strategies for effective DSM-IV diagnosis*. New York: Guilford Press.

National Institute on Drug Abuse. (1991). *The adolescent assessment/referral system manual* (DHHS Publication No. ADM 91-1735). Rockville, MD: U.S. Department of Health and Human Services.

National Institute on Drug Abuse. (1994). *Mental health assessment and diagnosis of substance abusers: Clinical report series* (NIH Publication No. 94-3846). Rockville, MD: U.S. Department of Health and Human Services.

Nunnally, J. C., & Bernstein, I. H. (1994). *Psychometric theory* (3rd ed.). New York: McGraw-Hill.

Ozonoff, S., Goodlin-Jones, B. L., & Solomon, M. (2005). Evidence-based assessment of autism spectrum disorders in children and adolescents. *Journal of Clinical Child and Adolescent Psychology*, *34*(3), 523–540.

Pelham, W. E., Jr., Fabiano, G. A., & Massetti, G. M. (2005). Evidence-based assessment of attention deficit hyperactivity disorder in children and adolescents. *Journal of Clinical Child and Adolescent Psychology*, *34*(3), 449–476.

Potter, C. C., & Jenson, J. M. (2007). Assessment of mental health and substance abuse treatment needs in juvenile justice. In A. R. Roberts & D. W. Springer (Eds.), *Social work in juvenile and criminal justice settings* (3rd ed., pp. 133–150). Springfield, IL: Charles C Thomas.

Rahdert, E. R. (1991). *The adolescent assessment/referral system manual* (DHHS Publication No. ADM 91-1735). Rockville, MD: U.S. Department of Health and Human Services, National Institute on Drug Abuse.

Saleebey, D. (Ed.). (1997). *The strengths perspective in social work practice* (2nd ed.). New York: Longman.

Shaffer, D., Fisher, P. W., & Lucas, C. P. (1999). Respondent-based interviews. In D. Shaffer, C. P. Lucas, & J. E. Richters (Eds.), *Diagnostic assessment in child and adolescent psychopathology* (pp. 3–33). New York: Guilford Press.

Shaffer, D., Fisher, P. W., Lucas, C. P., Dulcan, M., & Schwab-Stone, M. E. (2000). NIMH Diagnostic Interview Schedule for Children, Version IV (NIMH DISC-IV): Description, differences from previous versions, and reliability of some common diagnoses. *Journal of the American Academy of Child and Adolescent Psychiatry, 39*, 28–38.

Shaffer, D., Lucas, C. P., & Richters, J. E. (Eds.). (1999). *Diagnostic assessment in child and adolescent psychopathology.* New York: Guilford Press.

Silverman, W. K., & Ollendick, T. H. (2005). Evidence-based assessment of anxiety and its disorders in children and adolescents. *Journal of Clinical Child and Adolescent Psychology, 34*(3), 380–411.

Springer, D. W. (1998). Validation of the Adolescent Concerns Evaluation (ACE): Detecting indicators of runaway behavior in adolescents. *Social Work Research, 22*(4), 241–250.

Springer, D. W., Abell, N., & Hudson, W. W. (2002). Creating and validating rapid assessment instruments for practice and research (Pt. 1). *Research on Social Work Practice, 12*(3), 408–439.

Springer, D. W., Abell, N., & Nugent, W. (2002). Creating and validating rapid assessment instruments for practice and research (Pt. 2). *Research on Social Work Practice, 12*(6), 768–795.

Springer, D. W., & Franklin, C. (2003). Standardized assessment measures and computer-assisted assessment technologies. In C. J. Jordan & C. Franklin, *Clinical assessment for social workers: Quantitative and qualitative methods* (2nd ed., pp. 97–137). Chicago: Lyceum Books.

Springer, D. W., McNeece, C. A., & Arnold, E. M. (2003). *Substance abuse treatment for criminal offenders: An evidence-based guide for practitioners.* Washington, DC: American Psychological Association.

Tarter, R., & Hegedus, A. (1991). The Drug Use Screening Inventory: Its application in the evaluation and treatment of alcohol and drug abuse. *Alcohol Health Research World, 15*, 65–75.

U.S. Congress, Office of Technology Assessment. (1991). *Adolescent health* (OTA-H-468). Washington, DC: U.S. Government Printing Office.

Vega, W. A. (1990). Hispanic families in the 1980s: A decade of research. *Journal of Marriage and the Family, 52*, 1015–1024.

Vega, W. A., & Gil, A. G. (1998). *Drug use and ethnicity in early adolescence.* New York: Plenum Press.

Vega, W. A., Gil, A. G., Warheit, G. J., Zimmerman, R. S., & Apospori, E. (1993). Acculturation and delinquent behavior among Cuban American adolescents: Toward an empirical model. *American Journal of Community Psychology, 21*, 113–125.

Wasserman, G. A., Jensen, P. S., Ko, S. J., Cocozza, J., Trupin, E., Angold, A., et al. (2002). Mental health assessments in juvenile justice: Report on the consensus conference. *Journal of the American Academy of Child and Adolescent Psychiatry, 42*, 752–761.

Wasserman, G. A., McReynolds, L. S., Lucas, C. P., Fisher, P., & Santos, L. (2002). The Voice DISC-IV with incarcerated male youths: Prevalence of disorder. *Journal of the American Academy of Child and Adolescent Psychiatry, 41*, 314–321.

Wolkind, S. N. (1977). A child's relationships after admission to residential care. *Child: Care, Health, and Development, 3*, 357–362.

World Health Organization. (1992). *International classification of diseases and health-related problems.* Geneva, Switzerland: Author.

Youngstrom, E. A., Findling, R. L., Youngstrom, J. K., & Calabrese, J. R. (2005). Toward an evidence-based assessment of pediatric bipolar disorder. *Journal of Clinical Child and Adolescent Psychology, 34*(3), 433–448.

Chapter 14

INTERVENTION WITH ADOLESCENTS

Craig Winston LeCroy

Adolescents in today's society face significant risks that can compromise their health and well-being. The developmental period of adolescence is recognized as more difficult and dangerous than it has been in the recent past. A significant difference is that modern adolescents begin exposure to risky behavior at a much earlier age than adolescents of the past. Many youth begin experimentation with risky behaviors such as cigarette use and sex during their early adolescent years (Carr, 2002). Dryfoos (1990), in a survey of adolescent risk behavior, estimates that half of all youth are at moderate to high risk of engaging in problem behaviors. Carr (2002) estimates that between 10% and 20% of adolescents will suffer from psychological problems serious enough to warrant treatment. A frequently quoted statistic is that at least one in five youth suffers from a current developmental, emotional, or behavioral problem (see Evans & Seligman, 2005; U.S. Department of Health and Human Services, 1999). Even those adolescents who are not considered to be at risk must navigate through adolescence—a period easily characterized as a playing field of obstacles and barriers to healthy development.

Those interested in interventions for adolescents have become increasingly focused on programs that can promote positive youth development, reduce risk factors, and remediate adolescent problem behaviors and disorders. Better assessment tools and better interventions have paved the way for improving the quality of the mental health and well-being of adolescents. An increasing emphasis on best practices, research-based practice, and evidence-based practice (EBP) is being supported and promoted by varying groups of professionals (see, e.g., Carr, 2000, 2002; Evans et al., 2005; Hibbs & Jensen, 2005; Kazdin, 2000; Rutter & Taylor, 2002; U.S. Public Health Service, Office of the Surgeon General, 2004). Furthermore, advocacy groups, parents, and local government are also putting a renewed emphasis on effective interventions for adolescents (Hoagwood, 2005).

This chapter reviews current issues and problems facing adolescents and examines prevention and intervention strategies and programs designed to improve adolescent mental health and well-being. The central concern is which interventions are effective with adolescents. This chapter also examines treatment delivery factors that influence outcomes.

OVERVIEW OF ISSUES AND PROBLEMS FACING ADOLESCENTS

Developmental characteristics of adolescents are important considerations in the design and implementation of effective interventions. During early adolescence, physical changes occur more rapidly than at any other time in the life span except infancy (Ashford, LeCroy,

& Lortie, 2006). The production of sex hormones, puberty, and appearance of secondary sex characteristics are significant changes that take place in adolescence. During adolescence, the shift from concrete to formal operational thinking takes place, and adolescents begin to think more abstractly. This has significance for the design of interventions because young adolescents or troubled adolescents often have difficulty linking thoughts, feelings, and behaviors. Identity formation and self-development come to the forefront of the adolescent's attention and can lead to positive or negative behaviors. Peers are an important source of support and stress. Pressure by peers for approval and conformity are directly related to engagement in risky behaviors. Last, emotional development is maturing and adolescents often experience a wide fluctuation of emotional reactions. Learning how to cope with negative emotions is important in developing a positive sense of well-being. An important skill in working with adolescents is being able to identify common developmental problems, issues needing closer observation, and developmental observations requiring attention (Table 14.1).

While adolescence is a time for significant rapid development, it is also the time that many of the major mental disorders begin. Furthermore, after onset many of these disorders persist into adulthood that leads to significant impairment in adulthood. Beyond mental disorders many adolescents engage in at-risk behavior or are exposed to social conditions that impact their development. These high-risk behaviors often pave the way for dysfunctional adult behavior such as substance abuse and unprotected sex.

Table 14.1   Developmental Considerations in Conducting an Assessment with Adolescents

Routine Observation	Developmental Issues (Not Problems)
Brain development and abstract thought	Excessive concern with body image
Peer groups	Spending too much time alone
Body image	Negative peer influence
Sense of morality	Decreased interest in school
Independence	Academic difficulties
Sexual identity	Moodiness
Romantic involvements	Sexual behavior
Focus on physical appearance	Transition to middle school
Increased caloric intact	Parent conflict
Hormonal changes	Late maturing girls
Menstruation (girls) and nocturnal emission (boys)	Risk behaviors (e.g., automobile safety)

Strengths and Landmarks of Development	Developmental Observations Requiring Attention
Increased resilience	Eating disorders
Development of autonomy and independence	Depression (stability of moods)
Increased influence of peers	Pregnancy
Enhancing parent-adolescent relationships	Sex abuse and rape
Peer support	Violent behaviors and exposure to violence
Egocentrism	Firearm exposure/use
	Conduct disorder and delinquency

It is now understood that many problem behaviors and mental disorders are common in adolescence (Table 14.2). Epidemiological studies of adolescents have obtained a better understanding of the likelihood of occurrence of such behaviors and disorders.

Of particular concern is the rising prevalence of mental disorders in children and adolescents over the years. Perhaps better assessment and detection can account for some of this, but the stressful and difficult environments that many adolescents experience is also likely to contribute. Another important factor is that adolescence is a longer time period than in the past. Indeed, many believe a new phase of "emergent adulthood" is needed to address the lengthening time period many adolescents find themselves in (Arnett, 2004). But the critical consideration is that the availability of potentially harmful environments (exposure to drugs, poverty, and homelessness) that can take their toll on young people (Evans & Seligman, 2005).

Adolescent interventions can be categorized according to two main types. The first refers to the "absence of dysfunction in psychological, emotional, behavioral, and social spheres"

Table 14.2   Prevalence Rates for Selected Behavior Problems and Disorders

Behavior Problems and Disorders	Prevalence Rates

Drug use	Have been drunk in the past 30 days:
	   21% of 10th graders
	   33% of 12th graders
	 By high school graduation:
	   54% have used illicit drugs

Sexual behavior	Birth rates for 15- to 19-year-old females:
	   57 per 1,000
	 Pregnancy rate per year:
	   About 10% of 15- to 19-year-old females
	   About half of adolescents are sexually active before they graduate from high school.

School dropout	*Status dropout rate:* the percentage of an age group that is not enrolled in school and has not earned a high school diploma. Approximately 11% of 16- to 24-year-olds (who were out of school without a high school diploma).
Suicide	Overall suicide rate of 8% to 9% within 2% to 3% of the attempts requiring medical attention.
Depression	Depression rates range from 1% to 6%. When all kinds of depressive disorders are included the rate is about 10%.
Anxiety disorders	Overall rate for all kinds of anxiety disorders ranges from 6% to 15%.
Eating disorders	About 3% to 4% of the adolescent female population suffer from eating disorders Anorexia

Autism Spectrum Disorder	Rates have shown increases in the last 30 years.
	 Recent estimates are:
	   16.8 per 10,000 for autism
	   45.8 per 10,000 for other pervasive developmental disorders

(Kazdin, 1993, p. 128). Dysfunction is defined as impairment in everyday life. Mental health disorders such as anxiety disorder, depression, and autism are examples of dysfunctions. Adolescents who suffer from disorders such as these are impaired in their everyday functional abilities (e.g., social relationships, school performance) and their dysfunction is likely to influence their well-being (e.g., suicide attempts, substance abuse). As Kazdin (1993, p. 128) notes it is important to recognize that "a variety of behaviors in which adolescents engage (e.g., substance use, antisocial acts, school dysfunction) and conditions to which they are exposed (e.g., poverty, homelessness, physical abuse) are dysfunctional because they impede the quality of current functioning and often portend deleterious physical and psychological consequences."

The second main type of adolescent intervention focuses on optimal functioning or well-being in psychological or social domains (Kazdin, 1993). Well-being is the presence of strengths that promote optimal functioning—it is not just the absence of impairment. The strengths perspective and positive psychology promote social competence, coping skills, and positive attachments to significant others—all are a part of optimal functioning. Social competence is considered a key concept that directs attention to adolescents' ability to cope with the demands of the environment by using cognitive and social skills to achieve positive outcomes.

These two approaches are part of a continuum of interventions with adolescents but suggest different conceptualizations, models of treatment, and intended outcomes. Promoting optimal functioning or positive mental health is fundamentally based on promoting certain competencies (Kazdin, 1993; LeCroy, 2006). The goal of these interventions is to build strengths, teach coping skills, and learn new social skills to enhance everyday functioning. In addition to being more socially competent, adolescents may benefit from these approaches because they limit clinical dysfunction (Kazdin, 1993). In contrast, interventions designed to address dysfunction are based on the diagnosis of disorders and the administration of certain interventions to reduce impairment. More intensive interventions are often needed such as long-term therapy, residential treatment, hospitalization, and medication. Table 14.3 lists some of the major at-risk problems and clinical disorders evident in adolescence.

To address the problem behaviors and clinical disorders so many adolescents confront, adolescent interventions are based on promoting competencies and positive functioning in prevention or the clinical treatment of specific disorders in treatment.

Table 14.3   Some Common Adolescent At-Risk Problems and Diagnoses

Anxiety disorders
Conduct Disorder and delinquency
Depression
Eating disorders
Substance use and abuse
Sexual abuse
Sexual behavior
Running away from home
Oppositional Defiant Disorder
School problems and dropout
Cutting behavior
Suicide risk

PROMISING PROGRAMS OF PREVENTION AND INTERVENTION

For this chapter, *promising programs* are defined as research-based programs that have some demonstrated positive outcomes. Programs were identified through multiple sources including literature reviews, recent books on EBP (e.g., Nathan & Gorman, 1998, *A Guide to Treatments that Work;* Carr, 2000, *What Works with Children and Adolescents;* Evans et al., 2005, *Treating and Preventing Adolescent Mental Health Disorders: What We Know and What We Don't Know;* Fonagy, Target, Cottrell, Phillips, & Kurtz, 2002, *What Works for Whom? A Critical Review of Treatments for Children and Adolescents*), and federal web sites. Programs identified as effective or promising are by no means inclusive of all effective programs. Also, in this chapter there is not a distinction between well-established treatments and probably efficacious treatments as discussed by the Task Force Report on Promoting and Dissemination of Psychological Procedures (1995). At the time of this report, only three programs were considered well established and none were specifically directed at adolescents. Since this report, a ground swell of new data have entered the field and additional reviews have contributed to what constitutes "evidence-based," "promising," or "empirically supported" treatments. As a result, there is no clear agreement on criteria and standards and different judgments are made in regard to studies that can be classified under the empirical rubric.

PROMOTING THE DEVELOPMENT OF COMPETENCIES AND THE PREVENTION OF DISORDERS

Prevention programs are described according to the Institute of Medicine (IOM, 1994) definitions. In this report, prevention refers to interventions that occur before the initial onset of a disorder. Universal prevention is defined as efforts that are beneficial to a whole population or group. As such, they target the whole population or group that has not been identified as being at risk for the disorder being prevented. Selective prevention is defined as efforts that target individuals or groups of the population whose risk of developing a disorder is higher than average. Indicated prevention is defined as efforts to identify high-risk individuals who have detectable signs or symptoms that predict the disorder.

SUBSTANCE ABUSE PREVENTION PROGRAMS

In discussing interventions for prevention of dysfunction, two of the more common problems adolescents confront are substance use and sexual behavior. These programs are often applied at either the universal prevention or selective prevention level.

Substance Abuse Prevention

The Midwestern Prevention Program (Chou et al., 1998; Pentz et al., 1990; Perry et al., 1996, 2000) is a multifaceted approach to the prevention of smoking, alcohol, and drug use. It targets whole school populations. The program includes the following: 10-session classroom-based resistance skills training component; a parent training component on parenting skills, parent-adolescent communication, and substance abuse prevention policy; a community component to organize leaders for a drug abuse task force; and a mass media campaign. Outcomes for the program have been consistently positive. For example, compared with controls program youth, participants showed a reduction in smoking, alcohol use, and marijuana use after 1 year. Three-year follow-up showed reduced rates of smoking and marijuana use (Johnson et al., 1990).

Project Nothland was similar and involved several components: skills training in the classroom, a family-based component, a peer group component, and a community-based component. The classroom component involved learning resistance skills, life skills, and modifying norms regarding substance use among peers. Other active parts of the program included developing prosocial alternatives to substance use and developing a play about avoiding substance use. Peer leaders conducted the sessions. Parents were involved with the program through newsletters offering information about prevention and evening parent sessions at the school that addressed substance use prevention. The community component focused on recruiting and training staff for a drug abuse prevention task force. Efforts were made to include a wide range of community members such as police, school officials, health officials, clergy, and adolescents. The task forces typically address the sale of alcohol to minors, incentives for avoiding substance use, and developing substance-free alternative activities for youth. Results of an outcome study found that when compared with controls adolescents in the treatment program had reduced alcohol use, more negative attitudes toward alcohol use, and better family communication about alcohol use. The program did not affect cigarette smoking.

Other similar projects such as Life Skills Training (Botvin, 2001; Botvin, Baker, Busenbury, Tortu, & Botvin, 1990) have found similar results and have been applied to diverse low-income populations (Botvin, Schinke, Epstein, & Diaz, 1994). Research by Hansen, Graham, Wolkenstein, and Rohrback (1991) using a resistance skills program and normative education (addressing misconceptions about drug-using norms among peers) found that without normative education, resistance training was not effective in reducing drug use. Table 14.4 presents the key intervention strategies for substance abuse prevention.

Table 14.4   Key Intervention Strategies for Substance Abuse Prevention

Target risk factors for substance abuse.
Use peer leaders to implement curriculum.
Use parent and family involvement to strengthen outcomes.
Address parent-adolescent conflict and communication.
Broad-based programs can be effective.
Use normative education to correct misconceptions and create conservative drug norms.
Promote alternative prosocial behaviors to substitute for drug use.
Use situations that elicit drug use to teach resistance skills.
Focus on culturally relevant situations.
Promote explicit skills for addressing peer pressure.
Teach good nonverbal communication skills.
Teach coping and stress management skills.
Teach general problem-solving and decision-making skills.
Ensure that the curriculum is developmentally appropriate for the age group.

Pregnancy, Sexually Transmitted Diseases, and HIV Prevention

Life skills was one of the early programs for prevention in this area (Schinke & Gilchrist, 1983). Using cognitive-behavioral strategies, this program applied problem-solving and assertiveness skills to sexual behavior. The approach focused on four fundamental aspects: having access to information on which to base decisions, understanding the information to make decisions, personalizing the information to maximize decision making, and applying behavioral skills to implement decisions in social situations. Later versions used a four-step problem-solving model: Stop, Options, Decision, and Action. Results found that compared to a control group, participants had fewer incidences of unprotected sexual intercourse at a 1-year follow-up. An additional study found that those in a health educator-led program had greater gains on outcomes than those in a self-directed program (Schinke, Gordon, & Weston, 1990).

Most subsequent programs have used intervention strategies that focus on psychoeducation, communication, and skills training (Carr, 2000). The main intervention includes: didactic methods and group discussion for psychoeducation; communication skills for initiating safe sex discussions using role plays, rehearsals, and feedback; and skills training for confronting difficult sexually risky situations and for buying and using condoms. Programs benefited from the AIDS risk reduction model. This model addresses three stages that people transition through in changing their behavior with respect to using condoms (Catania, Kegeles, & Coates, 1990). The first stage is where people become aware that unprotected sex may lead to AIDS. The intervention focuses on increasing knowledge about AIDS transmission and prevention. The notion that "It could happen to me" sinks in with awareness and the severity of the consequences become real when people realize "It could be fatal." In this phase, individuals review their past lives and evaluate the degree to which their past behavior placed them at risk for AIDS. The second stage is a commitment to use condoms in the future. The intervention focuses on the decision-making process that reinforces the notion that a condom is effective in preventing HIV infection. Barriers to condom use such as embarrassment about buying or using them are addressed. Enactment is the third stage. The intervention focuses on helping people take active steps to prepare to use condoms. Knowing how to use them, having access to them, and communicating with partners about them is part of this stage. Addressing barriers to condom use such as being overwhelmed by high levels of sexual arousal is also addressed. Research has found that all stages of the risk reduction model of condom use are associated with eventual condom use (Sheeran, Abraham, & Orbell, 1999). Results from multiple studies suggest these prevention programs can influence sexual behavior and prevent pregnancy, sexually transmitted diseases (STDs), and HIV (Table 14.5; Barth, Fetro, Leland, & Volkan, 1992; Jemmott, Jemmott, & Fong, 1992; St. Lawrence, Jefferson, Alleyne, & Brasfield, 1995).

PROMISING TREATMENT PROGRAMS

Treatment programs refer to programs that attempt to reduce dysfunction in psychological, emotional, behavioral, and social functioning. These are interventions that are directed toward addressing impairment in everyday life. As such, these interventions are typically conceptualized in response to *DSM-III-R* psychiatric disorders. As Kazdin (1993) notes, prevention and treatment are a continuum and prevention can minimize maladjustment and

Table 14.5   Key Intervention Strategies for Prevention of Pregnancy, STDs, and HIV

Target risk factors for adolescent pregnancy, STDs, and HIV.

Teach facts about STD and AIDS transmission, pregnancy, and contraception.

Promote the notion that peers and partners accept condoms.

Promote mutual monogamy and partner reduction.

Encourage treatment for STDs of sexual partners.

Teach the skill of carrying condoms with you.

Teach condom use skills.

Teach communication skills with partners.

Use situations that elicit sexual behavior to teach condom skills.

Teach coping behaviors related to combining drug use and sexual behavior.

Focus on culturally relevant situations.

Teach good nonverbal communication skills.

Teach coping and stress-management skills.

Teach general problem-solving and decision-making skills.

Ensure that the curriculum is developmentally appropriate for age group.

clinical dysfunction in adolescence. Treatment is reserved for cases for which preventive efforts did not succeed.

Adolescent Coping with Depression Course

The adolescent coping with depression course is a widely recognized evidence-based treatment developed for adolescents. It is grounded in cognitive and behavioral treatment of depression and is a modified version of a treatment program that was developed for adults (Clarke & Lewinsohn, 1984). The overall strategy of the intervention is to intervene in dysfunctional cognitions—hopelessness and helplessness—and change how adolescents interact with their environment so it is more reinforcing—with more pleasant activities and more social engagement. The course revolves around key understandings of why adolescents are likely to suffer from depressive episodes. Adolescents are often deficient in social skills so the course teaches conversation, planning social activities, and friendship-making skills. Adolescents learn to increase pleasant activities and are taught self-change skills such as self-monitoring, setting realistic goals, developing a plan for change, and self-reinforcement. In order to help adolescents decrease their anxiety, the program emphasizes learning relaxation training. Similar to more well-known cognitive therapy strategies, the course teaches identifying, challenging, and changing negative thoughts and irrational beliefs. The program devotes six sessions to communication and problem solving where adolescents learn active listening and problem solving along with negotiation skills. Last, the final two sessions integrate the skills and examine how to anticipate and plan for future problems. Each participant develops a life plan and set of goals. Table 14.6 presents the skills and content that is covered in the course. Research studies (Lewinsohn, Clarke, Hops, & Andrew, 1990) found that more adolescents in the treatment group no longer met *DSM* criteria for depression compared to a control condition. Treatment gains were maintained at a 2-year follow-up assessment. An additional study (Clarke, Rohde, Lewinsohn, Hops, & Seeley, 1999) replicated the finding and examined the impact of adding a parent involvement component. Results found that parent involvement was not associated with enhanced improvement.

Table 14.6   Skills and Content in the Coping with Depression Course

Skill	Content
Mood monitoring	Examining feelings and understanding how to assess your mood
Social skills	Learning conversation skills, social planning skills, and making friends
Pleasant activities	Learning self-change strategies such as setting goals
Relaxation	Learning how to decrease anxiety using relaxation
Constructive thinking	Learning how to reduce negative cognitions related to depression, replacing self-defeating thoughts with self-enhancing thoughts
Communication	Learning how to resolve conflict, how to communicate clearly, and use active listening
Negotiation and problem solving	Learning how to negotiate, applying problem-solving skills to situations
Maintenance of gain	Integrating the skills, developing a life plan, setting goals, and developing a relapse plan for what to do

Based on "The Adolescent Coping with Depression Course: A Cognitive-Behavioral Approach to the Treatment of Depression" (pp. 219–238), by P. Rohde, P. M. Lewinsohn, G. N. Clarke, H. Hops, and J. R. Seeley in *Psychosocial Treatments for Child and Adolescent Disorders: Empirically Based Strategies for Clinical Practice*, E. D. Hibbs and P. S. Jensen (Eds.), 2005, Washington DC: American Psychological Association.

Multisystemic Therapy

Multisystemic therapy (MST) is a broad-based therapy that has been used for adolescents who engage in "willful misconduct" (Henggeler & Lee, 2003). The most frequent applications of this treatment have been with youth who suffer from conduct disorder, are classified as juvenile offenders, have substance abuse problems, or have experienced a psychiatric crisis. The overarching goals of multisystemic therapy are to decrease antisocial behavior, improve psychosocial functioning, and reduce out-of-home placements. This multifaceted intervention is based on ecological theory and attempts to influence factors within adolescent, family, school, peer group, and community spheres that can have a positive impact on the youth. A typical application of MST would target an adolescent's social and academic skills. Family work might include improving family communication, parental supervision, and parent management skills. Peer interventions may address limiting contact with deviant peers and substituting new nondeviant peer groups. School-focused interventions might examine educational placement and enhance parent-school communication.

Henggeler and Lee (2003) discuss some critical aspects of the design and implementation of MST noting the following: multidetermined nature of serious clinical problems (behavior is multidetermined and individual, family, peer, school, and community factors need to be considered); caregivers are key to long-term outcomes (the focus is on developing the caregiver's ability to parent effectively and facilitating support systems for the family); integration of EBPs (MST is based on incorporating evidence-based treatments such as family therapy, parent management training, and use of medications); intensive services that overcome barriers to service access (intense services are provided to overcome barriers using a home-based treatment model and low caseloads); rigorous quality assurance system (systems are in place to promote treatment fidelity such as protocols, workshops on the treatment model, weekly consultation, and off-site consultants). Although general, nine treatment principles are often presented as the foundation of MST (Table 14.7). Research studies from eight published articles (Henggeler & Lee, 2003) have found positive outcomes when compared to control group subjects on criminal behavior, substance abuse, and emotional disturbance.

Functional Family Therapy

This intervention model evolved from an early effort to use a family system's conceptual framework with delinquent adolescents (Alexander & Parsons, 1982). Functional family therapy (FFT) has a strong social learning focus but uses systems theory and behavioral and cognitive strategies to influence functioning. The functional part of FFT is that problems are examined in terms of the function they serve for the individual adolescent and the family system. In general, family members are helped to change their communication patterns, increase parental supervision, and use new parenting skills to alter behavior. The fundamental approach is based on earlier studies that showed delinquents have more defensive communication, less supportive communication, and less supervisions when compared with nondelinquents. The intervention involves conjoint family treatment. Initial treatment focuses on teaching communication skills, problem-solving skills, and negotiation skills. Reframing is used extensively to reduce blaming and help parents perceive problem behavior as maintained by environmental contingencies rather than intrinsic factors. As treatment progresses, the emphasis is on contingency contracts whereby parents and adolescents exchange behaviors that they each would like to see more of. Several studies (see reviews

Table 14.7   The MST Treatment Principles

Treatment Principle	Description
Finding the fit	Using ecological notions to deliver treatment across appropriate social domains
Positive and strength focused	Emphasizing the positive and focusing on family strengths, building hope and enhancing confidence
Increasing responsibility	Using interventions to promote responsible behavior
Present focused, action oriented and well defined	Setting clear goals and determining measurable outcomes
Targeting sequences	Using interventions that target sequences of behavior within and between multiple systems that help to maintain the problems
Developmentally appropriate	Using interventions that fit the developmental needs of youth
Continuous effort	Using ongoing interventions that require daily or weekly effort by family members to maximize the change process
Evaluation and accountability	Evaluating interventions continuously from multiple perspectives
Generalization	Using interventions that promote treatment generalizations and maintenance of change

Based on *Multisystemic Treatment of Antisocial Behavior in Children and Adolescents*, by S. W. Henggeler, S. K. Schoenwald, C. M. Borduin, M. D. Rowland, and P. B. Cunningham, 1998, New York: Guilford Press.

by Carr, 2000; Fonagy & Kurtz, 2002) have found that FFT was effective in improving communication, reducing conduct problems, and out-of-home placement, and reducing recidivism rates in delinquent adolescents as well as their siblings.

Problem-Solving and Social Skills Training

Research has documented that the capacity to use problem solving for social and interpersonal problems is an important aspect of adaptive functioning. Indeed, deficits in problem-solving abilities are related to both dysfunctional difficulties and clinical disorders. For example, problem-solving deficits are related to delinquent behaviors (Kazdin, 2003), depression (Lewinsohn & Gotlib, 1995), and coping with stress (Compas, Benson, Boyer, Hicks, & Konik, 2002; Compas, Connor-Smith, Saltzman, Thomsen, & Wadsworth, 2001). Without social skills, adolescents are more likely to experience friendship difficulties, inappropriately expressed emotions, and an inability to resist peer pressure (LeCroy & Wooton, 2002). Problem-solving and social skills training are widely used interventions that focus on either learning how to generate and use more effective solutions to situational conflicts or learning the skills needed to respond effectively to situational conflicts. Sometimes these interventions are used separately and sometimes they are combined, for example, when problem solving is conceived of as an accessory social skill. Problem solving is a cognitive-behavioral strategy that teaches thought processes to help adolescents confront difficult interactions. Social skills training is a behavioral strategy that teaches new behaviors or skills for addressing difficult situations. Implementing problem-solving interventions typically follows the primary components of problem-solving skills (D'Zurilla & Nezu, 1990):

- Problem definition and formulation.
- Generating alternative solutions.
- Decision making and selection of a solution.
- Implementation and evaluation of a solution.

Application of problem-solving interventions was spearheaded by the classic work of Spivack and Shure (1976) using the interpersonal cognitive problem-solving (ICPS) model that included three basic skills: alternative thinking, which is generating alternative solutions to a problem; consequential thinking, which is the ability to examine the short- and long-term consequences of a decision; and means-ends thinking, which is the ability to plan a sequence of goal-directed actions in order to avoid obstacles and solve problems in a timely manner. The intervention process is described by Kazdin's (2005) program of problem-solving therapy for aggressive and antisocial youth as presented in Table 14.8.

Social skills training is typically presented in a small group format using behavior group therapy principles and strategies for teaching specific skills. The group format provides support and a reinforcing context for learning new response and appropriate behaviors in a variety of social situations. The group allows for extensive use of modeling and feedback that are successful components of group treatment. Table 14.9 presents a summary of the steps used in social skills training.

Research studies support the use of problem-solving therapy. Kazdin (2005) reviews 10 studies that document a variety of outcomes in comparison with control groups. In particular,

Table 14.8   Strategies for Implementing Problem-Solving Therapy

Problem solving is taught in a systematic step-by-step process.

Adolescents learn how to approach situations that can use problem-solving skills.

Adolescents learn to make self-statements that focus attention on the process.

Solutions are selected that are deemed important to the youth and significant others.

Modeling and reinforcement are used to promote prosocial behaviors.

Structured tasks like games, activities, and stories are used to teach the skills.

Applications of problem solving move from canned versions to real-life applications.

Problem-solving abilities are modeled by applying statements to particular problems.

Cues are used to prompt the use of the problem-solving skills.

Feedback, re-rehearsal, and praise are used to train adolescents in the use of the skills.

Essential ingredients include modeling, practice, role-plays, feedback, and praise.

Based on "Child, Parent, and Family-Based Treatment of Aggressive and Antisocial Child Behavior" (pp. 445–476), by A. E. Kazdin, in *Psychosocial Treatments for Child and Adolescent Disorders: Empirically Based Strategies for Clinical Practice,* E. D. Hibbs and P. S. Jensen (Eds.), 2005, Washington, DC: American Psychological Association.

the studies find significant reductions in antisocial behavior and increases in prosocial behavior. Combining problem-solving therapy with parent management treatment tends to increase the effectiveness. Many studies add to the evidence of problem solving if you consider studies that include elements of problem-solving therapy in their overall model.

Research on social skills training is more varied and has been examined in prevention and with specific clinical disorders. In the prevention field, social skills training is often the key component, for example, resistance skills training in substance abuse and pregnancy

Table 14.9   Steps for Teaching Social Skills

Step	Description
Present the social skill taught	Solicit an explanation of the skill and get group members to provide rationales for the skill.
Discuss the social skill	List the skill steps and get group members to give examples of using the skill.
Present a problem situation and model the skill	Evaluate the performance and get group members to discuss the model.
Set the stage for role-playing the skill	Select members for role-playing and get group members to observe the role-play.
Group members rehearse the skill	Provide coaching if needed and get members to provide feedback on verbal and nonverbal elements.
Practice using complex skill situations	Teach accessory skills, (e.g., problem solving and get members to discuss situations and provide feedback).
Train for generalization and maintenance	Encourage practice of skill outside of the group and get members to bring in their own problem situations.

Based on "Social Skills Training" (pp. 126–169), by C .W. LeCroy, in *Handbook of Child and Adolescent Treatment Manuals,* C. W. LeCroy (Ed.), 1994, New York: Free Press; and "Designing and Facilitating Groups with Children" (pp. 595–602), by C. W. LeCroy in *The School Services Sourcebook: A Guide for School Based Professionals,* C. Franklin, M. B. Harris, and P. Allen-Meares (Eds.), 2006, New York: Oxford University Press.

prevention programs. There are many evidence-based prevention programs that emphasize social skills training. With clinical disorders, social skills training is much more of a component of the treatment. For example, with delinquent adolescents, social skills training may be one part of a comprehensive treatment package. In general, studies have supported the use of social skills training as an effective component (Carr, 2000; Kazdin, 2005; LeCroy, 2006).

ONGOING TREATMENT AND CASE MANAGEMENT

As noted earlier, interventions for adolescents form a continuum from brief structured treatments to longer, ongoing treatment strategies. These longer ongoing interventions are designed for adolescents with persistent and long-term conditions. Typically, multimodel interventions will be directed at youth such as residential treatment, special education, ongoing family treatment, medication management, and special education. An important aspect of intervention at this level is the awareness and understanding that the problems being confronted are serious and chronic. In many respects, the mental health system has not adapted an approach to intervention that acknowledges and responds to these chronic conditions.

Multidimensional Foster Care

This model of care was designed as an alternative to placement in group care settings and uses a series of multicomponent, multilevel interventions that occur in family, school, and community settings (Chamberlain, 1994; Chamberlain & Smith, 2005). This model assumes that problems are determined by multiple causes and effects and therefore the intervention focuses on multiple settings. This program has been used with a variety of adolescents, including adolescents leaving mental hospitals (Chamberlain & Reid, 1991), adolescents with low cognitive functioning and inappropriate sexual behavior (Chamberlain, 2003), and adolescents with behavioral and emotional problems (Smith, Stormshak, Chamberlain, & Bridges Whaley, 2001). This program recruits foster families and trains and supervises them to provide daily care of the adolescents placed with them. A major aspect of the intervention is training foster parents in the social learning, parent training model. It integrates six service elements including individual therapy and skill training, family therapy with biological relatives, school consultations and school-based interventions, consultation with parole or probation officers, psychiatric consultation, and case management services to coordinate all aspects of the program. Regular home visits are conducted throughout the youth's placement where the goal is to return the adolescent to his or her family of origin following placement in the Multidimensional Treatment Foster Care (MTFC) program. The placement usually lasts 6 to 9 months. Research results from three studies (see Chamberlain & Smith, 2005, for a review) of MTFC using comparison or control groups have found promising outcomes. For example, one study (Chamberlain, Ray, & Moore, 1996) reported outcome data favoring the intervention over the control group noting significantly fewer arrests, self-reported delinquent behavior, fewer days incarcerated, and fewer instances of running away. Cost-benefit data also suggest the program is cost effective. A similar program is multiple family group (MFG) treatment although it is not long term. MFG interventions have been increasingly offered as a treatment for clinically diagnosed youth (Fristad, Goldberg-Arnold, & Gavazzi, 2003; McKay, Harrison, Gonzales, Kim, &

Table 14.10   Commonly Used Treatment Manuals and Resources for Prevention and Intervention

Alexander, J., & Parsons, B. (1982). *Functional family therapy.* Monterey, CA: Brooks/Cole.

Botvin, G. (2001). *Life skills training manual.* New York: Cornell University Medical Center.

Chamberlain, P. (1994). *Family connections: A treatment foster care model for adolescents with delinquency.* Eugene, OR: Castalia Press.

Clarke, G., & Lewinsohn, P. (1984). *The Coping with Depression Course—Adolescent Version: A psychoeducational intervention for unipolar depression in high school students.* Eugene, OR: Castalia Press.

Dishion, T. J., & Kavahagh, K. (2001). *Intervening in adolescent problem behavior.* New York: Guilford Press.

Fairburn, C., & Wilson, G. (1993). *Binge eating: Assessment and treatment.* New York: Guilford Press.

Feindler, E., & Ecton, R. (1985). *Adolescent anger control: Cognitive-behavioral techniques.* New York: Pergamon.

Forgatch, M., & Patterson, G. (1989). *Parents and adolescents living together: Part 2. Family problem solving.* Eugene, OR: Castalia Press.

Henggeler, S., & Bordvin, S. (1990). *Family therapy and beyond: A multisystemic approach to treatment the behavior problems of children and adolescents.* Pacific Grove, CA: Brooks/Cole.

Kendall, P., Chansky, T. E., Kane, M. T., Kim, R. S., Kortander, E., Ronan, K. R., et al. (1992). *Anxiety Disorder in youth: Cognitive behavioral interventions.* Needham Heights, MA: Allyn & Bacon.

LeCroy, C. W., & Daley, J. (2001). *Empowering adolescent girls: Building skills for the future with the Go Grrrls program.* New York: Norton.

Mufson, L., Moreau, D., Weissman, M., & Klerman, G. (1993). *Interpersonal psychotherapy with depressed adolescents.* New York: Guilford Press.

Robin, A., & Foster, S. (1989). *Negotiating parent-adolescent conflict.* New York: Guilford Press.

Robin, A. (1998) *ADHD in adolescents: Diagnosis and treatment.* New York: Guilford Press.

Szapocznik, J., & Kurtines, W. (1989). *Breakthroughs in family therapy with drug abusing youth.* New York: Springer.

Quintana, 2002). The program offers family meetings and addresses multiple goals such as psychoeducation, information exchange, parent support, parent management, family communication, supervision, and household rules. Studies have found that MFG leads to better outcomes than treatment as usual and engages more families in treatment.

This chapter presents a limited number of evidence-based interventions with adolescents. Table 14.10 presents some of the more commonly used treatment manuals and resources for prevention and intervention.

CONSIDERATIONS IN SERVICE DELIVERY

A critical issue in service delivery with adolescents is their ability to find and accept help when they deem it necessary. Although adolescence is a time when some serious problems can emerge, it unfortunately is also a time when adolescents face acute barriers to accessing the help they need. Adolescents all too often do not know where to go for help or who they can trust to get help. Consider the following scenarios: the adolescent girl who is raped but too ashamed to tell her friends or parents, an adolescent trapped in a sexually intimate relationship with no birth control or STD protection, the adolescent who has depressed moods and feels hopeless, or an adolescent who feels trapped by a gang into illegal behavior.

Given their level of need, adolescents vastly underutilize systems of care. Research studies have found that adolescents seek care less than any other age group (Cypress, 1984). The key factors in this underutilization of services are cost, poor organization of services, lack of availability, and concerns regarding confidentiality (Millstein & Litt, 1990). Furthermore, many of the serious problems confronted by adolescents such as mental disorders, sexually transmitted diseases, and abuse are not covered by many health insurance plans or the coverage is so restrictive and complex that access to help is impeded (Ashford et al., 2006; National Research Council, 1993).

Interventions or systems of care must become more sensitive to adolescents' concerns about their privacy and confidentiality (LeCroy & Daley, 2001). Survey results reveal that under conditions where medical treatment would be confidential, adolescents would be significantly more likely to seek care for depression, birth control, STDs, and drug use (Council on Scientific Affairs, 1993). One study (Kobocow, McGuire, & Blau, 1983) administered personal interviews requiring substantial self-disclosure to a group of 195 seventh- and eighth-grade students and found that "56.8% of females and 38.6% of males listed assurance of confidentiality as the most important statement made to the interviewer prior to the interview" (p. 422). These results illustrate the high value that adolescents place on confidentiality, as well as the need for increased sensitivity to adolescents' strong concerns about their privacy. If we want to help young people in trouble or at risk, we need to pave a road for them that is easy to follow and will lead to a successful outcome. Access to professionals who are specifically trained with adolescents is only one component of successful intervention for youth in trouble. Youth who need help must feel cared for and respected by a network of people.

MOTIVATION FOR TREATMENT

A distinguishing feature of interventions with adolescents, as compared with adults, is that often the client has not sought help on his or her own accord. Many adolescents end up in treatment because they were arrested, a parent found drugs in their room, or a teacher reported behavior problems. Although we have stressed promising or evidence-based interventions with adolescents, all are dependent on engagement in the treatment. Engagement is a significant issue for both adolescents and their families, if doing family therapy.

Increasingly, engagement is being addressed as a significant aspect of delivering effective services. The popularity of motivational interviewing (Miller & Rollnick, 2002) is related to awareness of the need for proper engagement in treatment. The stages-of-change model (Prochaska & DiClemente, 1986) also helped focus intervention efforts on motivation. For example, the majority of people who quit smoking do so on their own—once they are in the proper stage of change and motivated to take action toward the problem. Dishion and Kavanagh (2003) discuss initial strategies for engaging adolescents in treatment. Table 14.11 presents a summary of those ideas.

Table 14.11   Strategies for Engaging Adolescents in Treatment

Strategy	Description
Respect privacy and space	Adolescents often begin treatment with a sense of mistrust. Empathize with their reluctance to participate in the treatment.
Normalize experiences	Try to normalize the adolescents need for help—for example, "This can be a difficult time and a lot of young people have found talking with someone helpful."
Advocate the adolescent's interest	Be clear about your relationship with the adolescent. Communicate about how you perceive their situation and describe what the benefit is for their involvement.
Link interests and services	Adolescents are more engaged if they see the connection between their concerns, the assessment, and the intervention.
Create optimistic reframes	The extent of an adolescent's engagement in treatment is related to the use of positive reframes.
Keep it brief, start slow	Don't make the mistake of being too friendly or too confrontive, or both, too early in treatment. Adolescents may be better helped in a brief time period like 30 minutes rather than the standard 50-minute session.

Based on *Intervening in Adolescent Problem Behavior: A Family Centered Approach,* by T. J. Dishion and K. Kavanagh, 2003, New York: Guilford Press.

CONTEXT AND FOCUS OF TREATMENT

Typically when an adolescent is identified as needing help, the most common provision of treatment is the individual adolescent. And while this may be appropriate for many situations, focusing only on the adolescent ignores the context—the various systems that can influence one's functioning. Environmental factors play an important role in understanding and intervening in adolescent problem behaviors. The adolescent's individual and cognitive functioning are important, interpersonal relationships and peer relationships are considered critical in adolescence, the school system provides an important context for understanding difficulties, and the community and neighborhood can have a direct influence of functioning. Many adverse contextual features have been shown to have direct implications for adolescent functioning and clinical disorders. For example, factors such as sexual abuse or participation in a peer drug culture are going to directly impact an adolescent's functioning. As a contextual factor, poverty limits access, participation, and the effectiveness of interventions. These multiple influences raise the question, "To whom should the treatment be directed?" (Kazdin, 2000). Interventions can occur at the individual, family, peer, school, and neighborhood level. A common error is to limit the intervention to just the individual level (LeCroy, 1992). Family and peer interventions are sometimes needed to produce desired outcomes. Many of the evidence-based programs reviewed in this chapter stress a multidimensional approach to treatment. At the prevention level, neighborhoods and communities are reasonable targets for change. Increasingly, researchers and practitioners are embracing the value of an ecological perspective for intervention.

CONCLUSION

Progress in developing and implementing interventions for adolescents that achieve measurable benefit has been substantial (Carr, 2000; Kazdin & Weisz, 2003). This limited review has presented a variety of programs that represent different strategies for intervention. The strategies vary from prevention to intervention and suggest a continuum of intervention. Figure 14.1 depicts the ecological context showing at the center the adolescent, family, peer, neighborhood, and community context. Factors that can have impending influences are identified at each level. Interventions can range from universal prevention to ongoing

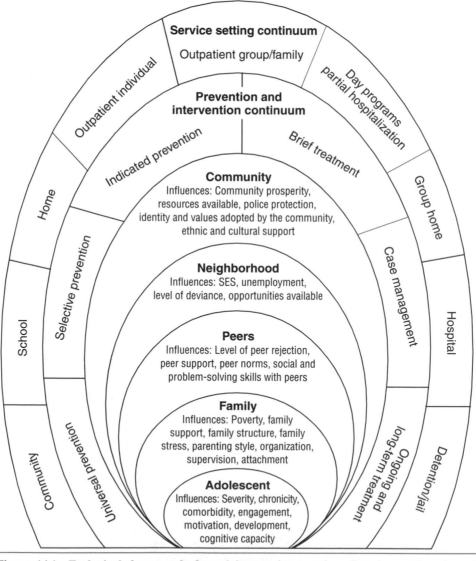

Figure 14.1 Ecological framework for adolescent intervention. Based on Mrazek and Haggarty (1994); Stroul and Friedman (1986); and Weisz, Sandler, Durlak, and Anton (2005).

and long-term treatment as suggested by Figure 14.1. The figure also depicts the multiple intervention settings where interventions occur, such as school or community settings.

Adolescents face critical issues in today's complex society. Too often, adolescents face risks that they are not prepared to cope with. However, interventions for adolescents suggest promising new developments, and there is new evidence for the effectiveness of these interventions. Implementation issues such as access to services and motivation for treatment are also being acknowledged, and ongoing knowledge of these factors can enhance the interventions being used with young people.

REFERENCES

Alexander, J. F., & Parsons, B. V. (1982). *Functional family therapy*. Monterey, CA: Brooks/Cole.

Arnett, J. J. (2004). *Emerging adulthood: The winding road from the late teens through the twenties*. New York: Oxford University Press.

Ashford, J., LeCroy, C., & Lortie, K. (2006). *Human behavior in the social environment: A multidimensional perspective* (3rd ed.). Pacific Grove, CA: Wadsworth.

Barth, R. P., Fetro, J., Leland, N., & Volkan, K. (1992). Preventing adolescent pregnancy with social and cognitive skills. *Journal of Adolescent Research, 7*, 208–232.

Botvin, G. (2001). *Life skills training manual*. New York: Cornell University Medical Center.

Botvin, G., Baker, E., Busenbury, L., Tortu, S., & Botvin, E. (1990). Preventing adolescent drug abuse through a multimodal cognitive behavioural approach: Results of a three year study. *Journal of Consulting and Clinical Psychology, 58*, 437–446.

Botvin, G., Schinke, S., Epstein, J., & Diaz, T. (1994). Effectiveness of culturally focused and generic skills training approaches to alcohol and drug abuse prevention among minority youths. *Psychology of Addictive Behaviours, 8*, 116–127.

Carr, A. (2000). *What works for children and adolescents? A critical review of psychological interventions with children, adolescents and their families*. New York: Routledge.

Carr, A. (2002). *Prevention: What works with children and adolescents? A critical review of psychological prevention programmes for children, adolescents and their families*. New York: Taylor & Francis.

Catania, J., Kegeles, S., & Coates, T. (1990). Towards an understanding of risk behaviour: An AIDS Risk Reduction Model (ARRM). *Health Education Quarterly, 17*, 53–72.

Chamberlain, P. (1994). *Family connections: A treatment foster care model for adolescents with delinquency*. Eugene, OR: Castalia Press.

Chamberlain, P. (2003). *Treating chronic juvenile offenders*. Washington, DC: American Psychological Association.

Chamberlain, P., Ray, J., & Moore, K. J. (1996). Characteristics of residential care of adolescent offenders: A comparison of assumptions and practices in two models. *Journal of Child and Family Studies, 5*, 259–271.

Chamberlain, P., & Reid, J. B. (1991). Using a specialized foster care treatment model for children and adolescents leaving the state mental hospital. *Journal of Community Psychology, 19*, 266–276.

Chamberlain, P., & Smith, D. K. (2005). Antisocial behavior in children and adolescents: The Oregon Multidimensional Treatment Foster Care Model. In A. E. Kazdin & J. R. Weisz (Eds.), *Evidence-based psychotherapies for children and adolescents* (557–574). New York: Oxford University Press.

Chou, C., Montgomery, S., Pentz, M., Rohrback, L., Johnson, C., Flay, B., et al. (1998). Effects of a community based prevention program on decreasing drug use in high risk adolescents. *American Journal of Public Health, 88*, 944–948.

Clarke, G., & Lewinsohn, P. (1984). *The Coping with Depression Course—Adolescent Version: A psychoeducational intervention for unipolar depression in high school students.* Eugene, OR: Castalia Press.

Clarke, G., Rohde, P., Lewinsohn, P. M., Hops, H., & Seeley, J. R. (1999). Cognitive-behavioral treatment of adolescent depression: Efficacy of acute group treatment and booster sessions. *Journal of American Academy of Child and Adolescent Psychiatry, 38,* 272–279.

Compas, B. E., Benson, M., Boyer, M., Hicks, T. V., & Konik, B. (2002). Problem-solving and problem-solving therapies. In M. Rutter & E. Taylor (Eds.), *Child and adolescent psychiatry* (4th ed., pp. 938–948). Malden, MA: Blackwell.

Compas, B. E., Connor-Smith, J. K., Saltzman, H., Thomsen, A. H., & Wadsworth, M. E. (2001). Coping with stress during childhood and adolescence: Progress, problems and potential. *Psychological Bulletin, 127,* 87–127.

Council on Scientific Affairs, American Medical Association. (1993). Confidential health services for adolescents. *Journal of the American Medical Association, 269,* 1420–1424.

Cypress, B. K. (1984). *Health care of adolescents by office-based physicians: National Ambulatory Care Survey, 1980–1981* (DHHS, NCHS Publication, No. 99). Washington, DC: U.S. Government Printing Office.

Dishion, T. J., & Kavanagh, K. (2003). *Intervening in adolescent problem behavior: A family centered approach.* New York: Guilford Press.

Dryfoos, J. G. (1990). *Adolescents at risk: Prevalence and prevention.* New York: Oxford University Press.

D'Zurilla, T. J., & Nezu, A. M. (1990). Development and preliminary evaluation of the social problem-solving inventory. *Psychological Assessment: A Journal of Consulting and Clinical Psychology, 2,* 156–163.

Evans, D. L., Foa, E. B., Gur, R. E., Hendin, H., O'Brien, C. P., Seligman, M. E. P., et al. (2005). *Treating and preventing adolescent mental health disorders: What we know and what we don't know.* New York: Oxford University Press.

Evans, D. L., & Seligman, M. E. P. (2005). *Introduction.* In D. L. Evans, E. B. Foa, R. E. Gur, H. Hendin, C. P. O'Brien, M. E. P. Seligman, et al. (Eds.), *Treating and preventing adolescent mental health disorders: What we know and don't know* (pp. xxv–xi). New York: Oxford University Press.

Fairburn, C., & Wilson, G. (1993). *Binge eating: Assessment and treatment.* New York: Guilford Press.

Feindler, E., & Ecton, R. (1985). *Adolescent anger control: Cognitive-behavioral techniques.* New York: Pergamon Press.

Fonagy, P., & Kurtz, A. (2002). Disturbance of conduct. In P. Fonagy, M. Target, D. Cottrell, J. Phillips, & Z. Kurtz, (Eds.), *What works for whom? A critical review of treatments for children and adolescents* (pp. 106–192). New York: Guilford Press.

Fonagy, P., Target, M., Cottrell, D., Phillips, J., & Kurtz, Z. (2002). *What works for whom? A critical review of treatments for children and adolescents.* New York: Guilford Press.

Forgatch, M., & Patterson, G. (1989). *Parents and adolescents living together: Pt. 2. Family problem solving.* Eugene, OR: Castalia Press.

Fristad, M. A., Goldberg-Arnold, J. S., & Gavazzi, S. M. (2003). Multi-family psychoeducation groups in the treatment of children with mood disorders. *Journal of Marital and Family Therapy, 29,* 491–504.

Hansen, W., Graham, J., Wolkenstein, B., & Rohrback, L. (1991). Program integrity as a moderator of prevention program effectiveness: Results for fifth-grade students in the adolescent alcohol prevention trial. *Journal of Studies on Alcohol, 52,* 568–579.

Henggeler, S. W., & Bordvin, S. (1990). *Family therapy and beyond: A multisystemic approach to the treating the behavior problems of children and adolescents.* Pacific Grove, CA: Brooks/Cole.

Henggeler, S. W., & Lee, T. (2003). Multisystemic treatment of serious clinical problems. In A. E. Kazdin & J. R. Weisz (Eds.), *Evidence-based psychotherapies for children and adolescents* (pp. 301–322). New York: Guilford Press.

Henggeler, S. W., Schoenwald, S. K., Borduin, C. M., Rowland, M. D., & Cunningham, P. B. (1998). *Multisystemic treatment of antisocial behavior in children and adolescents*. New York: Guilford Press.

Hibbs, E. D., & Jensen, P. S. (2005). *Psychosocial treatments for child and adolescent disorders: Empirically based strategies for clinical practice* (2nd ed.). Washington, DC: American Psychological Association.

Hoagwood, K. (2005). Family-based services in children's mental health: A research review and synthesis. *Journal of Child Psychology and Psychiatry: Annual Research Review, 46*, 690–713.

Institute of Medicine. (1994). *Reducing risk for mental disorders: Frontiers for prevention intervention research*. Washington, DC: National Academy Press.

Jemmott, J., Jemmott, L., & Fong, G. (1992). Reductions in HIV risk-associated sexual behaviours among Black male adolescents: Effects of an AIDS prevention intervention. *American Journal of Public Health, 82*, 372–377.

Johnson, C., Pentz, M., Weber, M., Dwyer, J., Bear, N., MacKinnon, D., et al. (1990). Relative effectiveness of comprehensive community programming for drug abuse prevention with high risk and low risk adolescents. *Journal of Consulting and Clinical Psychology, 58*, 447–456.

Kazdin, A. E. (1993). Psychotherapy for children and adolescents: Current progress and future research directions. *American Psychologist, 48*, 644–657.

Kazdin, A. E. (2000). *Psychotherapy for children and adolescents: Directions for research and practice*. Oxford: Oxford University Press.

Kazdin, A. E. (2003). Problem solving skill training and parent management training for conduct disorder. In A. E. Kazdin & J. R. Weisz (Eds.), *Evidence-based psychotherapy for children and adolescents* (pp. 241–262). New York: Guilford Press.

Kazdin, A. E. (2005). Child, parent, and family-based treatment of aggressive and antisocial child behavior. In E. D. Hibbs & P. S. Jensen (Eds.), *Psychosocial treatments for child and adolescent disorders: Empirically based strategies for clinical practice* (pp. 44–476). Washington, DC: American Psychological Association.

Kazdin, A. E., & Weisz, J. R. (2003). *Evidence-based psychotherapy for children and adolescents*. New York: Guilford Press.

Kendall, P. T. E., Chansky, M. T., Kane, R. S., Kim, E., Kortander, K. R., Ronan, F. M., et al. (1992). *Anxiety disorder in youth: Cognitive behavioral interventions*. Needham Heights, MA: Allyn & Bacon.

Kobocow, B., McGuire, J. M., & Blau, B. I. (1983). The influence of confidentiality conditions on self-disclosure of early adolescents. *Professional Psychology: Research and Practice, 14*, 435–475.

LeCroy, C. W. (1992). Enhancing the delivery of effective mental health services to children. *Social Work, 37*, 225–233.

LeCroy, C. W. (1994). Social skills training. In C. W. LeCroy (Ed.), *Handbook of child and adolescent treatment manuals* (pp. 126–169). New York: Free Press.

LeCroy, C. W. (2006). Designing and facilitating groups with children. In C. Franklin, M. B. Harris, & P. Allen-Meares (Eds.), *The school services sourcebook: A guide for school based professionals* (pp. 595–602). New York: Oxford University Press.

LeCroy, C. W., & Daley, J. (2001). *Empowering adolescent girls: Building skills for the future with the Go Grrrls Program*. New York: Norton.

LeCroy, C. W., & Wooton, L. (2002). Social skills groups in the schools. In R. Constable, S. McDonald, & J. P. Flynn (Eds.), *School social work: Practice, policy, and research* (pp. 441–457). Chicago: Lyceum Books.

Lewinsohn, P. M., Clarke, G. N., Hops, H., & Andrews, J. (1990). Cognitive-behavioral group treatment of depression in adolescents. *Behavior Therapy, 21*, 385–401.

Lewinsohn, P. M., & Gotlib, I. H. (1995). Behavioral theory and treatment of depression. In E. E. Beckam & W. R. Leber (Eds.), *Handbook of depression* (pp. 352–375). New York: Guilford Press.

McKay, M., Harrison, M., Gonzales, J., Kim, L., & Quintana, E. (2002). Multiple family groups for urban children with conduct difficulties and their families. *Psychiatric Services, 53,* 1467–1469.

Miller, W. R., & Rollnick, S. (2002). *Motivational interviewing: Preparing people for change* (2nd ed.). New York: Guilford Press.

Millstein, S. G., & Litt, I. F. (1990). Adolescent health. In S. Feldman & G. R. Elliott (Eds.), *At the threshold: The developing adolescent* (pp. 213–223). Cambridge, MA: Harvard University Press.

Mrazek, P. J., & Haggerty, R. J. (1994). *Reducing risks for mental disorders: Frontiers for preventive intervention.* Washington, DC: National Academies Press.

Mufson, L., Moreau, D., Weissman, M. W., & Klerman, G. L. (1993). *Interpersonal psychotherapy with depressed adolescents.* New York: Guilford Press.

Nathan, P., & Gorman, J. (1998). *A guide to treatments that work.* New York: Oxford University Press.

National Research Council. (1993). *Losing generations: Adolescents in high-risk settings.* Washington, DC: National Academy Press.

Pentz, M., Trebow, E., Hansen, W., MacKinnon, D., Dwyer, J., Johnson, C., et al. (1990). Effects of program implementation on adolescent drug use behaviour: The midwestern prevention. *Project Evaluation Review, 14,* 264–289.

Perry, C. L., Williams, C. L., Komro, K. A., Veblen-Mortenson, S., Forster, J. L., Bernstein-Lachter, R, et al. (2000, February). Project Northland High School Interventions: Community action to reduce adolescent alcohol use. *Health Education and Behavior, 27,* 29–49.

Perry, C. L., Williams, C. L., Veblen-Mortenson, S., Toomey, T., Komro, K., Anstine, P., et al. (1996). Project Northland: Outcomes of a community wide alcohol use prevention programme during early adolescence. *American Journal of Public Health, 86,* 956–965.

Prochaska, J. O., & DiClemente, C. C. (1986). Toward a comprehensive model of change. In W. Miller & N. Heather (Eds.), *Treating addictive behaviors: Processes of change* (pp. 3–27). New York: Plenum Press.

Robin, A. (1998). *ADHD in adolescents: Diagnosis and treatment.* New York: Guilford Press.

Robin, A., & Foster, S. (1989). *Negotiating parent-adolescent conflict.* New York: Guilford Press.

Rohde, P., Lewinsohn, P. M., Clarke, G. N., Hops, H., & Seeley, J. R. (2005). The adolescent coping with depression course: A cognitive-behavioral approach to the treatment of depression. In E. D. Hibbs & P. S. Jensen (Eds.), *Psychosocial treatments for child and adolescent disorders: Empirically based strategies for clinical practice* (pp. 219–238). Washington, DC: American Psychological Association.

Rutter, M., & Taylor, E. (2002). Clinical assessment and diagnostic formulation. In M. Rutter & E. Taylor (Eds.), *Child and adolescent psychiatry* (pp. 247–272). Malden, MA: Blackwell.

Schinke, S., & Gilchrist, L. (1983). Coping with contraception: Cognitive with behavioral methods with adolescents. *Cognitive Therapy and Research, 7,* 379–388.

Schinke, S., Gordon, A. N., & Weston, R. E. (1990). Self-instruction to prevent HIV infection among African-American and Hispanic-American adolescents. *Journal of Consulting and Clinical Psychology, 58,* 432–436.

Sheeran, P., Abraham, C., & Orbell, S. (1999). Psychosocial correlates of condom use: A meta-analysis. *Psychological Bulletin, 125,* 90–132.

Smith, D. K., Stormshak, E., Chamberlain, P., & Bridges Whaley, R. (2001). Placement disruptions in treatment foster care. *Journal of Emotional and Behavioral Disorders, 9,* 200–205.

Spivack, G., & Shure, M. B. (1976). *Social adjustment of young children.* San Francisco: Jossey-Bass.

St. Lawrence, J. S., Jefferson, K. W., Alleyne, E., & Brasfield, T. L. (1995). Comparison of education versus behavioral skills training interventions in lowering sexual HIV-risk behaviour of substance-dependent adolescents. *Journal of Consulting and Clinical Psychology, 63*, 154–157.

Stroul, B., & Friedman, R. (1986). *A system of care for severely emotionally disturbed children and youth.* Washington, DC: Georgetown University, CASSP Technical Assistance Center.

Szapocznik, J., & Kurtines, W. (1989). *Breakthroughs in family therapy with drug abusing youth.* New York: Springer.

Task Force on Promotion and Dissemination of Psychological Procedures. (1995). Training in and dissemination of empirically validated psychological treatments: Report and recommendations. *Clinical Psychologist, 48*, 3–23.

U.S. Department of Health and Human Services, Office of the Surgeon General. (1999). *Mental health: A report of the surgeon general.* Rockville, MD: U.S. Department of Health and Human Services.

U.S. Public Health Service, Office of the Surgeon General. (2004). *Report of the Surgeon General's conference on children's mental health: A national action agenda.* Rockville, MD: Author.

Weisz, J. R., Sandler, I. N., Durlak, J. A., & Anton, B. S. (2005). Promoting and protecting youth mental health through evidence-based prevention and treatment. *American Psychologist, 60*, 628–648.

Chapter 15

ASSESSMENT OF ADULTS

Elaine Congress

Individual assessment, although fundamental in planning interventions with adults, is a challenging endeavor. While there are a variety of definitions of social work assessment, this chapter is based on the following definition from the *Social Work Desk Reference*:

> Assessment is the process of systematically collecting data about a client's functioning and monitoring progress in client functioning on an ongoing basis. Assessment is defined as a process of problem selection and specification that is guided in social work by a person in environment systems orientation. Assessment is used to identify and measure specific problem behaviors as well as protective and resilience factors, and to determine if treatment is necessary. Information is usually gathered from a variety of sources (e.g., individual, family member, case records, observation, rapid assessment tools and genograms). Types of assessment include bio-psycho-social history taking, multiple dimensional crisis assessment, symptom checklists, functional analysis, and mental statues exams. (Roberts & Greene, 2002, p. 830)

Using the social work framework of person in environment, a successful assessment involves not only understanding the individual as an physical and psychological entity, but also in relationship to both micro- and macro-environments. In looking at the intersection of this person in an environmental matrix, the social worker is in the best position to complete a comprehensive client assessment. While many regard social work assessment as focusing on problems and diagnosis, the assessment of strengths and resilience is equally as important in completing a comprehensive assessment of the client. Other common features of current social work assessment models outlined by Jordan and Franklin (2003) include the following:

- Social work assessment models are eclectic and integrative and are not based on one underlying theory.
- Long history taking is de-emphasized, and there is a focus on seeking only relevant history that is related to the function of service. For example, a social worker in a medical setting might be most interested in physical health past and present, while a social worker in a family therapy agency might focus on the history of family relationships past and present.
- Social work assessment involves a collaborative process between client and worker. Using an evidence-based practice (EBP) approach, the client is actively involved in sharing information with the goal of deciding on the best possible treatment. Involving the client in a short-term active participatory approach to diagnosis is the best way to ensure that the client continues to participate in treatment.

- Assessment and treatment are seen as a unified whole. There is no longer a lengthy assessment period during which clients' needs and problems are held in abeyance. Having a short-term focused assessment enables the client to see the relevance of assessment and helps to ensure that the client will remain in treatment. A corollary of this is that assessment does not end before intervention begins. Assessment continues throughout the treatment process. With an ongoing assessment process, the social worker can modify treatment based on new information that emerges from the ongoing assessment process.

A comprehensive client assessment includes many factors, both in terms of the individual—appearance, developmental history, past and current physical health, cognitive ability and style, intellectual capacity, mental status, psychiatric diagnosis, and cultural/racial identity, as well as the individual relationship to environment—role within family, family history, physical environment of home and neighborhood, and relationship to the outside community. An important part of the assessment process involves focusing not only on the deficits that a client presents but also the client's strengths and resilience.

There are many challenges to completing a comprehensive assessment of a client. First, in a managed care environment with short-term treatment models, a thorough assessment is often not possible. Clinicians frequently focus only on information needed to complete forms or to select an intervention. In fact, many EBP models look primarily at the client's participation in the choice of intervention and minimize the assessment process. Yet, a thorough assessment is most helpful in making the best intervention decision.

Another challenge has been that assessment is often accomplished with a singular focus. Some assessment models favor an individual psychological assessment, while others look more at environmental factors influencing the client. The best assessment involves an integrative approach that uses a broad lens for assessing clients from both biopsychosocial and person-in-environment perspectives. Often, a rating scale such as the one developed by Pomeroy, Holleran, and Franklin (2003) is helpful in providing a comprehensive individual assessment.

Another frequent criticism of assessment is that it often relies on a deficit model. The assessment of a client often involves diagnosis using *DSM-IV*. Applying only a *DSM-IV* diagnosis to a client focuses on a psychiatric problem and pathology and neglects strengths that should be viewed as important aspects of assessment and intervention with clients.

HISTORICAL BACKGROUND

Psychosocial Diagnostic Assessment

From the birth of the social work profession, many different assessment models have been used. Perhaps the most well known is the psychosocial or diagnosis approach first developed by Hollis. This model relies heavily on family and developmental history to reach a psychodiagnostic assessment of the client. An ego psychology framework (Goldstein, 2002) is fundamental to this approach. While initially this approach focused to a large extent on a client's developmental history, now the person/client in relationship to the current environment is stressed. According to a psychosocial ego psychology perspective, the assessment process has the following steps: (1) assessing the client's interactions with his or her environment in the here and now and how successfully he or she is in coping effectively with major life roles and tasks; (2) assessing the client's adaptive, autonomous, and conflict-free areas of ego functioning, as well as ego deficits and maladaptive functioning; (3) evaluating the impact of a client's past on current functioning; and (4) examining environmental obstacles that impede a client's functioning (Goldstein, 2002; Hollis & Wood, 1981). According to a psychosocial diagnostic approach, information for client assessment was collected in a variety of ways including: (a) psychiatric interviewing to determine a diagnosis, (b) the use of standardized and projective testing to support diagnostic assessment, (c) current psychosocial assessment and study of prior development and adjustment to identify problem areas, (d) use of standardized interviewing to assess problem areas and current functioning, and (e) study of the client social work relationship to ascertain client's patterns of interactions (Jordan & Franklin, 2003).

The psychosocial assessment model is well suited to today's medical model that involves the study, diagnosis, and treatment format. Many medically based behavioral health settings use this approach. Furthermore, the focus of many behavioral health centers on clients' return to more adaptive functioning is also compatible with a psychosocial diagnostic ego psychology model. A *DSM-IV* diagnosis is usually a requirement for beginning treatment and thus the detailed study using a psychosocial approach is often helpful in arriving at a diagnosis. Structured assessment tools such as the eco-map (Hartman & Laird, 1983) and the genogram (McGoldrick, Gerson, & Schallenberg, 1999) are also helpful for practitioners in completing assessments. There is a need for more outcome-focused research, however, on the effectiveness of using these instruments. Finally, the development of standardized semistructured interviews using a psychosocial approach is most helpful in promoting current evidence-based assessment.

Problem-Solving Assessment

Another major assessment model was the problem-solving assessment originally developed by Helen Harris Perlman in 1957. This model is based on the psychosocial diagnosis model described earlier and the functional model that focuses on growth and potential as well as agency function. Perlman saw assessment as an eclectic model with four Ps—Person, Problem, Place, and Process—as a way to organize information about the client. In terms of person, the social worker should think of the client's personality characteristics and what interactions with the environment are significant. A second area involved a focus on problem. How can the problem be defined? Is it a crisis, a repetitive issue? What other ways has the client sought to resolve the problem? The third category is place or agency. What concerns does the client have about contact within the agency? What is most helpful and what is most harmful about the agency in the process of client assessment? The fourth relates to process. What intervention will be most successful? What will be the consequences of a particular choice of treatment?

Current assessment still relies a great deal on the problem-solving approach to assessment. First, a very quick assessment tool such as that outlined by Perlman is most helpful in the current social service environment with its focus on short-term assessment and intervention. Another advantage especially for culturally diverse clients who may be fearful of interaction with the agency is the inclusion of Perlman's third P—Place—in the assessment process. This approach encourages the social worker to look at how the fears and feelings that clients may have about the agency affect the assessment process. This may be especially true for undocumented clients who are apprehensive that social workers will use their power and authority to report their immigration status.

There are two major concerns about the problem-solving approach as used in current assessment practice. First, there is limited attention to the person's strengths and resilience in resolving the problem. Modern assessment models seek to focus specifically on the strengths a client brings to the situation. The client's definition of the "problem" and what strengths he or she can use and has used in the past to address the problem are considered key. Another major concern about the problem-solving approach is that it is based primarily on practice wisdom with limited empirical research to support its use. With the emphasis on EBP, research is needed to ascertain the effectiveness of this assessment model as a foundation for treatment interventions with diverse clients.

Cognitive Behavior Assessment

Cognitive behavior assessment models have made a major contribution to current practice and research about assessment. Meichenbaum (1993) outlines three metaphors that have guided this complex model—conditioning, information processing, and constructive narrative. Early cognitive behaviorists focused primarily on conditioning as the way certain behaviors were learned. Then the focus shifted to a greater emphasis on cognitions, social learning, and the development of belief systems. Most recently, the focus has been on the use of client narratives and life stories as part of the assessment process.

Jordan and Franklin (2003) identify four attributes of cognitive behavior assessment that are particularly useful in today's practice:

1. Because much of today's practice focuses on short-term intervention, the focus on rapid assessment and treatment is particularly useful. Assessment includes history only as it is related to the client's current functioning, while the main focus is on identifying the faulty learning and cognitive patterns that have contributed to current maladaptive behavior.

2. Much research has been conducted on outcomes of cognitive behavior approaches. This is particularly useful with today's emphasis on evidence-based assessment and treatment.

3. Many assessment and treatment manuals for use with assessing a number of identified client problems such as depression, substance abuse, personality disorders, and Posttraumatic Stress Disorder have been developed using the cognitive-behavioral approach.

4. Ongoing assessment has been stressed as essential in evaluating the effectiveness of treatment. The integration of assessment with treatment is very much part of current beliefs about assessment.

Life Model Assessment

The life model assessment (Germain & Gitterman, 1996) uses an ecological framework that focuses on the client's interactions with the environment in three main areas—life transitions, environmental pressures, and maladaptive interpersonal processes. Major aims of this theory are to link closely person and environment, stress the client's perspective, and provide linkages among direct service, administration, and policy planning.

There has been some concern that the life model assessment does not guide current practice interventions very well (Wakefield, 1996). With the need for short-term evidence-based assessment and intervention, the weakness of this link is problematic. The ecological model, however, has served as a foundation for developing multisystematic therapy, an evidence-based therapy that has proven to be useful with youth and families (Henggeler, Schoenwald, Borduin, Rowland, & Cunningham, 1998). An assessment tool such as the eco-map (Hartman & Laird, 1983) that is based on the life model ecological approach has been useful, although research on this has been limited. Computer software programs may help practitioners use this assessment tool more effectively, standardize its use, and provide more opportunities for research about its effectiveness.

Task Centered Assessment

The task centered assessment model developed by Reid (1988) focuses on specific target problems and their desired outcomes. Major steps in this model include task planning, implementation, and review. Task planning builds on initial problem formulation. The client's perception of the problem is considered most important, and the practitioner helps the client in exploring, clarifying, and specifying the problem. Task centered assessment focuses on a thorough understanding of the client's problems and goals, prioritizing problems, and the development of a specific contract to achieve the defined goals. This approach is most useful in practice today with a focus on time-limited and evidence-based outcomes.

Solution Focused Assessment

A major new assessment model is the brief solution focused therapy assessment developed by De Jong and Berg (2001) for work with mandated clients. With this model, assessment is part of the intervention process. Franklin and Moore (1999) have identified the following methods for conducting a solution focused assessment:

- Tracking solution behaviors or exceptions to the problem.
- Scaling the problem.
- Using coping and motivation questions.
- Asking the miracle question.

This approach is very client centered and focuses on client's strengths—what clients can do and want to do, not on their deficits and failures. Franklin (2002) identifies positive features of this model with mandated clients:

- Using a nonjudgmental approach in understanding client problems.
- Making the congruence between what the client wants and what services can be provided as close as possible.
- Emphasizing clients' choices as much as possible.
- Providing education to clients about what treatment will involve.

- Developing specific goals with clients.
- Discussing what is nonnegotiable from the agency's standpoint

Although research on the use of this model has been positive, more work in this area is necessary to evaluate its effectiveness.

Strengths Perspective Assessment

A final perspective that has had a major influence on current assessment practice is the strengths perspective developed by Saleeby (1997). This perspective is fundamental to the values-based perspective of social work in that all people are seen as having dignity and worth as individuals, as well as the right to self-determination. Using this approach, the practitioner looks for knowledge, competencies, hidden resources, and resilience in each and every client who comes for treatment. The practitioner moves away from identifying only deficits or diagnosing pathology with *DSM-IV* toward a broader understanding of person-in-environment client functioning. The strengths perspective has had a significant impact on mental health services. Yet the strengths perspective is often seen as only one aspect of a comprehensive assessment with a diagnostic *DSM-IV* having more importance in a behavioral health service delivery system. There have been various attempts to develop standardized measures to assess strengths and competencies (Jordan & Franklin, 2003) and also to incorporate a strengths approach into a more traditional psychosocial assessment. With the current emphasis on evidence-based assessment and practice, much more empirical research is needed on outcomes with strengths-based assessment.

SUMMARY OF CURRENT EVIDENCE-BASED ASSESSMENT FOR INDIVIDUALS

There are a number of sources of information that a social worker can use in completing assessments on individual clients. These sources include:

- Background information on clients from case records.
- Verbal reports from clients about their feelings, history, and problems.
- Direct observation of nonverbal behavior.
- Observation of interaction with family members and others in clients' environment.
- Collateral information from families, relatives, physicians, teachers, employers, and other professionals.
- Tests or other assessment instruments.

Social workers often begin to work with clients after reading lengthy case records. While there are advantages to having a preliminary understanding of a client before contact is made, the major disadvantage is that case records may unduly influence the social worker's perception of the client. Case records are often written from a deficit perspective. Frequently, a *DSM-IV* diagnosis is included that may not be current. This may be especially true in mental health settings when the client has had a long history of mental health treatment. Research on whether the assessment process is helped or hindered by the social worker's prior perusal of a case record is needed.

The primary source of information for assessment should come directly from the client. The practitioner needs to be a skilled interviewer to elicit information that is particularly relevant to the client's problem. Previously, client assessment was a very lengthy process often spanning several interviews. The current trend is brief assessment to learn information that is particularly pertinent to the client problem and what will be most helpful in future work. A thorough assessment usually includes the following categories (Cooper & Lesser, 2002):

- Identifying information.
- Referral source.
- Presenting problem.
- History of the problem.
- Previous counseling experiences.
- Family background.
- Developmental history.
- Educational history.
- Employment history.
- History of trauma.
- Medical history.
- Cultural history.
- Spirituality/religion.
- Mental status and current functioning.
- Mental status exam.
- Multiaxial *DSM-IV* diagnosis.
- Recommendations and goals for treatment.
- Plans to evaluate.

Including an evaluation plan provides an empirical foundation for the assessment process.

A major source of information for assessment comes from the social worker's observation of nonverbal behavior. What demographic information do we learn nonverbally—sex, age, race? How is the client dressed? How does the client answer questions? How does the client relate to the worker?

Often, the social worker has an opportunity to observe the individual client in interaction with others—family members, friends, group members, or other professionals. This can be an important source of information about the client's challenges in personal relationships with others.

The social worker can learn important information about the client from collateral contact with others including family and other professionals. It is important, however, that the social worker not rely too much on negative reports of family members. Family members may present distorted views of clients based on their own interests. Reports from others should only be a *secondary* method for receiving information to use in a client assessment.

The final method of gathering information for assessment is through tests or assessment instruments. Because many of these instruments have been standardized, assessment through these measures is considered important in promoting EBP.

Assessment Scales and Tools

The next section explores some of the scales and assessment tools that have been used in assessment of individual clients.

The person-in-environment (PIE) testing scale developed by Pomeroy et al. (2003) is helpful in that each area is considered either as a problem or strength. The categories are appearance, biomedical/organic, use of substances, developmental issues/transitions, coping abilities, stressors, capacity for relationships, social functioning, behavioral function, sexual functioning, problem-solving/coping skills, creativity, cognitive functioning, emotional function, self-concept, motivation, cultural and ethnic identification, role functioning, spirituality/religion, and other strengths. Not only is the individual client assessed on these different areas, but each area is also studied in relationship to family, friends, school/work, community, and social work intervention. The value of the PIE rating scale is that it provides an organized systematic way to acquire important information about the client.

Cultural Assessment

One area of much importance in today's practice is that of cultural and ethnic identification. An increasing number of urban, suburban, and rural clients are either first- or second-generation Americans (U.S. Census, 2000). Understanding a client's cultural background is very important in completing an assessment. The culturagram (Congress, 1994, 2002; Congress & Kung, 2005) has been useful in assessment with people of color (Lum, 2004), victims of domestic violence (Congress & Brownell, 2007), older people (Brownell, 1997), children (Webb, 1996), and clients with health problems (Congress, 2004). Making use of a paper and pen diagram, the culturagram (See Figure 15.1) looks at reasons for immigration,

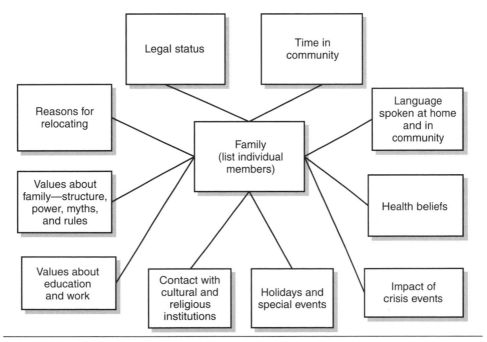

Figure 15.1 Culturagram—2000

length of time in the United States, legal status, language spoken at home and in the community, health beliefs, crisis events, holidays, contact with religious and cultural institutions, beliefs about education and work, and beliefs about family structure and roles. As the United States becomes increasingly diverse, it will be even more important to develop and use assessment tools to better understand clients from different cultural backgrounds.

Suicide Assessment

Suicide assessment and prevention is an important part of any comprehensive assessment process. The number of suicide attempts is on the rise especially among adolescents. The following factors have been cited as associated with high risk of suicide (Hepworth, Rooney, Rooney, Larsen, & Strom-Gottfried, 2005):

- Feelings of despair and hopelessness.
- History of previous suicide attempts.
- Concrete, available, and lethal plans to commit suicide.
- Family history of suicide.
- Ruminations about suicide.
- Lack of support systems.
- Feelings of worthlessness.
- Belief that others would be better off if one were dead.
- Age—very old or adolescent.
- Substance.

In completing a comprehensive assessment in which the client speaks of feelings of hopelessness, the social worker should not avoid introducing the discussion of suicide because it is a misconception that talking about suicide will give a client the idea.

There have been a number of scales developed to ascertain suicide risk for adults such as the Hopelessness Scale (Beck, Resnik, & Lettieri, 1974); the Scale for Suicide Ideation (Beck, Kovacs, & Weissman, 1979), and the Suicide Probability Scale (Cull & Gill, 1991). The Children's Depression Scale (Kovacs, 1992) and the John Hopkins Depression Scale (Joshi, Capozzoli, & Coyle, 1990) are helpful instruments in assessing children's and adolescents's risk of suicide.

DSM-IV Assessment

In behavioral health settings, social workers are frequently expected to understand and make a *DSM-IV-TR* diagnosis. The following categories are included in *DSM-IV* (American Psychiatric Association, 1994):

- Disorders Usually First Diagnosed in Infancy, Childhood, or Adolescence.
- Delirium, Dementia, and Amnestic and other Cognitive Disorders.
- Mental Disorders Due to a General Medical Condition.
- Substance-Related Disorders.
- Schizophrenia and Other Psychotic Disorders.
- Mood Disorders.

- Anxiety Disorders.
- Somatoform Disorders.
- Factitious Disorders.
- Dissociative Disorders.
- Sexual and Gender Identity Disorders.
- Eating Disorders.
- Sleep Disorders.
- Impulse-Control Disorders Not Otherwise Classified.
- Adjustment Disorders.
- Personality Disorders.

These diagnoses are descriptive in nature and not tied to any theoretical framework. A *DSM-IV* diagnosis has five axes:

Axis I: Primary Clinical Disorder
Axis II: Personality Disorder or Mental Retardation
Axis III: Medical problems
Axis IV: Psychosocial issues
Axis V: Global Assessment of Functioning

Many settings only made use of Axis I. While reliability and validity are seen as important in the use of any scale, there is a question about whether *DSM-IV* has satisfied this criterion. Kutchins and Kirk (1997) are particular concerned about the lack of reliability, while Neimeyer and Raskin (2000) see *DSM-IV* as based on social political processes rather than evidence-based research. Social workers, however, are most concerned that *DSM-IV* is based on a deficit model with no focus on the context or environment in diagnostic assessment. To increase understanding of diagnosis as related to person and environment, the National Association of Social Workers (NASW) has published the PIE system developed by Karls and Wandrei (1994), which looks as roles and conflicts in roles as crucial in assessment.

Use of the multiaxis approach in *DSM-IV* is most compatible with social work's focus on PIE. While Axes I, II, and III are psychiatric or medical classifications, Axis IV and Axis V consider context and social environment. There is some concern, however, that Axis I receives the most attention. Another positive factor about *DSM-IV* is the inclusion of the Appendix I Outline for Cultural Formulation and Glossary of Culture Bound Syndromes. This demonstrates recognition that there are psychiatric disorders other than the ones most frequently known in American culture.

A very useful diagnostic tool in evaluating mental functioning is the mental status exam. The Mini-Mental State Examination (MMSE) that has been published by Parveza, Cohen, and Blaser (1990) addresses the following issues:

- Orientation to time and place.
- Registration (how much repetition is needed to understand a concept).
- Attention and calculation.
- Recall and memory.
- Language.

The practitioner asks the client certain structured questions with a cut-off score of 23 that is considered acceptable for both cognitive and mental health functioning, although those tested with less education, who are older, or from different ethnicities may show different results (Fillenbaum, Heyman, Williams, Prosnitz, & Burchett, 1990).

Depression and Anxiety Tests

There have been a number of tests developed to measure mental health disorders in adults. In practice, social workers frequently encounter clients with depressive disorders including Major Depressive Disorder and Dysthmic Disorder. The most widely used measurement for assessing depressive symptoms in adults is the Beck Depression Inventory (Beck, Steer, & Brown, 1996). This test consists of 21 items rated on a 4-point scale ranging from 0 to 3 that measures the intensity of depressive symptoms. A score of 0 to 13 indicates normal level of depression; 14 to 19, mild to moderate level; 20 to 28, moderate to severe levels; and 29 to 63, extremely severe levels of depression. The client fills out this depression inventory in a short period of time. Since the Beck Depression Inventory was first developed in 1951, there have been numerous research studies. It has been shown to have excellent reliability with a test-retest coefficient of .90, as well as concurrent and criterion validity.

Clients self-administer the Beck Depression Inventory, and the Hamilton Rating Scale for Depression (Hamilton, 1967) is completed by the interviewer. It consists of 18 items measured on a 5-point Likert scale and contains items on depressed mood, suicide, anxiety, general somatic symptoms, and loss of interest in work and social activities. The Hamilton Rating Scale has been widely used with the elderly, people with HIV/AIDS, and adults with minor depressive disorders.

A number of instruments have been developed to measure anxiety disorders, especially trauma and phobia. The State Trait Anxiety Inventory (STAI) is a standardized self-report instrument with 20 questions in the State section and 20 questions in the Trait section. The scale has been validated and reported to have coefficient alpha reliability coefficients ranging from .86 to .95 (Spielberger, 1983).

To evaluate Posttraumatic Stress Disorder (PTSD), the Trauma Symptom Checklist (TSC-33) is useful. A client rates 33 items such as insomnia and feeling isolated from others from 0 (never) to 3 (very often). The scale has been shown to have internal consistency with an alpha of .89 (Briere & Ruentz, 1989).

The Fear Questionnaire (FQ) developed by Fisher and Corcoran (1994) is a 24-item instrument designed to assess target phobias as well as general fears. The instrument has an alpha of .82 for the three subscales and .92 for target phobias.

Personality disorders (Axis II on *DSM-IV*) have long been difficult to assess in only one interview. Often the client with a personality disorder does not have any other mental disorder and may be of above average intelligence. In contrast to other psychiatric disorders, those people with personality disorders may not experience much discomfort and often do not seek mental health treatment except in crisis. When a client has repeated difficulties in work and personal relationships, the possibility of a personality disorder should be considered. Personality disorders include Borderline Personality Disorder, Antisocial Personality Disorder, Paranoid Personality Disorder, Narcissistic Personality Disorder, and Obsessive-Compulsive Personality Disorder. Since personality disorders may be difficult to recognize in clients, social workers can help ensure the accuracy of the diagnosis by the use of standardized, structured interviews such as the Structured Clinical Interview for Diagnosis (SCID-II; Garb, 1998). Because clinicians tend to over diagnose or under diagnose clients, the use of a structured interview often yields more reliable results (Wood, Garb, Lilienfeld, & Nezworski, 2002).

The Minnesota Multiphasic Personality Inventories (MMPI and MMPI-II) developed by psychologists in the 1940s are well established standardized tests for assessing personality disorders (Jordan & Franklin, 2003). Other standardized personal assessment tests including the Millon Clinical Multiaxial Inventory-III (Millon, 1997) and the California Psychological Inventory (McAllister, 1996) are also useful standardized personality assessment measures. It is important for social workers who want to make the assessment process more evidence based to learn more about these standardized psychological tests that measure personality disorders.

Substance Abuse Assessment

A social worker who is asked to assess adults often misses a diagnosis of alcohol abuse and dependence. Part of the challenge is that alcohol is a legal substance and also a very accepted part of social interactions. *DSM-IV* has very specific diagnoses for alcoholism, but often social workers think primarily of another diagnosis. Frequent alcohol use may result in the development of symptoms (anxiety, depression, medical conditions, cognitive difficulties) that may suggest diagnoses other than alcohol abuse. Furthermore, many adults with other psychiatric disorders attempt to self medicate by drugs or alcohol with the result of a dual diagnosis of alcohol abuse and another psychiatric disorder. A contributing factor is that few clients directly state that they have a problem with alcohol as denial is frequently used in an attempt to cover up a substance abuse problem. The social worker must often act as a detective in looking at signs that may indicate an alcohol problem. During the assessment process, often a client who indicates work difficulties because of frequent absences or encounters with the law because of domestic violence or driving violations may be signaling a problem with substance abuse.

There are a number of assessment instruments that have been developed to measure the presence, extent, and severity of substance abuse problems. Two widely used assessment tools are CAGEii developed by Ewing (Mayfield, McLeod, & Hall, 1994) and the Michigan Alcohol Screening Test (MAST) (Selzer, 1971). CAGEii makes use of four questions related to desire to cut down on drinking, response of others to drinking, guilt feelings about drinking, and time of drinking. A positive response to two or more questions signifies a possible substance abuse problem and need for further investigation. The MAST makes use of 25 items to ascertain alcohol use or abuse. More comprehensive than the CAGEii, the MAST is often used to find out more information about the extent or severity of a client's substance abuse. A version of this test Drug Abuse Screening Test (DAST) has also been used to detect drug abuse.

Assessment of Older People

As social workers frequently encounter older people in their practice, assessment issues for older people need special attention. Depression is frequently an emotional disorder experienced by older people, yet frequently under diagnosed. The Geriatric Depression Scale (GDS) is most helpful in assessing depression in older people (Brink et al., 1982).

There are a number of versions of this test ranging from 1 to 30 items. This test is very helpful as an initial screening tool to assess depressive symptoms among the elderly.

Another frequently used assessment tool with older adults is one that assesses functional status. There are numerous assessment tools that evaluate functional status. Some of the issues covered in functional assessment instruments include the following areas: ability to use the telephone, shopping, food preparation, housekeeping, laundry, use of laundry, medication responsibility, and financial management.

In summary, the social worker should probably best begin with a general psychosocial assessment report including the diagnosis that was outlined previously. As part of the assessment report the social worker can use or consult with other professionals about standardized assessment instruments for depression, anxiety, substance abuse, and functional ability.

LIMITATIONS OF THE EVIDENCE

As apparent from the proceeding information, there are many general assessment formats. Yet empirical research on these different methods is very limited. Efforts to gather general assessment information through specific software computer programs or a semistructured interviews, however, represent an attempt to standardize information taken for assessment. While standardized general assessment tools are in their infancy, in contrast, there are a number of well-researched inventories for specific disorders such as depression and anxiety. Reliability and validity has been well established for many of these diagnostic instruments. One challenge, however, is that these diagnoses must be identified before a client can be given a specific test. Another challenge is that these tests focus on a specific disorder and that there is no provision for strengths that a client may have in coping with the psychiatric disorder or social support systems that can help mitigate the negative effects of the mental disorder.

IMPLICATIONS FOR SOCIAL WORK ON MICRO-, MEZZO-, AND MACROLEVELS

The importance of a comprehensive assessment for individual clients is evident. No treatment intervention can begin before there is assessment as to the nature of the problem and what strengths the client brings to resolving the problem. The nature of the problem is not only psychological, but often familial and social. The social worker must also look to the family and community for strengths and resources in addressing the problem. Accurate assessment is probably more challenging than ever for microlevel practice because with short-term treatment social workers are very limited in the amount of time that can be spent in the assessment process. Although assessment tools to examine the severity of mental disorders have been well documented, a continual challenge has been the limited amount of well-researched, general assessment instruments. Since cultural background is such an important component in the assessment process, more attention needs to be given to research on quickly administered assessment tools that address this factor.

Mezzolevel practice is designed to change the systems that most directly affect the client, namely the family, peer group, and classroom (Hepworth et al., 2005). A social worker completing a comprehensive assessment considers not only the individual, but also the environment surrounding the client. In order to understand the psychological functioning of the client, it is important to understand the impact of the family, school, or work environment. The multiple focus of the PIE rating scale (Karls & Wandrei, 1994) can be helpful in assessment on a mezzolevel.

How is assessment related to the macrolevel of practice? First, most agencies require a structured proscribed assessment form that may vary in length. Sometimes a *DSM-IV* diagnosis receives much more attention than the assessment of the client's strengths. At other times, the required assessment may be so lengthy and irrelevant that clients do not connect with their social workers during the assessment process thus impeding future treatment interventions.

A faulty assessment process is problematic for several reasons. First, an important problem to include in treatment planning may not be recognized. This may happen when the social worker has to make speedy assessments with very limited time. Second, if too much time is spent on unnecessary assessment then the client may leave before treatment has begun. In today's practice, assessment and intervention are frequently interwoven. This speaks to the importance of a focused relevant assessment if the treatment intervention is to be helpful.

CONCLUSION

Individual assessment of adults continues to be as important for social workers as in the early days of psychosocial diagnostic assessment. Much has changed though. The assessment process is much shorter and focused on the problem at hand. Often, assessment is not separate from intervention. While we have developed well-documented specific tests to assess the presence of specific mental disorders, general assessment instruments have not been subject to such empirical investigation. With the current focus on EBP, it is crucial that we apply the same standards to the assessment process. Because assessment continues to be an essential first step in engaging and understanding clients, empirical evidence to support decisions about assessment models and methods is much needed.

REFERENCES

American Psychiatric Association. (1994). *Diagnostic and statistical manual of mental disorders* (4th ed.). Washington, DC: Author.

Beck, A., Kovacs, M., & Weissman, A. (1979). Assessment of suicidal intention. *Journal of Counseling and Clinical Psychology, 47*, 343–352.

Beck, A., Resnik, H., & Lettieri, D. (Eds.). (1974). *The prediction of suicide*. Bowie, MD: Charles Press.

Beck, A., Steer, R., & Brown, G. (1996). *Manual for the Beck Depression Inventory* (2nd ed.). San Antonio, TX: Psychological Corporation.

Briere, J., & Ruentz, M. (1989). The TSC (TSC-33): Early data on a new scale. *Journal of Interpersonal Violence, 4*, 151–163.

Brink, T., Yesavage, J., Lum, O., Heersema, P., Adley, M., & Rose, T. (1982). Screening tests of geriatric depression. *Clinical Gerontology, 1*, 37–44.

Brownell, P. (1997). The application of the culturagram in cross-cultural practice with elder abuse victims. *Journal of Elder Abuse and Neglect, 9*(2), 19–33.

Congress, E. (1994). The use of culturagrams to assess and empower culturally diverse families. *Families in Society, 75*(9), 531–540.

Congress, E. (2002). Using culturagrams with culturally diverse families. In A. Roberts & G. Greene (Eds.), *Social work desk reference* (pp. 57–61). New York: Oxford University Press.

Congress, E. (2004). Cultural and ethnic issues in working with culturally diverse patients and their families: Use of the culturagram to promote cultural competency in health care settings. *Social Work in Health Care, 39*(3/4), 249–262.

Congress, E., & Brownell, P. (2007). Application of culturagram to assess and empower culturally and ethnically diverse battered women. In A. Roberts (Ed.), *Battered women and their families* (2nd ed., pp. 387–404). New York: Springer.

Congress, E., & Kung, W. (2005). Using the culturagram to assess and empower culturally diverse families. In E. Congress & M. Gonzalez (Eds.), *Multicultural perspectives in working with families* (pp. 3–21). New York: Springer.

Cooper, M., & Lesser, J. (2002). *Clinical social work practice: An integrated approach* (2nd ed.). Needham Heights, MA: Allyn & Bacon.

Cull, J., & Gill, W. (1991). *Suicide Probability Scale (PS)*. Los Angeles: Western Psychological Services.

De Jong, P., & Berg, I. (2001). Constructing cooperation with mandated clients. *Social Work, 46,* 361–374.

Fillenbaum, G., Heyman, A., Williams, K., Prosnitz, B., & Burchett, B. (1990). Sensitivity and specificity of standardized screens of cognitive impairment and dementia among elderly Black and White community residents. *Journal of Clinical Epidemiology, 43,* 651–660.

Fisher, J., & Corcoran, K. (1994). *Measures for clinical practice: A sourcebook* (2nd ed.). New York: Free Press.

Franklin, C. (2002, March/April). Becoming a strengths fact finder. *Family Therapy Magazine,* 39–46.

Franklin, C., & Moore, K. (1999). Solution-focused brief therapy. In C. Franklin & C. Jordan (Eds.), *Family practice: Brief systems methods for social work* (pp. 105–141). Pacific Grove, CA: Brooks/Cole.

Garb, H. (1998). *Studying the clinician: Judgment research and psychological assessment.* Washington, DC: American Psychological Association.

Germain, C., & Gitterman, A. (1996). *The life model approach to social work practice: Advances in theory and practice.* Storrs: University of Connecticut.

Goldstein, E. (2002). *Object relations theory and self psychology in social work.* New York: Free Press.

Hamilton, M. (1967). Development of a rating scale for primary depressive illness. *British Journal of Social and Clinical Psychology, 6,* 278–296.

Hartman, A., & Laird, J. (1983). *Family-oriented social work practice.* New York: Free Press.

Henggeler, S., Schoenwald, S., Borduin, C., Rowland, M., & Cunningham, P. (1998). *Multisystemic treatment of antisocial behavior in children and adolescents.* New York: Guilford Press.

Hepworth, D., Rooney, R., Rooney, G., Larsen, J., & Strom-Gottfried, K. (2005). *Direct social work practice* (7th ed.). Pacific Grove, CA: Brooks/Cole.

Hollis, F., & Wood, M. E. (1981). *Casework: A psychosocial therapy* (3rd ed.). New York: Random House.

Jordan, C., & Franklin, C. (2003). *Clinical assessment for social workers.* Chicago: Lyceum Books.

Joshi, P., Capozzoli, J., & Coyle, J. (1990). The Johns Hopkins Depression Scale: Normative data and validation in child psychiatry patients. *Journal of the American Academy of Child and Adolescent Psychiatry, 29*(2), 283–288.

Karls, J., & Wandrei, K. (1994). *Person-in-Environment System: The PIE classification system for social functioning problems.* Washington, DC: National Association of Social Workers Press.

Kovacs, M. (1992). *Children's Depression Inventory manual*. Los Angeles: Western Psychological Services.

Kutchins, H., & Kirk, S. (1997). *Making us crazy: DSM—The psychiatric bible and the creation of mental disorders*. New York: Free Press.

Lum, D. (2004). *Social work practice and people of color: A process-stage approach* (5th ed.). Belmont, CA: Brooks/Cole.

Mayfield, D., McLeod, G., & Hall, P. (1994). The CAGE Questionnaire: Validation of a new method. *American Journal of Psychiatry, 131*, 1121–1123.

McAllister, L. (1996). *A practical guide to California Psychological Inventory interpretation*. Palo Alto, CA: Consulting Psychologist Press.

McGoldrick, M., Gerson, J., & Schallenberg, J. (1999). *Genograms: Assessment and intervention*. New York: Norton.

Meichenbaum, D. (1993). Changing conceptions of cognitive behavior modification: Retrospect and prospect. *Journal of Consulting and Clinical Psychology, 61*, 202–204.

Millon, T. (1997). *The Millon inventories: Clinical and personality assessment*. New York: Guilford Press.

Neimeyer, R., & Raskin, J. (2000). *Constructions of disorder: Meaning-making frameworks for psychotherapy*. Washington, DC: American Psychological Association.

Parveza, G., Cohen, D., & Blaser, C. (1990). A brief form of Mini-Mental State Exam for use in community care settings. *Behavior, Health, and Aging, 1*(2), 133–139.

Perlman, H. (1957). *Social casework: A problem-solving process*. Chicago: University of Chicago Press.

Pomeroy, E., Holleran, L., & Franklin, C. (2003). Adults. In C. Jordan & C. Franklin (Eds.), *Clinical assessment for social workers* (pp. 155–197). Chicago: Lyceum Books.

Reid, W. (1988). Brief task-centered treatment. In R. Dorfman (Ed.), *Paradigms of clinical social work* (pp. 96–219). New York: Brunner/Mazel.

Roberts, A., & Greene, G. (Eds.). (2002). *Social workers desk reference*. New York: Oxford University Press

Saleeby, D. (1997). *The strengths perspective in social work practice* (2nd. ed.). New York: Longman.

Selzer, M. (1971). The Michigan Alcoholism Screening Test: The quest for a new diagnostic instrument. *American Journal of Psychiatry, 127*, 89–94.

Spielberger, V. (1983). *Manual for the State-Trait Anxiety Inventory*. Palo Alto, CA: Consulting Psychologists Press.

U.S. Census. (2000). *Mapping census 2000: The geography of U.S. diversity*. Available from www.census.gov/population/www/cen2000/atlas.html.

Wakefield, J. (1996). Does social work need the ecosystems perspective? Is the perspective clinically useful? *Social Service Review, 70*(1), 1–32.

Webb, N. (1996). *Social work practice with children*. New York: Guilford Press.

Wood, J., Garb, H., Lilienfeld, S., & Nezworski, T. (2002). Clinical assessment. *Annual Review of Psychology, 53*, 519–543.

Chapter 16 ————————————————

INTERVENTION WITH ADULTS

Bruce A. Thyer

This chapter reviews contemporary developments and advances regarding the effectiveness of various psychosocial interventions and assessment methods used by social workers who serve adult clients. Clinical social workers are the largest discipline providing psychotherapy services to adults in the United States, outnumbering psychologists and psychiatrists by a considerable margin. By virtue of our mere numbers, if not our sense of professionalism, it is crucial that members of our discipline keep abreast of the latest information on psychotherapy effectiveness. The term *psychosocial* treatment or therapy will be used throughout this chapter because it is more inclusive than psychotherapy, case management, and other terms for interpersonal helping. Barker (2003) provides the following definition of psychosocial therapy:

> A relationship that occurs between a professional and an individual, family, group, or community for the purpose of helping the client overcome specific emotional or social problems and achieve specified goals for well-being. (p. 349)

It is used here in a much broader sense than that employed by Hollis (1964) in describing a particular theoretically based approach to social casework. It is juxtaposed to other major methods of intervention, such as medications, surgery, hospitalization, or changes in laws or social policy. It involves both intrapersonal and interpersonal processes, as well as a person's physical environment. Although much of this chapter's focus will be on psychotherapies, the principles discussed apply to all forms of psychosocial intervention. Occasional reference will be made to these other modes of helping, for example, case management, advocacy, mediation, and so on. In this chapter, persons chronologically older than the teenage years are referred to as *adults*.

HISTORICAL BACKGROUND

In the past decade and a half, there have been two substantial initiatives to identify the evidentiary foundations of various psychosocial interventions. They began roughly at the same time, in the early 1990s, as independent efforts, and have continued on to the present. They are discussed sequentially, but this does not imply any sense of priority or authoritativeness.

Task Force on Promotion and Dissemination of Psychological Interventions

The first one to be addressed was developed at the initiative of Martin Seligman, then president of Division 12, the Division of Clinical Psychology, one of over 50 divisions within the American Psychological Association. Seligman established a *Task Force on Promotion and Dissemination of Psychological Interventions,* primarily composed of major players who supported the scientist-practitioner model of psychological training. This group was charged with three distinct tasks. The first was to identify some set of evidentiary standards that could be used to assess the effectiveness of different psychological treatments when applied to help clients with discrete and specific so-called mental disorders. The second assignment was, once these evidentiary guidelines were established, to actually apply them in evaluating the evidence related to the effectiveness of these various interventions and to prepare and publish lists of such well-supported treatments. The third assignment was to prepare a list of treatment manuals for these presumptively well-supported interventions, including information as to how these manuals could be obtained and where clinicians could gain supervised experience in learning to use them. A treatment manual was defined as a written document that provided sufficient detail so as to permit a competent clinician to replicate the treatment. As you might imagine, none of these tasks was undertaken without considerable discussion, and indeed controversy (see Chambless & Ollendick, 2001), but the original task force continued their work through several successive presidents of Division 12 and was largely successful in completing their assignments.

The first task was perhaps the most contentious, and in the interests of space and time I will simply refer to the final set of criteria, reproduced in Chapter 5, Table 5.1 in this volume. On the face of it, these criteria seem relatively modest, but they certainly engendered a storm of controversy, mostly stemming from two overlapping camps. The psychodynamically, phenomenologically, and humanistically inclined psychotherapists were anxious that their preferred treatments may not meet these seemingly (to them) stringent standards and that this could negatively affect the credibility of their services. The second group of opponents were those who advocated postmodernist perspectives and repudiated the idea that certain forms of evidence (e.g., experiments) should be given greater credibility than other ways of knowing (e.g., case studies or other forms of qualitative inquiry). The behavior analysts, who rarely employed randomized controlled trials in their evaluations of therapy, successfully insisted that a series of well-controlled single case studies could also provide convincing evidence related to the effectiveness of psychological treatments, hence the inclusion of Criteria II in Table 5.1.

Acceptance of the evidentiary criteria listed in Table 5.1 was helped through a recognition that the task force was clearly committed to identifying genuinely effective psychotherapies, irrespective of theoretical orientations, and also that these standards were modeled after those used by the U.S. Food and Drug Administration in the process to approve the safety, efficacy, and use of new medications. These suggested standards appeared in various publications (Chambless et al., 1998; Task Force, 1995) and the language softened from referring to "empirically validated" to "empirically supported" treatments in order to provide some distance from any implication that research on a given psychotherapy was concluded.

Once the bar had been set, members of the task force began assembling reports on what psychological treatments met these standards appearing in Table 5.1 and developed lists

Table 16.1   Examples of Empirically Validated Treatments

Well-Established Treatments

Beck's Cognitive Therapy for Depression
Behavioral Marital Therapy
Cognitive Behavior Therapy (CBT) for Panic Disorder with and without Agoraphobia
CBT for Generalized Anxiety Disorder
Exposure Therapy for Phobias
Exposure Therapy and Response Prevention for Obsessive-Compulsive Disorder
Group CBT for Social Phobia
Interpersonal Psychotherapy for Bulimia
Token Economy Programs for the Chronically Mentally Ill

Probably Efficacious Treatments

Brief Psychodynamic Therapies
Dialectical Behavior Therapy for Borderline Personality Disorder
Lewinsohn's Psychoeducational Treatment for Depression

Based on "Training in and Dissemination of Empirically-Validated Psychological Treatments," by the Task Force on Promotion and Dissemination of Psychological Procedures, 1995, *Clinical Psychologist, 48*(1), pp. 3–23.

of them. Once such list is partially reproduced in Table 16.1. The original list is longer, listing about 25 therapies, and also includes citations to the intervention research justifying the treatment's inclusion. Updates to this list appeared in later publications that collected a list of the treatment manuals describing the well-established interventions and provided information as to where they were published or could otherwise be acquired (Chambless et al., 1998; Woody, Weisz, & McLean, 2005). Further publications appeared (Sanderson & Woody, 1995; Van Hasselt & Hersen, 1996; Woody & Sanderson, 1998). Some members of the task force went on to produce books describing these empirically supported treatments, which have proven to greatly enrich the treatment literature (e.g., Nathan & Gorman, 1998, 2007; Weisz, 2004), and a later initiative (Woody et al., 2005) was to conduct a survey of APA-accredited doctoral and internship training programs in clinical psychology in the United States and Canada, assessing the extent to which these programs were providing training in task force identified, empirically supported treatments, and to compare changes in such training opportunities over the past decade (1993 to 2003). The picture was mixed. In 2003, the modal number of empirically supported treatments that students were trained in during graduate school was zero (!), and the mode for providing supervised training during the internship was also zero (!). The mean numbers of ESTs taught dropped from 11.5 (1993) to 9.5 (2003); but the responding programs differed from the two surveys, so this is not a reliable index. Only four ESTs were taught by more than 50% of the internship programs. "Most of the treatments that have robust empirical support are not taught (in a supervised way) by the majority of training programs" (Woody et al., 2005, p. 9), a rather embarrassing finding considering the conspicuous manner in which psychology says it is distinguished from other mental health fields by its rigorous adherence to a scientist-practitioner model of training.

The original task force has since been renamed the Committee on Science and Practice, within Division 12 of the APA, and continues its work although in less striking ways. The standards of evidence found in Table 5.1 remain in play, but the list of ESTs is periodically (and appropriately) amended to reflect advances in clinical research (Nathan & Gorman, 1998, 2007). This latter volume is immodestly titled *A Guide to Treatments that Work*, but it really does live up to its name. It was claimed that "This volume emanates from a task force of the board of directors of Division 12 (Clinical Psychology) of the American Psychological Association (APA) established in 1993 during my Presidency of that division" (Seligman, 1998, p. v). Seligman wanted this book to be an interdisciplinary, state-of-the-science summary of what is known to work in terms of psychological (what we social workers would call psychosocial) and pharmacological treatments, disorder by disorder by disorder. "The work was to be a disinterested review of outcome studies, not a lobbying effort: These volumes are intended to be scientific documents of a high order. It is essential that their integrity be unimpeachable" (Seligman, 1998, p. vi). There could be no involvement of researchers who received funding from pharmaceutical companies or who had other financial conflicts of interest, and there was to be no editorial control from either Division 12 or the APA at large. The mandate to the clinician-scholars invited to author various chapters was clear and compelling:

> The purpose of these chapters is to present the most rigorous, scientifically based evidence for the efficacy of treatments that is available. At the same time, it is clear that for some disorders there are treatments widely recognized by experienced clinicians to be useful that may not have been subjected to rigorous investigation for a variety of reasons. Our aim is to be clear with readers what treatments have been scientifically validated, what treatments are felt by a large number of experts to be valuable but have never been properly scientifically examined, and what treatments are known to be of little value. (Nathan & Gorman, 1998, p. x)

This project was carried out as proposed, with the first edition appearing in 1998 and undated editions in 2002 and 2007. It is an invaluable resource for social workers seeking guidance about effective interventions relevant to adult clients who meet the formal diagnostic criteria for a mental disorder.

Keep in mind that Division 12 is but one of over 50 divisions within the APA, and the APA as the host organization has taken great pains not to endorse this initiative of Division 12, due to the sensitivies of the larger community of psychologists, many of whom are decidedly not enamored with efforts such as these. Indeed the first edition contained a legal disclaimer that lawyers within the APA insisted be included in *A Guide to Treatments that Work,* stating that:

> This book does not represent an official statement by APA, or any of its divisions, but rather the personal views of the authors based upon their review of the scientific literature relative to therapeutic techniques and drugs for various psychological disorders. The book recites the literature and describes the controlled outcome studies relative to therapies but it is not intended to recommend "treatments of choice," establish standards or guidelines for "care" or provide advice on the efficacy of the therapies listed . . . health care providers and members of the public are advised that this book should not be definitively relied upon in making choices for appropriate care and treatment. (Seligman, 1998, p. vii)

So much for Seligman's hope that there would be no outside editorial control! Recently, the APA has begun using the language of evidence-based practice (Norcross, Beutler, & Levant, 2006), reflecting the more profound influence of this initiative, originating outside of psychology, and described next, but unfortunately in doing so they blurred the distinction between the concept of empirically supported treatments (e.g., identifying interventions supported by a certain level of evidence) and the process of evidence-based practice.

Evidence-Based Practice

The term *evidence-based medicine* first appeared in print in a 1992 article by Gordon Guyatt, a physician concerned with promoting the greater use of scientifically reliable research findings in the practice of health care. Guyatt, allied with a number of medical doctors with similar views began publishing a series of papers in the *Journal of the American Medical Association* (JAMA), the *British Medical Journal* (BMJ), and other leading medical journals, describing the basic tenets of what came to be called *evidence-based practice,* a more broadly based term reflective of the application of these principles to all health-care disciplines, not just medicine. The best-selling textbook *Evidence-Based Medicine: How to Practice and Teach EBM* has gone into its third edition (Strauss, Richardon, Glasziou, & Haynes, 2005), from which much of the content in this section of this chapter is drawn.

The definition of evidence-based medicine is deceptively simple:

> Evidence-based medicine (EBM) requires the integration of the best research evidence with our clinical expertise and our patient's unique values and circumstances. (Strauss et al., 2005, p. 1)

This three-component sentence often has the second and third elements overlooked, in favor of an almost exclusive emphasis on the first element, research evidence. In other words, many misconstrue EBP to simply mean locating research evidence (e.g., best-supported interventions) and then applying them to practice. This is clearly a false representation of EBP since the definition involves three equally important elements, research evidence, clinical expertise, and client's values and circumstances. Anyone who equates EBP solely with applying empirically supported techniques has a gross and fundamental misunderstanding of this process of learning, teaching, and practicing.

EBM arose due to some realizations among its originators:

- Clinicians have a great need for valid information about a client's problem, prognosis, effective ways to assess and diagnosis, how to treat clients, and how to prevent problems.
- The traditional ways of communicating such information is inadequate. Books and journals are frequently out of date, wrong, ineffective, overwhelming, or simply convey bogus information.
- There are often growing disparities between our clinical skills, empirically based knowledge, and practice effectiveness.
- There are serious limitations as to how much time clinicians can spend in tracking down clinically relevant and valid information.

However, there are some technological developments that make it possible to overcome some of these factors inhibiting genuinely effective practice:

- New ways to track down information efficiently.
- The creation and availability of systematic reviews (of which more will be said later) of the effects of health care and psychosocial interventions.

- The development of evidence-based journals that reprint summaries of genuinely useful Information from recently published journals (e.g., *Evidence-Based Mental Health,* see http://ebmh.bmj.com).
- The development of improved ways to learn about research evidence, clinical skills, and assessment methods.

Evidence-based practice is best viewed as a process of learning or of locating information and acting upon it, rather than locating empirically supported treatments and applying them. EBP is seen as having five steps, including:

1. Converting the need for information (about prevention, diagnosis, prognosis, therapy, causation, etc.) into an answerable question.
2. Tracking down the best evidence with which to answer that question.
3. Critically appraising that evidence for its validity (closeness to the truth), impact (size of the effect), and applicability (usefulness in our clinical practice).
4. Integrating the critical appraisal with our clinical expertise and our patients' unique biology, values, and circumstances.
5. Evaluating our effectiveness and efficiency in executing Steps 1 to 4 and seeking ways to improve them for next time (Steps 1 to 5 are quoted from Strauss et al., 2005, pp. 3–4).

Strauss et al. (2005) and related primary resources spend a good deal of space on each of these five steps, and the reader interested in learning more about EBP within social work is strongly urged to begin with Strauss et al. and other small books central to the EBM movement (e.g., Guyatt & Rennie, 2002; Moore & McQuay, 2006) *before* delving into the related literatures on EBP to be found in social work (e.g., J. Corcoran, 2000; Cournoyer, 2004; Gibbs, 2003; O'Hare, 2005; Roberts & Yeager, 2006; Thyer & Kazi, 2004; Thyer & Wodarski, 2007).

Concurrent with the establishment of the EBP movement within medicine, an international group of health-care professionals established an organization called the Cochrane Collaboration (CC; www.cochrane.org). I strongly urge you to sign on to the Cochrane web site and take some time perusing what it has to offer and to become familiar with this highly influential organization. The Cochrane Collaboration is named after a distinguished British epidemiologist, Archie Cochrane. The CC is both international and not for profit and is "dedicated to making up-to-date, accurate information about the effects of health care readily available worldwide. It produces and disseminates systematic reviews of health care interventions and promotes the search for evidence in the form of clinical trials and other studies of interventions. . . . The major product of the Collaboration is the *Cochrane Database of Systematic Reviews* which is published quarterly. . . . Those who prepare the reviews are mostly health professionals who volunteer to work on one of the many Cochrane Review Groups, with editorial teams overseeing the preparation and maintenance of the reviews, as well as application of the rigorous quality standards for which Cochrane Reviews have become known" (all quotations are from the Cochrane web site, and downloaded on March 16, 2007).

Health-care professionals from a variety of disciplines (including social work) located around the world volunteer to serve on Cochrane Review Groups (CRGs), of which there are dozens, such as the Childhood Cancer Group; Depression, Anxiety, and Neurosis Group; Drug and Alcohol Group; HIV/AIDS Group; Pain, Palliative, and Supportive Care Group; Pregnancy and Childbirth Group; and the Schizophrenia Group, to list a few of particular relevance to social work. There are also various methods groups and many bricks-and-mortar Cochrane Centers located around the world. The CC hosts an annual international conference and many regional or national meetings, such as Summer Institute (open to social workers!) for Evidence-Based Practice (held in San Antonio, Texas, in July 2007).

On their web site, you can also locate the *Cochrane Manual*, a detailed guide to designing and evaluating systematic reviews (SRs) of high quality research on health-care interventions and methods of assessment, roughly categorized by the subject matter of the various review groups (see Table 16.2). There are free summaries of these SRs available on the web site, and your local university library most likely subscribes to the CC library, allowing you free access to these invaluable resources. In terms of timely, comprehensive, and minimally biased appraisals of the effects of various treatments, the CC SRs represent the state of the art. The CC does admittedly focus on physical health conditions, which includes mental illnesses; and the majority of the reviews deal with medical interventions, not psychosocial ones, but categorizing issues as either medical problems and psychosocial ones, or as medical treatments versus psychosocial treatments, is not always easy. A

Table 16.2   What Is a Systematic Review?

A systematic review uses transparent procedures to identify, assess, and synthesize results of research on a particular topic. These procedures are explicit, so that others can replicate the review, and are defined in advance of the review and include:

Clear inclusion/exclusion criteria specify the study designs, populations, interventions, and outcomes that will be covered in the review.

An explicit search strategy is developed and implemented to identify all published and unpublished studies that meet the inclusion criteria. The search strategy specifies keyword strings and sources (i.e., electronic databases, web sites, experts, and journals) that will be included in the search.

Systematic coding and analysis of included studies' methods, intervention and comparison conditions, sample characteristics, outcome measures, and results.

Meta-analysis (when possible) to estimate pooled effect sizes (ES) and moderators of ES.

How Are C2 Systematic Reviews Different from Other Systematic Reviews?

C2 reviews must include a systematic search for unpublished reports (to avoid publication bias).

C2 reviews are usually international in scope.

A protocol (proposal) for the review is developed in advance and undergoes careful peer review by international experts in the substantive area, experts in systematic review methods, and a trial search coordinator.

Study inclusion decisions and coding decisions are accomplished by at least two reviewers who work independently and compare results.

C2 reviews undergo peer review and editorial review.

Completed C2 reviews are published in C2-RIPE and may be published elsewhere.

From "What Is a Systematic Review?" by Social Welfare Group, Campbell Collaboration. Retrieved March 16, 2007, from www.campbellcollaboration.org/SWCG/reviews.asp.

recent issue of the *British Medical Journal* contained a fascinating report of a randomized controlled trial of the effects of providing insulation in homes on the health and well-being of residents (Howden-Chapman et al., 2007). The 4,407 low-income participants lived in 1,350 households, half of which were randomly selected to receive upgraded insulation (to keep the homes warmer). The provision of more insulation produced improved health, fewer days absent from work or school, and fewer visits to the doctor. Is this a "medical" intervention? Regardless, the implications for social work clinical and community practice seem clear; and studies such as this, which will eventually be incorporated in CC SRs, make it worthwhile for social workers to become familiar with this database of information and reports on treatments for disorders that afflict adult social work clients.

The Campbell Collaboration (C2; see www.Campbellcollaboration.org), named after psychologist Donald Campbell, is closely modeled after the work, operation, and products of the Cochrane Collaboration. Unlike CC, the C2, founded in 1999, focuses on preparing SRs in the fields of education, criminal justice, and social welfare. It, too, hosts an annual conference, supports a variety of centers around the world, devises methodological standards, and encourages international social work scholars to propose topics for SRs, to develop research protocols related to those titles, and then to actually carry out these protocols and to publish the SRs. At present, there are more proposed titles and protocols (representing SRs in development) than there are completed SRs, but the list of published SRs will expand greatly over the next few years. The approach taken by the C2 with respect to systematic reviews is outlined in Table 16.1. Strenuous efforts are made to control for or minimize bias when completing these reviews, and they can be said to represent the most methodologically rigorous and comprehensive evaluations of the literature dealing with EBP-style answerable questions that are available to contemporary social workers. Both the Cochrane and Campbell Collaborations are inclusive organizations, and they are always looking for competent social workers to volunteer to serve on their various review groups or even to undertake SRs in various areas of social welfare. Do not be bashful in contacting them to see if you can help.

Practice Guidelines

You may have heard of the intriguing term *practice guidelines*, and it may be useful to review what is meant by this phrase:

> [D]efined as "systematically developed statements to assist practitioner and patient decisions about appropriate care for specific clinical circumstances" (Institute of Medicine, 1990, p. 27), practice guidelines are recommendations for clinical care based on research findings and the consensus of experienced clinicians with expertise in a given practice area. Practice protocols, standards, algorithms, options, parameters, pathways, and preferred practice patterns are nuanced terms broadly synonymous with the concept *clinical practice guidelines*. (Howard & Jenson, 1999b, p. 285)

There has been little discussion of the relevance of practice guidelines within the social work literature. Matthew Howard and Jeffrey Jenson (1999b) guest edited a special issue of the distinguished journal *Research on Social Work Practice* devoted to the topic of practice guidelines and clinical social work, and Aaron Rosen and Enola Proctor (2003) edited a book titled *Developing Practice Guidelines for Social Work Interventions: Issues, Methods, and Research Agenda,* based on a conference sponsored by the George Warren

Brown School of Social Work at Washington University. To date, I am unaware of any practice guideline developed by social workers within and for the profession of clinical social work, and our discipline's contributions to practice guidelines appear to be meager. The National Association of Social Workers (NASW) is a conspicuously absent player on the scene of practice guidelines and lacking major organizational initiatives; it seems that relatively little will be forthcoming.

There is a very large interdisciplinary and disciplinary literature of practice guidelines, however, for many hundreds of mental illnesses and other psychosocial problems, some of which are obviously potentially applicable to social work intervention with adults. But these almost always share a glaring problem that you may have overlooked in the definition quoted earlier, namely that practice guidelines are usually based on an amalgamation of scientific research findings and the consensus of experts. It is this latter feature that contaminates, in the view of many, the credibility of practice guidelines. Those guidelines hammered out behind closed doors, crafted in smoke-filled rooms by the Machiavellian mavens of mental illness, lack the virtues of transparency associated with the APA's task force or the SR protocols of the CC or C2. You can assign weights to different levels of evidence when crafting an SR, so much for a randomized controlled trial, so much less for a quasi-experiment, and so on. And use independent raters to assure us of the reliability of such judgments. But you cannot do that when the pristine purity of transparently conducted published research findings are contaminated with the dross of expert consensus. It is like adding a drop of ink to a glass of clear water. The weighty and distinguished voice of senior authority figures, wedded to a given model of practice to which they have devoted their life's work, may overwhelm the timid research-based (but valid) appraisals of the more junior clinical researcher.

Be that as it may, practice guidelines are available for many adult disorders, and those of the American Psychiatric Association have some of the widest currency. The American Psychiatric Association began publishing practice guidelines in 1991. These are initially published in issues of the *American Journal of Psychiatry,* the flagship journal of the American Psychiatric Association and are later made available for purchase at the web site (www.psych.org/psych_pract/treatg/pg/prac_guide.cfm). The guidelines have a notation as to when they were initially published, and if your university subscribes to the *American Journal of Psychiatry* you will very likely be able to download it directly from the journal at no cost. Also available on this web site is the American Psychiatric Association's Guideline Development Process, which describes how their practice guidelines are crafted. In it is noted that:

> The evidence base for practice guidelines is derived from two sources: research studies and clinical consensus. Where gaps exist in the research data, evidence is derived from clinical consensus, obtained through board review of multiple drafts of each guideline.... Both research data and clinical consensus vary in their validity and reliability for different clinical situations; guidelines state explicitly the nature of the supporting evidence for specific recommendations, so that readers can make their own judgments regarding the utility of the recommendations. (Steering Committee on Practice Guidelines, 2006, p. 4)

This approach differs significantly from that used by the APA task force and the CC and C2, each of which largely exclude any role of so-called expert consensus in the crafting of the evaluative reviews. Although the American Psychiatric Association will indeed describe the

University of Michigan School of Social Work. The IOM periodically issues reports on various topics, some of which pertain to social work practice with adults; and while these reports lack the transparency and comprehensiveness of SRs, they nevertheless can be a useful source of information that contribute to social care.

SUMMARY OF EMPIRICALLY SUPPORTED INTERVENTIONS

So far I have not addressed the actual availability of information about empirically supported practices that social workers can consult in regards to their providing services to adults. The available resources are impressively large, relative to what was available only a couple of decades ago, but perhaps discouragingly meager considering the seriousness, complexity, and vastness of needs.

The periodical publications that emerged from the Division 12 *Task Force on the Promotion and Dissemination of Psychological Interventions*, for example, Chambless et al. (1996, 1998), Sanderson and Woody (1995), Task Force (1995), Woody and Sanderson (1998), and Woody et al. (2005) are all available for free on the Division 12 web site (www.apa.org/divisions/div12/journals.html#ESTs/). But frankly a much better resource is Nathan and Gorman's (2007) *A Guide to Treatments that Work*. Each chapter is a comprehensive research synthesis about what is known regarding the psychosocial or pharmacological treatment for clients with a discrete diagnosable mental illness. There is also a summary table at the beginning of the book (some excerpts from this table are reproduced in Table 16.3). In the left column is a specific syndrome, next is a list of empirically supported treatments, the standards of proof used to make this determination, and last, on the right, some references to research supporting the inclusion of this particular treatment. There are 29 diagnosable mental illnesses for which the authors have provided comprehensive appraisals. The social worker seeking information on effective treatments will find this resource of great value.

Nathan and Gorman's (2002) book is a summary of research and can point social workers in the direction of effective treatments, but Van Hasselt and Hersen (1996) provide actual treatment manuals for 17 adult psychosocial and medical problems. These are listed in Table 16.4. These treatment manuals describe interventions in sufficient detail so as to enable a skilled clinician (social worker, psychologist, psychiatrist, etc.) to deliver these services to clients. The interventions are all well supported, as defined by the Division 12 task force criteria and consulting these manuals would be a great first step for a social worker to begin acquiring clinical skills in delivering these empirically supported psychosocial interventions. The articles by Sanderson and Woody (1995) and Woody and Sanderson (1998) provide another listing of treatment manuals and how to obtain them but not copies of the actual manuals themselves.

The Campbell and Cochrane Collaborations are another exceedingly useful resource for learning about the evidentiary status of various interventions potentially useful to social workers serving adult clients. If you turn to the web sites of these two organizations, you will find a long list of proposed topics (to be the subject of future systematic reviews), a shorter list of protocols proposed by various research teams that have been approved by the respective collaborations, and an even shorter list of actual systematic reviews. But although limited in number, these SRs probably represent the most scientifically credible and up-to-date

Table 16.3 Summary of Treatments That Work

Syndromes	Treatments	Standards of Proof	Chapters in Nathan & Gorman (2002)
Bulimia Nervosa (BN)	*Several different classes of antidepressant drugs* produce significant, short-term reductions in binge eating and purging.	A large number of Type 1 and Type 2 randomized clinical trials (RCTs), utilizing placebo as comparison.	Wilson & Fairburn, Chapter 22, pp. 559–592
	Manual-based cognitive-behavioral therapy (CBT) is currently the treatment of choice. Roughly half the patients receiving CBT cease binge eating and purging. Long-term maintenance of improvement appears to be reasonably good.	A very substantial number of Type 1 and Type 2 RCTs.	
Schizophrenia	*Behavior therapy and social-learning-token-economy programs* help structure, support, and reinforce prosocial behaviors in persons with schizophrenia.	Many Type 1 and Type 2 RCTs and a very large number of Type 3 studies of behavior therapy and social-learning-token-economy programs.	Kopelowicz, Liberman, & Zarate, Chapter 8, pp. 201–228
	Structured, educational, family interventions help patients with schizophrenia maintain gains achieved with medication and customary case management.	Over 20 Type 1 and Type 2 RCTs of educational family interventions.	
	Social skills training has enabled persons with Schizophrenia to acquire instrumental and affiliative skills to improve functioning in their communities.	More than 40 Type 1 and Type 2 RCTs of social skills training.	
	Pharmacological treatment has had a profoundly positive impact on the course of Schizophrenia. The recent introduction of *atypical antipsychotics* has been promising because of their reduced side effects and enhanced efficacy in some refractory patients.	A very large number of RCTs over 40 years.	Bradford, Stroup, & Lieberman, Chapter 7, pp. 169–199
Specific phobias	*Exposure-based procedures, especially in-vivo exposure,* reduce or eliminate most or all components of specific phobic disorders.	A very large number of Type 1 RCTs	Barlow, Raffa, & Cohen, Chapter 13, pp. 301–335
	No pharmacological intervention has been shown to be effective for specific phobias.		Roy-Byrne, & Cowley, Chapter 14, pp. 337–365

Table 16.4   Treatment Manuals for Adult Disorders Available in Van Hasselt and Hersen (1996)

Panic Disorder and Agoraphobia
Obsessive-Compulsive Disorder
Cognitive-Behavioral Treatment of Social Phobia
Social Skills Training for Depression
Cognitive-Behavior Therapy for Treatment of Depressed Inpatients
Biobehavioral Treatment and Rehabilitation for Persons with Schizophrenia*
Community Reinforcement Training with Concerned Others
Cognitive-Behavioral Treatment of Sex Offenders
Treatment of Sexual Dysfunctions
A Comprehensive Treatment Manual for the Management of Obesity
Lifestyle Change: A Program for Long-Term Weight Management
Managing Marital Therapy: Helping Partners Change
Insomnia
Cognitive-Behavioral Treatment of Body-Image Disturbances
Cognitive-Behavioral Treatment of Postconcussion Syndrome
Trichotillomania Treatment Manual
Anger Management Training with Essential Hypertensive Patients

*This manual was co-authored by a social worker, Stephen E. Wong, PhD.
Source: Sourcebook of Psychological Treatment Manuals for Adult Disorders, by V. B. Van Hasselt and M. Hersen (Eds.), 1996, New York: Plenum Press.

summaries of the research literature regarding the usefulness of various interventions and assessment methods. Table 16.5 lists a selection of completed SRs that you can locate on these collaborations' web sites. The last one listed, *Work Programs for Welfare Recipients*, was completed in August of 2006 and is an analysis of randomized controlled studies, quasi-experimental outcome studies, and cluster-randomized controlled trials of welfare-to-work programs for persons receiving public assistance, such as Temporary Assistance for Needy Families (TANF). The analysis of the research literature involved 46 programs encompassing over 412,000 participants, with outcomes reported for up to 6 years. The free document is 122 pages long. You can see how a systematic review of this nature is potentially far more informative than reading a single study appearing in a journal; and if you are a social worker involved in serving TANF clients, a review of this comprehensive a nature could prove enormously useful for you in learning about what aspects of welfare-to-work programs are genuinely helpful, versus those that are less beneficial.

Think of the implications of having information of this high a quality available, both for social work practice as well as for education. No longer does an individual social worker have to search aimlessly through journals, vainly hoping to locate some potentially useful studies. Other very well-qualified scholars have already culled the literature, separated the credible research from the less useful, and summarized the results, for your independent review and analysis of its applicability to your practice situations and clients. Think of the absurdity of teaching social work practice courses using one or more theories as the guiding framework to structure the class when you and students have access to actual outcomes research about various psychosocial treatments readily used by social workers active in various areas of practice such as schizophrenia, depression, anxiety disorders, and so on. If we are in the business of educating students to practice in these various areas, these

Table 16.5   Examples of Completed Systematic Reviews Addressing Psychosocial Interventions for Adults

---

From the Cochrane Collaboration (www.cochrane.org)
Screening and Case Finding Instruments for Depression
Marital Therapy for Depression
Short Term Psychodynamic Psychotherapies for Common Mental Disorders
Interventions for Helping People Recognize Early Signs of the Recurrence of Bipolar Disorder
Psychological Debriefing for Prevention Post Traumatic Stress Disorder (PTSD)
Psychological Treatment of Post Traumatic Stress Disorder (PTSD)
Individual Psychotherapy in the Outpatient Treatment of Adults with Anorexia Nervosa
Interventions for Vaginismus
Alcoholics Anonymous and other 12-Step Programs for Alcohol Dependence
Psychotherapeutic Interventions for Cannabis Abuse and/or/Dependence in Outpatient Settings
Family Intervention for Schizophrenia
Token Economy for Schizophrenia
Cognitive Behavior Therapy for Schizophrenia
Hypnosis for Schizophrenia
Life Skills Programmes for Chronic Mental Illnesses
Art Therapy for Schizophrenia or Schizophrenia-Like Illnesses
Supportive Therapy for Schizophrenia
Individual Behavioural Counseling for Smoking Cessation
Group Behaviour Therapy Programmes for Smoking Cessation
Strategies for Increasing the Participation of Women in Community Breast Cancer Screenings
Reminiscence Therapy for Dementia
Psychological Treatments for Epilepsy

From the Campbell Collaboration (www.campbellcollaboration.org)
Cognitive Behavioral Programs for Juvenile and Adult Offenders: A Meta-Analysis of Controlled Intervention Studies
The Effectiveness of Incarceration-based Drug Treatment on Criminal Behavior
Interventions for Learning Disabled Sex Offenders
Work Programmes for Welfare Recipients

Note: Available on the web sites of the Cochrane and Campbell Collaborations.

systematic reviews published by the Campbell and Cochrane Collaborations could (should?) be a very important component of such instruction. Yet, sadly, many social work students and practitioners have yet to come into contact with these incredibly useful resources.

The IOM is another resource, arguably less comprehensive than the work of the Campbell and Cochrane Collaborations, but still potentially valuable in learning about interventions for use with adult clients. A few of its reports with applicability to our field include the following titles, all available at www.iom.edu:

- Improving the Social Security Disability Decision Process.
- Posttraumatic Stress Disorder: Diagnosis and Assessment.
- Improving the Quality of Health Care for Mental and Substance-Use Conditions.
- WIC Food Packages: Time for a Change.
- Improving Palliative Care: We Can Take Better Care of People with Cancer.
- Taking Action to Reduce Tobacco Use.

The American Psychiatric Association has produced a series of practice guidelines for selected mental illnesses, and these are available for purchase as PDF documents at their web site (www.psych.org/psych_pract/treatg/pg/prac_guide.cfm) for the following disorders:

- Acute Stress Disorder and Posttraumtic Stress Disorder.
- Alzheimer's Disease and Other Dementias of Late Life.
- Bipolar Disorder.
- Borderline Personality Disorder.
- Delirium.
- Eating Disorders.
- HIV/AIDS.
- Major Depressive Disorder.
- Obsessive-Compulsive Disorder.
- Panic Disorder.
- Psychiatric Evaluation of Adults.
- Substance Use Disorders.
- Suicidal Behaviors.

You may also be able to print them out for free from the applicable issues of the *American Journal of Psychiatry* via your local university library. Keep in mind that these practice guidelines typically overemphasize pharmacological treatments at the expense of psychotherapeutic or psychosocial services, and they involve elements of the consensus clinical opinions of presumptive experts, but even with these caveats, they are still informative.

LIMITATIONS OF THE EVIDENCE

You can view the glass as half full or half empty. Do we know much more now, in terms of genuinely effective psychosocial interventions for use with the adult clients of social workers, than we did say 2 or 3 decades ago? Absolutely! But it is undeniable that large gaps exist, and for many important areas of social work practice the interventive map remains labeled *terra incognita*. For several dozen of the major mental illnesses, significant strides have been made, and new advances appear in the clinical research literature on a weekly if not daily basis. Keep in mind that the process of evidence-based practice, or the lists of empirically supported treatments, do not exclusively insist on a reliance on an accumulation of pristine randomized controlled trials before social work practitioners can decide what to do. We need to decide what to do every day and cannot defer making important decisions about the nature of the services we offer our clients. Evidence-based practice does point out that certain forms of evidence, such as randomized controlled trials, meta-analyses, and systematic reviews, can provide us with more credible information about the effectiveness of services, but if that level of evidence is unavailable, then you should act by taking into account the highest quality evidence that is available. This may be quasi-experiments not involving the random assignment of clients to various treatment conditions; it may be time-series studies, case-control investigations, economic analyses, single-subject experiments; or even qualitative research like narrative case studies. The point is to make a conscientious effort to seek out the highest quality available information and integrate this with your own clinical skills and the clients' values and circumstances in making decisions about potential services to offer. It may be that the highest quality evidence suggests one course of action (e.g., cognitive therapy for depression), but your own background provided you with insufficient training in this method to be able to offer it. You can opt to provide something else (e.g., nonspecific supportive counseling), but at least you are doing so with the conscious recognition that this is likely to be a less-than-optimal service for your client. Or you may be prompted on the basis of your analysis of the evidence to seek out additional training and supervision of an evidence-based intervention that your clients may need or to refer your client to a service provider who can better meet the client's needs.

It is widely recognized that many of the psychosocial interventions that are empirically supported are based on studies in which people of color and other historically oppressed groups are underrepresented. This presents us with the problem of generalizing findings obtained from largely Caucasian client samples to these other groups. There is no need to assume that the treatments will be ineffective with other groups, but it is a far better strategy for findings demonstrated to be valid with one group (Caucasians) to have been successfully replicated in other groups (African Americans, Hispanics, etc.). This is slowly being accomplished.

It is also well known that treatments demonstrated to be useful in tightly controlled studies involving clients who meet the diagnostic criteria for only one disorder, with services provided by atypically highly trained and supervised therapists, may not yield similarly positive benefits when implemented in other practice settings. In the real world, services are likely to involve clients who meet the diagnostic criteria for multiple disorders, who experience impoverished environments, have additional stressors impacting them, who attend appointments less regularly, and who get services from less-than-stellar clinicians. This problem, too, is being vigorously addressed through translational research studies examining the "transportability" of empirically supported services into routine care.

There are also significant gaps in the literature related to the disciplinary contributions specific to social work. In the field of psychotherapy, clinical social workers are the largest discipline providing such services in the United States, with far more practitioners than clinical psychology or psychiatry; yet social workers are sadly underrepresented in terms of designing, conducting, and publishing high-quality outcome studies. There are many reasons for this. Clinical psychology emerged from an academic discipline that had many decades of an experimentalist tradition in its history; whereas social work came from the Settlement House, the church, and the community organization society, not the laboratory. To be recognized as a psychologist, you must have completed a doctorate—in most cases, a research-based doctorate; whereas in social work we made the disciplinary decision to lower-the-bar so to speak, back in the mid-1970s, by admitting BSWs into our professional ranks (prior to that time, a master's degree was required). We continue to wrestle with defining what the profession of social work actually is and who a social worker is, and these issues make it difficult to carve out our discipline's unique niche in the human services and health-care fields (Thyer, 2002). State departments of children and family services rarely have a career ladder specific to BSWs and MSWs and usually open up their child welfare and other human services jobs to persons who have completed a wide array of undergraduate or graduate majors. There is actually very little sound evidence, for example, that BSWs make better child protective service workers than non-BSWs (Perry, 2006a) or that social workers are better supervisors in the human services than persons without the social work degree (Perry, 2006b). We see life coaches, care coordinators, discharge planners, nurses, philosophical counselors, clinical sociologists, and so on, all undertaking tasks formerly largely conducted by members of our profession. All these issues make it difficult to convincingly assert a unique and specific role for social work and social workers. Those who argue that we somehow possess a value base and ethical system that sets us apart from other fields usually make this argument in ignorance of the considerable attention being given to issues of social justice, the alleviation of poverty, and of providing services to historically oppressed groups by psychologists, nurses, and psychiatrists. One has but to compare the massive outreach and service efforts of the APA to the people of New Orleans following Hurricane Katrina, compared to the minimal responses of the much larger NASW, to see that psychologists were walking the walk, not merely talking the talk.

This is not to conclude that the profession of social work is not incredibly valuable. It is. Indeed there are many aspects of our field that are noble and inspiring. But the services we provide and the theories we learn about are primarily shared with, if indeed not derived from, other disciplines. If we are to become more than the "utility players" of the human services, we must take a much more active role as creators and disseminators of the evidence-based knowledge that is increasingly being seen as an important aspect of social care. This leads to the next section.

IMPLICATIONS FOR SOCIAL WORK AT THE MICRO-, MEZZO-, AND MACROLEVELS

What should we do with the information presented thus far? Here are a few suggestions.

Micro- and Mezzolevel Practice

The focus of most of the preceding content has been on micro- and mezzolevel social work practice, interventions with individuals, families, small groups, and agencies (Barker, 2003, p. 272) and the implications of this information should be pretty clear. Individual social work students should regularly seek out the evidentiary foundations of what they are being taught. Politely ask, with a bright smile, the instructors of your direct practice classes if they can point you to any systematic reviews or randomized controlled studies demonstrating that what you are being taught is really capable of helping clients. Honest instructors should be able to do this right away, or do so in a few days, or else forthrightly tell you that there is no such evidence. The intellectually corrupt ones will tell you that randomized controlled studies are incapable of measuring the subtle but nonetheless powerful effects of these interventions and that scientific analyses have little place in the evaluation of social work interventions. The morally corrupt ones will angrily inform you that you have no right to ask such questions and that you should accept what they teach without question, on the basis of their clinical experience and theoretical knowledge. Reinforce with smiles, attention, and words of encouragement, instructor efforts, minimal though they may initially be, to teach about empirically supported treatments and the process of evidence-based practice. And use your course evaluations to provide corresponding feedback, organizing your classmates to do the same.

Established practitioners can investigate the intellectual resources described in this chapter to learn more about empirically supported treatments related to the fields of practice you are engaged in. Obtain empirically supported practice guidelines and treatment manuals and attempt to acquire skills in these interventions. Locate sources of qualified supervision in these methods and consider getting formal advanced training via workshops and continuing education programs. Contact your local NASW chapter and ask them to sponsor CEU programs related to evidence-based practice and empirically supported treatments. Social work faculty who teach direct practice classes should begin integrating the principles and resources described in this chapter into their classroom instruction and clinical supervision. Purge your syllabi of outmoded or superceded theory and replace it with readings and texts related to EBP and empirically supported treatments.

Macrolevel Practice

At the macrolevel, meaning political action, community organizing, public education, and the administration of agencies (Barker, 2003, p. 257), there are a number of possible implications for social work practice. Within our major professional organizations, the NASW could amend its code of ethics to include something along the following lines:

> Clients should be offered as a first choice treatment, interventions with some significant degree of empirical support, where such knowledge exists, and only provided other treatments after such first choice treatments have been given a legitimate trial and shown not to be efficacious.

and

> Clinicians should routinely gather empirical data on clients' relevant behavior, affect, and reports of thoughts, using reliable and valid measures, where such measures have been developed. These measures should be repeated throughout the course of treatment, and used in clinical decision making to supplement professional judgments pertaining to the alteration or termination of treatment. (Thyer, 1995, p. 95)

The NASW could also greatly expand on the laudable standard they established as far back as 1992, in their statement on reparative therapies:

> Proponents of reparative therapies claim—without documentation, many successes. They assert that their processes are supported by conclusive scientific data which are in fact little more than anecdotal. NCOLGI protests these efforts to "convert" people through irresponsible therapies ... empirical research does not demonstrate that ... sexual orientation (heterosexual or homosexual) can be changed through these so-called reparative therapies. (National Committee on Lesbian and Gay Issues, 1992, p. 1)

If one particular therapy is deemed by the NASW as unethical at least in part because it lacks a sufficient empirical foundation, this has the appearance of a precedent-setting standard that could be extended to other, similarly nonempirically supported treatments. It is unclear why gay and lesbian clients should be afforded protection against ineffective treatments and not other social work clientele.

This series of recommendations would involve a two-pronged approach: promoting the use of the empirically supported treatment and discouraging the use of that which has been shown not to be useful. This should be done cautiously. Absence of evidence is not evidence of absence. Many interventions have not yet been adequately tested and may ultimately prove helpful. So an initial focus on treatments that are pretty clearly harmful (e.g., rebirthing therapy, boot camps, primal scream therapy) or useless (thought-field therapy, neurolinguistic programming, therapeutic touch, hypnosis for chronic mental illness, etc.) would be a good way to shape the field.

Another leverage point the NASW could apply, as could the various state licensure boards, is to require the providers of continuing education units for social workers to list the evidentiary foundations supporting the assessment and treatment methods they are disseminating. There is much that is useless and bogus being purveyed by the providers of CEUs, and by declining to endorse these programs, in favor of those with a focus on empirically supported treatments, the entire field would be enhanced.

Apart from the NASW, other social work interest groups could provide education to third-party payers such as insurance companies and managed care firms so that they would no longer reimburse social workers who provided interventions known to be bogus or ineffective. Turning off the funding stream that fertilizes the weeds found in private or agency-based practice would be another useful way to improve the discipline.

The CSWE could revise its accreditation standards mandating, as does psychiatry and clinical psychology, that BSW and MSW students be provided training in empirically supported treatments, and it could lessen its emphasis on teaching theoretical content of dubious validity (Thyer, 1994, 2001). Instead, favor more of a problem-focused approach, wherein students take courses in given areas of practice (e.g., child abuse and neglect, domestic violence, chronic mental illness) and are taught about assessment methods and psychosocial interventions that are empirically supported, irrespective of the theoretical orientation they are derived from. If they are helpful to clients, students should be taught about them. Textbooks should be similarly structured around helpful interventions for specific problems (e.g., O'Hare, 2005; Thyer & Wodarski, 2007), not by an overarching theory or collection of theories.

In general, greater attention needs to be given to training in specific methods of clinical intervention (see Thyer, 2007), as opposed to a generalized model of supportive engagement with clients, focusing solely on skills such as empathy, warmth, genuineness, and unconditional positive regard. This traditional model, based on the naive premise that somehow, with the cheerleading of a supportive social worker, clients will be able to dig deep within themselves to solve their own problems, has been incredibly destructive to the effectiveness and credibility of professional social work. These clinical skills are indeed important and need to be taught and mastered by our students, but they are insufficient preparation by themselves for one to be an effective clinician, absent competence in providing one or more empirically supported treatments effective for clients with specific problems.

Another source of change could involve some benevolent patron underwriting the legal expenses of one or more clients seen by licensed social workers, and who were provided with a nonempirically supported therapy for the treatment of a condition for which one or more empirically supported treatments have been clearly established. These clients would sue their social worker, alleging malpractice in that the social worker failed to provide them (or at least offer) these empirically supported treatments. The patron would provide sufficient funding to ensure that these cases went to court, where they would be hopefully settled in favor of the plaintiff, and thus begin establishing the legal precedent that social work clients should have the right to effective treatment, where it is known to exist (see

Myers & Thyer, 1997). Oddly, and embarrassingly, this standard does not appear to be established at present (see K. Corcoran, 1998).

CONCLUSION

There is much to be positive and optimistic about. Our profession has access to powerful tools for effective social work practice with adults. The evidentiary foundations undergirding major areas of practice are rapidly expanding, and the values of transparency and scientific rigor are assuming an ever-greater importance. These developments are most evident in the fields of mental health and to a lesser extent the general domain of clinical social work. Many long-cherished interventions used within our field are being subjected to rigorous testing. Some are being supported; others are being shown to be of little value; many remain underresearched. These rapidly expanding developments require intellectually nimble social workers committed to a lifetime of professional learning and of keeping abreast with the newest developments. Advances in information technology, such as the computerized searching of journal databases and access via the Internet to international consortia such as the Campbell and Cochrane Collaborations, make it possible for virtually every social worker to remain current and continually refresh his or her repertoire of effective clinical skills. This is not only a good practice for the individual social worker, but essential for the long-term survival of a profession that is being increasingly challenged to demonstrate its capability to prevent and remedy significant interpersonal and societal problems.

At present, faculty in MSW programs reportedly strongly endorse providing students with training in evidence-based practice and in empirically supported treatments (Rubin & Parrish, 2007). Yet, curiously, our MSW programs only rarely provide graduate students with training and clinical supervision in the provision of empirically supported treatments (Bledsoe et al., 2007). Training programs in clinical psychology and psychiatry are doing better in this regard. We can and must improve the empirical foundations of what we teach and practice.

REFERENCES

Barker, R. L. (Ed.). (2003). *The social work dictionary* (5th ed.). Washington, DC: National Association of Social Workers Press.

Bledsoe, S. E., Weissman, M. M., Mullen, E. J., Betts, K., Gameroff, M. J., Verdeli, H., et al. (2007). Empirically supported psychotherapy in social work training programs: Does the definition of evidence matter? *Research on Social Work Practice, 17*, 449–455.

Chambless, D. L., Baker, M. J., Baucom, D. H., Beutler, L. E., Calhoun, K. S., Crits-Critsoph, P., et al. (1998). Update on empirically validated therapies (Pt. II). *Clinical Psychologist, 51*(1), 3–16.

Chambless, D. L., & Ollendick, T. H. (2001). Empirically supported psychological interventions: Controversies and evidence. *Annual Review of Psychology, 52*, 685–716.

Chambless, D. L., Sanderson, W. C., Shoham, V., Bennet Johnson, S., Pope, K. S. Crits-Cristoph, P., et al. (1996). An update on empirically validated therapies. *Clinical Psychologist, 49*(2), 5–18.

Corcoran, J. (2000). *Evidence-based social work with families.* New York: Springer.

Corcoran, K. (1998). Clients without a cause: Is there a legal right to effective treatment? *Research on Social Work Practice, 8*, 589–596.

Cournoyer, B. R. (2004). *The evidence-based social work skills book.* New York: Allyn & Bacon.

Gibbs, L. E. (2003). *Evidence-based practice for the helping professions.* Pacific Grove, CA: Brooks/Cole.

Guyatt, G., & Rennie, D. (Eds.). (2002). *Users' guides to the medical literature: Essentials of evidence-based clinical practice.* Chicago: American Medical Association.

Guyatt, G., & Rennie, D. (Eds.). (2006). *Users' guides to the medical literature: Essentials of evidence-based clinical practice* (2nd ed.). Chicago: American Medical Association.

Hollis, F. (1964). *Casework: A psychosocial therapy.* New York: Columbia University Press.

Howard, M. O., & Jenson, J. M. (1999a). Clinical practice guidelines: Should social work develop them? *Research on Social Work Practice, 9,* 283–301.

Howard, M. O., & Jenson, J. (Eds.). (1999b). Practice guidelines and clinical social work [Special issue]. *Research on Social Work Practice, 9*(3).

Howden-Chapman, P., Matheson, A., Crane, J., Vigers, H., Cunningham, M., Blakely, T., et al. (2007, February 27). Effective of insulating existing houses on health inequality: Cluster randomised study in the community (DOI:10.1136/bmj.39070.573032.80). *British Medical Journal.*

Institute of Medicine. (1990). *Clinical practice guidelines: Directions for a new program.* Washington, DC: National Academy Press.

Moore, A., & McQuay, H. (2006). *Bandolier's litte book of making sense of the medical evidence.* New York: Oxford University Press.

Myers, L. L., & Thyer, B. A. (1997). Should social work clients have the right to effective treatment? *Social Work, 42,* 127–145.

Nathan, P. E., & Gorman, J. M. (Eds.). (1998). *A guide to treatments that work.* New York: Oxford University Press.

Nathan, P. E., & Gorman, J. M. (Eds.). (2002). *A guide to treatments that work* (2nd ed.). New York: Oxford University Press.

Nathan, P. E., & Gorman, J. M. (Eds.). (2007). *A guide to treatments that work* (3rd ed.). New York: Oxford University Press.

National Committee on Lesbian and Gay Issues. (1992). *Position statement on reparative therapies.* Washington, DC: National Association of Social Workers Press.

Norcross, J. C., Beutler, L. E., & Levant, R. F. (Eds.). (2006). *Evidence-based practices in mental health: Debate and dialogue on the fundamental questions.* Washington, DC: American Psychological Association.

O'Hare, T. (2005). *Evidence-based practices for social workers: An interdisciplinary approach.* Chicago: Lyceum Books.

Perry, R. E. (2006a). Do social workers make better child welfare workers than non-social workers? *Research on Social Work Practice, 16,* 392–405.

Perry, R. E. (2006b). Education and child welfare supervisor performance: Does a social work degree matter? *Research on Social Work Practice, 16,* 591–604.

Persons, J. B., Thase, M. E., & Crits-Christoph, P. (1996). The role of psychotherapy in the treatment of depression. *Archives of General Psychiatry, 53,* 283–290.

Roberts, A. R., & Yeager, K. R. (Eds.). (2006). *Foundations of evidence-based social work practice.* New York: Oxford University Press.

Rosen, A., & Proctor, E. (Eds.). (2003). *Developing practice guidelines for social work interventions: Issues, methods, and research agenda.* New York: Columbia University Press.

Rubin, A., & Parrish, D. (2007). Views of evidence-based practice among faculty in MSW programs: A national survey. *Research on Social Work Practice,* 110–122.

Sanderson, W. C., & Woody, S. (1995). *Manuals for empirically validated treatments: A project of the Task Force on Psychological Interventions, Division of Clinical Psychology, American Psychological Association.* Retrieved March 13, 2007, from www.apa.org/divisions/div12/est/MANUALSforevt.html.

Seligman, M. E. (1998). Foreword: A Purpose. In P. Nathan & J. Gorman (Eds.), *A guide to treatments that work* (pp. v–vii). New York: Oxford University Press.

Social Welfare Group, Campbell Collaboration. (n.d.). *What is a systematic review?* Retrieved March 16, 2007, from www.campbellcollaboration.org/SWCG/reviews/asp.

Steering Committee on Practice Guidelines. (2006, May). *Practice guideline development process.* Washington, DC: American Psychiatric Association. Retrieved March 16, 2007, from www.psych.org/psych_pract/treatg/pg/prac_guide.cfm/.

Strauss, S. E., Richardson, W. S., Glasziou, P., & Haynes, R. B. (2005). *Evidence-based medicine: How to practice and teach EBM* (3rd ed.). New York: Elsevier.

Task Force on Promotion and Dissemination of Psychological Procedures. (1995). Training in and dissemination of empirically-validated psychological treatments. *Clinical Psychologist, 48*(1), 3–23.

Thyer, B. A. (1994). Are theories for practice necessary? *Journal of Social Work Education, 30,* 147–151.

Thyer, B. A. (1995). Promoting an empiricist agenda within the human services: An ethical and humanistic imperative. *Journal of Behavior Therapy and Experimental Psychiatry, 26,* 93–98.

Thyer, B. A. (2001). What is the role of theory in research on social work practice? *Journal of Social Work Education, 37,* 9–25.

Thyer, B. A. (2002). Developing discipline-specific knowledge for social work: Is it possible? *Journal of Social Work Education, 38,* 101–113.

Thyer, B. A. (2003). Social work should help develop interdisciplinary evidence-based practice guidelines, not discipline-specific ones. In A. Rosen & E. Proctor (Eds.), *Developing practice guidelines for social work interventions: Issues, methods, and research agenda* (pp. 128–139). New York: Columbia University Press.

Thyer, B. A. (2007). Social work education and clinical learning: Towards evidence-based practice. *Clinical Social Work Journal, 35,* 25–32.

Thyer, B. A., & Kazi, M. A. F. (Eds.). (2004). *International perspectives on evidence-based practice in social work.* Birmingham, England: Venture Press.

Thyer, B. A., & Wodarski, J. S. (Eds.). (2007). *Social work in mental health: An evidence-based approach.* Hoboken, NJ: Wiley.

Van Hasselt, V. B., & Hersen, M. (Eds.). (1996). *Sourcebook of psychological treatment manuals for adult disorders.* New York: Plenum Press.

Weisz, J. R. (2004). *Psychotherapy for children and adolescents: Evidence-based treatments and case examples.* Cambridge: Cambridge University Press.

Woody, S. R., & Sanderson, W. C. (1998). *Manuals for empirically supported treatments: 1998 update.* Retrieved March 17, 2007, from www.apa.org/divisions/div12/est/manual60.pdf.

Woody, S. R., Weisz, J., & McLean, C. (2005). Empirically supported treatments: Ten years later. *Clinical Psychologist, 58*(4), 5–11.

Chapter 17 —————————————————————

ASSESSMENT OF THE ELDERLY

Gregory J. Paveza

Comprehensive Geriatric Assessment (CGA) has emerged as an important method for helping social workers address the needs of older adults particularly as the number of older adults and their need for services continues to grow within the United States.

Comprehensive Geriatric Assessment is a process of engaging in a total evaluation of older adults. It requires the practitioner to gather information in multiple areas of client functioning including medical history, cognitive status, emotional well-being, the ability to perform activities of daily living (ADLs) and instrumental activities of daily living (IADLs), the person's social support system, the physical environment in which the person lives, and many other areas of the older person's life. Such a process requires that the social work practitioner have a broad command of all areas of aging practice. One must understand how to effectively gather medical information, assess current cognitive status, the emotional well-being of the client, ADLs and IADLs, the person's social support system, and to conduct an effective and thorough assessment of the older adult's physical environment (Gallo & Bogner, 2006). Finally, the social work practitioner must be able to comprehensively link the findings from the assessment to an intervention plan for the individual client (Gallo, Fulmer, Paveza, & Reichel, 2000).

Since the process of comprehensive geriatric assessment is not a single subject, but rather an amalgamation of several areas, this chapter of necessity addresses both the broad subject as well as the specific elements that comprise a comprehensive geriatric assessment. This chapter details a process for gathering and organizing information rather than a specific intervention or method of engaging in practice. As such, this chapter is organized differently than other chapters in this book. This chapter reviews each of the elements that comprise a comprehensive geriatric assessment, discusses some of the instruments that may be of assistance for obtaining information in that area of the assessment, summarizes some of the unique issues encompassed in that area of the assessment process, and looks at the import of the area for arriving at a care plan. The chapter concludes with a discussion concerning the integration of the elements of the assessment into a whole that informs a recommended care plan for the client and a review of the literature on effectiveness of the process.

The elements that are recommended for inclusion in a comprehensive geriatric assessment have broadened over the past several years. This is evident when one reviews any text on geriatric assessment with multiple editions. A perfect example is the *Handbook of Geriatric Assessment*. The first edition, published in 1988, consisted of 10 chapters totaling 231 pages of text and index, with a single contributed chapter (Gallo, Reichel, & Andersen, 1988). By the second edition, published in 1995, the book still had 10 chapters, but it had expanded to 257 pages of text and index, with two contributed chapters (Gallo, Reichel, & Andersen, 1995). The third edition of the *Handbook* consisted of 13 chapters with 361 pages of text and index, with five contributed chapters (Gallo et al., 2000). The latest edition of the *Handbook,* the fourth edition, has expanded to 20 chapters with 473 pages of text and index, and 18 of the chapters include authors other than the editors of the book (Gallo, Bogner, Fulmer, & Paveza, 2006). These changes in the *Handbook* suggest that both the amount and complexity of information has so expanded that no single group of authors can adequately address the topic.

As stated at the beginning of this chapter, comprehensive geriatric assessment is not an intervention technique, but rather it is a process for gathering comprehensive information on older adults within the context of the older person's environment. Given the breadth and depth of this biopsychosocial environmentally cognizant approach to gathering information on older adults, one might suspect that the approach was developed by social workers to address their work with older adults. Unfortunately, there is no substantive evidence to support this contention. Rather, this approach seems to be built on the experiences of early geriatric physicians. They discovered that when working with older adults in in-patient settings, information beyond that of the medical history and presenting medical problems was required in order to effectively create a treatment plan for their older patients (Gallo et al., 1988).

HISTORICAL BACKGROUND

Comprehensive geriatric assessment is a direct outgrowth of the earlier movement within geriatric medicine to develop Comprehensive Geriatric Assessment Units (GAUs). GAUs identified the need for a comprehensive assessment process usually beginning with a physical exam and medical history and then adding information on functional status, that is, the ability to perform basic activities of daily living, mental health, size of the social support network, and interactions that support network, economic needs, and environmental considerations (L. A. Rubenstein, 1995). These domains with some modifications continue to remain the focus of comprehensive geriatric assessment (Mouton & Esparza, 2006). A comprehensive assessment should consist of assessment in at least six areas: mental status, functional assessment, social and environmental assessment, nutritional and health practices review, medical history and treatments, and assessment of emotional well-being (Paveza, 1993). The consistency across authors and across disciplines in identifying the areas essential to the assessment process suggests that there is a generally accepted concept of the information that needs to be gathered to adequately address the care needs of the older adult patient whether that person is in the hospital or residing in the community.

Moving from this historical perspective, let us begin a more in-depth discussion of the elements comprising the assessment process. Each of these elements is discussed from the perspective of how the element helps us understand the current biopsychosocial status of the older adult, techniques and instruments the practitioner can use to assess an element of the comprehensive assessment, potential problems with using some of the discussed instruments, and the relationship of that element of the assessment to care planning for the older adult.

available research evidence in their practice guidelines, the reader is still left unclear as to the extent expert opinion was blended with a dispassionate appraisal of empirical research. This renders the American Psychiatric Association's practice guidelines less credible in the view of those who subscribe to more of a science-orientation as opposed to an artistic perspective on practice.

One problem that psychologists in particular have noted with respect to the American Psychiatric Association's practice guidelines is that they seemingly overemphasize the use of psychotropic medications at the expense of possibly more efficacious psychosocial treatments (see Persons, Thase, & Crits-Christoph, 1996). This is perhaps understandable since the psychiatrist's unique contribution to the care of the mentally ill largely resides in his or her ability to provide biological assessments and treatments, whereas the practice of psychotherapy is provided by all of the other legally regulated mental health professions. Does the field of psychiatry's considerable investment (sometimes literal) in psychopharmacological treatments affect the therapy recommendations found in its practice guidelines? Does the field of clinical psychology's investment in psychological treatments bias its appraisals of the research literature so they it favors nonpharmacological interventions? Like Casablanca's Inspector Reynaud finding out that gambling was taking place in *Rick's Café Americain,* you, too, might be shocked to discover that pecuniary considerations could influence the crafting of scientific documents. Shocked perhaps, but also not so naive as to dismiss the possibility.

Various writers have suggested that clinical social work should undertake the development of practice guidelines crafted by social workers for use in social work treatment. This strikes me as absurd, and I have said so previously, in more modest language (Thyer, 2003). We have psychiatrists creating practice guidelines for help with people with schizophrenia, psychologists are doing the same thing, as are the nurses, and so on. What seems more legitimate and useful is for social workers to proactively advocate for having clinical social workers well represented on expert panels that craft *interdisciplinary practice guidelines,* not disciplinary ones. No single field, certainly not social work, can provide genuinely comprehensive care for adults with mental disorders. Psychiatry, psychology, nursing, and clinical social work all have useful and sometimes admittedly overlapping roles to play. Creating interdisciplinary practice guidelines for use by *all* the major players and professions, ones that take into proper and judicious account the biological and the psychosocial research literature, would seem far more useful for adults with mental illnesses that having distinct disciplinary practice guidelines for each of the major fields.

Howard and Jenson (1999b) list a wide array of resources that social workers can consult in tracking down clinical practice guidelines, but to reiterate, the methodological quality of practice guidelines is uneven. Some are based solely on expert consensus and are not the usual resource one would seek out for state-of-the-art-and-science information on helping adults.

Institute of Medicine

The Institute of Medicine (IOM) is a branch of the National Academies, federal entities charged with providing the government with science-based, independent, and authoritative advice on matters related to biomedical science, medicine, and health (see www.iom.edu). A very few social workers belong to the IOM, including Paula Allen-Meares, dean of the

ELEMENTS OF THE COMPREHENSIVE ASSESSMENT

I have already suggested that the comprehensive assessment process should address some common areas, including current medical problems and medical history, assessment of the person's ability to perform the basic activities of daily living, assessment of emotional problems, and social and economic issues (Gallo et al., 1995; Mouton & Esparza, 2006; Paveza, 1993; L. A. Rubenstein, 1995). Beyond these basic elements, authors differ on the other elements to be included in the assessment. Several authors when discussing the assessment of functional status also suggest that in addition to basic activities of daily living that the assessment of functional status must include the instrumental or independent activities of daily living (Older Americans Resources and Services [OARS] Methodology, 1978). The addition of assessment for elder mistreatment has also recently been suggested as important to a thorough and complete assessment (Fulmer & O'Malley, 1987; Gallo et al., 2000; VanderWeerd, Firpo, Fulmer, & Paveza, 2006). The need to assess values and the impact of those values on "Do Not Resuscitate" directives and durable power of attorney for health care have also been added to the growing list of items to be covered in the assessment process (Doukas, McCullough, & Crane, 2006). Additional areas suggested for incorporation into the process include older adults' ability to continue to drive, their use of alcohol and drugs, and pain assessment (Carr & Rebok, 2006; Richardson, 2006; Zanjani & Oslin, 2006). Some of these special areas of concern were originally considered to be part of one of the broader categories such as medical history, social history or environmental assessment, the assessment for elder mistreatment being a perfect example. In an earlier edition of the *Handbook of Geriatric Assessment,* the discussion of elder mistreatment is included in the chapter on social assessment, but in the latest edition it merits a chapter of its own (Gallo et al., 2000; VanderWeerd et al., 2006). While these special areas are addressed in this chapter, most are included under broader headings to more appropriately place them in the context of the assessment process. This chapter also discusses the elements of comprehensive geriatric assessment using a modification of my previously mentioned framework. The elements of the assessment are discussed under six broad areas: mental status, functional assessment, medical history, and treatments including nutrition and health practices review, emotional/psychological well-being, and social and environmental assessment (Paveza, 1993).

MENTAL STATUS

The assessment of mental status should be one of the initial components, if not the initial component, of the comprehensive assessment. While the social work practitioner needs to be cognizant that clients may be somewhat taken aback by the introduction of this item as the first element of the interview, I have argued consistently that after establishing initial rapport, starting the remainder of the assessment process with the mental status review is essential to avoid engaging in an information gathering process that could yield little or no useful information while taking up a significant number of both the client's and practitioner's time and money (Paveza, Cohen, Blaser, & Hagopian, 1990; Paveza, Prohaska, Hagopian, & Cohen, 1989).

Gathering information on a client's mental status has generally been described as requiring the practitioner to assess at a minimum the client's level of consciousness, her or his orientation to time and place, and her or his attention and memory (Gallo & Wittink, 2006a). Additional areas that may be covered include information concerning language, the ability to engage in abstract thinking and constructional ability (Chodosh, 2001; Gallo & Wittink, 2006a; Scalmati & Smyth, 2001). Each of the domains covered in a mental status exam can provide important information concerning the client's ability to provide historically accurate information, to engage in conversations that require abstract thinking, and to consent to or reject care plans or elements of care plans (Paveza, 1993; Paveza, Cohen, Hagopian, et al., 1990; Paveza et al., 1989).

Gathering mental status information has become relatively standardized. This means that a social work practitioner can quickly ask the questions needed to obtain information in this area. Included among the instruments commonly used are the Folstein Mini-Mental Status Exam (the MMSE; Folstein, Folstein, & McHugh, 1975), Pheiffer's Short Portable Mental Status Questionnaire (SPMSQ; Pheiffer, 1975) as well as the six-item Orientation-Memory-Concentration Test (Katzman et al., 1983). Other tests that can provide additional information are category fluency sets and the clock-drawing test. These two instruments provide some additional benefits over those more typically used for screening, with the set test generally being seen as less offensive to older adults than the more traditional screens (Gallo & Wittink, 2006a. Moreover, the clock-drawing test can provide useful information about the ability of the older adult to transition between abstract and concrete thinking and his or her use of judgment as he or she draws the clock and puts in the required elements (Gallo & Wittink, 2006a). Mental status screening has been well researched, and a general description of some of the problematic issues with these screens can be found in the *Handbook of Geriatric Assessment,* fourth edition (Gallo & Wittink, 2006a), the *Geropsychology Assessment Resource Guide* (National Center for Cost Containment, 1993), and *Measuring Health: A Guide to Rating Scales and Questionnaires* (McDowell & Newell, 1996).

In general, issues of importance when interpreting a mental status screen focus on the level of formal education of the older adult, with those having less formal education often scoring lower than their actual level of cognitive functioning and those with high levels of education often appearing to do better than the actual level of cognitive functioning (Gallo & Wittink, 2006a). For this reason, as well as others discussed in the literature, the clinician should never use the results of any single mental status assessment to arrive at a diagnosis of dementia, nor should a client accept this diagnosis based solely on a mental status screen. The diagnosis of dementia must be arrived at in a manner that addresses all criteria established either in the *Diagnostic and Statistical Manual of Mental Disorders*, fourth edition (American Psychiatric Association, 1994) or in the NINCDS-ADRDA Consensus Criteria (McKhann et al., 1984). The purpose of the mental status exam is to assist the clinician in determining whether the client can provide useful information for planning, consent to treatment, and for planning care and whether the client needs referral for a complete neuropsychological exam.

FUNCTIONAL ASSESSMENT

Probably the most critical element of the assessment is determining the client's functional ability. Functional ability is the capacity of the individual to perform certain personal care behaviors that are seen as essential to being able to care for him- or herself independently in a community living environment. The original six behaviors seen as essential to being able to function in the community, and usually referred to as activities of daily living, were feeding, bathing, grooming, dressing, continence, toileting, and transfer (Gallo & Paveza, 2006; Katz, Ford, Moskowitz, Jackson, & Jaffe, 1963). Eventually to these six behaviors were added an additional set of behaviors usually referred to as the instrumental activities of daily living. These behaviors were seen as more complex and demanding than the ADLs but still important for a person who wanted to reside independently in the community (OARS Methodology, 1978). The behaviors initially included in the IADLs were telephone usage, the ability to travel around town, go shopping, prepare his or her own meals, do housework, take needed medications, and manage his or her own money. While over time this initial set of IADLs has been modified for various reasons (Fillenbaum, 1995; Paveza Cohen, Blaser, et al., 1990; Paveza et al., 1989), in general the behaviors included in the IADLs have remained relatively stable.

As with the other areas of the comprehensive assessment process, a number of different standardized instruments have been developed to measure either separately or in combination ADLs and IADLs. These assessment instruments use different metrics to arrive at the determination of functional ability, but all offer a quick and easy method to obtain this information (Fillenbaum, 1995; Katz et al., 1963; Paveza et al., 1989). Some, such as the Direct Assessment of Functioning (DAF) which was developed for use with dementia patients (Lowenstein et al., 1989), were designed for use with specific types of clients.

The importance of a well-conducted functional assessment cannot be overstated. The measure of functional ability has been shown to be the best single predictor of cost of community-based services (Paveza, Mensah, Cohen, Williams, & Jankowski, 1998) and is the essential component for developing a care plan for that identifies those client behaviors most likely requiring intervention (Gallo & Paveza, 2006; Paveza et al., 1989).

The assessment of mental status and functional status set the first two elements of the assessment process. With these two elements completed, the next most logical step is to gather medical history and information on nutritional and health practices.

MEDICAL HISTORY AND NUTRITIONAL AND HEALTH BEHAVIORS ASSESSMENT

The next elements of the comprehensive assessment focus on obtaining an accurate medical history and gathering information about the person's nutritional well-being and other health practices that may impact the client's well-being or quality of life. The medical history needs to gather information about both current and past medical conditions. One of the easiest ways to obtain information on medical conditions is to use a body-systems approach. Information concerning both past and current medical conditions for each of the body's systems serves as a reference point for a set of questions about various medical conditions that might occur in that bodily system. One seeks information then on the circulatory system, for example, by asking questions that address likely medical conditions a client may have or have had, such as hypertension, angina, heart attack, and other diseases of the circulatory system. By taking this structured approach to obtaining medical history, it is less likely that the clinician will forget to ask questions about likely medical conditions or that a client will forget to provide information on a specific illness (Paveza et al., 1989). Included as part of gathering information about medical conditions is obtaining information about the medications that are being taken. This includes both physician-prescribed medications as well as all over-the-counter medications and includes vitamin and mineral supplements, herbal and other homeopathic remedies, aspirin and other nonsteroidal anti-inflammatory agents (NSAIDS), cold and flu medications, and anything else that the client may use on a regular basis. It is important to recognize, however, that many clients may be unsure about which medication is for which medical condition. To assist the client in providing and the social work practitioner in obtaining accurate information in this area, it is often helpful to work with the client to complete a drug inventory.

The drug inventory is conducted by asking the client to bring all prescribed medications, over-the-counter medications, herbal medicines, and vitamin and mineral supplements to a common area. When assembled, the clinician first reviews all of the prescribed medications, writes down the name of the medication, the date that it was prescribed, and the doctor who prescribed it. Then all other medications and supplements are recorded. After the completion of the interview, the clinician should work with a knowledgeable pharmacist to ensure that there are no potential interactions either between the prescribed medications or between any of the prescribed medications and the other medications and supplements taken. Should potential interactions be discovered, the clinician should contact the client or caregiver and raise the concern with them as well as including this information in the care plan.

Having completed the medical history and drug inventory, it is also important that the clinician gather information concerning nutritional status and health practices. A simple procedure for obtaining information on nutritional status is to use the Nutritional Screening Initiative Checklist. This simple 14-item questionnaire gathers information about issues that impact older adults' ability to stay nutritionally healthy including financial, emotional, and logistic ability to identify, purchase, and prepare appropriate foods as well as identifying the potential impact of medications and psychological illness on food intake (Wallace, Shea, & Guttman, 2006). In addition to the nutrition screening, it is important for the clinician to seek information from the client concerning the use of alcohol, smoking behavior, the amount of exercise engaged in, whether he or she is experiencing any problems with sleep, and whether the older adult has been able to obtained various recommended immunizations. Each of these areas has the potential to impact both the older adult's risk of mortality as well as his or her quality of life. An area that is often overlooked, but needs to be included in this portion of the assessment is the current sexual activity and practices of the older adult. This area is often overlooked because of the clinician's discomfort in seeking this type of information from the older adult. Yet, unless some time is spent talking about this important area of functioning—an area of potential emotional distress and risk-taking behavior in some older adults—will be missed (Nicklin, 2006).

The clinician should also include in this section an assessment of pain. Many older adults experience pain from the same causes as younger adults, to which can be added the pain impact of many chronic illnesses. While it was once believed that older adults did not experience pain with the same intensity as younger adults, recent literature suggests this is not true. Moreover, older adults are often given the impression that they should be able to tolerate the pain they are experiencing based on this mistaken notion that their qualitative perception of pain is diminished. Simple assessments of pain include the Numeric Rating Scale, in which a client is asked to rate his or her pain on a scale from 0 to 10, with 0 equaling "no pain" and 10 equaling "the worst pain the person can imagine." A Visual Analog Scale in which a 10-cm line is shown to the client, with one end being labeled "No Pain" and the other end labeled as "Worst Imaginable Pain" on which the client then indicates where his or her pain falls is another alternative for quickly assessing the current level of pain experienced by the client. While both of these measures are useful for monitoring pain because they can be used to detect small changes in the client's experience of pain, it is important to remember that these scales will not provide information on changes in psychological distress or physical function that may be caused by pain (Richardson, 2006).

To assess pain in areas other than intensity, one must consider the use of a multidimensional pain scale such as the McGill Pain Questionnaire (MPQ). This instrument assesses pain in sensory, affective, and evaluative areas. While the MPQ has been used in a variety of settings, it can take up to 20 minutes to complete and may not be appropriate for use during the initial assessment of the client. Rather, the clinician may wish to indicate that as part of the care plan that a more comprehensive assessment of the client's pain be conducted with referral to a pain clinic.

Having completed this portion of the medical history and assessment of health behaviors and practices, it is important for the clinician to include recommendations in the care plan that will help mitigate or remove the impact of any deficiencies (Wallace et al., 2006).

The final area to cover as part of the medical history and assessment of health behaviors and practices is an assessment of emotional well-being.

ASSESSMENT OF EMOTIONAL WELL-BEING

The assessment of emotional well-being as part of the comprehensive assessment should focus at a minimum on the presence of depression and/or anxiety. However, if at all possible, the clinician should explore a range of psychiatric symptoms and the psychiatric illnesses associated with those symptoms.

The assessment for depression in older adults is probably the most easily accomplished because of the amount of clinical anecdotal information on the frequency of depression in older adults, the research suggesting that rates of depression in older adults are higher than for younger populations, or the belief that depression is considered to be among the more treatable of emotional conditions experienced by older adults (Gallo & Wittnik, 2006b). Regardless of the reason for this focus on depression, it is important that it be assessed. Because of the amount of attention paid to depression, the availability of aids to assist in determining the presence of depression is extensive. A discussion of those aids occurs in almost any book addressing the care of older adults, as well as those that specifically address mental health issues with this population (Blazer, 1995, 1998; Chiu & Ames, 1994; Gallo et al., 2006; Kurlowicz, 2001, Schneider, Reynolds, Lebowitz, & Friedhoff, 1994). What the clinician must remember is that whichever aid he or she chooses, the focus should be on ease and simplicity of administration during an extended information gathering process.

Assessment of anxiety is also important with older adults, and Blazer (1998) probably provides one of the more cogent discussions of the need for assessing this area of emotional well-being in older adults. One particular reason for assessing anxiety is the fact that in older adults depression and anxiety can present with similar symptom pictures. Thus, an appropriate differential diagnosis assessment of both becomes important (Blazer, 1998; Diffenbach, 2001).

Additionally, should the older adult present with symptoms or describe symptoms to the social work practitioner that suggests the presence of other psychiatric illnesses, the clinician should assess for that emotional problem as well, or at the very least refer the older adult for a complete psychiatric evaluation.

Once the clinician has completed gathering information on medical history, nutritional status, health practice and behaviors, and emotional well-being, the focus of the interview should turn to obtaining information on the social, economic and environmental, well-being of the older adult.

ASSESSMENT OF SOCIAL, ECONOMIC AND ENVIRONMENTAL, WELL-BEING

The assessment of the social, environmental, and economic well-being of the older adult client as part of a comprehensive geriatric assessment encompasses a wide range of topics. It is also during this part of the interview that the clinician will interview those providing care to the older adult to determine the stability of the caregiving relationships and the stress that those providing care may be experiencing (Morano & Morano, 2006). This is the area of assessment where the social work practitioner is likely to be most comfortable since it mirrors those areas of assessment in which the social worker has received extensive training and had the most practice experience.

Social Assessment

The focus of the social assessment should be on both the extent of the social system or social network that surrounds the older adult and on the quality of that system. The clinician needs to determine the number of persons who make up the support system; the number of persons in the support system that the client identifies as significant; the relationship to the older adult of each person who is identified as significant; and the amount, intensity, and quality of contact that the older adult has with those as identified as significant. Some sense of the amount and quality of contacts with those identified as less significant should also be determined. The clinician needs to particularly identify those serving as caregivers to the older adult and determine the amount of care that each is providing. Once this information has been obtained from the client, the clinician should seek permission from the client to, at a minimum, meet and talk with those providing care.

Interaction with the caregivers should focus on the medical conditions, ADLs, IADLs, and other areas where care is provided, the amount of care required by the client in terms of hours per day, how the caregiving load is distributed among the various caregivers, the extent to which each caregiver experiences providing care as a burden, and the degree to which each of the caregivers derives satisfaction from the caregiving experience. Morano and Morano (2006) provide an excellent discussion of these elements of social assessment.

Unique areas included with the social assessment of older adults include specific assessment for the presence of elder mistreatment, assessment of spiritual well-being, and values clarification to assist with advanced directives. The assessment for elder mistreatment should focus on determining whether the older adult has been or is the victim of physical abuse, caregiver or self-neglect, psychological abuse, and financial exploitation

(VanderWeerd et al., 2006). Assessing for the possibility of elder mistreatment is particularly important when conducting an assessment where the older adult has a dementing illness because the research suggests that the presence of elder mistreatment in these families is significantly higher than in the general population (Paveza et al., 1992).

In addition to assessing for elder mistreatment, the clinician should spend some time assessing the spiritual well-being of the older adult. This is a time in the older adult's life when he or she may rekindle his or her spirituality. Other older adults, who may have always been spiritually active, find themselves cut off from those activities that have been part of their spiritual life (Morano & Morano, 2006). For this reason it is important to determine previous level of spiritual activity, current level of activity, and desired level of activity, as well as some understanding of the general importance of spiritual beliefs and activity in the older adult's life. Building on this, the clinician should determine whether there has been a change in the level of activity, information concerning the older adult's perception of the importance of such activity in his or her life, and any impact that a change in participation may be having on the older adult's quality of life (Morano & Morano, 2006).

The exploration of the importance of spirituality in the older adult's life can also serve as a good starting point for a discussion of values and a clarification of values related to the older adult's wishes concerning end-of-life care. What are the older adult's beliefs concerning the use of heroic measures to being kept alive, are there circumstances where the older adult would not wish to be resuscitated, what are they specifically? It is also important to explore whether the older adult has designated health-care surrogates and whether the appropriate documents are in place to permit his or her wishes concerning end-of-life health care to be acted on. It is important to determine if the older adult has shared with the health-care surrogates his or her wishes about health-care choices so that if the older adult is no longer able to make those decisions the health-care surrogate can effectively act for the older adults.

If this discussion has not occurred, then the information obtained during this part of the assessment can be used as part of the care-planning process to engage family members around these wishes and to have everyone who might have an interest in the well-being of the older adult clearly aware of what the person's wishes are concerning end-of-life care. In far too many instances, the older adult may have in place a "Do Not Resuscitate" document, a durable power of attorney for health care and possibly for finances, and a living will; but the older adult has never had a conversation with family members about these things. With a lack of clear direction from the older adult, family members often end up disagreeing about the type and level of care to be provided. Significant animosity can and does develop in families around such decisions often resulting in lifelong disruptions in family relationships. With a little planning and preparation, the older adult can be assisted by the clinician to engage with other members of the family about the specific type and level of care he or she desires under various circumstances. This information can then be reduced to a written document that is provided to all relevant members of the family. While not a perfect solution, it is likely to reduce the frustration that family members experience when having to make health-care decisions for their parents or siblings (Doukas et al., 2006).

With the completion of the assessment of the social network and related elements, the clinician can turn his or her focus to the final two areas of the assessment process, economic well-being and environmental assessment.

Economic Well-Being

Assessment of economic well-being involves not only determining how much income the older adult has, but also the number of persons dependent either completely or in part on that income. But economic well-being goes beyond a simple accounting of income and those dependent on it. The assessment needs to determine what demands are placed on that income in terms of expenditures and whether the older adult perceives that income to be sufficient to meet his or her needs and those of the persons dependent on that income (Fillenbaum, 1988; Morano & Morano, 2006). A thorough review of the older adult's economic well-being permits the clinician to have a clear sense of what types of economic assistance the older adult might need and how willing to accept help the person is.

Environmental Assessment

The final area for review in the comprehensive assessment is the assessment of the older adult's physical living environment. This requires the clinician to visit the place where the older adult lives, whether this is an independent living situation, an assisted living facility, or a long-term care facility. If the clinician is conducting an assessment prior to a hospital discharge, it will be important for the clinician to consider making a visit to the place to which the older adult will be initially discharged and also to the place where the client will permanently live, if it is different.

Environmental assessment should include a complete tour of the residence, with the clinician paying particular attention to elements in the environment that may impact on the quality of life for the older adult or pose a physical impediment or hazard for the older adult. Elements that the clinician needs to observe, for instance, are the presence of hand-rails and grab-bars in bathing and toileting areas, presence of stairways and how often they must be used by the older adult. Additionally, the clinician should note the presence of throw rugs and/or electrical extensions that may pose a hazard to the older adult with mobility problems. Attention should be paid to whether heating, cooling, and ventilation are adequate for both summer and winter, whether lighting is adequate to permit objects to be seen and recognized, whether knobs on faucets can be turned easily and water temperature adjusted without the older adult being scalded or burned, and whether door knobs can be easily opened and closed as well as some general sense of the atmosphere of the living environment. Morano and Morano provide an excellent checklist in the *Handbook of Geriatric Assessment*, fourth edition (Morano & Morano, 2006). A consideration during this review should be determining the number of persons who occupy the physical environment. The clinician needs to determine whether there is ample room for all to live adequately and for all to have some privacy when needed.

Once the clinician has completed the review of the older adult's actual living quarters, attention needs to be directed to the surrounding environment. Things to be considered include the safety of the neighborhood, ease and access to transportation including a through review of whether the older adult is still driving, and whether this is still in the older adult's best interest (Carr & Rebok, 2006; Morano & Morano, 2006). Other items of interest should be the availability of sidewalks and their state of repair in relation to the impact this might have on the older adult's mobility. Depending on the information obtained during the review of the client's total environment, important recommendations may need to be included in the care plan concerning modifications to the living environment and its surroundings, the older adult's ability to continue driving, and transportation alternatives that can help ensure that the older adult can obtain food, pay bills, and keep doctor's appointments (Carr & Rebok, 2006).

THE CARE PLAN

On conclusion of the assessment process, the clinician needs to compile a complete report that summarizes all of the relevant findings from the assessment. What specifically should be included in the report will depend on what the clinician uncovers during the assessment process. At a minimum, information from all of the areas explored should be included in the care plan including findings on mental status, functional ability, medical history, nutrition and health practices, social network, economic well-being, and the living environment. The plan should report on the older adult's ability to function in the community and on the older adult's quality of life as well as provide information that supports the recommendations for services or assistance. A person reading the report should be able to connect any intervention recommended as part of the care plan to a clearly stated finding from the assessment process by referencing specific links to elements of the assessment (Gallo et al., 2000). The format of the report should be such that both a layperson, most likely the older adult, the caregiver, or some other family member, as well as paraprofessionals working in the health-care and social service fields and professionals working in a variety of medical care and social service settings can all easily understand the recommendations and the information that brought the clinician to those recommendations. Such a report will make it easier for the clinician to negotiate and advocate for the older adult as the clinician seeks appropriate services for the older adult.

In making recommendations, the clinician needs to be prepared to draw from a wide range of potential interventions particularly when working with community-dwelling older adults. Recommendations might include education for family caregivers to assist them with improving their skills in caring for the older adult, family counseling to help the family cope with the stress of their situation, community-based health and social services including home health care, adult day care, and other services. Also included in the services to be considered is placement in either an assisted-living facility or other more intense long-term care living arrangement. The clinician needs to be prepared to support and assist the older adult and the family members as they review the recommendations and make their choices. The clinician must always remember that the ultimate choice in selecting interventions belongs to the older adult and those providing care to that older adult—not to the person doing the assessment and making recommendations.

CONCLUSION

In concluding this chapter, I wish to briefly discuss the literature that provides some insight into the effectiveness of comprehensive geriatric assessment. Findings concerning the effectiveness of comprehensive geriatric assessment have been mixed. Several studies have raised question about the effectiveness of comprehensive geriatric assessment, with Ruben and colleagues (Ruben et al., 1995) clearly showing that such assessments did not improve the health or survival of hospitalized geriatric patients and Siu and his coworkers showing that assessments carried out prior to hospital discharge did not improve outcomes for frail elderly (Siu et al., 1996). On the other hand, Rubenstein and his fellow researchers, Struck and associates, Alessi and her colleagues, and Naylor and associates all provide evidence for the effectiveness of comprehensive assessment in improving outcomes, delaying disability in older adults, helping to identify new problems when assessment is repeated annually, and in fewer recurring hospitalizations (Alessi et al., 1997; Naylor et al., 1999; L. Z. Rubenstein, Stuck, Siu, & Wieland, 1991; Stuck, Zwahlen, et al., 1995). The meta-analysis of several studies clearly suggests that while the evidence might be divided, the majority of the studies included in the meta-analysis and the meta-analysis itself concludes that comprehensive geriatric assessment enhances implementation of care recommendations and client adherence to those recommendations (Stuck, Wieland, Rubenstein, Siu, & Adams, 1995).

Conducting a comprehensive geriatric assessment as described here is likely to improve the care provided to older adult clients and result in delaying more negative outcomes.

REFERENCES

Alessi, C. A., Stuck, A. E., Aronow, H. U., Yuhas, K. E., Bula, C. J., Madison, R., et al. (1997). The process of care in preventive in-home comprehensive geriatric assessment. *Journal of the American Geriatrics Society, 45*(9), 1044–1050.

American Psychiatric Association. (1994). *Diagnostic and statistical manual of mental disorders* (4th ed.). Washington, DC: Author.

Blazer, D. (1995). *Depression.* In G. L. Maddox (Ed.), *The encyclopedia of aging: A comprehensive resource in gerontology and geriatrics* (2nd ed., pp. 265–266). New York: Springer.

Blazer, D. (1998). *Emotional problems in later life: Intervention strategies for professional caregivers* (2nd ed.). New York: Springer.

Carr, D., & Rebok, G. W. (2006). The older adult driver. In J. J. Gallo, H. R. Bogner, T. Fulmer, & G. J. Paveza (Eds.), *Handbook of geriatric assessment* (4th ed., pp. 45–58). Sudbury, MA: Jones and Bartlett.

Chiu, E., & Ames, D. (Eds.). (1994). *Functional psychiatric disorders of the elderly.* Cambridge: Cambridge University Press.

Chodosh, J. (2001). Cognitive screening tests: The mini-mental status exam. In M. D. Mezey (Ed.), *The encyclopedia of elder care: The comprehensive resource on geriatric and social care* (pp. 142–144). New York: Springer.

Diffenbach, G. (2001). Anxiety and panic disorders. In M. D. Mezey (Ed.), *The encyclopedia of elder care: The comprehensive resource on geriatric and social care* (pp. 61–63). New York: Springer.

Doukas, D. J., McCullough, L. B., & Crane, M. K. (2006). Enhancing advanced directive discussions using the values history. In J. J. Gallo, H. R. Bogner, T. Fulmer, & G. J. Paveza (Eds.), *Handbook of geriatric assessment* (4th ed., pp. 59–75). Sudbury, MA: Jones and Bartlett.

Fillenbaum, G. G. (1988). *Multidimensional functional assessment of older adults: The duke older Americans resources and services procedures.* Hillsdale, NJ: Erlbaum.

Fillenbaum, G. G. (1995). Multidimensional functional assessment. In G. L. Maddox (Ed.), *The encyclopedia of aging: A comprehensive resource in gerontology and geriatrics* (2nd ed., pp. 653–654). New York: Springer.

Folstein, M., Folstein, S., & McHugh, P. (1975). Mini-mental state: A practical method for grading the cognitive state of patients for the clinician. *Journal of Psychiatric Research, 12,* 189–198.

Fulmer, T. T., & O'Malley, T. A. (1987). *Inadequate care of the elderly: A health care perspective on abuse and neglect.* New York: Springer.

Gallo, J. J., & Bogner, H. R. (2006). The context of geriatric care. In J. J. Gallo, H. R. Bogner, T. Fullmer, & G. J. Paveza (Eds.), *The handbook of geriatric assessment* (4th ed., pp. 3–13). Sudbury, MA: Jones and Bartlett.

Gallo, J. J., Bogner, H. R., Fulmer, T., & Paveza, G. J. (Eds.). (2006). *Handbook of geriatric assessment* (4th ed.). Sudbury, MA: Jones and Bartlett.

Gallo, J. J., Fulmer, T., Paveza, G. J., & Reichel, W. (Eds.). (2000). *Handbook of geriatric assessment* (3rd ed.). Gaithersburg, MD: Aspen.

Gallo, J. J., & Paveza, G. J. (2006). Activities of daily living and instrumental activities of daily living assessment. In J. J. Gallo, H. R. Bogner, T. Fulmer, & G. J. Paveza (Eds.), *Handbook of geriatric assessment* (4th ed., pp. 193–240). Sudbury, MA: Jones and Bartlett.

Gallo, J. J., Reichel, W., & Andersen, L. M. (Eds.). (1988). *Handbook of geriatric assessment.* Rockville, MD: Aspen.

Gallo, J. J., Reichel, W., & Andersen, L. M. (Eds.). (1995). *Handbook of geriatric assessment* (2nd ed.). Rockville, MD: Aspen.

Gallo, J. J., & Wittink, M. N. (2006a). Cognitive assessment. In J. J. Gallo, H. R. Bogner, T. Fulmer, & G. J. Paveza (Eds.), *Handbook of geriatric assessment* (4th ed., pp. 105–151). Sudbury, MA: Jones and Bartlett.

Gallo, J. J., & Wittnik, M. N. (2006b). Depression assessment. In J. J. Gallo, H. R. Bogner, T. Fulmer, & G. J. Paveza (Eds.), *Handbook of geriatric assessment* (4th ed., pp. 153–173). Sudbury, MA: Jones and Bartlett

Katz, S., Ford, A. B., Moskowitz, R. W., Jackson, B. A., & Jaffe, M. W. (1963, September 21). Studies of illness in the aged. The index of ADL: A standardized measure of biological and psychosocial function. *Journal of the American Medical Association, 185*, 914–919.

Katzman, R., Brown, T., Fuld, P., Peck, A., Schechter, R., & Schimmel, H. (1983). Validation of a short orientation-memory-concentration test of cognitive impairment. *American Journal of Psychiatry, 140*, 734–739.

Kurlowicz, L. H. (2001). Depression measurement instruments. In M. D. Mezey (Ed.), *The encyclopedia of elder care: The comprehensive resource on geriatric and social care* (pp. 210–212). New York: Springer.

Lowenstein, D. A., Amigo, E., Duara, R., Guterman, A., Hurwitz, D., Berkowitz, N., et al. (1989). A new scale for the assessment of functional status in Alzheimer's disease and related disorders. *Journal of Gerontology: Psychological Sciences, 44*(4), P114–P121.

McDowell, I., & Newell, C. (1996). *Measuring health: A guide to rating scales and questionnaires* (2nd ed.). New York: Oxford University Press.

McKhann, G., Drachman, D., Folstein, M., Katzman, R., Price, D., & Stadlan, E. M. (1984). Clinical diagnosis of Alzheimer's disease: Report of the NINCDS-ADRDA work group under the auspices of department of health and human services task force on Alzheimer's disease. *Neurology, 34*, 939–944.

Morano, C., & Morano, B. (2006). Social assessment. In J. J. Gallo, H. R. Bogner, T. Fulmer, & G. J. Paveza (Eds.), *Handbook of geriatric assessment* (4th ed., pp. 241–271). Sudbury, MA: Jones and Bartlett.

Mouton, C. P., & Esparza, Y. B. (2006). Ethnicity and geriatric assessment. In J. J. Gallo, H. R. Bogner, T. Fulmer, & G. J. Paveza (Eds.), *Handbook of geriatric assessment* (4th ed., pp. 29–44). Sudbury, MA: Jones and Bartlett.

National Center for Cost Containment. (1993). *Geropsychology assessment resource guide.* Milwaukee, WI: Department of Commerce, National Technical Information Service.

Naylor, M. D., Brooten, D., Campbell, R., Jacobsen, B. S., Mezey, M. D., Pauly, M. V., et al. (1999). Comprehensive discharge planning and home follow-up of hospitalized elders: A randomized clinical trial. *Journal of the American Medical Association, 281*(7), 613–620.

Nicklin, D. (2006). Physical assessment. In J. J. Gallo, H. R. Bogner, T. Fulmer, & G. J. Paveza (Eds.), *Handbook of geriatric assessment* (4th ed., pp. 273–317). Sudbury, MA: Jones and Bartlett.

Older Americans Resources and Services (OARS) Methodology. (1978). *Multidimensional Functional Assessment Questionnaire* (2nd ed.). Durham, NC: Duke University Center for the Study of Aging and Human Development.

Paveza, G. J. (1993). Social services and the Alzheimer's disease patient: An overview. *Neurology*, *43*(8, Suppl. 4), 11–15.

Paveza, G. J., Cohen, D., Blaser, C. J., & Hagopian, M. (1990). A brief form of the mini-mental state examination for use in community care settings. *Behavior, Health and Aging*, *1*(2), 133–139.

Paveza, G. J., Cohen, D., Eisdorfer, C., Freels, S., Semla, T., Ashford, J. W., et al. (1992). Severe family violence and Alzheimer's disease: Prevalence and risk factors. *Gerontologist*, *32*(4), 493–497.

Paveza, G. J., Cohen, D., Hagopian, M., Prohaska, T., Blaser, C. J., & Brauner, D. (1990). A brief assessment tool for determining eligibility and need for community-based long-term care services. *Behavior, Health and Aging*, *1*(2), 121–132.

Paveza, G. J., Mensah, E., Cohen, D., Williams, S., & Jankowski, L. (1998). Costs of home and community-based long-term care services to the cognitively impaired aged. *Journal of Mental Health and Aging*, *4*(1), 69–82.

Paveza, G. J., Prohaska, T., Hagopian, M., & Cohen, D. (1989). *Determination of need revision: Final report*, Vol. I. Chicago: University of Illinois, Gerontology Center.

Pheiffer, E. (1975). A short portable mental status questionnaire for the assessment of organic brain deficit in elderly patients. *Journal of the American Geriatrics Society*, *23*, 433–441.

Richardson, J. P. (2006). Pain assessment. In J. J. Gallo, H. R. Bogner, T. Fulmer, & G. J. Paveza (Eds.), *Handbook of geriatric assessment* (4th ed., pp. 319–329). Sudbury, MA: Jones and Bartlett.

Ruben, D. B., Borok, G. M., Wolde-Tsadik, G., Ershoff, D. H., Fishman, L. K., Ambrosini, V. L., et al. (1995). A randomized trial of comprehensive geriatric assessment in the care of hospitalized patients. *New England Journal of Medicine*, *332*(20), 1345–1350.

Rubenstein, L. A. (1995). Geriatric assessment units: Their rationale, history, process and effectiveness. In G. L. Maddox (Eds.), *The encyclopedia of aging: A comprehensive resource in gerontology and geriatrics* (2nd ed., pp. 403–406). New York: Springer.

Rubenstein, L. Z., Stuck, A. E., Siu, A. L., & Wieland, D. (1991). Impacts of geriatric evaluation and management programs on defined outcomes: Overview of the evidence. *Journal of the American Geriatrics Society*, *39*, 8–16.

Scalmati, A., & Smyth, C. (2001). Cognition instruments. In M. D. Mezey (Ed.), *The encyclopedia of elder care: The comprehensive resource on geriatric and social care* (pp. 137–139). New York: Springer.

Schneider, L. S., Reynolds, C. F., III, Lebowitz, B. D., & Friedhoff, A. J. (Eds.). (1994). *Diagnosis and treatment of depression in late life: Results of the NIH consensus development conference.* Washington, DC: American Psychiatric Press.

Siu, A. L., Kravitz, R. L., Keeler, E., Hemmerling, K., Kington, R., Davis, J. W., et al. (1996). Post-discharge geriatric assessment of hospitalized frail elderly patients. *Archives of Internal Medicine*, *156*(1), 76–81.

Stuck, A. E., Wieland, D., Rubenstein, L. Z., Siu, A. L., & Adams, J. (1995). Comprehensive geriatric assessment: Meta-analysis of main effects and elements enhancing effectiveness. In L. Z. Rubenstein, D. Wieland, & R. Bernabei (Eds.), *Geriatric assessment technology: The state of the art* (pp. 11–26). Milano, Italy: Editrice Kurtis-Milano.

Stuck, A. E., Zwahlen, H. G., Neuenschwander, B. E., Meyer Schweizer, R. A., Bauen, G., & Beck, J. C. (1995). Methodologic challenges of randomized controlled studies on in-home comprehensive geriatric assessment: The EIGER project—Evaluation of in-home geriatric health visits in elderly residents. *Aging-Clinical and Experimental Research*, *7*(3), 218–223.

VanderWeerd, C., Firpo, A., Fulmer, T., & Paveza, G. J. (2006). Recognizing mistreatment in older adults. In J. J. Gallo, H. R. Bogner, T. Fulmer, & G. J. Paveza (Eds.), *Handbook of geriatric assessment* (4th ed., pp. 78–101). Sudbury, MA: Jones and Bartlett.

Wallace, M., Shea, J., & Guttman, C. (2006). Health promotion. In J. J. Gallo, H. R. Bogner, T. Fulmer, & G. J. Paveza (Eds.), *Handbook of geriatric assessment* (4th ed., pp. 331–368). Sudbury, MA: Jones and Bartlett.

Zanjani, F., & Oslin, D. (2006). Substance use and abuse assessment. In J. J. Gallo, H. R. Bogner, T. Fulmer, & G. J. Paveza (Eds.), *Handbook of geriatric assessment* (4th ed., pp. 175–192). Sudbury, MA: Jones and Bartlett.

Chapter 18 ————————————————————

INTERVENTION WITH THE ELDERLY

Michael J. Holosko and John Heckman

This chapter presents an overview of issues related to interventions with the elderly. Geron-tological social work is predicted to be one of the high-demand future job markets for our profession, as we in the United States are rapidly becoming an aging society (U.S. Bureau of Labor Statistics, 2004). Thus, it seems both relevant and timely to include a chapter about this area of social work practice. Prior to presenting the materials that assess the efficacy of evidence-based interventions with the elderly, a brief historical background provides the context and rationale for understanding this information.

HISTORICAL BACKGROUND

The Demographic Reality

In most industrialized countries of the world, a demographic population explosion has occurred among those aged 65 and older. This is primarily attributed to improved med-ical treatment, earlier changes in lifestyle, reduced mortality rates, increased financial independence, old age pensions, governmental assistance, advances in technology, greater mobility and access to health and social services, and formal and informal support networks (Holosko & Feit, 2004).

For the past 40 or 50 years, U.S. policy makers at federal, state, and/or local levels have both witnessed and acknowledged this exponential growth, but don't quite know how to deal with it. For example, in an article written by A. Otten in the *Wall Street Journal,* on Monday, July 10, 1984, a three-part series was titled: "The Oldest-Old: Ever More Americans Live into Their 80's and 90's and Cause Big Problems" [Part I]; "The Strain on Social Services and Relatives Will Rise: Should Care Be Rationed?" [II]; and, "A Five-Generation Family" [III]. Concerns about how to reconcile or address this reality are a longstanding and ubiquitous feature of our society. Breaking these data down a bit further provides additional insights into some interesting and challenging policy and practice realities for social workers practicing in this area.

Although there is some disagreement in the literature about what constitutes an el-derly person, policy makers deem 65 as the present age benchmark (Holosko & Leslie, 2004). From a formative or "Level I" life span perspective, persons over 65 represent the fastest growing age group in the United States. Projections are that by the year 2030, over 70 million Americans will be at least 65 years of age (Administration on Aging, 2003). At a "Level II" perspective, this subgroup is further broken down by current health, aging, and lifecycle markers as: "Young-Old" or 65 to 75, "Moderately-Old" or 75 to 90, and "Old-Old" being 90+ years. Indeed, since about 1988, the fastest growing cohort on our lifecycle continuum is the 85+ year-old category (Feit & Cueuves-Feit, 1991, 2004).

From a "Level III" demographic perspective: (a) There are and will continue to be more women than men who live beyond age 65 in the United States; (b) more of the 65+ age group will come from ethnically diverse groups; (c) more elderly will be actively employed in the future; (d) more elderly will be residing in urban centers rather than rural settings; and (e) more elderly will become meaningfully involved in our day-to-day lives, for example, in arts, literature, movies, athletics, politics, educational and economic institutions, and so on. Indeed, as indicated by Holosko and Holosko (2004), as a society, we can no longer take an "out-of-sight . . . out-of-mind" mentality with the elderly because they are and will continue to be in plain sight and clearly in our minds. Just where and when these three growth trends will subside, or even plateau, is nowhere to be seen on our current society's horizon.

Practice Implications

In attempting to discern how these trends may impact on social work practice with the elderly, the first author conducted a literature search on emerging practice issues about the elderly from 1975 to 2006. Tables of contents for main teaching texts written by social workers, as well as training institute workshops offered by the Council on Social Work Education (CSWE) and the National Association of Social Workers (NASW), served as the database for this cursory review. One rather interesting finding emerged. The so-called "emerging practice issues" cited early on in documents by Lowry (1979); Schneider, Decker, Freeman, Messerschmidt, and Syran (1984); and Greene (1988) were the same emerging practice topics listed by the Hartford Foundation's Gero-Education Group at a recent CSWE Conference (www.Gero-EdCenter.org), almost verbatim circa 1988.

To the nascent reader of these admittedly rather spurious comparative data, it would appear that practice issues that were deemed on the forefront some 20 years ago by our profession are still on the forefront today. However, what has changed is not the issues themselves but: (a) the sheer numbers of elderly; (b) their various subgroups; (c) their health and psychosocial problems, and the context in which they present; (d) the variety of interventions we offer to deal with these issues; and (e) our ability to assess the efficacy of our interventions. Sadly, what else has not changed (in this brief chronological snapshot) is the dire shortage of social workers educated and trained to practice in this area (Hooyman & Kayak, 2002; Lowry, 1979). A recently released NASW National Workforce Study of licensed social workers reported the number of new social workers providing services to older adults is decreasing, despite the projected increases in the number of older adults who will need social work services (NASW, 2006).

Defining and Assessing the Evidence-Based Practice Interventions

Social workers' decade-long affair with evidence-based practice (EBP) has been significantly tempered (Gambrill, 2006). This is due in large part to the profession's inability to realistically define the concept and practitioners' inability to implement it in practice (Thyer & Kazi, 2004). An evolving and much more realistic definition of EBP is "the conscientious and judicious use of current best practice in making decisions for individual treatment" (Howard, McMillan, & Pollio, 2003; Pollio, 2002, 2006; Sackett, Richardson, Rosenberg, & Haynes, 1997). This less stringent definition is used in this chapter.

As a result, the information reviewed herein included both quantitative and qualitative research as well as evaluation research studies. In short, as long as empirical data were systematically collected to either inform or direct practice, they were retained for subsequent analyses. Figure 18.1 presents a three-cohort conceptualization of these data-driven studies.

Figure 18.1 shifts the perceptual lens of more traditionally delimiting definitions of EBP to a looser definition of "social work practice [in this case with the elderly] based on empirical data" or the actual evidence per se. Thus, published articles, studies, chapters, texts, or monographs not grounded in this way were not retained for analyses for this chapter.

Nonempirically based studies, historical reviews, frameworks (conceptual, theoretical, treatment) not based on empirical data, studies about gerontological workers themselves, policy analyses, critiques of practice, opinion pieces, and trend analyses were consequently excluded. Ironically, this latter literature accounted for approximately 35% of the published critical mass captured by the initial search parameters. Further, in order to keep this chapter relatively current, only literature from 1995 onward was reviewed. Key words used in

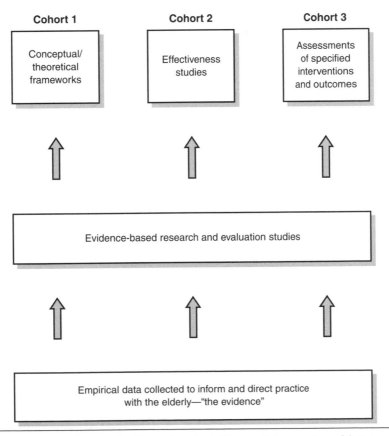

Figure 18.1   Three cohorts of evidence-based studies used in a review of interventions for the elderly

searching these literature sources were: *gerontology, interventions, outcomes, social work practice, effectiveness, assessing practice,* and *evidence-based practice.*

In addition, we attempted to seek out EBP literature and present it in ways that emphasized the practice ↔ evidence linkage. After a presentation of the summarized evidence-based intervention studies, as indicated in the three cohorts in Figure 18.1, a model for integrating such evidence into practice is then presented.

SUMMARY OF CURRENT EVIDENCE-BASED INTERVENTIONS WITH THE ELDERLY

Cohort 1—Conceptual/Theoretical Frameworks

Too often in overviews of the literature of this nature, published accounts are summarily dismissed if they do not include a readily identifiable "Method" section or empirical data, for example, tables of statistics. This nascent approach unfortunately delimits a host of important literature that, on further investigation, has an empirical basis to it. Figure 18.1 conceptualized literature in Cohort 1 as having an empirical basis to it. That is, empirical data were used to develop these conceptual and/or theoretical frameworks that guided gerontological social work practice.

Three criteria were used to determine literature suitable for inclusion here. First, all of these published accounts clearly had to be empirically linked to practice interventions with the elderly. This was operationalized in one of two ways: (1) greater than 50% of the references cited at the end of the chapter/article had to have analyzed/cited primary or secondary data, and/or (2) case examples were used in the document as the basis for the proposed conceptual/theoretical framework. For the most part, such chapters/articles grounded the rationale for the proposed framework in empirical studies that, in turn, presented the basis for their subsequent development.

As previously mentioned in this chapter, elders are living longer, proliferating in number, and incurring escalating costs of care. Ironically, many of these potential clients did not expect to live as long as they presently are, and their resources have significantly diminished as their lives are extended. As such, residential long-term care and end-of-life planning were prevalent topics among many studies considered for inclusion in Cohort 1 (Table 18.1).

Thus, the quality of life in long-term care facilities is becoming a more salient issue. Solomon (2004) explored providing for quality of life in long-term residential homes for elderly clients by suggesting nine criteria that have a positive contributive influence. These were good physical care, pleasant environment, autonomy/choice, attentive staff, respectful treatment, personal meaning, engaging activities, opportunities for significant relationships, and interdisciplinary collaboration. Revisiting a common intervention for clinical practice with elderly populations (group work) with a unique taxonomy, Solomon presented four group types: self-government, support, educational, and resident volunteer. By using case examples, this study showed how providing for quality of life in residential homes can improve over-all health status, increase self-determination within the residents, foster interprofessional collaboration, and decrease misunderstandings that may occur among providers and recipients of this care modality.

Table 18.1 Conceptual/Theoretical Frameworks: Interventions for the Elderly

Reference	Title of Citation	Target Group	Main Variables	Other Comments
Haight & Gibson (2005)	A Social Work Perspective	Nursing home elderly, cognitive and sensory alert and impaired elderly	Multidisciplinary misunderstandings, conflict, and interactions Elderly group work dynamics Special issues	Role-play exercises for interprofessional collaboration. Case example: self-determination and relevant participation in group work
Nasw.org (2004)	End-of-Life Care	Older adults	Efforts to increase research and translate findings A list of end-of-life references	Series of all studies empirical studying showing effectiveness for these protocols
Pinquart, Sörenson, & Peak (2004)	Helping Older Adults and Their Families Develop and Implement Case Plans	Older adults who have no care plan, those with unrealistic plans, families in conflict about care plans	Response styles regarding approaching need for care or help Influences on preparation Positive effects of preparing in advance	Section on intervention strategies: three contexts for intervention, eight-step process model of strategies. Case example for process model application
Solomon (2004)	The Role of the Social Worker in Long-Term Care	Residents of homes for the aged and other long-term facilities	Nine primary qualities for a good life in a nursing home, (e.g., having autonomy and choice, new relationships inside and outside the institution)	30 days (following hospital discharge)
Naleppa & Reid (2003)	Case Management	Elderly in need of multiple services	Three components of the task-centered case management practice model Research conducted to evaluate and develop the model	Includes a small-scale, hospital study

(continued)

Table 18.1 *(Continued)*

Reference	Title of Citation	Target Group	Main Variables	Other Comments
Bisman (2003)	Rural Aging: Social Work Practice Models and Intervention Dynamics	Rural elderly	Three central social work components: assessment and case theory, biopsychosocial perspective, and self-awareness/use of self Four theoretical models and ideas to guide intervention	Five theoretical models: Social support, family systems, group work, case management, and community practice; many authors cited in section on intervention ideas
Graziano (2003)	Trauma and Aging	Older adults who have experienced trauma at any point in the life cycle	Trauma response manifestation theories Partial list of those at risk for reemergence of traumatic stress symptoms Suggestions for incorporating a trauma framework into practice	Three case examples representing different trauma experiences across the life cycle and differences in trauma responses
Li & Blaser (2003)	Rural Program Planning and Development for Older Adults	Rural elderly	Description of social care systems model Description of the nature and use of informal support networks and formal services Strategies for rural service and program development	
McInnis-Dittrich (2002)	Alternative Interventions in the Socioemotional Problems of Elders	Older adults, those with Alzheimer's disease	Music therapies Art therapies Drama therapies Animal-assisted therapies	Web sites are listed at the end

Peck (2001)	Looking Back at Life and Its Influence on Subjective Well-Being	Older adults	Model of subjective well-being and explanations of key concepts Psychosocial development influences Social work interventions	Interventions: Life review therapy, environment-focused interventions
Hobart (2001)	Death and Dying and the Social Work Role	Older adults	Death and dying laws (e.g., Patient Self-Determination Act) and implication 2001 Ethnographic Study Solutions for problems in advance care planning and end-of-life medical decision making (e.g., combining advance directive forms into one document)	6 months (included seven 1-hour sessions and weekly SSS support from psychiatric nurse)
Leon, Altholz, & Dziegielewski (1999)	Compassion Fatigue: Considerations for Working with the Elderly	Older adults	Compassion fatigue definition Contributing factors (e.g., the labor intensive yet short-term nature of the work) Effects on the worker (e.g., feelings of incompetence) Preventive measure (e.g., learning to identify signs)	A case example is used to illustrate variables contributing to compassion fatigue (e.g., worker's age, personal dynamics, agency factors)

Similarly, Pinquart, Sörenson, and Peak (2004), recognized the familial imperative to develop a realistic care plan for later life relatives. They provided a strategic eight-step process model designed to support older adults through the preparatory development of their future care needs. Additionally, they suggested three contextual opportunities for intervention (i.e., educational settings, direct referrals, and discharge planning). This framework assists a social worker in enhancing a client's right to self-determination, sense of wellness, and affect some alleviation of stress for the client's extended family. It was shown that being knowledgeable about phenomena and tendencies common to older adults and their families related to the approaching need for care enables practitioners to better assist these clients.

Another study in this cohort addressed a social worker's role in issues of death and dying. Hobart (2001) explored the ever-expanding role of the social worker in advance care planning and end-of-life decision making. The complexity of this advocacy role is highlighted as well as the obligatory responsibility of the social worker to be well versed on issues, legislation, policy, providers, and patient's rights. Additionally, being able to navigate through the quagmire of psychosocial currents is crucial for the efficacy of the social worker's praxis. Hobart discussed Advance Directive Education (ADE), "Right to Die" legislation, the Patient Self-Determination Act of 1991 (PSDA), and argued for ethnographic sensitivity in one's approach to issues of death and dying. The conceptual framework provided here reminds us of the multiplicity of skills and working knowledge one must bring to the person in their environment. Among these studies, is a NASW "End-of-Life Care" protocol. This helpful study compiles, summarizes, and delimits a multitude of critical studies on end-of-life care that will prove advantageous to a clinician in his or her professional endeavors. Over 20 articles were presented in this review covering the broad gamut of issues relating to caring for this population as they prepare for the end of life.

Cohort 1 studies also included interventional theoretical frameworks for working with the elderly within a particular sociocultural situatedness, namely, rural settings (Bisman, 2003; Li & Blaser, 2003). These studies highlight the unique challenges that social workers face when intervening with rural elderly populations. The "lower-than-average" general health, the narrow range of available services, the economic stratification of the clientele, the limited access to formal and diverse service providers, and the concomitant geographic isolation often exacerbate the presenting problems of this treatment group. Bisman (2003) suggested four theoretical models for intervention with rural elderly clients: social support, family systems, group work, and case management/community practice, thus reinforcing the ubiquitous modality for practice with the elderly. This article is efficacious to a practitioner and contains helpful information for further reading and research.

The Li and Blaser (2003) study moves beyond the micro- and mezzolevels of social praxis and into macrolevel social work. These authors suggest an integrative social care systems model for rural program planning with older adults that amalgamates both formal and informal sources of care, community leaders and residents, and culture and creativity. This model seeks to provide for both the client as well as the community. Through the use of case studies, Li and Blaser (2003) illustrate the essential strategies that are fundamental to success in rural program planning and development for older adults.

The last intervention area of these studies relates to the uniqueness of working with this population. Here, numerous conceptual/theoretical frameworks are provided that address issues of compassion fatigue (Leon, Altholz, & Dziegielewski, 1999), trauma as it relates to aging (Graziano, 2003), elder morbidity and subjective well-being (Peck, 2001), alternative socioemotional interventions for depression (McInnis-Dittrich, 2002), and task-centered case management (Naleppa & Reid, 2003). The task-centered case management practice model is for work with the elderly in need of multiple services. The model has three components: a core intervention model, parallel intervention functions, and alternative intervention modules. Each of the studies has important clinical implications that could benefit practitioners working in this area.

Leon et al. (1999) used case examples to reinforce the inherent danger to clinicians who work with elderly populations. Social work burnout can occur because of the short-term nature of the labor-intensive work with the elderly. Some contributive factors to compassion fatigue noted were feelings of incompetence, the experiences of secondary traumatic stress disorder, the misperception that the elderly client's life cannot be improved (by interventions), the scarcity of resources for this treatment group, and the latent existential angst about the inevitability of aging and declining in health that the practitioner realizes for him- or herself. This study presented an eight-step process that could possibly prevent compassion fatigue.

The articles in Cohort 1, although not necessarily having specified outcomes, targeted populations, and rigorous evidence-based methodological designs, are evidenced-based, by the previous definition provided, and are important to gerontological social work practitioners. They present numerously empirically derived conceptual/theoretical frameworks for interventions with the elderly that, more often than not, have worked elsewhere. These modalities of intervention range from service among rural populations, residential populations with physical and/or cognitive impairment, and emotional/spiritual penury. Additionally, some of the studies in this cohort serve a perfunctory role in improving the quality of self-care in the social worker; advocacy for the client; and service to, with, and among elderly populations.

Cohort 2—Effectiveness Studies

The effectiveness studies in Cohort 2 (Table 18.2) illustrate the necessity of using multifaceted interventional strategies for multidimensional presenting problems of the elderly.

As the ever-burgeoning elderly population expands, a social worker's knowledge of efficacious interventions must remain commensurate with the anticipated needs of these potential clients. Ascertaining what has worked for other clinicians can be of benefit to any social work practitioner. Essentially, the nature of the presenting problems within this cohort fell into one or more of the following categories: acute/chronic pain, depressive symptoms, social isolation, declining biopsychosocial health, and/or cognitive impairment (e.g., dementia, Alzheimer's). The interventions reviewed in Cohort 2 ran the gamut of education, physiotherapy, pharmacological treatment, community-based and home-based therapy, care through the medium of technology, and alternative rehabilitation through Eastern meditative practice and existential empowerment. Collectively, these studies did not specify designated, and/or anticipated outcomes, but rather, sought to determine the efficacy of the interventions. Additionally, the time frame or duration of the interventions varied in part because of the absence of targeted outcomes specified prior to the study. Their methodological criteria allowed these studies to be dichotomized into two practice effectiveness categories, namely, those interventions that worked and those that did not.

Table 18.2 Effectiveness Studies of Interventions with Elderly Populations between 2006 and 1995

Reference	Interventions Provided	Presenting Problems	Populations	Duration/ Occasion of Interventions	Outcomes	Effectiveness of Interventions
Abrahamson & Khan (2006)	ED	Osteoarthritis patients with low trauma fractures	15	6 months	Significant improvements in standardized scores, e.g., osteoporosis questionnaire, functional independence measure, and mini mental state examination	Osteoporosis education in elderly rehabilitation inpatients with fractures is effective, but requires adequate patient cognitive skills.
Stinson & Kirk (2006)	SRT, SSS	Assisted living female residents with depression	24 (control group and intervention group)	6 weeks	Reminiscence has no significant decrease in depression and increase in self-transcendence	The study revealed an inverse relationship between depression and self-transcendence suggesting a need to research alternative therapies for treatment of depression in the older female. Reminiscence offers a possible intervention for treatment of depression in older women.
Wright, Hickson, & Frost (2006)	Eating in supervised dining hall with nursing assistant	Acutely ill patients who eat alone in their rooms	48	Lunch time in cafeteria	Intervention group gained weight	Food intake can be improved by using a supervised dining room, and this will potentially lead to weight gain and corresponding improvements in nutritional status and rehabilitation.
Gutheil & Heyman (2005)	STEP, ED, SSS	High-functioning, CDS and their potential or designated health care agents	27 dyads (person and agent = 54)	2 months (3 sessions)	Intervention group outcomes, e.g., higher scores in communication, knowledge of health options, and positive attitude toward end-of-life planning	The STEP intervention can help high-functioning CDS with end-of-life planning, acquiring greater knowledge of health-care roles, responsibilities, and options and foster greater communication skills.

Authors	Intervention	Sample	N	Duration	Outcomes	Conclusions
Mo-Kyung, Belza, LoGerfo, & Cunningham (2005)	ED, PT	EKI in senior citizen home	13	12 weeks	Improved outcomes on muscle strength, agility/balance, blood pressure, exercise adherence, and self-satisfaction	The exercise program was successful and should be evaluated on a larger population and in populations of other ethnic minorities.
Leff et al. (2005)	Hospital-at-home model of care	Acutely ill CDS patients receiving Medicare-managed care at two VA sites	455	22 months	Subjects had a shorter length of stay and lower mean costs of treatment compared to acute hospital care	The hospital-at-home model is feasible, safe, and efficacious for certain older patients with selected acute medical illnesses.
Mittelman, Roth, Coon, & Haley (2004)	RCSG, SSS	Spouse-caregivers of Alzheimer's patients	406	9 years, 5 months	Outcomes achieved, (e.g., caregiving skills increased, mobilized support from family networks increased, and depressive symptoms decreased)	Counseling and social service support lead to sustained benefits for elderly spouse caregivers of Alzheimer's patients.
Ciechanowski et al. (2004)	RCT, CIHBT, PST, PEARLS, CBT	Patients with minor depression and/or dysthymia	138	29 months	Outcomes, decrease in depressive symptoms and increase in quality of life	The PEARLS program, a community-integrated, home-based treatment for depression, significantly reduces depressive symptoms and improves health status.
Kapasi, Ouslander, Schnelle, Kutner, & Fahey (2003)	Random CCT, functionally oriented endurance and resistance exercise training	Frail nursing home residents	190	32 weeks	Intervention did not bring beneficial or detrimental effects on immune parameters in the study population	The interventional exercise program has no demonstrable effect on immunity in frail elderly residents in nursing homes.

(continued)

Table 18.2 (*Continued*)

Reference	Interventions Provided	Presenting Problems	Populations	Duration/Occasion of Interventions	Outcomes	Effectiveness of Interventions
Tsang, Mok, Au Yeung, & Chan (2003)	RCT, ECG, *Qigong* (The Eight Section Brocades)	Patients with subacute chronic physical illnesses and depression	50	12 weeks	Control group expressed improvement in physical, psychological, and general health	*Qigong* may prove to be an alternative treatment for subacute chronic physical illnesses and depression.
Solomon, Adams, Silver, Zimmer, & DeVeaux (2002)	CCT, pharmacological, MMSE	CDS with no memory impairment	230 (203 completed the intervention)	6 weeks	Control group (who received the Ginkgo pharmacological treatment) showed no improvement in memory or cognitive function	Ginkgo provides no measurable benefit in memory or related cognitive function to adults with healthy cognitive function.
White et al. (2002)	RCT, Internet education and access	Volunteers from residential congregate housing sites and nursing facilities	100	6 months 2-week intervention (9 hours of small group training over 6 days)	Outcomes, (e.g., reduced depressive symptoms/ loneliness)	The Internet may prove to be of psychosocial benefit (i.e., reduction of loneliness and depressive symptoms) to seniors who learn how to use it and have access to it.

Author (Year)	Intervention	Setting	N	Duration	Outcomes	Conclusions
De Leo, Buono & Dwyer (2002)	PST, SSS, TeleHelp-TeleCheck service	Users of a telephone help line and emergency response service	18,641	10 years	Outcomes, fewer suicide deaths among elderly service users	The study confirms the initial promise of the TeleHelp-TeleCheck service over a much longer time period.
Kochevar, Smith, & Bernard (2001)	NT with exercise program	Native-American CDS in urban area	22	6 weeks	Significant decrease in blood pressure and respirations	Physical and emotional health can improve among Native-American seniors as a result of exercise and nutritional training.
Kuhn & Mendes de Leon (2001)	ED intervention	Alzheimer's caregivers	58	6 months	Modest benefits in knowledge of disease and coping	Study data suggests that knowledge of Alzheimer's can assist caregiver coping.
Camberg et al. (1999)	Personalized simulated presence, MMSE	Nursing home residents with ADRD	54	Ongoing	No significant change as a result of intervention	Simulated presence may prove to be effective in enhancing well-being and decreasing problem behaviors in nursing home settings.
Inouye et al. (1993)	CCT, PCS, NCEP	General medicine wards at teaching geriatric hospital—frail elders	216	Ongoing	Beneficial effects, (e.g., reduction of delirium, functional impairment, incontinence, and pressure sores, were achieved without increasing per-day hospital costs)	NCEP appears effective to decrease functional decline in targeted elderly hospitalized medical patients.

(continued)

Table 18.2 (*Continued*)

Reference	Interventions Provided	Presenting Problems	Populations	Duration/Occasion of Interventions	Outcomes	Effectiveness of Interventions
Campbell et al. (1997)	RCT, PT, home exercise program of strength and balance retraining exercises, ECG	Female general practice patients in New Zealand who are at risk for falling	233	12 months	Rate of falls was lower in the exercise than in the control group and balance improved	An individual program of strength and balance retraining exercises improved physical function and was effective in reducing falls and injuries in women 80 years and older.
Banerjee, Shamash, Macdonald, & Mann (1996)	RCT, PGT, AGECAT, pharmacological	Depressed disabled people receiving home care	69	6 months	Outcome, significant recovery within the treatment group	Depression is treatable in elderly people receiving home care.

ADRD = Alzheimer's disease and related dementia; AGECAT = Automatic geriatric examination for computer assisted taxonomy; CBT = Cognitive behavioral therapy; CCT = Controlled clinical trial; CDS = Community-dwelling seniors; CIHBT = Community-integrated; home-based treatment; ECG = Educational control group; ED = Education; EKI = Elderly Korean immigrants; MMSE = Mini mental state examination; NCEP = Nursing-centered educational program; NT = Nutritional training; PCS = Prospective cohort study; PEARLS = Program to encourage active rewarding lives for seniors; PGT = Psychogeriatric team; PST = Problem solving therapy; PT = Physiotherapy; RCSG = Random controlled support group; RCT = Random clinical trial; SRT = Structured reminiscence therapy; SSS = Social service support; SSW = Session with social worker; STEP = Start talking early program; VA = Veterans Administration.

At first glance, you might think that the needs of the elderly have remained quite consistent over the past 20 years. However, the studies in Cohort 2 (and the subsequent Cohort 3) reveal that the presenting problems of the elderly have become more complicated than before. The cost of adequate care has escalated far beyond the economic viability of the client group. Even though technology has created the possibility of instantaneous digital interactivity, it appears that social groups and communities have become more polarized and collectivities have become ever more stratified (Dunlop & Holosko, in press). With these societal changes anonymously thrust on the variegated collectivities that make up our culture, we witness the exacerbation of the numerous presenting problems of the elderly. Thus, interventional strategies have become more strategic, multidimensional, and time framed as needs arise.

These studies sought to ascertain the efficacy of various interventions ranging from education to structured reminiscence therapy, from physical therapy to supervised eating in social settings, from Eastern Chinese meditative/movement oriented practices to pharmacological interventions for depression. The wide array in Cohort 2 exemplified the clinician's creativity and willingness to experiment in order to address the presenting problems within the elderly community. Some tested educational curricula while others investigated the utility of technology and physiotherapy. These studies were selected, in part, because they satisfied the criteria of our search, and also because they represented a considerable range in interventional approaches in a variety of settings both locally and internationally. Some were clinically based, while others were community- or home-based interventions.

Among the clinically based interventions, Abrahamson and Khan (2006) found that osteoporosis education among elderly patients with low trauma fractures significantly improved the functional independence and psychological well-being of the patients. This educational intervention did not reduce levels of actual pain experienced by the subjects. However, the interrelated connection between cognitively understanding the disease and cultivating strategies to manage the pain of the disease resulted in both greater physical confidence and decreased depressive symptoms. This study demonstrated the direct corollary between the experience of pain and declining ambulatory function to depressive symptomology.

Tsang, Mok, Au Yeung, and Chan (2003) also recognized the correlation between pain and depression in their study of the efficacy of *Quigong*. From the Chinese words *Qi* [chi] which means energy and *gong* [kung] which means skill, this ancient practice merges meditation and deliberate movement. *Quigong* is famous in China for reducing stress, lowering blood pressure, and fostering a better attitude about life. Tsang et al. (2003) found that elderly patients with chronic subacute physical illnesses and pain also experienced depressive symptoms. The control group that received the *Quigong* intervention for 12 weeks showed significant improvement in physical, psychological, and general health well-being. The results of this study suggested that alternatives to pharmacological interventions for pain and depression exist.

The relationship among acute illness, pain, recovery, and the propensity to socially isolate oneself was addressed in the Wright, Hickson, and Frost (2006) study. They evaluated a nurse-aided supervised dining intervention. Generally, acutely ill nursing home patients have a tendency to eat alone in their rooms. This self-imposed social isolation has a corroborative negative effect on recovery, weight-loss, and general health. Their intervention involved encouraging these elderly residents to go to the formal dining hall during lunch time rather than eating alone in their rooms. The simple act of communal dining, rather than socially isolating, resulted in increased food intake, healthy weight gain, and corresponding improvements in nutritional status and rehabilitation. The effect of communal interactivity on the general health status of the geriatric client cannot be overstated.

Community-based interventions were also quite common among the studies reviewed (Ciechanowski et al., 2004; Kochevar, Smith, & Bernard, 2001). Both studies sought to explore the correlation between physical and general health and the biopsychosocial wellness of the subjects. Kochevar et al. (2001) utilized nutritional training and a physical exercise program among Native-American urban elders for 6 weeks. As result of this intervention, the physical and emotional health of the subjects significantly increased. Ciechanowski et al. (2004) evaluated an educational program, Program to Encourage Active Rewarding Lives for Seniors (PEARLS), among 138 elderly patients with minor depression and/or dysthymia. PEARLS proved to be an efficacious community-integrated, home-based treatment for depression by significantly reducing depressive symptoms and improving the general health status of the participants.

Several studies employed technology, for example, telephones, computers, Internet, and recording devices, as an integral part of their interventional strategy (Camberg et al., 1999; De Leo, Buono, & Dwyer, 2002; White et al., 2002). These interventions ranged in duration from 6 months to 10 years. Cohort 2 studies also included professional and semiprofessional practitioners in the administering of their interventions.

Other studies integrated physiotherapy and education (Campbell et al., 1997; Kapasi, Ouslander, Schnelle, Kutner, & Fahey, 2003; Kochevar et al., 2001; Mo-Kyung, Belza, LoGerfo, & Cunningham, 2005; Tsang et al., 2003). The duration of these interventions ranged from 12 to 32 weeks. Some addressed specific ethnic groups, that is, elderly Korean immigrants (Mo-Kyung et al., 2005), while others focused on specific impairments and risks, that is, elderly frail women who are at-risk of falling (Campbell et al., 1997). Regardless of the population, merging physiotherapy and education proved to be efficacious among geriatric clients, in general.

One final trend to highlight within gerontological work and these studies was the aging-in-place model. The ubiquitous modality of care in the past was the institutionalization of the elderly in personal care/residential homes. For the past 2 decades, however, the devolution of health care has challenged the federal role in domestic health and human services policy. Consequently, in light of the contextual verities of the managed care movement, the sociodemographics of aging, and the preferential biases of the elderly to die at home, a new paradigm for elder care is emerging.

In North America, much of the decision making in health-related issues has been devolved to local authorities. The raison d'être behind such a new model of care emerges from three areas of concern: (1) the governmental expectation for equitable care; (2) the providers' economic, social, and health-related interests; and (3) the clients' health care-related preferences and needs (Lomas, Woods, & Veenstra, 1997). The aging-in-place model has transpired as a new model for care, particularly among aging populations, as a response to the escalating costs of care, the scarcity of adequate space for an ever-increasing population of elderly, and in response to the expressed desires of the elderly to die at home (Groth-Juncker & McCusker, 1983).

Two of the studies in Cohort 2 addressed the aging-in-place model (Banerjee, Shamash, Macdonald, & Mann, 1996; Leff et al., 2005). The fact that these two studies were conducted nearly a decade apart demonstrates that the aging-in-place model of health care continues to be prototypical of present and future modalities of treatment. Banerjee et al. (1996) involved 69 disabled patients suffering from depression. For a period of 6 months, the subjects received a multifaceted intervention combining pharmacological aides and automatic geriatric examination for computer-assisted taxonomy assessment (AGECAT) from a psychogeriatric team in the clients' home setting. The treatment group experienced significant alleviation of depressive symptoms and an overall increase in their general health status.

In the Leff et al. (2005) study, 455 acutely ill community-dwelling seniors received the hospital-at-home model of care for 22 months. As a result, the subjects had a shorter length of stay and lower mean costs of treatment compared to acute hospital care. This study demonstrated the efficacy of the hospital-at-home model as feasible, safe, and cost effective for certain older patients with selected acute medical illnesses. The aging-in-place paradigm underlying this study will continue to be an important impetus in future interventional strategies, particularly among aging populations.

Cohort 3—Specified Intervention and Outcome Studies

Cohort 3 represents a summarized collection of studies retained from the hundreds reviewed that satisfied certain criteria.

Namely, these studies (Table 18.3) contained clearly identified interventions, specified populations, particular time frames within which the interventions were conducted, and targeted, and/or specified outcomes. They employed a range of practitioners including professionals, semiprofessionals, health-care agents, and family members of the subjects examined. Additionally, interventions were offered in clinical and nonclinical locations and in an array of social settings, including urban, suburban, and rural, both in the United States and abroad.

The collective interventional framework of the studies in Cohort 3 can be generalized into two overlapping spheres, mental health and physical health. This may be due to the fact, in part, that the presenting problems of many elderly patients/clients are diametrically related to the unique transitions of later life, for example, declining health, chronic and acute pain, increased limitations in physical performance, loss of social connections and relationships, sociocultural isolation, cognitive changes, the escalating cost of health care, and anxiety and depressive disorders. And many of these are interrelated. As the unprecedented increase in the number of elderly continues to proliferate and the life expectancy of older adults extends, empirical evidence-based research on efficacious interventions will continue to be an essential tool to the social work practitioner (Cummings & Kropf, in press). Curiously, of the hundreds of studies reviewed here, most of the discipline-specific social work publications failed to meet the stringent intervention-outcome identified criteria in Table 18.3.

Many of these study designs included interdisciplinary, and/or multi-interventional strategies to address presenting problems (Caplan, Willaims, Daly, & Abraham, 2004; Poon, Hui, Dai, Kwok, & Woo, 2005; Rich, Gray, Beckham, Wittenberg, & Luther, 1996; Slaets, Kauffmann, Duivenvoorden, Pelemans, & Schudel, 1997). Multidisciplinary teamwork in treating the elderly is the norm and appears to be the most effective interventional stratagem. Perhaps this is due in part to the complexities that are concurrent to later-life

Table 18.3 Specified Interventions and Outcomes with Elderly Populations between 2006 and 1995

References	Interventions Provided	Presenting Problems	Specified Populations	Duration of Interventions	Targeted Outcomes	Effectiveness of Interventions
Engelhardt, Toseland, Gao, & Banks (2006)	RCT, GEM	Males who were above-average users of outpatient VA services	160	48 months	Although no increase in survival of patient indicated, intervention achieved outcome, (e.g., costs of services decreased at the 24- to 48-month period)	The GEM program can reduce the costs to senior citizen veterans who are proven to be above-average users of outpatient VA services.
Hunkeler et al. (2006)	RCT, CCM (IMPACT– CBT, PST, ED, pharmacological)	Patients with major depression, dysthymia, or both in primary care clinics	1801	36 months	Outcomes achieved, (e.g., depressive symptoms, physical functioning, quality of life, self-efficacy, and satisfaction of care)	The IMPACT model may show the way to less depression and greater, overall health in older adults.
Thomas et al. (2005)	Random CCT, Tai Chi exercise, resistance training	Chinese subjects	180	12 month longitudinal study	Outcomes not achieved, (e.g., no cardiovascular risk from Tai Chi)	Tai Chi as an intervention is no more or less beneficial to cardiovascular risk in the elderly.
Poon, Hui, Dai, Kwok, & Woo (2005)	RCT, CBT, MDT, telemedicine, CBP, FTFG, video-conferencing, SSS	CDS with mild dementia and mild cognitive impairments in China	22	12 weeks	MMSE, RBMT, HDS showed higher scores, (e.g., attention, memory, spatial construction, and language)	Telemedicine is a feasible and acceptable means in providing cognitive assessments and interventions to elder persons with mild cognitive deficits.
Enguidanos, Davis, & Katz (2005)	RCT, PCCBT, PST, and pharmacologic aids	Moderately/severely depressed patients referred to Geriatric Care Management service	153	19 months	PCCBT efficacious, (e.g., significantly reduced depressive symptoms)	Education, PST, and PCCBT can help moderately/severely depressed seniors to reduce depressive symptoms—case study approach used.

Author	Intervention	Sample	N	Duration	Outcomes	Findings
Tse, Pun, & Benzie (2005)	Affective images during PT	Patients suffering from chronic pain	15	6 weeks	Outcomes achieved, (e.g., subjects reported increase in health-related quality of life)	Affective images may provide moderate, nonpharmacological intervention for elderly persons with chronic pain.
Ryan-Woolley & Rees (2005)	RCT, concordance, use of medicine organizer, ED	Sheltered housing residents in United Kingdom	62	12 months	Outcomes achieved, (e.g., more prescription change, decrease in the number of prescriptions, less waste of medicine)	Pharmacists using concordance and medicine organizers can reduce medicine waste and misuse.
Caplan, Williams, Daly, & Abraham (2004)	RCT, MDT, CGA, DEED II program	Patients discharged home from emergency department in urban area, Australia	739	30 days (following hospital discharge) and 18 month follow-up	Outcomes achieved, (e.g., lower rate of emergency admissions, greater degree of mental and physical function, lower costs of care for patients)	DEED II, a multidisciplinary intervention, can improve health outcomes for the elderly and lower rates of readmission to hospitals.
Cummings (2003)	GT (remotivation and supportive therapy techniques)	Depressed assisted-living residents	17	10 sessions, 5 weeks	Outcomes achieved, (e.g., participants experienced significant decrease in depressive symptoms and reported higher degree of life satisfaction)	GT can increase life satisfaction and decrease depressive symptoms in assisted-living elderly with depressive symptoms.

(continued)

Table 18.3 (*Continued*)

References	Interventions Provided	Presenting Problems	Specified Populations	Duration of Interventions	Targeted Outcomes	Effectiveness of Interventions
Dipko, Xavier, & Kohlwes (2003)	ECG, ADE, SSW, DPAHC, LW	Outpatients in primary care clinic	203 (ECG) and 13,913 (comparison group)	33 months	Outcomes achieved, (e.g., ECG was twice as effective as SSW, patients were more likely to complete advance directives independent of education strategy)	Group education is an effective and time- and cost-effective social work tool for completion of advance medical directives for elderly patients.
Ball et al. (2002)	RCT, CBT, ECG	Independently living residents in six metropolitan areas	2,832	46 months	Outcomes achieved, (e.g., significant improvement in speed of processing, in reasoning, and of memory, cognitive improvement)	Results support the effectiveness and durability of cognitive training interventions in improving targeted-cognitive abilities in the elderly.
Gill, Baker, & Gottschalk (2002)	RCT, ECG, and competency-based exercise program to increase balance	Physically frail patients of primary care practices who live at home	176	12 months	Outcomes achieved, (e.g., treatment participants demonstrated improvement in physical functioning)	In physically frail older people, a home-based intervention reduced the functional decline in subjects.
Dougherty et al. (2002)	RCT, CBT, biofeedback, and pelvic muscle exercise	Rural women with urinary incontinence	178	24 months	Outcomes achieved, (e.g., participants reported less urine loss and greater quality of life)	In older rural women with urinary incontinence, a behavioral management approach for continence intervention reduced urine loss.

Study	Design/Intervention	Sample	N	Duration	Outcomes	Conclusion
Schonfeld et al. (2000)	CBT, psychoeducation (GET SMART)	Outpatient veterans with substance abuse problems	110	16 weeks	Outcomes achieved, (e.g., increase in abstinence among patients 6 months later and longer time between relapses reported by patients)	GET SMART can be an effective intervention with elderly subjects with substance abuse problems.
Mazzuca, Brandt, Katz, Hanna, & Melfi (1999)	CCT, self-care, ED	Rheumatoid arthritis and osteoarthritis	211	48 months	Outcomes achieved, (e.g., education reduced frequency and cost of primary care visits)	Education can benefit seniors in management of pain from arthritic conditions and reduce health costs.
Proctor et al. (1999)	RCT, CBT, SSS	Residents in nursing homes in United Kingdom who displayed depression and organic symptoms	120	6 months (included seven 1-hour sessions and weekly SSS support from psychiatric nurse)	Outcomes, (e.g., organic and depressive symptoms improved but behavioral and physical disability did not)	Behavioral outreach (CBT) teams can assist elderly with depressive and organic symptoms but are not efficacious to the improvement of behavioral or physical symptoms.
Keefe, Caldwell, Baucom, Salley, & Robinson (1999)	RCT, spouse-assisted CBT	Osteoarthritis knee pain	88	12 months	Outcomes achieved, (e.g., overall higher self-efficacy, lower levels of psychological and physical disability, and improved pain levels)	Spouse-assisted CBT is effective in increasing self-efficacy and managing pain in seniors with osteoarthritis-related knee pain.
Tennstedt et al. (1998)	RCT, CBP, ED	Adults from 40 senior housing sites in urban area who reported fear of falling	434	12 months (6-week, 6-month, and 12-month follow-ups)	Outcomes, (e.g., immediate but not statistically significant improvement in mobility, social functionality, and mobility control)	Community-based education to reduce fear of falling in older adults has modest beneficial effects.

(continued)

Table 18.3 *(Continued)*

References	Interventions Provided	Presenting Problems	Specified Populations	Duration of Interventions	Targeted Outcomes	Effectiveness of Interventions
Glasgow et al. (1997)	RCT, ED with emphasis on goal setting and PST	CDS with type 2 diabetes	206	12 months	Outcomes achieved, (e.g., significant improvements in food habits, caloric consumption, serum cholesterol levels, and percentage of fat)	Educational health programs with emphasis on goal setting and problem solving can work with elderly patients with type 2 diabetes.
Fries, Carey, & McShane (1997)	RCT, mail-delivered ASMP	Rheumatoid arthritis and osteoarthritis	375	6 months	Outcomes achieved, (e.g., decreased pain, global vitality increased, joint count improved, and clinical visits decreased)	Self-management courses can improve the health of the elderly and decrease costs of clinical care for pain.
Sharpe et al. (1997)	ED and physical activity program with emphasis on strength, balance, motor-coordination, and mobility	Adults in rural congregate nutrition sites	110—treatment group (61) and comparison group (49)	12 months (twice-weekly sessions)	Outcomes achieved, (e.g., greater improvements in physical functioning over the previous year than the comparison group)	Low-intensity exercise can benefit the overall health and physical functionality of elderly subjects.
Slaets, Kauffmann, Duivenvoorden, Pelemans, & Schudel (1997)	MDT, PSYG team, CBT, and SSS	Medical inpatients with poor physical functioning	237—treatment group (140) and control group (97)	12 months (following discharge)	Outcomes achieved, (e.g., improvement in the physical functioning of the treatment group participants)	Combining elements from psychiatric, social service, and geriatric consultation with elements of unit-driven service improves physical functioning among the elderly.

Study	Methods	Subjects	Sample	Duration	Outcomes	Conclusions
Rich, Gray, Beckham, Wittenberg, & Luther (1996)	RCT, MDT, NT, ED, and SSS	CHF patients with poor behavioral medication compliance	156—intervention group (80) and conventional care group (76)	30 days (following hospital discharge)	Outcomes achieved, e.g., medication compliance in patients increased	A MDT can improve medication compliance during first 30 days following discharge from the hospital in elderly patients with CHF.
Maisiak, Austin, & Heck (1996)	RCT, telephone monitoring and counseling	Rheumatoid arthritis and osteoarthritis	405	9 months	Outcomes achieved, e.g., better health status scores, number of medical visits decreased	Elderly patients with rheumatoid arthritis and osteoarthritis are responsive to telephone counseling and support for pain.
Rich et al. (1995)	PRT, Nurse-directed MDT, NT, ED, and SSS	CHF patients with poor behavioral compliance to treatment who were at risk for re-admittance to hospital following discharge	282—treatment group (142) and control group (140)	90 days (following hospital discharge)	Outcomes achieved, e.g., hospital readmission was significantly reduced	Nurse-directed MDT can improve the quality of life and reduce both hospital use and medical costs for elderly patients with CHF.
Bailly & DePoy (1995)	ADE, ECG	Clients at a family medical care practice in rural area	10	2 weeks	Statistically significant increase in knowledge of ADE was not reported	Authors suggest that ADE may be a family issue rather than solely an individual issue.

ADE = Advance directive education; ASMP = Arthritis self-management program; CBP = Community-based group; CBT = Cognitive behavioral therapy; CCM = Collaborative care management; CCT = Controlled clinical trial; CDS = Community-dwelling seniors; CGA = Comprehensive geriatric assessment; CHF = Congestive heart failure; DEED II = Discharge of elderly from the emergency department program; DPAHC = Durable power of attorney for health care; ECG = Educational control group; ED = Education; FTFG = Face to face group; GEM = Geriatric evaluation and management program; GET SMART = Geriatric evaluation team: substance misuse/abuse recognition and treatment program; GT = Group therapy; HDS = Hierarchical dementia scale; LW = Living will; MDT = Multidisciplinary team; MMSE = Mini-mental state examination; NT = Nutritional training; PCCBT = Patient-centered cognitive behavioral therapy; PRT = Prospective randomized trial; PST = Problem solving therapy; PSYG = Psychogeriatric; PT = Physiotherapy; RBMT = Rivermead behavioral memory test; RCT = Random clinical trial; SSS = Social service support; SSW = Session with social worker; VA = Veterans Administration.

experiences and its respective host of challenges. Among the uniqueness of gerontological practice is the biopsychosocial holistic approach to using interventions with the client. Using a multidisciplinary approach is one way of addressing the whole person in his or her environment.

Cohort 3 studies clearly reveal an eclectic methodological range in their interventions. These interventions range in duration from 2 weeks to 48 months and every possibility in between. Some synthesized pharmacological and therapeutic stratagems to address presenting problems of severe depression in the elderly subjects (Enguidanos, Davis, & Katz, 2005; Hunkeler et al., 2006). Others utilized a collaborative approach of technology and therapy to address presenting problems ranging from cognitive impairment to chronic pain, from depression to arthritis, and from urinary incontinence to dementia (Dougherty et al., 2002; Poon et al., 2005; Tse, Pun, & Benzie, 2005).

Since the 1950s, the ubiquitous modality for treating the elderly is group work. This approach continues to be apparent, having success in both achieving desired outcomes (Ball et al., 2002) and nonsuccess in accomplishing specified outcomes (Bailly & DePoy, 1995; Gill, Baker, & Gottschalk, 2002). Thus, from these data, group work/therapy remains an efficacious interventional stratagem within the elderly population. Many of such interventions included problem solving, remotivational, and/or cognitive-behavioral therapy (Ball et al., 2002; Cummings, 2003; Dougherty et al., 2002; Enguidanos et al., 2005; Glasgow et al., 1997; Hunkeler et al., 2006; Keefe, Caldwell, Baucom, Salley, & Robinson, 1999; Proctor et al., 1999; Schonfeld et al., 2000). This finding was recently corroborated in another review of evidence and outcome literature with this population (Kolomer, in press).

The eclecticism of these interventions demonstrates the expediency of taking more than one approach to a presenting problem. In short, they suggest that multifaceted presenting problems require multimethodological interventions. Rich et al.'s (1996) study on congestive heart failure patients who demonstrated poor behavioral compliance to their treatment were at risk of readmission to the hospital, thus increasing the cost of care and potentially exacerbating their physical ailment. By utilizing a nurse-led multidisciplinary team that provided nutritional training, education, and social service support, hospital readmission was significantly reduced among those in the treatment group, thus reducing the costs of care and increasing the general health of these subjects.

Further, upon examining the overall cohort, we recognize that the variegated interventions are quite similar in their recognition of the inextricable connection between pain and depressive symptoms. Acute and chronic pain have the potential to lower health status scores, quality of life, self-efficacy, and social functioning of elderly clients/patients. These studies show that many of the targeted outcomes of the interventions were consistently related to the symptomatic experiences that are concomitant to chronic and acute pain. For example, Maisiak, Austin, and Heck (1996) conducted a study on elderly patients suffering from rheumatoid arthritis and osteoarthritis. The chronic and acute pain of these conditions lowered the health status scores of the study group and increased the number of medical visits, thus increasing the cost and inconvenience of health care for these 405 subjects. The 9-month intervention of telephone monitoring and counseling bettered the health status scores, decreased the number of medical visits, and decreased the concomitant costs of care for these subjects. This study showed that elderly patients with rheumatoid arthritis and osteoarthritis are responsive to telephone counseling and support for pain.

Overall, the studies in Cohort 3 suggest that the greater the specificity of the target group, the more precise the interventional strategy, the more defined the desired/targeted outcomes, the greater likelihood of success. Additionally, they reveal that the complexities of experiences in later life necessitate interdisciplinary multi-interventional strategies that synthesize several methods toward specific and desired outcomes. The implication for the social work practitioner is that he or she must become more adept at reviewing, conducting, and using evidence-based empirical research and become acquainted with a variety of disciplines in order to navigate the quagmire of the biopsychosocial experiences of elderly clients (Cummings & Kropf, in press).

In these studies, the specified targeted outcomes ranged from the very broad; for example, reduction of depressive symptoms, increase in degree of life satisfaction, improvement in physical functioning, and/or increase of knowledge about end-of-life planning, to the very specific; for example, reducing the loss of urine, lowering serum cholesterol levels, completion of advance directives, and/or lowering costs for outpatient services over a 48-month period. These studies also reflect the well-known bias of published literature, that is, treatments that work. Nevertheless, the contributive importance of these studies along the continuum of practice presented in this chapter help social workers understand the inimitable synergistic value of using EBP for their intervention strategies.

LIMITATIONS OF THE EVIDENCE

As with any overview chapter of this nature, the search process used to collect the articles/chapters/published accounts of EBP interventions may not have captured all of the available published literature. For this we apologize. Second, the processes used to define evidence-based practice and the subsequent conceptualization of it depart somewhat from more traditional notions of its use in reviews of this nature (e.g., Cummings & Kropf, in press).

Despite these limitations and based on Figure 18.1, we collected and analyzed literature according to three cohorts: (1) conceptual/theoretical frameworks for treatment, (2) effectiveness studies, and (3) specified intervention and outcome studies. Prior to a discussion of these subsections, the limitations and conceptualization of how the residual published accounts were retained is discussed.

What became apparent in this overall review is the need for the social work profession to develop a more relevant definition of EBP. This has been noted before (Gambrill, 2006; Holosko, 2004; Pollio, 2002, 2006; Sackett et al., 1997; Thyer & Kazi, 2004). Such a definition should embrace the practice reality of professionals working in our field, have an empirical basis to it, and should inform and direct practice in meaningful ways. All of the submissions offered in this chapter meet these minimal criteria.

IMPLICATIONS FOR SOCIAL WORK AT MICRO-, MEZZO-, AND MACROLEVELS

If we were to look at various practice trends in the field of gerontology, four main trends prevail. First, there are and will continue to be a shortage of trained personnel to work in this area. Second, education and training needs far exceed the ability for practitioners working in this area to provide adequate, timely, and much needed care. Third, practitioners are

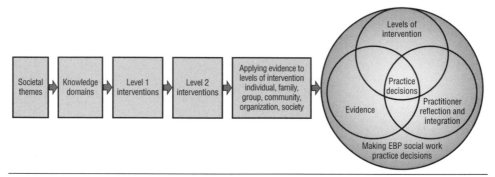

Figure 18.2   Minimal knowledge and skills necessary to use evidence-based practice with the elderly

required to integrate specialized knowledge, skills, and interventions in order to be effective in working with the elderly. Fourth, social work practitioners must embrace the principles of advanced generalist practice and move fluidly and seamlessly in providing competent interventions to their clients. The latter implies that the micro/mezzo/macro distinction delimits our ability to be effective with such clients (Holosko, White, & Feit, 2004).

In an effort to illustrate how EBP underpins practice in this field, Figure 18.2 illustrates how a cumulative progression of societal issues, levels of intervention, and the application of such evidence to practice results for better-informed practice decisions. Rather than illustrating *what* evidence should be used to affect practice, this figure shows *how* evidence directs and informs our practice. In each step of Figure 18.2, a series of current and minimal knowledge requirements are identified. Then, the assumptions underpinning each will be identified followed by a brief discussion.

Societal Themes Issues

Social workers require a formative contextual knowledge of what's going on in society and in my community with the elderly? Having such awareness, allows us to understand how broader issues truly impact day-to-day practice realities in working with the elderly. These current themes are presented in Table 18.4.

Table 18.4   Current Societal Issues/Themes

The escalating number of elderly and their unique and specialized health, mental health, and social issues

"Aging-in-place" or supporting individuals to reside in their homes and communities for as long as possible

Not enough resources to adequately serve and treat the demands of this subpopulation

The impact of new technologies that can be used to better serve and treat this subpopulation

The systematic devolution of federal and state monies and supports to local community-based initiatives

Out-migration of elderly person from rural to urban centers to avail themselves of services

Long-standing and prevailing ageism challenges our ability to practice in this field

The main assumptions around these cornerstone societal issues or themes are (a) as society evolves, these themes will inevitably change, (b) they systemically interrelate with each other, and (c) all gerontological practice in any "community of care" is shaped by broader societal issues that frame such practice.

In regard to the latter, workers need to (a) understand how to work creatively in limited resources; (b) demystify stereotypes typically presented about elderly persons; (c) understand policies, procedures, and best practices that shape how and what they do; and (d) not practice in a contextual vacuum. Indeed, gerontological social work has been a forerunner in recognizing and responding to the political, societal, and practice realities of the elderly today. Our longstanding work with the marginal and vulnerable populations of society has perhaps made us more prepared and clearer about how to effectively approach practice in a time of limited and rationed health and social services (Holosko & Holosko, 2004).

Basic Knowledge Areas

The minimal knowledge areas in quadrant 2 (Figure 18.2) for social work practitioners working with the elderly are presented in Table 18.5.

The main assumptions underpinning Table 18.5 are (a) each involves core knowledge, values, and skills that are differentially applied to each client or client situation; and (b) there are minimal knowledge requirements in each area that practitioners need in order to offer responsible and ethical practice (Vourlekis, Zlotnick, & Simons, 2005).

As a precursor to the application of interventions with the elderly, these then are deemed as the basic knowledge domains of any gerontological social work practitioner. Indeed, there is much to learn here, and a healthier reframe might be to look as these as a process of career professional learning and systematically developing and accruing knowledge about each area on a case-by-case basis. Seeking and finding relevant empirical evidence to understand such knowledge and integrating it into day-to-day practice are challenges that every worker faces in his or her unique way.

Level 1—Intervention Skills

As indicated in the numerous studies previously reviewed in this chapter, a variety of interventions often multiplied and differentially applied are the norm, not the exception, for

Table 18.5   Basic Knowledge Areas for Working with the Elderly

Biopsychosocial holistic approach
Formal and informal support systems
Grief and loss
Death and dying
Sexuality
Medical conditions unique to the elderly
Mental health conditions unique to the elderly
Social and family situations and conditions unique to the elderly
Spirituality
Diversity and culture
Unique family situations

practitioners who work in this field (see Tables 18.1, 18.2, and 18.3). These are referred to as "Level 1—Skills" because they are the basic or minimal ones necessary to work at the entry levels of practice with the elderly. As Figure 18.2 also illustrates, they are cumulative in nature or build on a practitioner's ability to integrate both the previously described societal themes and formative knowledge domains. These are presented in Table 18.6.

In today's practice reality, these Level 1 skills are typically provided in any accredited BSW program in North America. It is *how* they are used with the elderly, however, that characterizes their uniqueness for practitioners working in this field. Two underlying assumptions about their current use with the elderly include: (1) all need to be grounded in a strengths-based perspective, and (2) they require an overt client-centered focus in their application.

From a strengths-based framework, the notion is to apply such interventions to promote factors of successful aging. These include the avoidance of disease and disability, involvement in society, continued high cognitive and physical impairment, and maintained or acquired sense of purpose and autonomy (Rowe & Kahn, 1998). As society gives responsibility for care back to individuals, families, and communities, clearly there is renewed support for a client-centered focus with the elderly. The elderly person then, despite capacity, physical abilities, and financial resources is to be considered *as the person with the resources to make changes in his or her situation to be more functional* (Holosko & Holosko, 2004, p. 37).

Level II Intervention Skills

Building on the previous areas, Table 18.7 presents a list of minimal Level II intervention skills that gerontological practitioners require. Again, many of these were mentioned in the numerous evidence-based studies previously reviewed in Tables 18.1 to 18.3 that assessed practice efficacy.

Table 18.7 presents a set of skills that clearly delineate specialization criteria for social workers working with the elderly. Although such skills are more likely to be offered in our MSW, rather than BSW curricula (Holosko, 1995), they require more knowledge, specialized training, and education than these curricula currently offer. The two assumptions on which they stand are (1) you must be an advanced generalist practitioner in order to be effective in this field, and (2) instilling hope with each client and client situation and needs to become integrated into each intervention offered.

Table 18.6   Level 1 Intervention Skills

Assessment
Counseling
Discharge planning
Treatment planning and monitoring treatment
Case management
Group work
Advocacy and brokering
Community outreach coordination
Education

Table 18.7   Level II Intervention Skills

Defining what is unique about social work practice with the elderly
Complex ethical decision making
Capacity assessment
Caregiving dynamics
End-of-life protocols and caring
Working in multisystem levels
Working effectively and creatively with minimal resources
Anchoring all interventions in the best available evidence
Routinely evaluating one's own practice effectiveness

Gerontological social worker practitioners epitomize the essence of advanced generalist practice. Staying current with new developments in the field, working simultaneously and fluidly with all levels—micro/mezzo/macro—and evaluating their practice are the norm, not the exception, for such practitioners (Holosko & Feit, 2004; Vourlekis et al., 2005). It is at this level that one begins to see how judiciously using empirical data, seeking and using current literature and case material and the best available evidence, and judiciously using these data to direct and inform practice are "part-and-parcel" of everyday gerontological practice. Thus, there is no option for not integrating empirical data into practice, whether it is secondary or primary data collected by the practitioners themselves or learned from the literature (Rosen, 2003).

The issue of the instillation of hope into each client, client situation, intervention, and so on becomes a formidable challenge for practitioners working in this field. We cannot rely solely on the outcomes of our interventions, for example, "most clients should do better after the 12 weeks of treatment," to be the only indicator of our intervention successes or failures. Neither can we "buy in" to self-pitying clients or colleagues who have given up hope on themselves or their situations. These challenges are consistently confronted in areas such as advanced stages of dementia, chronic physical disease, and/or end-of-life transitions.

Applying Evidence to Render Better Practice Decisions

The final grid and circle synthesizing the integration of these areas in this cumulative process implies applying evidence to impact a better practice decision. Whether such evidence results in a better set of practice questions (Gibbs, 2005), it is the synergy of the application of the available evidence through an intervention that results in better-informed practice decisions. This then becomes the culmination (in this model) of the evidence-informing practice process.

One of the three intersecting circles in Figure 18.2 involves "Practice Reflection and Integration." Thus, having the evidence and knowing how to apply it requires some "practice wisdom," as we used to say. This is truly where the "art" side of practice meets the "empirical" side and both are necessary to render better-informed practice decisions. The perennial false dichotomy that has polarized these two areas of social work (for a number years) is, therefore, rooted in this synthesis model.

For instance, if social work practitioners use the best available evidence to render a practice decision as such, they cannot be accused of dismissing either side of the "science-art" continuum. It is the precise synthesis of their interaction that is the trigger for the eventual practice decision. However, if a practice decision is made without this synthesis, it would be deemed unethical and irresponsible by default (Gambrill, 2006).

This critical intersect is the very place where (a) a looser definition of EBP can be rationalized (as is argued in this chapter); (b) statistical and clinical significance can be deemed as equally relevant; and, most importantly, (c) practitioners working in this field can render an empirically based practice decision in a reflective, individualized, and integrative knowledge-based fashion—evidence-based practice defined in gerontological social work practice.

CONCLUSION

This chapter presented an overview of EBP interventions with the elderly. At the onset, it was suggested that understanding the context in which these interventions occurred may help social work practitioners to better understand the literature and data presented herein. These broader contexts included: the demographic reality of a rapidly growing aging society, social policies or so-called best practices that shape current gerontological practice and practice implications.

A model (Figure 18.1) based on a less stringent definition of EBP categorized these literature/studies into three related cohorts. Cohort 1 was called "Conceptual/Theoretical Frameworks," Cohort 2 was called "Effectiveness Studies," and Cohort 3 was "Intervention and Outcome Studies." The parameters of each of these and their conceptual rationale were presented prior to a discussion of the data within them.

After a discussion of these data, a second figure (Figure 18.2) configured a relationship about not *what* this evidence was, but *how* it could be used in a practice model. Thus, the integration of evidence into gerontological practice was then discussed.

Based on this chapter, the question becomes—*What do social work practitioners need to know about evidence-based interventions with the elderly?* There are a few things that seem important.

First, despite the fact that more social workers are practicing with the elderly than ever before and considerable progress has been made in the profession's ability to conduct more research and evaluation (Padgett, 2005), we must strive to continue to evaluate our practice interventions with the elderly. Morrow-Howell and Burnette (2001) indicated that the top priority identified by gerontological social workers and researchers was the development and tending of psychosocial interventions with the elderly.

In a recent review of literature about evidence-based practice with the elderly, Cummings and Kropf (in press) concluded their insights review by stating:

> Researchers acknowledge that greater understanding about how different intervention approaches promote beneficial outcomes within the diversity of the older population is required. Since limited evidence exists in many areas of practice with older adults, researchers have abundant opportunities to conduct research that will add to the knowledge base about effective intervention approaches.

Indeed, continuing to build a social work research agenda about practice interventions is seen as being essential to developing timely knowledge about our practice efforts.

Second, as is argued in this chapter, the social work profession has acknowledged that it requires a more relevant definition of evidence-based practice (Gambrill, 2006). This definition should guide and inform practice and be able to be easily operationalized in the practice worlds of our practitioners (Pollio, 2006). The integrative model (Figure 18.2) presented a case supporting this contention. The cohort definitions on which this model was based (Figure 18.1) further argued for a new definition of EBP. Indeed, as is presented throughout this chapter, the nexus for understanding the relationship between research/evaluation and practice is first how research/evaluation data guides/directs/informs practice. Second, how it becomes integrated into day-to-day practice activities is where "the real proof is in the pudding"—to quote an old English proverb.

Overall, Tables 18.1, 18.2, and 18.3 taken together revealed that:

- Social work is not the only profession taking a leadership role in assessing practice efficacy with the elderly.
- Inherent internal and external validity threats, for example, history, maturation, subject and experimenter expectancy, and generalizability are "part and parcel" of conducting research/evaluations of practice interventions with this population.
- Multidisciplinary team interventions are the norm for practitioners working in this field.
- Group work intervention is still the prevailing practice modality for providing intervention to the elderly.
- Multiple intervention strategies targeting specific multifaceted problems are the current practice in this field.
- Empowerment and strengths-based approaches have significantly influenced social work practice with the elderly.
- Issues, problems, and concerns of the elderly are slowly being reframed as normalized, not pathological.
- Describing and measuring our practice outcomes in more precise ways has resulted in ameliorating specific problems of clients, "better time framed" treatment protocols, sharper interventions, and better-informed practice decisions.

Finally, gerontological social work practice holds a promising future for our profession. It is a field rife with both challenges and opportunities in which social work can take an active leadership role. Basing our practice and interventions on empirical evidence that directs and informs judicious practice decisions is an important way for us to impart such leadership. Social work has the necessary knowledge, values, and skills to affect such responsible and ethical practice.

REFERENCES

Abrahamson, S. J., & Khan, F. (2006). Brief osteoporosis education in an inpatient rehabilitation setting improves knowledge of osteoporosis in elderly patients with low-trauma fractures. *International Journal of Rehabilitation Research*, 29(1), 61–64.

Administration on Aging. (2003). *A profile of older Americans*. Retrieved March 23, 2004, from www.aoa.gov/prof/Statistics/profile/2003/profiles2003.asp.

Bailly, D., & DePoy, E. (1995). Older people's responses to education about advance directives. *Health and Social Work, 20*(3), 223–229.

Ball, K., Berch, D. B., Helmers, K. F., Jobe, J. B., Leveck, M. D., Marsiske, M., et al. (2002). Effects of cognitive training interventions with older adults: A randomized controlled trial. *Journal of the American Medical Association, 288*(18), 2271–2281.

Banerjee, S., Shamash, K., Macdonald, A. J. D., & Mann, A. H. (1996). Randomized controlled trial of effect of intervention by psychogeriatric team on depression in frail elderly people at home. *British Medical Journal, 313*(7064), 1058–1061.

Bisman, C. D. (2003). Rural aging: Social work practice models and intervention dynamics. *Journal of Gerontological Social Work, 41*(1/2), 37–58.

Camberg, L., Woods, P., Ooi, W. L., Hurley, A., Volicer, L., Ashley, J., et al. (1999). Evaluation of simulated presence: A personalized approach to enhance well-being in persons with Alzheimer's disease. *Journal of the American Geriatrics Society, 47*(4), 446–452.

Campbell, J. A., Robertson, M. C., Gardner, M. M., Norton, R. N., Tilyard, M. W., & Buchner, D. M. (1997). Randomized controlled trial of a general practice program of home based exercise to prevent falls in elderly women. *British Medical Journal, 315*(7115), 1065–1069.

Caplan, G. A., Williams, A. J., Daly, B., & Abraham, K. (2004). A randomized, controlled trial of comprehensive geriatric assessment and multidisciplinary intervention after discharge of elderly from the emergency department: The DEED II Study. *Journal of the American Geriatrics Society, 52*(9), 1417–1423.

Ciechanowski, P., Wagner, E., Schmaling, K., Schwartz, S., Williams, B., Diehr, P., et al. (2004). Community-integrated home-based depression treatment in older adults: A randomized controlled trial. *Journal of the American Medical Association, 291*(13), 1626–1628.

Council in Social Work Education. (2006, February). *Gero-Ed Forum* [Abstract]. Chicago. Retrieved October 17, 2007, from www.Gero-EdCenter.org.

Cummings, S. (2003). The efficacy of an integrated group treatment program for depressed assisted living residents. *Research on Social Work Practice, 13*(5), 608–621.

Cummings, S., & Kropf, N. (Eds.). (in press). Evidence-based psycho-social treatments for older adults [Special edition]. *Journal of Evidence-Based Social Work.*

De Leo, D., Buono, D., & Dwyer, J. (2002). Suicide among the elderly: The long-term impact of a telephone support and assessment intervention in northern Italy. *British Journal of Psychiatry, 181*(3), 226–229.

Dipko, L., Xavier, K., & Kohlwes, R. (2003). Advance directive group education in a VA outpatient clinic. *Social Work in Health Care, 38*, 93–106.

Dougherty, M. C., Dwyer, J. W., Pendergast, J. F., Boyington, A. R., Tomlinson U., Coward, R. T., et al. (2002). A randomized trial of behavioral management for continence with older rural women. *Research in Nursing and Health, 25*(1), 3–13.

Dunlop, J., & Holosko, M. J. (in press). Technology and evidence-based practice [Special guest edition]. *Journal of Evidence-Based Social Work Practice, 3*(3/4).

Engelhardt, J. B., Toseland, R. W., Gao, J., & Banks, S. (2006). Long-term effects of outpatient geriatric evaluation and management on health care utilization, cost, and survival. *Research on Social Work Practice, 16*, 20–27.

Enguidanos, S. M., Davis, C., & Katz, L. (2005). Shifting the paradigm in geriatric care management: Moving from the medical model to patient-centered care. *Social Work in Health Care, 41*(1), 1–16.

Feit, M. D., & Cuevas-Feit, N. (1991). An overview of social work practice with the elderly. In M. J. Holosko & M. D. Feit (Eds.), *Social work practice with the elderly* (2nd ed., pp. 3–27). Toronto, Ontario, Canada: Canadian Scholar's Press.

Feit, M. D., & Cuevas-Feit, N. (2004). An overview of social work practice with the elderly. In M. J. Holosko & M. D. Feit (Eds.), *Social work practice with the elderly* (3rd ed., pp. 3–27). Toronto, Ontario, Canada: Canadian Scholar's Press.

Fries, J. F., Carey, C., & McShane, D. J. (1997). Patient education in arthritis: Randomized controlled trial of a mail-delivered program. *Journal of Rheumatology*, *24*(7), 1378–1383.

Gambrill, E. (2006). Evidence-based practice and policy: Choices ahead. *Research on Social Work Practice*, *16*(3), 338–358.

Gibbs, L. (2005, October). *Using research to make life-affecting judgments and decisions.* Keynote address at the 17th National Symposium on Doctoral Research, Ohio State University, Columbus.

Gill, T. M., Baker, D. I., & Gottschalk, M. (2002). A program to prevent functional decline in physically frail, elderly persons who live at home. *New England Journal of Medicine*, *347*(14), 1068–1074.

Glasgow, R., La Chance, P., Toobert, D., Brown, J., Hampson, S., & Riddle, M. (1997). Long term effects and costs of brief behavioral dietary intervention for patients with diabetes delivered from medical office. *Patient Education and Counseling*, *32*(3), 175–184.

Graziano, R. (2003). Trauma and aging. *Journal of Gerontological Social Work*, *40*(4), 3–21.

Greene, R. (1988). *Continuing education for gerontological careers.* Washington, DC: Council on Social Work Education.

Groth-Juncker, A., & McCusker, J. (1983). Where do elderly patients prefer to die? Place of death and patient characteristics of 100 elderly patients under the care of a home health care team. *Journal of the American Geriatric Society*, *31*(8), 457–461.

Gutheil, I. A., & Heyman, J. C. (2005). Communication between older people and their health care agents: Results of an intervention. *Health and Social Work*, *30*(2), 107–128.

Haight, B., & Gibson, F. (Eds.). (2005). *Burnside's working with older adults: Group processes and techniques* (4th ed.). Sudbury, MA: Jones and Bartlett.

Hobart, K. R. (2001). Death and dying and the social work role. *Journal of Gerontological Social Work*, *36*(3/4), 181–192.

Holosko, M. J. (1995). The inclusion of gerontology consent into undergraduate social work curricula in Australia and New Zealand. *Gerontology and Geriatrics Education*, *15*(4), 5–20.

Holosko, M. J. (2004). Evidence-based practice in Canada. In B. Thyer & M. Kazi (Eds.), *International perspectives: Evidence-based practice in social work* (pp. 61–78). London: Venture Press.

Holosko, M. J., & Feit, M. D. (Eds.). (2004). *Social work practice with the elderly* (3rd ed.). Toronto, Ontario, Canada: Canadian Scholar's Press.

Holosko, M. J., & Holosko, D. A. (2004). What is unique about social work practice with the elderly? In M. J. Holosko & M. D. Feit (Eds.), *Social work practice with the elderly* (3rd ed., pp. 27–49). Toronto, Ontario, Canada: Canadian Scholar's Press.

Holosko, M. J., & Leslie, D. R. (2004). Social policies that influence practice with the elderly. In M. J. Holosko & M. D. Feit (Eds.), *Social work practice with the elderly* (3rd ed., pp. 119–151). Toronto, Ontario, Canada: Canadian Scholar's Press.

Holosko, M. J., White, L., & Feit, M. D. (2004). Gerontological social work practice in 2005 and beyond. In M. J. Holosko & M. D. Feit (Eds.), *Social work practice with the elderly* (3rd ed., pp. 549–557). Toronto, Ontario, Canada: Canadian Scholar's Press.

Hooyman, N. R., & Kayak, H. A. (2002). *Social gerontology: A multi-disciplinary perspective* (6th ed.). Upper Saddle River, NJ: Pearson Education.

Howard, M. D., McMillan, C., & Pollio, D. (2003). Teaching evidence-based practice: Toward a new paradigm for social work education. *Research a Social Work Practice*, *13*(2), 234–259.

Hunkeler, E. M., Katon, W., Tang, L., Williams, J. W., Jr., Kroenke, K., Lin, E. H., et al. (2006). Long-term outcomes from the IMPACT randomized trial for depressed elderly patients in primary care. *British Medical Journal*, *332*(7536), 259–262.

Inouye, S. K., Wagner, D. R., Acampora, D., Horwitz, R. I., Cooney, L. M., & Tinetii, M. E. (1993). A controlled trial of a nursing-centered intervention in hospitalized elderly medical patients: The Yale Geriatric Care Program. *Journal of the American Geriatrics Society*, *41*, 1353–1360.

Kapasi, Z. H., Ouslander, J. G., Schnelle, J. F., Kutner, M., & Fahey, J. L. (2003). Effects of an exercise intervention on immunologic parameters in frail elderly nursing home residents. *Journal of Gerontology: Series A, Biological Sciences and Medical Sciences, 58*(7), 636–643.

Keefe, F. J., Caldwell, D. S., Baucom, D., Salley, A., & Robinson, E. (1999). Spouse assisted coping skills training in the management of knee pain in osteoarthritis: Long-term follow up results. *Arthritis Care and Research, 12*(2), 101–111.

Kochevar, A., Smith, K., & Bernard, M. (2001). Effects of a community-based intervention to increase activity in American Indian elders. *Journal of the Oklahoma State Medical Association, 94*(10), 455–460.

Kolomer, S. (in press). Evidence-based psycho-social treatments for grandparent caregivers. *Journal of Evidence-Based Social Work.*

Kuhn, D., & Mendes de Leon, C. (2001). Evaluation of an educational intervention with relatives of persons in the early stage of Alzheimer's disease. *Research on Social Work Practice, 11*(5), 531–548.

Leff, B., Burton, L., Mader, S. L., Naughton, B., Burl, J., Inouye, S. K., et al. (2005). Hospital as home: Feasibility and outcomes of a program to provide hospital level care at home for acutely ill older patients. *Annals of Internal Medicine, 143*(11), 798–808.

Leon, A. M., Altholz, J. A. S., & Dziegielewski, S. F. (1999). Compassion fatigue: Considerations for working with the elderly. *Journal of Gerontological Social Work, 32*(1), 43–62.

Li, H., & Blaser, C. J. (2003). Rural program planning and development for older adults. *Journal of Gerontological Social Work, 41*(1/2), 75–89.

Lomas, J., Woods, J., & Veenstra, G. (1997). Devolving authority for health care in Canada's provinces: Pt. 1. An introduction to the issues. *Canadian Medical Association Journal, 56*, 371–377.

Lowry, L. (1979). *Social policies and programs on aging.* Lexington, MA: Lexington Books.

Maisiak, R., Austin, J., & Heck, L. (1996). Health outcomes of two telephone interventions for patients with rheumatoid arthritis or osteoarthritis. *Arthritis Rheumatology, 39*(8), 1391–1399.

Mazzuca, S. A., Brandt, K. D., Katz, B. P., Hanna, M. P., & Melfi, C. A. (1999). Reduced utilization and cost of primary care clinic visits resulting from self-care education for patients with osteoarthritis of the knee. *Arthritis Rheumatology, 42*(6), 1267–1273.

McInnis-Dittrich, K. (2002). *Social work with elders: A biopsychosocial approach to assessment and intervention.* Boston: Allyn & Bacon.

Mittelman, M. S., Roth, D. L., Coon, D. W., & Haley, W. E. (2004). Sustained benefit of supportive intervention for depressive symptoms in caregivers of patients with Alzheimer's disease. *American Journal of Psychiatry, 161*(5), 850–856.

Mo-Kyung, S., Belza, B., LoGerfo, J., & Cunningham, S. (2005). Evaluation of a community-based exercise program for elderly Korean immigrants. *Public Health Nursing, 22*(5), 407–413.

Morrow-Howell, N., & Burnette, D. (2001). Gerontological social work research: Current status and future directions. *Journal for Gerontological Social Work, 36*(3/4), 63–79.

Naleppa, M. J., & Reid, W. J. (2003). *Gerontological social work: A task-centered approach.* New York: Columbia University Press.

National Association of Social Workers. (2006). *National study of licensed social workers 2006.* Retrieved November 14, 2006, from http://workforce.socialworkers.org.

National Association of Social Workers. (2004). *End-of-life care.* Retrieved November 14, 2006, from www.socialworkers.org.

Otten, A. (1984, July 10). The oldest-old (3 Pts.). *Wall Street Journal*, pp. 1–2.

Padgett, D. K. (2005). The Society for Social Work Research at 10 years of age and counting: An idea whose time had come. *Research on Social Work Practice, 15*(1), 3–7.

Peck, M. D. (2001). Looking back at life and its influence on subjective well-being. *Journal of Gerontological Social Work, 35*(2), 3–21.

Pinquart, M., Sörensen, S., & Peak, T. (2004). Helping older adults and their families develop and implement care plans. *Journal of Gerontological Social Work*, *43*(4), 3–23.

Pollio, D. (2002). The evidence-based group worker. *Social Work with Groups*, *25*(4), 57–70.

Pollio, D. (2006). The art of evidence-based practice. *Research on Social Work Practice*, *16*(2), 224–232.

Poon, P., Hui, E., Dai, D., Kwok, T., & Woo, J. (2005). Cognitive intervention for community-dwelling older persons with memory problems: Telemedicine versus face-to-face treatment. *International Journal of Geriatric Psychiatry*, *20*(3), 285–286.

Proctor, R., Burns, A., Powell, H. S., Tarrier, N., Faragher, B., Richardson, G., et al. (1999). Behavioral management in nursing and residential homes: A randomized controlled trial. *Lancet*, *354*(9172), 26–29.

Rich, M. W., Beckham, V., Wittenberg, C., Leven, C. L., Freedland, K. E., & Carney, R. M. (1995). A multidisciplinary intervention to prevent the readmission of elderly patients with congestive heart failure. *New England Journal of Medicine*, *333*(18), 1190–1195.

Rich, M. W., Gray, D. B., Beckham, V., Wittenberg, C., & Luther, P. (1996). Effect of a multidisciplinary intervention on medication compliance in elderly patients with congestive heart failure. *American Journal of Medicine*, *101*, 3270–3276.

Rosen, A. (2003). Evidence-based social work practice: Challenges and promises. *Social Work Research*, *27*, 208–210.

Rowe, J. W., & Kahn, R. L. (1998). *Successful aging*. New York: Pantheon Books.

Ryan-Woolley, B. M., & Rees, J. A. (2005). Initializing concordance in frail elderly patients via a Medicines Organizer. *Annals of Pharmacotherapy*, *39*, 1–6.

Sackett, D. L., Richardson, W. S., Rosenberg, W., & Haynes, R. B. (1997). *Evidence-based medicine: How to practice and teach EBM*. New York: Churchill Livingstone.

Schneider, R., Decker, T., Freeman, J., Messerschmidt, L., & Syran, C. (Eds.). (1984). *Specialized course outline for gerontological social work education*. Washington, DC: Council on Social Work Education Press.

Schonfeld, L., Dupree, L. W., Dickson, F. E., Royer, C. M., McDermott, C. H., Rosansky, J. S., et al. (2000). Cognitive behavioral treatment of older veterans with substance abuse problems. *Journal of Geriatric Psychiatric and Neurology*, *13*, 124–128.

Sharpe, P. A., Jackson, K. L., White, C., Vaca, V. L., Hickey, T., Gu, J., et al. (1997). Effects of a one-year physical activity intervention for older adults at congregate nutrition sites. *Gerontologist*, *37*, 208–215.

Slaets, J. P., Kauffmann, R. H., Duivenvoorden, H. J., Pelemans, W., & Schudel, W. J. (1997). A randomized trial of geriatric liaison intervention in elderly medical inpatients. *Psychosomatic Medicine*, *59*(6), 585–591.

Solomon, P. R., Adams, F., Silver, A., Zimmer, J., & DeVeaux, R. (2002). Ginkgo for memory enhancement: A randomized controlled trial. *Journal of the American Medical Association*, *288*, 835–840.

Solomon, R. (2004). The role of the social worker in long-term care. *Journal of Gerontological Social Work*, *43*(2/3), 187–202.

Stinson, C. K., & Kirk, E. (2006). Structured reminiscence: An intervention to decrease depression and increase self-transcendence in older women. *Journal of Clinical Nursing*, *15*, 208–218.

Tennstedt, S., Howland, J., Lachman, M., Peterson, E., Kasten, L., & Jette, A. (1998). A randomized, controlled trial of a group intervention to reduce fear of falling and associated activity restriction in older adults. *Journal of Gerontology: Series B, Psychological Sciences*, *53*, 384–392.

Thomas, G. N., Hong, A. W. L., Tomlinson, B., Lau, E., Lam, C. W. K., Sanderson, J. E., et al. (2005). Effects of Tai Chi and resistance training on cardiovascular risk factors in the elderly: A 12-month longitudinal, controlled intervention study. *Clinical Endocrinology*, *63*, 663–669.

Thyer, B., & Kazi, M. (Eds.). (2004). *International perspectives: Evidence-based practice in social work*. London: Venture Press.

Tsang, H. W. H., Mok, C. K., Au Yeung, Y. T., & Chan, S. Y. C. (2003). The effect of Qigong on general and psychosocial health of elderly with chronic physical illnesses: A randomized clinical trial. *International Journal of Geriatric Psychiatry, 18*(5), 441–449.

Tse, M. Y., Pun, S. P. Y., & Benzie, I. F. F. (2005). Affective images: Relieving chronic pain and enhancing quality of life for older persons. *CyberPsychology and Behavior, 8*(6), 571–579.

U.S. Bureau of Labor Statistics. (2004). *Occupational employment statistics*. Retrieved November 21, 2004, from www.bls.gov/OES/.

Vourlekis, B., Zlotnick, J., & Simons, K. (2005). *Evaluating social work services in nursing homes: Toward quality psychosocial care and its measurement*. Washington, DC: Institute for the Advancement of Social Work Research.

White, H., McConnell, E., Clip, E., Branch, L. G., Sloane, R., Pieper, C., et al. (2002). A randomized controlled trial of the psychosocial impact of providing internet training and access to older adults. *Aging and Mental Health, 6*(3), 213–221.

Wright, L., Hickson, M., & Frost, G. (2006). Eating together is important: Using a dining room in an acute elderly medical ward increases energy intake. *Journal of Human Nutrition and Dietetics, 19*(1), 23–26.

Chapter 19

ASSESSMENT OF FAMILIES

Robyn Munford and Jackie Sanders

The focus of this chapter is the assessment of families. Because it is typically the first point of contact between a client and a social worker, assessment is a key component of relationship building with clients. In the social work literature and in the actual practice of social work, there are contrasting perspectives about the purpose of assessment, its definitions, and where it is located within the helping relationship (Parton & O'Byrne, 2000). There are also differing perspectives on the roles of clients in the assessment process; these perspectives are influenced by our view of clients as recipients of the services of social workers but also as the key change agents in the helping process (O'Neil, 2003).

We begin with an overview of the history of assessment within social work practice. This leads into a discussion of the current views of assessment and some of the challenges to these views. The remainder of the chapter explores the assessment process at the micro-, mezzo-, and macrolevels of practice.

The knowledge social workers use to assess and work with families is closely connected with views about the nature of families and family life (Munford & Sanders, 1999). Factors such as social workers' understanding of the diversity of family life and the ways in which social work can effectively respond to this diversity can determine the success of interventions with families. The organizational and practitioner response to diversity will influence the degree of success of any resulting intervention. The values that social workers bring to the helping relationship will inform how effectively they can utilize their knowledge and skills to produce accurate and sensitive assessments on which sound social work plans can be built. Their ability to develop a realistic understanding of the contexts of families and how they come to seek help will contribute to the achievement of effective outcomes for families (Healy, 2005).

Assessment in most social work settings is an integral part of good social work practice. It usually provides the first opportunity for social workers and the client and family to spend a period of focused time together exchanging information and looking to the future. In many social work settings, it will be difficult to separate assessment from the overall intervention because some early intervention will start in the assessment meetings. For instance, concrete needs that become apparent during these first meetings may be able to be addressed and guidance may be given over legal and procedural issues the family may be facing. The assessment may be restricted to one or two meetings given the social work setting, but it may also be a flexible process where the entire family or only certain members are involved at different points in the assessment process. Once an intervention has commenced, future assessments may well take place as new issues emerge and as the social worker and family pause to consider what has been achieved and to indicate any new directions for the work. Our discussion recognizes the permeable boundaries to assessment and to intervention processes.

Professional practice requires social workers to continually reflect on the nature of effective practice with families and the way in which their practice makes a difference in the lives of families. Writers such as Margolin (1997) remind us that social work is not removed from the operation of power and control. On a daily level, social workers juggle the challenge of mediating the demands of professional practice and agency requirements with the desire to work in a way that can genuinely engage with, and challenge, the structures and the discourses that prevent clients from participation and from taking control of their own lives. Social workers recognize that assessment can be used as a rationing device to limit client numbers and to determine who is eligible to receive services. Resource issues such as this can create major difficulties where agency requirements may directly conflict with a social worker's value base.

The assessment of families has also been concerned with the wider social work issue of the definition of social work as an art or science (Thompson, 2002) and how this influences the way we work with families. There can be a tension between clinical social work assessment tools and the more relationally based strategies social workers need to use to come to a full understanding of the family. The use of more formal measures must be balanced with insight and considered holistic reflection on family functioning. While social workers must always be aware of risk and safety concerns, they must also know how to situate the family at the center of the assessment because it is the family who will ultimately make the changes. As Holland (2004), Milner and O'Byrne (2002), and Thompson (2002) suggest, effectively balancing the collection of information and applying measurement-based assessment tools with the sensitized interaction with a family involves knowledge and skill and a commitment to a reflective approach. Combining these very different skill sets enables the social worker to select from a range of approaches to achieve a comprehensive assessment that enables a deeper understanding of the family (Milner & O'Byrne, 2002; O'Hare, 2005). Assessments may also draw on other professionals' skills and knowledge. Effective assessments enable the social worker to create a sound foundation on which the intervention can be based. Historically, the nature and success of these assessments has often depended on the availability of resources, services, and support mechanisms and on the willingness of social workers to be creative in their advocacy for clients.

HISTORICAL BACKGROUND

The ideas just discussed are reflected in a recent history of social work (Johnson & Yanca, 2004) and in the historical accounts of work with families (Lightburn & Sessions, 2006; Thompson, 2002; Warren-Adamson & Lightburn, 2006). The historical debates underpinning social work with families parallel those in other fields of social work practice. Changes in the assessment of families over time have been closely aligned with the way families have been viewed by professionals and with how resources and services have been developed and allocated. Service provision for children with disabilities and their families illustrates this point. There have been dramatic changes to the assessment procedures used with families with children with disabilities. Early services to these families were focused on protection and asylum. Children with disabilities were removed from their families to live in institutions and often had little contact with their family. The focus of social work with the family was often on assisting them to "forget" about the child with the disability and to channel their energies into taking care of other family members (Ferguson & O'Brien, 2005). Deficit-based assessment that highlighted what people with disabilities were unable or incapable of doing were prominent historically, and one of the most common service interventions involved exclusion and removal from mainstream society. However, challenges from families and from the disability rights movement has brought about a transformation in perspectives and services, and now assessments typically focus on identifying support and resources so that families can care for their children with a disabilities at home and encourage participation in all community activities. Social work is now focused on providing advocacy, support, resources, and services to families so that their child can fully participate in their community (Sullivan & Munford, 2005), and assessment has accommodated this significant reorientation.

This example demonstrates the complex factors that have influenced the way that social work has been constructed. As will be noted throughout this chapter, changes in the way social work occurs produces fundamental shifts in the nature, focus, and delivery of assessments (Milner & O'Byrne, 2002). Significant changes to social work practice are closely connected to changes in the political and economic context and to societal expectations of the social work role (Dominelli, 1996; Healy, 2000, 2005; Ife, 1997, 2001). These changes are also linked to the belief systems that define and assess certain populations and groups and determine their rights to have support and to participate in their communities (as is illustrated in the example of families caring for children with disabilities).

Social work began in most Western countries as a voluntary activity, often located within religious and charitable organizations that saw the need to address the consequences of poverty and urbanization (Johnson & Yanca, 2004). There has always been a tension between providing charity, philanthropy, and support and the need for control and protection. There have been consistent debates throughout the profession's history about how the recipients of services are to be identified and defined and about the client's right to determine how services should be delivered. The service user's voice has become stronger in more recent times as social work has continued to reflect on the balance between rights and obligations and on complex issues around matters of risk and safety (Ellis & Dean, 2000).

Alongside the debates of how to organize the delivery of care and support and who should have the responsibility for ensuring the well-being of families, social workers have also debated their role and their knowledge base (Allan, Pease, & Briskman, 2003; Healy, 2005; Stepney & Ford, 2000). Historically, this debate has moved from a benevolent support approach to an approach that focused on professional and expert knowledge where social workers could effectively target assessments and interventions. While work in the community and neighborhood and the support of self-help groups remained important interventions, casework became a predominant activity for social workers (Johnson & Yanca, 2004). Social workers located their work within agencies and worked with other professionals to provide services to children and families and other client groups (R. W. Roberts & Nee, 1970). Alongside this work (as is evident in most Western nations) were debates about how much the state should intervene to eradicate poverty and to provide welfare services to families (Stepney & Ford, 2000). Social workers, however, have maintained their commitment, through social work education programs and their national associations, to work to enhance human potential and to promote social change, problem solving in human relationships, and the empowerment and liberation of people in order to achieve well-being. As the international definition of social work has asserted: Central to social work practice is an understanding of the principles of human rights and social justice. Indigenous and local knowledge should define the context of social work and the key social work task is to embrace humanitarian and democratic ideals addressing injustices and inequities through their daily practice (www.ifsw.org).

The international view that social work should have a primary interest in the principles of social justice and human rights has been comprehensively debated within the profession. The key issues have been concerned with how social work contributes to these principles at what level of practice. The role of social work with all client groups will remain hotly contested (Dominelli, 1998) as will the theoretical frameworks utilized to inform our practice. These debates will also continue to influence the way that assessment processes will be constructed and the types of evidence that will be adopted in order to assess effectiveness in all aspects of social work practice with families.

CURRENT EVIDENCE ON THE ASSESSMENT OF FAMILIES

The evidence on the assessment of families and what approaches have been predominant in the field comes from a range of sources including: research and evaluation using a range of methods informed by specific paradigms on the purpose and nature of the research and evaluation task (Dolan, Canavan, & Pinkerton, 2006), literature that has documented practice, and information from the field through practitioner and client accounts (Parton, 2000). There are many debates about what constitutes robust and sound evidence (Healy, 2005; O'Hare, 2005; Parton, 2000; A. R. Roberts & Yeager, 2006). These often focus on the authenticity of the perspectives and the knowledge paradigms being used to measure this effectiveness (A. R. Roberts & Yeager, 2006). For example, some would argue that tightly controlled and regulated scientific investigations, such as random controlled trials, are best equipped to allow social workers to assess the effectiveness of interventions. Others would argue that these take a too narrow approach and may not take into account the context of social work practice ignoring the important role of critical thinking in social work practice (O'Hare, 2005). The focus on measuring variables that can be controlled may ignore key aspects such as the processes and contexts that flow through clients' lives. An effective social worker should be aware that the achievement of positive outcomes with clients requires them to respond to uncontrollable events and to know how to make the best use of knowledge from research and evaluation and from the practice domain (Healy, 2005; A. R. Roberts & Yeager, 2006).

Clegg (2005) argues that evidence is a contested domain and that a conceptual shift to a critical realist approach is required where positivist models of evidence are not seen as the only measure of evidence. A critical realist approach defines "evidence as work that can give insight into the structures, powers, generative mechanisms and tendencies that help us understand the concrete worlds of experience" (p. 421). This approach recognizes the transformative nature of social action, such as social work, and the centrality of human agency in change processes. These approaches focus on the need to be sensitive to the realities of practice and to the complexities of the experiences of the participants involved in the practice environment (Clegg, 2005; McNeill, 2001). There is recognition of the dynamic interplay between practice and research (Healy, 2005; A. R. Roberts & Yeager, 2006) and an acceptance that evidence must be derived from multiple sources using multiple methods that can accommodate a wide range of practice situations (O'Hare, 2005).

These ideas on the nature of evidence and the approach taken by authors such as O'Hare (2005) have informed this discussion on assessment and the need to work with multiple information sources across a range of settings. While one can argue that there are many views on how to classify current frameworks for assessing families, a number of key themes have emerged over time. These are connected to the role of the social worker in the change process and understandings about the nature of the social work task. These are intricately connected to the perspectives held about family life and the complex ways in which wider contexts influence outcomes (Cooper, 2001; Holland, 2004; McCartt Hess, McGowan, & Botsko, 2003). Dominelli (1998) suggests that the broad categories of social work can be classified as therapeutic helping approaches, maintenance approaches, and emancipatory approaches. Therapeutic helping approaches to assessment and intervention assist individuals, families, and groups to address their life circumstances by exploring strategies for problem solving. In the family therapy field, a number of therapeutic approaches in a range of settings have been adopted including structural family therapy, narrative approaches, multisystemic therapy, just therapy (Sessions & Lightburn, 2006), and psychosocial approaches that connect the inner self to wider environment and systems issues (Dominelli, 1998). Some of these approaches have attempted to locate the family within the community and work with wider issues outside the family system (Waldegrave, 1990); however, most of these remain focused on a therapeutic approach and the interactions within the family (Sessions & Lightburn, 2006). Researchers such as Sessions and Lightburn (2006) are advocating for a stronger connection between the work done within families and the wider systems and propose that the most effective location for this work is within community-based settings.

Maintenance approaches represent another major strand in social work practice and family work. Here social work is often labeled as practical and pragmatic (Dominelli, 1998) with the focus of the assessment being on the identification of practical and concrete needs; the social worker assists the client to procure resources and to solve problems. This approach is not usually associated with intense therapeutic work, focusing often instead on the here and now and the immediate resolution of problems. A range of assessment and intervention strategies are used including task-centered approaches and behavior management strategies. Ecological and systems perspectives can be included in these approaches and focus on assisting clients to achieve balance in their networks. They can also involve an adaptation of behavior and the development of more effective coping strategies.

There has been criticism of both therapeutic and maintenance approaches by some social workers who argue that neither address power imbalances. That may be the fundamental reason why clients and families are facing challenges (Finn & Jacobson, 2003). Emerging out of this critique has been the development of structural and critical approaches and more recently poststructural perspectives. These newer approaches explicitly focus on power, a critique of systems, and a commitment to achieving personal and social change. Assessment strategies emphasize understanding how the troubles that families face are embedded within structural conditions. Dominelli (1998) classifies these perspectives as emancipatory and includes within this category any approach that has a commitment to social justice and to making explicit work with clients that focuses on exposing power relations and the root causes of conditions such as poverty, abuse, gender inequality, and racism. Clients are encouraged to make links between their personal troubles and public issues. Feminist social work, anti-oppressive practice, radical social work, community work, advocacy and empowerment, and indigenous approaches are commonly found in the emancipatory group.

Assessment strategies depend on which approach to social work is taken. However, the focus is not always clearly delineated with theoretical concepts often being utilized in more than one of these approaches. While it is relatively easy to identify the boundaries between the different approaches on paper, practitioners frequently draw from more than one theoretical approach in their work. For example, the principles and concepts of strengths-based work with clients are present in therapeutic work with families and in emancipatory approaches. In a similar way, the assessment tools used vary across settings and with the mandates held by the social worker. The status of the client as either voluntary or involuntary will have a significant influence on the nature and approach taken to assessment. So, for instance, a family who comes voluntarily to a community-based mental health setting to address relationship issues will present different assessment challenges and require a different approach than the family who is under investigation by a child protection agency.

Thompson (2002) suggests that social workers need to have a strong repertoire of assessment knowledge, including tools and strategies, and be able to use their knowledge across settings and populations. Working with a young person within a family will require a different focus and understanding than working with the parent of this young person. Thompson asserts that being clear about the key elements of the social work assessment process and one's key role in this process will assist the social worker in being more effective. He argues for a reflective approach that enables the social worker to know how assessment fits within the other aspects of the helping process and to be explicit about the ideas that are informing assessment decisions.

A reflective approach also requires the social worker to know how to use the evidence available and to make informed decisions about problems and possible solutions. It also demands that the social worker use processes such as supervision to evaluate practice and to continually develop their competence and critically reflect on their practice. Thompson (2002) identifies a number of factors to be aware of when reflecting on one's assessment practice. These include: being aware of how to form helping partnerships with clients, knowing how to use a broad range of evidence about assessment, balancing a focus on the problem with a focus on solution finding, being creative in seeking solutions, being explicit about the system and organizational barriers that interrupt the assessment process, and focusing on the holistic needs of the family, not only on the individuals within it.

Assessment of families requires attention be given to the immediate family needs as well as broader issues. Epistemological issues such as the nature and status of knowledge also need to be carefully considered when thinking about the assessment of families. Assessment is fundamentally about the construction of the "official" story about a family, its needs and strengths; and decisions are usually made about access to resources, relationship issues, and care of children. Power relations and issues around the control of knowledge often feature in social work debates about assessment; it is not a neutral, fact-gathering exercise that can be executed by the application of a value-free set of skills. In this connection, Holland (2004) reminds us to be vigilant about the helping role and the way in which knowledge is socially, culturally, and historically constructed within the helping relationship. In terms of approaches to assessment, it is important that social workers seek a range of evidence and work to identify what it is that clients bring to the helping relationship and how this can assist in finding solutions to the problems they bring to social workers (O'Hare, 2005).

LIMITATIONS TO THE EVIDENCE ON THE ASSESSMENT OF FAMILIES

The failure to take a broad approach to seeking evidence about best practice in assessment constitutes some of the major limitations in this area of practice. The ideas explored in the previous section underline the importance of the use of evidence in assessment processes but focus also on the contested nature of this evidence and encourage the social worker to be constantly aware of how knowledge is constructed and how it will reflect the exigencies of particular contexts. Constructivist approaches attempt to address these issues (Parton & O'Byrne, 2000) and assert the view that social workers should be able to work with the conflicting interpretations of the issues that families bring to the helping relationship and to work with the family to identify solutions that reflect and address the complexities of family life. This requires flexibility, an open approach to your practice, and an ability to continually question the foundational and current social work practice knowledge.

A key element that has not received due consideration in the evidence on what constitutes good practice in assessment is the way in which the diversity of family life is understood and how this can be incorporated into your practice and inform the strategies used in the assessment of families. Thompson (2002) argues that there are "dangers of adopting an uncritical, reductionist approach to the family as a social institution and the basis of so much social work practice" (p. 45).

Thompson (2002, pp. 45–46) asserts that while the term *family* is regularly used in social work practice "it is often used in a vague and ambiguous way, with little clarity about what we mean by the term or why it is deemed to be so important." To counteract a reductionist and simplistic view of families and family life the assessment process must explicitly allow for the family to articulate its own sense of family and to identify the key values they have as a family unit. Cultural competence then becomes a core competency for social workers who undertake family assessments. They need to understand the many different ways in which families operate and to be able to differentiate differences from problems. Traditionally some of the literature has failed to identify this diversity and has not situated assessment and intervention strategies within specific historical, social, political, economic, and cultural contexts (Munford & Sanders, 2001, 2005). This has often resulted in a mismatch between the needs of clients, service provision, and social work interventions. Moreover, this has at times, resulted in families being blamed for unsuccessful interventions that have failed to recognize that the knowledge systems informing practice have no relevance for the belief systems and contexts of these families (Munford & Sanders, 2005).

This challenge to how family life is perceived is located within wider challenges to dominant paradigms. Writers have argued that the dominant paradigms such as systems and ecosystems approaches construct the social environment as a neutral concept (Finn & Jacobson, 2003). These paradigms do not reveal how "the dominant political and economic order directly contributes to social problems" (p. 61). Diversity is not just about local difference; it also concerns external forces such as globalization, inequality and uneven economic development, advances in communication for selected communities and the precariousness of human rights (p. 57). Central to these concerns is the need to recognize the diversity of family life from a global perspective and "the multiple constructions of social reality" (p. 60). The social work profession has in recent times been challenged to foreground the rights of indigenous populations (Corwin, 2006; Dei, Hall, & Rosenberg, 2000) and now, with the increasing movement of populations across the globe, social workers are needing to incorporate new knowledge frameworks that challenge previous accepted discourses on practice (Nash, 2005).

When working within families and assessing needs, we need to take a broad approach that recognizes how the family environment and the context in which they live "may open up or restrict life opportunities" (Munford & Sanders, 2005, p. 160). The key challenge here is to recognize how the common themes of making available material and social resources and achieving health and well-being for all family members are constructed within the global economy and have different meanings across different contexts (Parton & O'Byrne, 2000).

The challenges take on a particular character when we consider the way in which assessment of families fits within the wider social work process. Fook (2002) provides an insightful critique of assessment processes and locates this critique within a critical reflective approach to practice that challenges the domination of knowledge systems recognizing multiple and diverse constructions and creates inclusive structures through shared dialogue and knowledge building (pp. 40–41). Fook asserts that the ways we assess problems are "integrally connected with the ways in which we construct knowledge of our world and more generally our place within it" (p. 115).

Fook (2002) suggests that social workers need to build multiple interpretations of issues and problems that include the views of all participants in the change process. Assessment is not a linear process that simply gathers together the facts about a situation. Facts are contested and typically open to multiple interpretations and any information about a family requires careful consideration in order to test out the social worker's assumptions about the family situation. Some of the material on assessment has implied a neutral, systematic process of fact gathering; this view ignores the complexity of the assessment process and its strong connection to the way knowledge and discourses are constructed about family life (Milner & O'Byrne, 2002). Take the earlier example of disability; in order to achieve a comprehensive assessment of the family who is struggling to support a child with a disability, a social worker needs to understand the discourses that have functioned historically to define disabled people and their families. This has included the medicalization of disability as well perspectives that have pathologized disability and prevented disabled people from participating in their communities. The social worker must be aware of how professionals have contributed to upholding negative practices that have functioned to exclude disabled people. People's experiences often vary across environments (Fook, 2002); they may be active participants in one environment, while in other environments the entire family may be excluded because their child with disabilities is not encouraged to participate in a community activity. Comprehensive social work assessments take account of the way in which families' experiences differ across contexts and in so doing incorporate understanding of the way in which context shapes both experience and possibilities for change.

Fook's (2002) arguments direct social workers to understand knowledge frameworks that have been previously ignored or misinterpreted. This argument connects with the recognition that family life is diverse. An example from practice in Aotearoa/New Zealand underlines this point and involves the foregrounding of indigenous knowledge to inform work with families. Indigenous frameworks and understandings, as well as a desire to develop what it means to practice in bicultural ways, have exerted a powerful influence over the way in which social and community work practice has developed. In Aotearoa/ New Zealand for example, this bicultural context has resulted in new ways of working with families. For example, the Whare Tapa Wha model (Durie, 1995) provides an indigenous interpretation of health and well-being. It encompasses spiritual, psychological, physical, and kinship dimensions of family life and can be used to assess families seeking support from state agencies, health services, and community-based services. These models have been used to work with other cultural groups who bring diverse knowledge to the assessment process.

The expansion of social work practice frameworks to include new social and cultural understandings of families and the nature of effective support has resulted in improved professional responsiveness and effectiveness in both assessment and intervention. These new understandings have often emphasized the centrality of meaning making and interpretation in the social work task and in the lives of families. While the opening of social work to these new approaches has not always been smooth, it has resulted in more responsive professional practice and an emphasis on respecting, understanding, and responding directly to diversity at all levels of practice.

THE ASSESSMENT PROCESS WITHIN SOCIAL WORK PRACTICE—MICRO-, MEZZO-, AND MACROLEVELS

Social work takes place at a number of levels. All of these levels require the social worker to have knowledge and skills to work with "a narrative construction process [where] workers may experiment with different ways of framing a situation, in order to explore multiple perspectives and build up a picture of changing contexts and their influences" (Fook, 2002, p. 124). This process will be facilitated within a values framework that recognizes the strengths and strategies clients bring to the change process (Munford & Sanders, 2005). Context is central to the helping process and, as discussed in previous sections, social workers are being challenged to incorporate previously ignored or misinterpreted knowledge frameworks into their practice (Parton & O'Byrne, 2000). For example, in Aotearoa/New Zealand there is a commitment to embrace new ways of working as part of a search for processes that more effectively support families and communities. The emphasis is on finding local solutions by validating local stories and knowledge in order to build engaged communities that find strength in utilizing their own energy, resources, and local talent (Mataira, 2002, p. 5).

Current social work practice has seen the emergence of new perspectives on family work. A strong influence has been those perspectives informed by critical social work and constructivist approaches (Allan et al., 2003; Finn & Jacobson, 2003; Parton & O'Byrne, 2000). These approaches encourage social workers to interrogate power relations, to appreciate how knowledge is constructed, and to critically examine the relationship between clients and social workers. They provide a foundation for discussion in this chapter on the assessment of families; central to these views is an understanding of how theory and practice interact with one another and contribute equally to knowledge development (O'Hare, 2005; Parton, 2000). The constructivist approach challenges social workers to foreground the authority of clients as "engaged" subjects and to understand that clients "will be undertaking their own active synthesis and interpretation of the social work intervention" (Cooper, 2001, p. 724). This view transforms the way we perceive assessment and intervention processes, where the definition of clients moves from seeing them as passive recipients of help, where the social worker as expert controls the change process, to a view that sees clients as active participants in the change process and experts on what will work in their lives (Ife, 2001). Strength-based approaches are encompassed within the constructivist paradigm and emphasize a focus on what it is that enables clients to survive and grow as well as those matters that may stand in the way (Corcoran, 2005; Saleebey, 2002). These approaches focus on hearing stories differently in order to find solutions and create positive change (Munford & Sanders, 1999). Strengths-based approaches to assessment, as with many of the emerging models, move away from a focus on deficits and on the dysfunctional aspects of family life (Corcoran, 2005), opening up new possibilities for finding solutions to the problems clients bring to social workers.

This following consideration of the micro-, mezzo- and macrolevels of assessment practice is informed by the current thinking on assessment that incorporates strengths approaches and that also acknowledges the need for critical thinking around meaning, context, power, history, and possibility for clients (Finn & Jacobson, 2003). While not minimizing the enormous difficulties families may face, such as abuse, poverty, poor health, and the loss of hope (Dawson & Berry, 2002), the strengths-based approach to assessment focuses on the competencies families have used to overcome and survive difficult circumstances (Munford & Sanders, 2001).

The microlevel is concerned with direct work with the family. The focus is on working with the family system and its networks. Assessment considers the family and includes an exploration of the systems that impact on family life in all its diversity. The mezzolevel expands the assessment process to include organizations, communities, and neighborhoods. The worker pays attention to identifying the capacity of wider systems around the family and developing intervention plans at this level on behalf of families. The macrolevel involves an assessment of the structures and policies that impact family life and may involve the social worker in advocacy roles and in policy analysis and critique.

The key themes informing assessment processes with families include:

- A commitment to the belief that families bring strengths and resources to the helping relationship, and these can be harnessed in finding solutions. This means that the assessment can provide opportunities for exploring both problems and resources within the family.

- An understanding that a focus on strengths does not diminish the importance of identifying risk and safety issues and finding ways to protect clients from harm and causing harm.

- A move to a focus on strengths challenges some of the traditional approaches that have focused on deficits and problems (Corcoran, 2005; Saleebey, 2002). These approaches have been criticized for focusing on the dysfunctional aspects of families and holding a narrow view of the family who requires assistance from formal service systems. The competencies of these "failed" families have often been ignored with the social worker missing key information that will demonstrate how these families have in fact survived and managed to achieve success despite the challenges (Gilligan, 2000, 2004; Norman, 2000).

- A consistent challenge to social workers to think about what it is that enables families to survive and grow and how to identify the moments where positive change was achieved. Social workers need to be aware of the impact of service systems that may function to further alienate families and to mask the possibilities for change.

- A focus on help-seeking behavior as a positive event representing the beginning of a process that locates the family as the key agent of change. This will be achieved through the establishment of strong relationships and partnerships between clients and social workers.

- An understanding that in the wider environments and networks of clients there are resources that can assist in the change process. There are informal networks available that can be harnessed as key components of the change process. Social workers need to adopt a perspective that enables them to be creative in seeking out resources. This may also require them to understand that they are not the only experts in the change process.

These ideas inform all levels of assessment practice. The goal is to have a wide-ranging repertoire of assessment, planning, and intervention strategies that are developed within an action and reflection cycle that has a strong solution-focus. While the focus in this chapter is on assessment, the strategies outlined are intricately linked to the other phases of the helping relationship. It should be noted that assessment is present in all phases of social work interventions given the need to continually reflect on intervention strategies and to seek further information and clarification if these strategies are not successful. The evidence on the phases of assessment is vast (Thompson, 2002). The following discussion represents a synthesis of the key ideas and is informed by those perspectives that conceive social work as socially constructed within a relationship between clients and social workers who both have connections with a wider context that impacts on the nature of the helping relationship (Parton & O'Byrne, 2000).

The discussion begins with the microlevel and the assessment processes that are considered to be effective at this level. The knowledge and strategies used at this level will also be present at the mezzo- and macrolevels of practice, such as the importance of understanding context and the way this influences how social work relationships will be constructed (Healy, 2005).

The Microlevel

The key phases to be addressed in working directly with families at the microlevel include: engaging with the family and forming a helping partnership and identifying possible solutions and planning for positive change.

Engaging with the Family and Forming a Helping Partnership

This phase of the assessment process provides a foundation for subsequent phases, and the success of these will depend on how well this first phase can be achieved. When entering the world of a family the social worker must take the time to understand the broader influences that may determine how families live their lives (Munford & Sanders, 1999). Families are likely to have difficulty identifying their competences and abilities when they are immersed in challenging times. During assessment, the social worker has a central role in assisting families to tell their stories in ways that enables them to identify positive aspects of their experience and to build on this to create a vision for the future. Issues in the wider environment (e.g., the meeting of basic needs such as income and shelter) may have to be addressed alongside other family issues.

Before social workers engage with families, they must be clear about the mandate for the helping relationship and the expectations of their organization. This includes understanding the principles on which the organization is based and the philosophies it holds about work with families. While it is expected that the social worker will have the appropriate value base, skills, and knowledge to work effectively with families, it is also expected that social workers will be aware of the practical and material resources they can mobilize to assist the family. Even while in the assessment phase, social workers may need to assist the family in dealing with these issues before they can focus on other issues such as addressing challenges in family relationships, including matters such as parenting issues.

It is important for social workers to engage in context-sensitive work (Healy, 2005). This requires understanding how including the political, economic, religious, and cultural contexts informs the helping relationship. A key example is that of culture (Corwin, 2006). The beginning phase of the assessment process must take into account the cultural frame-works that underpin family decision making and how these influence the construction of family relationships. If the social worker ignores these influences, he or she is likely to miss key information that will assist in the assessment process. The worst possible scenario would see the social worker unable to form a positive partnership with the family in this crucial first phase of relationship building. The social worker may also miss opportunities to harness informal networks that can assist the family in finding a solution. For example, the use of extended family members to support the care of children and young people may well be an appropriate early support to draw on.

There are some specific strategies social workers can use to facilitate this phase of assessment. The first includes active listening and fully engaging in the stories being presented by the family. This may require social workers to suspend judgment; this is especially relevant for those families who have been labeled as "multiproblem families" that have been the focus of many social service interventions from many agencies. The suspension of judgment does not deny the existence of risk and safety issues, but allows the social worker to see the issues from new perspectives, and it is from here that fresh insights may emerge. This is particularly important for families where social workers have not been able to support them to address supposedly intractable issues. As Thompson (2002) suggests, we can utilize assessment tools that are focused on information gathering to provide a description of the family and the issues they are facing. However, social workers must also reflect on whether this description leads them to explore different questions so that they can achieve a deeper understanding of the issues, disrupt taken-for-granted assumptions, and assist the family to be creative in their solution finding.

Social workers who are engaged in active listening also work to disrupt notions of the "expert" and to critically examine how they view the knowledge and experience that clients bring to helping relationships (Munford & Sanders, 2003; Sanders & Munford, 2003).

Forming constructive partnerships requires a genuine sharing of ideas and an understanding from the social worker's perspective that clients have critical knowledge that can be harnessed in the change process (Fook, 2003). Social work is facilitative not directive and families need to maintain control and identify priorities for what they want to achieve in family life (Cooper, 2001; Egan, 2002). This partnership is based on an understanding that clients may hold narratives that portray themselves as incompetent and without agency over their circumstances. A skilled worker is able to draw out the strengths in these narratives and assist the family to develop alternative meanings and interpretations of their situation.

One of the major challenges in work with families is to identify how a social worker can work with the whole family system and also with individuals within it. One of the challenges is to ensure that the needs of all family members are being addressed. To achieve this goal, social workers may need to change both direction and focus at different times throughout the assessment and intervention processes. The goal is to ensure that the social worker provides many opportunities to explore the multiple interpretations of issues and solutions taking into account the perspective of all family members. Fook (2002) asserts that discovering meaning requires a commitment from the social worker to work with families to construct a narrative about their situation that may change as the helping partnership develops. Given that the issues that families bring to the social worker are likely to be complex, the assessment process will also be complex, and at times interpretations of issues by different family members may be contradictory. The social worker needs to take care to ensure that there are no missed opportunities and that contradictory messages from family members are thoroughly explored because they often contain information that will assist in the finding of solutions.

Some of the assessment tools used in this phase include:

- *Systems assessment:* Here the focus is on the social worker's understanding that what happens in the everyday lives of families face may prevent them from finding solutions (Morison Dore, 1993). For example, many parents struggle to parent their children well, not because they do not desire to, but because there are factors that prevent them from doing so. They may struggle with the daily tasks associated with being a parent. They may be poor, experience ill health, parent alone, or have negative experiences that prevent them from developing effective solution-finding strategies. Here social workers listen to the stories about how families organize their daily lives and what it is that works for them in their daily routines and what it is that gets in the way.

- *Assessment of family history:* Past experiences influence the current everyday experiences of families. For example, parents' negative experiences in childhood may prevent them from developing positive strategies with their own children and with other adults in the family. These past experiences may also prevent them from having aspirations and dreams for their family.

- *Asking questions differently:* The social worker can support the family to tell its story and to reflect on all of the factors that have influenced family life. Many families have not had the opportunity to explore what family life is about for them and how they would like it to be for all family members. Taking time on this enables the family to build trust and confidence in the social worker that will provide a strong foundation for subsequent interactions and interventions.

- *Discovering successful change strategies:* Social workers need to understand how hard it can be for families to believe that change is possible. Families may have internalized the discourses that have labeled them as difficult families and unable to care for each other. Moreover, families who are struggling to find the basic resources for survival often feel marginalized and isolated and unable to fully utilize the resources available to them. This strategy involves working with the family to identify where and in what situations they have been successful. This information is then used to identify strategies for addressing current issues.

These factors remind us that the assessment process is not just about what families are not able to do and what is getting in the way, but it is a process that enables families to identify what it is that they have achieved despite difficult circumstances. It is important that the assessment does not become a checklist for what has gone wrong in the past but rather that it provides a framework for thinking differently and creatively about what it is that has enabled families to survive despite these difficulties. Many families have been continually assessed, and this has often not resulted in any positive outcomes for the family. Norman (2000, p. 2) challenges social workers to resist working with clients to find "evermore sophisticated formulations of their problems" while ignoring the factors that will be significant for achieving and sustaining positive change.

Identifying Possible Solutions and Planning for Positive Change

In the process of hearing the family's story, the social worker and the family are identifying strengths and finding solutions. Planning takes place throughout the assessment phases and into the intervention phase and through until termination. A reflective approach to practice means that at times plans will need to be revised and new strategies identified. Central to the planning process is the focus on analysis and being prepared to explore a range of alternative meanings and interpretations (Milner & O'Byrne, 2002). The supervision of social work practice is critical here, and social workers can use this opportunity to test out interpretations and strategies. Unlike some of the traditional approaches where clients have not been actively involved in the assessment process, constructivist processes are built on the key principle that assessment involves the development of a shared understanding of issues and solutions and that the client is central in this process (Cooper, 2001). Assessment work is completed together within a strong partnership between worker and client. The success of this phase will have a significant influence on the success of intervention strategies (Milner & O'Byrne, 2002).

Planning involves making short- and long-term goals, outlining a pathway and direction for the change process, and identifying intervention strategies. This process can provide an opportunity for social workers and families to test out possible intervention strategies and the accuracy of assessment observations. For example, families who are unable to see possibilities for change may work with the social worker to try out alternative ways of operating. Take the example of parents who are having difficulty relating to their teenager. The worker may assist the parents to find a moment in the day to be with this teenager where there are no expectations other than to be together for 15 minutes. When this is achieved, the parents may be able to work to find other times when they have been able to relate positively with their teenager. The focus here is on a reframing of a difficult situation where everything appears to be negative to one where there are glimpses of what is possible in this relationship. Discovering how and where success has been achieved can disrupt the overwhelming feeling of incompetence felt by many families. The reframing and reinterpretation of everyday activities, routines, and relationships within the family and the achievement of small changes can assist families to find out how seemingly intractable issues can be addressed and long-term positive change achieved.

Planning for positive change must have a realistic focus for families and be connected to what they can manage at any point in time. For example, the parents of children with disabilities often find that the demands of support services are too great and often expect too much of all family members (Hughson, 2003; Saleebey, 2006). Many cite the example of the demands placed on them to ensure that their children are fully involved in a range of educational, recreational, and social activities. In this situation, the needs of family members conflict, and unrealistic expectations may be placed on siblings whose own activities then become disrupted. While not wanting to abandon the belief that success is possible and solutions can always be found, social workers must also listen to their clients' genuine concerns about balancing the needs of all family members as they seek solutions to their current issues.

As with the first phase in the assessment process, the planning phase also requires the social worker to be creative in supporting the family to explore alternative meanings about the issues presented and to find solutions to these. The themes identified in the previous phases also have relevance for this phase. In addition, consideration must be given to identifying and planning for solutions. This particular aspect has some key characteristics and includes some specific tools and strategies:

- *Understanding context in the planning process:* The social worker needs to reflect on meaning frameworks and context and how this influences planning for solutions. For example, if working with a cultural group other than one's own, alternative knowledge frameworks must be acknowledged and incorporated in all phases of the helping process. Recognizing the diversity that families bring to the helping relationship is a powerful strategy that allows the social worker to harness different strategies and utilize a wide range of resources. This may include using interpreters and cultural advisors who can assist the social worker to have fresh perspectives on the issues being presented. Taking care of the traditions that cultures have around important activities such as greeting and welcoming visitors, forming relationships, and acknowledging ancestors and others who are part of extended family networks will bring richness to the helping partnership and enable the social worker to form authentic relationships with clients.

- *Multileveled interventions:* The previous point is closely connected to social workers' abilities to work on a number of levels. They need to be able to assess the availability of resources both within and external to the family. Often they will work with social workers involved at other levels of practice to ensure that family needs are met, for example, those working in advocacy roles. At other times, they will be working at an organizational level to ensure that services remain relevant for families and can contribute positively to the change process (Sanders & Munford, 2003).

- *Identifying multiple intervention strategies:* In planning for the intervention, social workers need to be familiar with a wide range of strategies and if necessary seek assistance with these. For example, in working on parenting issues with a family who is supporting a child with mental health issues, securing some home support so parents can have some time out may become an important and effective strategy to initiate during the assessment phase. Comprehensive assessments and planning processes incorporate holistic approaches and include: practical assistance (such as organizing child care and home support and transport to support groups), environmental change (arranging for adaptation to the home environment so a child with disabilities can learn to cook), and service provision (arranging for a medical assessment to ensure that a child's challenging behavior is not connected to a health-related issue).

- *Maintaining a reflective stance:* In forming a partnership with the family, the social worker would have responded effectively and sensitively to the factors that contribute to the way in which family life is organized. This continues into the intervention phase. The planning process provides another opportunity to reflect on one's responsiveness to the family and to identify what barriers may emerge in the intervention phase. For example, the social worker may have noticed that tension was developing in the way he or she had related to a young person and to the parents. For example, the parents, given the way they run their household, may want all contact and communication between the social worker and the teenager to be first approved by them. If the social worker makes an assessment that this may create some difficulties in the intervention phase, the planning process can provide an opportunity to address this matter.

- *Evaluation of family support networks:* An effective planning process should include a review of how families are going to be supported to utilize their own networks in the change process. This strongly connects to the principle that social workers must not be seen as central in families' lives and that they must not disrupt the naturally occurring support networks that families have developed over time (Munford & Sanders, 1999). A strategy for the social worker is not to be the replacement for these networks but to support families to reactivate networks that may have become inactive or to develop alternative networks. For example, families may need to establish new networks as their children move through the education system and develop new interests and connections. Families may also need to be assisted to find more productive and nurturing networks if those they currently have are harmful to their well-being, such as gang associations. The central point here for the social worker is to remain focused on the principle that families are at the center of their own change process (Gilligan, 2004) and that one of the social worker's key tasks is to assist families to fully utilize the resources within their own contexts.

This section focused on the microlevel and direct work with families. This work is closely connected to work on the mezzolevel where workers will carry out interventions in the environments that will impact on family life including organizations, communities of interest, and neighborhoods. In the discussion on the microlevel, connections to the mezzolevel were introduced; we now turn to a discussion of the mezzolevel.

The Mezzolevel

This work is often based within community organizations that have a mandate to work alongside families to improve community environments and to develop more effective organizational responses to the needs of families. Many of the factors that are present in direct assessment work with families are also evident at the mezzolevel. For example, the close connection between theory and practice and the way one informs the other is often recognized in work at the mezzolevel, as is the foregrounding of local knowledge and the harnessing of the experiences of communities and their past history in resolving issues. Context is also important, and typically this involves social workers recognizing that families live their everyday lives within particular contexts and that these will influence how they can exercise agency over the matters that impact on family life. Social workers must also acknowledge the connections between the local and the global and the way in which global issues impact daily lives within neighborhoods and other communities of interest. The key theoretical approaches informing this work have historically been based on critical approaches (Fook, 2003; Ife, 1997); those that focus on empowerment and structural change; feminist and radical approaches; and, in more recent times, indigenous approaches.

There are a number of factors that inform assessment processes within community and organizational settings. These include linking the personal troubles of families to public issues, working with diversity in family and community life, and building strong and nurturing communities.

Linking Personal Troubles to Public Issues

This involves an analysis of the connections between the personal troubles families face and public issues. Structural conditions will have a major influence on family life, either positively or negatively. Take the example of a mother living in public housing, parenting alone, and having difficulty meeting the electricity payments. The community worker after working with her on an assessment of the situation discovers that the public housing agency is not meeting its obligations to its tenants. Here the social worker can assist the mother to intervene at this level to effect change. In these circumstances, the client may choose to join the social worker in addressing this immediate need and may also join in working for better conditions for public housing tenants more generally. This will always be a choice on the part of the client. Community workers should have no expectations that clients who are dealing with difficult everyday issues will have energy to give to wider issues. However, for some of these clients, becoming involved in these issues can enhance their self-efficacy and self-determination as they discover that others are facing similar difficulties as a result of structural conditions and as they begin to see that through action they can change some of their material circumstances.

In the process of linking the personal and the political, social workers and clients can develop alternative scenarios for understanding how issues are constructed (Allan et al., 2003). This can provide opportunities for clients to address the factors that have caused them to internalize some of the negative labels (e.g., the assumption that single parents will have parenting challenges and struggle to be good enough parents) and to join with others to gain an understanding of the discourses that have functioned to maintain them in marginalized positions. At this point, they may choose to become actively involved in wider social change processes. It is here that the skilled social worker working from a community base is able to assist clients to reexamine the meanings attached to their current positions and to share knowledge as part of the collaborative social change process.

Working with Diversity in Family and Community Life

Assessment at the mezzolevel also involves an understanding of how difference and diversity is constructed within community life. As in direct work with families, social workers must be aware of the different contexts within the community and how these will impact the life events of the family. Take, for example, the position of different cultural groups in the community. It is important for the social worker to know how they are positioned in relation to each other and the way in which different positions may be linked to different resources. This will involve an assessment of historical trends regarding these groups and how the movement of new groups into the community has transformed the cultural and social landscape (Nash, 2005). It will also involve an understanding of the positioning of indigenous groups within dominant structures and how this has influenced the participation of these families in community life and the way in which community level decisions are made.

Communities are increasingly socially and culturally diverse, drawing people from very different places and with very different backgrounds together. While in many ways this diversification is positive, it does raise some specific issues for social workers who work at the mezzolevel. In particular, knowing how to build an understanding of the social ecology of neighborhoods and communities and assess the impact of neighborhood characteristics on family life is an essential competency for contemporary social workers. For example, migrant families often find themselves unable to participate fully in community life because the dominant cultural frameworks uphold the position of certain belief systems and practices that marginalize their belief systems. Take also the discourses around disability and the inclusion of people with disabilities in community life. Physical environments that do not facilitate easy access are likely to see people with disabilities become increasingly marginalized and isolated. Assessment examines the impacts of these factors on family life, how they may restrict opportunities for families, and how they impact on well-being and quality-of-life issues (Beilharz, 2002).

Building Strong and Nurturing Communities

Social workers operating at the mezzolevel are concerned about how communities enhance or hinder family life. Family life is likely to be enhanced when children are cared for in well-resourced families and communities (in a range of domains such as social, cultural, and economic) and when a range of opportunities are freely available (Munford & Sanders, 2001). Assessment here involves the worker in an examination of how communities are able to provide support to those families who may be isolated and who have restricted informal networks of support. The challenge for social workers in impoverished communities is to identify how formal helping systems can develop innovative strategies that facilitate the establishment of support networks within the local neighborhood. The focus is on providing locally based services and networks that are accessible, identifying and supporting the development of local solutions, and creating local environments that are family friendly.

The building of strong and nurturing communities parallels work with families in that its goal is to strengthen the capacity of communities to respond to issues and to nurture all of their members. It is also strongly connected to approaches that focus on developing strengths within communities (Beilharz, 2002) and strategies that support communities to become self-determining. Many of the major issues confronting families can be addressed on a wider community level (Sanders & Munford, 2001). For example, providing safe environments and community programs for children that underline the importance of nurturing adults being able to participate in children's lives. As Masten and Coatsworth (1998) suggest:

> Successful children remind us that children grow up in multiple contexts—in families, schools, peer groups, baseball teams, religious organizations, and many other groups—and each context is a potential source of protective as well as risk factors. (p. 216)

Community strategies that focus on communities and social change combined with family and individual intervention can have a major impact on key issues and can strengthen family and community life.

The assessment tools used at the mezzolevel include:

- *Community profiling:* The social worker carries out an assessment of the naturally occurring networks, local resources, and social ecology of communities and identifies how well these are utilized by community members and how these can be enhanced (Munford & Sanders, 1999). This also includes documentation of changes to the neighborhood over time and how these changes impact family life. Key areas include an evaluation of the physical environment, an analysis of population profiles and changes to this, an analysis of historical changes in the community and their impacts on community life, and an examination of the functioning of community networks and how well these are operating to support families (Munford & Walsh-Tapiata, 2000).

- *Organizational mapping and profiling:* The social worker evaluates the contributions formal organizations are making to family and community life and how well they are working together to support families. It involves tracking service delivery and responsiveness and mapping the interactions and collaboration between organizations. Social workers working within organizations may also use this tool to assess how well their own organization is supporting social work practice with families. Here the social worker may focus on organizational health and well-being (Zunz & Chernesky, 2000) and may facilitate such activities as reviewing how much effort is spent on organizational matters that interrupt direct work with families and the time given to reflective practice.

- *Asset-based inventories:* Emerging directly out of strengths-based approaches (Kretzman & McKnight, 1997), these tools enable the worker to assess the resources, capacities, and strengths of a community. This information is then used to identify intervention strategies that use community capacity and capability to address communitywide issues. The inventory enables the social worker to identify how current capability can be used to address new issues. For example, as part of an initiative to address the needs of young people in the community who are living on the margins of community life, an asset-based inventory can be compiled that identifies the resources available to young people and also considers the acceptability of each of these to specific subgroups. The inventory can also be used as evidence to support the lobbying for changes to existing services or the development of new targeted activities.

- *Structural analysis approaches:* The social worker uses a structured process for bringing groups together to work on a social change project. The assessment continues throughout the project via a continuous feedback and action and reflection cycle (Munford & Walsh-Tapiata, 2005). The assessment focuses on process and task goals including assessment of group cohesiveness and how to enhance this throughout the project, analysis of the factors contributing to the identified issue, review of possible intervention strategies, and planning for change.

The work carried out at the mezzolevel is closely connected with work at the microlevel. The issues addressed at the community level often emerge out of direct work with families.

For example, addressing violence against women and children within direct work often leads to public education and the development of programs designed to involve the community to develop strategies that will respond to the issue from a wider perspective. Organizations may also be involved in contributing to positive change for families more generally as links are made between the personal experiences of clients and the wider contributing factors. Social work organizations can provide valuable information and support to those working on family issues at the community level. Work at the mezzolevel can be closely aligned to the macrolevel where assessment is concerned with the structures and policies that impact on family life.

The Macrolevel

Work at the macrolevel will connect closely to that done at the mezzolevel (e.g., advocacy typically arises at the mezzolevel, but often targets macrolevel decision makers). However a key role at the macrolevel involves work in policy analysis and development as well as research and evaluation carried out in a number of key areas in federal, state, regional, and community organizations. For many social workers, this may become the focus of their work, and they may move out of direct practice to engage in these roles. Here the knowledge they have developed in working directly with families and within communities enables them to critically evaluate the impact of policy development and implementation. Other social workers will remain in direct practice but will be aware that decisions at the macrolevel will have implications for practice and will determine how family services are to be resourced and delivered. These social workers may take on roles at the macrolevel within their direct delivery roles. This may involve activities such as advocacy for or against policy and practice developments including submission writing and meetings with key stakeholders.

Work at the macrolevel begins with a perspective that acknowledges that what is happening in the daily lives of families is strongly influenced by wider forces (Munford & Sanders, 1999). This work often draws on social justice perspectives (Finn & Jacobson, 2003) that seek to address the needs of the family within a framework that incorporates an understanding of the factors that may prevent families from participation and from finding ways to address their immediate concerns. The work at the macrolevel will be informed by work at other levels. For example, organizations can have a key role in documenting the impact of policy on service provision and delivery and with this evidence can demonstrate both positive and negative outcomes of these policies. This work at the macro level assists families to see that their issues may not be caused by their actions and relationships, but may be connected to wider factors. For example, the closure of a key industry in their town, housing policies that increase the rents of public housing, education policies that decrease the support given to children with challenging behavior, and welfare policies that expect mothers and fathers to be in the paid workforce but do not provide enough financial resource for the delivery of quality child care services. These examples illustrate that changes in local economies and punitive government policies can result in inadequate resources for families and can together in turn make it difficult to focus on creating changes in patterns of family relations. The social worker may choose to become part of the process of challenging these policies while assisting families to mediate the effects on family life. Social work is "on the boundary between private lives and public concerns" and what happens within "individual, specific applications" is strongly connected to wider issues (Cooper, 2001, p. 722).

Assessment tools at the macrolevel include:

- *Policy analysis, development, and critique:* Policy development and implementation is assessed for the impact on family life. Those working within organizations charged with developing policy for families must engage in consultation processes that involve the ideas of key stakeholders such as families and social workers. There will be pressure on these workers to assess the costs and benefits of policies from all perspectives often within a tightly constrained fiscal environment. This pressure can make it difficult to retain a focus on what types of policies are beneficial for families.

- *Advocacy:* This is a key role at the macrolevel and may include class advocacy focused on particular issues or case advocacy on behalf of clients. Assessment involves the gathering and synthesizing of information from a range of sources. It will also include historical and comparative investigation so that successful strategies adopted in earlier issues and cases or in other jurisdictions can be used to inform current advocacy processes.

- *Research and evaluation:* Assessment is focused on researching and evaluating the outcomes of programs and services and developing or synthesizing new ideas. Social workers need skills in gathering and investigating information from a range of sources. This will include working with social workers and clients to assist them to present their information on services and programs and to become involved in the evaluation of these. This work can be strongly connected to reflective practice where social workers are encouraged to make links between their everyday experiences of clients and the factors that enhance or hinder the achievement of well-being.

It can be argued that effective social work assessment will include knowing how to achieve deep understandings of family life in a range of contexts on a range of levels—the micro, mezzo and macro. While not all social workers will be involved at all levels, it is essential that they understand how the relationships within these levels and the interactions between them will impact on the everyday experiences of families.

CONCLUSION

This chapter has taken a broad approach to the assessment of families and has examined social work at the micro-, mezzo- and macrolevels of practice. It began with a discussion of the historical perspectives on the assessment of families. This revealed that over time theoretical perspectives informing assessment processes had changed in response to a range of demands including those from the profession, clients, and the wider society. The discussion on the evidence about what constitutes best practice in assessment demonstrated that practice is influenced by changes in the contexts of family life and in social work practice. An underlying theme in this chapter has been that assessment processes must be sensitive to and respond appropriately to the diversity of family life and be able to accommodate new frameworks of knowledge that will continue to influence the development of social work practice in the future.

REFERENCES

Allan, J., Pease, B., & Briskman, L. (2003). *Critical social work: An introduction to theories and practice*. Sydney, Australia: Allen & Unwin.

Beilharz, L. (2002). *Building community: The shared action experience*. Bendigo, Australia: St. Luke's Innovative Resources.

Clegg, S. (2005). Evidence-based practice in educational research: A critical realist critique of systematic review. *British Journal of Sociology of Education*, 26(3), 415–428.

Cooper, B. (2001). Constructivism in social work: Towards a participative practice viability. *British Journal of Social Work*, 31, 721–737.

Corcoran, J. (2005). *Building strengths and skills: A collaborative approach to working with clients*. New York: Oxford University Press.

Corwin, M. D. (2006). Culturally competent community-based clinical practice: A critical review. In A. Lightburn & P. Sessions (Eds.), *Handbook of community-based clinical practice* (pp. 99–110). New York: Oxford University Press.

Dawson, K., & Berry, M. (2002). Engaging families in child welfare services: An evidence-based approach to best practice. *Child Welfare League of America*, 81(2), 293–317.

Dei, G. J. S., Hall, B. L., & Rosenberg, D. G. (2000). *Indigenous knowledges in global contexts: Multiple readings of our world*. Toronto, Ontario, Canada: University of Toronto Press.

Dolan, P., Canavan, J., & Pinkerton, J. (2006). *Family support as reflective practice*. London: Jessica Kingsley.

Dominelli, L. (1996). Deprofessionalising social work: Anti-oppressive practice, competences, and postmodernism. *British Journal of Social Work*, 26, 153–175.

Dominelli, L. (1998). Anti-oppressive practice in context. In R. Adams, L. Dominelli, & M. Payne (Eds.), *Social work: Themes, issues, and critical debates* (pp. 3–22). Houndmills, England: Macmillan.

Durie, M. (1995). *Whaiora, maori health development*. Auckland, New Zealand: Oxford University Press.

Egan, G. (2002). *The skilled helper: A problem-management and opportunity-development approach to helping*. Pacific Grove, CA: Brooks/Cole.

Ellis, K., & Dean, H. (2000). *Social policy and the body: Transitions in corporeal discourse*. Houndmills, England: Macmillan.

Ferguson, P., & O'Brien, P. (2005). From giving service to being of service. In P. O'Brien & M. Sullivan (Eds.), *Allies in emancipation: Shifting from providing service to being of support* (pp. 3–18). Melbourne, Australia: Thomson.

Finn, J. L., & Jacobson, M. (2003). Just practice: Steps toward a new social work paradigm. *Journal of Social Work Education*, 39(1), 57–78.

Fook, J. (2002). *Social work: Critical theory and practice*. London: Sage.

Fook, J. (2003). Critical social work: The current issues. *Qualitative Social Work*, 2(2), 123–130.

Gilligan, R. (2000). Family support: Issues and prospects. In J. Canavan, P. Dolan, & J. Pinkerton (Eds.), *Family support: Direction from diversity* (pp. 13–34). London: Jessica Kingsley.

Gilligan, R. (2004). Promoting resilience in child and family social work: Issues for social work practice. *Social Work Education*, 23(1), 93–104.

Healy, K. (2000). *Social work practices: Contemporary perspectives on change*. London: Sage.

Healy, K. (2005). *Social work theories in context: Creating frameworks for practice*. New York: Macmillan.

Holland, S. (2004). *Child and family assessment in social work practice*. London: Sage.

Hughson, A. (2003). Evaluation research in social programmes: The centrality of families. In R. Munford & J. Sanders (Eds.), *Making a difference in families: Research that creates change* (pp. 171–192). Sydney, Australia: Allen & Unwin.

Ife, J. (1997). *Rethinking social work: Towards critical practice*. Melbourne, Australia: Longman.

Ife, J. (2001). *Human rights and social work: Towards rights-based practice*. Cambridge: Cambridge University Press.

Johnson, L. C., & Yanca, S. J. (2004). *Social work practice: A generalist approach*. Boston: Pearson.

Kretzman, J., & McKnight, J. (1997). *A guide to capacity inventories: Mobilizing the community skills of local residents*. Chicago: ACTA Publications.

Lightburn, A., & Sessions, P. (2006). Community-based clinical practice: Re-creating the culture of care. In A. Lightburn & P. Sessions (Eds.), *Handbook of community-based clinical practice* (pp. 19–35). New York: Oxford University Press.

Margolin, L. (1997). *Under the cover of kindness*. Charolottesville: University Press of Virginia.

Masten, A., & Coatsworth, D. (1998). The development of competence in favourable and unfavourable environments: Lessons from research on successful children. *American Psychologist, 53*(20), 205–220.

Mataira, P. J. (2002). Treaty partnering: Establishment of a charter for Maori community based programmes. *Te Komako, Social Work Review, 14*(2), 5–7.

McCartt Hess, P., McGowan, B. G., & Botsko, M. (2003). *Nurturing the one, supporting the many: The Center for Family Life in Sunset Park, Brooklyn*. New York: Columbia University Press.

McNeill, F. (2001). Developing effectiveness: Frontline perspectives. *Social Work Education, 20*(6), 671–687.

Milner, J., & O'Byrne, P. (2002). *Assessment in social work*. London: Macmillan.

Morison Dore, M. (1993, November). Family preservation and poor families: When "homebuilding" is not enough. *Families in Society*, 545–556.

Munford, R., & Sanders, J. (1999). *Supporting families*. Palmerston North, New Zealand: Dunmore Press.

Munford, R., & Sanders, J. (2003). *Making a difference in families: Research that creates change*. Sydney, Australia: Allen & Unwin.

Munford, R., & Sanders, J. (2005). Working with families: Strengths-based approaches. In M. Nash, R. Munford, & K. O'Donoghue (Eds.), *Social work theories in action* (pp. 158–173). London: Jessica Kingsley.

Munford, R., & Sanders, J. (with Andrew, A., Butler, P., Kaipuke, R., & Ruwhiu, L.). (2001). Aotearoa/New Zealand: Working differently with communities and families. In C. Warren-Adamson (Ed.), *Family centres and their international role in social action* (pp. 146–162). Aldershot, England: Ashgate.

Munford, R., & Walsh-Tapiata, W. (2000). *Strategies for change: Community development in Aotearoa, New Zealand*. Palmerston North, New Zealand: Massey University.

Munford, R., & Walsh-Tapiata, W. (2005). Community development: Principles into practice. In M. Nash, R. Munford, & K. O'Donoghue (Eds.), *Social work theories in action* (pp. 97–112). London: Jessica Kingsley.

Nash, M. (2005). Responding to settlement needs: Migrants and refugees and community development. In M. Nash, R. Munford, & K. O'Donoghue (Eds.), *Social work theories in action* (pp. 140–154). London: Jessica Kingsley.

Norman, E. (2000). *Resiliency enhancement: Putting the strengths perspective into social work practice*. New York: Columbia University Press.

O'Hare, T. (2005). *Evidence-based practices for social workers: An interdisciplinary approach*. Chicago: Lyceum Books.

O'Neil, D. (2003). Clients as researchers: The benefits of strengths-based research. In R. Munford & J. Sanders (Eds.), *Making a difference in families: Research that creates change* (pp. 113–129). Sydney, Australia: Allen & Unwin.

Parton, N. (2000). Preface. In P. Stepney & D. Ford (Eds.), *Social work models, methods and theories* (pp. v–vi). Dorset, England: Russell House.

Parton, N., & O'Byrne, P. (2000). *Constructive social work: Towards a new practice.* Houndmills, England: Palgrave.

Roberts, A. R., & Yeager, K. R. (2006). *Foundations of evidence-based social work practice.* New York: Oxford University Press.

Roberts, R. W., & Nee, R. H. (1970). *Theories of social casework.* Chicago: University of Chicago Press.

Saleebey, D. (2002). *The strengths perspective in social work practice.* White Plains, NY: Longman.

Saleebey, D. (2006). A paradigm shift in developmental perspectives? The self in context. In A. Lightburn & P. Sessions (Eds.), *Handbook of community-based clinical practice* (pp. 3–18). New York: Oxford University Press.

Sanders, J., & Munford, R. (2001). *Heart work and hard mahi: A report on the first 18 months of the Highbury Whanau Resource Centre's Alternative Education Programme.* Palmerston North, New Zealand: Massey University.

Sanders, J., & Munford, R. (2003). Strengthening practice through research: Research in organizations. In R. Munford & J. Sanders (Eds.), *Making a difference in families: Research that creates change* (pp. 151–170). Sydney, Australia: Allen & Unwin.

Sessions, P., & Lightburn, A. (2006). What is community-based clinical practice? Traditions and transformations. In A. Lightburn & P. Sessions (Eds.), *Handbook of community-based clinical practice* (pp. 3–18). New York: Oxford University Press.

Stepney, P., & Ford, D. (2000). *Social work models, methods and theories.* Dorset, England: Russell House.

Sullivan, M., & Munford, R. (2005). Disability and support: The interface between disability theory and support: An individual challenge. In P. O'Brien & M. Sullivan (Eds.), *Allies in emancipation: Shifting from providing service to being of support* (pp. 19–34). Melbourne, Australia: Thomson.

Thompson, N. (2002). *Building the future: Social work with children, young people and their families.* Dorset, England: Russell House.

Waldegrave, C. (1990). Just therapy. *Dulwich Center Newsletter, 1,* 6–47.

Warren-Adamson, C., & Lightburn, A. (2006). Developing a community-based model for integrated family center practice. In A. Lightburn & P. Sessions (Eds.), *Handbook of community-based clinical practice* (pp. 261–284). New York: Oxford University Press.

Zunz, S. J., & Chernesky, R. H. (2000). The workplace as a protective environment: Management strategies. In E. Norman (Ed.), *Resiliency enhancement: Putting the strengths perspective into social work practice* (pp. 157–176). New York: Columbia University Press.

Chapter 20

INTERVENTION WITH FAMILIES

Cynthia Franklin, Catheleen Jordan, and Laura Hopson

The ecological systems perspective that guides social work practice calls for intervention on multiple levels to achieve treatment goals. For this reason, social work practice often engages families in sessions rather than working with an individual alone. Family intervention takes many forms, and the definition of the family may vary widely. The family is the center of attention (Hartman & Laird, 1983). In some cases, family therapy may consist primarily of an individual and their spouse or significant other. In others, parents, children, and grandparents may all be involved in sessions. It is helpful to involve any family member who is connected with or influences a client's reason for seeking help. Even when individuals seek social work services for help with an issue that they view as their own individual problem, the ecosystems perspective calls for engaging family members who have an important connection with that individual. In other situations, clients may begin by seeking help as a family unit, involving parents, children, and other family members from the first session.

The ecosystems perspective theorizes that intervening to change dynamics in one part of a system can improve functioning in other parts of the system. Thus, intervening to improve relationships within the family system can improve the functioning of the individual family members (Franklin & Jordan, 1999). Improving the communication between an individual and their estranged parent may result in improved communication between the individual and a spouse or child, as well. The stress that is alleviated by improving family interactions can result in improvements in school performance and mental health status. Because social workers understand the importance of working with an individual within their environment, family intervention has become a valuable tool in social work practice. This chapter reviews the development of family therapy, the existing research evidence on the effectiveness of various approaches, and the importance of family intervention for social work practice at the micro-, mezzo-, and macrolevels.

HISTORICAL BACKGROUND

Although understanding family history and characteristics was highly valued among the earliest social workers, family intervention did not become a formal mode of treatment until the 1950s. Before that time, practitioners worked primarily with the individual (Janzen, Harris, Jordan, & Franklin, 2005). Early social workers performing casework, or case management, roles often worked through organizations called "family service" agencies.

Yet, the progression from working with individuals to working with families did not occur until later. The emphasis on psychoanalysis and the mental hygiene movement was on rehabilitating the individual. Thus, social workers and other mental health practitioners did not typically focus on the family. Even when practitioners recognized the value of working with the family, the traditional psychoanalytic model did not lend itself well to this practice (Hartman & Laird, 1983).

As social workers began to shift from working with individuals to families, they began to change the way they viewed the presenting problem. A difficulty experienced by the individual was viewed as an issue involving family dynamics. The behavior of a child who was disruptive in school, for example, was no longer viewed as simply a child with disruptive behaviors. Instead the social worker might explore family interaction styles, including household rules, discipline, consistency, and communication styles of the parents in defining the goals for intervention.

The development of systems theory as a general orientation that guided social work practice provided a framework for working with families more effectively. Systems theory is concerned with the social, structural, and interactional foundations of behavior. The focus is on problematic patterns of family communication or interaction rather than deficits of a particular family member. Early practitioners of systemic approaches drew on general systems theory and sociological theories, such as structural functionalism, to guide their interventions. Later theorists incorporated ideas from cybernetics and ecological theory resulting in approaches such as Hartman and Laird's "family-centered" ecological systems model (Franklin & Jordan, 1999; Hartman & Laird, 1983). Systems theory posits that behavior is a result of interactions with others in the environment. The structure and patterns of interaction within a family will influence the behavior of each family member (Franklin & Jordan, 1999). Practice consistent with systems theory calls for working with the family as well as considering the environmental factors affecting the family (Hartman & Laird, 1983).

Structural family therapy, developed by Salvador Minuchin in the 1970s, was one of the earliest family intervention models. This perspective views family functioning as a result of structure, subsystems, and boundaries. These structural components drive patterns of interaction between family members. Every family has spoken or unspoken rules that govern these interactions. Family subsystems are defined as family members who are joined to perform particular family functions (Janzen et al., 2005). Parents, for example, are a subsystem whose purpose is to raise the children in the family. Boundaries are conceptual barriers to interactions within the family. A boundary commonly exists between the subsystems of children and parents. A helpful boundary between parents and children may be evidenced by the parents' ability to communicate family rules and feelings of love and support to children while refraining from discussing other topics, such as stress within the parental subsystem resulting from financial difficulties or relationship problems. Structural family therapy greatly influenced social work practice by defining the way presenting problems were conceptualized and guiding techniques used with families.

Other early family therapy approaches that influenced social work family practice include the gestalt approach, developed by Kempler, and the communicative-interactive approach, developed by Satir. These and other influential models view family functioning in terms of connections and separations from various family members (Janzen et al., 2005). When difficulties arise within the family, the practitioner explores whether connections or alliances between family members are contributing to the presenting problem. It may also be that the absence of connections between family members is contributing more to the problem than existing connections. When the mother is estranged from the father in a family, for example, the result may be behavior problems in the children.

Tools that developed out of early treatment approaches and are still commonly used to understand family interactions are roles, rules, homeostasis, and triangulation. *Family roles* are the positions each member holds in the family that govern their interactions with the other family members. If the mother's role is that of the caretaker, she may be designated as the family member who takes the children to school and doctor's appointments and is expected to take time off from work when the children are ill. One parent may take on the role of primary decision maker. When important family issues are discussed, the other parent will typically defer to the decision maker, who will make the final decision (Janzen et al., 2005).

Homeostasis refers to a tendency among family members to balance out efforts to change interactions. If a child's behavior problems serve a function within a family system by distracting parents from their own relationship difficulties, they may behave in subtle ways that encourage the ongoing behavior problems because improving the child's behavior would disrupt the family equilibrium. Closely related to the example used earlier, *triangulation* occurs when two people in a family focus energy on a third to relieve tension. In the previous example, the parents relieve tension by triangulating the child and focusing their attention on the child's behavior problems rather than their own relationship difficulties (Janzen et al., 2005).

Rules are spoken or unspoken agreements about the behavior and interactions of family members. A spoken family rule could include a child's responsibility to help prepare a meal or care for a younger sibling after school while the parents are at work. Often, the most powerful rules are unspoken. There may be an unspoken family rule that a grandparent's problem with alcohol abuse is never discussed. This has important implications for family intervention because, often, the intervention will require discussing and potentially changing unspoken family rules (Janzen et al., 2005).

The techniques and concepts developed through the early family intervention models continue to appear in modern family interventions. One primary difference in the current climate, however, is the emphasis on providing evidence for the effectiveness of intervention techniques.

SUMMARY OF CURRENT EVIDENCE-BASED INTERVENTION WITH FAMILIES

In today's practice environment, social workers and other helping professionals are increasingly called on to demonstrate the effectiveness of their interventions. Many family intervention models have been well researched and are effective in achieving positive outcomes, such as reduced behavior problems and improved family interactions.

In order to obtain funding from state and federal agencies, community-based organizations must demonstrate that they are using evidence-based practices (EBP). In addition, practitioners are often called on to demonstrate that their interventions with clients are resulting in positive outcomes that are tied directly to treatment goals. Often, they are required to deliver interventions that can produce positive change within a brief period of time (Franklin & Jordan, 1999). They may be required to provide explanations for continuing work with a particular family for more than 2 to 3 months, for example.

Because managed care is commonly used to finance health and mental health care, it has greatly influenced the delivery of services. In order to maximize efficiency and contain costs, managed care companies typically pay only for treatments that are proven to be brief and effective (Franklin & Jordan, 1999). Managed care has changed family therapy interventions by encouraging the use of outcome measures in evaluating interventions with clients, group rather than individual interventions, goal-oriented treatment planning, and time-limited rather than long-term therapy (Franklin & Jordan, 1999).

Evidence-Based Practices

Though many definitions of EBP saturate the literature, we offer two definitions that most closely define our understanding of the concept and serve to explicate our vision of EBP:

> The use of the best available scientific knowledge derived from randomized controlled outcome studies, and meta-analyses of existing outcome studies, as one basis for guiding professional interventions and effective therapies, combined with professional ethical standards, clinical judgment, and practice wisdom. (Barker, 2003, p. 149)

> . . . the integration of the best research evidence with our clinical expertise and our patient's unique values and circumstances. (Strauss, Richardson, Glasziou, & Haynes, 2005, p. 1)

We realize that the debate about EBP is sometimes polarized, but we offer definitions of EBP broad enough to take into account its limitations. For example, critics have charged that there is not enough available evidence to guide practice; therefore, the few available evidence-based micro- and macrolevel interventions would be too limited to be of use to clients. However, we take this into account and agree with Gray (2001) who says "the leading figures in EBP . . . emphasized that clinicians had to use their scientific training and their judgment to interpret (guidelines) and individualize care accordingly" (p. 26).

Though there is some disagreement in the literature regarding the definition of EBP, the field of family treatment is informed by rigorous standards. According to the most rigorous standard, an intervention is considered evidence-based if it has been evaluated in a well-controlled experimental design in which participants were randomly assigned to treatment and control conditions, and the intervention resulted in statistically significant positive outcomes for participants. Often, the designation requires that the positive outcomes have been replicated in other well-controlled research. Because such a design is often difficult or impossible to achieve in community organizations that provide mental health services to families, less well-controlled research, quasi-experimental designs have been deemed as acceptable for defining an intervention as evidence based. Quasi-experimental designs are often used when it is not possible to randomly assign families to intervention and control conditions due to agency rules and standards for treatment. The evidence-based interventions described next include those that have been evaluated using well-controlled experimental designs, and those evaluated using strong quasi-experimental designs.

Evidence-based interventions have many common characteristics regarding the format in which services are delivered and the content included in the curricula. A list of these elements includes:

Format of Effective Practices

- Use of group and/or family sessions rather than relying on individual sessions alone.
- Brief in duration, lasting approximately 6 weeks.
- Limited number of sessions (10 to 15).
- A written manual that provides step-by-step guidelines for each session.
- Use of multiple approaches to changing behavior (i.e., instructional and skill building components).
- Intervening on multiple ecological levels (i.e., child, parent, teacher).
- Family approaches that have foundations in cognitive behavioral, structural, or strategic therapy.

Content Included in Effective Practices

- Program content addresses general life skills or knowledge and skills related to drug use.
- Opportunities to practice newly learned skills such as modeling and practicing behaviors and completing homework assignments, such as practicing skills at home with family members.
- Emphasis on the importance of family, school, and community support to create a culture that promotes shared accountability for change.
- Programs promoted a consistent prevention message that is communicated by families, schools, and community members.
- Student strengths rather than deficits as the program's focus.
- Programs that serve ethnically and culturally diverse youth tailored materials for the target group and often used bicultural facilitators. Simply translating a curriculum into another language was insufficient in promoting intervention effectiveness with minority youth (Schinke, Brounstein, & Gardner, 2002).
- Communication and problem-solving skills.
- Behavioral goal setting.
- Target changes in different systems (e.g., family, school, peer group).
- Providing feedback about behavior (Roans & Hoagwood, 2000; Schinke et al., 2002).

Before discussing family interventions with solid research support, we will identify clinical assessment techniques, as well as treatment planning techniques, that help us to arrive at the correct intervention. These concepts—assessment, treatment planning, and intervention—are necessarily linked and cannot stand alone. Following a discussion of each, we discuss the final element of a complete approach to family treatment, treatment monitoring.

Family Assessment

Assessment techniques inform treatment planning and selection; these techniques may be qualitative, quantitative, or a combination of the two approaches. Levine (as cited in Jordan & Franklin, 2003) identifies common features of social work assessment models:

- *Social work assessment emphasizes both individuals and their social environments*: Viewing clients in their contexts of families, groups, and communities is the preferred approach to assessment.

- *Social work assessment includes the strengths and resilience of clients*: It is equally important to assess competencies and strengths as it is to address problem areas and pathologies. The goals of most approaches include increasing the self-efficacy of clients, restoring or supporting their inherent problem-solving capacities, and returning clients to their best adaptive functioning.

- *Most social work assessment models are integrative and rely on more than one underlying theory*: The theory base of social work practice is extremely eclectic. Social work models combine multiple theories in their assessment and practice focuses. Social work is interprofessional by nature, and social workers usually are employed in host settings. Knowledge from several fields is also integrated into social work assessment and practice.

- *Assessments de-emphasize long history taking*: Overall, history for the sake of history taking has been de-emphasized, even in models such as the psychosocial that traditionally focused on this information. Instead, only relevant history is used in a more strategic manner to understand presenting problems and needed interventions.

- *Assessments are organized around task-centered planning or goal orientations*: The purpose of assessment across models is to resolve presenting problems or to move clients toward desired goals. Assessments across social work models focus mostly on the present contexts and future behaviors that client's desire.

- *Social work assessments share common types of information*: Even though different tools and methods are used across models for gathering information from clients, social work models appear to share in common the types of information that are valued in constructing assessments. Problem definitions, identified strengths specific goals, intervention planning or solution building, and outcome monitoring are shared by all models.

- *Social work assessments use a collaborative process between client and practitioner*: Social Work models all show a preference for collaborative work with clients in gathering information and goal construction. Shared power and client-centered perspectives are important to the clinical assessment process. This stands in contrast to more authoritative approaches where the practitioner is seen as the only expert on the client and his or her problems.

- *Assessments in social work emphasize brief, time-limited perspectives*: The preference for brevity and short-term assessments and interventions is acknowledged by all practice models reviewed. This is perhaps driven by the current-day realities of the practice environments in which practitioners work as well as the applied and human problem-solving nature of social work practice (pp. 37–38).

Assessment as we have described it fits in nicely with an EBP approach. Assessment using this approach is integrative and follows theoretically, with Lazarus's technical eclecticism that "assumes that practice methods from different underlying theoretical models may be used together . . . choice is based on research support for the technique or the best available practice wisdom" (Jordan & Franklin, 2003, p. 38).

Corcoran and Franklin provide a rationale for using quantitative measurement in assessment and identify assessment techniques that inform treatment planning and intervention selection, as well as provide guidelines (Jordan & Franklin, 2003, pp. 71–96). Quantitative assessment methods are used because they (1) help practitioners improve treatment by providing feedback about treatment progress, (2) enable practitioners to contribute to the clinical research literature, (3) provide information to ensure practice evaluation and accountability, and (4) allows social workers to increase their repertoire of skills and compete with other helping professionals in doing independent client assessments.

Seven types of quantitative measures helpful for family work are discussed here. First is *client self-recording and monitoring*. These measures are used by the client to collect and record his or her thoughts, feelings, or behaviors. Self-recording refers to retrospective data collected (i.e., remember the number of arguments you had with your dad last week) versus monitoring that refers to data collected on the spot (i.e., record information about an argument when it occurs). The format of this type of recording can be in the form of a log or diary as seen in Table 20.1. Note that more than one family member can independently complete such a log so that the social worker obtains the differing members' perspectives.

Self-anchored and rating scales are a second type of measurement technique. These measures are constructed by the social worker and client family together when a standardized scale is not available. They are brief and use the client's own behavioral indicators as the "anchors." Table 20.2 shows an example of a log used to assess family members' communication at dinnertime. Each family member fills out a self-anchored scale after dinner to rate the level of communication that took place.

Third, *questionnaires* can be used to collect various types of information. Questionnaires may be obtained from publishers or may be designed by the practitioner to obtain information of a specific or of a global nature, depending on the information needed. For example, questionnaires exist to measure children's behavior problems, marital and family relationship quality, and so forth. These questionnaires are helpful in providing a systemic view of family problems that informs treatment planning rather than to monitor change.

A fourth type of quantitative measure is *direct behavioral observation*. The specific behavior in question is observed and recorded in this type of measurement. Direct observation is most used in residential or institutional settings due to the expense and time required to do it. In family treatment, a child's school problems might be operationalized and measured

Table 20.1   Client Log—Completed by Teenage Son

Date	Time	Duration	Situation	Thoughts
Sunday	11:00 p.m.	1 hour	Dad yelled at me when I came home after curfew.	Very angry. Wanted to hit him. Thought about running away.

Table 20.2 Client Self-Anchored Scale for Communication—Completed by All Family Members

Instructions: Circle the Number that Applies Every Day after Dinner.

Family communication good.	1 2 3 4 5 6 7
Family communication broke down.	1 2 3 4 5 6 7
Pleasant conversation at dinner.	1 2 3 4 5 6 7
One or more members did not participate in the conversation or were angry, rude, etc.	1 2 3 4 5 6 7
Everyone was respectful to others.	1 2 3 4 5 6 7

by the teacher. For example, if the child is disruptive in the classroom by talking and getting out of his seat, the teacher can record these incidents.

Related to behavioral observation, *role-play and analogue situations* are a fifth type of quantitative measurement. These are enactments of the families' problems allowing the practitioner to observe the problem (e.g., family arguments) as they are reenacted. As the practitioner observes the scene, she may record the number of sarcastic remarks versus the number of appropriate requests for feedback, for instance.

Sixth are *goal-attainment scaling* measures. This is a measurement of client change as defined by the treatment goals. For instance, a teenage family member's school avoidance problem might be the focus of treatment. Table 20.3 gives an example of how the goals would be used to collect information in this way.

Finally, a seventh type of quantitative measure are *standardized measures*. These measures are not only ready made and available for most family problems, they have uniformity of scoring and interpreting. The best ones have cutoff scores so that problems may be compared with a reference group of clinical and/or nonclinical individuals. For example, several standardized measures measure family satisfaction using various indicators of satisfaction. One measure might focus on the behavioral indicators of satisfaction (i.e., "My family members always treat each other with respect"), while another measure might focus on the family members' feelings (i.e., "I feel like no one in my family really loves me"). It is important to match the standardized measure with the family's way of viewing the problem. Jordan and Franklin (2003) provide more information about these and other types of assessment techniques.

Table 20.3 Goal Attainment Scale—To Measure Teenager's Staying at School

Scale Attainment Level	Scale: Staying at School
Most unfavorable (−2)	Left school, picked up by police
Less than expected (−1)	Left school
Expected level (0)	Stayed at school all day
More than expected (+1)	Stayed at school all day, did homework
Best anticipated success (+2)	Stayed at school all day, did homework, participated in a group

Guidelines for developing a measurement system include:

- *Use of multiple methods to measure client behavior:* Ideally, both a self-report and a report of another rater should be used. Multiple clients are available to observe or record information in family work.
- *Development of a baseline indicator:* Baseline refers to the information collected before treatment begins. The baseline information should establish the need for intervention and indicate the seriousness of the problem. It can be used as a comparison with treatment data collected in order to monitor treatment progress.
- *Use of at least one repeated measure:* This refers to collection of data several times during assessment and intervention in order to track progress. More will be said about this approach later in this chapter.
- *Incorporate both specific and global measures:* Using this approach, you will be more likely to capture both the breadth and depth of the client's problem(s). In sum, an ideal measurement system might include: (a) a self-report measure, (b) a behavioral observation measure, and (c) a report measure filled out by a significant other. To illustrate, a family with communication/anger problems might each complete a self-anchored scale on their own communication (a), be observed in a communication role-play situation (b), and complete a rating scale of their family members' communication attempts (c).

Ultimately, assessment is the link between research and practice. It informs treatment planning.

Treatment Planning

Jordan and Franklin (2003, pp. 59–68) review the treatment planning process, or moving from assessment to intervention. Steps are assessing client readiness, assessing alternative interventions, and using a treatment planning framework. Finally, treatment monitoring is an essential aspect of the approach.

Client readiness may be assessed by considering the quality of the relationship between the family and the practitioner. If barriers to open communication exist, these must be addressed before intervention begins. Also, baseline information should be collected before intervention begins so that the nature and extent of the problem is known.

Several *alternative interventions* may exist to treat a particular family problem and the practitioner must choose in which direction to proceed. An important consideration is the evidence base of the particular treatments. Which treatments have the most evidence to support their use with the type of family and type of family problem that is the focus of interventive efforts. If more than one treatment meets this critical evaluation of evidence, practitioner and client preference may then help to determine the best choice. For instance, some treatments may be outside of the training of the practitioner and would not be the appropriate choice until the practitioner has the appropriate supervision, certification, and so forth to perform the treatment. Or one treatment may appeal to the client family more than alternative treatments, so clients should be given a choice whenever possible. For example, one family may prefer an educational approach where a second family would be happier with an experiential approach.

Table 20.4   Treatment Plan—Family with Communication Problems

Problem Selection

1. Poor communication

Problem Definition

Poor communication equals communication style characterized by angry arguments with yelling and screaming; disagreements remain unresolved.

Goal

1. Improve couple's communication.

Objectives

1a. Improve communication as measured by an improvement on the Primary Communication Inventory (Navran, 1967).

1b. Improve communication skills as measured by practitioner in role-play.

Intervention

Communication training: The therapist will focus on teaching the couple both verbal and nonverbal communicating skills. Verbal skills include the use of "I" statements to communicate needs, active listening, correct timing of message delivery, expression of feelings, and editing of unproductive communications. Nonverbal tools include appropriate facial expressions to match verbal content, posture, voice, and physical proximity to partner. In addition, anger control techniques like recognizing escalating anger, taking a time-out, admitting one's own part in the argument, and problem solving will also be taught.

From *Clinical Assessment for Social Workers: Quantitative and Qualitative Methods* (pp. 66–67), by C. Jordan and C. Franklin, 2003, Chicago: Lyceum Books. Adapted with permission.

Use of a *treatment planning framework* provides the final linkage between assessment and intervention. Steps are problem selection, problem definition, goal development, objective construction, intervention creation, and diagnosis determination (if appropriate). Table 20.4 provides a basic treatment planning framework.

We mentioned *treatment monitoring* earlier in this chapter. In this section, we describe this process, also sometimes called single subject design, as described by Jordan and Franklin (2003, pp. 57–59). This approach assumes repeated measures of the targeted problem in order to track progress of the intervention. The steps of single subject design are:

1. Measures are administered repeatedly, usually weekly or daily.
2. Baseline data is collected before the formal intervention begins.
3. Data is collected in phases, usually baseline, intervention, and follow-up. These phases are graphed, and data is compared across the phases. The intervention must be clearly defined. It is important to know when the intervention is being applied and when it is not so that its success or failure may be assessed.
4. The data is analyzed. Success or failure of the intervention can be determined by looking at the slope and trend of the data in each phase or using statistical procedures such as the celeration line or Shewhart chart approaches.

Single subject designs have other uses in addition to tracking client problems. They may be used by supervisors to help improve the interventive efforts of their staff. Data from caseloads may be aggregated and provided to funders in order to show success and obtain funding for services or further research.

The linkage has now been made from the beginning assessment, through client readiness, treatment selection, planning, and monitoring. Let's turn to an examination of some of the interventions with the strongest evidence base.

Family Interventions with Solid Research Support

The following section describes some of the *family interventions* that have solid research support for their effectiveness, such as multisystemic therapy, as well as approaches that are promising in their growing research support and are in common use, such as solution-focused brief therapy.

Brief strategic family therapy (BSFT) was developed by Jose Szapocznik to address conduct and behavior problems, including drug use in families with an adolescent between the ages of 12 and 17. Families typically meet for 12 to 15 sessions, which focus on building communication and problem-solving skills. The practitioner works to promote parental leadership, mutual support between parents, effective communication, problem solving, clear, consistent rules and consequences, nurturing, and shared responsibility for family problems (Substance Abuse and Mental Health Services Administration [SAMHSA] Center for Substance Abuse Prevention, 2005). BSFT has been found to be effective in multiple well-controlled studies with minority and nonminority youth (Santisteban et al., 2003).

The Incredible Years is an intervention for families with younger children developed by Carolyn Webster-Stratton. The intervention employs three curricula for parents, teachers, and children. Facilitators use videotaped scenes to structure the content and stimulate group discussion. Sessions focus on improving communication and social skills and reducing behavioral and emotional problems in children between the ages of 2 and 8. The Incredible Years has been evaluated in multiple randomized control group studies with children diagnosed with oppositional defiant disorder or conduct problems. Findings demonstrate that over half of the children diagnosed with oppositional defiant disorder before the intervention no longer carried this diagnosis after participation (SAMHSA Center for Substance Abuse Prevention, 2005).

Family psychoeducation may be offered to individual families or to multiple families meeting as a group. The model has demonstrated effective outcomes with families affected by mental illnesses, such as depression, Bipolar Disorder, and Schizophrenia (Anderson et al., 1986; Brennan, 1995; Holden & Anderson, 1990; Schwartz & Schwartz, 1993). The approach was influenced by structural family therapy, which emphasized joining with the family and enhancing boundaries. The practitioner begins by building a strong working alliance with the family and discussing resources as well as past attempts to cope with the illness. Early in the course of the intervention, the practitioner provides current information about the illness and treatment, including information about symptoms, medication, warning signs of relapse, and coping strategies (Anderson et al., 1986).

Psychoeducation also focuses on understanding and building a support network for families. Other families, church groups, family members, or friends who are affected by mental illness may be included in the concept of a family's social network. Through modeling and rehearsing social skills, the practitioner assists the family in learning skills that will help them maintain strong support networks (Franklin & Jordan, 1999).

Multifamily psychoeducational groups include the members of multiple families and their social support network in the intervention. Research demonstrates that this approach effectively helps families manage negative symptoms of Schizophrenia (Voss, 2003). Another study found that the approach results in improved knowledge about mood disorders and more positive family interactions (Fristad, Goldberg-Arnold, & Gavazzi, 2003; Hoagwood, 2005). The group allows different families to share their stories and find commonalities among families' experiences. The practitioner encourages positive interaction between families in which they share their feelings and can offer each other suggestions (Janzen et al., 2005; McFarlane, 2002).

Multisystemic therapy (MST), developed by Scott Henggeler, is another well-researched family intervention. This home-based intervention aims to decrease delinquency, antisocial behavior, and substance abuse among juvenile offenders between the ages of 12 and 17. The intervention works with the parents to provide guidance and intervenes on multiple system levels to effect changes in adolescents' behavior within their own environment. Multiple well-controlled studies evaluating MST demonstrate that it is effective in reducing substance use and antisocial behavior among juvenile offenders.

The practitioner aims to empower parents and help them develop structure and discipline needed for effective parenting while increasing family connectedness. Children are encouraged to reduce contact with peers who exert a negative influence through drug use or delinquency. Practitioners also work to establish collaboration between parents and school staff. The approach is characterized by a comprehensive approach that addresses issues on multiple environmental levels, although practitioners tailor the intervention to meet the specific needs of each family (Randall & Cunningham, 2003). The following are the nine principles of MST (Multisystemic Therapy Services, 1998):

1. Understanding the fit between problems and their systemic context.
2. Emphasizing strengths.
3. Designing interventions that promote responsible behavior and decrease irresponsible behavior.
4. Focus on the present, remain action-oriented, and target problems that are well-defined.
5. Target behaviors that maintain identified problems.
6. Choose interventions that meet youths' developmental needs.
7. Require effort from family members on a daily or weekly basis.
8. Continuously evaluate the effectiveness of intervention.
9. Promote treatment generalization and long-term maintenance of positive changes by empowering caregivers.

Multidimensional family therapy, developed by Howard Liddle, aims to reduce substance use and delinquency among adolescents. The approach combines individual sessions with the adolescent and parents as well as family sessions. Studies have been conducted with ethnically diverse youth between the ages of 11 and 18 in a wide variety of settings. Research demonstrates that adolescents in families that receive the intervention reduce marijuana use, depression, anxiety, and delinquent behaviors compared with families who receive another form of intervention.

Multidimensional family therapy has demonstrated effective outcomes for adolescent substance abusers in multiple controlled studies and has been named as an effective program by the U.S. Department of Health and Human Services, the National Institute on Drug Abuse (NIDA), and the Substance Abuse and Mental Health Services Administration (SAMHSA; Dennis et al., 2002; Liddle et al., 2001, 2002).

Multidimensional family therapy consists of five core components:

1. Intervention with the adolescent to address developmental issues, such as identity formation, peer relations, and drug use consequences.
2. Intervention with the parent(s) to improve monitoring and limit setting.
3. Intervention to change the parent-adolescent interaction to encourage the parents' participation in the teen's life.
4. Interventions with other family members to develop the motivation and skills to interact in more positive ways.
5. Interventions with systems external to the family to develop collaborative relationships among all other systems in which the adolescent is involved, such as school or the juvenile justice system.

COGNITIVE BEHAVIOR THERAPY WITH PARENT COMPONENT

Functional family therapy (FFT) is a prevention/intervention approach that aims to decrease behavior problems for youth between the ages of 11 and 18. Practitioners work individually or in two-person teams with clients in their homes and in clinical settings (Center for the Study and Prevention of Violence, 2006). The model aims to reduce risk factors and promote protective factors and includes the following processes:

- Engagement, to prevent dropping out of treatment before completion.
- Building motivation for working toward sustained behavior change.
- Assessment, to clarify relationships among family members and with larger systems.
- Behavior change, through communication training, behavioral tasks, parenting skills, contracting, and evaluating costs and benefits of communication patterns.
- Generalization, which includes case management to assist the family in addressing environmental constraints and accessing resources (Center for the Study and Prevention of Violence, 2006).

FFT has been evaluated in multiple clinical trials and has been found to be effective with adolescents diagnosed with Conduct Disorder, Oppositional Defiant Disorder, Disruptive Behavior Disorder, and those who abuse substances. The approach has also been effective in preventing placement in more restrictive settings (Alexander et al., 1998; Center for the Study and Prevention of Violence, 2006).

Parent-child interaction therapy was developed by Eyeberg and colleagues for children with Conduct Disorder and their families. The approach is based on the assumption that by improving the interactions between parents and children, the child's behavior will improve. Parents are taught skills to interact with children in a warm, responsive manner. The parents learn to praise positive behaviors, ignore negative behaviors, and provide consistent consequences (Child Anxiety Network, 2006). Multiple studies evaluating the model demonstrate that the outcomes of the approach include positive changes in interaction styles, increased compliance from children, and reduced behavior problems (Child Anxiety Network, 2006; Eyberg & Robinson, 1982; Foote, Eyberg, & Schuhmann, 1998).

Parent management training (PMT) aims to train parents to manage problem behaviors in the home and at school. Practitioners provide information about social learning principals and techniques and models the techniques for parents. Parents learn to define behaviors through observation and recording and to change behavior through reinforcement of prosocial behaviors and punishment of negative behaviors (Feldman & Kazdin, 1995). Through numerous studies evaluating the effectiveness of PMT, it has demonstrated effectiveness in decreasing oppositional and aggressive behaviors and increasing prosocial behaviors (Feldman & Kazdin, 1995). The approach has demonstrated therapeutic change for both children and parents and reduced barriers to parent's success in treatment (Hoagwood, 2005; Kazdin & Whitely, 2003).

Emotionally-focused therapy (EFT) was developed by Greenberg and Johnson (1988). Problems in the relationship are defined as a failure to provide a secure attachment base for one or both of the partners. EFT assumes that negative patterns of interaction cycles result from fear of losing one's primary object of attachment. The resulting communication is often characterized by withdrawing, attacking, being overly rational, discounting the partner's concerns, or criticizing. The intervention often begins with individual sessions before moving on to couple or family sessions. The practitioner helps couples identify and communicate their own emotions, understand how they evoke negative responses in their partners, and change their interactions to be more genuine and positive (Greenberg & Johnson, 1988; Janzen et al., 2005) Although there is only limited research on the effectiveness of EFT, a few studies demonstrate that it improves the quality of relationships (Dunn & Schwebel, 1995; Janzen et al., 2005).

Solution-focused brief therapy is another intervention that has a growing body of research support but has not been rigorously evaluated in numerous well-controlled research studies. However, it is an approach that is used with families in many community organizations. Practitioners communicate respect for the client by telling them that they are the expert in resolving their problems. The assumption is that clients have the knowledge, strength, skills, and insights to solve their own problems (Berg, 1994). Four underlying assumptions guide solution-focused therapy sessions:

1. Each client and family is unique;
2. Clients already possess the strength and resources to achieve their goals;
3. Change is constant, and a small change in one part of a client or family system can produce bigger changes or changes in another part of the system; and
4. Sessions should focus on the present and future because it is impossible to change the past (Lipchik, 2002).

Throughout the intervention, the therapist defines the situation and goals using clients' perceptions and language. The practitioner continuously emphasizes clients' strengths and compliments them for every success.

Although more research is needed to prove the efficacy of solution-focused brief therapy, studies demonstrates that it results in positive outcomes for clients on improving self-esteem and coping (LaFountain & Garner, 1996), reducing behavior problems (Corcoran & Stephenson, 2000; Franklin, Biever, Moore, Clemons, & Scamardo, 2001; Franklin, Corcoran, Nowicki, & Streeter, 1997; Newsome, 2002), attaining goals (LaFountain & Garner, 1996; Littrell, Malia, & Vanderwood, 1995; Newsome, 2002), and improving social skills (Newsome, 2002). Among criminal justice populations, solution-focused brief therapy has demonstrated efficacy in reducing recidivism (Lindforss & Magnusson, 1997) and adolescent antisocial behavior (Seagram, 1997, as cited in Gingerich & Eisengart, 2000). Research has also demonstrated that SFBT results in positive outcomes for improving parenting skills (Zimmerman, Jacobsen, MacIntyre, & Watson, 1996).

LIMITATIONS OF EVIDENCE-BASED FAMILY INTERVENTIONS

Overall, the number of rigorous studies evaluating the effectiveness of family treatments is too small to conclude that family treatment is an effective approach for improving children's mental health. However, the approaches that have been evaluated demonstrate positive outcomes in children's behavior, understanding of mental health issues, and family interactions (Hoagwood, 2005). Additional research is greatly needed to further support the effectiveness of well-research interventions and to demonstrate the effectiveness of other approaches that are widely used in the community.

Despite the availability of family treatment approaches that have demonstrated positive outcomes in methodologically strong research studies, these interventions are having a limited impact on work with families in the community. Organizations have a multitude of evidence-based practices from which to choose, and organizations such as SAMHSA provide information on these interventions, outcomes of efficacy trials, target population, and training requirements, among other things. Yet, despite the availability of effective programs and clearinghouses of information, few community organizations use evidence-based practices consistently. Those that do implement the recommended programs often do not implement them as intended, and they cannot replicate the same positive outcomes demonstrated in the well-controlled studies. Multisystemic therapy, for example, is one of the few approaches that has been evaluated repeatedly in community settings. These community-based studies demonstrate smaller effect sizes than those found in the rigorous research trials, suggesting that the program is less effective when implemented in the community (Henggeler, 2004).

There are many possible explanations for the lack of evidence-based curricula implemented in the community and for their diminished effectiveness: Researchers and program developers may not understand the needs and priorities of the community setting. A research-based curriculum may call for working with clients in groups, but the community organization may believe that individual sessions are more helpful for their clients, for example. The practitioners may feel that the curriculum is not appropriate for clients in their community because of cultural differences between the community members and curriculum developers (Franklin & Hopson, 2005).

When considering research supporting an EBP, practitioners are often concerned that the intervention was not tested with clients similar to those seen in community settings.

Some EBPs were tested only with clients that meet the criteria for a particular diagnosis, but social workers more typically work with clients who have co-occurring disorders. Families served by community organizations may be more diverse than study samples with respect to culture, ethnicity, and socioeconomic status. Clinicians may perceive that an EBP does not adequately address complex problems that their clients face, such as abuse, neglect, poverty, or parental drug use (Robbins, Bachrach, & Szapocznik, 2002).

In order for an intervention to succeed in a community organization, clinicians need to have a positive attitude about the intervention and believe they have the skills to implement the new intervention (Rohrbach, Graham, & Hansen, 1993). Some social workers may not have the necessary skills to implement a particular EBP. Many evidence-based interventions require competency in providing the intervention as well as skills in using behavioral or cognitive behavioral approaches to changing behaviors. Clinicians may also require extensive knowledge of mental health issues that the intervention addresses in order to confidently deliver the program. Social workers in community settings may represent a range of competency levels in each of these areas (Corrigan, Steiner, McCracken, Blaser, & Barr, 2001).

Practitioners have difficulty adopting interventions supported by research evidence because they receive less training in the effective interventions than they do in other methods that are not supported by research (Myers & Thyer, 1997). In order to increase research-based practice, Myers and Thyer (1997) recommend that social workers be trained in techniques that are based on research evidence to the fullest possible extent. Continuing education for practitioners should also consist of empirically based knowledge.

The type of training provided to practitioners is important for implementing effective practices. Onsite trainings tend to be more effective than videotaped instructions or written materials for teaching skills and promoting the use of EBPs (Basen-Engquist et al., 1994). Including ongoing consultation in addition to training for practitioners facilitates the sustained use of EBPs as well (Corrigan et al., 2001; Kelly et al., 2000; Marinelli-Casey, Domier, & Rawson, 2002). This ongoing, personal consultation also helps motivate clinicians to learn and use effective interventions (Corrigan et al., 2001; Kelly et al., 2000; Proctor, 2003). Ongoing support has also been helpful in encouraging clinicians to use outcome measures in assessing their own practice (Close-Goedjen & Saunders, 2002). Combining this type of training and consultation with treatment manuals appears to be the most effective strategy for encouraging the sustained use of EBPs in the community (Kelly et al., 2000; McFarlane, McNary, Dixon, Hornby, & Cimett, 2001). Incentives, such as monetary bonuses or vacation time, can also encourage practitioners to implement and sustain a new intervention (Corrigan et al., 2001).

The success of an EBP in the community may depend greatly on characteristics of community-based organizations. These characteristics include the size of the organization, staff turnover, salary level, caseload size, and availability of resources (Chillag et al., 2002; Schoenwald & Hoagwood, 2001). High caseloads affect the time and energy a practitioner can devote to learning and implementing a new approach. Although EBPs are typically evaluated with practitioners who have manageable caseloads, clinicians in community settings typically work with a large number of clients (Shoenwald & Hoagwood, 2001). The clinicians may be unable to dedicate the necessary time to learning and implementing the new intervention without compromising their work with clients. Hutchinson and Johnston

(2004) found that factors promoting the use of EBPs among nurses included availability of more time to review research reports and implement new practices.

Often, implementation of an EBP may call for coordinating services within a team of service providers. This can become difficult for community organizations because they may have to devote disproportionate resources to implementing one program and devoting fewer resources to other important programs. Working with a team of service providers requires skills in collaboration. These skills require training in order to collaborate successfully, and many social workers may not be accustomed to working within a team to plan treatment goals, for example (Corrigan et al., 2001).

The philosophy of the organization and the culture of the surrounding community also influence whether a new intervention will be accepted. Before organizations adopt an intervention, they evaluate the intervention's compatibility with the organization's philosophy and with values of the local community. Organizations prefer to adopt programs that fill an unmet need in the community (Miller, 2001). The intervention must also be relevant to the organization's mission, feasible within the agency setting, and compatible with the opinions of agency consumers (Miller, 2003).

Inadequate funds for purchasing a curriculum may also serve as a barrier. Evidenced-based practices, such as multisystemic therapy and brief strategic family therapy, often have high costs for training and ongoing consultation services (e.g., Henggeler, Melton, Brondino, Scherer, & Hanley, 1997; Henggeler, Schoenwald, Liao, Letourneau, & Edwards, 2002). Many community-based organizations may have difficulty obtaining the necessary funds (Aos, Phipps, Barnoski, & Lieb, 2001).

The gap between social work research and practice is due to a large extent to differing perceptions about the utility of research findings. Researchers value strong methodology and are likely to question any findings that result from a poorly designed study. Practitioners, on the other hand, are more interested in learning about treatments they can use with their clients. They may focus little attention on methodological issues and attend only to the results and discussion sections of articles. This results in a disconnect between the interventions that researchers and practitioners view as empirically based (Franklin, 1999).

Researchers often argue that practitioners should more closely analyze research literature to determine whether the intervention is effective. Yet, such an analysis is difficult and time consuming and is not feasible for most social work practitioners in school settings. Although social work researchers are actively working to increase research support for school-based social work interventions, this research will do little to benefit the profession if social work practitioners do not implement these interventions. Social workers, like many other professionals, are unlikely to use evidence-based interventions because they have little time for reading research articles. In addition, research articles are often written in a style that is difficult for nonresearchers to understand, and there is a lack of attention to aspects of the school setting that may affect the adoption of research-based practices.

Research reports often leave practitioners unsure about the specifics of the intervention and how it is implemented. Researchers can help bridge the gap between social work practice and research by providing clear summaries of efficacy research that are short and easily understood by practitioners. Providing a summary of the research literature, however, is not adequate to close the gap between research and practice. Interventions must be described in a way that is easy for practitioners to replicate. Treatment manuals, for example, can help practitioners better understand the intervention and implement it correctly (Franklin, 1999).

In considering whether new interventions can succeed in community settings, social work researchers and program developers will need to collaborate actively with practitioners and other key agency staff. This will help researchers understand the issues that practitioners address on a daily basis and will result in interventions that are more likely to meet their needs. Researchers also need to consider the staff who will be responsible for conducting the intervention, the conditions under which the intervention will be implemented, and the effect the intervention is likely to have on the target population. The intervention should be a good fit for the organizational setting, practitioners within the setting, and those whom the intervention is intended to benefit. If an intervention requires specialized training and particular skills, the researcher should consider whether practitioners in the setting can be realistically trained to provide the intervention and whether they are likely to conduct the intervention as the researcher intended. Researchers will also need to consider whether the intervention is consistent with the philosophy and goals of the organization. If an intervention intended for a school has no benefit related to educational outcomes, for example, the school administrators may have difficulty justifying the time and money required to sustain the intervention (Schoenwald & Hoagwood, 2001).

Producing strong outcome studies does not, in itself, bridge the gap between social work practice and research. Even in fields that have a strong record of evaluating their interventions, the research does not adequately demonstrate that effective interventions will remain effective in naturalistic settings. Much of the psychology research on psychosocial interventions for children has been conducted in clinical settings. Since successful outcomes of research in such settings often do not result in consistent effects when applied to naturalistic settings, there is a great need to evaluate the interventions in the real world (Brestan & Eyberg, 1998). This is important because if interventions shown to be effective in clinical settings do not work for practitioners in schools and community mental health clinics, they do little to increase practitioners' faith in evidence-based interventions.

IMPLICATIONS FOR SOCIAL WORK PRACTICE

Family intervention has implications for social work practice at multiple ecological levels. The ecological systems perspective defines an individual's environment using three systemic levels: the microsystem, the mesosystem, and the macrosystem. The levels exist along a continuum defined by the amount of direct interaction between the individual and the systems within each level. The microsystem is defined by influential others with whom an individual has regular face-to-face contact, such as family and friends (Heffernan, Shuttlesworth, & Ambrosino, 1992). Microsystem interventions work with the individual directly and may include those with whom the individual has direct contact, such as family members or teachers (Hepworth, Rooney, & Larson, 1997). The mezzosystem is defined by relationships between the microsystems that do not include the individual but affect the individual's behavior. The mezzosystem includes interactions between a child's parents, between parents and teachers, or between a child's peers (Heffernan et al., 1992). It may also include schools, school boards, community organizations, and local government. Mezzosystems interventions aim to change systems, such as family or peer group, that affect the individual (Hepworth et al., 1997). The macrosystem is defined by societal factors, such as cultural values and social policy. Macrolevel interventions include social planning and community organization (Heffernan et al., 1992).

Family interventions have implications for each systemic level. The practitioner is concerned with characteristics of individual family members, such as a child's behavior in school, or a parent's diagnosis of depression. These issues may be explored with an individual member of the family. However, the family practitioner always takes the next step of understanding how the characteristics of individual family members are influenced by family dynamics and how they influence the family system. Much of the work occurs on the mezzosystems level.

The mezzosystems level of the ecological systems framework involves interactions among those with whom an individual has closest contact (Heffernan et al., 1992). Family therapy interventions are consistent with interventions that aim to affect change at the mezzosystems level because they aim to change patterns of interaction among family members. Family practitioners work to improve family relationships and communication patterns. These improvements in the dynamics of a family system can change individual behavior. Family interventions, for example, have been associated with reduced risk behavior among adolescent family members (Borduin, Henggeler, Blaske, & Stein, 1990; Santisteban et al., 2003).

The mezzosystem also consists of settings in which an individual does not participate directly but which affect the individual or those who directly interact with the individual. These systems include schools, school boards, community organizations, and local government. Interventions work to affect change on a systems level by changing the culture within an organization or school, for example (Heffernan et al., 1992). Although family interventions focus primarily on changing family dynamics, practitioners may have to also address organizational factors that influence the effectiveness of their practices. In order to be successful, interventions need to be compatible with the organization's philosophy and with values of the local community. Organizations prefer to adopt programs that fill an unmet need in the community, but they also consider the feasibility of introducing a program given the available money and personnel (Miller, 2001). This is relevant for promoting the use of effective family interventions in the community because organizations need to feel that the intervention meets the needs of their community and clients before investing in the training and resources required for many evidence-based interventions.

It is important that practitioners acknowledge the mezzosystem factors that influence family functioning. The stress resulting from poor housing conditions or difficulty paying utility bills can greatly affect how family members relate to each other. A school's disciplinary practices may affect family dynamics. If a child diagnosed with ADHD is sent to the principal's office every day for disruptive behavior, a parent may feel that the school is insensitive to the needs of the child and that the child is missing out on important educational experiences. This can create a great deal of tension between the school and the parents in a family system that can affect the functioning of the family as a whole. A parent's place of employment often affects the amount of time that the parent can spend interacting with children and providing consistent. Mezzosystem factors may also determine the resources available to the family. If a family belongs to a church or community organization that provides a network of supportive friends, they may be better able to cope with stressors.

The macrosystem is defined by societal factors, such as cultural values and social policies (Heffernan et al., 1992). Family practitioners need to be aware of macrosystem factors that affect their work with families. As discussed earlier, the influence of managed care means that social workers are often expected to use EBPs and time-limited interventions. Social policies may play a large role in family functioning. Families served by social workers may be affected by welfare legislation, policies on subsidized housing, and education policies. Social workers may have to help families understand policies and advocate on behalf of families that are negatively affected by policies.

If a social worker focuses only on the micro- and mezzolevel issues, the therapeutic relationship may suffer greatly. Practitioners need to be constantly aware of cultural issues that can affect the process of family intervention. Families from one particular ethnic group may have a negative view of seeking mental health services and may experience shame in meeting with a social worker. Those from other cultural backgrounds may feel no shame at all. Cultural factors often determine the roles that family members take. On some cultures more than others, older siblings may assist in caretaking for younger siblings. Cultural factors may influence the father's level of involvement in child rearing. Culture influences the approach to raising children and disciplinary practices.

Social work researchers are uniquely qualified to affect change at multiple systemic levels, given the profession's grounding in the ecological systems perspective. They can intervene to change organizational systems in which they work or those with which their clients interact. A social worker can educate school administrators about the importance of school culture for student success, for example, or work to change an organizational policy that makes it difficult to serve families living in poverty, such as billing rules.

CONCLUSION

Family intervention has grown in importance during the past 50 years and has become integral to social work practice. This chapter has reviewed the historical background of family interventions and the growing need to demonstrate the effectiveness of interventions. The growing body of research on evidence-based family intervention has the potential to greatly improve social work services with families, but the interventions can only benefit families if community organizations put them into everyday use. This next step is critical for improving services delivery. Yet, it will require a great deal of collaboration and communication among practitioners, researchers, and program developers. This collaboration can result in evidence-based practices that are more relevant for community organizations and user-friendly for practitioners.

REFERENCES

Alexander, J., Barton, C., Gordon, D., Grotpeter, J., Hansson, K., Harrison, R., et al. (1998). *Blueprints for violence prevention: Book three. Functional family therapy.* Denver: Colorado Division of Criminal Justice.

Anderson, C. M., Griffin, S., Rossi, A., Pagonis, I., Holder, D. P., & Treiber, R. (1986). A comparative study of the impact of education versus process groups for families of clients with affective disorders. *Family Process, 25,* 185–205.

Aos, S., Phipps, P., Barnoski, R., & Lieb, R. (2001). *The comparative costs and benefits of programs to reduce crime* (Version 4.0). Olympia: Washington State Institute for Public Policy. Retrieved June 11, 2004, from www.wa.gov/wsipp/.

Barker, R. L. (2003). *The social work dictionary*. Washington, DC: National Association of Social Workers Press.

Basen-Engquist, K., O'Hara-Tompkins, N., Lovato, C. Y., Lewis, M. J., Parcel, G. S., & Gingiss, P. (1994). The effect of two types of teacher training on implementation of smart choices: A tobacco prevention curriculum. *Journal of School Health, 64*, 334–339.

Berg, I. K. (1994). *Family-based services: A solution-focused approach*. New York: Norton.

Borduin, C. M., Henggeler, S. W., Blaske, D. M., & Stein, R. (1990). Multisystemic treatment of adolescent sexual offenders. *International Journal of Offender Therapy and Comparative Criminology, 35*, 105–114.

Brennan, J. (1995). A short term psycho educational multiple family group for bipolar clients and their families. *Social Work, 40*(6), 737–743.

Brestan, E. V., & Eyberg, S. M. (1998). Effective psychosocial treatments of conduct-disordered children and adolescents: 29 years, 82 studies, and 5,272 kids. *Journal of Clinical Child Psychology, 27*, 180–189.

Center for the Study and Prevention of Violence. (2006). *Blueprints model programs: Functional family therapy*. Retrieved September 29, 2006, from www.colorado.edu/cspv/blueprints/model/programs/FFT.html.

Child Anxiety Network. (2006). *Specialized programs: Parent-child interaction therapy*. Retrieved September 29, 2006, from www.childanxiety.net/Specialty_Programs.htm.

Chillag, K., Bartholow, K., Cordeiro, J., Swanson, J. P., Stebbins, S., Woodside, C., et al. (2002). Factors affecting the delivery of HIV/AIDS prevention programs by community-based organizations. *AIDS Education and Prevention, 14*(Suppl. A), 27–37.

Close-Goedjen, J. L., & Saunders, S. M. (2002). The effect of technical support on clinician attitudes toward an outcome assessment instrument. *Journal of Behavioral Health Services and Research, 29*(1), 99–108.

Corcoran, J., & Stephenson, M. (2000). The effectiveness of solution focused therapy with child behavior problems: A preliminary report. *Families in Society, 81*, 468–474.

Corrigan, P. W., Steiner, L., McCracken, S. G., Blaser, B., & Barr, M. (2001). Strategies for disseminating evidence-based practices to staff who treat people with serious mental illness. *Psychiatric Services, 52*(12), 1598–1606.

Dennis, M., Titus, J. C., Diamond, G., Donaldson, J., Godley, S. H., Tims, F. M., et al. (2002). The Cannabis Youth Treatment (CYT) Experiment: Rationale, study design, and analysis plans. *Addiction* (Suppl. 1), 16–34.

Dunn, R. L., & Schwebel, A. I. (1995). Meta-analytic review of marital therapy outcome research. *Journal of Family Psychology, 9*, 58–68.

Eyberg, S. M., & Robinson, E. A. (1982). Parent-child interaction training: Effects on family functioning. *Journal of Clinical Child Psychology, 11*, 130–137.

Feldman, J., & Kazdin, A. E. (1995). Parent management training for oppositional and conduct problem children. *Clinical Psychologist, 48*(4), 3–5.

Foote, R., Eyberg, S. M., & Schuhmann, E. (1998). Parent-child interaction approaches to the treatment of child behavior disorders. In T. H. Ollendick & R. J. Prinz (Eds.), *Advances in clinical child psychology* (pp. 125–151). New York: Plenum Press.

Franklin, C. (1999). Research on practice: Better than you think? [Editorial]. *Social Work in Education, 21*, 3–10.

Franklin, C., Biever, J., Moore, K., Clemons, D., & Scamardo, M. (2001). The effectiveness of solution-focused therapy with children in a school setting. *Research on Social Work Practice, 11*(4), 411–434.

Franklin, C., Corcoran, J., Nowicki, J., & Streeter, C. (1997). Using client self-anchored scales to measure outcomes in solution-focused therapy. *Journal of Systemic Therapies*, *16*(3), 246–265.

Franklin, C., & Hopson, L. (2005, February). *New challenges in research: Translating community-based practices into evidence-based practices.* Paper presented at the annual program meeting of the Council on Social Work Education, New York.

Franklin, C., & Jordan, C. (1999). *Family practice: Brief systems methods for social work.* Pacific Grove, CA: Brooks/Cole.

Fristad, M. A., Goldberg-Arnold, J. S., & Gavazzi, S. M. (2003). Multi-family psychoeducation groups in the treatment of children with mood disorders. *Journal of Marital and Family Therapy*, *29*(4), 491–504.

Gambrill, E. (2006). Evidence-based practice and policy: Choices ahead. *Research on Social Work Practice*, *16*(3), 338–357.

Gingerich, W. J., & Eisengart, S. (2000). Solution-focused brief therapy: A review of the outcome research. *Family Process*, *39*, 477–498.

Gray, J. A. M. (2001). The origin of evidence-based practice. In A. Edwards & G. Elwyn (Eds.), *Evidence-informed client choice* (pp. 19–33). New York: Oxford University Press.

Greenberg, L., & Johnson, S. (1988). *Emotionally focused therapy for couples.* New York: Guilford Press.

Hartman, A., & Laird, J. (1983). *Family centered social work practice.* New York: Free Press.

Heffernan, J., Shuttlesworth, G., & Ambrosino, R. (1992). *Social work and social welfare: An introduction.* Minneapolis, MN: West.

Henggeler, S. W. (2004). Decreasing effect sizes for effectiveness studies—Implications for the transport of evidence-based treatments: Comment on Curtis, Ronan, and Borduin. *Journal of Family Psychology*, *18*, 420–423.

Henggeler, S. W., Melton, G. B., Brondino, M. J., Scherer, D. G., & Hanley, J. H. (1997). Multisystemic therapy with violent and chronic juvenile offenders and their families: The role of treatment fidelity in successful dissemination. *Journal of Consulting and Clinical Psychology*, *65*, 821–833.

Henggeler, S. W., Schoenwald, S. K., Liao, J. G., Letourneau, E. J., & Edwards, D. L. (2002). Transporting efficacious treatments to field settings: The link between supervisory practices and therapist fidelity in MST programs. *Journal of Clinical Child Psychology*, *31*, 155–167.

Hepworth, D. H., Rooney, R. H., & Larson, J. A. (1997). *Direct social work practice: Theory and skills* (5th ed.). Pacific Grove, CA: Brooks/Cole.

Hoagwood, K. (2005). Family-based services in children's mental health: A research review and synthesis. *Journal of Child and Family Psychiatry*, *46*(7), 690–713.

Holden, D., & Anderson, C. M. (1990). Psychoeducational family intervention for depressed clients and their families. In G. I. Keitner (Ed.), *Depression and families: Impact and treatment* (pp. 57–84). Washington, DC: American Psychiatric Press.

Hutchinson, A. M., & Johnston, L. (2004). Bridging the divide: a survey of nurses' opinions regarding barriers to, and facilitators of, research utilization in the practice setting. *Journal of Clinical Nursing*, *13*(3), 304–315.

Janzen, C., Harris, O., Jordan, C., & Franklin, C. (2005). *Family treatment: Evidence-based practice with populations at risk* (4th ed.). Belmont, CA: Thomson Learning.

Jordan, C., & Franklin, C. (2003). *Clinical assessment for social workers: Quantitative and qualitative methods.* Chicago: Lyceum Books.

Kazdin, A. E., & Whitley, M. K. (2003). Treatment of parental stress to enhance therapeutic change among children referred for aggressive and antisocial behavior. *Journal of Consulting and Clinical Psychology*, *71*, 504–515.

Kelly, J. A., Somlai, A. M., DiFranceisco, W. J., Otto-Salaj, L. I., McAuliffe, T. L., Hackl, K. L., et al. (2000). Bridging the gap between the science and service of HIV prevention: Transferring effective research-based HIV prevention intervention to community AIDS service providers. *American Journal of Public Health, 90*, 1082–1088.

LaFountain, R. M., & Garner, N. E. (1996). Solution-focused counseling groups: The results are in. *Journal for Specialists in Group Work, 21*(2), 128–143.

Liddle, H. A., Dakof, G. A., Parker, K., Diamond, G. S., Barrett, K., & Tejeda, M. (2001). Multidimensional family therapy for adolescent drug abuse: Results of a randomized clinical trial. *American Journal of Drug and Alcohol Abuse, 27*(4), 651–688.

Liddle, H. A., Rowe, C. L., Quille, T., Dakof, G., Sakran, E., & Biaggi, H. (2002). Transporting a research-developed adolescent drug abuse treatment into practice [Special edition]. *Journal of Substance Abuse Treatment: Special Edition on Transferring Research to Practice, 22*, 231–243.

Lindforss, L., & Magnusson, D. (1997). Solution-focused therapy in prison. *Contemporary Family Therapy, 19*(1), 89–103.

Lipchik, E. (2002). *Beyond techniques in solution-focused therapy*. New York: Guilford Press.

Littrell, J. M., Malia, J. A., & Vanderwood, M. (1995). Single-session brief counseling in a high school. *Journal of Counseling and Development, 73*, 451–458.

Marinelli-Casey, P., Domier, C. P., & Rawson, R. A. (2002). The gap between research and practice in substance abuse treatment. *Psychiatric Services, 53*, 984–987.

McFarlane, W. R. (2002). An overview of psychoeducational multifamily group treatment. In W. R. McFarlane (Ed.), *Multifamily groups in the treatment of severe psychiatric disorders* (pp. 71–103). New York: Guilford Press.

McFarlane, W. R., McNary, S., Dixon, L., Hornby, H., & Cimett, E. (2001). Predictors of dissemination of family psychoeducation in community mental health centers in Maine and Illinois. *Psychiatric Services, 52*, 935–942.

Miller, R. L. (2001). Innovation in HIV prevention: Organizational and intervention characteristics affecting program adoption. *American Journal of Community Psychology, 29*(4), 621–647.

Miller, R. L. (2003). Adapting an evidence-based intervention: Tales of the hustler project. *AIDS Education and Prevention, 15*(Suppl. A.), 127–138.

Multisystemic Therapy Services. (1998). *MST treatment model: Multisystemic therapy at a glance*. Retrieved October 14, 2004, from www.musc.edu/fsrc/overview/atreatmentmodel.htm#treatmentmodel/.

Myers, L., & Thyer, B. (1997). Should social work clients have the right to effective treatment? *Social Work, 42*(3), 288–298.

Newsome, S. (2002). *The impact of solution-focused brief therapy with at-risk junior high school students*. Unpublished doctoral dissertation, Ohio State University, Columbus.

Proctor, E. K. (2003). Evidence for practice: Challenges, opportunities, and access. *Social Work Research, 27*(4), 195–196.

Randall, J., & Cunningham, P. B. (2003). Multisystemic therapy: A treatment for violent substance-abusing and substance-dependent juvenile offenders. *Addictive Behaviors, 28*, 1731–1739.

Roans, M., & Hoagwood, K. (2000). School-based mental health services: A research review. *Clinical Child and Family Psychology Review, 3*(4), 223–241.

Robbins, M. S., Bachrach, K., & Szapocznik, J. (2002). Bridging the research-practice gap in adolescent treatment: The case of brief strategic family therapy. *Journal of Substance Abuse Treatment, 23*, 123–132.

Rohrbach, L. A., Graham, J. W., & Hansen, W. B. (1993). Diffusion of a school-based substance abuse prevention program: Predictors of program implementation. *Preventive Medicine, 22*, 237–260.

Rowe, C. L., Liddle, H. A., & Dakof, G. A. (2002). Classifying adolescent substance abusers by level of externalizing and internalizing symptoms. *Journal of Child and Adolescent Substance Abuse, 11*(2), 41–66.

Santisteban, D. A., Coatsworth, D., Perez-Vidal, A., Kurtines, W. M., Schwanz, S. J., LaPerriere, A., et al. (2003). The efficacy of brief strategic family therapy in modifying Hispanic adolescent behavior problems and substance use. *Journal of Family Psychology, 17*, 121–133.

Schinke, S., Brounstein, P., & Gardner, S. (2002). *Science-based prevention programs and principles.* Rockville, MD: U.S. Department of Health and Human Services.

Schoenwald, S. K., & Hoagwood, K. (2001). Effectiveness, transportability, and dissemination of interventions: What matters when? *Psychiatric Services, 52*(9), 1190–1197.

Schwartz, A., & Schwartz, R. (1993). *Depression: Theories and treatments.* New York: Columbia University Press.

Strauss, S. E., Richardson, W. S., Glasziou, P., & Haynes, R. B. (2005). *Evidence-based medicine: How to practice and teach EBM* (3rd ed.). New York: Churchill Livingstone.

Substance Abuse and Mental Health Services Administration Center for Substance Abuse Prevention. (2005). *SAMHSA Model Programs.* Retrieved December 10, 2005, from www.modelprograms.samhsa.gov/matrix_all.cfm.

Voss, W. D. (2003). Multiple family group (MFG) treatment and negative symptoms in schizophrenia: Two-year outcomes. *Dissertation Abstracts International: Sciences and Engineering, 63*(11B), 5541.

Zimmerman, T. S., Jacobsen, R. B., MacIntyre, M., & Watson, C. (1996). Solution-focused parenting groups: An empirical study. *Journal of Systemic Therapies, 15*(4), 12–25.

Chapter 21 ———————————————————————

ASSESSMENT OF GROUPS

D. Mark Ragg

Group-level thinking develops through the careful observation of group interactions and the application of group-focused knowledge. This two-step process requires social workers to develop an awareness and appreciation of the interpersonal dynamics occurring among people. Social workers must then access knowledge to help explain their observations. Eventually, the knowledge can be applied toward understanding the dynamic forces that occur when people gather into groups.

Social work knowledge about groups has developed over the past century. Such knowledge emerged through many simultaneous processes. Initially, social workers and other professionals observed group phenomenon. Observations lead to potential understandings through the development of theories that can be shared. Such theories provide the foundation for many group articles and textbooks. This level of knowledge is often referred to as "grounded theory," meaning that the theoretical understandings are based on careful observation.

After theory development, knowledge building requires increasingly more rigorous observation. Such observations occur through empirical studies. These studies require social scientists to develop methods for careful and precise observation. In recent years, the technology for this level of observation has increased, resulting in multiple empirical studies of group dynamics. This level of knowledge building allows social workers to contrast grounded theory with rigorous observations.

This chapter operates in concert with the next chapter to highlight empirical observations that can solidify our understanding of groups. This chapter briefly explores the history of our theoretical understanding and common themes. The common themes are presented as considerations that can be used to assess group dynamics. These considerations provide a framework for understanding and applying the empirical information.

HISTORICAL BACKGROUND

Our understanding of group dynamics is heavily influenced by the sociotechnical systems movement, the recreational movement, and the group psychotherapy movement. While there are other influences, these three movements have been instrumental in building our knowledge of how groups operate. A brief discussion of each movement is provided to identify diverse contributions and common dynamics that can be used for assessment.

The sociotechnical systems movement has a long history of using groups to humanize industrialized work settings. This movement began with the Hawthorne studies when researchers studied how the organization of work and working conditions influenced worker productivity (Mayo, 1933; Roethlisberger & Dickson, 1939). These studies found that the use of work groups enhanced loyalty to the organization and resulted in superior productivity. Based on these findings, researchers recommended using groups in the workplace to counterbalance the dehumanizing aspects of industrialization.

A team at the Tavistock Clinic in England expanded the Hawthorne findings by conducting experiments on how groups can support workers and compensate for work conditions (Emery, 1978). These researchers argued that the workplace should be democratized by allowing teams of workers to cross-train for any job (on the team) and make critical production decisions (Herbst, 1962; Trist, Higgin, Murray, & Pollock, 1963). This democratization of production maximized interdependence, investment, decision making, and mastery among the workgroup members (Emery & Emery, 1974; Trist et al., 1963).

After the Tavistock contributions, much of the industrial group-work research focused on issues of leadership. Using groups to enhance productivity was an underlying theme of most sociotechnical systems research. Critical elements emerging from this knowledge base include valuing participation, democracy, self-direction, and mastery. Such concepts, while initially divergent in their application, are consistent with social work values. In the earliest application of group work, social workers were also interested in using democratic group processes and fighting the dehumanizing influence of industrialization (Konopka, 1963).

The second movement, recreational group work, focused initially on youth-focused social and recreational groups (Coyle, 1948). Social workers were using groups in their community and shelter practices to help youth and immigrant families adjust to the United States. Social workers subscribed to Dewey's (1933) assertions that small leisure groups should be part of a progressive educational system and Follett's (1920) arguments that groups are central to solving community problems. Social work allied easily with these philosophical positions and incorporated group work into community level activities.

As the recreational movement progressed, the work of Kurt Lewin (1935) provided theoretical constructs to understand the group-level dynamics. Authors such as Grace Coyle (1948) carefully observed youth groups and solidified some of the principles of group-based recreation so they could be communicated to future workers. Coyle paid close attention to types of groups and how they formed. She took a particular interest in the facilitation of cohesion in the group.

Concurrent with Coyle, group theorists focused on how to effectively intervene with groups. Wilson and Ryland (1949) and Konopka (1963) outlined general principles of group intervention. Such authors provided program media and shared records of practice to illustrate the most effective methods for understanding and influencing group processes. The focus of many group workers at this time was on group-level dynamics such as climate, subgroups, values, and democratic processes within the group (Coyle, 1948). Social work became heavily involved in expanding the grounded theory for understanding and influencing groups.

With the level of group knowledge expanding, Papell and Rothman (1966) identified three models of group work prevalent in social work: the reciprocal, remedial, and social action groups. The distinctions outlined in this article identify three critical influences in the group movement: groups seeking to change individuals, groups focused on empowerment and social change, and groups traditionally associated with the re-creational movement. The inclusion of remedial groups was a reflection of the third movement starting to influence social work practice.

This third movement is referred to as the *group psychotherapy movement*. This movement was heavily influenced by the writings of Freud (1922). While the re-creation movement focused on the group as a whole, group psychotherapy focused on the individuals and how they responded in the group. Freud noted that the leader influences the group members and they, concurrently, influence each other. Many group therapists adopted a leader centric based on an assumption that the leader must be strong to harness the volatile psychic energies of the group members.

Bion (1961) blended a focus on group dynamics with the leader-centric focus. Bion assumed that the group members experienced a need for a protective leader. Therapeutic influence emerged from the discovery that the leader could not meet the group members' needs producing a subsequent shift toward self-reliance. The group therapist focused on the transference relationship between the members and the leader because members re-create earlier life conflicts through the group relationships (Foulkes & Anthony, 1957).

When group workers joined the National Association of Social Workers (NASW) in 1955, there was an increased exposure to clinical caseworkers and subsequent interest in clinical work. At this time, group psychotherapy was gaining momentum, providing a clinically focused group method for social workers to explore. Many group workers began using the group method to change individual group members (Gilbert & Specht, 1981). The increased clinical focus drew many group workers away from using groups to mobilize collective group action. Papell and Rothman (1980) consequently revised their initial typology to include group psychotherapy, structured group approaches, and the mainstream model of group work.

The convergence of these three movements provides social work with a rich foundation of group knowledge with multiple potential applications. Each movement provides a specific perspective on knowledge. Sociotechnical systems focus on promoting outcomes, group psychotherapy expands knowledge on member experiences, and the recreational approach advances our knowledge on working with the whole group. These contributions notwithstanding, most of our historical knowledge remains grounded in theory. To continue the knowledge building, this chapter draws on empirical literature to provide additional evidence for group assessment.

The remainder of the chapter uses the overlaps and convergences among the three movements as a framework for discussing group dynamics. Given that these dynamics are so central to understanding groups, this chapter discusses empirical evidence associated with each dynamic and explores how the evidence can be used to assess social work groups. The dynamics used throughout the chapter include:

- Group engagement.
- Group cohesion.
- Group climate.
- Group interaction.
- Group leadership.
- Group development.

SUMMARY OF CURRENT EVIDENCE AND APPLICATIONS TO GROUP ASSESSMENT

To organize the available group knowledge to assess groups, this section is organized into nine subsections based on well-established group dynamics. Each group dynamic is presented as a consideration during group assessment. While this framework presents each consideration separately, it is important to remember that group dynamics are interrelated. As you read each consideration, try to integrate your understanding of previous subsections to understand the interrelationships between the group dynamics. The nine considerations include:

1. *Group definition:* Groups can fail because they do not constitute a workable group. Workers must sometimes assess whether or not the collective meets the criteria for a group.

2. *Group pragmatics:* Planning decisions can make it difficult for group members to participate. Workers must sometimes assess the timing and structure of the group to identify barriers to group success.

3. *Group composition:* Often, the array of people entering a group creates dynamics that inhibit group success. Workers need to understand how the members' traits can influence the experience of group members and subsequent dynamics.

4. *Group engagement:* Members must find a reason to continue attending the group and form a commitment to shared goals. If multiple people drop out or attendance is inconsistent, it is difficult for other group dynamics to develop.

5. *Group identity/cohesion:* When people form a group, a shared identity and sense of closeness develops. The shared identification and relationships keep the group membership committed to the group.

6. *Group climate:* An interpersonal atmosphere develops among the members, reflecting the emotional elements of the group. Workers tune into this group climate to understand the shared emotion among the members.

7. *Group interactions:* The exchanges among the group members form patterns. Some patterns indicate problems in the group while others reflect group health. Workers monitor interaction patterns to identify potential group problems.

8. *Group leadership:* The formal group leader and the members themselves all play leadership roles in a group. Group leadership refers to both the emergent leadership and the approach that professionals assume when leading a group.

9. *Group development:* The group dynamics change over the life of the group. Group development is the term used to describe the normative patterns of change associated with the passage of time in a group.

Group Definition

When assessing group level problems, it is helpful to first consider whether you have a group. There are collectivities that do not achieve the criterion for a group. We are all thrust into situations where we are with other people (e.g., in an elevator) but do not have enough in common to be considered a group. Consequently, identifying whether your collectivity makes the criterion for group consideration is used here as the first level of group assessment.

Finding evidence-based practice (EBP) for assessing group criteria is difficult because there have been no studies addressing this specific question. There have been studies where researchers exclude groups that do not achieve some basic criteria of "groupness." This section draws on two studies that identified criteria for group consideration. There are four simple criterion that can help make this determination:

1. *Minimum size:* It is commonly accepted that there should be at least three people in the group. If the number falls below three, there are not enough relationships to achieve the dynamics common to groups. If the group you are assessing does not have enough members to be considered a group, you may want to address the membership issues before using group dynamics to assess the problems.

2. *Common interest:* Groups have a shared or common interest. Group members share this interest and have an investment in the group outcomes (Kenny & LaVoie, 1985). When assessing a group, try to identify the common interest or investment. If there is no commonality at this level, you may not be assessing a group.

3. *Shared beliefs:* Groups have some shared values or beliefs that help identify members of the group from those outside of the group (Moritz & Watson, 1998). These beliefs may cause problems for the members or may be a source of pride. For example, in a staff group there will be shared professional beliefs and values while in a group of batterers, there will be a different set of shared beliefs that help identify the group.

4. *Interdependence:* Groups work together to accomplish some goal or outcome. Members' efforts combine to achieve the outcome in a way where each person must contribute for the group to be successful (Moritz & Watson, 1998). If each person can go off and do his or her own work with no consideration of the others, it is unlikely that a group has been formed. This is often a problem in student projects where groups simply divide up the work. In the final product, some members are upset because other people have not made their efforts interdependent with others.

When using these criterion to assess group problems, it is useful to first screen for the existence of criterion. If criteria are identified, then other group assessment considerations can be useful for understanding group problems. If the group criteria are not evident, you will likely need to consider the decisions and priorities that were used when establishing the group. Most often, if the collectivity you are assessing does not achieve the criterion for a group, problems will be associated with decisions made when forming the group. Consider the decision making carefully; if there are competing priorities used to establish group membership, you may need to explore the implications of each set of priorities.

Group Pragmatics

Often social workers plan group sessions based on agency considerations such as room availability and worker schedules. While such considerations are important, they are not shared concerns with group members. The timing of group meetings can influence group member motivation and attendance. Several researchers have found that establishing a suitable meeting time was one of the most common challenges to participation (Bogenschneider, 1996; Spoth & Redmond, 1996; Tolan & McKay, 1996).

Pragmatic concerns include client travel, childcare, and language (Spoth, Redmond, Hockaday, & Chung, 1996; Tolan & McKay, 1996). Programs that plan around client realities (e.g., needing childcare or using public transportation) tend to be more successful in terms of attendance and participation (Kirchenbaum, 1979; Lengua et al., 1992). Similarly, group programs that accommodate minority status and language differences also appear to enhance member attendance and participation in the group program (Herrera & Sanchez, 1980).

Group members' pragmatic concerns are accentuated if they have lower incomes or are otherwise disadvantaged (Home & Darveau-Fournier, 1990). Several researchers have identified problems in attendance, participation, and outcomes when group members experience economic or functional social disadvantages (Andra & Thomas, 1998; Dumas & Wahler, 1983; Lorion, 1973; Lorion & Felner, 1986; Ross, Mirowski, & Cockerham, 1983). The implications for social work groups are profound given that we traditionally work with disadvantaged populations.

Pragmatic problems most often are observed in attendance rates, dropout rates, and level of active participation (Andra & Thomas, 1998; Dumas & Whahler, 1983; Kazdin, 1990; Webster-Stratton, 1985). The assessment implications of these findings focus primarily on the structure of the group program or planning decisions. There are four types of issues to consider carefully when assessing a group program. These include:

1. *Motivation issues:* Motivation levels are associated with the group member's life situation. If the client situation is prone to lower levels of change motivation (e.g., court referred, addicted), group pragmatics will become an excuse for dropping out of the group program because there is minimal potential investment in the group. It is important to schedule meetings when deterrents are minimized (e.g., not during rush hour or after public transportation has ended). It may also become necessary with problems that have fluctuating motivation (e.g., substance abuse treatment) to use motivational enhancements such as prompts and reminders (Lash, Burden, Monteleone, & Lehmann, 2004).

2. *Life stress issues:* Depending on group members' life situations, motivation and attendance will change. For example, parents with younger children do not often like attending meetings in the evening because of childcare concerns. Similarly, parents of school-aged children often resist committing to meetings right after work.

3. *Pattern of life issues:* There are times of the day, week, month, and year that make it more difficult for group members to attend. For example, during summer people often take vacation and during late December people have family obligations.

4. *Cultural issues:* There are language, values, and other barriers to service based on cultural differences between the agency, staff, and clients. You will often have to consider the cultural groups in your community and assess your program decisions based on the experience of clients within each cultural group.

While pragmatic concerns are not the only considerations that influence absenteeism and dropout rates, these considerations are easy to assess because the information needed for assessment is readily available. You will already know the time, location, decision-making priorities, and information on client needs. If it appears that group concerns are associated with pragmatic issues, you can immediately explore options for renegotiating these elements of the group program.

Group Composition

While many agencies do not screen potential members before including them in the group, the research literature indicates that group composition decisions can influence group functioning. In a study of 99 undergraduate teams, Molleman (2005) found that groups often divide based on cultural identity, ability, and personality traits. When such divides become structural in a group, they often disrupt group effectiveness (Molleman, 2005).

Composition considerations begin with the group worker's demographic traits. Two studies have found that people assume reciprocity when a group leader shares an identity group membership (e.g., race) with a subgroup of members. However, people with no shared identity with the group leader assume fair treatment simply based on their joining the group (Duck & Fielding, 1999; Tanis & Postmes, 2005). These findings suggest that the initial impressions based on leader traits begin unspoken expectations that must be navigated with care.

Concurrent with group leader traits, many studies have explored diversity issues among group members. A laboratory study of work groups comparing Chinese and Caucasian leadership behaviors found that Caucasians are more likely to assume the group leadership roles (Kelsey, 1998). Studies have concluded that race-related issues of status and power are a consideration for minority group members when they join a group (Lucken & Simon, 2005). After joining the group, racial balance fluctuations influence decisions to leave the group (Prislin & Christensen, 2005) and levels of enjoyment for minority group members (Paletz, Peng, Erez, & Maslach, 2004).

Gender also emerges as a composition consideration. In laboratory studies with students, researchers find that increases in the proportion of men in the group correspond to increased levels of interrupting and power displays (Karakowsky, McBey, & Miller, 2004). In similar research, a laboratory study of gender composition and gender-related attitude found that the gender composition influences the conflict resolution strategies used by the group (Becker-Beck, 2001). This same study found that gender attitudes can polarize the group when traditional values are in conflict with more liberal attitudes. In a study of group risk tolerance, researchers found that men are more influential than women in making risk-taking decisions (Karakowsky & Elangovan, 2001).

Status and power are important considerations when assessing the group composition (Tyler & Blader, 2002). Group participants tend to share more with people perceived as having equal (or less) power than they themselves (van Dijke & Poppe, 2004). Group members may set higher expectations for higher-status members. One study found that group members assume that higher-status people are more competent (Lovaglia, 1995). Concurrently, behavioral breaches of higher status members (e.g., false representation) receive higher levels of condemnation by lower-status group members (Birchmeier, Joinson, & Dietz-Uhler, 2005).

A final membership consideration is group member personality. There have been multiple studies on the impact of personality on group dynamics. The following emotional and personality traits are found to influence group dynamics:

- Emotional stability, agreeableness, and confidence are associated with participation, collaboration, and positive outcomes in the group (Halfhill, Sundstrom, Lahner, Calderone, & Nielsen, 2005; MacNair-Semands, 2002; Oetzel, 2001; Perrone & Sedlacek, 2000).
- Personality variability is associated with conflicted criterion for success, poorer task accomplishment, and conflict in the group (Halfhill et al., 2005; Mohammed & Angell, 2003; Priola, Smith, & Armstrong, 2004; Schei & Rognes, 2005).
- Personality differences influence the preferred structure for the group with intuitive members preferring a loose structure and analytic members working better with imposed structures (Priola et al., 2004).
- People high in power needs speak more often (Islam & Zyphur, 2005), overrate the level of conflict, and underrate the level of group support (MacNair-Semands & Lese, 2000).

Diversity-related problems appear to be associated with group balance and openness. There is a tendency for people to prefer homogeneous group membership that reflects their own personal traits (Kruglanski, Shah, Pierro, & Mannetti, 2002). When this tendency causes some group members to homogenize the group based on their personality traits, group problems will occur (Halfhill et al., 2005). When there is sufficient shared experience and common ground, diversity can be positive and promote group creativity (Choi, Price, & Vinokur, 2003; Miura & Hida, 2004).

Group composition issues have implications for group leadership. First, the group leader is charged with ensuring that there is sufficient common ground by balancing the membership (Halfhill et al., 2005; Miura & Hida, 2004). This often requires conducting selection or orientation interviews prior to the group to address and preempt potential problems (de Jager & Strauss, 1998; Evensen & Bednar, 1978). Group leaders must also monitor the potential for schisms so early intervention can occur.

Group Engagement

Group composition gives rise to engagement considerations as the members meet each other and must make a commitment to the group. Evidence of engagement by the fourth session is associated with positive group outcomes (Ogrodniczuk & Piper, 2003). In a study of engagement and therapeutic alliance, researchers found that engaged members with a high initial alliance who increase their alliance over time and patients with low initial alliance who decrease their alliance (but remain engaged) both have positive outcomes (Piper, Ogrodniczuk, LaMarche, Hilscher, & Joyce, 2005). The critical element in this study appears to be that engagement, as indicated by a willingness to grapple with group issues, promotes positive outcomes regardless of the therapeutic alliance.

Engagement is most often indicated by continued attendance and participation. Engagement occurs early in the group based on member expectations and initial experiences in the group program (Kivlighan & Jauquet, 1990; Klein & Carroll, 1986; McCallum, Piper, Ogrodniczuk, & Joyce, 2002; Ogrodniczuk & Piper, 2003; Parloff, 1961). Initial experiences of acceptance and openness are associated with a commitment to the group (de Cremer & Tyler, 2005). When people don't feel they can share with the other group members, don't fit in, or are uncomfortable with the leader's style, they are more likely to drop out of the group (Parloff, 1961; Van Vugt, Jepson, Hart, & De Cremer, 2004; Yalom, 1966).

In the early group experiences, group members must form a confidence that the group will meet their needs (Baker, 2001; Pescosolido, 2001). When individual members feel empowered and believe that the group can achieve its goals, a broader group level confidence can develop (Jung & Sosik, 2002; Marmarosh, Holtz, & Schottenbauer, 2005). Group confidence is associated with increased intermember communication (Oetzel, 2001), group cohesion (Sargent & Sue-Chan, 2001), and group performance (Jordan, Feild, & Armenakis, 2002; Lee, Tinsley, & Bobko, 2002, 2004). If members form a belief that the group cannot meet their needs or develop negative feelings about the group, attendance tends to suffer (MacNair-Semands, 2002; McCallum et al., 2002; McKisack & Waller, 1996; Westra, Dozois, & Boardman, 2002).

To enhance engagement potential, group leaders often screen potential members to ensure that they understand the purpose, opportunities, and expectations associated with group treatment (Riva, Lippert, & Tackett, 2000). Some programs use orientation groups to enhance engagement and attendance (France & Dugo, 1985). Another engagement enhancement technique is to use phone contacts, providing prompts and feedback to the members (Lash & Blosser, 1999). In a survey of 75 randomly selected group leaders, researchers found that most workers used a selection strategy to enhance engagement and prevent group problems (Riva et al., 2000).

When assessing groups for engagement problems, it is likely that assessment will be prompted by poor attendance, high dropout rates, or poor participation. These dynamics are often symptomatic of procedural problems. The following list may help identify the nature of group elements that underlie engagement problems:

- *Intake procedures:* Consider how the group leader makes contact and explains the group to the potential members. Procedures that involve some pregroup contact that explains the group, provides feedback, and builds a pregroup relationship seems to enhance engagement (France & Dugo, 1985; Lash & Blosser, 1999).
- *Leadership style:* Given that people will tend to leave the group if they feel the leadership style does not fit for them (van Vugt et al., 2004), consider the leadership approach and reflect on the leader's methods as they might impact group members.
- *Messages about the group:* Given the importance of group efficacy, consider the messages relayed to the members when they first come to the group. Remember that members need hope that the group can meet their needs (Jordan et al., 2002; Westra et al., 2002).
- *Emergent leadership:* When group members assume leadership and express confidence in the group, group efficacy increases (Pescosolido, 2001; Yamaguchi & Maehr, 2004).

Consider how the group program makes it possible for group members to assume leadership roles and influence the group.

- *Early group sessions:* Given that engagement occurs early in the group (Baker, 2001; Pescosolido, 2001), reflect very carefully on the early group sessions to ensure that members feel accepted and respected by the leader and other members (de Cremer & Tyler, 2005).

Group Identity/Cohesion

Cohesion refers to the sense of "we-ness" and the intermember bonds that cause members to remain in a group (Anderson, 1997; Cartwright & Zander, 1968). As the group becomes cohesive, there is an increase in caring among the members and a feeling that they are all in the same boat together. This is the dynamic that provides feelings that the group is different from the rest of life and important in achieving the group members' goals. There are several group features commonly used as indicators of cohesion:

- *Affect:* Members feel closeness to the group as a whole (Pollack, 1998; Rugel, 1987). There are feelings of wanting to come to the group and that the group is meeting some important need.
- *Openness:* Members feel comfortable in the group and decrease their attempts to manage other people's impressions (Pollack, 1998; Roark, 1989). They are able to be honest and forthright with the other members about their feelings and situations.
- *Investment:* Members identify part of themselves with the group and want to see the group members achieve their goals (Beech & Hamilton-Giachritsis, 2005; Rugel, 1987). Members are willing to risk and take action to ensure that the group and members are successful.
- *Focus/alliance:* The purpose and goals of the group are clear to the members and they are committed to fulfilling the group purpose (Marziali, Munroe-Blum & McCleary, 1997; van Andel, Erdman, Karsdorp, Appels, & Trijsburg, 2003).

Cohesion is considered by many to be one of the most important group dynamics. In outcome research, group cohesion is associated with the accomplishment of group goals (Allen, Sargent, & Bradley, 2003; Chang & Bordia, 2001). This finding is consistent in work groups (Pollack, 1998), treatment groups, (Beech & Hamilton-Giachritsis, 2005; Marziali et al., 1997; Tschuschke & Dies, 1994), and student seminar groups (Meredith, 1987). While the association between cohesion and successful outcomes is consistent, some findings suggest that the indicators of cohesion may change depending on the type of group (Stokes, 1983).

Beyond simply promoting positive outcomes, cohesion is associated with the member-group relationship and development of positive group processes. Several studies find positive influences of group cohesion:

- A study of 105 workers in 19 service groups found that cohesion is associated with a sense of belonging to the group (Pollack, 1998).
- A study of exercise classes found that cohesion is associated with a shared group vision (Burke et al., 2005).

- Studies of treatment and student groups found that higher levels of cohesion are associated with verbal risk taking, here-and-now interaction, self-disclosure, and reductions in problem-maintaining thinking (Beech & Hamilton-Giachritsis, 2005; Rosenfeld & Gilbert, 1989; Slavin, 1993).

- Several studies found an association between high group cohesion, individual efficacy, and group confidence (Chang & Bordia, 2001; Grabhorn, Kaufhold, & Overbeck, 2002; Marmarosh et al., 2005).

- A study of 22 play groups each with five to six children found that low cohesion was among the group dynamics associated with intermember aggression (de Rosier, Cillessen, Coie, & Dodge, 1994).

- A study of treatment groups found a lack of cohesion is associated with subgroups and schisms in the group (Sani, 2005).

When assessing a group for potential problems, it is important to consider the potential indicators of low cohesion. The literature provides six clear indicators that there are problems with cohesion. These indicators include:

1. *Negative emotion:* High levels of negative emotion in a group are associated with the development of schisms and factions that interfere with group cohesion (Sani, 2005). If negative emotion seems prevalent in the group, monitor for subgroups and factions.

2. *Social loafing:* Members who participate very little and allow others to do the work are referred to as social loafers. In a laboratory study of high, moderate, and low cohesion groupings, researchers found that high cohesion groups had less social loafing (Karau & Hart, 1998).

3. *Poor outcomes:* Groups that have high cohesion tend to have superior outcomes. In a study that observed 50 self-managed work teams (military officers) for a 5-week period, researchers found that cohesion contributed to group performance (Jordan et al., 2002). Likewise, a laboratory study of 57 undergraduate groups produced similar findings (Allen et al., 2003).

4. *Low interpersonal sharing:* Cohesive groups tend to have higher levels of sharing and personal interaction. In a study of 78 teams with a total sample size of 1,000 subjects, researchers found that frequent sharing was associated with higher levels of group cohesion (Carron et al., 2004).

5. *Low consensus:* Groups that don't agree on goals, methods of goal achievement, and direction tend to have lower levels of cohesion. In a study of exercise classes, researchers found that groups with shared goals and demonstrated action toward meeting their goals had higher levels of cohesion (Burke et al., 2005).

6. *Low interdependence:* Groups that have little in common or avoid working together on their goals tend to have low cohesion. Situational interdependence (e.g., all members experiencing similar situations) is associated with increased participation and cooperation among the members (Oetzel, 2001). A study of 57 work teams also found that task interdependence (members working collaboratively toward a goal) is associated with group cohesion (Kirkman & Shapiro, 2000).

Whenever problems are evident in a group, there will likely be threats to cohesion. However, cohesion is associated with engagement, composition, interactions, and other group elements. Consequently, an assessment of cohesion may require renegotiating leadership patterns or altering the interaction to increase sharing and interdependence. One may also want to intervene preemptively by meeting with potential group members ahead of time to promote a positive group identity (Marmarosh & Corazzini, 1997).

Group Climate

The group climate refers to the nonverbal, interpersonal feeling in the group (Alissi, 1982; Shaw, 1971). The relational climate is often the most commonly mentioned factor when members speak of their group experience in therapy groups (Johnson, Bulingame, Olsen, Davies, & Gleave, 2005; Shechtman & Gluk, 2005), work groups (Bain, Mann, & Pirola-Merlo, 2001), and training groups (Choi et al., 2003). Concurrent with influencing the member experience, the climate of the group is associated with innovation, confidence, and group outcomes in many types of groups (Bain et al., 2001; Bierhoff & Muller, 2005; Choi et al., 2003; Harper & Askling, 1980; Schiff & Bargal, 2000).

The group climate has an emotional and interactive element. A recent study of 43 student groups found that a climate of emotional openness and stability predicted performance (Bond & Ng, 2004). Conversely, a study of 33 group casualties identified a lack of support as the most frequent harmful dynamic (Smokowski, Rose, & Bacallao, 2001). A climate of persistent negative emotion and competitiveness in the group is associated with aggression in children's groups (de Rosier et al., 1994). While emotion is a critical element of group climate, findings suggest that emotional elements are mediated by here-and-now exchanges, openness, and risk taking in the group (Bond & Ng, 2004; Kivlighan & Jauquet, 1990).

Several group dynamics are associated with the group climate. First, group climate appears to be associated with engagement. Early studies of group dropout rates found that individuals who perceive themselves as having a poor relationship with the group tend to drop out of treatment (Parloff, 1961; Yalom, 1966). The group climate is also associated with perceptions of group efficacy (Choi et al., 2003; Schiff & Bargal, 2000). Additional studies find an association with group cohesion (Dimmock, Grove, & Eklund, 2005; Pollack, 1998). Finally, group climate is associated with outcomes (Bain et al., 2001; Choi et al., 2003).

When assessing the group climate, there are several indicators of potential problems. These indicators are both verbal and nonverbal in nature. Group workers must often monitor the unspoken elements of the group to identify potential problems. The following five indicators can help identify climate problems. When using these indicators, remember that some indicators may pertain to more than one group dynamic.

1. *Negative tensions:* Pervasive negative tensions in the group can indicate climate problems (Bond & Ng, 2004). It is important to monitor for consistent anxiety, anger, hostility, competitiveness, and other negative emotions.
2. *Evasiveness:* If group members are not openly sharing, it may indicate problems with group support (Smokowski et al., 2001). People are not likely to share unless the group feels safe.
3. *Attendance problems:* When people do not feel comfortable in the group, they tend to stop attending (Yalom, 1966). If attendance is not consistent or there are dropouts, a group climate problem may be impacting engagement.

4. *Here-and-now risk-taking:* Group members must be able to address the interactions, relationships, and attitudes among the group members. These interactions require risk taking. Such risk taking is a sign that the climate is good (Kivlighan & Jauquet, 1990). A lack of such risk taking, especially in the later stages of the group, may indicate climate problems.

5. *Hopelessness:* A positive group climate is associated with group efficacy (Choi et al., 2003). If group members indicate a lack of hope in the group there may be problems in the group climate.

Interactive Processes

All groups contain interactive processes. Frequent and evenly distributed interaction among group members is beneficial to the group (Holtz, 2004). In a laboratory study of 189 students, researchers found that equal participation and respect among the members was associated with group satisfaction (Oetzel, 2001). An 18-month study of adults in group therapy found that speaking out in the group was associated with better outcomes (Fielding, 1983). Similar findings were found in a study of undergraduate students in learning groups (Olivera & Straus, 2004).

Groups appear to have internal systems for managing the interactions of the group members. Within the group, there is a tendency for the interactive patterns to self-organize around the context of the group (Pincus & Guastello, 2005). One study found that in groups that value evenly distributed group attention, members tend to balance themselves by waiting longer to talk after a lengthy disclosure (Kuk, 2000). Such reciprocal exchanges are associated with higher levels of trust and affective commitment in groups (Molm, 2003).

Group interactions often cluster around themes of conflict and closeness (Pincus & Guastello, 2005). Closeness themes of agreeableness and helpfulness are associated with increased collaboration among group members (Halfhill et al., 2005). Closeness themes are also associated with group cohesion (Bierhoff & Muller, 1999; Bond & Ng, 2004). Joking cultures (group-related inside jokes) can develop in groups helping to establish group boundaries, build affiliation, and control group members (Fine & de Soucey, 2005).

Conflict themes can be harmful to both the group and the individuals in the group. A study of 33 group casualties found that confrontation, criticism, pressuring, fighting, and nonhelpful feedback were the most commonly mentioned damaging interactions (Smokowski et al., 2001). In a study focused on group functioning, researchers categorized groups based on functional levels. This study found that conflict was a common theme in the least functional groups (Wheelan & Williams, 2003).

Conflict sets up reciprocal exchanges where one member's attack results in a counterattack (Pincus & Guastello, 2005). A study of group conflict identified primary provokers (those who initiate problematic interactions) and secondary provokers (those who respond) in the problem sequences. Primary provokers tend to produce both friendly and hostile interactive themes. Conflict is most disruptive when the focus of the conflict is based on a lack of tolerance for demographic or personality differences (Bayazit & Mannix, 2003). Task-related conflict can be disruptive if avoided and allowed to escalate and interfere with problem solving (Becker-Beck, 2001). Researchers indicated that task-related conflict must be addressed early in the group.

Methods of nonconflictual decision making can also be problematic. Majority-rule methods of making decisions or resolving problems (e.g., voting) often fail to protect the group as these methods inherently exclude some group members (Schei & Rognes, 2005). In a meta-analytic study of group decision making, Orlitzky and Hirokawa (2001) found that evaluating the negative outcomes of alternatives, problem analysis, and having clear criteria for the solution were the critical components of positive outcomes.

When assessing group interaction, the previous findings provide indicators of potential problems. The following list of seven indicators can be used to assess the group interaction. Like other group dynamics, these indicators are not mutually exclusive and may also indicate problems with other dynamics:

1. *Unequal sharing* (Holtz, 2004; Oetzel, 2001; Olivera & Straus, 2004): When some members never speak and others monopolize the group discussion, there may be interactive problems (Fielding, 1983).

2. *Lack of support* (Molm, 2003; Smokowski et al., 2001): When group members speak and other members respond with judgmental feedback rather than providing support, there may be problems in the group.

3. *Emotionally volatile expressions* (Bayazit & Manniz, 2003; Bond & Ng, 2004): When group members exhibit high levels of emotional variability in their interaction, there may be problems. This is particularly true with themes of hostility and dependence.

4. *Personal attacks* (Bayazit & Mannix, 2003; Smokowski et al., 2001): When members attack each other with a focus on personality or personal traits, there are likely problems in the group interaction.

5. *Pressuring members/intolerance for differences* (Smokawski et al., 2001): If group members pressure others or focus on specific members due to personality or demographic differences, there may be and intolerance of differences governing the interactions.

6. *Avoidance of problems* (Becker-Beck, 2001): When group members avoid bringing up differences or other tension provoking issues, there may be a problem in how the group approaches problems.

7. *Voting rather than reaching for consensus* (Schei & Rognes, 2005): When decisions are made by a majority rule, subgroups are compromised in the group rather than being engaged in the decisions. This can become divisive in the group.

Group Leadership

There are two types of group leadership: formal and emergent (or indigenous). Formal group leadership refers to the actions used by the group worker to help the group achieve its goals. Emergent leadership refers to members assuming leadership roles in response to the needs of the group. Formal leadership has a strong influence on the climate and outcomes of the group (Bierhoff & Muller, 2005). Some group leader traits account for much of this influence. A study focused on task groups found that the leader's self-efficacy determines task strategies influencing group outcomes (Kane, Zaccaro, Tremble, & Masuda, 2002). The approach adopted by the leader also influences member attrition. A recent study found that autocratic leadership was associated with group member decisions to leave the group (van Vugt et al., 2004).

Some group level problems are an indication of member responses to leader actions. A study of "good" versus "bad" group sessions tracking themes of dominance and friendliness in leader-member interactions found that during "good" sessions leaders were variable but balanced. In sessions identified as "bad," leaders tended toward extreme positions in the areas of dominance versus submission and hostility versus friendliness (Kivlighan, Mullison, Flohr, Proudman, & Francis, 1992). A comparative study of 33 group casualties and 50 participants from groups with no casualties found that the leader pressuring members was the strongest discriminator (Smokowski, Rose, Todar, & Reardon, 1999). Other problematic leader behaviors included monopolizing the group, low support, criticism, and unhelpful feedback/advice.

Autocratic leadership is identified as the most problematic style of group work. Autocratic group leaders tend to instruct, judge, limit the group focus, and control the criteria of success (Fiene, 1979; van Vugt et al., 2004). Such styles are associated with negative affect in the group, poor outcomes, and higher attrition rates (Bierhoff & Muller, 2005; van Vugt et al., 2004). Even when leaders consult with members, it is possible to withhold power from the group. A laboratory study of 144 subjects in three-way negotiation exercises found that leaders who caucus (selective feedback for decision making) retained power while joint decision making decreased leadership power (Mannix, 1993).

When leaders exert too much power over the group, interactive and emotional group processes are compromised. A study of 26 undergraduate task groups found that leader-power orientation strongly influences the negotiating latitude of the group members (McClane, 1991). A similar study of 216 students found that during group conflict, leaders with high power needs inhibit the affective expressions of group members (Fodor, 1995). Research indicates that while both verbal and nonverbal leader-power expressions influence the group, the nonverbal expressions yield the strongest negative affect in the group members (Driskell & Salas, 2005).

In contrast to autocratic leadership, democratic group leadership is frequently considered a superior approach. Demographic leadership is typically identified by leader actions that encourage and support group member input. A study of 33 college students found that leader support and encouragement was associated with increased member participation (Harper & Askling, 1980). This same leadership style is associated with member satisfaction (Foels, Driskell, Mullen, & Salas, 2000; Kushell & Newton, 1986; Meredith, 1987; Stitt, Schmidt, Price, & Kipnis, 1983). Satisfaction is strongest for female group members who tend to react most strongly to autocratic styles of leadership (Kushell & Newton, 1986).

Two elements of democratic leadership—encouragement to voice opinions and support—both receive support in the empirical literature. In a study of 169 training groups attending a 5-day workshop, researchers found that supportive leadership is associated with increased group self-efficacy and outcomes (Choi et al., 2003). A study focused on group stability found that when the leader creates an atmosphere where members feel that they have permission to voice dissent, negative emotion, subgrouping, and schisms are moderated (Sani, 2005).

A dynamic made possible in democratic groups is emergent leadership. Emergent leaders are identified by high level of group participation (Kelsey, 1998). A study of children's groups found that emergent task and relationship leadership is positively associated with group regulation, participation, and cohesion (Kelsey, 1998; Yamaguchi & Maehr, 2004). Emergent leaders often enhance the atmosphere of the group by promoting group self-efficacy and highlighting positive group elements (Pescosolido, 2001; Yamaguchi & Maehr, 2004).

In work groups, the concepts of autocratic and democratic leadership are seldom used. The most commonly used positive leadership style is transformational leadership, that increases members' commitment to, and identification with, the group. In a study of 47 workgroups from Korean firms, this style of leadership was related to member empowerment, group cohesiveness, and group effectiveness (Jung & Sosik, 2002). In studies of transformational leadership agreeableness, showing interest, reinforcement, and validation of the members promotes group cohesion and effective decision making (Gardner & Cleavenger, 1998; Rozell & Gundersen, 2003). These tenants of transformational leadership are strikingly similar to descriptions of democratic leadership.

There is sufficient evidence to conclude that group leadership style can inhibit or promote helpful group processes. The following list of indicators may be used to assess the potential for leader related problems in a group. When using these indicators, remember that they may be associated with multiple problems given that group processes are interrelated. The indicators include:

- *Infrequent, limited, or strained member disclosures* (Harper & Askling, 1980; Kivlighan et al., 1992): If members are reluctant to share or respond to others in the group, changes may be needed in how the group is lead.
- *Drop-outs and absenteeism* (van Vugt et al., 2004): If members are not attending group meetings or are leaving the group, this may indicate dissatisfaction with the leadership style.
- *Acquiescence/conformity* (Grabhorn et al., 2002): Group members who feel they cannot speak their minds or fear repercussions may respond by conforming rather than voicing dissent.
- *Negative mood/dissatisfaction with the group* (Meredith, 1987; Sani, 2005): A pervasive negative mood or atmosphere in the group may indicate that the members are unhappy but are unable to openly express their discontent.
- *Development of subgroups of schisms* (Sani, 2005): While there are many possible reasons for subgrouping and schisms, use of power and inhibiting dissent can contribute to these dynamics.

When using these indicators, it is important to also consider the composition of the group. In a study of marathon groups, Kilmann and Sotile (1976) found that internalizers work better with an unstructured group approach while externalizers required more structure in the group. One might consequently expect externalized members to be more tolerant of an autocratic style. While females are less likely to engage in emergent leadership, they have more reactions to autocratic leaders (Kushell & Newton, 1986; Yamaguchi & Maehr, 2004). Such membership dynamics may influence the group responses to leadership style.

Group Development

Group development is the final consideration because development involves subtle changes in all other group dynamics with the passage of time. Many discussions of group development are based on grounded theory. These discussions typically outline a model of stages and predictable changes that occur through the life of the group. There are also empirical studies that have assessed group changes over time. This section outlines some of these findings.

Three studies have identified developmental influences on engagement. The first study using a multivariate analysis of variance (MANOVA) found that members became more engaged, adopted realistic expectations, and demonstrated less avoidance as the group progressed (Kivlighan & Jauquet, 1990). A study of violence abatement programs found that early in treatment members prioritize problem awareness and understanding and later emphasize the emotional and interactive elements of the group (Roy, Turcotte, Montminy, & Lindsay, 2005). A similar study found that individual attributes are valued early in the group while the structure of the group is identified as important in the later group stages (Lin, Yang, Arya, Huang, & Li, 2005). All three studies demonstrate a shift from individualistic and safe pursuits to an increased collective and personal focus.

Concurrent with studying engagement, research has found developmental changes in the group climate. Kivlighan and Lilly (1997) assessed group climate changes by surveying 52 group members at scheduled time intervals. Findings indicated climate changes at the beginning, middle, and end of the group. The most significant changes were noted in the areas of engagement and conflict, with engagement decreasing in the middle stages of group development while conflict peaked in that same stage. This study found that group dynamics shift differentially depending on the stage rather than through linear increases over time.

Studies have also identified developmental changes in cohesion. A study of 89 group members in 12 short-term treatment groups found that member-specific indicators of cohesion change as the group progresses (Budman, Soldz, Demby, Davism, & Merry, 1993). Another study of 38 men in violence abatement groups found that group cohesion develops after universality has been achieved (Schwartz & Waldo, 1999). In a similar study of short-term psychotherapy groups ($N = 154$ members), Kipnes, Piper, and Joyce (2002) found that intermember and member-leader cohesion increased across the 12 sessions while the member-group cohesion decreased. This suggests that the intermember bonds become stronger over the life of the group.

Some studies have identified interaction changes associated with group development. A study of self-disclosure and perceptions of closeness found that both self-disclosure and feelings of closeness increase with group development (Bunch, Lund, & Wiggins, 1983). The content of interaction also appears to change. A more recent study tracked the percentage of statements focused on dependency, fight, and flight across time, finding that work-focused statements increased with the passage of time while dependency, fight, and flight statements decreased (Wheelan, Davidson, & Tilin, 2003).

A final set of studies focused on changes in therapeutic factors. A study of 15 clinical groups used the Therapeutic Factors Inventory to assess developmental change, finding that perceptions of the group and therapeutic factors changed with elapsed time. In particular, guidance and catharsis increase in value at the latter stages of group development (MacNair-Semands & Lese, 2000). These findings are consistent with earlier studies (Freedman & Hurley, 1980; Kivlighan & Goldfine, 1991; MacKenzie, 1983).

The general patterns in the research suggest that early stages of development involve individually focused and shallower exploration. In these stages, members focus on increasing awareness and understanding. These are cognitive and individually focused pursuits.

As the group progresses, there is more conflict and more engagement. During the later stages, sharing and work increase. During these latter stages, there is an increased focus on the other members as intermember relationships elevate in importance and members spend more time guiding and supporting each other.

When assessing the group development, monitor for changes occurring across time. If changes are not evident, there may be developmental problems. It is also useful to contrast changes with what can be considered developmentally normal. The following list of indicators can be used to identify potential problems with group development. When problems are detected, it is usually necessary to consider the other dynamics to understand what may be interfering with development. Consequently, use these indicators to identify a problem and then use the other considerations to understand why the problem is emerging in the group. The indicators that can assist monitoring for developmental problems include:

- *Increases in self-disclosure* (Bunch et al., 1983): As the group progresses members should start sharing more of their personal stories and experiences.
- *Increases in closeness/intimacy* (MacNair-Semands & Lese, 2000): Group members should be more comfortable expressing emotion and taking risks as the group progresses.
- *Increases in work focus* (Wheelan et al., 2003): As the group progresses, distractions should start to decrease as more attention is focused on achieving the group goals.
- *Decreases in emotional dependency themes* (Wheelan et al., 2003): Early in the group, there is more impression management and efforts to be liked; these indicators of emotional dependency and insecurity should diminish as the group progresses.
- *Decreases in conflict* (Kivlighan & Lilly, 1997): While conflict is common in the early to middle stages of group development, it should diminish as the group progresses. If conflict persists, there may be problems.

IDENTIFIED NEEDS FOR NEW RESEARCH

The current findings are consistent with many of the grounded theories in the field of social work. As such, past group wisdom about group dynamics is validated. However, there are practice developments that highlight a need for new knowledge. In particular, there are two movements in social work practice influencing how social workers conduct groups. The first is the managed care movement, creating financial priorities and limitations on group treatment. The second movement is evidence-based treatment, promoting manualized approaches to group programming.

The first movement, managed care, influences group practice in two ways. First, third-party reimbursement systems often limit the number of sessions and level of involvement. Consequently, many members will drop out of treatment not based on the utility of treatment but rather based on financial considerations. The second influence is for agencies to promote group programs because they can receive funding for multiple clients attending the group with a minimal personnel expense. Financial incentives can overshadow knowledge-based decisions through causing agencies to adopt procedures that maximize financial rather than treatment outcomes.

As a result, of these managed-care outcomes, organizations and agencies may have hidden agendas when groups are formed or dissolved. While financial considerations are legitimate, they must not interfere with achieving group outcomes. One of the outcomes of administrative priorities is to admit all potential group members to the group with little consideration as to how the group members will function as a group. Concurrently, agencies may forgo pregroup screening and orientation sessions. One can expect problems with achieving group criterion, engagement, and climate if screening and orientation concerns are overshadowed by financial considerations. More research is needed to identify the impact of different member-selection strategies. Practitioners need researchers to explore the impact of these agency decisions so they can more effectively advocate for clients and ensure the most effective treatment.

The second need for new research is due to an unintended consequence of the evidence-based treatment movement. This consequence is that many groups are adopting manualized treatment approaches, shifting the emphasis from the group worker's skills to model fidelity. Some agencies purchase treatment packages, offering the program using specially trained paraprofessionals or volunteers. Such group leaders are trained in the manualized package rather than in understanding group dynamics and outcomes.

There is very little research on the group dynamics occurring within manualized programs and how leaders manage the group dynamics concurrent within the program structure. One may expect problems in leadership, cohesion, and group climate as the following the program overrides member concerns. As the field is increasingly influenced by manualized approaches, research into the ideal balance between group dynamics and the program is needed to guide practitioners. It is also important to understand the level of group knowledge needed by practitioners using manualized packages.

These two areas of concern have important implications for assessing groups. Our current research on group dynamics is grounded in groups that do not use a manualized system and are outcome, rather than financially, driven. Using the criteria outlined in this chapter for assessing other types of groups may be difficult because one must assume that all groups are equivalent. There may be other dynamics in manualized groups that promote success. Likewise, there may be dynamics associated with managed care that either inhibit or promote group success. Research is needed to test the nature of these influences on groups so social workers can be ready to assess and conduct all types of groups.

REFERENCES

Alissi, A. S. (1982). The social group work method: Towards a reaffirmation of essentials. *Social Work with Groups, 5*, 3–17.

Allen, B. C., Sargent, L. D., & Bradley, L. M. (2003). Differential effects of task and reward interdependence on perceived helping behavior, effort, and group performance. *Small Group Research, 34*, 716–740.

Anderson, J. (1997). *Social work with groups.* New York: Longman.

Andra, M. L., & Thomas, A. M. (1998). The influence of parenting stress and socioeconomic disadvantage on therapy attendance among parents and their behavior disordered preschool children. *Education and Treatment of Children, 21*, 195–208.

Bain, P. G., Mann, L., & Pirola-Merlo, A. (2001). The innovation imperative: The relationships between team climate, innovation, and performance in research and development teams. *Small Group Research, 32*, 55–73.

Baker, D. F. (2001). The development of collective efficacy in small task groups. *Small Group Research*, *32*, 451–474.

Bayazit, M., & Mannix, E. A. (2003). Should I stay or should I go? Predicting team members' intent to remain in the team. *Small Group Research*, *34*, 290–321.

Becker-Beck, U. (2001). Methods for diagnosing interaction strategies: An application to group interaction in conflict situations. *Small Group Research*, *32*, 259–282.

Beech, A. R., & Hamilton-Giachritsis, C. E. (2005). Relationship between therapeutic climate and treatment outcome in group-based sexual offender treatment programs. *Sexual Abuse: Journal of Research and Treatment*, *17*, 127–140.

Bierhoff, H. W. & Muller, G. F. (1999). Positive feelings and cooperative support in project groups. *Swiss Journal of Psychology*, *58*(3), 180–190.

Bierhoff, H. W., & Muller, G. F. (2005). Leadership, mood, atmosphere, and cooperative support in project groups. *Journal of Managerial Psychology*, *20*(6), 483–497.

Bion, W. R. (1961). *Experiences in groups*. London: Tavistock.

Birchmeier, Z., Joinson, A. N., & Dietz-Uhler, B. (2005). Storming and forming a normative response to a deception revealed online. *Social Science Computer Review*, *23*, 108–121.

Bogenschneider, K. (1996). An ecological risk/protective theory for building prevention programs, policies, and community capacity to support youth. *Family Relations*, *45*, 127–138.

Bond, M. H., & Ng, I. W-C. (2004). The depth of a group's personality resources: Impacts on group process and group performance. *Asian Journal of Social Psychology*, *7*, 285–300.

Budman, S. H., Soldz, S., Demby, A., Davism, M., & Merry, J. (1993). What is cohesiveness? An empirical examination. *Small Group Research*, *24*, 199–216.

Bunch, G. J., Lund, N. L., & Wiggins, F. K. (1983). Self-disclosure and perceived closeness in the development of group process. *Journal for Specialists in Group Work*, *8*, 59–66.

Burke, S. M., Carron, A. V., Patterson, M. M., Estabrooks, P. A., Hill, J. L., Loughead, T. M., et al. (2005). Cohesion as shared beliefs in exercise classes. *Small Group Research*, *36*, 267–288.

Carron, A. V., Brawley, L. R., Bray, S. R., Eys, M. A., Dorsch, K. D., Estabrooks, P. A., et al. (2004). Using consensus as a criterion for groupness: Implications for the cohesion-group success relationship. *Small Group Research*, *35*, 466–491.

Cartwright, D., & Zander, A. (1968). *Group dynamics: Research and theory* (3rd ed.). New York: Harper & Row.

Chang, A., & Bordia, P. (2001). A multidimensional approach to the group cohesion-group performance relationship. *Small Group Research*, *32*, 379–405.

Choi, J. N., Price, R. H., & Vinokur, A. D. (2003). Self-efficacy changes in groups: Effects of diversity, leadership, and group climate. *Journal of Organizational Behavior*, *24*, 357–372.

Coyle, G. L. (1948). *Group work with American youth: A guide to the practice of leadership*. New York: Harper & Row.

de Cremer, D., & Tyler, T. R. (2005). Am I respected or not? Inclusion and reputation as issues in group membership. *Social Justice Research*, *18*, 121–153.

de Jager, W., & Strauss, R. (1998). The selection of young adolescents for group therapy: Working towards cohesion. *Southern African Journal of Child and Adolescent Mental Health*, *10*, 133–139.

de Rosier, M. E., Cillessen, A. H. N., Coie, J. D., & Dodge, K. A. (1994). Group social context and children's aggressive behavior. *Child Development*, *65*, 1068–1079.

Dewey, J. (1933). Education and our present social problems. *Education Method*, *12*, 385–390.

Dimmock, J. A., Grove, J. R., & Eklund, R. C. (2005). Reconceptualizing team identification: New dimensions and their relationship to intergroup bias. *Group Dynamics: Theory, Research, and Practice*, *9*, 75–86.

Driskell, J. E., & Salas, E. (2005). The effect of content and demeanor on reactions to dominance behavior. *Group Dynamics: Theory, Research, and Practice*, *9*, 3–14.

Duck, J. M., & Fielding, K. S. (1999). Leaders and subgroups: One of us or one of them? *Group Processes and Intergroup Relations*, *2*, 203–230.

Dumas, J. E., & Wahler, R. G. (1983). Predictors of treatment outcome in parent training: Mother insularity and socioeconomic disadvantage. *Behavioral Assessment, 5*, 301–313.

Emery, F. (1978). Characteristics of socio-technical systems. In F. Emery (Ed.), *The emergence of a new paradigm of work* (pp. 38–86). Canberra: Australian National University, Centre for Continuing Education.

Emery, F., & Emery, M. (1974). *Participative design.* Canberra: Australian National University, Centre for Continuing Education.

Evensen, E. P., & Bednar, R. L. (1978). Effects of specific cognitive and behavior structure on early group behavior and atmosphere. *Journal of Counseling Psychology, 25*, 66–75.

Fielding, J. M. (1983). Verbal participation and group therapy outcome. *British Journal of Psychiatry, 142*, 524–528.

Fiene, J. F. (1979). Elements of leadership which impede creativity. *Creative Child and Adult Quarterly, 4*, 30–39.

Fine, G. A., & de Soucey, M. (2005). Joking cultures: Humor themes as social regulation in group life. *Humor: International Journal of Humor Research, 18*, 1–22.

Fodor, E. M. (1995). Leader power motive and group conflict as influences on group member self-affect. *Journal of Research in Personality, 29*, 418–431.

Foels, R., Driskell, J. E., Mullen, B., & Salas, E. (2000). The effects of democratic leadership on group member satisfaction: An integration. *Small Group Research, 31*, 676–701.

Follett, M. P. (1920). *The new state.* New York: Longmans, Green.

Foulkes, S. H., & Anthony, E. J. (1957). *Group psychotherapy, the psychoanalytic approach.* London: Penguin Books.

France, D. G., & Dugo, J. M. (1985). Pretherapy orientation as preparation for open psychotherapy groups. *Psychotherapy: Theory, Research, Practice, Training, 22*, 256–261.

Freedman, S. M., & Hurley, J. R. (1980). Perceptions of helpfulness and behavior in groups. *Group, 4*, 51–58.

Freud, S. (1922). *Group psychology and the analysis of the ego.* London: International Psychoanalytic Press.

Gardner, W. L., & Cleavenger, D. (1998). The impression management strategies associated with transformational leadership at the world-class level. *Management Communication Quarterly, 12*, 3–42.

Gilbert, N., & Specht, H. (1981). *The emergence of social welfare and social work* (2nd ed.). Itasca, IL: Peacock.

Grabhorn, R., Kaufhold, J., & Overbeck, G. (2002). The role of differentiated group experience in the course of inpatient psychotherapy. In S. P. Shohov (Ed.), *Advances in psychology research* (pp. 141–154). Hauppauge, NY: Nova Science.

Halfhill, T., Sundstrom, E., Lahner, J., Calderone, W., & Nielsen, T. M. (2005). Group personality composition and group effectiveness: An integrative review of empirical research. *Small Group Research, 36*, 83–105.

Harper, N. L., & Askling, L. R. (1980). Group communication and quality of task solution in a media production organization. *Communication Monographs, 47*, 77–100.

Herbst, D. D. G. (1962). *Autonomous group functioning.* London: Tavistock.

Herrera, A. E., & Sanchez, V. C. (1980). Prescriptive group psychotherapy: A successful application in the treatment of low income, Spanish-speaking clients. *Psychotherapy Theory, Research and Practice, 17*, 169–174.

Holtz, R. (2004). Group cohesion, attitude projection, and opinion certainty: Beyond interaction. *Group Dynamics: Theory, Research, and Practice, 8*, 112–125.

Home, A., & Darveau-Fournier, L. (1990). Facing the challenge of developing group services for high risk families. *Group Work, 3*, 236–248.

Islam, G., & Zyphur, M. J. (2005). Power, voice, and hierarchy: Exploring the antecedents of speaking up in groups. *Group Dynamics: Theory, Research, and Practice, 9*, 93–103.

Johnson, J. E., Bulingame, G. M., Olsen, J. A., Davies, R. D., & Gleave, R. L. (2005). Group climate, cohesion, alliance, and empathy in group psychotherapy: Multilevel structural equation models. *Journal of Counseling Psychology, 52*, 310–321.

Jordan, M. H., Feild, J. S., & Armenakis, A. A. (2002). The relationship of group process variables and team performance: A team-level analysis in a field setting. *Small Group Research, 33*, 121–150.

Jung, D. I., & Sosik, J. J. (2002). Transformational leadership in work groups: The role of empowerment, cohesiveness, and collective-efficacy on perceived group performance. *Small Group Research, 33*, 313–336.

Kane, T. D., Zaccaro, S. J., Tremble, T. R., Jr., & Masuda, A. D. (2002). An examination of the leader's regulation of groups. *Small Group Research, 33*, 65–120.

Karakowsky, L., & Elangovan, A. R. (2001). Risky decision making in mixed-gender teams: Whose risk tolerance matters? *Small Group Research, 32*, 94–111.

Karakowsky, L., McBey, K., & Miller, D. L. (2004). Gender, perceived competence, and power displays: Examining verbal interruptions in a group context. *Small Group Research, 35*, 407–439.

Karau, S. J., & Hart, J. W. (1998). Group cohesiveness and social loafing: Effects of a social interaction manipulation on individual motivation within groups. *Group Dynamics: Theory, Research, and Practice, 2*, 185–191.

Kazdin, A. (1990). Premature termination from treatment among children referred for antisocial behaviour. *Journal of Child Psychology and Psychiatry, 31*, 415–425.

Kelsey, B. L. (1998). The dynamics of multicultural groups: Ethnicity as a determinant of leadership. *Small Group Research, 29*, 602–623.

Kenny, D. A., & LaVoie, L. (1985). Separating individual and group effects. *Journal of Personality and Social Psychology, 48*, 339–348.

Kilmann, P. R., & Sotile, W. M. (1976). The effects of structured and unstructured leader roles on internal and external group participants. *Journal of Clinical Psychology, 32*, 848–856.

Kipnes, D. R., Piper, W. E., & Joyce, A. S. (2002). Cohesion and outcome in short-term psychodynamic groups for complicated grief. *International Journal of Group Psychotherapy, 52*, 483–509.

Kirchenbaum, D. S. (1979). Social competence intervention and evaluation in the inner city: Cincinnati's social skills development program. *Journal of Consulting and Clinical Psychology, 47*, 778–780.

Kirkman, B. L., & Shapiro, D. L. (2000). Understanding why team members won't share: An examination of factors related to employee receptivity to team-based rewards. *Small Group Research, 31*, 175–209.

Kivlighan, D. M., Jr., & Goldfine, D. C. (1991). Endorsement of therapeutic factors as a function of stage of group development and participant interpersonal attitudes. *Journal of Counseling Psychologist, 38*, 150–158.

Kivlighan, D. M., Jr., & Jauquet, C. A. (1990). Quality of group member agendas and group session climate. *Small Group Research, 21*, 205–219.

Kivlighan, D. M., Jr., & Lilly, R. L. (1997). Developmental changes in group climate as they relate to therapeutic gain. *Group Dynamics: Theory, Research, and Practice, 1*, 208–221.

Kivlighan, D. M., Jr., Mullison, D. D., Flohr, D. F., Proudman, S., & Francis, A. M. R. (1992). The interpersonal structure of "good" versus "bad" group counseling sessions: A multiple-case study. *Psychotherapy, 29*, 500–508.

Klein, R. H., & Carroll, R. (1986). Patient characteristics and attendance patterns in outpatient group psychotherapy. *International Journal of Group Psychotherapy, 36*, 115–132.

Konopka, G. (1963). *Social group work: A helping process.* Englewood Cliffs, NJ: Prentice Hall.

Kruglanski, A. W., Shah, J. Y., Pierro, A., & Mannetti, L. (2002). When similarity breeds content: Need for closure and the allure of homogenous and self-resembling groups. *Journal of Personality and Social Psychology, 83*, 648–662.

Kuk, G. (2000). "When to speak again": Self-regulation under facilitation. *Group Dynamics: Theory, Research, and Practice*, *4*, 291–306.

Kushell, E., & Newton, R. (1986). Gender, leadership style, and subordinate satisfaction: An experiment. *Sex Roles*, *14*, 203–209.

Lash, S. J., & Blosser, S. L. (1999). Increasing adherence to substance abuse aftercare groups. *Journal of Substance Abuse Treatment*, *16*, 55–60.

Lash, S. J., Burden, J. L., Monteleone, B. R., & Lehmann, L. P. (2004). Social reinforcement of substance abuse treatment aftercare participation: Impact on outcome. *Addictive Behaviors*, *29*, 337–342.

Lee, C., Tinsley, C. H., & Bobko, P. (2002). An investigation of the antecedents and consequences of group level confidence. *Journal of Applied Social Psychology*, *32*, 1628–1652.

Lee, C., Tinsley, C. H., & Bobko, P. (2004). An investigation of the antecedents and consequences of group-level confidence: Erratum. *Journal of Applied Social Psychology*, *34*, 2656–2658.

Lengua, L. J., Roosa, M. W., Schupak-Neuberg, E., Michaels, M. L., Berg, C. N., & Weschler, L. F. (1992). Using focus groups to guide the development of a parenting program for difficult-to-reach, high-risk families. *Family Relations*, *41*, 163–168.

Lewin, K. (1935). *A dynamic theory of personality*. New York: McGraw-Hill.

Lin, Z., Yang, J., Arya, B., Huang, Z., & Li, D. (2005). Structural versus individual perspectives on the dynamics of group performance: Theoretical exploration and empirical investigation. *Journal of Management*, *31*, 354–380.

Lorion, R. P. (1973). Socioeconomic status and traditional treatment approaches reconsidered. *Psychological Bulletin*, *79*, 263–270.

Lorion, R. P., & Felner, R. D. (1986). Research on mental health interventions with the disadvantaged. In S. L. Garfield & A. E. Bergin (Eds.), *Handbook of psychotherapy and behavior change* (pp. 739–775). New York: Wiley.

Lovaglia, M. J. (1995). Power and status: Exchange, attribution, and expectation states. *Small Group Research*, *26*, 400–426.

Lucken, M., & Simon, B. (2005). Cognitive and affective experiences of minority and majority members: The role of group size, status, and power. *Journal of Experimental Social Psychology*, *41*, 396–413.

MacKenzie, K. R. (1983). The clinical application of a group climate measure. In R. R. Dies & K. R. MacKenzie (Eds.), *Advances in group psychotherapy: Integrating research and practice* (pp. 159–170). Madison, CT: International Universities Press.

MacNair-Semands, R. R. (2002). Predicting attendance and expectations for group therapy. *Group Dynamics: Theory, Research, and Practice*, *6*, 219–228.

MacNair-Semands, R. R., & Lese, K. P. (2000). Interpersonal problems and the perception of therapeutic factors in group therapy. *Small Group Research*, *31*, 158–174.

Mannix, E. A. (1993). The influence of power, distribution norms and task meeting structure on resource allocation in small group negotiation. *International Journal of Conflict Management*, *4*, 5–23.

Marmarosh, C. L., & Corazzini, J. G. (1997). Putting the group in your pocket: Using collective identity to enhance personal and collective self-esteem. *Group Dynamics: Theory, Research, and Practice*, *1*, 65–74.

Marmarosh, C. L., Holtz, A., & Shottenbauer, M. (2005). Group cohesiveness, group-derived collective self-esteem, group-derived hope, and the well-being of group therapy members. *Group Dynamics: Theory, Research, and Practice*, *9*, 32–44.

Marziali, E., Munroe-Blum, H., & McCleary, L. (1997). The contribution of group cohesion and group alliance to the outcome of group psychotherapy. *International Journal of Group Psychotherapy*, *47*, 475–497.

Mayo, E. (1933). *The human problems of an industrialized civilization*. New York: Macmillan.

McCallum, M., Piper, W. E., Ogrodniczuk, J. S., & Joyce, A. S. (2002). Early process and dropping out from short-term group therapy for complicated grief. *Group Dynamics: Theory, Research, and Practice*, *6*, 243–254.

McClane, W. E. (1991). The interaction of leader and member characteristics in the leader-member exchange (LMX) model of leadership. *Small Group Research*, *22*, 283–300.

McKisack, C., & Waller, G. (1996). Why is attendance variable at groups for women with bulimia nervosa? The role of eating psychopathology and other characteristics. *International Journal of Eating Disorders*, *20*, 205–209.

Meredith, G. M. (1987). Attributes of group atmosphere as predictors of students' satisfaction in seminar-format classes. *Psychological Reports*, *61*, 79–82.

Miura, A., & Hida, M. (2004). Synergy between diversity and similarity in group-idea generation. *Small Group Research*, *35*, 540–564.

Mohammed, S., & Angell, L. C. (2003). Personality heterogeneity in teams: Which differences make a difference for team performance? *Small Group Research*, *34*, 651–677.

Molleman, E. (2005). Diversity in demographic characteristics, abilities and personality traits: Do faultlines affect team functioning? *Group Decision and Negotiation*, *14*, 173–193.

Molm, L. D. (2003). Power, trust, and fairness: Comparisons of negotiated and reciprocal exchange. In S. R. Thye & J. Skvoretz (Eds.), *Advances in group processes* (Vol. 20, pp. 31–65). Oxford: Elsevier Science.

Moritz, S. E., & Watson, C. B. (1998). Levels of analysis issues in group treatment: Using efficacy as an example of a multilevel model. *Group Dynamics: Theory, Research and Practice*, *2*, 285–298.

Oetzel, J. G. (2001). Self-construals, communication processes, and group outcomes in homogeneous and heterogeneous groups. *Small Group Research*, *32*, 19–54.

Ogrodniczuk, J. S., & Piper, W. E. (2003). The effect of group climate on outcome in two forms of short-term group therapy. *Group Dynamics: Theory, Research, and Practice*, *7*, 64–76.

Olivera, F., & Straus, S. G. (2004). Group-to-individual transfer of learning: Cognitive and social factors. *Small Group Research*, *35*, 440–465.

Orlitzky, M., & Hirokawa, R. Y. (2001). To err is human, to correct for it divine: A meta-analysis of research testing the functional theory of group decision-making effectiveness. *Small Group Research*, *32*, 313–341.

Paletz, S. B. F., Peng, K., Erez, M., & Maslach, C. (2004). Ethnic composition and its differential impact on group processes in diverse teams. *Small Group Research*, *35*, 128–157.

Papell, C. P., & Rothman, B. (1966). Social group work models: Possession and heritage. *Journal of Education for Social Work*, *2*, 66–77.

Papell, C. P., & Rothman, B. (1980). Relating the mainstream model of social work with groups to group psychotherapy and the structured group approach. *Social Work with Groups*, *3*, 5–22.

Parloff, M. B. (1961). Therapist-patient relationships and outcome of psychotherapy. *Journal of Consulting Psychology*, *25*, 29–38.

Perrone, K. M., & Sedlacek, W. E. (2000). A comparison of group cohesiveness and client satisfaction in homogenous and heterogenous groups. *Journal for Specialists in Group Work*, *25*, 243–251.

Pescosolido, A. T. (2001). Informal leaders and the development of group efficacy. *Small Group Research*, *32*, 74–93.

Pincus, D., & Guastello, S. J. (2005). Nonlinear dynamics and interpersonal correlates of verbal turn-taking patterns in a group therapy session. *Small Group Research*, *36*, 635–677.

Piper, W. E., Ogrodniczuk, J. S., LaMarche, C., Hilscher, T., & Joyce, A. S. (2005). Level of alliance, pattern of alliance, and outcome in short-term group therapy. *International Journal of Group Psychotherapy*, *55*, 527–550.

Pollack, B. N. (1998). The impact of the sociophysical environment on interpersonal communication and feelings of belonging in work groups. In J. Sanford & B. R. Connell (Eds.), *People, places and public policy* (pp. 71–78). Edmond, OK: Environmental Design Research Association.

Priola, V., Smith, J. L., & Armstrong, S. J. (2004). Group work and cognitive style: A discursive investigation. *Small Group Research, 35*, 565–595.

Prislin, R., & Christensen, P. N. (2005). The effects of social change within a group on membership preferences: To leave or not to leave? *Personality and Social Psychology Bulletin, 31*, 595–609.

Riva, M. T., Lippert, L., & Tackett, M. J. (2000). Selection practices of group leaders: A national survey. *Journal for Specialists in Group Work, 25*, 157–169.

Roark, A. E. (1989). Factors related to group cohesiveness. *Small Group Behavior, 20*, 62–69.

Roethlisberger, F. J., & Dickson, W. J. (1939). *Management and the worker.* Cambridge, MA: Harvard University Press.

Rosenfeld, L. B., & Gilbert, J. R. (1989). The measurement of cohesion and its relationship to dimensions of self-disclosure in classroom settings. *Small Group Behavior, 20*, 291–301.

Ross, C. E., Mirowski, J., & Cockerham, W. C. (1983). Social class, Mexican culture and fatalism: Their effect on psychological distress. *American Journal of Community Psychology, 11*, 383–400.

Roy, V., Turcotte, D., Montminy, L., & Lindsay, J. (2005). Therapeutic factors at the beginning of the intervention process in groups for men who batter. *Small Group Research, 36*, 106–133.

Rozell, E. J., & Gundersen, D. E. (2003). The effects of leader impression management on group perceptions of cohesion, consensus, and communication. *Small Group Research, 34*, 197–222.

Rugel, R. P. (1987). Achieving congruence in Tavistock groups: Empirical findings and implications for group therapy. *Small Group Behavior, 18*, 108–117.

Sani, F. (2005). When subgroups secede: Extending and refining the social psychological model of schism in groups. *Personality and Social Psychology Bulletin, 31*, 1074–1086.

Sargent, L. D., & Sue-Chan, C. (2001). Does diversity affect group efficacy? The intervening role of cohesion and task interdependence. *Small Group Research, 32*, 426–450.

Schei, V., & Rognes, J. K. (2005). Small group negotiation: When members differ in motivational orientation. *Small Group Research, 36*, 289–320.

Schiff, M., & Bargal, D. (2000). Helping characteristics of self-help and support groups: Their contribution to participants' subjective well-being. *Small Group Research, 31*, 275–304.

Schwartz, J. P., & Waldo, M. (1999). Therapeutic factors in spouse-abuse group treatment. *Journal for Specialists in Group Work, 24*, 197–207.

Shaw, M. E. (1971). *Group dynamics: The psychology of small group behavior.* New York: McGraw-Hill.

Shechtman, Z., & Gluk, O. (2005). An investigation of therapeutic factors in children's groups. *Group Dynamics: Theory, Research, and Practice, 9*, 127–134.

Slavin, R. L. (1993). The significance of here-and-now disclosure in promoting cohesion in group psychotherapy. *Group, 17*, 143–150.

Smokowski, P. R., Rose, S., & Bacallao, M. L. (2001). Damaging experiences in therapeutic groups: How vulnerable consumers become group casualties. *Small Group Research, 32*, 223–251.

Smokowski, P. R., Rose, S., Todar, K., & Reardon, K. (1999). Postgroup-casualty status, group events, and leader behaviour: An early look into the dynamics of damaging group experiences. *Research on Social Work Practice, 9*, 555–574.

Spoth, R., & Redmond, C. (1996). A theory-based parent competency model incorporating intervention attendance effects. *Family Relations, 45*, 139–147.

Spoth, R., Redmond, C., Hockaday, C., & Chung, Y. (1996). Barriers to participation to family skills preventive interventions and their evaluations: A replication and extension. *Family Relations, 45*, 247–254.

Stitt, C., Schmidt, S., Price, K., & Kipnis, D. (1983). Sex of leader, leader behavior, and subordinate satisfaction. *Sex Roles, 9*, 31–42.

Stokes, J. P. (1983). Components of group cohesion: Intermember attraction, instrumental value, and risk taking. *Small Group Behavior, 14*, 163–173.

Tanis, M., & Postmes, T. (2005). A social identity approach to trust: Interpersonal perception, group membership and trusting behaviour. *European Journal of Social Psychology*, *35*, 413–424.

Tolan, P. H., & McKay, M. M. (1996). Preventing serious antisocial behavior in inner-city children: An empirically based family intervention program. *Family Relations*, *45*, 148–155.

Trist, E. L., Higgin, G. W., Murray, J., & Pollock, A. B. (1963). *Organizational choice capabilities of groups at the coal face under changing technologies.* London: Tavistock.

Tschuschke, V., & Dies, R. R. (1994). Intensive analysis of therapeutic factors and outcome in long-term inpatient groups. *International Journal of Group Psychotherapy*, *44*, 185–208.

Tyler, T. R., & Blader, S. L. (2002). Autonomous vs. comparative status: Must we be better than others to feel good about ourselves? *Organizational Behavior and Human Decision Processes*, *89*, 813–838.

van Andel, P., Erdman, R. A. M., Karsdorp, P. A., Appels, A., & Trijsburg, R. W. (2003). Group cohesion and working alliance: Prediction of treatment outcome in cardiac patients receiving cognitive behavioral group psychotherapy. *Psychotherapy and Psychosomatics*, *72*, 141–149.

van Dijke, M., & Poppe, M. (2004). Social comparison of power: Interpersonal versus intergroup effects. *Group Dynamics: Theory, Research, and Practice*, *8*, 13–26.

van Vugt, M., Jepson, S. F., Hart, C. M., & De Cremer, D. (2004). Autocratic leadership in social dilemmas: A threat to group stability. *Journal of Experimental Social Psychology*, *40*, 1–13.

Webster-Stratton, C. (1985). Predictors of treatment outcome in parent training for conduct disordered children. *Behavior Therapy*, *16*, 223–243.

Westra, J. A., Dozois, D. J. A., & Boardman, C. (2002). Predictors of treatment change and engagement in cognitive-behavioral group therapy for depression. *Journal of Cognitive Psychotherapy*, *16*, 227–241.

Wheelan, S. A., Davidson, B., & Tilin, F. (2003). Group development across time: Reality or illusion? *Small Group Research*, *34*, 223–245.

Wheelan, S. A., & Williams, T. (2003). Mapping dynamic interaction patterns in work groups. *Small Group Research*, *34*, 443–467.

Wilson, G., & Ryland, G. (1949). *Social group work practice: The creative use of the social process.* Boston: Houghton Mifflin.

Yalom, I. D. (1966). A study of group therapy dropouts. *Archives of General Psychiatry*, *14*(4), 393–414.

Yamaguchi, R., & Maehr, M. L. (2004). Children's emergent leadership: The relationships with group characteristics and outcomes. *Small Group Research*, *35*, 388–406.

Chapter 22

GROUP WORK: A CRITICAL ADDITION TO THE SOCIAL WORK REPERTOIRE

Lena Dominelli

Group work has long been considered one of the three key methods in social work along-side casework or one-to-one work and community work (Younghusband, 1978). It has offered social work practice a way of moving beyond casework to link individuals to their social surroundings and networks, a feature that can be traced to Victorian Britain and the Settlement Movement (Breton, 1990).

Group work involves people coming together to achieve particular ends. It can be considered a method of social interaction that digs deep into humanity's past if one takes the view that it was rooted in social interactions that occurred in daily life between two or more individuals. Helen Bosanquet expressed the importance of this dimension in family-based group relationships, particularly in providing stability and good role models for children in 1906. Based in daily life routines, family and community relations provide specialized forms of groups that I call *groups in everyday life practices* (GELPs). Many of these will be informal, and some will be taken for granted in ways that might leave their group nature implicit. Key to this is the absence of explicit recognition of how power relations play out among group members. Families are classical depictions of this in that gendered relations or the power that men hold over women in the family were not acknowledged until feminists exposed these through their theories and practices in the 1960s (Millet, 1969). Similarly, adultist relations—the power that adults hold over children and capacities to make decisions on their behalf—were not appreciated until feminists gave these a name, usually in the context of the sexual and/or physical abuse of children (Dominelli, 1989).

In this chapter, I examine group work's historical development and its current significance to the profession. I focus less on the GELP types of groups than on those that are formulated as a method of social work intervention that explores social interactions involving several individuals working together to achieve particular objectives. Although the range of groups that exists is vast, I emphasize the British origins of, and developments in, group work linked to "the social" or the interactive arena of social relations and touch on those of other countries because its group work models were transported elsewhere through imitation, as occurred in the case of the United States under Jane Addams and colonial development in parts of the old and new Commonwealth under the British Empire. Countries whose historical antecedents lie elsewhere have their own specific stories to tell, but I do not cover these here. There are a number of typologies used for groups, for example, Papell and Rothman's (1980) models, but I have recategorized these as therapeutic groups, educational groups, community groups, and identity-based social action groups. There are a number of variations within each category, for example, cognitive behavioral groups fall within the therapeutic grouping and feminist groups are part of the identity-based one. Explicit literatures exist for each category, but there is not enough space to consider these in this chapter.

GROUP WORK: A NEW METHOD OF INTERVENTION WITH DEEP HISTORICAL ROOTS

Younghusband (1978) identified group work as one of the three methods of social work that had a history that went back to late Victorian Britain. Before it became encompassed within the social work practice repertoire, working with groups of people was a part of associational life that depicted formal attempts at bringing groups of people together to achieve specific ends. These became the progenitors of the groups used in social work. They included a huge array of activities that ranged from recreational clubs and educational, trade union, guild, and cooperative endeavors aimed at helping working-class people improve their life circumstances (Rose, 2002). The key thing that linked these associational efforts was their being premised on *self-help*, or the idea that people could organize collectively to enhance their potential of successfully achieving certain goals. Their significance from a social work perspective is rooted in their moving away from individual pathologies and underlining how collective action of some sort could produce changes in both individual behavior and social conditions. This element of group work remains significant today, particularly in the field of social work known as youth work. Within social work, groups can be seen as efforts premised on achieving the social integration of wayward individuals, assisting them in therapeutic recovery, or introducing structural changes in political practice and social relations (Grief & Ephross, 2005; Malekoff, 1997). The development and importance of groups is a major concern of this chapter.

The Victorians had a number of denominational groups that were established as key mechanisms through which to spread evangelical messages (Eagar, 1954). These often involved moralizing and pathologizing those who disobeyed moral injunctions, particularly those associated with having children out of wedlock and engaging in criminal activities. They combined clerical and volunteer inputs and made receiving assistance contingent on good behavior, especially for girls and unmarried mothers. Their moralizing tendencies should not obscure the important forms of assistance they provided to destitute people in the absence of a welfare state, particularly in the form of food, clothing, and schooling often associated with religious education. Their involvement actually provided resources for poor people who would have otherwise been left to fend for themselves. And, they reinforced charitable almsgiving and philanthropy, particularly among the middle classes who then set themselves up as role models for the "deserving" poor to emulate, a characteristic that Leonard and Corrigan (1979) and Mullender (1990) decried in modern practice.

Additionally, Sunday schools, according to Smith (1988) provided important foundations for the youth work that continues to echo in town hall settings. The relationship basis of these groups laid the foundations for what later became known as relational social work. Then, as now, the workers used relationships as conduits for changing human behavior, albeit not necessarily rooting it in its structural context. The Victorians realized the limitations of these types of groups and the failure of charity and denominational schools to meet the broader needs of working class children. This realization led to the creation of the Ragged Schools (Eagar, 1954).

Ragged Schools targeted children and young people living in deprived urban areas, particularly in the slums of big cities like London, Glasgow, Birmingham, Manchester, and Newcastle and used educational achievements as the road to social advancement. Groups as a means for changing behavior and improving one's life were central to their operation. Besides teaching the "4 rs" of reading, 'riting, 'rithmatic, and religion, their remit extended to acquiring shelter, hostel accommodation, reading and coffee rooms, savings clubs, and holiday schemes. Thus, these early groups had a pedagogic remit that sought to address the needs of poor people more holistically than casework interventions and based their analyses on systemic shortcomings in social organization (Barnett, 1898). The Ragged Schools became the forbearers of Evening Institutes and Youth Institutes as occurred, for example, in Long Acre, London, in 1870. The Institutes offered a wider range of educational and recreational opportunities to working-class men and boys and sought to widen possibilities for leading more rewarding lives than those obtainable under the daily grind of poverty.

Girls clubs, organized separately from those of the boys, provided similar openings for girls, although these were often focused on domesticity and preparing girls to become good wives and mothers. Women like Maud Stanley who worked in the Covent Garden area of London created important resources for young girls through these clubs. However, she was less keen on self-directed groups than on the more paternalistic model of groups being run for poor people by skilled workers who had their "best interests" at heart. Her approach was challenged by Emmeline Pethick and Mary Neal who offered alternative models by creating cooperative ventures formulated on more democratic principles that emphasized member participation. These principles could be seen as precursors to feminist ways of organizing that dominated the latter half of the twentieth century (Dominelli & McLeod, 1989; Donnelly, 1986). Pithick and Lily Montagu also created camping groups that prefigured the outward bound groups, highly favored by intermediate treatment initiatives used to teach social skills and appropriate ways of interacting with others to young offenders during the 1960s, 1970s, and 1980s. These aimed to produce "good citizens" who could participate in, and contribute to, community life.

Disagreements about how to organize and run groups prevailed then as now. Pelham (1890), for example, strongly emphasized small groups in which personal relationships could flourish. Small groups form the foundation of much community-based activity today. Pelham argued that members should become involved in running these groups, a point now used to encourage the development of organizational and practical skills across the membership of a group. This point was later developed by feminists into the rotation of roles to ensure that all group members acquired similar skills (Frankfort, 1972). Although Pelham favored small groups as the basis for this engagement with others, one of his contemporaries, Charles Russell, preferred larger clubs that could provide more resources even though this resulted in much of the relational dimension of the work being subordinated to organizational ends. Russell also favored the expertise of the professional or worker over that acquired by experience among the group membership. Today, we would recognize this in the debates between those favoring professional knowledge and expertise and those highlighting user experiential knowledge and expertise (Belenky, Clinchy, Goldberg, & Tarule, 1997) grounded in "subjugated knowledges" (Foucault, 1991). Feminist groups take this point to argue against the invisibility of marginalized groups and the failure of their voices to be heard in important discourses about social change (Dominelli, 2004). Russell did, however, argue that these workers should be committed to the people that they were working with and demanded that they focus on bringing out the best in them as safeguards to ensure that the workers did not abuse their power over weaker others. Today, we acknowledge these tendencies as externally generated interventions in other-directed groups (Northen, 1998).

The boys and girls clubs constituted another formal source of group work in Victorian England. These focused on both schooling and recreational endeavors and laid much of the groundwork for what later became youth work. These clubs also had a pedagogic dimension, although this was tempered with activities that sought to develop both mind and body simultaneously. These groups aimed to benefit members and focused on people as social beings who could work together effectively if given adequate encouragement. The task of a group leader was to encourage group members in working together. This placed the issue of leadership and group processes—power relations and relationships between different group members, in the frame of both theory and practice—points later developed by Coyle (1935), but now also covered in systems theories, psychodynamic and psychosocial theories, task-centered theories, and learning theories.

The most significant development of late Victorian times for group-based *social work* interventions was the Settlement Movement (Smith, 1988), which brought group work into public focus both as a method of intervening in poor people's lives and as a way of highlighting social inequalities that could be addressed in the drive to social reform. Through this philosophical approach, the methods of working that prevailed in the Settlement Movement contrasted sharply with those in the Charity Organization Society (COS). Both were struggling for supremacy over the terrain of social work at the time; but the COS, which advocated philanthropic and individualized forms of interventions as the way toward poverty alleviation, won out. Consequently, it gave rise to the method known as casework or one-to-one individual work and set the tone for the individualization and fragmentation of social problems that continues to be a strong tradition in social worker interventions (Dominelli, 1997, 2004). The caseworkers working in the COS were also moralizing and pathologizing in their approach to those in need, an approach eschewed by those involved in the Settlement Movement.

The Settlement Movement represented community-based, action-oriented forms of organizing that brought together middle-class university students and working-class residents of urban slums. Samuel and Henrietta Barnett set up the first Settlement House, Toynbee Hall in Whitechapel in London in 1884. This was based on the idea that research into social problems and education to improve the mind could generate possibilities for a better life and leadership for local communities (Barnett, 1898). This orientation, we would recognize today in many group- and community-based initiatives. As it grew, the Settlement Movement became diverse and included denominational influences, for example, Oxford House, also created in 1884 to focus primarily on working with boys and men. Later, the Passmore Edwards House created playgroups for children and saw these as important elements in stimulating young minds and bodies. This particular organization became Mary Ward House and gave a special impetus to those providing schooling for disabled children. Its lead on what is now called play therapy was followed by the Bermondsey Settlement's Guild of Play that taught children under 10 years of age to sing and play music. Mary Ward

House eventually became the home of the National Institute for Social Work (NISW) that hosted many crucial developments including community action in the United Kingdom and social policy initiatives, particularly around diversity, until the government closed it down to form the Social Care Institute for Excellence (SCIE) in 2001. NISW also produced literature for social work educators, much of which focused on group work and community work. Creating resources and literature of use to social work educators and practitioners is being followed by SCIE, and its resources are currently being used to enhance the quality of social work education and research in the United Kingdom.

The Settlement Movement created many other resources for poor people, some continue to the present. Among these were the Workers Educational Association (1903), Workers Travel Association (1921), Youth Hostel Association (1931), Community Service Volunteers (1962), and National Gifted Children Association (1981). The Settlement Movement emphasized friendship, community links, and fellowship—items that we would now recognize as the bridging parts of social capital (Putnam, 1993, 2000); the use of groups to promote social interactions; cultural awareness of the diversities evident in communities; and the use of experience in working with people. The latter two were key elements of Jane Addams' work in the Settlement Movement in the United States. Social capital has three forms: bonding capital, bridging capital, and linking capital. The first form refers to forms of support among a tightly knit, homogeneous group. It is considered inward looking and "exclusive" because it does not seek links with others. Bridging capital is outward looking and seeks connections to others who may or may not share similar characteristics. But it aims to enhance the social capital held by the group. Linking capital carries bridging capital further by connecting to existing networks or forming new ones that extend the exchange and formation of limited resources among those participating in the network (Woolcock, 1998).

The philosophy of Toynbee Hall emphasized pedagogic principles and collective action in promoting connections between individuals and their communities to tackle structural inequalities, particularly poverty. Its prime efforts focused on education, housing, welfare provisions, and economic development. The Settlement Movement spread from Toynbee Hall, across the United Kingdom and, when Jane Addams visited London, across the Atlantic. She planted its seeds in the United States, and these were harvested in practice when she opened Hull House in Chicago in 1889. The user groups that the Settlement Movement targeted encompassed both the indigenous working class and immigrant settlers. The latter had sought to improve their social circumstances through migration, but they experienced discrimination at many levels, particularly in education, jobs, and housing. These were the areas that the community and group workers associated with the Settlement Movement, including Addams (1910) organized around. Ironically, Toynbee Hall was where John Profumo went to do "good works" and spend the rest of his days (4 decades) after the scandal of the Profumo Affair—his relationship with Christine Keeler, a sex worker who simultaneously had a relationship with Profumo—a British Cabinet Minister—and a Russian spy. In 2006, Toynbee Hall was threatened with destruction in favor of housing developments that would lead to a gentrification of this part of London and the consequent loss of badly needed resources for working-class people. It remains to be seen whether this historic landmark and an essential ingredient in the history of social work is saved.

As self-help endeavors, these early groups did not rely on state support. Instead, they drew on voluntary efforts provided by individuals and other organizations in what we would now call *civil society*. These groups shared a commitment to social reform and humanity—then called "brotherhood"—and moral and social development. The self-help component encouraged workers to engage fully with those participating in these groups to ensure that they became involved in group discussions and decision-making processes. The group processes emphasized involvement, democracy, and solidarity among people (Coyle, 1935). As their popularity grew, these groups provided a favored working method adopted by the early socialists, including the Christian Socialists and Fabians who sought to make society better and offered some critique of capitalist social relations (Webb & Webb, 1897).

An example of this broader dimension to group work development was evident in the Workers Educational Association (WEA) that was formed in 1903 as the product of the adult education initiatives of the mid-nineteenth century. The WEA emphasized the use of fellowship and democratic processes in discussions as *the* method of proceeding in group-based teaching. Emphasizing greater equality among group members and teachers, small tutorial classes were a key forum for working in these groups. Further developed by R. H. Tawney in Rochdale, we would recognize these approaches in the social work classroom at the beginning of the twenty-first century. Basil Veaxlee and Edward Lindeman began to theorize these developments and provided the basis for subsequent analyses and theories of group work, giving pride of place to democratic participation and involvement in group activities, as central to educational ventures, especially among adults (Reid, 1983).

At the beginning of the twentieth century, many of the analyses focusing on understanding and theorizing group-work processes emanated from the United States. Some were linked to developments in the social sciences, others with the growth of psychological theories, especially those linked to social interaction, but as experienced by individuals, and others to the feminist movement. Vital among these were George Herbert Mead who identified the "social" self, Robert McIvor who focused on the idea of community and intergroup relations, and Charles Horton Cooley who theorized small groups, and women activists who sought to provide services designed by women and run by women for the benefit of women (Frankfort, 1972). Feminist theorists also problematized group dynamics, identifying the dangers of leaders usurping group powers and skills for their own purposes, and the dangers of the "false equality trap" that women fell into when they downplayed the importance of difference in the interests of pursing commonalities to promote collective action (Barker, 1986; Dominelli, 2002). This was a particular concern for women of African descent who felt marginalized and excluded by the women's liberation movement, especially in the United States (Collins, 2000).

Within the group work movement itself, Grace L. Coyle, a former settlement worker, wrote several influential texts while holding a lecturing post at Case Western Reserve University. These were *Social Process in Organized Groups* (1930), *Group Experience and Democratic Values: Group Work with American Youth* (1948). These emphasized the interactive and participative nature of groups and the impact of members on each other in creating their own roles and establishing leadership positions. Gertrude Wilson and Gladys Ryland's, *Social Group Work Practice* (1949) quickly established these models for use in teaching situations both in the field and the classroom. Through the activities of these theoreticians, the *experiences of being in a group* began to be seen as formative in group structures and development at both organizational and individual levels. Their innovations also helped to integrate the social and the personal. Coyle also started the first university-based course on group work in the Social Work Department at Case Western

Reserve University. And, the National Conference of Social Work in the United States in 1935 included group work.

At around this time, the therapeutic dimension in group work became formalized and systematized through the expansion of psychodynamic theories that aimed at individual empowerment, often within group settings. These contrasted with group development as such and downplayed the centrality of structural inequalities as barriers to daily life and their impact as major impediments to progressive social change. Therapeutic interventions aimed to improve individual functioning and prepare a person for a position in the labor market. This strategy has not gone away, despite being relegated to the fringes of social action during the 1960s and 1970s as a result of the War on Poverty in the United States and the Community Development Projects in the United Kingdom. These focused on declining local economies and their destruction as the basis for disadvantage and emphasized social reform rather than individual change. However, the idea of working one's way out of poverty is enjoying a resurgence. In the United Kingdom, for example, this approach is now evident in the use of groups under New Labour's New Deal. These prepare people for paid work, albeit often in low paid jobs that cannot lift them out of poverty (Millar, 2000). Ehrenreich (2002) articulates similar claims about the failure of the market economy and neo-liberal social policies to alleviate poverty in the United States. In the United Kingdom, groups formed under the New Deal have also been heavily influenced by demand that outcomes be used to evaluate the effectiveness of group interventions or progress (or lack of it) in altering individual behavior. Performance-based evaluations like these continue to contribute to narratives that individualize and fragment social problems (Abels & Abels, 1999; Dominelli, 2004). Narrative-based interventions also allow group workers to focus on meanings, address complex identity issues, and focus on people. However, as they focus on a series of points or conversations, narratives can fragment social initiatives (Garvin, Guttierez, & Galinsky, 2004).

While formal group work teaching declined in the United States during the 1960s in response to generic social work, it spread in practice through the new social movements. To counter this development, the First Annual Symposium for the Advancement of Group Work was organized by concerned group workers in Canada and the United States in 1979. They eventually formed the Association for the Advancement of Social Work with Groups. The 1960s, 1970s, and 1980s saw the burgeoning of group work initiatives that set the scene for the development of identity-based social action groups in a whole range of spheres: the women's movement, the civil rights movement, the disability movement, movements among mentally ill people, and the homosexual movement (Henry, East, & Schmit, 1999; Toseland & Rivas, 2005). Group work in the latter half of the twentieth century has promoted cultural diversity, an examination of hierarchy in oppressive structures, a questioning of the boundaries of inclusiveness to show how inclusive structures like communities can be exclusionary, and a challenging of dichotomous thinking and doing. It also revealed that groups can be used to deny people their entitlement to human growth, human rights, and progress. Some groups, for example, Fathers for Justice, also sought to promote their rights at the expense of women by demanding a reinstatement of fathers' rights over and above those of women—a return to old-fashioned patriarchy, if you like.

The women's movement was crucial in developing new group work models during this period. Of vital importance among these were the consciousness-raising groups and therapeutic health groups that brought women together in collectives to ensure that the

"personal became political." These rooted personal woes in social contexts and social relations. They also challenged professional orthodoxies, whether this was in the arena of health,
drugs, medical care, caring work, child bearing and minding, domestic violence, sexual
abuse, or political organization (Cohen & Mullender, 2003; Dominelli & Jonsdottir, 1989;
Dominelli & McLeod, 1989). Additionally, feminist groups questioned group hierarchies
and processes to demand greater accountability and involvement of group members in all
group activities and respect for subjugated knowledge and expertise. Black women, disabled women, and lesbians also highlighted the importance of social differentiation and
body image in any collective endeavors that sought to universalize the specific experiences
of one individual or group (Begum, 1992; Collins, 2000; Lorde, 1984).

These diverse threads have combined to give group work its variety and commitment to
empowerment strategies (Mullender & Ward, 1991). Despite the richness of group work's
legacy and its durability, group work has been a dwindling element of the social work
curriculum in the United Kingdom, especially once community work was divorced from
generic training during the mid-1980s. However, stalwarts of the method have fought hard
to retain it in some way or other. An examination of reading lists relating to social work
courses on the Web demonstrate the marginality of group work teaching and learning
in today's curricula. The need for such knowledge among practitioners today becomes
ever greater, if they are to gain the skills and knowledge necessary for dealing with the
complexities of current practice in a globalizing world that has seen the internationalization
of social problems (Dominelli, 2004). Despite these setbacks, the relevance of group work
is being recognized in the new Children's Trusts as an effective way of engaging with
troubled and troubling young people. Unlike Anti-Social Behavior Orders (ASBOs; court
orders to refrain individuals from acting in ways that cause nuisance or offense to others)
that focus on individual pathology, therapeutic approaches use group dynamics to change
individual behavior, although they often obscure the social origins of much of young
people's alienation. Probation and prison have used therapeutic groups for some time,
especially as cognitive behavioral therapy to work with groups of violent men and sex
offenders (McCulloch & Kelly, 2007).

GROUP WORK MODELS FOR PRACTICE

In this brief excursion into the history of group work, I have identified five key types of
groups that social workers can utilize in their practice. I build on Papell and Rothman
(1980), but reformulate their typology to take into account new developments since theirs
was developed including the mainstreaming of their models in some way, especially to
lower costs in the welfare state in the United Kingdom. These, I depict as follows:

1. The GELP.
2. Therapeutic.
3. Educational.
4. Community action-oriented.
5. Identity-based social action groups.

These groups have different structures and values, but they follow many of the same
processes of organization for groups described in Table 22.1, namely, recruitment, group

Table 22.1   Group Processes: Commonalities across Group Typologies

Group work processes and principles of organization today would not seem unfamiliar to the early pioneers developing more participative forms of engaging with members. Then as now, these focused on:

Recruitment
The criteria for group composition and size of group are key aspects in recruitment or encouraging people to join a group. A group's membership can be open or closed, depending on the decisions made about its size and composition.

Group purpose
Identifying the group's purpose is central to its capacity to function effectively and relates to its purpose or raison d'être.

Type of group
Theories and models of group work are important in facilitating discussions about the type of group being formed and how it will operate. These are typically defined as the: remedial, reciprocity and mainstream models (Papell and Rothman, 1980). I would add the groups based in everyday life practices (GELP) and identity-based social action groups to their typology.

Group action
The settings in which groups operate, define what constitutes success and where action plans are formulated. They comprise pivotal points in group decision-making processes. Evaluating group activities is essential in maintaining and developing groups, including learning from mistakes.

Group dynamics and processes
The barriers and opportunities to member involvement impact on length of meetings and the internal dynamics of a group, particularly those determining how it operates. These are central to a group's capacity to realize its ambitions (or to end in failure). For small groups, Alissi (2001) has identified these processes as centering on democratic values, collective decision making, needs-focused interventions, individual and social betterment, and working with and not for groups.

Leadership
Determining who will be the leader, how a leader will be chosen, and what leadership style is to be followed is also crucial to a group's ability to operate effectively. Leadership styles usually follow patterns: authoritarian, democratic, or laissez-faire (Reid, 1997). Each has its strengths and weaknesses. Authoritarian leaders make all the decisions and retain firm control of the group. Democratic leaders have various styles in encouraging participation among members. These range from consultation to full involvement in decision making. Laissez-faire leaders can abrogate responsibility for leading and/or managing the group.

Membership building and maintenance
Recruiting members to a group is a first step. Membership needs to be constantly reviewed, maintained, and renewed. Groups can wither and die through lack of attention to maintaining group morale and membership concerns. Movement in and out of a group, with at times a small core group that maintains stability, is not unusual.

(*continued*)

Table 22.1 *(Continued)*

Emotional work

Working with members' feelings in and emotional reactions within groups, including other members and their leaders, is an often neglected but crucial dimension of social work intervention. It needs careful consideration and nurturing if its dynamics are not to undermine or impede a group's development and potential to meet its targets (Dominelli, 1990, 2006). Responding to group diversity is a particularly taxing dimension of emotionality in group work and crucial to maintaining morale, extending group membership, or coping with losing group members and fluctuations in membership. Addressing emotionality is vital to successfully promoting inclusivity in multicultural societies and facilitating the integration of individuals within the larger whole.

Evaluation

The group should always evaluate its work. This should be seen as a continuous process rather than a single instance and will have informal as well as formal elements. Getting verbal feedback by asking members what they think about the group's plan of action is an informal evaluation method. Asking people to complete questionnaires and systematically evaluating the questionnaires is a formal evaluation method.

---

purpose or objectives, group type or model including the theoretical base on which it is formulated, group action, group dynamics and processes, leadership role, membership maintenance, emotional work, and evaluation. The type of group formed also depends on the values held by its members including the leaders and establish the ways in which groups define themselves, evolve their structures, and undertake action. These can be authoritarian, participative (to varying degrees), and egalitarian. The formation of groups and their evolution as dynamic entities depends on settings, values, and purposes. Table 22.2 lists key questions for group workers and members to consider whether working with individuals or groups. These questions are useful in organizing any group.

Group Work Models for Social Work Practice: Key Features

Groups Based in Everyday Life Practices

Social workers often use GELPS when working with children and families and older people and their caregivers. They exemplify informal, self-help types of groups. Group members pay little attention to group dynamics and processes, and they tend to build on taken-for-granted ways of relating to people. Group membership is voluntary although it membership initially has "blood" connections linked to the family of origin. Group dynamics are usually hierarchical, with divisions according to gender and age overlaid with an ideology of equality that is not always evident in reality in Western democracies. These groups represent a form of bonding capital that social workers traditionally utilize in facilitating caring relationships between group members.

Therapeutic Groups

Therapeutic groups aim to change individual behavior and enhance individual coping strategies, especially in traumatic situations. They are found in many settings and are ameliorative and proactive rather than concerned with structural change. There is huge variety in their

Table 22.2   Questions to Consider When Organizing and Running Groups

Objectives (issues to be thought about before beginning the recruitment process)
Why set up a group?
Who is the group for?
What will the group seek to achieve (or what problem(s) is it intended to solve)?

Group membership (issues to be thought about before beginning the recruitment process)
Who will join the group?
What size will the group be?

Group name (issue to be thought about before beginning the recruitment process and afterward when the membership is known)
What will the group be called?

Decision-making process (part of the membership maintenance process and power relations between members and leaders)
How will the group make decisions?
What role will members play?
What role will the leaders play?
Will there be an executive committee, and what role will it play?

Group atmosphere (part of the group maintenance and emotional work process)
How will members of the group be made to feel comfortable with each other?
How will group morale be maintained (individually and collectively)?
How will conflict be handled?

Group actions (part of the group maintenance and evaluation processes)
Who will organize group activities?
How will group visibility be achieved?
How will the membership be kept on board?
How will success be measured?
Who will evaluate the actions and ensure that lessons are learned for future actions?

Resources (part of the group maintenance and evaluation processes)
What resources does the group have (include networking with other groups)?
How will additional resources be obtained?
Who is responsible for obtaining further resources?

form. This ranges from psychodynamic counseling to cognitive behavioral groups. They are often used to address trauma in individuals involved in armed conflict situations, especially children (Stewart & Thomson, 2005). These groups focus on the internal self rather than social structures and although there is some sensitivity to power issues, even if following a Rogerian approach, for example, the expert is firmly in control. They are popular in professions other than social work, especially psychology and psychiatry. They are often expert-led with hierarchical group dynamics as occurs in the case of reminiscence groups for older people or can cover some self-help voluntary groups, for example, Alcoholics Anonymous.

Educational Groups

Educational groups focus on developing peoples' understanding of the world and improving and utilizing their knowledge and skills base. They cover a wide variety of topics and can be formal or informal. Informal groups use stories and oral histories while formal ones draw on pedagogic processes to engage students in teaching and learning. These groups are often, but not always, hierarchical and expert-led. Formal educational groups often take place in classroom settings (Silver, 1983). Their aim is to improve the mind and so can be seen as having an element of consciousness-raising within them.

Community Action-Oriented Groups

Community action-oriented groups tread a middle ground between therapeutic groups and identity-based social action ones. Its members engage in changing policies and practices as well as social problems. These groups are situated in a community and involve people living in a geographic area coming together to address a common problem. They cover a number of issues and vary in size and can be based on individual concerns or collective ones. They also tend to create insiders (those in the group) and outsiders (those excluded from it). These groups can be led by experts, volunteers, or activists. Their group dynamics are also varied and relationships within them can be authoritarian, participative, or democratic. These groups can be very heterogenic and those prone to a degree of intragroup conflict as well as intergroup controversies.

Identity-Based Social Action Groups

There are a number of identity-based social action groups. Formed mainly by members of the new social movements mentioned earlier and now include environmentalists. Each has their priorities and concerns. In this chapter, I focus only on the key principles of feminist group work which problematized many aspects of expert-led groups; developed innovative methods of conducting groups, for example, consciousness-raising; brought new social problems into the public arena, for example, men's violence against women; made structural social change a group objective; and initiated new forms of critical scholarship (Cohen & Mullender, 2003; Dominelli, 2006; Dominelli & McLeod, 1989). Processes of participation are central to feminist group work. These encourage group members to work in more egalitarian relationships and draw connections between the lives that individual women lead and their social position, thus making connections between the personal and the structural, raising consciousness of these links and undertaking social action that improves women's lives.

Self-directed, consciousness-raising techniques and viewing politics as power in both intimate and public relationships enabled women in these groups to devise their own means for understanding their world and securing change in it. In that sense, feminist groups also provide a specific form of self-help groups. Its collective way of working also gave feminist groups both personal and political change objectives and prioritized networking as a way of extending the resources and support that women could access. Feminist politics is not always about party politics, although it can be, for example, Kwenna Frambothid, a feminist party in Iceland during the 1980s and 1990s (Dominelli & Jonsdottir, 1989). Most often, it is about power relations among people, realizing how these can work to the advantage some people at the expense of others and changing that state of affairs. Consequently, feminists tend to prefer groups with minimal structures and rotate positions. This gives everyone a chance to learn the same skills and prevent any individual from usurping the group processes for their self-advancement (see Table 22.3).

Table 22.3   Chart of Group Models

Type of Group	Primary Focus	Leader	Group Dynamics	Social Capital
GELPS	Individual	Volunteer	Paternalistic	Bonding
Therapeutic	Individual	Paid expert	Hierarchical	Bonding
Educational	Individual	Volunteer or paid	Participative	Bonding or bridging
Community action-oriented	Individual or collective	Volunteer, paid, or activist	Participative	Bonding or bridging
Identity-based social action	Individual, collective, and network	Volunteer or paid	Democratic and collective	Bonding, bridging, and linking

CONCLUSION

Group work has been effective in enabling people to understand the social contexts of their lives and its links to individual functioning, identify the strengths of oppressed and/or marginalized people, and acting to solve social problems. Running a group requires expertise in group dynamics and knowledge of the broader social world within which groups operate, including policy and practice frameworks. The importance of group work in dealing effectively with the problems that social workers encounter today should not be underestimated (Sharry, 2005). It is regrettable that so many institutions of higher education have failed to give this topic the profile it merits on social work courses. However, practice has a way of letting its needs become known, not least through connections to research and field placements. Combined with the internationalization of social problems, this changing social context is already demanding that group work teaching and learning be reinstated in a mainstream position in the curriculum. For this to happen, group workers and members have to play a stronger role.

REFERENCES

Abels, P., & Abels, S. (1999). Narrative social work with groups: Just in time. In S. Henry, C. L. Schmitz, & J. East (Eds.), *Social work with groups* (57–74). Binghamton, NY: Haworth Press.

Addams, J. (1910). *Twenty years at Hull House with autobiographical notes.* London: Macmillan.

Alissi, A. (2001). The social group work tradition. *Social Work Practice Foundation Occasional Papers*, 1–25.

Barker, H. (1986, Summer) Recapturing sisterhood: A critical look at "process" in feminist organizations and community action. *Critical Social Policy*, *16*, 80–90.

Barnett, S. (1898). University settlements. In W. Reason (Ed.), *University and social settlements* (pp. 11–26). London: Methuen.

Begum, N. (1992). Disabled women and the feminist agenda. *Feminist Review*, *40*, 71–84.

Belenky, M. E., Clinchy, M. B., Goldberger, R. N., & Tarule, M. J. (1997) *Women's ways of knowing: The development of self, voice, and mind.* New York: Basic Books.

Breton, M. (1990). Learning from social group work traditions. *Social Work with Groups*, *13*(3), 21–34.

Cohen, M., & Mullender, A. (2003). *Gender and group work*. London: Routledge.

Collins, P. H. (2000). *Black feminist thought: Knowledge, consciousness and the politics of empowerment*. London: Routledge.

Coyle, G. (1935). *Social process in organised groups*. New York: Richard Smith.

Dominelli, L. (1989). Betrayal of trust: A feminist analysis of power relationships in incest abuse. *British Journal of Social Work, 19*(4), 291–307.

Dominelli, L. (1990). *Women and community action*. Birmingham: Venture Press.

Dominelli, L. (1997) *Sociology for social work*. London: Macmillan.

Dominelli, L. (2002). *Feminist social work theory and practice*. London: Palgrave.

Dominelli, L. (2004). *Social work: Theory and practice for a changing profession*. Cambridge, England: Polity Press.

Dominelli, L. (2006). *Women and community action* (2nd ed.). Bristol, PA: Policy Press.

Dominelli, L., & Jonsdottir, G. (1989). Feminist political organising: Some reflections on the experiences of kwenna frambothid in Iceland. *Feminist Review, 30*, 36–60.

Dominelli, L., & McLeod, E. (1989). *Feminist social work*. London: Macmillan.

Donnelly, A. (1986). *Feminist social work with a women's group* [Monograph]. Norwich, Norfolk, England: University of East Anglia.

Eagar, W. (1954). *Making men: The history of the Boys Clubs and related movements in Great Britain*. London: University of London Press.

Ehrenreich, B. (2002). *Nickled and dimed in America*. London: Grantham Books.

Foucault, M. (1991). Governmentality. In G. Burchell, C. Gordon, & P. Miller (Eds.), *The Foucault effect: Studies in governmentality* (pp. 87–104). Hemel Hempstead, London: Harvester/Wheatsheaf.

Frankfort, I. (1972). *Vaginal politics*. New York: Quadrangle Books.

Garvin, C., Guttierez, L., & Galinsky, M. (Eds.). (2004). *Handbook of social work with groups*. New York: Guilford Press.

Grief, G., & Ephross, P. (2005). *Group work with populations at risk*. Oxford: Oxford University Press.

Henry, S., East, J., & Schmit, C. (Eds.). (1999). *Social work with groups: Mining the gold*. Binghamton, NY: Haworth Press.

Leonard, P., & Corrigan, P. (1979). *Social work under capitalism*. London: Macmillan.

Lorde, A. (1984). *Sister outside*. New York: Crossing Press.

Malekoff, A. (1997). *Group work with adolescents: Principles and practice*. New York: Guilford Press.

McCulloch, T., & Kelly, L. (2007). Working with sex offenders in context: Which way forward? *Probation Journal, 54*(1), 2–21.

Millar, J. (2000). *Keeping track of welfare reform*. New York: Joseph Rowntree Foundation.

Millet, K. (1969). *Sexual politics*. Garden City, NY: Doubleday.

Mullender, A. (1990). The Ebony Project and transracial foster parents. *Social Work with Groups, 13*(4), 23–42.

Mullender, A., & Ward, D. (1991). *Self-directed groups: User action for empowerment*. London: Whiting and Birch.

Northen, H. (1998). Ethical dilemmas in social work with groups. *Social Work with Groups, 21*(1/2), 5–17.

Papell, C., & Rothman, B. (1980). Relating the mainstream model of social work with group to group psychotherapy and the structured group approach. *Social Work with Groups, 3*(2), 5–23.

Pelham, T. (1890). *Handbook to youths' institutes and working boys' clubs*. London: London Diocesan Council for the Welfare of Young Men.

Putnam, R. (1993). *Making democracy work: Civic traditions in modern Italy*. Princeton, NJ: Princeton University Press.

Putnam, R. (2000). *Bowling alone: The collapse and revival of American community*. New York: Simon & Schuster.

Reid, K. (1983). *From character building to social treatment: The history of the use of groups in social work*. Westport, CT: Greenwood Press.

Reid, K. (1997). *Social work practice with groups*. Pacific Grove, CA: Brooks/Cole.

Rose, J. (2002). *The intellectual life of the working-classes*. New Haven, CT: Yale University Press.

Sharry, J. (2005). The principles of solution-focused group work. In *Solution focused group work*. Thousand Oaks, CA: Sage.

Silver, H. (1983). *Education as history*. London: Methuen.

Smith, M. (1988). *Developing youth work*. Milton Keynes, United Kingdom: Open University Press.

Stewart, D., & Thomson, K. (2005). "The FACE YOUR FEAR Club: Therapeutic group work with young children as a response to community trauma in northern Ireland." *British Journal of Social Work*, *35*, 105–124.

Toseland, R., & Rivas, R. (2005). *An introduction to group work practice*. Boston: Allyn & Bacon.

Webb, S., & Webb, B. (1897). *Industrial democracy*. London: Fabian Society.

Woolcock, M. (1998). Social capital and economic development: Towards a theoretical synthesis and policy framework. *Theory and Society*, *27*, 151–208.

Younghusband, E. (1978). *Social work in Britain: 1950–1975*. London: Allen & Unwin.

Chapter 23 ⸻

ASSESSMENT OF COMMUNITIES

Don M. Fuchs

This chapter is one of two chapters in this volume that looks at social work practice with communities. This chapter focuses on social work practice approaches to the community assessment. This chapter presents and examines the theoretical foundations that underpin, shape, and direct the concepts of community and community social work practice and the assessment approaches used. It discusses the historical background, context, and emerging issues relating to community assessment. In addition, it examines the evidence base of the current approaches to community assessment and intervention. Finally, it discusses the implications of the current state of this knowledge for micro-, mezzo-, and macrolevel practice and presents some conclusions that suggest future directions for integrating technology policy, practice, and research.

HISTORICAL BACKGROUND

Two different, but related, streams of thought flow from the literature relating to community social work practice. These two approaches have influenced how community assessment is perceived and how different assessment approaches have been developed and applied in community practice. One body of literature has emerged out of the history of social work as involved with the marginalized and socially excluded. It has its roots in the Settlement House Movement. Ross and Lappin (1955) were some of the first social work scholars to formulate differential social work approaches in community practice. Out of this tradition, a body of literature developed that identified three different approaches to community organization: community development, social planning, and social action and advocacy (Rothman, 1999a, 1999b; Rothman, Tropman, & Erhlich, 2001; Rubin & Rubin, 2001). A second body of literature builds on the generalist theories that identify social work practice as a macrolevel practice (Kirst-Ashman & Hull, 2006; Netting, Kettner, & McMurtry, 2004; Pincus & Minahan, 1973). This approach is grounded in an ecosystemic, planned changed paradigm of social work practice that has emerged to address the social justice concerns that arose out of the civil rights movement in the 1960s (Germaine, 1991; Pincus & Minahan, 1973). In addition, many of the macrolevel practice theorists are grounded in a more detailed complex expansion of the Rothman model interwoven view of the mixed and phased modes of community intervention. They look at social work practice with larger social units, organizations, and service delivery systems, for example, the child welfare system, the criminal justice system, and government and other policy-setting bodies (Kirst-Ashman, & Hull, 2006; Netting et al., 2004).

Hardcastle, Powers, and Wenocur (2004, p. 3) maintain that in the generalist model, community practice is the core of social work and necessary for all social workers, whether generalists, specialists, therapists, or activists. Social work claims an ecological perspective as one of its major perspectives: Individuals are part of social ecologies, and social ecology is about community. They maintain that social work practice is about using naturally occurring and socially constructed networks within the social environment to provide social support, empowerment, and social efficacy. They maintain that while community practice is often only seen as community organization, community development, social planning, or social action, it has come to be understood and defined more broadly in generalist social work practice. Hardcastle et al. define community practice as the application of practice skills to alter the behavioral patterns of community groups, organizations, and institutions or people's relationships and interactions with these entities.

Hardcastle et al. (2004) contend that the macrolevel social workers (the community organizers, planners, and social activists) and the direct service or clinical practitioners may differ in perspective, but they are working toward the same end. The community organizer assumes that if the community, with its organizations and institutions and behavior patterns, can function more effectively and be more responsive to its members, the members of the community will be healthier and happier. Both micro- and macrolevel practitioners require knowledge of community structures and behavior changes in some part of the community. Both sets of social workers generally use a similar problem-solving strategy. Additionally, social workers often engage in both sets of practices, either simultaneously or sequentially. They work directly with clients and, at the same time, develop community resources.

Further building on the generalist framework for macrolevel practice, Weil and Gamble (1995) divide their tripartite community practice prototype of community organization, community development, and social action into an eight-component model that combines practice acts with the purposes of the practice. The unifying features of their list of components are empowerment-based interventions to strengthen participation in democratic processes, assisting groups and communities in advocating for their basic needs, and organizing for social justice, thereby improving the effectiveness and responsiveness of human service systems (p. 577).

Weil and Gamble maintain that community practice has traditionally occurred in a focused number of domains. The domain in which the community practice is occurring plays a major role in guiding and determining the approach to community assessment taken by the social work practitioners. The model's eight practice domains are (1) neighborhood and community organizing, (2) organizing functional communities, (3) community social and economic development, (4) social planning, (5) program development and community liaison, (6) political and social action, (7) coalitions building and maintenance, and (8) social movements (pp. 580–589). Their model specifies a range of social work roles or skills necessary to fulfill the domains: organizer, teacher, coach, advocate, negotiator, broker manager, researcher, communicator, facilitator. Most significantly, these are roles that cut across all social work practice domains.

COMMUNITY THEORY: AN ESSENTIAL COMPONENT IN SHAPING APPROACHES TO COMMUNITY ASSESSMENT

The definition of community is critical to community assessments in social work intervention. There are many different definitions and theories of community (Fisher, 2005; McKnight, 1997; Rubin & Rubin, 2001). The community social work practitioners' understanding of a wide range of definitions and theories of community is an important prerequisite for conducting effective community assessments and interventions. Communities are always the context, if not the content, of social work practice. Communities and community practice have been central to social work's history and development. Understanding, intervening in, and using the client's social environment as part of the helping process are skills consonant with the profession's ecological foundation (Netting et al., 2004). Social systems, especially communities, strongly influence the ways people think and act. Communities can be nurturing environments and provide basic social, economic, and emotional supports to individuals and families. Conversely, communities can be hostile places where there are inequities that contribute significantly to the oppression and social exclusion of individuals and families. An individual's identity is developed through involvement in and identification with social and community groups (McMillan, 1996; Miller & Prentice, 1994).

Community theories explain what communities are and how communities function. Community theories tend to be complex because the concept is ephemeral, intricate, ideological, and multifaceted, covering a wide range of social phenomena (Weil, 2005). There are many approaches to defining community. Communities can be understood either as geographic entities or as groups that share a special concern or identity. Although a geographic community can range from a small neighborhood to a large city and environs, most of the existing community research begins at the neighborhood or territorial level.

Netting et al. (2004, p. 126) contends that no matter what definition is selected, concepts such as "space, people, interaction and shared identity are common elements." Netting suggests the most commonly cited definition is "that combination of social units and systems that perform the major social functions relevant to meeting people's needs on a local level" (R. L. Warren, 1978, p. 9). Community, according to Warren, means the organization of social activities that affords people access to what is necessary for day-to-day living, such as the school, the grocery store, the hospital, the house of worship, and other such social units and systems. We customarily think of social units as beginning with the domestic unit, extending to the neighborhood or to a voluntary association, and on to the larger community. A community may or may not have clear boundaries but is significant because it performs important functions necessary for human survival.

Fellin (2001) contends that community occurs when "a group of people form a social unit based on common location, interest, identification, culture, and/or activities" (p. 118). He distinguishes three dimensions of communities: (1) a place or geographic locale in which one's needs for sustenance are met, (2) a pattern of social interactions, and (3) a symbolic identification that gives meaning to one's sense of personal identity and sense of connectedness.

Geographical, spatial, and territorial communities vary in how they meet people's needs; how social interactions are patterned; and how collective identity is perceived. Local communities are often called neighborhoods, cities, towns, boroughs, barrios, or some other name. Smaller geographic spaces are nested within communities such as neighborhoods that are portions of towns or public housing developments within cities.

Communities of identification and interest are not necessarily geographically based. Netting (2004) suggests that these "nonplace" communities are often referred to as functional, relational, or associational communities, communities of affiliation or affinity, and even communities of the mind. These nongeographical or functional communities bring people together based on ethnicity, race, religion, lifestyle, ideology, sexual orientation, social class, profession, or workplace. They create a sense of personal identification and are connected to the functional community.

Functional communities are examples of communities that are based on identification and interest that are formed when "people share a concern about a common issue, which ranges from advocacy for the needs of children with disabling conditions to environmental protection" (Fellin, 2001, p. 128).

In assessing communities for social work interventions, it is important for social workers to recognize and understand communities that are formed around shared concerns, such as AIDS, gun control, terrorism, and political loyalties. Currently, it is even more important to recognize that these communities reflect a mutuality of deeply held beliefs and values that may conflict with those of other communities. For example, faith-based communities may be in conflict with gay and lesbian communities. Communities of interest are becoming increasingly active and special interest groups can often polarize communities.

Further, Fellin (2001) identifies communities that are focused on a collective relationship that gives meaning to one's identity. In a complex society, people establish their own constellations of relationships based on place and nonplace considerations. For example, a social worker may be a member of an association of social workers (a nonplace place community), live in a neighborhood (a place community), and have close relationships with individuals scattered around the world (a personal network). Because each person will have a particular constellation of relationships, each person's definition of community will be distinctive. Often viewed as networks or webs of formal and informal resources, these relationships and what they mean to the person's sense of community are very important for social workers to recognize, respect, and understand. Network analysis and ecological mapping help reveal how individuals perceive their communities.

Netting et. al. (2004) in providing an overview of community theory observes that community structure and function have dominated how communities are viewed. When functions are not adequately performed, communities are seen as dysfunctional or incompetent in meeting the needs of their members. Five community functions have been identified: (1) production, distribution, and consumption; (2) socialization; (3) social control; (4) social participation; and (5) mutual support (D. I. Warren, 1981; R. L. Warren, 1978). Netting et al. (2004, p. 158) added two more functions: defense and communication. According to these approaches, it is when the economic function breaks down that communities fail.

Community power, politics, and change are hallmarks of social work practice (Homan, 2004). Social workers often view communities as political arenas in which the power of dominant groups necessitates a change so that the needs of underserved populations can be addressed. Understanding the politics of different communities is critical to social workers as they interact with diverse groups.

Weil (2005, p. 11) contends that current theory and practice still grapple with the complexities and changes in the connections of the individual to society and with heightened concerns about the decline in influence of face-to-face communities. This is accompanied by increasingly mechanistic, technological effects on formal economic, social, and political structures that further distance people from their local and larger geographic communities (Fiqueria-McDonough, 2001). Now we face the added challenge of viewing the individual in a global context, facing further decline in the supportive community and the impact of international and global economic and political forces on the local community (Fiqueria-McDonough, 2001; Rifkin, 2000).

Classical theory and sociological approaches have been increasingly critiqued by critical theorists as being culture bound, vested in current political power structures, ignoring many aspects of power, providing little if any focus on women's actions and contributions in society and most typically not making efforts to hear or understand the views of groups that have been marginalized. Weil (2005) contends that current scholars and practitioners need to be engaged in continual examination and modification of the theories to take account of changing political, economic, and social conditions.

New areas being developed in contemporary community practice include resilience, empowerment, capacity building, and asset mapping. Cohen (1985) emphasized the degree of personal identification and symbolic construction of community by people. He conceives of community as "a system of values, norms and moral codes which provide a sense of identity with a bounded whole to its members" (Cohen, 1985, p. 68).

Weil (2005) argues that communities are the context of all social work practice and community practice is recognized as a major means to carry forward the profession's long-standing ethical commitment to social justice. She indicates that social justice implies commitment to fairness in our dealings with each other in the major public aspects of our lives—the political, economic, social, and civil realms. Social justice should foster equal human rights, distributive justice, and a structure of opportunity and be grounded in representative and participatory democracy. This would indicate the need for the development of increased participatory mechanisms to foster inclusive, participatory, action-oriented community assessment processes.

Fiqueria-McDonough (2001) argue that community assessment processes as part of community practice must contribute to improving the quality of life for and with people and communities related to direct work to build resources and develop social and political power. A practical extension of Rawls' (1970) discussion of distributive justice work argues for providing the most attention, redress, and resources to those who are least advantaged.

Weil (2005) argues that community practice encompasses four central processes: development, organizing, planning, and action for progressive social change. Together, these processes form social work's major method of actively working for social justice. Community practice emphasizes working mutually with citizens groups, cultural and multicultural groups, and human service organizations to improve life options and opportunities in communities and to press for the expansion of human rights, political equality, and distributive justice. These efforts range from grassroots work to social action and legislative advocacy to change oppressive systems.

Fisher (2005) adds that community practice is "grounded in values of democratic process, citizen participation, group determination, empowerment, and multicultural and leadership development" (p. 64) Democratic revitalization and building civil society is a central purview of community practice in all its forms and processes, including community assessment. This is expressed through transformation that supports social and economic development and brings complex political economies and administrative structures under democratic scrutiny through increased citizen knowledge and understanding of economic and political problems.

Community assessment/intervention improves quality of life and increases social justice through social and economic development, community organizing, social planning, and progressive social change. It is a cooperative effort between practitioners and affected individuals, groups, organizations, communities, and coalitions. Improving the quality of life for impoverished and vulnerable persons and communities means helping people help themselves to build resources and develop social and political power (Weil, 2005).

ASSESSMENT IN PRACTICE: DISCOVERING AND DOCUMENTING THE LIFE OF A COMMUNITY

There are many different perspectives on the role and approaches taken toward assessment as part of community social work practice. Hardcastle et al. (2004) sees assessment in community practice as discovering and documenting the life of a community. Once the process of defining and understanding the approach to the focal community is completed, the process of community assessment can begin. Usually community assessment proceeds on two levels: One looks at existing studies that have been done on the focal community and the other conducts a specific assessment of the community.

Hardcastle et al. (2004) suggests that there are four major types of community studies used in community assessment and discovery: (1) field studies (original research using informal interviewing and observation to describe firsthand a particular locality, culture or network); (2) community power structure study (original research compared with a previous study of community power if available); (3) community analysis study (secondary sources plus original data from informal interviews and observation); and (4) problems and services study (secondary sources plus input from meetings, interaction with service providers, and users surveys).

Assessment is very much related to the approach taken to community practice: Different types of community interventions, community development, community organizing, social planning, social action, and social change models all involve different types of data collection, community engagement/mobilization processes, and methods of assessment (Weil, 2005, p. 151). Assessment is an important part of community practice intervention. In the initial stages of community practice, assessment frameworks can serve as a means of planning or a vehicle for information exchange as part of formal problem solving and as a way to determine which services are needed by whom.

Assessment can be viewed broadly as a social study or analysis and as a resource-oriented needs evaluation. More narrowly, assessment could be viewed as fitting the pieces together for a particular system. Lauffer (1984) saw community needs assessment as focusing on the examination of what is, on what is likely to be, or on what can or ought to be. Until recently, community assessment has focused on identifying problems, issues, and deficiencies. More recent application of ecologically based generalist approaches to community practice has led to a shift from an emphasis on a need-deficiency-problem assessment to an emphasis on asset-capacity problem solving that focuses on strengths and community assets mapping (Johnson & Grant, 2005; Johnson & Yanca, 2001; Kirst-Ashman & Hull, 2006).

ASSESSMENT FRAMEWORKS

Netting et al. (2004) contends that there are three reasons why macrolevel practitioners need a framework for assessing communities: (1) to ensure that person-in-environment perspectives are taken into account, (2) communities change and professionals need a framework for understanding these changes, and (3) macrolevel change requires an under-standing of the history and development of a community as well as an analysis of its current status.

Further, Netting et al. (2004) maintains that, in macrolevel social work practice, com-munity assessment provides one method of analyzing what has occurred and is occurring within the designated practice arena. Skilled macrolevel practice requires (a) focused and precise data collection; (b) analysis of historical trends; and (c) a thorough understanding of qualitative elements that reflect human experiences, interactions, and relationships.

Kirst-Ashman and Hull (2006) assert that the assessment process begins with defining the target population before it moves on to examine the human service response and considers collective needs. Sources of help are then addressed including informal sources such as household, social networks, and mediating resources such as self-help groups and voluntary associations. Formal sources of services include nonprofit, public, and for-profit providers and both the nature and orientation of services may differ in important ways (Maguire, 1991). Determining the competence of these systems in combining to meet needs in an effective way is the final consideration.

Based on data and information accumulated in the process of assessing a community's human service system, the macrolevel practitioner must exercise judgment in evaluating the adequacy of resources devoted to the target population within the community (Kirst-Ashman & Hull, 2006). If the assessment has been thorough and productive, the practitioner will have gained enough understanding of what occurs within the community to identify and begin assessing needed change on behalf of the target population.

Hepworth and Larsen (1993) refer to the important variables/dimensions of assessment as (a) the nature of the problems, (b) the coping capacities of those involved, (c) the availability of needed resources, and (d) the motivation to resolve problems (p. 192).

Jeffries (1996, p. 110) maintains that practitioners want to be able to:

1. Size up the extent of change that is needed;
2. Determine its feasibility given the resources likely to be available in the community;
3. Understand the likely resistance to or support for such change both within the com-munity and from powerful decision makers who could be involved;
4. Determine how much scope the community and the workers have to make decisions about actions needed to achieve that change, either through participation in organized decision-making processes or through community organizations.

Community assessments are often either problem, need, or resources/capacity assess-ments. Hardcastle et al. (2004). and Spradly (1990) suggest that community assessments can take many different forms: (a) comprehensive assessments, (b) assessments of a familiarization nature, (c) problem-oriented assessments, and (d) assessments of subsystems. However, researchers seems to agree that some of the major elements for consideration in undertaking community assessments are the level of capacity participation, collaboration, the scope, the focus, and the purpose of the assessment (Weil, 2005).

Social community practice theorists indicate that community assessments can be further examined and explicated in terms of the scope, request initiator, and practitioner role, the beginning point of the analysis (e.g., from a social problem and or quality and comprehensiveness of services), service providers, and users (Fisher, 2005; Kirst-Ashman & Hull, 2006; Netting et al., 2004; Rothman, 2001).

In addition, there appears to be some agreement in the literature that a listening/learning/exploring style and philosophy should guide an initial community assessment process (Fisher, 2005; Kirst-Ashman & Hull, 2006; Weil, 2005). Practitioners need to critically reflect on their location (factors such as class, race, gender, ability, sexual orientation); their personal history with communities; and how these influence their values, perception, assumptions, beliefs, and attitudes in their approach to assessments.

To assist in assessing local communities, R. L. Warren (1978) developed a typology of six different types of communities based on the level of individual identifications, interactions, and linkages within and outside of the community:

1. *Integral communities* have high levels of identification by community residents, high levels of supportive interaction, and high levels of internal and external linkages. These tend to be the most adaptive and resourceful communities. People are active in larger communities outside their neighborhood, but at the same time they socialize and closely identify with their neighbors.

2. *Parochial communities* have high levels of identification and high levels of interaction, but low levels of external linkages. These communities often have a sense of separateness and self-reliance due to natural boundaries or a desire to preserve a distinctive set of values and lifestyles.

3. *Diffuse communities* are often homogenous in lifestyle. This area can range from a brand new subdivision to a large number of high-rise apartment dwellings in dense urban cities.

4. *Stepping stone/transitory community residents* have very limited commitment or identification with their local community and very limited interaction with other individuals in the neighborhood. There are cliques and clusters within the community, but these people go their own way, and the inner life of the neighborhood is limited and in decline. People look to family, friends, and associations outside of the local area for support and assistance.

5. *Mosaic community residents* have a low identification with the community, some interaction with small parts of the neighborhoods, and there is no connection between community residents and major political and economic organizations of the larger community or the broader social fabric.

6. *Anomic communities* have no sense of community. People are highly atomized and isolated. Fear and protective social barriers reflect great social distance between people. Local residents have no sense of local connections or identification with their

community and there is no interaction between community residents. Community residents are marginalized and socially excluded by the broader social community (R. L. Warren, 1978).

Netting et al. (2004, p. 163) have developed a four-step framework approach to community assessment that builds on a generalist approach to macrolevel practice at the community level. The approach has the following four tasks areas:

1. Focuses on identifying the local population, understanding the characteristics of the target population and assessing and mapping its needs, resources, capacity, and assets.
2. Determines the broader community characteristics identifying boundaries, community ethnic minority groups, profiles social problems in the community, and understands the dominant community values.
3. Identifies community differences. This involves identifying formal and covert mechanisms or structures that are oppressive or sustain oppression of minority groups.
4. Identifies community structures, organizations, and institutions by identifying and connecting with the community power structure and the available formal and informal helping resources. Further, it involves examining the health and social service delivery systems and mechanisms. In addition, it involves identifying patterns of resource control and allocation and service delivery activities. Finally, it involves examining the connections between formal and informal units of support and social service.

As these tasks are being completed, strategies are being planned and implemented to build and strengthen community capacity to meet needs and provide a safe and healthy context that contributes to the support and well-being of the residents. Part of the initial phases of community intervention may need to be directed at building the community capacity to participate in the assessment process. Netting and colleagues (2004) maintain that practitioners must adapt assessment processes to the needs, resources, and capacity of the community residents to participate meaningfully in the assessment process.

Fisher (2001) points out that there are many different approaches to community assessment. Some approaches use external assessors with specific types of expertise. For many community development and advocacy organizations, the community assessment is undertaken by community residents in collaboration with community workers as part of the community mobilization and need/resource assessment process of the intervention.

SOCIAL NETWORK AND SOCIAL NETWORK MAPPING

Increasingly, community practitioners have used social network analysis as an integral part of the community assessment process. This form of analysis is extremely useful as a tool for assessing dynamic relationships between individuals, groups, and organizations within the community context and for assisting with planning interventions aimed at empowering and strengthening communities (D. I. Warren, 1981). Social networks and social network intervention are inherent in social work's emphasis on a person-in-environment perspective and are an essential part of macrolevel social work practice with its emphasis on service coordination and holistic approaches to working with communities (Specht, 1986). Trevillion (1999) maintains that the more critical form of social network intervention for community residents is with their primary (immediate family and friends) and secondary order ties (neighbors, colleagues, fellow employees, other local community residents, and officials) that connect to others who provide the residents and the community with social support. Family friends and neighborhood organizations provide more help than tertiary or formal social agencies. Community members continually build and maintain social network ties as resources to address the day-to-day needs of residents and their families. Community residents are actively involved in seeking out others that they may be able to help. Residents of communities are continually involved.

Building on exchange theory, network analysis provides a useful tool for assessing the nature and efficacy of community adaptation (Maguire, 1984). Within the theoretical framework of social network analysis, social networks are defined as any set of ties between two or more social units. The social units can be individual, groups, organizations, neighborhoods, or communities that interact and engage in exchange to achieve their purposes (Maguire, 1991; e.g., social action coalitions, neighborhood parent support networks, neighborhood watch, and women's health networks). Social networks require social and human interaction for bonding and cohesion. Networks and support resource systems exist in any situation involving the exchange of resources across social units. Resources exchanged can be tangible, such as money and clients, or intangible, such as information, emotional support, or legitimatization. Networks can be personal, professional, and organizational; and network linkages can be interpersonal between individuals, groups, organizations; and interorganization between organizations and service agencies (Trevellion, 1999). Not all network units need be in direct contact with all other networks. Networks are collection of social contacts. Client referral systems between agencies and service coordination agreements between two or more agencies are examples of networks.

Trevillion defines *networking* (or social network intervention at the community level) as the assessment, development, and maintenance or mobilization of the action sets of a social network. It involves actual exchanges. It involves actual exchanges, particularly those that provide social support. It involves the creation of conditions for and the actual exchanges of material and instrumental, advice and guidance resources, and affective social support resources.

The building of social action organizations/coalitions or the negotiations of the service coordination agreement between two or more agencies are examples of network intervention. They involve identification and mapping of the network units and building linkages between the social units at the neighborhood level to assess the social units. Assessment at the neighborhood/community level involves identification and mapping the social connections between individuals, groups, and organizations in the community to identify the composition, structure, function, and content of the social network ties within the community. Identification of the composition involves identification of the actual types of social units within the networks that are the individuals, groups, and organizations that are directly connected within the neighborhood network. In addition, it also involves assessing the number of social units in the network. Structural dimensions involve assessing the nature and number of ties including directionality and density of the ties between the social networks.

Network analysis assists in developing an empirically grounded understanding of the various functions the networks serve within neighborhoods and communities. Neighborhood networks serve various functions within communities. At times, networks are established to provide support for families (Venkatesh, Nosovitch, & Miner, 2004). At others times, they may serve to coordinate the social service agency to provide a specific type of service to a particular consumer population, such as a women's health network or interagency network of child and family service providers. Or they mobilize a particular set of formal or informal helping ties to provide service or to take action, for example, a health action network.

Finally, community workers can use social network analysis to identify sources of stress/support and risk and to map the flow of social support resources and risk over the social network (Trevillion, 1999). This provides the community practitioners with a basis to intervene to strengthen existing neighborhood networks or to mobilize different action sets of social ties within communities or neighborhoods (Fuchs, 2000, p. 32). It also assists community social workers to intervene to construct new social network ties and to build new social networks in anomic and marginalized communities or communities where there is significant in- and out-migration (Fuchs, 1995).

ROLE OF TECHNOLOGY IN COMMUNITY ASSESSMENT

The rate of change within communities has been accelerating at an unprecedented rate. One of the major drivers of change has been global growth in the accessible computer technology. This has and will continue to have a profound impact on how communities interact internally and externally. In addition, this rapid growth in the application of computer technology is transforming community social work practice and has greatly extended and transformed how community assessments are understood and are being carried out.

Communication technology has had major impacts on the nature and structures and definitions of communities. Day and Schuler (2004a) have indicated that because of the revolutionary changes occurring within our information society, there is a need to view community practice in a new context. In addition to the broad sociological definition of society, there is need to distinguish three distinct but interrelated senses of community, each of which is broad and flexible enough to accommodate the subjectivity of most interpretations, and each of which is relevant to the network society context-descriptive community as value and active community. The descriptive community leads to definition and valued identification leads to action. The collective community comprises individual community members that have developed an inherent interest in each other. In addition to sharing the same geographical space and experiences in healthy communities, members learn to respect and celebrate the richness and diversity of human interests. Diversity then distinguishes the individual from the collective but at the same time contributes to that collective.

It is through this sense of belonging to—identifying with—local communities that people engage in community activities. The active community refers to collective action by community members embracing one or more communal values. Such activities are normally undertaken purposively through the vehicle of groups, networks, and organizations that constitute a community's social capital, which are significant to any assessment of community.

Although community and voluntary sector groups are the cornerstone of community life, the daily pressures for survival on such groups often means that enabling active communities is a major task and a shared value base between citizens and community policy makers. Day and Schuler (2004b) suggest that distrust of bureaucrats and politicians often means that achieving this shared value base is problematic, especially between citizens/community groups and the mechanism of local governance. They maintain that by assessing and understanding what community means to local people at the local level, it should be possible to develop policies that are meaningful and germane to people in those communities.

Community policy frameworks are essential to guide community assessment and intervention planning. Marginalized or socially excluded peoples often require more direct involvement from community policy mechanisms than other populations in more adaptive communities. Despite the need for support, community policy mechanisms should be predicated on the notion that community practices (i.e., services, activities, functions, and processes) need to be embedded in the aspirations, needs, and culture of the people involved. Ownership and identity are crucial elements in building healthy communities.

The following policy framework provides a focus for community assessment in a rapidly changing technological driven society. Community policy should (a) understand and meet community needs; (b) work in partnership with active community groups and organizations; (c) be based on one or more community value, that is, solidarity, participation, and coherence; (d) prioritize the needs of the community's socially excluded marginalized disadvantaged and oppressed; (e) valorize and celebrate cultural diversity; and (f) reflect a commitment to the objectives of community autonomy and responsibility for community initiatives (Day & Schuler, 2004c, p. 9).

Community practice that flows from community policy assists in providing the context and a holistic approach to practice. Day and Schular (2004c, p. 14) assert that community practice is a method for promoting policies that encourage the planning, building, and sustainability of healthy communities and usually involves some or all of the following components: (a) the sustained involvement of paid community workers; (b) a broad range of professionals who are increasingly using community work methods in their work; (c) the efforts of self-managed community groups themselves; and (d) managerial attempts at reviving, restructuring, and reallocating services to encourage community access and involvement in the planning and delivery of services.

In this approach, community practice practitioners use technology as assessment tools to assist in the gathering of community assessment data but also to engage and mobilize the community members in the change process. In policy-driven community practice, Day and Schular (2004c) indicate that there are three approaches to community practice: a focus on community services, community development, and community action. They indicate that no matter what the composition of local partnership or the complexion of the approach employed, community practice should be viewed as a framework of these three interrelated elements that assist in identifying, understanding, and fulfilling community need. Within a networks society context, collaborative community practice requires the subordination of information technology systems, artifacts, and services to meeting those needs as a crucial contribution to building a healthy empowered and active community.

Day and Schuler (2004a, p. 19) indicate that there is a rapidly increasing and evolving application of information technology in community practice. The nature of the medium and its potential for inexpensive and ubiquitous access to information and communication will transform the processes and make more data available to assist in community assessment for mobilizing communities and community practice. Many forms of community technologies are emerging as communities seek to achieve a diverse range of social goals. Social movements across the world are utilizing information technologies to support and sustain their communication, organization, mobilization, and activation processes to foster local action and global interaction.

Information technology needs to be seen as a tool used by the community to work toward change at the local community level. For effective community practice, communities must be able to direct the application of the technology; and community practitioners must increasingly be involved in the development of the community's capacity to use technology and to incorporate it into all aspects of community practice intervention processes. The uses must be developed in a manner that could be extended long after the life of the project.

LIMITATIONS OF THE EVIDENCE

A thorough review of the literature pertaining to assessment in social work practice at the microlevel or mezzolevel yielded primarily descriptions of various approaches to assessing communities. Much of the literature at best describes the application of assessment approaches or frameworks as used in community development, organizing, and planning, and social action interventions aimed at progressive social change. Usually the literature provides little if any analysis of the effectiveness or usefulness of the assessment frameworks. Most of the literature provides anecdotal descriptions of how to apply a particular method specific to a particular type of community or community need or problem. There is little literature on the research of approaches to community assessment. In addition, much of the literature that describes the approaches to community assessment is sector specific, for example, health, criminology, child welfare, and education. They are usually very narrowly focused on assessing needs, assets, or the prevalence of particular medical, social, or environmental conditions.

Plescia, Koontza, and Laurent (2001) found in their public health research that geographic-based assessments help target specific community needs and promote community participation. This echoes the research about community assessment that indicates that it is particularly important to see that community assessment involves community members to ensure reliability and validity of the assessment process and data at the geographic community level (Clark et al., 2003; Coulton, Korbin, Chan, & Su, 2001; Williams & Yanoshik, 2001). In addition, much of the literature indicates that the community assessment process is an important intervention tool for mobilizing communities to address and to work toward effective social change at the community level. However, there is a dearth of research indicating which assessment tools are effective for this purpose (Coulton, 2005).

After an extensive review of the research literature on social work community practice, Coulton (2005) concluded what is needed is a knowledge base of community change built on much more convincing evidence. Social workers need to take greater advantage of the many research tools that could be used to build the knowledge base of effective community practice. More research using rigorous designs has to be done to examine the effectiveness of social work community intervention. More use must be made of econometric analysis and not only limited to psychometric measures. Relevant community intervention evaluation approaches such as empowerment evaluation and participatory action research need to be developed and used more broadly to determine the effectiveness of community-based interventions (Fetterman, Kaftarian, & Wandersman, 1996; Fetterman & Wandersman, 2005).

Research on community assessment must be part of an overall strategy of research in the area of community social work practice. Coulton (2005) and Connell, Kubisch, Schorr, and Weiss (1995) maintain that moving forward on a community research agenda requires more collaborative work across communities because constructing a knowledge base requires the testing of similar interventions in multiple places. Community assessment and intervention research depends on collaboration with community partners built on established relationships and deep knowledge of place. To implement strong designs in which communities are matched or profiled beforehand, researchers need to draw on an infrastructure of community measures and data. It is seldom feasible to establish a baseline trend, for example, unless systems for gathering and storing data about communities are in place in various locales (Coulton et al., 2001). Without comparability of studies, it is difficult to accumulate knowledge. With growing numbers of new research tools available, social workers are being called on move community assessment and intervention research forward.

IMPLICATIONS FOR SOCIAL WORK ON MICRO-, MEZZO-, AND MACROLEVELS

The person-in-environment or ecological framework of social work practice (Germaine, 1991; Kemp, Whittaker, & Tracey, 1997) provides the foundation for the generalist approach to community social work practice. It provides an extremely useful perspective for social work practice with communities because it greatly assists in understanding the relationships between micro, mezzo and macro factors for planning implementing community interventions. It allows social workers to individualize intervention efforts in the context of the community environment. It assists social workers to understand the relationship between the individual and the community. It provides the context for empowering and mobilizing individuals to effect social change at the mezzo- and macrolevels of their lives. Specifically, this framework aims at assessing the physical environment of the community both built and natural and its impacts on individuals. In addition, it looks at assessing the social interactional organizational environment at the neighborhood and community level. Also it aims to assess the institutional and organizational environment with the communities, the sociopolitical and cultural environment, and the community environment as constructed in individual and collective systems of meaning and belief (Kemp et al., 1997, p. 86). The person-in-environment or ecological perspective provides a theoretical framework that assists in understanding the interrelationships between individual/personal factors (microlevel) and neighborhoods/community (mezzolevel) and the societal/political (macrolevel).

Community practice in addition to its traditional focus must also address three critical contexts that are reshaping our world. These contexts are major changes sweeping the globe and include: (a) the increase in multicultural societies worldwide; (b) the expansion of rights for women and children and further expansion of human rights; (c) globalization of the major economic, political, and social shifts occurring throughout the world and creating complex interactive effects (Weil & Gamble, 2005, p. 121).

FUTURE DIRECTIONS

There are five central practice issues that need to be addressed. These issues necessitate more equalitarian collaborative empowering approaches in the community assessment process. They necessitate greater social inclusion, participation, and access in community intervention approaches beginning with assessment. The central issues that must be addressed are:

1. Expanding and refining practice approaches that can build toward social and economic justice.
2. Focusing practice on the expansion of basic human rights to marginalized groups of women, children, and men.
3. Building opportunity structures for disadvantaged populations and working to build multicultural strategies and coalitions for positive social change based on specific situations and common human needs.
4. Focusing community practice activities on social and economic development strengthening civil society and enlarging civic and political participation.
5. Finding effective multinational approaches to reducing absolute poverty (Weil, 2005, p. 4).

CONCLUSION

Approaches to community assessment are evolving to be more focused on dynamic iterative processes that are inextricably connected to the intervention process. Community practitioners need to become allies to the community residents in mobilizing, engaging, and building their capacity early in the assessment process. The rapid growth in communication and information technology is incorporated into the assessment process to include marginalized minority groups in our increasingly more diverse communities. However, the rapid growth of technology has the potential for either extending the effectiveness of community social development practices or for perpetuating oppressive community structures. The challenge for community social workers continues to be one of reducing oppression and promoting a social justice orientation in the context of rapidly changing communities, societal values, and global contexts.

REFERENCES

Clark, M. J., Cary, S., Grover Diemert, M. S., Ceballos, R., Sifientes, M., & Atteberry, I. (2003). Involving community in community assessment in. *Public Health Nursing, 20*(6), 456–463.

Cohen, Y. (1985). *Neighborhoods and friendship networks. A study of three residential areas of Jerusalem.* Chicago: University of Chicago Press.

Connell, J., Kubisch, I. A., Schorr, I., & Weiss, C. (1995). *New approaches to evaluating community initiatives: Concepts, methods and contexts.* New York: Asperi Institute.

Coulton, C. J. (2005). The place of community in social practice research: Conceptual and methodological developments. *Social Work Research, 29*(2), 73–85.

Coulton, C. J., Korbin, J., Chan, T., & Su, M. (2001). Mapping residents' perceptions of neighborhood boundaries: A methodological note. *American Journal of Community Psychology, 29*, 371–383.

Day, P., & Schuler, D. (2004a). Community practice: An alternative vision of the network society. In P. Day & D. Schuler (Eds.), *Community practice* (pp. 1–20). New York: Routledge/Taylor & Francis.

Day, P., & Schuler, D. (2004b). *Community practice in the network society: Local action/global interaction*. London: Routledge/Taylor & Francis.

Day, P., & Schuler, D. (2004c). Integrating community practice policy and research. In P. Day & D. Schuler (Eds.), *Community practice in the network society: Local action/global interaction* (pp. 216–254). London: Routledge/Taylor & Francis.

Fellin, P. (2001). Understanding American communities. In J. Rothman, L. Erlich, & J. E. Tropman (Eds.), *Strategies of community intervention* (6th ed., pp. 118–132). Itasca, IL: Peacock.

Fetterman, D. M., Kaftarian, S. J., & Wandersman, A. (Eds.). (1996). *Empowerment evaluation*. Thousand Oaks, CA: Sage.

Fetterman, D. M., & Wandersman, A. (Eds.). (2005). *Empowerment evaluation principles in practice*. Thousand Oaks, CA: Sage.

Fiqueria-McDonough, J. (2001). *Community analysis and praxis: Toward a grounded civil society*. Philadelphia: Brunner-Routledge/Taylor & Francis.

Fisher, R. (2001). Social action community organization: Proliferation, persistence, roots, and prospects. In J. Rothman, L. Erlich, & J. E. Tropman (Eds.), *Strategies of community intervention* (6th ed., pp. 53–67). Itasca, IL: Peacock.

Fisher, R. (2005). History, context, and emerging issues for community practice. In M. Weil (Ed.), *The handbook of community practice* (pp. 34–58). Thousand Oaks, CA: Sage.

Fuchs, D. (1995). Preserving and strengthening families and protecting children: Social network intervention. In J. Hudson & B. Galaway (Eds.), *Child welfare in Canada research and policy implications*. Toronto, Ontario, Canada: Thompson.

Fuchs, D. (2000). Social network theory, research and practice: Implications for family group conferencing. In G. Burford & J. Hudson (Eds.), *Family group conferencing: New directions in community-centered child and family practice* (pp. 131–139). New York: Aldine de Gruyter.

Germaine, C. (1991). *Human behavior in the social environment: An ecological perspective*. New York: Columbia University Press.

Hardcastle, D. A., Powers, P. R., & Wenocur, S. (2004). *Community practice theories and skills for social workers* (2nd ed.). New York: Oxford University Press.

Hepworth, D. H., & Larsen, J. A. (1993). *Direct social work practice*. Pacific Grove, CA: Brooks/Cole.

Homan, M. S. (2004). *Promoting community change: Making it happen in the real world* (3rd ed.). Belmont, CA: Brooks/Cole-Thomson Learning.

Jeffries, A. (1996). Modeling community work: An analytic framework for practice. *Journal of Community Practice, 3*(3/4), 101–125.

Johnson, J. L., & Grant, J. R. G. (2005). *Community practice casebook series*. New York: Allyn & Bacon.

Johnson, L. C., & Yanca, S. J. (2001). *Social work practice* (7th ed.). Boston: Allyn & Bacon.

Kemp, S., Whittaker, J., & Tracey, E. (1997). *Person-environment practice: The social ecology of interpersonal helping*. New York: Aldine de Gruyter.

Kirst-Ashman, K. K., & Hull, G. H., Jr. (2006). *Generalist practice: With organizations and communities* (3rd ed.). Belmont, CA: Thomson Brooks/Cole.

Lauffer, A. (1984). Assessment and program development. In F. M. Cox, J. L. Erhlich, J. Rothman, & J. E. Tropman (Eds.), *Tactics and techniques of community practice* (2nd ed., pp. 60–75). Itasca, IL: Peacock.

Maguire, L. (1984). Newtorking for self-help: An empirically based guideline. In F. M. Cox, J. L. Erhlich, J. Rothman, & J. E. Tropman (Eds.), *Tactics and techniques of community practice* (2nd ed., pp. 198–208). Itasca, IL: Peacock.

Maguire, L. (1991). *Social support systems in practice*. Washington, DC: National Association of Social Workers Press.

McMillan, D. W. (1996). Sense of community. *Journal of Community Psychology*, 24(4), 315–325.

McKnight, J. L. (1997, March/April). A 21st century map for healthy communities and families. *Families in Society*, 117–127.

Millar, D. T., & Prentice, D. A. (1994). The self and the collective. *Society for Personality and Social Psychology*, 20(5), 451–453.

Netting, F. E., Kettner, P. M., & McMurtry, S. L. (2004). *Social work macro practice* (3rd ed.). New York: Pearson.

Pincus, A., & Minahan, A. (1973). *Social work practice: Model and method*. Itasca, IL: Peacock.

Plescia, M., Koontza, S., & Laurent, S. (2001, May). Community assessment in a vertically integrated health care system. *American Journal of Public Health*, 91(5), 811–814.

Rawls, J. (1970). *A theory of justice*. Cambridge, MA: Harvard University Press.

Rifkin, J. (2000). *The age of access: The new culture of hypercapitlism, where all of life is a paid for experience*. New York: Tarcher/Putnam.

Ross, M., & Lappin, B. (1955). *Community organization: Theory and principles*. New York: Harper.

Rothman, J. (1999a). Intent and content. In J. Rothman (Ed.), *Reflections on community organization: Enduring themes and critical issues* (pp. 3–26). Itasca, IL: Peacock.

Rothman, J. (1999b). A very personal account of the intellectual history of community organization. In J. Rothman (Ed.), *Reflections on community organization: Enduring themes and critical issues* (pp. 215–234). Itasca, IL: Peacock.

Rothman, J. (2001). Approaches to community intervention. In J. Rothman, J. Erhlich, & J. Tropman (Eds.), *Strategies for community intervention* (6th ed., pp. 27–64). Itasca, IL: Peacock.

Rothman, J., Tropman, J., & Erhlich, J. (2001). *Strategies of community intervention*. Itasca, IL: Peacock.

Rubin, H., & Rubin, S. (2001). *Community organizing and development* (3rd ed.). Boston: Allyn & Bacon.

Specht, H. (1986). Social support, social network, social exchange and social work practice. *Social Service Review*, 60(2), 218–240.

Spradly, B. W. (1990). *Community health nursing: Concepts and practice* (3rd ed.). Glenview, IL: Scott Foresman.

Trevillion, S. (1999). *Networking and community partnership* (2nd ed.). Aldershot, England: Ashgate.

Venkatesh, M., Nosovitch, J., & Miner, W. (2004). Community network development and user participation, In P. Day & D. Schuler (Eds.), *Community practice in the network society: Local action/global interaction* (pp. 186–199). New York: Routledge/Taylor & Francis.

Warren, D. I. (1978). *Neighborhood organizers handbook*. Notre Dame, IN: University of Notre Press.

Warren, D. I. (1981). *Helping networks*. Notre Dame, IN: University of Notre Press.

Warren, R. L. (1978). *The community in America* (3rd ed.). Chicago: Rand McNally.

Weil, M. (Eds.). (2005). *The handbook of community practice*. Thousand Oaks, CA: Sage.

Weil, M., & Gamble, D. (2005). Evolution, models and the changing context of community practice. In M. Weil (Ed.), *The handbook of community practice* (pp. 117–149). Thousand Oaks, CA: Sage.

Weil, M. O., & Gamble, D. (1995). Community practice modules. In R. L. Edwards (Ed.), *Encyclopedia of social work* (19th ed., Vol. 1, pp. 577–694). Silver Spring, MD: National Association of Social Workers Press.

Williams, R., & Yanoshik, K. (2001). Can you do a community assessment without talking to the community. *Journal of Community Health*, 26(4), 233–247.

Chapter 24

INTERVENTION WITH COMMUNITIES

Michael Reisch

Since the early nineteenth century, researchers have studied the role of local associations in promoting civic participation, strengthening democracy, and developing countervailing structures to those of the state. During the past 2 centuries, they have analyzed the ways in which these organizations have shaped social policies designed to assimilate an increasingly diverse population while enabling racial, ethnic, and religious minorities to resist the forces of institutional oppression. The interaction between these phenomena created the foundation of organized community intervention in the United States.

Community intervention has been known by a variety of names in social work (Weil & Gamble, 2005). Each name connoted a somewhat different orientation and emerged in a different context. The traditions of community intervention are rooted in such varied settings as settlement houses, the Charities Organization Societies (COS), rural development, democratic reform movements, and the organizing efforts of communities of color (Reisch, in press). Ross (1955) and Rothman (2001) were among the first to articulate its distinct forms and features. Rothman's tripartite typology of community/locality development, community planning, and social action continues, with modifications, to shape views of the field (Hyde, 1996; Rothman, 1996).

Scholars now identify eight models of community intervention: neighborhood and grassroots community organizing, organizing in functional communities and within existing service agencies, political and social action, community-based social and economic development, social planning, program development and community liaison, coalition work, and social movement work. They differ in their goals, targets, primary constituencies, scope of concern, and assigned practitioner roles (Hardcastle, Wenocur, & Powers, 1997; Weil & Gamble, 2005).

The literature on community intervention uses the term *community organization* interchangeably with concepts such as community development, citizen participation, citizen action, community planning, social action, and advocacy (Weil & Gamble, 2005). Yet, community intervention is actually a broader concept than community organizing since it encompasses the creation, implementation, and evaluation of community-based services and policies designed to affect the community as a whole.

The extensive literature on community intervention identifies a variety of broad purposes. Often, these reflect particular assumptions about the nature of community work and the ideologies of their proponents. Organizers from the Alinsky school, for example, focus on winning concrete reforms, changing power relations, and giving people a sense of their own power (Bobo, Kendall, & Max, 2001). They emphasize winning on a specific issue, building organizational capacity, developing power, and increasing people's sense of community and critical consciousness (Staples, 1984, 1997).

One overarching purpose of community intervention is to increase community competence—the ability of its members to identify their needs and solve problems (Brager & Purcell, 1967; Brager & Specht, 1973; Kahn, 1991). This perspective emerged from a social health model that seeks solutions to individual and social problems in both people and their environments (Lowe, 1997). In Warren's (1983) model of community development, community intervention is directed toward strengthening primary group relationships; community autonomy, viability, and control; the development of more equitable distribution of power and more widespread, democratic participation in decision-making; the creation of commitment among community members to their overall well-being; the promotion of diversity; and the effective management of conflict.

These different perspectives are reflected in the continuum of strategic goals for community intervention. At one end is the provision of social and psychological benefits to constituents, often through the creation of self-help and mutual aid programs. Further along the continuum is structural change to increase the effectiveness of existing services, programs, and policies. At the other end of the continuum is the goal of promoting institutional change, particularly around the distribution of power and resources.

Most scholars and practitioners agree, however, that the overall goal of community intervention is "to improve quality of life and increase social justice through social and economic development, community organizing, social planning, and progressive social change" (Weil, 2005, p. 10). It involves interpersonal, intergroup, and interorganizational cooperation and collaboration and focuses on the empowerment of those most affected by the systems and institutions that one is seeking to change (Reed, 2005; Sarri, 1997).

Because community intervention serves multiple functions, the role of theory in its development is complex and often synthetic. Reed (2005) identifies a wide range of theories that inform community practice including evolutionary, political economy, structural/functional, systems, ecological, conflict, symbolic interactionism, social learning, exchange, rational choice, co-construction, feminist and critical race theories, especially those that emphasize concepts of power and oppression (p. 89).

Conversely, the consequences of community intervention vary widely. They include the expansion of social or economic rights and benefits, greater access to existing services, public education about issues or the processes of promoting social change, resource development at the community or agency level, technical assistance, the formation of cross-cutting coalitions, participation in the electoral process, the creation of new or revised services, the development of community problem-solving processes, the enhancement of group or community identity, and the development of critical consciousness (Bobo et al., 2001; Fisher, 2005; Gutierrez, Lewis, Nagda, Wernick & Shore, 2005).

Focus of Community Intervention: What Does Community Mean?

In the sociological literature of the nineteenth and twentieth centuries, the idea of community, *gemeinschaft,* was frequently contrasted with that of society, *gesellschaft* (Tonnies, 1955). In this dual framework, community referred to commonly held values and behavioral prescriptions, the honoring of which are ultimately conditions of membership. In contrast, the cultural modernism of the mid- and late-twentieth centuries emphasized limited, partial, segmented, even shallow commitments to a variety of diverse collec-tivities—no one of which commands an individual's total loyalty. In contemporary scholar-ship, the idea of community has several dimensions: as a physical space (e.g., a neighbor-hood); as people with shared networks, culture, values, identity, norms, and institutions; as a social system or set of social systems with various rules for horizontal and vertical bound-ary maintenance between internal subsystems and external systems; as an arena of conflict; and as an "ecology of games" (Hardcastle et al., 1997). During the past 2 decades, some authors continue to prioritize the role of geographic communities, while others emphasize common issues or identity (Delgado, 1994).

Sometimes these approaches to community overlap since they share certain common characteristics. These include the importance of face-to-face communication with and among community members, reciprocal exchange of tangible and intangible "goods," and intra- and intergroup interaction (Fellin, 2001). In the twenty-first century, however, many of these characteristics are threatened by technological, political, economic, and social changes that distance people from each other (Reisch, 2005).

Conversely, different patterns of relationship exist within both geographic and functional communities. Vertical or *gesellschaft*-oriented relationships are concerned with structure and function and connected to systems outside of or above the community. Horizontal or *gemeinschaft*-oriented relationships involve the connections of community subsystems to each other and are concerned primarily with maintenance and process functions. In contemporary parlance, these different patterns of relationship are associated with the development of bonding and bridging social capital (see next).

In contrast to approaches to community intervention that emphasize consensus and stability, conflict theorists assume all social relationships have conflictual elements as well as integrative elements and that communities systematically generate conflict. This conflict manifests itself through opposing interests and resistance to hierarchical social and political relationships. Sometimes, it occurs over symbolic issues when the underlying issues cannot be made explicit, when contradictory goals exist, and when different means are proposed for achieving shared goals. It occurs most frequently over the distribution of scarce resources, including power (Coser, 1956; Warren, 1983).

From this viewpoint, conflict is a natural occurrence and not necessarily a negative force. In fact, some scholars suggest that conflict often serves a useful function, such as uniting previously unconnected people against a common enemy (Coser, 1956).

The dynamics of community conflict follow a particular pattern. It tends to move from specific to more general issues and, ultimately, to the emergence of new issues. Conflict can produce a polarization of social relations, the emergence of new leaders to lead disputes, and a change from formal to informal communication patterns (Coser, 1956; Warren, 1983). These different views of community change are reflected in the history of community intervention (Betten & Austin, 1990; Garvin & Cox, 2001).

HISTORICAL BACKGROUND

From de Tocqueville's (2004) study of U.S. civil society in the early nineteenth cen-tury, through contemporary research on civic participation (Putnam, 2000; Rich, 1999), community-based organizations have been regarded as institutions that help build civil society and foster participation in public life. Although community intervention has been a central feature of American social work since its inception, it "emerged less as a specific method . . . than as a means by which social service providers could develop [community] programs . . . and mobilize the resources needed to support and sustain them" (Wenocur & Reisch, 1989, p. 71). Initially linked with efforts to extend democracy into all phases of community life, the professionalizing impulse soon transformed community intervention from a cause-related method to "a function absorbed into the administrative structure of social work" (Lubove, 1965, p. 80).

The role of community intervention within social work grew most rapidly in three periods: the Progressive era, the Depression years, and the Civil Rights era. Yet, even during these periods, the pursuit of professionalism promoted the adoption of models of intervention that reflected the dominant values and goals of the financial and political supporters of social services—largely government, wealthy philanthropists, and foundations. For the most part, this precluded the development of widespread support for interventions that sought to change institutions through social action (Fisher, 1994; Reisch & Andrews, 2001; Reisch & Wenocur, 1986; Specht & Courtney, 1994).

In its early stages, community intervention developed on two distinct levels. One brought a rational, business-like approach to the field and focused on the creation or maintenance of social services. The other, at the grassroots level, stressed intragroup, intergroup, and interorganizational collaboration to strengthen natural helping networks and involve people in key decisions. The philosophical and theoretical roots of community intervention, therefore, included such varied sources as liberal political-economy, which focused on efficiency, anarchism, and the social gospel, which emphasized reciprocity, mutual aid, and collective self-interest (Simon, 1994).

During the Progressive era, community intervention occurred largely through settlement houses, the Charities Organization Societies (COSs), YM and YWCAs, the Boy Scouts and Girl Scouts, churches, self-help organizations, mutual aid societies, and community centers, which offered a combination of recreational, educational, and cultural programs. To a large extent, its methods were nonconfrontational and focused on community building efforts, including the improvement of intra- and intergroup communication (Betten & Austin, 1990; Fisher, 1994; Wenocur & Reisch, 1989).

Although they lacked a clear methodology and theoretical base, early practitioners of community intervention were still acknowledged as a separate, if lower, status category of social workers (Wenocur & Reisch, 1989). Despite this lower status, their underlying values and goals had considerable appeal. "[T]he . . . early prophets of community organization [believed that] . . . the future of democracy depended on the ordinary citizen's ability to regain control of his own destiny through intensive civic association [and] . . . cooperation with others, [thereby] . . . minimiz[ing] the demoralizing effects of community fragmentation" (Lubove, 1965, pp. 173–174).

In this period, the most ambitious effort to establish these democratic practices through community intervention was the "Social Unit Plan," founded in 1916. Based in part on the theories of Mary Parker Follett (1920), the proponents of a National Social Unit Organization believed that the neighborhood group was the cornerstone of a cooperative democracy that could break down the false distinction between private and civic life. Although its efforts at community education were somewhat successful, the block councils it created did not work as planned (Fisher, 1994).

At the same time, the COS also began to develop its ideas of community intervention. It hired a full-time organizer to organize other COSs or gather information about communities, but not to organize community residents. Ultimately, this approach led to the Community Chest (now United Way) movement. By the end of the 1920s, community intervention in social work had evolved to focus primarily on community planning, service coordination, evaluation, and fund-raising (Brilliant, 1990). This created a dilemma for practitioners of community intervention. The more they aspired to professional status, the less they were involved with social reform. The more they focused on systems change, the more difficulty they had in establishing a distinctive professional identity (Wenocur & Reisch, 1989).

The absence of a clear theoretical foundation for community intervention was not particularly helpful in resolving this dilemma. What theories existed centered on Dewey's (1916) ideas on progressive education, which stressed socialization and participation as a means to bridge the gap between the individual and the community. Through his work on the "community movement," Lindeman (1926) built on these ideas. He argued that "the fundamental task of community organization was to reconcile the 'democratic process' with specialists, agencies and institutions by means of recognized inter-relations" (Lubove, 1965, p. 179).

In sum, the integration of community intervention into the broader fabric of social service delivery, influenced by the ascendancy of financial federations and councils during the decade after World War I, obscured the boundary dilemmas of its methods. It was difficult to distinguish the activities of community organizers and planners within social work from those of like-minded individuals and groups outside of the profession, many of whom were volunteers. The absence of a clear, scientific basis for community intervention further exacerbated this situation.

By 1930, community intervention largely referred to the organization of donors and community agencies, not the residents of a community itself. The growth of public welfare during the New Deal and World War II, however, increased the planning dimension of community intervention and created new roles for experts. This rescued the field from professional oblivion, although not without problems and conflict—primarily over the role of social action. The Lane Report (1940), commissioned by the American Association of Social Work (AASW), attempted to paper over these differences by defining community intervention in terms that encompassed both its older planning functions and the newer occupational roles that government programs had created. While it appeared to give legitimacy to the pursuit of institutional reform, the report paid little attention to social action or social change at the grassroots level.

Nevertheless, community intervention emerged as a distinct method within social work during the 1930s and 1940s. In 1932, content on organizing was included in the AASW's minimum curriculum, and soon thereafter the first serious theoretical writing on the subject appeared within social work (Wenocur & Reisch, 1989). Concurrently, the left-wing Rank and File Movement, which was larger than the AASW in the mid-1930s, promoted the view that social workers should be organizers, much like those in trade unions. It sought to reconceptualize social work's focus by linking community intervention to what became known later as empowerment practice (Simon, 1994).

Although many social workers were politically active in the 1930s and 1940s, these activities diminished considerably in the post-World War II McCarthyism era. Mainstream social work leaders, like Kenneth Pray (1947), argued that organizers needed to abjure confrontation and class struggle. It was not until the 1960s that social work again adopted an activist community-oriented stance (Reisch & Andrews, 2001).

The distinction between social reform and social action of the postwar years suited the more conservative climate that emphasized profession building and conformity. The literature of the period defined community intervention as a helping process in the context of democratic values. At the same time, the concept of "community care" began to emerge. Buell and Associates integrated these strands (1952) into a public health model in which the organizer's role remained largely research and administration.

In the mid-1950s, primarily through the work of Ross (1955), the concept of community intervention gradually underwent another redefinition. Ross placed community intervention within a problem-solving mold to put it on a parallel plane with social casework. He also reintroduced the importance of community participation as a critical problem-solving mechanism that complemented, but was distinct from, the role played by community agencies. Through his influence, community intervention was linked closely with group work, emphasizing intra- and intergroup processes and the strengthening of social relationships, and the creation of what is now referred to as social capital. Although ideas about community power were introduced—largely as they related to planning processes—the work of activists outside of social work, like Alinsky, did not attract an audience within the field until the 1960s (Wenocur & Reisch, 1989).

During the 1960s, inspired by contemporary social movements, especially civil rights, and supported by government-funded Community Action Programs, community organizers created a wide range of grassroots, neighborhood-based, and social action programs. Although much of this activity occurred outside the social work profession, community organizers within social work achieved their greatest influence during this period (Fisher, 1994). The incorporation of activist principles into community intervention did not occur, however, without a struggle. Many liberals in social work were uncomfortable with some of the disruptive tactics activists used (Specht, 1969). Consequently, a split emerged during this period between grassroots organizers and advocates and policy analysts and planners that persists through the present.

After the movement-oriented activism of the 1960s subsided, community intervention took a different course. Local organizations with strong elements of direct democracy and populism emerged—again largely outside of social work. The community interventions they developed were more pragmatic and focused on addressing the material conditions of constituents' lives through the construction of durable organizations (Boyte, 1981). Three major styles of community intervention dominated this period: the Industrial Areas Foundation (IAF) model, created by Alinsky, which emphasized geographically based organizations and conflict-oriented strategies; a public interest model, influenced strongly by Ralph Nader, which stressed policy impact research and the use of the media; and constituency organizing around specific issues, such as the United Farm Workers under Cesar Chavez (Fisher, 1994).

During the last quarter of the twentieth century, critics of traditional models of community intervention bemoaned the absence of multicultural frameworks to guide practitioners. This influenced the ways in which practitioners defined problems and formulated strategies of intervention (Glugoski, Reisch, & Rivera, 1994). In response to such criticisms, social work scholars developed alternative models of community intervention that incorporated greater awareness of the significance of racial, ethnic, and gender diversity (Glugoski et al., 1994; Gutierrez & Lewis, 1998; Hyde, 2005; Rivera & Erlich, 1998; Weil, 2005). Since the late 1970s, the concept of empowerment has also emerged as a central feature of community practice (Gutierrez, Parsons, & Cox, 1998; Reisch, Wenocur, & Sherman, 1981; Solomon, 1976).

The Latin American concept of conscientization has had a complementary influence. Based on the work of Freire (1968, 1973), conscientization focuses on the collective process of enlightenment and the development of critical consciousness through dialogue, mutual problem posing, and problem solving. Stressing a dialectical relationship between reflection and action, it involves a new interpretation of the social environment, a transformation of community members from objects to subjects, and the creation of trust between community practitioners and community members.

During the past 3 decades, the field of community intervention has expanded considerably outside of the social work profession. It has created training institutions, publications, and its own culture. The link between activists and their university-based allies has become attenuated. This helps explain why the literature on evidence-based community intervention is much sparser than that for other social work methods.

CURRENT EVIDENCE-BASED INTERVENTION WITH COMMUNITIES

Because they emerged in response to the social consequences of industrialization, theories and methods of community intervention in the United States were shaped by common assumptions about its relationship to the political-economic environment. Despite their ideological differences, most community practitioners believe that some form of government-funded social provision is required to collectivize the social costs of a market-dominated economy. In this framework, community intervention helps convert private troubles into public issues and implement policies more fairly and effectively. Since the New Deal, therefore, most community practitioners have maintained a stance of cautious, if somewhat reluctant alliance with the state (Fisher & Kling, 1993).

For many decades, community or locality development has been one of the principal forms of community intervention practiced in the United States. Its core concepts have included the importance of democratic participation, intra- and intergroup dialogue, collaborative work, education, and capacity building. It focuses on the strengths of the community and its members, rather than their problems or deficits and involves the identification and validation of knowledge and skills (assets) that are often overlooked. Its practitioners play the role of learner, enabler, and facilitator (Rothman, 2001; Rubin & Rubin, 2004).

Rubin and Rubin (2004) define the goals of community development as individual and group empowerment, the production of social capital, and the creation of effective organizations through which people focus power to bring about changes in community conditions while acquiring and applying expertise in problem solving. In contrast to a social action approach, "community development . . . involves participants in constructive activities and processes to produce improvements, opportunities, structures, goods, and services that increase the quality of life and build member capacities" (Gutierrez et al., 2005, p. 345). It assumes that problems can be resolved through cooperation, consensus, and the identification of common interests and goals. Community development organizations take such forms as associations, congresses, advisory committees, neighborhood councils, community corporations, and government entities, which through collaboration and persuasion attempt to achieve both inclusive processes and concrete outcomes of benefit to constituents (Homan, 2004).

Scholars often use different criteria to identify the extent to which such interventions succeed in creating community well-being (Warren, 1983). Even the task of defining and measuring its attainment is difficult (Christakopoulou, Dawson, & Gari, 2001). Those who emphasize community power focus on community members' ability to influence social and political systems. Communitarians emphasize the enhancement of people's welfare through collective, community-based solutions (Etzioni, 1993).

Kretzmann and McKnight (1993) have articulated a different and influential perspective in this regard, sometimes referred to as the associational approach. Their model has two key features. One focuses on the voluntary nature of relationships among individuals who collectively determine how to identify and solve community problems. The other examines how individuals organize themselves and others to implement the solutions selected. The space created through this process is often called "civil society" (Putnam, 2000) or the domain of mediating structures (Berger & Neuhaus, 1977).

Proponents of the associational model assert that it produces a network of mutual support that enables citizens to negotiate everyday life. They argue that associations possess the potential to respond rapidly to local problems, individualize people's needs, recognize and utilize the unique gifts of community members, create arenas that promote the responsibilities and activities of citizenship, foster leadership development, and mobilize human capital (Fellin, 1998; McKnight, 1997). In this model, small groups play a key role.

Small groups have long been considered critical components of community intervention (Bakalinsky, 1984), and their functioning is, perhaps, the most thoroughly researched area of community intervention. The evidence obtained from these analyses can be applied effectively to community work with the caveat that intragroup behavior may not correlate with behaviors on a community scale. It can, however, help illuminate the interactions that occur between community members that are often mediated through groups (Green & Brock, 2005; Uslaner & Conley, 2003).

Through such vehicles as organizing committees, house meetings, issue committees, lobbying committees, and negotiating teams, small groups are the primary medium through which most community intervention occurs (Ephross & Vassil, 2004). Consequently, the literature—much of which is rooted in theories of adult education (Dewey, 1916; Freire, 1973)—focuses on group development to increase constituents' self-efficacy, and reflects "the belief . . . that [groups] are worth the struggle and effort that collective action requires" (Castelloe, as quoted in Gamble & Hoff, 2005, p. 179).

Recent scholarship on civic engagement and social capital analyzes how concepts like group identity might be applied to community-building efforts (Hutchinson, 2004; Hyman, 2002). Researchers have found that membership in groups and civic organizations correlates to constructive interaction with neighbors and the general level of social trust in a community (Claibourn & Martin, 2000; Putnam, 2000). Their findings assume that such trust is a precondition for effective participation in both private and public arenas (Etzioni, 1993; Fukuyama, 1995).

Through conscientization, a process that combines consciousness raising with social action (Freire, 1968), community intervention helps individuals connect personal and interpersonal circumstances to the wider environment (Bolland & McCallum, 2002). Most scholars agree that groups and intergroup networks with established norms and acknowledged social trust facilitate coordination, collaboration, and cooperation among their members for mutual benefit (Fukuyama, 1995; Newton, 2001; Putnam, 2000). These informal aspects of social relationships are reflected in what Putnam (2000) termed a community's level of "social associational engagement." There is near universal agreement that social capital can only be developed and used in a group context, although it is often difficult to measure (Orlitzky & Hirokawa, 2001).

In this context, community participation, also called citizen or civic participation or engagement, is defined as community involvement in the critical decision-making processes that affect the lives of community members (Daley & Marsiglia, 2000). It includes both rights (e.g., to vote) and responsibilities (to take an active role in decision making). Arnstein's (1969) "ladder of participation" characterizes such involvement on a continuum from citizen control to manipulation and underscores the role of power.

There is, however, persistent debate about the meaning of these somewhat ambiguous and overlapping concepts (DeFilippis, 2001; Edwards, Foley, & Diani, 2001; Skocpol & Fiorina, 1999; Wong, 2004). Schneider's (2007) distinction here is useful. She argues that civic engagement focuses outward to enhance the common good or that of the wider population of a defined community. In contrast, social capital focuses inward on sharing resources among members of a designated network.

The literature on social capital also makes a critical distinction between "bonding" and "bridging" capital (Portes, 2000). According to Putnam and Feldstein (2003), bonding social capital refers to the strengthening of close ties within groups to provide critical support and information for their members. In contrast, bridging social capital refers to the construction of reciprocal, horizontal, intergroup ties that transcend demographic boundaries. "Linking social capital" involves vertical ties, such as those among members of community-based organizations and government officials. Small group activities are critical components in both processes (Reisch & Guyet, 2006).

Considerable controversy also exists over the roles of culture and cultural identity in generating group and intergroup norms such as tolerance, mutuality, and trust and what types of intergroup relationships produce positive outcomes for the community as a whole (Claibourn & Martin, 2000). Some scholars argue that groups organized exclusively around cultural identity often produce negative outcomes for the community because of the exclusionary tendencies of group membership "rules" (Bargal, 2004; Wakefield & Poland, 2005; Woolcock, 2004). Others have sought to reframe the marginalization of some groups from a problem to an asset by focusing on the power that homogeneous cultural values can provide. They stress the critical role of "bonding social capital" in enabling group members "to successfully navigate the multiple worlds of family, school, neighborhood and community" (Farrell & Johnson, 2005, p. 502) or emphasize how culture, family, and spirituality can expand community engagement and build connections within communities (Gutierrez et al., 2005).

A recent innovation within the community intervention field is to develop new group structures—ranging from religious congregations to business cooperatives—that forge both bonding and bridging social capital. This approach assumes that such groups can help reduce intergroup tensions and overcome racial, ethnic, class, and religious divisions (Cnaan, Boddie, & Yancey, 2005). It harkens back to the "mutual aid model" of group development formulated by Schwartz (1986) in assuming that participation in collective action increases the likelihood of group members obtaining needed resources and acquiring "a sense of competence and efficacy" (Gitterman, 2004, p. 99).

These different goals are reflected in the differences between community development approaches that focus on community integration and those that emphasize community involvement. "Integration models" strive to strengthen internal community bonds and cohesion, while those that promote greater involvement concentrate on bringing the community into the larger decision-making process to ensure the sustainability of community change (Vidal & Gittell, 1998; Yabes, 2001). Both approaches regard these outcomes as means to empower community members, although the processes by which they are created differ substantially (Saegert & Winkel, 2004).

Some studies have found that homogeneous groups are more likely to generate stronger bonds of trust and collective power (Lopez & Stack, 2001). Groups also encourage more extensive participation in community activities and facilitate "people's capacity to prevent and solve ... problems" (Lelieveldt, 2004, p. 531). This is particularly true among disadvantaged populations. Other research indicates that creating a sense of shared values and goals where clear homogeneity among group members does not exist is crucial to the development of cooperation within the group (Wakefield & Poland, 2005). High levels of "bonding capital" in homogeneous communities can sometimes be detrimental to their overall well-being because the same factors that strengthen internal ties prevent the formation of linkages to external networks that possess critical resources and power (Uslaner & Conley, 2003).

The current literature contains few solutions to this dilemma. "Most analyses of neighborhood mobilization only focus on [its] structural dimension ... and pay relatively little attention to [issues] ... such as trust" (Bolland & McCallum, 2002; Lelieveldt, 2004, p. 533). There are few suggestions as to how the linkage between structures like networks and coalitions produces assets like trust, although the difficulty and importance of doing so across racial, ethnic, gender, and class lines are frequently emphasized (Chung Yan, 2004; Marshall & Stolle, 2004; Newton, 2001; Pearlmutter, 2002; Rivera & Erlich, 1998; Theiss-Morse & Hibbing, 2005; Uslaner & Conley, 2003).

Contemporary community planning efforts assume that community needs emerge from one or more of the following causes: resource deficiency, ineffective services, inappropriate structuring of services and resources, and the absence of institutional responsiveness (Weil, 2005). The purpose of this form of community intervention is to facilitate community members' involvement in defining their needs, determining the outcome goals of intervention, and developing criteria for measuring their attainment. Ideally, this involves the ongoing education of community residents and the provision of technical assistance in such areas as research and fund-raising (Adams & Nelson, 1997).

Among the central values of community-based social planning, Kahn (1969) lists maximum decentralization and dissemination of information at all stages of the process; the democratization of decision making through the use of a diverse array of planning devices; and the provision of greater control and power over the planning process to community residents, particularly in the areas of problem definition and evaluation. This requires a readiness to take risk, delegate authority, and, above all, create trust. Other critical features are the formation of ongoing collaborations at all stages, a focus on community strengths rather than deficits, the integration of cultural responsiveness, and the promotion of community building through participatory planning (North California Community Services Council, 1994).

Most models identify four basic steps in the community planning process: (1) The identification of community needs, (2) the development of alternative solutions, (3) the formation of detailed implementation plans, and (4) the determination and application of evaluative criteria. Recent literature has placed particular stress on the last step because of the importance of measuring intervention outcomes (O'Conner, 1995). Community planners now emphasize setting and maintaining standards, measuring performance through quantitative and qualitative techniques, and the ongoing monitoring of results.

Challenges in the field of community planning include the importance of distinguishing among effectiveness, efficiency, and effect (Lewis, 1985); the infusion of consistent values throughout the planning process; selecting methods of intervention to maximize effectiveness; developing indicators of effectiveness to be applied to the particular situation; applying standards and expectations to evaluate indicators; determining which organizational arrangements and processes best facilitate the attainment of effective outcomes; and mobilizing constituencies around effective performance criteria to maintain organizational autonomy (Weil, 2005).

One goal of community planning might be the generation of greater economic production through micro-enterprises or cooperatives. Another might seek to increase a community's economic capital by changing the lending practices of local financial institutions, attracting external sources of investment, and developing internal sources of capital (through peer lending, community loan funds, or individual assets accounts). A third goal might be the creation of more opportunities for local employment through the establishment of job training, skill development, or educational programs (Molina & Wallace, 1997).

There are various examples of such community intervention strategies in the United States and abroad. Perhaps the best known is the development of so-called Enterprise Zones, which focus on public/private cooperation and the relaxation of tax and environmental rules in economically depressed neighborhoods. Another is "Buy Black" initiatives, such as Recycling Black Dollars in Los Angeles. The most famous non-U.S. approach is the Grameen Bank, which emphasize micro-enterprise development. Some of its elements have been incorporated in assets-focused strategies in the United States (Sherraden, 2001).

An alternative model focuses on the neighborhood as a center of coproduction. It has several variations. In one, "natural helpers" or helping networks replace professionals and focus on specific issues such as crime prevention or child care. In another approach, the neighborhood association replaces the governance role of municipality. Examples include cooperatives, community development corporations, citizen planning boards, and neighborhood groups that focus on housing. In a third model, the delivery of a service is shared between a neighborhood entity and an external (professional or governmental entity) such as in the Hope VI Project during the 1990s. Such models differ from citizen participation in two ways. They allow communities to be more autonomous and focus not merely on replacing actors, but on changing systems.

An important research question in this area addresses the types of organizations that are most suitable for a particular community at a particular time (Delgado, 1994). Another analyzes what is the most effective role for community organizers or planners, especially in multicultural contexts. A third explores which strategies are most effective in different circumstances and which skills community members need to implement them (Kahn, 1991; Rothman, 2001; Trapp, 2004; Warren, 1975).

Community development and social action share a common belief in the possibility of successful change, the significant role played by organizers, the need to identify salient issues, and the importance of creating sustainable organizations. Staples (2004) describes this type of community intervention as "collective action at the grassroots level to address common problems and to bring about social change" (p. 344). Although social action has no clear ideological component, its advocates have generally been associated with the left wing of the social work field. Proponents of social action often assume that constituents are members of low-power groups or otherwise oppressed populations and that change efforts will be resisted by the defenders of the status quo. A goal of social action, therefore, is to accumulate sufficient power to pressure those who control critical resources to make concessions, negotiate, and redistribute societal goods. Fisher (2005) identifies several shared principles of social action organizing: (a) the organizer is a catalyst, not a leader, in the change process; (b) organizing focuses on the promotion of participatory democracy; and (c) the development of indigenous leaders is a critical component of social change (p. 47).

A primary emphasis in social action is on the importance of developing and implementing effective strategies and tactics. Most analyses, however, tend to be based on case or historical examples, rather than empirical research, and reflect authors' ideological and political biases. Since communities have unique histories and problems and since experimental designs are difficult to construct in the field of community intervention, it is more difficult to generalize about what constitutes effective social action than other forms of social work practice. It is widely accepted, however, that two critical factors are choosing the right target and selecting appropriate tactics.

Community intervention strategies are distinct from tactics in that they involve the overall plan of a group or organization to achieve its goals. According to Kahn (1991), the central question in the development of a strategy is, How are events and actions used to identify people's self-interests and to help people learn to struggle? A good strategy is thought out well in advance, builds on the experience of people, involves people in planning and implementation, is flexible and contextualized, has depth, is feasible, is based on people's culture, and is educational. Criteria for strategy selection include clarity about goals; identification of the forces to be defeated or neutralized and of potential allies; assessment of the most effective approaches to offset the opposition; recognition of the risks involved for people and the organization; evaluation of the potential aftermath of action (including its unintended consequences); and awareness of timing, context, and history (Netting, Kettner, & McMurry, 2001; Rubin & Rubin, 2004). The evidence indicates that certain guidelines are conducive for developing effective strategies. These include consistent communication with constituents, conducting ongoing research and evaluation, and emphasizing tangible gains and short-term goals (Homan, 2004).

A major distinction exists between proponents of consensus and conflict strategies in their assumptions, goals, purposes, means of communication, patterns of interorganizational relationships, and overall attitude toward systems or structural change. Generally, the former is associated with community development and planning and the latter with social action and advocacy. A consensus model is more suitable in situations of relatively equal distribution of power, where common ground exists, and when shared values, interests, and goals are either present or possible. A conflict model is used when there are power disparities, when resource distribution resembles a "zero sum game," and where sharp differences of values and interests are present (Sample, 1979). Both models assume that effective strategies require organizing *and* mobilizing community members.

Scholars of social action and social movements such as Morris (1984) point out that community mobilization often begins in "free spaces," such as beauty parlors and churches in the civil rights movement, YWCA's and consciousness raising groups in the feminist movement, and bath houses and bars in the LGBT movement. These spaces allow individuals to acquire a heightened sense of self and group identity and inspire people to defend their rights, traditions, and institutions. In the process, they also change their ways of learning and relating and acquire deeper self-definition and consciousness. The emphasis on organizational autonomy, symbolized by space and cultural freedom, stimulates a conflict between traditional and new modes of behavior (Delgado, 2000).

Most analyses of community mobilization take such group interest for granted. Yet, studies have determined that many organized groups fail to mobilize; some mobilized groups fail to act collectively; and some collective actors fail to contend for power or quickly disappear (Tilly, 1978). These findings produce several key questions.

First, how do we identify a group's interests to help formulate strategies? Most writers argue in favor of one of two approaches. The first infers the group's interests from its words and actions. This, however, leaves unanswered certain questions: To which part of the group do we pay attention and which of its actions are most significant? The second suggests inferring a group's interest from an analysis of the connections between its interests and social position. This requires a great deal of knowledge about the group, a challenge which is more complex in an increasingly multicultural society.

From an evidence-based perspective, there are problems with both approaches. First, groups are often unaware of their interests. Evidence is difficult to identify and synthesize and is often scarce or in conflict. Second, both approaches reflect the potential bias of outside organizers. There is also a conflict between a group's short-term and long-term interests that makes it difficult, if not impossible, to determine what constitutes the group's "real interest" (Skocpol & Fiorina, 1999; Tilly, 1978). A related problem is how to distinguish and act on differences between individual and group interests. One possible resolution is to recognize differences as a factor in the ability to identify and achieve collective interests. The greater the conflict, the more costly collective action is to participants.

Another important factor in strategy development is the legitimization of a group's issue, organization, or goals. It is critical here to recognize who is determining the effort's legitimacy and to understand legitimacy as a process that changes over time. Community intervention strategies acquire legitimacy largely on the basis of extrinsic factors, such as effectiveness, credibility and authority, and intrinsic factors, such as their ability to empower members to act and overcome helplessness and hopelessness.

Tactical legitimacy involves the relationship between a group's choice of tactics and its organizational legitimacy. In addition, the organization's relationship with other groups (e.g., coalitions) and leadership composition are significant. Finally, issue legitimacy occurs when the organization defines or frames the issue clearly and connects it to organizational or societal values, ethics, and morals. A recurrent dilemma for community organizations is how they can acquire legitimacy from external sources without adopting the value system of the structures they are trying to change (Bobo et al., 2001; Fisher, 1997; Fraser & Kirk, 2005).

Tactics are the specific activities carried out by an organization as part of its strategy (Netting et al., 2001). They are designed to create the pressures necessary to win on a particular issue and help build the organization through the participation of members (Kahn, 1991). Tactics relate to the manner in which a strategy is enacted and the tools that will be employed (Alinsky, 1971).

Kahn (1991) developed a useful categorization of social action tactics. "Social tactics" include marches, sit-ins, rallies, and demonstrations. "Real power tactics" can be either economic (boycotts, strikes) or political (civil disobedience). Less extreme power tactics, "political/normative tactics," include such mainstream activities as endorsing candidates, registering voters, mass lobbying, media advocacy, and testifying at public hearings. A "self-help tactic" includes the development of programs run by and for the organization's membership whose purpose is to establish separate or parallel institutions.

A final component of many tactics is often referred to as an "action"—a specific event designed to carry out a strategy and help an organization win on an issue. A series of actions comprise a campaign. Actions are the lifeblood of organizations, in which their underlying theories, analysis, structure, and resources are put into practice by communicating the organization's message to constituents, potential constituents, supporters, and opponents. They have two general purposes: to win a concession or obtain media exposure and to build the organization (Sampson). Nadler (1973) points out that militant action is not an end in itself. Unless it moves an organization closer to its objectives, it has failed because of the strain it puts on all parties to a community conflict.

In sum, studies of community intervention stress the importance of matching strategy and tactics to the target and goals. No tactic is ever used by itself but is always part of a carefully planned campaign and linked to a broader strategy. An action, therefore, is only one phase of many to achieve an organization's objectives. Other phases include building the organization, cultivating allies, and developing strategy.

As stated earlier, effective community intervention requires the identification of appropriate (i.e., winnable) issues around which to organize and mobilize communities. Factors that determine if an issue is winnable include the intensity of motivation among community members, the importance of positive reinforcement (e.g., through early "victories"), and the extent to which the intervention process emphasizes consciousness raising. The identification of issues, by definition, involves controversy. A problem may be widely shared, but an issue will be shaped by the specific solutions proposed, the resources used to solve it, and the political realities that affect solutions.

Several techniques have proven to be most effective in the successful identification of community issues. These include listening and encouraging people to talk about their hopes, anger, and fears. Another is visiting people in their homes, workplaces, and community sites and getting them to talk about what they think, pinning them down, exploring around what issues they would take action, who their friends and enemies are. Specific methods to obtain such information may include door-to-door canvassing or surveying or organizing small group meetings. These techniques help the community explore different ways the issue can be resolved, choose an acceptable resolution, and state the issue with increasing clarity and specificity (Trapp, 2004).

It is widely accepted that interorganizational relationships are critical to the effectiveness of community interventions. Such relationships provide access to resources and constraints on self-interest (Katz, Lazer, Arrow, & Contractor, 2004). These relationships occur through four types of linkages: (1) through informal systems, such as families, friends, and neighbors; (2) through quasi-formal and self-help or mutual aid systems; (3) through professional organizations; and (4) through such structured interorganizational relationships as collaboratives (Fellin, 2001; Reitan, 1998). In most communities multiple overlapping networks exists because group boundaries are not always clear (Kavanaugh, Reese, Carroll, & Rosson, 2005).

Recent research on the impact of intergroup relationships has produced "complex, and at times, contradictory findings" (Ziersch, Baum, MacDougall, & Putland, 2005, p. 81). For example, Uslaner and Conley (2003) and Green and Brock (2005) challenge Putnam's (2000) assumption that participation in *any form* of civic activities is what matters most. They argue that the *type of participation* may be more significant. Other research presents a more nuanced view of the impact and value of social groups within communities and society as a whole. There is widespread recognition that the presence of social capital can benefit one group while harming others (Lopez & Stack, 2001).

A prominent form of interorganizational collaboration is a coalition, usually defined as a time-limited organization of organizations that shares articulated goals, pools relevant resources, engages in conscious communication, develops joint strategies and tactics, and agrees on the distribution of benefits (Mizrahi & Rosenthal, 2001; Roberts-DeGenarro, 1997; Roberts-DeGenarro & Mizrahi, 2005). Such organizations take diverse forms and are often characterized by dynamic tensions. These tensions emerge because coalitions serve multiple, often conflicting purposes. These may include achieving political objectives that a single group cannot, building one's organization by "borrowing" power, or preventing a serious division between potential allies or rivals.

Research on coalitions reveals that combining two or more powerless organizations does not create power (Mizrahi & Rosenthal, 2001; Mondros & Wilson, 1994; Roberts-DeGenarro, 1997). Studies also suggest that successful coalitions contain most of the following features: broad geographic representation; large memberships with clearly defined roles; a distinctive ideology and attractive, clearly stated value positions; the ability to frame issues concisely; the use of a common language; ease of mobilization; large amount of tangible and intangible resources; and a dominant group of actors (Reisch, 1987; Roberts-DeGenarro, 1997).

Scholars have noted that potential problems may arise in forming a coalition due to differences over goals or ideology. They may appear because of differences in the level of commitment of the partners, disagreements about the distribution of power or responsibilities, organizational and personal styles or history, and the diversity of demographic characteristics. Studies also underscore the challenges of building and maintaining interracial coalitions and emphasize the importance of finding common issues to create such alliances (Crowfoot & Chesler, 1996).

Sustaining coalitions is equally challenging. All members must be provided with material, intangible, and ideological incentives. The coalition's structure and patterns of decision making must balance the needs of various organizational cultures while maintaining sufficient formality to be effective. It must focus on short-term projects while keeping in mind the relationships of these projects to the coalition's long-term goals. Finally, it must develop independent and reliable funding sources (Roberts-DeGenarro & Mizrahi, 2005).

Researchers have also identified a broad range of obstacles to successful community intervention. These include community members' fear of change; lack of time, energy, resources, skills, and information; cynicism regarding politics and community participation; pervasive individualism; lack of personal experience; lack of belief in one's ability to create change; and intra- and intergroup conflicts often based on class, racial, ethnic, cultural, and gender divisions (Fisher & Karger, 1997; Kahn, 1991; Rubin & Rubin, 2004). Recently, the community intervention literature has also stressed the need for practitioners to possess certain attributes to work effectively with racial and ethnic minorities.

In their provocative essay, Rivera and Erlich (1998) criticize the traditional profile of an organizer and posit an alternative set of essential characteristics. These include familiarity with the community's customs, traditions, social networks, and values; the possession of similar cultural and racial identification; an intimate knowledge of language and subgroup slang, and local leadership styles; a conceptual framework for political and economic analysis; knowledge of past organizing strategies, their strengths and limitations; use of conscientization and empowerment; knowledge of organizational behavior and decision-making and community psychology; skills in evaluation, participatory research, program planning, development and administrative management; and awareness of one's personal strengths and limitations (Bankhead & Erlich, 2005).

In contrast to traditional male-dominated models of practice, feminist models of community intervention are based on such principles as an emphasis on process, a focus on consciousness raising and praxis, attention to wholeness and unity of community work, a reconceptualization of power and empowerment, the democratic structuring of organizations, a recognition of the relationship between the personal and the political, and an orientation to structural change (Hyde, 2005; Weil, 1986). Most of the literature on feminist models of community intervention, however, is written from an advocacy perspective, and there is limited empirical research that supports its underlying assumptions and principles (Naples, 1998; Roth, 1998; Stall & Stoecker, 1998). Even feminists agree that "feminist community practice . . . must become more analytically robust . . . moving beyond descriptive modeling to critical self-reflection and evaluation" (Hyde, 2005, p. 367). They also agree it must become more multicultural.

In this regard, other scholars have proposed alternative approaches to community intervention that are more suitable to a diverse society, such as multicultural community organizing or MCO (Bradshaw, Soifer, & Gutierrez, 1994; Gutierrez, Lewis, Nagda, Wernick, & Shore,, 2005). Gutierrez (1997) defines MCO as "methods of practice that work toward the development of communities of color while creating mechanisms for greater intergroup interaction and change" (p. 250). It focuses on social change and social justice, not just the development of services. MCO emphasizes community empowerment and seeks to create horizontal linkages within communities, even as it strives to form extra-community alliances.

MCO is grounded in an "ethno-conscious" approach to practice that appreciates and recognizes strengths in communities of color. Its focus is on power and the confrontation of inequalities at all levels, and its primary goals are the development of partnership, participation, collaboration, and capacity building. To achieve its principal objectives, MCO adopts a four-level strategy that includes the identification of issues within specific communities, motivating behavioral change in individuals engaging in high-risk behaviors, organizing individuals within communities, and mobilizing community-based organizations and institutions to work together. These strategies are based on the assumption that building organizations within communities of color is a prerequisite for the construction of effective and viable multiracial coalitions that cross existing boundaries and forge new relationships (Gutierrez et al., 2005).

Even its proponents acknowledge, however, a lack of research evidence evaluating MCO methods. "The field of research on evaluating community organization methods has focused primarily on the effectiveness on changing individual-level outcomes [and] . . . has been primarily descriptive. . . . Only recently has [it] begun to look specifically at the effectiveness of methods for engaging citizens in community-level efforts or on strengthening community institutions" (Gutierrez, 2005, p. 256).

A final "alternative" model of community intervention, popular education, focuses on helping people understand and act on their social environment through consciousness-raising, praxis, and conscientization. It strives to develop specific skills to engage in power analysis, address power deficits, and increase power resources. It often uses cultural activities, such as theater, with considerable effectiveness (Boal, 1998).

Conceptually, popular education is similar to empowerment theory in its emphasis on the use of cocreated knowledge and dialogue and collective action, and its linkage of the personal and the political. Popular education exalts democratic participation, not as an abstract principle, but specifically "to preserve culture and insure that oppressive regimes . . . have little room to grow" (Finn, Jacobson, & Campana, 2005, p. 332). Groups become havens of security and stability, which instill a collectivist spirit through self-help and mutual aid. The group is a sanctuary for members to "experience new ways of acting and interacting" based on their new perceptions of self and the world (Breton, 2004, p. 60).

LIMITATIONS OF THE EVIDENCE

There are numerous reasons why it is difficult to measure the effectiveness of community interventions. First, there is frequently a lack of clarity regarding its goals. Second, the scope of interventions requires us to determine what constitutes effective practice in vastly different settings. Third, there is a need to differentiate between outcome and process results and apply these measures to different contexts.

Fourth, many forms of community intervention have an explicit or implicit goal of preventing community problems (or preventing them from becoming more severe). By definition, prevention efforts are harder to assess, in part because of the range of potential intervening variables (Christakopoulou et al., 2001; O'Conner, 1995; Orlitzky & Hirokawa, 2001). Fifth, in many community intervention efforts there is an unintentional conflation of long-term and short-term goals and objectives. This often leads to vague or conflicting definitions of "success." When multiple actors are involved, whose perspective on success should have priority?

An underlying source of difficulty in measuring the effectiveness of community intervention lies in the ambiguous meaning of frequently used terms, such as empowerment, agency, well-being, multiculturalism, and even the word "community" itself. There is also confusion over whether researchers are measuring the impact of intervention efforts on community participation or the attainment of substantive goals and objectives. As a result, there is often a lack of "multiple sources of scientific evidence" establishing what constitutes effective community intervention, particularly in the areas of grassroots organizing and social action where there has been little integration of "the best available research" with the equivalent of clinical expertise (American Psychological Association Presidential Task Force on Evidence-Based Practice, 2006).

There is more extensive literature on community planning and community development, particularly on issues related to civic participation and the self-concept of community members. Research on social capital and the role of groups in community intervention efforts is also more fully developed. Some of the findings of this research, however, are contradictory. Unfortunately, particularly given the current stress on evidence-based practice, many models of community intervention continue to be based more on ideology or unique case experience than generalizable empirical evidence.

This often makes it difficult for scholars and practitioners to think outside their "ideological boxes." Consequently, community intervention is often equated solely with certain types of activities which are syntonic with social work's dominant ideology. As a result, the educational value of the successful experiences of these groups is often considered irrelevant. Finally, the evaluation of community intervention is hampered by the shifting goals and by the many ethical dilemmas such interventions experience.

Another obstacle is that different theoretical approaches to community intervention define effectiveness or success in different ways. For example, the direct action model (Alinsky, 1971) focuses on organization-building, the acquisition of power and resources, and the attainment of tangible "victories" to inspire people. By contrast, the insurrectionary model developed by Cloward and Piven (1999) emphasizes spontaneous action rather than organization building. Social movement theory (Fisher, 1994; Gamson, 1975) examines the attainment of resources, power, rights, and access by community groups and their relationship to institutions of power. Complicating matters further, feminist organizing (Hyde, 2005; Weil, 1986) focuses on process issues such as enhanced participation and democratic (horizontal) decision-making that relies on consensus and consciousness-raising. In a similar vein, multicultural organizing stresses increased cultural awareness and matching community intervention methods to people's needs (Delgado, 1994; Gutierrez et al., 2005; Rivera & Erlich, 1998).

Equally difficult challenges exist in determining the effectiveness of planning efforts. Many of the underlying assumptions of the planning approach to community intervention, such as the possibility of retaining a "neutral" perspective, have been challenged (Weil, 2005). Other fundamental questions remain to be resolved. These include the relative impact of centralized or decentralized planning; the balance between expertise and democratic participation; the differences between short and long-term planning goals in assessing effectiveness; the significance of auspice for the goals established in the planning process and the criteria used to evaluate their attainment; and the relationship of community planning to social justice, social change, community self-determination, and empowerment (Fellin, 2001; Fraser & Kirk, 2005; Weil, 2005).

IMPLICATIONS FOR SOCIAL WORK

It is widely acknowledged that community intervention can be a means to integrate the delivery of social services into broader social change goals in three distinct ways. First, intervention efforts can create direct change in the community itself by creating new or revised services or advocating for greater accessibility to existing services. Through the involvement of community members in the planning and evaluation of services, people can acquire skills to effect change in the services they need (Adams & Nelson, 1997).

Second, the nature of the service delivery process itself can be designed to empower individuals and families (Gutierrez et al., 1998). Finally, services can be organized with a specific community change impact in mind. Thus, structural change can occur through the replacement of critical actors and the reallocation of existing roles within the service delivery organization or its affiliates (Hare, 2003). It can also occur by redistributing rights and obligations in the community's reward structure.

Although they have acknowledged the importance of state and national policies in addressing constituents' needs, community practitioners have focused primarily on practice at the local or neighborhood level during the past century. Common principles have included social justice, self-determination, democratic participation and leadership, and, more recently, empowerment, dialogue, and the creation of critical consciousness. During the past 20 years, tensions have emerged between a locality-focused model of community intervention and those based on common identity (Bankhead & Erlich, 2005).

Today, "the value base of community practice not only respects the dignity of the individual but focuses on the interdependence of families and communities . . . and the development of fairness, equity and equality (e.g., social justice)" (Weil, 2005, p. 125). Economic globalization, however, has created a new set of challenges to prevailing assumptions about community intervention. Its effects include the growing inability of communities to solve local problems whose sources are in the international arena; the withdrawal of government support for community development; the decline in influence of a long-time ally, organized labor; and changes in the role, culture, and status of nongovernmental (i.e., nonprofit) community-based organizations (Reisch, 2005).

Proposed responses to this challenge vary. Some community practitioners suggest the abandonment of geographically centered models of practice. Others focus on community self-sufficiency and promote the development of alternative or "counter" institutions at the local level. This issue has surfaced frequently in recent research on the role of social capital in community intervention and development, particularly in diverse communities (Claibourn & Martin, 2000; Colombo & Senatore, 2005; Hutchinson, 2004; Hyman, 2002; Uslaner & Conley, 2003). Thus, "the formation of a viable, community-based movement is hampered both by the existence of seemingly intractable racial, ethnic, and religious divisions and the absence of organizational structures that could unite the multiple, disparate community organizing projects currently underway" (Reisch, 2005, p. 541).

Many of the problems facing contemporary community intervention efforts, therefore, stem from dramatic shifts in the political-economic environment. In addition to economic globalization, these include ideological attacks on the concept of social welfare, the industrialization of social work practice, and the privatization of major features of community life (Fisher & Karger, 1997). Proposed solutions often include organizational reform or the use of alternative models of intervention to promote greater mutuality, less hierarchy, and increased control by community residents (Fabricant & Fisher, 2002; Farrell & Johnson, 2005; Kretzmann & McKnight, 1993).

Ironically, many of these change-oriented themes have now been incorporated, at least in rhetoric, into the core mission of the social work profession (National Association of Social Workers, 1996). Attempts to apply these principles in community intervention, however, have produced several significant contradictions (Reamer, 2006). One contradiction is between the application of principles of distribute justice and a "value-free" community practice. Another is between the emphasis on empowerment or self-determination and the use of an empiricist model of science that diminishes constituents' role in defining problems and solutions. A third is between democratic participation and empowerment and the antidemocratic or paternalistic tendencies of some organizers. A fourth is the potential conflict between community self-determination and social justice because of a lack of clarity about how the common good is defined and by whom. Finally, many community intervention practitioners face ethical dilemmas when they are forced to choose between equally unsatisfactory alternatives or confront political situations in which ethical principles conflict with legal or organizational obligations (Hardina, 2004).

CONCLUSION

Over the past century, practitioners of community intervention can point to numerous accomplishments. They have put items on the political agenda that had previously been overlooked or ignored. They have won important victories, particularly at the local level and have sometimes redressed the balance of community power. Their efforts have developed new leaders and, especially in recent years, have created multiple training grounds for youth (Checkoway & Gutierrez, 2006). Finally, community intervention has created more accountable decision-making processes and developed replicable models of community change, development, and planning. At the same time, community intervention efforts have been limited by a variety of factors including fragmentation within and between communities, particularly along racial, ethnic, and class lines; difficulty in determining who should be the targets of intervention and through what means; an inability to articulate a comprehensive, unifying vision of community development and change; and a perpetual lack of sufficient resources (Delgado, 2000).

In recent years, there have been several notable innovations in the field of community intervention that create guarded optimism for the future. They include the identification of new issues and the application of new methods of analysis; greater collaboration through training intermediaries with a particular impact on local leadership development; greater cooperation between community organizations and universities; the construction of new networks, often based on identity; and the use of new technologies such as the Internet (Hick & McNutt, 2002). In a different vein, Specht and Courtney (1994) propose reviving a model of community-based social care based on communitarian principles (Bellah, Madsen, Sullivan, Swidler, & Tipton, 1991; Etzioni, 1993). This approach, however, does not clarify how the "community" should be defined or whose conception of community should take priority.

Fisher and Kling (1993) have commented that change efforts are increasingly based in either geographic or interest communities rather than the workplace. Some of these efforts involve the development of interorganizational ties that transcend traditional boundaries of class, race, and culture (Bystydzienski & Schacht, 2001). To a greater extent, community struggles reflect contests over ideology and cultural or social identity. While different trends are emerging in different parts of the world, there is a now widespread reliance on strategies like community self-help and empowerment.

Others (Bankhead & Erlich, 2005; Rivera & Erlich, 1998) caution, however, that persistent issues have impeded the progress of community intervention in the past, in particular the effects of racism in all of its dimensions. They point out that the meaning of minority status in the United States is changing and becoming more complex as a consequence of recent immigration and intermarriage. Their agenda for community intervention in the twenty-first century emphasizes the need to build coalitions that confront inequality in all its forms through both traditional means (e.g., politics and legislative reform) and more innovative modes of community intervention, such as the use of the Internet. The effectiveness of such innovations, however, has yet to be fully assessed.

In their discussion of the future of community intervention, Wenocur and Soifer (1997) argue that many social movements rooted in the 1960s never really ended. With the assistance of liberal foundations, they have become increasingly professionalized, especially about fund-raising and training. Organizing efforts have also shifted from an emphasis on confrontation to collaborative partnerships with business and local government leaders particularly around community economic development. Like Delgado (1994), Rivera and Erlich (1998) and others, they acknowledge the shift among urban communities of color toward organizing on the basis of identity or interest rather than geography, largely outside of professional social work. The future of community intervention, therefore, might involve the formation of new coalitions, perhaps across national boundaries, a process enabled recently by technological developments.

Most authors agree that community intervention in the twenty-first century will be affected by such factors as economic globalization, demographic changes in urban centers, declining faith in the efficacy of the state, the growing importance of regionalism in the face of states' fiscal crises, and policy devolution. Other writers emphasize the growing influence of feminist models of organizing, the growing use of sophisticated databases, and greater awareness of the relationship between funding sources and strategy development. In the twenty-first century, many long-standing community intervention roles will continue to be useful, even if modified by changing contexts. "Community social workers will still be called on to help communities build democratic institutions, facilitate individual, group, and organizational development; and engage in facilitating inclusive methods and structures that will model democratic outcomes" (Weil & Gamble, 2005, p. 141).

REFERENCES

Adams, P., & Nelson, K. (1997). Reclaiming community: An integrative approach to human services. *Administration in Social Work*, *21*(3/4), 67–81.

Alinsky, S. (1971). *Rules for radicals*. New York: Vintage Books.

American Psychological Association Presidential Task Force on Evidence-Based Practice. (2006). Evidence-based practice in psychology. *American Psychologist*, *61*(4), 271–285.

Arnstein, S. R. (July, 1969). A ladder of citizen participation. *Journal of the American Planning Association*, *35*(4), 216–224.

Bakalinsky, R. (1984). The small group in community organization practice. *Social Work with Groups*, *7*(2), 87–96.

Bankhead, T., & Erlich, J. (2005). Diverse populations and community practice. In M. Weil, M. Reisch, D. N. Gamble, L. M. Gutierrez, E. A. Mulroy, & R. A. Cnaan (Eds.), *The handbook of community practice* (pp. 59–83). Thousand Oaks, CA: Sage.

Bargal, D. (2004). Groups for reducing intergroup conflict. In C. Garvin, L. Gutierrez, & M. Galinsky (Eds.), *Handbook of social work with groups* (pp. 292–306). New York: Guilford Press.

Bellah, R., Madsen, R., Sullivan, W. M., Swidler, A., & Tipton, S. M. (1991). *The good society*. New York: Vintage Books.

Berger, P., & Neuhaus, R. (1977). *To empower people: The role of mediating structures in public policy*. Washington, DC: American Enterprise Institute.

Betten, N., & Austin, M. J. (Eds.). (1990). *The roots of community organizing, 1917–1939*. Philadelphia: Temple University Press.

Boal, A. (1998). *Legislative theatre: Using performance to make politics* (A. Jackson, Trans.). London: Routledge.

Bobo, K., Kendall, J., & Max, S. (2001). *Organizing for social change* (3rd ed.). Santa Ana, CA: Seven Locks Press.

Bolland, J. M., & McCallum, D. M. (2002). Neighboring and community mobilization in high poverty inner-city neighborhoods. *Urban Affairs Review*, *38*(1), 42–69.

Boyte, H. (1981). *The backyard revolution*. Philadelphia: Temple University Press.

Bradshaw, C., Soifer, S., & Gutierrez, L. (1994). Toward a hybrid model for effective organizing with women of color. *Journal of Community Practice*, *1*(1), 25–41.

Brager, G., & Purcell, F. (Eds.). (1967). *Community action against poverty: Readings from the mobilization experience*. New Haven, CT: College and University Press.

Brager, G., & Specht, H. (1973). *Community organizing*. New York: Free Press.

Breton, M. (2004). An empowerment perspective. In C. D. Garvin, L. M. Gutierrez, & M. Galinsky (Eds.), *Handbook of social work with groups* (pp. 58–75). New York: Guilford Press.

Brilliant, E. (1990). *The United Way: Dilemmas of organized charity*. New York: Columbia University Press.

Buell, B., & Associates. (1952). *Community planning for human services*. New York: Columbia University Press.

Bystydzienski, J., & Schacht, S. (Eds.). (2001). *Forging radical alliances across difference: Coalition politics for the new millennium*. Lanham, MD: Rowman and Littlefield.

Checkoway, B. & Gutierrez, L. M. (Eds.) (2006). *Young people making community change*. Binghamton, NY: Haworth Press.

Christakopoulou, S., Dawson, J., & Gari, A. (2001). The Community Well-Being Questionnaire: Theoretical context and initial assessment of its reliability and validity. *Social Indicators Research*, *32*, 321.

Chung Yan, M. (2004). Bridging the fragmented community: Revitalizing settlement houses in the global era. *Journal of Community Practice*, *12*(1/2), 51–69.

Claibourn, M. P., & Martin, P. S. (2000). Trusting and joining? An empirical test of the reciprocal nature of social capital. *Political Behavior*, *22*(4), 267–291.

Cloward, R., & Piven, F. F. (1999). Disruptive dissensus: People and power in the industrial age. In J. Rothman (Ed.), *Reflections on community organization: Enduring themes and critical issues* (pp. 165–193). Itasca, IL: Peacock.

Cnaan, R., Boddie, S., & Yancey, G. (2005). Rise up and build the cities: Faith-based community organizing. In M. Weil, M. Reisch, D. N. Gamble, L. M. Gutierrez, E. A. Mulroy, & R. A. Cnaan. (Eds.), *The handbook of community practice* (pp. 372–387). Thousand Oaks, CA: Sage.

Colombo, M., & Senatore, A. (2005). The discursive construction of community identity. *Journal of Community and Applied Social Psychology*, *15*(1), 48–62.

Coser, L. (1956). *The functions of social conflict*. Glencoe, IL: Free Press.

Crowfoot, J., & Chesler, M. (1996). White men's roles in multicultural coalitions. In B. Owser & R. Hunt (Eds.), *Impacts of racism on White Americans* (2nd ed., pp. 203–229). Thousand Oaks, CA: Sage.

Daley, J. M., & Marsiglia, F. F. (2000). Community participation: Old wine in new bottles? *Journal of Community Practice, 8*(1) 61–86.

DeFilippis, J. (2001). The myth of social capital in community development. *Housing Policy Debate, 12*(4), 781–806.

Delgado, G. (1994). *Beyond the politics of place: New directions in community organizing in the 1990s.* Oakland, CA: Applied Research Center.

Delgado, M. (2000). *Community social work practice in an urban context.* New York: Oxford University Press.

de Tocqueville, A. (Ed.). (2004). *Democracy in America* (A. Goldhammer, Trans.). New York: Library of America.

Dewey, J. (1916). *Democracy and education: An introduction to the philosophy of education.* New York: Free Press.

Edwards, B., Foley, M., & Diani, M. (2001). *Beyond Tocqueville: Civil society and the social capital debate in comparative perspective.* Hanover, NH: Tufts University Press.

Ephross, P., & Vassil, T. (2004). Group work with working groups. In C. D. Garvin, L. M. Gutierrez, & M. Galinsky (Eds.), *Handbook of social work with groups* (pp. 400–414). New York: Guilford Press.

Etzioni, A. (1993). *The spirit of community: Rights, responsibilities, and the communitarian agenda.* New York: Crown.

Fabricant, M., & Fisher, R. (2002). Agency based community building in low income neighborhoods: A praxis framework. *Journal of Community Practice, 10*(2), 1–22.

Farrell, W. C., Jr., & Johnson, J. H., Jr. (2005). Investing in socially and economically distressed communities: Comprehensive strategies for inner city community and youth development. In M. Weil, M. Reisch, D. N. Gamble, L. M. Gutierrez, E. A. Mulroy, & R. A. Cnaan (Eds.), *The handbook of community practice* (pp. 494–507). Thousand Oaks, CA: Sage.

Fellin, P. (1998). Development of capital in poor, inner-city neighborhoods. *Journal of Community Practice, 5*(3), 87–98.

Fellin, P. (2001). *The community and the social worker* (3rd. ed.). Itasca, IL: Peacock.

Finn, J. L., Jacobson, M., & Campana, J. D. (2005). Participatory research, popular education and popular theater: Contributions to group work. In C. D. Garvin, L. M. Gutierrez, & M. Galinsky. (Eds.), *Handbook of social work with groups* (pp. 326–343). New York: Guilford Press.

Fisher, R. (1994). *Let the people decide: Community organizing in America* (2nd ed.). New York: Twayne.

Fisher, R. (1997). Social action community organization: Proliferation, persistence, roots, and prospects. In M. Minkler (Ed.), *Community organizing and community building for health* (pp. 53–67). New Brunswick, NJ: Rutgers University Press.

Fisher, R. (2005). History, context, and emerging issues for community practice. In M. Weil, M. Reisch, D. N. Gamble, L. M. Gutierrez, E. A. Mulroy, & R. A. Cnaan (Eds.), *The handbook of community practice* (pp. 34–58). Thousand Oaks, CA: Sage.

Fisher, R., & Karger, H. J. (1997). *Social work and community in a private world.* White Plains, NY: Longman.

Fisher, R., & Kling, J. (Eds.). (1993). *Mobilizing the community: Local politics in the era of the global city.* Newbury Park, CA: Sage.

Follett, M. P. (1920). *The new state: Group organization, the solution of popular government.* New York: Longmans, Green.

Fraser, J., & Kirk, E. (2005). Understanding community building in urban America. *Journal of Poverty, 9*(1), 23–43.

Freire, P. (1968). *Pedagogy of the oppressed.* New York: Seabury Press.

Freire, P. (1973). *Education for critical consciousness.* New York: Seabury Press.

Fukuyama, F. (1995). *Trust: The social virtues and the creation of prosperity.* New York: Free Press.

Gamble, D., & Hoff, M. (2005). Sustainable community development. In M. Weil, M. Reisch, D. N. Gamble, L. M. Gutierrez, E. A. Mulroy, & R.A. Cnaan (Eds.), *The handbook of community practice* (pp. 169–188). Thousand Oaks, CA: Sage.

Gamson, W. (1975). *The strategy of social protest.* Homewood, IL: Dorsey Press.

Garvin, C. D., & Cox, F. M. (2001). A history of community organizing since the Civil War with special reference to oppressed communities. In J. Rothman, J. L. Erlich, & J. E. Tropman (Eds.), *Strategies of community intervention* (6th ed., pp. 65–100). Itasca, IL: Peacock.

Gitterman, A. (2004). The mutual aid model. In C. D. Garvin, L. M. Gutierrez, & M. Galinsky (Eds.), *Handbook of social work with groups* (pp. 93–110). New York: Guilford Press.

Glugoski, G., Reisch, M., & Rivera, F. G. (1994). A holistic ethno-cultural paradigm: A new model for community organization teaching and practice. *Journal of Community Practice, 1*(1), 81–98.

Green, M. C., & Brock, T. C. (2005). Organizational membership vs. informal interaction: Contributions to skills and perceptions that build social capital. *Political Psychology, 26*(1), 1–25.

Gutierrez, L. M. (1997). Multicultural community organizing. In M. Reisch & E. Gambrill (Eds.), *Social work in the twenty-first century* (pp. 249–259). Thousand Oaks, CA: Pine Forge Press.

Gutierrez, L. M., & Lewis, E. A. (1998). A feminist perspective on organizing with women of color. In F. Rivera & J. Erlich (Eds.), *Community organizing in a diverse society* (3rd ed., pp. 97–116). Boston: Allyn & Bacon.

Gutierrez, L. M., Lewis, E. A., Nagda, B.A., Wernick, L, & Shore, S. (2005). Multicultural community practice strategies and intergroup empowerment. In M. Weil, M. Reisch, D. N. Gamble, L. M. Gutierrez, E. A. Mulroy, & R. A. Cnaan (Eds.), *The handbook of community practice* (pp. 341–359). Thousand Oaks, CA: Sage.

Gutierrez, L. M., Parsons, R. J., & Cox, E. O. (Eds.). (1998). *Empowerment in social work practice.* Pacific Grove, CA: Brooks/Cole.

Hardcastle, D. A., Wenocur, S., & Powers, P. R. (1997). *Community practice: Theories and skills for social workers.* New York: Oxford University Press.

Hardina, D. (2004). Guidelines for ethical practice in community organization. *Social Work, 49*(4), 595–604.

Hare, P. (2003). Roles, relationships, and groups in organizations: Some conclusions and recommendations. *Small Group Research, 34*(2), 123–154.

Hick, S., & McNutt, J. (Eds.). (2002). *Advocacy, activism, and the Internet.* Chicago: Lyceum.

Homan, M. S. (2004). *Promoting community change: Making it happen in the real world* (3rd. ed.). Belmont, CA: Brooks/Cole-Thompson.

Hutchinson, J. (2004). Social capital and community building in the inner city. *Journal of the American Planning Association, 70*(2), 168–175.

Hyde, C. (1996). A feminist response to Rothman's "The interweaving of community intervention approaches." *Journal of Community Practice, 3*(3/4), 127–145.

Hyde, C. (2005). Feminist community practice. In M. Weil, M. Reisch, D. N. Gamble, L. M. Gutierrez, E. A. Mulroy, & R. A. Cnaan (Eds.), *The handbook of community practice* (pp. 360–371). Thousand Oaks, CA: Sage.

Hyman, J. B. (2002). Exploring social capital and civic engagement to create a framework for community building. *Applied Developmental Science, 6*(4), 196–202.

Kahn, A. J. (1969). *Theory and practice of social planning.* New York: Russell Sage Foundation.

Kahn, S. (1991). *Organizing: A guide for grassroots leaders.* Silver Spring, MD: National Association of Social Workers Press.

Katz, N., Lazer, D., Arrow, H., & Contractor, N. (2004). Network theory and small groups. *Small Group Research, 35*(3), 307–332.

Kavanaugh, A. L., Reese, D. D., Carroll, J. M., & Rosson, M. B. (2005). Weak ties in networked communities. *Information Society, 21*(2), 119–131.

Kretzmann, J. P., & McKnight, J. L. (1993). *Building communities from the inside out: A path toward finding and mobilizing community assets*. Evanston, IL: Northwestern University, Center for Urban and Policy Research.

Lane, R. P. (1940). Report of groups studying the community organization process. *Proceedings of the National Conference of Social Work*. New York: Columbia University Press.

Lelieveldt, H. (2004). Helping citizens help themselves: Neighborhood improvement programs and the impact of social networks, trust, and norms on neighborhood-oriented forms of participation. *Urban Affairs Review, 39*(5), 531–551.

Lewis, H. (1985). Management in the nonprofit social services. In S. Slavin (Ed.), *Social administration: The management of the social services* (2nd ed., Vol. 1, pp. 6–13), Binghamton, NY: Haworth Press.

Lindeman, E. (1926). *The meaning of adult education*. New York: New Republic.

Lopez, M., & Stack, C. (2001). Social capital and the culture of power: Lessons from the field. In S. Saegert, J. Thomson, & M. Warren (Eds.), *Social capital and poor communities* (pp. 31–59). New York: Russell Sage Foundation.

Lowe, J. I. (1997). A social health model: A paradigm for social work in health care. In M. Reisch & E. Gambrill (Eds.), *Social work in the 21st century* (pp. 209–218). Thousand Oaks, CA: Pine Forge Press.

Lubove, R. (1965). *The professional altruist: The emergence of social work as a career, 1880–1930*. Cambridge, MA: Harvard University Press.

Marshall, M. J., & Stolle, D. (2004). Race and the city: Neighborhood context and the development of generalized trust. *Political Behavior, 26*(2), 125–153.

McKnight, J. L. (1997). A 21st century map for healthy communities and families. *Families in Society, 78*(1), 117–127.

Mizrahi, T., & Rosenthal, B. (2001). Complexities of effective coalition building: A study of leaders' strategies, struggles, and solutions. *Social Work, 46*(1), 63–78.

Molina, F., & Wallace, J. (1997, February 18). *The neighborhood jobs initiative: An overview of a community-based employment initiative for inner-city residents*. San Francisco: Manpower Demonstration Research Corporation.

Mondros, J., & Wilson, S. (1994). *Organizing for power and empowerment*. New York: Columbia University Press.

Morris, A. D. (1984). *The origins of the civil rights movement*. New York: Free Press.

Nadler, E. (1973). *Militant action and organizational development*. Unpublished paper. Brooklyn, NY: Author.

Naples, N. (Ed.). (1998). *Community activism and feminist politics: Organizing across race, class, and gender*. New York: Routledge.

National Association of Social Workers. (1996). *Code of ethics* (Rev. ed.). Washington, DC: Author.

Netting, E. F., Kettner, P. M., & McMurry, S. L. (2001). Selecting appropriate tactics. In J. Tropman, J. E. Erlich, & J. Rothman (Eds.), *Tactics and techniques of community intervention* (pp. 85–99). Itasca, IL: Peacock.

Newton, K. (2001). Trust, social capital, civil society and democracy. *International Political Science Review, 22*(2), 201–214.

Northern California Community Services Council. (1994). *Building healthy and safe communities: Principles for designing and delivering successful community programs*. San Francisco: Author.

O'Conner, A. (1995). Evaluating comprehensive community initiatives. In J. Connell, A. Kubish, L. Schorr, & C. Weiss (Eds.), *New approaches to evaluating community initiatives: Concepts, methods, and contexts* (pp. 23–63). Washington, DC: Aspen Institute.

Orlitzky, M., & Hirokawa, R. (2001). To err is human, to correct for it divine: A meta analysis of research testing the functional theory of group decision-making effectiveness. *Small Group Research, 32*(1), 313–341.

Pearlmutter, S. (2002). Achieving political practice: Integrating individual need and social action. *Journal of Progressive Human Services, 13*(1), 31–51.

Portes, A. (2000). The two meanings of social capital. *Sociological Forum, 15*(1), 1–12.

Pray, K. L. M. (1947). When is community organization social work practice? *Proceedings of the National Conference of Social Welfare,* 203–204.

Putnam, R. (2000). *Bowling alone: The collapse and revival of American community.* New York: Simon & Schuster.

Putnam, R., & Feldstein, L. (2003). *Better together: Restoring the American community.* New York: Simon & Schuster.

Reamer, F. G. (2006). *Social work values and ethics* (3rd ed.). New York: Columbia University Press.

Reed, B. G. (2005). Theorizing in community practice: Essential tools for building community, promoting social justice, and implementing social change. In M. Weil, M. Reisch, D. N. Gamble, L. M. Gutierrez, E. A. Mulroy, & R. A. Cnaan (Eds.), *Handbook of community practice* (pp. 84–102). Thousand Oaks, CA: Sage.

Reisch, M. (1987). From cause to case and back again: The reemergence of advocacy in social work. *Urban and Social Change Review, 19,* 20–24.

Reisch, M. (2005). Community practice challenges in a global economy. In M. Weil, M. Reisch, D. N. Gamble, L. M. Gutierrez, E. A. Mulroy, & R. A. Cnaan (Eds.), *Handbook of community practice* (pp. 529–547). Thousand Oaks, CA: Sage.

Reisch, M. (in press). From melting to multiculturalism: The impact of racial and ethnic diversity on U.S. social welfare. *British Journal of Social Work.*

Reisch, M., & Andrews, J. (2001). *The road not taken: A history of radical social work in the United States.* Philadelphia: Brunner-Routledge.

Reisch, M., & Guyet, D. (2006). Communities as "big small groups": Culture and social capital. In C. Milofsky & R. Cnaan (Eds.), *Handbook of community movements and local organizations* (pp. 163–178). New York: Springer.

Reisch, M., & Wenocur, S. (1986). The future of community organization in social work: Social activism and the politics of profession building. *Social Service Review, 60*(1), 70–93.

Reisch, M., Wenocur, S., & Sherman, W. (1981). Empowerment, conscientization, and animation as core social work skills. *Social Development Issues, 5*(2/3), 108–120.

Reitan, T. (1998). Theories of interorganizational relations in the human services. *Social Service Review, 72*(3), 285–309.

Rich, P. (1999). American voluntarism, social capital, and political culture. *Annals of the American Academy of Political and Social Science, 565,* 15–35.

Rivera, F., & Erlich, J. L. (Eds.). (1998). *Community organizing in a diverse society* (3rd ed.). Boston: Allyn & Bacon.

Roberts-DeGenarro, M. (1997). Conceptual framework of coalitions in an organizational context. In M. O. Weil (Ed.), *Community practice models in action* (pp. 91–107). New York: Haworth.

Roberts-DeGenarro, M., & Mizrahi, T. (2005). Coalitions as social change agents. In M. Weil, M. Reisch, D. N. Gamble, L. M. Gutierrez, E. A. Mulroy, & R. A. Cnaan (Eds.), *The handbook of community practice* (pp. 305–318). Thousand Oaks, CA: Sage.

Ross, M. G. (1955). *Community organization: Theory, principles, and practice.* New York: Harper & Row.

Roth, B. (1998). Feminist boundaries in the feminist-friendly organization: The women's caucus of ACT UP/LA. *Gender and Society, 12*(2), 129–145.

Rothman, J. (1996). The interweaving of community intervention approaches. *Journal of Community Practice, 3*(3/4), 69–99.

Rothman, J. (2001). Approaches to community intervention. In J. Rothman, J. L. Erlich, & J. E. Tropman (Eds.), *Strategies of community intervention* (6th ed., pp. 27–64). Itasca, IL: Peacock.

Rubin, H., & Rubin, I. (2004). *Community organizing and development* (3rd ed.). Boston: Allyn & Bacon.

Saegert, S., & Winkel, G. (2004). Crime, social capital, and community participation. *American Journal of Community Psychology, 34*(3/4), 219–233.

Sample, T. (1979). Consensus and conflict strategies. In F. M. Cox, J. L. Erlich, J. Rothman, & J. E. Tropman (Eds.), *Strategies of community intervention* (3rd ed., pp. 475–477). Itasca, IL: Peacock.

Sarri, R. (1997). International social work at the millennium. In M. Reisch & E. Gambrill (Eds.), *Social work in the 21st century* (pp. 387–395). Thousand Oaks, CA: Pine Forge Press.

Schneider, J. A.. (2007). Small nonprofits and civil society: Civic engagement and social capital. In C. Milofsky & R. Cnaan (Eds.), *Handbook of community movements and local organizations* (pp. 74–88). New York: Springer.

Schwartz, W. (1986). The group work tradition and the social work profession. *Social Work with Groups, 8*(4), 7–27.

Sherraden, M. S. (2001). Asset building policy and programs for the poor. In T. M. Shapiro & E. N. Wolff (Eds.), *Assets for the poor: The benefits of spreading asset ownership* (pp. 302–323). New York: Russell Sage Foundation.

Simon, B. L. (1994). *The empowerment tradition in American social work: A history.* New York: Columbia University Press.

Skocpol, T., & Fiorina, M. (1999). *Civic engagement in American democracy.* Washington, DC: Brookings Institution Press, and New York: Russell Sage Foundation.

Solomon, B. B. (1976). *Black empowerment: Social work in oppressed communities.* New York: Columbia University Press.

Specht, H. (1969). Disruptive tactics. *Proceedings of the 1968 National Conference on Social Welfare.* New York: Columbia University Press.

Specht, H., & Courtney, M. (1994). *Unfaithful angels: How social work has abandoned its mission.* New York: Free Press.

Stall, S., & Stoecker, R. (1998). Community organizing or organizing community? Gender and the crafts of empowerment. *Gender and Society, 12*(6), 729–756.

Staples, L. (1984). *Roots to power: A manual of grassroots organizing.* New York: Praeger/Greenwood Press.

Staples, L. (1997). Selecting and "cutting" the issue. In M. Minkler (Ed.), *Community organizing and community building for health* (pp. 175–194). New Brunswick, NJ: Rutgers University Press.

Staples, L. (2004). Social action groups. In C. D. Garvin, L. M. Gutierrez, & M. Galinsky (Eds.), *Handbook of social work with groups* (pp. 344–359). New York: Guilford Press.

Theiss-Morse, E., & Hibbing, J. R. (2005). Citizenship and social engagement. *Annual Review of Political Science, 8*, 227–249.

Tilly, C. (1978). *From mobilization to revolution.* Reading, MA: Addison-Wesley.

Tonnies, F. (1955). *Community and association.* London: Routledge/Kegan Paul.

Trapp, S. (2004). *Dynamics of organizing: Building power by developing the human spirit.* Chicago: National Training and Information Center.

Uslaner, E. M., & Conley, R. S. (2003). Civic engagement and particularized trust: The ties that bind people to their ethnic communities. *American Politics Research, 31*(4), 331–360.

Vidal, A., & Gittell, R. (1998). *Community organizing: Building social capital as a development strategy.* Thousand Oaks, CA: Sage.

Wakefield, S. E. L., & Poland, B. (2005). Family, friend, or foe? Critical reflections on the relevance and role of social capital in health promotion and community development. *Social Science and Medicine, 60*, 2819–2832.

Warren, R. (1975). Types of purposive change at the community level. In R. Kramer & H. Specht (Eds.), *Readings in community organization practice* (2nd ed.). Englewood Cliffs, NJ: Prentice Hall.

Warren, R. (1983). The "good community": What would it be? In R. Warren & L. Lyons (Eds.), *New perspectives on the American community*. Homewood, IL: Dorsey Press.

Weil, M. (1986). Women, community, and organizing. In N. Van Der Bergh & L. Cooper (Eds.), *Feminist visions for social work* (pp. 187–210). Silver Spring, MD: National Association of Social Workers Press.

Weil, M. (2005). Social planning with communities: Theory and practice. In M. Weil, M. Reisch, D. N. Gamble, L. M. Gutierrez, E. A. Mulroy, & R. A. Cnaan (Eds.), *The handbook of community practice* (pp. 215–243). Thousand Oaks, CA: Sage.

Weil, M., & Gamble, D. (2005). Evolution, models, and the changing context of community practice. In M. Weil, M. Reisch, D. N. Gamble, L. M. Gutierrez, E. A. Mulroy, & R. A. Cnaan (Eds.), *The handbook of community practice* (pp. 117–149). Thousand Oaks, CA: Sage.

Wenocur, S., & Reisch, M. (1989). *From charity to enterprise: The development of American social work in a market economy*. Urbana: University of Illinois Press.

Wenocur, S., & Soifer, S. (1997). Prospects for community organization. In M. Reisch & E. Gambrill (Eds.), *Social work in the 21st century* (pp. 198–208). Thousand Oaks, CA: Pine Forge Press.

Wong, R. S. K. (2004). Social capital: A theory of social structure and action. *Contemporary Sociology*, *33*(1), 24–26.

Woolcock, M. (2004). Social capital: A theory of social structure and action. *Social Forces*, *82*(3), 1209–1211.

Yabes, R. (2001). Community organizing: Building social capital as a development strategy. *Journal of the American Planning Association*, *67*(3), 344–345.

Ziersch, A. M., Baum, F. E., MacDougall, C., & Putland, C. (2005). Neighborhood life and social capital: The implications for health. *Social Science and Medicine*, *60*(1), 71–86.

Chapter 25

ASSESSMENT OF ORGANIZATIONS

Michael J. Austin and Catherine M. Vu

The majority of work carried out by social workers is done within a nonprofit or governmental organization. Therefore, it is important to understand the dynamics of organizations and how the skills and interests of staff, as well as clients, fit within the mission of the organization. Holland defines organizations as "formalized groups of people who make coordinated use of resources and skills to accomplish given goals or purposes . . . [with a] focus on promoting and enhancing the well-being of the people they serve" (as quoted in Gibelman, 2003, p. 19). This chapter focuses on assessing these organizations from different perspectives; in essence, where you sit influences what you see.

The capacity to perceive the organization from multiple perspectives is important because each perspective could lead to a different set of impressions. Therefore, the goal of this chapter is to develop a more holistic view that can inform decision making inside and outside the organization. The approach taken in this chapter is to assess organizations from four different perspectives: the direct service workers, middle and senior managers, external funders, and clients. The staff members who serve clients tend to view the organization from a bottom-up perspective in which they continuously search for a description of the "big picture" as a way of understanding decisions made elsewhere. Likewise, managers tend to view the organization from a top-down perspective, continuously searching for ways to understand how decisions have been implemented. Externally, funding organizations (foundations, United Way, government) search for multiple ways to understand the capacities of organizations to effectively utilize funds in the form of grants, contracts, or donations. And finally, clients often encounter and perceive human service organizations as "street level bureaucracies" (Lipsky, 1983) as they look for ways to understand the various levels of response and support to their initial and subsequent encounters. It is valuable to explore these four different perceptions in order to develop a comprehensive assessment of an organization.

The use of a systems framework for assessing organizations helps to focus on a multi-faceted and interrelated set of elements in dynamic relationships with one another (Schriver, 2004). For example, the internal organizational processes utilized by workers and managers are influenced by the external factors related to clients and funders. There is also a reciprocal interaction between all four perspectives and the systems perspective helps us see how organizations interact and adapt to these changing external factors.

WORKER'S PERSPECTIVE

Workers in human service organizations are exposed to a unique set of experiences that impact how they assess the organization. This section describes three different situations that workers might experience as they assess their workplace. The first situation involves the nature of the agency itself and how prospective employees might assess it in anticipation of accepting a position within the organization. In other words, what does the worker need to know about the organization before accepting the position? The second situation involves the organization's capacity for change. Here, workers are interested in knowing what they can do to facilitate improvements within the organization. The third situation relates to the fit between the worker and the organization and the shared values of the worker and the organization. In essence, what does the worker need to assess in order to decide if it is time to leave the organization?

Assessing the Organization on Entry

When workers first enter a human service organization, the most pressing concerns are the immediate aspects of their job's. This section describes three of those concerns: organizational structure and processes (the nature of the organization, its mission and goals), supervision (administrative, supportive, and educational), and the working conditions (rules/procedures, management structure, and compensation/benefits). The assessment of these concerns can provide workers with an understanding of what they might expect to find when they are employed by the organization.

Human Service Organizations

For workers to understand the nature of the human service organization, they need to know if it is public or private in nature because the distinction may help to explain the way services are provided. Gibelman (2003) defines public organizations and government agencies as those commissioned by the local, state, or federal governments to address the social welfare needs of the public. The mission and goals of these organizations are defined by the governing bodies and funded with tax dollars. Private organizations, on the other hand, include nonprofits (and in a few cases, for-profit agencies) that are also concerned with the public's well-being. While some private organizations may receive government funds, they are considered to be autonomous entities. It is important to know if the agency is public or nonprofit because it can affect a worker's assessment of the organization. For example, being employed at a government agency may have bureaucratic constraints, but may have better salaries and benefits. A nonprofit organization may have financial constraints, but its autonomy may allow for more rewarding and personally fulfilling work experiences.

The goals of a human service organization are also important. They provide staff members an understanding of the organization's mission and how it relates to their work. The mission of most human service organizations is to respond to the needs of individuals, families, and groups of people in the community (Gibelman, 2003). Developed by the governing body of the organization, a comprehensive mission statement includes the organization's goals, how it seeks to obtain them, the population to be served, and the expected outcomes. Given changes inside and outside the organization, mission statements need to be updated periodically in order to respond to these changes, especially those related to clients in the community.

Supervision

Social work is a profession that utilizes supervision to improve the quality of client services and promote the professional development of workers. Therefore, the nature of supervision can play a critical role in a worker's assessment of an organization. Competent supervisors foster supportive environments related to "risk-taking, collaboration, (service) outcomes, innovation, flexibility, adaptability, competitiveness, and ethical behavior" (Gibelman, 2003, p. 113). The authority of supervisors is derived from the mission and structure of the organization, and supervisors serve as a link between the worker and the higher levels of management.

The three main roles of supervision are administrative, supportive, and educational (Kadushin, 2002). In the administrative role, the supervisor allocates and monitors cases, oversees worker performance and evaluation, and shares information from management or other teams. The supportive role involves helping workers with stress management, sustaining morale, cultivating teamwork, building and sustaining loyalty to the organization, and addressing work-related problems of tension and dissatisfaction (Horejsi & Garthwait, 1999). The educational role includes sharing the knowledge and experience of the supervisor as well as providing support for professional development activities in order to improve practice skills and client services.

Supervisors in human service organizations are also responsible for assessing a worker's job performance. Both supervisors and workers need to share the same understanding of job expectations and criteria for evaluation in order for performance assessments to be beneficial to the individual and the organization. Useful assessment mechanisms include timelines for monitoring progress, regular feedback, and clear specifications of strengths and areas of improvement. These assessments may also lead to the identification of barriers within the agency that may affect the ability of workers to do their jobs. This important information ultimately needs to be shared with management and incorporated into the ongoing assessment of the organization.

Conditions of Work

The third area for a prospective human service worker to assess prior to entry relates to working conditions, such as the rules, procedures and policies that impact service delivery. For example, rules and procedures about the dress code, professional/client interactions, and safety measures are often described in the organization's personnel manual along with policies related to sexual harassment, discrimination, violence, and substance abuse. Understanding the organization chart is also important, especially the lines of authority needed to identify who or where a worker should go when a question or problem comes up. The clear communication of rules, procedures, policies, and structure is essential in helping workers understand their role in the agency.

The compensation, benefits, and career development opportunities are also important factors for workers to understand when assessing job offers. Fair compensation motivates workers to fulfill their job responsibilities to the best of their ability. If the salary is low, benefits such as child care, job sharing, flexible work hours, and career development opportunities are often used as incentives to attract and retain workers. Finally, opportunities to enhance employee knowledge, skills, and competence can be important factors when assessing the organization for its potential to provide challenging work, job satisfaction, promotional opportunities, and participation in agency decision making.

Assessing the Organization's Capacity for Change

Once inside the organization and working for a few years, workers begin to identify areas for improvement and therefore need to assess the organization's capacity for successfully engaging in change. The environment in which organizations exist continually changes and therefore organizations need to adapt in order to survive. To do so, the interactions between organizational employees, larger communities, key stakeholders, and interest groups can be influential in the success of the organization (Gibelman, 2003). This section describes the key players in the change process, how organizations respond to external and internal sources of change, and how they utilize coping strategies for promoting change.

Key Players in the Change Process

An organization's capacity to change is affected by its financial condition and those who occupy positions of power. Nonprofit organizations have the biggest challenge in terms of funding. While nonprofits can receive government funds to implement specific services and programs, these funds are often limited to the contract objectives of the public agencies. The traditional source of funding for nonprofits comes from charitable donations (foundations, corporate and individual contributions), joint ventures between corporations and nonprofits, and client fees (Gibelman, 2003).

Those who occupy positions of power/authority in human service organizations also need to be taken into consideration when assessing an organization's capacity for change. People in positions of authority are influential in organizations because they have the ability to promote or obstruct change. Identifying and assessing these people will help workers assess an organization's capacity for change. For example, organizational leaders who are concerned with maintaining the status quo are not likely to be interested in promoting change.

The type of governing bodies in a human service organization again depends on its nature. Public agencies are governed by elected officials or citizens appointed to advisory boards. Nonprofit organizations usually have a board of directors who carry out legal and policy-making functions. Although the governing bodies of public and nonprofit organizations have similar responsibilities, the focus of this section is on nonprofit organizations. The board of directors for nonprofit organizations is responsible for approving policies, defining services, tracking progress, and ensuring accountability to the community (Gibelman, 2003). They assume legal and policy-making responsibilities. Under the control of the board is the chief executive officer (CEO) or executive director who is hired by the board to ensure the sustainability of the organization by managing daily operations. The executive director is accountable to members of the board of directors and reports directly to them.

External Sources of Change

In addition to the financial status and governing structure of a human service organization, it is important to note the role of the external environment as it impacts the organization's capacity for change. Human service organizations operate as open systems where internal operations are affected by outside factors. The relationship between an organization and its external environment can define the characteristics of the organization in terms of its purpose, operations, clients, and services provided. Schmid (2000) defines the external environment as contextual elements outside of the organization that affect its performance. These contextual elements include funders, government agencies, policymakers, clients and community leaders as well as social policies (like state policies to deinstitutionalize the mentally ill), market forces (like managed care), and the changing systems of service delivery (like school-linked services). As these external factors change, organizations must also be able to change and adapt in order to survive. Since most nonprofit organizations receive a portion of their budget from government sources, the changing attitudes reflected in pubic opinion are important. Elected officials and the U.S. public have a history of ambivalence toward long-term commitments to social programs for disenfranchised populations (Gibelman, 2003). This general disposition leaves human service organizations at the mercy of policymakers who often have other priorities on their political agenda.

The patterns of service delivery often change as social policies dictate new procedures and funding limitations that impact an agency's capacity for change. The current trend in social policy is to privatize delivery systems where local and state governments rely on private organizations (both for profit and nonprofit) to provide human services for the public. This has a significant impact on the organizational environment of nonprofits because of increased competition between organizations for government funding. This often puts more pressure on the nonprofit organization to be more accountable for services provided and frequently requires the evaluation of services to determine if community needs are being met. The changing environment of human service organizations includes new public policies, the reduction in government spending on social services, the increasing popularity of cost containment philosophies, and the privatization of public services. The changes caused by external factors often have a profound impact on the organization and can lead to internal changes that impact both clients and staff members.

Internal Sources of Change

While some external factors may lead to organizational change, internal change can also emerge independently of the external environment. For example, when an executive director leaves the organization, a period of ambiguity can occur during the leadership transitions from one person to another. In this situation, staff members may feel insecure about their jobs, thereby increasing the stress levels within the organization (Ginsberg, 1997; Hernandez & Leslie, 2001). Another source of stress can emerge from reductions in agency budgets (leading to downsizing, restructuring, or outsourcing) as well as from budget increases (rapid expansion of staff and facilities expansion or the allocation of additional resources to existing programs). Internal change related to moving the organization to a different location can disrupt daily routines related to preserving relationships with old clients as well as cause the loss of clients that requires new efforts to reach out to new clients. The results of annual community needs assessments and/or program evaluations can also lead to organizational change. All these situations can lead to small or large scale organizational changes and often require careful planning in order to anticipate the effects of change and facilitate smooth transitions.

Coping with Change

External and internal sources of change can present challenges to those in the workplace. Just as workers use the strengths-based perspective, empowerment, and advocacy in working with clients, these same principles can be applied to improving organizations. The same strengths-based perspective that focuses on the ability of people to overcome adversity (Rapp, 1998; Saleebey, 1997) can be applied to helping organizations manage change by drawing on the strengths, assets, and resources of its staff to collectively develop strategies to address internal and external sources of change.

In a similar way, the concept of empowerment that includes the ability to obtain, acquire, or grant power to an individual or group (Gibleman, 2003) can be used in organizations to promote a positive mindset, renewed energy, or an eagerness to accept new responsibilities for action. Responding to internal and external sources of organizational change can also empower workers to become change agents themselves. Empowered workers can conduct needs assessments, develop program proposals, advocate for changes in administrative policies, participate in financial planning, design new intervention strategies, and organize staff and client groups. All of these empowerment strategies can be used to shape internal and external operations (Gibelman, 2003).

Understanding the internal and external sources of change and the associated strategies for managing change is important for workers to make their voices heard and to participate in organizational problem solving. Staff involvement can help to overcome resistance to change and promote improved communication between the staff and management.

Assessing Worker-Environment Fit

A thorough assessment of the fit between a worker's capabilities and the ongoing operations of an organization is rarely addressed in a comprehensive manner, except possibly at the point of termination. One reason it is often overlooked is the perception that people can adapt their styles and adjust their expectations to fit the changes in human services organizations. It is important to raise the question, what do workers need to assess to determine if there is still a good fit between their interests and skills and the changing nature of human service organizations? Some of the answers to this question can be found in an assessment of management styles, group functioning, and factors in the work environment.

The style of management can have a significant impact on an organization. The board of directors, senior management, and supervisors significantly impact the organization's culture (values, beliefs, symbols, and assumptions) in which workers carry out their responsibilities. They have the power to cultivate employee participation, risk-taking and problem-solving behaviors, and collaborative efforts. For example, "a participatory management style and a team approach for the effective coordination of consumer service, management, marketing, and support [can] achieve good communication, smooth flow of information and positive relations with external stakeholders" (Gibelman, 2003, p. 29).

The group dynamics of workers and staff in the agency are also related to management styles. Interpersonal support and open lines of communication allow for questions to be raised, ideas to be expressed, and feelings to be shared. This approach to teamwork and collaboration encourages workers to invest in organizational problem solving to address organizational issues and foster creativity and innovation (Rees, 1997). Creating a work environment that fosters relationship building and collaboration can increase staff morale, which in turn can increase feelings of personal effectiveness and productivity while decreasing levels of burnout (Austin & Hopkins, 2004; Gibelman, 2003).

Related to burnout are the specific employment factors of workload and time. Are there enough resources in the agency to create manageable workloads? Are workers overwhelmed by the amount of work they are expected to complete? Workers who are expected to do more than what is reasonable run the risk of "burning out" (a state of depression and irritability due to overwork). The nature of social services requires a high level of emotional involvement and can easily produce "compassion fatigue" leading to both physical and emotional exhaustion. This depletion in energy can negatively affect staff morale and can create a poor environment for delivering services.

The physical environment of office space and equipment can also impact worker performance as well as influence the client's perception of services. For example, a crowded and noisy office may inhibit a worker's ability to maintain confidential conversations with clients and thereby prevent them from effectively engaging clients and assessing their needs. Similarly, clients who must stand while waiting to be served due to lack of chairs and/or space may feel unwelcome or uncomfortable. With regard to equipment, time is wasted and efficiency reduced when workers must share a computer or operate with inadequate supplies. Without the proper environment to conduct meetings and do paperwork, workers may experience frustration that can affect their ability to serve clients.

As organizations respond to many internal and external sources of change, workers also need to develop realistic expectations about the capacities of their organization. For example, seeking advice from peers, colleagues, and/or mentors can help determine whether there is a good fit between the worker's capabilities and the current climate and culture of the organization. When organizational improvement seems unlikely and the fit between workers and organization is not good, workers may need to change jobs by seeking opportunities inside or outside of the organization. A career in social work often involves movement from one organization to another (Gibelman, 2003). This personal decision is often determined by the level of job satisfaction and one's career objectives.

In summary, while workers can have an impact on organizational change, they often need to work collaboratively with management to achieve success. A supervisor can be an advocate for the client-centered recommendations of line workers, especially when issues related to decision making and program implementation are being addressed by top management. As noted in the next section, knowing about the different roles and concerns of managers can assist workers in promoting change and advancing the mission of the organization.

MANAGEMENT'S PERSPECTIVE

Just as workers have their own perspective when assessing human service organizations, managers also assess organizations in the context of their experiences from entry into the organization to exit (Austin, 1989; Austin & Gilmore, 1992). They also recognize the impact of their predecessor and how the past history of the organization influences the present and future (Austin, 1996). While the exploration of these issues is beyond the scope of this chapter, they have an important impact on the two major domains of managerial work; namely, internal operations and external relations with other organizations and the community.

When assessing human service organizations, effective managers continually search for ways to diagnose the efficiency and effectiveness of the organization to ensure that it is functioning at its optimal level and to find approaches to solve problems, meet challenges, or enhance performance (Harrison, 2005). Diagnosis of an organization can also inform managerial decision making when improvement and adjustments are needed to adapt to changing environments. This section describes organizational assessment from the manager's perspective in the context of an open systems model of organizational functioning. The section features two approaches to assessing organizations; namely internal operations assessment and external relations assessment.

Open Systems Model

The interaction between organizations and their environments is described by Harrison (2005) in terms of an open systems (OS) model that includes the following:

1. Inputs: Resources such as raw materials, money, people, and information that organizations acquire from their environment and use to produce their outputs.
2. Outputs: Products, services, and ideas that are outcomes of organizational action.
3. Organizational behavior and processes: Prevailing patterns of interaction between individuals and groups that contribute directly or indirectly to transforming inputs into outputs.
4. Technology: Tools, equipment, and techniques used to process inputs and transform them into outputs.
5. Environment: Two types of environments:
   • Close (task) environment: External organizations and conditions that are directly related to the operations of a human service organization.
   • Remote (general) environment: Institutions and conditions that have infrequent or long-term effects on the organization and its close environment, including the economy, the legal and political systems, the state of scientific and technical knowledge, social institutions such as the family, population distribution and composition, and local or national cultures.
6. Structure: Enduring relations between individuals, groups, and larger units.
7. Culture: Shared norms, values, beliefs, and assumptions and the behavior and artifacts that express these orientations, including symbols, rituals, stories, and language.
8. System dynamics: Feedback of information and demands from inside and outside the organization. (pp. 34–35)

Applying the OS model to organizational assessment has several advantages. First, it takes into consideration the environment in which an organization operates. Second, it helps managers focus their data gathering on those components of the system that need attention or need to be changed. Since the OS approach emphasizes the interactions between system components, managers are better able to anticipate the impact of change on one or more components. With the OS model as a foundation for organizational assessment, it is possible to identify the primary indicators for assessing internal operations and external relations.

Assessing Internal Operations

The internal operations of an organization consist of organizational performance indicators and staff performance standards. Managers who are interested in producing positive client outcomes must take both of these dimensions into consideration when determining the most appropriate ways to measure them. This section identifies the factors of internal operations related to organizational and employee job performance, the compatibility of system components, and organizational politics.

Internally, managers have a vested interest in the job performance of staff members because poor performance in providing client services can undermine the agency's goals and objectives. Externally, organizations that are unable to meet their goals and objectives may experience difficulties in obtaining the resources needed to continue operations. The bottom line is that worker performance can affect the funding of the agency and thereby have a substantial impact on the whole organization. Therefore, one of the responsibilities of managers is to help workers and teams develop or modify their approach or intervention methods to ensure effective service delivery. Managers of human service organizations often focus on at least five areas to measure performance: client outcomes, productivity, resource allocation, efficiency, and staff morale (Rapp & Poertner, 1992).

Client outcomes involve the benefits received by clients. This can be measured by affective changes (changes in mood and/or feelings), learning (changes in the way people think about themselves, others, or a situation), behavior changes (adopting new behaviors or eliminating undesirable behaviors), status maintenance or change (maintaining or changing an individual's social or economic position), and environmental modifications (improvement in living conditions, affect policies, or impact public values and beliefs; Rapp & Poertner, 1992). These client outcomes are only a few of the many outcomes that managers can measure to assess organizational performance.

Productivity is another measure that can be used to evaluate performance. Rapp and Poertner (1992) define productivity within the context of client-centered administration in four different ways: (1) client counts (the number of people who receive services), (2) service episodes (a complete period of service provision from intake to termination), (3) service events (a count of the specific actions taken by either the worker or the client, or both), and (4) elapsed time (the amount of time taken to deliver a specific service). Productivity measures can be used to improve client outcomes by assessing specific client outcomes, consistently examining these events, and relaying the information back to staff. This systematic monitoring of productivity can be a useful mechanism for demonstrating the relationship between worker behaviors and client outcomes (Rapp & Poertner, 1992).

Managers need to measure resource allocation as it relates to improving client outcomes. According to Rapp and Poertner (1992), resources can be defined as funds (money that is obtained through grants, legislative testimony, fund-raising, and program advocacy), personnel (with consideration based on personal characteristics, qualifications, and skills), technology (information and training), clients (a consistent flow of appropriate referrals), and public support and influence (engaging key players in the community for the benefit of the organization and its clients). A manager's ability to acquire such resources is another way to assess organizational performance in relationship to client outcomes.

Efficiency is a performance area measured by the ratio between the amount of resources obtained and the outcomes produced. This can be done by determining the dollar cost per unit of service, the amount of time a worker spends on direct client interaction or collateral contact (related to productivity), or the percentage of clients served out of a total target population.

Staff morale involves the job satisfaction of workers. This measure is important because dissatisfied workers who are tired, frustrated, or burned out are unlikely to contribute to improved client outcomes. As a part of their leadership role, managers in human service organizations need to monitor staff experiences related to satisfying and fulfilling work because these experiences can have a direct impact on client outcomes.

In addition to worker performance, managers are also concerned with other internal operation issues such as the fit between system components and the political environment of the organization. As Harrison (2005) notes, "fit refers to the extent to which the behavioral or organizational requirements and constraints in one part of a system are compatible with those in other parts" (p. 77). For example, the culture in human service organizations that values empowerment and promoting client strengths requires an organizational structure that allows workers to openly express their observations and ideas within the organization. The lack of fit between values and organizational structure can lead to poor individual, interpersonal, and group outcomes. Without an accurate and balanced assessment of internal operations, staff can experience considerable frustration and tension, whether blamed for a lack of competency or unsuccessful in convincing others about the impact of dysfunctional systems on their work.

The political environment of an organization is another component of internal operations, especially when it focuses on the different levels of leadership within organizations that can be used to empower others to address organizational goals. Managers can encourage staff to assume the leadership roles needed to facilitate teamwork and shared responsibility for accountability. Central to the issue of leadership and power delegation is the ability of managers to empower others to advocate for changes that will benefit the organization as well as external stakeholders (Menefee, 2000).

The next section addresses the importance of assessing individual and group behavior in the context of organizational processes; namely, the processes of problem identification/ resolution, the different venues and levels where it occurs, and different ways to assess these processes.

Assessing Individual and Group Behavior

Managers need to pay attention to strategies, standards, and goals that influence individual and group behavior because their impact can help improve coordination and teamwork, clarify the division of labor within and between groups, and modify the nature of team and individual tasks (Harrison, 2005). The effectiveness of individuals depends largely on "the degree and quality of worker efforts, their level of initiative, cooperation with other employees, absenteeism, lateness, and commitment to the job" (p. 57). The quality of work life (QWL) involves the interrelationship between the workplace factors and the material and psychological well-being of staff. Managers can affect individual productivity by ensuring that the work environment addresses the needs of workers. An open and communicative atmosphere is beneficial to both the supervisor and supervisee, especially related to clarifying standards for individual performance requirements. QWL issues include the physical working conditions, level of compensation, job security, interpersonal relationships and support, and interesting and fulfilling work.

In addition to QWL for individual workers, QWL also relates to group composition, structure, and technology that can impact organizational performance. Team members reflecting a diversity of social experiences, education, and occupation can foster both innovation as well as conflict (Milliken & Martins, 1996). Deficiencies in both organizational structure and process can also lead to ineffective group behavior. Other factors that may influence group efficiency are communication, personal conflict/tension between members, and group norms and values. Managers who are able to create a supportive environment to address such issues can increase the productivity of both individuals and group performance. This productivity can facilitate the achievement of organizational goals and objectives.

The performance of group tasks can be assessed in terms of organizational and group conditions. Hackman (1987, 1991) developed the action model for group task performance that includes three critical group processes: (1) group efforts to achieve adequate levels of performance, (2) application of skills and knowledge, and (3) use of strategies that are culturally and organizationally relevant. These processes are affected by four factors: (1) the organizational context in which the group functions (goals, rewards, information, and training), (2) group design and culture (challenging objectives, shared responsibility, assigned accountability) and features of group composition (clear roles, relevant members, norms to guide behavior, and diverse training and experiences), (3) outside help (coaching and consulting from others leaders and experts within the organization or from external groups and organizations), and (4) material and technical resources that can impact group processes in performing tasks.

Assessing External Relations

For the manager engaged in organizational assessment, external relationships are as important as internal operations. Hasenfeld (1983) notes that human service organizations are dependent on both external financial resources as well as the local community for its legitimization and clients. This dependency relationship on external relations can make organizations vulnerable and less independent. The external environment can be viewed in terms of a set of resources needed for survival and a set of limitations requiring adaptation in order to provide effective services. Thus, the ability of an organization to provide adequate services is a reflection of its strategies to manage relations with its external environment.

This section provides an overview of managerial concerns related to assessing external relations. The external relations include elements in the task environment (competing agencies, funding organizations, or public regulatory bodies) and the general environment (economic conditions, national politics, and new information and technology). Assessing the interactions between the organization and these elements in the task and general environment can help managers to improve decision making and planning so that the organization can adapt to changes in the environment. One aspect of the task environment is the funding organization that is addressed in the next section. The general environment is the primary focus of this section.

General environmental factors can have a major impact on human service organizations, including the current economy, national politics, as well as the support of funders and the information and technology available to managers. Current economic conditions are an important part of the general environment because they impact the amount of resources available to organizations. For example, if economic conditions are favorable, individuals and corporations, as well as government agencies, are more likely to invest in the delivery of human services. If economic conditions are unfavorable, less money will be available for services. In addition, the economy has a direct impact on the number of clients needing services from organizations. In times of economic downturn, people may lose their jobs, creating a higher need for human services due to reduced income and related problems. Therefore, managers need to be prepared for the combination of a decrease in funding from outside resources and increased clients needs due to adverse economic conditions.

National politics is also a part of the general environment of an organization. Public policies tend to reflect the mood of society in its efforts to address the needs of communities. Government guidelines and changing policies can impact the behavior of organizations, especially when nonprofits under contract with government organizations must adapt to new rules and regulations in order to provide client services. Therefore, effective environmental assessment includes up-to-date information on social policies and the maintenance of communication systems needed to keep workers informed about new regulations.

Assessing the general environment for new information and technology is important for identifying promising practices that can improve service delivery and control costs, especially when new technology can increase organizational efficiency. Another way to respond to changes in the organization's environment is to create internal adjustments that minimize disruptions in the organization (e.g., employ temporary staff and/or reallocate resources), alleviate the impact of sudden surprises, and aid in planning for future change. And finally, assessing the external environment can provide managers with information in order to intervene in the environment itself to address the needs of the organization. This can be done through political participation (e.g., lobbying), using economic power (e.g., organizing boycotts), media outreach to influence demand and attitudes, forging relationships with other organizations in the environment, and altering services to enter new markets and niches. Any one of these responses needs to be assessed in terms of the quality and quantity of resources acquired, the organizational adaptation required, the costs associated with a proactive stance, and the increased capacity to innovate (Harrison, 2005). Effectiveness can also be assessed in terms of the organization's ability to create favorable changes in the external environment.

Managers have the important task of balancing the functioning and performance of internal operations with external relations, both of which have a significant impact on organizational capacity building. The ability of an organization to expand its current resources demonstrates to funders that it is effective in gaining other forms of community support. Managers who are knowledgeable about the mission of their funding institution(s) will be able to connect the priorities of funders with the needs of their clients.

FUNDER'S PERSPECTIVE

Funders who provide organizations with grants also use assessment tools in their decision-making process. An increasing number of grant-making institutions are creating, modifying, or adopting assessment tools that are used to determine strengths and limitations of the organizations they seek to fund (Bartczak, 2005).

This section describes the funder's point of view in assessing organizations as they seek to understand the overall performance of the agencies they fund. By conducting an assessment of an organization, funders are able to identify the capacity-building strategies needed for strengthening organizations that they seek to fund. By focusing on the funding of nonprofits, it is important to note that they rely heavily on grants from government agencies, philanthropic organizations and charities, and individual donors.

Assessing Organizational Capacity

Organizational capacity building is a key element in a funder's decision-making process. Assessing capacity provides the grant-making institution with information on how organizations are operating in changing and competitive environments. Capacity has been defined as a "continuous process of attracting and managing finite board-ensured resources (both human and capital) in a rapidly changing landscape to produce projects, programs, services, and activities that are demonstrably appropriate to the nonprofit's mission" (Freeman & Roming, 2005). This section is divided into two areas that capture the funder's perspective: (1) reasons to conduct an organizational assessment and (2) organizational activities and indicators of success.

From a funder's point of view, there are four major reasons to conduct an organizational assessment (Gurthrie & Preston, 2005). The first reason is to strengthen the nonprofit sector by building the capacity of individual nonprofits. Organizational assessments can increase the funder's knowledge about grantee capacity and help both grantor (fund provider) and grantee (recipient of funds) identify strengths as well as areas for improvement. The second reason is to assist the grantee in further understanding its own organizational capacity. Assessments have been shown to expand grantee knowledge of their organization because it points out components of capacity that previously may not have been considered (Gurthrie & Preston, 2005). In addition, assessments can act as a mechanism through which change can occur. Third, assessments can be used as a catalyst for planning future organizational improvement and capacity building interventions. Because strengths and areas for improvement are often revealed during assessments, these assessments can lead to the development of new ideas and resources as well as the development of future goals and objectives. Finally, assessment tools can be used to monitor change over time. An annual analysis of organizational indicators can help to identify persistent concerns and as well as assess the impact of previous interventions. Successful assessments are tailored to the individual needs of the specific organization, account for the challenges facing the organization, and document the impact of the rapidly changing environment in which the organization is located.

Assessment tools often identify several key areas of organizational activity and their indicators of success. These areas include (a) leadership; (b) mission, vision, and strategy; (c) program delivery and impact; (d) strategic relationships; (e) resource development; and (f) internal operations and management (Connolly & Lukas, 2002). Table 25.1 provides examples of each area and an array of categories for assessment.

Leadership and governance in nonprofit organizations relate to the board of directors where members are responsible for overseeing policies and programs, reviewing strategic goals, financial status, and executive leadership performance (Connolly & Lukas, 2002). Funders look at the degree of involvement of the board of directors to assess their level

Table 25.1   Organizational Activities and Indicators of Success from a Funder's Perspective

I. Leadership

1. Board of Directors

    Composition, commitment, involvement, and support

    Governance structure

    Committee participation

    Fund-raising involvement

    Strategic planning role

    Training and orientation

2. Management

    Team composition, collaboration, and leadership

    Communication

    Decision making

    Financial experience and expertise

    Personal/interpersonal effectiveness and analytical and strategic thinking

    Leadership related to passion and vision

    Orientation to outcome assessment and utilization

    Involvement of senior management team

II. Mission

1. Vision

    Clarity of vision

    Boldness of vision

2. Mission

    Overarching goals

    Monitoring of landscape

    Knowledge management

    Shared values and beliefs

3. Strategy

    Strategic plan and planning skills

    Overall strategy and operational planning

    Performance targets

    Decision-making framework

    Use and development of organizational processes

    Interdepartmental coordination

    Shared practices

III. Program Delivery and Impact

    Assessment of community needs and environment

    Communications strategies and outreach effectiveness

    Public relations and marketing

    Influence on policy making

    New program development

    Performance measurement

Table 25.1 *(Continued)*

IV. Strategic Relationships

    External relationship building
    Local community presence and involvement
    Development and nurturing of partnerships and alliances

V. Resource Development

1. Financial management
    Assets and expenditures
    Financial planning and budgeting
    Financial operations management
    Use of financial and operations data
2. Revenue streams
    Diverse revenue sources and funding model
    Fund development strategy and activities
    Fund development staff, budget, and skills
    Private revenue sources (nonfoundation or contract)

VI. Internal Operations and Management

1. Organizational performance
    Data analysis skills and staff
    Performance management and use of benchmarking
    Performance analysis and program adjustments
    Program relevance and integration
    Program growth and replication
    Organizational design
    Performance as a shared value
2. Human resources
    Recruitment, development, and retention of management and general staff
    Human resources planning (staff and volunteers)
    Organizational processes and use of development
    Incentives
    Individual job design
    Staffing levels
    Senior management team
    Management of legal and liability issues

Based on "CCI Building Capacity Self-Assessment Tool," "McKinsey Capacity Assessment Grid," and "SVP Organizational Capacity Assessment Tool" *A Funder's Guide to Organizational Assessment: Tools, Processes, and Their Use in Building Capacity,* by L. Bartczak, 2005, St. Paul, MN: Fieldstone Alliance.

of participation in agency activities. Consistent board participation is important in order to maintain a current understanding of agency operations. Since board members are not the persons interacting directly with clients or operating the agency, they need to be aware of how their decisions and recommendations impact clients and staff. Active and informed board members demonstrate to the grantor that the organization is being guided by policy makers who understand the dynamics of the agency operations.

In addition to the leadership responsibilities of the board, the quality of program management is also important for funders to assess. Clearly defined lines of authority and effective management at each level are critical for assessing organizational productivity, capability, and potential for growth. An organization's mission, vision, and strategy reflect its purpose and identity. They need to be current in order to reflect the changing needs of clients as well as the changing demands of social and political environments. In addition, funders look for "results-oriented, strategic, and self-reflective planning that aligns strategies with the mission and organizational capacity" (Connolly & Lukas, 2002). The review of an organization's mission should involve input from stakeholders, including board members, management teams, and line workers, as well as the community (clients and leaders). Communications between all stakeholders of the organization can strengthen organizational operations and the provision of effective community services. For organizations to be effective, they must be informed about the problems they seek to resolve. For example, if an organization is seeking a grant related to housing, it must be knowledgeable about current public policies, relevant statistics about housing, and the programs already in place.

The ultimate social impact of an organization can be captured by assessing services and outcomes and their effect on the populations being served. The results of services delivered should be tangible and well documented in order to demonstrate to funders that their money is being put to good use. The use of formal evaluations, such as surveys, focus groups, and interviews are often used to assess organizational performance. The use of evaluations reflects positively on organizations as it indicates the organization's commitment to providing quality services.

The organization's level of community involvement is another aspect of a funder's assessment, especially its reputation and level of participation in the community (Connolly & Lukas, 2002). If the agency is successful in serving clients, its reputation in the community should be positive. Community organizations need to establish connections with one another if collaboration between staff members is to be successful. An agency's ability to collaborate with other agencies is a sign of capacity building where knowledge and resources can be expanded through sharing with other agencies. Capitalizing on community connections with clients and other agencies helps to advance the goals of the organization and expand its influence in the community.

A significant part of a funder's assessment of organizational capacity is an organization's ability to manage its finances. Responsible planning and budgeting measures are reassuring to funders when they try to anticipate how their funds will be managed. Financial reporting is important to funders because it provides transparency with respect to the grantee's financial position, the results of its activities, cash flows, and external accountability (Freeman & Roming, 2005). Without proper financial monitoring, an organization is unable to sustain its operations. From the grantors' perspective, funds are unlikely to be given to organizations that operate with poor financial accounting systems.

In addition to the funding provided by the grantor, funders also look at the ability of an organization to develop and obtain grants from other resources. Support from a variety of sources ensures that revenues are diversified, consistent, and adequate to accomplish the organization's mission, long-term goals, and strategic direction (Connolly & Lukas, 2002). A capacity to develop resources indicates to the foundation that an agency has the ability to attract funds other than those given by the grantor.

The internal functioning of the agency affects the quality of services provided to the community. If the agency is not functioning effectively, it limits its ability to build capacity and effectively utilize funding from foundations and other sources. Grantors seek to fund agencies that provide appropriate programs and services, and grantees who receive these funds need to demonstrate positive outcomes or run the risk of losing funding support in the future.

The funders of human service organizations seek to impact the lives of clients by investing in programs and services. Therefore, it is also important to include the perspective of clients when assessing organizations. In addition to the views of staff, management, and funders, a client perspective is important for developing a comprehensive assessment of any human service organization.

CLIENTS' PERSPECTIVE

The fourth dimension of our framework for providing a comprehensive view of organizational assessment is the client perspective. As Hasenfeld (1983) notes, there are at least three definitions of clients served by human service organizations: (1) either a voluntary or involuntary recipient or consumer of services, (2) a dependent recipient of services whose behaviors need to change in order to meet society's values and expectations, and (3) a participant in the organization's activities who cooperates with the prescribed rules and procedures of a particular intervention.

Hasenfeld (1983) observes a power imbalance between the client and the organization. He concludes that the power advantage of human service organizations results in significant control over the lives of service recipients. The power differential can lead to a struggle between clients and organizations where each tries to maximize payoffs while minimizing costs. Despite the power disparity between client and organization, there is much value in considering the client's influence on the organization-client relationship. Human service organizations could not exist without clients, and clients might find it difficult to survive without accessing the resources of human service organizations. This interdependent relationship supported by tax and philanthropic funds from the community entitles service recipients to receive the highest possible quality of customer service. Even though some clients may not have the opportunity to take their "business" elsewhere, these clients should be treated with the same respect as if they did have that choice (O'Neil, Hassett, & Austin, 1995).

This analysis of the client perspective begins with a brief description of some of the problems that clients can experience when seeking help from human service organizations. Second, some of the characteristics of client satisfaction are described in terms of reliability, responsiveness, assurance, empathy, and tangibles. And finally, different ways of assessing service quality from the client's perspective are identified.

Rapp and Poertner (1992, p. 11) describe several difficulties that clients may experience when seeking help from human service organizations:

> Clients bring their problems, needs, pain, and suffering to the human service agency seeking help, direction, relief, and an increased sense of control and power. Too often their feelings of impotence are exacerbated in the face of rules, policies, and protocols seemingly unresponsive to their problems. At times the process is dehumanizing whether because of the physical setting or because of personnel behavior. Too often our services are ineffective; they fail to produce benefits for the clients.

Clients can also experience obstacles such as long waits, excessive intake processes, and multiple stressful experiences when seeking or continuing services. Similarly, service providers can experience frustration when trying to balance the needs of clients with the limitations of the organization's resources. In addition, insufficient training and inadequate supervisory support can result in different types of worker behavior that can negatively impact the client.

Given that the goal of human service organizations and their workforce is to help clients improve or change their situation, the assessment of client satisfaction has become an important aspect of organizational assessment. Drawing on the organizational performance research in the for-profit sector, Zeithaml, Parasuraman, and Berry (1990) identified five major factors related to customer satisfaction: reliability, responsiveness, assurance, empathy, and tangibles. They found that *reliability* was ranked the highest among the five quality dimensions of customer service. Reliability refers an organization's ability to provide service in a consistent manner with little or no variation between customers over time. The second highest quality dimension is *responsiveness,* especially the amount of time customers must wait for service or for phone calls to be returned. Ranked third most important, *assurance* relates to employee attitudes when interacting with customers (e.g., friendliness, warmth, and hospitality), especially the attitudes of telephone operators and receptionists.

Empathy is the fourth most important dimension of quality. It includes the employee's understanding of the customer's situation and the provision of specific services that are tailored to the customer's needs. Empathy is directly related to assurance because it encompasses an attitude of compassion and kindness rather than treating customers as numbers.

The last dimension of quality relates to such *tangibles* as the appearance and décor of the office space as well as the equipment, personnel, and publications used by the organization. While most clients prefer to be served in pleasant and comfortable settings where they are made to feel welcomed by employees who present themselves in a professional manner (dress, language, expression, etc.), it is important to note that tangibles are ranked lowest among the five dimensions of quality customer service in for-profit organizations.

The same five dimensions of quality (reliability, responsiveness, assurance, empathy, and tangibles) in the for-profit sector are also relevant when clients assess human service organizations. For example, a study of client satisfaction in the public social services sector (O'Neil et al., 1995) identified six categories (in-person techniques, general techniques, telephone techniques, personal techniques, physical environment, and employee support techniques) where staff in human service organizations could improve services to clients. These categories overlap with the quality dimensions identified in the for-profit sector. For example, similar to customers of for-profit organizations, clients also expect high quality service provided in the same manner each time they interact with the organization (Martin, 1995). When greeted with a warm welcome over the phone or in person in human service organizations, clients who are anxious about receiving assistance can feel more comfortable and less stressed. Competent staff who are informed about their programs and resources and warmly greet clients are providing assurance and thereby affect the perceived quality of services.

O'Neil et al. (1995) identified the following ways to improve reliability in human service organizations: (a) understand all procedures and policies, (b) give clear and concise explanations and directions and verify the client's understanding, and (c) when possible, do everything right the first time. Understanding the inner workings of an organization enables the worker to give consistent information to clients. Giving clear and concise explanations and directions also helps to facilitate reliability with respect to client perceptions of service quality. To prevent misunderstandings between the worker and the client, assurance is enhanced when workers verify a client's understanding, thereby ensuring that both parties have the same understanding.

Responsiveness in human service organizations includes responding quickly to client issues or inquiries, making sure to return phone calls or answering waiting callers quickly, and explaining any delays in services. By giving clients a timely response to their concerns, staff display diligence in managing their cases. Returning phone calls promptly and keeping the client on hold for a minimal amount of time demonstrates the worker's active involvement and interest in helping the client. Explanations about delays can also reassure clients about their status and shows that attention is being paid to their case.

Assurance is related to the quality of responsiveness. O'Neil et al. (1995) found that staff in human service organizations need to pay more attention to acknowledging the client's presence, welcoming the client by smiling, making eye contact, addressing the individual as Ms. or Mr., and handling private matters confidentially. Recognizing the client's presence and providing a warm and hospitable welcome demonstrates respect for the client. Keeping client matters confidential is also a sign of respecting and honoring the personal affairs of clients.

Empathy can be demonstrated by human service workers when they display an understanding of the client's perspective or frame of reference (especially related to race, ethnicity, gender, age, ability, and sexual orientation), asking how they can help, and developing and practicing listening skills. Workers who can show sympathy and understanding of the client's situation are able to engage clients more successfully and establish rapport. When workers ask clients how they can be of assistance, it allows clients an opportunity to express their needs so that workers can help them tailor specific interventions to address their situation. During this process, workers can also expand their listening skills to better serve their clients.

O'Neil et al. (1995) also found that the environment in which clients are received also impacts their assessment of the organization. Tangibles, such as clear and multicultural language on signs and materials, comfortable and clean waiting areas, and child-friendly environments can reflect the organization's commitment to quality client services. Offering language-appropriate directions or reading materials indicates a recognition of the populations being served. Inviting waiting rooms or offices make the visit to the organization a more pleasant experience. A child-friendly area where young children can be occupied demonstrates the organization's sensitivity the needs of parents. In addition, workers who are well dressed and conduct themselves in confident manner help clients to trust that their concerns will be handled in a professional nature.

Martin (1995) defines a customer-driven human service agency (the terms *client* and *customer* are often used interchangeably in the human services) as one that "willingly reorders its priorities so that customers and customer satisfaction are placed at the top of the list of major agency concerns" (p. 167). In order to effectively address the needs of clients, human service organizations need to monitor the perceptions of clients by regularly asking them for their views. The array of organizational mechanisms includes the periodic review and analysis of items appearing in a "suggestion box," conducting client focus groups, and the use of client satisfaction surveys. The most comprehensive approach to assessing client satisfaction is the combination of all three approaches.

In summary, this section identified some of the issues that client's face when entering and assessing a human service organization. While staff members of the organization may be preoccupied with internal operations and delivering services, clients care about the *quality* of services provided. When clients assess the performance of organizations, they often consider the following dimensions of quality: reliability, responsiveness, assurance, empathy, and tangibles. These dimensions are broad categorizations for assessing the quality of human services and are not meant to be exhaustive. Ultimately, organizations must tailor their assessment of service quality to the needs of their clients. One way to identify these changing needs is to involve both clients and staff members in the collection and analysis of accurate data.

CONCLUSION

The driving force of human service organizations is its client population. The social, economic, and political structure in the United States ensures that people will always have human service needs such as finding a job, seeking welfare assistance, and/or securing mental health services. Government and philanthropic funds are provided to community organizations to assist clients with their needs. The needs of the clients lead to the development of social policies and programs and help to motivate donors and foundations to address them.

As a result, government or philanthropic funders must choose or contract with human service organizations that have the capacity to deliver services within an established mission and set of goals that reflect the interests and values of the funding institutions. When assessing human service organizations, funders look for the leadership, mission, vision, and strategy, program delivery and impact, strategic relationships, resource development, and internal operations and management to base its decision for funding. The ability of an organization to demonstrate competency in these areas makes them attractive to funders who are able to provide resources for organizations to do their work.

Managers of organizations must keep both the interests of clients and funders in mind when managing internal operations and maintaining external relations. By working with individuals and groups, managers seek to ensure that the work done within the organization is not only accomplishing organizational performance goals, but that it also meets the expectations of funders in achieving the same objectives. Organizations that are able to demonstrate capacity receive a continuous flow of financial resources that support the staff in meeting the organization's performance targets.

Management seeks to influence workers' assessment of the organization by providing the necessary leadership and support for implementing its mission, providing supervisory support, and fostering open and supportive working conditions. Managers who foster an environment that encourags workers to engage in problem solving and organizational change are often successful in retaining workers and preventing burnout. They also monitor the degree to which the mission of the organization is in alignment with workers' understanding and expectations of the organization in order to prevent miscommunication and negative impacts on clients.

Performance is a concern for both managers and workers. Managers are interested in achieving the highest performance from workers when assessing client outcomes. Workers are interested in addressing organizational expectations in order to meet the needs of clients and grow professionally. The shared concern for high levels of organizational performance needs to be monitored on an ongoing basis.

Workers who are satisfied with their jobs are able to provide quality service. These workers are committed to helping clients solve their problems in a manner satisfactory to service recipients. To clients of human service organizations, the provision of quality service relates to reliability, responsiveness, assurance, empathy, and tangibles. Workers who keep these dimensions of quality in mind are able to empower clients to make changes to their lives that can lead to positive client outcomes.

The four perspectives (clients, funders, managers, and workers) described in this chapter and illustrated in Figure 25.1 are needed in order to acquire a comprehensive understanding of organizational assessment. It is critical to note that each party "sits in a different position" inside or outside of the organization and therefore develops an assessment based on different perceptions, assumptions, experiences, and interests. The ongoing (e.g., annual) monitoring of these different perspectives, using different mechanisms (e.g., surveys, focus groups, interviews) provide the elements needed to pursue organizational excellence. The influence of each perspective on another provides an agenda for future dialogue among staff and

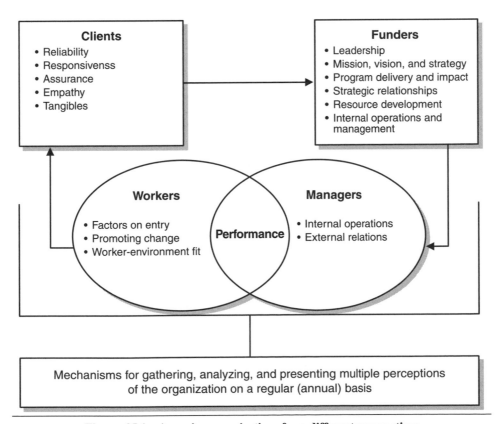

Figure 25.1   Assessing organizations from different perspectives

investigation for researchers. For example, one pattern of influence noted in Figure 25.1 begins with clients' needs influencing funders who, in turn, influence managers and workers who seek to maximize organizational performance related to meeting clients' needs. Other patterns of influence could also be identified.

A major goal for the staff and managers of human service organizations and their funders is the achievement of organizational excellence. Organizational assessment is a key ingredient in achieving excellence. As Kettner (2002) notes, excellence includes a client-focused mission statement for the organization, an organizational culture that promotes consistency and commitment to quality services, and an organizational climate of teamwork that values the views of clients and staff members. As human service organizations seek to measure themselves against national standards located in agency accreditation processes, they will find that assessment is a central feature of the organizational self-study process used by accreditation organizations in the fields of child welfare, mental health, health-care, and aging services. In essence, organizational assessment is the first step down the road to achieving organizational excellence.

REFERENCES

Austin, M. J. (1989). Executive entry: Multiple perspectives on the process of muddling through. *Administration in Social Work, 13*(3/4), 55–71.

Austin, M. J. (1996). Planning for organizational change: Linking the past with the present and future. *Journal of Jewish Communal Service, 73*(1), 44–52.

Austin, M. J., & Gilmore, T. (1993). Executive exit: Multiple perspectives on managing the leadership transition. *Administration in Social Work, 17*(1), 47–60.

Austin, M. J., & Hopkins, K. (Eds.). (2004). *Supervision as collaboration in the human services: Building a learning culture.* Thousand Oaks, CA: Sage.

Bartczak, L. (2005). *A funder's guide to organizational assessment: Tools, processes, and their use in building capacity.* St. Paul, MN: Fieldstone Alliance.

Connolly, P., & Lukas, C. (2002). *Strengthening nonprofit performance: A funder's guide to capacity building.* St. Paul, MN: Fieldstone Alliance.

Freeman, D. E., & Roming, L. (2005). The Unity Foundation's CQ: Capacity benchmarking and capacity building. In L. Bartczak (Ed.), *A funder's guide to organizational assessment: Tools, processes, and their use in building capacity* (pp. 97–111). St. Paul, MN: Fieldstone Alliance.

Gibelman, M. (2003). *Navigating human service organizations: Essential information for thriving and surviving in agencies.* Chicago: Lyceum Books.

Ginsberg, S. (1997, August 24). When departure produces uncertainty: Chief executives are being replaces more frequently than before causing anxiety among employees at all levels. *Washington Post,* p. H4.

Gurthrie, K., & Preston, A. (2005). Building capacity while assessing it. In Bartczak (Ed.), *A funder's guide to organizational assessment: Tools, processes, and their use in building capacity* (pp. 29–60). St. Paul, MN: Fieldstone Alliance.

Hackman, J. R. (1987). The design of work teams. In J. Lorsch (Ed.), *Handbook of organizational behavior.* Englewood Cliffs, NJ: Prentice Hall.

Hackman, J. R. (Ed.). (1991). *Groups that work (and those that don't).* San Francisco: Jossey-Bass.

Harrison, M. (2005). *Diagnosing organizations: Methods, models, and processes* (3rd ed.). Thousand Oaks, CA: Sage.

Hasenfeld, Y. (1983). *Human service organizations.* Upper Saddle River, NJ: Prentice Hall.

Hernandez, C. M., & Leslie, D. R. (2001). Charismatic leadership: The aftermath. *Nonprofit Management and Leadership, 11*(4), 493–497.

Horejsi, C. R., & Garthwait, C. L. (1999). *The social work practicum: A guide and workbook for students*. Boston: Allyn & Bacon.

Kadushin, A. (2002). *Supervision in social work* (4th ed.). New York: Columbia University Press.

Kettner, P. (2002). *Achieving excellence in the management of human service organizations*. Boston: Allyn & Bacon.

Lipsky, M. (1983). *Street-level bureaucracy: Dilemmas of the individual in public service*. New York: Russell Sage Foundation.

Martin, L. (1995). Customer satisfaction in the social services. In G. Burton & P. McCallion (Eds.), *Total quality management social services* (pp. 165–181). Albany, NY: Rockefeller College Press.

Menefee, D. (2000). What managers do and why they do it. In R. Pati (Ed.), *The handbook of social welfare management* (pp. 247–266). Thousand Oaks, CA: Sage.

Milliken, F., & Martins, L. (1996). Searching for common threads: Understanding the multiple effects of diversity in organizational groups. *Academy of Management Review, 21*, 402–433.

O'Neil, R., Hassett, S., & Austin, M. J. (1995). Clients as customers: A county social service agency listens to its primary customer. In B. Gummer & P. McCallion (Eds.), *Total Quality Management (TQM) in social services: Theory and practice* (pp. 275–284). Albany, NY: Rockefeller College Press.

Rapp, C. A. (1998). *The strengths model: Case management with people suffering from severe and persistent mental illness*. New York: Oxford University Press.

Rapp, C. A., & Poertner, J. (1992). *Social administration: A client-centered approach*. New York: Longman.

Rees, F. (1997). *Teamwork from start to finish*. San Francisco: Jossey-Bass.

Saleebey, D. (Ed.). (1997). *The strengths perspective in social work practice* (2nd ed.) New York: Longman.

Schmid, H. (2000). Agency environment relations: Understanding task environments. In R. J. Patti (Ed.), *Handbook of social welfare management* (pp. 133–154). Thousand Oaks, CA: Sage.

Schriver, J. M. (2004). *Human behavior and the social environment: Shifting paradigms in essential knowledge for social work*. San Francisco: Pearson.

Zeithaml, V., Parasuraman, A., & Berry, L. (1990). *Delivering quality services*. New York: Free Press.

Chapter 26

INTERVENTION WITH ORGANIZATIONS

Charles Glisson

Human service organizations generally and social service organizations in particular vary greatly in the work environments they create for social workers and others who provide services and interact with clients. This is important because there is evidence that these organizations' work environments (e.g., organizational structure, culture, climate, and work attitudes) affect employee turnover, service provider interactions with the people they serve, service quality, and service outcomes. Service providers in social service organizations with more positive work environments are less likely to quit their jobs, deliver higher quality services, and produce better outcomes (Glisson, 1978, 2007; Glisson & Durick, 1988; Glisson & Green, 2006; Glisson & Hemmelgarn, 1998; Glisson & James, 2002; Glisson, Landsverk, et al., in press; Glisson, Schoenwald et al., in press). A recent study of child welfare systems by the U.S. General Accounting Office (2003) concluded that increased workforce stability and positive organizational climates are critical to improving services in those systems. Moreover, a number of writers argue that the work environments of both mental health and social service organizations are important to service outcomes because they affect whether best practices are adopted, how they are implemented, and whether they are sustained and effective (Glisson, 2002; Glisson, Landsverk et al., in press; Glisson, Schoenwald et al., in press; Hoagwood, Burns, Kiser, Ringeisen, & Schoenwald, 2001; Hohmann & Shear, 2002; Jensen, 2003; Schoenwald & Hoagwood, 2001).

For these reasons, studies of child welfare systems that examined the effects of work environment characteristics on service quality and outcomes concluded that future efforts to improve children's service systems should focus on creating positive organizational climates (Glisson, 2007; Glisson & Hemmelgarn, 1998; U.S. General Accounting Office, 2003). However, little is known about effective methods for developing positive work environments within mental health and social service systems. This is because organizational intervention strategies that have been used to improve work environments and performance in other types of organizations are rarely used in mental health and social service systems (U.S. General Accounting Office, 2003). Moreover, almost no controlled studies of organizational intervention strategies have been conducted in mental health and social service systems, and only one randomized controlled study to date has tested whether an

This research was supported by NIMH research grant number R01-MH66905. Correspondence concerning this article should be sent to Charles Glisson, PhD, Children's Mental Health Services Research Center, The University of Tennessee, Knoxville, TN 37996-3332; phone: (865) 974-1707, fax: (865) 974-1662, e-mail: cglisson@utk.edu.

organizational intervention strategy can improve organizational climate and reduce service provider turnover in these types of systems (Glisson, Dukes, & Green, 2006).

In the world of business management and administrative practice, examples of organizational change efforts are common, and a wide variety of efforts to make organizations more effective or efficient could be included under the heading of organizational interventions. For example, these efforts might include selection (e.g., boards of directors firing an existing CEO and hiring a new one); organizational lumping and splitting (i.e., lumping previously separated organizational units or divisions together into one division, or splitting a single division or unit into separate units); the use of surveys to provide feedback to the administration on employee attitudes about their jobs; or the implementation of new technologies (e.g., computerized management information system). These are just a few of the many examples of efforts to improve organizations that are attempted on a routine and ongoing basis by a variety of organizations nationwide, frequently with disappointing results. The deficits in many of these efforts are rooted in the fact that each activity is insufficient when used alone, without benefit of an overall, comprehensive change model and strategy. More comprehensive strategies are rarely used because boards of directors, CEOs, and organizational members generally like the notion of improving effectiveness and efficiency, but also want to avoid the pain of disrupting familiar, well-worn paths of behavior, expectations, and attitudes that define the fundamental nature of their organization. That is, it seems to be common among organizations, as well as individuals, to want things to work better without doing anything different. This is the major barrier that confronts any organizational intervention or change effort.

The resistance to organizational change is rooted in the inclination to use familiar "well-worn paths," the need to avoid the potential embarrassment of failing at a new strategy, and the frustration of having gone through the disruption of previous change efforts that resulted in little substantive improvements. Although the previously mentioned examples of organizational change efforts could be, and frequently are, implemented with the hope of improving an organization's performance and success, the efforts are doomed to failure when they are undertaken without benefit of systematic organizational intervention strategies that have been previously shown to work and without the type of comprehensive, longitudinal intervention plan that is required to improve the performance of a complex organization.

Although the term *best practices* is used pervasively throughout the organizational literature as well as the practice world, there is little effort to define the criteria that must be met to qualify an organizational intervention or change strategy as a "best practice," and almost no change strategies have been tested in controlled experimental trials (Pfeffer & Sutton, 2006). Moreover, most organizational change efforts in the world of practice are conducted in a piecemeal, unsystematic, and reactive way, without regard to what has been shown to work in other organizations or without a guiding model of organizational behavior and change.

Change efforts that use an integrated array of intervention strategies simultaneously, not just one or two, implemented within a comprehensive model of change, and guided by specific goals and principles of organizational behavior, are surprisingly rare. This is important because there is a growing body of research that suggests such planned, comprehensive interventions may be the most successful. However, much of the existing information about interventions in organizations comes from the broad organizational literature that has focused primarily on business and industrial organizations and, to a less extent, on government organization. As a result, the conceptual and empirical basis for interventions in social service and mental health organizations depend heavily on literature from business and government. This chapter reviews the broader organizational literature and describes a comprehensive, planned intervention model that integrates and adapts much of the broader literature on organizational intervention for social and mental health services.

SOCIAL, STRATEGIC, AND TECHNICAL DIMENSIONS OF ORGANIZATIONAL CONTEXT

Organizational change experts agree that successful interventions must be guided by a comprehensive model of organization change that addresses social, strategic, and technical factors in organizations (Farias & Johnson, 2000; Robertson, Roberts, & Porras, 1993; Woodman, 1989; Worren, Ruddle, & Moore, 1999). These three dimensions define and encompass the elements of organizational context that are most important for work performance and organizational effectiveness. Moreover, these three dimensions are all malleable, and there is evidence that they can be shaped by planned interventions.

Social context defines the human dimension of an organization and characterizes the expectations, affective tone, and behaviors that capture how employees interact with, and react to, their work environment and their clients. An organization's social context includes the norms and values that shape the organization's culture (i.e., proficienty, rigidity), the climate created by the psychological impact of the work environment on the individual workers (i.e., engagement, stress), and the work attitudes (i.e., job satisfaction, commitment) that characterize employees' affective responses to their work environment (Glisson, Landsverk, et al., in press). Although traditional organizational development techniques focused on social context, and it could be argued that social context is the most important of the three for organizational effectiveness, there is evidence that the most successful interventions address all three (Farias & Johnson, 2000; Robertson et al., 1993; Woodman, 1989; Worren et al., 1999).

The technical dimension of organizational context, what has been termed its core technology, includes the knowledge, skills, and tools that are used to create the product or provide the service that is the organization's raison d'etre. In social service organizations, these factors define the practice knowledge and models, assessment tools and protocols, intervention approaches, and monitoring measures that are used by individual social workers in their efforts to serve clients. Compared to the type of hard-core technologies used in many business and industrial organizations, social service technologies are softer and more easily molded by the social context in which they are implemented. As a result, social service technologies can be described as *vulnerable* technologies that adapt to fit the structure, culture, and climate in which they are implemented (Glisson, 1978, 1992, 2002).

The strategic dimension of organizational context is composed of the plans and tactics that organizations use to survive, achieve stated goals, improve, and grow. Strategies in service organizations can focus on interactions with elements in the organization's external environment (e.g., clients, funding agencies, regulatory agencies, advocacy groups, and competing organizations) and on internal processes (e.g., changes in service capacity, deployment of personnel, focus of employee evaluations). Again, there is evidence that the most effective organizational interventions address social, technical, and strategic factors to ensure that change efforts in each dimension are complementary.

WORK ENVIRONMENTS OF SOCIAL SERVICE ORGANIZATIONS

The nature of the social workers' responsibilities; the seriousness of the behavioral and emotional problems experienced by the children and families they serve; and the demands of judges, attorneys, advocates, and others make social work in many service systems stressful, indeterminate, and complex. These work environment characteristics explain why previous studies of mental health, child welfare, and juvenile justice systems found that indicators of organizational climate such as case overload, role conflict, emotional exhaustion, and depersonalization affected case managers' work attitudes, the quality of care they provide, and service outcomes (Glisson, 2007; Glisson & Durick, 1988; Glisson & Hemmelgarn, 1998; Glisson & James, 2002; Glisson, Schoenwald, et al., in press).

These work environment characteristics also help to explain why many mental health and social service systems develop resistant and rigid cultures that erect barriers to innovation and resist new practices that could potentially improve the quality and outcomes of services. These cultures require excessive documentation, overly restrictive supervisory approval, and rigid conformity to procedural specifications such as protection against public criticism, administrative sanctions, and litigation. Such cultures promote reactivity rather than responsiveness to serving clients because social workers in rigid and resistant service cultures create strategies to avoid assuming responsibility for children and families with the most serious problems out of fear that bureaucratic or legal sanctions will result if examples of failed services become public (Glisson & James, 1992; Nugent & Glisson, 1999). As a result, proficient organizational cultures that emphasize performance, competence, and innovation are difficult to develop, and social workers in many mental health and social service systems follow well-worn and familiar organizational paths of behavior regardless of the implications for service quality or outcomes (Martin, Peters, & Glisson, 1998).

USING PLANNED INTERVENTION TO CHANGE ORGANIZATIONAL CONTEXTS

Almost no organizational intervention research has been conducted in social service organizations, but there is empirical evidence from hundreds of studies in a variety of organizations that organizational interventions can build the types of cultures and climates that make organizations more effective (Burke, 1993). A meta-analysis of 126 studies by Neuman, Edwards, and Raju (1989) and a meta-analysis of 98 studies by Guzzo, Jette, and Katzell (1985) concluded that organizational interventions can improve work attitudes and performance. A meta-analysis of 52 additional studies by Robertson et al. (1993) found that organizational interventions that target multiple organizational dimensions (e.g., social, technological, and strategic) are the most effective. They also found that among interventions that target a single dimension, those that target social context (e.g., culture and climate) are the most effective.

Affirming the value of targeting multiple dimensions, Worren et al. (1999) argued that traditional development models that focus only on work relationships are less effective than broader systems-based models. Systems interventions introduce new strategies to guide the organization's interactions with its external environment, implement innovative technologies, and change specific work behaviors. Most recent intervention models take a broader systems perspective (Woodman, 1989). That is, they focus on the technology and strategies used by the organization as well as facilitate positive social contexts and work relationships (Farias & Johnson, 2000).

Both traditional organizational development models and more recent intervention models that focus on an array of organizational factors acknowledge the central role in change efforts played by the social context of an organization. Studies in a variety of organizations confirm the importance of an organization's social context in implementing state-of-the-art technologies and forming strategic responses to evolving or turbulent external environments. For example, hospitals with "psychologically safe" climates are more likely to implement new cardiac surgical technologies successfully (Edmondson, Bohmer, & Pisano, 2001). Successful strategic and technical changes in an information technology firm are linked to organizational social contexts characterized by support and trust (Huy, 2002). And a study of a children's residential treatment facility identified social context factors that presented barriers to strategic change and technological innovation aimed at improving services (Kahn, Cross, & Parker, 2003).

Studies also indicate that successful organizational interventions must focus on small groups or teams within an organization. This is because resistance to change and innovation in an organization forms at small group levels. It is within these work groups that the social processing of information, social interactions devoted to understanding the work, the development of shared schema, and other interpretative processes occur (George & Jones, 2001). For this reason, Weick and Quinn (1999) argued that change at the organizational level is rooted in group-level change. Similarly, general systems theories of organizational performance explain that group-level changes affect the entire organizational system within which the groups are embedded (Katz & Kahn, 1978; Whelan-Berry, Gordon, & Hinings, 2003).

HISTORICAL BACKGROUND

The evolution of planned organizational intervention for improving organizational performance and the implications of that evolution for social work and social services are reflected in the changes in the focus and orientation of the intervention models over several decades. This evolution provides an important background for understanding the origins of the models that guide current organizational intervention research and practice.

From Scientific Management to Human Relations

The focus and nature of efforts to improve organizational effectiveness experienced a profound change in the twentieth century. That change reflected a tension between two opposing ideas about how organizations should be viewed. One view described an organization as a machine with interconnected parts that could be operated or modified in a way to maximize its performance, based on the expertise of the "operator" or "driver" (e.g., CEO). The other view described an organization as a psychosocial organism that develops a life and direction of its own and has to be "guided" rather than "driven" to maximize effectiveness. The mechanistic model of organization spawned "scientific management" techniques and related strategies that sought improved organizational performance by (a) breaking down the core work of the organization into the smallest possible increments or tasks, (b) determining how each incremental task could be accomplished in the most efficient manner, (c) training workers to perform each of the tasks in the most efficient way, and (d) then monitoring each task to make sure it was performed in exactly the same way. Contemporary assembly lines and time-motion studies evolved from these ideas as industrial organizations became entranced with the idea of "man as machine," an idea that was famously satirized by Charlie Chaplin in a 1936 film that focused on assembly line work, titled *Modern Times*.

In the middle of the twentieth century, a new approach to improving organizational performance gained attention. The new approach emphasized the nature of human relations and human interactions within an organic model. Studies of strategies for creating more humane working conditions, improving work relationships, expanding work responsibilities, and developing the "human side of enterprise" proliferated (McGregor, 1960).

From Individual Workers to Social Context

Structure has long been synonymous with formal organization and has been studied empirically for more than half a century (March & Simon, 1958). In its simpler form, organizational structure describes the configuration of the organization in terms of its horizontal layers and vertical divisions. In a more complex form, structure can be viewed as reflecting an integral part of organizational culture by prescribing the amount of discretion, flexibility, and innovation granted to individual workers.

In the earliest literature on structure, a disproportionate emphasis was placed on identifying the optimal way for all organizations to structure in terms of the number of layers or divisions and the number of employees within each. Scholars later abandoned the search for the "one best way" to structure all organizations and directed their attention to understanding the contingencies on which the optimal structuring of particular work activities depended. For example, Woodward (1958, 1965) identified the core technology of an organization as the most important contingency and spawned several decades of research into the relationship between structure and technology. Some of this research focused on human service and mental health organizations (Glisson, 1978, 1992). These and other efforts viewed the nature of the core technology of an organization (e.g., mental health treatment) as critical to understanding how the organization should be structured. Moreover, it was determined that the more an organization's structure complemented and supported the work conducted in the organization's core technology, the more effective the organization. However, as described in subsequent sections, this relationship was found not to be as straightforward as it first seemed.

Culture and Climate as Distinct Constructs

The organizational research literature has included the concepts of organizational culture and climate for several decades, but until the past decade, the research literature on each construct developed independently (Glisson, 2000; Reichers & Schneider, 1990). Moreover, as their popularity increased, multiple definitions evolved for each construct. But a recent content analysis of the organizational literatures on culture and climate identified a core concept for each construct (Verbeke, Volgering, & Hessels, 1998). The core concepts described *climate* as the way people perceive their work environment and *culture* as the way things are done in an organization (Verbeke et al., 1998). Using this distinction, climate is defined as a property of the individual and culture is defined as a property of the organization. This difference has been suggested for over a decade and characterizes the definitions of the two constructs presented here (James, James, & Ashe, 1990).

Culture is defined as the norms and expectations that drive work behavior in an organization or work unit. These norms and expectations guide the way work is approached and socialize new employees in the priorities of the organization (e.g., Does paperwork or client well-being come first?). Organizational culture is often described in "layers," with behavioral expectations and norms representing an outer layer and values and assumptions representing an inner layer (Rousseau, 1990). Stated in another way, Hofstede (1998) described behavior as the visible part of culture and values as the invisible part. For this reason, culture is sometimes described as a "deep" construct. Although Stackman, Pinder, and Connor (2000) pointed out that it is not clear what "deep" means in an organization, the description of the "deep" aspects of culture parallel the "inner layer" described by Rousseau (1990) and the "invisible" part of culture described by Hofstede (1998).

Culture appears to be transmitted among employees more through behavioral expectations and normative beliefs than through "deeper" values or assumptions (Ashkanasy, Broadfoot, & Falkus, 2000; Hofstede, 1998; Hofstede, Neuijen, Ohayv, & Sanders, 1990). This is because individuals in an organization can comply with behavioral expectations without necessarily internalizing the values and assumptions that lie at the core of those expectations. Expectations and norms may reflect the values and assumptions of organizational leaders, but not other members of the organization. Or expectations and norms may be determined by the job demands and realities that workers face on a daily basis, regardless of the values and assumptions of top management (Hemmelgarn, Glisson, & Dukes, 2001). But it is the "visible" expectations and norms that are most explicit and shared, while the deeper assumptions and values held by management or reflected in the behavior of the workplace may be less obvious (Glisson & James, 2002).

The distinction between *psychological* climate and *organizational* climate, shown in Figure 26.1, provides a basis for understanding climate and the role it plays in linking organizational properties to mental health service provider attitudes and behavior (Glisson & James, 2002; James & James, 1989; James et al., 1990; James & Jones, 1974). Psychological climate is the individual's perception of the psychological impact of the work environment on his or her own well-being (James & James, 1989). When workers in the same organizational unit agree on their perceptions, their "shared" perceptions can be aggregated to describe the organizational climate of their work unit (Jones & James, 1979; Joyce & Slocum, 1984). The psychological climate of a work environment is measured as multiple dimensions (e.g., stress, engagement, functionality), a single, higher-order, general psychological climate factor is believed to underlie these dimensions (Glisson, Landsverk et al., in press). This general factor represents the worker's overall perception of the positive or negative psychological impact of the work environment on the worker (James & James, 1989; James et al., 1990). Several studies identified a single psychological climate factor

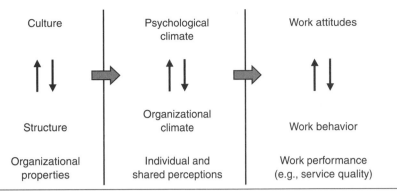

Figure 26.1   Conceptual model of organizational social context

that represents the overall psychological "safety" of the work environment for the individual worker (Brown & Leigh, 1996; Glisson & Hemmelgarn, 1998; Glisson & James, 2002). At the same time, there is also evidence that the overall climate of a work environment can be represented by multiple second-order factors (Glisson et al., 2006; Glisson, Landsverk, et al., in press).

Work Attitudes

Work attitudes in organizational research most frequently include job satisfaction and organizational commitment (Glisson & Durick, 1988). Both have been studied extensively for many years. Locke (1976) defined job satisfaction as the positive appraisal of one's job or job experiences. Mowday, Porter, and Steers (1982) described organizational commitment as a willingness to exert considerable effort on behalf of the organization and a strong desire to remain a member of the organization. So commitment was viewed as an employee's attachment to the organization, whereas satisfaction focused on the employee's specific tasks and duties (Mowday et al., 1982; Williams & Hazer, 1986). Although the two variables would be expected to be correlated, an employee who is attached to a specific organization might be unhappy with certain aspects of a specific job within that organization and vice versa. A half-century ago, Viteles (1953) suggested that employee morale was a function of both satisfaction and commitment. That is, employees with high morale have an attachment to their organization and a positive reaction to their specific job within the organization (Glisson, Landsverk, et al., in press).

From Organizational Development to Change Management

There is evidence that organizational development strategies that address the social context of services can contribute to effectiveness, but that broader strategies that integrate social, strategic, and technological factors are even more effective. These findings prompted some writers to challenge the effectiveness of narrowly focused organizational development strategies and to advocate the use of change strategies that use a broader array of interventions. Worren et al. (1999) argued that traditional models of organizational development that merely facilitate positive human relations are less effective than broader systems-based models that introduce new strategies for guiding an organization's interactions with its external environment, implement innovative technologies to improve the quality of the product or service, and target specific work behaviors for improvement. Although interventions vary widely, many of the development models take a broader systems perspective (Woodman, 1989). That is, they focus on the technology, strategies, and social context of organizational systems as well as target specific work behaviors in active change efforts that go beyond the facilitation of positive work relationships (Farias & Johnson, 2000). In the ARC (availability, responsiveness, and continuity) organizational intervention model described later, multiple intervention components are integrated within a broader system perspective and adapted for use with organizations that provide social and mental health services (Glisson et al., 2006).

From Intra-Organizational to Both Intra- and Inter-Organizational Strategies

Intra-organizational intervention strategies address the needs of service providers (e.g., therapists, caseworkers) and involve them in organizational policy decisions and in the design of organizational processes that affect their work (e.g., the provision of services). The majority of the studies of organizational interventions have focused on intra-organizational issues. Although almost no organizational change research has been conducted in social service or mental health service organizations, there is empirical evidence that organizational interventions in other types of organizations can build the types of intra-organizational contexts that make organizations more effective (Burke, 1993). Intervention models that include interorganizational strategies are less common, but there are organizational domain development strategies that suggest interorganizational issues can complement or constrain efforts at meaningful organizational change.

Interorganizational domain development strategies used in the ARC model create alliances among service providers, organizations, local opinion leaders, and community stakeholders for the purpose of addressing targeted problems and supporting effective children's services that respond to those problems within a particular community. Although less research has been conducted on domain development than on organizational development strategies generally, success with domain strategies has been documented in a variety of community contexts (Gray, 1990; Patton & Cissell, 1990; Trist, 1985). Molgaard (1997) concluded that community-level development strategies are especially useful in rural communities to support the implementation of new mental health programs. Research indicates that informal community-level alliances are critical to mental health service delivery in rural areas and that these alliances in rural areas are most likely to be formed at the county level and not at lower (e.g., town) or higher (e.g., multicounty) levels (Fried, Johnsen, Starrett, Calloway, & Morrissey, 1998). ARC development strategies focus on county-level government, community groups, businesses, and key community opinion leaders such as judges, principals, and ministers.

From Business Organizations to Human Services

The business and industrial world's enthusiasm about organizational social context originated with Peters and Waterman's (1982) book, *In Search of Excellence*. Using America's most successful businesses as case studies, Peters and Waterman inspired a nationwide infatuation with culture and climate among business and industrial leaders. Osborne and Gaebler's (1992) *Reinventing Government* provided a popular extension and expansion of Peters and Waterman's work to include government agencies by demonstrating the importance of organizational social context to the performance of public agencies. Schorr's (1997) *Common Purpose* built on Osborne and Gaebler's work to explain the role that organizational social context plays in child welfare and family service systems and provided a number of case examples of how the effectiveness of service systems was affected by the norms, expectations, perceptions, and attitudes that comprise the social context of the organization.

The social context created by an organization includes interpersonal relationships, social norms, behavioral expectations, individual perceptions, attitudes, and other psychosocial factors that govern how organizational members approach their work, interact with others in their organization, interpret their work environment, collaborate with members of "referent" organizations, and how they feel about their jobs. For many decades, scholars of business and industrial organizations recognized the importance of psychosocial factors that comprise the "human side of enterprise" (McGregor, 1960). And over the past half-century, a number of studies examined the adoption and implementation of new technologies and organizational effectiveness as a function of organizational social context. Several studies concluded that the dimensions of organizational social context that are particularly important to innovation and effectiveness are its culture, climate, structure, and domain (see reviews in Glisson, 1992, 2000; Gray, 1985, 1990; Michela & Burke, 2000; Rogers, 2003; Sorensen, 2002).

An organization's culture, climate, structure, and domain are important because they create a social context that invites or rejects innovation, complements or inhibits the activities required for success, and sustains or alters adherence to the protocols that compose the organization's core technology. Research on these constructs can be used by researchers to understand and study the dissemination and implementation of efficacious mental health treatments, adherence to treatment protocols, and service effectiveness. To date, this work has been useful in several studies that examined how organizational context affects the quality and outcomes of children's services (Glisson, 2000, 2007; Glisson & Green, 2006; Glisson & Hemmelgarn, 1998; Glisson & James, 2002; Hemmelgarn et al., 2001). Several key characteristics of organizational social context are reviewed here and included in a conceptual model (shown in Figure 26.1) that is used to discuss the importance of organizational context for the outcomes of children's mental health services.

THE ARC MODEL AS A FRAMEWORK FOR IMPLEMENTING ORGANIZATION INTERVENTION

The ARC intervention strategy depends on general systems theory (Katz & Kahn, 1978), diffusion of innovation theory (Rogers, 2003), sociotechnical models of organizational effectiveness (Rousseau, 1977; Trist, 1985), traditional models of organizational development (Burke, 1993; Porras & Robertson, 1992; Tichy, 1983), and interorganizational domain development (Trist, 1985). General systems theories describe organizations as linking inputs from their external environments to technical processes to create outputs in the form of products or services (Katz & Kahn, 1978). Those outputs complete a cycle of exchange between the organization and its external environment. Although *technical* and *strategic* processes produce these outputs, general systems, sociotechnical, diffusion of innovation, and change management models argue that the effectiveness of technical and strategic processes depends on the *social* context in which they are embedded (Robertson et al., 1993; Rogers, 2003; Rousseau, 1977; Trist, 1985; Worren et al., 1999). These models are supported by social cognitive theory that describes the effect of social context on cognitive processes that affect both attitudes and behavior (Bandura, 1986). This effect explains why traditional models of organizational development focus on organizational social contexts (Burke, 1993; Michela & Burke, 2000; Porras & Robertson, 1992).

The Use of Trained Change Agents

ARC change agents work with service teams, administrators, key opinion leaders, and community stakeholders to help remove barriers to performance created by bureaucratic red tape, turf wars, misinformation, ineffective procedures, poor communication, and mistrust (Beer, 1980; Bennis, 1966; Blake, Shepard, & Mouton, 1964; Callister & Wall, 2001; French & Bell, 1984; Porras & Robertson, 1992; Robey & Altman, 1982; Rogers, 2003). Change agents help organizations overcome such barriers to adopt best practices, develop new service strategies, and design successful work processes and structures (Burke, 1993; French & Bell, 1984; Pasmore, Francis, Haldeman, & Shani, 1982; Porras, 1986; Steel & Shane, 1986; Walton, 1987).

The ARC model does not prescribe a priori solutions to organizational barriers to effectiveness but instead provides the structure and process through which service systems can "learn" to improve by first identifying barriers and then developing individualized strategies for addressing those barriers. The ARC model depicts organizations as comprised of the three primary dimensions mentioned above: social context (e.g., culture, climate, work attitudes), strategies (e.g., plans, tactics), and core technologies (e.g., knowledge, skills, tools). Further, the multiple intervention components that comprise the model address all three dimensions.

The intervention components that focus on social context are designed to build a constructive organizational culture and healthy psychological climate that promote the social support and psychological safety required for successful collaboration and innovation. There is evidence that service organizations with proficient, flexible cultures, and healthy, engaged climates encourage and support the types of service provider attitudes and behaviors that contribute to learning, innovation, and improvement efforts. We know, for example, that among health, mental health, and social service providers in high-stress work environments, those who work in proficient cultures and healthy climates are less likely to quit their jobs or experience burnout and more likely to adopt innovative technologies, exhibit the level of commitment required to solve tough problems encountered on the job, provide higher quality service and achieve better service outcomes (Edmondson et al., 2001; Glisson & Durick, 1988; Glisson & Green, 2006; Glisson & Hemmelgarn, 1998; Glisson & James, 2002; Glisson, Schoenwald, et al., in press; Jaskyte & Dressler, 2005). The ARC model was developed to develop those types of cultures and climates in mental health and social service organizations.

Intervention in Organizations as a Team-Based Process

A significant portion of the ARC organizational intervention is team based because research indicates that culture, climate, and work attitudes can vary within an organization by team or small work unit; resistance to change is based in team or small group processes; and that efforts to support innovation and change are most successful when they focus interventions at the team or small group level. It is within work groups that the social processing of information, social interactions devoted to affective sense making, the development of shared schema, and other interpretative processes occur (George & Jones, 2001). For this reason, Weick and Quinn (1999) argued that change at the organizational level is rooted in group-level change. Similarly, general systems theories of organizational performance explain that group-level changes affect the entire organizational system within which the groups are embedded (Katz & Kahn, 1978; Whelan-Berry et al., 2003). Our preliminary research indicates that the social context of child welfare and juvenile justice organizations vary by service team and that ARC intervention can improve the social context of targeted teams within a larger organizational context (Glisson et al., 2006; Glisson & James, 2002).

Stages in Organizational Intervention

As shown in Table 26.1, the ARC intervention components are grouped in three stages (collaboration, participation, and innovation) and implemented over four phases. The first stage focuses on the interorganizational domain and includes components designed to facilitate collaboration with other organizations, stakeholders, and networks (Gray, 1985, 1990). These collaborations provide sources of information, technical expertise, and

Table 26.1   Stages, Components, and Phases of the ARC Organizational Intervention Model

	Phases			
Stages and components	I Problem Identification	II Direction Setting	III Implementation	IV Stabilization
Collaboration				
1. Leadership development	■			
2. Personal relationships	■			
3. Network development	■	■		
Participation				
4. Team building	■	■		
5. Information and training	■	■	■	
6. Feedback	■	■	■	■
7. Participatory decision making	■	■	■	■
8. Conflict management	■	■	■	■
Innovation				
9. Goal setting		■		
10. Continuous improvement			■	■
11. Job redesign			■	■
12. Self-regulation				■

political support required to improve services through innovation and change. The second stage includes the components required to build the level of participation within the social context of the organization needed to develop proficient, flexible cultures and healthy climates that support innovation and change. Building the participation required to develop the organization's social context is a team-based effort. These components also generate a need for innovation by stimulating a "tension for change" through information, feedback, and participation. Components in the final stage identify barriers to improved services and address those barriers with redesigned service protocols, new treatment models, improved assessment strategies, and other innovations.

Guiding Principles for Intervention in Organization

All organizations are guided by principles although those principles are frequently implicit and counterproductive. The ARC organizational model for collaboration, participation, and innovation depends on the implementation of five principles that were adapted for social and mental health service organizations from Osborne and Gaebler's (1992) model of effective public service organizations. These principles are introduced in the first stage of the collaboration and repeatedly emphasized through the participation and innovation stages to guide discussions, inform decisions, and support action in all three stages. These guiding principles state that effective service organizations are:

1. *Mission-driven not rule-driven:* All service provider actions and decisions should contribute to the well-being of clients and the appropriateness of any action or decision should be assessed on that basis. This principle addresses the threat posed by the well-documented "iron cage of bureaucracy" that emerges in large organizations to restrict service provider discretion with increasingly rigid rules that ignore the unique characteristics of specific clients and inhibit service provider responsiveness to emergent client needs.

2. *Results-oriented not process-oriented:* Performance is evaluated at the individual service provider, treatment team, program, and organizational levels on the basis of improvements in the well-being of clients. This principle addresses deficits in service caused by the common practice of evaluating performance on the basis of process criteria such as the number of clients served, number of client contacts made in a given time period, or the extent to which required paperwork is completed.

3. *Improvement-directed not status quo-directed:* The organization must continually look for new ways to further improve the well-being of its clients and avoid complacency with the organizational status quo. This principle addresses the tendency of established organizations to abhor change and to cling to established protocols whether or not the protocols promote effective service.

4. *Relationship-centered not individual-centered:* Successful social and mental health services are supported by a network of interorganizational relationships and successful clients are supported by a social network of relationships within which they are embedded (e.g., family, school, community). This principle focuses change efforts on the social context within which services are provided and within which clients must function.

5. *Participation-based not authority-based:* An organization's absorptive capacity for new knowledge and openness to innovation is a function of the active participation of staff in identifying barriers to services and in designing approaches for removing those barriers. This principle counters the practice of top officials prescribing efforts to improve services without benefit of the experience, practice knowledge, and input of the frontline service providers.

Phases in Organizational Intervention

Consistent with the multicomponent and phased nature of organizational and inter-organizational intervention strategies shown to be effective in meta analyses (Barraud-Didier & Guerrero, 2002; Burke, 1993; Guzzo et al., 1985; Neuman et al., 1989; Porras & Robertson, 1992; Robertson et al., 1993; Rogers, 2003; Trist, 1985; Worren et al., 1999), the model of collaboration, participation, and innovation uses 12 intervention components through four phases: (I) problem identification, (II) direction setting, (III) implementation, and (IV) stabilization.

I. Problem Identification Phase

In the first phase, leaders, organizational networks, and stakeholders are identified and recruited to help improve services. Important goals in the first phase are to develop personal relationships between members of the collaborating organizations, form collaborative teams (e.g., form new advisory and action groups), and use existing data or gather new data about the impact of the problems of interest that are relevant to the collaborators.

II. Direction Setting Phase

In the second phase, collaborative groups, leaders and participating teams examine interests, articulate values, and develop initial agreements that address targeted issues. The goal is to establish a shared understanding of how targeted issues can be addressed (Gray, 1990). Collaborative groups and treatment teams implement ARC principles and use information (e.g., organizational surveys, feedback systems) to understand and target areas for change.

III. Implementation Phase

A primary objective is to ensure that agreed on activities and patterns of interaction among the collaborating organizations, leaders and teams occur (e.g., in newly formed advisory and action groups, or in existing treatment teams). The possibility of informal power redistribution may meet resistance and barriers that are based on fundamental differences in the way a targeted problem is understood can also emerge. Early in this phase, ARC principles are applied and potential conflicts identified and discussed to minimize the effects of resistance and barriers on agreements and trust.

IV. Stabilization Phase

In this phase, the goal is that the organizations develop strategies for sustaining efforts to collaborate, and to monitor and improve services that address targeted problems and issues. For example, training work team leaders to implement ARC strategies over an extended ARC intervention period is designed to support the stabilization phase.

ARC Strategies in Organizational Intervention

The organizational and interorganizational domain literature concludes that multiple intervention components are needed to develop effective organizational responses to identified problems (Barraud-Didier & Guerrero, 2002; Burke, 1993; Guzzo et al., 1985; Neuman et al., 1989; Porras & Robertson, 1992; Robertson et al., 1993; Rogers, 2003; Trist, 1985; Worren et al., 1999) This is because multiple factors affect the success of an organizational change effort, and the relative importance of each factor in a specific effort is difficult to predict a priori (Robertson et al., 1993; Worren et al., 1999). The five ARC principles described earlier guide the implementation of three stages of 12 intervention components across the four phases. Two of the components, organizational leadership and goal setting, were originally subsumed under 10 components in the initial articles on ARC, but have since been identified as separate components (for a total of 12) as a result of two preliminary studies. Selected on the basis of their demonstrated effectiveness in other industries, the content of the multiple organizational and interorganizational domain development components was adapted for ARC to include specific examples from social and mental health services. The intervention strategies are guided by the *ARC Training Manual* and *ARC Facilitator's Guide* developed by the Children's Mental Health Services Research Center to include detailed steps for implementing the intervention components listed next (Glisson et al., 2006).

As shown in Table 26.1, these components are grouped in three stages, implemented in four phases, and are listed here in a prescribed order. However, the order of implementation must be flexible to respond to the needs of the participating organizations. In addition, experience to date with the ARC model indicates that some components may have to be continued beyond their respective phases:

- *Leadership development* enables leaders to use the ARC principles to communicate a clear vision for change, set high performance standards related to that vision, and create a healthy climate for implementing new technology and polices. Initial work includes sharing information with staff, forming a participative structure to implement the ARC model and guide the interorganizational collaboration (e.g., forming stakeholder advisory groups or interorganizational action groups). Organizational leadership establishes rewards and incentives for meeting performance standards related to improving the well-being of clients (Edmondson et al., 2001; Green, 1998; Gustafson et al., 2003; Meyers, Sivakumar, & Nakata, 1999; Murphy & Southey, 2003; Young, 2000).

- *Cultivate personal relationships* among members of collaborating organizations, opinion leaders, and stakeholders to provide the foundation for communication, sharing information, and solving problems that emerge during the development effort (Rogers, 2003). Personal relationships are formed through one-on-one meetings, quid pro quo activities that are valued by stakeholders and organizational members, and arranging meetings that focus on service issues and barriers that are of interest to the organization and others. Personal relationships are important to negotiating and reframing the meaning of an innovation and adoption of identified best practices (Backer & Rogers, 1998; Ferlie, Gabbay, Fitzgerald, Locock, & Dopson, 2001).

- *Access and facilitate networks* for boundary spanning among change agents, other service providers, opinion leaders, and stakeholders. Members of collaborating organizations provide opportunities for information and idea exchange, service provider access to experts, and stakeholder participation (Goes & Park, 1997; Rogers, 2003). Innovation is influenced by the structure and quality of social networks that influence perceptions, provide information, and offer support (Edmondson et al., 2001; Ferlie et al., 2001). Organizations that promote the development of boundary spanning networks (e.g., through the participation of members of collaborating organizations, access to existing networks, newly formed advisory and action groups that include members of collaborating organizations, and including treatment team leaders in ARC boundary spanning) are more likely to assimilate innovations and best practices (Barnsley, Lemieux-Charles, & McKinney, 1998; Ferlie et al., 2001; Tushman, 1977).

- *Build teamwork* within newly formed action groups and treatment teams selected for the ARC intervention to facilitate participation, information sharing, and support among members. The emphasis here is on helping new or existing teams use their collective expertise and resources to improve services and increase participation and social support to reduce the perceived risks associated with learning new techniques and implementing innovations (Baer & Frese, 2003; Dyer, 1977; Edmondson et al., 2001; Ensley & Pearce, 2001; Higgins & Routhieaux, 1999; Patten, 1981; Rentsch, 1990; Rentsch & Klimoski, 2001). For example, teamwork is developed in selected treatment teams by team leaders who have been trained to apply the ARC model of team problem solving to actual cases and service issues identified by team members.

- *Provide information and training* about the ARC model, the meaning of best practices, and data management strategies to treatment teams to address barriers to innovation and support efforts to improve services (Barraud-Didier & Guerrero, 2002; Green, 1998; Gustafson et al., 2003; Meyers et al., 1999; Pasmore et al., 1982; Rogers, 2003; Tasi, 2001). For example, treatment team leaders trained in ARC strategies help treatment teams understand how to use outcome data to establish baselines and monitor progress in addressing identified barriers to service (Barraud-Didier & Guerrero, 2002; Pasmore et al., 1982; Rogers, 2003; Tasi, 2001). As discussed previously, the subjective perceptions of an innovation (e.g., a new treatment previously, assessment tool, or information system) is as important to its adoption and implementation as its objective attributes (Dearing & And, 1994). Information and training address factors shown to be important to these perceptions. These include demonstrating the relative advantage of an innovation, explaining ARC principles (e.g., improvement directed) that support innovation, offering opportunities to experiment with a new practice, reducing uncertainty associated with innovation, and providing technical support (Dirkson, Ament, & Go, 1996; Ferlie et al., 2001; Meyer & Goes, 1988).

- *Establish a feedback system* (e.g., new assessment and information system) to provide performance information to therapists, treatment teams, programs, and administrators. Feedback about performance is a key factor contributing to the successful adoption of new practices and other improvements by creating a "tension for change" (Burke, 1993; Green, 1998; Grimshaw et al., 2004; Merlani, Garnerin, Diby, Ferring, & Ricou, 2001; Meyer & Goes, 1988; Porras, 1986; Rogers, 2003; Scanlon, Darby, Rolph, & Doty, 2001). In addition, the feedback is necessary to the continuous quality improvement activities described later that are used to guide innovation and change efforts. Following ARC principles, performance feedback is aggregated at different levels so that treatment teams and programs can use the information in their improvement efforts.

- *Implement participatory decision making* within newly formed action groups and ARC treatment teams to create support, increase clarity about innovations (e.g., new treatment models or information systems), and provide the opportunity for input into problem-solving efforts that affect the way services are delivered (e.g., referral procedures, designated service areas, adoption of best practices). Participatory decision making is central to conflict resolution, goal setting, continuous quality improvement, teamwork, and other components of the intervention (Bennis, 1966; McGregor, 1960; Meyers et al., 1999; Porras, 1986; Terziovski, 2002; Yousef, 2000). The use of participatory decision making in the identification of an innovation such as an evidence-based practice is central to developing social support for its subsequent implementation.

- *Resolve conflicts* at the interpersonal, intra-organizational, and interorganizational levels to mediate differences in opinions and competing interests that threaten service effectiveness. Use information sharing, clarification of issues, prioritizing, and established procedures for identifying implicit schema that drive behavior in newly formed interorganizational action groups and existing service teams to moderate or resolve conflicts that are identified in the intervention effort (Alper, Tjosvold, & Law, 2000; Caldwell & O'Reilly, 1982; Callister & Wall, 2001; Rentsch & Klimoski, 2001; Walton, 1987).

- *Goal setting* procedures use data provided by feedback (e.g., from new performance information system) to identify goals using performance criteria that are shared and can be monitored (e.g., treatment team identifies the goal of keeping a specific proportion of outpatient children from entering residential care within a 6-month period). The treatment teams and interorganizational action groups set both short-term and long-term performance goals using participative decision-making procedures described previously. These goals should be difficult to reach and represent actual challenges for the treatment teams and collaborative groups related to service improvement, learning, and innovation (Durham, Knight, & Locke, 1997; Gibson, 2001; Knight, Durham, & Locke, 2001; Sue-Chan & Ong, 2002; Weldon & Yun, 2000).

- *Use continuous quality improvement* techniques to provide the means for changing organizational practices (e.g., referral procedures, transportation policies) and identify potential innovations (e.g., best practices) to facilitate and support the work of the frontline service providers. Recommendations for improvements originate from the ARC treatment teams using databased procedures that identify barriers to care and monitor results of improvement initiatives (Berlowitz et al., 2003; Lemieux-Charles et al., 2002; Shortell, Bennett, & Byck, 1998; Shortell et al., 1995; Steel & Shane, 1986). As a result of these activities, it is expected that the ARC treatment teams will recommend innovations and changes that address identified service deficits and that service improvement plans will include the identification of best practices that could be implemented by treatment teams, as well as changes in existing organizational procedures.

- *Redesign job characteristics* to eliminate service barriers by revising job characteristics (e.g., redefine responsibilities) and teaching new skills (e.g., treatment team leader trained in ARC will teach teams to use standardized assessment profiles in clinical decision making) for specific positions. Job redesign requires that treatment teams be given the opportunity to make suggestions about how their members approach their work and implement new skills for assessment, treatment, and monitoring (French & Bell, 1984; Hackman & Oldham, 1980; Terziovski, 2002).

- *Ensure self-regulation and stabilization* of innovations by providing information and training to facilitate the independent use of the previous components so that the innovations are maintained after the organizational intervention is discontinued (Porras, 1986; Rogers, 2003). Team leaders trained in the ARC model are given progressively more responsibility for implementing these components with their treatment teams. Training service team leaders to implement ARC strategies and the associated lengthened intervention period is expected to contribute to and self-regulation and stabilization.

Intervention Component Summary

The 12 intervention components reflect the most widely used intervention strategies in organizational change efforts. They were selected, adapted, and assembled for the ARC model to address the conclusions of studies that the phased introduction of multiple interventions components maximizes the probability of success in organizational change efforts. The components therefore represent a comprehensive list of organizational change strategies as well as the components of the ARC change model.

LIMITATIONS OF THE EVIDENCE

As explained, studies of organizational interventions have proliferated over many decades and include several meta analyses of almost 300 studies that support the use of planned organizational interventions in improving organizational performance (Guzzo et al., 1985; Neuman et al., 1989; Robertson et al., 1993). At the same time, there are limitations to this evidence that must be considered in evaluating the current knowledge of organization interventions and the roles such interventions can play in improving mental health and social service systems:

- *Poor specification of intervention strategies* characterize these studies when compared to the level of specification found in the best studies of psychosocial interventions with individuals and families. Many of the studies characterize the interventions in general terms without the detail necessary to replicate the intervention. That fact that organization intervention targets large social systems and addresses human relationships, personal attitudes, and behavior, creates a level of complexity and challenge that requires specific intervention strategies that can be replicated and tested. The level of specificity and testing has not been achieved to date.
- *The prevalence of case studies* of single organizations reduces the generalizability of the findings. Although these case studies tend to provide descriptions of the personal and social characteristics of specific individuals and systems that are addressed in development efforts and document successes and failures for the individual cases, there is little that can be generalized, both because the intervention strategies are

rarely described in adequate detail and the detail that is provided concerns idiographic characteristics that are not easily transferred to other organizations. Although case studies make interesting reading and can be helpful in providing insight into the challenges and barriers encountered in change efforts, few generalizable and specific intervention strategies have emerged from these studies.

- *The high number of qualitative studies* relative to quantitative studies of organizational intervention limits the level of evidence about outcomes to anecdotal statements about improvement in many of these studies. The lack of outcome measures and the inability to rule out type I errors limits the confidence with which development efforts are evaluated.

- *Randomized controlled trials* with multiple organizations are needed to address limitations in both the internal and external validity that characterize most of the organizational intervention studies to date. Although expensive and difficult to implement, such studies are needed to identify which organization interventions improve organizational performance.

- *Intensive studies of change within organizations using validated, quantitative measures are needed* to understand the specific mechanisms that link organization interventions to performance and outcome criteria. These types of intensive studies would follow change at the work group and individual levels within organizations to better understand how performance is affected during and following the implementation of each intervention strategy.

- *Finally, studies in mental health and social service organizations are needed* to understand which organization intervention strategies work best in these types of organizations. The vast majority of studies have been conducted in business organizations, so there is still much to be learned about the knowledge from these studies that can be applied to mental health and social service organizations. At this point, we do not know which of the strategies that have been developed in business organizations can be transported successfully into mental health and social service organizations.

IMPLICATIONS FOR SOCIAL WORK PRACTICE

The most important implications of organizational intervention for social work practice are related to service outcomes. Based on evidence to date, these interventions would necessarily improve work environments as well. The most valuable organizational interventions for social service organizations, therefore, would be able to improve both the work environments for service providers and the outcomes of the services they provide. That is to say that the interventions would result in social workers experiencing less job-related stress, a greater since of accomplishment, and being less likely to quit their jobs. Poor work environments and high turnover plague many social service organizations, and there is evidence that these factors play roles in poor service quality and outcomes.

Following the sociotechnical model of organizational effectiveness and innovation diffusion theory, interventions that create organizational social contexts characterized by proficient cultures and engaged climates should be more likely to *adopt innovative technologies*. These technologies would include evidence-based practices, new management information and decision support systems, assessment tools, and related core technologies designed to improve service quality and outcomes.

In addition, organizational interventions that change organizational social contexts (e.g., culture, climate) can also be used to improve *fidelity to practice and treatment protocols* once the new technologies are adopted. Low fidelity plagues attempts to implement new technologies, and there is evidence that most organizations adapt new technologies to fit their existing social contexts rather than adapting their social contexts to support the new technologies. Organizational interventions can be coupled with the adoption of new technologies to improve fidelity and retain the characteristics of the new technology that contribute to its effectiveness.

Finally, there is evidence that organization interventions can create positive social contexts that contribute to *the development of therapeutic relationships.* Organizational studies indicate that employees who experience lower stress, greater engagement, and are able to place the well-being of their clients first are more likely to develop service relationships that their clients perceive as supportive and positive. In addition, there is evidence from clinical research that both children and adults value relationships with individuals whom they perceive to be available, responsive, and characterized by continuity. Therefore, organizational interventions that create social contexts that increase the *availability, responsiveness, and continuity of services* provide support for the development of effective service relationships valued by both service providers and clients.

CONCLUSION

Organizational interventions to improve performance have a long history with a literature that can be traced back to the first decades of the last century (e.g., Taylor, Weber). Since the middle of the last century, a variety of organizational interventions have been applied and studied systematically in a wide range of business and industrial settings. Within the past 2 decades, more attention has been given to developing interventions for governmental and human service organizations. The research to date suggests that the most effective strategies in all types of organizations rely on broad-based systems models and include multiple interventions components with an emphasis on changing the organization's social context (e.g., culture, climate, work attitudes).

Although several meta-analyses conclude that organizational interventions can change social contexts and improve organizational performance, the research relies heavily on qualitative methods, case studies, and nonexperimental designs with few controls of threats to internal and external validity. Moreover, relatively few studies address human service organizations and almost none have been conducted with mental health and social service organizations.

One organizational intervention model labeled ARC for availability, responsiveness, and continuity, has been developed specifically for mental health and social service organizations and includes 12 intervention components that are implemented over three stages and four phases using change agents that work with organizational leaders, community stakeholders, and service teams. The 12 components were selected from the organizational literature to provide a comprehensive array of intervention strategies that organizational studies to date suggest can be used to develop positive work environments and improve performance. A randomized controlled trial indicates the ARC intervention model successfully reduced turnover and improved the work environments in multicounty child welfare system.

Although we have a number of best practices and evidence-based treatment models shown to efficacious in clinical studies, few best practices, including evidence-based treatments, are implemented effectively in actual community-based mental health and social service settings. Moving from a science of treatment efficacy to a science of implementation effectiveness requires evidence-based organizational strategies that can help build community-based service systems that promote the adoption of best practices, fidelity to best practice protocols, positive working alliances between service providers and consumers, and service availability, responsiveness, and continuity.

REFERENCES

Alper, S., Tjosvold, D., & Law, K. S. (2000). Conflict management, efficacy, and performance in organizational teams. *Personnel Psychology, 53*, 625–642.

Ashkanasy, N. M., Broadfoot, L. E., & Falkus, S. (2000). Questionnaire measures of organizational culture. In N. M. Ashkanasy, C. P. M. Wilderom, & M. F. Peterson (Eds.), *Handbook of organizational culture and climate* (pp. 131–146). Thousand Oaks, CA: Sage.

Backer, T. E., & Rogers, E. M. (1998). Diffusion of innovations theory and work-site AIDS programs. *Journal of Health Communication, 3*, 17–29.

Baer, M., & Frese, M. (2003). Innovation is not enough: Climates for initiatives and psychological safety, process innovations and firm performance. *Journal of Organizational Behavior, 24*, 45–68.

Bandura, A. (1986). *Social foundations of thought: A social cognitive theory*. Englewood Cliffs, NJ: Prentice Hall.

Barnsley, J., Lemieux-Charles, L., & McKinney, M. M. (1998). Integrating learning into integrated delivery systems. *Health Care Management Review, 23*, 18–28.

Barraud-Didier, V., & Guerrero, S. (2002). Impact of social innovations on French companies' performance. *Measuring Business Excellence, 6*, 42–48.

Beer, M. (1980). *Organization change and development: A systems review*. Santa Monica, CA: Goodyear.

Bennis, W. G. (1966). *Changing organizations*. New York: McGraw-Hill.

Berlowitz, D. R., Young, G. J., Hickey, E. C., Saliba, D., Mittman, B. S., Czarnowski, E., et al. (2003). Quality improvement implementation in the nursing home. *Health Services Research, 38*, 65–83.

Blake, R. R., Shepard, H. A., & Mouton, J. S. (1964). *Managing intergroup conflict in industry*. Houston, TX: Gulf.

Brown, S. P., & Leigh, T. W. (1996). A new look at psychological climate and its relationship to job involvement, effort, and performance. *Journal of Applied Psychology, 81*(4), 358–368.

Burke, W. W. (1993). *Organization development* (2nd ed.). Reading, MA: Addison-Wesley.

Caldwell, D. F., & O'Reilly, C. A. (1982). Boundary spanning and individual performance: The impact of self-monitoring. *Journal of Applied Psychology, 67*, 124–127.

Callister, R. R., & Wall, J. A. (2001). Conflict across organizational boundaries: Managed care organizations versus health care providers. *Journal of Applied Psychology, 86*, 754–763.

Dearing, J. W., & And, O. (1994). Portraying the new: Communication between university innovators and potential users. *Science Communication, 16*, 11–42.

Dirkson, C. D., Ament, A. J., & Go, P. M. (1996). Diffusion of six surgical endoscopic procedures in The Netherlands: Stimulating and restraining factors. *Health Policy, 37*, 91–104.

Durham, C. C., Knight, D., & Locke, E. A. (1997). Effects of leader role, team-set goal difficulty, efficacy, and tactics on team effectiveness. *Organizational Behavior and Human Decision Processes*, *72*, 203–229.

Dyer, W. G. (1977). *Team building: Issues and alternatives*. Reading, MA: Addison-Wesley.

Edmondson, A. C., Bohmer, R. M., & Pisano, G. P. (2001). Disrupted routines: Team learning and new technology implementation in hospitals. *Administrative Science Quarterly*, *46*, 685–716.

Ensley, M. D., & Pearce, C. L. (2001). Shared cognition in top management teams: Implications for new venture performance. *Journal of Organizational Behavior*, *22*, 145–160.

Farias, G., & Johnson, H. (2000). Organizational development and change management. *Journal of Applied Behavioral Science*, *36*, 376–379.

Ferlie, E., Gabbay, J., Fitzgerald, L., Locock, L., & Dopson, S. (2001). Evidence-based medicine and organizational change: An overview of some recent qualitative research. In L. Ashburner (Ed.), *Organisational behaviour and organisational studies in health care: Reflections on the future* (pp. 18–42). Basingstoke, Hampshire, England: Palgrave.

French, W. L., & Bell, C. H. (1984). *Organization development: Behavioral science interventions for organization improvement* (3rd ed.). Englewood Cliffs, NJ: Prentice Hall.

Fried, B. J., Johnsen, M. C., Starrett, B. E., Calloway, M. O., & Morrissey, J. P. (1998). An empirical assessment of rural community support networks for individuals with severe mental disorders. *Community Mental Health Journal*, *34*(1), 39–56.

George, J. M., & Jones, G. R. (2001). Towards a process model of individual change in organizations. *Human Relations*, *54*, 419–444.

Gibson, C. B. (2001). Me and us: Differential relationships among goal-setting training, efficacy and effectiveness at the individual and team level. *Journal of Organizational Behavior*, *22*, 789–808.

Glisson, C. (1978). Dependence of technological routinization on structural variables in human service organizations. *Administrative Science Quarterly*, *23*, 383–395.

Glisson, C. (1992). Structure and technology in human service organizations. In Y. Hasenfeld (Ed.), *Human services as complex organizations* (pp. 184–202). Beverly Hills, CA: Sage.

Glisson, C. (2000). Organizational culture and climate. In R. Patti (Ed.) *The handbook of social welfare management* (pp. 195–218). Thousand Oaks, CA: Sage.

Glisson, C. (2002). The organizational context of children's mental health services. *Clinical Child and Family Psychology Review*, *5*, 233–253.

Glisson, C. (2007). *The association of organizational climate with service outcomes in child welfare agencies*. Manuscript submitted for publication.

Glisson, C., Dukes, D., & Green, P. (2006). The effects of the ARC organizational intervention on caseworker turnover, climate, and culture in children's service systems. *Child Abuse and Neglect*, *30*, 855–880.

Glisson, C., & Durick, M. (1988). Predictors of job satisfaction and organizational commitment in human service organizations. *Administrative Science Quarterly*, *33*, 61–81.

Glisson, C., & Green, P. (2006). The effects of organizational culture and climate on the access to mental health care in child welfare and juvenile justice systems. *Administration and Policy in Mental Health and Mental Health Services Research*, *33*(4), 433–448.

Glisson, C., & Hemmelgarn, A. L. (1998). The effects of organizational climate and interorganizational coordination on the quality and outcomes of children's service systems. *Child Abuse and Neglect*, *22*, 401–421.

Glisson, C., & James, L. R. (1992). The interorganizational coordination of services to children in state custody. In D. Bargal & H. Schmid (Eds.), *Organizational change and development in human service organizations* (pp. 65–80). New York: Haworth Press.

Glisson, C., & James, L. R. (2002). The cross-level effects of culture and climate in human service teams. *Journal of Organizational Behavior*, *23*, 767–794.

Glisson, C., Landsverk, J., Schoenwald, S. K., Kelleher, K., Hoagwood, K. E., Mayberg, S., et al. (in press). Assessing the Organizational Social Context (OSC) of mental health services: Implications for implementation research and practice. *Administration and Policy in Mental Health and Mental Health Services Research.*

Glisson, C. Schoenwald, S. K., Kelleher, K., Landsverk, J., Hoagwood, K. E., Mayberg, S., et al. (in press). Therapist turnover and new program sustainability in mental health clinics as a function of organizational culture, climate, and service structure. *Administration and Policy in Mental Health and Mental Health Services Research.*

Goes, J. B., & Park, S. H. (1997). Intraorganizational links and innovation: The case of hospital services. *Academy of Management Journal, 40*, 673–696.

Gray, B. (1985). Conditions facilitating interorganizational collaboration. *Human Relations, 38*, 911–936.

Gray, B. (1990). Building interorganizational alliances: Planned change in a global environment. *Research in Organizational Change and Development, 4*, 101–140.

Green, P. S. (1998). Improving clinical effectiveness in an integrated care delivery system. *Journal for Healthcare Quality, 20*, 4–8.

Grimshaw, J. M., Thomas, R. E., MacLennan, G., Fraser, C., Ramsay, C. R., Vale, L., et al. (2004). Effectiveness and efficiency of guideline dissemination and implementation strategies. *Health Technology Assessment Report, 8*(6), 1–84.

Gustafson, D. H., Sainfort, F., Eichler, M., Adams, L., Bisognano, M., & Steudel, H. (2003). Developing and testing a model to predict outcomes of organizational change. *Health Services Research, 38*, 751–776.

Guzzo, R. A., Jette, R. D., & Katzell, R. A. (1985). The effects of psychologically based intervention programs on worker productivity: A meta-analysis. *Personnel Psychology, 38*, 275–291.

Hackman, J. R., & Oldham, G. R. (1980). *Work redesign.* Reading, MA: Addison-Wesley.

Hemmelgarn, A. L., Glisson, C., & Dukes, D. (2001). Emergency room culture and the emotional support component of family-centered care. *Children's Health Care, 30*, 93–110.

Higgins, S. E., & Routhieaux, R. L. (1999). A multiple level analysis of hospital team effectiveness. *Health Care Supervisor, 17*, 1–13.

Hoagwood, K., Burns, B. J., Kiser, L., Ringeisen, H., & Schoenwald, S. (2001). Evidence-based practice in child and adolescent mental health services. *Psychiatric Services, 52*, 1179–1189.

Hofstede, G. (1998). Attitudes, values and organizational culture: Disentangling the concepts. *Organization Studies, 19*(3), 477–492.

Hofstede, G., Neuijen, B., Ohayv, D. D., & Sanders, G. (1990). Measuring organizational cultures: A qualitative and quantitative study across twenty states. *Administrative Science Quarterly, 35*, 286–316.

Hohmann, A. A., & Shear, M. K. (2002). Community-based intervention research: Coping with the noise of real life in study design. *American Journal of Psychiatry, 159*, 201–207.

Huy, Q. N. (2002). Emotional balancing of organizational continuity and radical change: The contribution of middle managers. *Administrative Science Quarterly, 47*, 31–69.

James, L. A., & James, L. R. (1989). Integrating work environment perceptions: Explorations into the measurement of meaning. *Journal of Applied Psychology, 74*, 739–751.

James, L. R., James, L. A., & Ashe, D. K. (1990). The meaning of organizations: An essay. In B. Schneider (Ed.), *Organizational climate and culture* (pp. 40–84). San Francisco: Jossey-Bass.

James, L. R., & Jones, A. P. (1974). Organizational climate: A review of theory and research. *Psychological Bulletin, 81*, 1096–1112.

Jaskyte, K., & Dressler, W. W. (2005). Organizational culture land innovation in nonprofit human service organizations. *Administration in Social Work, 29*, 23–41.

Jensen, P. S. (2003). Commentary: The next generation is overdue. *Journal of the American Academy of Child and Adolescent Psychiatry, 42*, 527–530.

Jones, A. P., & James, L. R. (1979). Psychological climate: Dimensions and relationships of individual and aggregated work environment perceptions. *Organizational Behavior and Human Performance*, *23*, 201–250.

Joyce, W. F., & Slocum, J. W. (1984). Collective climate: Agreement as a basis for defining aggregate climates in organizations. *Academy of Management Journal*, *24*, 721–742.

Kahn, W. A., Cross, R., & Parker, A. (2003). Layers of diagnosis for planned relational change in organizations. *Journal of Applied Behavioral Science*, *34*, 259–280.

Katz, D., & Kahn, R. L. (1978). *The social psychology of organizations* (2nd ed.). New York: Wiley.

Knight, D., Durham, C. C., & Locke, E. A. (2001). The relationship of team goals, incentives, and efficacy to strategic risk, tactical implementation, and performance. *Academy of Management Journal*, *44*, 326–338.

Lemieux-Charles, L., Murray, M., Baker, G. R., Barnsley, J., Tasa, K., & Ibrahim, S. A. (2002). The effects of quality improvement practices on team effectiveness: A meditational model. *Journal of Organizational Behavior*, *23*, 533–553.

Locke, E. A. (1976). *The nature and causes of job satisfaction*. New York: McGraw-Hill.

March, J. G., & Simon, H. A. (1958). *Organizations*. New York: Wiley.

Martin, L. M., Peters, C. L., & Glisson, C. (1998). Factors affecting case management recommendations for children entering state custody. *Social Service Review*, *72*, 521–544.

McGregor, D. M. (1960). *The human side of enterprise*. New York: McGraw-Hill.

Merlani, P., Garnerin, P., Diby, M., Ferring, M., & Ricou, B. (2001). Quality improvement report: Linking guideline to regular feedback to increase appropriate requests for clinical tests: Blood gas analysis in intensive care. *British Medical Journal*, *323*, 620–624.

Meyer, A. D., & Goes, J. B. (1988). Organizational assimilation of innovations: A multilevel contextual analysis. *Academy of Management Journal*, *31*, 897–923.

Meyers, P. W., Sivakumar, K., & Nakata, C. (1999). Implementation of industrial process innovations: Factors, effects, and marketing implications. *Journal of Product Innovation Management*, *16*, 295–311.

Michela, J. L., & Burke, W. W. (2000). Organizational culture and climate in transformations for quality and innovations. In N. M. Ashkanasy, C. P. M. Wilderom, & M. F. Peterson (Eds.), *Handbook of organizational culture and climate* (pp. 225–244). Thousand Oaks, CA: Sage.

Molgaard, V. K. (1997). The extension service as key mechanism for research and services delivery for prevention of mental health disorders in rural America. *American Journal of Community Psychology*, *25*(4), 515–544.

Mowday, R., Porter, L., & Steers, R. (1982). *Organizational linkages: The psychology of commitment, absenteeism, and turnover*. New York: Academic Press.

Murphy, G. D., & Southey, G. (2003). High performance work practices: Perceived determinants of adoption and the role of the HR practitioner. *Personnel Review*, *32*, 73–92.

Neuman, G. A., Edwards, J. E., & Raju, N. S. (1989). Organizational development interventions: A meta-analysis of their effects on satisfaction and other attitudes. *Personnel Psychology*, *42*, 461–489.

Nugent, W., & Glisson, C. (1999). Reactivity and responsiveness in children's service systems. *Journal of Social Service Research*, *25*, 41–60.

Osborne, D., & Gaebler, T. A. (1992). *Reinventing government*. Reading, MA: Addison-Wesley.

Pasmore, W., Francis, C., Haldeman, J., & Shani, A. (1982). Sociotechnical systems: A North American reflection on empirical studies of the seventies. *Human Relations*, *35*, 1179–1204.

Patten, T. (1981). *Organizational development through team building*. New York: Wiley.

Patton, R. D., & Cissell, W. B. (1990). *Community organization: Traditional principles and modern applications*. Johnson City, TN: Latchpins Press.

Peters, T. Y., & Waterman, R. (1982). *In search of excellence: Lessons from America's best run corporations*. New York: Warner Books.

Pfeffer, J., & Sutton, R. I. (2006). *Hard facts, dangerous half-truths, and total nonsense: Profiting from evidence-based management*. Boston: Harvard Business School Press.

Porras, J. I. (1986). Organization development. In G. E. Germane (Ed.), *The executive course: What every manager needs to know about the essentials of business* (pp. 261–293). Reading, MA: Addison-Wesley.

Porras, J. I., & Robertson, P. J. (1992). Organizational development: Theory, practice, and research. In M. D. Dunnette & L. M. Hough (Eds.), *Handbook of industrial and organizational psychology* (2nd ed., Vol. 3, pp. 719–822). Palo Alto, CA: Consulting Psychologists Press.

Reichers, A. E., & Schneider, B. (1990). Climate and culture: An evolution of constructs. In B. Schneider (Ed.), *Organizational climate and culture* (pp. 5–39). San Francisco: Jossey-Bass.

Rentsch, J. R. (1990). Climate and culture: Interaction and qualitative differences in organizational meanings. *Journal of Applied Psychology, 75,* 661–668.

Rentsch, J. R., & Klimoski, R. J. (2001). Why do "great minds" think alike? Antecedents of team member schema agreement. *Journal of Organizational Behavior, 22,* 107–120.

Robertson, P. J., Roberts, D. R., & Porras, J. I. (1993). Dynamics of planned organizational change: Assessing empirical support for a theoretical model. *Academy of Management Journal, 36,* 619–634.

Robey, D., & Altman, S. (1982). *Organization development: Progress and perspectives*. New York: Macmillan.

Rogers, E. M. (2003). *Diffusion of innovations* (5th ed.). New York: Free Press.

Rousseau, D. M. (1977). Technological differences in job characteristics, employee satisfaction, and motivation: A synthesis of job design research and sociotechnical systems theory. *Organizational Behavior and Human Performance, 19,* 18–42.

Rousseau, D. M. (1990). Assessing organizational culture: The case for multiple methods. In B. Schneider (Ed.), *Organizational climate and culture* (pp. 153–192). San Francisco: Jossey-Bass.

Scanlon, D. P., Darby, C., Rolph, E., & Doty, H. E. (2001). The role of performance measures for improving quality in managed care organizations. *Health Services Research, 36,* 619–641.

Schoenwald, S. K., & Hoagwood, K. (2001). Effectiveness, transportability, and dissemination of interventions: What matters when? *Psychiatric Services, 52,* 1190–1197.

Schorr, L. B. (1997). *Common purpose*. New York: Doubleday.

Shortell, S. M., Bennett, C. L., & Byck, G. R. (1998). Assessing the impact of continuous quality improvement on clinical practice: What it will take to accelerate progress. *Milbank Quarterly, 76,* 593–624.

Shortell, S. M., O'Brien, J. L., Carman, J. M., Foster, R. W., Hughes, E. F. X., Boerstler, H., et al. (1995). Assessing the impact of continuous quality improvement/total quality management: Concept versus implementation. *Health Services Research, 30,* 377–401.

Sorensen, J. B. (2002). The strength of corporate culture and the reliability of firm performance. *Administrative Science Quarterly, 47,* 70–91.

Stackman, R. W., Pinder, C. C., & Connor, P. E. (2000). Values lost: Redirecting research on values in the workplace. In N. M. Ashkanasy, C. P. M. Wilderom, & M. F. Peterson (Eds.), *Handbook of organizational culture and climate* (pp. 37–54). Thousand Oaks, CA: Sage.

Steel, R. P., & Shane, G. S. (1986). Evaluation research on quality circles: Technical and analytical implications. *Human Relations, 39,* 449–468.

Sue-Chan, C., & Ong, M. (2002). Goal assignment and performance: Assessing the medicating roles of goal commitment and self-efficacy and the moderating role of power distance. *Organizational Behavior and Human Decision Processes, 89,* 1140–1161.

Tasi, W. (2001). Knowledge transfer in intraorganizational networks: Effects of network position and absorptive capacity on business unit innovation and performance. *Academy of Management Journal, 44,* 996–1004.

Terziovski, M. (2002). Achieving performance excellence through an integrated strategy of radical innovation and continuous improvement. *Measuring Business Excellence, 6,* 5–14.

Tichy, N. M. (1983). *Managing strategic change: Technical, political, and cultural dynamics*. New York: Wiley.

Trist, E. (1985). Intervention strategies for interorganizational domains. In R. Tannenbaum, N. Margulies, & F. Massarik (Eds.), *Human systems development* (pp. 167–197). San Francisco: Jossey-Bass.

Tushman, M. (1977). Special boundary roles in the innovation process. *Administrative Science Quarterly, 22*, 587–605.

U.S. General Accounting Office. (2003). *Child welfare: HHS could play a greater role in helping child welfare agencies recruit and retain staff* (GAO-03-357). Washington, DC: Author.

Verbeke, W., Volgering, M., & Hessels, M. (1998). Exploring the conceptual expansion within the field of organizational behaviour: Organizational climate and organizational culture. *Journal of Management Studies, 35*, 303–329.

Viteles, M. S. (1953). *Motivation and morale in industry*. New York: Norton.

Walton, R. E. (1987). *Managing conflict: Interpersonal dialogue and third-party roles*. Reading, MA: Addison-Wesley.

Weick, K. E., & Quinn, R. E. (1999). Organizational change and development. *Annual Review of Psychology, 50*, 361–386.

Weldon, E., & Yun, S. (2000). The effects of proximal and distal goals on goal level, strategy development, and group performance. *Journal of Applied Behavioral Science, 36*, 336–344.

Whelan-Berry, K. S., Gordon, J. R., & Hinings, C. R. (2003). Strengthening organizational change process. *Journal of Applied Behavioral Science, 39*, 186–207.

Williams, L. J., & Hazer, J. T. (1986). Antecedents and consequences of satisfaction and commitment in turnover models: A reanalysis using latent variable structural equation methods. *Journal of Applied Psychology, 71*(2), 219–231.

Woodman, R. W. (1989). Organizational change and development: New arenas for inquiry and action. *Journal of Management, 15*, 205–228.

Woodward, J. (1958). *Management and technology*. London: Her Majesty's Stationery Office.

Woodward, J. (1965). *Industrial organization*. London: Oxford University Press.

Worren, N. A. M., Ruddle, K., & Moore, K. (1999). From organizational development to change management. *Journal of Applied Behavioral Science, 35*, 273–286.

Young, G. J. (2000). Managing organizational transformations: Lessons from the Veterans Health Administration. *California Management Review, 43*, 66–83.

Yousef, D. A. (2000). Organizational commitment: A mediator of the relationships of leadership behavior with job satisfaction and performance in a non-western country. *Journal of Managerial Psychology, 15*, 6–28.

Chapter 27

ASSESSMENT OF INSTITUTIONS

Heather K. Horton, Katharine Briar-Lawson,
William Rowe, and Brian Roland

Institutions as we define them in this chapter are formal establishments identified with social purpose and permanence organized to provide a service. They may be public or private, large or small, insular or semipermeable. Social workers have been involved with institutions long before the profession was organized. In fact, some social work pioneers helped to establish many of the institutions that continue to provide service today. Some of these include hospitals, mental health facilities, long-term care residential facilities for children or adults, correctional facilities, residential schools, and other service-related institutions with a specific focus such as substance abuse.

This chapter is concerned with the assessment of institutions for the purpose of relevance, viability, and quality assurance. For many years in human services, institutions were not assessed at all. In fact, because they were often run by religious orders, charitable institutions, and state and federal governments, there was an erroneous assumption that their essential purpose was to be helpful to the individuals, families, and communities that they served. The major exception to this was correctional facilities because of their social control and protection function, but even these often started out with the intention of reforming the inmates to become productive and peaceful citizens. The workhouse, the orphanage, and the asylum all started out with the best of intentions given the knowledge and resources available.

As we look at the evolution of assessment and quality assurance, it becomes evident that these functions are critical if society is going to continue to use institutions to provide ethical human services. To understand the evolution of assessment processes, it may be helpful to review some examples to depict the various types of investigations and rudimentary assessments that were employed in the past.

With the advent of the asylum, institutions became the primary means for serving individuals who were unable to care for themselves. Many institutions provided, above all, care and custody. Rehabilitation was secondary to the custodial function and the recovery movement is a relatively new paradigm. Thus, results-oriented evaluation and quality assurance systems in place in the past several decades are the by-product of paradigmatic changes regarding the possible conditions that led persons to an institution in the first place. Thus, mental disorders and co-occurring challenges of substance abuse, alcoholism, intellectual disabilities, which in the past might have been treated with a custodial approach, are now subject to data-driven outcomes charting, evidence-based principles for services, and quality assurance systems that demand evidence of ongoing improvement.

While custodial functions might serve some wider community purpose—such as boundary maintenance—to protect the public from the behaviors of persons deemed as deviant, some forms of custodial care may have exacerbated behavioral problems, calling into question the value of the institutional experience. Thus, assessment plays and has played in past decades an extraordinarily important role in measuring the human benefits as well as the cost effectiveness and cost benefits of institutional care.

HISTORICAL BACKGROUND

In the mid-nineteenth and early twentieth century, parallel events occurred in the United States, Canada, and Great Britain that set the conditions for assessment and quality assurance of institutions. These were led by reformers who were pioneers and early professionals. Their work was followed by consumers such as Clifford Beers whose personal stories also served to advance reform and to showcase another early form of institutional assessment.

Dorothea Dix

In the United States, during the nineteenth century, Dorothea Dix, social reformer and social work pioneer, campaigned for the care and safety of the mentally ill. Dix began assessing the degrees of mental illness in the prison systems and found that these institutions were not equipped to provide necessary, quality treatment to the mentally ill. She was instrumental in the effort to decriminalize the mentally ill and appropriately place them in institutions other than prisons and almshouses. She protested against the practice of criminalizing mental illness, arguing that it would be better for both the mentally ill and society as a whole if they were treated in hospitals, in as humane a setting and manner as possible (Gilligan, 2001).

Dix addressed several state legislatures as well as Congress in an attempt to encourage state and federal governments to create public hospitals in which mentally ill patients could receive treatment in therapeutic settings. Dix was so remarkably successful that asylums for the mentally ill and mentally retarded were established and operated by state governments in almost all of the states by the late 1800s (McPheeters, 1977).

Dix also advocated for the national government to take a primary role in the care of the mentally ill population. In 1848, she sent a document to Congress asking the national government to donate 5 million acres of land to build hospitals for the mentally ill. Although her efforts with national government were unsuccessful, she sparked a movement in which services for the mentally ill population were brought into the social and political arenas. Over 3 decades, her advocacy led to the founding of 32 hospitals in 18 states (Sharfstein, 2000). Despite Dix's work to build hospitals for the mentally ill and to foster more effective treatment, they were still substandard.

Dix used tools that were essential to other social reformers—observations, documenting what was seen and then appealing to the public, the media, policy makers and other professionals to promote quality improvements. Some of the exposes by early reformers, such as Jane Addams, involved taking the media with them to take pictures and write stories about what their investigation had uncovered. Tools of rigorous research and evaluation now required in quality assurance and effectiveness studies were not employed. Some of the work of these tenacious reformers created a rudimentary but nonetheless iterative type of, quality improvement process. The assessment process of early reformers involved exposing problems rather than designing programs framed by rigorous outcome evaluation. Tools and frameworks for designing assessment to ensure ongoing program improvement and effectiveness were to come later.

John Langmuir

Paralleling the work of Dix was John Langmuir—a Canadian pioneer civil servant. He was appointed inspector of prisons, asylums, and public charities in 1868. As it turned out, Langmuir was a talented administrator, actively writing numerous recommendations for reform. He improved conditions in the field of corrections, care of the mentally ill and mentally handicapped, and for the education of the blind and the deaf. He also supported the advancement of many voluntary institutions that housed and cared for the medically ill, elderly citizens, homeless children, and unwed mothers.

One of Langmuir's routine orphanage inspections in Toronto in 1877 revealed that 40% of the infants who had been taken in during the past year had died. He immediately established an infirmary within the orphanage to provide special medical care and within 1 year the mortality rate had fallen by 14%. When Langmuir became inspector in 1868, there were few societal resources to help marginalized populations. Jails were used to accommodate young male and female offenders as well as both male and female hardened criminals. Jails were also used to house the mentally ill and the elderly. By 1882, he had established intermediate prisons with sentences up to 2 years, "a reformatory for women with a separate section for girls under 16, and mental hospitals or asylums" (Bellamy & Irving, 2001, p. 105). Langmuir had clearly established the idea that inspection/assessment could lead to positive reform.

Great Britain

The development of institutions in Great Britain has a long and checkered history. Subsequent to the feudal system, most social welfare was centered in the church. After the dissolution of the monasteries and convents in the 1500s, the government was forced to assume a larger role. The workhouse and the almshouse became the primary institutions for dispensing social welfare under the poor laws. In 1873, the board of guardians determined that wives deserted by their husbands, wives and families of convicted prisoners, single women with illegitimate children, and able-bodied widows with one child were required to seek relief in the workhouse (De Schweinitz, 1943). The reform movements of the late nineteenth century forced a reconsideration of these practices and a series of committees were set up to oversee the needs of young children, the sick and permanently incapacitated, the aged needing institutional care, and the mentally defective. These included the education committee, the health committee, the asylums committee, and the pension committee. These committees determined placements in various specialized institutions such as schools, hospitals, and asylums but could also determine what amounted to community care as they deemed appropriate.

ASSESSMENT AND EARLY INSTITUTIONS

Given these few historical examples of how human service institutions were created, it is easy to see that the assessment of such institutions would be as varied as the institutions themselves. In the early days, assessments were almost always internal and, more often than not, driven by financial concerns. Key issues were physical plant, equipment, staffing, and funding to operate whatever human service was being offered. Private institutions, especially church-affiliated ones, were additionally concerned with how the institution and its services fit with their particular religious perspective whereas government services more often had simple mandates, that is, home for orphans, care for the incapacitated, convalescent sanatorium's for those with tuberculosis, and care and treatment of the mentally ill. Concerns about mission, program, objectives, outcomes, staff credentials, health, safety, and nutrition are more recent.

Equally important to what was being assessed was who was doing the assessment and what would become of the results. Often assessments were simply internally motivated by a complaint or problem. As such they could be self-serving or worse, used to cover up inadequate practices. Sometimes politicians or even reporters initiated external reviews. Seldom were consumers or families consulted or included in such reviews.

Assessment Based on Inspections

Much of the assessment work of our professional forbearers relied on inspections rather than on ongoing studies of effectiveness. While inspections might be high profile and involve some of the tools of evaluation research (such as observation and recording), observations alone could not guarantee systematic data on outcome effectiveness. However, a case example might be used to arouse public concern and expose risk factors. Inspections might include, for example, a limited or potentially biased sample of observed conditions and behaviors. Thus, when Dorothea Dix, Jane Addams, and other social reformers made their observations, sometimes with the media in tow, their "assessments" were more like exposes than empirical studies. Nonetheless, such approaches were effective in galvanizing public opinion and policy leaders about the ongoing need for change and improvement.

Record keeping in institutions had been underway for several centuries. Statistics that were maintained comprised data on institutionalized populations, on their movements and changes (such as new ward or program assignments). These were not necessarily used as evaluative tools. However, they might be used to buttress exposes, the findings from investigatory probes, or in later decades class-action lawsuits.

Consumer Guided Assessment

Consumer perspectives on institutions also played a role in assessment and improvement processes. While many had written stories about their experience, for example, in asylums, none had the impact of that of Clifford Beers. Shortly after the turn of the century, Clifford Beers, a recent graduate of Yale, became suicidal after his brother died from epilepsy. Beers was hospitalized for 3 years in private nonprofit and for-profit asylums, as well as in a state mental hospital. While hospitalized, he had a vision about writing a book that would shape the future of mental health treatment and advocate that recovery is possible. Indeed, while others had exposed the deficiencies of mental institutions, his book, *A Mind that Found Itself,* was highly influential in fostering a reassessment of mental hospitals and even the need for community-based prevention and early intervention (Foley & Sharfstein, & Butler, 1983). Above all, Beers' work demonstrated recovery was possible.

Beers then became known as a reformer, bringing attention to ineffective mental hospitals across the country. Since evaluations and assessments were not undertaken of mental hospitals, his book served as one example of how to document and to assess these institutions (Friedman, 2002). Beers went beyond the exposes of early reformers as he documented his experiences of inhumane treatment and his concerns about untrained, underpaid, and often abusive staff. This influential book along with Beers' advocacy helped to pave the way for a national movement and the establishment of the National Committee for Mental Hygiene.

The National Committee collected data on the conditions of mental hospitals. Subscribing to the idea that recovery is possible, the National Committee also inspired the child guidance movement as Beers and colleagues were able to link adult mental disorders to the need for childhood supports. His work also helped to spawn the development of psychiatric social work (Friedman, 2002) and the recovery movement.

From Inspections to Surveys

Like Dix, Julia Lathrop, another early social reformer and social worker, documented the conditions of asylums in Illinois. Many had children thrown in with the mentally ill who were detained along with the physically ill. All ages were warehoused in these asylums. Her early inspections of these facilities led her to join Clifford Beers as a charter member of the National Committee for Mental Hygiene. By 1912, the National Committee for Mental Hygiene received funds to do surveys on the care of the mentally ill and those deemed mentally retarded (Deutsch, 1949). Such surveys were foundational to the development of the movement and were advancements in the development of assessment tools.

Lathrop, like Beers, decried the lack of trained staff to serve those institutionalized. In 1909, she founded the first mental hygiene clinic for children. She went on to be appointed in 1912 as the first head of the U.S. Children's Bureau and was influential in fostering prevention and community-based care for children and families.

Lathrop was part of the emerging leadership in social work that sought to promote scientific approaches to social problems. This scientific framework was central to the rise of social casework and philanthropy. It reinforced the development of assessment processes and tools.

EMERGING FEDERAL ROLE IN INSTITUTIONAL REFORMS AND ASSESSMENT

World War I brought home lessons that underscored Beers' personal saga. Some mental illness could be cured, and some of those with mental disorders linked to the trauma of war could be treated (Foley et al. 1983). Institutional surveys increased, exposes continued, and abuses of patients were often cited (Rothman, 1980). Through this period, it was the Harrison Narcotics Act that required federally funded research on addictions, immigrants, and crime and delinquency. In 1929, two federal hospitals were built to address addictions, and the Public Health Service was launched to conduct studies on mental illness prevalence and incidence (Foley et al., 1983).

The health-care sector was the first to establish formal care standards. In 1917, the American College of Standards developed a one-page document outlining minimum standards for hospitals. In 1918, only 89 of 692 hospitals surveyed met the requirements of the minimum standard (Joint Commission, 2007).

The Great Depression, with its suicides and great human despair, helped to reinforce the belief that the federal government should play a central role in addressing mental disorders. Despite such growing readiness to federalize some of the responsibilities and quality assurances regarding the treatment of mental disorders, such emergent ideas were sidelined by the time of World War II.

It was not until the end of the World War II that national public debates returned to the need for alternatives to current mental hospitals. Such views coincided with the return of veterans from World War II and public concern over the need to help those with war-related mental disorders (Foley et al., 1983). Nevertheless, the post-World War II era witnessed increased institutionalization in prisons, mental hospitals, and facilities for the mentally retarded (French, 1987). During this period, there was an influx of patients receiving health care in facilities, consequently creating overcrowding resulting in poor treatment and deplorable conditions.

In 1955, when numbers of patients in state hospitals reached their highest point, 559,000 persons out of a total national population of 165 million were institutionalized in state mental hospitals (Lamb & Bachrach, 2001). Once the failures of the public mental hospital system became undeniable and widely recognized, both the legal community and the medical and mental health professions decided these institutions were doing more harm than good (Gilligan, 2001).

CHARACTERISTICS OF ASYLUMS

Augmenting the anti-institutionalization movement were writings by Erving Goffman, a sociologist who worked in a mental hospital. In his book, *Asylums,* he depicts many facilities such as mental hospitals, prisons, and hospitals as "total institutions." Such asylums routinize treatment of those served creating dependency, passivity, and powerlessness (Goffman, 1962). Identities are stripped; numbers are often given to each inmate for identification rather than using names. Although patient or inmate needs and conditions require differentiated approaches, as argued for several decades by social workers and many others, total institutions, depicted by Goffman, were seen as having undifferentiated approaches to those institutionalized. Activities are portrayed as meeting the needs of the institution and not those it served. Dehumanizing aspects were detailed, and the institution was seen to be causing or aggravating the condition it was to treat. The total institution revealed by Goffman was a closed system and society with its own rules, rule monitors, and expectations. All facets of care were addressed from morning until night.

The asylum often served as a "dumping ground" for those whose behaviors violate social norms. And for some, asylums imposed order from the outside in the hope that it would be internalized. Thus, the mentally ill and others (such as those in prison) deemed to have deviated from social norms of acceptable behavior were seen as prime candidates for externally imposed structures to foster personal transformation.

Goffman's writings coincided with the rise of the anti-institutionalization movement. They helped to underscore the fact that institutions shared common dimensions despite their divergent missions. Such integrative thinking also helped to reinforce evaluative measures that could be applied to institutions serving diverse purposes and populations.

Goffman's depiction also helped to give vivid images of what some in the field call institutionalization. This includes ambivalence or resistance to leaving the institution (Patrick, Smith, Schleifer, Morris, & McLennon, 2006). Goffman's work was reinforced by that of Foucault (1983) who saw institutions as defining the individuals they were to treat and dehumanizing them in the process.

THE ANTI-INSTITUTIONALIZATION MOVEMENT

The anti-institutionalization movement brought with it many theories and rhetoric about the benefits of community-based care systems. These alternative community-based systems were to be augmented by the availability of psychotropic drugs. It was believed that the new medications could address symptoms. Moreover, institutional diversion programs and greatly restricted access to institutions were enacted (Talbott, 2004). For example, to be admitted to a mental hospital, one had to demonstrate grave or imminent danger to self or others. As a result of the deterioration of state mental health institutions, the deinstitutionalization movement accelerated in the 1970s. This movement, reinforced in part from the costs of care, advocated for a decrease in the number of patients receiving institutional care in state facilities.

Deinstitutionalization involved two elements: the discharge of existing state hospital patients to the community and a decrease in new admissions to the state facilities (Talbott, 2004). Sharp ideological shifts and ongoing exposes made confinement more difficult. What was once an average length of stay in a mental hospital of 6 months now averaged 15 days (Markowitz, 2006).

Tenets of the deinstitutionalization movement included beliefs that community care is better than institutional care, that costs are lessened, and the "least restrictive" setting would provide a higher quality environment (Talbott, 2004). Many of the community systems of care and facilities envisioned during the deinstitutionalization movement never eventuated. Thus medical, mental health, social services, nutrition, vocational supports, and rehabilitation services that might have been accessed in an institution did not follow the discharged into the community. Even now, they are not readily available. In effect, no system of care was created to replace the "total institution."

NORMALIZATION, THE LEAST RESTRICTIVE ENVIRONMENT, AND RECOVERY

While deinstitutionalization goals of normalization and individual choice were met with enthusiasm by human rights advocates and grassroots recovery movements (Farone, 2006), they became compromised in their implementation.

Concepts of "normalization" and "least restrictive environment" were introduced as part of the deinstitutionalization movement. Normalization implies having conditions similar to one's home. Being in the least restrictive environment suggests that the individual be able to enjoy maximum freedom in daily living and pursuits. The idea of the least restrictive environment has pervaded public policy across all service sectors including those with mental disorders, the aged, children, and adolescents in institutional care.

While deinstitutionalization may not have spawned the systematic community-based systems of care, there has been an increase in boarding homes, half-way houses for those with drug and alcohol abuse or mental disorders, along with nursing homes, group homes, and residential treatment for children and youth.

Policies fostering the least restrictive environment continue to evolve from the 1963 when Congress authorized funds for community mental health centers. For example, in 1980, PL 96-272 required that "reasonable efforts" be demonstrated to enable children who had been abused and/or neglected to stay in their own homes rather than be removed and placed in foster homes or institutions. More recently, the Olmstead Act requires that the aged and those with disabilities be provided with community-based care, and if some form of out-of-home care is warranted, it should meet the criteria for the least restrictive environment.

Effects

Deinstitutionalization promoted a shift from institutionalization to community-based services in which patients were integrated back into their local communities. Although the goals of deinstitutionalization are to prevent chronic disability, protect patients' rights, and reduce the cost of care, hospitalized mental patients have been moved to communities without the provision of supportive networks in the community (Segal, 1979). The principles guiding deinstitutionalization were theoretically sound, but large failures occurred within the application process. Patients in institutions were discharged without available community services in which they could receive adequate treatment, care, and support.

Deinstitutionalization was more than the removal of patients from hospitals. It also fostered the decentralization (Freshwater & Westwood, 2006) and devolution of responsibility for the mentally ill to local communities.

Moreover, over the past several decades, it is apparent that there is an inverse relationship between prison and psychiatric hospitalization. Increased proportions of the mentally ill are incarcerated, and there has been a recriminalization of mental illness. The mentally ill are overly arrested and warehoused in jails. Currently, there are more mentally ill housed in jails than in mental hospitals. Police are often the main sources of referral (Markowitz, 2006).

What was billed as a human rights movement had several effects. The first was to create a sharp increase in homeless mentally ill persons. Currently, it is estimated that as many as 3.5 million people in the United States experience homelessness (National Law Center on Homelessness and Poverty, as cited on www.pbs.org, retrieved March 10, 2007). The federal Substance Abuse and Mental Health Administration (1996, as cited on www.pbs.org, retrieved March 10, 2007) found that up to 25% of the homeless population in the United States reported some form of serious mental illness. The second effect was to recreate the asylum with sharp increases in the mentally ill and mentally retarded in jails and prisons. The third effect was that of increasing caregiver burdens especially for women (Briar & Ryan, 1986).

Talbott (2004) decries the movement as a disaster; funds did not follow the deinstitutionalized to the community. He argues that what transpired was not the intended deinstitutionalization but transinstitutionalization as patients shifted from one facility to another, such as a nursing home or jail or prison. Indeed, the deinstitutionalization movement achieved moving the mentally ill from the hospitals back onto the street, subsequently creating a population of homeless mentally ill. Those who lived on the streets often turned to substance abuse and many became inappropriately incarcerated.

Paralleling the rise of community-based service for the deinstitutionalization has been the ongoing development of the recovery movement. This movement unites those with mental disorders with others in recovery (substance abusers, alcoholics). Such consumer-based recovery leaders and activists argue that the medical and rehabilitation model of treatment is not sufficient to ensure recovery. Consumer-delivered services have emerged as complements to more traditional rehabilitation approaches. In consumer-led services, a "whatever it takes" service ethic may prevail. Consumers serve as role models for one another as they address barriers that might not be part of traditional rehabilitation programs.

Despite the consumer recovery movement, the full effects of deinstitutionalization have brought us full circle. Just as Dorothea Dix decried the criminalization of mental illness and the presence of mentally ill in prisons, we now find that the bulk of mental health services are provided in prison and jails. With no other pathway available, prisons and jails have replaced many of the earlier mental hospitals as the new asylum. Indeed, wings of jails and prisons are entirely devoted to the mentally ill. The criminalization of mental illness and related disorders such as intellectual disabilities has reemerged. Ten to 15% of persons in jails and prison are deemed mentally ill (Lamb, Weinberger, & Gross, 2004). Other reports run as high as 25% or more (Torrey, 1995). Some argue that there are more mentally ill in U.S. jails and prisons than in mental hospitals (Honberg & Gruttadaro, 2005). In many cases, mental illness co-occurs with substance abuse, further complicating the assessment and quality assurance process in institutions, especially jails and prisons. Incarcerated youth may have even higher rates of mental disorders, estimated to range from 60% to 75% (Honberg & Gruttadaro, 2005).

As discussed in the next section, jails and prisons are not subjected to the same quality assurance reviews that mental hospitals face. In fact, the assessment process and the requirements for quality assurance are at great variance with those imposed on mental hospitals. We now look at these assessment processes involving mental hospitals and other institutions, remembering that many of the mentally ill who are removed from the community lack these quality assurance systems. Moreover, some of the negative by-products of mental hospitals—institutionalism and dependency—may now be experienced by those in jails and prisons.

CURRENT FRAMEWORKS FOR ASSESSING INSTITUTIONS

The assessment of institutions has a long and complicated history. In part, reactions to unacceptable conditions led to the development of standardized assessments. Deinstitutionalization, class-action lawsuits, and the demand for least restrictive environments created the need for organized approaches to standards of care across all types of human services.

With the tremendous expansion of social programs during the 1960s, assessment became an integral part of policy making, planning, and administration (Rossi & Freeman, 1982, p. 22). The Government Performance Results Act of 1993 required all federal agencies to work with the states to establish performance goals and monitor performance results for all federal programs (Office of Management and Budget, 2002).

To ensure that our institutions, in contrast to individuals, are delivering safe and effective services, several accreditation or quality assurance institutions have been established. Some of these institutions have long and distinguished histories in the health field whereas others are more recent. For some institutions, mental health is a very small part of their responsibilities, whereas others (e.g., the Commission on Accreditation of Rehabilitation Facilities or CARF) offer more specialized accreditation pertinent to mental health care providers. For example, CARF provides accreditation for programs related to disabilities, rehabilitation, vocational services, and mental health.

In 1951, the Joint Commission on Accreditation of Healthcare Institutions (JCAHO) was created to improve the quality of care provided to the public by setting standards and evaluating the performance of institutions against those standards. Today, JCAHO evaluates and accredits more than 15,000 health-care institutions including some 5,200 hospitals and 10,000 other health-care institutions (long-term care institutions, clinical laboratories, ambulatory care institutions, behavioral health institutions, and health-care networks, including HMOs; O'Malley, 1997).

Another accrediting body is the National Committee for Quality Assurance (NCQA). NCQA is an independent, nonprofit organization established in 1979 that reviews and accredits health maintenance institutions of all types. The NCQA represents the interests of purchasers, consumers, and health-care institutions, and its accreditation survey teams consist primarily of physicians.

The Health Plan Employer Data and Information Set (HEDIS) is a "report card" mechanism used by the National Committee for Quality Assurance (NCQA). The HEDIS report card mechanism is currently not required as part of the JCAHO or NCQA survey process, but may be in the future. The report card mechanism was created to standardize the way in which health plans calculate and report information about their performance, thereby enabling comparisons among plans. NCQA believes that the ability of purchasers and consumers to compare the quality of plans through HEDIS will result in competition in the market and lead managed care institutions to improve the care and service they provide. HEDIS includes eight performance domains: effectiveness of care, access to and availability of care, member satisfaction, health plan stability, use of services, cost of care, informed health-care choices, and health plan descriptive information (O'Malley, 1997).

In a similar fashion, performance among the nation's prison systems is monitored by the Association of State Correctional Administration (ASCA). In 1999, the ASCA identified standards for correctional performance that represent the most important elements of institutional correctional processes (e.g., public safety: escapes from within secure prisons, escapes from outside secure facilities; institutional safety: victims of prisoner-on-prisoner attacks, prisoner-on-staff attacks). A national performance measurement system has facilitated cross-jurisdictional assessments of the best and most efficient practices (Wright, 2004).

A recent survey found that 20% to 25% of the nation's prisons have strategic management systems that can create integrated information systems to monitor performance; the remaining 75% to 80% have a more limited capacity to measure and report on ASCA key indicators. The one exception is in the area of substance abuse and mental health measurement. "Because the records are collected by health units of prison systems, even the integrated information systems often lack detailed information to respond to the ASCA indicators in this area" (Wright, 2004, p. 56). This is problematic given the earlier discussion about the fact that one-third of the inmate population is mentally ill. Moreover, up to 80% of jail populations have a substance abuse disorder (Califano, 1998). In the social and welfare sector, as opposed to the health and prison sector, standardized care plans create a challenge. Human service institutions vary in ways that make the development of national monitoring systems difficult. For example, most welfare institutions differ widely in the kinds of treatments provided. Among other things, treatments vary in context (e.g., generalist versus specialist), setting (e.g., inpatient, outpatient, and residential), and funding streams (public versus private). Accrediting bodies in the domain of human services must specialize the standards of quality to meet the needs of providers whose services vary widely in terms of the range of possible services, interventions, and outcomes.

The child welfare sector is a human service domain that has attempted to develop national standards by requiring each state to submit data regarding child protection and welfare. The *Child and Family Services Review* assesses state outcomes in three domains: safety, permanency, and family and child well-being. The data profiles allow each state to compare safety and permanency data indicators with national standards determined by the U.S. Children's Bureau (Courtney, Needell, & Wulczyn, 2004). These standards have been criticized in part because of their broad base. The measures were adopted (in part) because the federal data system can only manage data that is cross-sectional. As such, changes in state performance over time cannot be measured, and even more problematic is the superficial nature of the data this is collected.

CARF is an accrediting body that serves the human service sector and mental health services in particular. CARF was founded in 1966 as an independent, nonprofit accreditation service in the areas of rehabilitation, employment, child and family, community, and aging services. CARF currently accredits more than 4,900 providers at more than 17,000 locations in the United States, Canada, Western Europe, and South America. There is an ongoing competitive process in the accreditation of human service institutions as a similar agency, the Council on Accreditation (COA), vies with CARF for the right to monitor the quality of social and welfare agencies across the country, and increasingly, around the world. Ultimately, all accrediting agencies have an overarching goal of improving the quality of services that enhance the lives of the persons served.

An organization seeking accreditation for a mental health program from CARF must demonstrate through policy and practice the following: a partnership with consumers in the development of treatment services, service design and delivery mechanisms that focus on the needs of the persons served, a multidisciplinary service approach, program accessibility and the assignment of qualified staff members, and outcome evaluation procedures (CARF, 2007).

The health-care standards employed by HEDIS, alternatively, permit researchers and consumers to evaluate extensive data at the level of specific procedures as well as by particular diseases. For example, the administration of adolescent immunizations, appropriate medications for people with asthma, breast cancer screenings, and cervical cancer screenings. The ability of purchasers and consumers to compare the quality of plans through

HEDIS may result in competition in the market and lead managed care institutions to improve the care and service they provide (O'Malley, 1997).

The way in which quality is evaluated in U.S. institutions is addressed in more depth later in the chapter. The construct of quality and its indicators are described as well as the empirical literature concerning quality assurance, quality improvement, and the newest form of assessment—continuous quality improvement. Next, specific models of organizational effectiveness and quality assessment are delineated. With the current institutional demand for effective and efficient services, it is critical that researchers have a conceptual framework for analyzing those factors that influence evaluations of effectiveness in their particular domain of service (Scheid & Greenley, 1997). How an institution will approach the process of assessment varies by type of institution, purpose of evaluation, level of analysis, and perhaps most importantly, how effectiveness and quality are operationalized.

ORGANIZATIONAL EFFECTIVENESS

The study of organizational effectiveness (OE) has a complex history. In contrast to the quality approaches described in the next section, OE approaches to the assessment of institutions focus on higher level indicators that measure overall achievement, for example, resource acquisition, size, and growth indicators.

The way in which researchers and practitioners define the OE construct is continually evolving. In general, OE refers to human judgments about desirability of the outcomes of organizational performance from the vantage point of the varied constituencies directly and indirectly affected by the organization (Zammuto, 1984, p. 614). Current models of the assessment of institutions can be linked back to goal-based approaches to effectiveness that view institutions as rational and oriented toward achieving a goal (Barnard, 1938; Perrow, 1965; Price, 1972). This approach has its roots in a purely mechanistic view of institutions in which effectiveness is measured by the degree of goal achievement. In goal-attainment models, effectiveness is operationalized in terms of productivity and/or efficiency (D'Aunno, 1991), and measures typically include the quantity and quality of goods and services produced and the efficiency with which goods or services are produced. This is the model behind the current emphasis on assessment and is best suited to institutions focusing on *outputs,* such as quality of life. The approach, according to D'Aunno (1991), is most useful when institutions have goals that are measurable, relatively few in number, and widely agreed on (Cameron, 1986; Hasenfeld, 1983).

A growing sense of dissatisfaction with goal-attainment models became apparent in a series of critical reviews during the mid-1970s (Campbell, 1977; Campbell, Brownas, Peterson, & Dunnette, 1974; Dubin, 1976; Steers, 1975). The major criticism concerned the idea that institutions encompass multiple, ambiguous, noncomparable, and inharmonious goals that cannot be specified completely (Starbuck & Nystrom, 1983, p. 137). Following these reviews, new themes emerged in the effectiveness literature in the form of *system resource* and *multiple constituency* (MC) models. Some writers present the system resource model as the first alternative to arise from the dissatisfaction with goal-oriented approaches and the MC approach as being subsequent to, or an alternative to, the system approach (D'Aunno, 1991; Forbes, 1998; Scheid & Greenley, 1997). Other writers describe the MC approach as an extension of the goal attainment model (Herman & Renz, 1998; Zammuto,

1984). In either case, these newer models allowed the complexity of social and political environments in which institutions are embedded to be taken into consideration during assessment.

System Resource Model of Effectiveness

The system resource approach (Georgopolous & Tannenbaum, 1957; Yuchtman & Seashore, 1967) defines effectiveness as the degree to which an organization can preserve its internal integration (i.e., acquire and exploit resources), adapt to the environment and, therefore, survive (Eisinger, 2002; Scheid & Greenley, 1997). In other words, the approach defines effectiveness as viability or survival (Forbes, 1998). Steers (1975) found that the most commonly utilized systems criteria of effectiveness were organizational adaptation and flexibility. Variations of this approach involve contingency theory that posits that those institutions whose internal structures "fit" the demands of their technology or task environment are effective (Scott, 1992). For example, the characteristics of an institution's culture and environment should coincide with the type of service being provided in order to be judged effective. In general, system resource models are best suited for institutions where formalization (adherence to rules and procedures) is low or environmental turbulence (uncertainty and complexity) is high because in these contexts, it is typically the case that *system* effectiveness precedes and is a prerequisite for *goal* effectiveness (Scheid & Greenley, 1997). A good example of such a system is a mental health institution. In this case, service providers must continually work to satisfy external stakeholders (e.g., funders and family members). The effort necessitates a process that first and foremost provides real services to real people. Only subsequent to the provision of services can such an institution measure its internal effectiveness.

Multiple Constituency Model of Effectiveness

The MC approach (Tsui, 1990) to measuring effectiveness also emphasizes the relationship between the organization and its environment. The MC approach proposes that an organization is successful to the degree that it satisfies the interest of multiple stakeholders who are identified by tracing various resource exchanges with the organization(s) of interest (D'Aunno, 1991; Scheid & Greenley, 1997). Stakeholders include clients, client family groups (e.g., National Alliance for the Mentally Ill [NAMI]), professional advocates, state hospitals, psychiatrists, as well as funding officials, government agents, and board members. The multiple constituency approach to determining organizational effectiveness concerns the degree of fit between participants' interpretations and the reality of environmental demands. As such, an organization is successful if it satisfies the interests of multiple constituencies or stakeholders (Baruch & Ramalho, 2006; D'Aunno, 1991; Scheid & Greenley, 1997).

   Over time, researchers and practitioners have recognized that stakeholders use different criteria to evaluate effectiveness (Herman & Renz, 1998). Because institutions and their environments are evolving, effectiveness must be viewed in the context of change (D'Aunno, 1991). Specialist institutions, like those serving people with chronic mental illness, are a good example of institutions with higher levels of environmental demands because they must conform (or at least appear to conform) to a wide variety of potentially contradictory demands from participants, as well as multiple external constituencies (Scheid & Greenley, 1997). The environmental demands are evolving over time and sometimes openly conflict with each other. For example, one of the longstanding critiques of mental health care has been that services are fragmented and uncoordinated, resulting in a lack of access and gaps in care (Dill & Rochefort, 1989). As demonstration sites began to address these concerns, there was little evidence of client improvement. As such, the environmental demand for more integrated services came in conflict with the basic needs of the primary beneficiaries of those services (Lehman, Postrado, Roth, McNary, & Goldman, 1994).

Institutional Theory Model of Effectiveness

The final model of effectiveness is institutional theory. Institutional theorists distinguish between two kinds of environmental pressures: efficiency and effectiveness in the production of goods or services and *expectations* about how institutions should behave with regards to structure and process (D'Aunno, 1991). Some argue that human service institutions face more pressures for conformity to widely held beliefs (e.g., community-based care is more compassionate than institutionalized care) than demands for efficiency or effectiveness in production (Meyer & Scott, 1983). Mental health hospitals and schools are examples of institutions in which the quality, as well as the cost of services, is hard for consumers to evaluate. Institutional theory predicts that when there is high uncertainty about the technology for achieving specific outcomes or when outcomes are difficult to measure, institutions are likely to emphasize approved procedures to achieve or maintain their legitimacy (Dimaggio & Powell, 1983; Meyer & Rowan, 1977). As such, some institutions are rewarded for standardization and replication, even when the services they are providing may not meet traditional standards of quality.

Institutional theorists also posit that widely held beliefs and rules in the environments of institutions influence their structure and behavior irrespective of their technologies and resource exchanges (Scott, 1987; Zucker, 1987). To illustrate, the effectiveness of drug abuse treatment institutions is influenced by a widely held set of beliefs concerning the Alcoholics Anonymous model. D'Aunno (1991) explains that

> alcoholism and substance abuse are believed to be diseases that can be treated only when clients abstain completely from alcohol and drugs and take responsibility for helping themselves. All clients have the same problem and can be treated through the same methods. Effective treatment can only begin after individuals recognize that they are ill and have the desire to recover. (p. 352)

As other technologies and models of treatment are developed (e.g., psychosocial models), treatment centers have found themselves facing conflicting beliefs about how to treat their clients. If conformity to external demands is the key to acquiring legitimacy and the resources needed for survival, as institutional theory predicts, then treatment centers will blend their approach and become what D'Aunno (1991) referred to as "hybrid" programs. Mental health programs that deviated from traditional mental health practices in order to serve substance abusers received less external support (e.g., funds) from the mental health sector because they were no longer conforming to expectations about appropriate structure and process (just as institutional theory would predict).

Social Constructionist Model of Effectiveness

The concept of effectiveness and quality with regard to institutions is important to both practitioners and researchers alike. The way in which effectiveness is conceptualized and research objectives pursued in the study of effectiveness has changed over time. New models are emerging that define effectiveness as a social construction: "[A]n achievement of organizational agents and other stakeholders in convincing each other that an organization is pursuing the right objectives in the right way" (Herman & Renz, 1998, p. 25). Researchers have started directly employing a social constructivist approach to models of effectiveness that emphasize issues of process over measurement (Forbes, 1998). In this case, *perceptions* of effectiveness are evaluated internally, at each level of the organization (from the board of directors to frontline workers), as well as externally (e.g., funders) and are compared to other organizational characteristics (e.g., age, financial data). Such a perspective views effectiveness as a set of judgments that are an outcome of a stream of interactions and impressions that may change frequently. Both institutional theory and the social constructivist approach remind us that institutions are social inventions created to satisfy human needs (Zammuto, 1982).

In addition to organizational effectiveness approaches, quality assurance approaches to the assessment of institutions are also concerned with viability and success at the highest levels; however, the assessment procedures relate more directly to regulatory processes and program evaluation. Recent policy and research initiatives have drawn widespread attention to gaps in the quality of care (Patel, Butler, & Wells, 2006) and, increasingly, the importance of accurate reporting, especially when the most vulnerable segments of the population are at issue.

QUALITY

Quality assurance efforts in the first half of the twentieth century were restricted to a reactive approach—evaluating bad outcomes. With limited staff time for chart review, only the more egregious outcomes could routinely be investigated, resulting in a case-by-case rather than a systemwide perspective (Bellin & Dubler, 2001, p. 1513).

Throughout the Western world, health-care costs have risen dramatically, provoking political bodies to mandate methods of reducing costs. Concurrently, institutions are confronted with demands to improve the quality of products and services. Making the situation more complicated is that the present system of quality assurance is characterized by multiple, competing, and usually contradictory health-care management corporations and accrediting bodies. The accreditation industry is big business. Yet, there is little evidence that this activity produces better outcomes for consumers (Bickman, 1999). Systematic research on accreditation is sparse, but there is data suggesting that differences between accredited and nonaccredited hospitals have reported only weak relationships between certification and indicators of quality of care (e.g., Hadley & McGurrin, 1988, as cited in Bickman, 1999). At least one study has found no difference (Bravo, Dubois, Charpentier, De Wals, & Emond, 1999 as cited in Bickman, 1999). Thus, the relationship of accreditation to client outcomes must await additional research.

Given the importance of quality, it is not surprising that a long but unsuccessful search has been conducted for a global definition of the construct. It has been suggested that such a global definition does not exist and that different definitions of quality are appropriate in different circumstances (Reeves & Bednar, 1994, p. 440). As such, it is likely that comparative and cumulative research results about quality can only be obtained by focusing on the fundamental nature of an institution's output and using a definition of quality suitable for that output (Reeves & Bednar, 1994). For example, personal social service institutions (e.g., nursing homes, mental health institutions) are the intense end of the regulatory spectrum (Challis, Day, Klein, & Scrivens, 1994) and, therefore, have quality standards that are among the most detailed (Johnson, Jenkinson, Kendall, & Blackmore, 1998). In particular, the development of quality measures for mental health care has been in a stage of proliferation. The strength of this process is that it has produced many measures covering a wide range of quality domains, clinical conditions, and types of treatment (Hermann et al., 2000).

Research supports the idea that definitions of quality should focus on an institution's particular outputs (e.g., employment retention and increased housing stability versus children's permanency in living situations). In addition, to differentiate between different forms of care, multiple methods of quality assessment are called for that focus on structure and process as well as outcome (Cotter, Salvage, Meyer, & Bridges, 1998).

Bellin and Dubler (2001) identify three patterns of deficient care that should be identified by quality assurance systems: (1) a dramatic deviation from the expected outcome (e.g., unexpected death), (2) a reasonable outcome despite a less-than-optimal process (e.g., serious delays in the emergency room triage system), and (3) a reasonable outcome with an acceptable process (e.g., earlier discharge for patients with conditions shown to rarely need intervention after a certain point) (p. 1514). Bellin and Dubler describe the way in which the quality assurance process naturally encourages continuous assessment because it is committed to using the results to immediately inform the process of care: "This feedback loop, with its expectation of responsiveness, motivates and legitimates continuous quality improvement reviews. Statistical rigor and sound methodology further enhance the ethical legitimacy of continuous quality improvement" (p. 1514).

Continuous Quality Improvement

The renaming of the quality assurance process to continuous quality improvement (CQI) reflects the recognition that the process is one of continued improvement in the context of error rather than an idealized, unachievable notion of perfection (Bellin & Dubler, 2001, p. 1514). CQI is described as a philosophy of continual improvement of the processes associated with providing a good or service that meets or exceeds customer expectations (Shortell, Bennett, & Byck, 1998, p. 594). CQI implies the use of total quality management techniques developed in manufacturing and service industries. It has been described as a paradigm shift that "applies the scientific method to organizational work processes" (Chowanec, 1994, p. 789).

Bellin and Dubler (2001) explain that a continuous quality improvement process is able to (a) query the electronic record and identify cohorts of patients who have received substandard care or who have not responded to treatment as expected, (b) review internal time to the delivery of specific services, and (c) identify process failures that have not yet led to sentinel events (p. 1512). The CQI process can also plan prospectively to implement and evaluate corrective strategies.

CQI and similar models can lead to change but only if based on accurate measures of important structures, processes, and outcomes (Hermann et al., 2000). The process requires that those involved understand the linkages between the processes and the outcomes of care, that they systematically collect data on these linkages, and that they create an atmosphere at all levels of institutions that supports the implementation of changes in treatment based on observed linkages (Bickman, Noser, & Summerfelt, 1999; Deming, 1982, 1986; Dickens, 1994).

Although many support the application of CQI in health-care settings, there have been very few demonstrations of its implementation, much less its success, in other human service fields. Dickens (1994) has noted the popularity of CQI in education (Edwards, 1991; Ivancevitch & Ivancevitch, 1992), government (Swiss, 1992), and health care (Fried, 1992; Graham, 1995) but not in mental health care. Although the potential for outcomes monitoring and feedback to improve the quality of mental health services is recognized, there is little empirical evidence that this type of feedback improves quality of care (Bickman, 1999). Clearly, measurement-based quality improvement can be only as good as its measures. Further testing, development, and consensus will be needed to realize the possibilities of CQI and related efforts (Hermann et al., 2000).

As health care moves more firmly into a competitive marketplace with ongoing pressures to lower costs, raise efficiency, and improve quality, formalized methods of quality assessment and quality improvement are becoming increasingly important. There are several major barriers to the improvement of services that must be dealt with if we are going to achieve progress in the delivery of quality mental health services. Testing the effectiveness of our current approaches to assuring quality and effectiveness is one step. We need to have standardized treatments that have been shown to work in the real world. This will require more research on identifying effective treatments in community settings. We need to establish valid and reliable measurement of both processes and outcomes in service settings, and we need research on practice to understand the factors that affect the delivery of services. With the proper resources, commitment, and training, service institutions should be able to lead this movement, in partnership with academic researchers, to create truly effective mental health service (Bickman, 1999).

Following are the results of numerous studies that provide a beginning basis for the available evidence in institutional assessment.

SUMMARY OF CURRENT EVIDENCE-BASED ASSESSMENT OF INSTITUTIONS

In general, the long-term goal of assessing institutions is to improve institutions' effectiveness and ultimately client outcomes. However, assessment also has short-term goals such as improving the client intake process, increasing the effectiveness of treatment or interventive technologies, and cost-savings. Institutions tend to label this process differently; some call it quality assessment or assurance, others refer to it as outcomes or evaluation research, and still others term it as credentialing or quality improvement. The differences in nomenclature usually refer to differences in systems and processes for assessment; however, many of the same systematic processes are labeled differently. This certainly adds to confusion in discussing processes and prohibits replication between and among institutions. Essentially, effective institutional assessment involves measuring institutional performance on several indicators including the organization's structure, process, and outcome (Donabedian, 1980). Structure refers to stable characteristics of the providers of care, for example, financial resources, the physical setting, and the organizational setting. An assessment of structural factors includes an examination of the physical amenities of the facility and qualifications of the staff and the administrative organization. An analysis of the stable characteristics of institutions can be viewed as a proxy for quality rather than an actual measure of quality (Cotter et al., 1998). Process refers to the set of activities that takes place in the care setting. For example, this may include peer review of care practices, observing what actually happens between staff and consumers/patients (Cotter et al., 1998), access to care, program delivery, community collaboration, and resource acquisition. Outcome refers to aspects of the consumer's well-being that can be linked directly to the care provided. For example, this may include health and well-being after intervention or care, consumer satisfaction, and other quality-of-life indicators. Donabedian (1992) argues that there is not a one-to-one correspondence between outcomes and quality of an organization's performance. An evaluation of outcomes only permits inferences to be made about the quality of the care delivered. To be able to make more meaningful (i.e., valid) statements concerning quality, it is necessary also to examine structure and process (Cotter et al., 1998, p. 258). Structure, process, and outcome indicators in the context of an organizational effectiveness approach to the assessment of institutions will be summarized first, followed by findings from the quality assurance literature.

Studies of Organizational Effectiveness

Scheid and Greenly (1997) evaluated 29 mental health programs in Wisconsin. The agencies were purposely chosen from among those with good reputations. The goal was to determine which service approach was most effective. Effectiveness was operationalized by asking program directors and staff to rate their agency's quality of care, access to care for those in need, innovativeness, efficiency, and overall effectiveness. The subjective assessment of institutional effectiveness by members of the internal environment is the same measure that has been utilized by other organizational researchers (D'Aunno, 1991; Tsui, 1990). There was strong support for the idea that environmental conformity (e.g., providing particular services to particular client groups as articulated by a variety of stakeholders) is associated with a higher level of organizational effectiveness (as rated by constituents internal to the organization). Mental health agencies that offered specialized services to those with chronic mental illness, for example, were more likely to evaluate themselves as effective compared to generalist mental health programs, in part, because of their more narrowly defined goals.

In other words, mental health institutions that specialize in services and meet the institutional expectations of what constitutes appropriate mental health care evaluated themselves as more effective and efficient than institutions that did not exhibit these processes of institutional conformity (Scheid & Greenley, 1997).

Herman and Renz (1998) evaluated 64 nonprofit institutions. A large portion were health and welfare charities, the remaining institutions were designed to serve customers with developmental disabilities. The authors created a measure of organizational effectiveness that included nine indicators encompassing structure, process, and outcome-related factors: financial management, fund-raising, program delivery, public relations, community collaboration, working with volunteers, human resource management, government relations, and board governance. The purpose of the study was to examine the relationship between board effectiveness and organizational effectiveness. Results indicated that especially effective institutions have highly effective boards (as judged by stakeholders), have boards with higher social prestige, use more practitioner identified "correct" management procedures (e.g., strategic planning, measures of customer satisfaction), and use more change management strategies (e.g., enhancing legitimization, seeking new revenue sources). This study contributes to an emerging literature regarding frameworks for considering assessment, quality, and effectiveness indicators from a social constructivist perspective. The authors emphasize the idea that a single organizational reality does not exist. Rather, different stakeholders create effectiveness on the basis of the criteria and impressions they deem most relevant (p. x).

While most researchers studying organizational effectiveness conceptualize the construct as a dependent variable, a careful study by Yoo and Brooks (2005) investigated the influence organizational variables have on service effectiveness among a total of 3,883 children and 13 networks of institutions. The independent variables employed in their study were similar to the variables we have conceptualized comprising organizational effectiveness itself (see Figure 27.1). In particular, perceptions of effectiveness, as determined by workers from each organization, were associated with better outcomes for clients. Institutions characterized by their workers as having greater routineness of work (i.e., formalization), supervisor and coworker support (i.e., positive institutional environment), and strong leadership qualities (i.e., positive institutional environment) were related to fewer occurrences of out-of-home

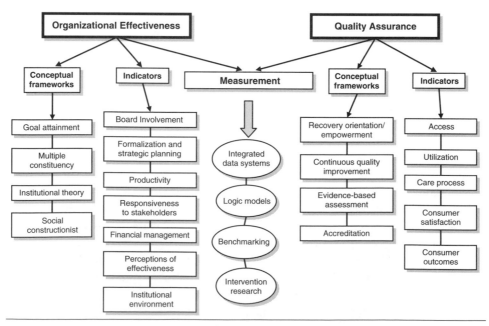

Figure 27.1   The assessment of institutions

placement for children who participated in family preservation programs. The authors conclude that management practice has an important role in service effectiveness.

Studies of Quality and Mental Health

Decisions about the delivery of services typically involve technical competence, cost efficiency, and client outcomes (Scheid & Greenley, 1997). Access to community-based mental health services, in particular, has been an important concern of program evaluators and advocates for decades. In 1975, the National Institute of Mental Health (NIMH) required all federally funded community mental health centers to evaluate their performance in terms of accessibility of services (NIMH, 1977). Measures of access to mental health services have appeared among the performance measures proposed by the American College of Mental Health Administration (ACMHA) Santa Fe Summit on Behavioral Health (1998), and the National Association of State Mental Health Program Directors (NASMHPD), and President's Task Force on Performance Measures (1998).

In mental health services research, quality of care is typically divided into three distinct domains: access to care, the treatment process, and treatment outcomes. Within the access domain, utilization rates are recognized to be one of the most direct and efficient measures of this broad concept (Styles, Boothroyd, Snyder, & Zong, 2002). Indicators of access to care include subjective perception (consumer satisfaction), geographical location of services, economic factors (the ability to afford services), and how people are treated and by whom (cultural sensitivity) (Pandiani, Banks, Simon, Van Vleck, & Pomeroy, 2005). Concerns about quality of care, accessibility, and affordability of services have shaped the debate about health care for more than 2 decades and are relevant both to the overall health-care system in general and to behavioral health care in particular (Blumenthal, 1999).

Valenstein et al. (2004) evaluated mental health care providers perceptions of widely used indicators for quality monitoring in mental health services. The results indicate that frontline mental health workers believe that feedback about widely used indicators would be valuable in improving care. Frontline mental health workers ($n = 684$) were most positive about indicators in the satisfaction domain: 79% felt these indicators might be helpful in efforts to improve care, 70% felt able to influence these indicators, and 34% were willing to take incentives/risks for performance. In general, mental health workers were more positive about domains regarding process and access than utilization and outcome. Perhaps this is because workers felt least able to influence outcome domains compared to the other domains. Such information may be useful in efforts to increase the relevance and effectiveness of quality improvement activities in mental health institutions.

Shaller (2004) studied the barriers to using quality measures for children's mental health services. He conducted semistructured interviews with 40 opinion leaders drawn from four groups: (1) funders of quality-measurement development and implementation, (2) developers of quality measures, (3) users of quality measures, and (4) providers of children's mental health services. All four groups acknowledge the importance of developing a robust set of quality measures that can serve multiple objectives and multiple audiences. One of the most commonly cited measures across all groups included the Health Plan Employer Data and Information Set (HEDIS) that was noted to be a successful measurement tool in the field.

The major challenges cited by funders and developers were the lack of trained field staff to conduct needed research and development and the lack of compelling evidence that quality measurement and improvement actually results in better outcomes for children. Shaller (2004) concludes that child health quality leaders will need to manage the tension between standardization and innovation to maintain an appropriate balance between the benefits of both.

Chowanec (1994) describes the implementation of the CQI approach on a unit for chronically mentally ill patients at a state psychiatric facility. He first notes that to be effective in the long run a program for implementing CQI should proceed in four steps, "focusing first on the CQI attitude, then on the CQI approach, and then on the CQI process" (p. 790). Only after these elements are in place can the organization introduce a CQI plan (the fourth step) that will serve as a blueprint for continuous organizational improvement. The development of a plan is perhaps the most challenging part of the process because it involves deciding what to measure and how it should be measured.

The CQI *attitude* is described by the idea that frontline workers can only be as good as their organization allows them to be. The belief is that quality problems are not caused by a worker's lack of effort but by the way the work is organized. The CQI *approach* is a rational way to solve problems that can be applied to improve outcomes, regardless of the nature of the problem. As described earlier, it is a framework for applying the scientific method to the workings of an organization (Chowanec, 1994, pp. 790–791). Finally, the CQI *process* involves systematic monitoring, evaluation, and "improvement of the effectiveness and efficiency of work procedures rather than on inspection of the finished project" (p. 791).

In an institution like a state psychiatric hospital, the staff was hesitant to embrace what was first perceived as the latest evolution of the "much resented QA" (Chowanec, 1994, p. 790). At some point in the process, the staff and administrators accepted that the focus was on planning future improvements rather than critiquing past efforts and worked together to improve the overall quality of care. Chowanec was a consultant to the hospital unit as well as the director of the psychology department. He emphasized the particular efforts that made the implementation of CQI a success in the context of a unit for people with chronic mental illness: All staff participated in formulating a shared mission; overall treatment goals were based on the patient's needs, the unit's resources, and the role the unit played within the total hospital system; and quantitative data were used to monitor progress toward the goal.

The assessment of quality in institutions ultimately rests on improved patient outcomes and increased patient satisfaction. CQI involves understanding the relationship between the procedures by which human services are provided to patients and patient outcomes and satisfaction (Chowanec, 1994, p. 791). Clearly, quality assessments will contain elements that are specific to the type of institution or type of service that the institution provides. There are some central elements to best practices for institutional assessment that can be adapted to specific situations.

Limitations of the Evidence

The primary limitation of the evidence regarding the assessment of institutions revolves around the fragmented research literature. As shown in Figure 27.1, the literatures regarding OE and QA do not have obvious points of intersection. The purpose of the research and indicators used to understand key relationships differ at the level of analysis as well as ultimate use in the field of assessment.

IMPLICATIONS AT MACRO-, MEZZO-, AND MICROLEVELS

Social work can play a leading role in the fostering of quality assessment of institutions. At the macrolevel, such leadership requires a research engine to drive the organization. Issues involving both organizational effectiveness and quality assurance need to be addressed. As Figure 27.1 suggests, the macro leader will be concerned with both the quality assurance process and with organizational effectiveness. While these two approaches, as noted earlier, are not integrated in the literature, they must be integrated at the macrolevel to achieve institutional effectiveness and quality assurance.

For example, to address organizational effectiveness macro leaders will need to satisfy multiple constituencies such as funders, board members, staff, family members, and other stakeholders that goals of service are ensured with the funds and related staff resources available. In some cases, turbulent environments involving changing funding streams, or unexpected capital expenditures may destabilize the organization or institution. Macro leaders may need to advance new funding strategies to ensure that the resources are in place to achieve desired outcomes. Sometimes deprofessionalization occurs to reduce costs in service delivery. This along with other types of cost containment may, in the short run, balance the books but in the long run may undercut effective and efficient services.

Ideally, macro leaders will be able to sustain goal achievement in their attention to organizational effectiveness and move to systems of quality assurance as a best practice requirement for CQI. Such quality assurance frameworks can be built on integrated information systems, benchmarks for desired outcomes, and measures that can be used to chart progress. Leadership skills to build research and information systems are critical to institutional viability. Financing such systems may be challenging for some unless incentives are fostered by federal- or state-level investments. Thus the macro leader must be a visionary in fostering investments from private sources or public funding streams so that research engines of renewal and effectiveness are in place. Sometimes the repositioning of staff to be quality assurance facilitators may reculture the organization so that all begin to focus more on outcomes rather than services alone.

At the macrolevel, the executive leadership needs to develop a logic model that maps the framework for services, programs, and the desire for outcomes and indices of success. Logic models are increasingly adopted by institutions that specify goals, assumptions, target populations, services programs and related interventions, the short- and long-term outcomes expected, and indicators for these.

Critical to quality assurance are data systems that provide reliable information on performance and that can track cohorts of service users through the system of care. From this, those who have not benefited from services, not responded as expected, or who have experienced substandard care can be identified. Program failures can be identified and the variables that led to the events can be examined. These systems often require integration so that data gathered about one set of outcomes, such as length of stay or system reentry, can be linked to other kinds of data, such as caseload size. From this information, corrective improvement can be tested and evaluated.

To date much quality assurance work addresses deficits and problems. Like the old expose/deficit assessment of past centuries, the assessment process has not moved to a best practice system. Rather than focusing on the deficit or problem-based corrective strategy, macro leaders can also focus such quality assurance systems on fostering creative improvements and models for best practices. For example, program outcome data along with cost data may provide the basis for creative new programming and budget neutral expenditure shifts. An illustration might be that stepdown services (less restrictive) can be provided with wraparound support in the community as effectively and efficiently as institutionally based service. Thus, length of stay might be reduced with improved community-based integration and quality outcomes.

The macrolevel social work leader will be focused on developing a data systems infrastructure so that the relevant variables are used to chart progress. The macro social work leader plays a key role in advancing the need for progress charting so that data entry, at the frontline, is not seen as an anathema to service delivery but instead part of the process.

Above all, the macrolevel social work leader will be focused on client-based outcomes. What difference the services, program, or entire institutional experience makes for client improvements is the most critical feature of the quality improvement process. These client outcome improvement goals translate into institutional level outcome goals.

Some social work leaders will find that results-based accountability has taken on new dimensions in recent years with high stakes dynamics. For example, those who lead child welfare systems and institutions or public schools will find that with the Child and Family Service Reviews, or the educational policy of No Child Left Behind fiscal sanctions are possible if thresholds for successful outcomes are not met.

Macrolevel social work leadership can also spearhead evidence-based practice and services. Thus, close partnerships with local universities and schools of social work will help with research reviews, access to new studies, and research literature. The macrolevel leader will also need to be attentive to benchmarking. This is based on external standards, derived by consensus among experts as to the desired programs or outcomes expected within the organization. Ongoing surveys measure progress and cross-site comparison helps leaders compare their success against others. Improvements can be charted and such benchmarking measures can be integrated into ongoing quality assurance efforts (Pecora, Seelig, Zirps, & Davis, 1996).

At the mezzolevel, social work supervisors and managers must balance tasks that foster organizational effectiveness and quality assurance efforts. The supervisor or middle manager will oversee client access to services, practices, and sometimes costs. It is also the job of the mezzolevel social worker to spot problems and to invent solutions so that on a daily basis there may be many "in-flight" quality assurance efforts operating to ensure smooth delivery of services and programs. In the aggregate, quality assurance data on client cohorts and their success or failure may mask the daily corrective action that the mezzo or frontline (microlevel) social worker enacts. Like the macrolevel leaders, mezzolevel social workers can use quality assurance not just for deficit-based problem identification and solutions but as an opportunity to design innovative programs and services to advance and approximate desired goals of highly successful outcomes. Thus mezzolevel manager roles are critical to the innovation process on which organizational effectiveness and quality assurance depend. Moreover, mezzolevel managers and supervisors are often the inventors of pilots and demonstration projects, testing new ways to deliver services. These can be undertaken with special grant funds, budget neutral expenditure shifts (especially if addressing least restrictive stepdown services that may be more effective and less costly), or repositioning of staff and related resources (volunteers, peers, parents).

At the microlevel, frontline staff are ideally "clinician scientists," capable of charting progress with each client served while being attuned to consumer preferences for timing and options for service. Every practice act may be a research act with documentation of progress becoming a normalized part of the direct service function. Issues related to client satisfaction can also become feedback guided by frontline staff as they work on improved quality of treatment, intervention assessment, and intervention effectiveness. Some frontline social work staff may not have access to the Internet or to electronic record keeping. This may impede their access to updated information about the growing body of promising or best practices, model programs and evidence-based interventions. Mezzo- and macrolevel social work leaders will need to foster the research tools and culture that help to reinforce the inventive frontline social worker. Frontline staff may also be supervisors of fieldwork students from local schools of social work. These fieldwork students can also be key collaborators in research reviews, intervention modification, and testing.

Ideally, it is on the frontline level where innovations in practice and interventions strategies can be designed. The earlier themes on recovery and the need to break away from the deficit and medical model of treatment and quality assurance should inspire frontline social workers to learn from their own effectiveness and practice innovations. This means that frontline and mezzolevel staff will be examining ways to use single subject research design approaches to create quasi-experimental conditions in order to test effectiveness. Such single-subject designs may be pivotal strategies as effective practices are then "scaled up" to larger groups of consumers who may benefit from the intervention.

CONCLUSION

The recovery movement and the discoveries of Clifford Beers and the National Mental Hygiene Committee remind us that it is continually possible to move beyond the deficit-oriented medical model to invent solutions to the most pressing challenges facing populations in care. Custodial or even rehabilitation models may not approximate the more optimistic recovery benchmarks that consumer movements warrant. Organizational survival and compliance with federal standards and benchmarks are not the same as embracing a developmental approach to the creation of model programs and institutions.

As research becomes more rigorous, with greater attention to the understanding of why particular strategies work and the factors that augment or interfere with their success in different institutions, we believe that a number of strategies will prove effective at promoting evidence-based assessment. One promising practice is seen in the high-performing learning organization where it is recognized that institutions and programs must be continually evolving. Such institutions are data driven, using outcomes to generate improvements and innovations. Add to this the notion of consumer guided change and improvement and we greatly increase the likelihood of the organization's ability to remain relevant, as well as effective.

As in the rest of social welfare, however, these effects will generally be modest. Unless we adjust our expectations, the continued quest for the perfect tool or mechanism to evaluate the quality and effectiveness of institutions will result in missed opportunities to make consistent, incremental improvements in the way we provide services to our constituents (Shojania & Grimshaw, 2005, p. 150).

REFERENCES

Barnard, C. (1938). *The functions of the executive.* Cambridge, MA: Harvard University Press.

Baruch, Y., & Ramalho, N. (2006). Communalities and distinctions in the measurement of organizational performance and effectiveness across for-profit and nonprofit sectors. *Nonprofit and Voluntary Sector Quarterly, 35*(1), 39–65.

Bellamy, D., & Irving, A. (2001). Pioneers. In J. C. Turner & F. J. Turner (Eds.), *Canadian social welfare* (4th ed., pp. 104–105). Toronto, Ontario, Canada: Allyn & Bacon.

Bellin, E., & Dubler, N. N. (2001). The quality improvement-research divide and the need for external oversight. *American Journal of Public Health, 91*(9), 1512–1517.

Bickman, L. (1999). Practice makes perfect and other myths about mental health services. *American Psychological Association, 54*(11), 965–978.

Bickman, L., Noser, K., & Summerfelt, W. T. (1999). Long term effects of a system of care on children and adolescents. *Journal of Behavioral Health Services Research, 26*, 185–202.

Blumenthal, D. (1999). Health care reform at the close of the 20th century. *New England Journal of Medicine, 340*(24), 1916–1920.

Briar, K., & Ryan, R. (1986). The anti-institution movement and women caregivers. *Affilia: Journal of Women in Social Work,* 20–31.

Califano, J. A. (1998). *Behind bars: Substance abuse and America's prison population.* New York: Columbia University, National Center of Addiction and Substance Abuse. Retrieved February 11, 2007, from www.casacolumbia.org/supportcasa/item.asp?cID=12&PID=108/.

Cameron, K. (1986). Effectiveness as paradox: Consensus and conflict in conceptions of organizational effectiveness. *Management Science, 32*(5), 539–553.

Campbell, J. P. (1977). On the nature of organizational effectiveness. In P. S. Goodman & J. M. Pennings (Eds.), *New perspectives on organizational effectiveness* (pp. 13–55). San Francisco: Jossey-Bass.

Campbell, J. P., Brownas, E. A., Peterson, N. G., & Dunnette, M. D. (1974). The measurement of organizational effectiveness: A review of relevant research and opinion. *Navy Personnel Research and Development Center.* Minneapolis, MN: Personnel Decisions.

Challis, D., Day, P., Klein, R., & Scrivens, E. (1994). Managing quasi-markets: Institutions of regulation. In W. Bartlett, C. Propper, D. Wilson, & J. Le Grand (Eds.), *Quasi-markets in the welfare state: The emerging findings* (pp. 10–32). Bristol, Avon, England: School for Advanced Urban Studies.

Chowanec, G. D. (1994). Continuous quality improvement: Conceptual foundations and application to mental health care. *Hospital and Community Psychiatry, 45*(8), 789–793.

Commission on Accreditation of Rehabilitation Facilities. (2007). *Who are we?* Retrieved February 11, 2007, from www.carf.org/consumer.aspx?content=content/About/News/boilerplate.htm.

Cotter, A. J. E., Salvage, A. V., Meyer, J. E., & Bridges, J. (1998). Measuring outcomes of long-term care for older people. *Reviews in Clinical Gerontology, 8*, 257–268.

Courtney, M. E., Needell, B., & Wulczyn, F. (2004). Unintended consequences of the push for accountability: The case of national child welfare performance standards. *Children and Youth Services Review, 26*(12), 1141–1154.

D'Aunno, T. (1991). The effectiveness of human service organizations. In Y. Hasenfeld (Ed.), *Human services as complex organizations* (pp. 341–361). Newbury Park, CA: Sage.

Deming, W. E. (1982). *Quality, productivity, and competitive position.* Cambridge, MA: MIT Press, Center for Advanced Engineering Study.

Deming, W. E. (1986). *Out of the crisis*. Cambridge, MA: MIT Press, Center for Advanced Engineering Study.

De Schweinitz, K. (1943). *England's road to social security*. New York: Barnes.

Deutsch, A. (1949). *The mentally ill in America: A history of their care and treatment from colonial times*. New York: Columbia University Press.

Dickens, P. (1994). *Quality and excellence in human services*. Chichester, West Sussex, England: Wiley.

Dill, A., & Rochefort, D. (1989). Coordination, continuity, and centralized control: A policy perspective on service strategies for the chronic mentally ill. *Journal of Social Issues*, *45*(3), 145–159.

Dimaggio, P. J., & Powell, W. W. (1983). The iron cage revisited: Institutional isomorphism and collective rationality in organizational fields. *American Sociological Review*, *48*, 147–160.

Donabedian, A. (1980). *The definition of quality and approaches to its assessment*. Ann Arbor, MI: Health Administration Press.

Donabedian, A. (1992). *Lecture outlines and illustrative materials* [Seminar on quality assessment and assurance]. Oxford: Oxford University, National Institute for Nursing, Brasenose College.

Dubin, R. (1976). Organizational effectiveness: Some dilemmas of perspective. *Organization and Administrative Sciences*, *7*, 7–14.

Edwards, E. (1991). Total quality management in higher education. *Management Services*, *35*(12), 18–20.

Eisinger, P. (2002). Organizational capacity and organizational effectiveness among street-level food assistance programs. *Nonprofit and Voluntary Sector Quarterly*, *31*(1), 115–130.

Farone, D. W. (2006). Schizophrenia, community integration, and recovery: Implications for social work practice. *Social Work in Mental Health*, *4*(4), 21–36.

Foley, H. A., Sharfstein, S. S., & Butler, R. N. (1983). *Madness and government: Who cares for the mentally ill?* Washington, DC: American Psychiatric Press.

Forbes, D. P. (1998). Measuring the unmeasurable: Empirical studies of nonprofit organization effectiveness from 1977 to 1997. *Nonprofit and Voluntary Sector Quarterly*, *27*, 183–202.

Foucault, M. (1988). *Madness and civilization: A history of insanity in the age of reason*. New York: Random House.

French, L. (1987). Victimization of the mentally ill: An unintended consequence of deinstitutionalization. *Social Work*, *32*(6), 502–505.

Freshwater, D., & Westwood, T. (2006). Risk, detention, and evidence: Humanizing mental health reform. *Journal of Psychiatric and Mental Health Nursing*, *13*(3), 257–259.

Fried, R. A. (1992). A crisis in health care. *Quality Progress*, *24*(4), 67–69.

Friedman, M. B. (2002). *Clifford Beers: The origins of modern mental health policy*. Retrieved February 3, 2007, from the Mental Health Association of Westchester web site:www.mhawestchester.org/advocates/beers802.asp/.

Georgopolous, B., & Tannenbaum, A. (1957). The study of organizational effectiveness. *American Sociological Review*, *22*, 534–540.

Gilligan, J. (2001). The last mental hospital. *Psychiatric Quarterly*, *72*(1), 45–61.

Goffman, E. (1962). *Asylums: Essays on the social situation of mental patients and other inmates*. Chicago: Aldine.

Graham, N. O. (1995). *Quality in health care, theory, application and evolution*. Gaithersburg, MD: Aspen Press.

Hasenfeld, Y. (1983). *Human service organizations*. Englewood Cliffs, NJ: Prentice Hall.

Herman, R. D., & Renz, D. O. (1998). Nonprofit organizational effectiveness: Contrasts between especially effective and less effective organizations. *Nonprofit Management and Leadership*, *9*(1), 23–38.

Hermann, R. C., Leff, H. S., Palmer, R. H., Yang, D., Teller, T., Provost, S., et al. (2000). Quality measures for mental health care: Results from a national inventory. *Medical Care Research and Review*, *57*(2), 136–154.

Honberg, R., & Gruttadaro, D. (2005). Flawed mental health policies and the tragedy of criminalization. *Corrections Today*, *67*(1), 22–27.

Ivancevitch, D. M., & Ivancevitch, S. H. (1992). TQM in the classroom. *Management Accounting*, *74*(4), 14–15.

Johnson, N., Jenkinson, S., Kendall, I., & Blackmore, M. (1998). Regulating for quality in the voluntary sector. *Journal of Social Policy*, *27*(3), 307–328.

Joint Commission. (2007). *Our history.* Retrieved February 11, 2007, from www .jointcommission.org.

Lamb, H., & Bachrach, L. (2001). Some perspectives on deinstitutionalization. *Psychiatric Services*, *52*, 1039–1045.

Lamb, H., Weinberger, L. E., & Gross, B. H. (2004). Mentally ill persons in the criminal justice system: Some perspectives. *Psychiatric Quarterly*, *75*(2), 107–126.

Lehman, A. F., Postrado, L. T., Roth, D., McNary, S. W., & Goldman, H. H. (1994). Continuity of care and client outcomes in the Robert Wood Johnson Foundation program on chronic mental illness. *Milbank Quarterly*, *72*(1), 105–122.

Markowitz, F. E. (2006). Psychiatric hospital capacity, homelessness, and crime and arrest rates. *Criminology*, *44*(1), 45–72.

McPheeters, H. (1977). Mental health programs. *Proceedings of the Academy of Political Science*, *32*, 159–169.

Meyer, J. W., & Rowan, B. (1977). Institutionalized organizations: Formal structure as myth and ceremony. *American Journal of Sociology*, *83*, 340–363.

Meyer, J. W., & Scott, W. R. (Eds.). (1983). *Organizational environments*. Beverly Hills, CA: Sage.

National Association of State Mental Health Program Directors & President's Task Force on Performance Measures Technical. (1998). *Draft recommended operational definitions and measures to implement the NASMHPD framework of mental health performance indicators*. Washington, DC: National Association of State Mental Health Program Directors.

National Institute of Mental Health. (1977). *1977 standards for accreditation of managed care organizations*. Washington, DC: National Committee for Quality Assurance.

Office of Management and Budget. (2002). *Government Performance and Results Act of 1993*. Retrieved February 11, 2007, from www.whitehouse.gov/omb/mgmt-gpra/gplaw2m.html.

O'Malley, C. (1997). Quality measurement for health systems: Accreditation and report cards. *American Journal of Health-System Pharmacy*, *54*(13), 1528–1535.

Pandiani, J. A., Banks, S. M., Simon, M. M., Van Vleck, M. C., & Pomeroy, S. M. (2005). Access to child and adolescent mental health services. *Journal of Child and Family Studies*, *14*(3), 431–441.

Patel, K. K., Butler, B., & Wells, K. B. (2006). What is necessary to transform the quality of mental health care? *Health Affairs*, *25*(3), 681–693.

Patrick, V., Smith, R. C., Schleifer, S. J., Morris, M. E., & McLennon, K. (2006). Facilitating discharge in state psychiatric institutions: A group intervention strategy. *Psychiatric Rehabilitation Journal*, *29*(3), 183–188.

Pecora, P. J., Seelig, W. R., Zirps, F. A., & Davis, S. M. (1996). Quality improvement and evaluation in child and family services: Managing into the next century. Washington, DC: CWLA Press.

Perrow, C. (1965). The analysis of goals in complex organizations. *American Journal of Sociology*, *26*(6), 854–866.

Price, J. (1972). *Organizational effectiveness: An inventory of propositions*. Homewood, IL: Irwin.

Randall, K. (2003). A social contract for deinstitutionalization. *Journal of Social Philosophy*, *34*(3), 475–486.

Reeves, C. A., & Bednar, D. A. (1994). Defining quality: Alternatives and implications. *Academy of Management Review, 19*(3), 419–445.

Rossi, P. H., & Freeman, H. E. (1982). *Evaluation: A systematic approach.* Newbury Park, CA: Sage.

Rothman, D. J. (1971). *The discovery of the asylum.* Boston: Little, Brown.

Rothman, D. J. (1980). *Conscience and convenience: The asylum and its alternatives in progressive America.* Boston: Little, Brown.

Santa Fe Summit on Behavioral Health. (1998). *Santa Fe Summit on Behavioral Health: Preserving quality and value in the managed care equation* [Final report]. Pittsburgh: American College of Mental Health Administration.

Scheid, T. L., & Greenley, J. R. (1997). Evaluations of organizational effectiveness in mental health programs. *Journal of Health and Social Behavior, 38*(4), 403–426.

Scott, W. R. (1987). The adolescence of institutional theory. *Administrative Science Quarterly, 32,* 493–511.

Scott, W. R. (1992). *Organizations: Rational, natural, and open systems.* Englewood Cliffs, NJ: Prentice Hall.

Segal, S. (1979). Community care and deinstitutionalization: A review. *Social Work, 26*(6), 521–527.

Shaller, D. (2004). Implementing and using quality measures for children's health care: Perspectives on the state of the practice. *Pediatrics, 113*(1), 217–227.

Sharfstein, S. S. (2000). What ever happened to community mental health? *Psychiatric Services, 51*(5), 616–620.

Shojania, K. G., & Grimshaw, J. M. (2005). Evidence-based quality improvement: The state of the science. *Health Affairs, 24*(1), 138–150.

Shortell, S. M., Bennett, C. L., & Byck, G. R. (1998). Assessing the impact of continuous quality improvement on clinical practice: What it will take to accelerate progress. *Milbank Quarterly, 76*(4), 593–632.

Starbuck, W. H., & Nystrom, P. C. (1983). Pursuing organizational effectiveness that is ambiguously specified. In K. S. Cameron & D. A., Wheelton (Eds.), *Organizational effectiveness: A comparison of multiple models* (pp. 135–161). New York: Academic Press.

Steers, R. M. (1975). Problems in measuring organizational effectiveness. *Administrative Science Quarterly, 10,* 546–558.

Styles, P., Boothroyd, R., Snyder, K., & Zong, X. (2002). Service penetration by persons with severe mental illness: How should it be measured? *Journal of Behavioral Health Services and Research, 29*(2), 198–207.

Swiss, J. E. (1992). Adapting total quality management to government. *Public Administration Review, 52,* 356–362.

Talbott, J. A. (2004). Deinstitutionalization: Avoiding the disasters of the past. *Psychiatric Services, 55*(10), 1112–1115.

Thomson O'Brien, M. A., Oxman, A. D., Davis, D. A., Haynes, R. B., Freemantle, N., & Harvey, E. L. (2000). Audit and feedback: Effects on professional practice and health care outcomes. In *Cochrane Database of Systematic Reviews* (Vol. 3, CD000259). Chichester, West Sussex, England: Wiley.

Torrey, E. F. (1995). Jails and prisons: America's new mental hospitals. *American Journal of Public Health, 85*(12), 1611–1613.

Tsui, A. S. (1990). A multiple-constituency model of effectiveness: An empirical examination at the human resource subunit level. *Administrative Science Quarterly, 35,* 458–483.

Valenstein, M., Mitchinson, A., Ronis, D. L., Alexander, J. A., Duffy, S. A., Craig, T. J., et al. (2004). Quality indicators and monitoring of mental health services: What do frontline providers think? *American Journal of Psychiatry, 161*(1), 146–153.

Wright, K. N. (2004). As assessment of the capacity to measure performance among the nation's prison systems. *Federal Probation, 68*(1), 51–58.

Yoo, J., & Brooks, D. (2005). The role of organizational variables in predicting service effectiveness: An analysis of a multilevel model. *Research on Social Work Practice, 15*(4), 267–277.

Yuchtman, E., & Seashore, S. (1967). A system resource approach to organizational effectiveness. *American Sociological Review, 32*(6), 891–903.

Zammuto, R. F. (1982). *Assessing organizational effectiveness: Systems change, adaptation, and strategy*. Albany: State University of New York Press.

Zammuto, R. F. (1984). A comparison of multiple constituency models of organizational effectiveness. *Academy of Management Review, 9*(4), 606–616.

Zucker, L. G. (1987). Institutional theories of organizations. *Annual Review of Sociology, 13*, 443–464.

Chapter 28

INTERVENTION WITH INSTITUTIONS

Leon Fulcher

Social work intervention with institutions covers a wide range of clients, organizational configurations, service systems, and policy contexts. Whether operating as components of the health-care, education, social welfare, or criminal justice sectors, institutions of different size, design, and purpose have participated in the delivery of social work services since the earliest days of the profession. To address each aspect of social work intervention with institutions—across all four of society's resource sectors and with clientele across the life span—would require far more space than is available here. For that reason, attention is drawn to particular evidential issues that are highlighted with respect to care services for children, young people, and their families whether intervening with large institutions, smaller residential group living arrangements, or indeed, the range of day-care services that operate alongside or as contemporary alternatives to institutional care. The generic term *client* is used where arguments are thought to apply across the human life span whereas children or young people are used when the evidence is more client specific.

Working definitions are also important because not all places in the world refer to interventions with institutions through the lens of social work (Fulcher, 2003). In the United Kingdom, for example, the terms *social care* and *residential child care* are commonly used alongside social work, whereas elsewhere—as in Canada and to some extent South Africa—the more client-specific terminology of *child* and *youth care* is used regardless of whether interventions with institutions are targeted specifically (Anglin, 2003). Another issue surrounds use of the term *institution* because this draws attention to only one of the historically significant patterns of service delivery while excluding other important services that share organizational and design characteristics. The term *group care* is thus used to delineate a discrete field of practice and occupational focus that

> incorporates those areas of service—institutional care, residential group living (including, but not necessarily requiring, 24-hour, 7 days per week care) and other community-based day services (covering lesser time periods)—that supply a range of developmentally enhancing services for groups of consumers. Locating a service in the group care field results from identifying how each type of service places emphasis on shared living and learning arrangements in a specified center of activity. (Ainsworth & Fulcher, 1981, p. 8)

An essential requirement of responsive practice is the need to locate the perspectives of clients at the center of service planning and policy formation. Such an approach challenges

---

Leon Fulcher is a social work and group care research and training consultant with experience in the United States, Canada, the United Kingdom, Ireland, New Zealand, Malaysia, China, and the United Arab Emirates. He is also an honorary fellow in the School of Social and Political Studies at the University of Edinburgh.

traditional "expert" models that assume an inability on the part of clients and their families to participate fully as partners in decision making about care and treatment processes. The literary device of metaphor is used in what follows to introduce six "voices"[1] that explore what Garfat called "the effective child and youth care intervention" (1998, p. 1). Each voice speaks its own language and offers distinctive justifications for the care and treatment of prospective clients (Hudson & Nurius, 1994, pp. 3–4). The *first voice* belongs to the *specific people* for whom health and welfare services purport to operate. This voice communicates graphic accounts of life in and out of care, or indeed, in and out of schools, work, or families. While lip service is often given to locating the voices of clients at the center of care service planning and policy formation, it is too often the case that other voices speak louder; sometimes with unfortunate consequences. The *second voice* speaks through encounters with *family and extended family members* often articulating very clear preferences about the shared care of family members, whether family participation in care planning and decision-making processes are taken seriously or not. A *third voice* of *health, education, and welfare professionals* frequently introduces discordant tones of formality and technical jargon when explaining complex diagnostic outcomes and treatment processes. Whenever professionals come together to plan for the needs of children or young people requiring "extra" care—beyond that which is readily available from families—then the voices of experts commonly speak louder than others. The contemporary Family Group Conference—with its legacy in Maori culture—was enshrined in New Zealand child welfare law nearly 2 decades ago to ensure that all three of these voices are heard in formal decision making about the care and supervision of children or young people (Fulcher, 1999).

Special interest groups, politicians, policy makers, and the media represent a *fourth public voice* that speaks about prospective clients in all parts of the world. This voice has significant economic influence at local and national levels, shaping marketing strategies both nationally and internationally. Whether tuning in to this voice via MTV images, or through profiles of children, young people, and families living in London, Chechnya, Tokyo, Jakarta, Lagos, or Sao Paulo beamed daily to the world via CNN or BBC World, such images contribute toward social policies that are frequently shaped through reactions to community disasters, court proceedings, or public outrage around social behavior in given circumstances. A *fifth voice* speaks through *regulatory policies and procedures* that shape contemporary practices in human service organizations. This voice uses a technical language of behavioral competencies, evidential outcomes, and evaluative transparency to regulate "duty of care" and "minimum standards" under contract law, proscribing service mandates that fund and regulate health and welfare organizations.

Finally, there is a *voice of scholars, researchers, and theorists*—mostly from Europe and North America (Payne, 1997)—but also from Africa (Bukenya, 1996), Asia (Yahya, 1994), and other Southern Hemisphere countries (Te Whaiti, McCarthy, & Durie, 1997). For the past half-century, this voice has authenticated or refuted claims to a knowledge base for responsive social work and social care practice.[2] This voice of research and scholarship

---

[1] In choosing this term, the writer has relied on the *Scottish Chambers Dictionary* for an ancient definition of French derivation—where *voice* means "to act as mouthpiece of: to give utterance or expression to: and to endow with voice."

[2] The author wishes to acknowledge limitations associated with the way this review was restricted due to being "Other-Than-English Challenged," making it impossible to decipher much written material voiced in languages other than English. This is a significant limitation.

has, at times, argued that nothing works when it comes to social work intervention with institutions or that out-of-family care almost always produces negative consequences for children, young people, and their families. It is through this sixth voice that the chapter unfolds, first considering practice ideologies that have significantly shaped social work interventions with institutions during the past half-century. Then a review is offered of evidence supporting responsive practices with clients in receipt of group care services, followed by a short discussion of limitations associated with that evidence. Finally, implications for social work practice are discussed using Bronfenbrenner's (1979) micro-, meso-, exo- and macro levels of intervention.

HISTORICAL BACKGROUND

For the past half century, all Western economies have been dominated by a handful of practice ideologies—*normalization, de-institutionalization, mainstreaming, minimal intervention, diversion,* and *use of the least restrictive environment*—that have dramatically reshaped interventions with and within group care institutions, especially for children and young people. Each practice ideology developed as the result of work carried out mostly in the United States between 1950 and 1980 in health and welfare services concerned with developmental disability, special education, psychiatric care, and criminal justice services (Fulcher & Ainsworth, 2006). Combined with economic notions of free market trade and globalization (Scull, 1977), these practice ideologies have been used to dramatically reshape health, education, social welfare, and criminal justice services internationally:

- Social work in the field of developmental disability began promoting normalization as a practice ideology that shaped professional involvement with handicapped children and adults, necessitating significant reorganization of mental retardation services or services for handicapped people that existed prior to the 1970s.
- Social work in the mental health and mental retardation fields began promoting de-institutionalization and the development of community care, arguing that with few exceptions, people are better off living outside an institution than within one.
- Social work in the special education field began promoting mainstreaming and the idea that optimal learning environments for children and young people involve people learning together, where the strengths of some learners support the limitations of others and where life skills and academic learning are combined.
- Social work in the criminal justice field began promoting nonintervention or minimal intervention, advocating for diversion of young people away from the criminal justice system, and using the least restrictive environment when providing direct services, based on the notion that most young people grow out of their troublesome phase, and it is best to keep kids out of the system wherever possible.

Zealous pursuit of practice ideology when combined with public sector economics often resulted in dramatically reduced availability of services for at-risk children and young people (Fulcher & Ainsworth, 1994). In many respects, child welfare policy came to reflect a policy orientation of laissez-faire and patriarchy "broadly identified with the nineteenth century but [an orientation that] enjoyed some renaissance in the late twentieth century" (Fox-Harding, 1991, p. 10):

> The terms laissez-faire and minimalism describe the view that the role of the state in child care should be a minimal one, while the privacy and sanctity of the parent-child relationship should be respected. . . . In extreme cases of poor parental care, state intervention is not only acceptable but preferably of a strong and authoritative kind, transferring the child to a secure placement with a new set of parent figures. Patriarchy refers to the power of adult males [to make decisions about what happens to] women and children, particularly in the family. (p. 13)

It is difficult to consider the six practice ideologies separately because in the course of their emerging influence on social work and social care services during the past half century, each has become interwoven and dependent on the other for justification. It is helpful, nonetheless, to look at each notion briefly so as to highlight the positive impact it has had on service reforms that have benefited clients and their families before examining their combined impact on policy reforms and social work interventions with institutions.

Policies That Targeted Developmental Disability and Mental Health Services

Normalization

The normalization construct was transported to the United States through the promotional efforts of Wolfensberger (1972). The origins of this idea lay in attempts to reform services for developmentally disabled or mentally handicapped children and adults in Scandinavia during the 1960s. The notion emerged in Denmark in the late 1950s (Banks-Mikkelson, 1969) but came to impact directly on services in other Scandinavian countries (Nirje, 1969; Pedlar, 1990). Simply stated, normalization promotes the use of

> means which are as culturally normative as possible to establish and/or maintain personal behaviors and characteristics which are as culturally normative as possible. . . . Within this framework, life satisfaction, self esteem and personal competence are viewed as products of involvement with mainstream activities of society. Also, participation in atypical, segregated or specialized environments [compounded by] affiliations with other socially devalued persons [are] considered detrimental to an individual's development. (Landesman & Butterfield, 1987, p. 810)

We can scarcely challenge the aims of normalization when the arguments that promote it are so simple and important. It is precisely *because* of these relatively simple truths that ardent believers and followers were attracted. Normalization thus offered justification for policy reforms and a rationale for reorganizing health, education, social welfare, and criminal justice services in virtually all Western economies. The normalization "movement" was aided by a research instrument that purported to measure coherence of services for developmentally disabled people when compared against a normalization ideal (Wolfensberger & Glenn, 1975; Wolfensberger & Thomas, 1983) along with a social role valorization theory (Wolfensberger, 1983).

De-Institutionalization

From the late nineteenth century onward—well before the idea of a welfare state—the response used in most Western economies with traditional social problems involved an *indoor relief* or institutional bias (Ainsworth & Fulcher, 1981; Jones & Fowles, 1984; Lerman, 1985). Such an historical preference expedited the construction of a range of traditional institutions including: lunatic asylums, mental hospitals, alms houses, orphanages, children's homes, residential schools, training centers for the retarded, and institutions for wayward and delinquent youths (Fulcher & Ainsworth, 2006). By the late 1950s, there was growing disillusionment with institutional solutions to many of these social problems, with populations of state mental hospitals and state schools for the mentally retarded reaching all time highs (Hunter, Shannon, & Sambrook, 1986). From that point onward, throughout the Western world, mental health and disability populations in institutional care began to decline (Scull, 1977), and the policy ideals of de-institutionalization and community care took on the trappings of a social movement.

Although aided by the discovery of psychotropic drugs (Gronfein, 1985), the more important influence promoting de-institutionalization was arguably that community-based services seemingly cost less than institutional care (Scull, 1977). Other influences included growth of the antipsychiatry lobby, questions about the effectiveness of particular treatments (such as lobotomies and electroconvulsive therapy), as well as human rights guarantees for all patients and inmates (Brown, 1981). Instances of inhumane and abusive practices in a range of institutional settings helped fuel the de-institutionalization and community care agenda (Biklen, 1979a; Wooden, 1976). Within a remarkably short period, institutional care was no longer the preferred intervention and instead became the *choice of last resort* for professional decision makers working in health-care, education, social welfare, and youth justice services. It is interesting to note how traditional boarding schools remained a clear exception to this pattern, retaining a prominent place in all Western countries providing for educational needs of the economic elite's young people.

Policies That Targeted Educational Services

Mainstreaming

Through its emphasis on the negative influence of segregated settings and the importance of culturally normative activities, normalization also helped promote the educational principle of mainstreaming—a policy ideal that claims that all individuals are capable of learning, including those who are developmentally delayed, disabled, or impaired. Mainstreaming argues that education for disabled or handicapped individuals should occur in regular community schools rather than in segregated special schools or classrooms (Connolly, 1990; Zigler & Muenchow, 1979). Community schools are expected to make special provision for all students, either within regular classrooms or—if absolutely necessary—in special education classrooms integrated with other normative school activities. Separation of disadvantaged students (however defined) into special classes should only be used as a last resort.

Use of the Least Restrictive Environment

In addition to mainstreaming, normalization also promoted use of the least restrictive environment. This became a legal principle in the United States from 1960s onward (Biklen, 1979b) leading to claims that all segregated settings are too restrictive. The notion of least restrictive environment is different from mainstreaming in that it refers to the optimal environment that brings a person closest to his or her learning potential while still providing for his or her unique educational needs. But the ideal and the actuality are frequently miles apart. For example, the Education for All Handicapped Children Act of 1975 (PL 94-142) guaranteed free, appropriate public education in the least restrictive environment for all American children. In reality, however, because of funding arrangements for local schools across the country, significant variations have continued to exist in the application of this laudable ideal. Litigation by parent and children's rights groups aimed at forcing the state to provide for excluded children became commonplace. In Australia, mainstreaming and use of the least restrictive environment were embraced enthusiastically and segregated special education centers were reassessed as being too restrictive. Handicapped children needed to be "mainstreamed" into ordinary classrooms. Those young people with behavior problems and who had difficulties coping with regular classrooms were frequently excluded from the education system. Similar developments occurred in New Zealand following introduction of the "Tomorrow's Schools" initiatives in the late 1980s that placed charter obligations on all schools to make provision for children with special needs. Government argued that resources were included within the bulk funding arrangements that enabled each Board of Trustees to decide how they responded to all students enrolled at their school. So long as charter obligations were seen to be addressed, there was no government interference in the way services were provided and intensive services for children with special needs largely disappeared. Many argued that services for these children became more limited than at any time since the 1950s.

Policies That Targeted Services for Criminal Justice Populations

Minimal Intervention

Disillusionment with the U.S. juvenile justice system became rampant in the 1960s and 1970s as many began questioning the capacity of this system to prevent delinquent children and young people from progressing to adult correctional facilities through the use of institutionally based services. High rates of recidivism, staff abuses of detained youths, and appalling conditions associated with solitary confinement (Wooden, 1976) generated serious questions about the extent to which the system had lost sight of its real mission. Institutions had become overcrowded, rigid, and custodial bureaucracies. The system as a whole was both expensive and stigmatizing, and there were far too many young people being institutionalized as neglected, incorrigible, or delinquent. There were claims that delinquent behavior was actually being reinforced in institutional settings, not reduced, so reform was inevitable and occurred dramatically in some places. In Massachusetts, for example, all state institutions for delinquents were closed abruptly during the course of a few weeks (Scull, 1977). In New Zealand, significant policy reforms were implemented in the late 1980s in response to the Ministerial Review of a Maori Perspective for the Department of Social Welfare (1986). In the United Kingdom, change was more gradual (Wagner, 1988), but the notion became prominent that state intervention in the lives of delinquent youths may serve only to compound the problem. Proponents of *radical nonintervention* claimed that if only adults will be patient, young people will cease being delinquent as they grow older (LeVine & Greer, 1984; Schur, 1965). Such a response is the correct one for many young people and minimal intervention rapidly gained popularity since the idea was less stigmatizing. The approach also cost less, giving it international appeal.

Diversion

In a policy environment informed by normalization, mainstreaming, and minimal intervention, it is easy to see why diversionary programs proliferated rapidly with the aim of keeping delinquent children and young people *out of the system*. Minimal intervention, diversion, and the use of alternatives to institutional care became a required strategy (Nelson, 1982) still popular nearly a quarter century later. Linked as it was to the policy ideal of de-institutionalization, diversion can be traced to the 1967 U.S. Presidential Commission on Law Enforcement and Administration of Justice that urged correctional authorities to develop diversionary programs where "the prevailing assumption [was] that by placing delinquents in noncoercive organizations outside the legal area, the negative effects of labelling will be decreased" (Parbon, 1978, p. 492). It was further argued that a consequence of such action would result in fewer juveniles progressing to adult correctional facilities. An extensive literature (e.g., Canagarayar, 1980; D. O'Brien, 1984; Pogrebin, Poole, & Regoli, 1984; Severy & Whitaker, 1984; M. Stewart & Ray, 1984) examines the variety of diversion programs introduced as the result of this 1967 policy. In New Zealand, the Children, Young Persons and Their Families Act (1989) gave statutory momentum to the diversion of children and young people away from institutions. While the statutory requirement of Family Group Conferences became internationally recognized as a significant development in the delivery of child, youth, and family services, the legislated ideal in New Zealand was dramatically eroded through fiscal limitations imposed by the treasury and a government preoccupied with reducing public expenditure. Fiscal constraint limited the extent to which extended family members could participate in decision making about the futures of their children. Diversion succeeded, however, in helping to reduce public expenditure on child and youth services with a

> reduction in the number of residential care beds available for young people from around 1000 beds in the late 1970s to around 100 beds by 1996 [*through emphasis being placed*] on family placements, kin-based care or family like situations in the community. By the mid-1990s it became apparent that the pendulum had swung too far, and that residential capacity was no longer adequate to meet demand. . . . In April 2002, reflecting its wish to minimise the number of young people held on remand in police cells because of inadequate residential options, Cabinet directed the Child, Youth and Family Service to review its 1996 Residential Services Strategy. (Child, Youth, and Family Services, 2003, p. 4)

In summary, all six practice ideologies—*normalization, de-institutionalization, mainstreaming, use of the least restrictive environment, diversion,* and *minimal intervention*—have featured prominently in the reform of social work interventions with institutional programs across health-care, education, social welfare, and criminal justice resource systems. Each practice ideology has become enshrined in legislative statutes. Normalization and de-institutionalization have been used to dramatically reduce the number of children and young people in institutions and, but for extreme circumstances, have limited the time that any young person can be held in an institutional placement. Mainstreaming and use of the least restrictive environment are core principles that now shape the education of children and young people. At the same time, minimal intervention and diversion have become justifications used to support families caring for their own children without government interference. In spite of these developments, however, institutional group care persists and continues to feature prominently in the delivery of specialist services for society's most vulnerable clientele, especially children and young people.

SUMMARY OF CONTEMPORARY EVIDENCE-BASED INTERVENTION WITH INSTITUTIONS

The metaphor of voice was introduced to highlight different perspectives that speak to the theme of social work interventions with institutions. That metaphor is now extended to give musical resonance for developmental and affective dynamics that are enmeshed in responsive interventions with clients in receipt of group care services. The soul, rhythms, and blues of evidence-based interventions are thus highlighted for consideration.

The Soul of Responsive Interventions

Thirty years of cross-cultural social work practice with institutions of one type or another—parenting, social work teaching, and group care research experience—has reaffirmed Maier's important arguments about why child and youth care should be considered "a method of social work" (1963). Maier articulated evidence-based concepts associated with child and adolescent development that inform responsive social work practices with children and young people, highlighting issues central to any managed care and treatment approach. At the start of the twenty-first century, that knowledge base (Maier, 1987; Milligan, 1998) continues to support responsive social work practices with children, young people, and their families at home or away from home. Maier provided early developmental evidence (1979) showing how *bodily comfort and physical safety* are key performance outcomes in the delivery of responsive social work services, starting with the question "Is this person safe now?" Proactive responses to bodily comfort and physical safety need to be consistently reinforced through daily practices with people in receipt of institutional services. This holds whether responding to an emergency or family crisis; whether formulating, implementing, and managing short- or medium-term plans with clients; or in developing care strategies that extend to young people beyond age 18 and emancipation (Fulcher & Fulcher, 1998). Claims to responsiveness by social workers are most clearly authenticated at the "*meeting place of practice.*" This is where all of the first three voices—those of clients, family, or extended family members, and health or welfare professionals—lay legitimate claims to being heard and to expectations that their respective contributions will be taken seriously.

At the core of a responsive service speaks a voice that resonates from the soul of each person in care. That voice always reflects a distinctive regional dialect and cultural history that shares the stories, visions, joys, and fears that touch the unique person in every potential client. The second voice at times speaks more quietly but often shouts from the souls of mothers, fathers, brothers, sisters, grandparents, aunties, uncles, cousins, and community members to express cultural and social preferences about the care of their particular family member (Fox-Harding, 1991). The third voice of health and welfare professionals—whether social workers, teachers, or health care providers—commonly expresses expert opinions about health care status, educational performance, or other social indicators of well-being

(Small & Fulcher, 1985), regardless of whether the technical language they speak is understood by clients and their families.

Central to Maier's thesis about the *Core of Care* for children at home and away from home was the recognition that *although each young person may be expected to achieve developmental milestones in terms of physical, cognitive, emotional, and social development, each is still different in their own special ways.* Such differences contribute to the soul of social work practices with group care services, whether group homes, residential schools, care centers, or larger institutions. Whether adapting to an abusive home environment or living rough in the jungle using a primitive language, children and young people go to enormous lengths to get their physical and bodily comfort needs met. Each young person learns to follow his or her own personal rhythms around hunger, toileting, personal space, dress, cold and warmth, sleep, illness susceptibility, moods, and habits. As Maier argued (1981, 1992), it follows that each person needs his or her own unique rhythms of caring to promote cultural safety, cognitive and emotional development, learning, social maturation, and enhanced personal well-being. Such rhythms connect with the soul of responsive social work and social care practices. It is through engaging proactively in rhythms of caring with particular clients—whether through nurturing care, teaching, therapeutic interventions, or behavioral supervision—that social work and social care gains professional and public endorsement for the service outcomes they help to produce (Ainsworth & Fulcher, 1981; Fulcher & Ainsworth, 1985, 2006).

Summary

The soul of responsive social work practice with people in receipt of institutional group care—regardless of age—is directly linked to the daily management and oversight of basic bodily comforts and personal safety needs. Because of developmental needs for physical safety and security, some people live temporarily in out-of-home placements while life plans are being reshaped and implemented. Second, the soul of responsive social work practice is touched through engaging with the unique character of each person receiving care. No matter how many developmental milestones are evaluated, it is still important to remember that all clients are different, each in their own special ways. Finally, the soul of responsive social work practice with group care services focuses on personal rhythms and opportunity events with clients, where sensitive engagement in caring relationships promotes personal development and social maturation through interactions that are, in many ways, autotherapeutic. The rhythms introduced between clients in care and their caregivers become fundamental to the successful delivery of quality service outcomes. To examine this further, we consider five important rhythms that frame responsive social work practices with clients in receipt of institutional care. Understanding (and heeding) the importance of these rhythms is fundamental to successful interventions with clients.

Rhythms of Responsive Group Care Interventions

A first set of *rhythms* that requires identification and proactive engagement are those *associated with family and extended family members*. These connect the client to rhythms of interaction with kinship networks that exist for each person received into care (Ainsworth, 1997; Bronfenbrenner, 1979; Burford & Casson, 1989; Garfat, 2003; Pennell & Burford, 1995). Family and extended family rhythms are closely associated with particular circumstances in each prospective client's home environment that may have resulted in their requiring health or welfare services and to their being admitted to an institutional care setting. Family rhythms contribute to the socialization and behavioral training a person has received before coming to the attention of health and welfare professionals. For all these reasons, it is essential that planned care and treatment give priority to the active participation of family and extended family members in decision making at virtually all levels. Active consideration needs also to be given to the kinship networks that help give people their social and cultural identities. It is difficult to ignore research evidence showing that despite what health and welfare professionals may wish or think, young people are still likely to resume contact and continue some involvement with family and extended family members after leaving care (Fanshel, Finch, & Grundy, 1990). Family connections and rhythms are closely associated with each person's sense of identity, helping to shape a unique personal and social character (Bronfenbrenner, 1979).

Next, it is important to identify each person's *learning and recreation rhythms*. These include both formal and informal rhythms associated with a person's capacity for learning, their formal educational activities and achievements, and recreational pursuits that con- tribute to large muscle and cardiovascular development, eye-hand coordination, and time structuring through leisure activities (Small & Fulcher, 1985). The learning and recreational rhythms will have been severely disrupted or underdeveloped for many people placed in institutions, as noted in Kendrick's (1996) study of Scottish young people. Paradoxically, these are the very *rhythms that connect* people to a peer group, giving opportunities for behavioral, social, and cultural learning so important to future development and longer-term achievement (Maier, 1975, 1987). Learning and recreational rhythms are clearly influenced through the purposeful use of activities in day or residential schools and institutional centers (VanderVen, 1985).

Play or occupational therapy, individual and small group leisure activities, and partic- ipation in community life offer people opportunities for activating and nurturing rhythms in learning and recreation. When children and young people experience predictability in caring and learning rhythms with their caregivers, it is then that they learn to trust and emotionally depend on personal relationships (Maier, 1979). Through managing relation- ships with prospective clients of any age, the emphasis can shift from institutional controls to personalized behavior training tailored to the needs of each person, whether living in a foster home, residential school, or institution (Garfat, 1998). Multiple learning opportu- nities are used to support personalized care plans that are sensitively planned around the developmental needs and performance of each person (Maier, 1981), giving soul to the rhythms of responsive social work and social care practice.

Rhythms associated with group living play an influential role whether attending summer camps or living in residential schools, group homes, or institutions (Beker & Eisikovits, 1991). When looking closely at the daily and weekly activities of people in care, one quickly finds that each day follows particular rhythms around food, sleep, work, or play—all re- quiring sensitive daily management (Fulcher, 1996; Redl, 1959). Rhythms of group living are concerned with differences that can be found between weekday routines and activities and events that happen on weeknights and weekends. Weekly and monthly rhythms in institutional group care can often be discerned through an examination of admission and discharge practices. These highlight whether a service provides short-term respite care, responses for people experiencing a crisis, or services offering longer-term supportive care, education, or residential supervision. Monthly and seasonal rhythms of institutional group care are also commonplace, especially when taking note of school, work, and holiday periods. Residential schools and care centers sponsored by religious organizations frequently employ weekly, monthly, and seasonal rituals in the delivery of care services, or as in Malaysia and other parts of Islam, religious practices require the offering of prayers five times a day. An examination of annual reports required of group care institutions quickly demonstrates how yearly rhythms of care are also important, most graphically seen when a young person reaches his or her 18th birthday and is reclassified an adult, often signaling the departure from care. At such times, support services that young people and families rely on are withdrawn, or they may be referred elsewhere, as in the case of a young person with developmental delays becoming the responsibility of health and disability services.

Responsive interventions with institutions need also to engage with a fourth set of rhythms associated with *community and peer group activities*. Responsive practices give attention to the needs of each person—regardless of age—for purposeful engagement in social experiences that help connect him or her to normative peer group activities (Fahlberg, 1990, 1991; Halverson, 1995). People in care, wherever they live, have frequently had their community and peer group rhythms disrupted as placement decisions get made without careful consideration for the unintended consequences of service decision making. As young people are moved from one setting to another or change schools, it follows that their friends are also displaced and important relationships get severed. Similarly, when an older adult is moved from his or her home into a care institution, such action frequently signals the loss of the home base and the loss of close neighbors and friends. Young people in care often become involved with others in care or engage in peer group activities that have a deleterious effect on their health and well-being, whether through alcohol and drug abuse, sexual abuse and neglect, or physical abuse. Unless new relationships are formed through the management of purposeful activities with alternative peers, then people in care have little choice but to rely on old friends and activities. These old relationships and patterns of behavior have frequently resulted in the untimely deaths of young people in care and "her stories" of struggle for survival in abusive relationships. Rhythms associated with peer group and communities of interest reach deep into the soul of people, regardless of where they live (Maier, 1985, 1990, 1992). Responsive interventions with institutions build from recognition of how these rhythms impact on people in care and how proactive engagement in community and peer group rhythms benefit people and their families (Maier, 1991).

Finally, one cannot ignore *cultural and spiritual rhythms of caring* that operate informally as well as formally in the delivery of responsive institutional care services. Elsewhere (Cairns et al., 1996; Fulcher, 1998; Tait-Rolleston, Cairns, Fulcher, Kereopa, & Nia Nia, 1997), it was shown how cultural rituals of encounter and exchange are commonly overlooked in the delivery of social work and child and youth care services (T. Stewart, 1997; Wilcox et al., 1991). Images, sounds, and smells of institutional care practice reflect cultural and spiritual rhythms of caring. These operate in any family or foster home, as well as in residential schools, group care centers, or institutions (Ramsden, 1997; Te Whaiti et al., 1997). Look again at people engaging and interacting with each other in an active institutional care service. Do people sit on tables, at tables, on the floor, or on chairs? Do they cross their legs such that the bottoms of their feet are visible? Are there smells of sweet grass burning or is incense burned as a symbolic gesture of welcome? Do young people eat with their right hand without utensils? Do they use chopsticks? Do people use a knife and fork in each hand or maneuver their way through dinner with a fork or spoon, except when cutting meat? Is pork served? Do young people drink alcohol under the supervision of adult caregivers? Do young people appear in public without arms and legs covered? Are rituals of fasting and prayer evident? Each of these questions draws attention to a cross-cultural dimension of practice that should never be ignored.

It is quickly apparent why minimal cross-cultural competencies are required if social workers are to avoid significant gaffs that leave some clients and caregivers feeling culturally unsafe (Fulcher, 2002a; Leigh, 1998; Rangihau, 1986, 1987; Shook, 1985). Rudolph Steiner Centers have taught the world a great deal about spiritual rhythms of caring and learning through seeking ways in which these rhythms can be carefully balanced for each child or for living and learning groups of young people. Successful outcomes for children, as well as adult children and families, have been achieved through thoughtfully matching the personal styles and learning attributes of different service participants in order to overcome performance deficits and achieve complementary outcomes. Practices elsewhere in the so-called developing world offer important illustrations of how cultural and spiritual rhythms of caring seek balance with behavioral representations of wellness (Cairns, 1991; Ibeabuchi, 1986; Rose, 1992; Sali, 1996).

Summary

Five different sets of rhythms have been identified as being important for responsive social work and social care interventions with institutions, rhythms that require sensitive management and oversight with out-of-home placements for people of all ages but especially for children and young people. Most people's lives are enmeshed within *rhythms that connect them with family and extended family members*—including kinship networks—that help locate each person with particular people, places, and a cultural identity.[3] *Learning and recreation rhythms*—both formal and informal—require sensitive management if people in care are to be offered a minimum guarantee that their lives should not be placed at greater risk as a consequence of having lived in a residential school, group home, or institution. *Rhythms associated with family and residential group living* can be monitored, recorded, and reported by hour, shift, weekday, weeknight, weekend, month, holiday period, sick leave, or year. *Community and peer group rhythms* offer opportunities that enable people to engage in purposeful activities and social learning opportunities. Finally, much is to be learned about the management of *cultural and spiritual rhythms of caring* that help give meaning to the lives of people in care. Cultural safety and personal well-being are recurring themes in the stories people have shared. Such stories reinforce the importance of pausing

---

[3] When encountering a young person for the first time in Scotland, one is frequently asked two important questions: *Where dae ya come fae?* (Where do you come from?) and *Where dae ya stay?* (Where do you stay?). The first question is prompted through hearing an accent that is "different," thus locating that person as being from somewhere else. The second question seeks to identify where that person lives now. Taken together, the two questions nicely illustrate meanings that locate parties to an interaction that are embedded in cross-cultural rhythms of exchange.

to acknowledge the emotional and physical pain experienced by children, young people, and adults in care, along with the tears they and their caregivers have shed over the years. Whether through frustration or relief, happiness or pain, such emotions are closely aligned to the challenge of providing *good enough* care and daily services that make a difference to the well-being and futures of those in receipt of institutional services.

The Blues of Social Work Intervention with Group Care Institutions

The blues of care are being experienced well before someone leaves their home and arrives at a residential school, group home, or institution (Kahan, 1989; Wagner, 1988). The *formal imposition of care, supervision, or custody*—whether by care and protection or place of safety order, criminal justice sentencing, or indefinite detention—follows from an important social history (Scarr & Eisenberg, 1993; Scull, 1977; Seed, 1973). Throughout that history, the voices of the person themselves, family and extended family members, neighbors, teachers, health or welfare professionals, and others may not have been heard clearly amid the *noise* of emotional turmoil. Most of the people for whom health and welfare organizations provide services have not been diverted away from a formal reception into care. If diverted initially to alternative community placements, boarding school, or extended family care, a care or supervision order may still have been issued subsequently.

As shown earlier, social work and social care have been reshaped for the past half century by practice ideologies that have impacted directly on the planning and management of contemporary institutional care services (P. O'Brien & Murray, 1997). These so-called *secondary influences* associated with the social policy environment, service organizations, and the delivery of agency services prompt a whole new line of discourse associated with managers and workers engaged in multiply restructured organizations delivering contemporary health and welfare services (Casson & George, 1995). It is against such an organizational backdrop that one must examine evidence from what few longitudinal studies are available about children and young people in care (Andersson, 2005; Patton, Goldfeld, Pieris-Caldwell, Bryant, & Vimpani, 2005; Poland & Legge, 2005; Viner & Taylor, 2005).

Viner and Taylor (2005) followed a British cohort of more than 13,000 young people from the age of 5 as part of a developmental study, collecting follow-up data for these young people at age 10, 16, and again at 30 years. A total of 343 young people or 3.6% of the sample population were found to have been in public care, with children of color more likely to have experienced out-of-home care placements. These authors concluded that public care of children was associated with adverse adult socioeconomic, educational, legal, and health outcomes in excess of that associated with childhood or adult disadvantage (Viner & Taylor, 2005, p. 895). Patton et al. (2005) reported that the number of Australian children on care and protection orders rose almost 50% between 1997 and 2004, with the rates six times higher for indigenous children. The proportion of Australian children placed in out-of-home care also rose from 3 per 1,000 children in 1997 to 5 per 1,000 in 2004 (Patton et al., 2005, p. 437). Andersson (2005) reported on a small follow-up study of 26 children placed when younger than 4 years of age in one Swedish children's home during the early 1980s, assessing outcomes at 3 and 9 months after leaving care, and with follow-up data collected after 5, 10, 15, and 20 years. The children's family relations—early attachments, later parental relationships, and the perception of who was their family—was highlighted as having been a prominent theme over the course of this longitudinal study. Three distinctive outcome clusters were identified: one for 10 children assessed as having had a "good" adjustment, a second for the 9 children considered to have had a "moderate" social adjustment and well-being, and another for the 7 children assessed to have experienced "bad" social adjustment and well-being, with drugs involvement, criminal behavior, and legal sanctions (Andersson, 2005). Andersson concluded "there is no doubt that family relations matter, whether a birth family or a foster family or alternate family combination . . . and to catch the meaning and significance of family relations, the children's voices are essential—at different points of time during childhood and again as young adults, looking back on childhood experiences" (p. 54).

Social workers are reminded of how they frequently operate at a "crash site" where the blues experienced by a person referred for placement in institutional care confronts discordant expectations of "The System" (Fulcher, 1988, 1994). Most contemporary health and social services operate in a policy environment that is overtly shaped by fiscal considerations. Agencies are expected to operate as business units that manage capital and human resources to produce quality outcomes for individual clients and their significant others (Knapp, 1984). One important feature of all this has been the growing recognition of work-related stresses and how professional fatigue impacts on teamwork in the delivery of social services (Fulcher, 1991). Maier noted (1979) how care for the caregivers is an essential characteristic of quality care guarantees made to children, young people, and their families (Burford, 1990; Fulcher, 1983). The professional identity and personal well-being of every worker or prospective worker influences the collective performance of social work and social care teams as a whole (Burford & Fulcher, 1985).

On arrival at a residential school, group home, or institution, a person is initially confronted with challenges to *personal and cultural safety* living among strangers (Dominelli, 1988; Fulcher, 1998, 2002a). Cultural safety—that state of being in which a person experiences that her or his personal well-being as well as social and cultural frames of reference are acknowledged, even if not fully understood—is highlighted each time a person starts engaging with others in a new care environment. "Are there any people like me here?" becomes a recurring emotional theme, along with questions like:

"Are there people who speak like I do?"

"Do they eat the way I do?"

"Do they eat the same food?"

"Why are these other people here?"

Rituals of group membership begin immediately when one enters the door of a group care institution (Fulcher, 1996). Responsive caregivers establish and maintain positive rituals of encounter that promote group membership for new members, students, care staff, domestic or catering workers, and other visitors to the center. In institutional group living situations, new residents may be assisted through the formal rituals of group membership. However, they must also establish their own personal location within subgroup hierarchies, coalitions, and alliances that operate in any resident group, while at the same time establishing purposeful relationships with staff. *Respect for individuality* connects with a client's personal identity and that sense of who they were before admission to care. This extends further to questions like:

"Who are/were their people?"

"Who cared about them and for them?"

"What was happening that resulted in their being placed in care?"

"What happens next?"

Personal and cultural safety, managing group membership(s), and reinforcing identity are all interwoven in responsive caring, reinforcing the importance of this aspect of intervention with institutions (Maier, 1991).

A third dimension of the blues is encountered whenever a person is placed in the position of *feeling shy, embarrassed, ridiculed, or unsafe,* whether attending school, camp, or living in a residential school, group home, or institution. *Shyness and embarrassment* have their own special meanings in the native languages spoken by people admitted into care. New Zealand Maori families experience *whakamaa* or embarrassment about a child or young person being placed in care, while in Malaysia, the parallel response involves feeling *malu.* The voice and dialect of each new resident or staff member is pinpointed very quickly through "*getting to know you rituals.*" Being made the brunt of jokes or feeling ridicule from resident group members are too often recurring themes. Social work practice needs to be ever vigilant about someone in care being made the subject of ridicule or abuse by staff. History has sadly documented an abusive legacy in institutional care practice, a history made prominent since World War II through media disclosures of abuse in all parts of the Western world (see, e.g., Canadian Royal Commission on Aboriginal Peoples, 1997; Commonwealth of Australia, 1997; Moore, 1996; Rangihau, 1986; Webster, 1998). When a client feels unsafe—whether culturally, spiritually, emotionally, or physically—then her or his voice sings a special refrain of the blues. Unless that voice and its special theme of the blues is heard by social work and social care workers prompting a sensitive response, clients such as these are placed at even greater risk than before. Responsive care practices need to guarantee that from the moment of first contact, no one placed in care will be made to feel unsafe or be left in unsafe situations.

A fourth rendition of the blues sings out *in anger, reacting to fear, or as survivors in the face of abusive relationships.* Young people frequently bring a lifetime of anger into out-of-home placements. And they are usually angry for very good reasons (Durst, 1992). Many young people feel anger toward teachers, parents or stepparents, boyfriends or girlfriends, and others for "letting them down." People also experience fear or apprehension when joining a new living or learning group. It is important to hear and respond with sensitivity to those voicing anger and fear. It is all too easy for these powerful emotions of group living to leave clients in abusive situations, whether as perpetrators, as victims, or as voyeurs with consequences that frequently last a lifetime. Legal obligations in the duty of care form the basis for minimum guarantees that no client shall be harmed nor become the victim of abuse of any kind while in receipt of state-mandated care (Fulcher, 2002b). Such expectations are also voiced by family and extended family members, by health and welfare professionals, by special interest groups and the media, and by those purchasing and administering cost-effective health and social services for clients and their families.

Finally, when a person becomes *isolated* from peers, from their caregivers, from family members, from friends, and from virtually everyone around them, it is important that social work and social care workers hear loudly and clearly the message of risk that requires immediate attention (Guttmann, 1991). Isolation and feelings of personal alienation should not be confused with times when someone seeks moments of solitude or time out. Isolation and alienation of the type referred to here are associated with fundamental questions of being and nonbeing and of suicidal ruminations. Burning preoccupations are sometimes tattooed in prominent places on person's hands, arms, chest, or face becoming symbolic reminders of painful moments that are etched as a *moko*[4] into their being for a lifetime. *Cutting* or *bruising* on someone's wrists, limbs, breasts, or genitals must always be a concern, and *body language* such as this should provoke action on the part of all social workers and care workers.

When *the principle of physical safety and security* is threatened through accidental or self-inflicted injury or through the death of a client in care, then the professional integrity of health and welfare services is called into question. It is important to remember that people can sometimes reach the stage—both emotionally and mentally—when *the very thought of expressing what they have done or experiences to which they have been subjected becomes either too worrisome or burdensome to contemplate*. At times like these, *attempted suicide or death through risk-taking* with drugs, alcohol, cars, motorcycles, or weapons becomes a stark alternative to the painful reality that engulfs their existence. Much can be learned in hindsight from the death of a client in care. Such instances remain salutary reminders to all social workers who continue to ask whether there might have been anything they could have done differently or whether anything might have saved that person. The messages from anyone who died in care must never fall on deaf ears nor cease to weigh heavily on the hearts and minds of those who were seemingly out of tune with the emotional pain of another person's life.

Summary

If social workers "tune in" and actively listen to what is going on, they will hear the blues sung every day by those for whom care, special education, treatment, supervision, or custody has been authorized (Garfat, 1998). Personal accounts of emotional suffering as well as the blues of survival in "the system" are common. Physical and cultural safety among the crowds of group living are easily overlooked during school camps and in residential schools, group homes, or institutions. Rituals of encounter associated with group membership and individuality are distinctive features of group living, whether planned or unplanned. Responsive social work interventions with clients in institutions require vigilance in situations where someone might feel embarrassed, shy, ridiculed, or unsafe. Other protocols need to be followed with someone who is feeling angry, scared, abusive, or abused. Finally, when someone becomes withdrawn, isolated, or perhaps other-worldly in their manner and temperament, it is important to recognize how they profile a person who may be seriously at risk of doing something that leads to death by suicide or risk taking with alcohol, drugs, cars, motorcycles, or weapons.

---

[4]Maori ceremonial tattooing of the face and body.

LIMITATIONS OF THE EVIDENCE

In spite of the social work profession having its earliest activities working in institutions such as those operated by the National Children's Homes in England during the late nineteenth century, there are still many challenges that social workers must face if their interventions with clients in care are to be responsive. Fundamentally, social workers must be capable of discerning when an institutional care placement may be in the best interests of their client, avoiding the trap of thinking that institutional care placements are to be avoided at all costs. Simplistic thinking such as this does very little to assist vulnerable clients or their families, nor does it help social workers respond adequately to people who are potential threats to the safety and well-being of family and community members. Social work interventions at other times need to approach institutional settings as client systems in their own right, promoting indirect social work interventions that nurture the health and well-being of clients through enabling care staff, supporting family participation in decision making, networking with other health and welfare professionals, and encouraging service accountability. The voices identified at the start of this chapter are used to highlight continuing limitations in the evidence associated with social work interventions with institutions.

Consumer Voices

With few exceptions, there are still not many longitudinal studies that examine outcomes associated with children and young people in receipt of group care services. Those studies that have been carried out, or are currently underway, in the United States, Canada, the United Kingdom, Australia, and New Zealand focus attention on trends in child and adolescent development. This broader focus is perhaps understandable. And yet, given that group care services are frequently used with these nations' most vulnerable children and young people, there is still little known about what happens in and during group care processes. Instead, available research has tended to "measure" characteristics prior to admission and then after discharge with the assumption being that all institutional placements are the same. This is simply not the case. To date, the voices of children and young people talking about their positive experiences in care are not systematically heard. With these voices silenced, the voices of those who have had negative experiences in care are potentially overstated.

Voices of Parents and Family Members

There is also limited research evidence that speaks about the positive experiences of parents and family members when involved with group care services. Such "evidence" is once again associated with examples of institutional abuse. There have been few attempts to examine this issue more objectively. Those providing group care services frequently offer anecdotal evidence about working in constructive partnerships with parents and family members, but such accounts are commonly dismissed as idiosyncratic and unscientific. Until longitudinal research of this kind is carried out, it is easy to see why ideologies commonly shape decision making about the use of group care services, irrespective of evidence or potential distortions in that evidence.

Voices of Health and Welfare Professionals

Poland and Legge (2005) offer one clear example of where health professionals have attempted to look systematically at the influence of out-of-home care services on the social adjustment and well-being of children and their subsequent development into adulthood. However, that research aggregated characteristics of 343 young people out of a sample population of more than 13,000 and then drew conclusions that public care—in and of itself—had deleterious effects on longer-term development. Without detracting from these important findings, the fact remains that little is known about the particular care services in question, how they operated or whether some of the children actually benefited from such experiences as found in the study reported by Andersson (2005). Such is the strength of ideological points of view that are hostile to group care services—generally speaking—it is not surprising that research of this kind is scarce. And yet placements in certain types of institution—such as prisons, youth secure detention facilities, and boarding schools—continue to increase; placements in other institutions—such as children's homes, adolescent psychiatric facilities, and youth justice training schools—have declined. There is little research that tracks the placement of young people from foster care to group care or vice versa, or across health, education, social welfare, and criminal justice systems. While part of the difficulty may be associated with funding, it is also the case that few scholars seem interested in pursuing such a complicated research undertaking. And in the absence of solid evidential research, practice ideologies remain dominant.

Voices of Public Interest Groups and the Media

These voices are ever poised to speak out when attempts are made to relocate a group care facility into a particular community or locale. The common response is "not in our town" or at least "not in our neighborhood." Smaller group home facilities are perhaps easier to accept although even these may generate public outrage. Webster (1998) reported how media attention has contributed to the evolution of a new kind of police investigation procedure conducted on a massive scale in Britain and at huge public expense to gather retrospective allegations of sexual abuse against residential care workers (p. 55). Moore (1996) offered a chilling illustration of how the voice of public opinion and media coverage could overrule all other voices associated with the Kincora Children's Home scandal in Northern Ireland, first receiving media attention in 1980 but surrounded by intrigue since one of the convicted sex abusers was a prominent Orangeman and an agent of the British intelligence service, MI5. One might conclude from these British accounts that the voice of public opinion and the media is rarely well informed by evidence but holds powerful sway over decision making about operational aspects of group care.

Regulatory Voices of Standard Setting, Accountability, and Transparency

For the past quarter century, it has been rare indeed to find a change in, or development of, health and welfare policies or practices that have not had to run the gauntlet of a long line of "But what does it cost?" questions. The economic problems that beset Western economies from the mid-1970s—precipitated by the so-called oil crisis—forced on public, private, and voluntary providers of care a degree of cost consciousness hitherto unknown in the postwar period. For years, each new policy initiative and each new extension of existing policies had to be evaluated within cost constraint, but such constraint was never as tight as the constraints faced from the start of the 1980s. Many an eminently reasonable policy change has been postponed, rejected, and at times even abused because it was felt to be too expensive. As a consequence, cost constraint became the subject of considerable criticism, and the penny-pinching politician, the short-sighted accountant, and the hard-headed economist came to be viewed as the chief villains of proactive change. Group care services were long felt to be the preserve of the social worker or the social policy advisor. These services, it was argued, should not be the testing ground for economic theories or cannon fodder for central government fiscal policies. Costs, in short, became an anathema to group care and the voice of cost accounting has thereafter prevailed. Cost-per-unit-of-service (whether measured by bed-day, hour, or treatment intervention) has become commonplace in most sectors. At the same time, there is still very little evidence of detailed cost-benefit analyses of differential responses for clients and their families (Knapp, 2006). This voice retains a dominant influence for social work interventions with institutions, a voice that cannot be ignored.

Voices of Scholarship, Professional Education, and Registration

Residential and institutional care workers worldwide remain a significantly poorly educated occupational group. This is ironic, given the complexity of tasks that care workers are asked to perform. Serious attempts have been made in some places to address the education and training needs of this important and often undervalued workforce, with formal child and youth care training courses now found across Canada, in Ireland, and the United Kingdom, as well as in Western and Northern Europe. The situation in the United States, Australia, New Zealand, and South Africa still remains patchy. Paradoxically, the richest and seemingly most advanced Western countries have failed to address this education and training issue in any comprehensive and coherent fashion. Instead, market forces have been left to shape workforce training policies with mostly adverse effects. Social work education and training is almost always directed toward working outside institutions, to target clinical support for clients or to involve boundary roles that support the planned arrival and departure of clients from institutions. Comparatively little is done by social workers to proactively influence group care life spaces or shape the client milieux of direct care services. The development of group care as an occupational focus has been thwarted by two distinct sources. The first source involves the limited way in which the field has been conceptualized, namely around settings (e.g., institutions or residential programs) or client groups (e.g., delinquency, autism, or ADHD). The second difficulty involves the absence of any clear practice formulations that identify the knowledge and skills required of those working in residential institutions, community-based group living programs, or day care. Hopes that a practice curriculum published in the early 1980s (Central Council for Education and Training in Social Work, 1983) might go some way toward responding to this second deficiency in the United Kingdom proved to be idealistic and illusory. Little has changed. Even the Scottish Institute for Residential Child Care at Strathclyde University remains dominated by faculties of education and social work that relegate group care for children and young people to the status of a minority interest in spite of limited pathways being offered toward specialist education and preemployment registration for practice in the group care field.

IMPLICATIONS FOR SOCIAL WORK PRACTICE

To conclude, the six voices introduced at the start of this chapter are used to highlight implications for social work practice in institutions with the aim of achieving increased responsiveness in the decade ahead. Each voice highlights the importance of planning and policy formation being much more tightly focused around the developmental needs of individual clients and their families. That there are at least six voices—all demanding to speak and be heard—gives evidence for the need to better understand complex organizational dynamics and interpersonal processes associated with responsive multidisciplinary practices in this field. Sadly, the combined output of all six voices frequently creates discord, with the more powerful voices dominating at the expense of others.

Intervention in Microsystems of Clients: "Walk the Talk"

People today—especially children and young people—are considerably more sophisticated than they were in previous generations, if only because of the range of stimuli available to them through the media, the Internet, and the twenty-first century challenges of daily life. Those involved with clients in receipt of group care services need to practice what they preach or teach, engaging in purposeful activity and direct-care services to clients and families in collaboration with other health, education, and welfare professionals. The five rhythms of proactive, responsive caring need to place clients at the center of planning and policy formulation. Think about how clients might participate in staff reviews of their performance week to week. A radical reframing of ideas is needed about the way service outcomes are monitored and evaluated with each client in receipt of care services and with family members of those in care. If social workers and managers are to lead by example, then clients need active encouragement to participate in decision making about what is happening or is about to happen in their lives.

Intervention in Mesosystems with Family, Extended Family, and Peers: "Think Outside the Box"

While lip service is often paid to family participation in decision making around the care, education, and supervision of family members, the realities of family participation often fail to match up with the rhetoric. Those engaged in the delivery of social work in institutions need to think and act more strategically with individual clients and families. This means exploring ideas about how to resource more responsive practice opportunities with particular clients and working in much greater partnership with family and extended family members, as well as peers, to achieve better outcomes. It also means thinking practically about the futures of each person in care and what those futures might hold when they reach age 18, 25, and older. There is ample research to show how family participation in decision making about children or young people placed in care helps to produce enhanced service outcomes

(Burford & Hudson, 2000). Whether relying on family group conferences or less formal protocols that encourage family participation, it is difficult to ignore the ways in which increased family participation usually means improved service outcomes and longer-term benefits for clients and their families.

Interventions in the Exosystem with Health and Welfare Professionals: "Get Real"

For all the advances in science, technology, and the arts gained during the past half century, there is still a paradox in how little has changed in direct practice encounters with clients at the coal face of caring in most group care services. The language of health and welfare professionals is still filled with jargon and big words used by different professional disciplines, drawing attention to knowledge maintained by experts whether communicated with clients and their families or not. Staff turnover in group care services still remains critically high and the research evidence is virtually nonexistent on how work rosters and staff-to-client ratios contribute to responsiveness and continuity in people's lives as they move through developmental life transitions. Status hierarchies continue to place frontline care workers at the bottom of organizational charts giving limited acknowledgment to strategic benefits arising from responsive practices employed with clients in care day by day. Peer supervision and formal supervision are all too frequently neglected or abandoned altogether, whether through work pressures or because of service reconfigurations driven by consultants lacking knowledge of the field and confusing professional supervision with management. Far from being a waste of public sector spending, time set aside for professional networking between health and welfare professionals is arguably the key to enhanced responsiveness in the delivery of group care services.

Exosystem Interventions with Regulatory and Fiscal Authorities: "Transparency of Costs and Accountability for Outcomes"

The last decade of the twentieth century saw group care services operating increasingly through purchase of service contracting arrangements with governments and public agencies. Services are now commonly monitored as business units that deliver specific performance outcomes to targeted clientele, with public sector accounting practices now shaping care service outcomes. Ironically, government services increasingly employ contract administrators—not practitioners—who expect more from the voluntary sector in exchange for funding than was ever expected of government services in the past. A result has been that voluntary and nongovernment organizations now spend as much time servicing the "new client" of government or ministerial expectations, distracting attention away from priorities of service responsiveness to "traditional clients" and their families. After all the contract jargon, technical language, and accountancy speak, the most important aspect of transparency is that which still focuses on the needs of clients in care. Accountability begins with family and extended family views about how a group care service assists with the care of their family member(s). For that reason, there is good evidence to support family group conferences being used at the beginning and end of each care order to reaffirm family participation at every stage of the service planning and evaluation process.

Interventions in the Macrosystem of Public Opinion: "Who's Caring?"

The future of responsive group care is closely aligned to investment in any nation's youth. Those claiming that "nothing works" in group care have seen this message snapped up by supporters of monetarist economics as justification for massive cuts in public investment in the futures of many countries' most vulnerable people. Few have bothered to explore "what works with which clients?" or "under which circumstances?" Then, as enquiry after enquiry documents the abuse of group care clients, public opinion becomes disparaging about there being anything that can make a difference. Social Darwinist views such as these end up blaming people for a DNA code that puts them beyond redemption. Having "failed the cure" of caring community services, many come to call for capital punishment for young adults, an outcome all too often seen as the logical solution for heinous crimes and ill behavior toward others. Advocates of targeted expenditure also fail to acknowledge the way that clients must now be labeled as "problems" before any assistance is justified; ignoring the unintended consequences of labeling on identity formation and self-esteem. Thus, while those lobbying for the corporate interests of industry and government employ millions to shape public opinion, few lobby for the interests of children, young people, and their families. The rhetoric of commitment rarely finds implementation in the realities of practice for those struggling to provide responsive health and welfare services.

Intervention in the Macrosystem with Research and Scholarship: "If You Pay Peanuts, You Get Monkeys"

If group care services are to gain formal recognition for the strategic role they play in support of a nation's most vulnerable citizens, there needs to be political commitment directly commensurate with that nation's strategic investment in the futures of children and young people. It has been said that New Zealand kept better records of its sheep population in the late nineteenth century than it did of its children. In the late twentieth century, zookeepers and horse racing attendants were often paid more than social workers, perhaps because of the heavy investment in bloodstock. Meanwhile, people in care remain very much at risk of underachievement, ill health, and court involvement because adults in many parts of the world lack the political will to invest in more responsive group care practices. Scandinavian examples throughout the past half-century have reaffirmed the importance of sustained political commitment to the professional registration of child and youth care workers. Recent disclosures of physical and sexual abuse in British residential homes only reinforce this point. It is not that more research is required to determine future directions for the development of group care services. The challenge lies in a radical reframing of policies and practices that implement what has already been documented with research evidence. This requires more than further restructuring for health and welfare organizations that have struggled through at least 3 decades of service reconfigurations while attempting to respond proactively to the contemporary needs of clients and their families. Planning needs to extend beyond the annual financial year. It needs to establish instead, strategic visions for the futures of people in care—their education, recreation, leisure, and sport—with 3- to 5-year time lines, updated yearly. Otherwise structural features of health and welfare bureaucracy will continue to undermine any nation's young people by failing to strategically invest in their sustainable futures.

CONCLUSION

There is much to be gained from social workers tuning in to all six voices that speak of responsive group care practices. All six voices require careful attention and active listening. The heart and soul of responsive group care are embedded in acts of caring that attend to bodily comforts and physical safety—acknowledging what makes each person unique. Each person follows her or his own personal rhythms around physical, cognitive, emotional, behavioral, and social development. Five distinctive rhythms of group care intervention were highlighted: family/extended family rhythms, learning and recreational rhythms, rhythms of daily living, community and peer group rhythms, and cultural/spiritual rhythms of caring. The blues of group care practice are heard through the social histories of each type of intervention; through engagement in rituals of group membership; during times of emotional vulnerability, anger, and pain; and during times of fear, withdrawal, and isolation. Proactive attention given to the soul and the rhythms of caring promotes health and well-being for all, helping to ameliorate the blues of group care practice that are heard daily. Significant gaps in the evidence supporting responsive group care practice require ongoing attention, but implications arising from the evidence that is already available point to important strategies for social workers seeking to make a difference in the lives of clients and interventions with institutions.

REFERENCES

Ainsworth, F. (1997). *Family centered group care: Model building*. Aldershot, Hampshire, England: Ashgate.

Ainsworth, F., & Fulcher, L. C. (Eds.). (1981). *Group care for children: Concept and issues*. London: Tavistock.

Andersson, G. (2005). Family relations, adjustment, and well-being in a longitudinal study of children in care. *Child and Family Social Work, 10*(1), 43–56.

Anglin, J. P. (2003). *Pain, normality, and the struggle for congruence: Reinterpreting residential care for children and youth*. New York: Hawarth Press.

Banks-Mikkelson, N. E. (1969). A metropolitan area of Denmark: Copenhagen. In R. Krugel & W. Wolfensberger (Eds.), *Changing patterns in residential services for the mentally retarded* (pp. 179–195). Washington, DC: National Committee on Mental Retardation.

Beker, J., & Eisikovits, Z. (Eds.). (1991). *Knowledge utilization in residential child and youth care work*. Washington, DC: Child Welfare League of America.

Biklen, D. (1979a). The case of deinstitutionalization. *Social Policy, 10*(1), 48–54.

Biklen, D. (1979b). The least restrictive environment: Its application in education. *Child and Youth Services, 5*(1/2), 121–144.

Bronfenbrenner, U. (1979). *The ecology of human development*. Cambridge, MA: Harvard University Press.

Brown, P. (1981). The mental patients' rights movement and mental health institutional change. *International Journal of Human Services, 11*(4), 523–540.

Bukenya, S. S. (1996). The Ugandan experience. *Realities and dreams: Plenary papers from the International Conference on Residential Child Care* (pp. 57–62). Glasgow Strathclyde, Scotland: Strathclyde University.

Burford, G. (1990). *Assessing teamwork: A comparative study of group home teams in Newfoundland and Labrador*. Unpublished doctoral dissertation, University of Stirling, Stirling, Scotland.

Burford, G., & Casson, S. (1989). Including families in residential work: Educational and agency tasks. *British Journal of Social Work, 19*(1), 19–37.

Burford, G., & Fulcher, L. C. (1985). Resident group influences on team functioning. In L. C. Fulcher & F. Ainsworth (Eds.), *Group care practice with children* (pp. 187–214). London: Tavistock.

Burford, G., & Hudson, J. (2000). *Family group conferencing: New directions in community-centered child and family practice*. New York: Aldine de Gruyter.

Cairns, T. (1991). Whangai: Caring for a child. In G. Maxwell, I. Hassall, & J. Robertson (Eds.), *Toward a child and family policy for New Zealand* (pp. 44–47). Wellington, New Zealand: Office of the Commissioner for Children.

Cairns, T., Fulcher, L. C., & Tait-Rolleston, W., Kereopa, H., Nia, T., Nia, P., et al. (1996). Puao-te-ata-tu (Daybreak) revisited. In D. J. McDonald & L. R. Cleave (Eds.), *Partnerships that work? Proceedings of the 1995 Asia-Pacific Regional Social Services Conference* (pp. 44–47). Christchurch, New Zealand: University of Canterbury.

Canadian Royal Commission on Aboriginal Peoples. (1997). *For seven generations: An information legacy of the Royal Commission on Aboriginal Peoples*. Ottawa, Ontario, Canada: Libraxus.

Canagarayar, J. K. (1980). Diversion: A new perspective in criminal justice. *Canadian Journal of Criminology, 22*(2), 168–175.

Casson, S., & George, C. (1995). *Culture change for total quality: An action guide for managers in social and health services*. London: Pitman.

Central Council for Education and Training in Social Work. (1983). *A practice curriculum for group care* (Paper 14.2). London: Staff Development in Social Services.

Commonwealth of Australia. (1997). *Aboriginal deaths in custody: Response by governments to the Royal Commission* (Vols. 1–3). Canberra: Australian Government Printing Services.

Connolly, R. E. (1990). Public law 94-142: The Education for all Handicapped Children Act. *New England Journal of Human Services, 9*(1), 21–27.

Department of Child, Youth, and Family Services. (2003). *Review of the residential services strategy 1996*. Wellington, New Zealand: Government Printing Office.

Department of Social Welfare. (1986). *Puao-te-Ata-tu (Daybreak): Report of the Ministerial Advisory Committee on a Maori Perspective for the Department of Social Welfare*. Wellington, New Zealand: Government Printing Office.

Dominelli, L. (1988). *Anti-racist social work*. London: Macmillan.

Durst, D. (1992). The road to poverty is paved with good intentions: Social interventions and indigenous peoples. *International Social Work, 35*(2), 191–202.

Fahlberg, V. (Ed.). (1990). *Residential treatment: A tapestry of many therapies*. Indianapolis, IN: Perspective Press.

Fahlberg, V. (1991). *A child's journey through placement*. Indianapolis, IN: Perspective Press.

Fanshel, D., Finch, S. J., & Grundy, J. F. (1990). *Foster children in life course perspective*. New York: Colombia University Press.

Fox-Harding, L. (1991). *Perspectives in child care policy*. London: Longman.

Fulcher, L. C. (1983). *Who cares for the caregivers? A comparative study of residential and day care teams working with children*. Unpublished doctoral dissertation, University of Stirling, Stirling, Scotland.

Fulcher, L. C. (1988). *The worker, the work group, and the organisational task: Corporate restructuring and the social services in New Zealand*. Wellington, New Zealand: Victoria University Press.

Fulcher, L. C. (1991). Teamwork in residential care. In J. Beker & Z. Eisikovits (Eds.), *Knowledge utilization in residential child and youth care practice* (pp. 215–235). Washington, DC: Child Welfare League of America.

Fulcher, L. C. (1994). When you're up to your neck in alligators, it's hard to remember that the original aim was to drain the swamp: Some lessons from New Zealand health sector reform. *Australian Social Work, 47*(2), 47–53.

Fulcher, L. C. (1996). Changing care in a changing world: The old and new worlds. *Social Work Review*, 7(1, 2), 20–26.

Fulcher, L. C. (1998). Acknowledging culture in child and youth care practice. *Social Work Education*, 17(3), 321–338.

Fulcher, L. C. (1999). Cultural origins of the contemporary family group conference. *Child Care in Practice*, 5(4), 328–339.

Fulcher, L. C. (2002a). Cultural safety and the duty of care. *Child Welfare*, 81(5), 689–708.

Fulcher, L. C. (2002b). The duty of care in child and youth care practice. *Journal of Child and Youth Care Work*, 17, 73–84.

Fulcher, L. C. (2003). The working definition of social work doesn't work very well in China and Malaysia [Special edition]. *Research on Social Work Practice*, 13(3), 376–387.

Fulcher, L. C., & Ainsworth, F. (Eds.). (1985). *Group care practice with children*. London: Tavistock.

Fulcher, L. C., & Ainsworth, F. (1994). Child welfare abandoned? The ideology and economics of contemporary service reform in New Zealand. *Social Work Review*, 6(5, 6), 2–13.

Fulcher, L. C., & Ainsworth, F. (Eds.). (2006). *Group care for children and young people revisited*. New York: Haworth Press.

Fulcher, L. C., & Fulcher, J. (1998). To intervene or not?—That is the question: Managing risk-taking behaviour in student halls of residence. *Journal of the Australian and New Zealand Student Services Association*, 11, 14–31.

Garfat, T. (1998). The effective child and youth care intervention. *Journal of Child and Youth Care*, 12, 1–178.

Garfat, T. (Ed.). (2003). *A child and youth care approach to working with families*. New York: Haworth Press.

Gronfein, W. (1985). Psychotropic drugs and the origins of deinstitutionalization. *Social Problems*, 32(5), 437–454.

Guttmann, E. (1991). Immediacy in residential child and youth care: The fusion of experience, self-consciousness, and action. In J. Beker & Z. Eisikovits (Eds.), *Knowledge utilization in residential child and youth care practice* (pp. 65–82). Washington, DC: Child Welfare League of America.

Halverson, A. (1995). The importance of caring and attachment in direct practice with adolescents. *Child and Youth Care Forum*, 24(3), 169.

Hudson, W. W., & Nurius, P. S. (1994). *Controversial issues in social work research*. Sydney, Australia: Allyn & Bacon.

Hunter, J. M., Shannon, G. W., & Sambrook, S. L. (1986). Rings of madness: Service areas of 19th century asylums in North America. *Social Science and Medicine*, 23(10), 1033–1050.

Ibeabuchi, G. B. E. (1986). *Developing child and youth care services in Nigeria: An analysis of contemporary problems and needs*. Unpublished doctoral dissertation, University of Stirling, Stirling, Scotland.

Jones, K., & Fowles, A. J. (1984). *Ideas on institutions: Analysing the literature on long-term care and custody*. London: Routledge & Kegan Paul.

Kahan, B. (1989). *Child care research, policy and practice*. London: Hodder & Stoughton.

Kendrick, A. J. (1996, September). *Residential child care in Scotland: A positive choice*. Realities and Dreams International Conference on Residential Child Care, Glasgow, Scotland.

Knapp, M. (1984). *The economics of social care*. London: Macmillan.

Knapp, M. (2006). The economics of group care practice: A reappraisal. In L. C. Fulcher & F. Ainsworth (Eds.), *Group care practice with children and young people re-visited* (pp. 259–284). New York: Haworth Press.

Landesman, S., & Butterfield, E. C. (1987). Normalization and deinstitutionalization of mentally retarded individuals: Controversy and fact. *American Psychologist*, 42(8), 809–816.

Leigh, J. W. (1998). *Communication for cultural competence*. Sydney, Australia: Allyn & Bacon.

Lerman, P. (1985). Deinstitutionalization and welfare policies. *Annals of the American Academy of Political and Social Science*, 5, 132–155.

LeVine, E., & Greer, M. (1984). Long-term effectiveness of the adolescent learning center: A challenge to the concept of least restrictive environment. *Adolescence, 19*(75), 521–526.

Maier, H. W. (1963). Child care as a method of social work. In *Training manual for child care staff* (pp. 62–81). New York: Child Welfare League of America Publications.

Maier, H. W. (1975). Learning to learn and living to live in residential treatment. *Child Welfare, 54*(6), 406–420.

Maier, H. W. (1979). The core of care: Essential ingredients for the development of children at home and away from home. *Child Care Quarterly, 8*(3), 161–173.

Maier, H. W. (1981). Essential components in care and treatment environments for children. In F. Ainsworth & L. C. Fulcher (Eds.), *Group care for children: Concept and issues* (pp. 19–70). London: Tavistock.

Maier, H. W. (1985). Primary care in secondary settings: Inherent strains. In L. C. Fulcher & F. Ainsworth (Eds.), *Group care practice with children* (pp. 21–47). London: Tavistock.

Maier, H. W. (1987). *Developmental group care of children and youth: Concepts and practice.* New York: Haworth Press.

Maier, H. W. (1990). A developmental perspective for child and youth care. In J. Anglin, C. Denholm, R. Ferguson, & A. Pence (Eds.), *Perspectives in professional child and youth care* (pp. 7–24). Binghamton, NY: Haworth Press.

Maier, H. W. (1991). An exploration of the substance of child and youth care practice. *Child and Youth Care Forum, 20*(6), 393–411.

Maier, H. W. (1992). Rhythmicity: A powerful force for experiencing unity and personal connections. *Journal of Child and Youth Care Work, 5*, 7–13.

Milligan, I. (1998). Residential child care is not social work! *Social Work Education, 17*(3), 275–285.

Moore, C. (1996). *The Kincora scandal: Political cover-up and intrigue in Northern Ireland.* Dublin, Ireland: Marino Press.

Nelson, G. (1982). Services to status offenders and delinquents under Title XX. *Social Work, 27*(4), 348–353.

Nirje, B. (1969). The normalization principle: Implications and comments. *Journal of Mental Subnormality, 16*(1), 62–70.

O'Brien, D. (1984). Juvenile diversion: An issues perspective from the Atlantic provinces. *Canadian Journal of Criminology, 26*(2), 217–230.

O'Brien, P., & Murray, R. (1997). *Human services: Towards partnership and support.* Palmerston North, New Zealand: Dunmore Press.

Parbon, E. (1978). Changes in juvenile justice: Evolution or reform. *Social Work, 23*(6), 494–497.

Patton, G. C., Goldfeld, S. R., Pieris-Caldwell, I., Bryant, M., & Vimpani, G. V. (2005). A picture of Australia's children. *Medical Journal of Australia, 182*(9), 437–438.

Payne, M. (1997). *Modern social work theory* (2nd ed.). London: Macmillan.

Pedlar, A. (1990). Normalization and integration: A look at the Swedish experience. *Mental Retardation, 28*(5), 275–282.

Pennell, J., & Burford, G. (1995). *Family group decision making project implementation report* (Vol. 1). St. John's, Newfoundland: Memorial University of Newfoundland, School of Social Work.

Pogrebin, M. R., Poole, E. D., & Regoli, R. M. (1984). Constructing and implementing a model juvenile diversion program. *Youth and Society, 15*(3), 305–324.

Poland, M., & Legge, J. (2005). *Review of New Zealand longitudinal studies.* Wellington: New Zealand Families Commission.

Ramsden, I. (1997). Cultural safety: Implementing the concept. In P. Te Whaiti, M. McCarthy, & A. Durie (Eds.), *Mai I Rangiatea: Maori wellbeing and development* (pp. 113–125). Auckland, New Zealand: Auckland University Press.

Rangihau, J. (1986). *Puao-te-Ata-tu (Daybreak): Report of the ministerial advisory committee on a Maori perspective for the department of social welfare*. Wellington, New Zealand: Department of Social Welfare, Government Printing Office.

Rangihau, J. (1987, October). *Beyond crisis*. Keynote address to the First New Zealand Conference on Social Work Education. Christchurch, New Zealand: University of Canterbury.

Redl, F. (1959). Strategy and technique of life space interview. *American Journal of Orthopsychiatry, 29*(I), 1–18.

Rose, L. (1992). On being a child and youth care worker. *Journal of Child and Youth Care, 5*(1), 21–26.

Sali, G. W. (1996). *Law and order in contemporary Papua New Guinea: An examination of causes and policy options*. Unpublished doctoral dissertation, Victoria University of Wellington, Wellington, New Zealand.

Scarr, S., & Eisenberg, M. (1993). Child research: Issues, perspectives, and results. *Annual Research Psychology, 44*, 613–644.

Schur, E. M. (1965). *Radical non-intervention: Rethinking the delinquency problem*. Englewood Cliffs, NJ: Prentice Hall.

Scull, A. (1977). *Decarceration: Community treatment and the deviant—A radical view*. Lexington, MA: Prentice Hall.

Seed, P. (1973). Should any child be placed in care? The forgotten great debate 1841–1874. *British Journal of Social Work, 3*(3), 321–330.

Severy, L., & Whitaker, J. (1984). Memphis-metro youth diversion program: Final report. *Child Welfare, 63*(3), 269–299.

Shook, E. F. (1985). *Ho'oponopono: Contemporary uses of a Hawaiian problem-solving process*. Honolulu: University of Hawaii Press.

Small, R., & Fulcher, L. C. (1985). Teaching competence in group care practice. In L. C. Fulcher & F. Ainsworth (Eds.), *Group care practice with children* (pp. 135–154). London: Tavistock.

Stewart, M., & Ray, R. (1984). Truants and the court: A diversionary program. *Social Work in Education, 6*(3), 179–192.

Stewart, T. (1997). Historical interfaces between Maori and psychology. In P. Te Whaiti, M. McCarthy, & A. Durie (Eds.), *Mai I Rangiatea: Maori wellbeing and development* (pp. 75–95). Auckland, New Zealand: Auckland University Press.

Tait-Rolleston, W., Cairns, T., Fulcher, L. C., Kereopa, H., & Nia Nia, P. (1997). He koha kii: Na kui ma, na koro ma—A gift of words from our ancestors. *Social Work Review, 9*(4), 30–36.

Te Whaiti, P., McCarthy, M., & Durie, A. (Eds.). (1997). *Mai I Rangiatea: Maori wellbeing and development*. Auckland, New Zealand: Auckland University Press.

VanderVen, K. D. (1985). Activity programming: Its developmental and therapeutic role in group care. In L. C. Fulcher & F. Ainsworth (Eds.), *Group care practice with children* (pp. 155–183). London: Tavistock.

Viner, R. M., & Taylor, B. (2005). Adult health and social outcomes of children who have been in public care: Population-based study. *Pediatrics, 115*(4), 894–899.

Wagner, G. (1988). *Residential care: The research reviewed*. London: Her Majesty's Stationery Office.

Webster, R. (1998). *The great children's home panic*. Oxford: Orwell Press.

Wilcox, R., Smith, D., Moore, J., Hewitt, A., Allan, G., Walker, H., et al. (1991). *Family decision making, family group conferences: Practitioner's views*. Lower Hutt, New Zealand: Practitioners Publishing.

Wolfensberger, W. (1972). *Normalization: The principle of normalization in human services*. Toronto, Ontario, Canada: National Institute for Medical Research.

Wolfensberger, W. (1983). Social role valorization: A proposed new term for the principle of normalization. *Mental Retardation, 21*(6), 234–239.

Wolfensberger, W., & Glenn, L. (1975). *Pass 3: Program analysis of service system—A method and qualitative evaluation of human services* [Field manual]. Toronto, Ontario, Canada: National Institute for Medical Research.

Wolfensberger, W., & Thomas, S. (1983). *Passing: Promoting service systems' implementation of normalization criteria and ratings manual* (2nd ed.). Toronto, Ontario, Canada: National Institute on Mental Retardation.

Wooden, K. (1976). *Weeping in the playtime of others*. New York: McGraw-Hill.

Yahya, Z. (1994). *Resisting colonialist discourse*. Bangi: Penerbit University Kebangsaan Malaysia Press.

Zigler, E., & Muenchow, S. (1979). Mainstreaming: The proof is in the implementation. *American Psychologist, 34*(10), 993–996.

Author Index

Greif, G. L., 219
Gresham, F. M., 232
Grief, G., 474
Griffin, S., 433
Griffith, J., 275
Grimshaw, J. M., 571, 606
Grimwood, C., 172, 173
Grinnell, R., 60
Grob, G., 145, 146
Grogan, C., 148
Grogan-Kaylor, A., 224, 229
Gronfein, W., 615
Gross, B. H., 590
Grotevant, H., 62
Groth-Juncker, A., 378
Grotpeter, J., 435
Grove, J. R., 458
Grover Diemert, M. S., 500
Grundy, J. F., 620
Grusky, O., 140
Gruttadaro, D., 590
Gu, J., 384
Guadagnoli, E., 202
Guardino, M., 164
Guastello, S. J., 459
Guba, E. G., 125
Guerrero, S., 569, 570, 571
Guess, H. A., 162
Gundersen, D. E., 462
Gur, R. E., 288
Gurthrie, K., 545
Gustafson, D. H., 570, 571
Guterman, A., 352
Gutheil, I. A., 372
Gutierrez, L., 223, 479, 506, 511, 513, 520, 521, 522, 523, 524
Guttman, C., 353, 354
Guttmann, E., 626
Guyatt, G., 3, 4, 5, 8, 10, 13, 106, 110, 111, 113, 331
Guyet, D., 513
Guzzo, R. A., 559, 569, 570, 573

Hackl, K. L., 438
Hackman, J. R., 543, 573
Hagan, T. A., 151
Haggerty, R. J., 304
Hagopian, M., 350, 351, 352
Haight, B., 367
Haldeman, J., 566, 570
Haley, J., 229
Haley, W. E., 373
Halfhill, T., 454, 459
Hall, B. L., 406
Hall, G. S., 268
Hall, P., 321
Halper, D. E., 206
Halverson, A., 621
Hamilton, J., 222, 223
Hamilton, M., 320
Hamilton-Giachritsis, C. E., 456, 457
Hampson, S., 384, 386
Hangan, C., 141
Hanley, B., 16, 18
Hanley, J. H., 439
Hanna, M. P., 383
Hansen, W., 292, 293, 438
Hanson, M., 127, 132, 438
Hansson, K., 435
Hardcastle, D. A., 84, 489, 493, 494, 505, 507
Hardina, D., 524

Harding, T., 165, 174
Hardy, G. E., 208
Hare, P., 523
Harper, N. L., 458, 461, 462
Harrigan, M., 62
Harrington, R., 229, 231
Harris, M., 145
Harris, N., 163
Harris, O., 423, 424, 425, 434, 436
Harrison, M., 300, 540, 542, 544
Harrison, R., 101, 435
Harrison, W. D., 129
Hart, A. Y., 206
Hart, C. M., 455, 460, 461, 462
Hart, J. W., 457
Hart, S. L., 218
Hartman, A., 220, 312, 314, 423, 424
Hartman, D. J., 78, 83
Hartsell, T. L., 94
Hartzema, A. G., 162
Harvey, E. L., 609
Hasenberg, N. M., 11, 16
Hasenfeld, Y., 543, 549, 593
Hasselblad, V., 189
Hassett, S., 549, 550, 551
Havassy, B. E., 151
Hawkins, J. D., 249, 274
Hawkins, K., 78
Hayes, R. J., 11
Haynes, B., 113
Haynes, K. S., 162, 166, 174
Haynes, R. B., 3, 4, 5, 8, 9, 15, 22, 105, 106, 192, 330, 331, 365, 387, 426, 609
Haynes, R. D., 7, 8
Haynes, R. M., 3, 5, 8, 9, 11, 12, 19
Hazer, J. T., 563
Healy, K., 399, 401, 402, 403, 409, 410
Heath, C., 21
Heck, L., 385, 386
Heersema, P., 321
Heffernan, J., 440, 441, 442
Hegedus, A., 275
Helmers, K. F., 382, 386
Helzer, J. E., 71
Hemmelgarn, A. L., 556, 559, 562, 563, 565, 566
Hemmerling, K., 359
Hendin, H., 288
Henggeler, S., 21, 255, 256, 296, 297, 301, 314, 437, 439, 441
Henin, A., 251
Henning, J. M., 189
Henry, S., 479
Hepworth, D., 46, 204, 217, 218, 224, 226, 318, 322, 440, 441, 494
Herbst, D. D. G., 448
Herkov, M., 72
Herman, R. D., 593, 594, 596, 599
Hermann, R. C., 597, 598
Hernandez, C. M., 537
Herrera, A. E., 452
Herrin, J., 12
Hersen, M., 106, 328, 336, 338
Hervis, O., 257
Herzog, P., 128
Hessels, M., 562
Hewitt, A., 621
Heyman, A., 320
Heyman, J. C., 372
Hibbing, J. R., 514
Hibbs, E. D., 288

Subject Index